STANDARD STORIES FROM THE OPERAS

STANDARD STORIES
FROM THE OPERAS

By

GLADYS DAVIDSON

Bibliophile Books

33 Maiden Lane
London W C 2 E 7 J S

All Rights Reserved
ISBN 0 370 00259 8
Printed in Great Britain for
The Bodley Head Ltd
9 Bow Street, London WC2E 7AL
by Redwood Burn Ltd
Trowbridge
First published 1944
Twelfth impression 1982

PREFACE

In this new combined edition of my *Standard Stories from the Operas*, the entire series contained in Volumes I and II have now been reset and issued in one combined omnibus volume. This has entailed the revising and the re-arrangement of the whole collection. I have, therefore, taken the opportunity of re-writing many of the longer stories in the earlier series in order to bring these into line with the more concise style adopted in the later stories comprised in Volume II issued in 1940. At the same time, the short Biographies of Composers have likewise been carefully revised and brought up to date; and the Alphabetical Index of Operas has been improved by the addition of much useful information regarding librettists and dates of production.

As explained in earlier editions, the subject of each opera selected is presented in the readable form of a short story, the various incidents being given exactly as they occur in the libretto. This, it is felt, makes for a more complete understanding and enjoyment of the music than can be gained from a mere synopsis of the plot. The long continued appreciation of my work in this direction has proved that the short story medium I have consistently adopted is a useful and popular one.

It will be noticed that many works of our own British composers have been dealt with; and that I have also included the stories of a considerable number of the more popular Russian operas, in which increasing interest is deservedly being taken.

Naturally, there will be found omissions in several spheres. Various reasons account for these, e.g. copyright difficulties; lack of space; the fact that two or more composers have dealt with the same subject; or that some stories are sufficiently well known in their original form. However, it is hoped that many of the stories now unavoidably omitted may yet be dealt with later in a supplementary work.

Meanwhile, it is hoped that in its present newly-revised and more compact form this representative collection of 154 Opera Stories will continue its good work of not only familiarizing lovers of music with the subject-matter of Grand Opera but also of providing the general reader with a budget of dramatic tales of infinite variety and interest.

G.D.

CONTENTS

AUTHOR'S ACKNOWLEDGMENTS

I wish to express my thanks to the following Composers, Authors, Publishing Houses, and holders of copyrights for their kind permission to include in this work the stories of the various operas selected, and for the courteous assistance they have given me regarding libretti, etc:—

Messrs. ASCHERBERG, HOPWOOD & CREW, LTD., London. (For Mascagni's *L'Amico Fritz* and *Cavalleria Rusticana*; Bizet's *Djamileh*; and Leoncavallo's *I Pagliacci*.)

SIR GRANVILLE BANTOCK. (For his opera *The Seal-Woman*.)

Major Hon. MAURICE BARING, O.B.E. (For *Fête Galante*, the libretto of which is based upon his short story of that title.)

LORD BERNERS. (For his opera *Le Carrosse du Saint Sacrement*.)

Messrs. BOOSEY & HAWKES, LTD., London. (For Bantock's *The Seal-Woman*; Benjamin's *The Devil Take Her*; Gounod's *Mirella*; Rimsky-Korsakov's *Sadko*, *The Snow-Maiden*, and *The Legend of Tsar Saltan*; Smetana's *The Bartered Bride*; Stanford's *Shamus O'Brien*; Stravinsky's *Mavra*; Auber's *Fra Diavolo*; Flotow's *Martha*; and Meyerbeer's *Robert the Devil*.)

RUTLAND BOUGHTON, Esq. (For his *Alkestis*, *The Immortal Hour*, *Bethlehem*, and *The Queen of Cornwall*.)

Messrs. BREITKOPF & HÄRTEL, Leipzig. (For Wagner's *Lohengrin* and *Tristan and Isolde*.)

Messrs. BROCKHAUS, Leipzig. (For Humperdinck's *Königskinder*.)

Messrs. CHAPPELL & CO., LTD., London. (For Gounod's *Faust* and Massenet's *Le Roi de Lahore*.)

Messrs. J. & W. CHESTER, LTD., London. (For Dvořák's *Rusalka*, and Goossens' *Don Juan de Mañara* and *Judith*.) Also for various Russian operas, as follows:—*Prince Igor*, *The Stone Guest*, *Boris Godounov*, *Khovantschina*, *Aleko*, *Francesca da Rimini*, *A Night in May*, *Ivan the Terrible*, *Mozart and Salieri*, *The Golden Cockerel*, *The Demon*, *The Nightingale*, *Eugène Onégin*, *Iolanta*, *The Queen of Spades*, *Mam'zelle Fifi*.

HAROLD CHILD, Esq. (For his libretto of *Hugh the Drover*.)

COVENT GARDEN MUSICAL PRODUCTIONS LTD., Royal Opera House, Covent Garden, London. (Through C. A. Barrand, Esq., General Manager.) For courteous assistance *re* libretti.

Messrs. CRAMER & Co., LTD., London. (For Offenbach's *Tales of Hoffmann*.)

Messrs. CURWEN & SON, LTD., London. (For Holst's *Savitri*, the music of which is published by this house. Also for Rutland Boughton's *Bethlehem*, and Dr. R. Vaughan Williams' *Hugh the Drover*.)

DURAND ET FILS, Paris. (For Debussy's *L'Enfant Prodigue* and *Pelléas et Mélisande*; Dukas' *Ariane et Barbe-Bleue*; Saint-Saëns' *Samson et Dalila*; and Ravel's *L'Heure Espagnole*.)

BARON D'ERLANGER. (For his opera *Tess*.)

Executors of the following :—
ARNOLD BENNETT. (Through Messrs. J. Pinker & Son, Ltd.) For *Don Juan de Mañara* and *Judith*.
THOMAS HARDY, O.M. (Through The Incorporated Society of Authors, Playwrights and Composers.) For *The Queen of Cornwall* and *Tess*.
SIR HENRY NEWBOLT. (Through Messrs. A. P. Watt & Son.) For *The Travelling Companion*.

Messrs. FÜRSTNER, LTD., London, W.1. For the following Operas by Richard Strauss :—
Feuersnot. Copyright 1901 and 1928, by Fürstner, Ltd., London, W.1.
Intermezzo. Copyright 1924, by Fürstner, Ltd., London, W.1.
Helen in Egypt. Copyright 1928, by Fürstner, Ltd., London, W.1.
Arabella. Copyright 1933, by Richard Strauss.

Herr ADOLPH FÜRSTNER, Berlin, W.10, and Herr S. FISCHER VERLAG, Berlin, W.57. (For Strauss's *Elektra*, *Rosenkavalier*, *Salomé*, and *Ariadne on Naxos*.)

(The story of *Elektra* is published by authorization of Herr Adolph Fürstner, Berlin, W.10, and Herr S. Fischer Verlag, Berlin, W.57. Copyright, 1908, by Adolph Fürstner, Berlin.)

(The story of *Rosenkavalier* is published by authorization of Herr Adolph Fürstner, Berlin, W.10. Copyright, 1909, by Adolph Fürstner, Berlin, W.10.)

(The story of *Salomé* is published by authorization of Herr Adolph Fürstner, Berlin, W.10. Copyright, 1905, by Adolph Fürstner. Also by permission of Messrs. John Lane, The Bodley Head, London, as holders of the English rights in Oscar Wilde's drama.)

(The story of *Ariadne on Naxos* is published by authorization of Herr Adolph Fürstner, Berlin, W.10. Copyright, 1912 and 1916, by Adolph Fürstner.)

Dr. Nicholas Comyn Gatty. (For his operas *Duke or Devil*, *King Alfred and the Cakes*, *Greysteel* and *Prince Ferelon*.)

Messrs. Goodwin & Tabb, London. (For kind assistance in connection with Mr. Holbrooke's works.)

Eugene Goossens, Esq. (For his operas *Don Juan de Mañara* and *Judith*.)

The Gramophone Company, Ltd., London. (Through Mr. V. Standbridge Homewood and Mr. C. B. Dawson Pane.) For courteous assistance *re* libretti and copyright matters.

Messrs. Frederick Harris, London. (For Verdi's *Il Trovatore*.)

Messrs. Heugel et Cie, Paris. (For Charpentier's *Louise*; Delibes' *Lakmé*; Massenet's *Thaïs* and *Le Jongleur de Notre-Dame*; and Thomas's *Mignon*.)

Josef Holbrooke, Esq. (For his *The Enchanter*, *The Stranger*, *The Snob*, and his Trilogy, *The Cauldron of Annwn*.)

Lord Howard de Walden. (For the stories of his poems forming the libretto of Holbrooke's Trilogy, *The Cauldron of Annwn*.)

Messrs. Hutchings & Romer, London. (For Wallace's *Maritana*.)

W. W. Jacobs, Esq. (For *The Boatswain's Mate*, the libretto of which is adapted from his short story, *Captains All*.

Messrs. John Lane, The Bodley Head, London. (For *Salomé*, as holders of the English rights in Oscar Wilde's drama of that title.)

George Lloyd, Esq., and William Lloyd, Esq. (For their operas —as composer and librettist, respectively—*Iernin* and *The Serf*.)

Messrs. Macmillan & Co., Ltd., London and New York. (For their permission as copyright-holders in the works of the late Thomas Hardy, O.M., to include the stories of *The Queen of Cornwall* and *Tess*.)

Sir Humphrey Milford and The Oxford University Press (Music Dept.), London. (For Dr. R. Vaughan Williams' *The Poisoned Kiss*.)

W. J. Miller, Esq. (For the story of his libretto to Mr. Philpot's *Dante and Beatrice*.)

Professor Gilbert Murray. (For the story of his translation of the *Alcestis* of Euripides, forming the libretto of Mr. Boughton's *Alkestis*.)

Messrs. NOVELLO & Co., London. (For Beethoven's *Fidelio*; Bellini's *La Sonnambula*; Meyerbeer's *Star of the North*; Verdi's *La Traviata* and *Rigoletto*; and Wagner's *The Flying Dutchman* and *Tannhäuser*. Also for Mr. Holst's *The Perfect Fool*; and for much courteous assistance *re* libretti.)

STEPHEN R. PHILPOT, Esq. (For his *Dante and Beatrice*.)

Messrs. RENDLE & Co., LTD., London. (For Bizet's *Carmen* and Gounod's *Philemon and Baucis*.)

Messrs. G. RICORDI & Co., LTD., London and New York. (For Boïto's *Mefistofele* and *Nerone*; d'Erlanger's *Tess*; Goldmark's *The Queen of Sheba*; Puccini's *Turandot*, *La Bohème*, *Madama Butterfly*, *Manon Lescaut*, *Tosca*, *The Girl of the Golden West*, *Gianni Schicchi*, *The Cloak*, and *Sister Angelica*. Also for Mascagni's *Iris*, and Verdi's *Don Carlos*.)

SADLER'S WELLS THEATRE. (Through the Secretary, Annette Prévost.) For much courteous assistance *re* libretti.

Messrs. SCHOTT & Co., LTD., London. (For Humperdinck's *Hansel and Gretel*, and Wagner's *The Mastersingers*, *The Nibelungs' Ring*, and *Parsifal*.)

MISS EVELYN SHARP (Mrs. Henry W. Nevinson). (For her libretto, *The Poisoned Kiss*.)

Mrs. WILLIAM SHARP. (For the story of Mr. Rutland Boughton's *The Immortal Hour*, the libretto of which is the allegorical poem of the late " Fiona Macleod " (William Sharp).)

Dame ETHEL SMYTH. (For her *Fête Galante*, *The Wreckers*, *The Forest*, and *The Boatswain's Mate*.)

SONZOGNO. (Casa Musicale Sonzogno, S.A.) Milan. (For Giordano's *André Chénier*.)

Messrs. STAINER & BELL, LTD., London. (For Gatty's *Duke or Devil* and *King Alfred and the Cakes*; and Stanford's *The Travelling Companion*.)

UNIVERSAL EDITION, A.G. Vienna. (For Jaromir Weinberger's *Schwanda the Bagpiper*; Delius' *A Village Romeo and Juliet*; and Offenbach's *The Goldsmith of Toledo*.)

DR. R. VAUGHAN WILLIAMS, O.M. (For his operas *Hugh the Drover* and *The Poisoned Kiss*.)

Herr J. WEINBERGER, Vienna. (For Wolf-Ferrari's *The Jewels of the Madonna* and *The Secret of Susanna*.)

Messrs. JOSEF WEINBERGER, LTD., London. (For Johann Strauss' *Die Fledermaus*, of which they are the owners of the stage performing rights.)

Messrs. JOSEPH WILLIAMS, LTD., London. (For Rutland Boughton's *The Queen of Cornwall*.)

It is also desired to acknowledge the source of *Mam'zelle Fifi*, the libretto of which is based upon Guy de Maupassant's well-known story.

STANDARD STORIES FROM THE OPERAS

FRA DIAVOLO *Auber*

ONE bright Easter Eve early in the nineteenth century, a lively troop of carbineers had gathered together in the inn at Terracina, near Naples, to drink success to the enterprise they were engaged upon. They were about to attack a band of brigands believed to be in that neighbourhood; and they expected to meet with many exciting adventures.

The leader of the outlaw band, known as Fra Diavolo, was the most dangerous bandit in Italy and fully justified his sinister name. His daring raids and impudent roguery had made him a terror to the country-side, so that the mere mention of his name caused alarm to all peaceful travellers. All previous attempts to capture this famous bandit had failed; but it was now hoped that he would soon be in the hands of the carbineers. The latter were impatient to begin the chase and to win the reward, for a high price had been set upon the head of Fra Diavolo. In eager haste, therefore, they tossed off the drinks poured out for them by Matteo, the innkeeper, and his pretty young daughter, Zerlina.

The captain of this gay troop, however, a handsome young brigadier named Lorenzo, sat alone at a side table, full of gloom; and his sadness deepened when the innkeeper presently invited all the company to attend the wedding of his daughter with a neighbouring farmer on the morrow. For Lorenzo was himself in love with Zerlina, who returned his affection; but his suit was not acceptable to her father. The latter would not hear of his attractive daughter marrying a poor brigadier with naught but his paltry pay to live upon. To settle the matter, he had hastily arranged a marriage for her with Francesco, a wealthy farmer; and the ceremony was to take place next day, on Easter morning, Zerlina now being bidden to say farewell to her portionless suitor.

While the lovers were whispering sadly together before the departure of Lorenzo and his troop, a sudden commotion was heard. Two richly-dressed travellers, a lady and a gentleman, hurried into the inn, talking excitedly. In a great state of agitation, they declared that they had just been attacked by a band of brigands, who had robbed them of all their jewellery; and they added that it was only by leaving the robbers in possession of their travelling carriage that they had been able to escape with their lives. The newcomers introduced themselves as Lord and

Lady Allcash, wealthy English travellers touring through Italy; and they explained that their postilion had been stopped by the bandits scarcely a mile away.

Lorenzo instantly called his men together, declaring that this must be the very band of brigands they were seeking; then, bidding a hasty but tender farewell to Zerlina, he dashed off with the soldiers, hoping to effect a capture.

While Zerlina now soothed the agitated lady, Lord Allcash, full of fussy importance, sat down to write out a notice, offering a handsome reward of one thousand ducats for the recovery of the lost jewels; and the paper was placed in a prominent position. Lady Allcash, who was young and sentimental, had observed with sympathy the tender parting between Zerlina and Lorenzo; and she expressed the hope that the handsome brigadier would win the reward.

Just then, a magnificent carriage drew up at the inn door; and a good-looking man of gay debonair appearance, stepped out and bowed gracefully to the English visitors. Lady Allcash returned his greeting with flattering delight; for the newcomer was seen to be a very charming fellow-traveller who had followed in her wake for some days past and with whom she had more than once indulged in a pleasant flirtation.

Her husband, however, was extremely annoyed; for, being somewhat dull himself, as well as self-important, he was already jealous of his coquettish wife's dashing new admirer. Hastily seizing her hand, he hurried her off to the private apartments he had already ordered to be prepared for their reception.

The newly-arrived guest, who gave his name as the Marquis of San Carlo, entered the inn and ordered a meal, announcing his intention of remaining the night there; and the innkeeper bustled about, blessing the good fortune that had brought two great lords to his hostelry on the same day. He apologized to the Marquis, however, for the fact that he himself would be absent from the inn until next morning, as he had promised to spend that night with his future son-in-law, who was to be married to his daughter early on the morrow; but he assured him that he would attend to all his honoured guests' needs before leaving.

So far from expressing annoyance at this announcement, the Marquis seemed pleased; and as he sat down to supper he asked for news of the neighbourhood. On being told of the recent escapade of the famous bandit, Fra Diavolo, he expressed interest and asked what sort of a fellow this brigand was; and when Zerlina was bidden by her father to sing to him a ballad descriptive of the dreaded robber, he was inclined to scoff at such a highly-coloured picture.

Later on, when the innkeeper had departed on his visit to the farmer, Francesco, a couple of swarthy, rough-looking men approached the Marquis as he sat alone and were soon talking confidentially with him. Though the innkeeper and the English travellers were ignorant of the fact, the so-called Marquis of San Carlo was none other than the dreaded Fra Diavolo himself, in disguise; and his present companions were two of his accomplices, Beppo and Giacomo. Being clever, witty, and elegant in appearance, the famous bandit had easily duped the wealthy English travellers, who had no idea of his true identity. During his flirtations with Lady Allcash, he had easily discovered the whereabouts of her jewels and also learned the pleasant fact that her husband was travelling with a large sum of money. He had then arranged with his gang to waylay the travellers on their journey to the inn at Terracina and to rob them of all their valuables, while he himself went on in advance to meet the pair again at the inn and to commiserate with them upon their loss.

He now learned from Beppo and Giacomo that though the robbers had secured the jewels and the carriage, they had not been successful in finding the large sum of gold which the English Milord was supposed to have with him. Perplexed and disappointed on hearing this, Fra Diavolo bade his accomplices to hide in the barn and await his further orders; and when they had departed, he remained in the parlour, thinking out a fresh plan for relieving the travellers of their gold.

Just then, Lady Allcash returned to the parlour, eager for a further flirtation with the gay Marquis, who was willing enough to amuse himself with such a charming lady; but they were quickly interrupted by the irate husband. The pretended Marquis, however, refused to quarrel, and cleverly inveigled the duped Milord into friendly conversation. By cunning flattery and sympathy, he soon learned all he wished to know. Lord Allcash, with conceited pride, declared that his own good wits had prevented his gold from being stolen. Having learned that bandits might be encountered on this journey he had changed all his gold into bank-bills, which he had caused to be sewn into the lining of the coat he was wearing and also into the voluminous sleeves of his lady's gown; and by this simple ruse, he had cheated the robbers.

While they were talking, and the disguised bandit was inwardly chuckling over the information he had just gained, Lorenzo and his soldiers returned in great triumph, declaring that they had rounded up the brigands and captured twelve of their number.

the rest having fled in panic. Better still, so far as the English travellers were concerned, Lorenzo himself had recovered from one of the gang all the jewels of which they had been robbed.

Zerlina was quickly in the arms of the young brigadier; and when Lady Allcash now declared that Lorenzo was entitled to the reward her husband had offered and handed to him a note for one thousand ducats, the lovers were filled with happiness, knowing that their troubles were ended. Since Lorenzo was now richer than Francesco, the innkeeper would no longer oppose their union. Flushed with his victory, Lorenzo declared that he would not be satisfied until he had captured the dreaded Fra Diavolo himself; and calling his men together once more, he dashed off with them to search for the brigand chief.

Meanwhile, the disguised Fra Diavolo was inwardly furious at the defeat of his band and was vowing vengeance upon Lorenzo; and after smilingly congratulating the English travellers upon the recovery of their jewels, still in his *rôle* as the elegant Marquis, he managed to slip away and made his way, unseen, to the barn, where his underlings, Beppo and Giacomo, were awaiting his coming. With them he arranged a plot for recovering the jewels and also for securing the bank-bills sewn into the clothing of Lord and Lady Allcash.

Having learned that the only means of reaching the English lord's apartments was through Zerlina's bedroom, the pretended Marquis concealed himself and his two rascals in an alcove adjoining this room, while the young girl was still attending to her duties in the parlour. They intended to remain hidden until all in the house had retired to bed, when they would be able to make their way through Zerlina's room into the apartment of Lord and Lady Allcash and effect the robbery of their jewels and money.

When she had conducted the distinguished visitors to their bedroom for the night, and the rest of the household had seemingly retired, Zerlina herself entered her own room and prepared for bed. She sang softly to herself as she undressed, happy in the thought that her father would no longer refuse her in marriage to her beloved Lorenzo, since the latter was now a man of considerable means. She even stopped for a few moments before her mirror, to admire her own pretty reflection therein, uttering aloud a charming compliment to herself; then she knelt down and said her prayers most devoutly. After putting out the light, she got into bed and was soon asleep.

The hidden bandits waited until the maiden's regular breathing assured them that she was soundly sleeping; then, on instructions from their chief, Beppo and Giacomo crept out from the alcove and made their way, softly and warily, towards the English Milord's chamber. As they passed Zerlina's bed, the young girl moved and murmured a few words; and Beppo instantly raised the dagger he carried, ready to stab her should she awaken. But Zerlina was only repeating in her sleep a few words of her simple childish prayer; and, conscience-stricken, the robber replaced his dagger and followed his companion towards the chamber beyond.

Just then a loud knocking on the door outside the inn announced the return of Lorenzo and his men; and all the household was quickly agog once more. Foiled by this unexpected interruption to his plans, the Marquis managed to cover the retreat of his underlings in the commotion which followed, during which Lorenzo explained that, having missed his quarry, he had brought his troop back for a short rest.

While Zerlina departed to set food before the tired soldiers, the gay Marquis found it necessary to explain his presence in the young girl's room, whence he had been seen issuing by both Lorenzo and the hastily-garbed Lord Allcash. He was equal to the occasion, however. With quick-witted readiness, he cleverly managed to convey to the English Milord that he was awaiting a tender meeting with the latter's flirtatious wife; and, at the same time, he took Lorenzo aside and led him to suppose that he was there at the invitation of Zerlina.

The young brigadier, overcome with grief at this seeming proof of his sweetheart's defection, instantly challenged the Marquis to a duel; a challenge which was promptly accepted by the latter, eager to avenge the rout of his band. He arranged to meet him at seven o'clock next morning in a rocky pass not far away; and then, having thus raised a hornets' nest satisfactory to his own interests, he managed, unobserved, to make his escape from the inn.

As Lord Allcash hustled his indignant wife back to their own apartment, pouring upraidings upon her for her supposed light conduct, Zerlina returned to call Lorenzo to the supper she had hastily prepared; but her lover met her with coldness and refused to speak to her. Having no knowledge of the cruel allegation made against her, she begged for an explanation; but this was denied to her, and the poor girl, with the mystery unsolved, had no alternative but to retire to her own room, where she passed the night in tears.

Meanwhile, Fra Diavolo quickly got in touch with his remaining outlaw band and lost no time in concocting a new scheme for robbing the English travellers and, at the same time, securing his vengeance against the young brigadier. It was arranged that when Lorenzo arrived for his duel at the rocky pass, he should be set upon and slain by the bandits. Then, a little later on, when the party from the inn had departed to the village church for Zerlina's wedding and the carbineers had gone in search of their absent leader, the brigand chief himself would make a quiet raid on the deserted hostelry and possess himself of the treasure he had so long coveted.

A note to this effect was conveyed to the two rascals, Beppo and Giacomo, who had been left in hiding near the inn to give warning should any unforeseen danger arise. Beppo was ordered to toll the bell of a small hermitage near by as soon as the wedding party had set forth, as the signal that all was safe.

Early next morning, Matteo the innkeeper arrived at the inn with the young farmer, Francesco, and the rest of the wedding party; and the unhappy Zerlina, who had vainly tried to learn the cause of Lorenzo's sudden coldness to her, was filled with despair. Seeing that the young brigadier was about to set forth with his troop to continue the search for Fra Diavolo and was making no attempt to prevent her marriage with Francesco, she ran to him once again and implored him to say in what way she had offended him. This time, Lorenzo, still believing her to be false, at last told her of the allegation made by the Marquis—that she had intended to receive the latter as her lover the night before. Then, remembering his appointment with the Marquis, he placed himself at the head of his troop and was about to depart when a sudden interruption came.

As the distracted Zerlina stood for a moment, speechless with dismay, she observed two suspicious-looking men drinking at a table outside the inn. These strangers were Beppo and Giacomo who, having received the note from their chief and thinking that all was going according to plan, were carelessly indulging themselves. As Zerlina now drew near, wondering who they might be, they became still more off their guard; and the foolish Beppo, recognizing her as the pretty girl he had seen admiring herself in her mirror the night before, laughingly repeated in a loud whisper to his companion the words she had then uttered.

Instantly realizing that some plot was afoot, Zerlina called upon the carbineers to seize the two strangers; and Lorenzo, hearing her cries of alarm, turned back as the men were dragged towards him. The note revealing the whole of Fra Diavolo's cunning plot was soon discovered; and Lorenzo now determined that the famous robber should not escape him this time, but should be caught in his own trap.

The wedding guests were bidden to retire within the inn for the time being, while the carbineers concealed themselves on the nearby hill-side down which Fra Diavolo intended to come when making his raid on the supposedly deserted inn; and the captive Beppo was compelled to toll the hermitage bell as the arranged signal that the wedding party had left for the church. Then, having hidden himself behind some bushes with Zerlina and the English travellers, Lorenzo eagerly awaited the result of his ambush.

Soon after the discomfited Beppo had begun to toll the hermitage bell, Fra Diavolo appeared on the hill-top; and although now attired in the gorgeous garb of a brigand chief, the hidden watchers instantly recognized him as the gay debonair Marquis who had so successfully deceived them all. Amazed at the discovery, Lorenzo's contrite eyes sought those of Zerlina in a silent appeal for forgiveness, whilst Lord and Lady Allcash joined hands in token of renewed good-fellowship.

Since the bell still continued to toll, Fra Diavolo concluded that all was well and gaily descended the hill-side with confidence; but, at a sign from Lorenzo, the carbineers sprang suddenly from their ambush and seized him ere he had time to realize his danger. In another moment, he was captured and bound; and as he was led away between two files of carbineers, a loud cry of triumph arose from the spectators now gathered around, who all rejoiced together at the capture of the dreaded bandit.

A few hours later, Zerlina's wedding was celebrated in the little village church; and the happy bridegroom who joined hands with her that day was not Francesco the farmer, but Lorenzo, the proud vanquisher of the famous Fra Diavolo.

PHŒBUS AND PAN _Bach_

PHŒBUS APOLLO—the glorious Sun-god, the God of Music and the Fine Arts and the beloved of the Muses—was so proud of his musical gifts and his wonderful singing that he could not bear to think he had a rival in the whole of the universe.

He had secured the first primitive lyre from the infant Mercury, who had cleverly invented the instrument by stringing sinews across an empty tortoise-shell and had then sold it to the great Sun-god for half a flock of cattle and the magic golden wand known as the Caduceus—thus early striking his first commercial bargain. Then the Sun-god set to work to improve upon it; and at last he produced an excellent musical instrument.

Upon this improved lyre, Apollo struck such perfectly harmonious chords and made such an exquisite accompaniment to his beautiful singing that his fame went forth to gods and mortals alike as the greatest of all musicians.

But, after awhile, to his indignant dismay, he discovered that he had a rival. Pan, the satyr, the God of Shepherds and Flocks and of the Woods, had also invented a musical instrument, and now dared even to set himself up as a competitor in the realms of music.

Pan had discovered how to make his musical instrument accidentally. Seeing the pretty water-nymph, Syrinx, on the riverside one day, he gave chase to her; but just as he was about to grasp her, she was changed by her sister nymphs—who had heard her cry for help—into a bunch of reeds. Pan, full of rage and disappointment, tore up the reeds and ran along by the riverside like the wild thing he was; and as he ran the breezes began to blow lightly through the hollow reeds and to make musical sounds. This so delighted Pan that he stopped to arrange the reeds more carefully; and thus there came to him the idea for a new musical instrument, which he perfected and called the Syrinx or Pandean Pipes.

Pan soon became a proficient player, so that his pipes gave great delight to the shepherds and nymphs who danced and sang to the lively music he thus made for them; and his fame went forth until at last it reached the ears of the great Apollo, who sent for his rival to give a command performance. At first the Sun-god professed to despise the satyr's instrument and his claim to be a musician on a level with himself. Later on, however, when he knew how popular Pan's music had become and how stoutly the latter defended the superiority of his own instrument over the lyre, he was compelled to recognize in him a serious rival, though he scoffed at the Shepherd King's claim that " Pan was the very Prince of Music ".

Constant strife between the pair now arose, and every time the protagonists met they wrangled about the superiority of their musical instruments and singing. At last, owing to the continued squabbles of the two music-makers, Mercury proposed that they should settle the matter once for all by holding a Contest of Song; and he also suggested that each should choose his own judge—a somewhat curious condition. This suggestion was agreed to by the rivals. Apollo selected as his judge Tmolus, the God of Mount Tmolus in Lydia, upon the slopes of which the famous river Pactolus had its source; and Pan chose Midas, the King of Phrygia, as his.

On the day appointed the contest took place in the presence of Mercury, Momus, and a large company of the personal supporters of Apollo and Pan. When the judges had taken up their positions and the audience had grouped themselves around, the contest began.

Phœbus Apollo, who had arrived in full state in his golden chariot of the sun, was the first to compete. As he stood forth, a noble and dazzling figure in his bright and glistening robes, he proudly gazed around the company, graciously acknowledging the greetings of his own judge, Tmolus; but he cast a disdainful glance of scorn upon Midas, whom he despised as a foolish King —who was, indeed, already behaving in a somewhat frivolously light manner. Then, taking up his lyre, he swept its strings with his delicate and inimitable touch and burst forth into an exquisitely sweet and tender song. In this he extolled the charms and grace of Hyacinthus, a beautiful Spartan youth greatly beloved by him, who, being one of the present company, now drew nearer to the Sun-god, whose glorious song he thus inspired to greater beauty still.

The company, and especially the supporters of Apollo, listened spellbound to the dulcet notes of the Sun-god; and when his wonderful song came to an end, he was led aside by the admiringly rapturous Tmolus, who could scarcely bring himself to listen to the efforts of the upstart rival.

It was now the turn of Pan, who, accompanied by a group of merry fauns and satyrs, entered the circle formed by the expectant audience and broke into a gay and hilarious song which opened with the enticing words: "To gladness from sadness song waketh the heart." As he sang in praise of joy and light-heartedness, the fauns and satyrs he had brought danced and capered about him, playing the pandean pipes with which he had supplied them. Every now and again he would cease singing and join them in their dance, playing upon his own instrument to show his amazing skill thereon.

This jovial song and the simple tuneful music of the Shepherd-god greatly pleased King Midas, who had been somewhat bored by the more elaborate and serious music of Apollo. It was all he could do to remain in his seat as became the dignity of a judge, while his feet constantly kept time with the rollicking notes which tickled his ears so pleasantly.

When Pan had finished his gay performance and had retired to one side with his fauns and satyrs, the judges came forward to make their award. Tmolus unhesitatingly gave his verdict in favour of the Sun-god's magnificent performance, declaring that,

B

compared with the strains of great Phœbus Apollo, the rustic pipes of Pan counted as nothing. And although the company had also enjoyed the merry tunefulness of Pan's more simple music, they agreed with this verdict.

But not so King Midas, who now came forward and declared that the palm should be awarded to Pan, whose lively music had pleased him much more and whose wind instrument he considered superior. He soon found, however, that it was not wise thus to offend the mighty Sun-god by not subscribing to his undoubted gifts. Apollo, scornful of such a verdict and despising what he considered the Phrygian King's stupid lack of real musical understanding, forthwith commanded him to wear a pair of ass's ears for the rest of his days—and with these awkward appendages he was immediately decorated.

Thus the contest ended disastrously for King Midas; and as the downcast Pan and his satyrs and fauns retired to the woods to recover their gaiety with more merry tunes, the radiant Sun-god drove away from the scene of his triumph amidst a fresh pæan of praise.[1]

THE BOHEMIAN GIRL   *Balfe*

ONE bright summer day, towards the end of the eighteenth century, high revels were being held in the Austrian city of Presburg. A troop of Austrian soldiers had just returned from the wars, flushed with victory and elated by their victorious invasion of the fair but unhappy land of Poland.

The gayest scene of all was taking place in the magnificent grounds of Count Arnheim, their leader. Here preparations were being made for a great hunt, and the retainers and peasants on the estate were merry-making in honour of their lord's return. When the Count presently joined them, accompanied by his nephew, Florestein, and his little daughter, Arline, a great shout

[1] This charming little opera was originally a satire. By Phœbus Bach indicated himself and the more serious and intellectual school of composers; and by Pan he symbolized the composers of the lighter music that appeals to the popular taste. By performances of the opera—regarded in his day as a musical satire—he was enabled to poke fun at several of his enemies. By the character of Midas, for instance, he ridiculed the musician and critic, Scheibe, of whose work he did not approve and who, in return, did not hesitate to criticize the master for the frequently complicated and occasionally almost incomprehensible passages in certain of his own compositions.

of welcome arose. Florestein was a conceited, foppish young man, whose gorgeous appearance was only surpassed by his foolish conversation; but little Arline, the heiress of Arnheim, was a lovely child and the joy of her widowed father's heart.

After acknowledging his guests' hearty welcome, the Count returned to the castle; then the gay hunting cavalcade set forth, to the merry sound of bugles and the cheering of the peasants who followed to watch the sport. Little Arline and her attendant nurse having also strayed off to the woods to watch the hunt from afar, the castle grounds were left deserted for a time.

Suddenly, a handsome young stranger, dressed in the garb of a Polish officer, ran into the gardens in a breathless and exhausted state, seeking a hiding-place. A band of Austrian soldiers, whose vigilance the proscribed fugitive could no longer elude, were already close upon his track and about to come into sight.

Unhappy Thaddeus of Poland! A scion of a noble family, he had bravely fought for the freedom of his country; but now, defeated and pursued, he wandered forth, homeless, without friends or fortune, his only hope to find some place of present shelter.

A statue of the Austrian Emperor near the entrance to the castle warned the fugitive that this was no safe haven for him; but before he had time to escape, a band of wild-looking gipsies suddenly swarmed into the grounds from the woodlands and quickly surrounded him. Seeing in these lawless gipsies a possible means of safety, Thaddeus begged them to let him join the band; and their leader, a light-hearted clever rogue aptly named Devilshoof, willingly agreed, being pleased with the good looks and boldness of the hapless fugitive.

As his new friends hastily stripped off his torn uniform and dressed him in gay gipsy garb, a sealed parchment fell to the ground. This document Thaddeus snatched up and concealed in his bosom. It was his commission, and the sole proof he now possessed of his noble birth.

Scarcely was his disguise completed than the pursuing Austrian soldiers arrived in the grounds, demanding news of the fugitive; but the wily Devilshoof was equal to the occasion. He declared that he had seen the runaway Polish officer making for a hill-side in the opposite direction; and as the soldiers dashed away on this wild-goose chase, the gipsies crowded triumphantly about their new comrade—Devilshoof, in particular, swearing to befriend him all his life.

Just then, there came excited cries from some of the merry-makers in the woodlands, who came running forth with the distressing news that the little Arline was being attacked by an infuriated stag. Without a moment's thought for himself, the chivalrous Thaddeus snatched up a gun from a seat near by and rushed off to her aid. He quickly reached the spot and killed the maddened animal; and then he returned to the grounds with the rescued child and her terrified attendant.

The Count was quickly on the scene and poured grateful thanks upon the pretended gipsy for having saved his beloved child; and after the little Arline had been taken into the castle to have a wounded arm bound up, he invited him to join in the festivities and to refresh himself with food and drink. Being exhausted, Thaddeus gladly accepted the invitation. When, however, he was handed a goblet of wine and asked to drink to the health of the Emperor, he proudly refused to do so and shattered the goblet at the feet of the royal statue.

Instantly there was a wild commotion, and the indignant guests would have slain Thaddeus had not Devilshoof rushed forward to the aid of his new comrade. At a sign from Count Arnheim, however, the two gipsies were separated and marched off in different directions by the retainers and huntsmen. Thaddeus was led away towards the woods, where he soon managed to break away from his captors and escaped to his gipsy friends; and Devilshoof was taken into the castle and locked in an upper room.

But Devilshoof was a slippery customer; and quickly making his escape through a window to the castle roof, he took a terrible revenge for his capture. Finding the room where little Arline was resting after her alarming adventure, he snatched up the child; then, making his way along a deserted passage, he escaped through a side door with his prize.

When, presently, the guests caught sight of Devilshoof, with Arline in his arms, hastening across a bridge that separated the castle grounds from the country-side, they gave chase and fired at him; but the cunning gipsy defiantly held up the child before him as a screen, and the pursuers were helpless. With a final triumphant yell, Devilshoof vanished into the depths of the forest, leaving confusion and dismay behind him; and the unhappy Count's heart was bowed down with grief for the loss of his beloved child.

Twelve years later, after many wanderings, the gipsy band once more encamped on the outskirts of Presburg. With them came Arline, now grown up into a beautiful young woman. The gipsies had brought her up as a member of their tribe, and she had no knowledge of her true birth. Their secret was known to none but Devilshoof and Thaddeus, both of whom kept it to themselves for their own sakes. Still a proscribed exile, Thaddeus had remained with the gipsies; and, as the years passed by, he and Arline had fallen in love. They now only awaited the pleasure of the gipsy queen, their tribal chief, to join their hands in marriage. But the gipsy queen was jealous, for she also loved the handsome Thaddeus; and she had not yet granted their request.

One night, soon after their return to the district, some of the gipsies, headed by the bold Devilshoof, accosted a party of drunken revellers returning late from an inn. Among the latter was Florestein, the nephew of Count Arnheim; and, instantly recognizing him, Devilshoof took particular pleasure in robbing him of a very richly-jewelled medallion he was wearing. His pleasure was short-lived, however.

Suddenly, a cloaked figure appeared, and the robbers fell back in dismay as they recognized in the newcomer their own beautiful chief, of whom they stood in the greatest awe. With an imperious gesture, the gipsy queen commanded her errant followers to return all the money and jewels of which they had just robbed the roisterers. Very sheepishly and reluctantly, they obeyed their ruler—with the exception of Devilshoof, who had slyly slipped away with his own prize as she arrived on the scene. When the Queen was told that Devilshoof had gone off with the most valuable jewel of all, she cunningly determined to make him give this up to her later on and to use it for her own purposes. She then returned to the camp with her crestfallen followers.

Meanwhile, Arline and Thaddeus were talking together happily in the moonlight just outside the tent of the gipsy queen. Arline was describing to her lover a strange dream she had just awakened from. She had dreamt that she dwelt in marble halls, amidst great riches and splendour, bearing a high ancestral name; that countless suitors sought her hand; but that, best of all, Thaddeus still loved her just the same.

When her story came to an end, she begged her lover to tell her the secret of her birth. She felt that he knew it, for he had already told her that a certain scar upon her arm had been caused by the attack of a maddened stag, from which danger he had himself rescued her years ago. For answer, however, Thaddeus only showered kisses upon her; for he knew that if he disclosed her true birth they must be parted for ever.

While they were thus folded in each other's arms, the gipsy queen suddenly returned. Furiously jealous at this charming spectacle, the gipsy ruler angrily demanded how the young girl dared aspire to the love of one who was the chosen lover of her queen. But Arline was not afraid of her rival's anger; and as Thaddeus proudly led her forward, while the other gipsies clustered around, she declared that it was their desire to be wedded.

Then Devilshoof, whose puckish delight it was to make mischief and to stir up jealousy, reminded the queen that it was her duty and obligation as ruler of the tribe to join the hands of those of her subjects who desired to be united; and the queen, afraid of losing her authority should she refuse, came slowly forward and haughtily placed the hand of Arline in that of Thaddeus, according to the gipsy custom of betrothal.

But she was full of inward rage and disappointment; and when the newly-betrothed lovers presently wandered off arm-in-arm, she turned upon the triumphantly smiling Devilshoof, and, passionately accusing him of having brought this evil hour upon her, declared that she would pardon him only on condition he yielded up to her the jewelled medallion he had stolen that night.

And now, Devilshoof himself was cornered; for, though he feared naught else, he dared not disobey the queen of his tribe, lest she should cast him forth as an outcast wanderer—an evil fate which no true gipsy cares to contemplate. Very reluctantly, therefore, he delivered up the medallion, as requested; but he vowed vengeance as he strode angrily away. The gipsy queen also thought of revenge; and as she hid the jewel in her dress, she laid a cunning plan for bringing trouble upon her rival by means of it.

Next day a great fair was held in Presburg, and all the gipsy tribe went to join in the revels. As Arline danced and sang with her companions for the amusement of the holiday-makers, she was secretly dogged by the gipsy queen, who soon found a chance for the downfall of her rival. Observing that Arline had successfully repulsed the unwelcome advances of Count Arnheim's foolish nephew, Florestein, who was once more among the revellers, she drew her aside and fastened the jewelled medallion around her neck as a reward for her very proper conduct. This evil ruse was instantly successful.

As Arline danced away merrily with the other Bohemian maids, she was once more accosted by the half-tipsy Florestein who, seeing that she was now wearing his jewelled medallion and eager to bring trouble upon one who had repulsed his advances, loudly accused her of having stolen the ornament from him. Arline indignantly defended herself; but, at the authoritative command of Florestein, she was quickly seized by the town guards and borne off to the Hall of Justice.

Here Count Arnheim sat, waiting to do justice on those offenders who should be brought before him that day; for his high position made him the Chief Judge of the district. The twelve years that had passed had aged him greatly; for all his efforts to trace his kidnapped daughter had been in vain, though he had never given up hope of finding her. He was thinking of her now, as the captured gipsy girl was dragged before him.

As the swaggering self-satisfied Florestein approached his uncle and accused Arline of having stolen his jewelled medallion, something in the beauty and innocent looks of the young girl so vigorously defending herself caused his heart to stir strangely within him. The chords of his memory were further touched as she continued to protest her innocence; and when the lovely gipsy presently drew a dagger and proudly declared that she would rather die than be accused of common theft, he sprang forward and seized her by the arm.

His action was so sudden that Arline's loose sleeve slipped back and revealed the rough scar upon her upper arm; and, tremblingly, the Count demanded how she had come by such a mark.

Full of surprise at his tone, Arline repeated the story of the maddened stag told her by Thaddeus; and Count Arnheim, knowing now beyond a doubt that this beautiful gipsy maiden was indeed his kidnapped child, clasped her in his arms with frantic joy, declaring to all the astonished bystanders that she was none other than his own beloved daughter.

. . . .

The pretty Arline was quickly restored to the high position to which she had been born; and very soon afterwards the proud and happy Count invited all the neighbouring nobility to a magnificent ball and banquet, that he might introduce his beloved daughter to his friends in fitting style.

On the night of the ball, however, Arline, now richly dressed and bejewelled, slipped away from her admiring guests and stood alone for a few moments in one of the splendid salons of the castle, feeling sad as she thought of her faithful lover, Thaddeus. She knew that, much as she already loved her newly-found and devoted father, she would never be really happy in her present gorgeous surroundings unless Thaddeus could be with her. She knew, too, that her foolish cousin, Florestein, whom she greatly despised, was already petitioning her hand in marriage; and she longed to escape from his importunities.

With a heavy sigh, her thoughts turned quickly to the free and happy past as she moved to return to her father's guests; and at that moment, Devilshoof, the gipsy, stepped through a window opening on to the balcony beyond, followed closely by Thaddeus himself. Instantly, the lovers were in each others' arms, swearing eternal fidelity. Almost immediately afterwards, the sound of approaching guests was heard; and Arline, realizing that this was not an appropriate time to present her gipsy lover to her father, hastily thrust Thaddeus into a curtained recess, whilst Devilshoof escaped through the window. In another moment, Count Arnheim entered the salon with a group of newly-arrived guests and, with a proud smile, took Arline by the hand and introduced her to his noble friends.

Meanwhile, the happy meeting between the parted lovers had been jealously watched by the gipsy queen from the balcony window; for she still loved Thaddeus and followed him closely wherever he went. Now, with bitter rage in her heart, she determined to make another attempt to discredit her innocent rival. She slipped into the salon through the window and approached Count Arnheim, to whom she revealed the compromising fact that his fair daughter's gipsy lover was even now concealed in the room.

As Thaddeus stepped forth from the alcove, the Count, bitterly disappointed, poured forth indignant reproaches upon the daughter he now felt to be unworthy of his love; but Arline fell on her knees before him, declaring that she would rather die than be parted from her beloved Thaddeus. When, however, the Count only exclaimed the more against the disgrace to his name should his daughter wed with an outcast gipsy, the ancestral pride of Thaddeus could no longer be restrained.

Caring naught for his own personal danger, he now haughtily declared himself to be of equally pure and noble birth as the Count himself, even though he wore the garb of a gipsy. He then told the whole story of his exile from Poland and his reason for joining the gipsy tribe; then, drawing forth his now priceless commission, from which he had never been parted, he handed it to the Count as the proof of his statement.

Count Arnheim was greatly moved by the sad story told by the exile who had once saved the life of his daughter; and when he had glanced at the commission parchment and read therein that Thaddeus was indeed of noble birth, he took him by the hand, saying that the feuds of their countries should now be forgotten and that they should be friends. He then placed Arline's hand in that of Thaddeus, and the lovers embraced with great joy.

While this happy scene was taking place, the queen of the gipsies, furious at the turn events were taking, had gone in search of a young gipsy she knew to be devoted to her service. Bidding the youth bring his musket and follow her, she once more crept round to the open window of the salon. With eyes gleaming with jealous hate, she watched for a moment the second embrace of the now joyful lovers; then, in a transport of rage, she bade the gipsy youth shoot Thaddeus instantly.

But Devilshoof had also followed closely upon her track, suspecting her murderous design upon the man with whom he had sworn eternal friendship; and, just as the musket was raised, by a dexterous movement, he diverted the young gipsy's aim and turned the muzzle upon the queen herself. There was a loud report and a shriek; and the queen of the gipsies fell to the ground, slain by the shot she had intended for her victim.

THE SEAL-WOMAN *Bantock*

THE moon was rising over the wild rocky coast of an islet in the Western Hebrides. It was midsummer, the time of enchantment and spells; and, though the islet was uninhabited, strange, sweet voices were plainly heard by the Cailleach, a lonely old crone, who sat on a low rock in the shadow of a cliff.

The Cailleach had spent the day on this lovely wild islet, and now awaited the return of the fishermen, whose boat would presently come round the bend of the bay to pick her up and carry her back with them to the mainland.

For this old crone was none other than the Hebridean poetess, Mary McClead, who had spent the whole of her life wandering from isle to isle, seeking material for the sweet songs she made and for which she was famous. The fishermen all knew her well; and to-day three of them were to call for her in the late evening at the turn of the tide by the Seal-Woman's Rock, where she now awaited them.

Though no other human being sat on this lonely rock, the old crone knew that she was not alone. True, none but the seals ever came thither—but were not the seals enchanted Princesses? Two of them, at least, she knew to be the spell-bound children of the King of Lochlann. Because these fair Princesses had been the happy possessors of greater beauty, wisdom, and courage than her own, their stepmother had become jealous of them; and so, having studied magic for many years, she had transformed the lovely sisters into seals.

Thrice every year these enchanted Princesses were permitted to cast aside their seal-robes and to become mortals again for a brief spell, until the next returning tide, when they must depart once more to their seal kith and kin in the sea. If, however, their seal-robes should be stolen or hidden away during the short time of their transformation, then must they remain mortal.

Well did the Cailleach know the spell-bound royal Seal-Sisters by the kingly look in their eyes. She was usually glad when they were about; but to-night when she heard their crooning songs at the back of the rock she sat upon, she felt a curious foreboding of some strange happenings about to befall.

She was relieved, therefore, when she saw the fishermen's boat drawn up on the shore some little distance away; for she knew they would presently arrive at her own lonely rock.

Meanwhile, the two fishermen and the Islesman, who was their companion, landed, the former to fetch some fishing-gear and the latter to set fresh nets. The Islesman bade the fishermen not to linger about their job, but to return at the turn of the tide. But his companions merely laughed at this warning, declaring that it was the Islesman himself who was more likely to be late, since he was known to be an incorrigible dreamer, ever seeing visions of lovely sea-maidens whom he longed to meet in the flesh.

This was true. When his friends had departed on their errand, the romantic young Islesman sat down on a rock and, while mending his net, sang a soft crooning love-song. He had a longing in his heart to behold the beautiful Seal-Woman of whom he had heard such charming legends and whom he desired to win as his bride. Then, reluctantly putting away from his mind such colourful thoughts for the time being, he hurried away to set his nets.

But his fate was nearer than he imagined. No sooner had the Islesman vanished into the shadows than the enchanted Seal-Woman and her young Seal-Sister appeared from behind the rocks and began to sing their wild sweet songs. Then, startled by the sudden return of the two fishermen, they hid behind the rocks once more.

Their song, however, had again been heard by the old crone, who now welcomed the two fishermen as they approached and invited her to get into their boat. They grumbled because the Islesman had not yet appeared, knowing well enough that he was probably still mooning about and dreaming of the mystic sea-maids he was always hoping to meet. As the tide was already on the turn, however, they decided to row away at once with the Cailleach and to return in the early morning for their errant companion.

When the boat had vanished out of sight, the Seal-Woman and her Seal-Sister appeared once more, now revealing themselves as lovely human maidens, since this was one of their hours of mortality. They were careful to leave their fur-covered seal-robes near the rock in readiness to be donned once more when they wished to return to the sea—since they would be earth-bound without them.

Then they sang songs and danced together gaily in the moonlight; and they talked about the spell of enchantment that still bound them and of their dual nature in which the Call of the Sea struggled constantly with their longing for mortal love.

So far, the Call of the Sea had always been the stronger, and was so still in the younger Seal-Sister, who never wished to be away from her seal kith and kin for long. But the elder sister, the beautiful Seal-Woman, knew of the inner longing of the mystic young Islesman to win her as his bride, ever since he had once beheld her bathing in the cove—and she already cherished a secret love for him, even though she knew that if she gave herself to a mortal lover her present life of joyous freedom must come to an end.

She was, therefore, disturbed and full of foreboding to-night, remembering the sad fate of a Water-Kelpie who had loved a mortal maid, only to be deserted by her.

While the Seal-Sisters were thus employing their precious mortal hour in singing and dancing and telling wonder-tales, the young Islesman returned from his wanderings and stood beside their discarded seal-robes, watching their movements with fascinated joy in his heart before they noticed his presence.

As soon as they beheld him, however, the transformed maidens tried to hide themselves once more; but the Islesman eagerly besought them to remain and to have no fear of him, pouring forth words of admiration for their loveliness.

While speaking thus, he trod upon the seal-robes lying at his feet; and as he lifted up the soft fur garments in amazement, the little Seal-Sister called out in fear and begged him not to keep their robes from them or they would be unable to return to the sea.

Then the Seal-Woman explained to the enthralled Islesman that they were indeed the enchanted daughters of the King of Lochlann, Seal-Maidens torn between their Sea-Madness and their Earth-Longing. That very night was one of the three times in the year when, at the full moon, they were compelled to return temporarily to their mortal state. Their time was already about to expire, but they would not be able to return to the sea unless he gave them back their magic seal-robes, in which case they must remain for seven years as mortals, a sad fate they did not desire.

The little Seal-Sister was already filled with despair at this thought; and she now passionately begged the Islesman to withhold no longer their precious seal-robes from them, since she was longing to get back to the laughter of the sea-breezes and the swirling joy of the waves.

But the Islesman, dazed by this magical visitation, could not take his burning gaze from the beauty of the Seal-Woman, whose long dark hair, pale face, and sea-blue eyes enthralled him; and he passionately besought her to stay with him and become his bride.

The Seal-Woman, though drawn to him in spite of herself by the strange mortal love that had already so quickly blossomed in her heart, knew that her ever-present sea-madness would never let her rest content for long in a mortal's arms; and she begged to be allowed to return to the sea. The Seal-Sister next tried coaxing, promising to provide rich hauls of fishes for his nets if only he would give up the seal-robes he now held so closely.

Then the Islesman, in his turn, pleaded for his own happiness to be considered. He had dreamed all his life of a lovely sea-maiden bride; and now, having found her and knowing that she returned his love, was he to be deprived of his joy?

Seizing the already half-yielding Seal-Woman by the arm, he now declared that if she would remain with him, her sister should go free. Hearing this, the Seal-Woman no longer hesitated, for she indeed truly loved this mortal who wooed her so passionately; and she bade him give her sister the seal-robe which was hers.

Gladly the Islesman tossed one of the seal-robes to the Seal-Sister, who quickly wrapped it around her and instantly plunged joyfully into the sea, singing a song of farewell from the waves.

Then the Islesman, realizing the sacrifice she had made for his happiness, knelt adoringly at the feet of the beautiful being who was to be his bride; and the Seal-Woman smiled joyfully upon him, for she also had chosen happiness in the arms of her mortal lover.

.   .   .   .

Seven years had gone by, and once more the Cailleach sat waiting for the return of the fishermen's boat. But now she sat outside the dwelling of the Islesman, though about to return to her own island.

When the fishermen arrived, she sang songs to them, and was

delighted when they declared them to be as sweet as any she had made in the days of her youth. Then, when the fishermen had gone to get their boat ready for departure, the old crone fell asleep and dreamed that she was visited by three Swan-Maidens, who also sang sweet songs to her.

From this pleasant dream she was awakened by the Islesman, who bade her welcome, and said his beloved wife would shortly return from her task of milking the cattle, when there would be a drink of warm milk for their honoured guest. He spoke very tenderly of his beautiful but mysterious sea-wife and of the love and sweet companionship she had always given in return to him and their fair child, Morag; and he begged the old crone to tell her island friends of his great happiness.

As he spoke, the Seal-Woman now appeared, with a pitcher of warm new milk, of which she begged the Cailleach to partake; and having greeted her tenderly, the Islesman departed to continue his work at the peat-stack, where he was piling up new peat and where the child, Morag, was playing as he worked.

The Seal-Woman and the old crone had a pleasant talk together; and they spoke of the seven years of true happiness which his sea-maiden bride had brought to the Islesman.

But the Seal-Woman added that her constant sea-longing had of late grown stronger, causing her sometimes to fear the future; and the Cailleach then uttered a blessing and prayed that no harm should befall this happy but humble home.

Soon the fishermen came to announce that their boat was ready; and the old crone went away with them, again calling down blessings upon her kind friends.

Left alone for a while, the Seal-Woman busied herself at her spinning-wheel, which she brought to the open doorway of her cottage home, singing a crooning spinning-song to accompany her skilful hands. Presently, however, she stopped and began to think once more of the strange sea-longing which now so constantly beset her after her seven long years of happiness. As she was wondering whether this " wound ", as she described it, would bring sadness to those she loved, her husband and their child Morag appeared, the Islesman having now finished his work at the peat-stack.

The pretty Morag ran happily towards her mother, who eagerly embraced her; but when she had enjoyed a drink of warm milk, the child ran back to play a little longer by the peat-stack.

For a while, the Islesman talked tenderly with his beloved wife, suggesting that, later on, when their child was in bed, they would wander down to the sea-shore, hand-in-hand, lovers still. Then he, too, went off to attend to his boat; and once more the Seal-Woman was left alone.

And now the spell-bound Princess could no longer keep back the secret shadow that had gradually been enveloping her soul—that her sea-madness was stronger than ever in her blood, bringing with it a passionate longing for her seal kith and kin which she now knew she could not withstand. Soon she was once more thinking rapturously of the blueness of the rippling waves and of the emerald depths into which she had once loved to dive—a joy she longed to recapture. Even as she stood thinking thus, she heard the magic call of her Seal-Sister and of her other seal kith and kin calling to her to return to them; and she was filled with foreboding.

At that moment the child Morag ran up again to the doorway towards her mother, carrying a cloak-like garment in her arms, which she excitedly declared she had found hidden behind the peat-stack as she played there. It was the seal-robe of the Seal-Woman, which the Islesman had hidden in that spot seven years ago, hoping it would never be found but not having had the heart to destroy it.

The finding of her long-lost seal-robe proved to the already distracted Seal-Woman that her forebodings were justified. This was fate, indeed; and she must act swiftly before the Islesman returned from his boat. The Call of the Sea was stronger than the Call of Mortal Love.

She passionately embraced the wondering Morag; then, wrapping the seal-robe closely around her, she hurried away towards the sea.

Now seeing her father returning from his boat, Morag ran to greet him; and at that moment, as the Islesman and his child stood together, hand-in-hand, the Seal-Woman appeared upon the cliff-top, outlined against the clear evening sky. As the Islesman gazed upon the scene, despairing but powerless, his lovely sea-bride, with an exultant cry, leapt joyfully into the waves. As a dream she had come; and as a dream she had passed out of his life for ever.

But the fair child Morag remained; and in Morag the deserted Islesman knew that his beloved Seal-Woman would live again to bring comfort to his sad heart.

FIDELIO
Beethoven

ONE warm summer day, during the eighteenth century, the sun was shining brightly in the courtyard of a certain Spanish prison fortress not very far from the city of Seville. Within this fortress there languished a number of political prisoners, several of whom, though innocent of crime, were the victims of despotic power, pining in captivity because some private enemy refused to speak the word that would have set them at liberty.

Among these innocent captives was a certain Don Florestan, a nobleman who, having had the misfortune to offend Don Pizarro, the Governor of the fortress, had been accused by him of some slight political misdemeanour and thrust into one of the deepest dungeons of the castle. Having thus got his hated enemy into his power, the crafty Governor let it be imagined that he had died shortly afterwards, so that he should not be released when his short term of imprisonment was over. Then, by keeping him closely chained in the deepest dungeon and slowly starving him, he hoped that the wretched man would really die eventually and that his own private vengeance would thus be satisfied without resort to actual violence.

However, his subtle plan was to be frustrated from an unexpected source. Don Florestan had a beautiful young wife, the Lady Leonora, who loved her husband with the utmost devotion. Suspecting that the report of his death was a false one, she determined to learn the truth at all costs and, if he still lived, to rescue him from the hands of his unscrupulous enemy.

Being of a brave and heroic disposition, Leonora was not afraid to risk her life for the sake of the man she loved; and she decided to carry out an adventurous plan in the disguise of a youth. Having donned plain and simple masculine attire, therefore, she boldly made her way to the fortress in which her husband pined in captivity. Having gained access to the chief jailer, she humbly requested the latter to engage her as his assistant, giving her name as Fidelio. In this way she hoped that she would at least learn how Don Florestan was faring, and possibly be able to find some means of escape for him.

Rocco, the jailer, being greatly struck with the pleasant looks and manners of the supposed youth, very willingly took the latter into his service; and since the new assistant was neat-handed, useful and obliging, he quickly became a favourite with all within the castle—to the great chagrin, however, of Jacquino, another youthful assistant who, being clumsy and somewhat dull, now found himself quite out of favour. Until now, young Jacquino had been smiled upon by the jailer's pretty daughter, Marcellina, who had been willing enough to look upon him as a possible sweetheart in the absence of a more dashing suitor; but the coming of Fidelio changed all that. The saucy Marcellina soon showed a preference for the newcomer, whose handsome face and air of melancholy attracted her fancy, causing her to treat her old sweetheart with disdain; and on discovering that his master, Rocco, also favoured his daughter's new choice, he felt more aggrieved still.

The disguised Leonora was greatly embarrassed by the coquettish behaviour of Marcellina, still more so on finding herself being looked upon as a likely son-in-law by Rocco. Although she had tried to ingratiate herself with the jailer's pretty daughter for her own dangerous purposes, she did not wish to pain the maiden in any way, nor upset the prospects of the jealous Jacquino.

However, she succeeded in hiding her embarrassment for the time being; and, by making herself more and more useful to Rocco, she gradually drew nearer to her goal. Although she was soon permitted to help with work connected with the more favoured prisoners, Rocco refused for a long time to let this new youthful assistant visit the deeper dungeons, declaring that the unhappy inmates of these dread abodes were no suitable sight for one so young. But, by judicial persistence, Leonora at last gained her heart's desire.

On the bright summer day upon which this story opens, the pretended youth, Fidelio, had persuaded the jailer, much against his will, to allow some of the more privileged captives to walk for a short time in the courtyard, that they might enjoy a breath of fresh air and sunshine; but the grateful pleasure of the chained prisoners was short-lived. Pizarro, the cruel Governor, unexpectedly appeared on the scene; and enraged by the spectacle of the captives walking in the courtyard, he poured forth angry abuse upon Rocco for daring to permit such an unorthodox act of mercy. The jailer, however, stopped this outburst by reminding Pizarro of the dark deeds he had assisted him to do in the past; and anxious to keep on good terms with one who knew so many of his wicked secrets, the Governor ceased to bluster, but gave orders for the captives to be locked up again.

When this had been done and Fidelio had also been dismissed, Don Pizarro tried to persuade Rocco to help him in the performance of yet another dark deed. Having received a despatch warning him that Don Fernando, a high Minister of State, intended to visit the fortress that same evening in the belief that certain victims of despotic power were still unjustly held captive there, the guilty Governor was filled with alarm. Not knowing how he should account for the presence of Don Florestan, so long believed to be dead, he decided to kill his hated victim within the next few hours. However, he did not intend to do this dreadful deed himself, if possible, but, instead, to make Rocco his instrument of vengeance.

Carelessly handing a purse of gold to the jailer, he hinted darkly that he desired the death of Don Florestan, the wretched captive now languishing in the deepest dungeon; but Rocco, recoiling from the thought of such cold-blooded murder, refused to do the deed. Then, afraid of going too far against the wishes of his unscrupulous superior by such sudden squeamishness, he reluctantly agreed to dig the victim's grave on condition that Pizarro himself struck the fatal blow. With this offer the Governor had to be content; and the two went their separate ways, having first laid their plans and arranged that the grave should be dug beneath an old disused cistern at the side of Don Florestan's dungeon.

Meanwhile, Leonora, having suspected from the dark looks of Pizarro that he intended ill to someone, had crept back to the courtyard, where she had remained hidden in such a position that she could overhear the conversation between the Governor and Rocco. Horrified on thus learning of the violent death so soon destined for her beloved husband, she determined to attempt a last-minute rescue of him even at the risk of her own life; and, reckless of danger, she hurried after Rocco, in order to be with him wherever he should go, so that she might wreck the dastardly plot.

Rocco, having little time in which to carry out his gruesome task, had no choice but to make use of his new assistant; and bidding the young Fidelio bring spades and pickaxes and follow him, he led the way to the deepest dungeon where the doomed captive lay.

Little dreaming that the one person in all the world he most longed to see, his beloved wife, was even now approaching, Don Florestan lay suffering upon the floor of his horrible cell, with despair in his heart; for he had been so long without food and was so terribly exhausted that he knew death could not be far off. Even now, however, the image of his beautiful Leonora shone brightly in his heart; and every now and again he would breathe her name tenderly or call out a passionate greeting to her, thinking in his wandering delirium that she indeed stood before him.

Just as he sank back after one of these flights of feverish fancy, Rocco the jailer entered the dungeon, followed by the trembling Leonora, who shivered as she felt the chill, damp air of the subterranean cell and glanced apprehensively at the huddled form on the ground. Rocco at once proceeded to the disused cistern situated at one side of the dungeon and, taking up his spade and pickaxe, began to dig the grave, calling to his assistant to do likewise. He spoke in gruff, but not unkindly tones, thinking that the youth's evident reluctance to begin the horrid task was due to the softness natural to his tender years, rather than to any deeper feeling.

At length, however, Leonora, in order to keep up her disguise, took her spade and began to assist in the work; but every now and again she turned her eyes upon the crouching form of the wretched captive, who appeared to be sleeping.

Presently, however, Don Florestan raised his head and addressed the jailer; and Leonora, at last beholding the pale, cadaverous face of her beloved husband and hearing his voice after so many sad months of absence, was so overcome that she sank back in a swoon. Rocco, not noticing the agitation of his assistant, approached the prisoner, who demanded, as he had already done in vain many times before, the name of the tyrant whose cruelty thus doomed him to a living death. Rocco, knowing that the unfortunate man was to die within that same hour, felt that there could now be no harm in granting this request; and he told Florestan that his enemy was none other than Don Pizarro himself, the Governor of the fortress.

The name of Pizarro recalled Leonora's wandering senses; and, still keeping her face hidden from Florestan, she tried to persuade Rocco to let her give the captive some bread she had brought with her for this purpose. Though the jailer at first refused, his own pity for the wretched prisoner at length got the better of him, and he gave his consent, even making him drink a little wine from a small flagon he had himself brought.

No sooner had Florestan eagerly partaken of the welcome food and drink, which quickly brought back some little strength to his emaciated frame, than the dreaded Pizarro entered the dungeon, his first words being to bid Rocco send his youthful assistant away. Leonora, however, though she pretended to obey, retired only into the shadows of the dungeon, and when the wicked Pizarro drew his dagger and sprang forward towards the captive, intending to stab him to the heart, she flung herself upon him and bade him desist. Then, as Pizarro, taken by surprise, drew back, she boldly declared herself to be the wife of his intended victim.

Florestan, now beholding the face of the supposed youth for the first time, was amazed to recognize his beloved Leonora; and full of joy even in this awful moment of mortal danger, the long-separated husband and wife embraced tenderly.

Pizarro, enraged at this untimely interruption of his evil plan and knowing that he had little time to lose, since his superior officer would arrive very shortly, again sprang forward, intending to wreak his vengeance upon both; but Leonora, in a flash, drew forth a loaded pistol she had concealed in her tunic and, covering him with it, declared she would fire if he moved a step farther.

Chagrined and completely nonplussed at this sudden turning of the tables upon him, Pizarro stood helpless, glaring furiously upon the brave Leonora; and as they stood thus, the sound of a trumpet was heard. Next moment, the young Jacquino, accompanied by several officers of the castle, appeared in the doorway, announcing that Don Fernando, the Minister, had just arrived and demanded an immediate interview with the Governor of the prison.

Pizarro, baulked of his prey and feeling that disaster was about to fall upon him, yet not daring to disobey the urgent command of his superior officer, turned angrily on his heel and left the cell.

When their enemy had left them, Florestan and Leonora again fell into each other's arms and rejoiced together, full of gladness at meeting once more and hoping that their troubles would now soon come to an end. Then, as soon as the exhausted nobleman had sufficiently recovered, Rocco escorted them both to the large court of the castle. Here, the Minister, Don Fernando, surrounded by soldiers and officers, was receiving the grateful thanks of many captives whom he had already ordered to be set free, knowing that they had been kept unjustly in bonds.

The jailer, now eager to bring his cruel master into disgrace, led Florestan and Leonora forward at once, appealing to the Minister for justice for them; and Don Fernando, astonished at thus beholding the rescued nobleman, whom all had believed to be dead, received him with great kindness and gave him a hearty welcome. Then, when he was told the whole story of Pizarro's infamous plot and how it had been frustrated by the intended victim's brave wife, he declared that Florestan was free from that moment; and he added that Leonora herself, the fearless Fidelio, should have the joy of removing the chains that had been put upon him so injustly.

When this pleasant task had been performed by the now happy Leonora, the whole assemblage were able to rejoice together, for all were glad at the downfall of the tyrant Pizarro, who had already been led away, now a captive himself. The released prisoners were glad because they were at liberty once more; Jacquino was glad because the attractive Fidelio could no longer rival him as a suitor to the pretty Marcellina; Rocco was pleased at the prospect of a new and less alarming master; and Florestan and his faithful Leonora were the most joyful of all, since they were restored to each other and a life of happiness.

NORMA   *Bellini*

IN Ancient Gaul, the Druids had gathered the people together in one of the Sacred Oak Temple Groves for a solemn ceremony.

The Roman invaders must be driven forth by a great uprising. Too long had the Gauls submitted to the power of Rome. There was now a sign of weakness to be noticed in the plans of the invading armies; and this was the time to strike a blow for freedom.

The signal for war could be given only by their beloved and powerful High Priestess, Norma, from the altar, after she had performed the sacred ceremony of cutting the mistletoe. All was ready for war, and they only awaited the signal.

But Norma still hesitated. With the golden sickle in her hand, after cutting the sacred bough, she refrained from giving the expected signal to the surprised people. Instead, the beautiful High Priestess—who was also a prophetess and the interpreter to the people of the will of their gods and oracles—declared that the time was not yet ripe for attempting to shake off the shackles of Rome. The oracle had revealed to her that this unwelcome fact was the will of the gods.

Then Norma went on sternly to denounce the Druids for their warlike blood-lust; and she prophesied that the Roman menace would presently vanish of its own accord. Already there were signs of internal dissension and weakness in Rome, which would increase until that mighty Empire fell.

When the Druids and people had retired from the Sacred

Grove, not entirely satisfied with her strange revelation of the oracle's message, Norma remained at the altar and prayed to the gods concerning a personal matter—for the return to her arms of the lover who had deserted her. For his sake she was averting the declaration of war.

For Norma had a dread secret which, so far, she had kept safely hidden from the knowledge of her people. Two or three years previously, she had conceived an unlawful passion for Pollione, the Roman Pro-Consul in Gaul, to whom, breaking her priestess vows of chastity and celibacy, she had become united and had borne two sons. Until recently, her happiness had been idyllic, since she loved the Roman soldier with all the intensity of a passionate nature. She and her enemy lover met in a secret part of her Temple home; and here her babes had been born and kept safely hidden from all but one faithful attendant.

Then, to her grief, Pollione began to visit her less frequently; and Norma, fearing she had a rival in his affections, but loving him still, prayed constantly for his return. But all to no avail.

Pollione, indeed, had already tired of Norma. He had now won the love of another young and lovely priestess, Adalgisa, whom he hoped to persuade to return to Rome with him on his now imminent recall thither.

But Adalgisa, though at first willing enough to abandon her religious vows, was soon troubled by her conscience—also by her deep reverence and devoted love for the High Priestess Norma, whom she did not wish to offend or distress by her sacrilege.

At last she felt impelled to confess to the latter the sinful passion she had conceived and her temptation to break her Temple vows; and this she did, with tears and prayers for forgiveness.

Norma, rendered the more sympathetic by her own unlawful love, was at first willing to release the young priestess from the Temple vows and even to find a means for the escape of the lovers. When, however, she discovered that Adalgisa's lover and her own were one and the same person, her sympathy changed to wrath and despair.

Rushing back to her secret apartment, Norma, in the madness of her grief, was about to slay the two little ones born to her and the faithless Pollione. But when the helpless babes awakened and smiled in her face, her maternal love for them rendered her incapable of doing such a deed.

While she wept over her children, Adalgisa, having followed her, entered to crave her forgiveness. The unhappy Norma now begged her rival to take the babes and deliver them safely into their father's keeping; for she, the sacrilegious High Priestess, now intended to expiate her sin upon the funeral pyre—this being the lawful punishment for those who broke their Temple vows.

But Adalgisa was horrified at such a terrible resolution. Her own lifelong devotion to Norma was even stronger than her unlawful love for the faithless Roman; and she now declared that she would try to persuade Pollione to return to his first love and to make her happy once more.

Pollione, however, enthralled by his new passion, refused to listen to the pleas of Adalgisa that he should renounce her and return to the mother of his children. Instead, he now attempted to snatch Adalgisa away by force, while she was actually serving in the Temple, hoping to carry her off to a vessel on the shore already awaiting his orders to sail for the coast of Italy. His sacrilegious act, however, was discovered, and he was captured.

And now, Norma, with the fury of a woman scorned, combined with the patriotic fervour she had suppressed so long, passionately struck the sacred shield that summoned the Druids and people to the Temple Grove. This was likewise the long-awaited signal for war.

When the people had gathered together at this clarion call, filled with fierce joy that at last they were to be allowed to rise against their Roman invaders, their joy quickly changed to horror and dismay.

When Pollione was brought for judgment before the High Priestess, Norma's anger against him quickly faded; for she still loved him. Now anxious to save him from the consequences of his rash act, she first of all demanded that he should renounce Adalgisa, when she would set him free. This he firmly refused to do.

Thus realizing that Pollione's love for her had indeed vanished, Norma was now determined to encompass her own death. Commanding the priests and votaries of the Temple to draw nearer, she announced to them that one of their own priestesses had broken her sacred vows of chastity; and she begged them to condemn the sinner to death.

Howls of execration broke forth at this announcement, all the people calling for the immediate death of the impious priestess. A huge pyre had already been built for an animal sacrifice in honour of the call to arms, and the furious Druids now demanded a human sacrifice instead. Let the sinful virgin mount the pyre.

Then, to their astonishment and grief, Norma snatched from her brow the sacred wreath of oak-leaves she wore as the symbol of her office and announced that she herself was the erring one;

and woeful groans broke out, for the High Priestess was beloved and revered by all.

Norma faced her people proudly, with sad resignation, and confessing the story of her sin to her sorrowing father, the Chief Druid, she entreated him to care for her lonely babes. Then, fearlessly, she mounted the pyre, which had already been set alight, and, spreading forth her hands, prayed to the gods for forgiveness.

But Norma did not die alone. When Pollione, her Roman lover, thus beheld her noble renunciation and generous shielding of her youthful rival, he felt a deep remorse and shame for his own faithless conduct, and his dormant love for the beautiful High Priestess revived. He now rushed forward and confessed before all his own share in her guilt. Then he calmly mounted the pyre and stood beside her, clasping her in his arms as the flames leapt up and encircled them both.

Thus, Norma, the High Priestess of Gaul, and her Roman lover were re-united in death.

I PURITANI   *Bellini*
(*The Puritans*)

DURING the great Civil War between the royal House of Stuart and the English Parliament, at the time when Charles II was a fugitive, the fortress of Plymouth was held by the Parliamentary Army. Here the commander of the fortress, Lord Walton, a Puritan sternly devoted to the side he had espoused, had brought his lovely young daughter, Elvira, that she might be safe from the many dangers of that troublous time.

The sweetness and grace of Elvira quickly gained her many admirers; for even the sombre Puritans were not proof against the enthralling charms of youth and beauty.

Amongst these admirers was Sir Richard Forth, a colonel in the Parliamentary forces; and being of good family and excellent repute among the Puritans, he met with a very favourable reception when he brought his suit to Lord Walton, who readily accepted him as his future son-in-law.

Elvira, however, had already, unknown to her father, given her heart to a Cavalier officer, Lord Arthur Talbot, who held a high position in the Royalist Army. When, therefore, she was told that the Puritan officer had been accepted as her suitor, she was filled with dismay, knowing such a loveless marriage could bring nothing but misery, yet believing that her father would never consent to her union with her Cavalier lover.

In this dilemma, she confided her troubles to her uncle, Sir George Walton, who, though a retired Puritan officer, yet remained in the fortress to assist his brother in the command. This gentleman, who loved Elvira as his own child, was so deeply moved by her passionate appeal for his aid that he promised to use every endeavour in his power to bring about her union with the man she loved.

At first, Sir George was not successful in his interview with his brother on Elvira's behalf; for the stern Puritan officer had no desire to connect himself with a Cavalier family and declared that he had already promised his daughter to Sir Richard Forth, who was in every way a suitable husband for her.

When, however, his brother, who cared less for political and religious distinctions, declared that Elvira's highly-strung system and loving nature could never bear the tragedy of a loveless marriage and that it would certainly break her heart should it be forced upon her, Lord Walton was no longer proof against such an appeal as this; for he was a devoted father and loved his daughter with very tender affection. He therefore agreed that the undesired betrothal with Sir Richard Forth should be set aside at once; and he also signified his consent to Elvira's marriage with Lord Arthur Talbot, giving instructions for the young Cavalier to be admitted into the fortress on the morrow that the nuptials might be celebrated there without further delay.

Elvira was filled with the utmost joy when her uncle brought her these glad tidings; and preparations for the wedding ceremony were commenced forthwith, so that a merry bustle was quickly set up in the sombre castle.

The young Cavalier was also overjoyed at this happy turn of events; and he needed no second bidding to prepare for his wedding with the beautiful maiden he loved so well.

On his arrival at the fortress next morning, Lord Arthur received a joyous welcome from all; for his many deeds of bravery and chivalry had won him universal renown, so that even the Puritan followers of Lord Walton had words of praise and admiration for this noble young Cavalier who was to be wedded to their leader's daughter that day.

A glad meeting took place between Elvira and her lover; and then, whilst the happy maiden retired to don her bridal robes, Arthur remained in the courtyard of the castle where his tender thoughts were unexpectedly diverted into another channel.

As he waited there, a captive lady, closely guarded, was brought out from the fortress into the courtyard, where she was informed by Lord Walton that she was about to be escorted to the Parliamentary tribunal, there to receive her sentence.

The despairing looks of the captive lady moved Arthur to deep pity; and on learning that she had been imprisoned several months in the fortress as one strongly suspected of being a spy in the Stuart cause and that she would certainly be condemned to the scaffold, the young Cavalier, as a fellow-adherent of the Royalists, determined to seek speech with her.

Therefore, whilst the attention of the officers and guards was turned in another direction for a short time, he managed to get sufficiently near the lady to enter into a low-toned conversation with her. Then, to his utter horror and dismay, he discovered that the captive was none other than the widow of the unfortunate Charles the First, Queen Henrietta. Whilst engaged in disguise on a secret enterprise on behalf of her fugitive son, she had been captured by her enemies and thrust by them into Plymouth fortress, where, though still preserving her incognito, she knew herself to be in the utmost danger.

Arthur, ever faithful to the Stuart cause, now felt it to be his sacred duty to rescue the unfortunate Queen from her desperate situation; and he told the unhappy Henrietta that he would do all in his power to save her.

At this moment, the bride and her maidens returned to the courtyard; and Elvira, whose tender heart could not bear that another should be in trouble when she herself was so full of joy, at once approached the captive lady—for whose sad fate she had many times grieved—and tried to cheer her with words of comfort. She even playfully removed her long bridal veil and draped it over Henrietta's dark locks, clapping her hands merrily at the effect and declaring the captive would make a beautiful bride; and the Queen, forgetting her sadness for the moment, was so charmed with the youthful grace and sweet innocence of Elvira that she indulgently suffered her artless playfulness.

The time for the ceremony was now almost due; and Elvira was hurried away to the chapel so quickly that she had not time to don her veil again, gaily calling to Henrietta to follow her with it, and forgetting in her eager excitement that the unhappy lady was a captive.

As the bridal party trooped into the chapel, Arthur slipped back to the courtyard, blessing the lucky chance which had left Henrietta in possession of the bridal veil; and bidding the Queen wrap it closely about her face and form, he hurried her to the gates of the courtyard, hoping that she might now be mistaken for Elvira and be thus permitted to pass through.

In spite of his anguish at being compelled to leave his beloved Elvira at the very moment of their wedding, Arthur was too loyal a Royalist to forsake his Queen in her extremity; and, crushing down the strong temptation to return to his waiting bride, he steadfastly conducted his royal charge to the fortress gates.

Here, to his dismay, he found Sir Richard Forth on guard; and the Puritan officer, severely smarting from the sudden cancellation of his betrothal with Elvira and believing the veiled lady to be the bride, refused to let them pass. Instead, he challenged his successful rival to mortal combat. When, however, Henrietta lifted her veil and in terrified accents bade the pair sheathe their swords, the Puritan saw that he had made a mistake; and he at once gave his permission for them to pass through the gates. He hoped that by reporting the secret departure of Arthur with the captive lady—whom he did not recognize—he would prove to Elvira the faithlessness of her Cavalier lover and thus further his own suit once more.

Arthur and the Queen thus escaped safely from the fortress; and as soon as the news became known, the greatest consternation prevailed. A number of Parliamentary soldiers were quickly sent out to search for the fugitives; but Lord Arthur cleverly succeeded in eluding them until he had placed the Queen on board a ship, in which she was safely conveyed to France.

Meanwhile, Elvira had received a terrible shock on learning of the desertion of her lover at the very moment of their marriage; and being led by the story of Sir Richard Forth to believe him faithless, her grief was so frantic that she completely lost her reason. The unhappy girl would wander out alone into the woods every day, now prattling childishly of happy days gone by and anon imagining herself in the company of her beloved Arthur; and all the inmates of the fortress were filled with sorrow at the terrible change that had taken place in her.

Lord Arthur Talbot was now proscribed and condemned to death by the Parliamentary Government for having effected the escape of a political prisoner.

However, after succeeding in eluding his enemies for several months, the young Cavalier managed to return to Plymouth, intending to enter the fortress once more, in spite of danger, and to claim his bride. As he hurried cautiously through the neighbouring wood, he happened to meet Elvira herself, who was aimlessly wandering there as usual, singing wild and plaintive ditties with the unmistakable air of one bereft of reason.

Terribly grieved and shocked at beholding his beloved one in such a condition, Arthur approached and gently folded her in his arms, uttering tender words of greeting. This sudden re-appearance of Arthur restored Elvira's mental balance. With great delight, she returned his embraces and listened gladly to the story of his adventures and his explanation as to the true identity of the captive lady whom he had thought it his duty to save from the scaffold.

Even as the restored lovers thus talked happily together, the Puritan search-party arrived on the scene, having learnt of Arthur's return to the neighbourhood and tracked him to the wood. Dragging the young Cavalier from the arms of Elvira, they bade him prepare for instant death.

At this distressing moment, however, another party came galloping up and ordered the immediate release of the prisoner; and as the search-party drew back in surprise, they were triumphantly informed that the Parliamentary forces had finally conquered the Royalists and that, in celebration of the event, all political prisoners were pardoned.

All was now peace and rejoicing; and Elvira, the Puritan maiden, completely restored to reason once more by the return of her lover, was united to the young Cavalier without further delay.

LA SONNAMBULA
(*The Somnambulist*) *Bellini*

In a certain pretty village in Switzerland, the light-hearted peasants were gathered together one summer evening on the shady green, talking in groups as they waited to witness the betrothal of Elvino, a prosperous young farmer, and his fair sweetheart, Amina, whose nuptials were to be celebrated on the morrow. The wreaths and garlands of flowers for the wedding decorations were being merrily set up by willing hands, and the village already wore a gala air. All were looking forward eagerly to the coming festivities—with the exception of one person, who alone refused to be joyful.

This was Lisa, the pretty young hostess of the village inn. Having once received attentions herself from the handsome Elvino, she had felt slighted when he fixed his affections upon Amina, whose beauty and sweet winning ways had made her

the belle of the village. Now, as she mingled with the merry
throng on the green, she was filled with envy for the happy fate
of the bride-elect and could do nothing but make spiteful remarks
about her rival, declaring her to be a mere nobody and not worthy
of so great a piece of fortune.

For Amina was a poor orphan, who had been brought up
by Dame Teresa of the Mill, a worthy woman who had loved
and cared for her as though she were her own child. In spite of
her unknown birth and dependent position, however, Amina was
beloved by all the villagers, whose hearts she had won by her
many deeds of kindness. But Lisa's jealousy would not allow her
to see any perfection in the gentle Amina; and so full of envy and
disappointment did she feel just now that to all the remarks made
to her by her own devoted admirer, Alessio, she only returned
snappish replies. These, however, disconcerted her swain but
little. For Alessio was a merry, lively fellow, full of fun and not
easily discouraged; and having conceived a great admiration for
the handsome but sharp-tongued Lisa, he was for ever coaxing
her to marry him. What was more, in spite of her many snubs,
he still felt confident of success in the end.

As they walked about the green this evening, he said
again : "Come, Lisa, let us also sign our marriage contract
whilst the Notary is here and save him the trouble of coming
again ! "

To this cool suggestion, however, Mistress Lisa merely tossed
her head and turned impatiently away; and Alessio, undaunted
began to join heartily in the merry wedding song he had himsel
composed in honour of the day and which the villagers had jus
raised as the pretty Amina appeared on the green, accompanied
by Dame Teresa.

When the song came to an end Amina thanked her friends fo
their kindly wishes; then, turning to Alessio and Lisa, she mis
chievously suggested that they should follow her example and
plight their troth with her that night.

" 'Tis just what I have been saying ! " cried the irrepressibl
Alessio gleefully. "Come, Lisa, say that you will, for I feel ·
must get married to-day, and if you won't have me, I'll have t
marry Dame Teresa ! "

All laughed merrily at this; but Lisa sulkily refused to join i
the fun, for Elvino had now arrived and the sight of his devotec
attentions to Amina caused her jealousy and disappointment t
smart afresh. The Notary having also now arrived with th
marriage contract, the guests gathered around a table which ha
been placed beneath the trees outside Dame Teresa's house; an

Elvino and Amina, having signed their names to the paper, their betrothal was thus formally concluded.

Just as the happy pair were receiving the congratulations of their friends, a strange cavalier—whose gay attire, aristocratic bearing, and deferential attendants proclaimed him to be a person of rank—approached and announced his intention of passing the night at the nearby inn.

On hearing this, Lisa, mindful of her duties as hostess, hurried forward officiously and offered her best accommodation to the stranger; then, having received some gallant compliments from her guest, who had an appreciative eye for a pretty face, she hastened within doors to make all ready, beaming with pleasure.

The stranger was, however, more greatly struck with the beauty of Amina, to whom he next addressed himself, declaring that she reminded him of someone whom he had long since loved and lost. So intense was his gaze that, after he had departed within the inn, Elvino, seized with a sudden pang of jealousy, reproached the maiden for having thus spoken with the newcomer. But Amina tenderly reassured her anxious lover, declaring that she loved but him alone; and the little cloud that had threatened to gather now quickly vanished.

As they moved away happily together, Alessio presently came running out to announce that he had discovered the stranger to be none other than the Count Rodolpho, whose château overlooked the village but who had not visited his native place since he was a child. Upon hearing this interesting news, the villagers were all filled with great excitement; and, as they trooped away to their homes, they arranged to assemble in the inn at break of day to sing a song of welcome to their lord and to show their joy at his arrival.

Some hours later, Count Rodolpho was conducted to the finest chamber which the old-fashioned inn afforded; and before he retired for the night, Lisa appeared at the door to ask if all his wishes had been attended to.

The Count, being a gay cavalier, felt that a flirtation with his pretty hostess would pass the time pleasantly; and Lisa was willing enough to accept his attentions. She was just about to depart, however, when a strange interruption came. A slight female figure, clad in a long white robe, softly entered the room and walked slowly across the floor, speaking aloud as though holding a conversation with some unseen person. To the great amazement of the Count and Lisa, they saw that this mysterious nocturnal visitor was Amina, who, although her eyes were wide open, saw them not, since she was walking in her sleep. Un-

known to anyone, and still less to herself, Amina was a somnambulist, and had quite unconsciously walked from her own
home and through the unfastened door of the inn; and as Count
Rodolpho now gazed in astonishment upon the maiden, whose
lovely face had so interested him earlier in the evening, he was
filled with a strange, deep emotion and listened eagerly to the
words she said. He gathered that she imagined herself speaking
to Elvino, since she spoke reproachfully of his having for a
moment doubted her faithful heart.

Lisa, though at first alarmed, quickly saw in this unforeseen
circumstance a means for satisfying her petty spite against the
orphan she despised. Quickly making her escape from the room,
she determined to seek out Elvino and prove to him that his
betrothed was base and unfaithful to him, since she had found
her in the chamber of the Count Rodolpho.

Meanwhile, Amina continued to speak in tender accents of her
love for Elvino; and unconsciously taking the Count's hand in
hers, she softly caressed it, repeatedly avowing her passion.

Count Rodolpho watched the sleeping maiden with increasing
emotion, feeling the charm of her ethereal beauty creeping over
him like a spell; and at last, fearful of awakening her and not
daring to trust himself longer in her sweet presence, he hastily
left the room. Leaving the inn at once, he made his way to his
own château.

After he had gone, Amina ceased to speak; and, presently sinking upon a couch, remained there in peaceful slumber.

It was now daybreak; and the peasants, in accordance with the
arrangement of the evening before, assembled in the inn, and,
making their way to the Count's chamber, began to sing a joyous
song of welcome, which they hoped would presently arouse him
from his slumbers. Soon afterwards, Lisa entered the room with
Elvino, whom she had brought to behold for himself his betrothed
slumbering in the chamber of the stranger, cruelly and unjustly
keeping from him the fact that Amina had walked there in her
sleep.

Elvino, who had indignantly refused to believe her story, now
uttered an exclamation of grief and despair on beholding what
appeared to him the proof of Lisa's statement; and at that moment
Amina, awakened by the singing, opened her eyes, and was
quickly filled with amazement on beholding her unaccustomed
surroundings. As she rose from the couch in bewilderment
Elvino burst forth into angry reproaches, declaring her to be
faithless and base; and in spite of the mystified Amina's piteous
assurances of innocence, since she could not explain how she came

to be found in such a compromising situation, he spurned her with scorn and departed in anger.

Amina, overcome with grief and despair, sank sobbing into the arms of Dame Teresa, who, though not understanding the mystery, yet believed her to be innocent and led her away with great tenderness; and the peasants then sadly dispersed, loath to think ill of the pretty maiden they loved so well, yet compelled to admit the evidence of their own eyes. But they were not satisfied; and later on in the day they set off to seek out the Count Rodolpho in his château to learn what he knew of this strange matter, and if he had indeed enticed the young girl to visit his room.

Meanwhile, Lisa was triumphant; and, having thus succeeded in bringing disgrace and ignominy upon her rival, she sought out Elvino, who had wandered into the woods near the château, and tenderly offered words of comfort to him. By encouraging his rage against Amina, she led him artfully to think of renewing his vows to herself; then, wisely refraining from becoming too importunate, she left him to his own reflections again and wandered alone down another glade. Here she was joined by the lively Alessio, who, after first bewailing the sad fate of Amina, made the brilliant suggestion that Lisa should marry him at once, so that the wedding decorations should not be wasted. This suggestion, however, was disdainfully flouted by the captious Lisa, who informed him that she already felt assured of eventually securing the more prosperous Elvino as a husband. Alessio, well used to such rebuffs, and not the least disconcerted by this surprising announcement, still pressed his own claims. Presently, however, seeing that the peasants were approaching from the château, the wrangling pair set off to join them.

Meanwhile, Amina, accompanied by the sympathetic Dame Teresa, had also sought solace for her woe in the woods; and presently coming face to face with the unhappy Elvino, she once more besought him to believe her innocence. Elvino, though filled with emotion at beholding the maiden whom he believed had wronged him, still refused to listen to her pleadings and, again turning from her with scorn and anger, hurried quickly away. As Dame Teresa vainly endeavoured to comfort the now heart-broken girl, the peasants came in sight, headed by Count Rodolpho, who, having heard from them of Amina's sad plight, had now come to prove her innocence.

Full of compassion, he approached the half-fainting girl; and, seeing that she was utterly exhausted by the strain that had been put upon her, he bade Dame Teresa take her into the nearby mill to rest for a while, promising that he would seek out Elvino and try to convince him of the innocence of his betrothed.

When Dame Teresa had led the unhappy Amina into the mill, the peasants went to seek Elvino and persuaded him to return with them. The Count now bade him be of good comfort and cease to mourn, since Amina was still worthy of his love. He then described to him how the maiden had entered his room the night before in her sleep, explaining that she was a somnambulist, and, as such, utterly unconscious of her actions at the time. Elvino and the simple peasants, however, never before having heard of this strange phenomenon, were scarcely yet convinced, finding it difficult to understand such a curious circumstance which had not come within their experience before.

But whilst they were still wondering at the story that had been told to them, they saw Amina softly approaching from the mill, passing them with wide-open, unseeing eyes and uttering Elvino's name in loving accents; and realizing that the maiden was again walking in her sleep, the Count explained this fact to the peasants and bade them remain quiet until she should awaken.

Elvino, overjoyed at this final proof of his beloved one's innocence, could scarcely restrain his happy feelings; and he watched the sleeping maiden's movements with eager interest. When she presently awakened to full consciousness, he clasped her in his arms with joy, beseeching her to forgive him for doubting her faith.

Amina, full of happiness on thus learning that Elvino still loved her and no longer believed her to be false, was soon restored to her accustomed gaiety; and the reunited pair were wedded that same day ere the sun went down, amidst the great rejoicings of the villagers, who were filled with delight because the fair maiden they loved so well was now cleared from all reproach.

THE LILY OF KILLARNEY   *Benedict*

ONE late summer evening, a gay company made merry in the salon at Tore Cregan, an ancient Irish mansion beautifully situated in the romantic district of Killarney. Hardress Cregan, the handsome young owner of the estate, was entertaining his friends with all the generous prodigality and light-hearted carelessness of his race. When, presently, a moonlight steeplechase was suggested in order to try the disputed merits of two thoroughbreds, it was hailed with zest; and the whole company trooped outside to watch the sport.

But Mrs. Cregan, the widowed mother of Hardress, remained behind in the deserted hall; and when a servant presently announced a newcomer, "Mr. Corrigan," her gaiety quickly vanished and a hunted look came into her eyes. For Corrigan was an agent, or "middleman", a low-bred, officious fellow who held a heavy mortgage on the Cregan estates. He was also ambitious and eager to make a position for himself in Kerry; so he did not hesitate to dictate insolent terms to the aristocratic family he thus had in his power. Knowing that the Cregans were considerably embarrassed for money and feeling that his chance of an early settlement of the payment due to himself was remote, he had curtly requested Mrs. Cregan to persuade her son to seek marriage with Miss Anne Chute, the richest heiress in Kerry, with whose wealth the matter of the mortgage could be comfortably disposed of. It was his unpleasant practice to intrude from time to time to learn how Hardress's suit was progressing.

To-night, however, he had a new and even more impudent suggestion to make. Being impressed by the still youthful looks and charms of Mrs. Cregan, he had the assurance to remark that, should Hardress not succeed in winning the heiress, he would himself be willing to accept the hand of the handsome widow in lieu of payment. To this suggestion, Mrs. Cregan, who despised and loathed the man, gave a proud refusal; but her indignant demeanour was quickly changed to dismay. Corrigan, angered by her scorn, declared that if she intended Hardress to settle the debt, she must keep a stricter watch upon him, since he was known to be indulging in a secret love-affair with a pretty peasant girl whom he kept hidden in a cottage on the opposite shore of the nearby lake.

Mrs. Cregan incredulously repudiated this statement; but Corrigan soon convinced her of its truth. As the song of a lake boatman now came to their ears, he declared this to be a signal for her son from his devoted follower, Danny Mann, who was evidently waiting to convey him to the opposite shore. Hastily drawing her into a curtained recess, he bade her watch the result of the boatman's signal. A few moments later, Hardress, having escaped from his guests, slipped furtively to the open window, where he flashed and shaded a lighted candle three times; then, hurrying down to the water's edge, he was rowed across the lake in Danny Mann's boat.

Mrs. Corrigan was filled with dismay by this proof of her son's intrigue; and Corrigan left the house in triumph, knowing that she would now hasten the negotiations for the marriage of Hardress with the heiress.

Meanwhile, in the cottage on the other side of the lake, the arrival of Hardress Cregan was eagerly awaited by Eily O'Connor, the Lily of Killarney, a lovely young Irish girl whose silky raven locks had won for her the name of Colleen Bawn. Not only was Hardress her lover, but he was her lawful husband also; for young Cregan had fallen so passionately in love with the beautiful peasant girl that, fearful of the opposition of his people, he had persuaded her to enter into a secret marriage with him. He had, however, bound her by a solemn promise not to reveal their true relationship for the time being, knowing that the prospect of his suggested marriage with the heiress, Anne Chute, was the only present means he had of keeping Corrigan from being too importunate regarding the mortgage payment.

Eily loved her high-born suitor too well to refuse his request, giving him the passionate devotion of her simple trusting nature; and at his bidding she kept herself hidden in a small cottage on the opposite lake-side, where she was guarded by a good old priest known as Father Tom. Here she was also frequently visited by a former peasant sweetheart, a smuggler outlaw named Myles-na-Coppaleen who, though knowing her to be the wife of Hardress Cregan, still showed his devotion to her by being always at hand and ready to serve her should the occasion arise.

To-night there were troubled hearts in the cottage when Myles arrived with a keg of smuggled spirits for his good friend, Father Tom. The latter, jealous of the good name of the pretty colleen over whom he exercised guardianship, was pressing Eily to persuade Hardress Cregan to acknowledge their marriage openly; but the young girl was reluctant to risk her present secret happiness by so doing, for of late her lover had shown signs of a disturbed mind.

When Hardress himself presently arrived, Eily quickly noticed that he was more anxious and upset than ever before; and her loving attempts to soothe him met with little response. Presently, he told her of the difficulty he was in regarding the mortgage on his estate; and he bluntly asked her to give up her marriage certificate to him, that he might be free to make the union his mother desired.

Eily's devoted love for Hardress was so deep that she was even willing to make the monstrous sacrifice he now demanded to save him from ruin; but Myles-na-Coppaleen and Father Tom indignantly interposed to prevent such a selfish design from being carried out.

Young Cregan, angry at being thus foiled, and equally ashamed of the base part he had felt compelled to play for the sake of his family welfare, now left the cottage in a rage, declaring that he would never visit it again and bidding the Colleen Bawn farewell for ever; and the unhappy Eily fell back overwhelmed with grief, heedless of the words of comfort uttered by her two faithful friends.

Hardress, though soon remorseful for his heartless conduct, now began to pay his addresses to Anne Chute with such success that their betrothal was presently announced; but the young man's thoughts constantly reverted to the deserted Eily, whom he still loved dearly and whose fair image he could not drive from his mind.

Soon, his troubled thoughts and embarrassing situation caused his devoted follower, Danny Mann, to suggest a desperate means for securing his freedom. Unscrupulous and lawless, the lake boatman now hinted that he himself would willingly resort to violence in order to remove the Colleen Bawn from his master's path Even when Hardress refused with horror and indignation to consider such a scheme, he still declared himself ready to do the deed at any time if Cregan sent him his glove as a token that he desired Eily O'Connor to vanish.

The unscrupulous but devoted Danny, however, soon found the opportunity he sought without the aid of Hardress. Skulking in the grounds outside Tore Cregan one evening, he observed an angry scene taking place in the salon within. The unpleasant agent, Corrigan, had again been pressing his unwelcome attentions upon Mrs. Cregan, when Hardress entered the room. Thus hearing for the first time of the agent's hateful alternative to his own proposed marriage with the heiress, the young man was so furious that he seized Corrigan by the shoulders and forcibly ejected him from the house.

While this struggle was still in progress, Danny Mann appeared at the window and attracted the attention of the agitated widow. In a whispered undertone, the wily boatman told her that he could arrange with Eily O'Connor that she would leave the neighbourhood and depart for America, if only he could show her one of Hardress's gloves as the token that he wished her to do so, and that he, Danny, was acting for him. Mrs. Cregan, still unaware of the secret marriage, eagerly hailed this suggestion, believing that, with the peasant girl safely out of the way, her son would then be willing enough to wed with Anne Chute; and she quickly produced one of Hardress's gloves as the token desired by Danny Mann, who went off with it in triumph.

Having crossed the lake once more, the old boatman stealthily made his way to the cottage of Eily O'Connor; and having made sure that she was alone, he entered and announced that Hardress Cregan had sent him to take her away at once. The unsuspicious Eily was filled with joy on hearing this, for she had seen and heard nothing of Hardress since the night he had left her in anger. With eager joy, she now stepped into Danny's boat, believing that her beloved one still loved her and was about to acknowledge her as his wife, after all. Nor did she have any doubts about trusting herself to the care of Danny Mann, who had always been her friend.

Too soon, however, her fears were awakened; for Danny Mann, instead of taking her to the opposite shore as she had expected, hastily rowed his boat to a dark and lonely water cave some distance away, where he roughly bade her step out on to a high rock. When she had tremblingly done so, he commanded her to deliver up to him the marriage certificate which he knew she now always carried in the bosom of her gown; adding in a threatening tone that if she refused to do so, he would fling her into the lake to drown.

The terrified girl, now fearing for her life, implored him to have pity upon her, declaring that she had sworn to the old priest, Father Tom, that she would never part with her marriage lines.

But Danny Mann was too passionately devoted to Hardress Cregan to be kept from his dread resolve by the tearful entreaties of the fair Lily of Killarney. Still believing that he was acting in the real interests of his beloved young master, he once more fiercely demanded to be given the marriage certificate; and when the distracted Eily again refused to part with it, he remorselessly pushed her into the deep water below.

Next moment, a shot was fired, and Danny Mann likewise fell into the water, mortally wounded by his unseen assailant.

This shot had been inadvertently fired by Myles-na-Coppaleen, the Colleen Bawn's peasant sweetheart, who used this solitary cave as a hiding-place for the contraband goods he smuggled from time to time. Swinging himself by means of a long rope into his secret domain at the very moment of Eily's fall into the water, he had seen a moving form on the rock above; and mistaking this in the half-darkness for an otter, he had taken aim and fired.

He was just chuckling over the excellent shot he had made, when he noticed a human form floating in the water; and soon. to his horror, recognizing this to be the form of his own beloved

Eily O'Connor, he instantly dived in to her rescue. After some little difficulty he reappeared with the now unconscious girl in his arms; and placing her tenderly in his boat, he hastily rowed away from the cave and conveyed her to his own cabin hut.

With tender care he restored the young girl to consciousness once more; and on learning from her that she had been thrust into the water by Danny Mann and that it must have been the latter whom he himself had shot in the cave in mistake for an otter, he suspected foul play. He determined, therefore, to keep the Colleen Bawn hidden in his own hut for the time being.

Meanwhile, Danny Mann, although mortally wounded, did not die immediately; and after a long and painful effort, he managed to crawl from the cave and reach a place of safety, where aid was forthcoming. He begged his rescuers to send for Father Tom, that he might confess to him before he died; and on the arrival of the old priest he told him the whole plot, declaring that he had drowned Eily O'Connor in the hope of being of service to Hardress Cregan.

The unaccountable disappearance of the Colleen Bawn confirmed his story, which quickly spread; and this information coming to the ears of Corrigan the agent, the latter cleverly turned it to his own purposes. He went before the magistrates and accused Hardress Cregan of complicity in the crime, maliciously triumphing in thus avenging himself upon the aristocratic Cregans for their contempt of him; and he was given a squad of guards to make an immediate arrest.

He led his men to the mansion of Anne Chute, where a gay company of guests had already assembled for the betrothal festivities, which were even now taking place. Even as the soldiers surrounded the house, however, Hardress Cregan, unable to keep up the deception any longer, drew the heiress away from her guests and revealed to her the story of his secret marriage with the Colleen Bawn for whose supposed tragic death he now deeply and sincerely mourned.

Anne Chute possessed a gentle and kindly nature; and instead of spurning him, as he had expected, she not only sympathized with his sorrow but generously expressed her forgiveness for his deception of herself.

It was just at this moment that the vindictive Corrigan entered with the officers of justice to arrest the unhappy young bridegroom-elect for his supposed complicity in the murder of Eily O'Connor; and a scene of consternation and confusion followed. Anne Chute and her guests declared stoutly that Hardress Cregan could not be guilty of such a horrible crime; but when Corrigan triumphantly produced the latter's glove which Danny Mann had obtained, declaring this to be the token agreed upon between the old boatman and his master that the unfortunate girl should disappear, the case certainly looked black against him.

Hardress indignantly denied that he had ever sent such a token, declaring that though Danny Mann had indeed made the dark suggestion to him, he had instantly repelled it with horror. Mrs. Cregan, who had been half dazed by the shock of her son's danger, now hastened forward and related how the old boatman had enticed her to give him the glove, thus proving beyond doubt that Hardress was entirely innocent in the matter.

Then, to the surprise and relief of all, there came a sudden and dramatic interruption to this distressing scene. Eily O'Connor herself entered the room, accompanied by Myles-na-Coppaleen, who, hearing of the dangerous position of Hardress Cregan, had judged this to be the right moment in which to produce the girl whose life he himself had saved.

With deep joy and thankfulness, Hardress clasped his beloved Eily in his arms; and then he proudly introduced her to the astonished company as his lawful wife. Seeing the turn affairs had taken, Corrigan the agent slunk quietly out of the room.

Nor had he again the power to annoy or persecute the Cregans; for, with generous magnanimity, Anne Chute insisted upon settling the matter of the mortgage as her wedding gift to Hardress and his lovely Colleen Bawn.

THE DEVIL TAKE HER   *Benjamin*

IF we are to believe all the fantastic folk-lore tales of the fifteenth century, the Devil must have been kept extremely busy in those days interfering with the lives of foolish mortals. Here is yet another tale of the Arch-Mischiefmaker's interference.

A young Poet sat writing a poem in his house in Cheapside one night. It was already ten o'clock, and the Poet worked feverishly by candle-light. The poem was a commission from a well-to-do neighbour, who wanted it as a song with which he might woo a certain wealthy widow. The latter, though middle-aged, was also romantic.

The Poet was at his wits' end for a rhyme with which to finish off his job—a rhyme which constantly eluded him.

He was still tearing his hair in poetic frenzy, when the neighbour came in to ask if the poem was ready.

Master Roger was portly and somewhat gross in mind as well as in body. When the Poet declared that the poem would be finished within an hour if only he could find the elusive rhyme he needed, his client, impatient to sing the lyric to his sentimental widow, suggested that the writer should go to his wife for inspiration.

On learning, however, that the Poet's wife was dumb, he at first commiserated with him, and then expressed the view that he was, perhaps, well off, after all, since a silent wife had her advantages. At least, she could not scold him! Then, bidding the Poet hasten with his song, he left him to work upon it.

While the worried Poet was still racking his brains for a rhyme, his dumb wife entered and stood beside him, laying her hand upon his shoulder. She was young and beautiful, and the Poet felt soothed by her touch. But he once more lamented her dumbness, longing to hear her speak and to know her thoughts. He sighed sadly because she must still remain to him a poem unread.

Nevertheless, her mere presence had revived his tired brain. Suddenly the rhyme he had been chasing all evening came rippling easily off his own tongue; and, with great joy, he now finished the poem.

Then, arm-in-arm with his silent wife, he went upstairs to bed.

.   .   .   .

Next morning, while Cheapside rang with street-cries—those of an orange-girl, a sweep, a bird-seller, a blind beggar—the Poet came running downstairs, elated and glad that his commission was satisfactorily finished. He sent off his maid, Lucy, to fetch Master Roger, that he might give him the poem and so receive the payment that was due.

When his dumb wife, Mistress Kate, came down, she seemed annoyed because the maid had been sent out so early; and she began, rather impatiently, to set the room to rights herself. When the maid returned, she indicated by signs that the latter must begin work at once; and she followed her out of the room to see her do so.

No sooner had the Poet settled down to write a new poem than his neighbour, Master Roger, came in with great news. Scarcely waiting to receive his finished poem, he announced that a strange doctor was outside in the street crying his wares and his marvellous capabilities, with the aid of a couple of loud-voiced attendants.

The Doctor was boasting that he could make the deaf hear, the blind to see, and the dumb to speak.

"This is your chance, my friend! Get him to make your silent wife speak the words you are always longing to hear!" cried Master Roger, quite excited.

The Poet flung down his pen with joy, and eagerly bade his client bring in this wonderful Doctor to see his wife.

The Doctor proved to be a fat and jolly old charlatan, most fantastically dressed in scarlet and black; and his attendants, who carried a bag containing phials and implements, likewise seemed very grotesque individuals.

When the Poet eagerly inquired his terms for loosening Mistress Kate's closed tongue and making her speak, the jolly Doctor at first demanded one hundred ducats. The mere mentioning of this huge fee caused the maker of verses to fall back in a faint, since this was the price of about two thousand of his own sonnets! He could never write so many, much less dispose of them!

When he had recovered somewhat, Master Roger now advised him to think no more about the matter, since no wife was worth so large a sum of money. He even added, very sagely: "A woman who is silent is better than gold!"

However, when the dumb wife presently entered the room, her beauty so greatly impressed the fantastically-dressed Doctor that he offered to perform the operation for fifty ducats. But silent Mistress Kate shook her head violently; then she held up one hand with its five fingers spread to indicate that five ducats only was the price she was willing to pay.

The merry old Doctor declared that, dumb or not, she was certainly keen on a good bargain. Then, still delighted with her charming looks, he invited her to make it ten ducats and he would do the job.

But the dumb wife still indicated that five was all she would give. So the Doctor agreed to cure her for five ducats, but with a kiss thrown in; and the bargain was thus made.

While Mistress Kate and her maid went into an upper room to make ready for the operation, the Poet, delighted at the thought that his beautiful wife would so shortly be talking to him, produced a bottle of old Canary wine and some goblets. He then invited the Doctor and his two attendants and Master Roger to drink with him to the success of the operation. Full of excitement, he called upon Æsculapius, the Father of all doctors, to show favour upon his wonderful disciple; but the latter—who certainly seemed more lively than serious—sang a gay drinking song instead.

Master Roger, though he joined heartily in the chorus of the Doctor's drinking song, was now somewhat dubious about the whole affair. He again warned his friend that the enterprise was a rash one, and reminded him that a silent woman was better than gold.

But the Poet was more eager than ever to hear his wife speak to him—to hold converse with his beautiful Kate, whose voice he had never yet heard, whose fair thoughts he longed to know. The operation should be carried out.

The strange Doctor was not long about his job. Soon there came shrieks of joy from upstairs, and the maid, Lucy, came running down with the wonderful news that her mistress could speak at last!

Next moment, the Doctor and his assistants brought in the Poet's wife between them, and set her down on a chair. The Poet rushed up to kiss and embrace her; and the maid poured out wine for her.

Mistress Kate demanded more wine to drink, and did not speak very much at first, her words being somewhat hesitant and stuttering.

The Doctor, very well pleased with himself, now demanded his fee; and the Poet slowly and reluctantly counted out five of his precious ducats. But when the Doctor next demanded the kiss likewise agreed upon, his patient indignantly called him " a ra-ra-rascal! " When he put his arms around her and tried to snatch the kiss which was part of his dues, she boxed his ears soundly and bade him begone.

Very ruefully, the Doctor and his assistants departed. Then the neighbour went home also, still shaking his head and wondering whether, after all, it would not have been better to have left the lady dumb. When the maid had likewise gone about her neglected household duties, the Poet at last found himself alone with his wife and able to test her new gift of speech.

And now the Poet was not long in discovering that Master Roger was right and that it would certainly have been wiser to leave Nature's work alone.

At first, Mistress Kate only repeated the last words of his loving remarks to her, as though trying out her newly-found voice; but very soon her stuttering accents ceased and she became fluent enough in her speech—in fact, much *too* fluent for the comfort of her dismayed husband.

When the latter wished to make love to her, she told him she was too busy with her household matters to waste time in love-making; and she spoke of his poems as " rubbish ". She likewise declared that for years she had been extremely bored by having been compelled to listen to his bad verses!

When she had rushed off to hustle her "idle maid", the poor Poet sat down in a dazed state—from which he was presently aroused by three gossiping dames who had come in to hear all about the wonderful cure. Was it true that his dumb wife could now speak?

But Mistress Kate, hearing their voices, came back into the room and soon proved to them that what they had heard was true and that she had voice enough to give them a good piece of her mind! She told them that she would have no gossips in her house; and she scolded them roundly for having flirted with her husband in the past, when she had not been able to say them nay. Then she drove them away with more vituperations; and the dames departed in a fright. They declared that the tongue she had found was a long and vitriolic one, indeed, and that the Doctor who had cured her must have been the Devil himself.

When a crowd now assembled outside, also calling for the Poet's wife to come forth and demonstrate her cure, Mistress Kate angrily seized a huge pitcher full of dirty water and poured its contents down upon the gaping folk from an upstairs window, together with a torrent of abusive words. Next, she scolded the maid, Lucy, for giving food to a beggar; and then she denounced her as a slut who had led her foolish master astray.

Such a terrible termagant did his wife prove herself to be, and so scurrilous was her newly-loosed tongue, that the unfortunate Poet greatly regretted the five ducats he had paid for such a result. He was nearly driven crazy by the shocking abuse she poured forth upon him. At last, in his despair, he cried out aloud: "I can stand no more! The Devil take you!"

Instantly there was a flash of lightning, and the Devil actually appeared, dressed in scarlet and complete with horns and cloven hoofs. He and the fantastic charlatan Doctor were one and the same person, as the gossiping dames had rightly suggested!

Mistress Kate, thinking that this new arrival was merely a dressed-up mummer or actor from the Blackfriars theatre, was more furious than ever at the intrusion of one she termed a "vagabond-rogue". She rained upon him such a cascade of vile names that even the Devil himself cowered from her wrath.

When the now thoroughly scared Poet entreated his diabolical visitor—whom he had not failed to recognize—to take his scolding wife away with him to the infernal regions, the Devil begged to be excused. Hell itself could not endure such a tongue. "Anything else I'll be glad enough to grant you—but keep your wife!"

he declared. "Then, take me instead! To live with her would be worse than Hell!" cried the distracted Poet.

So the Devil seized the Poet by the hand and vanished with him; and the termagant wife was left alone, sadly to reflect at her leisure that it was better to be dumb than to be a scold.

LE CARROSSE DU SAINT SACREMENT   *Berners*
(*The Coach of the Holy Sacrament*)

Lima, the capital of Peru, was probably as gay a city during the eighteenth century as at any time in its history. It was also a great religious centre. But the devout folk of Lima could be gay and lively, too.

Numerous festivals were held; gay caballeros amused themselves as gay caballeros do; and beautiful dark-eyed ladies graced the scene on every social occasion. In the height of the season nobody need be dull; and nobody wished to be absent from any Feast Day ceremony or from the gaieties that always followed. Even religious ceremonies were occasions for the display of wealth and grandeur.

Consequently, when the Spanish Viceroy found himself temporarily laid up with gout on one of these Church Festivals, he was extremely annoyed. Although he was now getting on in years, he did not care to miss any opportunity of appearing in public in his viceregal capacity.

On the present occasion he had a particular incentive to be present. Never before would he have cut such a dash! A magnificent State coach had just arrived for him from Madrid—so fine a coach had never yet been seen in Lima. He had been looking forward with keen anticipation for many weeks past to driving to Mass on this important Festival day in his resplendent new vehicle.

Instead of which, his old enemy, gout, had inconsiderately chosen this particular time to blaze forth in an unexpected attack. Not only was the Viceroy's foot on fire, his temper was likewise ablaze. His unfortunate secretary, Martinez, had to bear the first brunt of this ill-humour, on entering his master's room in the morning.

But Martinez was a young man of tact. He knew exactly how to bring the Viceroy back into a good mood once more. He had only to lead the conversation round to the subject of that fascinating young actress, La Périchole, his master's beautiful, if somewhat exacting, mistress.

For the Viceroy, though elderly, was still extremely susceptible to female charm. As a matter of fact, he worried considerably less about affairs of State than he did about the affairs of his enchanting mistress.

Naturally enough, the Périchole was equally fascinating in the eyes of other men. Though proud to be the mistress of the most important lord in the land, the latter was, undoubtedly, somewhat elderly. The Périchole, therefore, secretly indulged in flirtations with younger and more attractive caballeros. In consequence of these pleasant interludes, she had many enemies among the aristocratic ladies of Lima, who greatly resented losing so many of their own legitimate admirers to the popular actress.

It was by relating an amusing story of a mischievous prank she had played upon one of these haughty dames, the old Marquise d'Altamirano, that Martinez now restored his gouty master to good humour once more. The old Viceroy laughed heartily on hearing this racy story. Trust La Périchole to get the better of any would-be rival!

But his mood quickly changed on hearing that he himself had now a more serious rival than ever before. Forgetting his usual tact, Martinez went on to mention that La Périchole's *affaire* with Ramon, the handsome and famous Matador, had become the talk of the town.

The Viceroy fell into a great rage with Martinez on hearing this. " How dare you suggest that a Matador is my rival! " he shouted, indignantly, at the trembling secretary. " Get out of my sight! "

His rage only increased the stabs of pain in his gouty foot. When, therefore, the Périchole appeared in his room a few moments later, instead of storming at her, he received her coldly. But he was thunderstruck when he learned the object of her visit.

The Périchole had just had a bright idea. Would her exalted lover lend her the fine new State coach which had just arrived from Madrid, so that she might go to the Festival Mass in it? It would make her hateful enemy, the stuck-up old Marquise d'Altamirano, green with envy to see her riding in such royal state!

The Viceroy was shocked and horrified at the suggestion. The beautiful Périchole was delightful as a mistress to bring colour and comfort into his private life; but she must not expect to share his own semi-royal state. The Viceroy refused her request pointblank. Then he sternly reproved her for her scandalous intrigue with Ramon the Matador.

However, the Périchole had set her heart on enjoying this little triumph over her jealous detractors. She declared she simply *must* have the new State coach to drive in to Mass that morning. When her elderly lover again refused to oblige her, she began to storm and rage at him in her disappointment. She threatened to leave him for good and to take Ramon the Matador as her lover instead.

Now, the old Viceroy was really passionately devoted to the temperamental Périchole and was so accustomed to the charm and comfort of her presence that he could not bear the thought of living without her. It was his constant nightmare that she might some day leave him. He was well aware that his age would prevent him from holding her much longer, despite his wealth and high position. The Périchole's present threat touched him on the raw, as she had cleverly known.

Finally, he gave in. He agreed to let her use the new coach to go to Mass in, and promised to do anything she might desire if only she would not desert him.

Full of joy, the beautiful actress embraced her doting elderly lover with such seeming fervour that he was entranced. Then, bidding him take care of himself and his gout, she hurried away.

The Viceroy decided to make the best of a bad job and to get what entertainment he could, second-hand, from the first appearance in public of his new State coach—that wonderful coach in which he had himself hoped to make such a triumphal progress. He seated himself at the open window with a telescope, through which he would be able to follow the progress of the Périchole from the gateway of the viceregal mansion to the Cathedral, which he could see in the distance.

Out drove the magnificent new State coach, emblazoned with the royal coat of arms, drawn by six gaily-caparisoned pure-bred horses and complete with richly-uniformed bewigged coachman, footmen, and outriders—the most gorgeous equipage ever seen in Lima. Within it, in solitary state, decked in her handsomest silken robes of the latest fashion and her most dazzling jewels, sat the most beautiful woman in Lima—La Périchole, the famous actress.

How lovely she was! A somewhat expensive luxury, of course! But well worth it, in spite of her temperamental nature. How wise he had been to give in to her request! A woman in a thousand, thought the Viceroy proudly.

Great was the triumphant joy of the Périchole. In the crowded street, the people uttered cries of admiration. Then, quite soon, the splendid State coach passed the antiquated family vehicle of the Marquise d'Altamirano, lumbering along. The old Marquise stared in disconcerted amazement as the Périchole swept by in her fine equipage, staring in her turn with haughty insolence at her aristocratic enemy. Many others who had shown disdain for the lovely actress were likewise now repaid in their own coin.

It was, indeed, a triumphal progress for the Périchole. The Viceroy felt triumphant, too, and really proud of her. How he chuckled as he realized the outraged feelings of the jealous old Marquise and her haughty companions, as the beautiful actress swept past them in the magnificent State coach. How they would be gnashing their teeth!

But, all too soon, disillusionment came, and he was laughing on the wrong side of his face.

What was happening now? The Viceroy became agitated as, with the aid of the telescope, he continued to follow the progress of the State coach towards the Cathedral. A crowd had collected around the lumbering equipage of the Marquise d'Altamirano. In sweeping past at an accelerated pace—the coachman having evidently been instructed to this effect by his fair passenger—the State coach had neatly overturned that of the Marquise into the ditch.

The Viceroy put down the telescope in a great state of agitation. The Périchole had gone too far! It was all very well for her to triumph over her enemy by riding in a vastly superior vehicle; but to tip the Marquise into the ditch was quite another matter. The Marquise was an influential dame, who would certainly make trouble.

She did. All too soon, her chaplain arrived to inform the Viceroy that the angry Marquise intended to send a strong protest to Madrid about this insulting incident.

The now thoroughly alarmed Viceroy—whose gout had increased owing to the excitement of the morning—hardly knew what reply to make to this statement. He awaited the return of the Périchole with great misgivings.

He became even more excited when, presently, the Bishop of Lima was announced. Heavens! Surely the arrival of this important prelate so immediately after Mass could only mean trouble ahead!

But, to the Viceroy's amazement, the Bishop of Lima entered the room with a beaming countenance. He also most respectfully led by the hand the beautiful Périchole herself—the latter looking curiously meek, not to say angelic! Surely, wonders would never cease, thought the now bemused Viceroy.

The Bishop announced to him in gratified accents that the lady he had the honour to lead by the hand was now a humble penitent. What was more, as a proof of her renewed piety, she had presented to the Church the magnificent coach in which she had been driven to the Festival Mass that morning. It was to be used, she had said in presenting it, for conveying the priest who carried the Holy Sacrament to the sick in outlying districts.

In token of his gratitude for such a munificent gift, the Bishop now blessed the pious donor, as she stood before him with humbly-bowed head and modestly-lowered eyes; and he added: "Señora, this coach will be as the Chariot of Elijah, and will convey you straight to Heaven!"

Thus did La Périchole cleverly whitewash her triumph over her enemy. She also provided her doting old lover, the Viceroy, with much food for thought. She certainly *was* an expensive lady!

CARMEN   *Bizet*

ONE hot noontide during the early years of the nineteenth century a pretty young country girl, named Micaela, came shyly into a large public square in Seville. The square was full of bustling life; and numbers of light-hearted soldiers were joking and laughing as they lounged about near a cigarette factory. The girl-workers within this factory were expected to come out from work any moment; and the soldiers had sweethearts and friends among them.

Micaela was bewildered by this gay and noisy scene; and the bold glances and swaggering movements of the brilliantly-garbed soldiers seemed strange and even alarming to such a simple village maiden. However, she had a message for one of them, a young brigadier, Don José, who hailed from her own village; and she now sought him with hesitant diligence. Having learned that he was expected to appear presently when the guard was changed, she slipped into a sheltered corner to await his arrival, glad to escape from the many impudently-admiring advances made to her.

Just as the new guard entered the square, with Don José leading the men, there came a sudden interruption, which caused the shy

Micaela to remain hidden a little longer. The bell of the cigarette-factory clanged forth its noontide chimes; and next moment the girl cigarette-makers came pouring into the square, laughing, dancing, and jostling one another as they mingled with their friends outside.

Among this merry throng of newcomers was a beautiful young girl of gipsy birth, named Carmen, whose dark flashing eyes and scornful lips spoke of passionate emotions and reckless daring, and whose saucy sparkling glances proclaimed the born coquette. No sooner did she appear than a court of admiring youths instantly surrounded her, clamouring for her smiles and favours.

But the capricious beauty would have none of them this day, for her roving eye had fallen upon the handsome form of the young brigadier, Don José. Greatly struck with his dashing appearance, she presently went forward and boldly invited him to meet her when next he came off duty.

Don José, however, had been warned of the dangerous attractions of the lovely cigarette-maker and received her advances somewhat coldly; but when the saucy Carmen, as she laughingly tripped away, flung at his feet the red rose she had been wearing, he picked it up eagerly, enthralled by her dazzling glances in spite of himself.

Even when Micaela presently drew near and gave him his mother's message of entreaty to visit her at an early date, since she was ill and suffering, he could still think only of the fascinating Carmen; and when the village maiden had departed, sad at his seeming indifference, he still remained gazing at the gipsy's red rose so carelessly flung to him as a coquettish challenge.

A noisy commotion in the square suddenly interrupted his romantic thoughts. The hot-blooded Carmen had quarrelled with one of the other girl workers, and, in a fit of passion, had drawn a stiletto and aimed a blow at her. Although instantly seized by the soldiers, the reckless gipsy had no fear of remaining a captive for long. Don José was put in charge of the men who held her, pending an order for her imprisonment; and she hoped to be able to lure him to set her free.

Her hope soon became a certainty. Realizing only too well that she had attracted the handsome young brigadier—for whom a sudden answering passion had also sprung up in her own fickle heart—Carmen quickly determined to fascinate him still further, so that he should connive at her escape. With bewitching smiles, she declared she knew he already loved her since he continued to wear her rose; and when she entreatingly held out her bound hands, he surreptitiously slackened the cords.

The young brigadier was now completely bewitched by the enticing words of the beautiful coquette who thus tempted him to forget his duty. Full of the intoxication of sudden love, he whispered passionately that he would meet her at a certain border inn she had already mentioned to him if she would promise to love him in return.

Exultant at thus gaining her freedom and a new lover into the bargain, Carmen lightly gave her promise; and then the two quickly devised a plan of escape.

When the Captain of the Guard returned with the necessary prison order, the young brigadier promptly led off his captive. Ere they had gone a few steps, however, Carmen freed her hands from their already loosened cords and gave Don José a sudden jerk, so that he fell to the ground; and in the wild confusion that followed, the gipsy girl managed to make her escape through the crowd.

The tables were thus reversed; and as the daring Carmen gaily tripped away out of the square, singing, dancing, and waving her hand, Don José was himself seized and marched off to the guard-house under arrest for having openly allowed his prisoner to escape. Here he was detained for a few days; but all through his lonely hours he still thought only of the fascinating young beauty whom he now loved so passionately and with whom he was determined to keep his appointment as soon as he was released.

Meanwhile Carmen made her way to the border inn, the land-lord of which was one of a successful band of smugglers; and here, easily falling into gipsy ways once more, she gave her assistance to the illicit traffic, the dangers and risk of which strongly appealed to her daring spirit and love of adventure.

This border inn was the favourite resort of certain officers and soldiers in the town who, knowing nothing of the smuggling tendencies of the landlord, went thither to dance and amuse themselves with the pretty gipsy girls who frequented the place. On the day Don José was set at liberty, he sent a message to Carmen by one of these soldiers, announcing that he would visit her that same night.

It happened that a grand torchlight procession was being held that evening in honour of the most popular Toreador in Seville, a gay, handsome youth named Escamillo; and on passing the border inn the bull-fighter and his friends stepped within. Being instantly struck with the enticing beauty of Carmen, the dashing Escamillo made advances to her, seeking her good favour. The pretty gipsy, however, though much impressed with his handsome looks and careless charm, would neither accept nor refuse h' admiration, all her thoughts just then being centred on Don José, whom she expected to see that night.

When the Toreador, soldiers, and other customers had departed, the landlord and his smuggler friends discussed a new enterprise they were then engaged upon; and Carmen promised to persuade her new soldier lover to join them in this, bidding them wait for her in an adjoining room.

No sooner had the smugglers retired than she heard Don José's voice outside calling to her; and opening the door quietly, she was next moment clasped in her lover's arms. Then, while the newly-released young brigadier refreshed himself with the food and wine she placed before him, Carmen sang and danced in her most enchanting manner; and Don José, more enthralled than ever, applauded her with great delight.

Suddenly, however, an insistent bugle blast was heard outside, sounding the recall; and knowing this to be the signal for all soldiers to return to the barracks, Don José rose to bid his sweetheart farewell for the night. But Carmen did not mean him to go.

Employing her most practised seductive arts, she tempted him to desert his regiment and escape with her and her gipsy friends to the mountains, there to live the rover's life of freedom, excitement, and danger; and she declared that, otherwise, she would never see him again.

Just then the Captain of the Guard entered the room to look around for defaulters, and on encountering Don José, he sternly ordered him instantly to rejoin the now departing soldiers, who were again sounding the bugle call. The young brigadier, furious at the interruption, passionately refused to go; and next moment he had clashed swords with his superior officer.

Carmen, triumphant at her conquest, called aloud for help; and when the smugglers swarmed into the room, she made them seize and bind the unfortunate captain so that he should not interfere with their plans. Don José, unresistingly under the spell of Carmen's dangerous fascination, was next invited by the smugglers to join their enterprise; and when he had agreed to do so, the whole party made off to their rocky retreat in the mountains.

Here, amidst a wild, picturesque country, the smugglers plied their unlawful traffic with success for some time; and Don José, though often filled with remorse for his lost position and tortured by thoughts of his lonely mother, found relief in the frequent dangers he was exposed to and distraction in the constant society of Carmen. Despite the fact that she had caused him to desert his regiment and become a smuggler, he passionately loved the beautiful gipsy girl; but, to his mortification, Carmen's fickle affection grew cooler each day. Having lost the excitement of pursuit by conquest, she quickly tired of him and desired a new lover, already thinking tenderly of the handsome Toreador who had besought her favour at the inn.

As Carmen's love grew colder, the more passionately did Don José long to keep it; and in spite of her now frequent taunts and slights, he declared that he would never leave her side. All too soon, tragedy was in the air.

One early dawn as Don José was on guard at the entrance to the smugglers' haunt, Escamillo the Toreador suddenly appeared, declaring that he had come thither at the invitation of Carmen and implying that the lovely gipsy girl had already promised to accept him as her lover.

Mad with jealous anger at this cool announcement, Don José challenged his rival to a duel; and immediately, as the rising sun threw golden and crimson flashes over the picturesque gipsy encampment, the sinister clash of steel arose to dispel the peace of early morning. The gipsies soon came crowding round to applaud, their fierce natures ever eager for a fight; but Carmen rushed recklessly in between her rival sweethearts and separated them, calling furiously on her smuggler friends for assistance.

Having then made it plain that her preference now was in favour of the gay Escamillo, the Toreador departed joyfully, after gaining her promise to attend the bull-fight he was to take part in later that week and to bring her gipsy friends with her. An angry scene followed. Don José, stung to the quick by the passionate glances Carmen had bestowed upon her new admirer, upbraided her for her faithlessness; and he warned her not to torture him too much, declaring that he would kill her rather than she should accept his rival.

But the reckless Carmen cared naught for his threats, for she was brave, though fickle; but she was glad, nevertheless, when their quarrel was interrupted. Before Don José could expostulate further, a struggling girl was dragged into the camp by a group of the smugglers; and, to his amazement and dismay, the young brigadier recognized in this intruder his own village sweetheart, Micaela.

The simple peasant girl had journeyed to Seville a second time, bearing another sad message to the man she loved; and on being told of Don José's desertion and of the unlawful ways into which he had fallen, she had still determined to find him. Having learned that he was in the gipsy smugglers' camp, she had fearlessly made her way thither; and now, coming face to face with the object of her search, she implored him to return with her to his old home, where his lonely mother was still waiting and yearning for him.

Carmen, hoping thus to be rid of her now inconvenient lover, also added to this entreaty, saying that he would do well to go away since he was unsuited to a smuggler's life; but Don José, stung by her scornful taunt, swore that he would never leave her side, knowing well that she only desired his absence that she might pursue her new Toreador admirer.

Then Micaela, with tearful sympathy, told the passion-torn young man that his mother was actually dying and that unless he returned home immediately he would be too late to receive her forgiveness and last blessing. On hearing this, Don José was distracted with grief; and his filial love overcoming all other feelings for the moment, he now bade a hasty farewell to Carmen, declaring, however, that he would be with her again in a few days' time. He then departed hastily with Micaela.

The fickle Carmen, now thinking only of Escamillo, whom she already loved, returned next day to Seville with her gipsy friends, who had by this time finished their present enterprise and were eager to attend the bull-fight to which they had been invited. The gay Toreador soon found himself an accepted lover; and Carmen, now loving at last with the whole of her passionate nature, was radiantly happy with Escamillo.

On the day of the bull-fight, she accompanied him to the arena. When he had departed to begin the fight, she was just about to enter the enclosure in order to watch his expected triumph when she saw Don José hastily approaching. Her gipsy companions begged her to turn aside, fearing from his dark, gloomy looks that he meant to do her harm. But Carmen was brave; and, reckless of danger, she boldly went forward to meet her discarded lover with a cool and dauntless air.

Don José, chastened by grief for the death of his mother, at first gently took the beautiful girl's hand in his and besought her to return with him to his country home as his bride, that they might there live a new and better life together. He added that he loved her so dearly that he longed to save her from her present life of lawlessness.

But Carmen angrily freed herself from his eager grasp, saying that all was now at an end between them and that she could never love him again. Then, flinging at his feet the ring he had given her, she declared passionately that she now loved Escamillo the Toreador with her whole heart and would continue to do so until her last breath. Stung to madness by her repudiation of him, Don José's pent-up rage and jealousy now broke forth in all its fury; and, in a sudden frenzy of thwarted passion, he drew his stiletto and stabbed her to the heart.

As the beautiful Carmen sank lifeless to the ground, loud shouts of applause arose from the arena announcing the popular Toreador's new victory. Next moment, accompanied by a cheering crowd of admirers, Escamillo came forth from the enclosure, glowing with triumph and eager for the praises and greetings of his beloved one.

But those praises and greetings were never spoken; for the woman he loved lay dead at his feet.

DJAMILEH   *Bizet*

IN mediæval times, there lived in Cairo a rich young Turkish Prince named Haroun, who seemed to have experienced most of the joys of life at a very early age.

He lived in a splendid palace, with hundred of slaves to wait upon him; he had hosts of gay young friends who helped him to spend his money right royally; and he could feast, hunt, gamble, or otherwise amuse himself all day long.

But Haroun was not entirely happy. Although he could enjoy so many of the good things of life, there always seemed to be something that eluded him, just something lacking to give him that complete sense of satisfaction, contentment, and well-being, without which no man can be said to know happiness.

Although Haroun knew it not, that something which always eluded him and which alone could bring him true happiness, was love. So far, this luxurious young Prince—who was certainly one of Fortune's favourites—had only played with love. True, the beauty of women appealed to him very strongly; but he always resisted any likelihood of becoming entangled in the toils of love. He preferred to enjoy the easy freedom of one who plucked flowers for the brief joy of a single glance at their beauty, a single whiff of their fragrance, and was then free to cast them aside as of no more interest. He did not believe in real lasting love. His own father had been unfortunate in his marriage, having loved too well a faithless woman; and Haroun did not wish to meet with a similar misfortune.

Consequently, he would not marry. Instead, he ordered a new and beautiful slave-girl to be bought for him every month; and at the end of four weeks, he deposed her from his favour and amused himself with the next new charmer.

Knowing that their reign as harem favourite was to be so short, and that there was no likelihood of their being raised to the higher dignity of Princess, the lovely girls bought for Haroun's pleasure were careful not to let their own hearts become too deeply touched by the handsome looks and gay, charming disposition of their always kindly lord.

All but Djamileh, the most beautiful of them all, who, from her first introduction to the young Prince, had fallen deeply in love with him. But she was careful to keep her passion a secret from Haroun, whom she soon discovered desired only the lighter side of love and intended to keep his own heart untouched.

At first, Djamileh entered into the light and careless mood of her new master with complete success, entertaining him fully with her exquisite dancing and singing, so that he praised her talents on many occasions. When, however, she realized that her quite un-usual beauty and gifts had, apparently, made little impression upon Haroun, and that her love for him—expressed in many special acts of grace—obviously meant nothing to him, she was filled with a secret despair, knowing that at the end of a month her joy must come to an end.

But Djamileh's beauty and gifts had greatly attracted Haroun's secretary, Splendiano; and the latter, seeing that his master showed little interest in the lovely slave, hoped to win her for himself. His opportunity for broaching the subject occurred one day as he sat with his master, trying vainly to interest the latter in the over-heavy household accounts.

Haroun lay on a divan, lazily smoking and listening to the sweet singing of boatmen passing on the river outside. He was in a particularly dissatisfied mood just then, unable to understand why his life should seem so shallow and empty, when he was surrounded by so much luxury and had a rosy future ahead. When, therefore, Splendiano presently ventured to remind him that his vast fortune was diminishing and that it might soon be necessary to retrench somewhat, he scarcely heeded him. Even when the secretary added that the monthly purchase of beautiful slave-girls was becoming almost too expensive a luxury, suggesting that a halt might be called to this particular extravagance, he still paid little attention to him. Learning, however, that the beautiful Djamileh's month as his favourite was now at an end, he listlessly commanded the secretary to secure a new slave at once.

'This was Splendiano's chance. He humbly suggested that, since Djamileh's amazing beauty had evidently not particularly impressed his master, he, Splendiano, might be allowed to win her for himself. Haroun was startled, and hesitated a moment; then, almost reluctantly, he agreed.

The fact was that Haroun had been more moved by the beauty, gifts, and sweet nature of Djamileh than he was willing to admit; and the announcement that her month with him had already expired, had been a somewhat unpleasant shock. Nevertheless, he still wished to remain heart-free; and so he determined not to alter the now customary procedure he had himself instituted.

But when, presently, Djamileh came in to sing to him for the last time, he felt strangely stirred by her sad looks, knowing now that he would miss her sweet presence when she had left him. From her shy glances and her tender singing of the passionate love-song she had chosen, he also guessed her secret love for him, which he had already suspected.

At the end of the song, Djamileh seemed so hopelessly sad, that he felt a deep pity for her obvious distress, now knowing its cause. He sought to comfort her by announcing that he would grant her the freedom she must have always longed for; and he also hung a rich necklace around her neck as his parting gift. Then, afraid to trust himself longer in her presence, he hurried away to play dice with his friends. He still desired to have nothing to do with the trammels of love.

Before finally leaving her, however, he endeavoured to prove to her his own indifference to her charms by keeping her standing a few moments, still unveiled, while some of his waiting friends passed through the room to the gaming-table beyond. Djamileh was thus exposed to the latter's boldly admiring stares; and she was filled with distress, as he had hoped, that the man she loved should treat her thus so casually.

Presently, finding the unhappy girl alone and weeping, Splendiano took the opportunity to plead his own cause, declaring that he had their master's consent thus to approach her. He added that a new beauty was to be chosen that evening by Haroun, in accordance with his usual custom.

But Splendiano was not of an unkindly disposition; and when he now realized the despairing grief of Djamileh, he was willing to help her when she presently suggested a plan which had suddenly occurred to her.

The unhappy girl begged him to allow her, in disguise, to appear with the new group of slaves to be brought to the Palace that evening, from which their master would select a fresh charmer for the ensuing month. She hoped, by means of new dances, to enthral Haroun once more. If, however, she should not be chosen, then Splendiano might claim her as he desired. But Djamileh vowed secretly that, should she fail in this desperate enterprise, she would then kill herself rather than accept the love of another. Not knowing her sinister resolve, the secretary agreed to the scheme, feeling fairly hopeful that the result would be in his favour.

After the evening banquet was over, a slave-dealer arrived at the Palace with a number of lovely slave-maidens, who danced and sang before the young Prince and his lords. Among them appeared Djamileh, gorgeously attired, but disguised and closely veiled. Splendiano had kept his word, and, by means of a bribe, had persuaded the dealer to include the deposed favourite in his bevy of new charmers.

Haroun paid little attention at first to the performances of the new slaves; for he was feeling strangely sad and his thoughts kept wandering back to his last meeting with Djamileh. A curious warmth stole into his heart as he remembered the look of unconfessed love in her eyes and voice as she had sung to him. He could feel no interest in this new group of slaves brought for his delight—except, perhaps, in that one graceful veiled figure, whose movements were certainly more entrancing than any of the others. What a marvellous dancer she was!

Curiously enough, there was an alluring charm about every movement of this particular dancer that reminded the young Prince of his beloved Djamileh. His *beloved* Djamileh? Yes; he admitted it now—he loved her. But, foolishly, he had set her free; and she must now be far away!

Haroun was so occupied by these sad thoughts that when Splendiano presently became importunate for him to select his new slave, he impatiently bade the secretary choose for him. Then, calling him back, he declared that he would have the veiled dancer—solely because her graceful movements reminded him of Djamileh, though he did not admit this to Splendiano.

When, later on, the veiled dancer was brought to his room, Haroun at first showed little interest in her. Again he was thinking of the gentle girl to whom he had granted her freedom. But when the new slave suddenly unveiled and revealed herself as Djamileh, he was not only amazed but filled with an overwhelming joy.

Afraid of his anger, Djamileh now flung herself on her knees and passionately asked his forgiveness for the trick she had played upon him. Then she eagerly implored him to take back her freedom and to allow her instead to remain always with him as his slave. She would rather die than live without him.

And now, Haroun knew that happiness had come to him at last—that the love he had resisted so long was the one thing needed to crown his life. With great joy, therefore, he raised Djamileh from her lowly position and clasped her in his arms— beautiful, gentle, devoted Djamileh, who was to be his slave no longer but his beloved and honoured Princess.

MEFISTOFELE   *Boïto*

Prologue

THE Hosts of Heaven were singing praises before the Throne of the Almighty Ruler of the Universe. Legions upon legions of angels, cherubs, and seraphs all combined in rhythmic harmony in one overwhelming chorus of thanksgiving for the Goodness of God. Peace and Joy reigned with the King of Peace.

But a discordant note was presently heard. High up amidst the darkness of thunder-clouds soared the graceful but sinister form of Mefistofele, the Prince of Evil—that sardonic Spirit who had denied all good and desired only chaos, and who, because of his own arrogant pride and love of vainglory, had cut himself off from the Blest.

Hearing the angelic choir presently singing also of the virtue and simple faith of old Dr. Faustus, whose soul they hoped soon to welcome, Mefistofele called out a challenge to the Heavenly King he once had served. He would entice to evil the old learned Doctor and deprive the angelic hosts of the prize they hoped for.

His challenge was accepted; and Mefistofele, with a peal of sardonic laughter, departed amidst the blazing fire of lightning to seek out his earthly victim. By subtlety and cunning, he felt, in his pride, that he would certainly win his wager and claim the prize—the soul of Faust.

.   .   .   .

It was a festival day in Frankfort-on-Main during the Middle Ages. The streets were thronged with students, burghers, hunts-men, and pretty girls, all singing, dancing, and making merry. At a little distance, looking on at the gay scene, stood the venerable old Doctor, Faust, with his student companion, Wagner. Just behind them lingered a Grey Friar. When, presently, they strolled away, tired of the festival noise and bustle, the Grey Friar followed them.

When the old Doctor reached his humble lodging, he parted from his pupil and went inside. He climbed the steep stairs and entered his study and laboratory; and the Grey Friar slipped in behind him, unnoticed, keeping in the shadows.

Faust was not only weary with walking; he was also weary of life. His studies seemed to have brought him little satisfaction. But he could always seek comfort and peace from the Holy Book.

As he brought forth the latter, however, there came a shriek from the shadows. Mefistofele could not bear the sight of the Holy Book. He now flung off his friar's robe and revealed himself in the rich garb of a gay cavalier of the period. He invited Faust to join him in his pursuit of pleasure, promising to make the old man young again so that he might at last enjoy the delights of youth which he had foolishly missed by burying himself so closely in his books and laboratory studies.

Faust was strongly tempted—especially when Mefistofele next promised him wealth, power, and love, as well as youth. What was the price demanded? "Your Soul!" replied the Evil One.

Even that Faust was willing to barter—but not only for Youth and its joys. " Give me one hour of peace, one fleeting moment, when I may say ' Stop, for thou art blissful! ' Then, indeed, am I willing to die and to deliver my soul into thy keeping! "

Eagerly, Mefistofele promised such a seemingly simple request; and the bargain was completed. Triumphantly, Mefistofele now spread out his gay cloak and sped through the air with his hoped-for victim enclosed within its folds.

.   .   .   .

In her sweet-scented flower garden, Fair Marguerite wandered with her lover, Henry. He had suddenly appeared in her innocent life, a dashing, handsome cavalier, whose passionate love-making had quickly swept her off her feet.

Marguerite was completely overwhelmed by the excitement and intensity of this magical world of love in which she—a simple, pure, and gentle maiden—now found herself; and she gave herself willingly to her insistent lover, with no thought of evil to come. How could she know that her beloved " Henry " had, a short time ago, been known as Faust, a poor but learned old Doctor? All she knew was that " Henry " loved her, and that she loved him.

True, she was somewhat distrustful of his sardonic, but equally gay companion; but even he also played a helpful part in her wonderful romance. Did he not tactfully distract the attention of her mother, Dame Martha, so that the latter's usually watchful eye found more enticing occupation than gazing upon her daughter's every action?

Mefistofele, indeed, soon lured the still comely Martha into the entanglements of a flirtation as amusing to himself as flattering to the Dame—with the result that lovely Marguerite and her handsome cavalier had many opportunities for their secret and passionate love-making.

All too soon, however, Marguerite's entrancing romance came to an end. Mefistofele had no intention of bringing lasting happiness to her or to anyone else. Besides, he had another and far more alluring woman ready to stir the rejuvenated senses of Faust later on.

Therefore, he enticed his victim away from the clinging arms of the simple Frankfort maiden, and took him elsewhere to experience many other delights and wonders undreamed of even in his most fantastic imaginings.

Thus was Marguerite deserted by her lover and left to endure alone the consequences of her romantic dream.

.   .   .   .

The vainglorious Mefistofele could not resist displaying his own mighty power and grandeur to the rejuvenated cavalier whose soul he coveted.

Some time after the callous desertion of Marguerite, he transported Faust to the edge of the Brocken, a circle of rocky heights in the Hartz Mountains. Here, the Witches' Sabbath was being celebrated with the wildest orgies, in which demons and fiends from the nethermost regions of Hell joined with the witches in the most fantastic and horrible revels.

Lightning, thunder, and volcanic flames blazed and roared; and in the centre of the awe-inspiring scene, the flashing form of Mefistofele seemed to tower to a gigantic height as he thus gloried in the power of his magic. He called up demons of fearful aspect to pay homage to him as the Prince of Darkness; and the witches, as they circled around him in their whirling dances, likewise hailed him as Master, uttering wild eldritch cries of greeting.

Faust gazed upon this fantastic scene with mingled horror and fear; but presently his heart was filled with remorse, to the expulsion of all else. By means of a vision, called up by Mefistofele with satanic glee, he beheld his own recent victim, the unfortunate Marguerite, now languishing in prison under sentence of death and awaiting execution for having slain—in the delirium and anguish following upon her desertion—the child born to her and "Henry".

Grief-stricken at the havoc he had wrought, Faust implored the Demon to convey him quickly to the side of the betrayed maiden. This Mefistofele willingly enough did, hoping thereby to gain yet another victim—the soul of the condemned and demented Marguerite.

.   .   .   .

On entering the prison cell of Marguerite by the magical aid of his demon companion, Faust begged the distracted girl to fly with him and enjoy the pleasures of life once more in another sphere. At first, the now dying Marguerite seemed almost as though willing to do so, her heart once more responding for the moment to the magnetic presence of her lover.

Then seeing the sinister form of Mefistofele hovering in the background, she now knew the latter for what he was—the Spirit of all Evil. She withdrew instantly from her lover's arms and shrank back in shuddering horror, praying to Heaven for help and forgiveness.

Marguerite's prayers were heard; and as she drew her last breath, angelic voices were heard proclaiming her forgiveness and the salvation of her penitent soul.

.   .   .   .

Once more Mefistofele endeavoured to chain to himself more closely his hoped-for victim by means of a sensuous and soul-destroying passion.

He now transported Faust back through the Ages to the Homeric period of Classic Greece. Here, on the golden shores of the Peneus, in a flower-decked scene of surpassing beauty, with marble statues and graceful temples making a perfect background, Helen of Troy appeared in all the glory of her famous siren beauty to ravish the heart of Faust.

Forgotten now was the simple incident of gentle Marguerite. As he listened to this goddess-like being relating to him the romantic story of the devastating effect of her fatal beauty upon the heroes of Troy and Greece, Faust was enthralled indeed. He bowed down before this exquisite vision of female loveliness, hailing her as his ideal of beauty and wooing her with eager words as they wandered together in an earthly paradise of flowers.

But even the sensuous pagan passion of Helen of Troy could not bring true joy and contentment to the questing soul of Faust. And so the years went on. He had not yet experienced his one perfect hour of peace, his fleeting moment of truly satisfying bliss. The worldly joys, the power of riches, and the easy indulgence in selfish pleasures, provided so lavishly by the Tempter, did not bring him the happiness he sought. His rejuvenation had not been the overwhelming success that Mefistofele had promised.

Back in his shabby laboratory in Frankfort once more, Faust realized that his renewed life had not been worth while.

He was again an old man, feeble and tired, and death was fast approaching. He knew now that he had wasted the precious years that had gone by. To live for oneself was not the true meaning of life. The love of God and the love of one's fellows alone could bring true happiness.

He was repentant for his past sins and follies and full of remorse for the suffering he had caused to others; and now, at the point of death, he humbly prayed to Heaven for forgiveness. Yet once again he opened the Holy Book, and sought comfort from its pages as the sands of his life ran out.

And now, Mefistofele made yet another attempt to win the soul he had wagered for. Furious at seeing his coveted victim gleaning obvious comfort and contentment from the Holy Book—at the sight of which he cowered for a moment in abject fear—he once more endeavoured to ensnare him by magically thrilling sights and sounds. He showed him visions of entrancing sirens, and invited him to listen to sensuous, disturbing music, sung by seductive voices.

But such temptations had lost their power to move the remorseful Faust. Such ephemeral joys of the senses no longer appealed to the now sincere penitent, who sought only to be forgiven by the God against whom he had offended.

When, therefore, the foiled Demon, in a final gesture of pretended friendliness, spread out his cloak and invited the old man to fly with him once more into the vortex of worldly pleasures, Faust now turned from him with horror and loathing. He tottered over the Holy Book he had been reading, his fading eyes seeking its words of comfort yet once more. Already he heard the sound of angelic voices surrounding him; and as he drew his last breath, the heavenly chorus swelled to a glad triumphant anthem of rejoicing over the sinner who had repented and the soul that was saved.

As a shower of rose petals softly fell over the dead body of Faust in sign of heavenly forgiveness, the cowering form of the defeated Mefistofele vanished from sight. The King of Evil had lost his wager, and his challenge had come to naught.

NERONE
(*Nero*)

Boïto

NERO was Emperor in Rome, the most envied man in the whole of the civilized world. Young, handsome, ambitious, a genuine lover of the Arts, he was the popular idol of his people, who, ever seeking to please him by their flattery, worshipped him as a god.

It was, however, a far from god-like figure which ran, distracted, along the Appian Way on the night following the dreadful deed that had branded him a matricide; for Nero, though so lavishly gifted by Nature, was likewise vicious, cruel, and selfish. Despite the fact that it was his own mother, Agrippina, who had helped to make him Emperor in place of his half-brother, Britannicus, the rightful heir, he had since found her dominance too restraining to his love of absolute power; and, with unnatural callousness, he had murdered her with his own hands.

Then, with the cowardice of the true bully, he had become almost mad with fear lest the avenging Furies should haunt him for ever afterwards and lest his earthly glory should suffer eclipse because of his crime. In frantic haste, therefore, he caused the body of his murdered mother to be cremated that same night; and then, gathering up the ashes, he hastened in a distracted way to a certain grassy spot on the Appian Way, where he had given orders for a grave to be dug to receive them. Though he knew not remorse, he felt that only when these accusing ashes were safely buried would he cease to be haunted by his fears.

Even as he now fled, terrified, along the road that led to Rome, he believed that he was accompanied not only by the Furies but by the spectre of the murdered Agrippina herself; and though he tried to gain reassurance by declaring himself to be a second Orestes, the analogy was not convincing.

It was, therefore, a frenzied figure that presently reeled on to the moonlit grassy verge beside the open grave where his confederates were waiting.

One of the latter was Simon Magus, a High Priest of the popular Gnostic Temple in Rome, who practised his strange philosophy in its most degraded form and mingled it with the equally debased mythology of the Romans of that day. The vicious young Emperor had found this cunning, self-seeking Priest a useful ally on many unlawful occasions; and Simon Magus gladly pandered to his royal master's baser needs while carefully keeping an eye to his own main chance.

The other unlawful grave-digger was one of the Emperor's boon Court companions, Tigellinus, who likewise played up to his tyrant master's whims.

Just as the gruesome ceremony of burying the ashes of the murdered Agrippina had come to an end, there came the sound of approaching footsteps; and the form of a lovely woman, wrapped in a dark cloak and having a live writhing snake coiled around her neck and arms, drew near. All his guilty fears returning at this sudden apparition, Nero now fled to hide behind some nearby bushes, followed by the equally alarmed Tigellinus; and the ever-useful priest was left to deal with the newcomer. In the latter Simon soon recognized Asteria, a beautiful dabbler in magic and wonders, whose aid he had long wished to secure for his own Temple mysteries with which he impressed his superstitious congregations.

Being a recognized magician and worker of conjuring tricks himself, Simon Magus had no fear of Asteria and her hypnotized serpent; and, profiting by this encounter, he soon made a crafty offer to her. By his arts and from spying upon her movements, he had discovered that Asteria had conceived a great love for the young Emperor Nero and that she longed to have her love returned; and he determined to work upon her passion for his own ends. He now invited her to enact the part of a goddess at his next Temple ceremony, which the Emperor was to attend; and he promised that her exquisite beauty and close proximity to the latter during the Temple rites and orgies would quickly bring the susceptible Nero to her feet.

Enthralled by the prospect of thus finding a means of satisfying her audacious passion for one so far above her, Asteria eagerly consented to assist the High Priest in his grand ceremonies—though she now had little belief in these heathen deceptions and trickeries as practised by the latter. She was, indeed, somewhat attracted by the new gentle religion of the Christians, who were compelled to hold their simple services in hidden caves and other secret places because of their terrible persecution by the Romans.

One of these secret meeting-places of the Christians was near by on the Appian Way; and she knew of it. So did Simon Magus who was keeping this knowledge as another sop to offer his royal master at some convenient time.

Pleased to have secured the lovely Asteria for his grand Temple ceremony on the morrow, Simon Magus moved back a few yards to bury the tools he had just been working with, so that his gruesome deed might not be suspected; and next moment, another fair maiden of great beauty, robed in white, came by, softly reciting the new Pater Noster prayer of the Christians. This was Rubria, a Vestal Virgin who, though now a secret Christian, felt sad and sinful because she still continued her duties as a Vestal, fearing to be persecuted. Also, she was sad because she dearly loved Fanuel, a young Christian teacher and priest, who, however, was too enthralled by his holy mission to permit himself to be enslaved by an earthly love.

Asteria, who had remained, was so charmed by the sweetness of the simple Christian prayer recited by the white-robed Vestal that she approached and declared her own delight in the beautiful words; then, remembering her promise to join in the heathen rites of Simon Magus, she broke away suddenly and hastened along the Appian Way towards Rome.

Early dawn was now approaching, and as Rubria was about to continue her walk, the young Christian leader, Fanuel, came by, also praying; and, full of joy, the young girl spoke softly to him, hoping he would see how dearly she loved him. But Fanuel, though attracted by Rubria, was not to be lured from the thoughts of his present holy mission; and he spoke only of the converts.

As the two Christians spoke together, Simon Magus returned from hiding his tools. Knowing from his spy work that these two young people belonged to the new religious sect, another crafty idea instantly came into the brain of the heathen magician priest. He knew that the Christians gained great strength and powers of endurance from their new and simple religion; and also he had heard of the miracles performed by their Crucified Master and His Disciples. He, therefore, now boldly asked Fanuel to divulge the secret of his divine powers and to show him, Simon, how to perform miracles that would impress his own Temple worshippers. In return, he promised the Christian leader immunity from the present persecutions against his sect. Also, in like manner as the Devil had tempted Jesus in the Wilderness, he promised, by means of his own magic and influential earthly powers, to raise him to dazzling heights of glory in the Roman Empire.

Carried away by the vehemence of his own highly-coloured oratory and seeing himself as a world wonder-worker, with Fanuel as a well-trained tool to his hand, Simon Magus raised his voice almost to a clarion call; and the sound of his excited tones presently mingled with shouts and trumpet blasts which now could be heard approaching from the direction of Rome, whence a procession was obviously coming out from the City.

But Fanuel was not to be tempted by the alluring promises of a charlatan; and he sternly rebuked Simon with indignation, declaring that the strength and mighty deeds of the Christians came only from their God and could not be bartered for gold.

The young Christian priest now hurriedly departed on hearing the sounds of the procession drawing near, Rubria having already slipped away during this discussion; and Simon was left fuming at his failure to solve the mystery of the Christians' strength and mighty deeds and already planning an easy vengeance against them and their hated sect.

A great concourse of Romans now came marching along the Appian Way from the City as the first rays of the rising sun appeared over the Seven Hills—centurions, soldiers, lictors, musicians, trumpeters, nobles, citizens, and visiting strangers from oriental and other foreign countries. Banners were flying, Roman Eagles were glistening everywhere, wreaths and garlands were carried by slaves and children, and flowers were strewn on every side. In the midst of this joyful procession came a marvellous gilded triumphal car, at present empty—but the crowds were crying out eagerly : " Cæsar! Nerone! "

Nero, though he had been scared by his own terrible deed, was no fool; and while waiting for his murdered mother's ashes to be secretly prepared and buried, he had sent messengers back to Rome with the false story that Agrippina had been slain while in the act of planning his own death.

The people, overjoyed at the news of his escape, thus had come tumbling out from the city, soon forming into a gorgeous procession to bring back to Rome the Emperor they worshipped as a god . . . a worship cunningly engineered by himself.

When Nero presently heard the people clamouring joyously for him, he knew that his plot had succeeded; and he now came forth with Tigellinus from his hiding-place and proudly stepped into the triumphal car. Thus he drove back into Rome amidst the delirious acclamation of his cleverly deceived people.

.   .   .   .

In the gorgeous subterranean Temple of Simon Magus, mysterious and terrible rites were being performed before the altar of a huge brazen idol representing a goddess having powers over the demons of evil and darkness.

A vast congregation of worshippers was gathered in the Temple, overawed by the impressiveness of the scene, by the idolatrous actions of the richly-robed priests, and by the horrible libations of blood offered to the goddess through the brazen idol. The deceived worshippers knew not that the High Priest, Simon

Magus, joked behind the scenes with his colleagues; that he regarded them with cynical contempt for being so easily duped by his trickery; that the riches they brought as penances for sins or as payment for oracular statements went into the ever-capacious pockets of the priests, and that the mysterious voice of the goddess they heard was merely a very human one. To them the ceremonies were real and terrible.

But Simon Magus was playing for higher stakes to-day than the awe and cringing respect of his usual devotees. Knowing that Nero still suffered occasional qualms of conscience as a matricide, he had enticed him to attend this special Temple service, at which the royal murderer was to prostrate himself before the idol and so receive forgiveness from the goddess herself—whom he promised actually to produce in person at the altar by means of his magical gifts.

Just before the arrival of the Emperor, therefore, Simon made the love-sick Asteria pose gracefully at the foot of the altar to impersonate the goddess who should secure the obedience of her erring royal votary. But, strongly superstitious though Nero certainly was, his reaction to female beauty was stronger still—and Simon Magus now learned to his cost that he had overreached himself.

When Nero entered the Temple and approached the altar, he seemed, at first, awed and impressed; and he humbly bowed low before the gracious goddess, whom he had been led to believe had indeed appeared at the command of the magician, Simon Magus. Presently, however, as he beheld more clearly the loveliness of the so-called goddess, his passions became inflamed and he made as though to commit the sacrilege of snatching the divinity from before her own altar.

Full of alarm lest his fine scheme might thus fail, Simon now caused a thunderous voice to shout from the mouth of the brazen idol: "Nero! Begone!" In order further to scare his royal dupe, Simon also had many of the torches and mysterious lights extinguished; but, in this gloom, Asteria, realizing that her beauty had indeed kindled a temporary flame in the royal object of her love, crept closer to Nero and, winding her arms around him, kissed him passionately.

At first Nero eagerly responded; then he suddenly realized that he had been duped, that this was warm human flesh in his arms, no goddess, but a live and lovely woman whom he now thrust aside roughly. Next, he tested the pretended "voice" of the brazen oracle-idol by thrusting a blazing torch into its mouth; and hearing an undoubtedly human yell of pain issuing therefrom in response, he belaboured the statue madly with a huge mace which he snatched from the altar.

Now furious that he had thus been so ignominiously fooled, and eager to rid himself of one who knew too much about his own unlawful deeds, Nero called upon his guards to seize all the priests of the Temple and carry them off to await his cruel pleasure later on. For Simon Magus in particular, he planned a fearful fate. Once, in a foolish moment of expansive boastfulness, the charlatan priest had declared to his royal master that he could do anything—even fly. Nero now remembered this vain boast, and decreed that Simon should prove his flying powers at the next great Circus performance. He must mount to the top of the highest tower of the Oppidium and fly therefrom—like Icarus, who crashed to the ground when the sun melted his waxen wings.

Having thus sealed the fate of the trickster, Nero quelled the confusion and uproar in the Temple by mounting upon the battered altar and singing to the accompaniment of a sweet-toned lyre which was handed to him by a slave; and he was soon enjoying himself once more, singing to the acclamations of the crowd. He, Nero, would be their god.

.   .   .   .

Simon Magus, though he knew that he could not escape his fate, managed to put off the evil day a little longer by offering to disclose the position of the Christians' secret meeting-place. He and his priest-colleague were, therefore, allowed to lead the soldiers to this hidden spot on a night when it was believed the converts were likely to meet.

Fanuel, Rubria, and their Christian friends were, indeed, meeting that night to pray and to read their holy writings. They were all very contented and happy in their new simple faith. Only Rubria was sad; for her well-beloved Fanuel still remained nothing more than a brother to her and would not permit himself to think about the sweet love she had for him.

While the Christians were thus praying and rejoicing together, Asteria—who had escaped, unscathed, from the Temple upheaval—hastened into their midst with the dreadful news that Simon Magus had betrayed them and was even now leading the soldiers to their hiding-place. Terrible though this news was, the Christians, strong in their faith, remained calm and went on with their prayers; and they listened to Fanuel's words of comfort until the soldiers, led by Simon Magus, entered and made captives of them all.

Simon Magus made one more attempt to learn from the Christian leader the secret of his strange power; and he invited him to perform a miracle whereby he and his friends should escape the Circus doom that now awaited them, again promising him gold and riches as a reward. But Fanuel still proudly refused to buy his freedom; and the Christians were all marched off, still singing and praying, to await the dreaded hour when they would provide part of the fearful spectacle of a Roman holiday.

On the day of the Circus performance, there came a strange ending to one of the most magnificent shows of this horrible kind. The Circus was closely packed in every part, and Nero himself led and cheered on his people in an orgy of ferocious joy at the sight of the martyrdom of the Christians in the arena. The gladiatorial shows came first; and when it was time for the Christians to face their doom, there came an interruption. The Vestal Virgin, Rubria, sprang forward and, prostrating herself before Nero, entreated him passionately to spare the lives of these good and gentle people. Her pleading, however, was in vain, for the sadistic Emperor would not be deprived of his fearful entertainment—and because she had pleaded for them, Rubria herself was condemned to share the fate of her friends. Now openly declaring herself to be of their faith, Rubria gladly stood beside her beloved Fanuel; and the Christians were driven into the arena to fight with wild beasts, hailed with execrations by the crowds.

Meanwhile, Simon Magus, too, could not escape his fate; and from the top of the Oppidium tower, he was compelled to leap into the air as the fabled Icarus had done. But Simon had plotted a fearful revenge; and his friends, at his request, were even now setting fire to Rome. News of this plot, however, and the fact that Rome was already burning, had been hurriedly brought to Nero, who callously refused to stop the eagerly anticipated Circus performance for such a cause. Let Rome burn! He would build her up again, a fairer city than ever!

Nevertheless, the Circus performance did not continue much longer; for the crowd, presently seeing the heavy clouds of smoke rolling into the Colosseum, became panic-stricken and fled madly from the building in the hope of saving their homes.

All was confusion; and in the pandemonium that ensued, Fanuel, the young Christian leader, who had miraculously not yet been badly mauled in the arena, managed to make his escape through the dense clouds of smoke.

As Fanuel sought refuge in a lower part of the building, he was joined by Asteria, who had likewise been able to escape from the Circus pandemonium; and presently they found themselves in the Spoliarium, or crypt, where the dead bodies of the Circus victims were flung from above to await burial later on. They eagerly searched for the body of Rubria; and presently, after passing over the mangled corpse of Simon Magus, they found the Vestal's frail form. To their joy they discovered that, though dying, she still breathed and could speak to them.

And now, at last, when too late, Fanuel realized his own love for this gentle maiden; and he spoke to her in the tender accents she had always longed to hear. Thus, Rubria died happily in the arms of the man she loved, knowing that her love was returned. Also, there was peace in her soul, because, by her martyr's death, she had expiated her sin of continuing to serve as a Vestal Virgin while holding the Christian faith.

And Asteria, too, had found peace; for the events of that terrible day had driven away her passion for the evil Nero, and she had now accepted the simple faith of her Christian friends.

Meanwhile, the smoke and flames had now reached the vault; and Asteria just managed to drag Fanuel away from the corpse of his beloved one and hasten with him to a place of safety as the Circus walls fell in with a mighty crash.

PRINCE IGOR *Borodin*

ONE day, towards the close of the twelfth century, the great Russian Prince, Igor of Seversk, a mighty and renowned warrior, gathered his fighting men together in the market-place of Poltivle, his capital. He was about to lead them into battle with their hereditary enemy, the Polovtsy, a Tartar tribe equally renowned as themselves for bravery and prowess in the field.

A vast crowd of the townsfolk had also met in the square for the purpose of giving a rousing send-off to the departing warriors. On the steps of the palace stood Igor's wife, the beautiful Princess Yaroslavna, bidding a sad farewell to her royal husband and her son, the handsome young Prince Vladimir, who was to accompany his father to the wars.

The Princess had vainly endeavoured to prevent her husband from entering upon this expedition, having had a strange foreboding that it would end in disaster. The people also tried to hold the warriors in conversation in order to delay their departure, they, too, being depressed by a sense of approaching calamity.

While the expeditionary party thus tarried in the square an eclipse of the sun, which fell due that day, came on apace. As the light thus vanished and an uncanny darkness overshadowed the heavens, the superstitious people, taking this disturbance of Nature as a certain omen of disaster to their arms, fell upon their knees and implored their Prince to abandon his project and to remain with them.

Prince Igor, however, was not alarmed by signs and omens; and having learned that the Polovtsy had been driven by another rival prince into the Plains of the Don, he determined to go forward with his plan of meeting his foes there, expecting thus to take them at a disadvantage.

Having placed the affairs of state in the hands of his brother-in-law, Prince Galitsky, he bade a final loving farewell to his wife. Then, as the sun peeped forth once more from behind its enveloping shadow, he marshalled his warriors and, with his son riding beside him, set forth with them towards the plains.

In the weary weeks of waiting that followed, the Princess Yaroslavna had to face many difficulties and troubles. She soon found that her brother, Galitsky, always a dissolute and licentious prince, now intended to add treachery to his other bad qualities. No sooner did he enter upon his duties as Regent, than he began to plot for the usurpation of his brother-in-law's throne. In this piece of bare-faced villainy he was assisted by two clever rogues named Skoula and Eroshka, who, having deserted from Prince Igor's army, were willing enough to accept the bribes now offered them by the base Galitsky. As they were also famed as bards and skilful performers upon the native musical instruments of the period, they were welcome guests wherever they went. Thus were the deserter minstrels, while pursuing a seemingly innocent calling, able to carry the seditious messages of the treacherous Regent into the homes of those inhabitants of the city who were sufficiently base to listen to a scheme for the betrayal of their liege lord.

While hatching this dastardly plot, the intending usurper did not fail also to employ his powers as Regent in pandering to his own pleasures; and by indulging too freely in his libertine vices, he unconsciously brought about the discovery of his secret plot.

One day, as Igor's faithful wife, the Princess Yaroslavna, sat in the reception hall of the palace, sighing as she thought of her absent lord, a party of young maidens suddenly interrupted her musings. Flinging themselves at her feet and entreating her protection, they declared tearfully that one of their fairest com-

panions had been abducted for the amusement of the licentious
Regent, Prince Galitsky.

Yaroslavna was greatly distressed at the story told by the weeping girls; and, on instituting further inquiries, she now discovered the whole perfidious plot for the overthrow of her absent
lord which had been set on foot by the treachery of her brother.

When, therefore, Prince Galitsky presently entered the hall,
followed by the lords of the Court, she denounced him before
all as a traitor. After a stormy scene, in which she faced his
baffled fury unflinchingly, she deprived him of his authority
and drove him from the Court with indignation and contumely.

Even as this painful scene concluded, a terrified messenger from
the seat of war hastened into the presence of the Princess, bearing
the terrible news that the noble Prince Igor had met with disaster
to his arms, the Russian warriors having been utterly defeated
by the Polovtsy. Worst tidings of all, the Prince and his gallant
son Vladimir had been carried away with their remaining
followers as prisoners into the Tartar camp. Nor was this the
end of the alarming news. Elated with their victory, the Tartar
warriors were even at that moment marching on Poltivle, with
the object of sacking the city and reducing its inhabitants to
slavery.

At first, all were stunned by the fearful tidings brought by the
distracted messenger; but presently their patriotic feelings, stirred
by this national disaster and increased by the sight of their helpless,
grief-stricken Princess, roused the nobles into an outburst of loyal
devotion. Drawing their swords, they bade their liege lady not to
despair, swearing to defend her until death should claim them.

Meanwhile, the defeated Prince Igor lay chafing in the Tartar
camp, even though an honoured prisoner. His captor, the Khan
Khontchah, was an Oriental of the noblest and most chivalrous
type, and he treated the brave enemy now in his power with the
utmost courtesy and honour. The captive Igor, therefore, experienced no hardship or indignity but only suffered in spirit
from anxiety as to the fate of his fair city and of his beloved wife.

The gallant young Prince Vladimir was also treated as an
honoured guest; indeed, his woes were soon forgotten when he
was invited into the presence of the Khan's beautiful daughter,
Khonchakovna, with whom he quickly fell in love. Nor was it
long ere his love was returned. The Tartar maiden was instantly
attracted by the handsome young captive, and, with the fiery
ardour of the East, she readily responded to the eager wooing of
the Russian Prince.

With the magnanimity of a noble conqueror and the courteous

hospitality of the Eastern potentate, the Khan ordered a sumptuous banquet to be prepared in honour of his distinguished guests; and Igor and his son were astonished at the brilliant festivities thus provided for them, which far excelled any entertainment of the kind they had ever experienced before.

After the banquet, a number of beautiful dancing girls were introduced into the midst of the company to give an exhibition of the wild barbaric dances of the East, their performance being accompanied by skilful musicians who played exquisite airs upon their weird native instruments. The beauty of these maidens, the grace of their movements, and the wonderful music of the players, together with the blaze of jewels and the gorgeous costumes and tent decorations, lingered long in the memories of the Russian captives. The honour thus shown him helped Prince Igor to bear his woes with more resignation, though he still could not refrain from giving vent to his grief and shame from time to time.

On one of these latter occasions he was secretly approached by a renegade Polovtsy soldier, by name Ovlour, who happened to be a Christian, and who, eager to help a captive of his own religion, laid a plan of escape before the Russian Prince. But the noble Igor, appreciating the kindness and consideration with which he had been treated by the Tartar Khan, felt an equal honour within himself which forbade him to repay the latter's chivalry by thus breaking his parole; and, though sorely tempted, he proudly declined the offer. He continued, therefore, to endure his captivity with outward resignation, though inwardly chafing at the hard misfortune which had befallen him.

Meanwhile, the young Prince Vladimir and the lovely Tartar maiden, Khonchakovna, pursued their love-making under the most romantic conditions, oblivious of what the future might hold for them and living only for the joyful meetings each present day brought them.

Some weeks later, the victorious Tartar army returned to the Polovtsy camp laden with the rich treasures recently taken in the sack of Poltivle, and bringing in also many prisoners they had captured after breaking down the defences of the city; and upon their arrival even greater rejoicings than before were held by the victors, banquets were given, and the wildest orgies of dancing, feasting and drinking took place in every tent.

And now the temptation to escape was more than the wretched Igor could resist. The sight of his own men being brought into the enemy's camp as captives, together with the knowledge that his city had been sacked and that even his beloved wife might be in danger of captivity, stirred his chafing spirits to such a pitch

of despair that he determined to accept the renegade's offer of
facilitating his escape, feeling now that he was justified in
doing so.

He sent for Ovlour, therefore, and listened eagerly to the latter's
daring plans for his escape in company with young Vladimir.
It was arranged that the royal captives should steal out of the
camp that same night when the revels were at their highest; for
it was realized that it would be quite an easy matter to step past
the already drunken guards and thus reach the plains in safety,
where horses would be waiting for them.

All the elaborate plans made by Ovlour worked out satisfactorily; but just as the time arrived for the departure of the
runaways, there came an unexpected and unforeseen obstacle.

The Tartar maiden, Khonchakovna, seeking her lover in
accordance with her frequent custom, discovered the preparations
of the plotters just as they were about to set forth; and with true
Eastern fervour, she passionately entreated Vladimir not to leave
her to die of grief and despair, declaring that she could not live
without his love.

The young Russian Prince was now placed in a heart-rending
predicament, compelled to choose between love and duty; and
after a hard struggle he stifled for a few brief moments the yearning of his heart and yielded to the stern pleading of his father
who, already mounted, now spurred on his steed. He was about
to follow in filial obedience, when Khonchakovna flung herself
upon him and, winding her clinging arms around his neck, held
him back by sheer force, declaring fiercely that she would never
part from him while the breath of life remained in her. Nor did
the passionate maiden relax her detaining hold upon the lover
whom the vicissitudes of war had sent to her until Prince Igor
and Ovlour had successfully passed the camp's drunken sentries
and had vanished into the darkness beyond. No longer influenced
by his father's domination and realizing that his chance of escape
had gone, Vladimir yielded to the dictates of his heart and willingly enough returned to the revels with his beloved one, declaring
himself ready to live and even to die for her alone.

And death came very nigh to him within the next few hours.
When morning broke, the escape of Prince Igor was discovered;
and the Tartar soldiers, furious because their own careless revellings had made the escape possible and eager to vent their wrath
and disappointment upon the young Prince, seized Vladimir and
would have slain him then and there. But the dignified Khan,
still true to his benign and noble character, sternly ordered the
prisoner's release, observing with true Eastern philosophy that he

had a better plan for reconciling the young Prince to his captivity than putting him to death or even tightening his bonds. "The bonds of Love are stronger than iron bands," he added, as he placed the hand of Vladimir in that of Khonchakovna, "therefore, he shall be wedded to my daughter, who holds his heart in thrall and from whom he will have no desire to escape."

So the young Russian Prince was wedded to the Tartar maiden; and they lived happily together in the sunshine of each other's love.

Meanwhile, the unhappy Princess Yaroslavna pined and mourned in her lonely palace, which lay partly in ruins. Though she had escaped from indignity at the hands of the invaders by remaining in hiding until their departure, there now seemed nothing left for her to live for, since she felt that by this time her well-beloved lord and her gallant son were surely dead.

Every now and again, however, a faint hope would creep into her heart once more; and then she would take food with the few faithful attendants who still remained with her and would endeavour to cheer herself and them.

One day, after many weary weeks of waiting had gone by, Yaroslavna went out upon the terrace of the palace, on every side of which lay broken walls and loosened stones to bear witness to the sack of the city by the Tartar hordes; and as she gazed across the ruined city and over the bare fields beyond, she observed two horsemen approaching at a furious pace.

At first, fearing that these travellers might prove to be Tartar soldiers returning to effect her capture, she was about to fly to her former hiding-place when a second glance revealed to her astonished gaze and unbounded joy the fact that the leading horseman was her own beloved husband, Prince Igor. His sole attendant was the faithful Ovlour, who had so successfully arranged the escape.

A tender and truly thankful reunion took place between the royal pair, whose love and conjugal happiness had ever been of that ideal and edifying quality only enjoyed by the noblest natures; and after gathering their few scattered followers around them once more, the Prince and Princess entered the citadel to return thanks for their wonderful deliverance and to take up the reins of government once more.

As it happened, the two minstrel rogues, Skoulá and Eroshka, who had assisted the treacherous Prince Galitsky in his evil schemes, were skulking about the precincts of the historic edifice as the royal procession approached; and a clever idea now occurred to them. In order to save their own skins and to incline popular opinion in their favour should awkward questions be asked later on, they hastened to the belfry and set the bells ringing merrily—thus cunningly giving the impression of at least present loyalty by their eager haste to acquaint the scattered populace, by their joyful bell-ringing, of the happy return of the well-beloved Prince Igor.

ALKESTIS   *Boughton*

THERE was deep sorrow in the ancient palace of Admetus, King of Pheræ, in Thessaly, for the lovely and gracious Queen Alkestis was dying. She was about to give up her life to preserve that of her lord.

Admetus had been served for a period of nine years by the Sungod, Apollo, who, as penance for slaying Jupiter's Cyclops forgers of thunderbolts, had been condemned by the mighty King of Heaven to serve a mortal as bondman; and so gentle and considerate a master had the young Greek prince proved that Apollo had scarcely felt his thraldom at all but had come to love Admetus as a brother. When his period of service ended, therefore, he rewarded his late master by beguiling the Fates into granting him a great boon. When the appointed time came for Admetus to die, he was to be permitted to live on if he could find someone near and dear to him—his father, mother, or wife—to die in his stead.

Admetus was full of gratitude for the boon that had been wrested for him from the three Gray Sisters whom all mortals feared; for he loved life and all the good things thereof—the happiness of domestic bliss with a beautiful wife and fair children, and the earthly power of a princely position. But when, much sooner than expected, in the midst of his earthly glory, the time came for him to die and grim Death approached, he was faced with an unforeseen difficulty. Neither of his elderly parents—one or other of whom he had hoped might thus favour him, their sands of life being already well-nigh run out—would agree to take his place. The old retired King Pheres, indeed, told him in no measured terms that he considered such a request both selfish and unreasonable; and Admetus was filled with despair.

Then the beautiful Queen Alkestis, fearful lest her precious children should be left fatherless—a misfortune greatly dreaded in the heroic age—and eager to render the greatest service of all to the man she loved and to preserve a goodly King for the welfare of his people, nobly offered to make the splendid sacrifice herself; and Admetus, though torn between his desire to live and his love for the partner of his throne and the mother of his children, finally accepted this last supreme act of wifely devotion.

But when Alkestis began to weaken and droop before his anxious eyes and her last precious hours drew near, he was filled with agonized despair. Though he had selfishly brought himself to accept her monstrous sacrifice, it lacerated his truly affectionate nature when the time came for them to part. How he longed that someone else—less important to his comfort and happiness—might have been permitted to make the necessary sacrifice for him! Why should it be his adored Alkestis? All his life he had been beloved of the gods; why then, in this last blessing, should he be called upon to suffer so intensely? He had done no ill in his life to deserve it—thus he argued. But his railings of despair and his remorseful sorrow were unavailing. The Fates had accepted the sacrifice and it was now too late for him to prevent it; for the gentle Queen was already sinking fast and before the dawn of another day she would have departed to the Land of Shades.

It was now the mystic hour before the dawn; and as Apollo, the Sun-god, stood before the palace of Admetus, illuminating the black shadows with the radiance of his presence, he thought gratefully of the kindness he had ever received during his bondage from the young King and grieved because of his helplessness to prevent this present evil from falling upon him.

Even as he mused thus, Thanatos, or Death, drew near to the doomed house he was so soon to enter—a grim, crouching, black-draped, winged figure, who started back in revulsion on beholding the bright Sun-god, whom he hated for having already deprived him of Admetus as his lawful prey. Nothing daunted, however, Apollo put forth another plea for the innocent and gracious Alkestis, eloquently entreating that one so young and fair might be spared.

But Death refused the request, declaring cynically that the younger the soul the richer was his prize. Apollo, baffled for the moment, then departed, after prophesying a fall for the sinister victor and declaring that even now a mighty hero was approaching who should yet wrest the gentle prey from his grasp. Disdainful still, however, and announcing that Alkestis should certainly lie in the House of Hades presently, Death entered the palace to await the moment when he should take the prize for which he had come.

As the first streaks of dawn stabbed the sky, a group of the citizens of Pheræ appeared before the palace, sad and downcast, to inquire after their dying Queen and to utter songs of entreaty to the gods to spare her life even at this eleventh hour. When the weeping handmaid of Alkestis came out to them, they plied her with anxious questions. These simple folk loved their gracious royal lady dearly and wondered how Admetus could bear to let her die for him and thus cast such precious love away; and their tears fell fast as the handmaid told them of the resignation of Alkestis, of her calm preparations for death, of her many sad farewells, and of her sweet words of comfort for her sorrowing husband and children.

As they still wept and wondered, the doors were opened and the dying Alkestis, already clad in her funeral robes, supported in the arms of her unhappy husband and followed by her little son and daughter, came forth into the open. This was the appointed hour for her devoted soul to depart and she wished to die in the fresh soft air of the early dawn. And when the eagerly watching townsfolk beheld the grief-stricken aspect of their royal master, their reproaches died away and their hearts went out to him in sympathy.

As his beautiful Queen, weak and faint, sank upon the couch that had been placed for her, Admetus, overcome with woe, flung himself upon his knees beside her; but after comforting him awhile, Alkestis gently bade him rouse himself as she had one last request to ask of him. Having secured, by her own sacrifice, a father's continued care for her little ones, Alkestis now sought to strengthen their position and future happiness by entreating her lord, as her last dying request, not to bring another woman into his house as stepmother—perchance a woman who might be of less queenly spirit than herself and who might possibly ill-treat the children of a dead wife.

As Admetus broken-heartedly gave the promise she desired, Alkestis placed her weeping children in his arms; and then, with a last faint word of farewell, she fell back upon the couch and expired.

Loud cries of mourning arose from all as the body of the dead Queen was borne reverently into the house, where Death was waiting upon the doorstep, triumphant at having thus secured his prey. When the doors had closed upon the distracted husband and weeping children, the mourners still continued their songs of lament.

Presently, however, a stranger appeared in their midst—a man of mighty stature and noble bearing, who wore a lion's skin flung carelessly over his robe and carried a huge club across his shoulder. This was the great hero Herakles—or Hercules—who, travelling upon one of his great adventures, had just arrived in Pheræ and had come to claim hospitality from his friend, Admetus.

Upon beholding the stranger, the mourners ceased their songs of lamentation for the moment, while their leader held the newcomer in conversation. Presently, Admetus, having heard of his friend's arrival, came forth from the house to bid him welcome. Though filled with despairing remorse because of his wife's death, he determined at least to be true to the laws of hospitality; and endeavouring to hide his grief, he invited the tired and travel-stained hero to rest and feast within his gates.

At first Herakles refused the invitation, because of the obvious signs of mourning he saw around him; but Admetus carefully concealed his wife's death from him, declaring that the mourning was for a stranger who had died in the house and who was to be brought out for burial that evening. Seeing that Herakles was still loath to remain in a house of sorrow, Admetus—fearful lest he should depart and that the hospitality laws should thus be broken—added that the guest chamber and banquet-hall were far removed from that part of the house where lay the dead guest; and at length the tired and hungry hero agreed to remain, and was led within by the King. A splendid feast was immediately spread before the famous and honoured guest; and Herakles was thus so generously entertained that he soon forgot he was in a house of mourning and feasted and drank until at last he fell asleep.

Later on, as darkness fell, Admetus left his sleeping guest and crept quietly from the banqueting-hall. The funeral procession for the burial of Alkestis was then formed and set forth from the palace on its way to the tombs in the grove beyond.

Just as the mournful procession was proceeding on its way, another party appeared from the opposite direction, headed by Pheres, the old retired King of the land, who had come to offer sympathy to his son and to bring robes and other gifts to be buried with the dead according to the custom of the day. His words and offerings, however, were strongly resented by the grief-stricken Admetus, who was now half mad with woe and remorse; and a stormy scene at once ensued between the pair. Admetus poured forth recriminations upon his father for having refused to die for him; and Pheres scornfully reprobated his son's ignoble conduct in having permitted the gentle Alkestis thus to sacrifice herself. The truth of this accusation seared deeply into the remorseful heart of Admetus, though he replied furiously to the biting words of Pheres; and when the old King at last departed, full of anger because his gifts had been refused, he dropped his defiant attitude and with humbly bowed head gave orders for the burial ceremony to proceed.

When the mournful procession had passed out of sight, one of the household servants bidden to remain and wait upon the hero guest should he awaken, came out from the house. He was disgusted and distressed because the reveller—muddled with strong wine and still unaware of his host's tragic loss—was now awake and insisted upon continuing his carouse at this solemn instant when the well-beloved Queen was being laid in her tomb.

Even as the devoted slave gave vent to his feelings by an outburst of grief, Herakles himself came stumbling out through the door, arrayed in festive garments and rakishly crowned with a myrtle wreath, still flourishing a golden cup of wine in his unsteady hand; and beholding the weeping servant, he bade him dry his tears and make merry, laughingly proffering his own cup as he spoke. When the outraged youth dashed the cup from his hand, however, the well-feasted hero recovered himself somewhat; then, remembering the weeping crowd he had beheld on his arrival, he spoke more quietly and asked the slave for whom he mourned.

The servant, overcome by his sorrow and indignant at the guest's revellings, now told him the truth, despite his royal master's orders to the contrary. When Herakles thus realized that the inmates of the house of mourning he had come to were grieving for the death of the good Queen Alkestis herself, he was filled with dismay and real concern for the sorrow of his royal friend who had thus received and entertained him in the hour of his deepest woe.

Sobered by this revelation, Herakles was eager to make reparation for the unwitting pain he had caused. Amazed and filled with admiration at the wonderful devotion of Alkestis in thus giving her own life for that of her lord, he determined to set forth and seek out grim Death at the grave-side and there to wrestle with him for the noble soul about to be transported to the Land of Shades.

Herakles rushed forth impetuously to perform this heroic deed, while the servant, scared at his own temerity in having revealed his master's secret, hastened back into the house; and shortly afterwards the funeral party returned from the burial ceremony.

Although the citizens now endeavoured to comfort their unhappy King, their efforts were in vain; and Admetus, almost mad
with despair, flung himself upon the steps of the palace in a
paroxysm of grief.

As he still lay there, replying at intervals to the sympathetic
entreaties of his people, Herakles again appeared from the groves
beyond, slowly leading by the hand a silent woman closely veiled
from head to foot; and all the company drew back respectfully,
though gazing curiously upon the hero's strange companion and
wondering whence she came.

Leaving the veiled woman to be supported by the mystified
handmaidens, Herakles strode forward to the side of Admetus,
who arose at his approach; and after gently reproving him for
having hidden the truth of his real grief from him, he announced
that he must continue his interrupted journey at once. He then
asked the King to take charge of the woman he had brought until
he should return to claim her. He declared he had won her in a
contest against certain kings; but as he could not take her with
him upon his immediate difficult and dangerous task, he begged
Admetus to admit her into his own household for the time being.

Admetus, however, entreated his friend to take the woman he
had won elsewhere, declaring that he had no place in his household for her, since he might not put her in the men's hall, and
could not bear to have her in the women's chambers where once
his beloved wife had been. Then, as his grief again broke forth,
Herakles attempted to comfort him, even going so far as to
suggest that later on, as his grief wore off, he might take another
wife. However, Admetus' anger was so great on hearing this,
coming so soon after his promise to Alkestis, that the hero quickly
dropped the subject, not wishing to wound his friend unneces-
sarily, though he had joy in store for him. Instead, he again
implored accommodation for the prize he had won; and, after
many more refusals, Admetus at last consented, much against his
will, to take the woman into his household.

Herakles, well pleased with this success, now insisted that his
friend must himself lead the stranger into his palace; but upon
Admetus giving a shuddering refusal to this request, he seized
the latter's hand and placed it in that of the veiled woman. Then,
as the distracted King, who had covered his eyes that he might
not look upon the stranger though he trembled at her strangely
magnetic touch, Herakles snatched off her enveloping veil and
triumphantly bade his friend open his eyes and look upon—his
wife!

For Aikestis it was who thus stood revealed to all; and as

Admetus, now overcome with joy at this marvellous restoration of his beloved one, gazed upon her in reverential awe, Herakles related the story of how a few minutes ago he had fought and won a mighty battle for her with Death. Then, as Admetus wondered at the continued silence and stillness of his returned wife, the hero explained that, having been in the abode of Death, her voice must not be heard until her hours of purification were accomplished and she awakened on the third day, when all would be well with her.

Full of gratitude, Admetus entreated his friend to remain awhile and to share in the rejoicings that would now take place; but Herakles declared that he could stay no longer but must proceed on his way immediately.

And when Admetus had led away his beloved one—so miraculously restored to him—the hero flung his lion's skin over his back and lifted up his mighty club; and as he departed in search of further adventure and glory, then came Apollo, the glorious Sun-god, radiant and full of light, who once more passed over the threshold of the palace whence baffled Death had been driven as he had foretold.

BETHLEHEM *Boughton*

In the humble home of Joseph and Mary at Nazareth, a sound of heavenly singing broke the peaceful silence that reigned there. Softly it rose from a sweet low murmuring until it rang out as a triumphal chorus of glorious rejoicing.

Mary the Virgin, who was sitting alone in the house, happy and peaceful, looked up in wonder, knowing that such exquisite singing could come only from celestial hosts. But why should these triumphant heavenly voices fill such a humble home as hers and be heard only by the simple maiden wife of Joseph?

Soon she understood, however, and was filled with an even greater wonder. In the midst of a dazzling heavenly light, there now appeared before her the glorious shining form of the Angel Gabriel, who hailed her as the Most Blessed of Women and told her that she was to be the mother of the Second Person of the Godhead, for the Holy Ghost should alight upon her within that same hour—yet should she for ever remain in virginity.

As Mary trembled and fell to her knees, amazed on hearing

this mystery but humbly submissive to the Will of God, the glorious vision faded, the Angel Gabriel departed, and the heavenly voices died away.

Joy and wonder filled the simple maiden's heart, as she thus realized that she was to become the Mother of the Saviour of the World; and she remained as in a happy dream until aroused by the arrival of her husband, who presently entered the house, eager to greet the fair maiden whom he had married but recently.

But when Joseph heard Mary's wonderful news, he was at first angry, refusing to believe the strange story of her heavenly visitant or that the Child she was to bear was conceived of the Holy Ghost; and he retreated from her now drooping presence in sorrow and dismay.

As he turned and rushed blindly from the house, however, he also was greeted by a heavenly vision of the Angel Gabriel, who told him that this great matter had been ordained by God; and the Angel added that Mary's Child Who was presently to be born was, indeed, the Second Person in Trinity, and should be the Saviour of the World.

Gabriel also announced that the Holy Child should be named Jesus; then, again bidding Joseph not to be aghast, the Angelic Messenger departed.

Now filled with remorse for his first hard words, Joseph hastened back into the house to bring comfort and support to the pure maiden his wife. He fell humbly to his knees before the gentle Mary, craving her pardon for his doubt of her and worshipping her and the Holy Child she was so miraculously to bear.

Mary received her husband with gracious dignity and kindness, bearing him no ill-will for his first natural doubts; and they talked happily together of the miracle.

Then Joseph remembered that it would be necessary for him to go almost immediately to Bethlehem, in obedience to a decree of the Roman rulers in Judæa; and when he expressed his fears at leaving her alone, Mary announced her determination to accompany him. Had it not been prophesied that the Son of God, the Heavenly King of the Jews, the great Prince of the Royal House of David, was to be born in that little city of Judæa?

So Mary and Joseph set out for Bethlehem; and, in due time, the Holy Child was born there. But because all the inns and lodging-places in Bethlehem were crowded with other folk who had come thither to be taxed and numbered in accordance with the conquerors' new decree, Joseph could find no other resting-place for his weary wife and her precious burden than a stall or barn where cattle were housed. And thus it happened that the Son of God was laid in a manger as His first cradle.

. . . .

That night, on a hill-side near Bethlehem, shepherds were watching their flocks; and though the night was cold, they soon forgot their wintry discomfort as they presently beheld a mighty wonder.

A brilliant Star shone in the Eastern heavens more brightly than any star they had ever seen before. Presently, too, they heard the triumphant chorus of a mighty angelic host, announcing the birth of a Heavenly King and singing " Glory, Glory, in the Highest! " In the song, the Angels likewise announced the present humble abode of the newly-born Babe; and the shepherds were filled with amazement.

Then, as they marvelled together at this wonder, they remembered the prophecy of Isaiah that a Child should be born of a pure Virgin in the City of David and of David's line, who should be the Son of God and their King and Saviour; and they rejoiced greatly, as they realized that He whom all Judæa had expected so long had, indeed, come at last.

As the heavenly voices faded away, the shepherds hastened towards Bethlehem with eager steps. As they reached the humble stable, they heard the Angels again singing a joyous song and knew that their footsteps had been guided thither.

When they entered this lowly lodging, they found Joseph and Mary tending the Holy Child as He lay in a manger; and they knelt beside Him in humble worship.

Then the simple shepherds again sang for joy as they returned to their flocks on the hill-side.

. . . .

The shepherds were not the only folk who knew that the Mightiest Wonder of the World had happened on that wintry night in David's City.

A few days later, outside the splendid palace of Herod the Tetrarch in Jerusalem there waited three Wise Men—Zarathustra, Nubar, and Merlin—who were mighty kings in their own lands. They had travelled a great distance, each one separately but all for the same reason.

They had seen a brilliant Star in the East, which, it had been revealed to them, portended that a Heavenly Child had been born, a Child Who should be the greatest King the world had ever known and Who would be the Saviour of the World.

The three Wise Men had, therefore, come to worship this newly-born Child; and they had brought rich gifts to lay before

—gold, frankincense, and precious spices. They had followed the Star, which had moved before them; and they had now reached Jerusalem and had come to the palace for further news of the Heavenly King.

As they stood outside the palace, waiting for the gates to be opened and the curtains drawn back to reveal the splendid Herod, ready in audience, the three Wise Men spoke together of the Wonder they had come to see. They also listened to the talk of the people who were now gathering around.

The shepherds had already spread the joyful news of what they had seen and heard on the hill-side twelve nights ago; and some of the people were rejoicing because their long-expected King had come at last, while others doubted and spoke scornfully of the occurrence.

Presently, the doors of the palace were opened, and the rich heavy curtains drawn back; and the mighty Herod was seen seated within in great splendour and surrounded by his slaves and soldiers, all magnificently attired. Beside him sat his beautiful wife, Herodias; and the baby prince, her son, was likewise brought forth to receive the acclamations of the Court.

Herod was surprised and angered, therefore, when his herald, Calchas, presently announced that three mighty royal Wizards waited without. These strangers had travelled from their own distant countries to greet the newly-born Divine Kingly Child in his land, whose birth had been heralded to them by a dazzling Star which they had followed and which had led them to Judæa.

Nevertheless, though greatly disturbed by this news, Herod received the Wise Men graciously; and he was relieved when Zarathustra assured him that he need have no fears for himself or his own son, since the Star portended the birth, not of an earthly royal babe, but of a Divine Child.

Then Herod declared his eagerness to know more of this strange mystery; and he bade the three Wise Men to continue their journey, to follow the moving Star, and to find out if, indeed, any such Divine Child had been born. If this were so, he invited his distinguished visitors to return to him with their news, that he might likewise honour the Babe.

When the Wise Men had departed, however, Herod gave vent to his angry jealousy and declared that he would suffer no one to offend against his own greatness but would quickly take steps to drive out and destroy any rival to himself in Judæa.

The three Wise Men, on leaving Herod's palace, again followed the dazzling Star which had already led them so far from their own lands; and presently they arrived in Bethlehem and came to the stable where the Holy Family still remained.

Here, Joseph was at that moment listening to Mary with fear in his heart; for, as the Holy Mother sang lullabies to her Babe, she let fall prophecies regarding the sufferings He must endure later on. Soon, however, Joseph forgot his sadness in the presence of the splendid newcomers.

The three kingly Wise Men fell down before the Holy Child in reverence, awe, and worship, laying at His feet the rich gifts they had brought; and they hailed Mary as the Blessed Queen of Heaven.

While they thus worshipped in joyful wonder, the Angel Gabriel again appeared, warning them of the evil designs of Herod and bidding Joseph take Mary and the Child into the land of Egypt for safety.

With a final reverent greeting, the three Wise Men now departed; and having been warned by the Angel, they did not visit Herod again but returned secretly to their own lands.

Then Joseph and Mary, with the Holy Child, departed from the humble stable where they had known such joy and which they now left with regret; and they hurriedly journeyed towards the land of Egypt, where they might rest a while in safety from the jealous wrath of Herod.

And as the Holy Family went on their weary way, they were cheered once more by Angel voices carolling forth a mighty Chorus of Glory to God.

THE IMMORTAL HOUR *Boughton*

DALUA, Lord of the Hidden Way, came fatefully into a wild and beautiful forest glade at the rising of the moon. So mysterious and awful a spirit was he that he was dreaded and avoided even by the immortal folk themselves. He was feared even more by mortals. Forgetfulness fell upon all who passed within the dark shadow of his form; and his cold touch was death. Every mortal victim he secured filled him with triumph.

Half concealed among the trees on a high bank that overlooked the glade stood Dalua—a tall and awe-inspiring figure, sinister of aspect but having the splendid and supernatural beauty of the ancient gods. He awaited a new victim.

Though no human being was to be seen in the forest glade, Dalua was not alone. Amidst the purple and black shadows slashed by silvery shafts of moonlight, strange, elusive, intangible shapes appeared and vanished like phantoms; and ever and anon mysterious voices and mocking laughter were heard as though uttered from an invisible world—as, indeed, they were. For these unseen speakers were the voices of Elemental Spirits; and from time to time they hailed or taunted in mocking defiance the Watcher on the bank, who, however, was much too powerful for them seriously to defy or to divert from his present purpose.

Dalua had learned that Eochaidh,[1] the young High King of Ireland, was even now wandering in the forest alone, having tired of warfare and of kingly sports; and that he had come forth on a new adventure—to " woo the Immortal Hour " and to win an immortal maid as his bride. He also knew that Etain, a Faery Princess of the Shee or Hidden People, had wandered forth from her own land of the Young and the Heart's Desire, seeking for a new joy she could not name. Dalua had planned that these two should meet and wed—that the romantic young King should thus experience the " Immortal Hour " he craved for but that misfortune and sorrow should quickly follow. His faery bride must eventually return to the Land of the Young; and the life of her despairing mortal lover would then be claimed by the sinister spirit.

Having thus resolved, Dalua now caused the immortal Princess and the mortal King to meet him in turn in the forest at moonlight.

Etain came first in answer to the mighty influence that drew her to the spot as surely as though visibly led by the hand. Exquisite as the moonlight in her pale ethereal beauty, of nymphlike grace, lily purity, and white rose sweetness, starry-eyed and cloudy-haired, enthralling, elusive, mysterious, she moved slowly down the glade and seated herself beside a pool where grew snowy water-lilies no less fair than herself.

When Dalua approached and spoke to her, she was not afraid; and as he let the shadow of his hand sweep over her he knew that she had forgotten the Land of the Young and the sweet whispers of Midir, Prince of the Shee, who had loved her in those faery realms. When he told her of the mortal King she would presently meet and who would give her the strange new joy she sought, she was enraptured. He then bade her seek a huntsman's lodge near by; and Etain, unquestioning, moved away again like a sylph.

[1] Pronounced " Yochay ".

A little later, the young King Eochaidh likewise came down the glade; and he also stopped to gaze into the lily-pond where, by the magic arts of Dalua, he now beheld a vision of the lovely Faery Princess he sought. As he gazed, full of rapture, at this fair picture, Dalua now appeared and bade him follow in his footsteps if he would find his heart's desire.

Although the royal youth felt the sinister influence of the mysterious Dalua, he was so entranced by the lovely vision he had seen that he could not refrain from following him. But it was only a wild and weird voice he followed in the wake of, for Dalua had now become invisible and called his directions from various parts of the forest, often with mocking laughter. But the young King went on boldly to meet his fate.

. . . .

When Etain reached the huntsman's hut, she was at once admitted by the huntsman and his peasant wife, who both gazed upon her unearthly beauty with wondering awe. They did not know who she was; but they had expected her. A sinister-looking stranger of stern authoritative demeanour had called at the hut a short time before and had left with them some pieces of gold as payment for attending to the needs of two wanderers who would come, one after the other, to pass the night under their roof. The humble peasants had not dared to refuse the stranger's request; and now they were busy preparing supper for their guests.

A sudden storm had arisen, so that Etain shuddered slightly as she listened to the howling of the wind and the rolling of the thunder; and she pulled back the curtain in surprised alarm. As she dropped the curtain, a hunting-horn sounded and a voice called for admittance. Next moment, Eochaidh entered with a greeting for all and craved shelter for the night. The peasants bade him welcome, but shuddered slightly when, on touching his garments, they discovered, to their amazement, that they bore no traces of moisture despite the wild storm of rain he had just emerged from.

But Eochaidh knew nothing of the peasants' touch; for his eyes had met those of Etain and he was ravished by her exquisite beauty. He now knew why his steps had been so magically drawn thither—that those star-like eyes he had seen in his dreams had drawn him forward with the resistless strength of their magnetic beauty, and that the instantly answering love that now irradiated her face like moonlight was the long-sought hidden fire that was now flaming in his own heart.

Scarcely heeding the presence of the huntsman and his wife—

again awed by the royal bearing of their second stranger guest—
the wanderers sat down, side by side, and began to talk. When
Eochaidh introduced himself as the High King of Ireland, Etain
could tell him nothing of her own country because of the shadow
of forgetfulness cast upon her by the sinister Dalua. All she
knew was that she was a " daughter of the Lordly Ones ".

But swiftly love enveloped the pair with the great joy they both
had sought so long; and, full of happiness, they spoke of the glad
days they would spend together in Eochaidh's royal castle, when
Etain had become his Queen.

But even as they declared that their love for one another would
last for ever, there came a burst of mocking laughter from the
unseen spirits in the woods beyond; but the happy lovers heard
it not. A little later on, however, as they sat together while the
humble peasants slept, a strange far-away look came into Etain's
eyes. For a moment she had caught in the far distance the sound
of sweet singing—the Song of the Shee—which caused her to
remember dimly the Land of Heart's Desire, that beautiful Land
of the Young from which she had wandered :

> " How beautiful they are
> The lordly ones,
> Who dwell in the hills,
> In the hollow hills."

For an entranced moment she forgot the presence of the young
King. Then, as the Song of the Shee died away once more, she
fell back into the eager arms of Eochaidh, overcome by the joy of
her mortal love.

.   .   .   .

In the royal castle of Eochaidh, High King of Ireland, high
festival was being held in celebration of the anniversary of the
young King's marriage with the Faery Princess. A year had
passed by since Eochaidh had led home his beautiful stranger
bride—a year of perfect love and happiness, during which he had
experienced to the full the wonderful joy he had dreamed of and
so passionately craved for.

But now, as the King sat upon his throne, surrounded by the
Druid priests who were his counsellors, he was ill at ease, in
spite of the festival music and songs already being performed in
honour of his lovely Queen. Recently, a subtle change had taken
place in Etain. She had become restless, for dim memories of the
past were disturbing her with strange longings. The King's love
no longer filled her whole being as before, and she would start
from his embrace with a misty, far-away look in her eyes and with

parted lips, as though she heard distant music and whispering voices half recognized.

Eochaidh himself was troubled, too; for it seemed to him that his happiness was too perfect to last and that a shadow was already creeping over the sunshine of his joy—the shadow of Dalua, the mysterious Spirit of Shadowy Dreams. He was haunted by dreams and premonitions, and had heard sudden mocking laughter in the darkness; and sometimes he fancied he saw phantasmic shapes and shadowy hosts marching through the mists.

However, he endeavoured to shake off his sudden insistent sadness as the songs of the druids and bards arose around him on this festival evening; and when, presently, the Queen entered with her attendant women, he rose to meet her with gladness and to join in the song of greeting and loving welcome that burst forth as she appeared. With tender pride he led her to the throne beside him, an exquisitely dazzling figure in her regal robes and rich jewels; then he begged her to reply to her people's greeting and to speak a few gracious words to them.

Etain rose at once in answer to his plea; but she was abstracted and strange in her manner. After speaking a few gentle words of thanks to the expectant company, she passed her hand over her troubled brow as though trying to remember something. Then, declaring that she was weary, she bade them good night. Turning to the King, she also bade him a gentle farewell for the night, saying she was perplexed with strange dreams and with thoughts half forgotten and half remembered.

But Eochaidh, now more troubled than before, implored her to remain in the festival hall a longer time, now telling her of the strange thoughts and dreams that had also visited him recently. Again Etain spoke of the sweet delicate music and subtle whisperings that now constantly sounded in her ears, the "little lovely noise of myriad leaves". Then, adding that she was now too weary to remain longer, she once more bade him good night and left the hall.

Eochaidh, no longer in the mood for the festival music, now dismissed the Druids and Counsellors; and as the brilliant procession departed, a bright young stranger, wrapped in a green cloak, entered the hall. Having greeted the young King with princely dignity, the stranger, declaring that he had a boon to ask, now flung off his cloak and stood revealed in glittering garments of ruddy-gold, with sun-gold hair and a radiant countenance, and carrying himself with the faery grace of the Immortals.

He was Midir, the Faery Prince of the Shee and the Hidden

People, who had loved Etain in the Land of Youth and the Heart's Desire; and he had come to entice the wayward, wandering Faery Princess back to her own people.

Eochaidh, though no word was spoken of this, felt apprehension strike at his heart as he gazed fixedly upon the beautiful and bright stranger, fearing he knew not what but knowing now that his disturbing dreams and premonitions had not been without cause. Nevertheless, with quiet dignity, he asked his dazzling visitor to name the boon he had come to crave. Midir at once replied that it was but a small favour he asked—merely to touch the white hand of the Queen with his lips and to sing to her " a little echoing song "!

Eochaidh, though greatly disturbed by this strange request, would not refuse it; and he sent a young page-boy to bid the Queen return.

Etain soon appeared; and the King saw with surprise and apprehension that she had already discarded her queenly robes and was now clad in the same simple flowing garments in which he had first seen her. Though his sad fears grew with every moment, he led her to Midir and told her of the request the latter had made.

Etain, gazing lingeringly at Midir with a look of half-recognition in her eyes, slowly held out her hand to him; and when he had raised it gently to his lips, she begged him to sing to her the " little echoing song " he had come to sing.

Then Midir, keeping his eyes fixed steadfastly upon the Queen, took up a harp and began to sing the faery song of the Hidden People heard by Etain in the huntsman's hut in the forest:

> " How beautiful they are
> The lordly ones,
> Who dwell in the hills,
> In the hollow hills."

As Etain listened to the faery song the memory of long-forgotten things came back to her—the memory of the Land of Youth and of the Heart's Desire; and she now became insensible to her earthly surroundings, hearing only the enthralling Song of the Shee calling her to return to them.

With her eyes fixed upon his, she took the hand of Midir and began slowly to move away with him towards the open doorway; and when Eochaidh, now realizing with grief and despair that she was about to leave him, made a passionate movement towards her, she very gently repulsed him as though already almost a stranger to her.

Again Eochaidh moved forward, taking a threatening step towards Midir, who, with a proud majestic gesture, restrained him, so that he fell back again immediately, though still calling entreatingly to his beloved Queen.

As in a dream, Etain answered: "I cannot hear your voice so far away!" And once more, Eochaidh called wildly to her: "Come back! Come back! It is a dream that calls!"

> "Do not leave me, star of my desire,
> For now I know
> That you are part of me, and I the clay,
> The mortal clay that longed to gain
> And keep the starry Danann fire,
> The little spark that lives and does not die!"

But Etain heard only the call of Midir: "Hasten, lost love, found love! Come, Etain, come!"

Then, hand in hand, to the sound of the voices of the unseen singers in the far distance, the Faery Prince and the Faery Princess slowly left the royal hall and stepped forth into the darkness that led to Light to join "the Lordly Ones" who dwelt in the Land of the Heart's Desire.

With outstretched hands and a breaking heart, the baffled and distracted Eochaidh uttered a despairing cry: "My dreams! My dreams! Give me my dreams!"

In answer to his cry, Dalua, the mysterious King of Shadows, moved silently into the hall and laid his fatal touch upon him, saying: "There is none left but this . . . the Dream of Death!"

. . . .

Thus ended the Immortal Hour wooed by Eochaidh, High King of Ireland, who may be taken allegorically as representing the symbol of mundane life and mortal love, as Midir is a symbol of the spirit and Etain a symbol of the wayward but questing soul.

THE QUEEN OF CORNWALL *Boughton*

On the open terrace of the royal Castle of Tintagel, in fair Cornwall, a watchman passed to and fro, now looking out to sea for signs of stranger craft and anon scanning the paths that led up to the castle. King Mark had been out a-hunting with his Knights for several days past; but he was expected home at any moment now.

Even as the sound of approaching horsemen and the blowing of horns heralded the return of his royal master, Queen Iseult's woman attendant and confidante, Brangwain, hastened towards the watchman to know if, indeed, it was the King who approached.

Brangwain expressed relief that the royal chatelaine of the castle likewise had returned from a secret journey in time to greet her exacting and ever-jealous lord. For Iseult the Fair had just accomplished a rash and risky act.

During the temporary absence of King Mark she had received an urgent message from Iseult of Brittany—Iseult of the White Hands—the recently-made wife of Sir Tristram, her still passionately devoted lover, saying that the latter was ill of a fever and called constantly upon her in his delirium. Iseult of the White Hands, though fiercely jealous of her rival, the Queen of Cornwall—whom she knew only too well still held the heart of Tristram—yet herself loved the Knight so dearly that she could not deny his request.

Full of alarm at his fevered state and hoping that the presence of his beautiful Queen of Romance might restore his wandering reason, the distracted White Hands sent a messenger across the water to Cornwall to beg Iseult the Fair to come at once. If the returning vessel carried the Queen of Cornwall, it was to fly a white flag; but if she was not on board, a black flag was to hang from the mast. Already the sick Tristram began to recover at the happy thought that his beloved one would soon visit him. Then Iseult of the White Hands, seeing his joy, was once more filled with a raging jealousy, wishing she had never sent the message in that moment of alarm.

But the moment was propitious for the beautiful Queen of Cornwall, still pining for her lost lover. King Mark was engaged with his Knights in a big hunt; and there was just time for her to cross to Brittany and get back before his return. She set forth at once, therefore, flying a white flag, as directed.

But when Iseult of Brittany beheld the white flag on the approaching vessel, she was filled with deep misgiving and her jealousy flamed up once more, so that she determined to prevent the lovers from meeting, after all. As the boat touched shore, she now rushed forward to meet its royal passenger, declaring wildly that Tristram was already dead and that it was, therefore, useless for the Queen of Cornwall to land. The latter fell back swooning on hearing this tragic news; and she was already nearing the shores of Britain once more before she recovered.

Meanwhile, the sick Tristram was told by his wife that the ship from Cornwall had flown a black flag—the signal that his beloved one had not come to comfort and heal him; and he was once more plunged into despair. However, he learned the truth presently from one who had actually beheld the Queen on board the ship from Cornwall; and he furiously reproached his unhappy wife for her deceit.

Then, quickly recovering on thus realizing that Iseult the Fair still returned his love and had, in fact, risked the certain fury and vengeance of King Mark by coming to see him, Tristram, still weak but now jubilant, took ship and sailed for Cornwall himself. He donned the disguise of a minstrel in the hope of securing admission to Tintagel Castle. Though he knew it not, his equally despairing wife, Iseult of the White Hands, likewise boarded another ship and followed in his wake; for she could not bear thus to lose him to her rival.

Although the Queen of Cornwall had landed from her ill-fated journey just in time for the return of her royal lord, her attendant, Brangwain, was still full of anxiety lest her rash act should become known to the King; and her forebodings of ill quickly materialized.

No sooner had the royal hunter arrived in the entrance hall of the castle than he called loudly for the Queen, his jealous suspicions already aroused at her non-appearance in the hall to greet him. When Iseult presently entered, therefore, he angrily accused her of having seen her lover again during his absence; and inflamed further by his jealousy, he defied her to deny the accusation, since he had already learned from his spies that she had, indeed, taken a journey across the sea to Brittany.

Even when the unhappy Iseult, grieving for her lost lover, announced sadly that Tristram was dead, King Mark refused to believe her statement, declaring that the Knight had escaped death so many times that he would not trust him not to appear again; and he now announced that he would call a Council to be held, after he and his huntsmen Knights had banqueted, at which he would decide how best to deal finally with his wife's lover.

As the angry King disappeared within to feast with his Knights, the wretched Iseult wandered brokenly towards the terrace ramparts, wrapped in her sad thoughts. Presently, however, the remembrance of the King's rough, sneering words brought a sudden hope into her crushed heart. Could it be possible that her beloved Tristram indeed still lived, after all?

Had she been too ready to believe the hysterical words of his jealous wife?

This hope was increased when her attendant, Brangwain, on joining her, likewise expressed doubt about the veracity of Iseult of Brittany, who had certainly bidden the vessel turn about in frantic haste before the swooning Queen had time to recover.

Iseult the Fair now began to be buoyed up once more by the hope that her lover might still be alive, and to look forward with joy to meeting him once again—perhaps, even here in Tintagel, despite the presence of King Mark, whose jealousy and cold hatred would always be a menace to him. Although Mark no longer loved her, his pride would never permit him to relinquish his fair Queen or to bring a moment's happiness to the unfortunate lovers, even though he understood that their deep passion for one another had arisen through no fault of their own. It had, he knew, been the result of the love-potion they had both partaken of inadvertently at the hands of Brangwain. This had happened on board the vessel in which Tristram had escorted Iseult the Fair of Ireland to Cornwall, to become the bride of his royal master.

Even as hope thus revived for Iseult, there came the sound of sweet singing from without—a song such as Tristram himself had sung to her in the early days of their romance. Her heart gave a great leap of expectant joy—though she soon learned from Brangwain that the music came merely from an old harper, who craved alms at the gates.

The song of the minstrel had also been heard by the feasters in the banqueting-hall beyond; and King Mark impatiently sent out one of his Knights, Sir Andret, to give the beggar alms and bid him begone, since he was in no mood for music just then. Sir Andret, however, almost instantly had his suspicions aroused regarding the so-called " aged harper ", whose rather youthful steps did not seem entirely in keeping with his aged appearance. Being the confidant of the King, therefore, and eager to prove his zeal in the royal service, he slyly decided to return anon and to watch the movements of the newcomer from an unseen point of vantage.

Meanwhile, the " old harper ", finding himself dismissed, made his way to the entrance hall, where Iseult and Brangwain still sat alone; and, standing in the doorway, he removed his cloak and cap and revealed himself as the splendid Knight, Sir Tristram. With low cries of joy, the lovers rushed into each other's arms; and Brangwain, with a hasty look around to see that all was safe for the moment, left them to the ecstasy of their reunion.

When the first joy of their meeting was over, Iseult begged Tristram to tell her why he had allowed himself to be lured into accepting Iseult of the White Hands as his bride, when all his love was vowed to another. Tristram explained that during his unhappy wanderings after being driven forth from Cornwall by King Mark, he had fought for White Hands' father in Brittany, who had wished him to take as reward the greatest treasure of his land—his daughter; and thinking that his own beloved Queen was lost to him for ever, he had blindly taken the bride thus proudly offered. And though the listening Queen at first showed herself to be deeply wounded by this confession, she soon realized that never for a moment had Tristram ceased to love her; and soon, all her resentment was forgotten in the rapture of their reunion. They then made happy plans for a further stolen meeting that night.

The sounds of wild roistering already came from the Knights in the banqueting-hall beyond; and when their feasting came to an end they would be in no state to notice any unusual comings or goings. Towards cock-crow, too, the watchmen would grow drowsy and relax their vigilance. The hour before dawn, therefore, would probably provide their opportunity to meet again.

But the hopeful, if hazy, planning of the lovers, however, was doomed to failure, and their frail castle in the air soon came toppling to the ground.

Brangwain now rushed into the hall with the alarming news that a strange ship had just arrived at the jetty, from which had disembarked a closely-veiled and cloaked female figure. Fearful, as both realized that this stranger could be none other than Iseult of the White Hands, both Tristram and the Queen hurriedly departed from the hall—Iseult making her way to the gallery above, while Tristram hastened outside, hoping to intercept his inconveniently-arriving wife.

The first person to waylay the stranger, however, was the suspicious Knight, Sir Andret, who had already left the roisterers in the banqueting-room to spy upon the movements of the " aged harper ", of whose true identity he had little doubt. He intercepted the cloaked woman just entering the hall and learned from her that his suspicions had been well founded, that the harper was none other than Sir Tristram and that the stranger herself was the latter's injured wife.

Bidding Iseult of the White Hands enter the hall, Sir Andret hastened to the side of King Mark, to whom he told all he had learned. King Mark, in a fury of jealous rage, immediately rushed from the banqueting-room, with his drawn dagger in his hand; then, restraining his wrath for the moment, he decided first to spy upon his rival, moving from one hiding-place to another, in order to make sure of the right moment to strike his avenging blow.

Meanwhile, Tristram had returned to the entrance hall, where he found his wife, already weeping and begging his forgiveness for having followed him but declaring that she could not bear to be parted from him. Tristram poured bitter reproaches upon her, not only for now endangering his life by her untoward presence in Tintagel, but also for her former deceit in regard to the journey of her rival; but when White Hands again wept as she expressed remorse for this latter act, pitifully explaining that all was done because of her dear love for him, his heart softened towards her. He now realized that her love for him was as great as that of his other Iseult; and he was anguished at the strange workings of a cruel fate.

Now, when the equally distracted Queen of Cornwall, looking down upon this scene from the gallery above, saw that Tristram was softening towards his weeping wife, she could bear the strain no longer; and, heedless of danger, she hurried down to the hall to share in this really agonizing interview. But the sight of her husband's true love—his Queen of Romance, Iseult the Fair—now coming towards her, a vision of fatal beauty, was more than the over-wrought unloved wife could endure; and, with a cry of woe, she fell swooning at her rival's feet.

With gentle tenderness, Queen Iseult bade Brangwain carry the inert White Hands away to another chamber, and there to revive her with cordials and tend her with care; and then, irrationally, she turned and reproached Tristram for the fact that he was beloved by his own wife, as well as by herself. Soon, however, she realized the injustice of her reproaches; and once more declaring her own love for him, she listened eagerly to his new wild plans for their future.

All this time the lovers had been closely observed by the hidden King, who was jealously spying upon their every movement; and, unseen by either, he crept nearer and nearer, until he was within striking distance of his rival.

The once more enraptured pair, however, were first brought back to a sense of their danger, by the arrival of a messenger, who handed to them a scroll addressed by King Mark to his overlord, the mighty King Arthur, declaring his intention to slay Sir Tristram for his misdeeds. The messenger, having a regard for the luckless Knight, had thus risked much to warn him.

In frantic alarm, Iseult now implored Tristram to fly while he yet had time; but her lover made light of the matter. He declared that King Mark had been banqueting somewhat heavily that night, and that he had probably penned the scroll while under the influence of too much strong drink. In any case, he was grimly determined not to run away from his enemy. He, therefore, continued his wild wooing of his beloved Iseult, trying to soothe her anxieties with sweet, tender words.

But sadness and a feeling of impending disaster gradually enfolded the ill-fated pair; and the gathering darkness presently caused Tristram to wonder at the non-appearance of his enemy.

This was the moment for which King Mark had waited; and gliding swiftly from his hiding-place behind the still unwitting Tristram, he fiercely stabbed him to the heart.

As her lover fell dead at her feet, Iseult, stricken with woe, poured forth passionate recriminations upon the avenging King, who, however, turned away from her, unanswering, as though overcome by his own murderous deed.

Then, snatching the weapon from his now almost listless grasp, the frenzied Queen rushed upon him, and blindly drove the dagger into the heart of her lover's slayer.

Casting a last look of love upon the lifeless form of the onee splendid Tristram, Iseult the Fair, still in a frenzy of grief, now rushed out from the castle to the cliffs beyond; and, with a cry of welcome to the death that rose to greet her, she hurled herself into the seething waters below.

LOUISE   *Charpentier*

ONE evening in the spring-time, Louise, the beautiful young daughter of a Parisian artisan, stood at the open window of her parents' humble tenement dwelling waiting to greet her lover, Julien, an artist who had his studio in the house opposite. She was alone in the little home, but was fearful of interruption by her mother who might return at any moment; and she ran back to glance into the kitchen and to listen anxiously at the head of the stairs for the sound of approaching footsteps.

All was clear, but time was precious; and with radiant eagerness Louise hurried again to the window and out on to the tiny balcony beyond. To her relief, Julien already stood on the terrace outside his studio; and the lovers now greeted one another with

E

joy and were quickly absorbed in the delight of a stolen conversation.

Louise's parents did not approve of the handsome young artist's attentions to their pretty daughter; and they had forbidden all intercourse between the pair. Though poor, they belonged to the hard-working artisan class that took intense pride in living an honest and virtuous life, regarding severely the light pleasures of those who had time to idle away; and they distrusted the intentions of the romantic young artist who, coming from a higher grade in the social scale, had immersed himself in the care-free bohemian life of the Latin Quarter. Therefore, when Julien, sincerely in love with Louise, begged to be permitted to pay his addresses to her, he met with a cold reception and prejudiced disapproval.

But love is not easily denied; and the deep passion that had sprung up between the young people was strengthened all the more by opposition. They continued to meet almost daily in secret, on Louise's return from the city where she was employed as a midinette, seizing the few minutes while her mother was out buying food for the evening meal and before her father came back from his work.

This evening Julien reminded Louise of her promise to go away with him and leave her home for ever, should her parents continue to refuse sanction to their intercourse; and he added that he had already written another letter to her father as a last appeal.

Louise, torn between her duty to her devoted parents and her overwhelming love for Julien, now tried to divert her lover's thoughts into less dangerous channels. She entreated him to tell her how first he had come to love her; and the two were soon absorbed in a flood of happy recollections—how Julien had adored her on first beholding her upon the balcony in the sunshine; how he had showered rose-leaves upon her as she drew water in the courtyard below; and how, late one night while her parents were asleep, she had crept out to him and, folded in each other's arms, they had plighted their troth.

So enthralled were the lovers that they did not notice the entry of Louise's mother, returning with the provisions. The latter, overhearing the final portion of this pretty love-story and thus realizing with shocked dismay that the affair had gone further than she had imagined, hastened to the balcony and roughly dragged her daughter back into the room.

A violent scene quickly followed; but Louise boldly defended herself, declaring that she was compelled thus to deceive when her lover was denied permission to visit her openly as an accepted suitor. When her mother, however, began to abuse Julien as a loose-living vagabond who would certainly lead her astray, she angrily denied such a false accusation against the man she loved.

Louise's hot flow of words stopped suddenly upon the entrance of her father; and she quickly set about helping her mother, to prepare the evening meal. Later on, however, seeing that her father was reading the letter sent him by Julien, she begged him to consent at last to her lover's request and accept him as her suitor. Loving her father dearly, she fell readily into his inviting embrace and pleaded passionately for this happiness to be granted.

But her father loved her so devotedly himself that he was selfishly eager to keep her longer at his side that she might still be the light and joy of his home. To ensure this, and because of his real anxiety for her youthful welfare, he was ready enough to agree with his wife's scornful condemnation of Julien as a ne'er-do-well and a pleasure-loving fellow not suitable to become the husband of a quiet, modest working-girl.

It was in vain that Louise indignantly denied the vile aspersions cast upon the character of the young artist by her mother; she was still regarded by her doting father as almost a child who, lacking experience of life, regarded the future too rosily and did not understand that a fascinating love-dream might yet end in remorse and bitter tears. The intensity of her passion for Julien was unrealized by her father and unsympathized with by her mother; and the unhappy girl's entreaties were once more of no avail.

. . . .

Next morning, Julien, now realizing the futility of written appeals to her father, determined to intercept Louise on her way to work and to make another desperate attempt to persuade her to abandon her home and elope with him that same day.

At a very early hour, therefore, he made his way to the dress-making establishment where his beloved one was employed. It was situated in an open thoroughfare near the hill of Montmartre.

The scene was already a lively one. Ever since dawn there had been a constant succession of people passing along that way—rag-pickers, coal-gatherers, milk-women, junkmen, paper-sellers, street-sweepers, night-revellers returning home, and policemen coming on duty. As the sun rose, the street cries of hawkers were heard and city workers began to hurry along the streets to their places of employment.

Presently, the work-girls and midinettes began to arrive, arm-in-arm and joking with the gay youths who likewise now thronged the street; and Julien drew back into the shadows, waiting for his beloved one to appear. At last, when most of the other girls had already entered the building, Louise came along with her mother, who thus accompanied her pretty daughter lest she should be accosted by bold strangers.

Louise looked pale and unhappy after a night of weeping; but when her mother had departed she was quickly filled with joy once more as Julien slipped from his hiding-place and, intercepting her as she ran up the steps, clasped her in an eager embrace. Once again he passionately besought her to go away with him then and there; but Louise, though reassuring him of her tender love, struggled wildly from his grasp and fled in through the doorway.

So agitated was she, however, and so distractedly torn between her filial love and her passion for Julien that she could scarcely keep her attention upon her sewing work, despite the rallies of her merry companions.

Presently there came a sound of singing from the street below; and Louise became more agitated as she recognized the voice as that of Julien, who had thus boldly adopted the romantic methods of the gallants of a past age. Her gay companions ran to the window to wave and blow kisses to the serenader below who, however, seeing that Louise was not among them, gave them no encouragement but presently began to move away with downcast looks.

Then Louise, unable to struggle further against the surging tide of emotion that enveloped her, rose and flung down her work; and declaring herself to be overcome by the heat, she ran out of the room and down the stairs in feverish haste. Her companions were at first amazed at her sudden action; but when they presently beheld her walking away enfolded in the arms of the handsome young serenader, they considered it a great joke and laughed heartily.

But Louise was oblivious of their mirth; and as she wandered away with her lover's arms around her, she was filled with an ecstasy that bore her into the realms of enchantment, so that she counted the world well lost indeed.

.   .   .   .

In a pretty little house at the top of Montmartre, Julien and Louise lived together for many weeks in a happy world of their own. Their joy in one another was so complete that the days passed like a dream and no cloud arose to cast a shadow over their happiness.

Louise was quickly transformed by the radiance of love into the light-hearted joyous creature Nature had intended her to be. The narrow restrictions of her life at home, with the irksome severities of her mother's harsh rule and the over-anxious admonitions of her doting father, though not forgotten, had receded into the background. Nevertheless, whenever this subject of puritanical prejudice and parental tyranny was mentioned by the lovers, Julien would inveigh bitterly against such selfish suppression of the joys of youth. Sometimes, however, with a sudden pang of remorse, Louise would gently remind him that, possibly, the securing of one's own heart's desire might result in the breaking of those possessive parents' hearts; but Julien's tender embraces soon comforted her.

One evening after one of these self-reproachful outbursts on the part of his beloved one, Julien led Louise to their garden wall and bade her gaze down upon the wonderful city of Paris, where the gay lights of the night-time were already twinkling. Quickly their senses responded to the magic atmosphere of that most seductive city—Paris, the goddess of pleasure who, like an enchantress of old, had waved her wand over them to bring them love and now seemed to smile upon their joy with her dazzling illuminations and the ever-entrancing music of her streets. Realizing the freedom they had won and intoxicated by their happiness and the beauty of the night, the lovers involuntarily stretched forth their hands and invoked the protection of that same enchantress under whose irresistible spell they had fallen.

As they stood there, gazing down upon the night-time carnival frolics of Montmartre, a merry company of bohemian roisterers came pouring into the lovers' garden and insisted upon crowning Louise as their Queen of the Revels; and the fun soon waxed fast and furious.

Just as the merriment was at its height, there came a sudden interruption. A sombrely-clad working woman, severe of mien but obviously sad and anxious, appeared among the revellers and threaded her way through the various groups, oblivious of the curious glances cast upon her. It was the mother of Louise; and as she approached, Julien drew his beloved one into his firm grasp and defiantly faced the newcomer, at the same time motioning to his lively friends to depart.

When the revellers had withdrawn, the now sad and broken woman announced humbly that she had not come to quarrel but to entreat Louise to return home for a short time only. Her father, stricken with grief for the loss of his cherished and still deeply-loved daughter, had become dangerously ill; and now, in his delirium, he called so constantly for her that unless she returned at once to bring him peace of mind he would certainly die.

Louise was torn with anguish on thus learning that her beloved father's life was in danger and that she herself had caused his illness by leaving her home; but Julien, fearing to part with her even for such a dire necessity, first demanded a promise that she should be allowed to return to him when her father recovered.

The distressed mother, strangely softened by her grief and anxiety, readily gave the promise required; and Julien and the weeping Louise enfolded each other in a passionate farewell embrace.

Then the mother and daughter hurried away, Louise turning at the gate to throw a last longing kiss to her lover; and Julien was left alone with an aching heart.

. . . .

Once more Louise was back in her old home, chafing at the quickly renewed restraints of a narrow life. Like a singing-bird in a cage, she soon longed to escape once more and to regain the sweet freedom she had tasted for so short a time; and she pined for the comfort of her lover's arms and the joy of his all-sufficing presence.

Her father had begun to recover from his illness almost as soon as she had returned to him; but when he was restored to health and had started to work once more, the question of her return to Julien was shelved from day to day.

For a little while longer, Louise patiently refrained from insisting that her mother's promise should be kept. Then, at last, as she sat sewing by the open window one late evening, the entrancing lure of Paris once more stole over her senses; and a passionate longing to regain her freedom and to return to her waiting lover seized her as in a vice.

Her father sat gloomily regarding the drooping form of his daughter as he muttered a long complaining tirade against the woes of the poor in general. From this he went on to describe the disappointment of a loving parent who, having brought up a lovely daughter with stern care and in strict seclusion, had to suffer the injustice of having her enticed away by a honey-tongued stranger; and finally he began to call down curses upon the young artist who had thus brought such trouble upon his household.

Louise, unable to endure this unhappy situation longer, turned indignantly towards the table; whereupon her father, changing his tone, now entreated her not to leave her home again but to give him the continued comfort of her bright presence and to enjoy his own loving protection as of yore. But Louise declared that she wanted her freedom—freedom to live her own life. Again all the old arguments were brought up and arrayed before her, both parents declaring that the freedom she sought would only bring her sorrow and that their loving arms were safer than those of the lover she would return to.

All their arguments, however, failed to convince Louise, who again passionately demanded her freedom and the redemption of her mother's broken promise. Running back to the open window, she then invoked the City of Enchantment once more, calling upon it as upon a worker of magic to tear down the dreary prison walls around her and to restore her to the arms of her beloved one.

As she turned impetuously to escape from the room, her father barred her way; and when Louise, half mad with longing, called loudly upon her absent lover, he raised his arm as though to strike her. Then, suddenly giving up the struggle, he flung the door open himself and in a paroxysm of rage furiously bade her begone at once to drown herself in a life of sinful pleasure and never to darken his doors again.

As Louise, horror-struck at this savage outburst, hesitated to go now her father desired it and loath to part from him in such a storm of anger, her mother, also shocked at her husband's loss of control, pleaded with him not to thrust their beloved daughter out into the streets.

But the father, beside himself with rage, pushed his wife aside and again raised his hand threateningly towards the trembling girl; and Louise, now terrified, fled down the stairs and out into the street, running with all speed to seek the safety and shelter of her lover's arms.

No sooner had his daughter gone than the father's anger died away; and he rushed to the door, calling frantically to her to return. His cries, however, were unheard, for Louise had already vanished from sight. Prostrated with grief, he came back into the room and, stumbling towards the window, shook his trembling fist at the brightly illuminated city whose intoxicating lures had robbed him of his beloved daughter.

MAM'ZELLE FIFI   *Cui*
(*Mademoiselle Fifi*)

DURING the never-to-be-forgotten January of 1871, when the Franco-German War was raging and France was still suffering the terrible woes of invasion by her hated enemy, a party of

Prussians were in occupation of the pretty little village of Uville. Here, owing to bad weather conditions and the exigencies of the moment, they were compelled to remain for a much longer period than they had at first anticipated.

The invading officers had installed themselves in the fine old Château d'Uville as their headquarters; where, greatly to their disgust, they were compelled to pass many weary days of inactivity without amusements or distractions of any kind. The tempestuous weather and incessant rain made outdoor adventures impossible; and they quickly exhausted such amusement as was to be obtained by exploration of the château and interest in its many wonderful art treasures. In fact, they had no admiration, but only contempt, for the latter; they had even applauded the vandal-like behaviour of the youngest Lieutenant, Wilhelm von Eyrik, in wantonly destroying many of the most beautiful works of art in their temporary abode.

This latter degenerate youth passed by the name of "Mamzelle Fifi", owing to his effeminate appearance. This was accentuated by a fair complexion, a small slender figure pinched in at the waist, and a habit of expressing his scorn for things that did not meet with his approval by the contemptuous phrase " fi, fi donc ". He found real delight and continual amusement in defacing the treasures about him which had been collected during many years past by the former seigneurs of the château. Evidence of his wanton love of destruction was to be found in every room of the castle—more notably so in the large salon which served as the chief meeting-room of the officers.

In the salon in question he had allowed his vulgar fancy to run riot, and, out of pure wantonness, had slashed the priceless Gobelin tapestries on the walls into ribbons with his sword and cracked the crystal chandeliers and mirrors with well-aimed bullets from his pistol. Even the family portraits had been maltreated. Adding insult to injury, he had thought it a good joke to stick ugly German pipes into the canvases representing cardinals, judges and knights in armour, in order to vulgarize the aristocratic features painted thereon by various master hands. Upon the portrait of a proud lady he had sketched in charcoal a huge pair of German moustaches; and other flagrant examples of his insulting attentions were to be seen here and there.

In this apartment, one day after *déjeuner*, the commanding officer, Major the Graf von Farlsberg, sat smoking and drinking with his subordinates.

As usual, the junior officers soon began to grumble at the atrocious weather and the deadly dullness of their present monotonous existence. The Major commiserated with them good-naturedly, bidding them follow the example of their young companion, Lieutenant von Eyrik, who could always find some way of amusing himself, even if the results were disastrous. The young men, however, only showed further signs of restiveness, declaring that the childish amusements of "Mam'zelle Fifi" had no attraction for them. Even the story of Fifi's latest exploit— the exploding of a small mine in the art gallery of the château, full of famous pictures, priceless ceramics, carvings and other exquisite works of art, most of which had, in consequence of the explosion, been destroyed—did not restore their drooping spirits. Seeing that, evidently, they had some request to make, the Major bade them unburden their minds.

The Captain, Baron von Kelweingstein, pushed forward by the others as spokesman, now begged the Major to allow them to indulge in an evening of festivity and to invite some lively girls from the neighbouring town of Rouen to join them in making merry for a few hours.

So strong were their appeals that the good-natured Major— himself secretly pleased at the thought of what promised to be a pleasant respite from the weariness of inaction—agreed to the suggestion. The wily young Captain, fearful lest his senior should change his mind, immediately made arrangements for the revels to be held that night. He quickly sent a covered baggage-wagon into Rouen in charge of his own servant, who bore to a rakish officer friend there a note requesting the latter to select a party of the most charming of the light-living ladies of the town and to send them to the Château d'Uville in the returning wagon.

The Major, forbearing to reprimand the Captain for his precipitancy, directed the young men to go forward with their plans and to see that nothing was lacking for the pleasure of themselves and their lady guests. He then turned aside and gazed out through the open window at the soaked country-side and dripping trees. As his eyes fell upon the belfry of the little village church near by, he was reminded of the defiance of the brave old curé, the Abbé Chantovoine, who, as a protest against the invasion of the Prussians, refused to permit the church bell to be rung. The priest was willing enough to act as intermediary between the invaders and his flock, and, by his conciliatory conduct, saved the latter from many hardships and woes that might otherwise have befallen them; but he clung boldly and unwaveringly to this one mild form of resistance—the protest of a silent bell, by which he and the humble peasants upheld their national honour. Until the invaders had been driven forth and their land was free once more, the chimes of the village church should not be heard. Strange to say, the Prussian Major, hardened campaigner though he was and ruthless though he might be on other occasions, respected this peaceful protest of the good old Abbé, whose gentle courage irresistibly appealed to his better nature; and he had given instructions that the latter's wishes in this matter should be obeyed by his men.

This curious clemency on the part of his superior was greatly resented by the hot-tempered, intolerant von Eyrik, who was infuriated at the calm resistance of the old Abbé. Not only did he many times call upon the Major to let his men themselves ring the church bell merrily in acclamation of their conquest of the village, but, with all a bully's cowardly love of oppression, frequently begged to be allowed personally to chastise the curé and his village supporters for daring thus to resist the conqueror in their midst.

The Major, however, had refused firmly to allow his junior to interfere with the instructions he had given for the old Abbé's wishes to be respected. The church bell remained silent, and " Mam'zelle Fifi " perforce had to satisfy himself with his destructive amusements within the Château d'Uville.

By the time the Major's reverie was at an end, he found that the young men were making lavish preparations for their forthcoming entertainment and were already in riotous spirits. The large dining-table was invitingly laid out for an elaborate supper; and from the well-stocked cellars below an extravagant quantity of champagne and other rich wines of various kinds were brought up for the enjoyment of the revellers.

Scarcely were the preparations finished than the rumbling and bumping of an approaching baggage-wagon announced to the eagerly expectant Prussians that their guests, willing or not, had arrived. The officers, shouting with delight at the pleasure now within their grasp, hastened outside, and shortly returned to the room, each escorting a pretty lady upon his arm.

These girls of the town had, for the most part, come willingly enough. They had grown accustomed to the presence of the Prussians in their midst, and, with the philosophic good-humour of their class, were quite content to tolerate the amorous advances of even enemy admirers in return for a good supper and any further payment that might also be offered. Therefore, with one exception only, they entered whole-heartedly into the gaiety of the young men for whose pleasure they had been brought to the château, eating and drinking all that was offered to them. They even cheerfully endured the rough and frequently insulting caresses of their hosts, laughing loudly at the vulgar jokes and horseplay of the latter.

The only one among these free-and-easy "joy-girls" who resented the insulting attentions of her partner was a beautiful young Jewess named Rachel. Though she had joined the party of girls with seeming willingness and had even smiled and danced as she entered the room, Rachel had not come with them to the château for the purpose of merely amusing the Prussian officers. Having suffered much shame and loss at the hands of her country's foes, she had seen in this adventure a possible means of avenging herself.

Rachel had been handed over as a partner to the lively young subaltern, Wilhelm von Eyrik; and the insolent behaviour of this degenerate youth had quickly aroused her indignation. "Fifi", though pleased at having secured the most beautiful of the visitors as his prize, treated her with the utmost contempt and rudeness; and the sensitive, high-spirited girl quickly let him see that she hated and despised him for thus displaying his power as one of the conquering Prussians.

On parading round the room with her as his partner, the insolent youth had bent his head as though about to kiss her, but, instead, had blown a full puff of smoke from his cigar into her face. Rachel, angry at such an indignity, though remaining silent, had cast such a furious glance upon him that the Major, fearing lest the revel should be spoilt before it had scarce begun, called the young man to order and invited the party to seat themselves at the supper-table.

With the enjoyment of unaccustomed luxuries and the lavish supply of champagne, the fun waxed fast and furious; and it was not long before the revel developed into an orgy of excess and licence.

However, though her girl companions adapted themselves readily enough to the scene of levity into which they had been introduced, enduring the boorish attentions of their ill-mannered hosts with at least outward good-humour, Rachel stubbornly refused to submit tamely to the rough treatment she received at the hands of Lieutenant von Eyrik. The latter had as equal a talent for tormenting as for destroying; and seeing that the beautiful Jewess objected to his ill manners, it gave him pleasure to tease and aggravate her all the more.

Frequently the young officer was good-naturedly reprimanded by the Commandant, who endeavoured to keep the revel within bounds by calling for noisy drinking songs, in which all the party, with the one exception of Rachel, took part with great hilarity.

His partner's silence, however, evoked further unwelcome attentions from von Eyrik, who found the girl's increasing contempt both amusing and exasperating, while her dark beauty, enhanced tenfold by her flashing glances and scornful demeanour, became more and more alluring. Suddenly he snatched her in a close embrace and kissed her so long and violently upon the mouth that he even bit into the soft flesh, with the result that a streak of blood appeared on her chin when at last he released her. Furious at this outrage, Rachel again cast glances of hatred upon her brutal partner, as she dipped her handkerchief into water and bathed her bleeding lip; but she still maintained her silence.

As the evening advanced the boisterous noisiness of the party increased. A long series of toasts were now proposed, to which the young men drank so deeply that they soon threw off all restraint and treated their partners more roughly still.

Though the other girls joined noisily in the coarse hilarity of their hosts, Rachel still endeavoured to remain proudly aloof. The only effect of her disdainful glances, however, was to increase the irritation of " Mam'zelle Fifi ", who, rising unsteadily to his feet and raising an overflowing glass of champagne, drank to the continued success of the Prussian army and to the utter annihilation of the French, calling upon his companions to do likewise.

The other officers all honoured the toast noisily, but Rachel, her patriotic feelings wounded past further endurance, now broke her silence and hotly reminded von Eyrik that it was lucky for him no French soldiers were present, or those blustering words would have been crammed down his throat.

To this, the excited young Prussian replied contemptuously that the French were cowards and runaways and that all the men of France were in the power of the victorious invader. Then he added tantalizingly, as he set a glass of champagne on the head of the Jewess : " And all the women of France are our slaves and playthings, too! Even *you*, beautiful Rachel, came willingly for my pleasure and embraces, you spitfire Frenchwoman! "

" Don't dare to call me by the honourable name of Frenchwoman! " cried Rachel, her eyes blazing with wrath; and she raised her head so sharply that the wine-glass was dashed to the ground, and the champagne splashed in a golden shower over her black curls.

" What are you, then, you fury? " demanded her tormentor.

" I am what you brutal invaders have made of me—a creature of the streets! " cried Rachel, with bitter scorn : " yet am I good enough for a Prussian! "

Scarcely had she thus spoken than the young Lieutenant, stung to madness by her scorn, sprang up wildly and struck the girl a savage blow in the face. Immediately, Rachel fell upon him like a tigress and, snatching a knife from the table, stabbed him in the throat. As the young Prussian fell back in a dying condition, she dashed out through the open window which led on to the veranda and made her escape before the dazed and half-drunken officers had time to seize her.

The Major and his subordinates, sobered by this tragic end to their orgy, gathered round the fallen body of their comrade; and presently as they silently laid the dead body of " Mam'zelle Fifi " upon the hastily cleared table, to their amazement they heard the solemn tolling of the bell of the old village church.

Upon demanding of the Abbé Chantovoine, who entered the room later on, why the sacristan thus disobeyed the order of his superior, the good old man replied humbly : " I cannot refuse to bid him toll the bell for one who has passed away ! "

Then, falling upon his knees, he offered up a prayer for the soul of his dead enemy.

THE STONE GUEST *Dargomijsky*
(*Don Juan Story*)

ONE late evening during the seventeenth century, darkness was falling within the cloister enclosures of a famous monastery at the entrance to Madrid. Though most of the late strollers outside had already returned to their homes in the city, the gates of which would shortly be closed for the night, two silent cloaked figures still lurked within the holy precincts and kept themselves well hidden.

These two lingering intruders were Don Juan, the handsomest and most licentious of all the gay cavaliers of Madrid, and his confidential body-servant, Laporello. Their reason for thus lurking in the shadows to avoid chance passers-by was that the former was under a ban of exile from the fair city and might be arrested immediately if seen by the guards.

Not only was Don Juan famous for his amorous pursuit of numerous fair ladies; he had also gained an evil reputation for the deadly skill with which he slew his rivals and other opponents in the duels and frequent night encounters connected with his audacious love intrigues. At the present moment he was under the blackest cloud that had ever darkened his scandalous career. In one of his recent duelling encounters he had deliberately slain a Grandee of Spain—Don Pedro, one of the · most respected Commandants and highly-placed officials in Madrid; for which evil deed he had been exiled from the city.

Don Juan, however, was a light-hearted cavalier who cared nothing for danger and believed himself to have been born under a lucky star. Despite his sentence of banishment, therefore, here he was again at the entrance to Madrid, intending to slip into the city when a likely opportunity occurred. As a favoured courtier —the King himself had shared in some of his amorous adventures —he felt fairly safe from arrest from any wandering city guard who might happen to penetrate his identity beneath his voluminous and closely-wrapped cloak; and a small money bribe would certainly clinch the matter. Even when his somewhat fearful servant reminded him that the family of the late Commandant had sworn vengeance upon the murderer of their distinguished relative, having vowed to kill him should he ever fall into their hands, he merely laughed at such an unlikely possibility. Nothing should keep him from enjoying another night's adventure in fair Madrid.

" I intend to visit Laoura, the beautiful actress, as soon as we can get within these cursed gates! " he declared to his timorous henchman. " She loves me still and will give me a glad welcome, I know; and I will learn from her all the news of the town! How I pine for a goblet of wine and a fair woman's kiss! Come, let us see if we can make an attempt now to pass the guards, for darkness is drawing on apace! "

At that moment, however, a monk came strolling through the cloisters. Seeing the strangers lurking in the shadows, he asked their business. On being glibly told that they were strangers to the city, the monk became friendly and entered into conversation with them. To Don Juan's interest, he informed them that the body of Don Pedro, the murdered Commandant, had been buried in the grounds of this same monastery, and that a splendid monument, surmounted by a life-size statue of the late Grandee, had been erected there by his widow in honour of his memory. He added that the bereaved lady, Donna Anna, came thither every evening to visit the tomb and to pray for the soul of the good husband she had lost in such untimely fashion.

Astonished at this exhibition of wifely devotion—having heard the gossips say that the dead man was much older than his wife, to whom his behaviour had been jealously tyrannical—Don Juan inquired casually if the widowed lady was pretty. On being told by the monk that the late Commandant's wife was both young and extremely beautiful, but that she shunned intercourse with all would-be new admirers, he became intensely interested and desirous of making her acquaintance.

Almost as he spoke, a lady, clad in deep mourning garments, approached; and the monk informed the strangers that this new-comer was none other than Donna Anna herself coming to pray at the graveside of her husband, according to her usual evening custom. He went forward and, at her request, opened the gate leading into the monastery ground; and then he departed.

As Donna Anna also moved slowly forward, Don Juan felt a strange thrill pass through him. His inquisitive gaze had instantly discovered that her black draperies hid a form of voluptuous grace, that her eyes were wonderfully large and bright as in-distinctly seen through the heavy veil she wore, and that her undoubted beauty must certainly be of a very high order.

With his usual impetuosity, he would have followed her, had not his servant reminded him that the city gates were about to close. Inwardly vowing to make the acquaintance of this fascinating widow later on, Don Juan hastened to the city entrance; and wrapped closely in their dark cloaks, the two men managed to slip unnoticed through the gates just before they were closed and to pass on through the streets without being halted.

Bidding his servant to rejoin him later in a certain spot, Don Juan made his way alone to the abode of the beautiful actress, Laoura, who was at that time the toast of all Madrid. On arriving at her house, however, he was annoyed to find it brilliantly illuminated; and realizing that an entertainment was taking place within, he prudently decided to remain hidden in the grounds until the guests had departed. Bold and reckless as he always was, he knew that it would be foolish indeed to show himself in public while still under sentence of exile; so he waited about, chafing impatiently, until the guests began to leave. When it seemed to him that the last cavalier had departed and that the beautiful actress would now be alone in her private apartments, he slipped into the still open house and made his way thither.

But Laoura was not alone. Her latest admirer, Don Carlos, a near member of the late Commandant's family, had remained behind to declare his love. The fair actress, however, though pleased and flattered, had not immediately responded to his declaration, her thoughts being with her absent former lover.

When Don Juan suddenly strode into the room, therefore, Laoura uttered a cry of surprise and dismay; and Don Carlos emitted a curse as he instantly drew his sword and rushed upon the hated murderer of his revered relative. Don Juan, however, though furious at thus finding Laoura occupied with a new lover, was equal to the occasion. Whipping out his own sword, he instantly engaged in a deadly duel with his rival whom, owing to his wonderful dexterity as a swordsman, he soon stretched lifeless at his feet.

As Don Carlos fell, Laoura shrank back, covering her face with her hand; but as Don Juan, always an adept in such scenes, now drew her into a passionate embrace, she quickly fell again under the spell of his personal attraction and readily enough received him upon his old footing.

But Don Juan had not forgotten his sudden infatuation for the beautiful Donna Anna, whose half-hidden charms had so fired his imagination; and next evening he repaired to the monastery at the entrance to Madrid. Here, in the disguise of a monk, he hoped not only to make acquaintance with the fair widow but also to find a safe refuge from pursuit as the murderer of Don Carlos—for which new crime he was already being sought by the officers of justice.

With his usual cool daring, he put aside all thought of his own personal danger and gave himself up to the joy and excitement of the fresh conquest he hoped to make. This time, he took up his stand beside the monument of the late Commandant; and he was already admiring the excellent likeness and fine detail work of the surmounting statue when Donna Anna, still heavily veiled, drew near.

Although the pretended monk at first spoke humbly and reverentially to her, his quickly rising passion soon caused him to take on a more audacious and unmistakably admiring tone. Realizing that this was no monk but a bold new admirer who thus impudently dared to woo her at the foot of her late husband's statue, Donna Anna shrank back in alarm. However, the handsome looks and passionate glances of the young cavalier—who had now recklessly flung back his monk's cowl—caused her own heart to flutter strangely, even though she continued to reprove him coldly for his audacity. Almost against her own will, she raised her veil and revealed for a moment the full beauty of her exquisite features.

Don Juan, triumphant at thus realizing she was not indifferent to him, poured forth another flow of hot passionate words; but Donna Anna declared she could no longer listen to him there, adding that if he had anything of importance to say to her he might visit her at her house later on that evening.

Then, as though afraid of having acted too rashly, the fair

widow dropped her veil and hurried away; and Don Juan was left exulting in his conquest and joyful at the prospect of a new love affair.

As he turned away, he was now joined by Laporello who, with the easy freedom of an old servant, reproved him for thus shamelessly making love to the widow of the Commandant he had himself slain—and at the latter's memorial statue, too. For answer, Don Juan laughingly bade him turn back and invite the statue to be present at his forthcoming meeting with the lovely Donna Anna.

Laporello, entering into the joke, ran back and merrily delivered his master's invitation to the statue of the Commandant. Then, to his horror and dismay, he observed that the statue actually bowed its head gravely, as though in acceptance of the invitation. Trembling in every limb, he staggered back to his master and in terrified accents related to him the uncanny occurrence; but Don Juan, laughing gaily at his fears, likewise returned to the statue and himself repeated his impudent invitation in even more jocular fashion. He was sobered presently, however, when the statue again bowed its head in acquiescence.

Though somewhat subdued by this weird demonstration, Don Juan refused to be dissuaded by the more prudent counsels of his now thoroughly alarmed servant from keeping the assignation he had been given by Donna Anna, for whom his sudden infatuation deepened every moment. The curious chain of circumstances which had led to their meeting and the mystery connected with the strange movements of the Commandant's statue, pointing to supernatural agencies being at work, only added zest to what promised to be a delightful and exciting adventure.

Later that evening, therefore, he repaired with an eager step and the air of an expectant conqueror to the splendid mansion still occupied by Don Pedro's widow. He was immediately ushered into her presence; and he greeted her audaciously with all the fervour of an accepted lover.

Donna Anna received him kindly; but at first she seemed somewhat sad and tearful. However, when Don Juan presently expressed jealousy for the cause of her tears, she graciously declared that he need not be jealous since she only wept for the loss of a respected friend. She added that she had never felt a lover's affection for her late elderly husband, whom her parents had desired her to marry because of his wealth and important position, her own family being poor.

On hearing this, Don Juan was emboldened to further expressions of admiration for her dazzling beauty and of his delight in her sweet presence; and though the lovely widow declared that her bereavement was too recent for her to listen to such words from a new admirer, she was far from being displeased. Indeed, an answering passion was already stirring in her own breast.

At first Donna Anna was entirely unaware of the true identity of her visitor; but when Don Juan, in a sudden burst of unrestrained jealousy for her wifely devotion to the memory of her late husband, inadvertently revealed himself as the latter's slayer, she was filled with horror.

Her horror was but temporary, however; for when Don Juan, cunningly eager to impress her with a remorse he did not feel, poured forth words of humble contrition and begged her to take his dagger and slay him as a hated enemy, she declared herself unable to do so. Already the fascination of Don Juan's debonair personality and charm of manner was more than she could resist; and his present air of deep humility and well-simulated contrite penitence, coupled with his continuous protestations of love and devotion to herself, made such a great impression upon her that she soon found her righteous anger melting away. She even began to show anxiety for him to get to a place of safety, away from the fear of arrest, declaring that his presence in her house might be discovered at any moment should her friends or relatives appear unexpectedly.

Encouraged and further emboldened by her anxiety on his behalf, Don Juan now ventured to enfold her in his arms in a passionate embrace; and, to his triumphant joy, Donna Anna, unable to resist his passionate appeal and the promptings of her own long-starved heart, returned his embrace with an equal warmth. For one supreme moment, great happiness filled the hearts of both.

But their moment of delight was a short one. Even as they embraced, they heard the heavy measured tread of approaching footsteps, followed by a loud ominous knock upon the door.

After a brief pause of terrified silence and inward foreboding, Don Juan opened the door. There, upon the threshold, to the horror and amazement of the lovers, stood the now animated statue of the late Commandant, Don Pedro, with a fierce look of righteous wrath upon its marble face! As Don Juan stepped back involuntarily the statue said sternly: "You invited me to come hither to-night as your guest, and I have come! Vile murderer and libertine, your end is nigh! Do you not tremble?"

But Don Juan, for all his licentious wickedness, was no coward, and he replied boldly: "No! I am not afraid! I invited you

to come and witness my meeting with this fair lady whom I love!
I now bid you welcome! "

" Then shake hands with me! " commanded the Stone Guest
relentlessly; and the murderer, with bravado, but powerless to
resist, placed his hand in that of the animated statue, which
grasped it savagely and held it as in a vice.

Then Don Juan shrieked aloud with pain and terror as he now
realized that retribution was at hand and that he must at last
expiate his many crimes. As the Stone Guest held him in an
ever-strengthening remorseless grasp and he felt himself becoming
stiff and cold, he cried out with his last dying breath : " The end
has come! Farewell for ever, my beautiful and beloved Anna! "

PELLEAS AND MELISANDE
(Pelléas et Mélisande) *Debussy*

IN the sylvan depths of the great forest that stretched back from
the royal Castle of Allemonde, a strange and lovely maiden sat
weeping beside an old disused well in a clearing.

So absorbed was she in her grief that when a wandering huntsman, Prince Golaud of Allemonde, who had lost his way during
a boar-hunt, suddenly broke through the brushwood that bordered
the clearing, she still did not stir.

Golaud, a handsome man of middle-age, dark, and of a somewhat gloomy and stern countenance, was filled with amazement
at the sight of the weeping maiden beside the ancient well in that
lonely spot. He was instantly attracted by her strange air of
mystery—she seemed almost like one of the fabled Undines—
and by her extraordinary beauty, which was certainly almost unearthly in its ethereal quality. A mass of the finest golden hair—
as bright and fine as floss-silk—fell around her like a mantle of
sunshine.

When, presently realizing that she was no longer alone, the
maiden looked up with a startled gaze, her large wondering eyes,
darkly soft and dewy as the violets growing in the moss at her
feet, strangely thrilled the heart of Golaud and set it in a tumult
such as he had never before experienced.

Though of a rough and stormy disposition, he approached the
lovely maiden gently and, laying his hand softly upon her heaving
shoulders, inquired into the cause of her trouble, endeavouring to

discover the reason for her presence in such a lonely spot. At first the startled girl threatened to cast herself into the well, should he attempt to touch her; but when he instantly drew back, she became more reassured, though she would still tell him little or nothing of her antecedents. All he could learn from her was that her name was Melisande, that she had run away from some place already forgotten and had become lost in the forest, where she was now a friendless wanderer.

Declaring that it was not safe for her to remain alone in the forest, Golaud tried to persuade her to trust herself to him and to let him take her away with him. Realizing that she could not bear to speak of her past life, he wisely respected her silence and gradually won her confidence. Then he spoke to her of his own royal home, of his grandfather, King Arkel, his mother, Princess Genevieve, his half-brother Pelleas, and his little son Yniold—he, himself, being a widower. At length, to his great satisfaction, she consented to go with him to his hunting-lodge, where she presently became his bride.

Melisande, though grateful for her husband's love and protection, had not yet experienced love herself. When, however, after six months' absence, Golaud determined to return to his royal home once more, the true romance of her gentle life began— a romance doomed from the first to end in tragedy.

There was much speculation in the Castle of Allemonde as to the mysterious bride so eloquently spoken of by Golaud in a letter announcing his arrival. When, however, Melisande at length appeared in the royal family circle, she immediately won all hearts by her ethereal loveliness, her quiet but dignified timidity, and her gentle desire to please.

Then came her meeting with Pelleas, the young and well-beloved half-brother of Golaud—a slender youth of extreme beauty and charm and of a poetic and childlike simplicity of disposition. Now, all the world was changed for Melisande.

No sooner did Pelleas and Melisande behold each other, than a mutual and passionate love grew up within their hearts. They seemed made for one another; and in their simple-minded innocence they had no thought of, nor attempted any, wrong. They delighted in each other's company; and they loved to wander in the woods together gathering flowers, listening to the singing-birds, and rejoicing in the beauty and joy of life as children do.

They were so young and innocent of evil intent, that at first they did not realize that this sweet mutual joy and understanding was love. Even when they knew that they loved, they still did not speak of it.

But the jealousy of Golaud was quickly aroused, and he became more gloomy and morose each day. His former gentle consideration for the strange and rare being he had married—who seemed almost of a fairy nature—was gradually replaced by an attitude of unreasoning suspicion; and he constantly threw the pair together that he might have proof for his jealousy.

It was in vain that the unfortunate Melisande, despite her new joy in the love-revealing presence of Pelleas, endeavoured to avoid the latter, and desperately resolved to remain true to her husband. Fate and Golaud continually led them into forbidden paths and wove a mazy network of suspicion around them, through which they could not escape.

In the great park surrounding the Castle of Allemonde there was an old fountain which played into a very deep basin of water. Here, one very hot day at noon, Pelleas brought Melisande to shelter from the heat of the midday sun.

Melisande, glad to escape from the gloomy castle and its elderly inhabitants, became quite light-hearted and merry in this pleasant spot. She sat on the edge of the fountain, while Pelleas, young and ardent, lay at her feet and talked to her. He spoke of not very serious practical things, but of the things of youth, of joy—gazing the while into her eyes with his soul aflame, though never a word of love had yet passed his lips.

So happy was Melisande, yet withal so eager to have something to occupy her hands and her eyes—lest they should meet those other hands and eyes where danger lay—that she took off her betrothal ring and began to play with it. She tossed it up into the air and watched it glisten in the sunshine ere it fell back into her hands again. Up and down went the ring time after time. And then, too high a toss, too short a catch, and lo! the ring dropped into the fountain basin and vanished into the depths of the water below.

Melisande was full of distress at the loss of the ring given to her by her husband; and she returned with a heavy heart to the castle, fearful lest the wrath of the latter should fall upon her—which, indeed, proved to be the case.

Golaud was lying on a couch when she arrived, having met with a slight accident while hunting; and Melisande dutifully bathed his hurts and pressed her cool hand soothingly over his hot brow. Then, quite suddenly, overcome by the gloom of the darkened room and of her own undefined fears, she began to weep. Golaud, in his rough way, tried to comfort her. As he took her hand, however, he noticed that the betrothal ring he had given her was gone; and he asked what had become of it.

Melisande, afraid to tell him that the ring was already lost beyond recall, murmured confusedly that it must have dropped off when she was looking for shells for little Yniold in a cave on the seashore. Though she added that the tide was even then coming up, Golaud furiously bade her go back and search again for the ring, telling her to take Pelleas with her.

But though the two young people were compelled to go down to the cave on the wild shores, to support the story told by the frightened Melisande, the search, of course, was fruitless. Golaud's anger again had to be braved.

After this, the lovers tried hard to keep out of each other's way. Late one evening, however, as Melisande sat at her open chamber window, Pelleas passed below and whispered her name as he gazed up entreatingly. As Melisande leaned out in reply, her beautiful pale hair fell down in a golden shower on the upturned face of Pelleas, who, in a delirium of joy, took the shining locks in his hands and kissed them rapturously.

Scarcely had he murmured a few broken phrases, however, than a heavy step was heard, and Golaud approached. Melisande gathered up her hair hastily as her husband led his half-brother away, after pretending to scold them both for " playing as would a couple of children in the dark ".

But Golaud's furious jealousy had been aroused by this romantic scene; and next day, as a warning that he was not to be trifled with, he forced Pelleas to follow him into the grim and ghastly castle vaults, where one could pine and die in the damp, poisonous atmosphere. At a certain dangerous spot he seemed almost about to thrust his scared brother into one of the dark dungeons below, but as suddenly fought down the temptation. Pelleas was glad to come forth into the fresh free air once more.

Then Golaud turned on him and announced that he had over-heard his conversation with Melisande the evening before; and, though he spoke of it as childish playfulness, he now sternly warned him that it must not occur again. He added that Melisande was delicate and about to become a mother; and they must be careful with her.

But he was not careful with her himself; and the unfortunate Melisande now had to undergo many petty persecutions from her jealous husband. He even became violent at times, terrifying her by his passionate outbursts, first of love, and then of unreasoning anger.

On one occasion he burst into a room where she sat with old

King Arkel, and snatched up his sword as though to kill her. Then, flinging it away, he seized her by the hair—that lovely cloud of gold which had enveloped and intoxicated Pelleas on the evening when he had discovered them together—roughly twining the long shining locks around her body, and then forcing her to her knees. King Arkel interposed, deeply shocked and alarmed; and he calmed down once more. But Melisande was terrified, and wept.

In order to secure more definite proofs of his jealous suspicions, Golaud next compelled little Yniold, his son by his first wife, to watch the actions of the lovers. One late evening, he held the child up to a window outside the room where the pair were sitting together, and bade him describe what he saw there. The child's innocent description of the lovers, sitting silently, with the lamp between them, gazing at one another but coming no nearer, incensed him as greatly as though they had been in each other's arms—as did also little Yniold's truthful prattle that they liked him always to be with them and seemed afraid when he left them alone, as now.

Pelleas, now fearful for the safety of his beloved one because of the violence of her husband and afraid also to trust himself longer to restrain his already overwhelming passion, determined to leave the castle and to set forth upon a long sea journey. Having made his plans, he entreated Melisande to meet him just once more before he left.

When darkness fell, the lovers thus met for their last talk beside the fountain. There, as they bade each other farewell, they spoke of their love for the first time. As the joy and wonder of it enveloped them, they clung to one another in a rapture that could no longer be denied. In that one sweet moment of avowal, all the world, and even the pain of parting, was forgotten.

But, all too soon, their joy was shattered. Golaud, more suspicious than ever, had followed the pair to this fateful spot; and soon his approaching footsteps were heard and the flash of his sword was seen. In despair, the lovers embraced for the first and last time. Then as Melisande, pushed gently by Pelleas, fled terror-stricken, Golaud, in a wild passion of blind jealousy, sprang upon his brother and slew him.

. . . .

Later on, the sorrowing castle household gathered about the death-bed of Melisande, who was now sinking fast after the premature birth of her child.

Golaud knelt beside her with despair in his heart, full of remorse. But, even now, he could not refrain from questioning his dying wife regarding her love for Pelleas. Had it been a guilty love? Melisande, gathering together her failing strength, declared that her fidelity to her husband had never been at fault. She added simply that though she had, indeed, loved Pelleas with all her heart yet their unfortunate love had been innocent.

With these words, the gentle spirit of Melisande—frail, mysterious, elusive, elfin, and childlike—passed away. Then Golaud sank at her feet, overcome with grief and remorse that his violence had thus caused the deaths of the two beings he most loved in all the world.

THE PRODIGAL SON   *Debussy*
(*L'Enfant Prodigue*)

BENEATH the olive and fig trees in a beautiful sheltered spot near the Lake of Genezareth, stood Lia, the wife of Simeon, the richest man in the neighbouring village. She was alone and disconsolate. The sounds of light-hearted singing and rejoicing came ever and anon from the village and from the fields that surrounded her own homestead; for it was a festival day, and all the people were rejoicing and singing songs of praises to Jehovah, the God of Israel.

But the heart of Lia was too sad for rejoicing; and she had crept away from the festive throng to this quiet, peaceful spot, there to weep alone until the revellers should once more disturb her. Presently, they would all come past her retreat, dancing and singing on their way to feast in her husband's house near by. Meanwhile she was alone with her sorrow—a sorrow ever present and not to be denied, the sorrow of a mother's bleeding heart mourning for the loss of her youngest and best-loved child.

Where, oh where was Azaël, that dearly-loved but wilful younger son, so gay and so careless, who had been the light of the household? Tiring of restraint and longing to see more of the world, he had taken the portion allotted to him by his father and had wandered away to spend it in prodigal fashion abroad. He had never returned to that loving mother, whose heart bled constantly for the sight of him, not knowing whether he was dead or alive or to what depths of want and suffering he had fallen.

At a time of festival and rejoicing, as to-day, Lia's thoughts always turned to that lost and still precious child; and as the sound of merry-making drew nearer, her heart grew heavier still and her tears fell yet more abundantly. If only the fair and well-beloved Azaël could be there to gladden her heart by joining in the revels with the exuberant high spirits which had always been such a joy to her!

As Lia stood mourning beneath the trees, her husband, Simeon, appeared before the entrance of his house, leading his people and workers on their way from the fields to feast with him. Observing the unhappy looks of his wife and well aware of the reason for her grief, he drew near to her. Gently reproaching her for such indulgence in grief on this day of rejoicing, he bade her dry her tears, calling upon her to take her proper share in the festivities.

At the bidding of her kindly lord, Lia put aside her grief for the time being; and taking the hand of Simeon, she led with him the merry procession of festive folk now coming up from the fields. The gay young men and tender-eyed maidens, laden with flowers and fruits, danced and sang with happy light-heartedness, while the musicians accompanied them on harps and other musical instruments. Then a long procession was formed, and the merry company passed onward once more to another part of the village before returning to feast in the rich man's homestead.

As the lively procession departed a young man, travel-stained and clad in rags, foot-sore and weary, unhappy and despairing, stumbled from behind the bushes where he had been hiding. Limping forward, he fell helplessly to the ground beneath the olive trees. He had travelled day and night from a great distance, in pain and hunger and with sorrow and remorse in his heart, kept alive only by the hope of forgiveness.

This ragged and dishevelled wanderer was Azaël himself, the erring prodigal younger son of Simeon and Lia, whom the latter grieved for openly and constantly, and the former—though outwardly stern and unrelenting—secretly longed to behold again. Here he was at home once more, among his own people, yet not one of them, because of his voluntary exile and evil living—an outcast, lonely and despairing, in the sight of happy companionship, hope and plenty!

As the wretched Azaël sank weakly to the ground, remorse and self-pity seized him in its choking grasp.

He, too, might have been one of this joyous throng of merry-makers, among whom he had noticed his own fair young sister and elder brother, both still held in high honour and affection by his father's people. But, alas, he had foolishly cut himself off from the simple peaceful comforts of his home, the wise guidance and counsels of his father, and the wonderful love of his mother.

This last thought lacerated him most. The wonderful love of his mother! What had he gained to compare with that? Foolishly he had sacrificed his most precious gifts by leaving his home and by squandering his substance in riotous living in a distant land. Now, deserted in his hour of need by the idle companions who had shared his wild pleasures, he had wandered back to his parents to seek forgiveness.

In his anguish of body and mind, it seemed to him that he was about to die on the threshold of his old home and that he would never enter it again. Despairing as he realized how well he deserved that unhappy fate and with a last thought of his beloved mother, he fell back unconscious, overcome with physical weakness and mental agony.

As he lay there, Lia came back that way, having once more escaped from the revellers. Unable to conquer her sadness, always more difficult to bear at a time of rejoicing, her tears fell afresh as she thought that perhaps at this moment her beloved erring son might be lying, forsaken and dying, in a strange land.

Presently her eyes fell upon the huddled form lying beneath the olive trees; and she hastened to bring aid to the beggar thus fallen upon her threshold. Then, as she raised the drooping form, her heart gave a leap of joy as she saw that she held in her arms her own well-beloved Azaël. The erring one, for whom she had wept and prayed so long, had come back to her; and, holding him closely to her, she called upon him passionately to open his eyes and speak in answer to her fond call.

Azaël, recalled to consciousness by that well-remembered tender voice, opened his eyes; and when he beheld his mother and knew that he was forgiven and still loved by her, his joy and thankfulness knew no bounds.

As the mother and son rejoiced together, the repentant son humbly craving forgiveness and the happy mother showering words of love upon him, the merry-makers returned once more, headed by Simeon; and eagerly Lia called upon her husband to greet their returned son.

For a moment, Simeon, remembering the sins of the unhappy youth, hesitated; but soon, at the entreaty of Lia and his love conquering all, he hastened forward and clasped his repentant son in his arms with real joy in his heart. Azaël had done wrong, but he had repented of his sins and had suffered for them; surely then, forgiveness should be granted him? Had not he, Simeon, shed tears in secret for this erring son and prayed that he might return to the paths of righteousness and to his home once more? His prayers had been answered and his tears had not been in vain;

therefore he would condemn the sinner no longer, but instead would gladly pardon him.

Simeon, therefore, called upon his people to rejoice greatly because of the return of the wanderer, to kill the fatted calf for his refreshment, and to fill up their goblets at the feast in his honour.

Gladly the people responded to the call of Simeon; and the festival proceeded with renewed gaiety and gladness as the revellers rejoiced in the return of the repentant prodigal and in the joy and thankfulness of their lord.

LAKMÉ   *Delibes*

LONG after the Indian Mutiny, many of the more fanatical Hindu priests cherished a grudge against their British rulers and sought every possible opportunity of securing personal vengeance for real or imaginary wrongs.

One of the most dangerous of these rabidly fanatical priests was a certain Brahmin named Nilakantha. Because of a stupid blunder or of mistaken zeal on the part of those in authority, Nilakantha's pagoda-temple had once been attacked and desecrated by troops of the ruling white race, upon whom he had consequently vowed vengeance. He still served the half-ruined pagoda and had a considerable following of subordinate priests and Hindu partisans, to whom he had imparted his own fanatical hatred of the British. His dwelling was not far away from the temple, in a very lonely but beautiful part of India.

Here, early one morning, on the eve of a great religious festival, Nilakantha's followers joined him in his exquisite garden on their way to the pagoda. They often stopped thus for a moment to hear the prayers and receive the blessing of his daughter, Lakmé, who was also dedicated to the service of their gods.

The garden was a perfect fairyland of the wonderful flowers of India; and splendid trees cast a welcome shade over all. At one side of the garden stood the priest's house, almost concealed among the overhanging branches of the trees; and upon the door of the dwelling a lotus-leaf was carved, this being the emblem of one who served Brahma. Near the house stood a great statue of Ganeca—an idol with an elephant's head—the Indian God of Wisdom, which gave the mysterious habitation the air of a sanctuary. A stream flowed at the bottom of the garden.

In answer to the call of the priest and his followers, Lakmé, a beautiful Hindu maiden, came forth from the house and sang a prayer to Brahma, entreating for them his blessing and protection.

When the worshippers had departed on their way, Nilakantha announced to his daughter that he must follow them immediately and would not return until evening; and after bidding the house servitors to protect their mistress during his absence, he also departed.

Lakmé, though dedicated by her fanatical father to the service of Brahma, had all a pretty maiden's love of fine raiment and ornaments wherewith to enhance her beauty, even though none but temple worshippers might behold her. To-day, however, she soon relieved herself of the many heavy bracelets, necklaces, and chains of rich and sparkling jewels with which she was bedecked; and she piled these on a little stone table outside while she sang and played with her slave-girl, Mallika. Then the two girls stepped into a little boat moored at the bottom of the garden and rowed down the stream for a short distance.

Scarcely had they gone than a small party of English residents came by that way and peeped admiringly into the garden through the bamboos that hedged one side of it. These newcomers were two officers, Gerald and Frederick who, with Ellen and Rose, the young daughters of the Governor of the Province, had come out for a morning stroll and had wandered somewhat farther afield than usual.

The young people were full of curiosity regarding the dwellers in this little earthly paradise they had stumbled upon so unexpectedly; and Ellen and Gerald—who had recently been betrothed—were eager to enter and explore. As they pushed their way in through the bamboos, Frederick—who had lived longer in the district than Gerald—advised his fellow-officer not to intrude further. He then told them of the dangerous reputation of the Brahmin priest and of the risk they ran by thus entering the sanctuary of an unfriendly fanatic—especially one who possessed a beautiful daughter whom he kept hidden from all prying eyes.

Gerald, however, being of an adventurous and reckless nature, could not be kept back; and he was soon wandering about the garden, followed by the equally daring Ellen and the more timid Rose, despite the continued warnings of the prudent Frederick.

Presently they beheld the heap of jewels left upon the stone table; and Ellen was so enraptured with the design and exquisite workmanship of the ornaments that she entreated Gerald to make her a sketch of them that she might have the pattern copied.

This task Gerald was only too pleased to undertake, being enthralled with the beauty of the mysterious sanctuary they had lighted upon and willing enough to linger. To appease the anxious Frederick, however, he agreed to remain only on condition that the others returned to the Residency and left him alone to make the sketches. This being decided upon, Frederick—though still reluctant to leave behind one of the party in such risky surroundings—departed at once with the girls. Gerald then began to sketch the jewelled ornaments, his thoughts being greatly intrigued with the evidently charming owner of them, whose beauty had been so extolled by his friend.

While thus pleasantly engaged, he heard the gentle plash of oars; and the two Hindu girls landed from their boat and ran up the garden from the stream. As Lakmé came forward and he beheld her exquisite loveliness, Gerald could not refrain from uttering a cry of delighted admiration; but the startled vestal of the sanctuary was filled with alarm and dismay by his intrusion. In great agitation, she called to the servitors left in charge of her and bade them seek out her father at once.

When the attendants had departed, however, Lakmé's momentary fear vanished; and she was quickly enthralled by the fascination of the intruder, who was equally spellbound by her beauty. As the eyes of the young English officer met those of the lovely Hindu maiden, a mutual passion instantly sprang up between them. So overwhelming in its intensity was this sudden passion that, as they presently entered into happy conversation, enraptured with one another, they became oblivious of their surroundings. No thought of race hatred entered their minds at this supreme moment; all they were conscious of was that the transcendent gift of Love now wrapped them about as with a dazzling garment.

So deeply absorbed were the newly-made lovers that the rumblings of a sudden and quickly approaching thunderstorm were unheeded by them. Indeed, it was not until the sound of angry voices was heard and her madly furious father dashed into the garden that Lakmé sprang from Gerald's encircling arms and, in affrightened tones, entreated him to fly at once. Gerald now realized his extreme peril as the vengeance-vowing Brahmin, followed by a number of Hindu attendants, rushed towards him; and he quickly dashed through the hedge of bamboos into the thickly-wooded paths beyond and managed to make his escape, aided by the thunderstorm which now broke in great fury.

But though the young officer had escaped him for the moment, Nilakantha vowed a sacred vengeance against this imagined enemy of his race who had thus dared to invade his sanctuary and to make love to his beautiful daughter. Ignorant of the name and abode of Gerald, he resorted to a cunning stratagem in order to secure his victim. On the morrow a great feast-day was to be held in the nearby town, where festivities would take place in the streets; and knowing that the English residents frequently haunted the bazaars, booths, and open stalls of the market-place on such occasions, he determined to seek there for the young man whose life he meant to take. What was more, he compelled his unhappy daughter to accompany him thither as a decoy, both disguised in the humble garb of beggar-penitents—Lakmé terrified into submission to his will by the fanatical priest's angry railings at herself and his ferocious desire for the blood of her lover, who, however, she determined to save if possible.

This subtle ruse was successful. As Nilakantha had expected, a large number of English residents were wandering about the streets of the town next day, as interested spectators of the religious festivities connected with the Hindu feast-day. Among them were Gerald and Frederick, again escorting the young daughters of the Governor.

Gerald was not so interested in the proceedings as were the others, being still absorbed by his thoughts of the lovely Hindu maiden who had taken such sudden and complete possession of his heart; and he was much disturbed on presently learning from Frederick that their regiment was about to set forth on a punitive expedition to crush a native rebellion on the frontier, and that this would prevent him from seeing Lakmé again. When his friends had left the gay scene, he remained behind for a time, still dreamy and wrapped in thought.

Suddenly his attention was aroused by a song being sung by an entrancingly sweet voice which brought back to his sensitive mind the garden scene of the day before. Turning to observe the singer, he was amazed and delighted to recognize in her the beautiful Lakmé, even though thus clad in the dingy garments of a beggar-penitent. As he quickly began to make his way towards her through the throng, the cunning Nilakantha—who had hoped thus to entrap him—moved away stealthily to await a suitable moment for striking the fatal blow with the dagger he already held clutched in the folds of his humble garments.

Lakmé was at first overjoyed on seeing her English lover again so soon; but quickly remembering her father's evil designs against him, she begged him in agitated tones to leave her side immediately. Then, as Gerald passionately declared he must see her again before departing with his regiment, she told him that in the forest near her home there was a little bower made of bamboos, half-hidden among the trees and creepers, where they might meet for a short time.

Before Gerald had time to reply to this, however, Nilakantha sprang forward from his place of concealment and stabbed him fiercely with his dagger. Not waiting to see whether he had killed his victim or not, the vengeful Brahmin, eager now to save his own skin, quickly escaped through the crowd and made his way back to the sanctuary.

Lakmé, though horror-stricken as her lover fell beside her, did not lose control of herself. Seeing that Gerald was still alive and that his wound was not likely to be fatal, she called to the male slave who had followed in attendance upon the pretended beggar-penitents and who she knew to be devoted to herself; and she bade him carry the bleeding man out of the crowd. Having brought her wounded lover safely from the town, with the aid of the slave she managed to bear him to the little bamboo arbour in the forest of which she had spoken as a possible meeting-place. In this charming bower, smothered in flowers and creepers and shaded by trees, she bound up his wound with healing plants and nursed him back to consciousness, watching over him lovingly as he afterwards slept the long sleep of recovery.

When Gerald opened his eyes next morning and saw Lakmé sitting beside him in this forest bower of lovely blossoms, he felt at first that he had been transported to Paradise. Then, as memory came creeping back and he felt his wound—already almost healed by the wonderful herbs and healing leaves with which she had dressed it throughout the night—he was full of gratitude to her; and his sudden passion again flamed up as she bent over him with soft caresses and tender words.

For several hours the lovers talked happily together in this peaceful forest retreat. Then, fearing lest such perfect joy might not last, Lakmé ran off gaily into the jungle to bring a cup of holy water from a certain spring there which the Hindu maidens believed possessed the magic quality of making love eternal when a pair of lovers partook of it together.

As Gerald, left alone, lay resting contentedly and thinking of the sweet maiden whose beauty and tenderness had so completely thrown a spell of enchantment over him, he heard the sound of drums and fifes in the far distance, ever growing nearer; and a few minutes later he was astounded to see his friend Frederick approaching towards him. The latter had been out searching for him since early dawn, suspecting his sudden passion for the beautiful Hindu girl to be the cause of his disappearance.

Frederick was amazed on hearing the story of Nilakantha's murderous attack on his friend's life; but though touched by the loving devotion of Lakmé, he now entreated Gerald to leave the bower before the young girl returned and to rejoin his regiment which was even now setting forth upon the frontier expedition he had mentioned the day before. The fife music and marching of the troops could now be heard more plainly still as they neared the end of the forest which they had to pass on their way. There was still time for Gerald to join them as they came by; and his friend implored him to remember his duty to his country, his allegiance to his sovereign, and his pledged word to Ellen, his betrothed.

At first Gerald declared that his sudden passion for Lakmé and her love in return meant more to him than anything else on earth; but at length the earnest pleading of his friend prevailed. The call of race, of patriotism, of his own people—and possibly the voice of reason and conscience reminding him that the fair English girl Ellen was his true mate rather than the dark-eyed daughter of India—became too insistent to be denied. He therefore roused himself somewhat painfully and promised Frederick that he would join the troops when they came by; and as his friend dashed off in advance, he stood up and listened eagerly to the sound of the military music in the distance.

At that moment Lakmé returned, bearing a cup of holy water and calling joyfully to him to drink it with her. But as she looked upon her lover she knew at once that a change had taken place in him. Though he returned her loving greeting gently, she saw he was deeply moved by the sound of the distant music; and with quick intuition she thus knew instantly that the call of race meant more to him than his fleeting passion for her and that he was about to leave her.

Full of despair as she thus realized that her English lover was already lost to her for ever, she plucked a handful of poisonous flowers which grew among the luxuriant creepers, pressed out their juices and swallowed the liquid without a moment's hesitation. So quick was the action of the poison that she began to droop almost immediately; and as Gerald, too late to prevent her dread purpose, clasped her in his arms in a heart-broken, passionate embrace, she entreated him to drink with her the holy water she had brought.

Just as the lovers finished drinking from the cup, Nilakantha suddenly appeared before them, having compelled his slave to reveal the whereabouts of his erring daughter. Enraged at the sight of her in the arms of the hated Englishman—whom he had not expected to find still alive—he made a furious lunge at the young officer in a further attempt to slay him. But the dying Lakmé flung herself between the two, bidding her father to stay his hand since their offended gods would be appeased by the offer of one victim's life—her own!

With this last supreme gesture, the beautiful Lakmé fell back dead into Gerald's outstretched arms; and the father and lover, grief-stricken, mourned their dead together—the fanatical priest refraining from further vengeance against his enemy in the presence of death and accepting the last devoted sacrifice of his beloved daughter as a sufficient atonement to the gods he served.

A VILLAGE ROMEO AND JULIET   *Delius*
(*Romeo und Julia auf dem Dorf*)

ONE autumn morning, two rich farmers, Manz and Marti, were out ploughing their land on the beautiful country-side near the Swiss village of Seldwyla.

Between the two farm-lands lay a broad strip of hilly wilderness, luxuriously overgrown with a tangle of trees, bushes, and flowers; and as each farmer ploughed his furrow, he cast greedily longing eyes upon the rich soil of the wild land.

At one time the strip between the two holdings had been much broader; but as each ploughing season came round it became narrower. When Manz drove his plough upon the edge of the wilderness on his side, he surreptitiously made a deep broad furrow into the uncultivated ground and thus claimed it as his own; and when Marti furrowed the land on the opposite side, he also took in a goodly strip of the wilderness.

This wild land which both farmers coveted had lain unclaimed ever since the death of its last owner. The latter, a trumpeter, had left no heir but only a bastard son who had no rights in the eyes of the law and so could not inherit his father's property; and for several years nothing had been done in the matter.

At first the filching of portions of the wilderness, furrow by furrow, by Manz and Marti was so imperceptible as to be unnoticed by either. After a while, however, the decreasing strip between the holdings on both sides became an obvious fact, and the two farmers began to regard one another with uneasiness and sus-

F

picion. Before this demon of covetousness had seized upon them, they had been good friends; but greed was now alienating them, and to-day they noted each other's uneven furrows with secret anger.

Towards noon, while the farmers still ploughed, their children came merrily to a shady spot on the edge of the wilderness, bringing with them the midday meal of their parents. Sali, the young son of Manz, and Vreli, the pretty little daughter of Marti, loved one another with all the sweet and artless joy of childhood; and they lived such peaceful lives and their companionship was so perfect that no thought of sorrow over came into their heads.

Having spread out the midday meal for their respective fathers, the two children ran into the shady depths of the wild land to play. The two farmers now left their ploughs and came to the spot where the meal had been spread, greeting one another in somewhat surly fashion as they seated themselves upon the ground ready for their food.

Almost immediately afterwards the two children left their game to listen to the sound of approaching music; and presently a strange dark man appeared from the roadside, playing skilfully upon a fiddle and singing a merry song which fascinated the boy and girl.

As the Dark Fiddler drew nearer Marti announced to Manz that this stranger was the dead trumpeter's bastard son, who could not inherit his father's property because of the illegitimacy laws; and he added the further information that the unclaimed land had now been put up for sale.

Meanwhile, the Dark Fiddler continued to enchant the children with his fairy-like music; and in his song he told them that the wilderness was his, though he could not claim it but was doomed to the life of a wanderer and vagabond. He then invited the children to play in his untilled garden whenever they wished; but he added a prophecy to the effect that as soon as it was ploughed and levelled then happiness would fly from that peaceful region and trouble would take its place. These last words he gave as an obvious warning to the two farmers; and then he walked away into the wilderness, while the children gazed after him, awestruck.

Scarcely had the Dark Fiddler vanished than Marti and Manz began to quarrel. After declaring that the bidding for the trumpeter's land would certainly lie between them, since no one else would be likely to buy a narrow strip of holding hedged in by two large farms, they each accused the other of pilfering portions of the land mutually desired, announcing their intention to claim redress for every furrow stolen—rood for rood, ell for ell, and inch for inch.

As their angry voices grew louder and louder and their gestures became more violently threatening, the two children clung together in terror. Seeing this, each farmer seized his own child by the arm, roughly pulling them apart and forbidding them ever to speak to one another or to play together again. They then strode off with fury in their covetous hearts, dragging their grief-stricken children with them.

.   .   .   .

Six years later, the prophecy of the Dark Fiddler had been fulfilled. The two farmers' greedy squabbling over the coveted wilderness had resulted in litigation that had ruined them both and reduced them to extreme poverty. All their own rich farmlands had been sold, field by field, to pay for the cost of their constant law-suits. Their fine stocks of cattle and horses followed; and even their household furniture and effects were gradually disposed of.

Throughout all this sad trouble, however, Sali and Vreli had managed to meet occasionally in secret, though prevented by their family feud from open intercourse. And now, on the threshold of early manhood and womanhood, they were already declared lovers. Usually they met in the woods while their parents were at work or were pursuing their relentless litigation in Seldwyla.

One day, after a more lengthy separation than usual, Sali grew bolder in his agonizing longing to behold his beloved one, and ventured to visit her in her now dilapidated and poverty-stricken home. Vreli, however, was so terrified of the anger of her father should he happen to find them together, that the youth was compelled to depart in haste after securing her promise to meet him again later that same day.

Towards sunset, therefore, upon the disputed wilderness and amidst a blaze of poppies overgrown from the neighbouring cornfields, Sali eagerly awaited the approach of Vreli. When she arrived the lovers forgot their troubles for a while in the ecstasy of their meeting.

As they talked together almost as happily as of yore, the Dark Fiddler suddenly appeared from the woods and greeted them with apparent pleasure, expressing admiration of their youthful beauty and of their wisdom in thus seizing this stolen happiness despite their family misfortunes. He soon disappeared again; and though Vreli seemed somewhat fearful by the encounter, Sali soon comforted her once more. He then laughingly crowned her with a wreath of poppies and made her dance merrily with him.

Presently, however, they were seen by Marti, who had come spying upon his absent daughter; and he now dragged her away with angry cuffs. But Sali, beside himself with rage at this rough treatment of his beloved one, rushed impetuously upon Marti and struck him a heavy blow which stretched him senseless upon the ground. Quickly filled with remorse, however, he helped Vreli to revive her father; and between them they took the now subdued farmer back to his wretched home.

Some weeks later, Vreli sat musing alone at twilight before a small fire in the old farmhouse where she had lived all her life. This was the last night she would spend there; next day she must wander forth, a penniless outcast. Only that morning she had taken her father to an asylum in Seldwyla, his mind having given way under the weight of his woes; and a sense of deep loneliness fell upon her as she gazed around the room, empty now save for a bench and a small mattress, everything else in the house having been sold in payment of the many farm debts. To-morrow she would be a homeless wanderer.

But Love laughs at misfortune; and presently, Sali arrived and the lovers embraced with great joy. Together, they sat clasped in each other's arms before the flickering fire, talking of the happy days of their childhood and of the free gipsy life of the woods and country-side they would begin to enjoy together on the morrow. When at last, exhausted, they fell asleep, the same dream visited them both—a joyous dream in which they heard wedding bells pealing forth as though for their own marriage in the old village church of Seldwyla.

They awakened early next morning, greatly comforted by the dream that had come to them both—which they took as a happy omen. Hand in hand, they ran outside like merry children, eager to begin their new life of freedom.

They soon caught up with a stream of lively peasants in holiday attire; and on learning that they were bound for a fair in the next village, the happy lovers decided to follow in their wake.

When Sali and Vreli arrived at the fair, they found that the fun was already waxing fast and furious. A circus had been set up, and comical clowns and dainty columbines were playing their amusing antics and dancing to attract an audience. A huge crowd already thronged the merry-go-rounds and side-shows; and hustle, bustle, and merriment prevailed on every side.

Vreli and Sali were delighted with the gaiety of the scene; and though they had no money to spend upon visiting the shows and

booths, there was so much to be seen outside that for a long time
they were kept well amused. Arm-in-arm, they wandered about,
happily absorbed in their own inward joy and in the merriment
around them.

Later on, however, they became aware that many of the
peasants were staring at them in a very curious and somewhat
unfriendly fashion. At first they thought it was merely the poor-
ness of their clothes that attracted the attention and disdain of the
gaily-clad holiday-makers. Soon, however, they found that they
had been recognized by people from their own village who knew
the sad story of their family feud and were relating it to other
inquisitive folk.

When the lovers noticed that the villagers were whispering
about them, seeming to imply that they had no right to be there
together with their arms entwined as though betrothed—because
of their homeless, poverty-stricken condition and the fact that they
had not the means wherewithal to be married—they became
embarrassed and unhappy. Now eager to get away from a place
where they were known, Sali suggested that they should visit
another spot he knew of called the Paradise Garden, where no
one was likely to recognize them and where they might dance
happily together all the evening.

Vreli gladly agreed to this suggestion; and they were soon
walking hopefully along the path that led to their new destination,
their distress quickly forgotten.

It was now evening; and when they at length arrived at the
Paradise Garden, the sun had vanished and the soft summer
twilight had already set in.

The Paradise Garden was a beautiful spot that had become
wild and overgrown; and at one side of it there stood a dilapidated
little country house, now used as a cheap inn. At the back of
the garden a broad river flowed by; and a barge full of hay was
moored to the bank, together with several little pleasure-boats.
The river wound its way through a long valley, and in the
distance the snow-capped mountains could be seen.

The verandah of the inn was lighted by gay lanterns; and here
a group of wandering vagabond players were gathered, drinking.
The leader of the group was the Dark Fiddler; and as Sali and
Vreli entered the garden, arm-in-arm, he had just finished
regaling his companions with the story of the rich farmers'
struggle over the strip of land which should have been his had
he not had the misfortune to be born a bastard.

At first, not noticing the vagabonds, the lovers remained clasped
in each other's arms for a few moments, filled with the ecstasy of

their passion and rejoicing on finding themselves in this lovely spot where they imagined no one would know them. Their peaceful satisfaction, however, was quickly dispelled by the Dark Fiddler, who advanced towards them and greeted them once again, declaring he could see from their lover-like mien that he would soon be fiddling at their wedding.

He then invited them to join him and his vagabonds and to follow them to the mountains, the woods, and the country-side, there to live a life of freedom and unrestraint. Leading them to a table on the verandah, he introduced them to his vagabond friends; and then, calling for all the glasses to be refilled with wine, he bade the company drink to the health of the youthful lovers.

For a short time, Sali and Vreli were somewhat fascinated by the thought of the free life led by the vagabonds, who sang to them of the careless joys of a lawless life; but soon they realized that their own pure and perfect love was a very different thing from the free licence of these gipsy folk. The talk of the latter was often bitter with laughter that had a mocking tone in it; and they felt relieved when, presently, the party trooped into the inn for more drinks, the Dark Fiddler calling out to the lovers to think over his offer and to join the carousal later on.

But when the lovers were left alone in the Paradise Garden, they knew that the life of the vagabonds was not for them and that they must not expose their beautiful love to such an atmosphere. Once more they embraced lovingly; and as the moonlight now shone around them, a wonderful change seemed to come over the Paradise Garden as though it had been mysteriously touched by enchantment.

Just then the voices of the river barge-men were heard singing in the distance describing themselves in their song as " travellers passing by, drifting down the river ".

Instantly, the same thought seized upon the minds of Sali and Vreli. Should they also drift down the river—drift away for ever? Would this not solve their troubles? They were outcasts, unwanted, and friendless—too poor to be wedded, yet loving one another so dearly that their hearts would break if they were parted. If they could not live together, could they not at least die together? Yes! They would do so! In a boat as their bridal bed, they would drift down the river, which already seemed to be calling them to its pale silvery breast, upon which they would float into their last slumber to awaken in the real Paradise.

Rejoicing and happy in their resolve, the lovers immediately carried it out. Sali loosened one of the boats and helped Vreli into it; then, having withdrawn the plug from the bottom, he jumped in himself and pushed it off free from the bank.

Sinking down beside Vreli, Sali clasped his beloved one in his arms in a last passionate embrace as they drifted softly down the river. A little later, when the Dark Fiddler and his vagabonds presently came forth from the inn to learn if the lovers intended to join them or not, they were just in time to behold the boat sinking beneath the water in the middle of the stream.

THE DAUGHTER OF THE REGIMENT   *Donizetti*
(*La Figlia del Reggimento*)

DURING the occupation of the Swiss Tyrol by the French, the soldiers of the Eleventh Regiment of the Grand Army of Napoleon had many special opportunities for distinguishing themselves. Whenever they received orders to march against the enemy, therefore, the news was hailed with joy and the camp was soon full of the bustle of departure.

One of these gay departure days, however, was destined to bring forth much trouble to the soldiers of the Eleventh Regiment, and to mark an event which caused deep disturbance in their happy camp life. This trouble arose from their chance meeting with a party of travellers early in the morning.

It happened that a certain rich lady, the Marchioness of Berkenfeld, was driving through the Tyrol on a return journey to her château; who, on passing the camp of the Eleventh Regiment, was filled with dismay when her carriage was suddenly stopped by the soldiers. Her fears, however, were soon set at rest by the Sergeant in charge, an elderly man named Sulpice, who, on learning her name and destination, politely declared that no harm was intended her. On being invited to rest a while in the camp, she very gladly alighted from her carriage and retired to the tent indicated.

As the Marchioness retired, the soldiers raised a loud shout of welcome at the appearance of a pretty young girl, dressed in the garments of a vivandière, whom they all greeted eagerly as their beloved Marie, the Daughter of the Regiment. As the maiden tripped merrily amidst the men, Sulpice sighed deeply, for the unexpected coming of the Marchioness of Berkenfeld now reminded him of a certain duty in connection with this fair young girl.

The story of Marie's life was a strange one. When quite an infant, she had been discovered by Sergeant Sulpice on the battle-field; and since no one came to claim her, the Regiment had unanimously decided that she should be adopted by them and brought up in their camp. She was given the name of Marie; and as the years went on, she quickly won the hearts of all by her winning ways, so that she was tenderly cherished by her numerous adopted fathers and entitled by them the Daughter of the Regiment.

Marie had a loving and loyal heart, and returned the affection lavished on her with interest; and as she grew up to womanhood, she determined to repay her friends' kindness by serving them in the capacity of a vivandière. Never was there a merrier or more light-hearted maiden than Marie, the vivandière; and she was toasted everywhere as the truest comrade, the gentlest nurse, and the tenderest of comforters in times of woe.

When Marie had been first discovered on the battlefield by Sulpice, he found pinned to her clothing a letter, evidently written by her father, addressed to the Marchioness of Berkenfeld: but not having the means of delivering this letter at that time, the Sergeant had carefully hidden it away amongst his own posses-sions. Now, however, as this same Marchioness had at last so strangely and unexpectedly come into his life, he felt it to be his duty to give the document into her hands.

As this thought began to trouble him, he glanced tenderly towards the pretty Marie; and noticing that she looked somewhat sad and remembering that she had appeared less lively of late, he questioned her as to the reason. Marie, who loved Sulpice with the most filial affection, soon made a full confession to him; and the Sergeant was dismayed to learn that she had not only fallen in love, as he had rather suspected, but that the object of her affection was one whom she ought to have regarded as an enemy.

The girl related that one day quite recently she had been saved from great danger by a young Swiss named Tonio, to whom she had very quickly lost her heart. That her love was as ardently returned was proved by the fact that this young man had followed the Eleventh Regiment in all its movements ever since meeting her, in spite of the risk he thus ran by haunting the neighbour-hood of his country's enemies.

Even as the fair vivandière spoke, there came the sound of a commotion, and a party of soldiers dragged into the camp a young man whom they had just captured and apprehended as a spy. To her surprise and joy, Marie recognized in the prisoner her beloved Tonio.

To the astonishment of all she ran to embrace him; and when she had presently related the story of the service he had rendered her a short time ago, the men released him and welcomed him as a friend.

Tonio now boldly declared his love for Marie, and asked her hand in marriage; and when the elders of the Regiment saw that their beloved Daughter's happiness was bound up in this youth they gave their consent. They declared, however, that Tonio must join their ranks and serve Napoleon in future. Tonio willingly agreed to this condition, and thus became a soldier of the Grand Army. Nevertheless, he was not yet destined to enjoy the happiness he thought he had secured.

As he entered into sweet converse with his beloved sweetheart, the Marchioness of Berkenfeld came out from the tent where she had been resting; and Sulpice, unable to stifle the calls of his conscience, now entered into conversation with her on the subject of Marie, handing to her the letter which he had found pinned to the child's clothing.

When the Marchioness had read this letter, she became much agitated. Hurrying forward, she clasped Marie in her arms, declaring that the document proved the vivandière to be her own lost niece and the daughter of her sister, who had contracted a secret marriage with a young French captain.

As the soldiers listened to this declaration with dismay, the Marchioness next calmly announced that Marie must now return with her to her château, that she might be educated to fill the position to which she had been born. Though the young girl, horrified at the thought of leaving her beloved friends, entreated to be left with them, declaring that she had no desire to be a fine lady, her new relative was adamant in her resolve to remove her niece from such unorthodox surroundings.

The elders of the Eleventh Regiment were also compelled to admit that they had no right to keep the weeping girl from her own family; and, though they were heart-broken on being thus compelled to part with their darling, they gently persuaded her that she must leave them.

The Marchioness, afraid that further opposition might arise with delay, declared it was necessary for her to continue her journey at once and that she must certainly take her niece with her; and at last, Marie, on the advice of her friends, agreed to go. So the weeping vivandière took a tender farewell of her lifelong friends and kissed them all for the last time. When she came to Tonio, she embraced him passionately, declaring that, in spite of her altered position, she would always remain faithful to him.

As the sorrowful young man watched his sweetheart drive away with her aristocratic relative, he vowed that he would do great deeds and win for himself such an honourable name and position that he might be worthy to claim her yet.

On reaching the Château Berkenfeld, the Marchioness engaged masters and teachers to instruct her niece in all the accomplishments she considered necessary for the education of a young lady of high rank; and Marie, though finding such a life very cramping and irksome after the unrestrained freedom of the camp, endeavoured to please her aunt to the best of her ability.

But the girl's heart was with her military friends. Every now and again she would break out into enthusiastic reminiscences of her childhood and indulge in snatches of the merry regimental songs—to the horrified dismay of the decorous Marchioness, who was much shocked by such unladylike proceedings.

At the end of a year, Marie was declared by her masters to be vastly improved in her social demeanour; and the Marchioness, eager to establish her niece more firmly in her aristocratic circle, now arranged a marriage for her with the son of a Duchess. But Marie could not forget her soldier sweetheart, Tonio, whom she still loved as dearly as ever. In spite of her declarations that she could never wed with another, however, the Marchioness still continued her negotiations with the ducal suitor; and she even arranged the day on which the marriage contract should be signed.

It was about this time that Sergeant Sulpice was wounded in an engagement not many miles distant from the Château Berkenfeld, and was sent to the abode of the Marchioness to crave her hospitality for a while. The Marchioness received the Sergeant with much kindness, bestowing the utmost attention upon him; and when he had recovered somewhat from his wounds, she even permitted him free intercourse with Marie and told him of her plans with regard to the grand marriage she had arranged for her.

Sulpice at first could scarcely recognize the merry little Daughter of the Regiment in the richly-gowned and elegant young lady whom he was now bidden by his hostess to admire; but when Marie, forgetful of her recent lessons in deportment, rushed enthusiastically into his arms and hugged him with the most unmistakable joy, he knew that her faithful heart had not changed amidst her new surroundings.

The Marchioness was eager to show off her niece's new accomplishments to the Sergeant, and desired her to sing to him a sentimental ballad she had just received from Paris. She was greatly scandalized, however, when Marie, half-way through the ballad, suddenly broke out into the old rollicking regimental song she had always loved so well and roguishly went through a number of military evolutions as accompaniment.

But though Marie was cheered for a while by the arrival of the Sergeant, she soon grew unhappy again; for she could not prevent her aunt from carrying out the scheme of the grand marriage.

At last the day arrived upon which the marriage contract was to be signed; and Marie went out into the grounds of the château early in the morning with despair in her heart, feeling that she would now certainly be forced to carry out her aunt's wish. However, as she stood there with the sympathetic Sulpice, she suddenly heard the sound of distant drums and fifes; and as the merry "rataplan" drew nearer, she recognized with joy that it was the marching tune of her brave soldier friends.

It was indeed the Eleventh Regiment on their way from the war; and as they had to pass the Château Berkenfeld, they made a halt there in order to greet their adopted Daughter.

Marie was delighted by this happy meeting with her old comrades; and her crowning joy was the moment when she was clasped in the strong arms of her beloved Tonio, who was now commanding officer of the Regiment, having been thus rapidly promoted for his gallantry on the battlefield.

Tonio soon boldly announced that his new military rank now rendered him a fit suitor for Marie; and he at once asked her hand in marriage of the Marchioness—a request in which he was loyally supported by the whole Regiment, eager that its darling should wed the man she loved and not be forced into a marriage she detested.

But the Marchioness haughtily refused to give her consent, being bent upon her niece wedding into an aristrocratic family; and since the notary had already arrived, she declared that Marie must sign the marriage contract without further delay.

On hearing this cruel resolve Tonio stoutly declared that, contract or no contract, he should certainly carry off his sweetheart by force. Then the Marchioness, in order to avoid such a scandal, revealed to Marie that she was not merely her niece, but actually her own daughter. It now transpired that Marie was the child of a marriage the Marchioness had contracted in her early youth with a poor Savoyard Captain, at whose death she had concealed the whole affair, lest the knowledge of such a *mésalliance* should injure her in the good graces of her aristocratic relatives.

She therefore now claimed parental authority over her daughter; and Marie, feeling that she could not refuse to obey her own mother, consented to sign the marriage contract, at the same time declaring, however, that it would break her heart to part from her beloved Tonio.

The gentle submission of the despairing girl, however, at last overcame the hard resolve of her mother; and the sight of Marie's deep affection for her humbly-born lover brought back to the proud Marchioness the remembrance of those long-past happy days when she herself had loved. With tear-dimmed eyes and softened heart, she now called the lovers to her side; and placing Marie's hand in that of Tonio, she gave her consent to their union.

The contract with the son of the Duchess was thus promptly broken off; and whilst Marie and her lover rejoiced together, the delighted soldiers raised mighty cheers for the happiness of their beloved Daughter of the Regiment.

DON PASQUALE   *Donizetti*

DURING the early part of the nineteenth century, there lived in Rome a rather cantankerous old bachelor named Don Pasquale. Although extremely rich, he was decidedly mean and was always eager to secure more wealth for the family coffers.

Consequently, he was exceedingly annoyed, not to say enraged, when his nephew and heir, Ernesto, flatly refused to marry the rich, but plain and uninteresting, middle-aged lady he had chosen as a suitable match for him.

But Ernesto was young and handsome; and as he was also gay and romantic, such a marriage of convenience as that proposed by his uncle did not appeal to him in the least. What was more, he had fallen in love with a charmingly pretty young widow named Norina, who, though not rich, was as gay and romantic as himself. She returned his love, and he was determined to marry no one else.

When, however, his tiresome old uncle threatened to cut him off with the proverbial shilling unless he gave up all idea of marrying pretty Norina—whom the Don had refused even to look at—and agreed instead to accept the wealthy bride chosen for him, he was plunged into despair. For Ernesto led a pleasant life of security and moderate affluence as his uncle's heir, with the additional advantage of a fine fortune to look forward to later on; and he did not wish to give up such a comfortable existence. At the same time, he did not wish to relinquish his beloved Norina. So the young man was certainly in a quandary.

But luckily for Ernesto, he had a very good friend in a certain Dr. Malatesta, who was the friend and contemporary of Don Pasquale. Malatesta, though fond of his old friend, was fully alive to the latter's faults. Consequently, he had no compunctions about carrying out an amusing little plot, the idea of which presently occurred to him.

By means of this plot, Malatesta hoped to bring Don Pasquale into a more reasonable frame of mind and thus to gain his consent to the marriage of Ernesto with Norina. The old Doctor loved both these young people dearly, and was determined to make them happy—even at the expense of the friend of his own youth, whose obstinate meanness he felt deserved some such check as he now proposed.

He first of all went to Don Pasquale and pretended to sympathize with him in having such a headstrong nephew. Why not punish the young scamp by taking a wife himself, he next craftily suggested? Surely the Don was not yet too old to enjoy a fuller life? And think how pleasant it would be for him to have a kind and pleasant lady at the head of his house—one who would look after him well, obey his wishes in every respect, keep his extravagant servants in order and, by thus saving money for him, make his last days happy and comfortable. He could then afford to snap his fingers at his ungrateful nephew, should the latter continue to defy him by marrying against his will.

Don Pasquale was greatly taken with this idea, and declared that he would act upon it. Then Dr. Malatesta cunningly went on to say that he knew of exactly the right wife for him, one who possessed all the qualities he had just enumerated—his own sister, Sophronia. True, she was young and attractive, he added; but his friend was not yet too old to appreciate such helpful assets. He knew that his young sister would gladly accept so staid and still good-looking a husband.

Don Pasquale, greatly flattered, was now quite eager to see this young lady paragon; and despite his usual rather cantankerous attitude to women, he seemed rather pleased than otherwise that she had youth and good looks. He told his old friend to go forward with the betrothal contract, and to bring along the necessary Notary and the prospective bride as soon as possible.

Delighted with this initial success, Dr. Malatesta quickly put the second part of his plot in hand. He easily persuaded the sprightly Norina to pass herself off as his pretended young sister " Sophronia "; and he carefully coached her in the amusing part she was to play as the affianced wife of Don Pasquale—a very different type of wife from that which the latter was looking forward to.

Norina, who was witty and clever, looked upon the whole affair as a huge joke; and, being naturally an excellent actress, she readily agreed to carry out the part allotted to her.

Having made all the necessary arrangements, Malatesta duly arrived at Don Pasquale's house on the day appointed, together with "Sophronia" and a supposed Notary—the latter another of the old Doctor's lively friends who had likewise consented to masquerade in this legal character. This friend had entered into the farcical plot with as much glee as had the gay young Norina. He brought with him a bogus betrothal contract which he spread out with great solemnity on a table with quill-pens and ink-well, standing beside it in his lawyer's gown with a serious and dignified air.

Don Pasquale was delighted with the beauty of his proposed bride, though he had some doubts about burdening himself with so youthful a helpmeet. However, "Sophronia" stood so meekly and quietly beside her pretended elder brother, with such a modest and submissive demeanour and appeared so humble and willing to please, that his first qualms quickly vanished. Not for a single moment did he imagine that all was not in regular legal order or that "Sophronia" was a consummate actress, who would presently show him another and most disconcerting side to her versatile character.

When the time came to sign the betrothal contract, the unsuspecting Don Pasquale willingly enough put his signature to the imposing document; and "Sophronia" did likewise. Then came the witnesses; and among these, young Ernesto was duly called by his uncle—in order to drive home more deeply the meaning of the latter's punishment in the matter of his own delinquency.

Ernesto had been greatly shocked on learning only a few hours ago of his old uncle's decision to marry, knowing that his own prospects were certain to suffer in consequence. He now received a still greater shock. There had not been a chance for the plotters to let him into the secret beforehand. When, therefore, he now came forward to witness the document and recognized in his uncle's prospective bride his own beloved Norina, he was both amazed and horrified!

However, Malatesta and Norina both made frantic secret signs to him, from which he had the wit to gather that they had hatched some marvellous plot into which he would shortly be initiated.

Somewhat reluctantly, therefore, he duly witnessed the contract, as desired.

Malatesta and the pretended Notary then retired, taking with them the still puzzled Ernesto, to whom they soon revealed the plot they had hatched; and Don Pasquale was left with his newly-betrothed bride.

And now, to the old Don's surprise and alarm, there came a sudden transformation scene. Scarcely had the plotters retired after the signing of the betrothal contract than "Sophronia" completely reversed the quiet and demure air she had worn until that moment. As instructed by Malatesta, she now revealed herself in an entirely different character—as a woman of the wildest extravagance and of somewhat dubious morals.

As the contracted wife of a wealthy man, she soon proved herself to be a spendthrift. She sent out the servants to order the most expensive new decorations for the house, practically refurnishing it from top to bottom. Then she ordered milliners, dressmakers, and jewellers to come to her boudoir; and she selected dozens of the most fashionable gowns, hats, and mantles to be delivered at once, together with suitable jewels to match.

When her affianced husband, distracted by such ruthless expenditure, ventured to protest against this squandering of his fortune, she laughed gaily, declaring that as the wife of the famous Don Pasquale it was absolutely essential for her to keep up a magnificent appearance on all occasions.

She further announced that she intended to give splendid banquets, to attend all the grandest balls and theatre parties in Rome, and generally to live a life of unbounded pleasure and utmost luxury, now that she no longer needed to consider such mundane matters as lack of money and opportunity for spending.

Within the first hour or so of signing the betrothal contract, she had ordered goods worth a much larger sum than the fortune possessed by the unfortunate man she had promised to marry.

The prudent and even miserly Don Pasquale was quite dumbfounded by such reckless extravagance, and also by the outrageous behaviour of his newly affianced wife. Having filled her wardrobe to her satisfaction, the lively girl next proceeded to invite her friends to the house to admire her in her new grandeur; and during the next few hours, more shocks were forthcoming for the worried Don.

"Sophronia" soon proved to be of a skittish and flirtatious nature—her conduct now being the exact opposite of that of the quiet, modest, unobtrusive young person introduced by Dr. Malatesta. She laughed loudly and behaved in a coquettish manner with every male who appeared in the house. In particular, she carried on a hot flirtation with the Don's own scapegrace nephew, Ernesto, who, naturally enough, had quickly returned to enjoy the baiting of his miserly old uncle.

Very soon, love-letters, left openly in likely places, were discovered by the irate husband-to-be, who angrily accused his affianced bride of having a lover already concealed in the house. But laughingly impudent replies were all he gained from his accusations; and when he again protested loudly against her mad extravagance, she turned on him like a termagant and declared that he would certainly have to pay her bills, willy-nilly, since she was now the mistress of the house.

The disillusioned and really scared Don Pasquale now wished desperately that he had never contracted to marry such a capricious and extravagant girl as "Sophronia". In great distress, he presently sent for his old friend, Dr. Malatesta, and begged the latter almost tearfully to get him out of the difficulty in which he found himself.

Delighted by the success of his plot, Malatesta first suggested that his old friend should hand over his most unsuitable fiancée to his nephew Ernesto. This, he declared mischievously, might, possibly, be a better way of punishing the latter than troubling to get married himself. "But the betrothal contract is already signed and witnessed!" cried the now nearly frantic Don Pasquale.

Thus the way was paved for the revealing of the old Doctor's clever plot; and the relief of Don Pasquale was intense on now learning that the contract he had signed was not a legal document at all, but a bogus affair, and that the Notary who had brought it to the house was likewise a bogus official. He was amazed, too, on discovering that Ernesto's sweetheart, Norina, and his own flighty "Sophronia" were one and the same person. His greatest relief of all, however, was that the alarming bills run up by the latter had likewise been "arranged".

True, he was also at first furiously angry because of the trick played upon him; but his anger was quickly dissipated in his delight on finding himself a free bachelor once more, after his short but devastating experience as an affianced man.

Thoroughly exhausted by this nightmarish event, he was now only too willing to hand over the seemingly flighty and extravagant Norina to his delighted nephew, Ernesto. His good humour having thus been restored, he said no more about the dull but wealthy lady he had so recently insisted the latter should marry.

Within the last few hours he had learned—somewhat drastically, it is true!—that peace of mind and contentment were extremely important factors in any proposed marriage; and since the welfare of his nephew was really of interest to him, he was now willing to make him happy.

Dr. Malatesta, therefore, felt well pleased with himself for having brought his old friend, Don Pasquale, into this satisfactory frame of mind and for having at the same time brought happiness to his young friends, Ernesto and Norina.

A real Notary was quickly produced and a correct legal betrothal contract was signed by the young people; and a blessing upon their happy union was now gladly given by Don Pasquale, thankful for his own escape from an extravagant and flirtatious wife.

LUCIA DI LAMMERMOOR   *Donizetti*

DURING the turbulent times of the seventeenth-century revolution, many of the noble families of Scotland were plunged into poverty and ruin; and under the lax and uncertain rule of changing parties, many occasions arose for unjust oppression by the ambitious holders of powerful offices and for the pursuit of private feuds and motives of revenge.

Thus it came about that the Barons of Ravenswood, an ancient family who had dwelt for many centuries in the south-east of Scotland amidst the wild hills of Lammermoor, became gradually poor and lost the power they had enjoyed so long. Consequently, the young Lord Edgar, as the surviving Master of Ravenswood, found himself forced to struggle against overwhelming difficulties.

The young Edgar, enthusiastic and full of spirit, did not grudge the sharing of his country's troubles; but when most of his lands and possessions fell into the hands of the Ashtons, the long hated foes of his race and a less noble family than his own, his heart was indeed filled with bitterness.

By ingratiating themselves with the most powerful party then in office, the Ashtons had gained considerable influence in the southern provinces; and they did not fail to use their power by taunting and annoying the family of Ravenswood, whose hatred they returned with equal zest.

But whilst Edgar of Ravenswood, though shorn of his wealth, still managed to dwell securely in his crumbling old castle, his foes, in their ambitious flights and grasping pride, eventually overreached themselves; and Sir Henry Ashton, on coming into the estates, found himself faced with ruin. He had become entangled in a Government conspiracy; and suspicion having quickly fallen upon him, he knew himself to be in the utmost danger.

In this desperate situation one person alone could save him from the traitor's awful doom—his fair young sister, Lucy. For Lucy Ashton's exquisite beauty and gentle nature had gained her the admiration of Sir Arthur Bucklaw, a gay young nobleman who held high offices and whose great influence was sufficient to remove the danger which threatened the involved Henry.

This influence Sir Arthur was willing to exert if Lucy's hand were bestowed on him in marriage; and as Henry Ashton spoke of this matter one day with his henchman, Norman, and his chaplain, Bide-the-Bent, he anxiously sought to allay his fears thus.

Bide-the-Bent, who had been Lucy's tutor and loved her dearly, knowing that she had no affection for Sir Arthur, begged his master not to harass the maiden since she was still too young to think of such matters. Norman the henchman, however, laughed derisively on hearing this and declared that, so far from being too young to think of love, Lucy already had a devoted lover to whom she granted secret interviews in the grounds.

Henry, angry on hearing this news, demanded further information; and Norman declared that Lucy, when walking one day in the park, had been rescued from the furious attack of a wild bull by a handsome young stranger. She had straightway fallen in love with the latter and was now in the habit of meeting him frequently.

"And what is the name of this bold stranger who thus dares to woo my sister in secret?" cried Henry, pale with wrath; and Norman answered: "Edgar of Ravenswood!"

On hearing that Lucy's lover was none other than his own hated foe, Henry Ashton became furious and passionately vowed vengeance on the pair. Full of angry, uneasy thoughts, he now determined to hasten the alliance of his sister with Sir Arthur Bucklaw, after which he hoped soon to find means for vanquishing the disappointed lover.

Meanwhile, knowing her brother to be engaged with his followers, Lucy, attended by her maid, Alice, had crept down to the secret trysting-place in the park to await the coming of her lover, whom she expected that day. The henchman, Norman, had spoken the truth, and a deep love had indeed sprung up between Edgar of Ravenswood and the fair daughter of his enemies. Their trysting-place was an ancient fountain, around which a legend had grown up to the effect that a dead-and-gone Ravenswood had there slain a maiden who loved him and that her spirit still haunted the spot. Lucy now declared that she had herself recently beheld this wraith, which had made strange signs as though warning her against some unseen danger; whereupon Alice begged her young mistress no longer to continue her secret love meetings, since such a solemn warning evidently meant that trouble was in store for her.

But Lucy heeded her not; and seeing Edgar approach, she ran to greet him with great joy. Soon, however, when the first happy moments were passed, she noticed that her lover was anxious and somewhat preoccupied. On asking the cause, she was quickly filled with sorrow when Edgar announced that in a few hours he would be compelled to leave the country on a secret mission to France, a mission which had been entrusted to his care by the political party to which he belonged.

The young man also declared that he would now boldly seek an interview with Sir Henry Ashton, in order to secure his consent to their union. Lucy, however, fearing her brother's anger and knowing well that he would never consent to bestow her upon one for whom he bore such intense hatred, begged him to keep their love a precious secret until his return, lest evil should fall upon her during his absence.

Edgar's reply was a passionate tirade against the man who had so ruthlessly persecuted his race and brought ruin upon him; but quickly melted by the tears and entreaties of the gentle Lucy, he granted her request and comforted her with great tenderness.

The lovers now exchanged rings, as their solemn pledge of faithfulness to each other; and with many loving embraces, they at length bade one another farewell and parted with heavy hearts.

A sad and harassing time was now in store for Lucy. Sir Henry Ashton, beset on all sides with dangers and difficulties, was determined to save himself from utter disaster by wedding his lovely sister without further delay to Sir Arthur Bucklaw, who alone had the necessary influence to extricate him from the compromising political sea of trouble in which he had become immersed.

It was in vain that Lucy refused to agree to the marriage, even summoning courage to declare her plighted troth to Edgar of Ravenswood; her brother absolutely declined to consider her wishes in the matter, and ruthlessly resolved to sacrifice her happiness to his own selfish ends. He therefore made all the arrangements for her marriage with Sir Arthur Bucklaw to be carried out; and he proceeded to invite their relations and friends to attend the ceremony of signing the marriage contract and the wedding of the pair.

Lucy, finding herself helpless in the matter, could only hope that her beloved Edgar would return in time to claim her as his plighted bride and thus free her from her terrible position; but, to her sorrow, she received no replies to the letters she sent to her lover, and was soon plunged in despair. The fact of the matter was that Sir Henry's henchman, Norman, intercepted all the letters sent by the absent Edgar, and took them to his master. Between them, they also concocted a forged letter in which the Master of Ravenswood was made to announce that his affection for Lucy had waned and that he had taken another lady to be his wife.

This letter Henry Ashton kept as his last argument; and on the day on which the bridal guests were expected, he had a final interview with his sister, bidding her to be of more cheerful demeanour, since she must sign her marriage contract with Sir Arthur Bucklaw that day.

Again the unhappy girl declared that she could not marry Bucklaw since she had plighted herself to Edgar of Ravenswood, and she refused to heed her brother when he insisted that a vow made without the consent of her guardians was not binding upon her. Then, still finding her obdurate, Sir Henry produced the forged letter and bade her read it.

The hapless Lucy, believing the writing to be that of her lover, whom she was thus compelled to acknowledge as faithless, was now plunged into the deepest grief. Her brother, taking advantage of her dazed and helpless condition, besought her eagerly to turn her thoughts from such an unworthy object and to sign the contract of the brilliant marriage which had been arranged for her; and he added that he himself would certainly forfeit his life unless she would consent to wed Sir Arthur Bucklaw, who alone had the power to save him and was willing to do so on this one condition.

Lucy, thus basely deceived, felt that life had no further joy for her. Believing that it was her duty to save her brother from ruin, she fell into a state of wretched apathy and finally consented to the marriage, caring naught for what might befall her.

The wedding guests now arrived; and Lucy, at the stern bidding of her brother, signed the marriage contract with a trembling hand and in a dazed condition.

No sooner had she done the deed than a cloaked stranger dashed into the room; and, to the surprise and consternation of all, the intruder proved to be none other than Edgar of Ravenswood himself, who, having just returned from France, had come to claim his plighted bride.

For answer, Henry Ashton triumphantly showed him the signed marriage contract; and Edgar, thus seeing that Lucy had broken her troth, fell into a passion of rage and grief. Scorning all explanations from the distracted girl, he snatched her ring from his finger and returned it to her, passionately demanding his own back again.

Half-dazed with the shock of his sudden appearance, the unhappy Lucy, as in a dream, slowly and almost unwittingly drew the ring from her finger; and Edgar, after passionately trampling the love pledge beneath his foot, rushed from the room, uttering wild curses on the family of Ashton.

Hurrying to his crumbling and dismantled castle, the unhappy Master of Ravenswood remained plunged in the deepest grief. Here he was some hours later visited by the triumphant Henry Ashton, who came to announce that his sister's marriage with Sir Arthur Bucklaw had duly taken place. Passionate words passed between the two men, who had been implacable foes from childhood; and after proudly agreeing to settle their differences by a duel next morning, Henry Ashton returned to his mansion to join in the wedding festivities.

But woe was quickly to succeed to this forced merriment. Shortly after the bride and bridegroom had been escorted to their chamber, wild shrieks were heard, and the chaplain, Bide-the-Bent, rushed into the presence of the alarmed guests with a fearful story on his lips. Lucy, tortured and racked with the awful anxiety and sorrow of the last few weeks and utterly stunned and prostrated by the final shock of Edgar's return and passionate reproaches, had lost her reason; and in a paroxysm of frenzy, she had slain her newly-made husband.

Overwhelmed with horror, Henry Ashton and his guests hurried to the scene of this awful tragedy; but though they endeavoured to calm and restore the distraught girl, their efforts were in vain. The unhappy Lucy, worn out in body as well as in mind, died a few hours later.

Bide-the-Bent, and some other retainers of the family, quickly brought the sad news to Edgar Ravenswood, who, unable to rest, was passing the night in wretchedness amidst the tombs of his ancestors in a wild and craggy spot. When the unhappy lover thus heard of his beloved one's tragic death and now understood that he had wronged her, since she had been cruelly deceived, his woe was too great for him to bear. Determined not to live without her, he stabbed himself to the heart and fell dead at the feet of the horrified attendants.

LUCREZIA BORGIA   *Donizetti*

ONE summer day, at the beginning of the sixteenth century, a splendid *fête* was being held in the gardens of the Barberigo Palace in Venice; and amongst the gay company of guests thronging the fairylike grounds were many bearers of the proudest and most ancient names in Italy.

One of the chief guests was the brilliant young Duke Orsini, around whom there quickly gathered a group of lively friends, all of whom, with one exception, could boast of noble birth. Nor, strange to say, was this one guest of unknown ancestry despised by his companions; on the contrary, he was fêted and admired above all others present. For young Genarro, who knew nothing of his parentage and was not ashamed to reveal the fact that his early years had been spent under the guardianship of an old fisherman, had, on entering the Venetian army, quickly made a name for himself by his remarkable prowess in the recent warfare. Indeed, his heroic deeds, coupled with his handsome looks and charming disposition, had won for him great popularity and many friends, amongst whom even the aristocratic Orsini was proud to be numbered.

The principal subject of conversation amongst the guests was, as usual, the most recent atrocity committed by some member of the mighty Borgia family, who at that time held the chief power in Italy and were universally feared and detested for their unscrupulous conduct and deeds of cold-blooded cruelty. As the Orsini were amongst their most hated enemies, the young Duke did not hesitate to represent them in the worst possible light to his companions.

To-day, he dwelt on the many heartlessly cruel achievements of the Lady Lucrezia Borgia, who, although one of the most lovely and fascinating women of her time, had inherited her family's pride and love of power and, like her brother Cæsar, did not scruple to use violent means to satisfy her passions or ambitions. A thrust in the dark or a poisoned draught rewarded those who presumed to interfere with the schemes of the powerful Borgias; and their victims were of all ranks, from the lowest to the highest.

The young Genarro, fresh from deeds of honour and chivalry, soon sickened at the recital of deeds of treachery; and being overcome by the excessive heat, he presently stretched himself on the ground in a shady spot near the water and fell asleep. When he had thus left the group, Orsini, proud of his young friend, began to relate to his companions the stirring story of Genarro's heroic conduct in the recent battle of Rimini; and shortly afterwards they wandered away to another part of the grounds.

Presently, a gondola glided silently past the festive grounds; and a lady who sat within, noticing the sleeping form of Genarro on the bank near the water's edge, and being greatly struck with his exceeding beauty, landed and stepped lightly to his side.

This lady was none other than the notorious Lucrezia Borgia herself, who, though come on a secret mission to Venice, did not hesitate to enter boldly into the midst of her enemies merely for the sake of gratifying an impulse of the moment.

As she silently bent over the handsome sleeping youth, a feeling of great tenderness for him suddenly welled up within Lucrezia's heart. She now recognized him as her own son, the child born of a secret amour of her first early youth; and trembling with the excitement of her newly-awakened maternal love and her delight in the beauty of her offspring, she raised his hand and kissed it softly.

At her salute, the young man awakened, greatly confused on finding himself thus alone with such a dazzling stranger. Lucrezia was still young and beautiful; and her wonderful fascination was quickly felt by Genarro, who made friends with her at once and was soon engaged in pleasant conversation with her. He told her his story with all the trusting confidence of early youth; describing to her how he had been left as an infant with the old fisherman who had brought him up and how, after joining the Venetian army, he had seemed to lead a charmed existence, modestly refraining from dwelling upon his more recent exploits.

So delighted was the youth with the sympathy and kindness of his new friend that he begged her to reveal her name to him; but this Lucrezia refused to do. She did not wish to destroy his evident respect for her by disclosing her identity; nor did she dare to acknowledge her true relationship to him, having kept his birth a secret all these years.

As she presently turned and left him, Orsini and his companions came back to seek their friend; and instantly recognizing the departing lady, whose face was well known to all of them, they denounced her to Genarro as the detested Lucrezia Borgia whose hateful deeds they had so recently described to him.

Though Genarro was shocked by this announcement, he had already so completely fallen under the fascination of Lucrezia that he took every opportunity that arose of seeing her; and his friendship with her was strengthened by frequent meetings.

Their evident affection for each other was ere long noticed by Lucrezia's husband, the Duke Alphonso of Ferrara, in whose breast jealousy was quickly roused to such a pitch that he vowed vengeance upon the pair and eagerly watched for an opportunity of satisfying his wrath.

The young Duke Orsini and his companions were also greatly disturbed by their young friend's infatuation for one of the hated Borgia family; and they did all in their power, by means of scoldings and taunts, to draw him away from Lucrezia's wiles, knowing only too well that such an intimacy would certainly end disastrously for the young man.

But Genarro, who felt himself attracted by some mighty force towards the beautiful woman who showed such tender affection for him, although unable to define the feeling he had for her, continued his new intimacy in spite of the warnings of his friends. At times, however, their taunts stung him bitterly, for he knew well the evil character which Lucrezia had earned for herself; and he would then despise himself for allowing her to exercise such a strange fascination over him.

On one such occasion as this, having met his friends in the public square in front of the Borgia Palace at Ferrara and been taunted by them more bitterly than usual, he gave vent to a passionate outburst of anger against Lucrezia; and, heedless of consequences, he dashed up to the palace door and recklessly struck off the first letter of her family name with the short dagger he wore, leaving only the equivocal word " orgia ".

This rash deed was observed by the Duke of Ferrara himself, who at once ordered his attendants to make the young man a prisoner and hold him in the palace. He then caused the defacing of the family name to be made known to Lucrezia who, unaware that the deed had been committed by Genarro and only feeling rage at the insult, demanded that the culprit should be seized and put to death. The Duke, gloating over the chance that had at last put his supposed rival in his power, declared that her wish should be immediately carried out; and he ordered the prisoner to be brought into the room for sentence.

Then, when Lucrezia saw that it was her own beloved son whom she had thus so carelessly condemned to death, she was filled with dismay and horror and at once began to plead with her husband for his life.

But the Duke remained obdurate; and he furiously denounced Genarro as her lover, who should now die in her presence. In spite of the frantic woman's entreaties and passionate tirades, the most he would grant was that she should choose the mode of his death.

Lucrezia was for the moment filled with despair, not daring to vindicate herself by revealing her true relationship to Genarro. Then suddenly her quick wit devised a way out of the difficulty, and she declared that she was willing for the prisoner to die by drinking a draught of the famous poisoned wine of the Borgias.

The Duke, well pleased that his own strong will should have, as he supposed, conquered the proud spirit of his wife, triumphantly produced a cup of poisoned wine which he handed to the unfortunate Genarro, compelling him to drain it to the last drop; then, with a mocking laugh, he left the pair to take a last farewell of each other. But he had forgotten for the moment that the Borgias had the power to cure as well as to kill with the subtle poisons they used. When he had departed, Lucrezia hastily produced an antidote to the fatal draught which Genarro had just taken, so that the young man, by swallowing this, was thus saved from an untimely end.

Having seen that the antidote was taking good effect, Lucrezia hurried the still half-dazed Genarro out of the palace through an unfrequented passage; and bidding him betake himself to Venice, she hoped he was safe from further harm.

Being no longer occupied with the engrossing pleasure of her newly-found son's society and freed from the softening influence which he had exercised over her, Lucrezia became once more involved in her political schemes and personal intrigues. Having vowed vengeance upon the young Duke Orsini and his four companions for their denunciation of her to Genarro, she determined to carry out her deadly intention at a splendid banquet to be held at the palace of the Princess Negroni, a lady whose entertainments were always attended by the victims she had marked out.

When the night of the banquet arrived, the cunning Borgia managed to poison a flagon of rich wine which she caused to be served to the five nobles whose deaths she desired; and then she concealed herself, to await the consummation of her plan.

As the revels waxed more boisterous, Orsini, exhilarated by the rare wine he had been served with, entertained the company by singing a gay drinking song. Amidst the applause which followed his performance Lucrezia made her appearance and, revealing herself to Orsini and his companions, announced with cruel triumph that they had all partaken of poisoned wine and that in a few minutes they would be dead. At her command, the attendants showed the five victims the coffins in which they would shortly lie. At this moment, however, when her vengeance was just consummated, she was suddenly prostrated with horror. For Genarro—who, neglectful of her bidding, had remained in Ferrara—now suddenly appeared before her; and announcing that he also, as a guest at the banquet, had partaken of the poisoned wine, he sternly desired her to provide a sixth coffin for his remains when he should presently breathe his last.

The revellers, overcome by this tragic interruption to their mirth, left the banqueting hall one by one, with pale faces and trembling steps; and the mother and son were left alone.

Lucrezia was filled with the utmost horror on thus discovering that she had once again caused her beloved son to be poisoned. Quickly producing the antidote, with tears and entreaties she begged him to swallow it instantly; and her anxiety for his extreme danger was so great that, unable to control her feelings, she now revealed herself to him as his mother.

But Genarro refused to accept the antidote; for he was stunned by the announcement that this terrible woman, whose cold-blooded murder of his friends repelled him with horror, was his mother. It was in vain that Lucrezia, seeing that the poison was already taking deadly effect upon her now gasping son, entreated him passionately to take the antidote which she offered to him and which alone could save his life. Genarro was determined not to live since his friends were doomed to die; and, regardless of his mother's despair, he thrust the antidote aside and a few moments later fell back in her arms, dead.

At this moment, the Duke Alphonso entered the room; and Lucrezia, in a paroxysm of grief and wild despair, revealed to him the true relationship in which she had stood to Genarro.

The Duke had scarcely time to grasp the meaning of her distracted words, when the wretched Lucrezia herself fell gasping to the floor. The shock of having unwittingly murdered her own son was greater than she had strength to bear, and with a last despairing cry of woe and remorse, she also drank of the poisoned wine and fell dead beside the still form of her beloved Genarro.

ARIANE ET BARBE-BLEUE
(Ariadne and Blue-Beard)

Dukas

THIS is the old story of Blue-Beard, transformed into an allegory.

In mediæval times, there lived in a certain dismal castle a mysteriously sinister individual known as Blue-Beard, because of the bluish tinge, in his long shaggy beard.

The peasants who lived in the district around this gloomy castle had no love for Blue-Beard, whom they believed to be a murderer. It was known that every few months a lovely lady was taken into the castle by Blue-Beard to become his bride; but she was never seen again. It was supposed that she had been murdered.

But this was not actually the case. Blue-Beard did not murder the wives he married; he merely kept them as captives. So long as they obeyed his every wish and were dutiful wives—and, though regarded as a monster by the peasants, he could be quite attractive when he chose—all was well with them. If, however, they disobeyed his commands or showed signs of independence, he imprisoned them in horrible dungeons.

He tested all his wives in the same way. He gave them seven keys—six made of silver and one of gold—which fitted the locks of seven different rooms. They were at liberty to use the silver keys if they so desired—which they always did. But the golden key fitted the lock of a secret chamber, which they were forbidden to enter. It was because their natural curiosity had led them to disobey this last tantalizing command that they had met with such a sad fate.

When Blue-Beard married his sixth wife, Ariane, however, he met his match.

Ariane had heard all about the previous wives who had so mysteriously disappeared; and she was determined to find out what had happened to them. She was beautiful, brave, and strong; and she had no fear of Blue-Beard. But she was clever enough to know that she must be careful if she would solve the mystery. She did not wish to come to grief herself. She believed that the five wives declared by the peasants to have been murdered might not be dead after all. Probably they were hidden in dungeons; and if this proved to be the case, she hoped to set the captives free.

No sooner had Ariane been given the seven keys by the cunning Blue-Beard, than she set to work to unravel the mystery.

At the first favourable opportunity, she slipped away with the old Nurse who had come to the castle with her as her attendant and began to explore the subterranean halls and passages which might be likely to lead to dungeons and hidden rooms.

She soon found herself in a magnificent hall, illuminated by candles and having high windows opening on to an inside gallery. Three small doors were to be seen on either side of the entrance. From the open windows came the sound of menacing voices from a crowd of peasants gathered outside, who were ready to break into the castle and come to the assistance of the new bride they believed was about to be murdered; but Ariane scarcely heard them. She was so eager to find a keyhole which would fit the golden key she had been forbidden to use that she flung the six silver keys on to the floor as of no account.

The old Nurse, however, knew that great treasures and bridal gifts were probably hidden behind the small doors; and she begged permission from her mistress to have these opened first. Ariane impatiently gave consent; and the Nurse fitted a silver key into the first door. It fitted the keyhole, and the door instantly flew open. Out fell a shower of sparkling purple amethysts; and as the astonished women entered, they found that the room contained hundreds of bracelets, belts, rings, necklaces, tiaras, and chains, all set with these pretty stones.

The next silver key opened a room from which fell a shower of rubies; the third produced a cascade of emeralds; the fourth contained wonderful pearls; the fifth, turquoises and sapphires!

When the sixth door was reached, the Nurse seemed afraid and hesitant; but when Ariane, delighted at the treasures already revealed, commanded her to do so, she fitted the sixth silver key and opened the door. Instantly Ariane and her attendant were almost blinded by such a dazzling light that they seemed to be gazing straight into the heart of the sun. This room contained thousands of glittering diamonds, which flashed and scintillated on every side; and soon Ariane, ecstatic at such dazzling beauty, had not only crowned herself with diamonds, but had clasped so many bracelets and chains about her slender form that she positively blazed with the precious stones.

The Nurse was now thoroughly frightened by this dazzling scene, and cowered back in dismay. But Ariane had seen a little door at the end of the diamond room; and she hurried towards it with her golden key, which exactly fitted the lock. Although she could now hear the cries of the peasants outside, calling out a warning to her to remember the fate of the five previous wives, whom they declared had been murdered, she did not heed them.

Nor did she heed the entreaties of the old Nurse, who begged her to remain safely among the dazzling jewels. She eagerly turned the golden key in the keyhole of the seventh door, and flung it open. It was as dark as night!

This, then, was the Secret Chamber she had been forbidden to enter. From its gloomy vault-like depths, came the sound of weak voices chanting a sad song—the voices, surely, of the five lost wives! How she longed to set them free!

But before Ariane had time to enter the forbidden chamber, she was now accosted by Blue-Beard himself, who had crept upon her unawares. The Nurse was terrified; and she sought wildly for an opening through which she could admit the howling peasants outside, who were clamouring to get in and kill the "Monster" who owned the castle.

Ariane, however, was not afraid; and she turned and boldly faced Blue-Beard, denouncing him for his cruelty and declaring that she now intended to set his victims free. Blue-Beard was at first astounded by her defiance of him, and somewhat admiringly offered to forgive her disobedience entirely if she would close the seventh door and return with him. But Ariane scornfully refused to give up her quest; and she held him at bay until the peasants at last burst into the hall and he was then obliged to flee before their rage. The peasants would have killed him then and there; but Ariane calmly held them back, declaring that he had done her no ill.

The brave girl then closed the door upon the rabble; and while the peasants were seeking elsewhere for Blue-Beard, she entered the Secret Chamber, followed fearfully by the Nurse.

Here, at last, she found the five lost wives, not corpses, as had been declared, but pale and emaciated dungeon captives, ill-kempt and half starved. With great joy she brought them forth and comforted them, learning their names and hearing their stories—the latter all very much alike. When the released captives asked how she had managed to disobey the law of Blue-Beard and yet live to set them free, she declared she had put her faith in a higher law than that of this inhuman monster.

Then she led them out into the light of day once more and was filled with joy when she saw them wandering forth into the sunshine, singing happily.

A little later, when the freed wives had returned to the hall, she helped to array them in fine clothes and gave them their choice of the dazzling jewels she had unearthed; and for a while they were all very happy together, singing, feasting, and dressing themselves like princesses.

But soon there came the sound of a great uproar. The peasants had broken into the castle once more and had discovered Blue-Beard's hiding-place. They now brought him, wounded, exhausted, and bound with thongs, into the hall where the six wives had gathered together. They set him down in their midst, in great triumph, waiting for them to give the word for his instant death.

To the surprise of the peasants, however, this expected command was not given. Instead, Ariane began to bandage up the prisoner's wounds; and the five other wives eagerly helped her, running to fetch water and soothing his stiff limbs with tender hands.

The gaping peasants were further amazed when Ariane gratefully thanked them for having thus acted as the saviour of her sister-wives and herself—then led them quietly to the entrance and shut the door upon them!

Meanwhile, the five wives who had been treated so badly were now making a great fuss over their former tyrant. They even expressed dismay and horror because the " horrible peasants " had given him so many hurts. They were greatly delighted when Ariane now cut the cords that bound him and set him entirely free.

But when Ariane next bade farewell to Blue-Beard and invited her sister-wives to leave him and the castle with her and never return thither, they one and all refused to do so.

Though the door was open and they were now at liberty to wander forth into a new world of freedom and hope, they shook their heads. They still preferred captivity with the man who had enslaved them—even with such a man as Blue-Beard!—to freedom in a lonely world without him. So Ariane wandered forth alone.

From this allegory we are invited to believe that five women out of every six, given such a choice as that of the released wives, would do as they did. But the sixth, like Ariane, cherishes freedom as the greatest gift of all.

RUSALKA   *Dvořák*
(*The Water-Nymph*)

ONE night of dazzling moonlight, a lovely Water-Nymph sat sighing on a willow branch overhanging a peaceful lake.

She was so engrossed with her own sad thoughts that she did not even notice a group of merry little wood-elves, who presently came dancing down the moonlit glade behind her; nor did she seem aware that the cottage of an old Witch stood near the entrance to the glade. So wrapped up was she in her sorrow that she saw and heard nothing.

The wood-elves took no notice of the sad nymph. They had come to the water-side, full of mischief, eager only to tease the old Water-Sprite who was the guardian of the lake. They danced wildly on the edge of the lake, calling him playful names, hoping thereby to disturb him and rouse his ire. But the Water-Sprite was a good-natured old fairy fellow; and when he heard the teasing songs of the elves, he most obligingly arose from the depths of the waters to scold them. Then, still laughing and singing their teasing song, the mischievous elves danced away to the woods.

And now the old Water-Sprite's attention was drawn to a more serious matter. The lovely Water-Nymph sitting so droopingly on the willow-bough, began to pour out to him the sad story of her woe. She had fallen in love with a handsome young Prince, whom she had seen several times lately bathing in the lake; and she now longed to take on human form and to become a beautiful maiden, that the royal youth might love her in return.

At first the Water-Sprite was shocked and dismayed on hearing this; and he advised the nymph to think no more about her mortal lover. If she took on human form, more troubles would be in store for her. It would be better for her to remain happy in her own watery world.

But the Water-Nymph declared she was so deeply in love she cared not what suffering it might cause her if only she could gain her heart's desire. Seeing that she was determined, the Water-Sprite now told her to seek the aid of the Old Witch, who was capable of granting her wish. He then sank back into his own well-loved watery depths, with a final warning to her to give up the idea of such fatal folly.

His words fell on heedless ears, however; for the Water-Nymph eagerly called upon the Old Witch to come forth from her cottage. When the crone appeared and announced that it was within her power to grant her desire, she was filled with joy. Even when the Old Witch warned her of the price she must be prepared to pay, she was almost too impatient to listen to the conditions named, which were certainly terrible enough. When she became a human maiden, she would be dumb; and if her human lover should prove false to her, a curse would fall upon her, whereby she would have to return to the depths of the waters for ever. What was more, in the latter case, the mortal she loved would likewise fall under the curse.

Despite these ominous conditions, the Water-Nymph still persisted in her desire to become a human maiden, feeling sure of the power of her own love to retain that of the mortal she desired. So she followed the Old Witch into the latter's cottage, where the transformation was to take place. As she departed, wails arose from the old Water-Sprite and the other nymph denizens of the lake, who feared for her ultimate fate.

Meanwhile, as the Witch's spells were being completed, the glorious young Prince with whom the Water-Nymph had fallen in love came hastening down the glade. He was looking for a fair white doe he had been chasing all the day, which, after bringing him to this spot, had now disappeared. The sound of hunting-horns could be heard in the distance, where the Prince's followers were still enjoying the chase. A little nearer the song of a huntsman was more plainly heard—the words of which contained a curious note of warning to the royal youth, bidding him beware of danger.

The young Prince, however, took no heed of the huntsman's song, for he seemed strangely attracted to this glade. As he drew near to the lake, he remembered that he had bathed in its cool waters on several occasions. Just then, as he turned to walk back to the glade, the door of the Witch's cottage opened and out came the loveliest maiden he had ever beheld. It was the transformed Water-Nymph. Her beauty was so dazzling that the young man was completely enthralled, and a sudden passion for her burned within him. Even when he discovered that she was dumb and could not reply to the words of love and admiration he poured upon her, he was still entranced. The beautiful maiden smiled sweetly upon him, the light of a passionate love shining in her deep blue eyes; and when he held out his arms to her, she fell gladly into the warm human embrace for which she had craved.

Completely entranced with one another, the lovers wandered arm-in-arm along the glade towards the royal hunting-party, which now rode off to the Prince's castle. They were followed by the mournful songs of the water-nymphs, bewailing the loss of their beloved but misguided sister.

.   .   .   .

In the royal castle, great celebrations were held in honour of the wedding of the Prince to the lovely maiden he had found in the woods. The castle was full of guests—among them a very proud and magnificent Princess from a foreign country. This royal lady did not approve of the Prince's choice of a dumb bride of whose antecedents nothing was known. She had hoped to marry the Prince herself.

Even the servants gossiped about the mysterious stranger who was unable to speak to any of them, and who, though sweet and gentle, they were inclined to think had probably bewitched their royal lord. It was also whispered among them that the Prince's passionate love for the beautiful maiden was already beginning to wane; and they knew that he was troubled in his mind and was beginning to regret his hasty action.

This was true. On one of the festive evenings, the Prince came walking through the splendid palace gardens with the former Water-Nymph, whose exquisite human beauty no longer satisfied him. Because she was dumb, he could learn nothing from her of her former life; nor could she reply to his own loving words. He had not found in her such a burning passion as he had hoped; there was something lacking in her human make-up that disappointed him. She was still a mystery to him; a mystery of which he had already tired.

Unable to reply to her beloved one's unreasonable complaints, the nymph-maiden looked pleadingly with eyes of love upon him, as though entreating him to a renewed content in her. She could not bear to think that her human happiness could have ended so soon—even before the wedding celebrations were over. But the Prince broke away from her clinging arms impatiently; and seeing the foreign Princess approaching, he hastened forward to greet the latter with exaggerated words of admiration and homage. Bidding his chosen bride retire to her chamber and dress herself in her most gorgeous garments for the evening entertainment just now beginning, he took the hand of his royal guest and led her away towards the castle. The unhappy bride departed, alone, with despair in her heart.

The grand illumination of the gardens now began, to the sound of trumpets and music; and presently the royal guests began to come out to join in these final festivities.

In the midst of the gardens there was a deep pond; and while the evening festivities were at their height, the old Water-Sprite, guardian of the lake in the forest, suddenly arose from its waters. He had come thither to help the misguided Water-Nymph who had left her watery home in human form because of her love for a mortal. Already he had noticed that the Prince's love for the maiden had waned and that the foreign Princess was now the object of his passion; and the kindly old Water-Sprite mourned for the tragedy about to happen.

As the wedding festival songs and dances continued, he knew that the woe of his beloved nymph must deepen, since her short-lived happiness was already doomed. He realized, however, that, in her sorrow, she would instinctively make her way to her natural element, water; and he anxiously awaited her arrival at the pond.

The old Water-Sprite was right. Now realizing only too well that her human romance was almost over, the Water-Nymph maiden presently drew near to the pond, being attracted to the water in her grief as though by a magic spell. Here she was greatly comforted to find her old friend; and now, as she touched her natural element, her lost gift of speech returned to her.

She soon poured forth the story of her sorrow—how her own deep love had failed to keep that of the Prince, whose heart had instinctively turned to one of his own race.

Even as the two fairy folk spoke together, the Prince was seen near by with the foreign Princess, to whom he was already making ardent love. So enthralled with his new passion was the royal youth that he scarcely glanced at his chosen bride when she presently appeared before him with her arms outstretched imploringly, her lips once more locked as she came away from the water.

And now the old Water-Sprite rose up majestically from the depths of the pond, a weird and menacing figure. He sternly warned the young Prince that though he now declined the loving invitation of his nymph-bride, yet was he eventually doomed to accept her embraces. The curse laid upon her when she made her sacrifice for the sake of winning his love would also fall upon him.

Then, seizing the scorned nymph-bride by the hand, her fairy champion plunged with her into the depths of the pond.

The Prince, startled by these mysterious happenings, knew now that he was caught in the net of enchantment; and he turned for comfort and help to his royal visitor, who had so willingly accepted his protestations of love. But, to his surprise and dismay, the foreign Princess had no desire to have anything to do with magic or the supernatural, and, in great disdain, she left him and hurriedly departed from the castle.

Thus, in the midst of his wedding celebrations, the royal youth found himself alone, having lost the fair wood-maiden he had once loved so passionately as well as the haughty Princess for whom he had deserted her.

Once more the Water-Nymph was back in her own domain.

She sat on a willow-bough overhanging the lake in the forest, as formerly. But now, as part of the price to be paid for having loved a mortal, she had been transformed into a will-o'-the-wisp, so that a dancing flame played about her head. Not yet could she become as her sister-nymphs in the water. She must suffer the pangs of unrequited love.

No one in the forest could lessen her woe. It was no use entreating the Old Witch to help her again; nor could the friendly old Water-Sprite do anything more for her. Only by the life of her mortal lover, willingly laid down in atonement for her, could she be set free from her sorrow and find peace. Rather than that, however, she preferred to go on suffering and to endure the pain of her grief and her broken heart. Her pure and wonderful love had not changed. She would not harm her beloved one. With a heart-rending sigh, she plunged into the lake, to hide herself and her woe.

No sooner had she vanished from sight than two of the Prince's retainers came hurrying down the forest glade and called forth the Old Witch from her cottage. They had come to seek her help in finding their beloved Prince, who had wandered away from the castle in a distracted state and was now lost.

They were soon driven away again, however, by the old Water-Sprite, who rose up in anger from the lake and shouted curses upon them, in which he was joined by the cackling laughter of the Old Witch. They would have nothing more to do with mortals in their peaceful glade.

Nevertheless, another human figure now came staggering down the glade when silence had been restored. This was the Prince himself, distraught and exhausted. Filled with remorse for his cruel and heartless conduct, he had come to seek out the lovely nymph-maiden he had betrayed, having again followed a white doe to this spot; and he now called wildly for her to appear.

Slowly a light began to flicker over the surface of the lake—a will-o'-the-wisp's dancing flame; and the Water-Nymph, crowned with light, sadly rose up from the water, and came towards the edge. Gently she reproached the Prince for his betrayal of her and for the doom he had thus brought upon her. Yet she longed deeply to be embraced by him once more and to bestow her own kisses upon him, but, because of the curse which had fallen upon her, her kisses could only bring death to him.

But the Prince wished only to atone for his betrayal of her; and his love had now returned double-fold. In spite of her warning, he rushed forward eagerly and clasped her drooping figure in his arms, kissing her passionately and imploring her to kiss him in return. At last she yielded to his entreaty.

Immediately the Prince fell back, dead. The curse had come upon him, as fore-ordained. But the death of the Prince did not release the Water-Nymph from her own doom. She was compelled to return to the depths of the lake for ever. Never again would she know mortal love.

Nevertheless, the Water-Nymph was satisfied. It had been a joy to her to know that the Prince's love had come back to her at last, and that she had been permitted the ecstasy of receiving his kisses once more. The price she had paid was not too heavy for this perfect joy for which she had craved.

Tenderly, and for the last time, she kissed her dead lover. Then, slowly and with contentment, she vanished into the depths of the lake.

TESS   *D'Erlanger*

IT was early dawn on May-Day in Wessex—that peaceful, ethereal hour between darkness and light, when life seems at a standstill and under a magic spell.

But disenchantment had already taken place at the cottage of Jack Durbeyfield in Blackmoor Vale. His lovely daughter, Tess, with considerable difficulty, had ruthlessly awakened her young brother, Aby, who was now sleepily getting into his rough clothes while his energetic sister ran down to feed the old horse, Prince— the mainstay of this extremely poor household—in readiness for an early jog-trot into the neighbouring market-town. Her mother, Joan Durbeyfield, soon joined her; and the two women managed to get the still grumbling lad off to market with his meagre load of vegetables.

Then Tess, always cheerful and happy, despite the poverty in which she lived, ran off to begin her usual household duties— though, at her mother's pleading, she had stopped with her for a few moments to watch the other country folk passing by to work in the fields, singing as they went.

Meanwhile, her father, Jack Durbeyfield, had also got to work, busying himself with his accounts, which were in a very bad way and gave him no satisfaction. He was, indeed, almost in despair, and wondered dismally how he should meet the debt he owed to Toronton, a dealer who supplied him with ce tain necessary commodities. At that moment, his wife, Joan, in alarm, hurried in to tell him that the man he feared to face was even then approaching the cottage; and he rose to greet his unwelcome visitor with blank dismay.

Toronton, however, was in a curiously amiable mood. He was not a pleasant fellow, being grasping and of a shifty turn, as the Durbeyfields well knew; and at first they distrusted his present amiability, when they had been expecting hard words because of the debt they were not prepared to meet just then.

To their amazement, Toronton greeted them both with mock respectfulness, doffing his hat and bowing before them, addressing Jack as " Sir John ", and Joan as " Lady D'Urberville ".

He then explained to the puzzled pair that among the " junk " accumulated in his business as a dealer, he had come across an ancient parchment in a library of old books he had just bought from a local parson. This parchment turned out to be a copy of the pedigree of the D'Urbervilles, an important and wealthy family living in the district; and from it he had traced a direct connection with his debtors, the Durbeyfields—the latter name being an obvious corruption of the more aristocratic one.

Toronton now suggested that Jack's handsome daughter, Tess, should be sent to claim cousinly kinship with the D'Urbervilles at their grand country house, where he happened to know they were requiring a " companion " or superior helper in the household. He added, with crafty facetiousness, that young Alec D'Urberville, the heir, was now at home; and thus, on his meeting such a beautiful new cousin, fate might be safely left to do the rest and bring about a match between the pair. With this reunion of the two families, the Durbeyfields' troubles would surely be ended.

Very pleased with what he considered his clever idea, Toronton departed quite gaily, declaring airily that the debt could now stand over until " Sir John " was ready to pay—as he certainly would be presently.

Jack and Joan Durbeyfield were likewise much puffed up with the idea of being far-off relations of the great folk of the district; and consequently, when Tess's admirer, Angel Clare, now appeared, they did not greet him with any enthusiasm. Before the great news brought them that morning, they had been well enough pleased that young Angel Clare, a parson's son and a gentleman student of farming in Wessex, should admire their handsome daughter; now, they felt, she might look higher still.

Angel Clare, however, heeded not their new coldness, but, when they had gone indoors, waited about the place until Tess should appear. Although his love of Nature had led him to engage in the practical work of farming, he was also a poet and a philosopher; and his love for Tess was of the worshipping kind. To him she was something divine to be revered for her innocent purity as well as loved for her beauty and sweet disposition.

Meanwhile, Tess, having finished her household duties, had now arrayed herself in her simple May-Day garb; for, poor though she was, she had been invited to join in the singing, dancing, and other festivities of the day with her friends. She was glad, therefore, when, on coming out in her festival attire, she was greeted admiringly by Angel Clare; and the sweethearts spent a few happy moments together before going off to join in the May-Day revels.

Later in the day, when Tess had returned from dancing on the village green, she was told the news brought by Toronton of her family's connection with the important rich D'Urbervilles and of the suggestion that she should seek out her new kin and fill the vacant position in their household.

But Tess loved her present simple life and was not afraid of poverty; and she begged her father not to send her away to her rich relatives, declaring eagerly that she would work all the harder at home, since she would be shy and unhappy with such grand strangers. Her mother, seeing how distressed she was, now took her part. She declared that her pretty Tess should not be made unhappy; but her husband, seeing his rosy dream of cousinly financial assistance fading away, was greatly disappointed.

He was still grumbling about the matter, when young Aby returned from market with a distressing story to tell. His country cart had been crashed into by the mail-coach, and Prince, their trusty old horse, had been killed.

All were thrown into deep consternation on hearing this dismal news; for old Prince had been their only remaining possession of any worth, so that their future outlook was now black indeed.

Then Tess, unable to bear the sight of her beloved parents thus hopeless and despairing, determined to sacrifice her own happiness; and, bidding them be of good cheer once more, she now declared her willingness to seek out their new connections. By taking up the position the latter had to offer, she would be able to earn money for them all and also to interest the rich D'Urbervilles in their poor relations.

. . . .

But Tess, as she had expected, was not happy, nor did she have the success hoped for, in her new abode. Although her recently discovered "cousins" had actually received her in their fine country home, they gave her only a menial position therein; and though described as a "companion" to the elderly mistress of the house—who was a rather severe and haughty dame—she was not treated as an equal, but was, indeed, merely another household servant. This vague position, however, the simple and practical Tess would gladly have endured, being only eager to earn money for her parents; but she soon found that the other servants were jealous of her slightly higher status, and that their envy even made them hate her.

One of the maids, in particular, made her new life unbearable. This was Dark-Car—who came of gipsy stock herself—who was likewise jealous of Tess's beauty, which she knew had attracted the attention of the young son and heir of the house, Alec D'Urberville. The latter sought the "cousinly companion's" society whenever this was possible; and because of this the sinister and madly-jealous girl did her utmost to bring trouble upon the newcomer.

One time, during the late evening, with the aid of the other servants, she caused Tess to be blamed for a breakage of valuable glass which she herself had deliberately thrown down; and when Tess ran out into the garden, wildly denying the unjust charge, Dark-Car followed and poured forth further abuse upon her—accusing her, in particular, of running after the young master. Then she squared her shoulders, doubled her fists, and challenged the now scared Tess to a fight.

As it happened, young Alec D'Urberville was also in 'the garden and saw and overheard all this little scene; and being, indeed, infatuated by his beautiful "cousin" ever since he had first set eyes upon her, he now stepped forth into the open and demanded an explanation of the trouble.

Tess, in tears, flung herself at his feet, imploring his protection; and Alec, dismissing the still angry Dark-Car, comforted his now reassured "cousin", openly showing his admiration for her beauty and promising to deal severely with anyone who should dare to offend her again.

When Alec had departed, leaving her to recover somewhat, Tess wandered farther into the garden, still troubled; and fearing that the young heir's bold admiration boded no good to her, she determined to return to her home at once before further ill befell her.

Just then she was accosted by her young brother, Aby, who came with further bad news for her. Her parents were in great distress and were, indeed, now so poor that there was no food in her old home that day; and Aby had come to beg help from his sister, upon whose new position such absurd hopes had been built by their foolish father.

In great distress, Tess now saw that she could not afford to give up her new work; and after sending Aby away with all the money she had already earned and with loving messages to her dear ones, she returned towards the great house to continue the life she hated.

It was now almost dark, and, to her horror, she found that the servants, in reprisal and further to damage her reputation in the eyes of their mistress, had locked and bolted the doors; and she was thus shut outside in the growing darkness of the garden.

Tess had been right in her fear that Alec D'Urberville's bold admiration and pretended kindness boded her no good. Knowing that his mother, little impressed by the "cousinship" claim, would never agree to his marriage with Tess, and having conceived a real passion for her, he determined to make her his mistress.

Consequently, this evening, he had watched with satisfaction from a hiding-place in the garden the bolting of the house doors, knowing that Tess was still outside and that she was thus at his mercy. When, therefore, the young girl now ran up and realized that she had been locked out, he once more stepped forward, as though to her assistance.

But his real vile purpose was soon made clear, when he began to make passionate love to the beautiful new "cousin" whom he had already marked down as his prey. With deep cunning, eager to secure her consent, he promised to assist her poverty-stricken parents if she would accede to his unlawful love.

It was in vain that Tess, entirely innocent but unable to hold her own against so experienced, determined, and ardent a wooer, endeavoured to save herself. She could not long resist him, knowing, as she did, that it would be at the expense of her beloved necessitous home folks. Thus, she was trapped by an unkind fate; and at last her resistance was broken down and she was compelled to yield herself to the importunities of Alec D'Urberville.

.   .   .   .

In the model dairy-house at Talbothays Farm, the hustle-bustle of cheery work was at its height; and cheese-makers, dairy-maids, and butter-churners all chattered and laughed together as they went about their simple tasks under the careful eye of Mrs. Crick, the proprietress.

Tess Durbeyfield, as beautiful as ever, but with the added indefinable charm of having known suffering, was there, busy among the cheese-wrappings, some of which she was mending; and near by stood Angel Clare, among the other cheese-workers.

For a year past, Angel had been away in another district, having been unable to bear Blackmoor after Tess had departed to her new " cousins " at the great house. He had now returned, and had been full of joy on finding his still beloved Tess working at the dairy-farm; and he had promptly applied for work there himself.

He had soon renewed his sincere wooing of Tess and had begged her to name a date for their marriage; but, so far, Tess had kept him at arm's length. Although she still loved him dearly, she now had a dreaded secret to hide from him. Angel had been away during the whole of her stay with the D'Urbervilles, and for some months afterwards; and he knew nothing of her innocent disgrace, nor of the child born to her and of the latter's recent death.

Knowing how idealistic was Angel's love for her, Tess dared not tell him of her misfortune—not lest he should blame her in any way, but lest his crystal-clear vision of her purity should be shattered. Nor did she dare to risk, after their marriage, the discovery of her wretched secret. She tried, therefore, to hold back the final giving of her word and the naming of a definite date for their wedding; and meanwhile she was happy in the knowledge of his love and had no wish to disturb it.

But Angel Clare could see no reason why their marriage should be delayed any longer; and he became so ardently eager for the consummation of his love that Tess knew she could not much longer deny him.

On this day, as they worked so near to one another, Angel found many opportunities for short conversations with Tess in the course of their work together; and each time he begged her to name the date for their marriage.

As Tess found herself alone towards the end of the day's work, Jack Durbeyfield, her father, hurried up to her, eagerly announcing that he had great news which could not await her return home that evening. He said that Alec D'Urberville was now free and willing to marry her, his martinet mother having recently died and left him entirely his own master; and he expected Tess to be joyful at this prospect of at last securing such a rich husband.

But Tess was not joyful—far from it. She declared that she hated her betrayer and would never marry him, whether he desired it or not; and she added that she loved only Angel Clare and was eager to wed with him but feared to do so because of her dreaded secret. Then she implored her father to take this task upon himself, and to tell the whole sad story to Angel; and Jack Durbeyfield, though disappointed at once again seeing his rosy dreams of a rich son-in-law vanishing, agreed to her request, being overcome, in spite of himself, by her vehement distress.

When her father had gone, Angel Clare again drew near and once more pleaded for her love and the naming of their wedding-day. This time, reassured by her father's promise, Tess gave way to her lover's pleading; and Angel rapturously clasped her in his arms.

.   .   .   .

It was late evening on Tess's wedding-day; and Angel Clare and his beloved one were alone in their bridal chamber.

The little room had been gaily decorated with garlands of flowers by the bride's girl-friends; and Aby had just laid her wedding-veil upon the white bed as a special adornment.

Overjoyed at finding himself alone at last with his lovely bride, Angel turned joyfully to clasp her in his eager arms; but Tess held back for a moment. Her heart was so full of deep gratitude because Angel had been willing to wed with her even after hearing from her father's lips the story of her innocent defilement, that she now flung herself at his feet, weeping with joy and declaring that he had raised her up from the sunset and darkness of shame and abasement to the daybreak and light of renewed purity.

But, on hearing this outburst, Angel Clare said he did not know what she meant by such strange words as "shame and abasement" in connection with herself; and his usually tender voice took on a sharp hurt tone as he demanded that she should reveal any dark secret she might hold from him and tell him the truth only.

Then, her joy turned to horror, Tess realized that her father had not kept faith with her, that he had not told the story of her shame, as promised, and that Angel Clare had, therefore, married her knowing nothing of her secret; and she uttered a loud cry of woe.

Equally overcome by an awful suspicion of some deadly deceit practised upon him, Angel roughly seized the hands of his trembling bride, whose sudden deathly pallor and deep agitation confirmed his fears; and he again demanded the truth from her.

The unhappy Tess begged him rather to let her die, declaring that her father had promised to reveal the story of what had happened to stain her purity and of her own real innocence in the matter; but he had broken his word to her and had failed to do so.

To this Angel bitterly replied that Jack Durbeyfield had probably been cautious on purpose; and the now distracted Tess saw that he did not believe she had even asked her father to do this thing. It was in vain for her to assert passionately her own entire innocence in this miserable affair . . . innocent or not, the purity of his bride had been besmirched, and his crystal-clear idyllic vision of her had been ruined for all time. He, Angel Clare, had worshipped at the shrine of a pure white lily—and that fair lily was no longer pure and white. He could love only a Tess who was as pure as she was beautiful; and the Tess who now stood before him was a stranger. His high ideal of purity was shattered, and his soul could not forgive. Heartbroken, he bowed his head and sobbed with anguish.

Tess, likewise heartbroken and despairing, but realizing clearly that she had, through no fault of her own, lost her beloved one for ever, made no further attempt to win his forgiveness. Cast out from Angel's heart, she could no longer remain as his bride. Her sentence was irrevocable; and the joys of love were not for her. Sadly, but firmly, she took off her wedding-ring and laid it on the bridal bed, beside which she knelt for a few moments to pray.

Then, proudly calm at last, and with unfaltering steps, she opened the door, cast one final look of love upon the bowed and sobbing form of Angel Clare, and passed out into the darkness of the night.

MARTHA   *Flotow*

THE Lady Henrietta was bored. She sat one summer morning in the gilded boudoir of her fine house at Richmond, and heaved sigh upon sigh. Although Maid-of-Honour to Queen Anne and the loveliest and most fascinating of all the Court beauties, she found no satisfaction in life. She was wearied of balls and routs, of the fulsome flatteries of her many admirers, and of the tiresome monotony of Court life. Satiated with pleasure, she had now retired to her own home for a few days' respite. Here, however, she was equally bored.

When her merry and resourceful little waiting-maid, Nancy, ventured to suggest: "If only your Ladyship could really fall in love!" the spoilt beauty did not even deign to reply. When, too, her staid cousin and would-be admirer, Lord Tristan Mickleford, was presently announced, his offer to escort her to any entertainment she desired was likewise frowned upon. She had little use just then for Lord Tristan, who was a middle-aged fop with stiffly-exaggerated Court manners and whose conversation was more boring than usual. Presently, however, she changed her mind.

Hearing sounds of merriment coming from without, she ran to the window to see what was afoot.

Groups of gay country maidens and youths were passing by on their way to the statute fair at Richmond, where they would presently stand in ranks to be hired as servants for the ensuing year, according to a local custom; and the sight of these merry rustics suddenly suggested a daring frolic to the bored Henrietta, who now exclaimed to her companions : " No more dull moments to-day! We will dress ourselves in peasant garb, Nancy, and go to the fair as country wenches seeking a master! Oh, what a frolic! And *you* shall come with us, my good Tristan, as our protecting brother! "

The foppish Lord Tristan was shocked and dismayed by the suggestion, protesting pompously that it was quite beneath his rank and courtly dignity to mingle with the motley crew at a fair. When, however, Henrietta declared she would never speak to him again unless he obeyed her sovereign will in this matter, he gave a feeble consent and grumblingly allowed himself to be garbed as a country bumpkin. By the time he was ready, his mischievous cousin joined him again with Nancy, both girls now attired in homespun, with short bright skirts, neat bodices, and quaint mob-caps—certainly the smartest and prettiest country maidens ever seen in those parts. Full of gaiety and eager excitement, they dragged off their unwilling swain to the fair.

When they arrived upon the scene, the business of the day was at its height; and quickly noting the long row of country wenches standing at one side waiting to be hired, Henrietta determined to join their ranks. She adroitly invented an excuse for ridding herself of the disgusted Lord Tristan for a short time; then, bubbling over with mirth, the two girls took up their stand amidst the serving-maids.

Among the busy crowd were two handsome, well-to-do young farmers, by name Plunket and Lionel, who, being in need of domestic help, had come to the statute fair to hire a couple of wenches. These two, though loving each other as such, were not brothers; but they had lived together since early childhood. Neither could recollect much of their first acquaintance, knowing little beyond the fact that Plunket's parents had rescued Lionel's father, a stranger and fugitive, from danger and destruction. Before dying, the mysterious stranger had bequeathed a ring to his orphan son, with the injunction that, should he ever be in distress, he should send it to the Queen, when his whole fate might be changed. Not being able to discover anything about the birth or rank of the orphan left in their charge, the honest farmer and his wife brought him up with their own son. Later on, when the farm eventually came into the hands of the young Plunket, the latter made Lionel share his inheritance with him.

As the young farmers now passed down the rows of country wenches, they were instantly struck with the good looks and smart appearance of Lady Henrietta and Nancy; and they offered to engage them at once, at higher wages than they had ever paid before. Henrietta, enjoying the frolic more and more, and delighted to see that the handsome Lionel was struck with her beauty, threw the latter a roguish glance and accepted his offer at once, giving her name as Martha. The merry Nancy, willing enough to follow where her mistress led, likewise accepted the offer made by Plunket, giving her name as Julia.

The young farmers, pleased by having secured two such attractive serving-maids, at once paid over to them the earnest-money, by which they were bound to them for a whole year's service. Then they desired the girls to follow them to the farm, that they might begin their duties.

But Henrietta and Nancy, laughing merrily, declared they had no intention of going to the farm, adding that the whole affair was merely a joke on their part. Soon, however, their merriment ended. The two young farmers, justifiably indignant, calmly informed them that, having taken earnest-money, they were bound by law to render service for a whole year, according to the custom of the district. The local sheriff who presided over the statute-hiring, ratified what the young farmers said, and ordered the girls to follow their new masters at once. Henrietta, now realizing that she had carried her escapade too far, was in great distress, not daring to disclose her true name and rank for fear of the scandal coming to the ears of the Queen.

When Lord Tristan presently arrived on the scene, he was powerless to help her then. The country folk, indignant because of their statute rule being questioned, set upon him at once and quickly drove him away.

Meanwhile, the two young farmers packed their newly-hired servants into a rough country wagon and drove them off to their farm without more ado; for Henrietta now thought it advisable to submit quietly to the indignity she had brought on herself, hoping to escape later on.

On arriving at the farm, however, the triumphant masters soon discovered that they had made a bad bargain as to the working capabilities of their new maids; for neither "Martha" nor "Julia" could do a stroke of domestic work. Nevertheless, their unusual charm quickly fascinated both the young men, so that they promptly fell in love with them.

While Plunket was vainly trying to instruct the mischievous and saucy Nancy in her duties in the kitchen—where she broke many dishes—Henrietta condescended to receive a lesson in spinning from the handsome Lionel, whose gentle manners and naturally aristocratic bearing had impressed her agreeably from the first. Lionel, whose admiration for the supposed "Martha" was developing into love at a most alarming rate, found his task a pleasant one; and he was thrilled by the touch of the soft white hand as he guided it through the intricacies of the spinning-wheel.

Elated by having made such an easy conquest of the young farmer, whose ardent glances soon betrayed the state of his susceptible heart, Henrietta quickly recovered her good spirits; and presently she offered to sing to the indulgent master who thus recklessly encouraged her in idleness.

So the bewitching Martha sang "The Last Rose of Summer" in a voice so soft and sweet that Lionel was enthralled; and when the song came to an end, he could not refrain from declaring his love for her. So far from being his handmaid, he now desired to make her his wife. Lady Henrietta, however, astonished and dismayed at the quick development of the passion she had so carelessly excited, took refuge in laughter; and the sensitive Lionel, seeing his genuine raptures thus treated with lightness, was deeply hurt.

Meanwhile, sounds of squabbling and the breaking of dishes came from the kitchen; and Plunket now returned with the saucy Nancy, whose outrageous behaviour had by this time nearly driven him frantic, though her tantalizing charms had already won his heart. As it was already getting dark, he ordered the two unsatisfactory servants to betake themselves to bed; and when the girls had gladly retired, he declared to the now wretched Lionel that he feared they had made a bad bargain.

During the night, as Lady Henrietta and Nancy were planning a means of escape, they heard the whispered voice of Lord Tristan calling to them from outside their window. He had discovered their whereabouts and had a carriage waiting at the bottom of the lane to take them away. The two girls eagerly clambered down from the low window; and their movements were so silent that they managed to make their escape unobserved.

The defrauded young farmers were full of indignation when they found that their pretty maids had flown; but though they eagerly searched the whole country-side for news of the runaways, their efforts were in vain.

Meanwhile, Henrietta had at first been glad enough to return to her Court life once more. But a strange sadness now frequently came over her spirits. The fact was that her heart had been more deeply touched by the honest affection of the handsome young farmer, Lionel, than she was willing to admit; and she longed to see him again, even though she knew the difference in their rank was an obstacle not easily to be overcome. Nancy, too, thought frequently of the sturdy Plunket, whose masterful ways had not been displeasing to her.

At last, after many weeks had passed by, the four young people met again.

One day, during a splendid royal hunt, Lady Henrietta withdrew a little apart from the gay company, and wandered off down a lonely glade, where she soon gave herself up to the melancholy thoughts that had lately taken possession of her.

Her attendant, Nancy, however, merry and lively as ever, went on with the rest of the party; and presently, to her surprise and utter consternation, she came face to face with the young farmer, Plunket, who happened to be strolling through Richmond forest that day on his way from the village.

No sooner did Plunket set eyes on Nancy than he recognized her instantly, despite her now formal dress, as his runaway maid; and accosting her without ceremony, he ordered her to return to his service at once. At first Nancy tried to put him off by laughing and pretending not to know him; but when Plunket seized her arm, gently but firmly, insisting that she should follow him, the girl was alarmed for her mistress's sake. Turning to the surprised ladies and gentlemen, she called on them to come to her aid.

Immediately the indignant party closed about Plunket, buffeting and belabouring him with their hunting-crops; and the unfortunate farmer was obliged to beat a retreat as best he could.

Meanwhile, Lionel, who was also walking in the forest not far away, had wandered unconsciously into the very same glade Henrietta had selected for her own lonely ramble. Presently approaching a lady of quality in the rich habit of a fashionable huntress, he recognized, to his utter astonishment, the beautiful features of his beloved Martha. In great delight, he hurried

forward with outstretched arms to greet her; and Henrietta, at
first overjoyed in spite of herself, uttered an exclamation of
pleasure. Then, recollecting that she would be disgraced should
the knowledge of her escapade become known at Court, and seeing that her companions in the chase were already approaching,
she suddenly turned cold and haughtily denied the young
farmer's acquaintance.

But Lionel, his passion enhanced on again beholding the object
of his affections, determined to assert his rights as a master;
and he commanded her eagerly to return to his employ. Then
Henrietta, afraid of what might follow, called out to her companions for help, declaring that Lionel was a madman.

Instantly, the rest of the hunting party crowded around; and
when Lionel now heard Henrietta being addressed on all sides
as " My Lady ", he saw in a flash that a trick had been played
upon him at the statute fair and that this fine Court beauty had
only been amusing herself at his expense. Realizing now that
his sincere love could never be requited, he was filled with disappointment and despair; and he began to pour forth such scornful, passionate reproaches that the huntsmen, thinking him mad
indeed, closed around and attempted to drive him away.

At this moment Plunket appeared on the scene once more; and
quickly joining in the fray he at length managed to drag his
friend away and to return with him to the farm.

Here the unhappy Lionel, overcome by grief and believing that
his beloved one was now lost to him for ever, quickly fell into a
delirious state bordering on frenzy; and Plunket, fearing for his
friend's life, at length sent a message to Lady Henrietta—whose
true rank and name he had presently discovered—entreating her to
visit the farm at least once again. With this message he also sent
the ring bequeathed to Lionel by his mysterious father, requesting the Maid of Honour to place it in the hands of the Queen.
He felt that this was a fitting time for the token to be presented,
since his unfortunate friend could not well be in greater distress
nor in more urgent need of help.

When Henrietta received the message, she was conscience-
stricken and filled with grief; for she had instantly regretted her
cruel treatment of Lionel in the forest and could no longer hide
from herself the fact that she loved him with her whole heart.
She determined, therefore, to visit the farm and to accept the love
of this faithful wooer; but first she visited the Queen with the
strange token sent to her.

A wonderful surprise was now in store for all. The carefully-
hoarded ring brought back a long-forgotten incident to the Queen

and proved to her that the young farmer, Lionel, was in reality the only son of the unfortunate Earl of Derby who, wrongfully accused of treason, had been forced to flee the country and had died in exile.

The royal lady determined to heal the wrongs inflicted on the father by restoring the son to his rightful rank and possessions; and the joyful tidings of this happy change in his fortunes was carried to Lionel by the fair Henrietta herself.

The young Earl was duly reinstated to the proper rank, wealth, and Court favour to which he was entitled; but, to the grief of Henrietta, the sufferings to which her thoughtless conduct had subjected him had unhinged her lover's mind and rendered his memory of all the incidents connected with herself a blank.

However, she presently determined to try a curious experiment. By staging the Richmond fair once more with the aid of her friends, she hoped to restore the balance of Lionel's disordered mind. The result was entirely satisfactory.

When Plunket led Lionel through the pretended show and down the ranks of pretty maids as he had done on the actual day of the fair, the light of memory gradually brought back the wandering reason of the young Earl and restored his mind to its normal state. The moment he beheld Henrietta in her dainty peasant dress, he recognized the beautiful Martha whose charms had won his heart; and a clear recollection of all the succeeding events likewise coming suddenly upon him, he hurried forward and clasped her in his arms with great joy, knowing now that there was no further obstacle to their union.

A short time afterwards, the young Earl of Derby, restored to reason and happiness, was married to the Lady Henrietta, whom he had learned to love so dearly as Martha the serving-maid. At the same time, Plunket took home his pretty bride, Nancy, to continue her bewitchment of him as the mistress of his farm.

DUKE OR DEVIL
Gatty

IN the early Middle Ages, the practice of Witchcraft and the supposed personal dealings of human beings with devils and the Powers of Evil were firmly believed in—and this not only by the poor and ignorant, but also by the priests and governing classes. Consequently, many innocent lives were tragically sacrificed to this curious belief, and burnings at the stake of persons accused of witchcraft took place from time to time in many Christian countries.

Sometimes, however, it happened that an amusing situation would result from a mistaken accusation of dabblings in the Black Art; the whole affair might then end in smoke of a less unpleasant kind.

This happened one day during the fifteenth century on the outskirts of Bologna, where superstition happened to be peculiarly rife and where excitement was at its height for two reasons.

The first cause for excitement among the townsfolk was the fact that the reigning Duke of Bologna was about to pay a State visit to his palace there for the first time in thirty years, having been absent since he was a child of twelve. He had passed all the intervening years amidst the grandeurs and beauties of Milan —which was certainly a much more interesting and a far livelier city than Bologna. But at last his conscience had awakened to the knowledge that it was his duty at least to visit the city of his birth and to make himself known personally to his people there —of whom he knew little beyond the pleasant fact that they added considerably to his revenue by means of taxes and by the cultivation of his land. So the visit was arranged, Bologna was decorated, and the Duke set forth.

The second cause of excitement in the district around Bologna was of a supernatural kind. Astrologers had recently declared that from their studies of the portents of the skies—in particular, an eclipse of the moon accompanied by seven shooting-stars—they had discovered that the Evil One was in their midst and that he boldly walked the streets of Bologna at night, wrapped in a long black cloak.

As evening drew on apace on the day on which this story opens, therefore, a couple of Watchmen had much to talk about as they drew near to the gates of the ducal palace where they were to light the lamps in readiness for the arrival of the Duke.

While these garrulous old cronies chattered of the tardiness of their lord's arrival and wondered whether he would come that day, after all, a pair of happy young lovers wandered past. The Watchmen recognized them as Pietro, the Blacksmith's son, with his sweetheart, Bianca, one of the prettiest girls in Bologna.

Scarcely had the young couple wandered away, arm-in-arm, than a thin, cadaverous, and particularly solemn-looking Priest appeared, with bowed head, counting his beads. The good Father was closely followed by Antonio the Blacksmith, who seemed in a very nervous state. Presently the latter accosted the Priest and inquired anxiously of him how he should know the Devil who was said to be walking the streets after dark and whose evil eye it was so necessary for all to avoid.

The Priest declared that the Evil Visitant would certainly be wrapped in a cloak black as his own deeds, and beneath it his cloven hooves would be visible. He added that when the Evil One spoke, no one should listen to him, but all back away from him in horror with the words: "Avaunt, Foul Fiend!"

Then, with an eye to the main chance, the Priest also added that it were well to give ten ducats to the charity funds as an extra precaution against the Evil Eye.

As the Priest passed on, Antonio—who seemed scared out of his wits by this news of the Devil in their midst—asked the Watchmen if they had seen his son Pietro. Upon learning that the latter was wandering in the wood with fair Bianca, he rushed off to find the couple and bring them safely home before they should be accosted by the roving Evil One.

When the Watchmen had lighted the lamps on the gates of the palace, they also departed hastily, fearing a like encounter.

No sooner had the old cronies vanished than a tall, dark stranger, wrapped in a long black cloak and wearing heavy riding-boots, approached the gates of the palace somewhat wearily. This stranger was none other than the long-expected Duke of Bologna who, instead of arriving in full state in a coach with outriders and lackeys, was entirely alone and unattended. About nine miles back, his fine coach had broken down, owing to the roughness of the country roads. He had decided, therefore, to leave the footmen and attendants to mend the ponderous vehicle and get it out of the muddy ruts, while he himself hurried along on foot—for he was now quite eager to behold the palace and people he had neglected so long.

The Duke realized with regret that he had been very foolish and remiss to put off attending to the duties and responsibilities of his high station in life until the present time. Experiencing a deep feeling of pride and even joy on thus beholding, after thirty years' absence, his fine palace, with his native city beyond, he now hastened eagerly towards the closed gates, ready to call out for admittance.

Before he reached the gates, however, the Blacksmith, Antonio, who had already been peeping fearfully at the stranger from behind a tree, now rushed forward, followed by Pietro and Bianca and a crowd of townsfolk, all crying out in horror and making such a clamour that the Watchmen soon returned to learn what was wrong.

Trembling with fright, the Blacksmith declared that the black-robed stranger gazing at them so boldly from the ducal gates was none other than the Evil One himself—since he was wrapped in the long black cloak mentioned by the Priest, while his huge riding-boots undoubtedly were worn to conceal his cloven hooves. The Priest, who had likewise now joined the throng, confirmed these suspicions, and led a horror-struck chorus of " Avaunt! Foul Fiend! Avaunt! "

It was in vain that the Duke, amazed and angered by this ridiculous reception of himself as the Devil, indignantly expostulated and endeavoured to explain his late and lonely arrival as due to the accident to his State coach. The superstitious Priest refused to allow anyone even to listen to him, declaring that every word spoken by the Evil One was fraught with danger. When the Duke, now enraged beyond measure, once more broke forth into explanations, the scared Holy Father ordered the Watchmen to gag him immediately to prevent any further utterances by him.

So the unfortunate Duke, despite his struggles and expostulations, was seized and gagged by the Watchmen, who held him firmly in their somewhat terrified grasp.

The only person among the gaping townsfolk who attempted to question this high-handed treatment of an absolute stranger in their midst was the pretty maiden Bianca. She begged the Priest to set his captive free, declaring that the stranger seemed quite pleasant-looking in her own eyes and that she felt sure he was merely a worthy gentleman who did not intend them any harm.

To this, however, the Priest, a fierce fanatic, solemnly announced that if she thus thought fit to defend the Evil One, then she must herself be in his power already; and he now commanded that this Devil in human form should instantly be thrown into the nearby river and drowned therein.

When Bianca, horrified by this order, again begged him to show pity upon the stranger, denying that any evil could be imputed to him since they knew nothing whatever about him, the Priest became angry because of this doubting of his authority; and both he and Antonio the Blacksmith began to upbraid her. Bianca, however, only the more vehemently pleaded for pity to be shown to the stranger; whereupon the Priest now menacingly accused the young girl of herself being a Witch in the power of the Evil One, for which crime she must be burned at the stake without delay.

On hearing this terrible accusation against his fair sweetheart, Pietro, the Blacksmith's son, declared indignantly that, so far from being a Witch, the lovely Bianca was a pattern of purity and goodness, from whose gentle conduct he had himself learned all his own lessons in Christian ways.

The fanatical Priest, however, now seized upon these words as a sign that Pietro also must be in league with the Evil One, since he based his conduct upon that of a Witch; and he commanded that the young man should likewise be burned at the stake that night, along with Bianca.

In vain did the now distracted Antonio plead for mercy to be shown to his son; and in vain did the helplessly gagged and bound Duke struggle to free himself and so to stop this coming tragedy—for the situation had now become extremely ugly. The townsfolk were likewise fired with the fanatical zeal of the Priest and clamoured madly for the evil stranger to be instantly drowned in the river, and for the Witch and her colleague to be burned at the stake that night.

Just as this clamour was at its height and the unfortunate victims were being dragged away by the fear-distracted crowd, there came a welcome interruption. The Duke's Gentleman-in-Waiting, Vincenzo, suddenly appeared on the scene, hot and weary, as advance guard to the now approaching mended State coach. Seeing his noble lord bound and gagged and hearing him described on all sides as the " Foul Fiend ", he roundly rated the Priest and the townsfolk for their stupidity, explaining angrily that the stranger was none other than their long-absent overlord, the Duke of Bologna.

He then quickly released and ungagged the exhausted Duke, while Pietro and Bianca, also instantly set free, fell on their knees before their ruling lord. The Priest and townsfolk quickly did likewise, fearing the consequences of their foolish mistake and rash conduct.

The Duke, however, had no desire to take vengeance upon them, as he well might have done. However, he declared that, after such a rough reception, he would not even enter his palace but would return immediately to Milan, since he had no liking for dolts. Bologna had seen the last of him.

The townsfolk begged him to forgive them and to stay with them at least a little while; but the Duke declined to favour them, and hastened towards his now waiting State coach. Before entering, however, he turned to the pretty Bianca and handed her his purse of gold as a wedding present and as some slight reward for having spoken so sweetly—and so dangerously—in his defence.

Then the Duke drove off in the lumbering but highly-decorated carriage as Pietro clasped his beloved Bianca in his arms. The people of Bologna were thus left to reflect upon their crass stupidity in not being able to distinguish between their own reigning Duke and a highly improbable Devil.

GREYSTEEL   *Gatty*
(*The Bearsarks Come to Surnadale*)

KOL the Bondman worked hard at his task of piling up kindling wood outside the farmstead of Surnadale, near Maeren in the far north of Norway; but as he worked, he sighed many times, for his heart was sad and full of bitterness.

He could not reconcile himself to his thraldom; he who had once been free to go and come according to his will, free to hunt, to perform mighty deeds of valour, to fight. Above all he longed to be free to fight and to gain renown with the aid of his beloved Magic Sword, Greysteel, now ignobly doomed to lie inactive and to taste the blood of foes no longer. But not to rust! No; Greysteel must be kept ever bright and shining, ready for the time when its owner should be free once more.

Even as the thought occurred to him, Kol went to the back of the heaped-up wood, where he kept the sword which his state of slavery now prevented him from using in battle; and drawing it forth with loving tenderness, he began to polish it with great care and pride. For Greysteel was no common sword. It had been forged by the dwarfs of Eld, and was a runic weapon of mystic and mighty power. It never failed to gain victory for its user, since it could cleave through tempered steel or other metal as though through snow.

Kol was the thrall of Ingibjorga, the beautiful daughter of Isi. The latter, as the blood foe of his own people, had come with a horde of warriors one day, defeated him in battle, burned his home, and enslaved him. However, Kol bore no grudge to the victor's fair daughter, but served her faithfully.

When Ingibjorga became the bride of Ari, the lord of Surnadale, Kol was sent with her. Though he had no love for his new master—who was of a boastful and selfish nature and moreover treated the thrall and his beloved Greysteel with scorn—he curbed his dislike for the sake of his gentle mistress, whose marriage he soon discovered was a loveless one.

He knew that she was unhappy, that her lord regarded her as merely a chattel of no value to him save to minister to his needs. He knew also that her love was given to her husband's brother, Gisli, a young lord of noble nature and great charm. The latter returned her passion with equal fervour, though the pair had never yet declared their love.

As Kol now polished his sword, Ingibjorga and Gisli came from the house, with happiness shining in their eyes because of the unspoken love in their hearts. Gisli was about to set forth to make a purchase of cattle upon the instructions of his brother; but he still lingered, knowing Ari to be abroad at his work and reluctant to part from Ingibjorga, whom he begged to come a part of the way with him. Ingibjorga at first refused, being anxious for him to depart before the return of Ari, whose midday meal she was about to prepare; but so persistent were the pleadings of Gisli, that at length she consented to go a little way towards the crest of the hill.

Scarcely had the undeclared lovers departed, than Ari appeared, none too pleased on finding his wife and brother both away.

Upon Gisli presently returning to fetch a halter he had forgotten in his eagerness to walk with Ingibjorga, Ari made scornful sport of the young man's forgetfulness of such an obviously necessary thing. When the latter had again set forth with the halter, somewhat confused by such unexpected badinage, his brother strode up to Kol and began vaingloriously to praise himself to the thrall as a vastly superior person to his seemingly dreamy and careless brother.

He received no answering praise, however, from Kol, who quickly changed the subject by announcing the news that the Bearsarks had made many raids in the neighbourhood recently and might now descend upon the farmstead of Surnadale at any moment, led by their ill-famed chief, Bjorn the Black. The Bearsarks were wild, lawless, piratical, wandering tribes of Northern Scandinavia, who, instead of making a living by honest toil, spent their time making raids on the peaceful farmer folk and rich lords, robbing them of their cattle, goods, and women, and committing many deeds of wanton cruelty and violence. Their leader was especially dreaded on account of his gigantic size and ruthlessness, and because of certain magic powers he was said to possess as the son of a witch woman.

Ari, however, boastfully declared that he cared nothing for the Bearsark raiders, but would give Black Bjorn a warm welcome, should he dare to attack him. Kol said no more; but he once more tenderly drew forth his magic sword and caressed it.

Soon after this, Ingibjorga returned, and Ari gave her many instructions about the preparation of the savoury meats for his meal—still in boastful vein, as though he alone understood such things—to all of which his patient wife replied submissively: " Yea, my lord! "

But when Ari had retired into the house, she did not immediately follow to perform her duties; for she had noticed the dark and discontented looks of Kol and desired to appease him. She now learnt from the thrall of his dislike for her boastful husband and his admiration for the nobler Gisli; and pleased by his praise for the man she loved, she spoke approvingly of the cherished sword, Greysteel, which Kol was now again fondling. Brandishing it in the air, Kol declared that the magic sword alone would save her when the Bearsarks descended upon the farmstead—which might be at any moment.

Even as he spoke, there came an ominous distant shouting, faint at first, but repeated ever and anon louder: " Hi! Hi! Below there! "

It was the war-cry of the dreaded Bearsarks; and as Kol clutched his weapon tighter and Ingibjorga listened, trembling, with her hand over her heart, the cry came again and yet again, each time nearer and clearer: " Hi! Below there! Bring out your wives and daughters! "

On the top ridges of the hills, the Bearsarks now appeared, brandishing their spears and clubs, clamouring for food, and ever repeating their terrible cries; and Ari quickly rushed forth into the open, furious because of this raid upon his peaceful dwelling.

As Ari came forth, Bjorn the Black, the terrible giant leader of the Bearsarks, also appeared on a rocky platform within speaking distance; and silencing his wild followers, he addressed himself to Ari. Declaring that news of the peerless beauty of Ingibjorga had gone forth far and wide, he insolently offered to engage in single combat with him for his fair wife, his thralls, and all his other goods and chattels, the fight to take place on the Combat Isle on the next fjord. Ari, eager to gain glory in such a fight as this, fearlessly accepted the challenge; and Bjorn and his Bearsarks withdrew to await him on the other side of the hill, bidding him hasten to prepare for the combat. With a coarse burst of laughter Bjorn also instructed him to bid his wife make herself ready to greet a new mate that evening, since her lord would not return to her alive.

Enraged by the Bearsark leader's insolent boast, Ari immediately prepared for battle, calling to his house carls to bring forth his shield and weapons and to follow him in attendance to watch the fight.

Kol, eager for the safety of his beloved mistress and having little faith in the boasted prowess of Ari, now implored the latter to make use of his magic sword "Greysteel" in this fateful battle, as victory then could not fail to be his. Ingibjorga also added her entreaties that he would thus meet the giant with the sword of sorcery, since nothing else was likely to avail with the son of a sorceress. But she soon found to her sorrow that her husband meant to fight not so much to preserve her honour and safety as to gain more glory and renown for himself. He scornfully refused to carry the magic sword which would have ensured her safety; and he rushed away, followed by the trembling carls, vaingloriously sure of his own victory. Kol also was about to depart to watch the fight when Gisli returned, unaware of what had happened; and he remained to tell the young lord of the Bearsark's challenge. He then rushed off, calling upon Gisli to follow also.

But Gisli was so overcome by the thought of Ingibjorga's danger and of Ari's vanity in seeking his own glory rather than endeavouring to ensure her safety by using the magic sword, that he could no longer restrain his long pent-up passion for his brother's wife; and when Ingibjorga presently drew near, he poured forth an eager avowal of his love. On hearing his declaration, Ingibjorga was secretly unable to deny the promptings of her own heart and was overjoyed by this proof that her own deep love was returned. Realizing their position, however, she scornfully reproached him for disloyalty to his brother, who was even now fighting to defend his home and honour.

At this moment, Kol appeared on the hill-side once more and called to Gisli to hasten to the scene of combat, if he would again see his brother alive; and, full of contrition for having delayed so long, Gisli rushed off. But even as he went, loud cries were heard from the hill-top: "Ari is killed!" And as the victorious cries of the triumphant Bearsarks rose on all sides, Ingibjorga called wildly to Kol to give her his dagger, since she would rather die than fall into the hands of Bjorn the Black.

But Kol bade her not despair since another life lay between her and her fate—the life of Gisli who loved her and would fight for her to the death. But this thought was agony also to the unhappy Ingibjorga, who could not bear that the man she loved should die for her.

Presently, to the sound of a sombre funeral dirge, the carls brought home the body of their dead master. With them came

Gisli who, forgetting all thoughts of jealousy and resentment against his brother and remembering only his fearless bravery, flung himself at the feet of the dead man, calling passionately for forgiveness and vowing to avenge his death.

Ingibjorga, on hearing this sincere outburst, realized that Gisli was worthy of her love and had redeemed his recent lapse from rectitude; and approaching him, she tenderly comforted him and resigned herself gladly to his eager embrace.

According to the custom of that time, she now belonged to Gisli who, as next of kin, became possessor of the dead man's goods and chattels, his wife and bondmen being regarded as part of these. Ingibjorga resigned herself very willingly in this case, since Gisli was the man she loved.

But Gisli still had to do battle for her with the blood-thirsty Bearsark; and Ingibjorga entreated him to make use of Kol's wonderful sword, since Bjorn's magic must be met with magic if he was to be defeated—mere brute strength and courage being insufficient in such an unequal contest, as had been proved by the defeat of Ari.

Gisli, despising no aid—not even that of magic—in his eagerness to save the woman he loved from falling into the hands of the spoiler, gladly took Greysteel in his hand. Then, when Bjorn the Black presently appeared with his Bearsarks, insolently announcing that he had come to take possession of the dead man's wife and chattels, the young lord rushed upon him furiously and engaged with him in mortal combat.

The duel did not last long, however; for with a few strokes of the magic sword, Gisli succeeded in slaying the terrible giant.

And now, as the astonished and dismayed Bearsarks bore away their dead leader, Ingibjorga and the victorious Gisli fell into each other's arms with great joy. The carls of Surnadale greeted their new lord and his beautiful lady with joyful acclamations, and a great feast was held.

And not the least thankful person at the festive board was Kol the Bondman, now made happy by receiving his freedom from Ingibjorga and Gisli in return for the great service rendered by his magic sword, Greysteel, which in future he would be able to use once more as a free man in open battle.

KING ALFRED AND THE CAKES . *Gatty*

WHEN the great King Alfred was ruling in England, the land was frequently ravaged by hordes of roving Danes who invaded the shores from their huge ships and spread terror and destruction wherever they went.

Nevertheless, the fierce pirates did not carry all before them; for they had mighty Alfred and his brave Saxons to reckon with. Alfred had no mind to let these heathen sea-rovers snatch his land from him.

When he first succeeded to the throne of Wessex—long before he became ruler over the whole of England—he had found the Danes firmly entrenched in many places; but he had vowed to drive them out. With a rough-and-tumble army, consisting mainly of humble but stout-hearted country folk, he fought many pitched battles with the invaders; and though he succeeded in bringing peace to his country at last, the greater part of his reign was occupied with such spasmodic warfare.

King Alfred gained great glory by his own personal bravery. Though he also met with many repulses, when he was forced to go into hiding for a time until he could gather his scattered forces together again, his name became as a mighty legend in the land, so that every Saxon capable of carrying arms was ready to fight and die for him.

It was while this noble-hearted King—known as " the Dragon " to his foes—was temporarily in retreat in Wessex one time awaiting a suitable opportunity for launching a fresh attack upon the invading Danes, that a curious adventure befell him.

Wessex could not be expected to look peaceful or richly culti-vated at this particular time. With most of the men away fighting the Danes, cultivation was bound to be neglected; and cattle and sheep had to be closely guarded lest the invading robbers should steal them away. Thus, it was a hard and anxious time for the women-folk left behind.

So thought Dame Oswyn, a neat-herder's wife, one day, as she stood at the table in her humble cottage in the Isle of Athelney. She was busily making up a batch of bread-cakes, just before going out to take food and mead to her husband. The latter was tending his herds at some little distance away, so that the Saxon soldiers might still have meat to give them strength.

This good dame was not in the best of tempers that day. She

was weary of the constant warfare, of the shedding of so much good Saxon blood, of the ravaging of the harvests year after year, and of the stealing of cattle. Even when she heard in the distance the thrilling cries of the Saxon warriors: "Alfred! Mightiest Monarch! Ours is the land!" she could no longer be roused to any great enthusiasm. This warfare was a bad business; and it was many a long year since she had known a quiet and peaceful summer in her once smiling land.

When, therefore, her fair young daughter, Osburga, ran in, full of excitement, with news of the fierce battle then raging around the little island and expressing anxiety for the fate of her youthful sweetheart, Adhelm, the already worried dame greeted her sharply.

Oswyn declared that young Adhelm, who was but a stripling, would do better to be minding the cattle, like her own good man, Edwy, instead of rushing off to fight for the King and preferring the excitement of danger to plain honest toil. Then, bidding Osburga get wood for the fire and afterwards remain to tend the cakes she was about to put down on the hearth to bake, she retired to the inner chamber to put on her head-dress prior to carrying out a meal to her absent husband.

Osburga, well knowing her mother's nerves to be overstrained, was about to obey without comment, when she heard the voice of her young sweetheart outside; and next moment, Adhelm, a handsome youth, entered slowly, leaning painfully on his long spear. He was bleeding from a gash in his arm; and Osburga, alarmed, hastened to bind up the wound, though he declared it to be of no account. The young man eagerly told his sweetheart that he had slain the Dane who had wounded him; but he added that the fighting was now over for the time being, that the Saxon warriors were scattered, and that their splendid King was in temporary retreat, alone, making secret plans for his next attack.

When Adhelm's wound had been dressed, he announced his resolve to go forth immediately to seek out his comrades in the recent fighting, in case they needed help; and Osburga, forgetful of her mother's instructions, went with him to help him on his way.

When Dame Oswyn returned, therefore, now wearing her head-dress, she grumbled once more because the maiden had not yet appeared with a new supply of wood and because she was not there to tend the baking of the cakes. However, she hastily put down the freshly-made bread-cakes to bake on the hearth among the ashes by the fire; then, taking up the bag of food and a jug of mead, ready to set forth on her errand to her goodman in the valley below, she waited at the open door for her daughter's return.

Instead of Osburga, however, a stranger came striding up to the door—a splendid-looking Saxon warrior, who carried a mighty spear in one hand, but held a sceptre in the other, hidden beneath his cloak. Though Dame Oswyn knew it not, this stranger was Alfred, the famous warrior-ruler of Wessex; and the King did not enlighten her as to his identity. He merely begged for a night's shelter, rest, and food. Oswyn—whose patriotic heart was in the right place, despite her grumblings—replied that, though she and her husband were but poor and simple folk, yet, seeing that the newcomer was a Saxon warrior, she was glad to grant his request.

Then a bright idea occurred to the good dame. Rather than waste any more time awaiting her errant daughter's return, she now begged the stranger to keep an eye on the cakes baking on the hearth and to turn them over from time to time. It would be for a short time only that he would thus be left in charge—until she or her daughter returned.

Alfred willingly promised to attend to the baking of the cakes; and after giving him further instructions on the matter—even threatening to " clap him on the pate " should he not mind his job carefully—the dame reluctantly departed on her errand, still somewhat anxious about her bread.

Left alone in the cottage, the weary King took off his cloak, laid down his sword and sceptre, and seated himself on a stool near the hearth. Here he fell a-thinking about the recent battle and about his secret plans for the immediate future.

At first he carried out his hostess's instructions, with some amusement remembering her sharp-tongued warning; and several times he carefully turned over the cakes as they began to bake in the warm ashes. Presently, however, he became more and more engrossed in his own anxious thoughts of the troubles and difficulties he had to solve; and then he forgot this unexpected domestic task which had been thrust upon him. So lost in deep reflection was he, indeed, that he did not even notice the shadows of two young people which presently darkened the doorway.

The newcomers were Osburga and Adhelm who, seeing a noble stranger sitting half-dozing before the fire, were at first surprised; but upon the young warrior instantly recognizing him as the King, they withdrew softly, deciding not to enter just then but to leave the royal warrior to his thoughts a little longer.

Meanwhile, too closely wrapped up in his new plans to have thought for anything else, Alfred still sat gazing into the glowing embers of the fire; and it was not until a sudden tongue of flame shot up from one of the now burning cakes that he was roused once more to a sense of his forgotten task.

It was then too late to remedy matters; for Dame Oswyn was already re-entering the cottage, having completed her errand to her neat-herd husband.

At the sight of her burning cakes, the irate dame began roundly to scold the stranger; and, not content with hard words, she rushed up to the culprit and boxed his ears with considerable vigour. At that moment, however, Osburga and Adhelm also re-entered the cottage and called fearfully upon the angry dame to forbear, since the stranger guest was none other than their liege lord the King.

Alfred now confirmed this statement of the young people, revealing his hidden sceptre to the astounded dame. When the latter now sank to her knees and humbly craved his pardon, however, he graciously granted it, adding smilingly that he certainly deserved a buffet for having neglected to perform the small task she had set him.

Then, admiring the fine looks and eager spirit of young Adhelm, the King declared that this brave youth, already wounded in his service, should at once become a member of his royal train; and he further desired Oswyn to give her consent to the young man's wooing of her fair daughter—which the now contrite dame gladly agreed to.

Then the little party settled down to eat and to rest; and as twilight fell, they gathered around the hearth and talked happily together about their beloved land of England and of the mighty doings of England's noble King, Alfred the Great.

PRINCE FERELON[1]   *Gatty*

IN the realm of fairy tales there once lived a beautiful Princess who had so persistently refused all the offers of marriage presented by innumerable suitors that at length her royal father, the King, wearying of her fastidiousness, determined to put an end to it. Having received intimation that on a certain day three more suitors intended to present themselves, he announced to his daughter that she must select a husband from among these, as this would be her last chance of choosing for herself. Failing her acceptance of one of the newcomers, the Court would be instructed

[1] This opera received the Carnegie Award in 1922.

to decide upon a husband for her, whom she would then be compelled to accept, willy-nilly.

Grand preparations were made for the reception of the three last suitors; and all the Court looked forward eagerly to the event, hoping that their beloved Princess would now satisfy the King by making the choice desired of her.

Just before the entry of the Court on the fateful day, the Princess's Maid of Honour, Meryl, appeared in the reception hall and began to arrange the draperies and cushions about her royal mistress's throne, singing a gay little tune as she did so. While she was thus engaged, a stranger entered the hall—a handsome young man dressed in the garb of a wandering minstrel and carrying a lute. Approaching Meryl, he declared he sought her aid, as he was a suitor for the Princess's hand. He revealed the fact that he was Prince Ferelon—a splendid Prince whom all had long desired would come forward as a suitor—but that he had adopted his present disguise for a special purpose he had in view.

Meryl, though overjoyed at the sight of the young Prince, sadly informed him that he was too late, since the list of suitors was closed.

But Prince Ferelon now declared that he himself would enact the parts of the three suitors who were to present themselves that day. Having fallen in love with the Princess, he had decided upon this plan of appearing before her in the guise of three different individuals, that he might thus have three chances of appealing to her instead of one. Begging Meryl to keep his secret, he asked her anxiously if the Princess's heart had yet been touched by love. To this question the Maid of Honour—now happy in the thought that her beloved mistress could not fail to accept this really charming suitor—saucily replied that he must discover this important fact for himself; and she bade him depart as the time of audience had arrived.

Scarcely had the young Prince left the hall than the Princess entered, clad in an exquisite robe but sad and unenthusiastic about the three suitors who were to present themselves. She declared that though all these aspirants for her hand called her beautiful, unrivalled, and peerless, they none of them loved her. They were enamoured only of her wealth, position, and beauty; and love was the one and only thing she desired.

Meryl, hugging to herself the secret knowledge of Prince Ferelon's confession of love, bade her take heart, saying that love would surely come to her yet; but the Princess only sighed the more deeply as she took her place and the Court began to assemble.

When the King—who was somewhat fussy and irascible, his patience having been sorely tried by his daughter's long-drawn-out selection of a consort—entered, he warned the fastidious Princess once again that this was her last chance of choosing a husband. Then, seating himself upon his throne, he commanded that the three suitors should enter in turn.

Prince Ferelon, disguised as an accomplished amateur musician, now appeared accompanied by a group of singers. Opening a roll of music he declared that he had composed a song in honour of the Princess; and he promised that if she would accept him he would regale her with similar sweet music every day. He then commanded the musicians to sing his song, which they did in affected style.

When the performance, which quickly bored the Princess, came to an end, the King and the courtiers were loud in their praises; and the King begged the Princess to consider carefully this honour done to her and to give a due and fitting answer. The Princess, however, said that though she had been taught to consider music as divine, so also was love; and turning to the musical suitor, she gently declined his offer. The King, angry and disappointed, declared she could not know her own mind, since these harmonies had delighted him and he had liked the composer; but the Princess persisted in her refusal, and the minstrel sadly departed with his singers.

When the second suitor was commanded to appear, Prince Ferelon again entered, this time in the disguise of a dress designer; and he was followed by a number of attendants carrying band-boxes and by mannequins wearing sumptuous garments. In a self-important and obsequious manner, he declared to the Princess that she always appeared in his thoughts arrayed in wonderful costumes of his own devising. After the mannequins had paraded across the hall, he entreated her to marry him that these lovely gowns might be hers and that he might behold her literally in his creations instead of merely looking upon them as empty shells.

The courtiers were full of praise for the elegance and taste of this suitor's work; and again the King begged his daughter to think carefully before she replied.

But the Princess proudly declared that she was a living soul not to be bought with clothes, and that she had no desire to fill the " empty shells " offered to her.

The King was very much annoyed that this second suitor, most desirable in his own eyes, should be sent packing; but his scoldings were in vain and the dress designer and his attendants retired in undignified haste.

Before there was time for the third suitor to be called, a group of dancers suddenly appeared and performed a wild and exhilarating ballet. Then Prince Ferelon rushed forward in yet another disguise, being clad in the careless and bizarre costume of the conventional " bohemian " artist-poet.

With an eager and over-enthusiastic manner and using exaggerated " high-falutin' " expressions, he sang the praises of the dance, inviting the Princess thus to speed through the years with him in joyful motion.

The Princess, however, unimpressed by his wild enthusiasm, declared that such exuberance belonged only to children and playful lambs in springtime; and she declared she would have none of it.

The King, angered by this third refusal of a likely suitor, after reproaching her violently, now commanded his chamberlain to prepare a ballot. He was determined that, since his daughter had refused to choose for herself, a husband should immediately be chosen for her.

The Princess, wildly declaring that they were all mad, blind, and unreasonable in not understanding the desire of her heart, came down from the throne in great agitation, covering her face with her hands; and Meryl, perplexed and in great distress at this final refusal of one she had hoped would win her royal mistress, endeavoured to comfort her.

Then, just as the ballot was about to be declared, Prince Ferelon hastened back into the hall, clad in his original disguise as a wandering minstrel and carrying a lute; and falling on his knees before the Princess, he declared that he had loved her from first beholding her. Having proved to his own satisfaction that she was not to be tempted by worldly goods, he now laid before her the offer of a truly loving heart.

As the Princess, overjoyed by this sincere offer of the simple unworldly love for which she had waited so long, moved forward and placed her hand in that of the seeming wandering musician, the King, in a blustering rage, called out for the intruder to be turned out; and the courtiers immediately endeavoured to obey his command. In the struggle, however, Prince Ferelon's outer cloak of disguise was torn off so that his royal garments were revealed beneath.

He was immediately recognized as Prince Ferelon, being well known to all; and the King, delighted that his daughter's choice had at length fallen upon such an eminently satisfactory suitor, immediately ordered the marriage feast to proceed. As Prince Ferelon embraced her, the happy Princess admitted that, despite

H

her former refusal, she had, nevertheless, been charmed with the music, the dresses, and the dancing. Then, to the surprise of all, the royal youth now revealed the fact of his three disguises, and ordered these pleasing appurtenances of his various characters to be brought in as gifts for his bride. An exquisite robe was placed upon the shoulders of the Princess, another one being handed to Meryl as a reward for her silence; and the music written by Ferelon specially for this event was played as the royal pair moved away to partake of their betrothal feast.

ANDRÉ CHÉNIER   *Giordano*
(*Andrea Chénier*)

ANDRÉ CHÉNIER, the distinguished French poet-patriot, lived during the stormy period of the Revolution. At first he had ardently supported the cause of the oppressed people against their tyrannical rulers, for their wrongs had his fullest sympathy. Later on, however, when the revolutionaries at last came into power, the frightful excesses of the new untried rulers in regard to the fallen aristocracy disgusted him. In particular, he was horrified by the merciless methods of Robespierre. Full of indignation, he wrote a number of brilliant pamphlets in which he uttered scathing indictments of this arch-tyrant as the inaugurator of the Reign of Terror.

For having thus offended the powerful Dictator, he was shortly afterwards denounced as a traitor, condemned, and executed—tragically enough, just before the Reign of Terror ended and his beloved country recovered its sanity.

In the following story, some of the actual incidents in the life of this patriotic poet-dreamer have been included.

.   .   .   .

Just before the French Revolution broke out in all its fury, a grand ball was held at the Château of the Comtesse de Coigny, near Paris. The entertainment was given on the usual lavish scale of the aristocrats, despite the rumblings of the coming conflict.

Although the Comtesse's chief servitor, Charles Gérard, dashed hither and thither, carrying out the orders of his haughty and exacting mistress, he already showed signs of having imbibed the new revolutionary spirit. In little ways and by certain of his actions, it was plain to see that he no longer served this *grande dame* so humbly and servilely as formerly.

The Comtesse, however, scarcely noticed the change in his behaviour, but merely scolded him roundly and, as usual, treated him as dirt beneath her elegant feet. But Gérard, as he sulkily went about his duties, stored up her haughty words as new grievances. He knew now that the Day of the People was at hand. He was secretly in love with Madeleine, the lovely daughter of his mistress; and though his passion was not even suspected, he put up with much ignominy for her sake. He hoped that some day soon the beautiful Madeleine might be glad to accept his attentions when faced with the disasters bound to come to her when the power of the nobility had been destroyed.

But Madeleine, a light-hearted, carefree girl, living only for pleasure, knew nothing of Gérard's secret passion—and would have cared less had she known. She had no interest in one so far below her in station.

She was, however, greatly intrigued by the flattering attention of a guest at the ball. This was André Chénier, the poet, a man of great fascination. At first, she made light-hearted fun of the poet's obvious admiration for her; and she laughed merrily at his poetic gift and even made light of the power of love to which he so frequently referred in his conversation with her.

But Chénier, with his poet's clear vision, recognized that sincerity, deep sympathy, and a sense of beauty lay dormant in the heart of this seemingly frivolous girl; and, having fallen passionately in love with her, he determined to awaken her better instincts. He drew her aside for a few moments and recited to her one of his most beautiful poems in honour of Love; and Madeleine, impressed in spite of herself by the beauty of the poet's thoughts, became ashamed of her foolish flippancy.

As Chénier had felt, there was true gold below the glittering sparkle of her careless surface gaiety. Before the ball came to an end, the young girl's newly-aroused interest in the poet's noble personality had already deepened into love.

The pair, however, did not meet again for nearly four years; for, almost immediately afterwards, the Revolution broke out. André Chénier quickly rose to a position of high importance among the revolutionaries; and for a time he was one of the best-loved leaders of the people.

Meanwhile, Madeleine de Coigny, after the death of her mother during the early days of the Revolution, had been carefully hidden and protected by her faithful old nurse, Bersi, a mulatto woman. Bersi herself was regarded as a harmless and patriotic citizeness, having shown herself in favour of the Revolution. Nevertheless, she loved the young aristocrat, Madeleine, so dearly that she would not betray her to the authorities then hounding down the nobility; instead, she kept her closely hidden in her own humble lodging in Paris.

Here, Madeleine had eagerly followed the career of the poet, Chénier, whom she had learned to love under happier circumstances; she even sent him letters of comfort and hope through all his many difficulties. She was careful, however, not to sign the letters—which were always personally conveyed to him by the faithful Bersi.

One day, while the Reign of Terror was at its height, André Chénier sat at a table outside a café in Paris, waiting for his friend, Roucher, who had gone to secure a passport for him. For the poet-patriot was already in great danger from the Revolutionary Party he had supported so nobly, but to whom he had now given dire offence by his denunciations of the savage Robespierre. Knowing that his work for the people was temporarily ended and that he might be arrested at any moment, he had been persuaded by his friends to make his escape from the country.

Unknown to the poet, he was constantly watched by a spy. The latter presently noticed a mulatto woman approach him as he now sat outside the café, hand to him a letter, and quickly depart. Chénier had cherished all the letters brought him by Bersi; for though they were unsigned, he knew they must come from one who loved him. This message, however, disturbed him. In it his unknown friend suggested that they should meet, since she was being spied upon; and she now craved his help.

When, therefore, Roucher presently returned with a passport for him—which he had had the greatest difficulty in obtaining—he refused to make immediate use of it, being determined first to keep the appointment made by his unknown correspondent. In spite of the warnings of his friend that every moment's delay was dangerous, he hastened to the meeting-place indicated in the letter. Here he was presently joined by the beautiful Madeleine de Coigny, in whom he instantly recognized the lovely maiden of the Château; and a joyful reunion took place.

But the spy, who had followed him furtively, had also recognized Madeleine as an aristocrat wanted by the Revolutionaries; and he hurried back with this news to his chief. The latter was none other than the late Comtesse de Coigny's servitor, Charles Gérard, who had now risen to a very high position under the Revolution. He had long sought the fugitive Madeleine, since his passion for her had not changed and he still longed to possess her. He now hoped to gain his wish.

Meanwhile, Chénier and Madeleine were once more declaring their love for one another; and the latter was also imploring her newly-discovered lover to protect her from the spies now dogging her every movement. While they were talking together, a wild mob passed by, cheering the powerful Robespierre who happened to be passing at the time; and the pair drew aside for a moment. They were, however, presently accosted by Gérard, brought thither by his spy; and he instantly challenged his rival in love to a duel.

The terrified Madeleine crouched back, knowing Gérard to be her enemy, not only politically, but because of his desire for her—of which she had learned before leaving the Château. She was greatly relieved, therefore, when Chénier, having wounded Gérard, seized her by the hand and succeeded in dragging her to a place of safety.

Their respite was but a short one. Gérard's spies were not long in capturing Chénier, who was quickly brought before the Revolutionary Tribunal. Gérard himself gloatingly signed the indictment against his rival: for, at last, the moment of his long-hoped-for triumph seemed to have come.

The distracted Madeleine, forgetful of her own danger, suddenly presented herself before Gérard and passionately pleaded with him to save her lover's life. But Gérard scornfully refused her request; instead, he declared his own love for her—which, he added, she could no longer afford to repudiate.

Then Madeleine, in desperation and knowing that nothing else would avail, declared herself willing to yield to his passion if, in return, he would use his powerful influence to save her beloved one from the guillotine.

When Gérard thus realized how beautiful a thing her love for his rival was, he was profoundly moved and his better nature prevailed. Renouncing all thought of his own desires, he now promised to do what he could to rescue Chénier; and he rushed off to the Tribunal, where the travesty of a trial was already taking place.

His efforts, however, were of no avail; and although he announced that the indictment was a false one, the infuriated mob were out for blood and refused to be deprived of their expected victim. Chénier was condemned to death, amid the howls of the mad populace.

When Madeleine realized that all hope of saving her lover was now at an end, she resolved to perish with him.

With the aid of Gérard—who vainly tried to dissuade her—she succeeded in gaining an entrance to the St. Lazare prison into which Chénier had been thrust. Here she bribed one of the warders to let her take the place of a young woman who had also been condemned to the guillotine and who was thus unexpectedly saved from death.

When dawn broke next day, therefore, and the prisoners were called one by one to the guillotine, André Chénier and his beloved and devoted Madeleine stepped forth calmly to meet their ·fate, joyful in the thought that in death they would at last be united.

THE QUEEN OF SHEBA   *Goldmark*

In the magnificent palace of King Solomon in Jerusalem, great preparations had just been completed for two important events— a Royal Visit and a grand State wedding.

Having heard of the almost incredible splendour of the King of Israel's abode and way of living and of his almost equally incredible wisdom, the Queen of Sheba had sent messengers to him expressing her desire to visit such a mighty King. She longed to behold his ivory and gold throne studded with gems, his rich silken draperies and embroideries, his works of Art, his dazzling Court and luxurious feasts, his stiffly-jewelled robes, his apes and peacocks and other rare and strange creatures from foreign parts.

This Queen herself was the ruler of a powerful country in the south-west of Arabia, but had found it difficult to believe the stories told of the royal magnificence of the King of Israel and of his amazing wisdom. Full of curiosity, therefore, she had determined to come and see for herself this wonderful King Solomon in all his glory.

When King Solomon knew that the beautiful Queen of Sheba was to visit him, he felt highly honoured. With great pride he sent out a magnificent troop of guards, headed by his favourite courtier, Assad, a handsome youth of noble birth, to meet and escort this important guest and her retinue.

The escort party expected to be away for several days; but immediately on his return Assad was to be wedded to the High Priest's daughter, Sulamith, whom he dearly loved.

Had Sheba's Queen not announced her resolve to make her

State visit to King Solomon just at that time, the marriage of these two important and well-beloved young people of Israel would already have taken place. The high mission of Assad, however, meant only a temporary postponement of the happy ceremony—which, it was hoped, the royal visitor would also grace with her presence.

When news of the returning escort was announced, intense excitement reigned in the palace. King Solomon was already seated on his magnificent throne, surrounded by his dazzling Court; and beside him stood the bride-elect, the lovely and gentle Sulamith, who could scarcely restrain her joyful eagerness to greet her returned lover so soon to become her husband.

Upon the entry of the young envoy, therefore, Sulamith ran forward happily with outstretched hands, eager for his greeting. To her surprise and grief, however, Assad drew back, pale and with lowered eyes, as though the sight of his betrothed dismayed him. Then, recovering himself somewhat, he hastened forward to the throne and announced to the King that his royal visitor, the Queen of Sheba, had arrived and was about to enter the palace.

Instantly aware, from his strange manner and distracted looks, that all was not well with the returned envoy, King Solomon questioned him; and Assad, sinking to his knees, made an amazing confession. While the escort guards were returning with the closely-veiled Queen of Sheba and her retinue, they had halted for some hours in the forest. Here, wandering alone in a cool watery glade, Assad had seen and been made love to by a nymph bathing in a well—a being of such exquisite beauty and beguiling charm that she had completely enthralled him so that he could think of no one else, not even of his fair betrothed. Her image still filled all his heart; hence his distress at the sight of Sulamith.

Now, King Solomon had had much experience in matters of feminine enticements. In his wisdom, therefore, he decided not to make too much of this irregular incident in the emotional life of his favourite young courtier. Consequently, he bade Assad think no more about his forest nymph but, having relieved his conscience by confessing his error, go forward with his marriage to Sulamith on the morrow, as arranged. The King hoped that the love of this pure young girl would stabilize him.

But even the wisdom of a Solomon sometimes has to bow to fate.

Even as the humbled Assad now turned to make his belated greeting to the puzzled Sulamith, the Queen of Sheba entered the audience hall with her splendid retinue; and as she approached the throne to greet the King, she graciously unveiled her face.

Until this moment, the royal visitor had kept herself closely covered in the presence of the Israelite escort; and so Assad had not yet beheld her face. It was with amazement and horror, therefore, that, as the royal lady now unveiled, he recognized in her his nymph of the forest well whose sensuous beauty had so bewitched him that he had forgotten his honour and his betrothal vow.

Overwhelmed once more by her enticing beauty and strangely possessive charm, Assad rushed forward with a glad cry of recognition. But he almost instantly fell back, abashed and confused; for the Queen of Sheba stared back at him without recognition and haughtily ignored him.

Then, with gracious dignity, the royal visitor turned to offer her homage to the mighty King Solomon; and she bade her slaves lay rich gifts at his feet while she sat beside him, eager to listen to his words of wisdom.

. . . .

But the Queen of Sheba did not intend to renounce her unlawful lover, despite her pretended unrecognition of him in the presence of King Solomon. When she presently learned that Assad was to be wedded next day to the daughter of the High Priest, she was suddenly filled with a raging jealousy; and she determined to enmesh him once more in the net of her own sensuous fascination.

That night, she sent her chief confidential slave, Astaroth, to Assad's apartment, with an invitation for him to meet her in the palace garden beside a fountain, which should remind him of their former meeting; and the young courtier, unable to resist this new temptation, hastened forth at her bidding. There, in the moonlight, at this secret meeting-place, the glamorous Queen, inflamed with desire for the handsome youth, soon found her seductive arts effective in once more arousing his still smouldering passion.

Forgotten was the gentle Sulamith, forgotten his honour; all was forgotten in the confused mind of Assad, lost in the maddening embraces of the siren Queen.

. . . .

Next day, in the magnificent Temple built by King Solomon to the Glory of God, all was prepared for the marriage ceremony of Assad and Sulamith. The High Priest, with his attendant Levites and a vast concourse of people, stood waiting at the time appointed; and when King Solomon himself arrived with his courtiers, all clad in gorgeous attire, the impressive ceremony began.

Sulamith, the sweet and gentle bride, stood near the altar with Assad—the latter still pale and agitated, but ready to keep his betrothal vow and hoping to find himself in calmer waters presently. But even as the wedding-ring was handed to the bridegroom by the High Priest to place upon the bride's finger, there came a fatal interruption.

At that same moment, another gorgeous procession entered the Temple, headed by the magnificently bejewelled Queen of Sheba, who carried in her hands a golden cup filled to the brim with priceless pearls—a wedding gift to her escort of the day before.

Once again overcome by the dazzling allure of the heathen Queen, the now almost demented Assad flung away the ring with which he was to have wedded Sulamith and, plunging forward, precipitated himself at the jewelled feet of his irresistible divinity, eagerly beseeching her to smile upon him and accept his love.

To his dismay, however, the Queen, once more on her guard and proudly desirous of maintaining her royal dignity before the King, received his protestations coldly and again disowned any previous interest in him; and all was confusion.

Then the High Priest and the Levites, thinking the young man had become suddenly mad, began the elaborate ceremony of exorcizing the evil spirit they believed had taken possession of him; and presently it seemed as though the unhappy Assad had become somewhat calmer.

But only for a moment; for the passion-racked Queen, unable to bear the sight of her victim once more standing beside his promised bride, called to him softly by name. Instantly Assad again flung himself at her feet, completely under her alluring spell; and he hailed her passionately as his beloved divinity and even prayed before her as though she were, indeed, a goddess.

Cries of horror arose from all the company at this idolatrous action. The High Priest and the Levites now declared furiously that Assad had desecrated the Holy Temple—for which crime the punishment was death.

The Queen, now realizing that her love of sensuous conquest had brought only disaster upon the object of her enticement, drew back, regretting her indiscretion. Meanwhile, the unhappy Sulamith collapsed in despair; and Assad now declared his willingness to die, since death alone could release him from his present pain.

Then King Solomon, though likewise angered by this desecration of his Temple, stayed the tumult with kingly dignity; and he announced that he alone would judge Assad for his lawless behaviour. If he decreed that death must be his punishment, then the young man should surely die; and with these authoritative words, the murmuring Priests had to content themselves.

King Solomon did not refrain from entertaining his distinguished, if disturbing, State guest in right royal style; and at a grand banquet he presently gave in her honour, he proved to her beyond doubt that the wonderful accounts she had heard of the magnificent splendour of his Court had been true indeed. The Queen was likewise deeply impressed by his extraordinary wisdom and learning. "The half was not told me!" she declared.

After the banquet, however, the King had soon to be on his guard; for the Queen of Sheba, now genuinely eager to save the life of the handsome youth she had seduced, did not hesitate to use her glamorous arts upon her royal host.

But Solomon could see through her guiles and refused to be enthralled thereby; and he let his beautiful guest see that her plea of disinterestedness in asking for the life of Assad to be spared was only that she might lure the unhappy youth once more into her dangerous toils. Furious that her secret purpose was thus plainly read by the wise King, the discomfited Queen of Sheba now left the royal palace with angry words, vowing vengeance and warfare upon Israel.

The unhappy and heart-broken Sulamith likewise pleaded passionately for the life of her lover to be spared—and with greater effect, for Solomon presently announced his royal decree that the sentence of death pronounced upon his favourite courtier should now be transmuted to banishment.

So Assad was driven forth into the desert, an exile who would gladly have welcomed death in any case. Then Sulamith, since earthly love was denied to her, entered an asylum of retreat on the borders of the desert, where dwelt other women and maidens who had likewise consecrated themselves to the service of God.

As Assad wandered on the edge of the desert, lonely and forsaken, a wonderful calm descended upon him. He now repented sincerely of his foolish and guilty passion for the beautiful but heathen siren Queen who had beguiled him with her enticements and had brought such misery upon him and upon the gentle Sulamith whom he had once loved so dearly.

As he thought of Sulamith, despair seized him; and he now longed above all things to live long enough to seek her out and plead for her forgiveness before he died. But this seemed unlikely, since he was already exhausted by his wanderings and was not far from death.

Although he knew it not, however, Sulamith was nearer to him than he supposed. Even as he thought thus tenderly of her, he had unconsciously drawn near to the desert retreat in which she had already sought and found refuge from worldly woes.

As he was about to enter the building to crave rest and shelter, however, a cavalcade came by—that of the Queen of Sheba returning to her own country.

The beautiful heathen Queen soon recognized and hurried to the side of the slowly-moving wanderer as he struggled wearily towards the building his dimming eyes had seen. Yet once again she used her seductive arts, trying to persuade him to return with her to her palace and live as her lover there.

But Assad was sincere in his repentance, and now understood only too well her beguilements and her falsity and, with proud dignity, he spurned her. He then rushed forth wildly into the desert, while his renewed will-power was strong enough to resist further temptations; and the Queen of Sheba, foiled, departed on her journey once more. Her passion for the handsome youth, however, was already fading; she had other lovers in plenty.

Meanwhile, another calamity befell Assad. As he struggled along towards the desert, exhausted by his wanderings, privations, and the excessive heat, he was overtaken by a devastating simoom which suddenly broke in great fury. Too weak to battle against the storm, he was quickly overcome and fell dying to the ground, half buried by the blinding sand.

Later on, when the storm had swept onward once more and the sky had cleared, the half-hidden and dying form of Assad was found by Sulamith, who had come out with her maidens for an early evening walk. Amazed, but full of joy on thus finding her lost lover so unexpectedly, she gently lifted him up and held him closely in her arms.

But her joy was short-lived and was all too quickly turned to despairing grief; for Assad, after weakly imploring her pardon and receiving it with deep content, almost instantly expired in her sweet and comforting embrace.

DON JUAN DE MAÑARA   *Goossens*

ONE evening, towards the end of the sixteenth century, the proud
and handsome young nobleman, Don Juan de Mañara, sat feasting with his friends in the Madrid palace of his father, the Duke
de Mañara, a rich and powerful Grandee of Castile.

The scene was a gay and brilliant one. The banqueting-hall
was magnificently furnished, the table lavishly spread; and the
guests—all of noble birth—wore the rich and bejewelled dress of
the period. Well-chosen musicians played soft music in the
gallery; and lackeys hurried hither and thither in eager attendance
upon the guests, under the careful eye of the very imposing major-
domo.

The feasting was now over; and while most of the lords and
ladies remained seated at the table, still sampling the priceless
wines, others danced together or flirted with the reckless gaiety
inspired by their pleasure-loving dissolute host.

Don Juan himself, however, stood somewhat apart. He was
tackling, with his accustomed skill, the delicate business of gracefully escaping from the entanglements of an old love while at the
same time flinging himself into the ever-fresh joys of a new one.

Both the fair lady recipients of his immediate past and present
attentions were guests at this entertainment; and for the first
time in his constant pursuit of fresh love experiences, Don Juan
found his " change-over " tactics not working so smoothly as he
had expected. Usually his discarded mistress was of a similarly
light disposition and was willing enough to accept the advances of
a new cavalier. In the present case, however, Doña Victoria had
unfortunately given her heart entirely to Juan; and she now
declared herself unable to love another, being full of despair at
losing him. Doña Carolina, the desired new mistress, on the
other hand, had quite gaily deserted her own former admirer,
Don Luis, in favour of the more desirable Juan.

Impressed by such constancy in Victoria, Juan—who, though
a libertine, was also an idealist, ever seeking, but never finding,
perfection in the women he loved—offered to make her a parting
gift. When Victoria eagerly begged for his dagger, secretly
intending to end her life by its aid, he willingly placed it in her
hand; and he declared that its many-jewelled hilt was worth as
much as a king's crown.

Then, turning to the laughing Carolina, he offered her, his new mistress, in return for a single kiss, all the castles in Spain so soon coming to him from his father, the Duke—who, even at that moment, lay dying in an apartment adjoining the banqueting-hall.

While his friends laughed at this extravagant outburst and while Carolina danced away gaily at the thought of the riches in store for her, Juan was suddenly plunged in gloom at remembering that these riches were not yet his. When, therefore, Don Luis suggested that, perhaps, his elder, but bastard brother, José, might prove to be the heir, after all—since the latter was the better-beloved of the old Duke for his more excellent moral qualities—he was filled with anger. His mood soon changed, however; and declaring that he, the legitimate son, was undoubtedly the heir, he announced his extravagant resolve to spend all the riches he succeeded to in searching for his ideal perfect woman until at last he found her.

While extolling this imaginary dream-woman, Juan was interrupted by the entrance of the major-domo, who announced solemnly that the old Duke now lay at the point of death in the ante-room beyond and that he had already sent for his priest-confessor, Dom Mortès.

On hearing this momentous news, Juan hastily dismissed his guests; and when the good Father presently arrived, he intercepted him eagerly. He was furious when Dom Mortès now revealed the unpleasant fact that the old dying Duke was about to sign a document making his illegitimate son, José, his heir.

Dazed for the moment by this news, so fatal to his own hopes, Juan hardly noticed the hasty departure of Dom Mortès. When his body-servant, Hussein, now announced that one of the departed guests, a veiled lady, had returned and desired speech with him, having sent his own jewelled dagger to reveal her identity, he impatiently bade him bring in the lady, knowing this could be none other than Victoria.

Before Hussein departed on his errand, however, Juan commanded the servant to draw back the heavy tapestries which separated the banqueting-hall from the ante-room beyond. His command was instantly obeyed, the curtains being drawn back to reveal the dying Duke just about to sign the document held before him by the priest, Dom Mortès.

Blindly enraged by the knowledge that, in another moment, his own fortune would have been signed away to the bastard brother he hated, Juan rushed into the ante-room and plunged the jewelled dagger he still held into the heart of the priest. The latter instantly fell dead at his feet, while the dying Duke, horror-struck by the sacrilegious deed, fell back unconscious upon the couch.

Thus assured of his own inheritance, Don Juan bade the equally horror-struck Hussein to draw the curtains once more, dispose conveniently of the priest's body, and attend to the expiring Duke. He then returned to the banqueting-hall; and, at that moment, Victoria entered, impatient at having been kept waiting so long.

Again his stricken mistress beseeched Juan to return to her arms. Then, finding that her pleading was in vain and learning instead that Juan intended to meet his new love, Carolina, in a summer pavilion on the morrow, she vowed that if he kept this rendezvous she would herself kill her rival with his own dagger. As she spoke, she snatched the jewelled weapon from her one-time lover and fled with it from the room.

While Juan stood for a moment dazed by the passion of jealousy he had aroused in so seemingly gentle a breast, he was accosted by another intruder. This was his bastard brother, Don José, who, knowing himself unwelcome, declared that he had come only at the earnest request of his beloved dying father, conveyed to him by the good priest, Dom Mortès.

Don José, though his mother had been of humble birth, had been well cared for by his grandee father and had grown up with a noble sense of duty towards his country; and he now tried to interest his half-brother in certain good works he wished to undertake when funds were available.

Don Juan, however, refused to talk of good works; but he invited his despised visitor to eat and drink instead, not wishing him yet to learn of the crime he had just committed.

As the two young men thus spoke together, José mentioned that though Juan's taste in fair ladies was famous throughout Castile, he was by no means the only judge of feminine charms. Then, rather foolishly, he added that he himself had a lovely mistress, named Inés, whom he had established at their father's castle at Villamayor, lent to him as a country home.

Fired by his bastard brother's vivid description of the beauty of the fair Inés and always eager for new delights, Don Juan secretly determined to seek out this lady himself that night and to steal her affections by his own superior charms. Then, having bidden the major-domo to conduct Don José into the presence of the dying Duke, he made a quick plan for the carrying out of his selfish desires.

Believing that José would not now leave his father until the latter had drawn his last breath, he commanded Hussein to have

horses and men brought to the gates immediately; and within an
hour he had set forth with his cavalcade for Villamayor.

.   .   .   .

In her handsome boudoir at the magnificent Castle of Villamayor, pretty Doña Inés sat awaiting the arrival of her lover,
Don José, whom she expected shortly to return from visiting his
dying father. She expected him to come back with news of his
new great riches as the favourite, though illegitimate, son of the
old Duke de Mañara; and she confidently hoped he would bring
with him as a gift for her some more of the lovely rubies she
loved so well, such as he had already lavished upon her, these
being her favourite jewels.

Meanwhile, during this waiting time, she amused herself by
teaching her maid Catalina how to use a fan with the true Spanish
art. Catalina, however, was more interested in telling her
mistress about the handsome cavalier she had seen earlier that
evening riding with twelve horseman servitors outside in the Mall.

While the lady and her maid thus talked together, they heard
the sound of a lover's sweet serenade being sung just below the
window. Inés was entranced, knowing the song to be addressed
to herself but realizing the voice not to be that of José. On now
hearing a knock at the door, she bade Catalina see who waited
without while she herself retired to her inner chamber.

Catalina, on opening the door, discovered Hussein outside, and
was easily persuaded by a purse of gold to leave her mistress's
chamber door and window unfastened; also to place a box of
jewels within her sight. When, therefore, curiosity caused Inés
presently to come forth from her inner chamber, she almost immediately discovered the jewel-box placed in a conveniently
prominent spot. Opening this, she took out a magnificent necklace of the glorious crimson rubies she loved so well.

Just as she was hanging this regal necklace around her neck
and admiring its dazzling effect against her fair skin, Don Juan
made a sudden entrance from the balcony window. Despite
Inés's cries of alarm, she was instantly attracted by the fascinating
looks and manners of Don Juan who, likewise attracted, began to
make passionate love to her, expressing his overwhelming admiration for her surprising beauty and begging her to accept him as
her lover.

Inés, flattered and swept away by such a lively passion, quickly
found her first resistance weakened; and she was almost ready to
yield to her new admirer's importunate pleading when the voice
of Don José was heard below, clamouring for his beloved mistress.

In alarm, Inés hid herself quickly in her inner chamber, while

Don Juan, cool and collected, stepped into the boudoir and confronted the astounded José. Before the latter could express his indignation on finding his libertine half-brother actually in the apartments of his own beloved mistress, Don Juan disarmed his first suspicions by pouring eager questions upon him regarding the condition of their dying father.

Under the strange spell of Juan's commanding presence and menacing attitude—for the libertine was furious at this unexpected interruption to his well-planned plot—José muttered that the old Duke was still conscious, though dying. Then he added accusingly that the good priest, Dom Mortès, had been found murdered in an outer courtyard of the palace; also, that the two beautiful ladies, Victoria and Carolina, were both dead. The former had met the latter in the summer pavilion awaiting her new lover and had stabbed her with Juan's own jewelled dagger; and then she had turned the weapon upon herself.

Knowing Juan to be the cause of these tragedies, José next was filled with fears for his own beloved mistress and demanded immediate access to her chamber; but Juan cynically declared that the lady now preferred himself, the better man, as her lover.

Angered by this insult and declaring it to be a lie, José drew his sword and rushed upon Don Juan who, however, being a famous swordsman, almost instantly disarmed him. Then, calling to his men to seize the fallen José—whom he now rejoiced to have in his power, having always regarded him as a hated rival—he commanded the lackeys to have him stripped and beaten with rods to humiliate him.

When José had been bound and dragged away, vowing to haunt his unnatural brother, Inés crept out from her hiding-place; but her would-be seducer now found her adamant instead of yielding, her better feelings having risen to the surface. When, therefore, the distracted Catalina next rushed in with the terrible news that her master, Don José, was being cruelly beaten by order of the strange cavalier, Inés fell swooning to the floor, overcome with horror.

But Don Juan instantly picked up the fainting lady in his arms and, calling to Hussein and his men, carried her outside to the waiting horsemen. A few moments later, the whole cavalcade rode off into the night towards Madrid, with the unconscious Inés in their midst.

．　　　．　　　．　　　．　　　．　　　．　　　．

Soon after these events, Don Juan became Duke of Mañara upon the death of his father; but though he still sought passionately for his ideal of perfection in his pursuit of beautiful women, tragedy dogged his every step. First, Don José, after having been beaten by lackeys, was too humiliated to face the world again and so took his own life. Then the lovely Inés followed his example. Rather than accept the embraces of her bandit lover, she flung herself from the high window of the lodging in which he had installed her and was drowned in the river below.

Still seeking pleasure and his ideal, Don Juan sought conquest after conquest but gained no satisfaction from any of the beautiful ladies he abducted. Finally, however, he met his match and was brought to his knees by supernatural means.

Coming one day to a popular inn in Madrid, Juan found his one-time roistering companion, Don Luis—from whose arms he had snatched the entrancing Carolina—and joined him in a game of dice. Don Luis had with him a new mistress, a beautiful girl named Pacquita, who quickly attracted the senses and admiration of Don Juan.

When, therefore, Luis presently lost not only all his money but his jewels and even his country house to the carelessly throwing Juan—who, however, seemed to have uncanny good luck that day —he declared that he had but one possession left, namely, his lovely mistress, Pacquita; and, in desperation, he offered to stake the latter on a single throw. Don Juan eagerly agreed—and won! Flinging insults now upon each other, the two cavaliers rushed into the street to fight a duel; and from this encounter Juan likewise returned triumphantly to claim his prize.

Meanwhile, Pacquita, on learning how she had been betrayed and soon knowing the tragic result of the duel, determined to slay her lover's murderer and herself. Taking a secret phial from the bosom of her gown, she dropped poison into two goblets of wine; then, when Don Juan returned to the room, victorious, to claim her as his prize, she feigned a gay acquiescence and offered him the one glass, while draining the contents of the other herself. Juan, however, refused to drink from the goblet set before him, being suspicious of her too eager offering; and he poured out fresh wine for himself.

At that moment Pacquita sank to the ground; and as she presently fell back dying in his arms and made confession of her grim deed, Juan felt remorse for the first time. It now seemed to him that this lovely girl came nearer to his ideal of perfection than any other woman he had yet met; and he grieved sincerely for her untimely death, of which he was the cause.

The dying Pacquita, realizing that the libertine's heart had been touched at last with a sense of guilt was eager now to save his soul from perdition. She begged him to seek out her sister,

Marta, a novitiate nun at the Convent of the Sacred Rosary and to entreat her to pray not only for her own erring sister but also for the soul of the now repentant cavalier before her; and Juan promised to do so.

.   .   .   .

Sister Marta, returning after Mass to the nave of the Church attached to the Convent of the Sacred Rosary to perform certain of her novice duties, noticed a stranger cavalier there who signed to her to stop and speak with him. It was Don Juan, who told her of the death of her sister and begged her to offer prayers for Pacquita's soul—also for his own. Then, struck by the young novice's surprising beauty, he began to plead with her to return with him to the world; but Marta, horrified, repulsed him, even though fascinated in spite of herself. Her temptation, however, was quickly ended. Even as the handsome cavalier spoke with her, an unearthly visitation took place before their awe-struck eyes.

The closed gilded gates of the richly-wrought screen which separated the nave of the Church from the choir and altar beyond, slowly opened without visible means; and, amidst a strange gloom, there issued forth the shadowy phantoms of all the victims of Don Juan's selfish passions, each chanting his or her own experience of his many misdeeds. These unearthly visitants were headed by the spectre of his much-injured brother, José. When this accusing phantom now sternly bade him repent, Juan, furious but undaunted, instantly drew his sword—upon which his supernatural visitant seized the stone sword of a guardian angel statue near by as though in defence.

In a lightning flash, Juan was disarmed and brought humbly to his knees. But the spectre of the injured Don José was merciful; and he declared that if a pure woman would offer her life in exchange for his, Juan's soul should be saved from perdition.

Juan, under no misapprehension regarding his own sinful life, knew only too well that this was, indeed, a forlorn hope; and he prepared to die. But when Sister Marta heard these words, she eagerly offered herself as the necessary sacrifice and flung herself willingly towards the spectre's stone sword of destruction. But the sword was no longer there, having been replaced instantly in the statue's outstretched hand once more; and the spectre of Don José announced that, having broken the pride of his erring brother, it were better for Sister Marta to live on and continue to pray for his soul.

This supernatural scene now came to an end; and as the phantoms vanished through the closing gates of the choir screen, a Monk drew near, offering a friar's rough mantle to the kneeling sinner. Truly repentant at last, the one-time libertine, after kissing the hem of holy Sister Marta's robe, wrapped round him the friar's gown which he humbly accepted; and then he followed the good Father who had brought it.

The world was to know Don Juan no more.

JUDITH *Goossens*

WHEN the Assyrian hosts 'set forth to conquer the Israelites, they soon found themselves up against a much greater and more far-reaching Force than they had expected. This was strange indeed; for their own armies were larger, stronger, and better equipped than those of the Hebrews, and their King—the glorious, godlike Nebuchadnezzar—was much more powerful and magnificent than any of the Kings of Israel had been since the wonderful days of Solomon.

Why was it, then, that so frequently small, but curiously opportune events happened to give unexpected victories to the almost hopelessly outclassed forces of Israel? At other times no such miraculous assistance was forthcoming; and then the downcast Hebrews seemed almost philosophical, as though they felt they deserved disaster. It was even whispered abroad that this was, indeed, actually the case . . . that it was the God of the Israelites, whom they declared to be the one and only God, who at times fought on their side but that He lent His aid only when they were obedient to His Laws.

The great Assyrian military lord, Prince Holofernes, the chief Commander of Nebuchadnezzar, who had been sent by his royal overlord to lay siege to Bethulia, the fair City on the Hills, began to think there might be something in this curious rumour— especially after a stormy late evening interview with one of his allies in the plains. Achior, Captain of the Ammonites, though himself an idolator, begged his military superior not to continue the siege of Bethulia any longer, since it was evident that the God of the Israelites was fighting on their side just then because of their present obedience to His Laws. But Holofernes was furious at the suggestion that he should raise the siege because the people of Bethulia were obedient to their God; and he added that the glorious King Nebuchadnezzar was the God he served, at whose behest he would slay all in that doomed city. He then ordered

Achior as a traitor to be bound to a stake outside the royal pavilion, to await further disposal.

Although Achior had thus endangered his life by defending a faith of which he knew but little, he soon learned that the rumour he had heard was a true one. Scarcely had Prince Holofernes hastened away angrily with his attendants to another part of the camp than a strange woman carrying a sack crept up to the tent opening, but started back in fear at the sight of Achior bound to a stake outside. In answer to his questions, the woman declared herself to be Haggith, the handmaiden of the Lady Judith, a noble matron of Bethulia—that unhappy city doomed to destruction so soon, where there was no water and where the people were already dying of thirst.

Even as she spoke, her mistress, the Lady Judith, likewise drew near stealthily—a woman of exquisite beauty, whose grace and noble bearing called forth a cry of admiration from the closely-bound Achior.

The latter, however, was horrified when he now learned from Judith that she had actually come to seek an interview with the great Prince Holofernes himself; and he tried to persuade her to return to her people, since the Assyrian General was cruel and ruthless and would certainly have her slain.

Then Judith, feeling that she could trust Achior, although he was not of her own faith, declared that she had come to save her people from the power of Holofernes—a mission she believed had been placed in her hands by the God of Israel, Who would give her the strength to carry it out. Because Achior had spoken as she would have had him speak, she declared that she would now set him free. Calling to Haggith, she took a great knife from the latter's sack and cut his bonds swiftly; and then she bade him fly for his life, while she and Haggith stood before the stake until he had vanished from sight.

A moment later a company of soldiers and slaves came up to the royal pavilion, headed by Bagoas, the Chief Eunuch of Prince Holofernes, who had come to provide for his lord's entertainment and feasting. Though angered at first by the presence of a strange Hebrew woman in the camp, Bagoas was immediately struck by the extreme beauty of Judith—whom, however, he was eager to keep away from the notice of his royal master, lest her charms should lure the latter into dealing less ruthlessly with the people of Bethulia or even keep him from making the expected attack on the early morrow.

He tried to lead her to his own tent; and he became furious when Judith declared firmly that Prince Holofernes was the only person in the camp she desired to speak with and that her message was for him alone. Fired by her beauty, too, he was about to snatch her away by force, when Holofernes himself returned, curtly dismissed Bagoas and led Judith into the interior of his most luxurious pavilion. Holofernes, accustomed though he was to female loveliness, quickly fell under the spell of Judith's regal beauty; and despite having been warned by the reluctantly-departing Bagoas that the Hebrew lady was as crafty as she was lovely, he threw precautions to the winds and gave himself up completely to the joys of the immediate moment. He ordered a feast to be spread, with rich wines; and he called for dancing-girls to entertain them both. When Judith meekly suggested that she would prefer to eat some of the special Hebrew food brought by her handmaiden, he commanded that Haggith should enter. But while, still at her request, he was pouring out cups of rich wine in which they were to pledge one another, Haggith drew out the great knife she had brought, and Judith hid this weapon among the cushions of the couch.

Judith, as though bent only upon pleasing her enemy host, told him how alarmed her people were at the sight of such mighty hosts of Assyrians in the plains below; but when Holofernes boastingly declared that they would be merely a useless rabble without himself as their leader, she smiled secretly to herself, well pleased to know this fact. She knew that, thanks to her own clever plot, this same rabble would certainly have no leader on the morrow, and that, consequently, her own people would triumph at last.

While she spoke soothingly and flatteringly to him, Judith carefully plied Holofernes constantly with the rich wines brought by the attendants; but of these she scarcely took a drop herself, though cleverly pretending to do so. Then, when the wine had done its work, so that the Assyrian leader's brain scarce followed the words she spoke and only his senses remained alert, she showed herself in a well-simulated loving mood.

But only for a few moments. As Holofernes fell back upon the couch from his first passionate embrace and as she bent once more over him as though inviting a second, Judith swiftly snatched up the knife she had concealed in the cushions and, with a mighty blow, killed him almost instantly. A superhuman strength seemed to have been lent to her for the carrying out of her mission—a fiery spirit which further enabled her to command the trembling Haggith, who now came forward from behind a curtain, to put the severed head in her sack and to follow her once more on the return journey to Bethulia. She, Judith, a beautiful daughter of Israel, had done the dreadful deed she had come to do. There would be no popular hero to lead the Assyrians to victory on the morrow; and Bethulia was saved.

FAUST   *Gounod*

IN a certain German town during the early years of the sixteenth century, a lonely life-long student sat in his laboratory late one evening. He mused on the vanity of all human knowledge and railed at the powerlessness of man to unravel the secret mysteries of Nature. He was an old man who had spent the whole of his life in the quest of learning; and not without considerable success. Faust the Alchemist, the laborious student of magic, mystery, and hidden wonders, had gained much repute among his fellows and was even looked upon with awe.

But the accumulation of knowledge had brought no satisfaction to his own soul, for the magic powers he sought were still withheld from him. As the old man sat in his silent chamber, lonely and unloved, he felt that his ceaseless toil had been in vain, inasmuch as, in the pursuit of learning, he had let the joys and beauties of life pass him by. All his vaunted knowledge could not bring back to him his lost youth with its faith, enthusiastic raptures and ambitions, and its fond dreams of hope and happiness.

Suddenly enraged by the impotency of the vain learning he had sacrificed his precious youth to attain, the old man seized a goblet containing a poisonous draught he had already prepared for himself. He was just about to drain its contents when the song of a band of merry young folk returning to their homes arrested him in the fatal act. Finding, however, that their song was all of love, hope, and prayer, he fell into another paroxysm of despair and called wildly on the powers of evil to come to his aid.

Instantly there was a blinding flash of unearthly light, a terrific crash of thunder, and the Prince of Evil himself stood before him!

Affrighted by this sudden answer to his rash invocation, Faust shrank back in horror; but the Demon—who, clad in brilliant red garments with a flashing sword at his side, had taken on the form of a gallant of the period and called himself Mephistopheles —approached his intended victim and demanded of him in mocking tones what he desired. Did he want gold? Or glory? Or a kingdom?

The old man shook his head, for none of these things had any charm for him; and he still feared his awful visitor. At last, however, tempted by the one fierce desire left to him, he could restrain himself no longer; and he passionately implored the Demon to bring back to him his lost youth, with all its entrancing delights and capacities for sweet enjoyment.

Mephistopheles replied that he had power to grant his wish and could instantly restore him to a glorious youth; but for one price only would he do this thing—the price of Faust's own soul! Then, as Faust drew back, fearful of entering into such a dreadful compact, the Demon cunningly tempted him further. By his supernatural powers he caused a wonderful vision to appear. As in a picture, Faust now beheld a beautiful maiden who sat spinning beside a cottage set in the midst of a flowery garden. The angelic looks of this lovely maiden filled the heart of Faust with a passionate desire to possess her. Upon the Tempter assuring him that this wish should also be gratified on accepting the terms demanded, the old man now seized his pen and recklessly signed the parchment contract already set before him.

As the vision slowly faded away, the Demon took up the discarded goblet of poison, changed its contents into a magic potion and bade his now secured prey to swallow the draught; and Faust eagerly did so.

Instantly he was transformed from an old man into a handsome youth of noble appearance, with quick young blood flowing through his veins and a heart throbbing with impulsive feeling and enjoyment of life. He found himself splendidly clad in the rich garments of a gay cavalier, with his pockets plentifully filled with gold; and resolving to enjoy to the full the pleasures now brought once again within his grasp, the rejuvenated Faust sallied forth with his evil companion.

.   .   .   .

Mephistopheles lost no time in taking Faust to the picturesque old city of Nuremburg, where the fair object of the latter's sudden passion dwelt in innocence and peace.

As the two strangers made their way into the city, they found that a fair was being held there. Gay students, pretty maidens, old men, and prim matrons, all clad in holiday attire, were laughing, chattering, and bargaining on every side. Outside a quaint old inn, a group of soldiers were standing under the trees drinking and bidding farewell to their citizen friends; for they were about to depart to the wars.

Among these soldiers was a young man named Valentine, who alone appeared grave amidst the merry throng. On being rallied for his dull spirits, he told his careless companions that his heart was heavy at the thought of leaving behind him his orphan sister, Margarita, a beautiful and virtuous young maiden who, though placed in the charge of a worthy woman, would thus be left for many months without a brother's loving care. Upon hearing this, a fair youth named Siebel who, though scarcely more than a boy, had already the dauntless spirit of a man, came forward and declared eagerly that he, Siebel, would guard and watch over Margarita as a brother in his stead. Valentine, somewhat comforted by this assurance, pressed his young friend's hand gratefully; and then he joined in the parting merriment of his companions.

While the soldiers were thus singing songs and drinking their farewell bumpers of wine, Mephistopheles suddenly joined the group and gave them a song. But the song he sang was a gaily mocking one, and the revellers drew back instinctively from the resplendent but evil-looking stranger. Siebel, in particular, felt him to be an enemy; and he shivered when the dark stranger, sensing his revulsion, seized his hand and pronounced that every flower he henceforth touched should immediately wither and die.

Then Mephistopheles, declaring that the wine offered to him was not worthy of the name, struck with his sword a small cask surmounted by an effigy of Bacchus which served as a sign to the inn. Instantly there gushed forth a stream of rich wine with which the revellers eagerly filled their cups—though they were startled when they felt the strange fluid coursing through their veins like liquid fire. Then Mephistopheles, laughing sardonically at their amazement and discomfiture, filled a goblet himself with the magic wine and drank it off to the toast of " Fair Margarita ! "

Enraged on hearing the name of his pure young sister thus lightly uttered by the sinister stranger, Valentine resentfully drew his sword and rushed upon him, followed by Siebel and the other gallants standing about. Mephistopheles, however, quickly drew a circle around himself with the point of his own weapon; and his would-be assailants then found themselves powerless, their swords instantly snapping in half when thrust within the magic circle. Seeing that infernal powers were being used against them, the gallants held up aloft the hilts of their swords; and before the Sign of the Cross, the Demon cringed abjectly and was compelled to retire.

The soldiers now made their final farewells and marched off

to join the departing regiment. Soon after they had gone, Mephistopheles again appeared with Faust, who was by this time all eagerness to see the fair object of his vision. In reply to his impatient demand, Mephistopheles indicated to him a fair-haired maiden now approaching them with a slow step and downcast eyes—a maiden of exquisite beauty, with the added charms of guileless innocence and perfect faith.

It was Margarita, the beloved sister of Valentine; and as Faust gazed upon her, he recognized with rapture the form and features of the lovely maiden revealed to him by the Demon in his laboratory vision.

With graceful ease he accosted her and begged to be allowed to escort her to her home. Margarita, however, was accustomed to treat such advances with coldness; and though her heart throbbed with sudden joy as her eyes met the ardent gaze of the handsome stranger, she replied modestly that she was but a humble maiden who needed no such escort. She then passed quietly on her way; and the discomfited Faust gazed after her with eyes of passionate admiration and tender longing, for an uncontrollable love for the sweet maiden was already surging in his heart.

.   .   .   .

Late that same evening, Mephistopheles led the willing Faust to the humble abode of Margarita, whose innocent soul the demon also hoped to secure as his prize.

As they approached the flower-laden garden, the young Siebel came forth and passed down the street; for this enthusiastic youth also loved Margarita and came to leave flowers for her every evening. On this particular evening, however, he had been filled with dismay because every flower he plucked had instantly withered in his hands; and he had shivered on remembering the words of the sinister stranger he had met that afternoon. Suddenly, however, he bethought himself to dip his fingers in a little bowl of holy water that stood within the porch of Margarita's cottage; then, to his joy, he found that the curse was powerless and that the flowers he gathered after this devotional act remained fresh. After laying his offering as usual upon a seat outside the porch, therefore, he came away. Immediately afterwards, Faust and Mephistopheles entered the garden.

Observing Siebel's flowers upon the rustic seat, Mephistopheles produced a casket of valuable jewels and placed it beside them; then he withdrew with Faust into the shadows to watch the result.

Presently the lovely Margarita came forth into the garden with a pensive air. She was still thinking of the handsome cavalier who had accosted her in the afternoon, whose passionate glances of admiration had thrilled her so intensely and had set her maiden heart throbbing so wildly. She soon noticed young Siebel's flowers and tenderly laid them aside with an indulgent smile; then, seeing the strange casket, she took it up wonderingly and opened it.

An exclamation of childish delight escaped her on beholding the dazzling jewels within; and unable to resist the temptation of adorning herself with them, she tremblingly clasped the many wonderful bracelets and chains about her snowy neck and arms. A mirror had been artfully laid within the casket; and as she gazed at the reflection of herself thus loaded with glittering gems and ropes of priceless pearls, she wondered what her noble gallant would think if he could behold her now, adorned as a princess.

Just then, Dame Martha, the worthy but not very vigilant guardian in whose charge Margarita had been left during her brother's absence at the wars, came forth from the cottage. Admiring the sparkling jewels, she declared that they must have been sent by some rich adorer.

At this moment, Faust and Mephistopheles came forth from the shadows to which they had retreated. The latter, declaring to Martha that he had important news for her, soon enticed the dame, with many flattering phrases, to leave her precious charge and to wander with him to another part of the garden.

Left alone with Margarita, Faust approached the beautiful maiden eagerly; and unable to control his feelings any longer, he passionately declared his love for her. Margarita, though she resisted his advances for some time, at length gave way to the answering love in her own heart and resigned herself to the tender embraces of the irresistible cavalier.

After this the enraptured lovers frequently met at dusk in this same flowery garden which thus became an enchanted spot for them. With remorseless insistence the fiendish Mephistopheles continually encouraged and aided Faust in his passionate but lawless pursuit of Margarita; and he never once relaxed his demoniacal temptations until the resistance of the passion-torn girl was broken down and her fair innocence destroyed.

.   .   .   .

The joys of a secret rapturous love were not long permitted to the betrayed Margarita. As the months went on and her dishonour became known, she had to submit to the scorn and sneers of her old companions, who showed little pity for the frailty of one whose virtue had always been held up to them as a pattern. All avoided her, except the faithful Siebel, who still sought to

bring comfort to the gentle maiden whose true and trustful love
had been her undoing.

Full of grief and remorse, Margarita sought comfort in prayer
and repentance; but even in the church the mocking Demon,
whose cruel temptation she had been unable to resist, would
seek her out and fill her heart with fear and despair.

It was while Margarita was humbly praying one evening in
the church near her cottage home that the soldiers returned from
the wars. Among them was the brave Valentine, who had
covered himself with glory in the campaign. Quickly escaping
from the congratulations of his friends, he hurried away to receive
the praises and greetings of his beloved sister.

At the door of the cottage, however, he was met by the unhappy Siebel, from whose agitated words he soon learned of the
betrayal of Margarita. Full of grief and anger, he hastened within
to pour forth reproaches upon the erring sister who had thus
brought a stain upon his name.

Siebel ran to the church to acquaint Margarita with her
brother's return. No sooner had the youth gone than Mephistopheles appeared with Faust, who was still unable to keep away
from the fair maiden he had betrayed. He was, however, sad
and remorseful; and it was his evil companion who, to entice
Margarita from her chamber, struck a guitar and sang a light
serenade beneath the window, leaving Faust standing near the
porch.

The serenade, however, was interrupted by Valentine, who
suddenly dashed out from the cottage, sword in hand. Realizing
that the betrayer of his sister stood before him, he challenged
Faust to combat. Instantly their blades clashed together; and
Faust, aided by the diabolical intervention of Mephistopheles,
quickly overcame his opponent, so that Valentine fell to the
ground mortally wounded.

At this moment, Siebel and Margarita came forth from the
church. Seeing what had happened, the unhappy girl, with a
loud cry of woe, flung herself upon the prostrate body of her
brother, beseeching him to pardon her. But Valentine roughly
flung her from him, declaring that her sin had slain him; and
with his last breath he cursed her passionately as he fell back
lifeless.

.   .   .   .

Horror-stricken by the awful calamity of which she had been
the cause, the unhappy Margarita was filled with unutterable
grief and despair. Her already harassed mind giving way under
the weight of woe now fallen upon it, in a sudden fit of mad

frenzy she took the life of the helpless babe soon afterwards born
to her. For this terrible though unconscious act, she was immediately flung into prison and condemned to death. Even as
she lay in the gloomy cell awaiting execution, however, her weary
soul, worn out with suffering and grief, was already preparing
to leave its earthly abode.

Faust was now filled with remorse and despair; and on the
night before the execution, aided by Mephistopheles, he gained
access to his beloved one's cell and eagerly besought her to fly
with him. But Margarita, seeing the sinister form of Mephistopheles in the background gazing upon her exultingly with eyes
like coals of fire, realized the danger of this new temptation; and
she spurned her lover's offer.

Before the return of Valentine she had begun to place her
reliance in prayer and repentance; and these holier feelings once
more gaining the ascendancy over her worldly desires, she fell
upon her knees to pray. It was in vain that the despairing Faust
implored her to escape with him and the exulting Demon
tempted her to yield. At last, with a final prayer for pardon and
mercy, she fell back upon her wretched couch and expired at
their feet.

Mephistopheles uttered a cry of fiendish triumph, hoping to
claim her soul as his; but at that moment a chorus of angelic
voices was heard proclaiming forgiveness for the repentant sinner,
whose faithful prayers had reached the Mercy-Seat on High.

Faust, awed and overcome with sorrow, sank to his knees in
prayer; and as the Demon, thus baulked of his expected prey,
shrank back in cringing defeat, the prison walls opened and the
released and ransomed soul of Margarita was borne upwards
to its celestial home.

MIRELLA   _Gounod_
(_Mireille_)

IN a large mulberry plantation of lovely Provence, a number of
merry girls were busily engaged in gathering up a rich harvest of
silk cocoons. As they worked, they sang and joked together,
happy in their fresh early youth and looking forward to sweetheart days ahead.

For this reason they did not favour the presence in their midst
of old Tavena, a country crone. In addition to having the reputa-

tion of being almost a witch—or, at least, a Wise Woman—old Tavena was also inclined to cast a gloom over their merriment by prophesying that, so far from continued joyous days ahead, there was more likely to be trouble and hard work in store for them when they were wedded to their sweethearts.

Nevertheless, though her youthful companions showed disfavour to old Tavena, this was not the case with Mirella, the lovely young daughter of Raimondo, the rich farmer and owner of the mulberry plantation. For Mirella was already seriously in love; and she knew that the reputed witch was wise and might be useful to her, since the course of her true love was not likely to run smoothly.

Mirella's sweetheart, Vincenzo, though a handsome youth, was merely a poor basket-maker; whereas her father was the wealthiest farmer in the district and was likely to wish his pretty daughter to accept a more important suitor.

Seeing the young girl standing alone and pensive, old Tavena drew near and warned her of this very thing she feared so much; and she advised her to give up all thought of ever wedding with Vincenzo, since she was never likely to gain her father's consent to the match. The Wise Woman added, however, that if she persisted in her resolve and trouble ensued, she, old Tavena, would be her friend.

When Tavena had departed, shaking her old head at the follies of youth, Mirella quickly forgot her friendly warnings. Seeing the handsome Vincenzo passing by, she hailed him joyfully; and the lovers spent a few blissful moments together. Vincenzo told Mirella that he had confided the secret of their love to his pretty and beloved sister, Vincenzina, who was eager to help the lovers in their quest for happiness.

Hearing her companions calling her back to work, Mirella was soon obliged to send her sweetheart on his way once more; but, in addition to a further declaration of their undying love, the pair first made a solemn pact together. They agreed that should Vincenzo's suit be refused by Mirella's wealthy father, they would then make a pilgrimage to the shrine and sanctuary of the Holy Virgin in the lonely desert plain of Crò, many miles away; and there they would renew their vows of love and invoke the aid of the gentle Madonna herself.

The lovers had not long to wait before learning of their fate. At a merry festival fair held a few days later in the ancient arena at Arles, where hundreds of revellers had gathered from all the towns and country places in the district, the handsome young Vincenzo carried all before him by winning most of the prizes in the dances, races, and games competitions; and Mirella felt very proud of her athletic sweetheart.

At the invitation of their gay young companions, the happy lovers sang a sweet song together, descriptive of their joy. But trouble was already at hand to cloud their sunshine.

When, presently, Vincenzo was called away to take part in another race and Mirella was left alone for a moment, old Tavena drew near and gave her disturbing news. She had just overheard a prosperous young bull-herder, named Urias, speaking of his love for the rich farmer's beautiful daughter; and she advised Mirella to consider this young man's suit, since he was likely to be more acceptable in the eyes of her father than the poor basket-maker.

But Mirella vowed fervently that she would never wed with anyone but her beloved Vincenzo. When, therefore, Urias—a powerfully-built and roughly handsome man of more mature years than her lover—appeared and presented his eager suit in person, her reply was the same. Even when the disappointed Urias indignantly declared that he had already received her father's consent, Mirella still firmly refused his eager pleading; and she moved away, sadly aware of trouble in store for her.

This quickly came to pass. Her father, the wealthy Raimondo, was likewise at the festival and had already seated himself at a table under the trees, where he was being served with wine by the attendants while awaiting the result of Urias's interview with Mirella; and he was furious when the crestfallen bull-herder now came up to him with the news of the refusal of his suit.

Raimondo was, therefore, in no favourable mood to listen to the humble basket-maker, Ambrogio, who now approached him in company with his son and daughter, and began to plead Vincenzo's cause, begging for his consent to the latter's marriage with Mirella—declaring that his son was so engrossed by his passionate love that he would surely die were his suit not granted.

But the angry Raimondo roughly refused to listen to the pleadings of the basket-maker and his son, unjustly accusing both of mercenary motives and declining to believe in the sincerity of Vincenzo's love; and when Mirella now appeared in some alarm on hearing the sound of raised angry voices, he sternly bade her to accept Urias, the man of his own choice, as her husband. Otherwise, he added threateningly, she must cease to regard herself as his daughter and would be cut off from his protection for ever.

But Mirella was staunch and brave; and standing beside the man she loved, she vowed again that him only would she wed. And Vincenzo, though his distressed old father now begged him to relinquish such a hopeless suit, also proudly declared that nothing should part him from his beloved one, even though poverty must be her lot.

On hearing this, and enraged beyond measure, the great man of the district raised his hand as though about to strike the daughter who had dared to thwart him. But Mirella, though distressed that she had caused him disappointment, fell on her knees and entreated him, in the name of her dead mother who he had once so dearly loved, to show pity for her daughter.

Even this final appeal, however, had no effect, since Raimondo was now beside himself with frustration and injured pride; and he declared Mirella to be no longer a daughter of his, but an outcast.

Full of grief, Mirella clung passionately to Vincenzo; and the two once more pledged their love, while the pretty Vincenzina sought to comfort them. Thus the festival, which had begun so happily, ended miserably for the lovers.

Now, however, they determined to renew and strengthen their vows by seeking divine aid at the shrine of the Virgin at Crò, as they had agreed to do in the event of their love being thwarted.

. . . .

The unhappy Mirella, having been forbidden her father's home, was the first to set off towards the sanctuary at Crò, which lay far out in the wild barren plains of a desert district; and next day, as the hours went on, the heat of the burning sun became so great that she was obliged to rest several times on her way.

At her first halt she came upon a shepherd boy, who, after playing a sweet tune upon his pipes, had fallen asleep while his sheep wandered away; and she envied him because he had no cares and could sleep in peace.

As she continued on her way, she was overtaken by old Tavena, who had hastened after her, bringing a message from Vincenzo. Her lover had been delayed, having had an encounter with his rival, the bull-herder, Urias, who had wounded him. The wound would not delay him long, however; and after he had had it bound up, he would follow on to their sanctuary meeting-place.

Then, having delivered her message, the Wise Woman announced her kindly resolve to return and to seek out Mirella's father, whom she knew to be already repenting of his harshness; and she hoped that when told of his despairing daughter's present dreary pilgrimage, he might be persuaded to forgive her.

When Tavena had departed on her self-imposed mission of help, Mirella continued her journey, which grew more wearisome and disheartening at every step she took into the wild, barren, desert-like plain; and the now blazing glare of the sun, and the lack of shade or cooling streams, soon caused her to feel faint and exhausted. She toiled on bravely, however, until at last she reached the Sanctuary; and here, before the shrine of the Virgin, she weakly sank upon her knees to pray and to invoke divine assistance in her present woe.

After what seemed to her an endless time, she was at last joined by Vincenzo, who made light of his wound; and the lovers rejoiced together and once more vowed their eternal love, upon which they now implored a divine blessing.

While they were thus invoking the Virgin's aid, Mirella suddenly fell back in a half-fainting condition, deadly pale; for the effort of having wandered in the blazing sun all day had now culminated in a kind of sunstroke.

Full of alarm and thinking her about to die, Vincenzo knelt distractedly beside her and held her closely in his arms; and at that moment, Raimondo, her father, rushed into the Sanctuary.

The wealthy farmer had, indeed, as stated by old Tavena, begun to feel remorse for his harshness towards his daughter; and when Mirella had not returned home the previous night, he had come out to search for her. On meeting the old Wise Woman and learning from her that the unhappy girl had journeyed out to the Virgin's Sanctuary in the desert plains to pray with her lover for divine assistance, he had followed her thither at utmost speed.

Now, on beholding his still well-loved daughter in an apparently dying condition, Raimondo knelt beside her, filled with belated compassion and remorse, imploring her forgiveness for his harshness; and he entreated her to live and become the bride of Vincenzo, whom he was now willing for her to marry.

These words acted as a magic charm upon the exhausted girl; and when Mirella presently opened her eyes and beheld her father and lover bending over her anxiously, eager for her to live and make them both happy, she soon began to recover.

Then Raimondo placed her hand in that of Vincenzo; and the now happy lovers knew that their prayers had been answered and that glad days were at last in store for them.

PHILEMON AND BAUCIS _Gounod_

ONE stormy evening, long ago in the mythical days of the gods and goddesses of the ancient Greeks and Romans, a couple of simple peasants named Philemon and Baucis were resting peacefully in their humble cottage on the borders of Phrygia, where they had lived together for many years of happy wedded life. They were now growing old; but although the shadows of life's eventide were fast deepening around them, they did not waste their remaining days in uttering vain regrets for departed youth. The love in their hearts was as fresh and green as ever and happiness was still theirs, in spite of poverty and old age.

There was a storm brewing outside; but the contented old couple scarcely heeded it as they continued to talk together happily until darkness fell. Not even a band of merry Bacchantes who presently danced past the cottage door on wildest revels bent, could draw from either a sigh of regret for the lost pleasures of youth.

Presently, however, Baucis went into an inner room to prepare a simple supper for them both—humble food that was sweeter to them than the luxuries of the rich, because it was the result of their own honest labour and was seasoned with love.

While she was absent, Philemon busied himself by making the fire burn more brightly; and presently he was interrupted by an imperative knock at the cottage door. By this time the storm was raging with great violence; and when, upon opening the door, he was accosted by two strangers who craved shelter from the wind and rain, Philemon at once invited them to enter. He expressed his distress that travellers should be out on such a wild night.

Unknown to good old Philemon, these two strangers were in reality Jupiter, the Father of the Gods, and Vulcan, the God of Fire and master of workers in metal. They were visiting the earth thus disguised in order to bring dire punishment upon the disobedient people of Phrygia, who had offended them by falling into evil ways. Having, however, been overtaken by this terrible storm—brought about by Jupiter's own commands as his means of punishment—they had sought refuge at the first homestead they came to, hoping that the owner might grant them shelter and thus prove himself more worthy than his neighbours, upon whom the angry gods' vengeance was now about to fall.

I

Their hopes were realized; for Philemon received them with great kindness and hospitality. He at once led them to the warm hearthstone, where he proceeded to divest them of their wet cloaks; and he declared it was a delight to welcome such noble guests, whom the gods must surely have sent.

Jupiter was very well pleased by this pleasant welcome; but Vulcan only grumbled and growled at having been dragged from his accustomed work against his will. He was, indeed, in an exceeding ill-humour; for he was still smarting from the recent intrigues of his beautiful wife Venus with the gods Mars and Mercury. He even called down curses upon these particularly fascinating gods who were the cause of his domestic woes. Upon hearing this, old Philemon, being a devout upholder of the gods he served so devoutly, was shocked; and he sternly reproved the stranger for thus speaking irreverently of the great Immortals. But Jupiter laughingly bade the peasant not to heed the ill-humour of his companion, who was in a strange mood that night.

When Philemon had retired to help his wife prepare a meal for their unexpected guests, Jupiter began to rally Vulcan on his gloomy looks and sulky temper. But the cross-grained, deformed god was not easily pacified; and he declared that he preferred to be left working with his faithful Cyclops in his subterranean forges, where nobody dared to poke fun at him for his ill-humours and ugly appearance and where he was not plagued by the sight of his faithless wife bestowing her bewitching smiles on other admirers.

Whilst Jupiter was laughing over his companion's complaints and gaily bidding him not to care for aught done by one so fair and fickle, Baucis entered the room. She carried a jug filled with goat's milk, which she placed on the table before the visitors, saying that Philemon would shortly follow with ripe fruits from their garden store.

Being even better pleased with the cheerful, kindly looks of old Baucis, Jupiter questioned her as to the reason for her evident contentment and happiness; and when she replied simply that this was due to the all-absorbing love she and her husband had for each other, which made them count poverty and old age as nothing, he was filled with amazement. When the great god next asked her whether she did not also long for riches, Baucis smiled as she shook her head and declared that Philemon's love was wealth enough for her. She added: "Love has been the guiding star of our simple lives; and now that our days are drawing to a close, our only regret is that we cannot begin over again and tread the same sweet path side by side a second time!"

At this moment, Philemon returned with a basket of fine ripe fruits from the garden and a vessel of sparkling water from the spring; and placing these on the table beside the goat's milk, he invited his guests to partake of the humble food which was, nevertheless, the best his poor home could offer.

Jupiter, delighted by the gracious hospitality of the good old couple, gladly accepted the invitation; and having drained the vessel of water to satisfy his own thirst, he bade Baucis to fill yet another goblet from the now empty flagon for Vulcan. Baucis was greatly surprised at this strange bidding; but on receiving the command from Jupiter a second time, she inclined the now empty vessel. To her utter amazement a stream of rich red wine immediately flowed into the goblet!

The simple peasants now realized that their strange guests were not ordinary mortals, and were in some fear as to who they might really be; but Jupiter, though still retaining his incognito, quickly reassured them, saying that he and his companion had been sent thither by the gods to bring dire punishment on the disobedient mortals in that neighbourhood who had offended them by doing much evil. He then bade them listen to the terrific thunderstorm which was now raging and would certainly destroy those on whom the gods' vengeance was about to fall. When the old couple began to tremble for their own safety, he told them to be of good comfort; for they would be spared because of the goodness of their lives and because of the hospitality and kindness they had shown to travellers in distress. He then bade the wondering pair to lie down in peace and rest securely until the morning, when they should awaken to reap the reward for their good deed—their heart's desire as revealed to him by Baucis.

Philemon and Baucis, now feeling a delicious drowsiness creeping over their senses, obeyed the god's authoritative command and gladly laid themselves down to sleep. Then, as they sank into a peaceful slumber, Jupiter cast a magic spell over them, whereby their beautiful youth was completely restored to them; and, at the same time, he transformed their humble cottage into a magnificent palace.

.   .   .   .

When morning dawned, the gods retired for a while and left the rejuvenated pair to make their wonderful discovery alone. Baucis was the first to awaken. Surprised at her unusual exhilaration of spirits and at feeling the blood coursing through her veins as in the days of her youth, she sprang to her feet; then, as she also beheld the new grandeur around her, she exclaimed: "I must be dreaming!" On approaching her still sleeping husband, she was further amazed to find him also young and handsome as in the days of yore, when he had first won her love; and running for a mirror her joy was complete when its reflection showed her that she likewise was restored to beautiful youth and was even fairer still than in the early flush of maidenhood long years ago!

"Philemon! Philemon! Awaken, my love, and rejoice!" she cried in delight. When Philemon arose immediately at the sound of her fresh young voice, he also was astonished to find himself within a palatial mansion; and he was utterly bewildered at the sight of the lovely maiden before him.

"Who art thou, fair one?" he asked in awestruck tones. "Thou art beautiful as my beloved Baucis was in the days of her youth!"

But Baucis held up the mirror before his eyes and bade him look at his own reflection; and when Philemon saw that he also had regained his handsome youth, his joy was unbounded.

The happy pair now knew that this marvellous transformation must have been brought about by the influence of the gods, whose messengers they had entertained the evening before; and overcome with gratitude and joy that the passion and delight of their youthful love was thus restored to them, they fell into each other's arms and rapturously embraced. Afterwards, hand in hand, the happy pair wandered from room to room in their new marble palace, full of wonder that such riches should be theirs; then they ran out into the most beautiful garden they had ever seen and enjoyed its scented flowers and the sweetness of its rare fruits.

For long the joyful lovers rejoiced in perfect bliss, regardless of time and heedless of the whole world; and then a cloud overshadowed their happiness. The gods returned to behold the result of their handiwork; and trouble immediately arose.

When Jupiter beheld the loveliness of the rejuvenated Baucis, he was so enthralled by her sweet fresh beauty that he suddenly desired to possess her for himself; and, god-like, he at once sought the means of gratifying his desire. Presently observing that Baucis was standing half-concealed by some flowering trees, playfully hiding from Philemon, he persuaded Vulcan to keep the handsome youth engaged for a while; and when the cross-grained God of Iron—still somewhat bad-tempered and aggrieved about his own domestic problems—had departed grumblingly upon this unwanted task, his flirtatious overlord impetuously began his new conquest.

Jupiter soon came face to face with the lovely maiden and began to address her in tones of admiration, at the same time giving her to understand his high estate; and when Baucis knew that it was the great god Jupiter to whom she was indebted for her restored youth and beauty and who now graciously condescended to admire her, she was so overcome that she sank humbly to her knees, trembling with fear. But Jupiter gently raised her from the ground, reassuring her in tender accents. Then, more and more enthralled by the maiden's exquisite grace and charm, he began to pour forth passionate protestations of love, even imploring her to accept his overtures.

At first, Baucis repulsed him, shrinking back with frightened mien; but at length her timidity was overcome. With a feeling of almost pardonable pride that her beauty was sufficient to cause the King of the Gods himself to plead for her love, she began to enjoy the situation and even to coquette with her exalted admirer. When, therefore, Philemon, having successfully escaped from the boring conversation of Vulcan, presently appeared on the scene, he was filled with amazement and indignation at beholding his beautiful wife in the arms of the stranger he had entertained the night before.

Baucis, quickly brought back to her senses by this timely interruption, instantly ran to her husband's side, begging him to curb his wrath; but Philemon's anger was not to be restrained and he broke forth into passionate reproaches. Jupiter, though furious that Vulcan's carelessness should have caused this unwelcome interruption to his own enjoyment, thought it prudent to retire for a while; and when he had departed, Philemon's torrent of reproaches fell faster than ever. Even when Baucis somewhat fearfully explained that it was the Immortal Jupiter who had thus honoured her with his admiration, the angry young peasant was not pacified; and at last the young girl herself grew angry and began to return his reproaches with equal passion.

Into the midst of this quarrel came Vulcan, who tried to make peace between them. He cynically bade Philemon be of good cheer since a matter of this kind was considered a mere trifle on Olympus, where faithlessness in love was the rule rather than the exception; and he added that the fair daughters of earth were not likely to excel where goddesses failed.

But Philemon was not to be reassured by any such doubtful comfort as this; and at last, in a paroxysm of jealous anger, he overturned the household gods—which, in the form of statuettes, adorned his new abode—and then rushed away wildly.

Baucis now began to weep bitterly, full of remorse that she should have so carelessly grieved the heart of her Philemon. Though a natural passing feeling of vanity in her re-born beauty had led her to be pleased with the admiration of the great god, her love for her husband had never for a moment wavered; and she was filled with despair at the thought that she might have forfeited his regard, which was her dearest possession.

After vainly trying to comfort the unhappy girl, Vulcan went off in search of Philemon, with whom he hoped to act the part of peace-maker; and no sooner had he departed on this difficult errand than Jupiter again returned. On beholding Baucis in tears, the amorous god hurried to her side, tenderly entreating her not to grieve but to accept his caresses and admiration instead; but Baucis, determined not to let such alluring flatteries again overcome her nobler instincts, quickly withdrew herself from his embrace. Then, falling on her knees before him, she passionately besought him to take her fatal youthful beauty away and make her old and wrinkled once more, that she might thus atone for the wrong she had done her faithful husband in listening even for a moment to words of love from other lips than his. She added: "What care I for beauty that but enthrals the hearts of others? I want my husband's love only, and that was mine when old! Therefore, my gracious lord, make me old again!"

As Baucis was pleading with Jupiter, Philemon approached with Vulcan; and on thus learning from her impassioned words that his wife still loved him only, he ran forward with great pleasure and clasped her in his arms. Then he knelt with her before the mighty god and added his pleadings to hers that they might both become old again.

Jupiter, though at first furious that a mere mortal should thus be preferred by a beautiful maiden before himself, the Ruler of the Gods, yet could not withhold his admiration for such perfect love as this.

Gradually, his anger melted away; and presently he announced to the faithful pair that they should still retain their youth and beauty and that he would no longer come between their affections but would pour blessings upon them instead.

Having thus restored harmony to the earthly home they had deigned to visit, the two gods returned to Olympus; and Philemon and Baucis were left in peace to rejoice in their renewed youth and in the perfect love that should again guide them surely along the path of happiness and contentment to their lives' end.

ROMEO AND JULIET *Gounod*

IN the city of Verona during the fourteenth century a fierce private feud had existed for many years between the two noble families of Capulet and Montague. To such a degree was this hatred carried that it was even shared by the servants, followers, and friends of the two rival houses—with the result that if a Capulet partisan met a Montague partisan, they invariably came to blows and did not hesitate to shed one another's blood.

One evening a banquet and masked ball was held at the palace of Lord Capulet; and to this festival all the chief lords and ladies of Verona were invited—with the exception, of course, of any members of the hated Montague family.

However, Lord Montague's son, Romeo, a handsome and daring young man of a romantic disposition, boldly announced his intention of attending, uninvited, the revels at the house of his family foe. Disguised in the dress of a pilgrim, therefore, and masked, he proceeded to the Capulet palace, accompanied by his bosom friends, Benvolio and Mercutio, likewise disguised. They were admitted, unquestioned, into the great hall, where they mingled freely with the invited guests; and for a while, no one suspected that a Montague was taking part in the revels.

Amongst the merry throng of dancers Romeo soon noticed a beautiful young girl, whose wonderful grace and charm strangely fascinated him; and drawing the attention of his friends to this fair maiden, he exclaimed enthusiastically: "I never saw true beauty till this night!"

This admiring remark was overheard by a kinsman of the Capulets, a fiery-tempered youth named Tybalt, who immediately recognized the voice as that of one of his detested foemen. Furious that a Montague should thus have dared to enter the house of Capulet, he drew his sword and challenged Romeo; and he would have slain him then and there had not Lord Capulet himself interfered. The latter, declaring that the laws of hospitality must be observed, sternly commanded his impetuous young kinsman to sheathe his weapon and announced that his enemy's son should remain that evening—having heard that he was a noble youth spoken of in the city with respect and honour.

Peace was thus temporarily restored; and presently Romeo secured an opportunity of speaking with the lovely maiden whose fair looks had so quickly enslaved his heart. He soon realized that her disposition was as sweet and gentle as her looks; and, to his joy, she returned his advances with many signs of favour.

Presently, the maiden was called away; and when she had departed, Romeo learnt that she was the daughter of Lord Capulet and that her name was Juliet.

Although filled with dismay that he had thus fallen in love with his enemy's daughter and that it was dangerous to make further advances to her, Romeo nevertheless determined to see the lovely maiden again. With this object in view, when the revels ended, he made his way into Lord Capulet's garden, absorbed in this new joy which had already filled his heart so completely.

To his delight, Juliet presently stepped forth on to the balcony outside her chamber window. She also was thinking of the strange sweet love which had so suddenly filled her whole being at the ardent gaze of the handsome young pilgrim who had conversed with her at the ball; and she wished to breathe her happy thoughts into the moonlit night.

But Juliet had already learnt that this noble youth whose eager words had so quickly and unresistingly won her heart, was the son of her family's foe and that she ought to hate rather than love him. As she thought of this troublesome difficulty in the path of her happiness, she murmured softly.:

> " O Romeo, Romeo! wherefore art thou Romeo?
> Deny thy father, and refuse thy name;
> Or if thou wilt not, be but sworn my love,
> And I'll no longer be a Capulet.
> 'Tis but thy name that is my enemy:
> Thou art thyself though, not a Montague.
> What's Montague? it is nor hand nor foot,
> Nor arm, nor face, nor any other part
> Belonging to a man. O, be some other name!
> What's in a name? that which we call a rose,
> By any other name would smell as sweet;
> So Romeo would, were he not Romeo called,
> Retain that dear perfection which he owes,
> Without that title: Romeo, doff thy name;
> And for thy name, which is no part of thee,
> Take all myself! "

On hearing these words, which proved to him that Juliet returned his love, Romeo crept softly forward and made his presence known to her by answering her spoken thought thus:

> " I take thee at thy word!
> Call me but love, and I'll be new baptiz'd;
> Henceforth I never will be Romeo! "

Juliet was filled with joy on thus beholding the object of her sweet reflections; and she gave him a tender greeting. For a long while the lovers talked happily together. In spite of the fact that Juliet had already been promised in marriage by her parents to a young man of noble family named Paris, she now gladly listened to Romeo's passionate declaration of love and vowed that she would wed none other than he. Several times their sweet converse was interrupted by Juliet's old nurse calling to her charge from within the chamber; and at last the maiden was obliged to tear herself away from the presence of her adoring lover and retire to rest.

Romeo did not return to his home immediately; and as dawn was already breaking, he made his way to a neighbouring monastery in order to seek the help of a good old monk named Friar Laurence.

The old Friar listened indulgently to the youth's rapturous recital of the love he had conceived for the beautiful Juliet; and when Romeo presently besought him to unite them in marriage that same day, he consented to do so, thinking that good might come of such a deed and possibly lead to the healing of the ancient feud between the two families.

Later in the day, therefore, a message was secretly conveyed to Juliet, who found means to visit Friar Laurence's cell, where Romeo was awaiting her; and there the old monk performed the rite of marriage for the loving pair and made them man and wife. Juliet then hurried back to her home with speed; and Romeo, after declaring that he would see her again in the Capulet garden after nightfall, went to join his friends Benvolio and Mercutio, whom he had arranged to meet in a certain street.

To his dismay, he found them engaged in a hot dispute with the fiery-tempered young Capulet, Tybalt, who still resented their intrusion of the previous night. Mercutio and Tybalt quickly drew their swords and engaged in a deadly fight, which ended in Mercutio receiving a mortal wound.

On seeing his friend fall in an expiring condition, Romeo, full of grief and indignation, at once made a furious onslaught upon Tybalt; and in the struggle which followed he killed the Capulet noble.

By this time the news of the encounter had spread in the city, and soon members of both the Capulet and Montague families hurried to the spot, together with the Prince of Verona himself who had been summoned by the watch. Cries of grief arose from both families; and the matter ended in the Prince declaring sentence of immediate banishment upon Romeo. Now full of despair, the latter concealed himself until nightfall in Friar

Laurence's cell, having resolved to see Juliet again before leaving the city.

When darkness fell, therefore, Romeo made his way once more to the Capulet garden and, scaling the balcony, bade a long and passionate farewell to the weeping Juliet. With the first signs of dawn, he was compelled to depart with a last fond embrace. Then, with a heavy heart and reluctant steps, he journeyed to Mantua, whence his messengers and friends could keep him acquainted with news concerning the fair young secret bride from whom he had been thus so cruelly parted.

After the departure of Romeo, Juliet found herself in a position of the utmost difficulty. Her parents determined that her marriage with the brilliant young Count Paris should now take place without further delay; and the nuptials were announced to be celebrated a few days hence.

It was in vain that the dismayed Juliet, not daring to reveal the fact of her secret marriage with the banished Romeo, pleaded her extreme youth, her indifference to Paris, and the family mourning for their kinsman, Tybalt. Her parents were only angered by her unwillingness and disobedience to their wishes; and they declared they would cast her off for ever should she fail to accept Paris as her husband on the day appointed.

Then the unhappy Juliet suddenly bethought her of the kind old monk who had wedded her to Romeo. Leaving her home with the utmost secrecy, she made her way to the cell of Friar Laurence, to whom she poured forth her tale of woe, beseeching him to counsel her in this terrible dilemma.

It happened that the old Friar had studied the properties of many valuable drugs; and he now provided Juliet with a certain potion which, if she drank it just before the wedding festivities began, would cause her to fall into a trance—with the result that her friends, thinking her to be dead, would place her on a bier in the family vault. Here, on awakening after forty-two hours had elapsed, she would be rescued by Romeo and secretly conveyed by him to Mantua, where they could dwell together in happiness.

The good old Friar promised to send messengers to Romeo, bidding him to come secretly at night to the vault to rescue her on her awakening; and Juliet gladly took the phial and departed to her home, much comforted.

She now no longer refused to wed Count Paris; and when the bridal day arrived, she moved quite calmly amidst the throng of lordly guests. But she had not forgotten the old Friar's potion, which she had been careful to take just before the ceremony began. In spite of the natural horror she felt at the thought of awakening in the gloomy family vault, in which her recently-slain cousin Tybalt was already lying, she had bravely conquered her fears and nerved herself to the ordeal; and she had secretly swallowed the contents of the phial with the whispered words: " Romeo, Romeo, Romeo! I drink to thee! "

Consequently, her parents and their guests were horror-struck when, soon after the wedding ceremony had begun, the lovely bride fell to the ground apparently dead; and the revels ended in the greatest confusion and dismay.

Lord and Lady Capulet were overcome with grief by what they supposed to be the sudden death of their fair young daughter; and with heart-rending tears and cries of woe, the unconscious form of Juliet was laid to rest on a bier in the family vault.

Friar Laurence, after waiting to hear how his plot had succeeded, despatched a messenger to Mantua to inform Romeo of all that had happened and to bid him come secretly to rescue his bride on her awakening. Unhappily, however, before the good father's messenger arrived in Mantua, Romeo had already heard from another source the terrible news of Juliet's supposed death.

Thus knowing nothing of the old monk's plan and believing his beloved one to be actually dead, Romeo was distracted with grief. Determined, however, to look at least once more upon the sweet face of Juliet, even though in death, he instantly mounted a horse and rode at a furious pace to Verona.

He reached the city at midnight of the second day since Juliet had been reported dead; and making his way at once to the churchyard, he secured a torch and a mattock and began fiercely to break open the tomb of the Capulets. He was just about to enter the vault when he was interrupted by Count Paris, who had also come to weep beside the remains of his lost bride. ·Not recognizing his rival in the darkness, Romeo, frantic with grief and refusing to be delayed in his quest, drew his sword and rushed upon the intruder. The two fought furiously until at last Paris fell mortally wounded. Then, when Romeo took up the torch to look upon his fallen antagonist and recognized the features of Paris, he was filled with remorse, knowing that this noble youth had also loved the dead maiden; and he laid him tenderly within the vault. After this, he knelt, overcome with grief and despair, beside the bier of Juliet, to gaze once more upon her fair and lovely form.

Romeo had already determined not to live on without Juliet; and he had broken his journey once in order to procure from an apothecary some deadly poison which would act instantaneously. He now bent down to bid his beloved one farewell and to kiss her cold lips for the last time; then, drawing forth the phial, he swallowed the poison, saying: "Here's to my love! . . . Thus with a kiss I die!"

The poison took effect immediately; and, with a sigh, Romeo fell dead beside the bier of his bride.

It happened that this was the hour at which Juliet was to awaken from her trance; and she now opened her eyes and looked around in wondering horror. Then her roving gaze fell upon the dead body of her beloved Romeo; and from the empty phial in his hand, she at once gathered that he had poisoned himself upon believing her to be dead. In an agony of grief, she came down from the bier to clasp her lover's limp form in her arms; and at that moment, there came the sounds of approaching steps and voices. The disturbance at the tomb had by this time attracted the notice of the watch, who were now hastily bringing both Capulets and Montagues to the churchyard.

On hearing the approaching sounds, Juliet knew that she must act quickly; for she was resolved to live no longer now her lover was dead. As she clasped Romeo in her arms, she kissed him passionately, hoping to imbibe some of the poison from his lips. Then, finding this unavailing, she drew forth the dagger which he wore and with it stabbed herself to the heart with these last words: "O happy dagger! This is thy sheath; there rust, and let me die!"

The kinsfolk of the two unfortunate lovers now rushed into the vault; and as the bereaved parents wept together over the dead bodies of their beloved children and understood that this sad tragedy had entirely arisen from their own selfish family feud, they humbly joined hands in token of mutual forgiveness and renewed friendship.

THE JEWESS   *Halèvy*
(*La Juive*)

TOWARDS the end of the fourteenth century, the Count de Brogni, Chief Magistrate of Rome, issued an Edict banishing all Jews from the sacred city. The persecuted people, knowing too well that delay meant torture and death, were compelled to submit to their enforced exodus and to seek refuge in other lands.

Before all had departed, however, the Neapolitans made a sudden raid on the city; and during the absence of de Brogni, his splendid palace was sacked and burnt. When the Chief Magistrate returned, therefore, after driving the raiders from the city, he found his home destroyed; and he was further informed, to his horror, that his young wife and infant daughter had been left to perish in the flames.

This was not entirely the truth, however. Though the mother had indeed been burned, the babe had been rescued by a Jew, named Eleazar. The latter, having thus saved the child by a sudden impulse, immediately carried her away with him to share his own fortunes, rather than restore her to the hated enemy of his race.

De Brogni, frantic at the loss of his beloved ones, sought solace by joining the Church; and having attained to the rank of a Cardinal, he quickly rose to great eminence and power in the service of Sigismund, Emperor of the West.

Meanwhile, Eleazar the Jew had journeyed with many of his exiled brethren to the city of Constance; and settling there, he engaged in the occupation of a dealer in gems, soon becoming very wealthy. The babe he had rescued was given the name of Rachel; and she was brought up as his own daughter and in his own religion.

As time went on, Rachel grew up to be a very beautiful maiden; and as she had always been taught to regard Eleazar as her father, she rendered him due reverence and obedience as such and proved herself to be a loving and devoted daughter. So the years passed peacefully enough for Eleazar and Rachel; but at last a change came, and woe fell upon them.

One day, in the year 1414, the city of Constance put on gala dress and the people prepared to celebrate a solemn but joyful festival in honour of recent war victories gained by their young Prince, Leopold. The Emperor Sigismund himself was to make a triumphal entry into the city during the day; consequently, all work was ordered to be suspended and the citizens prepared to receive their august ruler with loyal acclaim.

First of all, a solemn thanksgiving service was held in the chief church of the city. The latter was situated in a great square, at one end of which stood the famous jewel shop and dwelling of Eleazar the Jew. Presently it was noticed that work was obviously in progress within the Jew's abode, contrary to the decree that the day was to be observed as a sacred festival; and people began to gather in angry groups before the gem shop, shouting indignantly for the work therein to be stopped instantly.

Eleazar, having scorned to recognize the Christian festival as applying to himself, had decided to carry on with his occupation as usual; and now hearing the menacing cries of the outraged populace, he appeared fearlessly at the door of his shop. He was accompanied by his daughter Rachel and a handsome young man whom he had recently taken into his service as an artist, though a complete stranger to him.

This stranger was actually none other than the victorious young Prince Leopold, disguised as a humble worker in gems. On a former visit to the city, the young prince had seen the jeweller's lovely daughter and had straightway fallen in love with her. Knowing, however, that he would never be permitted to wed a Jewess, he had resorted to deception in order to satisfy the longings of his heart and to enjoy intercourse with the object of his affections. For this purpose he had left the Court a few weeks before the Emperor's entry into Constance, announcing that he would rejoin the royal party when the festival day arrived; for great honours were to be showered upon him on that occasion. Then, disguised in the simple garb of an artist-worker, he journeyed to Constance and introduced himself to Eleazar as a Jew, taking the name of Samuel.

Eleazar very willingly took the young man into his service because of the latter's natural artistic ability; and he accommodated him in his own home. Here the disguised prince quickly won the affections of Rachel and became her secret lover. Still realizing that he could never marry the beautiful Jewess, he persuaded her to keep their love for a while from the knowledge of Eleazar; for he could not bear the thought of parting from her so soon.

As the three now appeared at the shop door, the pretended Samuel quietly withdrew into the background, not wishing to be recognized; but the indignant mob roughly dragged Eleazar and his daughter outside, declaring they deserved to die by torture for their sacrilege of a solemn Festival Day. Despite Rachel's piteous plea for mercy, she and her father might have been quickly overcome had not an interruption occurred by the entry into the square of the powerful Catholic dignitary, Cardinal de Brogni, then passing on his way to welcome the Emperor.

On learning the cause of the disturbance, he gave orders for the persecuted pair to be released. He recognized Eleazar as one of the prominent Jews he had known in Rome; but he was quite unconscious of the fact that the beautiful Rachel was in reality his own daughter, whose loss he had never ceased to mourn. Compelled to obey the command of the all-powerful Cardinal, the crowd drew back sullenly, and Eleazar and Rachel returned in safety to their own home.

That evening a number of Hebrews met at the house of Eleazar to celebrate the solemn service of the Jewish Feast of the Passover; and just as the ceremony ended a loud clamour was heard at the entrance. Upon the door being opened, guards and attendants in the royal livery were seen without, escorting a richly-dressed lady, who entered the house alone and introduced herself as the Princess Eudoxia, niece of the Emperor. As she entered, Leopold hastily retired into the background and kept himself concealed from view; for he was affianced to this same fair princess and knew that ruin awaited him should he be discovered by her in this Jewish household.

The Princess stated that she had come to purchase from the gem-maker a handsome jewelled chain, which she wished to present to her betrothed, Prince Leopold, when the latter appeared at her uncle's Court on the morrow. Having chosen the most magnificent ornament of the kind which Eleazar had to offer, she bade him bring it to the palace next day; and then she withdrew with her escort.

The Jewish brethren having also by this time all departed, the pretended Samuel and Rachel found themselves alone. Observing her lover's pale face and agitated looks, the beautiful Jewess entreated him to tell her the reason for this. Then the young Prince, having been awakened by Eudoxia's visit to a sense of the wrong he was doing Rachel by thus seeking to win her love by deception, now remorsefully confessed that he was a Christian, though still not revealing his true rank.

Rachel, overcome with grief at this revelation, reproached him bitterly for having thus led her into the moral crime of having loved and sacrificed her honour to a Christian. However, when her father at that moment entered the room and, learning also of the stranger's deception, was about to stab the young man in his righteous wrath, her mood instantly changed. Flinging herself upon her knees between them, she implored Eleazar to have pity on them both and to permit them to marry.

"My father! Be not angry, but grant my wish!" she cried passionately. "I love Samuel, and he is all the world to me!"

Eleazar, who loved his adopted daughter with great tenderness, gently raised her from the ground; and in tones from which the anger had now vanished, he said that he would consent to the marriage, since her happiness depended upon it. But Leopold, knowing that he, a royal prince, could never enter into such a marriage, now felt himself compelled to repudiate the bride offered to him, madly though he still loved her. Declaring wildly that he, a Christian, could never wed with a Jewess, he rushed hastily from the house, despising himself for his own base conduct and followed by the furious curses of Eleazar.

Next day, the Jew and his daughter made their way to the royal palace, taking with them the splendid jewelled chain which the Princess Eudoxia had purchased the evening before. Here the Court was assembled with great magnificence; and Prince Leopold, seated on a throne beside his betrothed, was already receiving the congratulations and praises of the courtiers upon his success in the recent war.

When Rachel beheld the young Prince seated upon the throne, she at once recognized him as her false lover, Samuel, despite his now resplendent attire; and she determined to be avenged upon him for his cruel treatment of her. As the Princess Eudoxia was about to present her gift, the lovely Jewess sprang forward and snatched the chain away, passionately denouncing Leopold before the whole company as one who had committed the sacrilegious crime of having been the lover of a Jewess.

"I, Rachel, am the maiden he has sacrificed to his unlawful passion!" she cried in a voice that trembled with emotion. "And since I, too, have shared in his guilt, I am prepared to suffer for my sin!"

Upon hearing Rachel's denunciation, a wave of horror swept over the whole assemblage. The deed of which she accused the young Prince was regarded at that period as an unforgivable crime and was punishable by death; and as Leopold did not attempt to deny the accusation but bent his head in acknowledgment of guilt, all the company knew that he had indeed committed this act of sacrilege against his religion.

The Cardinal de Brogni, who was also present, now rose in indignation that such an outrage had been offered to the Christian Church; and he declared that, in accordance with the existing law, Leopold and Rachel must both suffer death for their crime, and that Eleazar should also share their fate as an accomplice. The condemned trio were then led away to prison, followed by the curses of the whole Court.

The Princess Eudoxia was overwhelmed with grief at this terrible frustration of her dearest hopes. In spite of Leopold's faithlessness, however, she still passionately loved him; and she determined, therefore, to make an effort to save him from death.

Having obtained permission to visit Rachel in prison, she besought her to save Leopold's life by declaring to the judges that he was not guilty of the crime of which she had accused him. Rachel, however, at first refused to help one who had so basely betrayed and repudiated her: but when Eudoxia fell on her knees and passionately pleaded with her again and again to save the man they both so dearly loved, she relented, unable to struggle longer against the promptings of her own heart, in which her false lover's image was for ever enshrined. She therefore promised Eudoxia to obey her wish.

Consequently, when brought before the judges later on, the devoted young Jewess boldly declared to them that Leopold was not guilty of the crime she had attributed to him, and that, in her mad jealousy, she had wrongfully accused him. The Cardinal de Brogni, rejoicing at this welcome news, now declared Leopold to be innocent and gave orders for his instant release; but Eleazar and Rachel, being now accused of having fabricated the whole story to entrap the royal Prince, were condemned for such high treason to the terrible death of being flung into a cauldron of boiling oil.

The Cardinal, however, feeling pity for the dreadful fate about to fall upon the lovely Jewish maiden, gave Eleazar the opportunity of saving his daughter by abjuring his faith and becoming a Christian. This suggestion, however, the staunch Jew scornfully repudiated, declaring that he preferred to die in his own faith rather than live to join the ranks of the Christians whom he hated. Then, having suddenly bethought him of a means of avenging himself upon one who had condemned him to so horrible a death, he revealed the story of how the Cardinal's infant daughter had been rescued from his burning palace years ago. He added that the maiden and her preserver were still living; and the Cardinal, who had never ceased to mourn for his lost child, now implored him to say where she was to be found, that he might cherish her once again.

But Eleazar refused to reveal the secret, having determined not to give De Brogni this information until Rachel was dead, that he might thus bring everlasting grief upon him for having condemned his own child to such an agonizing death; and though the proud Cardinal even humbled himself by kneeling in supplication before the Jew he despised, the longing of his heart remained unsatisfied.

However, when the day of execution arrived and the victims were brought out to meet their fate, the old Jew's resolution broke down as he and Rachel were left together for a few moments near the scaffold from which they were to be flung into the boiling oil. Now feeling horror at the thought of thus sacrificing the beautiful maiden he had loved as his own daughter to satisfy his private vengeance, he besought her with all his heart to become a Christian and so save herself from the awful death that awaited her.

But Rachel declared steadfastly that she would never renounce the faith in which she had been brought up and which she had learnt to love. Thus firmly resolved to wear the martyr's crown, she heroically sprang upon the scaffold and leapt into the seething cauldron with a cry of exultation.

Eleazar's moment of vengeance had now arrived, although he had sought to avert it. As his beloved Rachel vanished from sight and he sprang on the scaffold to follow her, he turned to de Brogni and cried in a frenzied voice in which triumph and anguish struggled for mastery: " Behold your daughter, proud Cardinal, now lost to you for ever! "

TRILOGY: THE CAULDRON OF ANNWN   *Holbrooke*
(*Part I. The Children of Don*)

THE myths of ancient prehistoric Britain teem with wonder stories of might and magic, when the gods were said to walk the earth as radiant beings ruling the forces of Nature and sub-duing Man to their own ends—yet ever and anon wedding with the daughters of Man and begetting half-divine heroes who, in their turn, subdued their fellows and gained great glory by performing mighty deeds of valour.

At last, however, Man began to war against the worship and power of the ancient gods. Religious evolution slowly but surely advanced with the years; and the old gods became discredited as Man began to drag from them and their cruel priesthood the knowledge they had so jealously kept from him.

About this time there arose among the people of ancient Britain a brave and half-divine hero, Gwydion, the Son of Don—the Earth Goddess or Goddess of Nature—who realized that knowledge was power and determined to wrest that power from the gods. He knew also that the source of a mighty power lay in a certain Cauldron possessed by Caridwen, the Goddess of Passion, who brewed in this vessel a magic liquid which caused all who inhaled its fumes to become the slaves of their dominant instincts —whether love, ambition, hate, revenge, avarice, or any other passion, they immediately became obsessed by the same to the exclusion of all other feelings. Every now and again there bubbled to the top of the Cauldron three drops of Wisdom; but all the rest was the deadly poison of passion.

Despite the fact that this Cauldron was set in the gloomy cavernous depths of Annwn, the Northern Underworld, where it was constantly served by the savage magic-working priesthood there, Gwydion determined to fetch it away to his own land. By possessing the Cauldron of Annwn, he believed that Man would be armed with its powers against the terrible gods of the ancient dynasty who now enslaved him. Therefore Gwydion, the dauntless hero, nobly sought thus to free the human soul to seek the Light of Knowledge; and he set forth bravely upon his mighty enterprise.

. . . .

In the great cavern Temple of the frozen Underworld of the North stood the seething Cauldron of Annwn upon the sacrificial altar-stone; and the priests prepared the human sacrifice they were about to offer up to their gods. A fair young virgin was dragged forth and bound upon the altar; and Arawn, King of Annwn, the Underworld, took up the sacrificial knife in readiness to strike the fatal blow.

But the blow did not fall. Gwydion, the Son of Don, stood suddenly within the entrance, announcing his title and declaring boldly that he had come to fetch away the magic Cauldron.

Furious that this audacious but god-like youth should thus dare to defy him, Arawn called upon the priests to seize the intruder and bind him likewise upon the sacrificial stone. But Gwydion, with grim fearlessness, fought his way through the angry priests and rushed upon Arawn with his long spear, soon stretching him dead at his feet. He then boldly seized the magic vessel and bore it away in triumph.

. . . .

Amidst the forest depths of Arvon, a procession of Druids conducted the magic Cauldron brought by Gwydion to their oak-shadowed temple. They were headed by Math Mathonwy, the Priest-King of Arvon, with whom walked Gwion, his chief Druid, a zealous but cruel and self-ambitious priest.

Gwydion watched them pass by into the Temple with a darkening brow and with disappointment and anger in his heart; for he already saw that his mighty deed of valour had been almost in vain. True, he had wrested the Cauldron from the Powers of Darkness; but now that the Druid priests had seized upon it, he knew they would use it only for their own power and glory and would still keep the mass of the people in ignorance and in abject submission to themselves. Where, then, was the freedom of knowledge which he had sought to bring for all?

Math—who was the mortal brother of the goddess Don—regarded Gwydion almost as a son; and he had named him as his heir to rule after his own death, even though he did not approve of the young hero's independent spirit. Because of the latter, he had always demanded his nephew's absolute submission to his own druidical authority. On his return now from the Temple, therefore, observing from Gwydion's dark looks that he was already rebellious, he boldly appointed him as the Guardian of the Cauldron and commanded him to refuse admittance to the sacred precincts to all save the Druids and the vestal virgins who attended on them—cunningly aware that the young man would not leave the terrible vessel unguarded but would be loyal to his charge.

Left alone to guard the Temple—practically a prisoner, since he dared not leave the Cauldron with its teeming evils to be meddled with by chance prying intruders—Gwydion fretted and pined. He now realized that he had been tricked by his crafty uncle, who had eagerly encouraged him on his adventurous quest in the hope of eventually securing the magic vessel for his own all-powerful priesthood. Presently, however, his gloomy thoughts were interrupted. As he strode away from the outer groves into the farthest recesses of the Temple to see that all was safe, his younger brother, Govannion, drew near. The latter was also angry and defiant for a more personal reason. Goewin, the beautiful maiden he loved and was betrothed to, had been compelled by Math against her will to serve in the Temple as a vestal virgin, instead of becoming his, Govannion's, bride.

Even as he muttered out his woe, Goewin came forth from her appointed place of service in the Temple to meet her lover; and the fatal fumes of the Cauldron having already intensified their love beyond control, they now clung to one another in a passionate embrace. Heedless of this violation of the sacred precincts, Govannion implored his beloved one to escape with him. While the latter hesitated to break her vestal vows, Govannion's sister, Elan, joined them and added her persuasions to those of her brother. Elan herself had conceived a violent love for her elder brother Gwydion, whom she had now come to seek. It had been foretold by the priests that she should bear a wonderful hero-son who would perform mighty deeds for their race; and she longed for Gwydion to be his hero father.

While the three thus spoke together, Gwydion returned from making his rounds as guard and sternly reproached them for thus desecrating the Temple with talk of their human passions.

Angrily Govannion hurled complaints at his brother for having caused their misery by his rape of the Cauldron—to serve which Goewin had been forced to dedicate herself as a vestal virgin—declaring that he had done an ill turn to their race by this useless deed; but Goewin and Elan only pleaded for his goodwill towards them.

At first Gwydion, in loyalty to the charge laid upon him by Math, would have retained his brother and sister for dire punishment as intruders and have bidden Goewin await her doom as an apostate; but quickly realizing that they could not resist the fatal fumes of the magic Cauldron which were already working within them, he decided to take their part. He therefore permitted the lovers to depart.

Elan, overwhelmed by her own passion, now entreated Gwydion to accept her love, reminding him once more of the prophecy regarding the hero-son to be born to her. But Gwydion bravely resisted her tempting pleas—his dominant passion for the general uplifting of man having been intensified by the Cauldron's fumes to the exclusion of all other human passions. Consequently, he gently but firmly commanded the passion-torn maiden to leave him; and when Elan, sorrowful and heart-broken by his refusal of her overwhelming love, had departed, he returned to the Temple to renew his vows of consecration.

.   .   .   .

Although Goewin had willingly given herself to Govannion with a great love that would not be denied, she could not forget the sacred office to which she had been appointed nor the powers of the Druidical priests. After a while she evaded her trysts with her lover and crept back to the forest Temple, full of remorse for the breaking of her vows as a vestal virgin and fearful of the consequences.

While she stood there, stretching out her arms in supplication towards the dread Cauldron and bemoaning that she was no longer fit to tend its ever-burning fires, Govannion entered, having tracked her thither after seeking her in all their trysting-places. Infuriated by her desertion, he poured forth reproaches upon her for thus denying the gift of love; but Goewin, torn between love and remorse for her lost innocence, was now afraid of her lover and would not respond to his pleadings.

As the sound of their voices reached him, Gwydion came out from the inner part of the Temple and again admonished them for desecrating the sacred grove with their earthly love; but once more he broke his own trust by giving them permission to depart, instead of holding them as captives to be punished. But both

Govannion and Goewin now turned upon him in anger for having brought the magic Cauldron thither to add to their woes; and while they thus wrangled together, their opportunity for escape was lost. At that moment, the Priest-King, Math, with Gwion and the other Druids, entered the Temple.

When Math sternly demanded why they stood there disputing instead of performing their appointed offices, Goewin now confessed that she was no longer fitted to serve as a vestal virgin— that Govannion had been her lover, and that Gwydion had permitted her to leave the Temple for her unlawful trysts. She then pleaded for mercy; but, in contempt, Math pronounced sentence of banishment upon her, commanding her to dwell in the woods alone, there to atone for her sin as an outcast.

As the unhappy Goewin went forth sorrowfully with bowed head, the furious priests now pronounced a terrible doom upon Gwydion for having failed in his trust as guardian of the Temple and precious Cauldron. They declared that such sin was too great for mercy; and they cruelly decreed that he should be cast from manhood and take on the form of a ravening wolf, together with the erring brother he had shielded. It was now dusk; and the brothers were quickly bound to the sacrificial stone to await full darkness, when their dreadful transformation would take place.

When the priests had withdrawn to work their magic spells, the fair Elan crept into the sanctuary and, eager to save the man she loved, would have cut the thongs that bound Gwydion; but the young hero, knowing that he could not escape his doom, even though freed from the sacrificial stone, would not permit her to do so. Instead, he bade her to fill a horn with magic liquid from the Cauldron, which she did in fear and trembling; and they drank of it together.

Almost immediately after, the voice of the great Sea-god, Lyd, was heard in the distance, uttering a spell by means of a yearning song of love; and Elan started up in great agitation. Mad with the poison of the gods and drawn irresistibly by the lure of the passionate song of the Sea-King, she forgot her love for Gwydion and rushed out of the Temple to meet the sea lover who thus enticed her.

Meanwhile, the magic spell of the Druids was consummated. As final darkness descended, wild red eyes suddenly gleamed amidst the forest trees; and, presently, two grey forms left the sacrificial stone and slunk forth into the open to mingle with the howling wolf pack outside.

.   .   .   .

Three years later the wolf pack again haunted that part of the forest where the Temple stood amidst the sacred groves of oaks; and among these savage wolves were Gwydion and Govannion. The presence of the wolves terrified the outcast Goewin, who was still living alone in the woods; but when she rushed into the Temple one day to beg for protection, she was cruelly driven forth once more by the fierce Druid Gwion. Almost immediately afterwards an agonized cry was heard, as Govannion, in his savage wolf form, set upon Goewin and devoured her.

Math, coming into the Temple also at this moment, reproached the vindictive Druid for his wanton cruelty, declaring that he himself had but banished the fallen vestal that she might repent of her sin in solitude. Then, though too late to save the unfortunate Goewin, he announced his intention of restoring Gwydion and his brother to their human forms once more. He needed the help of the hero-youth Gwydion, since his own powers were waning. Despite the angry remonstrances of Gwion—always jealous of the favoured Gwydion—Math summoned the wolf pack and, by means of his magic rites, bade Gwydion and Govannion step forth in their human forms.

As the spell thus fell from them, the Sons of Don appeared as men once more. Govannion slunk away among the trees; but Gwydion boldly faced the Priest-King, who now informed him that he must further atone for his sacrilege by finding another vestal maiden to take the place of the lost Goewin.

Gwydion at once remembered the beauty and purity of his own sister Elan, the fair daughter of Don, and suggested her for the sacred office; and he and Math at once set forth to seek her out and test her as a vestal.

.   .   .   .

Elan sat upon the rocks of a lonely sea-shore, wondering what would become of her little son, offspring of the Sea-King whose love-song had lured her to motherhood and who had since deserted her. Her sad thoughts were interrupted by Govannion who, having overheard the conversation between his brother and Math, had come to inform her that Gwydion had suggested her as a vestal virgin despite his knowledge of her former love for him. Elan, however, though she still loved Gwydion, declared herself willing to do anything to please the latter; and Govannion, who had hoped to bring about her refusal and thus to thwart the brother he still blamed for bringing woe upon him, now sulkily concealed himself near by to watch what befell.

Gwydion and Math now appeared; and Elan greeted her beloved one with great joy, telling him she was willing to accept the sacred office for which he had nominated her—thinking to please him thereby even though he could then never accept her love. She was soon filled with fear, however, when Math, not to be deceived by her apparent submission but determined to make sure of her virginity, drew with his staff a line upon the ground and bade her to overstep it as the sign he required—declaring this to be a magic line that could read the secrets of the heart.

Elan bravely made the attempt to pass the test; but the magic line, discerning her secret, seemed as a strong wall that barred her progress, so that she recoiled, mysteriously unable to cross it. At the same moment, a small boy—a beautiful fair-haired child, Dylan, son of the Sea-King—sprang up suddenly beside her; and with a cry of despair, Elan clasped her little one in her arms and sank to the ground with him, her shame revealed. In answer to Gwydion's amazed questions she reminded him of the night of his own wolf-transformation, when the magical song of the Sea-King had lured her forth from the Temple to meet the amorous God of the Waves.

Math, believing Gwydion to be the father of the child, called down curses upon him and upon all the children of Don, prophesying that they should never reign as kings in the land but that the Sons of the Sea should rule in their stead.

Gwydion, furious at this false accusation and determined to make a last desperate and supreme effort to save Man from the power of the Druids, now called upon Nodens—the oldest and most benevolent of the ancient gods of Britain—to befriend him; then he hurled himself upon Math and struck him a mortal blow with his spear.

As Gwydion, instantly remorseful, bent over the dying King and implored his forgiveness, Govannion crept silently towards the group and, snatching the little boy from Elan's arms, ran with him to the edge of the rocks and flung him into the sea. Then he returned and dragged the dazed and fainting Elan away with him.

This murderous deed, however, was frustrated. When Math had drawn his last breath, Gwydion promptly broke the dead King's magic wand, determined that the rule of magic should now cease in the land. Then again he called upon the god Nodens to help him in his hour of need.

In answer to his prayer, the fair child, Dylon, son of Elan and the Sea-King, presently clambered back from the foaming waters on to the rocks once more, safe and unhurt. At the same time there was heard a surging Song from the Waves proclaiming that they could not drown their Ruler's offspring—little Dylan, Son of the Wave, whom they would always love.

Gwydion now realized that Dylan was the Son of the Sea whom the dying Math had prophesied should be the founder of the new line of rulers in Britain. When Govannion presently returned, therefore, he took the child by the hand and announced to his brother that Dylan was his heir and the future King of their race. Govannion, however, was furious that he himself would thus be disinherited; and he passionately declared that he would fight his brother for his rights.

While this struggle was in progress, the Druids arrived on the scene, enraged by the death of their leader. The fierce Gwion, eager to be the latter's successor, vainly attempted to work the beast transformation spell once more upon the brothers; but he shrank back, cowed, when Gwydion triumphantly announced that he had broken the wand of Math and had thus destroyed the priestly powers of magic for ever.

Gwydion now commanded Govannion—whom he had overcome in their recent struggle but had generously refrained from slaying—to avenge himself upon the cruel Druid who, he now revealed, had driven forth the unhappy Goewin to be devoured by himself in wolf-form; and his horrified brother instantly hurled himself upon Gwion and slew him.

The other Druids, stunned by the slaying of their two leaders, made no further attempt at resistance, but shrank from the Children of Don in awe; and Gwydion held up the fair child Dylan and proclaimed that in him rested the fulfilment of every bright dream for the welfare of his race.

TRILOGY: THE CAULDRON OF ANNWN *Holbrooke*
(*Part II. Dylan, Son of the Wave*)

WHEN Dylan—son of Lyd the Sea-god and Elan, the beautiful daughter of Don the Goddess of Nature—was carried off by Gwydion to be his heir to the kingship of Britain, there was moaning and regret for his loss among the elements and spirits who were the subjects of Lyd. The Winds and the Waves never ceased to sing of the fair child thus torn from their embrace; and they called upon him, wherever he might be, to remember them always. " Dylan, Dylan, brother of the Waves, forget us not! "

was ever their cry. The Wildfowl, too, as they swept from the seas over the land in their strong swift course as lords of the air, ever sought to keep watch over the Sea-King's son and to bring news of him to those from whom he had been snatched and who still hoped that he would at last return to them.

But Dylan, though he never forgot the silvery realms and subjects of the Sea-King as the years went by and he grew up towards a beautiful manhood, was doomed never to return alive to the embrace of the ocean he loved so well.

.   .   .   .

In an orchard at eventide beside the walls of the Castle of Gwyddno, King of Ceredigion, sat Elan, the beautiful daughter of Don, still fair and desirable despite the years of sadness that had gone by. A few yards away sat Seithenin, the Keeper of the Dykes, with his harp, ready for a song. Gwyddno, who stood near by, bade him sing of mighty deeds and victories, because Gwydion, the hero High King of Britain, was to be their guest that night and was even now approaching with his hosts of conquering warriors.

Seithenin, however, who loved ease and the softer pleasures of life, declared that he would rather sing of the fairness of Elan, whose beauty was as the splendour of the moon; but Elan bade him not to sing of her, since she had known too much sorrow to be a theme for revelry. Seithenin, somewhat offended, withdrew into the castle, declaring that later on he would match himself with Dylan, the strange youthful bard now approaching with the hosts of Britain's King. Gwyddno then entreated Elan not to lament for ever because of her past griefs, but to rule with him and let him share her sorrows.

In reply Elan again shook her head sadly, declaring that there was no peace for her; and she warned Gwyddno to shrink from the children of Don, to whom he was about to give hospitality that night—for they had been touched by the black magic of Annwn, having breathed the fumes of the Cauldron of Caridwen, Goddess of Passion, which had been brought from that mysterious Underworld.

Even as she spoke, Govannion, her brother and Gwydion's, appeared on the path above and called forth a greeting to the King of Ceredigion, announcing himself as the herald of the gathered hosts outside sent in advance to know whether hospitality was to be offered them, or battle.

Gwyddno gave welcome to this haughty herald, and went forth at once to greet the mighty King without his gates.

Govannion then approached Elan, whom he had not seen since

the terrible day when he had flung her baby son into the sea and had dragged her forth to dwell alone in a secret bower after the slaying of Math Mathonwy by Gwydion. He now sternly demanded what she did in that place, insinuating that she had probably had many lovers since last they met. To this Elan replied that Gwydion, their brother, had bidden her meet him there; and she declared that, so far from comforting herself with new lovers, her heart had grieved constantly for the fair little son whom she still believed had been drowned when flung into the sea by Govannion. She had never been told that the Waves who loved him could not drown him, nor that Gwydion had taken him to be his heir.

Govannion, in whom the magic Cauldron had intensified the passion of jealousy, now gloomily declared that though coupled to Gwydion for life, yet hatred had been his mate throughout the years. While he and his sister still spoke together, the young Dylan presently appeared on the path above and drew near to the pair.

Fair and lovely was this royal youth, with his golden curls blowing in the breeze; and so fearlessly innocent and dreamy was the gaze of his deep blue eyes that they seemed to see far-off wonders and beauties hidden from the sight of ordinary mortals. Elan looked upon him with awe-struck admiration; and though she knew not that he was her own son, she felt strangely drawn towards him. There even came a clutching at her heart as the image of her Sea-King lover suddenly passed before her inner vision. When she asked her brother who the strange youth was, Govannion replied evasively that he was but a foolish bard and Gwydion's "love-child"; and turning to the young man, he asked him dourly if the feast was not marred that had not heard him.

Dylan, in a voice musical, sad, and mysterious as the softly rippling waves of summer seas, replied that he had indeed sung at feasts but that he loved better to sing to the wind-haunted forest, or to the silvery ocean his soul yearned for. He added that he was even now bound for the rocky shores where nature held her sway. Then, bidding Govannion tell those who inquired for him that he had cast off for ever the bondage they would hold him in and had gone to seek the freedom of nature he loved so well, he departed by the path that led to the sea-shore.

When he had gone, Elan cried out as though in pain, and implored her brother to follow the glorious youth and bring him back that she might speak with him. Govannion, though at first declining loftily to act as her messenger, was so fired by his own jealousy of Dylan and hatred for his brother that, realizing this to be his opportunity for ridding himself for ever of his supplanter as the latter's heir, he agreed to go in pursuit of him. He therefore set forth at once to follow him, intending to slay him.

While Elan still sat awaiting their return with eagerness, though filled with a strange presentiment of coming evil, Gwydion suddenly appeared before her. Surprised to find her alone, having himself sent Dylan into her presence—remorseful for having kept the mother and son apart so long—he asked anxiously whither Dylan had gone and why she had not kept him with her.

After greeting her beloved brother—whom she had once also desired as a lover—Elan replied that the stranger youth had gone forth to commune with nature in the gathering twilight. She added that the fair youth had a resemblance to her own lost Sea-King lover and that a strangely happy contentment had settled upon her in his presence; whereupon Gwydion replied that this was not strange, since he was her own son.

Then, as Elan uttered a cry of mingled amazement and joy on thus learning that her beloved son still lived, Gwydion revealed to her how the child had returned from the friendly Waves and how he had brought him up as his heir. He added regretfully that the hopes he had built up of him to reign as a mighty conquering king had been in vain; for Dylan had no desire for the pomps of kingship, but loved only to sing the poetry he made and to commune with nature. He had determined, therefore, to return him to his mother, though his heart was full of heaviness at losing him, for he loved him dearly.

When Elan now announced that at her request Govannion had followed Dylan to bring him back, Gwydion called out with a cry of agonized despair that she had sent death after her son in the form of Govannion, "the black hawk of the race", whose jealousy of the bright youth would certainly now cause him to take this opportunity of satisfying his jealous vengeance. Elan, full of woe at having thus found and lost her son in a few brief moments, begged him to seek some means of saving Dylan from his vengeful uncle. Gwydion, resigned to the inevitable, declared that nothing could save the youth, since the poison of the magic Cauldron was at its fell work once more; but he called out wildly to the Spirits of the Sea to speed their beloved Dylan to the waiting Waves, which alone might shield him from the jealous hate that followed to destroy him.

.   .   .   .

Meanwhile, Dylan, fair Son of the Seas, sped with eager steps along the cliffs and down the winding path that led to the wild rocky shore, glorying in his freedom and comparing the violet beauty of the quickly-gathering night with the torch-lit garishness of the feasting-hall. He called eagerly upon the gleaming silvery Waves to receive him, their beloved brother, who now returned to them like a glad lover to his secret love.

After him hastened Black Govannion, with hatred and jealousy in his heart and his spear held in his hand ready to strike the fatal blow. So far from bringing this sunny-haired, enchantment-born child of the kingly race back to the mother who longed for him, he now vowed to give reign to his still wolfish heart which called out so passionately and insistently for the blood of the god-like youth who stood between him and the power for which he craved. In silence and with snakelike movements, he crept after his unwitting prey, hovering above him with the sinister patience of the waiting hawk.

As he stood on the last high rock that led down to the sea, Dylan, with his pale gleaming hair streaming behind him in the gentle breeze, stretched out his arms and sang a happy yearning greeting towards the billowy ocean whose white-crested yielding breast he was now about to clasp in an everlasting embrace. But, even as the glorious son of the Sea-King sang out a poetic hymn of praise for the simple joys he loved, Black Govannion reached him with a sudden swift step and furiously drove his cruel spear into his back.

As Govannion strode away with his bloody spear, Dylan uttered a last murmur of farewell to the beautiful things of nature he had loved so well. Then, with a prayer of entreaty to the Sea-Folk and the Waves not to think of him as faithless because he could never now return to them, he fell back upon the rocks and drew his last breath.

During this time the air had become full of the sound of Sea-Birds in flight; and as the beautiful son of the Sea-King expired, thousands of Wildfowl hovered over him for a short time, crooning a sad and tender dirge. Then they rose into the air once more, spreading their powerful wings and stretching forth their long necks, and flew in a mighty array like a feathery fast-moving cloud into the midst of the ocean to bring the mournful tidings to the Sea-Folk, singing as they went: "Dead is Dylan! Dead is Dylan!"

In the haunts of the Sea-King, the Winds and the Waves and the Sea-Folk were still awaiting the return of Dylan, the well-beloved child they had once played with; and they sighed and longed to see him once more. The Sea-King himself also joined in their sighs and longings; for Dylan, the babe of his shore-snatched love, had been the pride and joy of his ocean realms.

As these sighs of yearning arose, the sound of flapping wings was heard, and the Wildfowl appeared as a cloud in the sky above. In answer to the Sea-Folk's call, " Where is Dylan? " the Wildfowl cried out in mournful shrieks, " Dead is Dylan! Dead is Dylan! "

Then as the wailing cries of the Winds and the Waves and the Sea-Folk rent the air, the Wildfowl related how they had seen the murderous blow struck. They had tracked Black Govannion —who thought that none had witnessed his fell deed—to his lair in the sea-girt Castle of Gwyddno, King of Ceredigion, where he now felt himself to be safe from justice.

Full of grief and a terrible wrath, the Sea-King arose and vowed vengeance upon the slayer of his son. He called up the Winds and the Lightning and Thunder, and all the elements in which he held mighty sway, commanding them to beat ruthlessly upon the rock-bound Castle of Gwyddno; and then, upon the seething boiling breast of a terrific and awe-inspiring Tempest, he rode in foaming rage to the shore.

. . . .

In the tower keep of the Castle of Gwyddno, Black Govannion and the Keeper of the Dykes sat carousing. Seithenin called repeatedly upon the gloomy guest to drink deeply; and he sang loudly to drown the noise of the fearful Tempest that raged outside and to smother the roar of the mighty Waves that beat upon the rocks and shook the foundations of the castle.

But Govannion would not sing; for the warring elements without struck terror into his guilty soul. It seemed to him that the crashing of the Thunder, the trembling of the earth, and the dashing against the castle walls of the ever-rising Waves were calling upon him in vengeance. Never before had such mighty seas beaten upon that rock-girt stronghold; and as he listened to their fearful raging, he now heard—first faintly in the distance and then loudly overhead—the wild screaming of the Sea-Birds, " Dead is Dylan! Dead is Dylan! " Thus he knew that his crime had been discovered.

As the drink-besotted Seithenin laid his head upon the table at last, Elan and Gwydion entered the room, Elan demanding the whereabouts of her son. When Govannion announced triumphantly that Dylan had gone where he would not return, she accused him of having murdered the youth; and he admitted the crime with fiendish satisfaction.

Full of grief and wrath, Gwydion seized his spear and prepared to do battle with his brother; but at that moment part of the wall gave way, the Waves began to dash into the room, and the Sea-King's voice was heard urging on his subject elements to their work of destruction. Another great volume of water rushed into the room, and Seithenin, attempting unsteadily to escape, was caught by it and overwhelmed; but Govannion, with stealthy tread, slunk away and hastened up to the battlements.

Gwydion would have followed to slay his brother, but Elan held him back, entreating that he and she might die together; and, hand-in-hand, they moved towards the breach in the wall and were enveloped by the Waves. But the Sea-King still sought the murderer of his fair son, and called upon the Waves to mount yet higher to the battlements where Govannion and Gwyddno stood. Black Govannion, seeing that there was now no escape for him, flung himself into the advancing sea; and then the Sea-King commanded the Waves to retire. He announced to Gwyddno that his race should be the inheritors of the state and glory that should have been Dylan's, of whom it was foretold that he should be reborn many times.

Then, as the Sea-King retired and the Tempest abated, the song of the Wildfowl was heard again in the distance, now singing a song of triumph in praise of their Lord of the Ocean.

TRILOGY: THE CAULDRON OF ANNWN *Holbrooke* (*Part III. Bronwen*)

IN this story, the third portion of the trilogy of " The Cauldron of Annwn ", the main characters of the two previous sections, " The Children of Don " and " Dylan, Son of the Wave " appear again, reincarnate in a different relation. They have been reborn for the fulfilment of their destiny and the working out of the terrible influence of the Magic Cauldron's deadly fumes which they had once inhaled, whose poison, intensifying their own predominant passions, they are doomed to exhale until it has run its course. Bronwen again endures the sorrows of Elan; Caradoc continues the religious and patriotic devotion and austerity of Gwydion, still sacrificing his love to his passion for his country; Evnissyen once more gives unbridled rein to Govannion's boundless ambition and wild jealousy, leading him, as before, to the murder of the innocent; and Bran, Taliessin, Cormac, and Gwern are respectively reincarnations of Math, Gwion, Arawn, and Dylan.

At the Rock of Harlech, in the early morning, Taliessin, the Druid-Bard and Avoucher of Britain, stood looking out to sea, awaiting great news from the Council of Princes then assembled. For the hand of Bronwen, the beautiful sister Queen of Bran, King of Britain, was sought by Matholoc, High King of Ireland; and this high matter of State was under discussion of the council, while Matholoc with his subject Kings of Ireland and his chieftains awaited their decision.

Hot from the Council came Caradoc, the splendid son of Bran. Caradoc was the Avenger of Britain and the guardian of the dread Cauldron of Annwn. In answer to the eager question of Taliessin he announced that the Princes had decided that it was expedient for Britain to be united to Ireland by marriage, so that the constant warfare between the two countries might thus cease and that there might be a lasting peace. But there was sadness in the heart of Caradoc as he gave this news; for he loved Bronwen with a great love which he knew was returned by her. It was hard that what was good for the welfare of their beloved country should bring such woe to them both.

Despite his devotion to Britain, Caradoc could not refrain from railing at the sacrifice he was thus called upon to make; but Taliessin reproved him sternly, bidding him think only of his duty. He also reminded him that if Bronwen did not become Ireland's queen, she might be required as an alternative to bestow her hand upon Evnissyen, the King's brother, who also loved her. According to the Pictish law, which permitted female descent, Bronwen's children would succeed to the Kingdom of Britain; and failing them, Evnissyen, as the King's younger brother, would be the next heir, all these being nearer the throne than the King's own son.

Evnissyen was a man in whom the passion of ambition ruled his every action, and in whose heart burned constant jealousy and a black hatred of all who stood in the path of his own advancement. Hence his great desire to wed with Bronwen, that he might thereby ensure his own wielding of the power he craved and the succession to the throne of Britain of his sons by her.

Caradoc, who knew the selfish ambitions of Evnissyen, groaned as he declared that any fate would be better for his beloved Bronwen than her marriage with his uncle. Better far that she should accept Matholoc and leave their shores for those of Ireland.

As he spoke thus with the Druid-Bard, Bronwen herself joined them to ask how her fate had been decided, proudly protesting that she should be the subject of such negotiations. Caradoc gently reminded her that she would not be forced into such a union against her will, but that as a queen she had freedom of choice in the matter. Eager for the welfare of Britain, and suppressing his own deep love for her, he then endeavoured to persuade her to accept the suit of the powerful Matholoc, whom he declared to be the noblest of all the mighty princes who had sought her in marriage. When Evnissyen presently appeared and, enflamed by his ambitions and his passion for the lovely queen, hotly pleaded his own cause with her, Caradoc sternly reproved him, bidding him remember that Bronwen had the freedom of her choice.

Evnissyen passionately resented the reproofs of Caradoc, and hotly challenged him to fight. At that moment, however, the two Kings and their chieftains arrived at the Rock of Harlech for the final decision to be announced; and the disputants put back their spears and awaited the announcement.

Matholoc, the handsome and splendid young King of Ireland, now formally demanded the answer of the Council to his suit, expressing his own great desire that their countries' long years of enmity might thus be ended by this happy union of himself with the fair " Lily of Britain ", the fame of whose beauty had gone far and wide. Bran, King of Britain, replied that this was also his hope, but that Bronwen had the freedom of her choice. Evnissyen, still eager to prevent the match, now sprang forward and demanded that the decision might be settled by single combat, offering himself as champion to meet Matholoc.

Bran, however, sternly bade him cease from strife; and turning to his beautiful sister, he gently requested her to make her choice. Bronwen, strongly influenced by Caradoc, the man she loved, nobly resolved to sacrifice her own feelings for the sake of the welfare of Britain; and placing her hand in that of Matholoc, indicated that her choice was made. Their nuptials were immediately celebrated, and a splendid marriage feast was held.

But Evnissyen, beside himself with raging jealousy, determined to make trouble. By calling their battle prowess into question, he first of all insulted Cormac, King of Connaught, and the other lesser Irish princes and chieftains as they sat at the feast. Later, when the newly-wed King and Queen had retired to their nuptial chamber, he added mortal blood insult to the High King of Ireland himself by going forth in the dead of night and defiling the

K

shields, flinging in uproar the sleeping or still feasting followers of Matholoc, and mutilating their horses.

Finally, in the sacred grove where stood the Magic Cauldron of Annwn, he met with Cormac—who had wandered thither to cool his anger at the personal insults to himself—and challenged him to fight, at the same time shouting out in a frenzy of jealous rage to Matholoc also to come forth and do battle with him. Matholoc, hearing his name thus called out in the night, left his sleeping bride and hastened to the grove, where, on hearing from Cormac of the deadly insult offered to him, he furiously thrust his subject King aside and prepared to do battle with Evnissyen himself.

At this moment, however, Caradoc appeared with his guards, who seized Evnissyen and held him captive. Bronwen and Bran also now appeared; and a wild scene ensued, all the warring passions of the Irish Kings and chiefs being aroused to madness by the blood insult against their High King, which they declared could only be wiped out by blood. Matholoc offered to release Bronwen from her marriage vows, should she desire it, since their countries must now be at war once again. But Bronwen declared that, having chosen to unite herself to him, she would go with him in all his ways; and Bran finally pacified the angry King by announcing that though he could not yield him the blood of his brother as demanded, yet he would banish Evnissyen there and then. He would also give to Matholoc the basins of gold, the silver wands, and double the number of horses maimed, which were the payments due by their ancient laws for a King's insult. But though Evnissyen was driven forth into banishment that same moment, Matholoc and his princes were not satisfied. They felt that the insult could only be wiped out with blood.

Then Bran said that as the greatest gift in his power, he would give them the Magic Cauldron of Annwn; and despite the passionate protests of Caradoc and Taliessin that their sacred treasure should thus be taken from their land, the Cauldron was brought forth from the sacred grove at the King's command.

Matholoc now expressed himself satisfied with this payment, though Cormac still called out for the blood atonement. Then the pacified High King set sail for Ireland, with Bronwen by his side, followed by his princes and chieftains with the fatal Cauldron, the poison fumes from which would henceforth stir up evil passions in his own land.

.   .   .   .

In Ireland a little son, Gwern—the reincarnation of Dylan, Son of the Wave—was born to Matholoc and Bronwen; and for a few short years the "Lily of Britain" was contented and absorbed with the joy of her child.

But, after a while, Cormac, King of Connaught, who had nursed in his heart vengeance against Britain, stirred up the other subject Kings in Ireland to demand the divorce of Bronwen on the ground of the old blood insult still unavenged. For a long time Matholoc refused indignantly to agree to the request of his angry chieftains, jealous for what they regarded as their tarnished honour; for he had come to love his beautiful Queen and her fair child dearly. But Bronwen was full of anxiety for the safety of her beloved son and fearful lest he should fall a prey to the ravening wolves of power; and being also alarmed lest her lord should lose his throne for her sake, she entreated that he would consent to her being put away from him. So insistent were her anxious pleadings, and so clamorous and dangerous the attitude of his chieftains, that Matholoc at last agreed to the divorce demanded. The news was first heard by the banished Evnissyen, who, still soaked in the poison of overwhelming ambition, cunningly sought his own restoration to power by making himself the bearer of these evil tidings to Britain. He found Bran and his chieftains sad and pining for news of Bronwen, of whom nothing had been heard for five years; and when he related what had now befallen her, a great cry of indignation arose from all the people for the disgrace that had been put upon their innocent and beloved Queen, the "White Lily of Britain".

Immediately, the hosts of Britain were gathered together and proceeded to invade Ireland, seeking redress for the wrongs of Bronwen. Bran first of all annulled the sentence of banishment from Evnissyen and restored him to his former position—which the crafty chief had fully expected would be the case. Caradoc and a certain number of chieftains and their hosts were left during the absence of her High King to guard Britain from the raiding hordes who ever and anon made war upon her.

In the great timbered hall of Matholoc's royal abode in Ireland, the two High Kings and their subject princes and chieftains met once more—a parley having been arranged before hostilities commenced by the gentle influence of Bronwen, who was eager to prevent bloodshed between those she loved. After much hot altercation, a more peaceful atmosphere prevailed among the chiefs; and Gwern, the son of Matholoc and Bronwen, was proclaimed as the next King of Ireland and the heir of Britain. The little prince lay in a cradle in one part of the Hall; and, at the request of Bran, Bronwen took up her child and placed him in the arms of her brother, who embraced him tenderly as he was acclaimed again and again by the chiefs.

Evnissyen was filled with violent anger at the acclamation of Gwern; and all his old raging jealousy broke out afresh, being intensified by the influence of the Cauldron of Annwn, which stood in the Hall. But now, by a mighty effort, he controlled himself somewhat, and asked that he, too, might hold the child in his arms.

Bronwen herself handed her little son to her former suitor, glad to imagine that he also wished well to her child; but, to her horror, the treacherous Evnissyen, in a sudden passion of mad jealousy, flung Gwern into the midst of the fire that surrounded the Magic Cauldron. With a loud cry of woe, Bronwen endeavoured to rush into the flames after her beloved child; but Bran tenderly but firmly held her back that she might not destroy herself, while Cormac and others drew out the charred body of Gwern from the flames.

In a fury of anger at this outrage, the two opposing parties now rushed out to seize their arms and to engage in deadly combat; and Matholoc, distracted by his grief and the disappointment of his hopes, spurned Bronwen and cursed all her race.

As the chiefs rushed out to fight, Evnissyen and Cormac met and engaged in a deadly duel, in which Cormac was slain. Then, seeing that all hope was lost, Evnissyen rushed towards the Cauldron and dashed it to pieces upon the altar; and, as a great spout of red flame arose from it, he fell dead beside the fragments.

The British and the Irish now fell furiously upon one another, fighting to the death until nearly all were slain. Bran received his death wound after fighting like a lion; and as he breathed his last in Bronwen's arms, he bade her return to Britain, where Caradoc awaited her.

. . . .

In Britain, dire misfortune had also fallen upon Caradoc; for a raiding party had overwhelmed him and the chieftains left to guard the land, and in the fray he had fallen mortally wounded.

He was leaning upon his spear looking out to sea when Bronwen, Taliessin, and the few surviving Britons from Ireland approached him.

Filled with woe at the terrible news they brought, he told them of his own disaster and mortal hurt; and then he spoke gently with Bronwen, who turned eagerly to him for comfort, glad of the sweet tenderness he had withheld from her so long. For a few moments the would-be lovers, parted by destiny, remained clasped in each other's arms in a passionate embrace; and then Bronwen —overwhelmed and broken-hearted by her many woes, the innocent victim of strange circumstances and doomed to be the cause of men's fearful warring—fell back and expired beside the man she had never ceased to love.

A few moments later, Caradoc also breathed his last; and as he died the air became filled with the sound of softly flapping wings and the song of birds was heard, bringing peace and the forgetting of sorrows.

THE ENCHANTER   *Holbrooke*
(The Wizard)

IN a wonderful fairy-like garden surrounding a turreted castle of high and frowning aspect, which stood in the midst of a forest, a wicked and powerful Wizard stood at midnight. He was weaving fresh spells and entertaining himself by compelling the unhappy people he had enchanted to dance for him. By means of his dark powers of magic, all travellers who drew near his grim and lonely castle he caused to become dumb and to serve him. These unfortunate captives were unable to escape, once within his toils; for if they attempted to cross the border of the garden they died.

To-night the Wizard had grouped some of his enchanted victims into the semblance of a fountain, and others as a heap of stones, where they remained petrified and unable to move. Then, standing apart—an awesome figure in his black robe, pointed hat, black hair, and long beard streaming out in the breeze—he waved his bright, flashing wand and sang forth his incantation with alternating cajolery, sternness, and demoniacal laughter, bidding his petrified captives awaken and dance for his pleasure.

One by one, the enchanted youths and maidens awakened from the sleep-spell laid upon them. In obedience to the commands of their master, they arose from the semblance of a fountain and heap of stones in their natural forms once more, singing and dancing in rhythmical and wildly mazy figures to the enthralling music he produced from no apparent source.

The Wizard then called forth one of the two lovely sister Princesses he held in thrall as his most treasured captives; and from the castle there came tripping the dainty Princess Patricia, who, against her will, was soon dancing and singing as madly as the others. Even when the Wizard, by means of his magic, raised up the demon spirits of fire to leap around him, the enchanted dancers still continued their wild gyrations, until at last their demon master, with a wave of his wand, dismissed them to their castle prison once more.

Left alone, the Wizard indulged in a boastful song in praise of his own mighty and terrible power. Then, as the dawn appeared and he heard the voice of an approaching wanderer calling in the distance, he retired to his own secret chamber within the castle, rubbing his hands gleefully at the thought of yet another victim.

Almost immediately afterwards, a young lord of the neighbouring Court, named Oscar, who had lost his way in the forest, appeared and made haste to approach the castle, rejoicing that, as he mistakenly imagined, aid was at hand. At that moment, however, the sprightly Patricia tripped into view, chasing a butterfly from flower to flower. Oscar, delighted with the beauty of the royal maiden, approached towards the magic garden, eager to speak with her. When Patricia beheld him, she, too, was attracted by the handsome youth, but drew away somewhat timidly. Instantly Oscar followed, now completely enthralled by the maiden's charm; and then, suddenly realizing the stranger's terrible danger, Patricia ran forward again, seeking, though under the spell of speechlessness, to warn him from entering the garden. She was too late, however; for the enthralled Oscar, eager to speak with her, rushed into the garden joyfully.

When, having crossed the magic line, he reached her side and clasped her in his arms, he found to his amazement and alarm that he had become entirely dumb and was unable to utter the hot words of love already on his lips. Patricia, full of distress, explained by means of signs the cause of his misfortune, which she also shared, indicating the magic castle and its Wizard owner.

Oscar, readily understanding the meaning of her signs, drew his sword and, seizing her by the hand, began to draw her away from the garden in haste.

Patricia, however, managed to stop his impetuous progress before he reached the border-line of the garden, explaining again by signs that it would mean death to both of them to step over the magic line after having once entered the garden. Then, in order to comfort him and to reconcile him to his present fate, she began to dance before him, the air being full of the music of enchantment. In a few moments, Oscar, intoxicated by her charm, also joined in the dance—the allurement of which quickly enabled the two young people to forget their sorrows and the difficulties before them in the joy of the present.

After a while, tiring of the dance, they wandered away together to seek the shelter of the trees from the now brightly shining sun.

As they disappeared from view, the elder Princess, Maria, a young woman of more surpassing loveliness than her sister, came into the garden, sighing as she thought of her hopeless captivity. She tried to comfort herself by remembering that her mother had once told her that Love was capable of conquering all the woes of the world. But how could Love ever reach her here in this enchanted garden?

Even as she thus sighed, however, the royal master of young Oscar, the handsome and adventurous Prince Anton, issued forth from the forest whither he had been wandering in search of adventures. No sooner did Prince Anton and Maria behold one another than a deep mutual love dawned in their hearts—Anton recognizing that this exquisite maiden was the ideal bride he had sought so long, and Maria knowing that this was the lover who should be her champion and save her from all her woes.

Nevertheless, eager to prevent another victim from falling beneath the Wizard's fatal spell, Maria—who, though unable to escape from the garden, had not been rendered dumb as had the other victims—drew back from the young Prince's pleading arms, entreating him not to enter the garden, explaining what would happen did he venture to cross the magic line and telling him of the evil enchantments of the Wizard. She further told him that her father, though a great king, had fallen into the power of this wicked Wizard who had destroyed him and had kept his courtiers and herself and her sister captives in this enchanted castle, leaving them, alone of all his victims, their speech, that he might enjoy the pleasure of hearing the human voice. Her sister, however, had since offended him and had been stricken dumb as a penalty; and all other strangers who entered the garden also became mute and died if they attempted afterwards to escape.

As the Princess's story came to an end, Patricia passed by with Oscar; and the Prince, recognizing in the latter his own chief friend, called eagerly to him. Oscar, however, owing to his enchanted state, had no recollection of his royal master; and the enthralled pair passed unheeding into the shadows again. Prince Anton was infuriated by the evil spells of the Wizard, whom he was valiantly eager to attack at once; but Princess Maria implored him not to enter but to seek aid before making any such attempt. So Prince Anton bade a tender farewell to the beautiful maiden, for whom he had already conceived a deep passion; and declaring that he would quickly return with the means of rescuing all the enchanted people, he hastened away to seek aid for his great adventure.

. . . .

In the palace of King Johann, a great festival was proceeding; but though the courtiers danced and sang and the Court Jester cut his funniest capers, the King refused to be entertained or even to smile. He declared that he could not be happy so long as his adventure-loving son continued to engage in dangerous and mad wanderings abroad.

Even as he grumbled, however, Prince Anton hurried into the festive hall, weary and travel-stained but full of eager excitement. Immediately after greeting his royal father, he poured forth the story of his last great adventure and begged for an army that he might destroy the wicked Wizard, release the enchanted people, and bring home the beautiful Princess with whom he had fallen in love.

To his great surprise and disappointment, this request was coldly refused by the King, who merely laughed at the story, declaring it to be the invention of a youthful brain. The Jester, following his royal master's lead, also laughed and made comical fun of the story told by the young Prince, adding wisely, however, that even if such a Wizard existed a mortal army would not be much use against his magic.

Prince Anton, furious at this unexpected treatment, again asserted the truth of his story and passionately called upon the nobles and soldiers to join with him in rescuing the lovely maidens he had seen.

As some of his own special friends were now beginning to range themselves on his side, a stranger entered the hall, who, by his long red robes, aged and dignified mien and flowing white beard, was recognized at once to be some great magician.

When the newcomer announced that he was Kaspar, one of the three Wise Kings of the East, all bowed down before him; and he then proceeded to prove to the company the truth of the young Prince's story.

With Anton's sword he described a circle with a triangle within it; and sprinkling a powder upon this, the room was suddenly plunged into darkness through which a pale greenish light began to glow. In the midst of this mysterious light, a vision of the Wizard's castle gradually appeared, with the beautiful Princess Maria first seen gazing wistfully through a barred window, and then in the garden, supported by a handsome young man, whom all recognized as Prince Anton himself.

When this vision had faded away, the lights returned once more; and the company were revealed in an attitude of wondering reverence and awe, even the Jester forgetting to cut his customary capers.

All were now fully convinced that there was black magic to be destroyed and beautiful maidens to be rescued; and all the nobles drew their swords and announced their willingness to set forth with their Prince at once upon this great adventure.

The King-Magician, however, declared that the Jester had spoken truly when he said that a mortal army was of no use against a wizard's spell. Declaring that magic must be met by magic, he announced that he and the young Prince alone should undertake this mighty enterprise—that the love of youth and the wisdom of age would be more potent than swords and spears. So the courtiers and soldiers were left behind; and with the blessing of the King and his people, the hoary Kaspar and the youthful Prince Anton set forth upon their quest.

.   .   .   .

Once again it was midnight, and the Wizard had brought his victims to dance in the moonlit garden before his grim castle.

As the whirling dance proceeded, Oscar appeared and mingled with the dancers, seeking the pretty Patricia, of whom he had become enamoured and who eluded him teasingly though longing to be with him. At length he caught her, and then, holding her closely, though still mute, entreated her by signs once again to escape from the garden with him, drawing her eagerly towards the magic border as he did so. But Patricia, afraid for the life of her lover, endeavoured to drag him back from the fatal line, expressing her wild terror on his behalf.

Oscar, however, laughed at her terrors and again passionately indicated his desire for her to risk all and follow him; and then, carelessly eager to prove his own fearless defiance of the Wizard's powers, he boldly stepped over the magic line, intending to jump back immediately to fetch her. But instantly, the Wizard's magic was at work; and the too bold young man staggered and fell upon the mound at the other side. At the same moment, violent thunder and blazing lightning ensued for a short time, while the Wizard appeared upon the battlements, uttering peals of demoniacal laughter as he rejoiced in the destruction of the victim who had so foolishly tried to escape his clutches.

Then, as the sudden storm ceased with the withdrawal of the Wizard from the battlements and the moonlight shone forth brightly once more, the body of Oscar was seen stretched dead upon the mound. Full of horror, the grief-stricken Patricia, seeing that her lover was thus lost to her for ever, resolved to join him in death. She therefore wildly sprang over the magic line; and as she fell expiring across the dead form of Oscar, the lightning and thunder once more burst forth in renewed violence. When this second storm ceased, the bodies of the lovers, together with all the enchanted dancers, had disappeared.

Soon afterwards, Prince Anton and Kaspar the King-Magician arrived before the castle. Much alarmed by the deserted scene which met his eyes, the royal youth called out anxiously and entreatingly for his beloved Maria to appear once more before his loving eyes.

The first to answer his call, however, was the Wizard, who flung open the door of the castle and angrily demanded who dared to call one of his fair maidens.

Prince Anton drew back involuntarily at the sight of the terrible Wizard, who cast baleful and malignant glances upon the intruder. But he boldly continued to call loudly for Maria, who now appeared. Though joyful at the quick return of her lover, she was filled with alarm by the presence of the Wizard and also by Anton's rashly eager steps towards her. Kaspar also tried to prevent the royal youth from rushing upon his doom; but Anton was so eager to clasp the beautiful Princess in his arms that he dashed heedlessly across the magic line. Instantly he became dumb, to the grief of Maria, who tenderly comforted him. She then told him, in answer to his signs, of the sad fate of Oscar and Patricia; and then the pair wandered off together in the moonlight.

Meanwhile, the evil Wizard and the good Magician began to pit their strength against one another, Kaspar boldly and calmly challenging the power of the worker of Black Magic. To prove his complete subjection of the evil spirits of darkness to his will, the Wizard uttered a terrifying and weird invocation and called up a host of demons whom he compelled to perform a fearful and terrifying devil dance, even commanding their awful master, Satan, to take part in it.

The Magician, however, remained calm and unalarmed throughout the whole ghastly performance; and then he responded with an appeal to the higher powers of Good. Drawing his sword, he described a circle around him and a triangle within it. Then, lifting up the sword, so that it appeared as an illuminated Cross and the symbol of Heaven, he caused the demons to cower before him and finally to return to their own abode with their evil master.

He next compelled the now terrified and trembling Wizard to retreat before him as he advanced towards the open doors of the castle with his illuminated and scintillating sword still held aloft.

As soon as the heavenly symbol of Good was brought within the portals of the castle, the turrets toppled and the castle fell in ruins, destroying the Wizard in its fall.

Then, as day began to dawn and the garden became visible in the soft, rosy light, blossoming with fresh and exquisite flowers, many people appeared from whom the spell of enchantment had now fallen, and who spoke, and sang, and danced as they rejoiced together. Among them came Prince Anton and the lovely Princess Maria, now happy lovers never to be parted again.

And when all had set forth upon their several ways once more, the beauty of the flower-laden garden was not entirely deserted or wasted. When the silver moonlight shone forth at night, the ethereal spirit forms of Oscar and Patricia appeared once more and with arms entwined flitted over the dewy lawns in a phantom dance—lovers still, whom death could not divide.

THE SNOB · *Holbrooke*

ON the roadside, about twelve miles from Marlborough Town, there was a copse with tall, spreading beech-trees which invited pleasant shade and rest from the glare of the dusty highway. Here one hot summer day, a couple of tramping gipsies had flung themselves down to rest on the edge of the copse—Bill Blizzard and his wife, Caroline. They had kindled a fire, upon which an old and blackened tin pot was already simmering. Beside them lay the sticks of a gipsy's tent and a bundle of straw for bedding, while a dilapidated, old-fashioned perambulator held a number of dirty bundles containing the ragged remnants of the family wardrobe and personal effects.

Caroline, a worn-out woman of middle-age, though still possessed of a certain handsomeness, was sun-burned to the last degree of which a white woman is capable, her hands being nearly black. She was clad in a ragged old black dress, almost falling to pieces and pinned together with rusty safety-pins. A dirty yellow bandanna handkerchief was knotted round her neck, and an old black and broken straw hat of the once popular sailor-shape was tied rakishly on to her rough head by a piece of torn veiling fastened under her chin. Her boots could scarcely be recognized as such, being merely bits of broken leather tied like bandages round her feet with string and rag; and she sat on the ground, hunched up and nursing her knees, with a look of utter dejection and misery.

Her husband, Bill, wore clothing in an almost equal stage of dilapidation—the relics of a labourer's corduroys, a ragged and dirty kerchief round his neck, a tattered cap on his head, and boots bursting at the toes. He was stretched full length on the grass, sucking at a tobaccoless pipe.

Presently, finding the latter but empty comfort, he produced a bent mouth-organ and began to play a topical tune upon it. This effort at cheerfulness under dismal conditions, however, only brought upon him the angry remonstrances of his wife—worn out to impatient irritability and exasperation by sore feet, hunger, and consciousness of the absolutely " stony-broke " condition of the family exchequer—who bade him in rough cockney accents to " Shut up, kawn't yer! "

Bill declared sulkily that his performance on the mouth-organ might earn them a " tanner " yet—only to be reminded witheringly by Caroline that a " tanner " was not likely to be forthcoming on a lonely country road, though she admitted it might serve them if they could reach Marlborough Town that evening. This last possibility, however, was a remote one, as her blistered feet would take her no further.

As the pair squabbled together—not without occasional bright gleams of cockney wit, despite their miserable condition—they were presently joined by a third tramp, whom they addressed as " Sparrow ", who had gone over the hill-side to accost a shepherd he had observed.

The newcomer, though likewise ragged, dirty, and unkempt, had all the characteristics of a broken-down, fifth-rate actor of the old school—moving with studied elegance, using exaggerated gestures, and making high-flown speeches in stilted elocutionary style though with a cockney accent. He was dressed in a rusty black suit with a tattered Inverness-cape buttoned up to his chin and a black slouched hat pulled well down over his shaggy grey locks.

When asked by Bill if he had met with any luck, he struck a tragic pose, making a mock heroic speech and describing the humble shepherd as a " varlet " from whom, however, he had managed to secure some tobacco, which he now produced. As Bill and Caroline eagerly seized upon the tobacco and filled and lighted up their pipes at once, Sparrow entertained them with a song, which he acted and sang in exaggerated style.

After this brief interlude of liveliness, the three tramps again relapsed into gloomy talk of the unlucky condition in which they found themselves, comparing their sad lot with the wealth and ease of Society folk.

Sparrow, however, being a philosopher, declared that the rich often envied the poor tramp his freedom; and presently he insisted on Caroline giving them a song lest their spirits should drop too low.

Then, as dismal thoughts once more settled upon the party, Sparrow announced that the Squire of the district was determined to hound all tramps off his property and that several parties of their own sort had been prosecuted and given twenty-one days' imprisonment as penalty. He added that this Squire—Mr. Cunningham, a *parvenu*, whom the county gentry declined to visit—was even now driving in his fine new motor-car, on the look-out for stray vagabonds. He was in touch with three keepers and a couple of policemen on bicycles who were searching the woods.

Even as Sparrow gave forth this disquieting news, the hoot of a motor-horn was heard and a car could be seen approaching in the distance.

Full of alarm, the tramps all sprang to their feet, Caroline gathering her bundles together in great haste, while Bill began to stamp out the fire. Sparrow, however, with great presence of mind, suddenly determined to save this dangerous situation by bluff, a bright idea having occurred to him; and quickly he divulged the scheme to his scared friends. They would pass themselves off to the approaching Squire as Society folk living the "simple life"—this being one of the latest fads of Mayfair. The free, unconventional pleasures of caravaning, or tramping like gipsies from village to village and camping out in lonely spots, had recently become a fashionable pastime of *blasé* pleasure-seekers of the wealthy and leisured classes. "You leave this to me!" cried Sparrow. "I haven't been on the boards for five-and-twenty years for nothing! Don't you speak a word till I give you the cue!"

The situation being desperate, the other two had no choice but to agree to this wild scheme. They had no sooner seated themselves once more, pulling at their pipes—Sparrow having stirred up the fire and flung on another log—than a splendid new car, painted a gaudy red, drew near and slowed up under the finger-post. It contained three passengers—Mr. Roger Cunningham, a stout, puffy-faced and arrogant little man of middle-age, dressed in a long dust-coat, a leather motor-cap and goggles; his wife, a short, stout and decidedly vulgar-looking woman, wearing a quantity of large and dazzling jewellery with her elaborately exaggerated motor attire; and his daughter, also fashionably garbed for motoring, who, though buxom and good-looking, wore an air of arrogance and ill-breeding as marked as that of her father. The chauffeur, in a brilliant uniform, though silent and outwardly respectful in manner, wore an expression on his face which revealed his inward contempt for his vulgar master and mistress.

Purple with rage, the new " Squire " descended from the car and, striding up to the tramps, roared out in a blustering tone : " Darn you! I've caught you at last! What's the meaning of this? "

Next, calling to his chauffeur he bade him note all that happened as he would be required to give evidence later on at the police court; and then, turning again to the wanderers, he bade them " Stand up! "

For answer, Sparrow, affecting a lazy, nonchalant air, merely stared at him as though he were some curious animal; and when Cunningham drew nearer and repeated his command, the old actor drawled out with calm impudence : " Who the devil do you think you're speaking to? "

Cunningham, amazed by this cool response, fell back a few paces, while his women folk stared at the party, mystified and open-mouthed, as Sparrow, addressing Caroline as " your ladyship ", suggested she should stroll away into the woods in case language might follow not suitable for her to hear.

Cunningham, an arrant snob and already fearful of having made another *faux pas*—a constantly annoying occurrence with him—now modified his tone somewhat. Speaking still with a pompous manner and affecting an exaggerated " Society " accent, he announced himself by name, suggesting that he and his country seat, Milden Grange, were perhaps known to this cool stranger whom he now addressed politely as " Sir ".

Sparrow replied with cold indifference that the name was unknown in the circles in which he moved. He then explained with unblushing plausibility that he and his friends were travelling thus as tramping gipsies for a few weeks and that they were even going so far as to affect the garb, manner, and speech of such lowly folk in order to keep up the delightful illusion. He added that they had tried caravaning at first, but had found that life too painfully respectable. He then stood up and introduced himself as the Hon. Cheyne Walker, and his friends as Lord and Lady Saffron.

Cunningham, overwhelmed on thus finding himself at last as he imagined in the presence of " real Society people " and snobbishly eager to ingratiate himself in their favour, apologized profusely for his "stupid blunder", declaring that he would never forgive himself. Sparrow, however, now blandly assured him that they were willing enough to accept his apologies and indeed took his former blustering conduct as a great compliment to their excellent disguise and histrionic ability. He then begged that the ladies might be introduced.

Full of fussy delight, Mrs. and Miss Cunningham alighted from the car and effusively shook hands with the three tramps. They declared that they were charmed to meet them and added that such an unconventional mode of life, with its freedom from care and social fetters, must be a pleasant change from the usual round of fashionable events—though, to be sure, this gipsy tramp life was all the fashion, too!

At these gushing remarks, Bill smiled painfully as he continued to puff at his clay pipe; and Caroline managed to say nothing, as she had been bidden, merely smirking in a manner half-friendly and half with a sinister leer.

Sparrow maintained a perfectly calm self-possession; and presently, to avoid further conversation, he invited "Lord Saffron" to sing them one of his lively songs. Bill did so in his best cockney street-style, his performance being loudly applauded by the "Squire" and his ladies.

When the song came to an end, Mrs. Cunningham invited the party to come away with them at once to stay a few days at the Grange—an invitation strongly supported by her snobbish husband, equally anxious to exhibit his wealth and the richness of his possessions to these fashionable "aristocrats".

But Sparrow, in spite of ecstatic pleadings on the part of Miss Cunningham, firmly declined the invitation, declaring that they had vowed not to sleep under a roof during the whole of their six weeks' journey. Even when the Cunninghams suggested that at least they might come along and dine that evening, and Caroline—prompted by her hungry condition—timidly expressed a desire to do so, the old actor reproachfully reminded her of her "wager made with the Duchess". He added that they were tramping to fixed mileage and places and were now on their way to Marlborough Town, but had been compelled to stop to rest a while because Lady Saffron was very footsore and tired. This, unfortunately, would make them considerably behind their scheduled time for that day.

On hearing this, Cunningham immediately offered to send them forward to Marlborough in his car. This invitation the wily Sparrow—well aware that his game of bluff could not be kept up much longer—accepted though still with pretended reluctance.

Immediately, the disgusted chauffeur was ordered to take on board his spotless car the broken-down perambulator and filthy bundles, tent sticks, blackened kettle, and other oddments of the tramps; while Mr. Cunningham handed the clumsy, but smirking, Caroline into the best seat with absurdly exaggerated deference, fussily arranging the fur rug over her knees and feet. When Bill and Sparrow had also taken their seats, Mrs. Cunningham and her daughter begged them eagerly to fix a date after their "amateur tramping" was over for a prolonged stay at the Grange. After much palavering and pretended calculations regarding other imaginary "country house visits", Sparrow gave a tentative, but still doubtful, acceptance for the first week in November.

The Cunninghams then, with hearty and exaggerated friendliness, shook hands with the three new disreputable-looking occupants of their gaudily-upholstered car; and as the motor glided away with a flourishing "honk" of the horn, the "Squire" remained standing with his hat in his hand, while his wife and daughter waved their handkerchiefs to their departing new acquaintances until they had vanished out of sight.

As they turned to walk home through the woods, congratulating themselves upon having so successfully saved the situation after their first unfortunate "mistake" and secured the promise of a visit from such "desirable and fashionable Society people", a couple of policemen, in the uniform of rural constables, approached them rapidly on bicycles. Dismounting from their machines the constables inquired if they had seen anything of "three of these tramping people"—two men and a woman—whom the county police had been trying to convict for months and had at last tracked to this spot on the information of a shepherd who had spoken with one of them. The constables then proceeded to describe "Lord and Lady Saffron" and the "Hon. Cheyne Walker" to the life, so that it was impossible for the shocked and chagrined Cunninghams not to recognize in this word picture of their new "smart fashionable friends" the vagabonds wanted by the local authorities.

To cover their confusion and to save themselves from ridicule, the Cunninghams declared they had noticed some tramps passing along the top of the downs half an hour ago, in the opposite direction to Marlborough. But when the constables had ridden off once more in the direction indicated the "Squire" and his ladies remained staring at one another, speechless with mortification and rage because of the clever trick played upon their gullible snobbishness by the plausible rogues now driving away so luxuriously from the clutches of the Vagrancy Act.

THE STRANGER
or Pierrot and Pierrette

Holbrooke
(An Allegorical Fantasy)

LOVE, Peace, and Contentment reigned in the pretty cottage home of Pierrot and Pierrette.

Pierrette was fair and charming, living only for the pleasure and delight of her beloved one; and Pierrot was a gallant and devoted lover.

Though their whole day was spent in sweet intercourse in the performance of necessary duties and the labours of Love, their greatest joy came in the late evening, when they wandered together in their little garden in the moonlight and listened to the magic music of Love played around them—that fairy music which can only be heard by those who truly love.

One day, however, there came a Stranger—the evil spirit of Vice—who had long desired to destroy their idyllic dream of Love; who, watching his opportunity, found Pierrot alone and tempted him into strange paths. He painted glowing word-pictures of the joys of the Town with its many enthralling pleasures; and such was his cunning skill that Pierrot was inflamed by a sudden desire for the unknown. Forgetting Pierrette, he was lured to the Town by the Stranger, who seized him in an irresistible grasp and plunged him forthwith into the mad whirlpool of unrestrained pleasure.

.   .   .   .

In the quaint old street of an eighteenth-century town, revellers were all gathered together for a gay festival. The scene was a charming one. Strange and curious houses of fantastic architecture were huddled together in picturesque confusion; and in the middle of the street there stood a tall clock-tower, brilliantly illuminated. There was something magical about this clock-tower, which served as an indication of the mind of the people; for in place of an ordinary clock-face, there shone forth now, at the beginning of the festival, the smiling face of an innocent child.

At the windows of the houses, women and pretty girls looked out with roguish, laughing glances; and upon the eager invitations of the handsomely-dressed cavaliers outside, they came dancing forth to join in the revels. All were in gala attire; and at first their amusements were innocent enough, and merriment and real enjoyment reigned as they danced their gay country dances or stately court measures.

And then as they separated into smaller groups, the Spirit of Pleasure entered into their midst in the form of a beautiful but elusive woman. As the Spirit of Pleasure danced insinuatingly amongst the revellers, she touched first one and then another lightly upon the shoulder; and each one upon whom she laid her magic touch left everything and followed her in a wild pursuit. When, after a mad chase, they all surrounded her with cheering cries, imagining that they had caught her at last, she suddenly vanished before their eyes, as elusive as ever. Then, as they gazed upon one another in amazement and with an empty sense of loss, a heralding chime clanged forth from the clock-tower, from which the innocent face of the child had also disappeared, having been replaced by that of a young girl.

For a moment the revellers halted; and then, as a bright and lovely Columbine appeared, they hailed her as their new Queen of Delight; and the revels were resumed again, the fun and frolics waxing faster and more furious as the moments passed.

To this scene of wild hilarity, the Stranger—whose robes concealed the Spirit of Vice—introduced the wondering and curious Pierrot, whom he had so successfully lured from his peaceful abode.

Introduced to alluring women and pretty girls by the sinister Stranger, dazzled by the lights and fascinated by the gay scene, Pierrot was instantly plunged into the whirlpool of pleasure, dancing with mad riotousness and indulging in many excesses he had never dreamed of before. Seeing that his victim seemed safely ensnared, the Stranger departed with a cynical laugh, determining now to seek out Pierrette and tempt her into this flowery path likewise.

At first Pierrot, missing his new companion, would have sought for him; but the gay women held him back with their clinging arms, loading him with flowers and garlands and using all their powers of enticement to keep him by their side. Once more there came a heralding chime from the clock-tower; and the revellers, stopping for a brief moment, saw that the face of the young girl was no longer there but that the face of middle-age now looked forth upon them instead.

They all shrank back and were a little awed; and then to drown their regrets they plunged into still livelier dances and louder gaieties. The Spirit of Pleasure suddenly returned and, seizing Pierrot in her clinging embrace, enticed him on to further excesses, ending by crowning him with flowers. Some of the revellers now appeared to have grown into old senile *roués* who, still in the toils of pleasure, continued to make love to the pretty girls. The latter while despising and laughing at aged admirers, nevertheless accepted the gold and jewels they offered. Presently, however, they returned once more to the arms of their youthful lovers and joined with them in deriding and driving away their elderly pursuers.

A comical clown now came capering into the midst of the throng, and the hilarity became greater still; and with the arrival of Harlequin also, who enticed the dancers to yet wilder excesses, the revel quickly developed into an orgy.

During the buffoonery of the clown, the solemn chiming of the clock-tower was again heard; and fearing to look now upon its ever-changing face, some of the revellers, ostrich-like, shrouded it so that it now appeared to be in shadow.

The dancers, who had suddenly become aghast and had shuddered at the warning chime of the clock, fearing that behind its shroud it now wore the face of old age, plunged into a wild bacchanalian dance, in which they whirled and gyrated madly, ever urged on to more violently reckless movements by the irresponsible Harlequin.

By this time, Pierrot, with his dress torn and dishevelled, and his garlands of flowers withered, was becoming satiated with this orgy of pleasure; but he still sought to join in the mad dance of the giddy throng. The pretty girls, however, had now wearied of their new admirer; and they turned aside, spurning him with scornful laughter as they fled from him in eager search for fresh excitement.

Hurt by their sudden rejection of him and disappointed with the fickle and unsatisfying nature of this orgy of pleasure, worn-out and weary, Pierrot made one more effort to join in the revels; but the dancers jostled him so roughly in their now unrestrained movements that he tottered and fell to the ground. No hand was stretched out to help him, the revellers merely laughing at his misfortune and then forgetting his existence; and poor Pierrot stumbled into a corner, alone and neglected.

Then, as the emptiness of his present pleasure-seeking life filled him with sadness, it seemed to Pierrot that he heard in the far distance—very faintly at first, but ever growing stronger—the sweet strains of that exquisite music he had always heard when wandering in the moonlight with Pierrette; and gradually the memory of his beloved one came back to him.

Realizing now that the mad, unrestrained pursuit of pleasure could never satisfy the longings of his heart and that true love alone was the shining light that led to happiness, Pierrot struggled to his feet, flinging away in disgust the now dead flowers with which he had been decorated; and, full of remorse for his lapse, he stretched out his arms to his unseen Pierrette. Determined to seek her forgiveness and the renewal of her love once more, he pushed his way through the wild, giddy revellers who surged and swayed around him, out into the cold darkness that was to lead him back once more to the warm light of love.

. . . .

Meanwhile, Pierrette had been grieving for the loss of Pierrot; but despite her grief, she would not forsake her allegiance to his memory, for she believed in the power of true love and did not lose the hope that he would return to her.

It was in vain that the sinister Stranger—having first of all bribed her nurse attendant, the Spirit of Deceit, into aiding and abetting him—endeavoured to tempt her to leave her retreat and likewise to seek the excitement of unrestrained pleasures.

To all his blandishments and glowing invitations, the faithful Pierrette turned a deaf ear, remaining true and steadfast in her love for Pierrot; and at last she cursed the Stranger for his deceit, and the chagrined Spirit of Vice was compelled to depart unsuccessful.

Then, when the moonlight shone forth, Pierrette went out into her little garden to wait and watch with hope in her heart. And there Pierrot, bruised and shaken, crept back to her, seeking forgiveness. He was gladly received into her outstretched arms; and the magic music of true love once more healed their wounded hearts and filled them with their former deep peace and contentment.

THE PERFECT FOOL   *Holst*

IN the dead of night, at a lonely spot where cross-roads met, a Wizard was performing his magic rites upon the rocky remains of an ancient sacrificial platform. A past master in the Black Art, he had no difficulty in raising up familiar spirits to assist him in his dark deeds; and to-night, having the most important task of his life on hand, he did not hesitate to invoke their aid.

He wished to make the strongest love-potion in the world—a potion so powerful that it should win for him the hand of the young Princess of the land, who was expected to choose a husband at that particular spot near the cross-roads early the following morning. This proud and beautiful royal lady—who was so fair that every man who beheld her loved her—had announced her intention of wedding that man only who could do the deed no other man could do. The conceited Wizard, though old, ugly, and extremely disagreeable, believed that he could perform the condition required by means of his magic arts. No one in the land but he could work spells and enchantments—therefore he could do what no other man could do.

Realizing, however, the disadvantages of his old age and unattractiveness, the worker of spells determined to be on the safe side by brewing an extra strong love-potion to aid him. To this end, therefore, he had kindled a fire, around which he drew a magic circle.

He now called forth the Spirits of Earth; and as crowds of goblins and gnomes came capering around him with fantastic leaps and antics, he commanded them to bring him a magic cup from the deepest cavern in the earth. When this had been done and the gnomes had departed, he called upon the Spirits of Water to fill the cup with the Essence of melting passionate Love. Finally, from the depths of the glowing embers, he brought forth the dazzling red-gold Spirits of Fire, who leaped like flames around him and whom he commanded to make the Essence of Love as a burning flame to set on fire the heart of his royal victim.

All the night through the Wizard continued his mystical rites; then, as the dawn began to appear, he dismissed his attendant spirits. His enchantments thus ended and the potion ready in the magic cup, he afterwards laid himself down behind the stones to rest a while.

As the Wizard slept, there came down the mountain path at daybreak a poor beggar-woman, dragging by the hand her only son. The latter was a loutish, half-witted youth, so stupid and foolish that he was of no use at all to his mother. What was more, he was so idle and sleepy that it was all she could do to keep him awake even for a short time; for he spent most of the twenty-four hours fast asleep. Yet, though this unfortunate mother constantly bewailed her bad luck in being burdened with such a useless son, she still persisted in dragging the poor Fool about with her from place to place because of a prophecy made at his birth. Certain Wise Men had come to her then and announced as they gazed at the vacant countenance of the babe:

> " He wins a bride with a glance of his eye,
> With a look he kills a foe;
> He achieves where others fail,
> With one word! "

As she now drew near to the rocky platform where, during the night just past, the Wizard had uttered his incantations, the weary Mother repeated the prophecy aloud with a hopeless sigh; for the loutish youth had already dropped down on the grass and, with a long and noisy yawn, had fallen asleep once more. How could this silly fellow win a bride with a glance of his eye, when he scarcely ever opened his eyes; how kill a foe with a look—except in his dreams!—and how achieve where others failed with one word, when he never spoke? Full of disgust at this thought, she shook her son roughly by the shoulder; but the sleepy Fool only yawned and fell asleep once more.

As the Mother turned away angrily, she suddenly caught sight of the sleeping Wizard; and seeing that this stranger, though old and ugly, appeared to be rich, since he was clad in handsome garments, she awakened him and entreated his aid.

The Wizard was at first furious on being disturbed. Then, seeing that it was but a harmless woman who had awakened him, he determined to make use of her as a dummy audience before whom he would rehearse the high-flown speech he intended to make before the Princess.

As the Mother stood timidly before him, spreading out her skirts and endeavouring to hide her sleeping son from sight, the Wizard now informed her that the Princess of the land was about to choose a husband that morning at the cross-roads; and he showed her the magic cup containing the love-potion he had brewed, adding that the liquid was so finely made that it was tasteless and pure as water. Full of vanity, he boasted that he himself could not fail to win the Princess since he alone could " do the deed no other man could do ".

The Mother, quickly divining that here also was the longed-for chance for her son to fulfil the prophecy pronounced at his birth, muttered over to herself once more the fateful words :

> " He wins a bride with a glance of his eye,
>   With a look he kills a foe:
>   He achieves where others fail,
>   With one word! "

Hearing these flattering words, the Wizard immediately took them as referring to himself; and he graciously commended the woman for her good opinion of him.

The Mother wisely kept her own counsel and still managed to hide her son—now likely to prove of some use to her at last, did she play her cards well. But when the man of magic began to recite his vainglorious speech before her, she was so scared by his mad gestures that, instead of acting up to him in the appreciative manner he desired, she shrank back in fear.

The Wizard, annoyed at her unresponsiveness, considered the idea of drinking a few drops of his potion to inspire her with a passion for him, thinking that a second and less important wife might prove useful. After scrutinizing her closely, however, he decided otherwise and declared disdainfully:

> " A man like me with a wife like that?
> No! It would not be proper! "

Then, not noticing the mortified looks of the Mother on hearing this rude remark, the conceited Wizard lay down to sleep once more behind the rocks, peremptorily bidding her awaken him as soon as the royal procession came in sight.

But the angry Mother cast vicious and menacing looks at the old Magician as he fell asleep; then, as her glance came back to her still slumbering son, hope grew up in her heart once more and she determined to secure for the poor Fool the wonderful prize sought by the clever man of magic. As luck would have it, at sunrise, three peasant girls came tripping down the mountain path carrying water-jugs to fill at the well in a hollow near by; and as they passed out of sight into the dell, singing of the beauty of pure, clear water, the Mother's last difficulty melted away.

Stealthily, the beggar-woman crept to the flat stone where the Wizard had carelessly left the cup containing his powerful love-potion; and snatching up the magic vessel, she returned to the side of her son, whom she shook violently until he sleepily opened his eyes and began to yawn. Quick as lightning, she poured the love-potion into his wide-open, yawning mouth; and when the Fool, too lazy to protest, had gulped it down she let him fall asleep again immediately.

When the three merry maidens presently came up from the well, their jugs full to the brim, she begged them to give her some water that she might quench her thirst. The girls willingly filled up the magic vessel with clear, sparkling water; and when they had departed on their way once more, the Mother carefully replaced the cup on the stone whence she had taken it. Next, hearing the sound of trumpets in the distance announcing the approach of the Princess, she awakened the Wizard as instructed. Then she crept back humbly to her sleeping son and sat down in front of him to await the carrying out of her plan.

A few moments later the Princess, with her courtiers, suitors, and attendants, arrived upon the scene; and as the royal party took up a stand upon the wayside by the cross-roads, a crowd of peasants also appeared from all sides and began to take a lively interest in the proceedings.

The Princess, clad in dazzling robes and lovely as a dream, at once announced that in accordance with her royal proclamation she stood there at the magic cross-roads to choose a husband—one who could do what no other man could do.

The conceited old Wizard immediately stepped forward, singing out his own praises and declaring himself to be the most wonderful man in the world. Then, when the surprised and unimpressed Princess replied calmly that he was much too old and ugly to make a suitable husband for her, the offended but cocksure Wizard announced that in a moment she would change her mind and, in an ecstasy of love, would then regard him as the handsomest and most splendid young man she had ever seen. As he spoke, he picked up the magic cup and, with many strange and conceited gestures, drank off its contents with much satisfaction and eager anticipation.

But, after repeating his fine speech, he was puzzled and dismayed because the Princess still remained indifferent and unchanged in her attitude towards him. Anxiously he asked her if she did not admire his now handsome and youthful looks and whether she did not already feel a passionate love surging within her as she gazed upon him. When the already bored Princess replied " No! " to these persistent questions, he became annoyed and attempted to press nearer to her side that she might the more closely admire him. Then, as the courtiers instantly drew their swords and formed a line of defence in front of their royal lady, he endeavoured to work the other part of the spell and to show the power of his terrible glance—which he confidently expected from what the vagabond woman had said would " kill a foe ".

But though he glared savagely at the courtiers and declared he would scorch and destroy them with his single glance, no flames appeared and no one was destroyed; and as the whole company now began to laugh his vaunted powers to scorn, he realized that his wonderful spell had failed. Suddenly catching sight of the Mother with a look of mocking triumph in her face, he accused her of being the cause of his plans going wrong; and his fury knew no bounds when the beggar-woman replied saucily to his accusations :

> " A man like you with a wife like that?
> No! It wouldn't be proper! "

Beside himself with rage and disappointment, the Wizard was about to hurl the magic cup at her head; but the courtiers flung themselves upon him and, after a wild struggle, drove him away from the spot amid the derisive laughter of the crowd. As he fled up the mountain-side, the man of magic rained curses upon the company, declaring that he would return shortly and bring a fearful fiery vengeance upon them after he had called up his familiar spirits to his aid. However, no one paid any heed to him; and when the laughter had subsided and peace was restored, the competition for the Princess's hand proceeded.

A Troubadour, who had just arrived, accompanied by a group of followers, immediately stepped forward and, striking an attitude of exaggerated admiration, begged to be allowed to sing forth his love. Announcing himself in high-flown terms as the greatest singer in the world, he attempted to sing a most elaborate cadenza passage which, however, proved too difficult for his self-vaunted gifts, so that he faltered and floundered many times. To add to his discomfiture, the Princess herself took up the refrain and proved by her bird-like rendering of the trills and high notes that her own vocal ability was vastly superior to that of this vain suitor.

When the crestfallen Troubadour had thus been compelled to retire from the contest, followed by the laughter of the rustic crowd, another competitor arrived. The new arrival—who wore a long dark cloak and carried a staff in his hand—announced himself in loud and sepulchral tones as a Traveller or Wanderer as he moved slowly and mysteriously towards the Princess. After extolling her beauty in high-flown fashion, he began to utter noisily a whole string of wild and meaningless phrases which none of the mystified audience could understand.

In his excitement and eagerness to produce a great effect, he stumbled over the sleeping Fool who, accustomed to being awakened by kicks and shakes, immediately sat up and stared stupidly straight in front of him. The first person he set eyes upon was the Princess; and immediately—to the inward triumphant satisfaction of the eagerly watching Mother—the spell caused by the magic potion he had swallowed began to work at once.

Slowly, as though in a trance or walking in her sleep, the beautiful Princess moved forward, passed the outstretched entreating arms of the Troubadour, the Traveller, and the other waiting suitors, and went forward, unfalteringly, to the Fool; and kneeling on the ground beside him, she began to fondle him and to call him by tender, loving names.

As the courtiers and simple rustics realized with amazement that their beloved Princess had thus fallen in love with a beggar, the Fool, heedless of the royal lady's passionate declarations, began to yawn once more. Despite his mother's shakings and scoldings, in another moment he had fallen asleep again. The Princess bade the Mother not to awaken him, declaring sweetly that it gave her joy merely to watch his sleeping form; and she continued her caresses and happy murmurings of tender love phrases.

So interested were the wondering beholders of this strange scene that they had scarcely noticed a curious darkness clouding the sky, accompanied by rumblings of thunder and other ominous sounds; but now they realized that a terrible storm was about to burst upon them.

In the increasing darkness, fiery flames began to appear on the horizon; and as the sudden conflagration drew nearer, the weird shapes of demons and evil spirits were seen to be wildly leaping and dancing in the rapidly encroaching flames. The terrified people entreated their beloved Princess to seek safety while there was yet time to do so and to help them in their need; for they believed that the powers of evil had been let loose in their midst.

The Princess, however, only smiled and declared that she was happy and at peace because her beloved one lay before her. Her oblivion in face of the immediate danger infuriated the people against the Fool, who they declared had bewitched their royal mistress; but when they would have dragged the sleeping youth away, the Mother drove them back fiercely. She declared that though others might fly, yet he must remain to face the danger because, having already won a bride with a glance of his eye, he would now kill the foe with a single look.

The people, however, were not reassured by this cryptic statement; and seeing that the Princess paid no heed to their entreaties and refused to stir from the spot, they resolved to go forth and fight the approaching foe themselves. Quickly they rushed away to call the soldiers to their aid; and as scared refugees from the outlying districts began to pour into their midst, the climax of the approaching catastrophe came.

Complete darkness now enveloped the skies, but the scene was brilliantly illuminated by the flames and the lightning that flashed on every side. In the midst of this ghastly fiery spectacle, surrounded by the leaping and dancing Spirits of Fire, appeared the Wizard, laughing hideously with evil triumph because of the terrible vengeance he was about to bring upon the Princess and the people who had flouted him.

His hoped-for revenge, however, did not materialize; and his much-vaunted magic recoiled on himself. The rustics all fled in terror; and only the Fool and his Mother and the Princes remained. The Mother had been anxiously waiting for this moment to arrive; and as soon as the furious Wizard appeared before the Princess, she roughly awakened the Fool once more and held up his head in such a position that he could not avoid looking at the man of magic.

No sooner did the glance of the sleepy Fool fall upon the Wizard than the latter wavered and fell, there was a terrific crash of thunder, and he vanished for ever amidst a huge tongue of flame that sprang up. Immediately the Spirits of Fire returned to their own element, the flames and burnings ceased, and the dark clouds of smoke began to roll away as the sun shone forth once more.

As the courtiers and rustics gradually returned on tiptoe to the spot where they had left their royal mistress, they found the latter still standing beside the Fool, now sleepily awake. In scornful tones, the Princess upbraided them for their cowardly conduct. Alone among them all, the poor Fool had remained to save her and to bring her peace. She then announced her intention of choosing the latter as her husband, and, turning to the Fool, begged him to tell her that he loved her.

But the Fool only stared at the beautiful maiden before him as though she were of no more account than any other woman; and the Princess, eagerly repeating her own declaration of love for him and her longing to have it returned, again asked him entreatingly whether he loved her. Then, to the amazement of all, the Fool grinned in a silly fashion and spoke just one word in reply: "No!"

The people were furious that a mere beggar should thus slight their beloved mistress, the most beautiful Princess in the world; but again the Mother intervened to prevent their attempted belabouring of her son by declaring that he had done the deed that no other man could do.

> "He has achieved where others failed,
> With one word!"

Then, turning to the Princess, she added in explanation : "For he is the only man who has ever looked upon your face and not loved you!"

The Princess was enraptured because she had thus secured a husband who entirely fulfilled her own conditions; and her people, also now rejoicing because the ancient prophecy had indeed come to pass, began to dance around the pair and to make preparations for the crowning of the beggar husband.

As the coronation procession approached, however, the Fool,

who had been growing sleepier and sleepier during these proceedings, now opened his mouth in a series of tremendous yawns; and then, sinking to the ground, he fell fast asleep once more before the High Priest could place the crown upon his head!

SAVITRI   *Holst*

THROUGH the deep recesses and the purple shadows of the Indian virgin forest, still tinged with the brief crimson-coppery afterglow of sunset, came Death, the dread Summoner, whose call all men must obey and whose law none can break.

As the Mighty One moved slowly and inexorably forward amid the solemn hush that preceded the darkness of night, and gradually drew nearer to the hut in the clearing where dwelt the Soul he came for, he sang out his summons to the young wife who sat within, announcing that he must take her beloved husband from her that night.

Savitri, dark and beautiful, with tender eyes as bright and shining as the stars which were even now appearing in the violet skies above, issued forth from the hut, pale and tearful, with grief already clutching at her heart. For she had clearly heard for several days and nights past in the far distance, at first faintly but ever growing plainer and surer, that fateful warning that her happiness must end—that Satyavan, her beloved one, must indeed be taken away from her.

Although the evening fire without the threshold was already burning brightly, she knew that its warmth could not preserve for her the precious life for which the Summoner was coming. The latter's grim form she could now dimly perceive drawing ever nearer through the shadowy trees. But Satyavan, lusty, full of life, and unaware of his quickly approaching end, was already returning from the forest depths, where he had been felling a tree with his mighty axe. There was no time, therefore, for the devoted wife to plead with the dread visitor not to cast his dark shadow over their perfect love.

As the light-hearted Satyavan, tall, lithe, and full of youthful strength and beauty, came bounding like a stag from the forest into the open clearing where stood the rustic dwelling he had built with his own eager hands, he, too, sang to Savitri; but his song had naught of woe in it, for it was the song of a happy lover, extolling the virtues and delights of his beloved one. " What wife in all the world is like to Savitri? " sang out the contented and joyous Satyavan.

But even as he flung aside the axe he carried and eagerly clasped his beautiful wife in his arms, the happy woodman noticed the tears and sad looks which she was unable any longer to hide from him; and he demanded anxiously: " What ails thee? "

Savitri, endeavouring to hide the truth from him, declared that she was troubled with dreams, illusions, and nameless fears and fancies of coming woe, which the forest, as a mirror, seemed to reflect before her timid inner vision. Satyavan's more material mind, however, could not be satisfied with such an explanation of her physical unrest and tremblings.

Instantly on the alert for her safety and suspecting a lurking foe in the shadows, he gently removed her clinging arms. Then, seizing his axe once more, he made as though to rush back into the forest to slay the enemy who thus dared to disturb his peace.

In despair, Savitri, now clearly beholding the fateful form of Death slowly approaching nearer, step by step, called fearfully and passionately to her beloved one not to seek the foe but to return to her loving arms; but Satyavan, his fears confirmed by her cries of alarm, continued to dash forward, swinging his axe high as he went, ready for a slashing lunge at the hidden foe.

Even as he raised his strong arm, however, the icy breath of Death, the Summoner, reached him. The axe fell limply from his paralysed arm, whence all the mighty strength had already departed; and he staggered back into the ready arms of Savitri, who led him gently to receive the warmth from the glowing embers of the fire burning upon the threshold of their home.

As Satyavan sank to the ground, feebly calling upon her with his dying breath, Savitri passionately clung to him in a last loving embrace, declaring that she would be with him wherever he might be, that his thoughts were hers as she watched over him, and that her spirit would dwell with him always. Then, as his eyes closed and his lifeless form fell from her tender grasp, she uttered a cry of woe, and sank, weeping and grief-stricken, upon the ground beside him.

Meanwhile, Death had approached so near that he now stood within a few yards of his victim; and Savitri once more heard the solemn announcement of his summons—that decree which no mortal had power to disobey when his time came. Savitri, imbued with the reverential resignation of her race to the inexorable decrees of fate, instead of indulging in futile recriminations, now arose and sang forth to Death a fearless song, in which she admitted the justness of his law in thus calling all men to his abode. She then declared that on every side she could see gentle faces, hear soft voices, and felt that even the air around her was holy.

To this Death replied that the holiness she felt was her own pure self, that the gentle faces she beheld were those of the many sufferers she herself had comforted, and that the voices she heard were the sweet words she had spoken—all the air had been made holy and sweet by the beauty of her love.

As he thus spoke in praise of the woman he had bereaved, Death became so deeply impressed by the beauty of such perfect mortal love that, seeking to comfort her bleeding heart, he offered to grant her a boon—then, anticipating her reply, he added, any boon save the life of her husband upon whom his icy breath had already fallen.

Savitri, quickly filled with great hope, called upon Death to grant her Life—that she might bring forth stalwart sons, and beautiful, bright-eyed daughters. She longed for Life, which was communion, since each one living lived for all; she would have Life, for Life was eternal. And then she began to plead also for the return of her husband, which was to her the gift of Life in its true fullness. Life without Love was no life at all—the life of woman was identical with wifehood and motherhood. If Satyavan were taken from her, then her voice would be mute and her feet could never tread the path of joy. She would be but a dream, an image floating on the waters of memory. He alone, her beloved one, could open for her the gate that led to the path of flowers—the path of a woman's real life. Therefore, Love to her was Life; and Life with its fullness of Love was the boon she craved.

Death, now finally overcome by the passionate appeal of Savitri, granted her the boon she had asked. Thus was the dread Summoner pushed back by the sheer force and beauty of a woman's wonderful love and compelled to depart without the victim for which he had come.

As Death vanished amid the shadows of the forest, Savitri bent over the prostrate form of Satyavan and in exultant tones besought him to open his eyes once more and to awaken to the joy of his home and his wife.

And presently, Satyavan opened his eyes and awakened, as though from a deep slumber, declaring that he had dreamt of a foe, and was glad to find that his troubles had vanished and that naught remained save his beloved one and her devotion—for Love alone was reality.

Then, as the re-united husband and wife retired, full of joy and gratitude, into their humble abode, Death passed away in the far distance, singing of how he had been conquered by Love—by one to whom he had granted the priceless boon of the fullness of Life.

HANSEL AND GRETEL   *Humperdinck*

IN the hut of Peter, the Broom-maker, Hansel and Gretel, his two children, had been left to work alone during the absence of their mother, Gertrude, who had bidden them to occupy themselves industriously until her return and not to idle or waste their time.

Hansel and Gretel were merry little folk despite the extreme poverty of their parents; and although they frequently went hungry to bed, they were so full of childish good spirits that they soon forgot their woes and always made the best of their simple lives.

So it happened that this afternoon they presently thought of a pleasanter way of enjoying themselves than by working hard and industriously as they had been bidden. Hansel was the first to fling down the broom he was binding. Then Gretel, after first scolding him for his laziness, put down her knitting and joined him in singing merry nursery songs and in dancing and playing about in the little kitchen-room that served as their dwelling-place.

They were very hungry; but Gretel comforted her brother by reminding him that at least there was a jug of milk on the table which their mother would be making into a pudding for their evening meal when their father returned from work. This happy thought cheered Hansel so much that he became more hilarious than before; and the two children began to spin one another round so gaily that they became dizzy and rolled over and over on the floor in their glee.

In the midst of this merry frolic, however, their mother, Gertrude, returned; and seeing that the children were playing instead of working as she had instructed them, she made a rush at Hansel, intending to box his ears for such disobedience. In her wrathful haste, however, instead of hitting Hansel, who saucily dodged out of her way, she struck the jug of milk so that it fell from the table and was spilled upon the floor.

Quickly the mother's anger cooled down on thus realizing that the only means by which she could make a meal for her hungry family that evening had now vanished; and only sorrow remained. However, well aware that it was no use crying over spilt milk, Gertrude soon recovered herself somewhat. Then, putting a basket into Gretel's hands, she bade both the children run out into the forest at once to gather wild strawberries, telling them severely not to play instead of working this time and not to return until the basket was filled with fruit for supper.

The children, glad to escape into the open air, set off at once, singing lively songs as they went; and Gertrude, sad and already regretting her hasty temper, sat down at the table and presently fell fast asleep from sheer weariness.

As the evening drew near, she was awakened by the cheerful singing of someone approaching the hut. This was Peter, the Broom-maker, who entered gaily, still singing as he unfastened a basket from his back. He had met with good luck that day, having sold all his stock of brooms in the neighbouring village, so that he had been able to buy some food; and he now triumphantly produced his basket filled with good things to eat.

" But where are our little ones? " he asked, as his wife roused herself and gladly set about getting a hot supper ready : " Where are Hansel and Gretel? "

When Gertrude replied that she had sent them out into the forest to gather wild strawberries, anxiously adding that they should have returned by this time, her husband was filled with horror. In one distant part of the forest there dwelt a wicked old Witch who enticed children into her abode by means of an array of sweetmeats on the outside of her house, and then baked them in a huge oven into gingerbreads, which she afterwards devoured. If Hansel and Gretel should have happened to lose their way, they might have fallen into the clutches of this terrible ogress.

Greatly alarmed by this fearful thought, the anxious parents, forgetting all about the meal they needed so much, hurried out into the forest to seek for their children, calling out their names as they went.

Meanwhile, Hansel and Gretel had spent a very happy evening in the forest. They were so delighted to have escaped from their irksome tasks and to be out in the beautiful woodlands, that they sang happily and played merry games with each other as they roamed about seeking for wild strawberries. Such frolics did they indulge in, indeed, that it was a very long time before th basket was even half filled. Every now and again they kept stopping to listen to the cuckoo, which they imitated in reply.

Then, while Hansel still searched for a few more berries to complete their task, Gretel plucked flowers and made them into a wreath, with which Hansel presently crowned her, bowing low before her as Queen of the Woods. Gretel was so pleased with this game that she rewarded her brother by popping first one strawberry and then another into his mouth; and presently both the children, now hungrier than ever, could no longer refrain from eating the remainder of the fruit, so that very soon the basket was empty once more.

By this time the sun had set and twilight was rapidly falling. In dismay, the children, realizing that it was too late to search for a fresh supply of strawberries, began to look for the path that led to their home; but they could not find it, and every step took them further into the depths of the forest. Knowing now that they were lost, Gretel began to cry for her father and mother; for she was full of fear and kept imagining that she beheld gnomes and goblins behind every tree. Though Hansel endeavoured to comfort her, he, too, was scared by the many strange noises he heard in the forest.

At last, darkness fell, and the two children were too weary to go another step; so they repeated their evening prayers and lay down on the mossy ground to rest, clasped in each other's arms. As they lay there, the Sandman, or Sleep Fairy, came and gently shook his magic dust in their eyes; and in a few moments they were fast asleep. While they slept a beautiful vision appeared to them; and they beheld fourteen guardian angels descending from the heavens above to keep watch over their sleeping forms. At daybreak, their dreams ended and the Dawn Fairy, rosy and bright, appeared and sprinkled dewdrops over them from a cluster of bluebells.

The Dawn Fairy and her attendants had scarcely vanished when Hansel and Gretel awakened and rubbed their eyes in surprise at finding themselves still in the forest instead of in their bed at home. Then as the mists rolled away and the sun shone forth, they beheld immediately in front of them a wonderful little house made of cakes and sweets of all kinds. It had a roof of chocolate cream, and windows of bright crystallized sugar. On one side of the house there was a large covered furnace oven, and on the other side stood a wooden cage; and the oven and the cage were joined to the house by a fence of gingerbread cut out into the figures of children. For this was the abode of the Ogress-Witch; and the figures on the fence were those of the unhappy children upon

L

whom she had cast her magic spell and had baked into ginger-bread.

Hansel and Gretel were amazed at this marvellous sight; and, delighted at the prospect of such pleasant food, the hungry children began to break off bits of sweetmeats from the cottage and to nibble them. When a voice from within called out: " Tip-tap, tip-tap, who raps at my house? " they answered merrily as they went on eating the delicious sweets: " The wind! The wind! The heavenly child! "

They were so busily munching chocolate that they did not at first notice the old Witch as she came creeping stealthily out of the cottage. Then, when they turned on hearing her cackling laugh, it was too late to run away; in a twinkling she had cast a rope around Hansel's neck and held him captive. She next put them both under a spell of enchantment by making strange gestures with a juniper bough and muttering mysterious words.

Having thus rendered both children helpless, she pushed Hansel into the cage, declaring that he must be fattened before she could cook him. She then disenchanted Gretel, who, alive to their great danger, very cleverly watched the whole performance, noticing the particular gestures and storing up in her mind the words used. When the Ogress ordered her into the house to work and make herself useful, she wisely did as she was told.

Having instructed Gretel to lay the table for a meal, the old Witch was so pleased at the prospect of the feast she was about to enjoy that she seized her broomstick and rode gaily round the cottage upon it. After thus careering about for some time, she went up to the cage in which she had placed Hansel, and, calling to Gretel to bring out a basket of food, proceeded to feed the boy through the bars of the cage. When she bade Hansel put out his finger to show the plumpness of it, the boy had the good sense to thrust forth a small bone; and the half-blind Witch, thinking that he must be nearly a skeleton, called to Gretel to bring still more food for him. While her back was turned, however, Gretel hastily snatched up the juniper bough; and by waving it and muttering in a whisper the words she had heard the Witch use, she disenchanted her brother so that all his strength came back once more.

The Witch now felt the arms and body of Gretel, and, thus discovering how plump she was, determined to make a meal of her first, since Hansel was not yet fat enough; so she went up to the oven and opened the door. Calling to Gretel, she ordered her to peep inside the huge furnace oven and tell her if the roaring fire within felt hot enough for cooking purposes—intending, of course, to push her inside. At this moment, Hansel, having managed with the help of his sister to escape from the cage while the Ogress was opening the oven door, also drew near without being observed by her.

Gretel now pretended to be very stupid; and declaring that she did not understand what she was meant to do, she begged the Ogress to show her. The old Witch, completely deceived, angrily hobbled to the open oven and, bending forward, began to feel the heat of it with her skinny hands. Instantly, Hansel and Gretel both rushed forward and bundled their enemy into the oven, shutting the door with a bang.

Full of joy at having thus disposed of the Ogress by roasting her in her own oven, the two children danced about in the highest glee. Then, as they once more began to eat the sweets off the cottage walls, there suddenly came a great crackling noise which ended in a loud explosion; and the oven fell to pieces. At the same time the figures on the gingerbread fence changed into real little boys and girls; for with the burning of the old Witch, the enchantment had also fallen from her victims and the gingerbread children took on their own forms once more. But as they were still motionless and their eyes were closed, Gretel kissed them and waved the juniper bough over them to complete the work of disenchantment.

Rejoicing at their happy release, the disenchanted children joined hands with Hansel and Gretel and danced, sang, and played all the merry games they could think of.

Just as the frolic was at its height, Peter, the Broom-maker, and his wife, Gertrude, arrived upon the scene, having sought their children sorrowfully all through the night; and it was with great thankfulness that they now clasped them in their arms once more. What was more, they were just in time to join in the crowning delight of pulling the body of the wicked old Witch out from the ruins of the oven in the form of a huge gingerbread cake into which she had herself been baked!

DIE KÖNIGSKINDER *Humperdinck*
(*Kings' Children*)

IN the midst of the dense Hella Woods, a small clearing had been made in one of the few sunny glades. Here, many miles away from the distant town of Hellabrunn, a mysterious old Witch had made her habitation. A rough tumbledown hut served her for shelter, summer and winter alike; and for companion she had a little maiden of royal birth whom she had kidnapped when the latter was but a tiny toddler.

The captive child, since babyhood, had never beheld any other human being; and she was not permitted to wander beyond sight of the hut. She knew that other people existed, however, having heard the old dame speak of the folk seen in her own wanderings to and fro.

In vain she asked for news of the bright world beyond the forest depths. In reply, she was only given a beating and harder tasks to perform; and she learned to hide her longings and to find pleasure in her secret thoughts.

The maiden's chief duty was to mind the old Witch's geese and prevent them from straying too far into the woodland depths. This was a task she loved; for then she could sit outside in the sunshine, and even deck herself with flowers and gaze at her own reflection in the sparkling streamlet.

The geese all loved her because she was gentle with them and regarded them as her friends; and it was the same with the other birds and timid wild creatures that dwelt in the woods.

One day the old witch departed into the forest depths beyond, to gather simples and also to seek for loathsome things for her magic potions and for the poisonous bread she made from time to time for sale to would-be murderers. Before going, however, she laid a temporary spell upon the trees and bushes near by, which would prevent her captive from straying beyond them during her absence.

As soon as the old dame had departed, the goose-girl's spirits rose at once, so that she began to dance and sing in the sunshine; and then, snatching up a wreath of wild-flowers she had made earlier in the day and hidden in a bush, she set it on her head and ran to gaze at her reflection in the lily-pond set in the cottage garden.

Though still clad in a short ragged gown, she was now in the first flush of fair young maidenhood; and she was possessed of a marvellous beauty, with the natural grace and noble bearing of a Princess. In spite of an old red kerchief which tightly swathed her head, a few stray golden locks escaped to betray the hidden wealth of her woman's crowning glory.

The charming picture she now beheld in the lily-pond delighted her; and she called to her beloved geese to come and admire her also. While she laughed at their obliging quacking and rejoiced in her own fair looks, she was suddenly addressed by a stranger. Turning in startled haste, she found herself face to face with a handsome youth who, though clad in garments torn and travel-stained, yet had the proud and kingly air of one of royal birth.

Though the terrified goose-girl at first stared in amazement at the stranger, her fear quickly vanished in wondering admiration and delight; and the young man was likewise enthralled by her own beauty. He had beheld many fair ladies before, but he had never yet been confronted with one of such dazzling loveli-ness as this ragged maiden.

He now told her that he was a king's son but that, dissatisfied with the emptiness of Court life, he had wandered forth from his royal home to seek adventures in the world and to gain renown alone and unaided. He added, however, that his good sword had gained him but little glory yet and that his wanderings had reduced him to the point of beggary.

After giving him water wherewith to quench his thirst, the goose-girl invited him to sit beside the lily-pond. Here the pair sat together and gazed into each other's eyes, still entranced by their mutual beauty; and overwhelming love quickly grew up in their hearts.

The King's Son could scarce believe his companion to be aught but a fairy, so fresh and fair were her looks. In answer to her wondering questions, he told her of the uses of his flashing sword, of the dull Court he had left, of his own yearnings and dis-satisfaction, and of his wanderings and adventures—how he had learned to brave dangers and to take a proud delight in freedom and the joy of living.

The beautiful goose-girl listened, enthralled and spellbound; and seeing that she already looked upon him with eyes of love, the royal youth clasped her in his arms and declared that she should presently wander forth with him.

Suddenly, a gust of wind blew off the maiden's wreath of flowers. The King's Son picked it up and thrust it into the bosom of his tunic, declaring he would keep it as a love token; and, in place of it, he drew forth a gold circlet from a small bundle he carried and offered to crown her with that instead. When, however, the young girl declared she was afraid of so grand an ornament and preferred her simple flowers, he flung the crown into the grass, put his arms around her, and began to lead her forth into the woodlands.

Happily the lovers strolled along—but for a few yards only. Presently there came another strong gust of wind, and the bushes —over which the witch had laid her temporary spell—now prevented the goose-girl from going even another yard. Terrified, the young girl stood still, while her pet geese came flocking around her, as though to entreat her not to leave them.

The King's Son, not understanding her terror or the cause of it, but thinking she cared more for her geese than for him, was offended by her now seeming desire to remain behind. When the scared maiden, still unable to move another step because of the witch's spell, now sank sobbing to the ground, the royal youth, beside himself with wrath and disappointment, reproached her bitterly; and he declared that she would never behold him again unless a miracle should happen—until a star of light should fall from the heavens above into the heart of one of the unopened lily-buds in her pond.

Then the angry youth rushed away into the forest and was quickly lost to sight; and the unhappy goose-girl was left to weep alone. In a short time, however, she saw the witch returning; and quickly she snatched up the fallen crown, slipped it over the head of her favourite goose, and drove the bird behind a bush just as the old dame appeared.

The witch, nevertheless, divined that a stranger had been with the girl; and she quickly dragged the whole story from her. Then, hearing the sounds of approaching music and voices, she roughly bundled the girl into the hut and slammed the door just as three more strangers issued forth from the wood.

The newcomers were a fiddler, a woodcutter, and a besom-maker, who announced that they had been sent to consult the Wise Woman—as they flatteringly called the witch—by the inhabitants of the neighbouring town of Hellabrunn. Their King had recently died without leaving an heir; and the counsellors of the town desired the worker of magic to tell them where they could quickest find a new ruler—who might be either a prince or a princess, but must be of royal birth and of the kingly kind.

The woodcutter and the besom-maker, being cowards at heart, were afraid to approach the witch, though they had been promised a high reward for doing so. The fiddler, however, was a seer who, having a brave and pure heart, had no fear of danger or evil influences; and he boldly marched up to the hut and knocked loudly upon the door. When the old witch appeared, angrily demanding his business, he gave his message at once.

Even as the fiddler spoke, however, he caught sight of the goose-girl peeping fearfully out of the window; and divining at once that she was of royal birth, he was filled with joy and knew that here he should find a queen, at least. The old witch, however, eager to be rid of her unwelcome visitors and remembering that the King's Son was bound to reach the town after passing through the wood, told the ambassadors that they and their friends might ring the joy-bells in Hellabrunn next day. She then prophesied that he who was of royal birth and worthy to be their King—even though he might come without pomp and in poor raiment—would be the first person to enter their town on the morrow at noon. She added cynically that the townsfolk were probably all fools and that, through their own stupidity, would as likely as not lose the good King they sought; and with this parting shot she retired into the hut and slammed the door once more.

The broom-maker and the woodcutter rushed off at once to bring this good news to their counsellors, hoping to secure the reward offered; but the fiddler, much disgusted by their mercenary natures, presently returned alone to the hut, determined to free the fair captive maiden he had seen, whom he felt sure was of royal birth.

He soon forced the angry witch to bring forth the goose-girl and to confess that the latter was indeed a princess who had been stolen in early childhood by the old dame herself. The fiddler then announced that the beautiful maiden must come away with him at once to reign as Queen in Hellabrunn, since she was worthy to be the bride of the King's Son who was to enter the town as its ruler on the morrow.

Full of joy on thus learning that she was a kingly child, the fair maiden quickly retrieved from her pet goose the crown she had refused to wear earlier in the day; and shaking down her long golden hair—which fell like a dazzling mantle around her —she placed the circlet upon her head.

Twilight had now fallen; and the goose-girl, longing for a sign that she should indeed behold her royal lover once again, fell upon her knees and prayed for a token to be given to her. To her joy, a star of light fell from the heavens above, hovered over the lily-pond, and fell into the heart of one of her beloved water-lilies, which opened at that moment to receive it.

Full of exultation as she remembered the words of the King's Son, the royal maiden, no longer afraid of the old witch, whose power over her was thus broken, now ran quickly into the dark woodlands. She was closely followed by the happy fiddler, who sang merrily to the cheerful music of his fiddle; and the angry old hag was left alone, cursing and grinding her teeth with rage.

.   .   .   .

Early next morning, the worthy folk of Hellabrunn were seen

to be bustling about, decorating their town and making preparations to receive their promised King. The broom-maker and the woodcutter had already received rewards for bringing the good news of the latter's coming arrival; and now, elated by their sudden importance, they boastfully gave out that the new ruler would come in a golden car, be clad in dazzling raiment, and be surrounded by a splendour of great glory.

Consequently, the King's Son was already in their midst before anyone knew of his arrival; for he had arrived late the evening before, footsore, ragged, and travel-stained, and had passed through the gates unnoticed, being merely regarded by the guards as a poor beggar. He passed the night sleeping behind a swine-pen, because he was too poor to enter the inn near the city gates; and early next morning, being too proud to beg, he asked the inn-keeper to let him work for his food. The latter agreed to accept him as a swine-herd; and the King's Son sat down outside the inn to rest a while before beginning his lowly tasks.

Meanwhile, the townsfolk, all in gala dress, were already assembling at the city gates in readiness to welcome their new King; and among them were the woodcutter and the broom-maker, both very pleased with the fuss now being made of them. Among the many children present was the broom-maker's little daughter, a pretty flaxen-haired child, whose natural kindness caused her to make friends at once with the weary young traveller and to invite him to play with her. The disguised and unrecognized prince, grateful for her welcome, now inquired the reason for the gay assemblage.

When the royal youth was told that the people were awaiting the arrival of a stranger of royal birth whom they meant to accept as their new King, he felt that he himself must certainly be the unknown ruler expected. He soon discovered, however, that these people of Hellabrunn were not worthy of him. When he asked the passers-by how they would receive their King should he appear before them in shabby garments and without any of the trappings of State, they were offended that such a suggestion should be made to them; and they declared snobbishly that they were only prepared to receive a ruler who came to them in gorgeous robes and in great State array, and who would be seated in a golden coach.

Feeling great contempt for such a small-minded, vulgar conception of kingship, the royal youth denounced the waiting folk as unworthy to be the subjects of a real King, declaring that a great ruler was known by his true nobility and kingly qualities rather than by his outward trappings.

Greatly enraged by this denunciation of them by a poorly-clad stranger, the townsfolk were about to set upon the latter and belabour him, when the hour of noon struck. The city gates were at once opened to the sound of clanging joy-bells; and all the people hurried forward eagerly to witness the entry of the royal stranger they expected.

To their amazement and disappointment, however, no gorgeously-clad King approached in a golden coach. Instead, there passed through the widely-opened gates the fair young goose-girl, still clad in her short ragged gown, but with a golden crown upon her long flowing locks. She was attended only by her flock of faithful geese, closely followed by the fiddler; and all the people stared in astonishment when, on beholding the newly-engaged swine-herd, she hastened to his side at once. Holding out her arms towards him, she announced that she was now worthy to wear his crown as a royally-born maiden; and she further declared that her love had cast out all her former fears and that she would evermore be true and faithful to him.

The King's Son, full of joy, clasped the beautiful maiden in his arms, pouring forth sweet tender words of love and devotion and addressing her as his Queen.

On hearing the poorly-clad strangers thus addressing one another as king and queen, the crowd burst forth into peals of derisive laughter; and though the fiddler eagerly declared that the loving pair were indeed of royal birth and entreated his neighbours to receive them as their rulers, bidding all to observe that they possessed the noble bearing that only belonged to kingly children, the stupid people of Hellabrunn would have none of them. Instead, they drove out the King's Son and the beautiful royal goose-girl with contumely from their town and closed the gates upon them.

Only one amongst them all believed the words of the fiddler. This was the broom-maker's little flaxen-haired daughter, who flung herself weeping upon the ground, crying out aloud because her foolish townsfolk had driven forth the noble and gracious royal pair who had been sent to rule over them. But no one paid any heed to the weeping child; for the angry people were already hustling off the staunch fiddler to the town gaol. Here they kept him several months as a captive and roughly ill-treated him because he had asked them to accept a couple of ragged strangers as their rulers. They also sent soldiers to arrest the old witch, declaring furiously that she had deceived them—whereas, for once in her life, the old dame had told them the truth. Nevertheless, they burnt her at the stake as a dealer in magic prophecy which was of no avail.

.　　　.　　　.　　　.　　　.　　　.

When at last the fiddler was released from gaol, it was winter-time; and he would certainly have starved had not the broom-maker's little daughter brought him food and helped him to reach the witch's deserted hut, where he could shelter in safety. He was greatly cheered when the little maid told him that she had already caused all the other children in the town to realize that the luckless strangers whom their undiscerning elders had so foolishly driven from their midst were indeed the expected royal King and Queen whose coming they had so eagerly awaited.

Next day, all the children came trooping out from the town through the snow to the hut, to entreat the fiddler to go forth with them to seek the royal lovers whom they believed were still wandering in the woodlands. As they made their plans, the broom-maker and the woodcutter also appeared with the news that the fiddler had now been forgiven by the townsfolk, who desired him to return and again make their hearts merry with his music. The fiddler, however, indignantly refused to dwell with people who were too stupid and mean-spirited to understand the meaning of true kingship and who had not the discernment to recognize a king even though he came before them in humble garments. He turned aside, therefore, and led the children away into the woods to begin their search; and the broom-maker and the woodcutter, afraid to return without the fiddler, took shelter for a while in the hut.

The Hellabrunn children were right in their belief that the royal wanderers were still in the forest; but they did not find them immediately.

Later on that same day, the King's Son struggled forth into the snowy glade near the hut, bearing in his arms the beautiful goose-girl, who was too exhausted and numb with cold to walk another step. During the months that had passed by the royal lovers had found sheltered spots in which to rest and partake of the scanty food which the woodlands provided; but now, at last, they had come to the end of their resources and were dying from want of food and from exposure.

Seeing that the hut was occupied, the young prince knocked hopefully at the door. When it was opened, he entreated the newly-arrived inmates for some food for his companion; but the stingy pair refused to part with anything without payment. Having no money, the royal youth brought forth from the bundle on his back the golden crown he had managed to preserve in his wanderings; and he offered half of it in payment for an ancient cake of dry bread left in a cupboard by the old witch and just found by the woodcutter. The latter, however, greedily demanded the whole of the crown; and the King's Son, thinking only of his beloved one's necessity, flung the golden circlet into the hut and received the stale hard cake in return.

The goose-girl revived for a while after nibbling some of the hard bread; and she insisted upon her companion eating some of it, too.. Then the weary pair talked happily for a short time longer in weak low voices, recalling the bright days of the autumn when they had sat together in the sunshine and had decked one another with flowers.

But the cake they had partaken of was a poisoned one, and the King's Son and the goose-girl soon knew that they were dying. As another storm began to blow and the snowflakes quickly covered them, the royal lovers kissed one another tenderly for the last time and softly sank into the sleep of death.

Here, on a frozen bank, covered with snow, they were found at last by the fiddler and the children of Hellabrunn, who all fell on their knees before them and wept for the sad fate of the fair young King and Queen who had come to a people unworthy to receive them.

I PAGLIACCI
(*The Players, or The Mountebanks*)   *Leoncavallo*

IT was the Feast of the Assumption, and the light-hearted inhabitants of a pretty village in Calabria had turned out in full force to make the most of the last day of a successful fair that had been held in their midst. The fair ground was crowded with holiday-makers, all bent on amusement, and a brisk business was carried on at the various shows and booths from morning till night.

A company of strolling players had been one of the chief attractions of the fair; and when during the afternoon, Canio, the master of the troupe, mounted the steps of his portable open-air theatre and, beating a noisy drum, invited the holiday-makers to attend a special performance to be given that evening, the announcement was hailed with great delight. The merry youths and maidens all signified their intention of witnessing the play;

and then Canio, assured of a good audience, went to spend the intervening time at the village tavern, together with his friend Beppo, the Harlequin of the company.

The travelling theatre had been set up close beside a high wall that separated the fair ground from the country road; and no sooner had Canio departed, than his pretty young actress wife, Nedda, came out from the booth and began to stroll towards this wall, as though expecting to see someone appear above it.

At the same moment, a hunchback named Tonio, who played the clown in the troupe's play, quickly approached and addressed her in endearing terms. Though distorted in mind as well as in body, the poor buffoon had yet fallen a victim to the charms of his master's wife and had long awaited this opportunity to declare his love. But the pretty Nedda, who hated and despised the hunchback, only laughed in derision at his protestations; and when the eager Tonio, rendered reckless by his passion, attempted boldly to seize her in his arms, she angrily snatched up a whip that was lying near and began to belabour him with it. The wretched hunchback was now obliged to make a hasty retreat; but, much enraged by her scornful treatment of him, he determined to avenge himself upon her and slunk off with evil in his heart.

As Nedda heaved a sigh of relief after watching Tonio vanish in the crowd, she heard her own name softly uttered in tender accents. Seeing the form of a handsome young man appearing above the wall, she hurried forward with delight, this second intruder on her solitude being as welcome as the first had been distasteful. For the pretty young actress had already wearied of her husband, whose more serious nature and almost savage love repelled her. Consequently, when Silvio, a rich young farmer in the district who had fallen in love with her at the theatre, found an opportunity to declare his passion, she had quickly returned his love, finding relief and pleasure in his gentler manners and softer moods.

The lovers met in secret at every opportunity; for Nedda, though constantly afraid of her husband's anger should he discover the intrigue, was yet daring enough to seek happiness at the risk of danger. Now Silvio had come for a last interview, knowing that the troupe were to depart on the morrow, since this was the final day of the fair.

The rustic youth quickly scaled the wall; and, clasping his sweetheart in his arms, he besought her to escape with him that night and leave a husband who was no better than a tyrant and a life that was distasteful to her. For a short time Nedda tried to resist Silvio's pleading, begging him not to tempt her; but at length.

overcome by his passionate entreaties, she yielded and promised to meet him that night after the last performance was over at the theatre, that they might depart together in secret.

Whilst the lovers were thus engrossed, Tonio returned, and watched this pretty scene for a few moments unobserved. Then, suddenly seeing in this incident a means of avenging himself upon Nedda for her disdainful treatment of his love, he crept softly away and departed to the village tavern to disclose to Canio the story of his wife's faithlessness.

On hearing the hunchback's tale, Canio was overwhelmed with rage and jealousy and instantly returned with him to the theatre. He arrived on the scene just in time to see Silvio disappearing over the wall and waving a tender farewell to Nedda, who answered him lovingly from below, repeating her promise to meet him after dark.

Enraged by this proof of his beautiful wife's infidelity, the injured husband ran forward to intercept the departing lover; but Silvio was already on the other side of the wall and beyond his reach. Canio then turned furiously upon the trembling Nedda; and roughly seizing her by the arm, he demanded the name of her lover. Nedda, though terrified by her husband's angry words and threatening aspect, boldly refused to betray the man she loved; and Canio, maddened by her refusal, impetuously drew his dagger from its sheath, declaring that he would kill her.

At this moment, Beppo appeared, having followed his friend from the tavern, fearing that something was wrong. Hearing Canio's threat, he sprang forward at once and, snatching the weapon from his hand, begged him to calm himself and prepare for the evening's performance at the theatre, since the holiday-makers were already clamouring for admission.

After an angry altercation, Canio was at length persuaded to remember the duties of his profession and to release Nedda, who quickly escaped to the back of the theatre; and having thus pacified his friend for the time being, Beppo began to make preparations for the approaching entertainment. The hunchback, too, begged his leader to dress for the play, cunningly suggesting that Nedda's lover would probably attend the theatre that night and thus give them an opportunity of attacking him. Canio, full of grief and despair—for he loved his wife passionately in his rough, savage way—was now persuaded to take his usual part in the comedy, although a tragedy was in his heart.

A lively audience of village folk now quickly filled the benches that had been placed before the open stage; and those who could not get seats stood on the rising ground at the back, all chattering together and eager for the play to begin.

Amongst those who managed to get a place near the front was the handsome Silvio, who, as Tonio had predicted, had not been able to resist the temptation of watching his sweetheart from afar; and when Nedda, now clad in her stage dress as Columbine—which part she took in the play—presently passed alongside the audience to collect the seat money, he whispered in her ear a tender reminder of their meeting later on.

By a strange coincidence, the play chosen for performance that night proved to be a burlesque of the very incidents the actors themselves had just experienced. The unsuspecting audience, though they little guessed it, were to be regaled with a page from real life, a repetition of the events that had occurred unobserved by them outside the theatre that afternoon—a comedy that was to end in a tragedy!

When the curtain went up Columbine—impersonated by Nedda—was discovered waiting for her lover, Harlequin—played by Beppo—whom she was about to entertain to supper during the absence of her husband, Punchinello. A half-witted servant, Taddeo—played by Tonio—entered after the opening speech, carrying food for the supper; and after placing the viands on the table, he began to make a grotesque declaration of love to Columbine, causing much laughter amongst the audience. Columbine, however, scornfully rejected his addresses and bade him begone; and Harlequin, who entered through the window at that moment, soon drove off the importunate servant and sent him to keep watch below. Harlequin and Columbine next went through an exaggerated love-scene, the faithless wife yielding to her lover's request to elope with him that night. Then, just as they settled down to enjoy the feast together, Taddeo ran into the room again, announcing in dramatic tones to Columbine that her husband had just returned home unexpectedly and was already vowing vengeance on her for entertaining a stranger during his absence. With a parting wave of the hand, Harlequin very ungallantly disappeared through the window, following the example of Taddeo, who had already decamped in another direction; and just as Columbine called out a tender farewell to her departing lover, Punchinello—impersonated by Canio—dashed into the room.

Until now, the play had been a most amusing burlesque and the audience had been kept in a state of constant laughter by the many ridiculous situations; but with the entrance of Punchinello, they quickly saw that serious drama was to follow. It happened that Nedda, as Columbine, in her farewell speech to Harlequin, had unconsciously made use of the very same words she had addressed to her real lover in the afternoon; and Canio, remembering only too well the speech that had brought such despair to his heart, gave vent to his jealous rage once more. Forgetting the words of the play, he seized his wife by the arm and again demanded the name of her lover. Nedda, surprised and alarmed by this unrehearsed incident of the play, went on with her Columbine speeches; and for a short time Canio returned to his part of Punchinello and the play proceeded. Columbine explained to her enraged spouse that it was only the foolish servant Taddeo who had been her guest at supper; and Taddeo, being discovered hiding in a cupboard, made a ludicrous speech, beseeching Punchinello not to doubt the fidelity of his wife and declaring in exaggerated terms that she would never deceive him. These play-book words caused Canio's suppressed passion to break out once more. Forgetting all but his own wrongs, he once more ordered Nedda to reveal the name of her lover, declaring passionately that he was Punchinello no longer but the husband she had deceived.

The audience had at first been delighted by what they considered the fine acting of the injured Punchinello, frequently giving vent to enthusiastic applause; but now they began to grow restless, feeling that such an intensity of passion could hardly be assumed. It was in vain that Nedda endeavoured to go on with the words of the play; and, seeing that her maddened husband was in deadly earnest, she only sought to defend herself. In spite of his threats, she utterly refused to declare the name of her lover; and at last, driven to madness by her refusal, Canio, in a frenzy of jealousy, drew his dagger and plunged it into her heart.

The audience, no longer deceived, but realizing that an actual tragedy was going on before their eyes, uttered loud shrieks of dismay; and Silvio, full of horror and despair, sprang upon the stage at a bound. Lifting his already dead sweetheart in his arms, he implored her in grief-stricken accents to speak to him once again. But Canio leapt upon him instantly, knowing now that the handsome young farmer was his rival and the cause of his woe; and with a second stroke of his dagger, he stretched the bereaved lover dead beside the fallen body of the hapless Nedda.

For a few moments, the frenzied Canio stood dazed and stupefied, gazing upon his dreadful handiwork; and then, as the spectators sprang forward to seize him, he yielded himself quietly into their hands, muttering tragically as they led him away: " The comedy is finished! "

IERNIN
Lloyd
(*A Celtic Tale*)

LONG after the Saxons had established themselves in England, many of the ancient Celtic princes still held sway in the wild hills and wide open spaces of Wales and in Cornwall. Here, though they were compelled to acknowledge the Saxon kings as their overlords, they continued for a number of years to rule over their own people and to keep them as a race apart from the alien invaders.

Among these proud Celtic princes was Bedwyr of West Penwith in Cornwall, whose ancestors had ruled in that part of the country long before King Arthur's days. So passionately eager was Bedwyr to keep the blood of his own race pure and untainted that when the time came for his beautiful daughter, Cunaide, to wed, he betrothed her to one of his own Cornish nobles, Gerent —although he knew that the Saxon King, his overlord, had already expressed the desire that her hand should be given to one of his own flaxen-haired Earls. Before any formal request for this alien alliance had been made, therefore, Bedwyr hurried on the marriage; and Gerent and Cunaide were well pleased enough, since they loved one another dearly.

On the day before his nuptials were to be celebrated, Gerent, accompanied by his friend, Edryn, another young Cornish noble, took part in a great hunt, this being the last entertainment of the kind he would enjoy as a bachelor. The hunting-party set off just before dawn, making their way to a wild and lonely spot on the moorlands, where stood a Circle of Stones known as the Nine Maidens. Here they intended to begin hunting in earnest as the first rays of the sun shone forth.

Before the huntsmen arrived, however, signs of life were already beginning to appear at this lonely spot. The Circle of Stones on Carn Galva, known as the Nine Maidens, had been regarded as a mysterious enchanted place longer than any man could remember. It was believed by the Cornish folk that in the earliest days of Christianity a wandering Saint had seen in that spot nine lovely Faery Sisters, who belonged to the magic Shining People of the Hills. They were dancing such a wild fantastic dance that he had feared for its pagan effect upon his recent converts, whom they were already seductively smiling upon. He had, therefore, sternly transformed the happy dancing sylphs into a circle of stones.

But folks who visited the enchanted spot at lonely times declared that mysterious sweet singing could sometimes be heard there— strange ethereal voices from the Faery World and from the invisible Shining People of the hills, woods, moorlands, and waterfalls.

At dawn to-day, not only Faery voices were to be heard. As the silvery voices rang out more clearly, as though to welcome the first rosy rays of the rising sun, one of the Stone Maidens in the enchanted Circle of Nine began to shiver and stir, and slowly to take on life. Gradually it assumed the shape and lovely ethereal features of Iernin, a Faery of the Hills, one of the Shining People and the most beautiful of the Nine Sisters who had been transformed into stone so many years ago.

So clear and strong had been the greeting of the Faery voices at dawn that day that Iernin had awakened from her long stony sleep and had come to life once more.

Full of rapturous joy on finding herself free again to sing and dance, Iernin invoked the hills and streams with her silvery voice, and with outstretched arms and dancing feet. Then, as she moved in and out among the eight remaining Stones, she suddenly remembered all that had happened to herself and these, her still cold and lifeless Sisters; and she became afraid. She called wildly upon her Faery kin; but the sweet voices had ceased to sing and there was no reply.

Instead, there now came the merry sound of mortal hunting-horns; and, full of terror, Iernin ran away to hide behind the bushes.

As Gerent and Edryn came hurrying up in advance of their friends to the Circle of Stones, they spoke happily together of the former's wedding on the morrow and of their mutual satisfaction that, by this alliance, Cornish folk would still be ruled by one of their own blood for many long years to come.

But their happy dream of the future was suddenly interrupted by a frightened cry; and next moment a group of huntsmen attendants hurried up to the Stone Circle, dragging with them the terrified Iernin, whom they had discovered hiding behind the bushes and whom they declared to be a witch, or an unholy being from another world who would cast an evil spell upon them all.

Seeing the wild, unearthly beauty of Iernin, Edryn likewise was filled with alarm lest his party had happened upon someone of magical or unlawful influence; and he was the more convinced that such was the case when he observed the strange effect of this uncanny encounter upon his friend.

Instantly on beholding one another, Gerent and Iernin had gazed into each other's eyes with the wondering delight of recognition, as though they had been lovers in some forgotten existence; and they seemed drawn to one another by a strong magical influence they were powerless to resist.

Tenderly and eagerly, Gerent spoke with the lovely Faery stranger who enthralled him so completely; and on learning her name, it seemed as familiar to him as his own.

But Edryn, now more alarmed than ever, declared that his friend must indeed be bewitched; and he bade the strange sylph-like maiden to depart. When Gerent indignantly inquired where could she go, since she was a wandering stranger, Edryn declared he cared not what happened to her so long as her disturbing presence was removed from their party; and he again sternly bade her begone.

The huntsmen, too, were convinced that the stranger was a witch and that evil would befall them if they came further under her magic spell; and, at a signal from Edryn, they loudly sounded their horns once more and dashed away to continue their interrupted hunting.

Gerent now seemed almost powerless to move of his own free will, being entirely under the spell of the lovely sylph; but when Edryn approached and took him by the hand, he allowed himself to be led away by his friend, though still as under the influence of a dream.

Thus was Iernin left alone, friendless and forsaken by the splendid mortal in whose eyes she had seen the light of love for her; and with a cry of woe, she fled away to hide once more, hoping for his return.

. . . .

That night in the Castle of Bosigran, Edryn related to Bedwyr the Prince the story of the strange encounter that had befallen the hunting-party that morning on the moor; and he also told him of the enthralment of Gerent.

Bedwyr, though declaring that the monks would deal with the sylph-maiden if she should prove to be a witch was, nevertheless, greatly distressed by the news; and he felt that some untoward fate was about to befall his house. He had misgivings now as to whether he had acted wisely in defying the Saxon King, his overlord, in the matter of his daughter's marriage; and he wondered whether misfortune would fall upon his beloved people in consequence.

But when, presently, his fair daughter, Cunaide, once more convinced him of her deep love for Gerent and of her desire to wed none other, the anxious Prince knew that her happiness, at least, was assured.

While they were talking on this matter, a Saxon Thane arrived at the castle with a message from his royal master, the Saxon King, demanding that the Princess Cunaide should be betrothed to the noble Earl, Æthelwulf.

Though this message was a haughty command from an overlord, disobedience to which might result in renewed warfare, it had the effect of rousing not only Bedwyr and Cunaide but all their followers to a great pitch of patriotic defiance. The latter were prepared to fight to the last man, if needs be, for the rights of their Prince and his fair daughter; and the discomfited envoy was bidden to return to his royal lord with the firm reply that his proposition was not acceptable.

.   .   .   .

Consequently, the marriage of Gerent and Cunaide went forward next day, as arranged.

Early in the morning, all the country folk of the district, dressed in festive attire, came flocking to the edge of the moors to see the wedding procession pass by. Here, at the cross-roads, an old Celtic Cross was to be seen in the background; and near this symbol of their faith, the simple people gathered in merry groups to gossip about the great folk now to be wedded and of the festivities in which they themselves would presently share. Bonfires would be lighted that night; and there would be feasting and merry-making for all at the castle and in the villages around.

The gossips had already heard of the bridegroom's meeting with the sylph-maiden; and they knew also that one of the Nine Maidens rocks had been removed, or had vanished. This led to much talk in awed tones of the mysterious Faery Shining People, of whom so many strange tales had been told in days gone by. Though such tales of enchantment were not approved by the monks and priests, the country folk still clung to their old superstitions. Better the Shining People, than the Saxon invaders, they felt.

When the grand wedding procession at last came by, complete with priests, monks, and lords and ladies in attendance on the bridal party, a great shout of greeting arose from the crowd. And when Prince Bedwyr called upon his people to stand by him should the Saxon King make trouble because of his defiance in this matter of his daughter's marriage, their shouts of acquiescence were mightier still; and they willingly swore before the Cross, at the command of the priests, obedience to their leal lord.

The excitement was still at its height and the wedding procession was just moving away—Cunaide smiling and happy, and Gerent calm, though still in a curious dream-like state—when there came a sudden interruption.

From behind some bushes, the sylph-like lovely form of Iernin came into view, moving slowly and uncertainly towards the bridal pair; and at the sight of this unearthly stranger, the procession stopped and the people pressed forward, staring in amazement and fear.

Iernin was also afraid and shrank back from the admiring glances cast upon her by some of the men; then, as her eyes fell suddenly upon the Celtic Cross, she uttered a shriek of terror at this symbol of a religion strange to one who hailed from pagan days. This cry seemed to prove to some of the crowd that the stranger must indeed be a witch; and they called on the priests for aid, while Iernin, distracted, invoked her own radiant Shining Ones, the Faery Folk, to help her.

Then, at last catching sight of Gerent in the centre of the bridal party, Iernin rushed forward and flung herself into his arms, hailing him joyfully as her lover and begging him to save her.

Full of horror, the people shrank back, while the priests raised their Crosses and declared the stranger maiden to be a witch and an outcast; and they added that anyone who gave her aid or spoke with her must likewise become an outcast.

But neither the stern denunciations of the priests nor the despairing reproaches of his fair bride, kept the unresisting Gerent from the Faery visitant who so enthralled him; and he declared that since he was to be regarded as an outcast and as one cursed by the priests, he was no longer a fit mate for the Prince's daughter.

Then, seizing the lovely Iernin by the hand, he hailed her as his bride and rushed away with her towards the moorlands beyond.

All the wedding-party fell back in horror and dismay; and the festival which had begun so happily, ended in confusion.

Clouds had been gathering all day; and when night fell, a great storm arose.

As it died away temporarily, two forms emerged from a sheltering bush and made their way towards the Nine Maidens Circle of Stones. They were Gerent and Iernin, returning irresistibly to the spot where they had first met; but happiness was not to be theirs for long.

Iernin already knew that they must part, that her beloved one could not thus cut himself off from his own kith and kin; and she now tried to persuade him to leave her and return to his home, since he was bound by the life that had given him birth.

But Gerent declared that as he had been cast off by his own people, he was now free and bound by no human law; and he added that he was hers for ever.

As the lovers thus spoke together, they were presently joined by Cunaide, who, though full of woe for her own sad heart, reproached Gerent solely for deserting his people in their time of need; and she begged him to return and to seek pardon at the altar he had desecrated. She believed that he was under a magic spell; and she had thus bravely sought him out secretly, hoping to save him yet, for she loved him still.

The coming of Cunaide proved to the unhappy Iernin that she had been right in persuading her mortal lover to leave her, and that the gulf between his world and her own was indeed too great for them to encompass.

But Gerent was still too deeply spellbound by his strange mad passion; and he refused the entreaties of both the women who loved him so dearly.

Then Iernin, realizing that nothing else would avail but her own disappearance, now broke away from her lover's side and once more took her stand in the empty space in the Circle of Stones. Here she invoked the supernatural powers of her own Faery World; and she called passionately upon the mighty Shining Ones to grant her the gift of forgetfulness—since she could never return to them after having loved a mortal—and to transform her once more to stone.

As she called forth a last tender farewell to her earthly lover, the storm broke again fiercely, so that in the renewed darkness she was lost to sight. Presently, however, when the storm-clouds had passed by and the pale moon shone forth again, it was seen that Iernin, the lovely sylph-maiden, had vanished for ever.

But the blank space in the Stone Circle was empty no longer; and where Iernin had last been seen, a rock-bound figure now stood again. The Nine Maidens were complete once more.

Then, as Cunaide led Gerent, still dazed and half-dreaming, back towards his home, knowing that her own tender love would heal his wounded heart in time, the Faery Voices of the Shining People were heard again, calling to one another—but not by Iernin, who had sacrificed all joy for evermore for the good of her mortal lover.

THE SERF   *Lloyd*

In the days of the early Norman Kings, England was far from being a peaceful country; and clashes between the victorious Normans and the conquered Saxons were frequent. Outlaw bands roamed the forests; and though the ranks of these were mainly made up of bold Saxons who defied the yoke of the Normans, they were sometimes joined also by discontented Norman rebels who made use of them for their own purposes.

This was especially the case during the stormy reign of King Stephen, when many of the outlaw bands joined forces with Matilda and her rebels. Among the chief of these was the Saxon, Sweyn—once a serf, but now a fearless outlaw who had wrested freedom for himself and had gathered a strong band of stout fellows around him, all sworn to defiance of the grasping Normans who had wronged them.

On the day on which this story opens, Sweyn and his men were eager to secure recruits for their band in Yorkshire; and for this purpose they were in hiding amidst the thick forests of the Hambleton Hills, near the village of Corsbi, where they had many sympathizers. They would not show themselves openly until evening, when the forest workers returned from their tree felling; meanwhile, in the village, life went on as usual.

Towards evening, their day's work done, the women of the village—all of them serfs—stood outside their poor dwellings awaiting the return of their men-folk. Among them was Sigrid, a beautiful young girl, who awaited the return of her lover, Cerdic, to whom she hoped to be betrothed on the morrow should the great Norman Lord of the Manor give his consent.

Sigrid was always anxious lest evil should befall her beloved one . . . his brother had been killed recently by a falling oak; and she knew not contentment now until Cerdic had returned safely each evening. She was afraid, too, that their Seigneur, the powerful Norman Lord de Fulke, might not consent to their betrothal.

Her mother, Githa, however, declared that de Fulke, though a Norman, was always just and kindly towards his thralls; and Sigrid was cheered somewhat by her words.

These two Saxon women were of a more superior bearing and appearance than the others around them, as though they came of higher birth, despite the fact that they were now serfs; and this was, indeed, the case. Githa's folk were of a royal race and had been free and prosperous before being enthralled by the conquerors; and she herself was still regarded with reverence in the village as a Seeress.

As Githa now soothed her anxious daughter, the men workers returned from the woodlands; and next moment Sigrid was happy in her lover's arms. Forgotten now were her anxieties, as she listened to Cerdic's praises of her beauty and of his joy in their coming betrothal.

But these peaceful moments were soon broken. A furtive figure was seen moving in and out among the trees; and presently the outlaw, Sweyn, sprang out into the midst of the villagers and greeted them cheerily. In particular, he greeted the handsome young Cerdic, whose strength and bravery he knew well; and he now invited the latter to join his bold band of outlaws, to cast off the bonds of thraldom that bound him, and to fight for his freedom.

But Cerdic did not respond readily to this enticing invitation, saying that, now he was about to be betrothed, he wished for a more settled life; an outlaw's den and a hunted life were not good prospects for any woman. The other villagers, too, were not easily roused from their apathy, for the Norman lord they served happened to be one of the nobler and more generous kind who treated his people well, so that they felt their thraldom less.

But when Sweyn mounted upon a huge oaken log and began to harangue them with all the vigour and eloquence of the born orator, they were at last impressed, in spite of themselves. For Sweyn gave them the dreaded news that though their present Seigneur—who was old and blind—had treated them well in the past, his son and successor had just returned from abroad, where he had imbibed much harder views regarding the conquered race. Why then, argued Sweyn, wait to feel the fangs of this young wolf?

So engrossed were the now thoroughly roused villagers that they scarcely noted the approach of a body of horsemen. But Sweyn's quick outlaw's eye, ever on the alert for danger, had seen and recognized the arms of the de Fulke followers; and firing an arrow into their midst as a sharp greeting and act of defiance from one who hated them, he sprang from his log and dashed furiously into the forest behind, where he was instantly lost in the dense undergrowth.

As the horsemen now drew rein, the villagers became silent, sullenly drooping their eyes and standing with the usual cowed mien of those in bondage.

The first of the new arrivals was the Reeve, or bailiff of their own Norman Seigneur, de Fulke; and he demanded angrily who had shot the arrow now sticking into the shield of one of his men. On learning that the arrow had been shot by a stranger who had fled, he dispatched a search-party into the forest—who, however, soon returned, empty-handed.

Meanwhile, the Reeve was presently joined by his newly-returned young lord, Robert de Fulke, with his squire and more fully-armed soldier-attendants. The haughty young lord, hearing of the incident, merely regarded the sullen serfs with contempt—until his roving eye fell upon Sigrid. Struck by the latter's beauty and unexpected dignity, he called her to his side and questioned both her and Githa, who stood beside her proudly. When he expressed amazement that one so full of natural grace should be living among serfs of coarser grain, Githa replied for both, declaring that, though now indeed serfs against their will, their ancestors had once been kings.

Robert bowed mockingly on hearing this statement; and with more admiring glances at Sigrid, who he declared was much too fair to be dwelling among such churls, he rode on with his men.

Cerdic, alarmed by the admiration and sudden look of lawless passion which had flamed in the dark eyes of the powerful young lord as he spoke with Sigrid, now begged her to remain no longer in the village, but to escape with him to join the outlaws, where she would at least be safe from this new danger which now threatened her. The young girl's own fears had likewise been aroused by this unwelcome encounter, though she was reluctant to leave her mother behind. When Githa added her own entreaties to those of Cerdic, however, she was about to bid her a hurried farewell when the Reeve, with some of Robert's soldiers, suddenly returned and declared that the young Seigneur had bidden them seize the fair maiden, Sigrid, and bring her to the castle.

Realizing that it was now too late to fly, Cerdic furiously attacked the first soldier to approach Sigrid and struck him to the ground with his axe; but before he could attack another, he was himself seized and bound by the other soldiers. The villagers, in protection of Sigrid, now wildly fell upon the remaining soldiers; and since the latter were in the minority, the Reeve called his men off and returned angrily to the castle, but carrying the wretched Cerdic with him, a captive.

Next day, the Reeve had a stormy interview with his young lord, to whom he brought the unwelcome news that Cerdic, the captive serf, might not receive the punishment desired for him

—namely, the loss of his hand, at least, if not a hanging. Robert
was also furious because the beautiful girl for whom he had conceived such a sudden passion had been denied him owing to her
lover's brave defence.

But the elder de Fulke, though he had not denied himself
similar unlawful pleasures in his own younger days, was a just
man. The soldier attacked by Cerdic had been wounded only,
and the serf's action was justifiable; hence the great lord had
decided to hear the whole case in his own Court of Justice at the
castle and to give judgment accordingly.

Curiously enough, this Norman nobleman had come to love
the conquered people he ruled over as dearly as though they had
been of his own race. His whole outlook on life, too, had changed
since he had visited the Holy Sepulchre as a Crusader some years
ago; and when, later on, he had become blind, his proud nature
had been subdued and his softened heart had become kindly.

So young Robert knew that his father was likely to deal at least
justly, if not indulgently, with the captive serf; and after curtly
dismissing the Reeve, he angrily paced the great hall of the castle,
feeling frustrated by such leniency and vowing himself to stern
harshness when his own turn came to rule.

His fuming was presently interrupted by an attendant now
ushering in a stranger, who desired to speak with him. The new
arrival proved to be Githa, the mother of Sigrid, who had come to
intercede for her daughter's lover and to plead with Robert and
his noble father to spare the young man's life. But Robert merely
laughed scornfully in her face, bidding her mockingly to call on
her royal ancestors for help.

Then Githa, who had occult gifts, fell into a sort of trance and
declared that, as in a vision, she could see three forms, one of
which lay dead and covered with a shroud—this latter the figure
of himself.

Robert, though inwardly alarmed, feeling that this strange
Saxon dame was, indeed, a Seer, pretended not to be impressed
by her statement; nevertheless, he rushed from her unwelcome
presence and, though laughing derisively, his laugh had a tinge
of fear in it.

.   .   .   .

When the elder de Fulke presently held his Court of Justice in
the great Hall of his castle, the proceedings were conducted with
as much open fairness and justice as though the prisoner, instead
of being merely a poor serf of the conquered race, had been a
noble Norman lord.

The blind Seigneur, wearing his impressive Crusader's garb,

was led to the raised dais by a page-boy; and the villagers were allowed to be present to see that justice was done to one of their own people and in accordance with their own laws of Edward the Confessor.

Even when, at times, the villagers became somewhat out of hand, so that young Robert haughtily begged his father to have them ejected, the latter insisted that they had every right to remain.

At first, Cerdic refused to defend himself or to give the reason why he had been provoked to strike the Lord Robert's man, wishing to spare his beloved one. But when things began to look black for him because of this, Sigrid herself rushed forward from her place among the other serfs and told the whole story plainly —how her lover had struck down the soldier who had been sent to abduct her for the pleasure of the newly-arrived young lord.

At the sound of the young girl's voice, the elder de Fulke seemed stirred as though by some half-forgotten memory; and when her mother, Githa, also stepped forth and added her evidence and entreaties for the release of Cerdic to those of her distracted daughter, his remembrance became clearer still—and he knew that a certain sin of his early youth had returned to reproach him. He was filled with grief and remorse; but first, justice must be done.

Having received a reluctant confirmation of this story from his now sullen son, de Fulke announced that as Cerdic's act had been the result of justifiable provocation he should be instantly released; and, not only this, but that he and Sigrid and Githa should receive their freedom and be serfs no longer.

Then, ordering the Court to be cleared of the now tumultuously triumphant and cheering villagers, but keeping back the chief actors in this episode, de Fulke questioned Githa more fully, having recognized her voice as that of one he had loved in the past though his blindness had prevented his recognition of her once admired features. From her replies, he then knew that his surmise was true and that the beautiful Sigrid was his own love-child by her.

But a stranger and more disastrous fact now also transpired —a fact which brought woe to the lovers. For de Fulke now announced that the ex-Serf was his son by another woman; and he sorrowfully added that, this being so, Cerdic and Sigrid were, therefore, brother and sister and so might never be united.

Now, full of despairing grief, the lovers were taken away by Githa, who wept with them for their woe; and presently they were followed by Robert, who quickly sought means of taking vengeance upon Cerdic for his defiance of him and likewise planned to secure Sigrid yet as his victim.

Meanwhile, the blind and prematurely-aged Seigneur was left alone in his Hall of Justice; and he now set up his dagger on the table as a Cross and knelt down humbly before it to pray, full of remorse for the tragic result of his early transgressions.

. . . .

In the forest near Lake Gormire, Sweyn and his outlaws had met for a final rally of recruits before joining forces with either Stephen the Usurper, or with Matilda the rightful claimant for England's troubled throne—it scarce seemed to matter which side they ranked themselves upon, since both factions provided them with equal chances of escape from their present hunted state.

Having made sure that his men were fed and ready for any emergency that might arise, Sweyn gave orders for the outlaw band to move off towards Thurso, where fighting was likely to begin shortly; but he decided to remain in the district himself with a picked band of men at no great distance and to return shortly in the hope of thus securing a few more last-minute recruits.

Scarcely had the outlaw band departed than Cerdic and Sigrid came hurrying through the forest, desperately seeking escape from the vengeful Robert, who they knew was already following them. They had hoped to be in time to join the outlaws, with whom they felt they might hide in safety; and when they now found the meeting-place deserted and knew that the outlaws had already departed, they were filled with despair.

The lovers were indeed in an unhappy plight; unable to be wedded, they could not bear to be parted. They had rushed off blindly into the forest—only to find that aid was denied them here.

Sigrid, distracted and weary, begged to be allowed to rest a while; but in their present danger, Cerdic dared not halt, being eager to push on in the hope of overtaking their outlaw friends.

Even as they paused a few moments to make this decision, Cerdic's fears were justified; for Robert and his men came dashing through the forest and bade them halt and return, since they were serfs on his land.

Cerdic called wildly upon Sweyn to come to his rescue, shouting his name loudly, as he felt the outlaws could not yet be very far away; and, to his relief, he heard an answering cry in the distance. He then turned upon the furious Robert and declared that the latter no longer had power over the movements of himself and Sigrid, since the elder de Fulke had already given them both their freedom; but Robert exultingly announced that no legal documents had yet been drawn up to this effect. Meanwhile, might was right, and he intended to enforce his own will.

He then gave orders for his men to bind Cerdic and to seize Sigrid. At that moment, however, Sweyn and his company of picked adventurers came dashing up to the rescue.

A wild encounter followed, in which Robert was slain by one of the outlaws; and his Norman followers were quickly routed.

A priest who had been following in the wake of the escaping lovers, now arrived upon the scene in the midst of this tumult; and he sternly commanded all to fall back before the Cross he held on high.

After praying for a few moments over the dead body of Robert, the priest then placed himself between the lovers, declaring that since they both were the children of one father they must now part for ever; and he bade them say farewell.

The unhappy pair, although they had blindly rushed away together into the forest, had known well enough that they must part; and Sigrid now begged Cerdic to leave her quickly, lest her will-power should fail her, after all.

And Cerdic, knowing that it was impossible for him to return to the village, having been the indirect cause of the young lord's death, now realized that he had no other choice than to join the outlaws' band.

The lovers, therefore, bade one another a tender farewell, with woe in their hearts.

Then Cerdic, tearing himself from his beloved one's arms, dashed forth into the forest with Sweyn and his men; and Sigrid, like one dead already, allowed herself to be led back to the village by the priest. Earthly joy was not for this unhappy pair; and of the sweet love of Cerdic and Sigrid, only a bright dream remained.

L'AMICO FRITZ *Mascagni*
(*Friend Fritz*)

IN sunny Alsace, in the early part of the nineteenth century, a Jewish colony had settled down very happily in a certain district; and here the members became prosperous, buying land and cultivating it with great success. While retaining their Jewish faith, they mingled well with their new Alsatian neighbours, who accepted them with ready friendliness. Indeed, the latter gradually imparted much of their own light-hearted gaiety into the lives of the adaptable settlers.

One of the wealthiest land-owners in this colony was a middle-aged bachelor named Fritz, who was also the most popular member of the community. Fritz had such a happy and generous disposition that everybody loved him. He helped the poor, he was good to all who worked for him, and he had hosts of friends —in fact, he was so much the friend of everyone that he was known all over that happy Alsatian district as " Friend Fritz ".

Yet, strange to say, this popular man had reached middle-age without any thought of marriage. Though any one of the many pretty girls in the colony would gladly have become his wife, Fritz had shown no inclination to choose one of them. At the same time, none could call him actually a woman-hater. He was kind and courteous to all; but he seemed resolved to remain a bachelor. He had never been in love; and he enjoyed his single-blessedness. But some thought he was acting unwisely.

The person most disturbed by this attitude of the richest bachelor in his flock was the jolly old Rabbi David, who happened to be an inveterate matchmaker. So keen, indeed, was the Rabbi to provide husbands for all the young girls of marriageable age in the district, that Fritz's constant refusal to become the happy principal in one of these contracts was a real source of worry to him. He even tried several little sly schemes to inveigle him into his matrimonial net; but Fritz was too wary for him. When the Rabbi came to beg of him the loan of a sum of money to provide one poor but pretty girl with a marriage portion, Fritz gladly handed the money over as a gift—but he did not offer to become the bridegroom, as the wily David had so innocently expected.

However, the old matchmaker did not give up hope; and when, presently, Friend Fritz gave a grand feast to celebrate his fortieth birthday, another chance arose.

Fritz, with his usual generosity, had invited all his friends, neighbours, and the workers on his estate, to attend his birthday feast; and he also invited a party of gipsies to come and provide lively music for his guests. Everybody was happy and jolly; and merry laughter was heard on every side.

Among the guests was the old Rabbi David, who sighed again because there was no mistress gracing the head of the table, though pretty maids abounded. Soon, however, his attention was drawn to a little incident which he hoped might prove to be the beginning of the romance he wished for.

Susel, the lovely young daughter of a farmer on the estate,

presently came up to her host and shyly offered him a modest posy of flowers as a birthday gift. Her flushed cheeks, her timid glances, and the sudden look of undeniable joy which shone from her eyes as Fritz smiled upon her, were sufficient signs to the ever-watchful David that this fair young girl secretly loved her host.

This was nothing new, of course. But what filled the old Rabbi with hopeful delight was the fact that the recipient of the posy looked with startled interest at Susel. Although he had seen her many times as a child, Fritz had never noticed before how beautiful she had become now that she was grown up. He could scarcely take his eyes off her; then, recovering himself, he invited her to sit beside him at table, and soon the pair were talking together very happily. Fritz next called to the chief gipsy performer, and bade him sing to them.

The gipsy, likewise sensing a romance, chose a melodious and very sentimental serenade; and coming close to Susel and Fritz, he seemed as though singing the honey-sweet ditty to them alone, while the rapt couple gazed happily into each other's eyes.

When the song ended, however, Fritz soon came back to earth; and seeing the quizzical glances of his friends, he began to join once more in their hilarious chatter and left Susel to join her own girl friends—which she did with considerable reluctance.

Later on, Fritz had to endure a good deal of teasing. His own especial young men friends declared slyly that he would soon be inviting them to his wedding feast, despite his laughing denials.

As for Rabbi David, he was full of eager glee, feeling certain that the heart of Fritz had at last been touched by Susel's fresh beauty and innocent charm. So convinced was he of this fact that he offered to make a wager that his bachelor friend would be wedded before another few weeks had passed.

Fritz, still good-humoured, but rather disturbed by the suggestion, gaily took up the challenge; and he wagered his best vineyard that the end of summer would find him still a confirmed bachelor. The terms of the wager were solemnly fixed by his friends; and the old Rabbi departed, well satisfied that he would be the winner, while Fritz laughingly declared that his vineyard would certainly remain his own.

But Friend Fritz's peace of mind had been shaken. To his dismay, he found himself thinking more frequently than he liked of the sweet, innocent charm of the girl who had presented him with a posy of flowers on his fortieth birthday. At such a staid age, surely he could not have fallen in love? But he wondered, all the same, full of perplexed doubts. Soon, however, he knew

Several times since the birthday party, he had found his way to the farm where Susel lived, with a flimsy excuse for visiting her father, who was his tenant. On one of these occasions, passing through the orchard, he found Susel perched up in a cherry tree, which she was busily stripping of its prettily dangling fruit.

Eagerly Fritz stopped to speak with the charming cherry-picker; and when Susel, thrilled by his notice, since she already loved him, threw down cherries for him to catch, he was amazed at the joy this simple but delightful game gave him. Nor could he help comparing the lusciously ripe red fruit with Susel's own rosy-red lips, just ripe for kissing. In fact, he realized that he was thoroughly enjoying himself; and he felt quite annoyed when some of his friends came along and called him off to another part of the estate.

Old David the Rabbi was also at the farm that day; and as he now rested for a while in the orchard, he slyly invited Susel to tell him once more the simple story of Isaac and Rebecca, which he himself had related to her many times when she was a child.

From Susel's artless eager telling of this ever-sweet love-story, the old Rabbi was now convinced of her own love for Fritz; and he was more determined than ever to bring about a match between the pair. To hasten the matter, he resorted to strategy.

Meeting Fritz, on the latter's return and when Susel had been called indoors, he told him with seeming satisfaction that he had now found exactly the right sort of husband for the farmer's pretty daughter—someone she could really love and respect. What was more, he added, her father was delighted with his future son-in-law.

To the matchmaker's satisfaction, his listener's reaction to this faked news was just what he had hoped and expected. Fritz was so greatly upset and crestfallen on hearing that Susel was to be married, that he hurried back home without another word—to the distress of Susel herself, who had hoped to see him again on her return to the orchard. She now felt that he could not be so interested in her as she had supposed.

A little later on that evening, the Rabbi visited Fritz in the latter's own home; and, quite casually, he informed him that the actual date of Susel's marriage had just been fixed. To his secret delight, Fritz now began to storm and rage, declaring that he himself did not approve of this marriage, whoever the bridegroom might be—in short, he should forbid the banns! He knew now that he loved Susel himself and that he could not bear another man to wed her.

The sly old Rabbi, seeing Susel now approaching—he himself

having cunningly given her instructions to bring a basket of cherries as a modest offering to her father's landlord—now ambled away once more, feeling that his own part in this charming romance was probably finished.

As Susel, sad and listless because of the doubts in her aching heart, came forward to present her basket of rosy fruit, Fritz scarcely acknowledged the gift. Instead, he asked her with studied coldness whether she had come to invite him to her wedding; and he added scornfully that he understood she had chosen the most eligible suitor among her many admirers.

Puzzled by this strange statement and deeply wounded by the contempt in his tone, the unhappy Susel was now entirely overcome; and, imagining that her sweet dream of love had come to naught, she burst into heart-rending sobs.

This was more than Fritz could bear. Not only did he now know beyond the shadow of a doubt that he dearly loved the weeping girl, but he felt that the Rabbi had probably made a mistake. Suddenly realizing that tears were surely strange in such circumstances, a great hope sprang up in his heart once more. He took Susel firmly in his arms and soon learned from her own lips that his hope was justified and that she returned his love with an equal fervour; and he embraced her rapturously.

With great joy, the now happy lovers went forth to greet their friends. And though Fritz had to bear much good-natured bantering from the latter for having lost his wager, he declared he did not care in the least. What was a mere vineyard compared with the joy of making lovely Susel his happy bride? He willingly handed over his best vineyard to Rabbi David.

But the jolly matchmaker had only wanted to see Friend Fritz, the most popular member of his flock, married at last to the prettiest girl in all Alsace; and he gladly presented the vineyard to sweet Susel as a wedding-gift.

CAVALLERIA RUSTICANA   *Mascagni*
(*Rustic Chivalry*)

IT was Easter morning, and the inhabitants of a certain pretty little village in the island of Sicily were wending their way towards the church to join in the customary special service of praise and thanksgiving in honour of the festival. They were light-hearted, peaceful peasants, who worked hard for their living and were glad to rejoice and be merry on feast days; and though shut off from the outside world, like other island folk they had considerable pride, and jealously guarded the honour of their native village. As they approached the church this bright Easter morning, their simple hearts were filled with joy and gratitude for the life of peaceful calm allotted to them. Though they knew it not, however, a tragedy was even now being enacted in their midst.

Turiddu, one of the handsomest youths in the village, had become a soldier, and before going off to the wars had obtained the promise of his sweetheart, Lola, to remain faithful to him, that they might be wedded on his return.

But the pretty Lola found the waiting time long and wearisome; and, at last, tiring of an absent lover, she accepted the advances of Alfio, the prosperous village carrier, who had a comfortable home to offer and who loved her dearly.

When Turiddu at length returned from his military service, therefore, he found his faithless sweetheart the wife of the happy Alfio; but though filled with disappointment and grief, he determined in his pride not to let Lola see that he cared aught for his loss. To this end, knowing that he was looked upon with favour by another fair village maiden, named Santuzza, he began to pay his addresses to her with much ardour; and he pursued his false wooing with such success that in a very short time he had not only stolen the young girl's heart, but her virtue, too.

When Lola saw that Turiddu had taken a new sweetheart in her place, she was filled with unreasonable resentment; and all her old love returning with the sting of jealousy, she sought to draw him back to her side once more, regardless of her wifely vows to Alfio. Nor did she find her task a difficult one. Turiddu's passion for her had never altered, although he had found comfort for a time in the smiles of Santuzza; and he gladly accepted her invitation to resume their old sweet intercourse.

Every day the lovers met in secret, being careful to keep their movements concealed from the unsuspecting Alfio; and for a little while they were able to rejoice in their lawless love.

But the secret did not long remain hidden from the betrayed and deserted Santuzza, who still passionately loved Turiddu; and when she discovered that the latter had returned to his old love she was filled with grief and jealousy. For a while, she kept the secret to herself, hoping to persuade the man she loved to come back to her and give up his dangerous intercourse with Lola; but when after many weeks had passed and still Turiddu came not, she determined to go and seek him out.

M

Having learnt from a neighbour that her false lover had been seen lingering near the abode of Alfio on the previous evening, she made her way, full of misery, to the abode of Turiddu's mother, Lucia, who lived in a cottage situated near the church in an open square. Here she waited until Lucia came out from the cottage, ready for church; and then, hurrying towards the good dame, she asked her where Turiddu was to be found.

Lucia replied that her son had gone a few days ago into the neighbouring town of Francoflute to fetch wine and had not yet returned; but Santuzza declared this could not be true, since he had been seen in the village only the evening before. On hearing this, Lucia was surprised and troubled; for, although she knew nothing of Turiddu's secret love intrigue, his movements had been mysterious to her of late and she had felt that all was not well with him.

Just then Alfio the carrier entered the square with his team, singing a merry song as he drove by. He stopped at the cottage to ask for a cup of wine, and upon the name of Turiddu being mentioned, he told Lucia, with a sudden frown, that her son had been lurking near his own cottage that very morning and had been seen there several other times of late. Lucia was about to say more on the subject when Santuzza, not wishing to betray her faithless lover, made a sign to her to desist. A few moments later Alfio went off with his team, but with a troubled look on his face; for a suspicion as to Turiddu's object in haunting his wife's abode now flashed across his mind for the first time.

When he had gone, Santuzza, unable to bear her grief in silence any longer, determined to take Lucia into her confidence. In despairing tones, she now poured out the whole wretched story to the dame—how Turiddu, in pique, had won her love and betrayed her, deserting her in order to return to his former sweetheart, Lola.

Lucia listened to this sad story with grief in her heart for the sin of her son and pity for the unhappy girl he had wronged; and when it came to an end, she folded Santuzza in her arms and said that she would offer prayers for her comfort even now. She then went into the church, which was already filled with worshippers singing their Easter anthem; but Santuzza remained weeping by the cottage door.

Presently, she saw Turiddu enter the square; and hurrying forward eagerly, she greeted him with reproaches, passionately imploring him to return to her love once more. But Turiddu, who had come to look for Lola on her way to church, was in no mood to hear the reproaches of Santuzza; and he declared that her pleadings were in vain to move him, for she was nothing to him and Lola's love was now all he wanted.

At this moment Lola herself came by, singing on her way to church. Seeing Santuzza and Turiddu together, a momentary wave of jealousy seized her. She began to mock them both for choosing the public square for their love-making; and when Turiddu tried to draw her away with him, she shook herself free and scornfully bade him stay with his beloved Santuzza. She then turned away with a careless laugh and went into the church; and Turiddu, rendered furious by her mocking words—which had been incited by the presence of her rival—turned angrily away from Santuzza and bade her leave him.

The wretched Santuzza, however, refused to be dismissed; and again she implored him to have pity and to return to her loving heart once more. But Turiddu declared cruelly that everything was now over between them, his love for Lola being all-absorbing; and when Santuzza clung to his arm in her wild eagerness, he flung her passionately from him and hastened into the church, heedless that she had fallen to the ground.

Santuzza lay for a few moments where she had fallen; and when she had recovered sufficiently to raise herself, she saw that Alfio the carrier had returned to the square again and was standing close beside her. Maddened by Turiddu's cruel treatment, she now determined to take revenge upon him; and turning eagerly to Alfio, she related to him the story of his wife's intrigue. She kept nothing back, not even Turiddu's betrayal of herself; and Alfio knew from her deep distress and passion that she spoke the truth, which his own recently awakened suspicions too surely confirmed.

The injured husband listened with grief and rage in his heart; and when the story came to an end, he exclaimed vehemently that all his love for his faithless wife was now changed to hate and that he would surely avenge himself speedily upon the betrayer of his honour.

Santuzza was terrified by the tumult of passion she had thus raised and would gladly have recalled her words, could she have done so; but Alfio flung her detaining arm from him and fled away to collect his agonized thoughts.

The service at the church was now at an end; and the worshippers came pouring forth into the square, laughing and rejoicing together, for the rest of the day was to be spent in merriment.

Turidu and the pretty Lola came out together with happy faces, for the careless girl's jealous outburst had quickly flown; and as they passed a little inn at one side of the square, Turiddu snatched up a cup of wine from a table that stood without and drank it off to the health of his sweetheart. Lola recklessly responded to the pledge; and then, Turiddu, carried away by the delirium of the moment, began to sing a lively drinking-song, in which he was heartily joined by the merry bystanders.

As the song came to an end, Alfio suddenly broke into the group; and from his pale, set face and the look of suppressed rage in his burning eyes, it soon became plain to all that some fearful act was in contemplation. The women drew together and began to whisper in frightened tones; but the men called out a friendly welcome to Alfio, who returned their greeting with calmness.

But when Turiddu, still keeping up his gay tone, offered the newcomer a cup of wine and boldly invited him to drink to their friendship, Alfio refused with the utmost scorn; and he declared in resentful tones that wine offered by Turiddu was to him but deadly poison. On hearing these words, Lolo uttered a cry of fear, knowing now that her wronged husband had discovered her intrigue; and, full of despair, she allowed herself to be led away by the trembling women, who quickly guessed that she was concerned in the quarrel and were eager to remove her from the scene.

Turiddu also saw that his secret was known to the man he had wronged, but he was not afraid to meet the consequences of his guilt; and seeing that Alfio meant to satisfy his honour by fighting, he went boldly forward and made the first challenge himself. This he did by biting the ear of his opponent, according to the local custom of the island; and at the same time, he took all the blame of the intrigue upon himself and begged Alfio not to deal harshly with Lola.

Alfio calmly accepted the challenge and, leading the way to a garden near by, bade Turiddu follow him, that they might fight there undisturbed. As Turiddu followed, he stopped at the door of his home and called for his mother; and when Lucia hurried out, alarmed at his excited tones, he begged her to guard and care for the unhappy Santuzza, whom he had so cruelly wronged. He also implored her to bless him and pray for his forgiveness; and then, with a last tender embrace, he drew his dagger and rushed into the garden to begin the duel.

Lucia was terrified by her son's aspect and realized at once what had happened; and when, at that moment, Santuzza ran up, asking wildly for her lover, she folded her in her arms with a sobbing cry.

Suddenly a loud shout of " Turiddu is slain! " came from those who had followed to watch the fight; and as the cry was taken up in the square, Santuzza, grief-stricken, sank senseless to the ground.

Thus was rustic honour satisfied and Alfio avenged of his wrongs; but the bright Easter morn that had dawned so joyously ended in gloom and the dark shadow of death!

IRIS   *Mascagni*

IN sunny Japan, the land of flowers and blue skies, pretty little Iris, the cherished and loving daughter of Cieco, the blind man, awoke one morning at dawn and appeared on the doorstep of her father's country cottage to greet the rising sun.

Though now on the threshold of a lovely maidenhood, Iris was as simple and innocent of the world as a child, having been kept away from the neighbouring town with its pleasures, frivolities, and temptations by a doting father, who also depended upon her aid in his own helpless condition of blindness. He needed her tender little hands to lead him about; and the sound of her sweet voice carolling happily about the house like a singing bird comforted and cheered him in the world of darkness in which he was compelled to live.

Gladly and charmingly did Iris minister to the needs of her stricken father; and her life was full of happiness as she sang about her simple household tasks or played with her dolls in true Japanese fashion.

So fair a flower as sweet Iris, however, was not allowed to blossom unseen, unknown, and unplucked. To-day, as she stood in her flowery garden, clad in a simple dainty kimono, stretching forth her little hands in admiration and adoration of the rising sun, she was observed and marked down as the prey of the spoiler.

Osako, a wealthy young nobleman, already world-weary and steeped in the excesses of pleasure, passed by that way with Kyoto, the owner of the richest house in the Yoshiwara. Beholding the lovely maiden absorbed in her invocations, the youthful *roué* was seized with a sudden longing to possess her, his jaded senses once more awakened by the sight of such ravishing beauty and sweet innocence.

The cunning Kyoto, greedy of gain and always eager to pander to the desires of his rich clients, immediately promised that Osako should become possessed of this charming prize within a few hours. He declared, however, that caution must prevail in pursuance of the scheme his quick brain had already concocted; for the maiden was timid and was also closely guarded by her father who, though blind, was yet strong enough to defend his beloved daughter. Eagerly the pair hurried away to arrange their evil plan forthwith.

Meanwhile, the little *mousmé*, unaware of her approaching danger, heard her father's call and hastened within doors; and presently she appeared again leading the blind man by the hand. She led him to a seat in the doorway of the cottage, that he might enjoy the warmth and brightness of the sun; then, having brought him his rosary, she left him to pray while she went out into the garden once more to caress her beloved flowers and to whisper her pretty thoughts to them.

Presently, a little company of players with a puppet-show, mountebanks, musicians, and geishas, followed by troops of admiring villagers, came into sight. As the players set up their miniature stage near the cottage and the villagers gathered around in a circle, the blind man called out to his daughter to come and stand beside him while this hubbub was proceeding.

Iris, however, was fascinated by the music and the puppet-show; and after reassuring her father by declaring that she was within hail of him, she wandered down to the hawthorn hedge to behold the entertainment at closer quarters, oblivious of the danger she thus incurred. For this little show had been quickly got together by Kyoto and Osako, who thus cunningly hoped to lure the pretty fairy of the cottage from her father's side; and as they caused their puppets to act, they soon saw that their ruse was succeeding.

Iris, never having beheld a performance of this kind before, entered into it with childish absorption, believing all the characters in the tragic story to be real. When Osako—who was possessed of an exquisite voice which thrilled and fascinated all who heard it—sang the song of the Sun-god who bore the dying heroine to his own glowing abode in the heavens, she was so entranced that she came shyly forth from a gap in the flowery hedge and moved nearer to the players.

Eagerly and excitedly, Osako watched the little starry-eyed maiden he desired thus enter the net he had spread for her; and at a sign from him the hired geishas now began to whirl in a mad dance around her while the music clashed and the gongs boomed louder than ever. Iris suddenly awakened from the romantic dream in which she had been absorbed, and gave a little cry of terror on thus finding herself in this wild crowd of dancers; but instantly her cries were stifled by a thick cloak which was now flung over her, and she was borne away by one of the mountebanks.

Kyoto, by order of Osako, crept back softly to the cottage and laid upon the doorstep—so noiselessly that he was unheard by the blind man—a little heap of gold coins. The latter were wrapped about with a note in which were cunningly written some words of farewell as though coming from Iris, stating that she had accepted the offer of a wealthy admirer to go with him to the city, there to live with him in splendour and gaiety.

Almost immediately the dance ended, the puppet theatre was taken down, and the pretended players departed for the city, while the village folk began to return to their own homes.

By this time the blind man, having called many times in vain for Iris, became alarmed by her continued absence from his side; and as the music died away in the distance, he stumbled down the garden, feeling his way helplessly and calling aloud for his daughter. As he fell outside the gap in the hedge, some of the pedlars and hangers-on who had formed part of the crowd, picked him up; and hearing of his trouble, they hastened into the cottage to look for Iris. Their search, however, was in vain; but discovering the gold coins and the note in the doorway, they brought these to the now frantic father and read the lying message out to him.

When the blind man thus heard that his beloved daughter— the light of his eyes and the joy of his heart—had gone to the city, even to the evil-reputed district of the Yoshiwara, and that, seemingly, she had gone thither of her own free will for the sake of pleasure and gain, his heart-broken grief changed to a furious anger. He cried out wildly that he would follow her with the returning crowd that he might seek her out to fling mud and ashes upon her and to disown her with curses. Seeing that the distracted Cieco was helpless, the pedlars, full of sympathy for his grief and wrath, took him by the hand and led him away, tottering and stumbling, towards the city in the wake of the ravishers.

When the unfortunate little Iris awakened to consciousness a few hours later, she found herself in a gorgeous chamber, more richly furnished than any she had imagined in her simple mind. Silken draperies woven with fantastic patterns in the gayest colours hung before the windows; and the walls were adorned with pictures of dragons and other curious monsters worked in enamel. Handsome vases of porcelain, and ornaments of beaten gold were elegantly posed here and there; carved censers in which fragrant oils burned were hanging from the decorated ceiling; and in one corner a Buddha smiled.

This was Kyoto's House of Pleasure in the Yoshiwara; and while Iris still slept, the panderer and his client, Osako, entered to gaze upon their stolen prize. The loveliness of the sleeping *mousmé* as she lay there upon the gilded couch, her beauty still further enhanced by the shimmering robes with which she had just been decked by the attendant geishas, caused Osako's sudden passion to burn more hotly still. He broke forth into an almost reverential panegyric of her many charms; and he even expressed a fear lest, experienced though he was in the pleasures of love, he might fail to woo so frail and precious a treasure willingly into his embrace.

The cunning and practical Kyoto, however, declared that as Osako was wealthy he could tempt and lure the maiden with rich gifts—gauzy garments, sparkling jewels, and exotic flowers; then seeing that their victim was about to awaken, the pair left her to open her wondering eyes alone in these new and strange surroundings.

Iris, on first awakening and finding herself in so rich and palatial a chamber, feeling the softness of her filmy garments and seeing the gilded sandals upon her feet, was filled with amazement and delight. Then, as the memory of the puppet-show, the whirling geishas, and the blackness that had suddenly descended upon her during the mazy mad dancing came back to her, she believed that she had died and was now awakening in Paradise.

As she rose and wandered about, she was filled with awe on beholding the many beautiful objects about her; and she softly touched some of them with wondering pleasure.

While she was thus happily engaged, absorbed in this new joy of the moment, Osako entered the room. Eagerly approaching the dainty maiden, he began to pour forth passionate protestations of love for her, praising her beauty and holding open his arms invitingly.

Recognizing the thrilling voice of the young noble as that of the puppet in the show representing the Sun-god, Iris at first believed that he must indeed be that bright and glorious being she had always worshipped as her Lord and King; but when Osako, intoxicated by his sudden passion, waxed bolder and became more violent in his love-making, she was alarmed and shrank back from his embraces and kisses. She was too innocently childlike to understand the meaning of his ardent expressions; and his passionate accents only mystified her.

Suddenly realizing that this strange but gaudy chamber was not the Paradise she had at first believed but that she was a captive in some dangerous place where all kinds of unimagined terrors might lurk, she fell upon her knees and entreated her would-be lover to send her back to her blind father, who was helpless without her aid—to the humble little cottage and pretty garden where she had been so happy. When Osako declared he would send money to her father and provide her with a palace and a fairy-like garden, bringing forth jewels and rich robes to tempt her, she only renewed her pleadings to be allowed to return to her own simple life.

At last Osako realized that she was merely mystified by his ardent love-making; and feeling almost awed in the presence of such childlike innocence, he called to Kyoto and, declaring that he had already tired of the pretty maiden, advised the panderer to send her back to her country home.

However, when Osako had departed, somewhat piqued by his failure, Kyoto made no attempt to follow out his parting command. Knowing that he might make much profit out of the lovely *mousmé* thus left on his hands, he determined to exhibit her in an open verandah overlooking the street—hoping to entice a likely client from the passing crowd.

Therefore, he called to his geishas to bring a still more dazzling robe in which to array the newcomer forthwith for the attraction of this verandah niche. When Iris, more terrified than ever, endeavoured to resist the geishas in their attempts to bedeck her, he dragged her roughly to a low window which revealed the fact that the house on this side stood upon the edge of a dark and deep precipice; and he threatened to throw her down into these fearsome depths if she disobeyed his commands.

As the scared girl shrank back in horror at the sight of the abyss, Kyoto, cunningly anxious to bring back her smiles for his own evil ends, now placed in her arms the doll which represented the Sun-god in the puppet play; and Iris, childishly pleased on thus possessing the doll that had so thrilled her, recovered somewhat. She now allowed herself to be dressed in the new and gaudy raiment and sat quietly in the window with the puppet in her hands, still utterly unconscious of the reason for her exhibition there.

Very soon, however, her unusual beauty attracted the attention of the pleasure-seekers in the streets, who crowded around the open verandah uttering cries of admiration and calling forth flowery compliments to her. Among these revellers was Osako who, stepping into the verandah, his passion once more inflamed by the sight of the childish beauty holding the Sun-god puppet in her arms, again poured forth a passionate protestation of love for her.

At this moment, there came a great commotion in the street. This was caused by the pedlars, who, unerring in their guess as to the whereabouts of the blind man's lost daughter, now appeared outside the verandah with the distracted Cieco in their midst.

As Iris shrank away again from the outstretched arms of Osako, she suddenly beheld her father approaching; and rushing to the edge of the verandah, she called to him eagerly to come and save her, joyfully expectant of his quick response and longing for the comfort and safety of his protective arms.

But the deceived Cieco, led to her side by the curious bystanders, still believed that his daughter had come to this ill resort of her own accord; and full of rage at her apparently voluntary degradation, he scooped up in his trembling hands dust and stones to fling in her face, at the same time uttering imprecations and calling down curses upon her.

Iris was maddened with grief by the curses and foul names hurled upon her by her beloved father; and feeling that she was an outcast indeed since he no longer loved her, she sprang back into the gilded chamber. Running to the open window beyond, she flung herself, with a wild cry of woe, down the precipice from which she had shrunk on its being revealed to her by Kyoto.

Osako, horror-struck, rushed forward too late to prevent this mad action of despair; and as the onlookers drew back, awed and speechless, a silence fell upon the crowd—broken only by the still angry blind man who, unconscious of the tragedy, continued to hurl dust and stones into empty space and to curse until he, too, became silent through sheer exhaustion.

. . . .

At the foot of the precipice throughout the night lay the broken form of little Iris. At dawn the rag-pickers came past that way and were about to rob her of her fine raiment, when they saw that she still breathed; and, full of terror, they fled away.

Then, as she uttered her dying groan, the sun shone forth in golden glory, as though to greet her. At the same time, tall, sweet-scented flowers sprang up on every side and enfolded her in their lovely embrace; and the body of the hapless little *mousmé* was lost to sight in their fragrant depths.

LE JONGLEUR DE NOTRE-DAME *Massenet*
(The Juggler of Our Lady)

ONE day during the fourteenth century, a poor Juggler came into the market-place of Clugny, in Burgundy. He was weary and worn; and at first he blinked his eyes and seemed almost dazed by the brightness of the sunshine and the gaiety of the scene that met his tired eyes.

For it was market-day in Clugny; and in the large square opposite the Abbey, a crowd of busy, merry folk had gathered around the stalls of the vendors of fruit, vegetables, and country produce. Many of the more youthful rustics, leaving their elders to attend to business, were amusing themselves with the younger townsfolk, dancing, chattering, and singing songs. They wore gaily-coloured garments; and as they danced and made merry together, the grey old square took on the appearance of a country fair.

So Jean the Juggler, though almost too tired to move, began to play on his hurdy-gurdy and prepared to show off his juggling tricks.

The merry folk gathered eagerly around the mountebank as soon as he appeared in the square, hoping for a jolly entertainment; but they soon drew back, disappointed with his worn-out looks. For poor Jean was thin and dingily-clad; and, in addition, being extremely hungry, his countenance was by no means cheerful.

Nevertheless, business was business; and seeing a merry crowd before him, the weary Juggler roused himself as best he could. He began to cut a few funny capers and, announcing himself as " the King of Jugglers ", made a brave show of his once excellent powers of entertaining.

The careless, light-hearted young revellers, however, only laughed at this toil-worn, broken " King of Jugglers "; and, very derisively, they called on him to choose his " Queen ", who might prove more amusing.

But Jean was not daunted by his adverse reception; and he capered in and out among the crowd with his wooden bowl, asking for stray coins and offering to perform his full juggler's entertainment. Still the crowd declared that they were tired of his stale old tricks, which they had seen so often that they knew them off by heart: as for his romantic songs, they were weary of them likewise. Nothing he had to offer seemed to meet with this gay crowd's approval.

At last, in desperation, Jean offered to sing a new drinking-song, an "*Alleluia du Vin*"—which he had hoped not to have to bring forth, as it was of a sacrilegious nature and the Juggler himself was sincerely devout. However, the people hailed his suggestion with joy and loudly acclaimed it when he sang it. Then they insisted that he should sing it again, but this time in the form of a sacred chant.

Jean, faint for want of food and knowing that this was his only chance of securing a few more coins with which to purchase a meal, agreed to the request of his careless audience. But, first of all, he bowed devoutly before a statue of the Virgin which stood above the door of the Abbey and craved pardon for his sacrilege, declaring humbly that he was at heart a good Christian and was forced by hunger only to do this deed. He then began to sing the new drinking-song in the form of a sacred chant; and the delighted crowd took it up gleefully and sang a roaring chorus to it.

Then there came an interruption. The door of the Abbey was opened and the Prior himself appeared, full of righteous indignation that this form of sacred music should be used for a drinking-song. With stern rebukes, he soon succeeded in driving away the crestfallen revellers; and then he poured forth maledictions upon the hapless Jean. The poor Juggler fell upon his knees and craved forgiveness; and he likewise entreated the Virgin to pardon him, declaring again that hunger only had caused him to commit such an offence.

The good Prior was now convinced of the Juggler's sincerity. He invited him, therefore, to save his soul alive by entering the Monastery as a brother and by renouncing his foolish juggling for ever.

At first, Jean was reluctant to give up his liberty. Though poor and travel-worn, he was still young; and he dearly loved the beauties of Nature he saw on his wanderings. He also had the affection of an artist for the poor trappings of his trade. He hesitated for a moment; then he caught sight of the monks' chief cook, Boniface, carrying into the Abbey some of the tempting food just purchased by him at the market stalls for the brethren. That decided Jean. The monks had generous meals; and his own pangs of hunger now made him gratefully accept the asylum offered him.

So Jean the Juggler followed the good Prior into the Abbey; but he was careful to take in with him his beloved hurdy-gurdy and his juggling-baggage, which he managed to conceal in a safe hiding-place.

.   .   .   .

After a while, in the Monastery, Jean felt better so far as his physical well-being was concerned. Rested, well-fed, and warmly-clad in his monk's rough robe, he looked a very different person. He was still weak and worn, however, and knew he had not long to live. Always pious, he loved the simple religious life; and he would have been very happy but for the fact that he seemed to have nothing to offer personally for the actual service of the Holy Virgin he worshipped so sincerely.

As he mingled with his brother monks in the Abbey Studio, he felt that his gifts were indeed poor. All the others were doing beautiful work with their hands and their brains. The Sculptor Monk had just completed a magnificent statue of the Virgin, which the Painter Monk was tinting. Other artist brothers were painting pictures to adorn the chapel. A Poet Monk had composed a new holy song, which his Musician brother was now setting to glorious music, while those with good voices were singing it over in readiness for its first performance.

All were engaged with some special work for the Virgin one day—the morning of the Assumption. Everybody was happy and busy, except the one-time Juggler. He sat disconsolate—and most uncomfortable in his unaccustomed heavy robe—grieving because he had nothing to offer to his beloved Virgin. He could not even join in the songs and prayers offered to her because he did not understand Latin, in which learned language they were all couched.

These clever brother-monks, however, were kind to the stranger in their midst; and each offered to teach him his own particular art. But, alas, they could not decide which was the most important art for Jean to be taught first; and they began to wrangle so loudly as to which was the highest art, that the humble pupil was quite glad when the Prior bade them take their newly-finished works to the chapel for dedication.

As Jean remained behind, still lamenting because he had no gifts to offer, the kindly Cook Monk, Boniface, came and spoke to him. On learning the reason for Jean's despondent looks, the jolly cook related to him the fable of the Sage Plant which, though not beautiful as the Lily, the Rose, or other lovely flowering plants, yet was useful and much prized in cookery. From this fable, Boniface added, one learned that the humblest action or offering was acceptable to the Virgin if offered sincerely as the best the giver had to offer.

These wise words brought much comfort to Jean, who now declared that he would die happy if the Holy Virgin would only bless him and accept a humble offering from him.

When Boniface had departed about his domestic duties, happy in his own useful art of cooking, a great light broke in upon the new monk's understanding and he was suddenly filled with excited happiness. He determined that he *would* make an offering to the Virgin, after all, the only offering possible to him, but an offering which would be of his best—his Juggling Entertainment!

He hastened cautiously to the hiding-place in which he had concealed his juggling-baggage and his hurdy-gurdy, and brought them into the studio. Quickly he doffed his monk's uncomfortable robe and attired himself once more in his tattered and soiled juggler's dress, arranging all his paraphernalia around him as of old.

He first of all bowed humbly before the statue of the Virgin which stood in a niche behind a *prie-dieu*, begging her to accept his gift and to bless him; and then he began his juggling entertainment before the statue.

Never before had Jean the Juggler played his hurdy-gurdy so gaily; never before had he danced and sang so well or cut such amusing capers; and his few poor juggling tricks seemed almost like real magic. He offered up his entertainment with true sincerity and gradually worked himself up into a state of feverish excitement and exaltation. His thin, worn-out body seemed scarcely able to bear such energy; and his weak heart beat wildly with ecstatic joy.

But again poor Jean seemed doomed to interruption from his superiors. The noise of his wild singing and dancing was heard in the chapel beyond; and the Prior and monks came hurrying back to the studio. They were quite scandalized by what they now beheld; for they considered the Juggler's antics before the statue of the Virgin to be an act of sacrilege.

They were about to rush upon the mountebank in horrified anger, when they were held in check by the gentle Boniface, who alone understood the reason for this strange scene; and he bade them listen and watch instead, for a miracle was taking place.

At that moment, a sound of Angel singing was heard and the statue of the Virgin seemed to come to life and to smile upon the fantastic figure below. Graciously the Divine Apparition extended her arms in a blessing over the Juggler's head in token of her acceptance of his gift, which the angelic voices went on to announce had opened to him the gates of Heaven.

The Prior and his monks, no longer proud of their own achievements, now knelt in humility before the blessed and honoured Jean and began to chant a song of praise for the Vision that had been vouchsafed to him and to them.

At first the Juggler did not realize what had happened, but was only filled with joy because he found he could now understand the Latin words in the Song of Triumph which the brethren had raised. But when he looked up and beheld the radiant apparition of the smiling Virgin with hands raised in blessing over him and realized that his poor gift of juggling—which was yet the best he had to offer—had been accepted, he was filled with holy ecstasy.

Utterly exhausted by the gigantic effort he had just made to give of his best, Jean now fell back, dying, but with a smile of peace upon his face, as the Holy Vision faded. At the same moment, Angel voices were heard once more, giving welcome to the soul of the humble Juggler whose sincerity of heart had gained for him the joys of Heaven. As these died away, the monks were left chanting a song of deep humility. They now realized that a Saint had been in their midst.

THE KING OF LAHORE   *Massenet*
(*Le Roi de Lahore*)

In the Temple of Indra at Lahore, one day during the eleventh century, there was a scene of great excitement. Vast multitudes of people were pressing towards the doors and trying to enter the already crowded edifice that they might also pray before the altar and image of the great god they worshipped.

The powerful Sultan Mahmoud had declared war against Lahore; even now, the terrible Mussulman hosts were advancing across the Indian desert.

Although their splendid young King, Alim, was bold and brave and had already determined to fight the invader, they were afraid. Only the gods—especially their own great god, Indra—could protect them; and they crowded to the Temple to pray.

Timour, the High Priest of Indra, with his attendant priests, tried to comfort and reassure the frightened people; and presently they calmed down somewhat.

Soon, however, the High Priest found himself involved in a still more difficult problem.

Scindia, the young King's chief adviser, called him aside. This official, a man of unlimited ambition and unbridled passions, had long cherished a secret love for Sita, one of the Virgin Priestesses attached to the Temple; and he longed to possess her. Having great power in the State, therefore, he now openly demanded that Timour should immediately release this beautiful maiden from her Temple vows that he might take her as his bride.

Horrified by the request, the High Priest rebuked him sternly for his presumption, declaring that the King alone could exercise this right—even then, it was not approved of. The priestess maidens were vowed to purity, celibacy, and service, and had nothing to do with earthly love.

Infuriated by this rebuff and the thwarting of his unlawful desires, Scindia now declared that Timour did not guard his virgins too well. The royal official had learned recently that a strange man, whose features were hidden by a cloak, secretly visited the Temple Sanctuary every evening to whisper words of love to beautiful Sita.

He quickly regretted having revealed this rumour, however. Timour, astounded by the news and filled with righteous anger, announced that if this indictment were proved, then Sita would have to suffer the penalty of death for her sin. Anxious to save the maiden he coveted, Scindia now insisted, in his character as Chief Adviser to the King, that he should be allowed to question Sita alone and so learn the truth from her.

Since he was a man of great power, the High Priest granted his request with reluctance—for he had no love for the minister; and Scindia was admitted to the inner Temple Sanctuary.

Here, Sita, a maiden of exquisite beauty and gentle disposition, was waiting with her companion virgin priestesses to perform the evening rites of their office. She received Scindia timidly, for, though he was her own relative, she feared him. When, therefore, he almost immediately began to make passionate love to her, she was still more afraid; and when she knew that he wished to take her away from the Temple and make her his bride, she shrank from him with undisguised loathing, firmly refusing to wed with him.

Stung by her refusal, Scindia now furiously accused her of receiving a stranger lover each evening; and the trembling Sita could not deny it. She told him that at the singing of the priestesses' evening song, a handsome stranger of noble mien came and stood near the altar and gazed on her with eyes of love. He even spoke tender words of love to her, but yet had never so much as touched her hand. She loved the stranger, too, but had no thought of breaking her Temple vows. Their love was pure.

Sita, though innocent, now realized the danger of her position; and she begged her relative to help and protect her from the anger of the priests. But Scindia was now beside himself with disappointment and jealous rage. He called in the High Priest and his attendant priests and, before them all, angrily accused Sita of receiving a lover during her altar duties.

A great outcry at such sacrilege arose from all present. Timour, the High Priest, sternly denounced Sita and declared that she must suffer the penalty of death for having broken her Temple vows.

It was in vain that the terrified young girl declared her innocence. She loved the stranger, but had not broken her vows. Nevertheless, all called out loudly for her to suffer the penalty of death.

In the midst of this uproar, however, there came an unexpected interruption. Alim, the young King of Lahore, suddenly entered from a nearby secret passage. Proudly he moved to the front.

As all now fell back in respectful, reverent silence, Alim announced calmly that Sita must live, since this was his royal will. He, himself, was the stranger who had visited the beautiful priestess; he loved Sita, and wished to make her his Queen.

Joyfully Sita recognized her beloved stranger, and went to stand beside him at his call. But fear was still in her heart. She had not known that he was the King.

Quickly her fears were justified. The King's decree could save her from death, but he himself could not escape punishment for breaking the Temple laws. The High Priest, though he loved his royal master, declared that he had committed a crime in thus profaning the Temple; and he sternly announced that, as penalty, he must now go forth in person to fight against the Mussulman invaders.

The young King proudly replied that he had already decided to lead his soldiers in battle; and he now humbly craved the High Priest to pardon him for his sin and to bless his enterprise—which Timour willingly did.

But Scindia's jealous heart was filled with black hate. He secretly vowed that Alim should die. He himself would strike him down in the battle, unknown to anyone. Then he would make himself King in Lahore and take the beautiful Sita as his bride, after all.

.   .   .   .   .   .

Although the vengeful Scindia followed the young King to the wars and fought boldly against the Mussulman hosts, he plotted in secret all the time. He won over the chiefs of the neighbouring districts and their followers to his side, poisoning their minds and those of the royal personal guards against Alim by putting a blacker and entirely false aspect upon the latter's Temple sacrilege.

Then, later on, in the midst of a fierce battle, he himself dealt the young King a fatal blow and called upon the now terrified defenders to retreat to Lahore.

At the time of this dastardly outrage, beautiful Sita was in the King's camp with her maidens, anxiously awaiting her beloved one's return from the desert battle; and she was filled with alarm when the retreating soldiers came rushing into the camp in disorder, on their way back to Lahore.

Her alarm was soon changed to despairing grief when Scindia next arrived with the dreadful news that Alim had been struck down and was dying. He added triumphantly that he himself would now be chosen King by the chiefs and that he would then force her to become his Queen.

For a moment the false treachery of Scindia seemed about to fail. Alim came staggering into the camp, pale and bleeding and, despite his deadly wounds, endeavoured to rally his men around him, declaring that he had not given the command to retreat and that the enemy could yet be defeated.

Even as he spoke these brave words, however, Alim fell gasping to the ground, and presently expired in the arms of the grief-stricken Sita.

The despairing girl was not left long with her beloved dead. Next moment, at a gesture from Scindia, she was seized by his personal followers and carried off by them to Lahore.

. . . .

In the sweet-scented Garden of the Blest, amidst the Paradise of the great god Indra, the Happy Departed Spirits of kings and heroes wandered blissfully. Flowers and magnificent vegetation surrounded them on every side, while the mighty mountain, Méron, formed a sheltering background.

When the Happy Spirits wished for entertainment, bright groups of exquisitely beautiful Houris danced lightly and seductively before them, to the piping of flutes played by some of the lesser deities.

The splendid god Indra sat on his dazzling throne of light, or moved graciously among his people. Wherever he moved, the Happy Spirits bowed down before him in adoration and gratitude.

Into this peaceful scene came the young King Alim after he had drawn his last breath on earth. He walked slowly and with a sad air; instead of rejoicing at his release from earthly woes, he seemed bowed down with grief.

He knelt humbly before the throne of Indra and begged that he might be permitted to return once more to earth and to his beloved Sita. His love for the beautiful priestess was so deep and all-embracing that it transcended even his joy in Paradise.

Realizing that the Departed Spirit of the young King would never know contentment in the Garden of the Blest without his beloved one by his side to share his joys, the great god took pity upon him, and, anxious to reward such perfect love, granted his request. But he made a condition. Alim must go back to earth shorn of his former power and wealth, not as a king but as a poor, obscure man of the people. And when Sita died, then he must also die again in that same moment.

Gratefully Alim accepted the conditions imposed upon him; and as he sank down to sleep in the midst of the Happy Departed Spirits and their Houris, the god Indra uttered an incantation over him, whereby he was wafted back to earth once more.

.   .   .   .

In Lahore a festive scene was taking place. The invading army of the Sultan had been driven back for the moment; and the treacherous Scindia had made himself King. This was his Coronation Day; and he was even now on his way from the Temple ceremony. Behind his own gorgeous procession there followed, at a little distance, the equally gorgeous procession of the Queen—the unhappy Sita, who had been thus ruthlessly compelled, against her will, to become the bride of the triumphant Scindia.

Before the King's procession arrived at the palace in Lahore, a poorly-clad traveller appeared in the square. It was Alim who, hearing the remarks and cries of the cheering crowds, now realized that his throne had been usurped by the same vile wretch who had betrayed him to his enemies and then had struck him down.

Fearful of the fate of his beloved Sita, Alim rushed madly up the steps into the palace, to seek for her. He did not penetrate far therein, however; the guards, thinking him to be merely a shabby stranger, soon seized him and roughly cast him out into the square once more.

At this moment, the dazzling coronation procession of the usurper arrived before the palace; and Alim, full of wrath, flung himself before Scindia and denounced him as a traitor, declaring himself to be the rightful King.

Scindia was at first filled with fear, thinking that the spectre of the young King he had murdered had indeed appeared before him and that he was about to suffer retribution for his regicidal deed. Then, recovering himself quickly, he furiously called upon his guards to strike down the travel-stained stranger as a madman who sought to slay him, the newly-crowned King.

But the High Priest and his attendant priests, and many of the people gathered around, were all amazed by the likeness of the shabby stranger to their late King; and declaring that he spoke as one inspired by the gods, Timour called for mercy to be shown to him.

As the tumult reached its height, the procession of the Queen arrived in the square, preceded by singing maidens who cast flowers and rose-leaves on every side.

At the sight of his beautiful Sita, arrayed as the Queen and bride of Scindia, Alim felt crushed to the ground with despair. He was about to be seized by the guards at a sign from Scindia, when Timour, still believing him to be at least a mystic messenger from the late King, commanded the priests to surround him and to bear him away to the Temple, where he might be hidden for a while from the maddened Scindia.

The latter now continued his interrupted royal progress and entered the palace, followed by the procession of his captive Queen.

.   .   .   .

In the Sanctuary of the Temple of Indra, a little later, a frantic figure rushed panting towards the colossal statue of the benign god, imploring protection.

It was Sita, who had managed to escape from the palace. Now, rather than submit to the hateful will of Scindia, she drew a dagger and was about to stab herself, when, from a hidden recess, the fugitive Alim appeared.

The lovers, in great joy, fell into one another's arms, their troubles forgotten in the ecstasy of reunion. But for a few moments only did they experience this earthly rapture. The jealous and thwarted Scindia had soon discovered the escape of his lovely bride and had followed her with his guards, hot-footed, to the Temple.

Furious at finding her in the Sanctuary with the stranger who had denounced him but an hour ago, Scindia called on his guards to seize the trembling girl.

But Sita, now in despair and seeing no further escape from her hated captor, just had time to draw her dagger once more; and, rather than become the forced bride of Scindia, she stabbed herself to the heart.

As she fell dying to the ground, Alim also staggered and fell. He was just able to drag himself to the limp form of Sita and to clasp her in his arms in a last loving embrace, when they both expired at the same moment.

Scindia, now overcome, in spite of himself, by the sight of this double tragedy, sank prostrate before the statue of the great god, realizing his own infamy and fearing for the divine vengeance to come.

.   .   .   .   .   .

Once more, in the Garden of the Blest, amidst the radiant celestial Paradise of Indra, came the Departed Spirit of Alim, once King of Lahore. But this time he was full of joyous ecstasy, for he did not come alone. Hand-in-hand with him walked the Departed Spirit of beautiful Sita, whom he had loved so dearly on earth and from whom he was now never to be parted.

As he led her in gratitude to the dazzling throne of Indra, a chorus of welcome arose from the great company of Happy Departed Spirits gathered around the god. Alim and Sita had found peace at last.

THAÏS   *Massenet*

In the early days of Christianity, a colony of Cenobite monks had set up their huts on the banks of the Nile at the edge of the Theban Desert. Here, one evening, just before sunset, the holy brethren sat outside in the open air at a long table, partaking of their frugal supper.

As they sat there, they spoke anxiously together of one of their number, Athanaël, who had taken a journey to the neighbouring city of Alexandria in the hope of gaining converts to the service of the one true God from among the pagans there; and they prayed for his safe return. Their leader, an old monk named Palémon, comforted them by announcing that he had been told in a vision that their brother would return that night. Even as he spoke, the wanderer appeared in sight and soon was in their midst.

Athanaël, young and handsome, had gone forth upon his mission full of fervent zeal; but now, on his return, weary and footsore, he was depressed and unhappy because he had failed. As the brethren crowded around him, eager to hear his tale, he told them that his task had been hopeless and that all the city was given up to sin and pleasure. The nobly-born youths, who were the leaders of this licentiousness, had all succumbed to the enthralling influence of the beautiful actress-courtesan, Thaïs, a priestess of Venus, whose loveliness and seductive charms none seemed able to resist. Day and night alike they spent in voluptuous pleasures, over which this fair siren reigned as Queen. So youthful was Thaïs that her life of sinful pleasures seemed all the more pitiful. So magnetic was the influence of the lovely temptress that Athanaël admitted, to his deep shame, he had himself been almost lured into seeking her presence. By earnest prayers and fasting, however, he had resisted the temptation and had since found peace once more in the desert on his return.

Old Palémon, anxious for the welfare of the zealous young monk, entreated him to give up his mission and not to return to the evil city again, lest he should ruin his peace of mind for ever; but Athanaël declared that he longed to rescue the soul of this sinful woman and that he would never rest until he had done so.

Later on as the night fell, when his companions had retired within their huts, Athanaël remained out alone in the deepening twilight, sad because of his failure. Presently, he beheld in a vision the form of the beautiful courtesan performing in the theatre before her lovers and admirers, posing, almost undraped, as Aphrodite, whose cult she practised as priestess. Full of shame and horror, as the vivid phantasm vanished, he called the brethren forth once more and declared passionately that he would return forthwith to the vicious city; and he vowed to take no rest until he had rescued Thaïs from her life of evil pleasure. He would then bring her forth as a penitent and convert to the service of God and present her as a sister to the White Nuns of a neighbouring convent, whose holy Abbess, Albine, he knew would receive her with joy.

Seeing that the young evangelist was determined to snatch this brand from the burning, despite the many dangers in his path, old Palémon did not seek further to dissuade him but gave him his blessing and prayed that this time he might succeed; and Athanaël set forth that night upon his mission, filled with holy exaltation.

.   .   .   .

On arriving in the great city of Alexandria, Athanaël immediately made his way to the home of Nicias, a rich and gay young noble whom he had known well in years gone by. He had also renewed his acquaintance with this friend of his youth on his recent mission to the city. Although pleased that Nicias still regarded him with affection as of yore, he had grieved, however, to find him given over to the life of a voluptuary, passing his days in a series of hectic pleasures and indulgences, according to the custom of the wealthy nobility of that city of luxury. Nicias, gay, irresponsible, and easy-going, only laughed at the reproaches of this friend of his student days, whose missionary zeal he could not understand and whose new religion he found dull and uninteresting compared with the licentious orgies of Paganism. But the two, nevertheless, remained good friends.

So it was to Nicias the young monk now bent his steps; and on approaching the splendid house where his friend lived upon the outskirts of the city, he found preparations for a great feast in progress.

At first, the servitor at the entrance refused to admit him, regarding him as a beggar because of the coarse, rough habit he wore; but at that moment Nicias himself appeared, leaning upon the shoulders of two pretty slave-girls, and gave him a glad welcome.

When Athanaël told him in eager, serious tones of the mission he had come upon, Nicias laughed incredulously at the monk's earnest intention to convert Thaïs, the Queen of Pleasure, to his own apparently gloomy paths of righteousness, declaring that failure stared him in the face. Nevertheless, he good-naturedly invited him to make his attempt that evening, as the banquet now being prepared was in honour of the lovely courtesan who was already on her way to his house, this being his own last night as her lover after a week of joy. He added, however, that it would be necessary for his friend to doff his monkish habit and to don a gala robe, which he offered to provide him with.

Athanaël was so full of zeal for the holy task he had set himself that he gladly accepted the invitation, agreeing willingly to the conditions; and then Nicias bade the slave-girls bring forth a splendid Eastern robe and prepare his friend for the banquet. As the girls dressed the young monk in the festive robes, they were full of admiration for his handsome looks and fine figure; and they did not hesitate to express their admiration openly, declaring that he was beautiful as a young god and even comparing him with Apollo—to the amusement of Nicias, who greatly enjoyed the shy discomfiture of his friend.

No sooner was Athanaël's toilet completed, than a tremendous acclamation arose from without, heralding the arrival of Thaïs, who was idolized by the populace as an actress and adored as the Queen of Love by all who were rich enough to buy her favours.

Accompanied by a crowd of revellers, Thaïs entered the banquet hall and was immediately led to her couch by Nicias; and the festivities were soon at their height.

Though astounded and almost overcome by the sight of the exquisite beauty of Thaïs, which caused his own heart to beat violently, Athanaël would not allow himself to join in the general chorus of adulation lavished upon her by the other guests, many of whom had been her lovers. Instead, controlling his racing pulses with a tremendous effort, he gazed upon her sternly as he sought for words of admonition.

Thaïs was instantly aware of the handsome stranger's severe gaze and was intrigued by his lack of complimentary phrases and the apparent sincerity of his disapproval of her. When he presently boldly accosted her and called upon her to repent of her sins and to renounce her loose life of pleasure, she did not resent his accusations; but she lightly tried to overcome his seriousness by her own charming allure, smiling brilliantly upon him and suggesting that he should consider the joys of love. She then saucily invited him to sit beside her on the couch, to crown himself with roses like her other lovers, and to realize that love was the only thing that mattered.

But Athanaël, though inwardly praying for strength to resist her enchanting beauty, continued courageously to upbraid her for her evil life. He implored her again and again to renounce her sensual lovers and to devote herself to the service of the one true God, declaring that the spiritual love of Christ alone could bring her lasting peace and comfort.

Thaïs, though she joined with her friends in laughing scornfully at the religious zeal of the bold stranger who thus dared to upbraid her in public, was impressed by his deep earnestness in spite of herself; and when he declared that he would follow her even to her own palace in his endeavour to save her soul alive, she invited him to do so.

Then, as the hilarious company began to dare him with loud bursts of ribald laughter, to venture thus to expose himself to the wiles of Venus, to brave Love in her own abode—a cry taken up scornfully by the beautiful courtesan herself—Athanaël lifted up his hands and fled in horror from this scene of licentious excess.

.   .   .   .

Late that night, towards dawn, when the orgy had ended, Thaïs returned to her own gorgeous palace. Having dismissed those favoured revellers who had escorted her home, she fell into a sad reverie as, weary to death and suddenly disenchanted, she realized the unsatisfying nature and soul-deadening effect of the life she led. The men she consorted with were brutal in their pursuit of selfish indulgence, while their women-folk were vain and wicked; and her own exquisite beauty would not endure for ever. As this last terrible thought came to her, she prostrated herself before a statue of Venus—whose priestess she was—and implored the goddess to preserve her dazzling beauty eternally.

At this moment, she heard a sound behind her. Turning, she beheld Athanaël, who immediately broke forth into glowing words of religious fervour, again imploring her to give up her present life of evil pleasures, to repent, and to accept instead the joys of Heaven.

For long he argued eloquently with her, bidding her to devote her radiant beauty to the service of God; and though Thaïs at first lightly twitted him for his compliments, she was again deeply impressed by his fervour, as at the banquet. When he begged her to save her soul for the life eternal, she begged him to tell her more about it.

Eagerly the zealous monk continued his exhortations; and though Thaïs again called upon Venus to shower delights upon her and declared that she was devoted only to the service of Love, she at last succumbed to the eloquent appeals of Athanaël. Flinging herself at his feet in a passion of repentant tears, she now begged him to take her away at once. Athanaël, full of joy at his victory, announced that he would take her away that night to journey through the desert to the Convent of the White Nuns, where she should spend the remainder of her life in acts of penitence for her many sins of the past. Then, as Thaïs, now completely won to repentance and exalted with the new spirituality that enveloped her, humbly expressed her willingness to obey her new religious teacher in all things, Athanaël sternly declared that she must destroy all traces of her old evil life. Thaïs the Courtesan must vanish and be forgotten, in order that Thaïs the Penitent might live and prepare for the life everlasting. All the treasures of her former life must be destroyed; and her palace must be consigned to the flames. As he began to throw down her beautiful treasures, however, Thaïs sought to keep an exquisite statuette of Cupid which Nicias had given to her; but Athanaël flung it to the ground and violently trampled it to pieces. Then, when Thaïs had unbound her hair and, discarding her jewelled raiment, had clad herself in a plain woollen robe, he took a torch and set forth with her from the palace.

At this moment, Nicias and a crowd of revellers appeared in front of the house, calling for Thaïs, their beloved idol, to come out to them, singing ribald songs and indulging in hilarious dances. An infuriated cry arose when Athanaël came forth from the now burning mansion, leading the sombrely-clad Thaïs by the hand and endeavouring to hurry her over the terrace above before their passage could be stopped.

Wildly the disappointed lovers called upon their idolized Thaïs not to leave them and hurled imprecations at the monk who thus bore her from their midst; but their clamorous entreaties were in vain, and Athanaël and his convert evaded them completely and escaped safely.

At an oasis in the Theban Desert, Athanaël and Thaïs at length arrived at midday, footsore and weary. The heat was intense under the blazing sun; and the glare of the scorching sand over which they had just passed made the shady palms and cool verdure of the oasis the more welcome to the tired travellers. Also the end of the journey was now in sight. Not far distant, on the other side of the oasis, the Convent of the White Sisters could be seen, its clustering white huts glistening in the dazzling sunlight.

Thaïs, unaccustomed to hardships and fasting and never having travelled on foot before, was completely worn out by this rough journey, which Athanaël had compelled her to perform in great haste, sternly forbidding her to rest by the way and exhorting her to bear her bodily discomforts and trials as a penitentiary punishment for her sins.

On reaching the edge of the oasis, however, Thaïs came to the end of her endurance, and stopped for a moment to rest on the welcome grass; but Athanaël severely commanded his penitent to rise and continue her way towards the Convent. Thaïs, humbly obeying, rose immediately and took a few more steps; but her weariness was so great that her limbs refused to support her further and, with a sigh, she sank again to the ground in a fainting condition.

Instantly, Athanaël was filled with compassion, his severity vanishing as though by magic. Kneeling beside her, he gently supported her drooping form in his arms, entreating her pardon for his harshness and addressing her with reverence and awe as a Saint.

He hastened to the well and brought back water and fruits which he found there, eagerly persuading her to eat and drink; and when, on recovering, she would have risen to continue the weary march, he gently prevented her from doing so. Instead, he bade her to hope and pray, which was all that could be expected of one in so weak a condition.

As they still rested there, the bells of the Convent were heard; and next moment, the Abbess Albine and her nuns were seen approaching them.

Athanaël then gently assisted Thaïs to rise; and leading her forward he gave her into the kindly hands of the White Sisters as a repentant sinner who wished to join their order.

Thaïs was now filled with the highest religious fervour; and a glow of ecstatic exultation seemed to envelop her as she was led away into the Convent after bidding Athanaël "farewell for ever".

On hearing the fatal words "for ever", a deadly chill struck at the heart of Athanaël; and, as the beautiful courtesan vanished from his sight, he realized suddenly in a flash that he loved her with that same overwhelming, irresistible earthly passion which he had just taught her to despise as a vile thing. Full of horror at his own defection, he now staggered from the oasis as one demented.

On his return to his brother monks that evening, he was overwhelmed with woe at this discovery; and he confessed to them that he now had no other thought in his heart but of Thaïs and his earthly love for her. He groaned when old Palémon sorrowfully reminded him of his wise warning to leave the evil city and its temptress alone.

Later on, when the monks had retired to their huts upon the approach of a storm, Athanaël wandered forth on the banks of the Nile, oblivious of the disturbing elements around him; and presently he beheld in a vision the form of his beloved penitent in a dying condition. Full of grief and alarm, the wretched monk immediately set forth for the Convent, heedless of the violent storm which now broke furiously and raged about him; and he never slackened speed until he reached the abode of the White Sisters.

Here he learned from the Abbess, to his despair, that his vision had been a true one and that Thaïs, having carried her fasting and deeds of penitence too far, was indeed at the point of death; and, grief-stricken, he entreated to be taken to her side.

Falling on his knees beside the dying penitent he passionately implored her to live and to smile on him, now declaring without shame or concealment his overwhelming love for her.

But Thaïs—once so ready to listen to the voice of love and whose dazzling beauty had enthralled the hearts of those who came beneath her sway—was already beyond all earthly passion. With her thoughts fixed steadfastly upon the eternal joys of Heaven, she passed away in peace; and the heartbroken Athanaël sank, despairing and heartbroken, at her feet.

THE HUGUENOTS
(Les Huguenots)

Meyerbeer

TOWARDS the close of an August day, in the year 1572, a festive scene was taking place in the Château de Nevers in the fair land of Touraine. The feuds between the Huguenot and Catholic parties in France had now reached the culminating point when an outburst between the two factions was daily looked for. It was in the interests of peace, therefore, that the Duc de Nevers, a Catholic nobleman of great wealth and vast estates, had included a young Huguenot gentleman, Raoul de Nangis, among the guests at the banquet he was now giving to his own Catholic friends.

At first the Catholic guests had somewhat resented the presence of a Huguenot in their midst; but Raoul's handsome appearance and noble air soon dispelled their usual contempt for those of the new faith. When toasts were presently drunk in honour of various fair ladies, it was noticed that the young stranger looked pensive; and he was rallied accordingly.

Raoul then related to the company an intriguing incident he had recently experienced. Wandering round the town one day, he had come across a group of hilarious and half-drunken students who had surrounded a curtained litter in which was seated a very beautiful young girl, who was greatly alarmed by their unwelcome and noisy attentions. Instantly drawing his sword, Raoul had quickly scattered the importunate loiterers, receiving the grateful thanks of the fair occupant of the litter. As she was borne away by her scared attendants, she had smiled upon her rescuer with such bewitching sweetness that he had promptly fallen in love with her; and he now declared that she was the lady of his heart for ever, though he had not beheld her since.

Though this pretty story met with the approval of the guests, the severe glances cast upon the latter by the stranger's puritanical old family servant, Marcel, caused them much annoyance. The old Huguenot, indeed, was quite horrified by the frivolity of the scene and did not hesitate to upbraid his young master for being in such careless company.

Just as Raoul was begging the guests to excuse his old retainer for his zealous severity, the Duc de Nevers was called from the room; and presently, de Nangis received a very unpleasant shock. Happening to glance through the window, he saw his host enter a nearby arbour with a veiled lady; and as the latter presently lifted her veil, he recognized the face and form of his own fair stranger of the litter incident—whose beauty had so enthralled him and whom he already loved.

Naturally imagining from the secrecy of their movements that de Nevers and the fair unknown must be lovers, Raoul was distracted with grief and disappointment. He was just about to make his excuses for an early departure when a page entered and handed to him a sealed note, declaring that it was a message from the Princess Marguerite de Valois, whose marriage to King Henry of Navarre was already imminent. In amazement, Raoul broke open the missive and found it contained a command from the young Queen-elect for him to attend her audience-chamber that evening.

Surprised that the young stranger whom they had been inclined to treat somewhat disdainfully was thus about to be so greatly honoured, the fickle guests now began to pour enthusiastic congratulations upon Raoul and to offer him marked respect; and the young Huguenot now found himself the centre of attraction until the revels ended.

The Princess Marguerite de Valois was eager to reconcile the warring religious factions of her country not only by her own forthcoming marriage with the Protestant King, Henry of Navarre, but also by endeavouring to arrange other marriages between certain noble Catholic and Huguenot families.

One such marriage to bring about religious union she hoped to arrange between her favourite lady-in-waiting, Valentine, daughter of the Comte de St. Bris, an influential Catholic leader, and the handsome young Huguenot, Raoul de Nangis. Although Valentine was already affianced to the Catholic Duc de Nevers, she believed that the latter would be willing to renounce her hand for such good reasons of State policy. To this end, wishing the matter to be settled before her own nuptials were celebrated, she had caused Valentine to seek a secret interview with the Duc de Nevers to bring about the cancelling of the contract between them.

Valentine had been willing enough to fall in with this plan, for she already loved Raoul, whom she had quickly identified with the gallant cavalier who had rescued her when annoyed by the drunken students; and she had conducted her painful mission with success—little dreaming, however, that her presence with the Duc de Nevers in the private arbour had been observed by her beloved one to the detriment of his own fair conception of her.

Marguerite de Valois was delighted to learn that de Nevers had agreed, though reluctantly, to release Valentine from her engagement to him; and she next secured the consent—also somewhat reluctantly given—of the Comte de St. Bris to the immediate betrothal of his daughter to the young Huguenot as a step towards reconciling the two religious parties.

When Raoul presently arrived in the royal audience-chamber, therefore, he was informed at once of the marriage it was the royal desire he should make. The young Huguenot, no longer caring to have any choice in such a matter, since the lovely maiden upon whom he had fixed his affections had proved unworthy, as he supposed, gave his consent readily enough; and the betrothal ceremony began.

The lords and officials of the Court now filed into the room, the Catholics ranging themselves on one side and the Huguenots on the other; and when, at the request of Marguerite, they had all vowed friendship and peace, the Comte de St. Bris led forth his daughter to present her in betrothal to the young Huguenot cavalier.

When Raoul, however, now recognized in his proffered bride the beautiful young girl he had rescued from the students and whom he had last seen in such seemingly compromising circumstances with the Duc de Nevers, he drew back with repugnance, declaring passionately that he would not wed with one so perfidious.

All was now confusion. Catholics and Huguenots alike were indignant at this outburst; and Valentine was filled with despair, for she had hoped that her love for de Nangis was returned by him. Raoul, however, still believing her to be base, again declared that he would not sully his ancient name by wedding with one so unworthy; and he departed without further explanation, leaving the company mystified as well as angry.

. . . .

Immediately after these events, all the participants in them moved to Paris, to take part in the celebrations in connection with the marriage of Marguerite de Valois with King Henry of Navarre. These festivities, however, were doomed to be marred; for the Catholic plot for a general massacre of the Huguenots was now quickly coming to a head, despite the genuinely sincere efforts of the young royal pair to avert such a catastrophe.

The Comte de St. Bris now lost no time in re-opening negotiations for his daughter's marriage with the Catholic Duc de Nevers, which he had always desired; and he also very promptly sent a duel challenge to Raoul de Nangis for satisfaction of the latter's insult to his daughter.

On the appointed day of her wedding, Valentine—who had broken-heartedly obeyed her father's wishes—entreated to be allowed to spend some hours in prayer in her favourite chapel on the banks of the Seine; and her request was granted. As it happened, this spot on the river bank was the meeting-place chosen for the forthcoming duel; and soon after entering the chapel, the unhappy bride-elect heard voices from without and recognized one of these as that of her father. At once on the alert, she now overheard St. Bris and his Catholic friends concoct a dastardly plot to murder de Nangis and his seconds when they presently arrived to keep their appointment for the duel; and she was filled with dismay.

As the conspirators moved away to collect their Catholic collaborators, Valentine crept forth from the chapel, determined to warn Raoul—whom she still loved, despite his strange repudiation of her. To her relief, the latter's faithful old servant, Marcel, came by at that moment; and telling him of the plot, she entreated him to warn his beloved master at once and to bring Huguenot soldiers to his assistance. She then returned to the chapel.

Shortly afterwards, Raoul and St. Bris arrived with their seconds; but no sooner had the duel begun than the Catholic followers of the latter also appeared, ready for their murderous assault. At the same moment, however, the Huguenot soldiers hastily gathered together by old Marcel likewise rushed forward; and a clashing skirmish ensued.

Just then, a third little company arrived. This was the newly-wed Marguerite de Valois, now Queen of Navarre, returning with her escort to her apartments in the royal palace. With an imperious gesture, the young Queen bade the combatants put up their weapons and inquired the cause of such unseemly strife during her wedding festivities. When Raoul's story was hotly contradicted by St. Bris, old Marcel came forward and verified his master's version, declaring that the warning of treachery to follow the legitimate duel had come from the lady who was even then issuing from the chapel.

Valentine, indeed, at that moment, came forward, overcome with anxiety for her lover's safety, yet full of confusion on being discovered intervening on his behalf. All were amazed at her appearance; and Raoul—who had not been able to quell his love for her, despite the fact that he had so scornfully spurned her—was bewildered on learning that she had been the means of saving his life and those of his friends. Doubtful now of his former suspicions, he asked why she had secretly visited de Nevers on the fatal evening of the banquet.

Queen Marguerite answered for the agitated girl, explaining that Valentine had gone at the royal request to de Nevers to implore him to renounce her hand; and when Raoul thus knew that Valentine's motive had been a pure and honourable one and not, as he had so jealously imagined, an unwotrhy one, he was filled with joy.

His joy, however, was quickly turned to grief once more on now learning that Valentine was already re-affianced to de Nevers and was to become the latter's bride that same evening; and at that moment there drew in to the shore a splendid barge, upon which stood the Duc, surrounded by his retainers. As de Nevers landed, St. Bris presented his daughter to him with pride, throwing a triumphant glance towards the despairing de Nangis; and, full of elation, the Catholic noble led his beautiful but now half-fainting betrothed to the waiting barge, in which they were conducted to his mansion, where their nuptials were celebrated a few hours later.

.   .   .   .

The unhappy Raoul, though almost stunned with grief for the loss of his beloved one, was determined to see Valentine once again, even at the risk of his life; and on the fatal eve of St. Bartholomew, he carried his resolve into effect.

Quite unsuspicious of the terrible fate about to fall upon those of his faith that night, the young Huguenot repaired at dusk to the mansion of de Nevers. Here he managed to make his way unperceived into the very room in which Valentine sat, lost in meditation and bemoaning her unhappy fate because of having been compelled to wed a man she did not love when her heart was given to another.

As Raoul broke in upon these sad reflections, she received him with a joy that could not be quelled; but soon she was filled with dire dismay. Scarcely had she greeted her distracted lover than she heard the approaching voices of her father and her husband; and she quickly realized that the discovery of de Nangis alone with her at that late hour would mean danger to him and disgrace to herself. Full of alarm, she begged him to escape whilst there was still time to do so; but Raoul declared that he cared not for danger but would gladly welcome death now that she was lost to him. Valentine, however, begged him not to be so rash, since his safety was dear to her; then, as the approaching voices were heard more clearly, she thrust him behind some heavy tapestries, bidding him, by their love, to remain in hiding until the danger was past.

Almost immediately afterwards, de Nevers, St. Bris, and a

number of other prominent Catholic lords entered the room and proceeded to hold a secret conference. When all were assembled, St. Bris unfolded to them the dreadful plot of Charles IX, the Catholic King of France and his Regent mother, the powerful Catherine de Medici—whereby, at the tolling of a bell that night, the Huguenots, one and all and irrespective of age, sex, or position, were to be massacred without mercy. Having received final instructions and tied white scarves around their arms to distinguish themselves from their intended victims, the conspirators departed on their awful mission, leaving the trembling Valentine alone.

No sooner had they left the room than Raoul sprang from his hiding-place, pale and filled with horror at the fearful plot that had, unknown to the assassins, been revealed to him. Hoping yet to be in time to warn his brother Huguenots of the calamity about to fall upon them, he would instantly have dashed from the house had not Valentine held him back. Wildly imploring him not to venture into the streets that night, she now declared passionately that she loved him dearly and that his life was precious to her.

Even in this moment of confusion and danger, Raoul's heart was filled with a deep joy on thus learning that his love was returned; and as he held the trembling girl in his arms, he was strongly tempted to remain safely with her.

But his nobler nature prevailed; and declaring that he must at all costs warn his doomed friends or perish with them, he unfolded her clinging arms and made his escape from the house as the clanging tocsin bell sounded.

Already the Massacre of St. Bartholomew's Eve had begun, and the streets of Paris were soon running with the innocent blood of the murdered Huguenots. Keeping in the background as well as he could, the horror-struck Raoul stumblingly made his way to the apartments in the palace set aside for the use of the newly-wed royal couple, King Henry of Navarre and his beautiful Queen, Marguerite de Valois. Bursting unceremoniously into the audience chamber, he implored the royal intervention and warned all the Huguenots present of their immediate danger, telling them of the terrible scenes he had already witnessed.

But it was now too late for this woeful calamity to be averted; and though Raoul fought his way bravely through the quickly increasing scene of carnage, trying to save as many of his friends and co-religionists as possible, he soon found his task a hopeless one.

N

To his joy, however, he presently came across his own faithful body-servant, Marcel, hiding in the alcove of a church; and the old Huguenot revealed to him the strange story of how he had been saved by the Duc de Nevers who, taking pity upon his helplessness, had thus been killed himself in defence of one of the hated new religion.

As they thus spoke together in agitated whispers, they were joined by Valentine, who had distractedly followed her lover from the house and sought him courageously through the dreadful streets of Paris. Overjoyed at having discovered him at last, she now entreated him to let her bind his arm with the white scarf she had brought that he might be taken for a Catholic and so preserve his life. She added that if he would renounce his unfortunate faith later on, she could obtain a free pardon for him and happiness might then still be theirs.

But Raoul, though now sorely tempted by the thought of future safety and joy, was too noble to save himself by denying the religion for which his companions in the faith were still sacrificing their lives; and, refusing the white scarf, he declared that he would remain with Marcel and await his fate.

When Valentine saw that he was thus resolved, she threw herself into his arms, tearing off her own white scarf and declaring that she would die with him as a Huguenot also, since, without him, she cared no longer to live. Then the doomed pair knelt together in the street, while old Marcel offered up a prayer of blessing upon them as the consecration of their love and devotion.

Even as they thus prayed together, a party of Catholic musketeers arrived on the scene and, seeing that the trio wore no white scarves, instantly fired upon them. The leader of this firing-party was the fanatical St. Bris, who soon received a terrible shock. As he approached nearer to gaze triumphantly upon the fallen victims, he realized, to his horror and grief, that he had slain his own beautiful daughter!

ROBERT THE DEVIL   *Meyerbeer*
(*Robert le Diable*)

A BRILLIANT scene was taking place in the port of Palermo one day in the beginning of the eleventh century. A large number of noble cavaliers and knights had lately arrived from various cities in Europe to take part in a grand Tournament to be held there; and all the company were talking about the great event as they greeted one another and quaffed wine together.

The Tournament was to be held under the auspices of the Duke of Messina, the hand of whose daughter, the beautiful Princess Isabella of Sicily, was offered as the prize of victory. It was for this reason that so many of the proudest knights in Christendom had determined to enter the lists, for the fair Princess was indeed a dazzling reward.

Amongst the latest arrivals was a handsome young knight, whose rich equipment and splendid train of attendants quickly attracted the attention of the assembled cavaliers and excited their curiosity as to who he might be. He was unknown to them, though not a stranger in Palermo. This newcomer was in reality Robert, Duke of Normandy, who had gained for himself the ill-famed title of "Robert the Devil"—a name which, though first bestowed on him from the supposition that his father had been a fiend, he had afterwards fully earned by his own recklessly wicked conduct. The latter had at length resulted in his expulsion from Normandy.

During his subsequent wanderings and adventures in Europe, Robert had made the acquaintance of the lovely Princess of Sicily, for whom he had instantly conceived a true and deep passion. Isabella, though knowing his evil reputation, had quickly returned his love, being irresistibly attracted by his handsome looks and the glimpses of a nobler nature which he exhibited when in her presence.

His wild and passionate disposition, however, quickly led Robert into a violent outburst of jealous rage against his beloved one's father, who did not encourage his suit; and not content with insulting the proud ruler, he also challenged all his knights to combat. This brought disaster upon him, for the Duke of Messina's angry knights were too powerful for him to overcome and soon compelled him to take to flight.

Robert was in despair at the result of his rash conduct, for Isabella was deeply offended. Though still secretly loving him well, she now seemed inclined to favour the addresses of the Duke of Granada, whose suit was constantly urged by her father. However, when the Tournament and its prize for victory were shortly afterwards announced, Robert determined to seek pardon of the Princess and enter the lists as a candidate. To this end he had arrived in Palermo with a gorgeous retinue, displaying every mark of extravagant splendour.

In all his evil pleasures and wild excesses, Robert had always been aided and encouraged by a sinister-looking knight, named Bertram, who was his constant companion and who, though he knew it not, was in reality his fiend-father. When he arrived in Palermo, therefore, this favoured friend was in close attendance upon the young Duke as usual.

Robert greeted the assembled nobles in a courtly manner; then, observing that some Norman troubadours were also in the company, he tossed a piece of gold to one of them and bade him sing a lay. The minstrel, whose name was Raimbaud, at once stepped forward; and little guessing that it was his royal master who stood before him, he announced to the expectant lords that he would sing to them the true story of Normandy's ill-fated young Duke known as " Robert the Devil ".

He then tuned his harp and began his lay, relating how the proud Princess Bertha of Normandy, after scornfully refusing many noble suitors, had at length accepted the love of a stranger prince, who was, in truth, a fiend in disguise. He went on to describe how the son of this strange marriage was young Robert, called the Devil because, inheriting a love of evil from his demon-father, he had constantly indulged in wicked excesses of every kind. Then, led away by the excitement of his theme, the minstrel portrayed the vices of Normandy's banished Duke in the glowing colours of popular dread.

Strange to say, Robert himself had never before heard the story of his supposed fiend-father; and as he listened to the minstrel's lay he became so full of rage that when it came to an end he could no longer restrain his feelings. Haughtily announcing that he himself was Robert of Normandy, he commanded his attendants to seize and hang the troubadour without delay. Instantly the wretched Raimbaud, realizing what a terrible mistake he had made, fell on his knees, entreating for mercy. He declared that he had not recognized his royal master, for whom he had brought an important message; and he added that he and his betrothed, a young village maiden, had come to Palermo together for this very purpose.

On hearing this, Robert now declared that he would take the village maiden in compensation for the minstrel's life; and ordering Raimbaud's release, he sent for the girl, promising her as a prize to his cavaliers. The unhappy Raimbaud uttered a cry of woe; but the gay cavaliers quickly surrounded the pretty maiden he had indicated, squabbling fiercely as to which should obtain possession of her.

The terrified girl cried aloud for mercy; but as she was helplessly dragged forward, Robert himself ran to her aid for he had instantly recognized her as his foster-sister, Alice, with whom he had played as a child in Normandy. He quickly released her from the rough hands of her lawless captors and, as the cavaliers fell back, grumbling at the loss of their prey, proclaimed that the maiden was under his protection; for the sight of her sweet, innocent face had roused within him once more the better feelings of his childhood days.

He then asked her how she came to be in Palermo; and Alice replied that she and her betrothed, Raimbaud, had deferred the day of their union, in order to bring a message to their royal master from his sainted mother. In answer to Robert's eager questions, she told him that Princess Bertha was now dead and that her last message to her erring son had been that as she had always prayed for him on earth, so would she also never cease to pray for him in heaven.

Full of grief on hearing of the death of his mother, Robert told Alice that naught was left to him but despair since he had also another woe to bear. On relating to her the story of his now hopeless love for Isabella, the village maiden comforted him greatly by declaring that she would seek out the Princess and implore her to pardon him. Then, suddenly catching sight of the sinister knight, Bertram, she trembled violently, saying that his dark face reminded her of a picture she had once seen of the Evil One; and seeing that he was about to approach, she crept away to rejoin her released lover.

Bertram now persuaded Robert to indulge in a game of dice with some of their new friends; and, encouraged by his evil companion to double and treble his stakes at each failure, the reckless young Duke quickly lost the whole of his fortune, even to his horses and armour.

Meanwhile, the gentle Alice had not forgotten her promise to her royal foster-brother. On the day of the Tournament she sought an interview with the Princess of Sicily as she sat beneath her gorgeous canopy and gave her a message from Robert, who implored pardon and humbly asked permission to contest for her hand in the lists that day. Isabella, who had never ceased to love Robert in spite of her displeasure at his wild conduct, was overjoyed to receive this contrite message. Readily granting the pardon he asked, she sent back a gracious invitation to him to accept the challenge of her principal suitor, the Duke of Granada, who proudly called on all rivals to meet him in open combat.

However, when at last the heralds blared forth the haughty Duke's challenge to Robert of Normandy, no response was made; and though the challenge was repeated again and again, still

Robert did not stand forth. Nor did he appear throughout the whole of the Tournament; and when, at the end of the contests, the Duke of Granada was declared victor and winner of the fair Princess's hand, Isabella returned to her apartments overcome with grief and despair, feeling that Robert had betrayed her trust and scorned her love.

Robert's absence from the Tournament had been cunningly contrived by the fiend-knight, Bertram, who had no desire for his victim to retrieve his character by gaining honour and glory in combat. Having lured him away from the scene by a phantom in the form of his hated rival, the Duke of Granada, his evil companion led him to a desert place outside the city.

Having induced him to enter a gloomy cave, where he intended to reveal a secret to him and also inquire of the spirits of darkness concerning him, Bertram returned for a moment to the open ground. Here, to his annoyance, he found Raimbaud the minstrel. The latter announced that he awaited Alice, his betrothed, whom he had asked to meet him there as they intended to be wedded that day.

Anxious for him to depart, the knight gave Raimbaud a handsome gift of gold, bidding him think no more of Alice but return to his wanderings once again—being now rich, he would quickly find many other pretty girls willing to love him. The minstrel, held for the time being under the spell of Bertram's evil influence, at once hurried back to the city where, however, better feelings prevailing again, he waited at the entrance for his betrothed.

Bertram now returned to the cave and invoked the evil spirits he knew so well. Whilst this invocation was going on, Alice appeared at the trysting-place and, full of disappointment that her lover had failed to keep his engagement, crept into the mouth of the cave to await him.

Here she was alarmed to see vivid flashes of lightning and to hear, amidst dreadful rumblings, the unearthly voices of demons calling a greeting to Robert. Fearing that her beloved foster-brother was in woeful danger, she was just about to spring forward to the spot where a flash of lightning presently revealed him to her sight, when Bertram suddenly blocked her path. He first attempted to address her in tones of gallantry; but the girl shrank back with a look of such unutterable horror in her eyes that the fiend knew at once she had guessed the secret of his true identity. Seizing her by the arm, he furiously declared that if she ever betrayed his secret or revealed aught of what she had seen and heard in the cave, she would die and would also bring death upon her lover and all whom she held dear; and Alice, though she longed to warn Robert, was so terrified by the awful aspect of Bertram that she dared not do so but departed quickly from the cave.

Bertram then returned to Robert and divulged to him an evil scheme, by means of which he hoped utterly to destroy his soul. He invited him to visit the spot where Princess Bertha had been buried and to pluck therefrom a certain magic bough that would give him resistless power; and Robert, deprived of the good influence of Alice, readily yielded to his solicitations. He therefore set off at once with his fiend-counsellor for the Convent of Rosalie, where his mother's remains had been laid.

This Convent had been founded by Princess Bertha for pure Christian worship; but the spot had soon been deprived of its sanctity by the nuns themselves who, forgetting their vows, had adored heathen gods and offered to them impious sacrifices. Where virtue had once been cherished, vice only now dwelt; and when Bertram and Robert appeared amidst the grave-stones, the evil spirits of the fallen nuns arose from all sides and, taking on the form of beautiful nymphs, assisted in the temptation of the victim.

For a short time Robert tried to resist the evil influences around him; but soon the insidious goading of Bertram prevailed and, plucking the magic bough, he rushed madly from the spot. His tempter quickly followed, bidding him to possess himself of the Princess of Sicily, whose innocence he might now destroy unhindered in revenge for the scorn with which her proud father had treated him; and roused to madness by the subtle suggestion, Robert instantly returned to Palermo to carry it out.

It was the day of Princess Isabella's nuptials with the Duke of Granada, whom she still disliked, though forced by her father to wed with him; and her attendants, attired in wedding garments, were already waiting in the ante-room to conduct the unhappy bride to the adjoining church as Robert entered.

By the power of his magic bough, the frenzied young Duke instantly caused all the attendants to fall into a charmed sleep; then, hurrying into the apartment beyond, he attempted to carry off the Princess by force. Isabella, quickly reading her ravisher's purpose in the evil passion that blazed in his eyes, fell on her knees and implored him by the pure love he had once felt for her to show mercy upon her helplessness. Robert, after a wild struggle with the evil desires within him, was at length overcome by her entreaties and, full of remorse, destroyed his talisman.

Instantly his magic powers vanished, so that the attendants, awakening from their charmed sleep in drowsy astonishment, suddenly beheld the intruder; and quickly divining his fell purpose, they rushed forward to seize him. Robert, however, taking to flight, escaped their hands; and the attendants, returning to the now grief-stricken bride, conducted her to the church in state, to await her bridegroom.

Robert found refuge in the cloisters of the church. Here he was soon joined by Bertram who, at last revealing himself as his fiend-father, now produced a parchment and begged him to sign it—by which act he would be bound to him for ever.

Though amazed to learn of the true identity of Bertram, Robert did not draw back in horror; in his hopeless misery, he still regarded the fiend as his best friend. He was just about to sign the contract, therefore, when the peasant girl, Alice, suddenly appeared in the cloisters and implored him to refrain from thus selling his soul; and she added that she had brought a joyful message for him.

She announced that Heaven watched over him and favoured his union with the woman he loved, for the proud Duke of Granada and his attendants had not been able to cross the threshold of the church; and she further announced that the beautiful Isabella, whose love was still his, now awaited him at the altar, hoping, by their union, to lead him to a better life.

On hearing this, Robert's despair became greater still, torn between the prospects of pure joys held out by Alice and the wicked enticements of Bertram; and a mighty struggle betwixt good and evil at once took place.

Alice, in her holy enthusiasm, no longer afraid of the fiend, fought desperately for the soul she longed to save. As her final effort, she produced a letter from the deceased Princess Bertha, in which the redeemed mother warned her son against the fiend who sought to destroy him and reminded him that she still prayed for him above.

This heavenly message at last prevailed over the wavering Robert and decided him to adopt the better course; and refusing to be tempted longer by the wicked Bertram, he joyfully allowed himself to be led away by Alice to join his waiting bride at the altar.

The defeated fiend, realizing that his cause was now lost for ever, instantly disappeared from the earth; and at the same moment a chorus of heavenly voices was heard rejoicing over the victory of a soul reclaimed from evil.

THE STAR OF THE NORTH   *Meyerbeer*
(*L'Étoile du Nord*)

ONE summer towards the end of the seventeenth century, a young
stranger worked for several months as a carpenter in the shipyard
of a little village in Finland. He seemed eager to learn all he
could about the art of shipbuilding; and he was such an excellent
worker that he often kept to his bench during the short spells of
relaxation following the noontide dinner-hour.

Though his fellow-workers and the villagers knew him as
Peter Michaeloff, that was not actually his name. He was in
reality none other than Peter the Great, the young Tsar of Russia.
With his customary energy of character and gift of thoroughness,
the youthful monarch had come thus disguised to the Finnish
shipyard to learn something for himself about the kind of
ships he required for his own navy. His love of adventure,
too, was served by the spice of danger entailed by this secret
enterprise.

Soon after his arrival in the Finnish village, Peter had fallen
ill, but had been nursed back to health by a fair maiden named
Catherine Skavronski. Having afterwards fallen deeply in love
with Catherine, whose beauty and strength of character exercised
extraordinary fascination over him, the young King lingered on in
the village long after the time he had appointed for his departure.
He was encouraged in this course by hearing Catherine declare
laughingly that her dead mother—who had possessed wonderful
gifts of prophecy—had foretold a brilliant future for her. He.
determined, therefore, to persevere in his wooing, realizing that
the maiden would certainly fulfil her destiny if she became his
bride. He loved to think of her as a bright star that shone for
him alone—his dazzling Star of the North, as he picturesquely
described her.

Although Peter, owing to his secret disguise, kept somewhat
aloof from the other shipyard workers, he had readily made
friends with a lively pastry-cook named Danilowitz, whose jollity
and kindliness appealed to his own warm-hearted nature. Danilowitz also liked the industrious young stranger, who had once
come to his aid at an awkward moment. While the pastry-cook
was selling his welcome wares during one of the dinner-hour
breaks, a shipyard worker began to sing a patriotic song in praise
of Finland and her protecting ruler, King Charles XII of Sweden.

Immediately afterwards, Danilowitz seized a goblet and raising it to his lips cried: "I pledge the Tsar of Russia, brave Peter the First!"

This daring toast, however, was not acceptable to the Finns and Swedes present, who, at that time regarded the Russians as their foes. Indignantly, they set upon the rash Danilowitz and would have mauled him badly had not the powerfully-built Peter intervened on his behalf and scattered his assailants with a few well-directed blows.

Realizing now that they were compatriots, Peter took a greater interest than ever in the pastry-cook; and without revealing his own identity, he promised him great advancement in the Tsar's army if he would join the Russian forces with him. Danilowitz eagerly agreed to his proposal, though he laughed good-humouredly at the idea of the honours Peter declared awaited him; and it was arranged that they should depart for Russia together when a suitable opportunity presented itself.

Usually, Catherine appeared in the shipyard at noontide, selling spirits to the workers, in which she did a good trade, earning enough money to keep herself and her brother, George Skavron-ski. The latter was a teacher of music who devoted himself mainly to his beloved art; and being of a somewhat weak nature, he allowed his clever and more energetic sister to take the lead in all matters connected with their welfare.

One day, soon after the toast-drinking incident, Catherine did not appear in the shipyard to fulfil her usual duties there; and, later on, Peter went to her home to learn the reason for her absence. He discovered that she had been making arrangements for the wedding that evening of her brother George with Prascovia, a pretty village maiden. Peter now took the opportunity of pleading his own cause once more with Catherine; but the latter only gave him merry rebuffs for answer. Although she had really loved him from the beginning of their acquaintance, she thoroughly understood the faults in his character; and she always laughingly declared that she would not marry him until he had learnt to keep his temper in control, to be less impatient and impetuous, and not to be so autocratic.

Although Peter greatly appreciated Catherine's clear insight into his character and knew that she admired his nobler qualities, he loved her so passionately that her home-truths hurt his pride and filled him with impatience; and now, as usual, he quickly lost his temper.

While this latest squabble was still in progress, the pretty little Prascovia came running up in terror, declaring that she had been chased by a party of wild Kalmuks and Cossacks, who were even now entering the village with evil intent.

Despite the general alarm at this disturbing news, Catherine boldly announced that all would still be well. She would play upon the superstitious nature of these rough tribesmen who were, she now revealed, her dead mother's kinsmen. When the Kalmuks came dashing up, therefore, the brave girl ran out fearlessly to meet them, bidding them in the name of their famous priestess of old, the Princess Vlasta, to depart at once—adding that the village they now sought to destroy was still under the latter's holy protection and that evil would befall them should they harm it.

On hearing her invoke this name—greatly revered by them—the troop immediately withdrew respectfully. To clinch the matter, however, the quick-witted Catherine now approached their leader, Gritzenko, with a mysterious air and prophesied that promotion quickly awaited him in the army of the Tsar; and thus filled with dreams of glory, the ambitious Kalmuk soon led his men away.

During this dramatic interlude, Peter, fearful lest the Kalmuks might recognize him, had kept well in the background; but he had grasped an axe in readiness to dash to the brave girl's aid, if necessary. Catherine had noted this; and she now told him tenderly that such anxiety on her behalf endeared him to her. Peter was filled with joy, realizing that his love was returned, even though the high-spirited maiden, exacting in her judgment of character, did not yet entirely respect him.

Now fired with a passionate desire to win her complete regard at all costs, Peter impetuously determined to return with the Kalmuks and Cossacks to his army and there to earn such renown as should compel her ungrudging admiration. Bidding her a hasty farewell, therefore, he hurried away to seek out Danilowitz and to return with him to Russia.

Meanwhile, further troubles seemed likely to fall upon the Skavronski household. Even as George's marriage with the pretty Prascovia was about to be celebrated, a military order was delivered at the house commanding the young bridegroom to leave the village that night with the Muscovite soldiers who had just arrived, as he was one of twelve chosen recruits who were to be pressed into the army of the Tsar. If a substitute could be found to take his place, however, he would thus be freed from serving.

Once more distress and confusion reigned; and once more Catherine's quick wit and boundless courage saved the situation. Accustomed always to bearing her brother's burdens upon her own strong young shoulders Catherine now boldly announced that she herself would take George's place as an army recruit for a fortnight, so that he might be married that night after all and also remain with his bride a short time before taking up his soldier's duties. Gratefully accepting her generous sacrifice, the happy bride and bridegroom now went forward with their marriage ceremony; and George promised to relieve his brave sister in a fortnight's time.

Catherine herself joined gaily in the lively wedding festivities, thinking only of the happiness of her beloved brother and quite regardless of the hardships and dangers she would shortly have to endure for his sake. When the merriment was at its height, however, she stole away unnoticed from the merry throng and, dressing herself in male attire, went off courageously to join the recruits who were to march with the Russian troops that night.

.   .   .   .

Many were the difficulties and hardships now endured by Catherine as a raw recruit; but the brave girl's wonderful powers of endurance and dauntless spirit carried her safely through them without misadventure or the discovery of her real identity.

A fortnight later the recruits reached the Russian camp, where they found the imperial forces gathered on the Finnish borders, ready to attack the armies of Sweden, upon which country war had now been declared by Russia. Here Catherine hoped soon to be relieved by her brother; but stormy days were ahead of her.

Her first adventure was with the Kalmuk, Gritzenko, who had already become a corporal, according to her easy prophecy. Gritzenko took a fancy to the boyish-looking new recruit and, wishing to impress the pretended lad with his own importance, chatted to him more frequently than was prudent—to the dismay of Catherine, eager to remain unnoticed.

Finally, the talkative soldier told the new recruit that he was being paid large sums of money for carrying documents from one highly-placed officer to another, conceitedly adding that they trusted him because he could not read. Thinking that the recruit was likewise ignorant—as, indeed, the latter cleverly pretended to be—he produced one of these documents as proof of his story. Catherine, however, being educated as well as quick-witted, quickly grasped that there was a conspiracy afoot in the camp unknown to the commanding officer; and having hastily read the document, she handed it back with a stupid air as though it meant nothing to her. Presently, however, when left alone, she wrote down the names of the mutinous officers involved and hid the paper in her tunic.

Later on that same evening, Catherine was ordered to mount guard outside a certain tent within which a couple of officers had just arrived to partake of supper. These newly-arrived officers were none other than the young Tsar Peter and Danilowitz—the latter already a colonel in the Russian army and rejoicing in the confidence of his companion, whose true identity was now known to him.

Peter, though in the dress of a plain captain, had been received respectfully as Tsar by the general in command but had immediately requested that his *incognito* should be strictly preserved for the moment. He had been told of the conspiracy in the camp and had boldly come in person to quell it, having already devised a scheme to that end. When the general had retired, astonished at the news, Peter and Danilowitz sat down to enjoy their supper, which was served to them by two pretty and lively little *vivandières*.

Peter, as he ever did in his moments of relaxation, gave himself up unreservedly to the pleasure of the moment. Casting aside for the time being the cares of State, he began to carouse gaily with Danilowitz, drinking deeply and flirting with the pert *vivandières* with all the accustomed licence of the times.

Catherine, passing to and fro outside the tent on sentry duty, was presently attracted by the sounds of hilarity from within; and, forgetful of her usual caution, she could not refrain from peeping through the opening. Instantly recognizing Peter in the person of the young captain, she was filled with joy on hearing her own name toasted by him at that moment. Her delight, however, was quickly turned to indignation on beholding her lover, heated by the wine he had drunk, snatch to him in a laughing embrace the merry *vivandière* who so constantly kept his goblet replenished. Just then, Gritzenko came by and, discovering the sentry thus neglectful of military discipline, instantly dragged the pretended youth away with threats of dire punishment.

Catherine, already upset by the scene within the tent and resentful of her rough handling by the Kalmuk, struck him angrily on the face—upon which, Gritzenko, furious at being thus defied by a mere recruit, forced the culprit into the tent before the officers and demanded reparation for such rank insubordination.

Peter, impatient at this unwelcome interruption of his pleasure and not even troubling to look at the offender, cried out carelessly: "Let him be shot!"

Catherine, now realizing the danger of her position, called out wildly as she was being dragged away to execution: "Peter! Peter! Save me! Do not let me be killed!"

Peter, though still half-bemused, recognized the voice as that of his beloved Catherine; and he sprang to his feet in bewilderment. Then, the shock of his discovery quickly restoring his clouded senses, he felt convinced that the young recruit was indeed the village maiden in disguise; and, overcome with horror that he had so carelessly given orders for her execution, he authoritatively commanded the pair to be brought back.

Gritzenko, however, returned alone to the tent, explaining with zealous pride that he had immediately attempted to carry out the first command—adding that when the prisoner had attempted to escape by jumping into the adjoining river, he had promptly shot him in the water. Well satisfied with what he had done, the Kalmuk handed Peter a note which he stated the young recruit had flung to him before plunging into the stream. Upon opening this missive, the now despairing royal lover saw that it contained the names of those officers concerned in the conspiracy; and at the end was a message of farewell, written in frantic haste by Catherine, bidding him use this information to advance himself in the service of the Tsar—of whose identity with Peter she was still ignorant.

As Peter stood grief-stricken at the thought that the brave maiden he loved so passionately was now lost to him for ever, the leaders of the conspiracy entered the tent. Regarding Danilowitz and the supposed young captain as belonging to their mutinous party, the newcomers began to talk over their plan of action, declaring that at a given signal they intended to join the ranks of the enemy against the Tsar, followed by all the men in the imperial army already disaffected by them.

Peter, roused from his grief by this treacherous threat to his arms, determined to turn the moment of danger to advantage by his own fearless daring. Despite the efforts made to restrain him by Danilowitz—who trembled for the safety of his beloved sovereign thus unprotected in the midst of traitors—he sprang forward and rebuked the officers passionately for thus seeking to avenge their own petty grievances when their country was in danger. Having worked them up into the wildest patriotic enthusiasm by his burning eloquence, he implored them first to drive away the enemies of Russia—after which he swore that he would himself deliver up the Tsar to them, unprotected and alone, to deal with as they chose.

The conspirators, already ashamed of their base designs by these scathing words, yet demanded who should be their guarantor for this; and Peter, without a moment's hesitation, answered fearlessly: "I, the Tsar, whom you were about to betray! Now, slay me if you will!"

For answer, however, the conspirators instantly fell on their knees, imploring pardon for their treachery—which Peter now magnanimously granted.

Thus, by a single bold action and the influence of his own noble personality did Peter quell the mutinous spirit which had threatened disaster to his arms; and having restored the patriotism of his men and their loyalty to himself as King, he was presently able to lead them on to victory.

. . . . . .

Some months later, when more peaceful days had come, Peter was once more plunged into despair as he thought of his lost Catherine. Nevertheless, he began to cling to the hope that she was not dead but that, though fired at in the water, she might possibly have escaped to land—for her body had never been recovered.

The faithful Danilowitz, at the request of his royal master and friend, undertook to seek her far and wide; and though at first his task seemed a hopeless one, his tireless efforts were finally crowned with success. Having received information that a poor peasant woman had rescued a wounded girl in soldier's clothing from the river about the time the tragedy had occurred, he ordered the now restored young woman to be brought to the Tsar's palace—where she was found to be indeed the long-lost Catherine. To the consternation of Danilowitz, however, he discovered that the shock of her wounds and the terrible hardships she had gone through had told heavily upon the brave girl's mental activities. Though robust once more in bodily health, her mind was affected to such an extent that she had completely forgotten all the circumstances connected with her love for Peter, the mention of whose name had no meaning for her.

For some days, Danilowitz kept her presence in the palace a secret from the young Tsar, being afraid to tell him the truth of the unfortunate girl's affliction. One day, however, Peter heard the sound of Catherine's sweet singing as he passed outside the room in which she sat. With overwhelming joy he instantly recognized her well-beloved voice—only to be plunged into grief once more on now learning from Danilowitz the sad news of her disturbed mental state and forgetfulness of himself.

Presently, however, renewed hope came to him. He now learned of cases similar to that of Catherine, whereby persons so affected had been restored to their normal state by being again brought into contact with scenes and incidents which had strongly impressed them in their happier days.

Peter determined to try this course with Catherine. By this time, her brother George, with his wife Prascovia, had arrived at the palace, seeking news of the lost Catherine through their old friend Danilowitz; and the young Tsar pressed them into his service for the carrying-out of his scheme, together with a number of peasants he also caused to be brought from the Finnish village where he had worked as a carpenter.

When the actors were all ready and the scene was set, Catherine was brought into the room to hear the peasants singing the songs they had sung at her brother's wedding, with George and Prascovia moving among them in their festive garb. Then Danilowitz, having donned his old pastry-cook's dress, likewise sang the songs he used to sing in the shipyard when selling his cakes; and finally, Peter himself, arrayed once more as a carpenter, took up his flute and played the airs Catherine had loved to hear him play when first they met.

As Catherine listened to this sweet music and gazed upon the happy scene, her memory was indeed gradually awakened, as her lover had hoped, until the cloud of forgetfulness was entirely lifted from her brain. Then, at last recognizing in the kingly figure so eagerly watching her the features of the man she had loved so dearly in the past, she moved forward with a glad cry and was clasped in his ready arms.

Full of joy that his beloved one was thus restored once more to her normal mental state Peter led her forward proudly to receive the homage of his friends and helpers; and one and all greeted her respectfully as their future Empress. Thus did the humble Catherine fulfil the brilliant destiny prophesied for her and become the bride and good genius of a great monarch, who always loved and revered her as his guiding star—his precious Star of the North.

BORIS GODOUNOV   *Moussorgsky*

WHEN the mighty Tsar Ivan the Terrible died in 1584, his son Feodor succeeded to the throne of Russia. As, however, the new Tsar was of weak intellect and almost an imbecile, a Regent was appointed in the person of Boris Godounov, one of the most powerful and distinguished nobles under the late monarch.

The next heir to the throne was Feodor's young brother, Dmitri, a handsome boy who early gave promise of brilliant achievements in the future; and Boris—who was intensely ambitious—knowing that the half-witted weakling, Feodor, was not likely to live long, soon came to regard the latter's fair young brother as the only obstacle to himself donning the purple in due course. Already he held the reins of power—judiciously strengthened by the marriage of his own young daughter, Xenia, to the royal moron; and though power was sweet to the ambitious man, the thought of kingship was sweeter still.

The consequence was that the young Dmitri was found dead one morning, stabbed by the hand of an assassin; and though for a short time suspicion pointed an accusing finger at the brilliant Regent, the latter was so popular and defended himself so ingeniously that his innocence came to be believed in and his powerful position was unassailed.

When, therefore, the weakly Feodor died in the year 1598, Boris Godounov had little difficulty in securing nomination as his successor—by virtue of his daughter's position as late consort and in default of a direct heir to the throne. He took the precaution, however, to send out his secret agents to gather the common people together in Moscow and to force them to utter supplications for him to become their Tsar—with the idea, chiefly, of impressing the Boyards, or nobles.

To give colour to the suggestion that sovereignty was being thrust upon him by the people against his own wish, he at first cunningly declined to become their ruler—so that their prayers of entreaty had to be renewed with greater fervour still. Then, finally, he feigned to give way to the insistent desires of the common people; and Boris Godounov was crowned Tsar of Russia amidst great pomp and splendour, being received afterwards by the bribed and threatened populace with tumultuous welcome and adulation.

But, although glory and the splendour of a powerful King were certainly added unto him, happiness and contentment never came to the remorseful soul of Boris Godounov. Ever and anon the memory of the innocent royal child, Dmitri, murdered in years gone by to pave the way for the attainment of his earthly ambitions, would rise up to torment his guilty conscience; and he never knew the joy of a peaceful mind. Though he kept his coronation vows sincerely, much of the good he desired to do turned to evil. He hoped to make a joyful second marriage for his beloved daughter, the young widowed Xenia; but misfortune overtook the proposed bridegroom, who met with an untimely death before the betrothal was consummated. His nobles plotted against him; famine and pestilence ravaged the land and drove his people to despair; and finally, after a troublesome reign of six years, a gigantic conspiracy arose in Poland, whence there marched a powerful army of rebels supporting an audacious Pretender to the throne of Russia, who succeeded in bringing disaster and death to the conscience-stricken usurper.

.　　.　　.　　.　　.　　.

In the Monastery of the Miracle, a pious old monk named Pimen sat up late one night after his devotions for the day were over, writing out his chronicles in feverish haste. Old Pimen was a great historian and the most industrious chronicler of his time; and he worked thus hard because of his fear that he might die before he had completed his great mission, which he believed had been divinely assigned to him—the mighty task of setting forth his country's history in all truth and faithfulness. As his task drew nearer to its close, he worked more continuously than ever, feeling his strength to be waning; and to-night he sat writing in his cell until the dawn and brought his chronicle up to the accession of the present ruler, Boris Godounov.

As old Pimen worked steadily through the night by the light of a solitary candle, a young monk named Gregory slept in a corner of the cell. Every now and again the sleeper would utter incoherent words and toss his arms high in agitation, as though excited by some strange dream—as, indeed, he was. Gregory's young and ardent spirit had not yet been crushed or subdued by his brief monastic life; and he had never been able to keep back his thoughts of the bright world without, where adventure, fame, glory, and love awaited those who sincerely sought such earthly delights. Often in his sleep he would dream of these forbidden joys.

Gregory was much attracted by the gentle old Pimen, who had taught him much of his own learning and whose former knowledge of the great world and of the history of the past had a strange fascination for him; and he would often pass the night in the latter's cell, listening eagerly as the old monk read out to him from his chronicle—until, from sheer youthful weariness, he fell asleep. This had happened on the night when Pimen had brought his chronicle up to date.

As he now awakened from his disturbing dream—the third night in succession that it had visited him—and saw old Pimen still writing by the light of the now guttering candle, he drew near to him and craved his blessing. He also told him of his

curious dream—that he had seemed to be standing on the pinnacle
of a tower with all the people of Moscow at his feet, at first
acclaiming him with rejoicing and later pouring execrations and
mocking laughter upon him, causing him such terror that he had
fallen from the tower to the ground. He then begged his revered
friend to tell him again about Ivan the Great—how the mighty
Tsar had loved beautiful women, had worn sumptuous garments,
and had eaten at splendid banquets. Old Pimen smiled indulgently at the eagerness of the youth, reminding him that such
earthly joys were but vanity and that even the magnificent Tsar
Ivan had known sorrow; and he added that their present ruler,
Boris, though outwardly glorious and seemingly to be envied,
was inwardly filled with the wretched and ever-present remorse of
a regicide.

But Gregory was not to be put off from indulging the natural
longings of youth by this last gloomy picture. He now eagerly
asked for further information about the murdered Tsarevich,
Dmitri, and of what age the latter would have been at the present
time; for Pimen had related all the supposed circumstances of this
crime—at present a secret known to no one else—to his young
companion, whom he desired should continue his chronicle after
he himself had been called to his long rest. The good Pimen
replied that had the young Dmitri lived, he would now have been
of the same age as Gregory himself. Then, as the voices of their
brother monks were now heard in the adjoining chapel chanting
their early morning prayers, the old chronicler, though weary
and tottering from his all-night labours, reached for his staff and
departed with his young companion to take part in the devotions
of the day.

But though Gregory knelt with the pious brethren and appeared
to be joining in their prayers and chants, his thoughts were far
away. An audacious scheme had suddenly presented itself to him,
and his quick, active brain was already planning how to carry it
out. The murdered Dmitri would now have been of his own age
had he lived—why, then, should not he, Gregory, appear in
Russia and impersonate that royal youth? It could be announced
that though news of the latter's untimely death had been circulated
years ago, he had not been murdered as then believed but had
been hidden in a monastery until the present time—when,
accidentally learning his true identity, he had effected his escape
and had come to claim the throne usurped by Boris Godounov.
Even though his representation would be a fraud, was not the
deception justified if he thus brought retribution upon the
criminal Boris? By means of the knowledge revealed to him in

old Pimen's chronicle, he now had the chance of avenging the assassinated royal youth and, at the same time, of fulfilling his own ambitions and aspirations. The culture and learning he had received at the monastery rendered him fit for such a task.

The more the adventurous Gregory considered this stupendous scheme, the more determined he became to carry it out. From the conversations he had held with old Pimen in regard to political matters, he decided that the most advantageous place for the launching of his career as Prince Dmitri would be Poland; for the Poles had ever been at variance with their Russian rulers and were at the present time in a state of great disaffection against the reigning Tsar, Boris. They would, therefore, be the more willing to accept the story he had concocted and to gather around him an army of rebel supporters to march against the usurper, whom they already hated. Having thus boldly planned, Gregory's first step was to find a suitable opportunity of escaping, unnoticed and unsuspected, from the monastery where he had lived since his early childhood.

After patiently waiting for some considerable time, a chance at length presented itself; and the young monk Gregory slipped out from the monastery in the dead of night and set forth upon his adventurous career as Pretender to the throne of Russia. Strange to say, so successful was his audacious imposture, so well-conceived were all his plans and so remarkably did circumstances play into his hands that he actually attained to the height of his ambition and sat upon the throne of Russia upon the death of Boris— reigning as Tsar for a short time until he, in his turn, was cast down from the pinnacle of glory to which he had so presumptuously aspired and was slain with his adherents. Thus was fulfilled the warning prophecy given to him in the strange dream that had visited him three times in succession before he set forth upon his mad adventure.

.   .   .   .

After escaping from the monastery, Gregory first of all fell in with a couple of roving friars, named Varlaam and Missail. The latter, though wearing the ragged garb of holy pilgrims and having probably once been attached to some monastery, were now merely vagabonds, wandering from place to place and securing a precarious living by begging alms and food at the homesteads and inns they passed on their journeyings to and fro.

These two vagrants were willing enough to admit Gregory to their companionship for a short time because his more respectable appearance was likely to secure them better hospitality than they were accustomed to enjoy. This proved to be the case; for when they reached an inn on the Lithuanian frontier, the hostess willingly admitted them at Gregory's request, treating all three as "holy hermits" for whom she professed great reverence. Moreover, she spread for them a generous meal, with rich wine in which to drink her health.

While the weary travellers were enjoying this good meal, however, there came an unpleasant interruption. A party of soldiers entered to ask the hostess about a "young heretic who had escaped from a monastery near Moscow and was suspected of conspiracy". They produced a document in which more details were given; but as they were unable to read, they requested one of the friars to decipher it for them.

Knowing well that this runaway could be none other than himself, Gregory eagerly seized the document and pretended to read the description it contained, cunningly painting the portrait of a person similar in appearance to the rogue Varlaam. The latter, however, was also cunning; and snatching the document in his turn, he slowly spelled out an amended description, which could be taken for no one but Gregory. Finding, therefore, that he could no longer deceive the guards, the young monk drew a dagger to defend himself and quickly made his escape through the window. Though the astonished soldiers pursued him for some distance, he managed to outrun and elude them.

Being now well advanced into Lithuania, he had no further fear of pursuit, but at once proceeded thence to Poland and set about his mighty task of establishing his false identity as the long-hidden Tsarevich Dmitri.

The Poles received the young stranger and his clever story with surprisingly credulous cordiality and accepted him willingly enough as Pretender to the throne of Russia; and the powerful nobles of Poland quickly gathered a large army together in support of his claim, being eager to march with him against the usurper Boris, whom they hated as an upstart.

Consequently, the enterprising young monk soon found himself a person of the greatest importance and settled down to the excitement of his new and dazzling position with the utmost ease and the keenest enjoyment, as though indeed born to such great honours. He was received all over Poland with astonishing acclamation; and as the months went on his strength and followers grew apace until at last he felt he might relax somewhat and take a short spell of rest and pleasure before making his final entry into Russia.

At this time the young Pretender was living quite royally in the gay city of Sandomir; and here he succumbed to the counter-attraction of love, which at one time threatened to turn him aside from the path of ambition. He fell passionately in love with Marina Mnichek, the beautiful and fascinating daughter of the Voyevode of Sandomir; and loving with all the ardour of early youth and an intensely romantic nature brought suddenly into contact with that all-devouring flame, he ceased for the time being to give even a thought to his mission. Content to experience only the lover's rapture of reciprocated passion, he would fain have dallied for ever in the company of the fair mistress who enthralled him.

But the beautiful Marina, though she returned his passion with equal intensity, was also extremely ambitious; and, with all the art and persistence of a clever woman, while returning her lover's caresses, she would not let him forget the brilliant future in store for him—which she meant to share.

In this effort, Marina was strongly supported by a fiercely fanatical priest, Rangoni by name, who desired her to become Queen that she might influence the new monarch in restoring the waning faith in Russia.

Her own ambition to reign as Queen thus encouraged by the demands of the Church, Marina, while accepting eagerly the passionate devotion of the pretended Dmitri, constantly referred to the great work that lay ahead of him. Even when her lover appeared to be hurt because his beautiful mistress seemed almost to care more for power than for his love, she had her answer. Flinging her arms around his neck, she would declare passionately that it was her great love that made her ambitious for him; and thus she would skilfully lead him back to the mighty enterprise he had embarked upon. At last she succeeded in bringing his period of relaxation to an end; and the young Pretender, Dmitri, at the head of a mighty army, set forth upon his daring and triumphant march into Russia, carrying all before him and gaining fresh adherents wherever he went.

.   .   .   .   .   .

While the great rebellion was thus progressing, Boris Godounov became more and more a prey to remorse and a guilty conscience. Even in the presence of his beloved children, he could not shake off the memory of his evil deed done in years gone by nor his dark forebodings of coming disaster. Gradually his mind became more and more disturbed; and his torturing thoughts gave him no peace.

One day he appeared suddenly in the apartment of his young son, and surprised the little Tsarevich in the midst of a merry clapping game with his old nurse; but though he smiled at the child's eager enjoyment the sight could not drive away his sadness. He endeavoured to comfort his beloved elder child, the widowed Xenia, who was also present; but he could not do so, and she left him, weeping.

While still endeavouring to listen to the artless prattle of his little son, he was presently interrupted by the hurried entrance of his chief adviser, Prince Shouisky, who came to announce in great agitation that he brought news of a serious rebellion. A Pretender had arisen in Poland and was already marching into Russia at the head of a gigantic army; and the minister added in awed tones that it was whispered among the common people that this bold adventurer was none other than the young Tsarevich Dmitri come back from the grave.

Turning pale as death, Boris quickly sent away his little son and fearfully demanded further particulars from the Boyard, whom he then dismissed; but as Prince Shouisky left the apartment he glanced back and beheld a strange sight. The conscience-stricken Tsar was crouching in a corner and, with outstretched hands, appeared to be trying to keep back some unseen person—the spectre of his own diseased mind, the murdered child, Dmitri, whom he now called upon in agonized tones : " Torment me not with the sight of thy wounds! Begone, and leave me in peace! "

.   .   .   .

The great rebellion now rapidly spread; and when the false Dmitri entered Russia at the head of his enthusiastic Polish army, thousands flocked to his standard. The oppressed peasantry received the Pretender with joyous acclamation and, defying the established authorities, indulged in many acts of lawlessness and licence. When opportunities occurred they seized the partisans of Boris and ill-treated them. In one village where an orgy of this kind was in progress, the vagabonds Varlaam and Missail took part in the tormenting of an elderly Boyard and some Jesuit priests—which vile entertainment was suddenly brought to an end by the timely arrival of the Pretender Dmitri himself, who sternly forbade the repetition of such excesses.

As the triumphant rebel army, conquering all before it, drew nearer to Moscow, a special meeting of the Duma was hastily summoned. As the Boyards gathered together, anxiously awaiting the arrival of Boris, whose counsel they eagerly desired in this moment of peril, Prince Shouisky entered in dismay to tell them that the Tsar appeared to be in an unbalanced state of mind. He then related to them the story of the strange mutterings and actions he had observed when last in his presence—the conduct of a man with a guilty conscience.

While they thus conferred together, Boris Godounov staggered into the council chamber in disordered attire. With wild gestures and distracted mien, he beat the air as though to shut out again from his sight some fearful vision, shrieking aloud in the tones of a madman : " Begone, thou bleeding child, Dmitri ! Who dares to say I murdered thee? They say thou art still living ! Why, then, dost thou haunt me so constantly? "

As the Boyards gazed upon their distraught monarch in amazement at this strange outburst, Boris gradually recovered somewhat and spoke to them in a more rational manner. When Prince Shouisky presently informed him that an old monk waited without and desired to speak with him, he commanded that the stranger should be admitted; for he hoped that the good old man of God might bring comfort to his tortured mind.

The stranger monk proved to be old Pimen who, gazing fixedly and accusingly upon the unhappy Tsar, related to him the story of a miracle that had just taken place. An old blind shepherd had recovered his sight upon uttering a prayer at the tomb of the murdered Tsarevich Dmitri, whose childish voice he believed had spoken to him from the grave.

On hearing this the conscience-stricken and remorse-worn Tsar fell back unconscious. Seeing that he was in a dying condition the Boyards gathered around him and sent for the young Tsarevich, at the same time calling upon the priests to administer the last rites to him and to cause the passing bell to be tolled.

The dying monarch recovered sufficiently to bestow his blessing upon his little son and to pray that the protection of heaven might rest upon him; and then, as the chants of the priests arose, with a last faint prayer for his own forgiveness, the soul of the unhappy but repentant Boris Godounov passed away.

KHOVANTSCHINA   *Moussorgsky*

DURING the early days of the mighty Tsar, Peter the Great, the Russian people suffered much, and misery and strife were rampant. During the long minority of this afterwards brilliant monarch and his brother Ivan—who at that time shared the throne with him, the two princes reigning as joint Tsars—many rebellions and changes of government took place.

During the year 1682 a crisis was close at hand, and the beautiful city of Moscow was rife with insurrection. Prince Galitsin, the Prime Minister, had for many years held the chief power in the land, ruling as the representative of the two youthful Tsars and enjoying the somewhat doubtful favour of their Regent sister, the Tsarevna Sophia, who had chosen him not only as her principal official but also as her lover. He had sought to consolidate his position and the authority bestowed upon him by his royal mistress by restricting the powers of the haughty and lawless nobles; but the latter furiously resented his ruthless curtailment of their ancient feudal privileges.

For several years the Boyards fretted and fumed under the yoke of the tyrant Minister; then, one of the strongest and proudest of them all, Prince Ivan Khovanstky—who traced his ancestry back to a Lithuanian sovereign—gathered a following of his own together in opposition to the rule of Prince Galitsin. He proved a formidable rival; for many of the nobles and the majority of the oppressed populace—who dared not do otherwise—joined his ranks. As Commander also of the famous Streltsy or Archer Guards, he engendered fear in the hearts of all who opposed him; for he permitted his own men unlimited licence, so that they committed all kinds of excesses in the name of order and were the terror of the whole community.

Khovanstky's handsome son, Prince Andrew, was a wild young libertine, willing to take part in any roistering carousal or vicious orgy; and the two Khovanstkys soon caused keen anxiety to the scheming Prince Galitsin who, with ill-concealed dread, saw them snatching at his own already waning powers.

But the sudden rise and wonderful success of the Khovanstkys had not been attained without bringing upon them the jealous hatred of most of the other great Boyards, who now found themselves smarting under the heels of two tyrants instead of one; and many of them retired to the country Court of the Tsarevna and began to plot there for the overthrow of their rivals and to ingratiate themselves with the youthful sovereigns by revealing the misrule and tyranny of both powerful parties. The head of these opposing nobles was the Boyard Shaklovity, who caused a letter to be sent to the Tsarevna, announcing that the Khovanstkys intended to overthrow the government with the aid of a certain religious sect known as the Old Believers, then to depose the two young monarchs and, finally, to set Prince Andrew Khovanstky on the throne in their stead.

On the day that the Boyard sent his incriminating letter to the Court, Prince Ivan Khovanstky arrived in the famous Red

Square of Moscow to show off the power and wealth of his splendid followers and to receive the fulsome praises and admiration of the cowed populace after he had addressed them. He was attended by his famous Archer Guards, the Streltsy, who stood around him as a threatening phalanx while he listened with a disdainful air to the fulsome song of welcome sung by the scared people in accordance with his command. When their song of terrified welcome came to an end, he called upon them to assist him in crushing the tyranny of the Prime Minister and the lawlessness of those Boyards who had not joined his own standard.

While the meek populace thus listened to the harangues of his father and obediently sang his praises, young Prince Andrew, in a quieter and less frequented spot not far distant, was enacting the tyrant in another way—the way of a licentious bully who sought to satisfy his selfish passions by brute force. He held in his arms a young girl, Emma, whose beauty and freshness had inflamed him with a sudden lawless passion; and although the unfortunate girl protested in agonized tones and struggled to escape from her tormentor, he only held her more closely and embraced her more fiercely.

Prince Andrew laughed derisively at his victim's pitiful requests to be released; for he had exercised considerable effort and cunning to put aside all obstacles in his pursuit of her. He had caused her father to be slain and her true lover to be exiled; and now he intended to compel her to yield to his desires, despite her desperate struggles.

Just as Emma's strength was beginning to fail, a sudden interruption occurred. There came past that way a young widow named Martha, who was a prominent member of the religious sect known as the Rasskolniki, or Old Believers. Only a few weeks ago this young woman had herself been the beloved mistress of Prince Andrew Khovanstky who, though he had once professed undying love for her—which she had passionately returned— had carelessly cast her aside when his infatuation waned. Seeing that he now held another struggling victim in his arms—and an unwilling one this time—Martha accosted him sharply, reproaching him for his faithlessness and for thus wantonly seeking the ruin of the unhappy and helpless Emma.

Stung and infuriated by the just reproaches of his cast-off mistress, Prince Andrew loosened his hold upon Emma, who quickly shrank back, still half-stunned with terror; then, furiously drawing a dagger, he flung himself upon the young widow and attempted to stab her.

Martha, however, was ready for him. Knowing well the

desperate character of her late lover, she, in her turn, swiftly drew
a dagger from the folds of her own garments and skilfully parried
the blow.

As Prince Andrew fell back, angry and baffled by this unexpected set-back to his murderous onslaught, the obsequious
supporters attached to his lawless father's retinue drew near,
followed by that haughty noble himself; and the young libertine,
unable to escape, was compelled to await the approach of the
party.

Prince Ivan Khovanstky greeted his son and Martha, recognizing in the latter an important member of the sect of Old
Believers, with whom he was anxious to ingratiate himself. Then,
observing the trembling Emma and being struck with her fresh
young beauty, he commanded one of the archers to seize the girl
and hold her in readiness for his own pleasure.

On hearing this, Prince Andrew passionately remonstrated with
his father, declaring that he loved Emma and had secured her for
himself; but seeing that Prince Ivan was not likely to yield to his
claim, he resolved that Emma should not be taken from him
alive. He was just about to stab the half-fainting girl when
Dositheus, the revered leader of the Old Believers, appeared on
the scene and, quickly grasping what was afoot, fearlessly took
matters into his own hands. Calmly bidding Martha to lead
Emma away to a place of safety, he waited until the two women
had departed; then he turned and sternly reproached the Princes
Khovanstky for their licentious behaviour.

Prince Ivan, inwardly fuming but not daring at the moment to
protest, since he desired the co-operation of the Old Believers in
his own political schemes, called upon his archers and retired
with the best dignity he could to the Kremlin, followed by the
angrily frustrated Prince Andrew.

That evening, Prince Galitsin, in his splendid mansion, was
sitting alone in a pleasant summer chamber that opened out into
a garden beyond, where shadows were already being cast by the
setting sun. His thoughts were dark and gloomy. Though he
held in his hand a love-letter he had just received from the
Tsarevna, it had brought neither joy nor comfort to his heavy
heart. He doubted the sincerity of its extravagant expressions
and reasoned, rightly enough, that with such a woman when
passion wanes, coldness and disfavour quickly follow—then woe
betide the unfortunate lover she has tired of!

Galitsin contemptuously decided not to be deceived or lured
nto rashness by the present warmth of the epistle he held in his

hand—little dreaming, however, that the fickle royal writer was already showing favour to his enemies and listening to their plots for his downfall. Just then, his attendant entered, ushering in the Old Believer, Martha, whom he had sent for, knowing that the young widow had a great reputation as a seer.

Because her foretellings of the future were always weirdly correct, the harassed Minister had sought the advice of Martha on several occasions, though he regarded her with considerable distrust, knowing her to be the mistress of the younger Khovanstky. As she now entered with her usual silent tread, he shivered slightly, but curtly bade her reveal to him his future destiny—for he hoped that her prophecy might possibly disprove his gloomy forebodings.

Twilight had now fallen, and a pale moonbeam fell upon the tall black-robed figure of Martha as she stood at a central table gazing into a silver bowl of clear water and making her incantation—which, however, brought no comfort to the anxious listener. She declared that he was surrounded by enemies who spoke fair words in his presence but plotted against him in secret; that an ignominious downfall awaited him; that he would be dragged in the dust of royal disfavour and end his days in wretched exile; and that the hopeless tears of woe he shed should teach him, the once powerful tyrant, the wonderful lesson of Divine justice.

Having thus delivered her prophecy, Martha glided silently from the room; but Galitsin sprang up and bade his attendant have her followed and drowned in a nearby sheet of water known as "the Marsh"—that she, at least, might be silenced for ever and bring no news of him to his enemies.

Almost immediately afterwards, Prince Ivan Khovanstky entered the room unannounced; and instantly a violent quarrel ensued between the rival tyrants. This was interrupted by the timely arrival of the aged Old Believer, Dositheus, who sternly rebuked them both and then bade them listen to a group of his own disciples in the ante-chamber singing a hymn of praise for the triumph of good over evil.

Prince Khovanstky, who tolerated the Old Believers only as his likely followers, listened with pretended respect to the fanatical chanting which now arose; but Galitsin was furious at their intrusion. He was just about to issue a sharp command concerning these unwanted singers when the young widow, Martha, rushed back into the room and, clinging to Dositheus, implored his protection. She declared that the Minister's servants had attempted to drown her in "the Marsh" and that she had only been saved by the timely arrival of a party of the Petrovsky or Royal Guards who had seized her would-be assassins and now held them captive.

The rival Princes heard of the presence of the Royal Guards with feelings of alarm, both realizing that their arrival boded ill to one or other of them. Next moment the fears of Prince Ivan were justified by the entry of the Boyard Shaklovity, who announced that the Tsarevna had caused a proclamation to be posted up to the effect that the Khovanstkys were believed to be conspiring against the State and that the young Tsar Peter had ordered an inquiry to be made into the matter.

During the confusion which followed, Martha and Dositheus were able to escape from the room and return to the district where they dwelt with the Old Believers; and Prince Ivan Khovanstky, still calm in his haughty arrogance, retired to his own mansion, refusing to resign his powers until the accusation against him had been proved.

The Boyard Shaklovity, however, did not let the grass grow under his feet, but determined to remove the hated tyrant without further delay. He visited Prince Ivan again, finding him feasting in his splendid banqueting-hall, surrounded by attendants and entertained by dancing-girls. Now announcing that the Tsarevna had called a Grand Council that day, the crafty Boyard added that the presence of Prince Ivan was required at this conference.

Khovanstky, though he feared treachery, boldly declared his willingness to attend the Council; and he called for his magnificent robes of state, ordering his attendants to array him in them and to load him with his most dazzling jewels. No sooner was he ready, however, and was about to pass over the threshold, than there came the sudden flash of a dagger—and the mighty Khovanstky fell to the ground, dead! The attendants fled in terror; but Shaklovity approached the corpse and gazed down upon it with mocking triumph, rejoicing in the fact that his plot had so far succeeded.

The downfall of the Prime Minister quickly followed this tragedy. The Tsarevna, tired of the lover she had raised to power, listened only too readily to the accusations made against him by her jealous counsellors—and the result was that the once powerful Prince Galitsin was deprived of all his dignities and was driven forth from his beloved country a disgraced and despairing exile. Thus was the prophecy of the young widow Martha fulfilled.

After the death of their chief, the followers of Khovanstky were quickly dispersed to the royal side; but Prince Andrew escaped for a time, though obliged to keep in hiding.

The Old Believers, learning that instructions had been given to the fierce Petrovsky Guards to slay every member of their sect, retired to an old hermitage in a wood near Moscow, there to await their end—but not at the hands of the soldiery. Old Dositheus, realizing that they could not now escape death, bade them build up and fire a huge pyre of wood, upon which they could mount and perish for the faith they held, as did the martyrs of old.

Whilst these sinister preparations were afoot, Martha had sought and found Prince Andrew, who, craven-hearted now that death threatened him on every side, gladly enough fled with his former mistress to the hermitage. Here he demanded news of the fair maid Emma, whom he still loved; but Martha told him that Emma was safe from his pursuit and would shortly be united to her own faithful lover, who had now been brought back from his unjust exile. Then, bidding the now distracted young man to think of earthly matters no longer but rather to bend his thoughts upon heaven, since his own death was nigh, she succeeded in persuading him by the power of her own love—which had never waned—to mount the now burning pyre with her.

When, therefore, the soldiers arrived at the hermitage, thirsting for the blood of their expected victims, they were greeted by an already blazing funeral pyre; and as the flames sprang up around them, the Old Believers, with the now repentant Prince Andrew in their midst, went cheerfully to death, singing a song of praise and thanksgiving, inasmuch as they were accounted worthy to suffer martyrdom for their faith.

COSI FAN TUTTE or THE SCHOOL FOR LOVERS   *Mozart* (*They All Do It*)

ONE day during the eighteenth century, in a café in Naples, two young cavaliers, Ferrando and Gratiano, were singing the praises of their betrothed ladies, declaring that they had the greatest faith in their fidelity, which would stand any test. On hearing this, their companion, Don Alfonso, a cynical old bachelor, declared that no woman was ever really faithful; and he laughed aloud at the young men's indignant protestations. He then suggested that they should allow him to put the ladies through a severe test to prove the truth of his statement; and Ferrando and Gratiano, thoroughly convinced that he would fail, gave him permission to do so, laying a substantial wager and agreeing to obey his directions implicitly for the following few days. Don Alfonso drew up his plan of campaign and the test began forthwith.

The two young men at once repaired to the abode of their betrothed ladies, Isadora and Dorabella, two beautiful Andalusian sisters; and presently they announced that they had been ordered to depart immediately with their regiments to Havannah, where fighting was proceeding. The two girls were full of grief and anxiety on hearing this disturbing news; and they parted from their lovers with tears and many protestations of undying fidelity.

A few days later, the two young men, having, in the meantime, completely changed their appearance and disguised themselves as officers of a foreign regiment, were introduced by Don Alfonso to Dorabella and Isadora as recently arrived strangers. The latter were completely deceived by the clever disguise adopted by Ferrando and Gratiano and failed to recognize them.

Acting upon the instructions of Don Alfonso, the newcomers proceeded to pay great attention to the young ladies, each making ardent and persuasive love to the betrothed of his friend.

Isadora and Dorabella, however, at first refused to be impressed or even interested in the "foreigners", and expressed great indignation at the violent love made to them by their new acquaintances. Their lovers were, consequently, greatly delighted and triumphed over Don Alfonso upon this proof of their ladies' fidelity. The wily old cynic, however, declared that he was not yet defeated but had arranged to carry the plot deeper still.

He then persuaded the young men to keep up their present disguise a little longer, and, at their next interview, to carry their despair at the ladies' indifference to the point of attempted suicide. The still completely confident lovers were willing enough to agree to this test also. To carry out their plan the more successfully, they managed to bribe Despina, the ladies' waiting-maid, to assist them by admitting them after they had, as "foreigners", been denied the house and grounds by her indignant mistresses.

In this plot, Don Alfonso, to his great satisfaction, felt that he was about to succeed. Despina, entering into the joke with great spirit, being already bored by the constant dolefulness of her ladies because of the absence of their lovers, found means to introduce the "foreigners" once more into the presence of Dorabella and Isadora.

At once, the disguised officers again made violent declarations of love, each to the betrothed of his friend as before, and announced that they were prepared to die rather than live without their sudden passion being returned. When the girls again indignantly refused to accept their addresses and expressed undying devotion to their "absent" lovers, the "strangers" then immediately produced phials of pretended poison and, swallowing the contents, fell upon the floor in a feigned dying condition.

This plan came dangerously near the point of succeeding. Isadora and Dorabella, being kind-hearted girls, were so concerned by the seemingly terrible result of their coldness that they became full of compassion and tried to comfort the suicidal young men with the tender words and caresses so cunningly played up for.

In answer to their frantic calls for help, Despina entered and, expressing pretended horror at the circumstance, bade her mistresses hold the love-sick swains carefully in their arms until she had fetched a doctor. This the girls did, tenderly soothing the limp forms they held—to the triumphant satisfaction of the gloating Don Alfonso, who had managed to conceal himself near by. Presently Despina returned, having meanwhile disguised herself in the black robes and wig of a physician; and making absurd mesmeric passes over the recumbent officers she pretended thus to overcome the action of the poison and to restore them to health once more.

After the revived strangers had departed, however, Despina's conscience pricked her, and she determined to remain loyal to her young mistresses after all. She sought them out, therefore, and revealed to them the whole plot, confessing how she had herself been bribed to take part in it.

At first, the two girls were very angry that such a trick should have been played upon them and that their lovers should have dared to wager upon their fidelity with the cynical and worldly old woman-hater, Don Alfonso. Then quickly recovering their good-humour, they determined to turn the tables upon them and to carry the war into the enemy's camp.

Enlisting the services of Despina in their turn, they arranged a very amusing counter-plot of their own. The next time their new suitors presented themselves, again making declarations of love and offers of marriage, they pretended to have suddenly fallen in love with them since the attempted suicides and boldly accepted them as their future husbands. They even went so far as to send for a notary and to sign the necessary marriage contracts— taking care, however, that these should be faked documents, the notary being impersonated by the versatile Despina in borrowed garments. The three girls acted so realistically that they succeeded in completely hoodwinking the young men and their old arch-plotter.

Furious that the fickleness of their *fiancées* should have been thus proved, as they imagined, the young men hastened away to discard their disguise, returning almost immediately in their ordinary garb and natural looks to pour forth angry reproaches upon the girls.

For some little time longer, Dorabella and Isadora kept up the deception; and then, taking pity upon the sincere distress of their lovers, they laughingly revealed the fact that they had cleverly turned the tables upon them.

The young men were greatly relieved at this turn of events; and now thoroughly ashamed that they should ever have pretended to doubt the fidelity of their chosen ladies, they very contritely sued for pardon.

This being readily granted the happy couples were re-united once more. The cynical old Don Alfonso, having lost his wager, was thus obliged to retire crestfallen, having failed to prove that fickleness and flirtation was second nature to every woman. Nevertheless, his " School for Lovers " had served its purpose—though not in the way he had intended!

DON GIOVANNI
(*Don Juan*)

Mozart

IT was night-time in Seville. A few distant lights were still calmly reflected in the peaceful river; but in the splendid palace of Don Pedro, the Commandant, darkness and silence reigned, for all the household had retired to rest. In the courtyard without, however, a man was crouching in the shadows.

This unsuspected intruder was Leporello, the confidential body-servant of Don Juan, the handsomest and most licentious young cavalier in the whole of Seville—indeed, the most famous libertine of the seventeenth century. Leporello was well used to midnight vigils of this kind, having kept watch in the chilly gloom many a dozen times while his gay master enjoyed a secret *rendezvous* within some fair lady's apartment. Usually the pair departed as quietly as they had come; but to-night this was not the case.

Suddenly the stillness of the night was broken by loud shrieks coming from within the building; and next moment Don Juan dashed from the palace out into the moonlit courtyard, closely pursued by a beautiful lady. This lady was Don Pedro's only daughter, the fair young Donna Anna who, discovering a strange cavalier in her chamber, had fled from him with shrieks of alarm. When the intruder, fearing that her cries would arouse the household, had retreated hastily to the courtyard, her courage had returned and she had bravely pursued him in order to discover his identity. Before she could do so, however, Don Pedro, disturbed by his daughter's cries, hastened out into the courtyard with a drawn sword in his hand.

Quickly grasping the situation, the Commandant furiously challenged the intruder to instant combat. Don Juan, finding there was no other escape for him, quickly crossed swords with his assailant; and, being a fatal adept in such encounters, he soon stretched Don Pedro dead at his feet. His servant Leporello now came forth from the shadows, and the pair hastily made their escape over the wall, still unrecognized.

As the grief-stricken Donna Anna bent despairingly over the dead body of the Commandant, her betrothed lover, Don Octavio, and several sleepy servants, also now appeared on the scene, attracted by the commotion and her loud cries for help. Comforting his beloved one as best he could, Don Octavio drew her gently away; but before entering the palace, Donna Anna implored him to swear that he would aid her in bringing vengeance upon the murderer of her father. Gladly the young cavalier gave his word; and in the courtyard beneath the moonlit sky, the lovers registered their solemn vow.

Meanwhile, Don Juan continued his life of selfish pleasure. His gay debonair nature made him careless of danger; and he went on from intrigue to intrigue with reckless lightheartedness. Sometimes, however, Nemesis followed him in the person of a discarded mistress.

This happened one day on coming out of a country inn adjoining his own estate on the borders of Seville. Seeing a veiled lady traveller standing near by, wringing her hands in evident distress, he stepped forward and accosted her with his usual gallant air. Then, to his dismay, as the distressed traveller flung back her veil, he recognized the features of a beautiful lady of Burgos, Donna Elvira, whom he had but recently betrayed and cast aside.

Donna Elvira immediately began to pour forth bitter reproaches upon the recreant lover who had so cruelly abandoned her; but Don Juan, callously familiar with such scenes, pushed forward Leporello, bidding him explain matters to her. Then, as Elvira eagerly approached the servant for the promised explanation, the heartless cavalier slyly made his escape.

Leporello treated his master's escapades as amusing interludes; and now waggishly bidding the abandoned lady be of good comfort since she was neither the first nor the last of his master's numberless victims, he produced a book from his pocket in which he had written the names of all the fair maidens who had been likewise deceived. Having read out a long list of names, with jocular comments upon each, the libertine's equally depraved servant suddenly took to his heels and ran away down the country road that led to his master's estate.

Elvira remained stunned for a short time; for she had loved Don Juan with her whole heart, having willingly yielded herself to him and trusted fondly in his false promises. Now, dishonoured and abandoned, she at last saw him in his true colours—a heartless libertine. Full of grief and just anger, she determined to avenge herself for her outraged affections and ruined life; and knowing that her betrayer's residence was in the neighbourhood, she hurried along the road taken by Leporello.

When Don Juan arrived at his mansion, he found that great revels were being held by the peasants on the estate in honour of the betrothal of a pair of rustic lovers; and seeing that the bride-elect, Zerlina, was an extremely pretty maiden, the gay lord of the soil determined to amuse himself with her. Consequently, when Leporello presently rejoined him, he bade the latter to conduct all the peasants immediately to the palace and to have them entertained with feasting and dancing within the banqueting-hall and garden—whispering an added injunction to keep the future bridegroom, Masetto, especially well occupied.

As the merry rustics, eager for this unexpected treat, trooped away willingly to the palace, Don Juan detained the pretty Zerlina and made violent love to her, cunningly endeavouring to lead her aside to a secluded woodland glade. The simple Zerlina, accustomed only to the clumsy wooing of a rustic clown, was greatly impressed by the ardent glances and sweet persuasive caresses of the great lord; and when the latter declared passionately that she was more fitted to become his own bride rather than that of the boorish Masetto, she coquettishly gave way to the dazzling thrill of the moment.

Just as Don Juan was about to lead away his charming prize, however, his base design was foiled by the sudden appearance of Donna Elvira, who, having made her way into the grounds, had watched and overheard the whole scene. She now hastened forward and revealed to the pretty rustic the truth about her new admirer—that he was but an evil deceiver who meant to ruin her. She then led the now horrified girl away, throwing a glance of scorn at the faithless gallant.

As the thwarted Don Juan turned angrily aside, he encountered a lady in deep mourning and a cavalier who had just entered the grounds. As he greeted them, he saw, to his additional discomfiture, that they were Donna Anna and her betrothed, Don Octavio. To his relief, Anna did not at first recognize him as her father's midnight murderer; and she calmly announced that she had come to ask his help in finding the villain who had brought such misery upon her.

But no sooner had the quick-witted cavalier cunningly promised them his aid, than Donna Elvira returned; and at once the distressed lady proceeded to reveal also to these newcomers his true character as a heartless spoiler. Don Juan now coolly announced that Elvira was a madwoman and pretended to soothe her frenzy —whereupon the latter, stung by this fresh outrage, repeated her knowledge of his sins and then, fearing she would not be believed, hurried away.

Don Juan, glad to escape, followed her by another path, saying with pretended anxiety that he wished to see she did herself no harm. When he had gone, Donna Anna declared to her betrothed that she now recognized Don Juan as her would-be ravisher and the murderer of her beloved father—adding that his agitated voice and angry gestures when disturbed by Elvira had further betrayed him.

Full of horror that they had thus unwittingly sought help from the very villain they wished to punish, the lovers hurried after the retreating Elvira, whom they soon overtook; and having heard the sad story she had to tell of her own woes, they willingly agreed to combine with her in bringing retribution upon Don Juan. They decided to begin their scheme by exposing him as a villain before his own assembled guests that night. Returning to the inn, therefore, they disguised themselves in long black dominoes and half-masks, having already learnt from one of the peasants that the revels were to end in a masked ball. Then they made their way back to the palace, which they entered with the other guests.

Meanwhile, the simple-minded Zerlina had easily been reassured by Leporello as to his master's flattering attentions, and went joyfully to the masked ball. Here she was soon secured by Don Juan as his partner in the merry dances that took place; and the bold libertine, determined to gratify his sudden passion for her, presently found an opportunity for drawing her towards a private inner room.

This secret manœuvre, however, was observed with indignation by Donna Anna and her two companions; and when Don Juan's fell purpose presently became patent to all, they pulled off their masks and denounced him before his own guests, relating the many evil things they knew of him.

The rustic bridegroom, Masetto, now roused to jealous fury, rushed forward to attack his false host, calling on his friends to help him; but Don Juan quickly drew his sword and, clearing a path for himself, managed to make his escape, quickly followed by Leporello.

.   .   .   .

Though their prey had escaped them for the moment, the avenging trio continued their quest. When Donna Anna and her betrothed returned to Seville, Elvira went with them, hiring a house in the city and taking the now subdued Zerlina with her as her maid.

Here, however, they were again discovered by the irrepressible Don Juan, who presently hatched another plot for the seduction of the pretty country girl. One dark evening, he exchanged cloaks and hats with the ever useful Leporello; and making his way to the house where Zerlina was hidden, he tried to abduct her by means of a trick.

When Elvira presently appeared at an upper window, her false lover called softly to her from out of the darkness below, declaring that he loved her still; and he implored her to come down and listen to his pleas for pardon and to receive his caresses once more. Quickly falling again under his irresistible spell, though against her better judgment, the susceptible Elvira was thus lured from the house to take a romantic stroll—but it was Leporello who led her away and who, wrapped in his master's cloak, she mistook for the man she still loved.

Don Juan now began to sing a charming serenade, which he hoped would quickly induce the timid Zerlina likewise to come forth—when he intended to carry her off at once. But this cunning scheme was frustrated by the unexpected appearance of Masetto and a group of other rustics, who had been on his track ever since the night of the ball and who now attacked him vigorously. Seeing, however, that they imagined him to be Leporello, since he wore the latter's cloak, Don Juan cunningly kept up the pretence and, expressing sympathy with their cause, soon sent them off on a wild-goose chase in search of their real enemy. Then, having enticed Masetto to remain behind under pretence of inspecting his weapon, he suddenly struck the un-suspecting peasant a heavy blow and ran off, leaving him helpless on the ground.

Zerlina, attracted by the noise of this scrimmage, now came forth from the house and helped the fallen man to rise. Recognizing her faithful lover with joy, she comforted him as best she could and afterwards accompanied him down the street in search of his companions.

Meanwhile, Elvira and the disguised Leporello had reached the courtyard outside the house of Donna Anna, where the versatile servant's true identity was quickly discovered by his indignant companion. At that moment, Anna and her betrothed came out to walk in the cool of the evening and hastened towards them on hearing Elvira's voice. Leporello tried to escape, but was met at the entrance to the courtyard by Masetto and Zerlina, who were still seeking their rustic companions. The fleet-footed maiden pursued and caught him; then, threatening him with a razor she had snatched up before leaving her mistress's house, she forced him to sit on a stone seat, to which she bound him firmly with cords. She then returned to her stiff and limping lover; and Leporello was left writhing and twisting vainly. Finally, however, he was released by a passer-by and was then able to rejoin his adventurous master once more.

   .   .   .   .   .   .

Leporello found Don Juan standing in the middle of a large square, where a splendid statue had recently been erected to the memory of the late Commandant, Don Pedro. Laughing at the grumbles of his long-suffering servant, Don Juan gaily related to him the story of yet another love adventure he had just experienced.

Suddenly, deep muffled words seemed to come from the stone Statue, warning the careless libertine that he would die before the morrow; and Leporello, terrified by this eerie circumstance, fell upon his knees. Don Juan, however, made fun of his fears and recklessly bade him rise and invite the Statue to attend the supper-party he was giving at his palace late that same night.

The frightened Leporello at first refused to do so; but upon a threatening gesture from his master, he rose and tremblingly uttered aloud the invitation he had been bidden to give. The Statue immediately bowed its head in response, as though in acceptance of the invitation, to the increasing alarm of Leporello who shrieked aloud. Don Juan, however, laughingly declared that the Statue's movement was merely fancy; and he dragged his quaking servant away and repaired to his palace.

But Leporello's fears were justified. As Don Juan sat at supper late that night with a gay company of guests, there came the ominous sound of heavy measured footsteps mounting the staircase; and as the door was flung open, the Statue of the murdered Don Pedro entered the banqueting-hall, with a stern look of righteous wrath on its marble face!

Full of terror, the guests fled from the room, while the scared Leporello hid beneath the supper-table; but Don Juan remained seated. Staring in astonishment at his strange visitor, he boldly demanded its business with him.

The Statue of the Commandant replied in sepulchral tones that it had come to the feast in answer to his own invitation—whereupon the gay host, still endeavouring to retain his self-possession, ordered Leporello to lay a fresh cover for the new arrival.

But as Leporello tremblingly crept forth from his hiding-place, the Statue declared that it had no need of mortal food; then, turning to Don Juan, it added, meaningly: " Thou badst me to thy banquet, and I, in turn, now invite thee to mine! Wilt come? "

Leporello, in terror, implored his master to refuse; but Don Juan, scorning to show fear, recklessly accepted at once and took the outstretched hand of his sinister visitor in pledge of the compact. When the icy-cold fingers of the Statue closed on his own in a vice-like grip, a shiver passed through the whole frame of the cavalier; and, feeling that his last hour had indeed come, he struggled vainly to free himself. The Statue, however, only held him the closer and in stern tones bade him repent while he yet had time.

But Don Juan, though now full of mortal fear, scorned repentance, and, in spite of the entreaties of Leporello and the further injunctions of the Statue, still shrieked out his defiance. Then the Statue, in an appalling voice, declared that his doom was sealed; and, letting its victim's hand drop, it suddenly sank through the flooring into the ground below.

At the same moment, fierce flames sprang up on all sides; and, from the deep abyss that had just engulfed the Statue, a host of demons leapt forth and seized Don Juan in their scorching grasp, springing back with him into the fiery depths below.

Then the flames died away, and the chasm closed; and when Don Octavio and his friends presently entered with the officers of Justice, the banqueting-hall had assumed its usual aspect once more. The giver of the banquet had vanished; and the new arrivals learned with awe from the still quaking Leporello that justice had already overtaken the criminal they sought.

THE MAGIC FLUTE
(*Die Zauberflöte*)

Mozart

IN the far-off days of ancient Egypt, mystery and magic were openly practised. According to the stories and traditions of those times, one could not wander far afield without encountering the strangest adventures in which magicians, enchantresses, necromancers, with their attendant genii, fairies and good and evil spirits, all took their parts.

This was certainly the case with the young Prince Tamino—a brave royal youth—who, while out hunting one day, became separated in the chase from his attendants and was lost in a vast and unknown wilderness. No sooner had he discovered himself to be alone, unprotected, and in strange surroundings, than a whole series of extraordinary and exciting adventures began to happen to him.

As he was wandering about in the forest jungle in which he found himself, the young Prince was suddenly attacked by a horrible serpent-dragon of such tremendous size that, brave though he was, he fled in terror before it. To his horror, the fearful monster quickly gained upon him; and the exhausted youth, giving himself up for lost, involuntarily uttered a loud cry for help, though no human being was in sight. He then fell to the ground in a swoon within a few feet of the serpent's jaws.

At that moment, however, three fairy-like maidens, attendants upon the Queen of the Night, an enchantress who dwelt in that wilderness, suddenly appeared upon the scene; and by exercising their magic arts, they slew the monster before it had time to seize its prey. They then restored the royal youth to consciousness once more; and they were so charmed with his handsome looks that each one wished to remain to guard him while the others returned to their mistress to bring her news of his arrival. Finally they settled the matter by leaving none of their number to talk to the handsome youth; and all three departed, declaring that they would quickly return with the Enchantress Queen.

Scarcely had the three fairy-like maidens departed, than another stranger appeared, as though by magic, before the astonished gaze of the young Prince. This new arrival was a very young sprightly being, full of lively chatter and merriment, who announced himself as a bird-catcher, Papageno by name; and as he was entirely clothed in gaily-coloured feathers, he was as curious to behold as he was amusing to listen to.

Tamino, who had only just fully recovered his senses—having scarcely been aware of the presence of the three maidens—immediately came to the conclusion that it was the newcomer who had slain the serpent-dragon lying dead beside him; and he poured forth grateful thanks to the stranger for having so promptly saved his life. The merry Papageno, with an eye to the main chance and having no objections to posing as a hero, did not attempt to undeceive the royal youth, but launched forth into a fine story of the great deed he had performed.

While he was still holding forth to this effect, the three maidens returned once more; and overhearing the boastings of Papageno, they magically closed his mouth for the time being, fastening it with a golden padlock, as a punishment for his fibs. They then showed to Tamino a portrait of their mistress's fair young daughter, Pamina; and the royal youth was so fascinated by the feminine loveliness thus revealed to him that he immediately fell in love with the pictured beauty.

He was aroused from his rapt gaze by the approach of the Enchantress Queen of the Night, whose dark beauty was also dazzling and who possessed a magic seductiveness not easy to resist. Just now she was in great distress. She explained to Tamino that her lovely daughter had been snatched away from her by a wicked magician named Sarastro—her most hated rival—who was keeping the maiden as a captive in his Temple of Magic, where he also practised the rites of a priest of Isis. The Queen of the Night then offered to release Tamino from her own power—into which he had fallen by entering her regions of enchantment—if he would undertake to rescue her captive daughter from Sarastro as the price of his deliverance. She promised further that, should he succeed in this difficult task, the hand of Pamina in marriage should be his reward.

Tamino willingly agreed to undertake this mission—being already deeply in love with the picture of the beautiful girl—and he declared that he would set forth at once and take with him as companion and assistant the lively Papageno, whom he still believed had slain the serpent. The three fairy attendants thereupon removed the golden padlock from the mouth of the merry bird-fancier, and brought forth gifts as means of aiding the pair in their difficult task. They presented a magic flute to Tamino, and a chime of magic bells to the bird-catcher, with which to make music in times of danger, when aid would immediately be sent them. The Queen of the Night also called up three young boy genii, whom she commanded to attend the knight-errant and his companion and to serve them as guides and advisers.

Tamino and Papageno, thus equipped and attended, set forth upon their mission at once; and in due course, guided by the genii, they came within sight of the splendid Temple Castle of Sarastro.

The gay Papageno skipped on in advance and arrived first, making his way to the courtyard of the castle. Here he was just in time to save the lovely Pamina from the unwelcome attentions of a hideous and unscrupulous Moorish slave named Monostatos. This servant, having been bidden to guard the captive, had sought during the course of his duties to ingratiate himself in her favour —to the great disgust of the fair maiden, who repulsed him with loathing.

He was just about to gain his ends by force, when Papageno suddenly appeared on the scene; and the sight of the bird-catcher, in his fantastic feather dress, so scared Monostatos that he fled from him to a safe distance. Papageno, on his part, was also much alarmed by the black skin of the Moor, whom he mistook for a devil; but conquering his fears, he related to Pamina the story of the young Prince who had fallen in love with her portrait, and entreated her to hasten away with him to meet her approaching lover. Pamina, thankful to escape from her Moorish persecutor, very gladly took the hand of Papageno and fled away with him. Monostatos, however, soon recovered from his fright and, calling the guards together, gave chase to the pair, quickly overtaking them. Papageno, in this moment of danger, remembered the magic bells given him by the Queen of the Night; and he began to shake them in the face of the pursuers. The effect was very amusing; for the merry tinkling of the magic bells was so irresistibly joyous that those who heard it immediately began to dance. All anger vanished at once; and the whole party, pursuers and pursued, returned together, gaily singing and dancing to the lively chimes of the fairy bells.

Meanwhile, Tamino had also arrived at the portals of the temple-castle, having been guided thither by the genii youths. Hammering furiously at the gates, he demanded of the solemn priest who opened it to be taken to the tyrant Sarastro, that he might compel him to release the fair maiden Pamina.

The under-priest was very indignant on hearing his master described as a tyrant, and he declared that Sarastro, the high-priest of Isis, was the wisest and most virtuous of men, who had the true welfare of Pamina at heart. For this reason he had taken her from the care of her enchantress mother—who was a spirit of evil—that she might be instructed in the ways of virtue and knowledge.

The priest declared that the maiden was already profiting well by her instruction and was performing her duties in the temple in a satisfactory manner.

Tamino was greatly relieved to hear this good news; and when Pamina presently appeared with the merry Papageno and his now dancing pursuers, he hastened to her side, anxious to introduce himself as one who desired to serve her as a devoted lover. Pamina, delighted with the handsome looks of the young Prince, was quick to return his affection; and the pair loved one another from that first meeting.

A great flourish of trumpets now announced the approach of the wise and wonderful magician, Sarastro who, magnificently robed and attended by a large company of priests, issued forth from the Temple to inquire into the reason for the disturbance.

On learning of the vile conduct of Monostatos, he ordered the latter to be punished for his misdeeds; and then he turned with fatherly benevolence to consider the case of the young lovers. He declared that they must first prove their love and faithfulness before being united, and for this purpose must go through many severe trials. Tamino boldly declared that no tests of endurance could shake his devotion to his beloved one; and, announcing himself ready to be initiated into the sacred rites of Isis and to go through all the trials necessary for his purification and spiritual elevation, he was led into the Temple at once to commence his trials.

Pamina was then taken away to continue her own duties and to receive instruction as before, being told by Sarastro that, by enduring such trials patiently and successfully, she would thus gain perfect happiness.

When the Queen of the Night heard of the high resolve of the lovers and that they had determined not to return to her own evil influences, she was furious; and she sought to avenge herself upon her arch-enemy Sarastro by all the means in her power. She first of all again got into touch with Tamino by means of her magic and endeavoured to prevent him from fulfilling his vows. She offered him many wonderful gifts and pleasures instead if he would return to her service; but the young Prince firmly refused to succumb to her cunning temptations, and bravely continued his ordeals.

Then she visited her daughter in the watches of the night and, leaving a dagger beside her, commanded her to slay Sarastro with it. She declared that she would cast her off for ever and cause evil to fall upon Tamino unless she obeyed; but Pamina, inspired by her lover's devotion, reiterated her resolve to follow his noble example.

The crafty Queen of the Night next tried her arts upon Monostatos, who readily fell in with her wicked plans, having already a grudge against Sarastro for the severe punishment meted out to him by the latter. He agreed, therefore, to make an attempt upon the life of the High Priest. When he found himself in the presence of the majestic Sarastro, however, the splendour and power of the latter's mere gaze were so awe-inspiring that the craven-hearted Moor could do nothing but slink away.

So the lovers went forward triumphantly through their many ordeals. At one time Pamina, finding the time of probation and separation extremely long, felt that her lover must have proved faithless, and became so full of despair that she wished to die. But the beautiful genii youths appeared before her with words of comfort, and her dark cloud of doubt vanished. She then begged Sarastro to permit her to join her lover, that she might share the same trials he was enduring; and her wish was granted.

After this, the lovers walked together through water and through a lake of fire, and endured other terrifying experiences; but in every test their love supported them. With the protection afforded them by the magic golden flute—which Tamino played upon in all their moments of trial—the sweet notes of which never failed to dissipate all dangers, they successfully passed through the period of probation and endured safely to the end. The Queen of the Night made one last attempt to frustrate the will of her magician enemy by making her way into the Temple of Isis when the lovers were on the point of completing their trials. Her scheme, however, was again frustrated, for Sarastro suddenly raised up a terrific tempest and she was driven forth by a great flood of water.

When their days of ordeal and purification had at last ended, the lovers were brought to the great outer Temple hall where the golden sunlight once more streamed upon them; and here all the powers of darkness and evil vanished, leaving them calm and full of a great joy. Then Tamino was permitted to take away the beautiful daughter of the defeated Queen of the Night; and he set forth with his beloved one to live a life of perfect happiness such as can only be attained by those who have passed through many trials and dangers.

Meanwhile, the merry Papageno had also been going through a very dismal time. His lively disposition suffered greatly when he was left by Tamino to wander in the wilderness by himself once more. He became sadder and sadder, and was at last so filled with despair, because of his lonely condition, that he resolved to hang himself. He was prevented from doing this fatal act by the appearance of the three genii youths who advised him to ring his magic bells. Quickly recovering his good spirits, Papageno did so; and as the merry tune of the bells chimed forth, lo! there suddenly appeared before him a charming little feather-clad maiden, as merry and fantastic in appearance as himself. She announced herself as Papagena; and the now happy bird-catcher gladly took her by the hand to dance with him through life—she was the very wife he had always longed for!

THE MARRIAGE OF FIGARO *Mozart*
(*Le Nozze di Figaro*)

ONE bright summer morning during the seventeenth century, a pleasant hum of excitement pervaded Count Almaviva's splendid castle near Seville. That evening, Figaro, the Count's confidential body-servant, was to be wedded to the Countess's pretty waiting-maid, Susanna; and the nuptials were to be celebrated with great festivities, in which not only the whole household but the peasants on the estate were to join.

But the happy bride and bridegroom-elect were fated to take part in several merry plots and harum-scarum adventures ere their wedding ceremony actually took place. Quite early in the morning, while arranging the furniture in their bridal chamber, Figaro was told by Susanna that their gay master—whose chief excitement in life was to engage in love-intrigues—had suddenly become infatuated with her own charms. This was disturbing news; but the valet, being a lively fellow whose keen wits had helped him out of many former difficulties, merrily assured his betrothed that he would soon concoct a scheme for thwarting the amorous Count.

However, Figaro's own good looks had brought him likewise an unwanted admirer who arrived at the castle that morning to bring further discomfiture upon him. This admirer was Marcellina, a dame from the neighbouring city who, though advancing in years, was of a skittish and sentimental disposition and had recently become enamoured of the handsome valet.

Owing to his extravagant habits, Figaro was often in need of money; and he had found the elderly Marcellina willing enough to lend him a considerable sum—but on condition that he signed a paper promising to marry her unless he refunded the money. Never dreaming that he would ever be called upon to keep either of these conditions, the needy valet had recklessly signed the document.

But Marcellina was in earnest, having got beyond the age when admirers were to be secured by her personal attractions; and she did not intend to let such a good chance of marriage slip through her fingers. Consequently, on learning that Figaro was about to be wedded to Susanna, she was much upset; and she had now arrived at the castle on the day of the wedding with the object of preventing the ceremony from taking place. As supporter, she had brought with her Dr. Bartolo, whose housekeeper she had been for many years—and with whom she had once indulged in a love intrigue. The latter likewise had a grudge against the popular Figaro for having thwarted him on a former occasion;[1] and he had willingly agreed to assist Marcellina in her claim. Having arrived in good time, the pair awaited a favourable opportunity to act.

Meanwhile, a third intrigue was afoot, which likewise involved the fascinating waiting-maid and her betrothed. While Susanna was busily occupied in her own private room, she was interrupted by the Countess's page, Cherubino—a handsome youth who adored his mistress, yet made love to all the maids in the castle—who sought her aid in a great state of agitation. He announced that the Count had just dismissed him from his service for flirting too outrageously with the gardener's young daughter, Barbarina; and he begged Susanna to intercede for him.

At that moment the Count himself was heard approaching; and, alarmed at the prospect of being discovered with the favoured lady's-maid, Cherubino hastily hid behind a large arm-chair as his master entered the room.

The enamoured Count Almaviva immediately began to make love to Susanna, entreating her to grant him a meeting in the garden at twilight; but the pretty bride-elect laughingly repulsed him, though unable to prevent him from snatching a kiss.

Just then, the voice of Basilio, a boring old music-master attached to the establishment, was heard approaching, singing as he came; and it was now the Count's turn to seek a hiding-place. Although he often used old Basilio to assist him in his love-intrigues, he did not wish to be discovered, even by a confederate,

[1] See *The Barber of Seville*.

in his present compromising situation; and he made a dash, therefore, towards the same big chair behind which Cherubino was already concealed. The sprightly page, however, saw him coming; and, in a twinkling, he adroitly slipped round to the other side and ensconced himself in the seat of the chair just as the Count crouched behind.

Susanna, trembling at this narrow escape, hastily flung a brocaded robe over the curled-up form of Cherubino; and no sooner had she done so than Basilio entered the room. The old scandal-monger had come to draw from Susanna all she knew of Cherubino's audacious calf-love for his mistress; and in spite of the waiting-maid's frantic efforts to stop him, he went on to declare that the page's infatuation was the talk of the whole household.

It happened that Count Almaviva, though frequently engaging in love-intrigues himself, was extremely jealous where the honour of his beautiful Countess was involved; and, infuriated by Basilio's words, he sprang from behind the chair—and at the same moment discovered the hapless page in the seat.

A wild scene of confusion now arose. The Count, doubly jealous, imagining that Cherubino had also been making love to Susanna, began to pour forth abuse on them both and declared that Figaro should be told of his bride-elect's duplicity; but Susanna, sure of the latter's trust in her, pleaded only for Cherubino's pardon, slyly reminding her master that the page had overhead his own words of love to her and should on that account be conciliated. Almaviva, thus compelled to a prudent course, then agreed to pardon Cherubino, though only on condition that the latter set off immediately for military service in the Count's own regiment; and the page was ordered to proceed to Seville at once.

.   .   .   .

Meanwhile, the Countess Almaviva had not failed to learn of her susceptible husband's infatuation for her confidential maid; but knowing that Susanna was too faithful to betray her, she presently bade the girl bring Figaro to her boudoir, hoping that the three of them might concoct a plot whereby the flirtatious young lord could be exposed and thus cured of engaging in such frivolous intrigues.

Figaro's fertile wits soon devised a merry scheme. An anonymous letter was to be sent to the Count, informing him that the Countess intended to grant a secret interview to a certain gallant at the revels to be held that night—which would rouse his jealousy to such a pitch that while he was endeavouring to prove his suspicions the wedding could take place before he had time to prevent it. To entangle him further, it was arranged that Susanna should grant him the twilight meeting in the garden which he had just requested, but that Cherubino—who had not yet departed—should take her place, dressed in her garments. Then the Countess was to surprise the pair and compel her husband, after thus discovering him in this compromising situation, to sue for pardon and return to her own affections.

This plan having been agreed upon, Figaro wrote the suggested letter and despatched it to the Count by old Basilio; and then he sent the page to the Countess's boudoir to be dressed for his part. Cherubino, delighted to be in the company of his beloved mistress once more, readily entered into the plot; and Susanna, after locking the door to prevent untimely interruptions, dressed him carefully in a gown and head-dress of her own, the page's fresh complexion and curling hair helping to make the disguise more complete.

Unluckily, just as Susanna had gone into an inner room to look for a ribbon, the Count himself knocked at the boudoir door and, finding it locked, became suspicious and angrily demanded to have it opened. Hastily locking Cherubino inside a dress cupboard, the Countess admitted her husband, who quickly observed her confused looks.

Remembering the anonymous letter he had already received, he declared that she had a lover hidden within the cupboard, having heard a sound of shuffling from its depths; and when the Countess tremblingly announced that it was only Susanna who had retired there, interrupted by his arrival in the act of trying on a new dress, he angrily called upon the maid to answer to her name. Cherubino, however, kept silent, and Susanna—who had returned unobserved and was now hidden behind a curtain—likewise dared not speak. The Count now felt that his suspicions were thus confirmed; and, in a storm of jealousy, he dragged off the Countess to get tools to break open the cupboard after taking the precaution of locking the doors of the boudoir and inner chamber to prevent the captive from escaping.

As soon as they were gone, Susanna came forth and quickly unlocked the cupboard with a duplicate key she carried in her pocket; and Cherubino dashed out, freed of his borrowed garments, which he had hastily discarded. Finding all the doors locked, he opened the window and sprang lightly into the garden below; and Susanna instantly took his place in the cupboard, fastening the door on the inside as the Count and Countess returned.

When the cupboard door was opened, therefore, and Susanna tripped forth, the jealous husband was compelled to sue for pardon. As Figaro just then entered to announce that the wedding guests were beginning to arrive, the situation might now have been saved but for another untimely interruption. Antonio the gardener came in with several broken flower-pots in his hands, declaring that these had been smashed by a man he had seen jump from the boudoir window into the midst of them only a few minutes ago; and again the Count's suspicions were aroused.

But Figaro, warned by the distracted looks of the Countess and Susanna, now mendaciously announced that it was he who had leapt from the window, making up a cock-and-bull story on the spur of the moment to account for his hidden presence in the boudoir.

His absurd explanation, however, did not satisfy the Count, who still felt he was being deceived. When, therefore, a few minutes later, old Dr. Bartolo and the housekeeper Marcellina entered and craved permission to speak with him, he was ready enough to listen to the charge they now brought against Figaro.

From the signed document produced by Marcellina, it was seen that Figaro was legally bound to marry the elderly housekeeper— for he was certainly never likely to be able to repay the large sum of money he had borrowed from her. But the quick-witted Figaro was not yet nonplussed; and he declared that he could not be wedded against his will without the sanction of his parents. Of the latter he stated he knew nothing, having been stolen from his home by gipsies when a very young child—adding that the only clue to his identity he now possessed was a curious mark that had been made on his arm in the form of a spatula.

On hearing this, Marcellina uttered a cry of joyful surprise; and next moment she clasped Figaro in her arms, declaring that he was her own dear son whom she had lost years ago and whose arm had been marked with a spatula in his infancy. It now transpired that this remarkable statement was the actual truth, Figaro indeed being the son born of the early love intrigue between Marcellina and Dr. Bartolo. What was more, the worthy doctor, forgetful of past grudges, announced that he would now marry his old housekeeper and recognize her lively son as his heir.

Figaro and Susanna were overjoyed to find that there was thus no bar to their union; and the Count, somewhat against his will, gave instructions that the wedding should take place that evening after all and that high revels should begin at once, the rustic guests having already assembled.

The giddy young page, Cherubino, was determined to join in the fun of the revels for a short time before departing to Seville to take up his military service. Eager that his master should not know of his continued presence, however, he persuaded Barbarina, the gardener's daughter—one of his numerous rustic sweethearts—to deck him in feminine garments once more and to introduce him to the company as her country cousin. Thus disguised, he gaily took part in the dancing on the lawn; and the Countess, greatly admiring the charming appearance of the pretended maiden, graciously kissed him on his being presented to her—to the delight of the saucy page.

At this moment, however, the Count appeared with Antonio the gardener who, having picked up Cherubino's feathered hat and cloak in his cottage, had discovered the ruse and had now brought his master in haste to unmask the young scapegrace. The Countess, disconcerted on thus learning that she had publicly kissed the page in mistake for a girl, now revealed, in her confusion, that it was indeed Cherubino who had jumped from her boudoir window that morning—adding that she and Susanna had been dressing him up to take part in a jest they had planned.

Having angrily dismissed the crestfallen page, the Count called upon Figaro for an explanation of his now obviously false version of the window-jumping feat—thinking to corner him. But Figaro's ever ready wit again prevented him from being at a loss; and he replied instantly that his own statement merely proved that both he and Cherubino had had the same fancy to leap through the window—which was not strange since it was well known that great wits often jumped together? With which merry quip he ran off to join in a country dance; and the Count was left with the perplexing thought that he was still being fooled.

Nor was the Countess satisfied. Although the betrothed pair were now happy and likely to gain their ends, she felt that her own purpose had not yet been achieved. Presently, therefore, she sought out Susanna and arranged another little plot with her. It was again agreed that the waiting-maid should now grant the Count the twilight interview he was so eager for, but that the Countess should take her place, dressed in her garments. Susanna, always ready for a joke, wrote a seductive note to her master, appointing a meeting at dusk in a certain quiet spot in the garden; and this she gave to Barbarina to deliver. The Count was delighted on receiving this missive, imagining that Susanna meant to accept him as a lover after all—or at least to grant him a last flirtatious interview before her wedding that night.

It happened that Figaro met Barbarina on her return after

delivering the note to the Count and gathered from her conversation that his bride-elect intended to meet their infatuated master that evening. Knowing nothing of the newly-hatched plot, he now imagined that Susanna had been deceiving him all along— and he jealously determined to watch her.

When twilight fell the Countess and Susanna exchanged clothes and hastened to the secluded glade agreed upon, where the waiting-maid presently retired among the trees, leaving her mistress in the open; and here they were observed by Figaro, who was already lurking behind the bushes.

By the merest chance, Cherubino, who had not yet departed, had likewise made an assignation in this same spot with the coquettish Barbarina; and seeing, as he imagined, Susanna approaching, he thought he might as well pass the waiting time by a little playful flirtation with the pretty lady's-maid. Consequently, approaching the trembling Countess and addressing her as Susanna, he began to make audacious speeches to her and even tried to snatch a kiss. At that moment, however, the Count suddenly appeared on the scene and, boxing the page's ears smartly, made him beat a hasty retreat.

Then, little dreaming that it was his own wife he was addressing, Almaviva began to make love to the seeming Susanna; and he presently led her into a small pavilion near by. No sooner had they vanished from sight than the real Susanna, disguised as the Countess, issued forth into the open; whereupon, Figaro likewise came out from his hiding-place and, much distressed by the scene he had just witnessed, began to pour forth his woes to the approaching lady—whom he mistook for his mistress. Upon Susanna laughingly revealing her true identity, however, he was joyfully relieved and readily agreed to assist her in this new plot.

When, therefore, the Count presently emerged from the pavilion for a moment to reconnoitre on hearing the sound of voices, Figaro instantly fell on his knees before the pretended Countess and began to utter extravagant protestations of love for her. Immediately rendered madly jealous on thus beholding what he supposed to be a clandestine meeting between his wife and a strange lover, the Count dashed forward furiously, calling loudly for his attendants in the adjacent garden to seize the intruder.

However, on the real Countess now emerging from the pavilion and revealing to him that the whole affair had been a playful ruse, his anger quickly evaporated; and realizing that his wife had got the better of him, having personally detected him in an actual intrigue, he humbly besought her pardon.

This was readily granted by the Countess, who had been

delighted to learn from her husband's genuine outburst of jealousy that he still loved her despite his propensity for flirtation—of which she hoped she had at last cured him. The mysteries and perplexities of the day having now been happily cleared up, all the plotters returned gaily to the castle, where the marriage ceremony of Figaro and Susanna at once took place amidst great rejoicings.

IL SERAGLIO   *Mozart*
(*The Seraglio*)

WITHIN the beautiful gardens surrounding the palace of Selim Pasha, a high official of the Turkish Court, a young Spanish nobleman named Belmonte was wandering disconsolately while seeking to remain hidden from sight. Although he knew himself to be in great danger and was even risking his life by his present enterprise, his own safety did not trouble him. His whole anxiety was on behalf of his betrothed, a beautiful lady named Constanza who, with her handmaid, Blonda, and Belmonte's own body-servant, Pedrillo, had been captured by brigands during an excursion into the country. The brigands had sold their captives as slaves to the rich Pasha, Selim, who had caused the two women to be lodged in his harem, intending to take Constanza as his own chief wife and to give Blonda to his vizier or chief steward, Osmin. Pedrillo he had installed as a gardener in the palace grounds, which extended to the shores of the Bosphorus.

Pedrillo, owing to his greater liberty, had manged to find the means of sending a communication to his master, informing him of the terrible adventure that had befallen the party and of their present whereabouts. Belmonte, who had been driven nearly distracted by the disappearance of his betrothed, had instantly hired a ship and set forth to attempt her rescue.

On arriving on the shores of the Bosphorus outside the Pasha's palace grounds, the young Spaniard, though furiously indignant because of this outrageous incident and eager to storm the abode of the Pasha, realized that caution was necessary. Before landing his men, therefore, he determined to spy out the land alone and then to formulate a plan of rescue.

With great difficulty and after patiently awaiting a favourable opportunity, Belmonte at length managed to make his way into the exquisite gardens of the palace; then, observing the strongly-guarded portals of the Seraglio, he became filled with despair at the thought of the almost hopeless task before him.

As he wandered about, however, concealing himself behind the dark cypresses and flower-laden bushes, Osmin, the elderly steward of the palace—an ill-tempered and uncouth-looking individual—came out into the garden and proceeded to gather a basket of ripe figs. Rough and grim though his appearance, Osmin was so pleased by the prospect of securing the fair handmaid, Blonda, as his share of this important capture that—although the newly-made slave had so far repulsed him with great disdain—he could not refrain from breaking forth into a little love-song as he performed his task.

At first Belmonte was somewhat amused as he listened to Osmin's deep gruff voice singing of a love that seemed so quaintly out of keeping with his uncouth looks; but presently, growing impatient, he issued forth boldly into the open and announced that he desired to speak with the new gardener, Pedrillo. At the mere mention of the latter's name, however, Osmin broke forth into a torrent of abuse and invective; for Pedrillo was Blonda's lover and, consequently, his own rival, for whom he had conceived a deadly hatred. At this moment Pedrillo himself appeared from another part of the garden; and old Osmin immediately turned upon him in a violent rage, pouring forth abuse upon him. Finally, he rushed away into the palace, so blinded by his sudden frenzied passion that he forgot for the moment all about the bold stranger who had dared to intrude into the grounds.

Belmonte now came forward and revealed himself to Pedrillo, who was overcome with joy at the sight of his beloved master. The latter immediately plied him with eager questions as to the welfare of his betrothed. Having learnt that Constanza was safe and well and that Selim Pasha, though already infatuated with her, had not yet pressed his attentions upon her unduly, Belmonte informed Pedrillo that he had a ship in waiting on the shore at the far end of the grounds; and the pair began to devise a plan to effect the escape of the two women. They decided that Belmonte should present himself as an artist and architect before the Pasha, who had a great desire to elaborate his estate by the creation of elegant buildings with interiors richly decorated with paintings. Then, having managed to get himself engaged in the capacity of adviser on these artistic questions, the adventurous young man would thus have a better chance of arranging a scheme for the escape of his betrothed.

Even as they arranged this somewhat precarious plan, Selim

Pasha was seen approaching from the river with Constanza, whom he was escorting from a river fête ordered for her entertainment; and Belmonte, though inwardly raging at the sight of his beloved one in the company of the Turkish lord, was drawn once more into hiding by the prudent Pedrillo to await a favourable opportunity of presenting himself.

As he led her towards the palace, followed at a respectful distance by a gorgeous retinue of attendants and musicians, Selim Pasha once more besought his beautiful captive to accept his love and devotion.

The thoughts of Constanza, however, were all with her absent lover; and, though grateful to the Pasha for his considerate treatment of her, she declared that her love was already given to a nobleman of her own country to whom she would ever be faithful.

As Constanza retired towards the women's quarters with Blonda and her attendants, Selim sighed deeply, realizing that it was hopeless to expect his fair slave to bestow her favours upon him of her own free-will. His unhappy thoughts, however, were now diverted by the approach of Pedrillo, who presented Belmonte to him as a famous artist who had just arrived with splendid ideas and plans for the embellishment of the palace and grounds. The young Spaniard was immediately engaged by the interested Pasha for this work—to the exceeding chagrin of old Osmin, who did all in his power to make the path of the newcomer anything but a bed of roses.

Having blusteringly vented his spite and ill-temper upon Belmonte and Pedrillo and effectually driven them out of his immediate vicinity for the time being, Osmin hastened into the portion of the garden that adjoined the women's quarters. Here he once more attempted to bully Blonda into showing him the respect and proper affection which befitted one who was to become his newest chattel. However, he found his match in the lively Blonda, who quickly turned on him like a little spitfire, treating his advances with the utmost disdain and laughing scornfully at his boorish love-making. She declared that if he dared to lay hands on her she would have no difficulty in getting him a good dose of the bastinado, since she and her mistress stood high in the favour of the Pasha.

When Osmin had been thus compelled by the pretty handmaid to beat an ignominious retreat, Pedrillo came out from a hiding-place near by; and Blonda gave this favoured admirer a very different reception—receiving him, indeed, with open arms and every sign of real affection.

She was filled with joy when Pedrillo informed her of the arrival of Belmonte and of the ship the latter had in waiting on the shore. Then Pedrillo arranged with her that she should join her mistress in the latter's apartment at midnight when the two lovers would arrive secretly at the open window with a ladder for their escape.

After this, Pedrillo sought out Osmin and managed to ingratiate himself into the latter's favour by offering him some very good wine at a moment when he was particularly thirsty. No sooner had the steward swallowed this long delicious drink that he became extremely sleepy; for the cunning Pedrillo had drugged the wine in order to render the steward incapable of interfering with their midnight plans. He then dragged the half-insensible Osmin away to sleep harmlessly upon his couch.

A little later on Constanza appeared in the garden, having learnt from Blonda the good news of her lover's arrival and longing to get a glimpse of the pretended artist. To her delight, Belmonte, also hopeful of a meeting, presently appeared from among the rose-bushes; and next moment the lovers were in each other's arms. Realizing, however, the necessity for extreme caution, they quickly parted once more with many protestations of love and devotion.

When midnight came, Belmonte and Pedrillo arrived in the garden outside the women's quarters and placed a ladder just below Constanza's open window; and the two excited but somewhat terrified girls immediately showed themselves in answer to the signal agreed upon.

No sooner had Constanza and Blonda, with much fear and trembling, managed to get safely down the ladder than there came an alarming shock for the little party. Old Osmin had, unfortunately, slept off the effect of the drugged wine much sooner than had been expected by Pedrillo; and hearing strange sounds in the dead of night, he made his way somewhat unsteadily to the spot whence the whisperings proceeded. Quickly sobered by the sight that met his gaze and realizing, despite his muddled brain, that the captives were attempting to escape, he called loudly for the guards. The latter at first mistook old Osmin himself for a midnight intruder and began to handle him roughly. Nevertheless, the angry steward, after many comical strugglings and rambling explanations, at length sent them chasing after their real prey, the escaped captives, who were quickly re-captured and brought back to the palace, together with their now despairing would-be rescuers.

Meanwhile, Selim Pasha had also been passing a sleepless night, sighing and full of self-pity because he could not win the voluntary love of his beautiful captive. Presently hearing loud cries from the guards and the sound of scuffling, he arose from his couch, just as Osmin, dishevelled but triumphant, entered the room to announce the attempted escape and re-capture of the fair slaves.

Furious on hearing this news, the Pasha gave orders for the captives to be brought before him immediately; and when they were roughly thrust into the room by the guards, he angrily declared that death was the punishment they must expect for such an attempt. Then, as his gaze fell upon the exquisite pale beauty of the trembling Constanza, his anger faded; and he declared that all should be forgiven her if she would now consent to become his chief wife.

But Constanza, full of a great courage inspired by her passionate love for Belmonte, now boldly declared that the pretended artist was her own devoted lover who had thus risked his life to save her from degradation; and she announced her brave determination to die with him rather than yield herself to the passion of another.

Then Belmonte, eager to save his beloved one, implored the Pasha to permit them both to be held to ransom, declaring that his father, the Governer of Oran, would gladly pay the sum demanded for their freedom. To this request, however, the Pasha replied that the Governor of Oran was a lifelong enemy of his; and he added that he was thus less likely to show mercy upon the pair on that account.

On hearing this, the lovers, now fully resigned to their fate and expecting any moment to be ordered to instant execution, fell into each other's arms and embraced one another tenderly. Uttering protestations of their undying love, they comforted themselves by declaring that, since a cruel fate thus prevented them from dwelling together in the life of joy to which they had looked forward, at least they would have the happiness of being united in death.

This exhibition of perfect love and devotion was more than Selim Pasha could witness unmoved; and since he really possessed a noble heart, he now announced that he would resign all claim upon the slaves he had bought, who were thus free to depart in peace. He even went further in his magnanimity and entreated for their future friendship. This request was readily granted by the two pairs of grateful lovers, who now set sail in Belmonte's waiting ship, full of joy and thankfulness that their terrible adventure had thus been brought to such a happy conclusion.

THE MERRY WIVES OF WINDSOR   *Nicolai*

THERE dwelt at Windsor during the reign of King Henry the Fourth a certain fat jolly knight named Sir John Falstaff; and in all fair England there was not a merrier old fellow than he. Many were the tales told of his mad escapades in company with gay Prince Hal; and many a round dozen of mischievous pranks and roguish tricks could be laid to the charge of the fat Knight of Windsor.

As may be readily guessed, one who led such a harum-scarum, careless life was not over-burdened with riches; but though Falstaff lived chiefly by his wits—and, be it admitted, occasionally by the depredations of his three rascally followers, Bardolph, Nym, and Pistol—his portly form did not grow less for lack of goodly cheer, neither did his thirst suffer for want of endless cups of sack.

Nevertheless, at one time, the gay old Knight found himself with a more than usually light purse; and appalled by the doleful prospect of restricted conviviality, he presently conceived the bright idea of providing himself with a couple of well-to-do sweethearts, in order to replenish his fallen fortunes.

Consequently, he wrote two flowery love-letters, word for word alike save for the names of the individual charmers; and he sent these missives to two comely housewives of Windsor, Mistress Ford and Mistress Page. Since the husbands of these worthy dames were prosperous and of good standing, he hoped that his love-making would secure to him many substantial gifts—to say nothing of providing him with a pleasant means of passing his time, since both ladies were still sufficiently young and well-favoured to prove attractive subjects for flirtation.

When Mistress Ford and Mistress Page had received these amorous effusions and, being friends and confidantes, had compared notes and discovered the letters to be precisely the same, they were at first very indignant that respectable dames should be thus addressed by such a well-known rake as Sir John Falstaff. However, soon guessing the reason for his sudden expressions of affection for them both, they set their quick wits to work to hatch a merry plan, whereby they should make the fat old Knight the laughing-stock of the town as a penalty for his audacity.

They determined to make a pretence of encouraging his advances, in order to bring on him the anger of their husbands.

With this object in view, they sent a letter to Falstaff, inviting him to visit Mistress Ford at her house next day—taking care to inform him that her husband, who was of a very jealous disposition, would then be safely out of the way.

Meanwhile, other little plots were also afoot in the two households. Mistress Page had a very pretty young daughter, charming Mistress Anne, who had at this time no less than three suitors for her hand. Her father desired her to wed a youth named Slender who, though foolish and a timid wooer, was rich; whilst her mother favoured a ridiculous and fussy old foreign admirer, Dr. Caius, a Frenchman. But pretty mistress Anne herself had already fixed her choice upon a somewhat poor but handsome young courtier named Fenton, whose sincere love for her she had quickly returned with as deep an affection; and, despite the machinations of her parents, she was resolved to wed none other than him.

In the Ford household, too, another plot was brewing. Master Ford, having been told by Falstaff's disreputable servant, Pistol—who had temporarily conceived a spite against his fat master—that the reprobate Knight was carrying on a lively flirtation with Mistress Ford, he became so madly jealous that he set about making plans for exposing the pair.

.   .   .   .

When the amorous old Falstaff appeared at Mistress Ford's house at the appointed time, he was coquettishly received by the lively dame, who pretended to accept his advances with every sign of favour. Very soon after his arrival, however, Mistress Page entered the room in haste and, with well-simulated fear, announced that Master Ford was approaching the house in a great rage, accompanied by Master Page and a number of other friends, all bent on dragging forth the lover whom they believed to be with Mistress Ford.

Falstaff, in a great fright, eagerly begged for protection, having no desire to meet the jealous husbands; and the two women promptly hid the scared Knight in a huge buck-basket—a receptacle for dirty clothes—which they had set ready for the purpose, gleefully stuffing his portly form in amongst the soiled linen. Then, covering him over with a cloth, they called two serving-men, to whom they gave instructions to carry the basket away to the meadow washing-ground . . . bidding them also in an undertone to tumble the contents into the river close by.

As the servants departed painfully with the heavy buck-basket, Ford entered the room, full of jealous fury and declaring that his wife had a lover hidden in the house; but his search for the ponderous Knight was in vain. Greatly mystified, he now decided to pay a visit to Falstaff in disguise, in order to learn the latter's further movements.

.   .   .   .

In the meantime, the elderly rake had received a very unexpected ducking in the river; but though this disagreeable experience damped his ardour for the time being, he soon became enthusiastic again next morning. As he sat with his boon companions in the Garter Inn, quaffing deep draughts of sack, he was handed a second letter from Mistress Ford, in which she invited him to visit her again that day, as her husband intended to go hawking.

Just as he fini-hed singing a jovial song in praise of good wine, Master Ford entered in disguise. Introducing himself by the name of Brooks, he asked the experienced Falstaff to help in a love affair, declaring that he had become infatuated with the charming Mistress Ford of Windsor, but was too timid to plead his own suit. He offered the Knight a well-filled purse for necessary expenses; and the needy Falstaff, nothing loath, accepted this unexpected windfall with great alacrity, boastfully declaring that he could easily arrange the matter since he would be seeing Mistress Ford that day.

Ford then retired, having thus gained the information he required; and Falstaff presently departed to keep his appointment with Mistress Ford, who once more received him with pretended favour. Very soon, however, as arranged between the two friends, Mistress Page again interrupted the roguish old Knight's lovemaking by running into the room with the news that Master Ford was returning in a greater rage than ever and declaring that if he could catch his wife's lover this time he would certainly kill him.

These alarming words put Falstaff into a woeful trembling, and he sought wildly for a hiding-place. This time the two dames quickly hustled him into an upper chamber, bidding him don the clothes of a certain fat old fortune-telling woman of Brentford, which they had borrowed for this purpose.

Whilst Mrs. Page hastily arrayed Sir John in the fortune-teller's gown and head-dress, Mistress Ford endeavoured to persuade her irate husband—who had now arrived on the scene—not to search the house, as he jealously insisted upon doing; and she declared that no other stranger was present save the Fat Woman of Brentford who happened to be visiting her that day.

This, as the wily dame had hoped, roused Ford's wrath all the more, as he had a special dislike for the old fortune-teller, whom

he had forbidden to enter his house again; and when Falstaff
presently appeared, dressed in the Fat Woman's clothes, he was
roughly seized by the angry husband and treated to a sound
cudgelling ere he was permitted to depart.

Both the merry wives were by this time convulsed with laughter
at the success of their plan; and they now told their husbands the
whole truth of the matter, so that Ford's jealousy quickly
vanished and he sought pardon from his wife for his doubt of her
integrity.

.   .   .   .

After peace had been thus happily restored, the two families
decided to carry the joke a little further still and give Falstaff a
third scare as a final penalty for his many misdeeds. It was
arranged that he should be lured into Windsor Forest at midnight
and there led to suppose that he was being attacked by fairies,
goblins, and other supernatural beings.

Consequently, a few days later, Mistress Ford invited her
ponderous admirer to meet her in the forest at midnight,
promising to lend him a pair of stag's horns as a head-dress,
that he might thus disguise himself as Herne the Hunter—in
which garb, should any of the townsfolk chance to see him, they
would quickly run away in terror, looking upon him as a ghost.
At that time there were plenty of superstitious folk to be found
who believed in the legend of Herne the Hunter, which was as
follows : In ages gone by, a certain famous hunter named Herne
had impiously slain a royal stag beneath the sacred oak tree, which
was then regarded as a place of refuge for hunted creatures. For
this misdeed, his disembodied spirit was condemned to wear the
stag's horns and to hunt at midnight in the forest of Windsor for
evermore, accompanied by a phantom train of fellow hunters and
dogs.

It was arranged that dainty Mistress Anne should appear in the
forest arrayed as the Fairy Queen, accompanied by a troop of
children disguised as elves and gnomes; and Page, Ford, Slender,
Dr. Caius and Fenton would also appear as various other
unearthly beings to assist in the teasing and tormenting of
Falstaff.

Master Page and his wife, unknown to each other, also determined to use this masquerade as a means for carrying out their
opposing wishes with regard to their daughter's marriage. So
Anne was first secretly commanded by her father to wear a red
gown, that she might thus be recognized by Slender, who meant
to run away with her, that they might be married that night by
the priest at Eton; and soon afterwards she was stealthily desired

by her mother to don a green robe, that she might be noted by Dr. Caius, with whom the crafty dame had arranged a similar elopement.

But merry Mistress Anne herself decided to wear bridal white garments, arranging with her beloved Fenton that he would know her thus and could slip away with her to the priest at Eton before the other suitors could find her; and in order to complete the confusion of the latter, she cleverly directed Slender to wear a green robe and Dr. Caius a red one in the masquerade—hoping that, in the darkness, they would elope with each other in mistake for herself.

On the appointed evening, Falstaff, disguised as Herne the Hunter, appeared under the Sacred Oak in Windsor Forest at midnight; and very soon afterwards, Mistress Ford and Mistress Page joined him. The two merry dames, enjoying the joke immensely, encouraged the fat Knight in his extravagant and absurd love-making. Then, hearing weird noises and seeing strange forms approaching, they pretended to be terrified and fled away shrieking, leaving the frightened Falstaff sprawling on the ground—for, in attempting to run away also, he had tripped and fallen.

The prostrate Knight was instantly surrounded by a band of pretended fairies, goblins and sprites, led by pretty Mistress Anne, attired in a flowing white robe as Titania; and they all sang and danced wildly around him. Falstaff was filled with alarm, believing that he was indeed in the midst of supernatural beings; and sharing the common superstitious notion that death would be the result of looking upon or speaking with fairy folk, he buried his face in his hands and lay motionless on the ground, hoping that they would presently vanish.

But the supposed Fairy Queen now sang out a further command to her sprites and goblins, bidding them to pinch and torment the old reprobate. At this command, her lively followers all set upon Falstaff, pinching and pummelling him and pricking him with their toy darts, uttering strange wild cries and indulging in loud peals of eldritch laughter; and the unlucky Knight, not daring to stir, and fearing he knew not what, soon began to bellow for mercy.

While this ludicrous scene was progressing, Fenton, in the guise of Oberon, drew near to Anne, whom he recognized by her white gown; and taking her by the hand, he hurried away with her to Eton, where the priest he had notified quickly married them. Slender and Dr. Caius, the one in green garments and the other in red, also joined hands and slipped away together—each believing the other to be Mistress Anne, in accordance with the instructions given them by the supporters of their suits.

When the merry wives were fully satisfied that their corpulent and audacious admirer had been thoroughly scared and had received a sufficiently severe pinching to teach him not to make love again to respectable married dames, they set him free, and revealed to him the true identity of the weird company of petty tormentors; and when all had enjoyed a hearty laugh at the fat old Knight's expense—in which the jolly Falstaff, bearing no malice, readily joined—the masquerade came to an end.

Then, to the amazement of Master Page and his wife, Slender and Dr. Caius both appeared, full of blustering wrath at the trick which had been played upon them by saucy Mistress Anne —which they had not discovered until they had reached Eton; and whilst the disappointed suitors were bewailing their loss, the two arch-plotters, Fenton and Anne, arrived also upon the scene to confess their successful ruse and to sue for pardon.

This was readily granted by the parents, who good-humouredly admitted that they had been outwitted by these determined lovers.

After this, the whole party trooped back to Master Page's house, to enjoy a wedding feast; and in deep draughts of his favourite beverage, Falstaff quickly drowned all remembrance of the teasing he had received at the hands of the Merry Wives of Windsor.

THE GOLDSMITH OF TOLEDO　　　　　*Offenbach*

TOWARDS the end of the eighteenth century, the citizens of Toledo were greatly disturbed and alarmed by a series of murders committed by a mysterious unknown assassin, who always chose the night-time for his ghastly work. The object of these murders was always the same; not money—which was invariably left untouched—but jewels of great beauty and fine workmanship. The bodies of the victims were always found stabbed in the back and lying in one particular spot near a fine statue of St. Sebastian, which stood in a shallow recess in a dark and lonely lane. By the position of the bodies and the nature of the wounds, it was suspected that the blows were all struck by the same hand—that of one who thus did foul murder for the sake of securing rich jewels.

Revellers bedecked with jewels began to be afraid of roaming the streets after dark; and stories of fresh murders cast a gloom over many festivities.

This was the case on a certain evening when a splendid entertainment was being held in the palace of the beautiful young Marquesa Dolores Almedina. As the guests were assembling in the salon, there came the news of yet another outrage, the victim being one of their own friends. Though greatly shocked, however, the guests determined to keep the matter secret, in order not to distress the Marquesa, who now entered to bid them welcome.

Dolores was immediately surrounded by her admiring guests, who vied with one another in showering complimentary speeches upon her; but though gracious to all, her most ardent glances fell upon Don Favero, a handsome cavalier, who had just returned from his duties as Ambassador at Braganza. Although not yet formally betrothed, Dolores and Favero already loved one another and were happy in their romance.

Seeing that their charming hostess seemed somewhat remote from them, as though her thoughts were elsewhere, her guests presently inquired the reason for this; and Dolores now related a curious story to them. That morning she had been seated in the Cathedral at her devotions before the shrine of the Madonna and Child, when suddenly a youth wrapped in a dark mantle and having his face concealed by a mask appeared at her side, put a golden casket into her hands and as suddenly vanished. On opening the casket, she found therein a necklace of the most exquisitely perfect pearls she had ever seen. On the lid of the casket these words were written: " Seek not for me, else will these pearls bring ill to thee! "

As the guests listened to this strange story, they were amazed; and when Dolores now produced the casket and placed the necklace around her neck, they exclaimed at the size and beauty of the pearls, declaring that only the most skilful goldsmith in the world could have produced such exquisite workmanship—Malaveda, a famous jeweller of their own city. They added that the pearls must certainly be a gift from some unknown admirer.

Don Favero was greatly disturbed about the matter, as he jealously feared a more wealthy rival; and when he presently found himself alone with Dolores, he implored her to have nothing to do with the strange gift, reminding her of the ancient proverb about pearls betokening tears.

But Dolores, though herself somewhat uneasy, her curious adventure having caused a chill dread to steal over her, could not resist the delight of teasing her lover by laughing at his fears and fanning his jealousy of an imagined rival; and after a lively passage of words which ended in a mild squabble, Don Favero impatiently departed to the dancing salon and left his charmer alone.

The Marquesa, feeling strangely weary, now ordered a servant to lower most of the lights; and, sending a message to her guests that she would rejoin them shortly, she lay back on a couch, glad to rest for a while.

As she fingered the necklace around her neck, the lustrous pearls suddenly began to gleam, now white as snow and then red as blood; but though disturbed by this strange phenomenon, she was so exhausted by the recent stirring of her emotions that presently she fell asleep.

A few moments later, while she still slept, a strange youth, masked and wrapped closely in a long black cloak, entered the room from behind the loggia curtains where he had been concealed and, creeping stealthily to the couch whereon the Marquesa lay, tried to unclasp the pearls from her neck. Before he had succeeded, Dolores awakened and recognized the intruder as the stranger from whom she had received the golden casket in the Cathedral that morning. She gave a cry of alarm and bade him begone, believing him to be an ill-omened phantom of her imagination.

The strange youth, however, commanded her to be silent, declaring wildly that unless she delivered up the pearls to him she would certainly lose her life. But Dolores was so terrified that she cried loudly for help; and the intruder had only just time to escape by the loggia as the alarmed guests ran in to the assistance of their hostess who, snatching the pearls from her neck and declaring that they were choking her, fell back fainting into the arms of the now remorseful Don Favero.

.   .   .   .

While these events were taking place in the brilliantly-lighted Almedina Palace, gloom and unhappiness reigned in the house of Malaveda, the celebrated Goldsmith of Toledo. The elderly jeweller had only just recovered from a severe illness; and though he was once more able to continue the exquisite craftsmanship at which he was such an adept, he was still somewhat weak and so strange in his manner that he was a constant anxiety to his pretty young daughter, Magdalena.

But it was the unhappy condition of Magdalena herself that mostly disturbed her constant companion, the kindly duenna, Teresa. For several months past the once light-hearted girl had been unusually sad; and to-night, as they sat working together in the goldsmith's large gloomy workshop—Magdalena at her spinning-wheel—old Teresa coaxed from her unhappy charge the secret of the trouble she had hidden so long. Magdalena confessed that she loved her father's handsome young assistant, Lenardo, who had at first returned her affection with an equal fervour; but she added sadly that latterly he had avoided her as though he no longer cared for her and appeared to be preoccupied with some dreadful secret.

While Teresa was endeavouring to comfort the distressed girl, there came a loud knocking upon the outer door; and hastily composing themselves, the pair went reluctantly down the passage, somewhat fearful as to who could be desiring admittance at such a late hour.

As they departed, Malaveda, the goldsmith, came forth from his inner chamber into the workshop; and unfastening a black chest against the wall, drew forth a large iron-bound box and staggered with it to the table. Unlocking the box with feverish haste, he opened it and took out a quantity of lovely jewels which glittered in the lamplight as he fondled them with childish delight. Hearing footsteps without, he quickly replaced the gems; and next moment his physician, Dr. Mendozza, entered the room and greeted him. The Doctor expressed surprise at his improved health and declared that, considering his dangerous condition of only a week ago, his sudden recovery seemed almost miraculous.

To this Malaveda replied seriously that a miracle had indeed been wrought on his behalf. Turning to a picture of the Madonna which adorned one of the walls, he said that on the previous evening, fearing he would not recover, he had invoked the aid of the Queen of Heaven—whereupon, the figure in the picture had seemed to glow with life. At the same time he had heard a voice saying that if he would give away his most valued and beloved treasure his health would be restored. In obedience to this command, therefore, early that morning he had handed to his assistant, Lenardo, a magnificent necklace of pearls in a golden casket—the most treasured of all the gems he possessed—and had bidden him go alone to the Cathedral and place the casket in the hands of the first woman he found kneeling at prayer before the Shrine of the Blessed Virgin. Lenardo having performed this office for him, from that hour he had been completely restored to health; and Mendozza soon satisfied himself that this was indeed the case.

Quite late that same night, Malaveda was again disturbed—this time by the Marquesa Dolores and her attendant cavalier, Don Favero. Apologizing for the lateness of her visit, Dolores, in some agitation, related the story of her adventure in the Cathedral; and handing the pearls to the goldsmith, she announced that she could not rest until she knew whether the necklace was the workmanship of Malaveda, as believed by her friends.

As Malaveda's eager hands closed lovingly over his precious pearls, a thrill of joy ran through him; but, nevertheless, he declared harshly that the necklace was not of his workmanship and that he had never seen it before. Then, in a wild burst of anger, he flung the pearls down and called frantically upon Dolores to take them out of his sight.

The visitors were surprised at this outburst; but putting it down to the after-effects of his recent illness, they bade the goldsmith farewell and departed, Dolores clasping the pearls around her neck once more.

When Malaveda was once more alone in his workshop, he fell into a great state of agitation. His longing for the pearls he had parted with for the sake of being restored to health was so intense that it became an agony to him; for he was possessed of a lust for beautiful jewels and could not bear to part with any gem that came into his possession. To comfort himself somewhat, he again opened his iron-bound box of jewels and began to gloat over its dazzling contents once more.

While thus engaged, he heard a slight sound. Turning, he beheld a panel in the wall slide back—this being the entrance to a secret passage leading out into the street, an exit which he had believed was known only to himself—and the cloaked form of his young assistant, Lenardo, stood before him.

As the goldsmith drew back with a cry of alarm, Lenardo announced in a stern accusing voice that not only had he discovered the secret passage, but that his recent suspicions as to its use had been at last confirmed by his master's own revelations uttered unconsciously in his presence when in a state of delirium during his illness. He now had clear proof that Malaveda had committed the recent murders in Toledo for the sake of possessing himself of certain coveted jewels. He added that, following the information given in his master's delirious ravings, he had made his way through the secret passage into the street where the outlet was concealed by the statue of St. Sebastian—which, on touching a hidden spring, moved aside sufficiently to permit of a single person to issue forth or return. Thus, unseen and unsuspected, the murderer had lurked in readiness to strike down his victims.

Malaveda, realizing the uselessness of denial, now confessed to the murders; and, in trembling and passionate tones, he declared that he was possessed of some evil demon that tempted him thus to do violence in order to secure the gems for which he craved. When he had made a beautiful jewel he could not bear it to pass out of his possession; and when he sold a costly trinket, he could not rest until he had slain the purchaser and thus snatched it back once more. Even as the unsuspecting customer went on his way down the quiet lane, the demon-possessed goldsmith would slip down the secret passage, silently slide aside the statue, slay his victim, and return in triumph with the jewel.

He now declared that it was a madness that possessed him and that, though he fought against it, he could not conquer his inordinate lust for the jewels he made. Above all, he loved pearls; and suddenly remembering the glorious necklace now in the possession of the Marquesa Dolores, he raved wildly that he could not bear her to have his cherished gems.

Fearing lest his demoniacally-possessed master should now be tempted to murder the beautiful young Marquesa, Lenardo sternly announced his intention of immediately delivering him into the hands of justice; but as he moved to the door with this object, Malaveda flung himself at his feet, entreating him to have mercy and to refrain from betraying him for the sake of Magdalena, who would die of grief were her beloved father condemned to death.

On hearing this appeal, Lenardo, who loved Magdalena deeply and sincerely was torn in twain. His recent avoidance of her and apparent coldness had been caused solely by his knowledge of her father's guilty secret. Either he must stifle his conscience and sense of justice by concealing his knowledge of the murders, or destroy the happiness and peace of mind of his beloved one. Seeing this, the crafty Malaveda renewed his pleadings; and Lenardo, unable to resist the promptings of his heart, gave way for the time being, though easing his conscience by secretly resolving to warn the Marquesa of her danger a second time—his first attempt at her festival having proved a failure.

Coming away from this painful interview, Lenardo was presently joined by Magdalena, whom he made happy once more by again declaring his love for her; and the reunited pair arranged to attend a masquerade to be held in the city next evening in celebration of a religious Feast.

Yet another belated visitor came to the house that night, when all had retired save the goldsmith himself. The latter was still in his workshop, feasting his eyes again upon his beloved jewels, when he heard an insistent knocking upon the outer door. Reluctantly admitting the visitor, he found this to be an artist named Carmona, who calmly announced that he had come for the

fine diamond ring he had left to be repaired several months ago—
which he now wished to present to a fair lady of whom he was
enamoured.

Malaveda, loath to give up this gem—for which he had conceived a passion—replied curtly that it was not yet ready to leave
his workshop; but the painter, suddenly catching sight of his ring
among the other jewels on the table, snatched it up eagerly.
Then, flinging down a purse of gold in payment for the work
done upon it, he hurried away in triumph.

But the happy lover's elation was short-lived. Even as he went
singing along the lane and passed the statue of St. Sebastian, a
sinister figure slipped out from a hidden opening behind the latter
—there was the flash of a dagger, a stifled shriek, and the painter,
Carmona, had breathed his last. A few minutes later, alone once
more in his workshop, the exultant goldsmith was gloating over
the much coveted diamond ring which now sparkled and flashed
upon his own trembling finger.

.   .   .   .

Next evening was the Feast of San Domingo; and after the
Cathedral services were over, the streets became crowded with
revellers.

Among the masqueraders were Lenardo and the pretty
Magdalena—the latter garbed as a gipsy and merrily eager to take
part in the revels. Lenardo, however, was somewhat weighed
down by the horrible secret he longed, yet feared, to reveal; and
before feeling free to enjoy himself, he knew he must find some
means of warning the lovely Marquesa of her ever-increasing
danger. He was relieved, therefore, when he presently caught
sight of Dolores, disguised in a mask and domino, coming forth
from her palace, alone.

Knowing that she would soon be joined by her favoured
cavalier, Don Favero, who had just been serenading her in company with a group of her other gay friends, he decided to act at
once—especially as he observed that she was wearing the fatal
pearls around her neck. He suspected, also, that his sinister
master, Malaveda, was lurking amidst the crowd, probably
already searching for the beautiful possessor of the pearls he
longed to re-possess; and he realized that there was no time to be
lost.

Seeing that the Marquesa had stopped on the other side of the
square, therefore, he produced a note he had already written and
addressed to her to await an opportunity of delivery; and handing
this to Magdalena, he begged her to cross the square and hand it
to the lady on the other side—not daring to approach her himself,

because of the terror with which he had inspired her on his first attemped warning.

Magdalena, though distressed on being asked to convey a letter from her lover to another woman, was so alarmed by Lenardo's sudden anxious excitement, that she agreed to do so. She was still further disturbed when Lenardo now hastened out of the square; but having given him her promise, she approached the masked lady at once and handed her the note.

Dolores, expecting merely a suggested assignation from one of her admirers, read the message out aloud. This entreated her to meet the writer at midnight near the St. Sebastian statue, and to wear her recently received pearl necklace that he might recognize her immediately by this means.

As Magdalena now uttered a cry of distress on thus learning that Lenardo desired to meet another woman alone at midnight, Dolores sought to comfort her. On discovering her identity and learning that the sender of the message—which she took to be merely a merry joke excusable at a time of carnival—was the girl's lover, she quickly devised a plan for playing a trick upon this seemingly saucy reveller.

She suggested to Magdalena, therefore, that they should exchange garments, pointing out that the latter—in domino and mask and wearing the revealing pearls—would then be in a position to befool her roving swain to her heart's content.

Magdalena, now relieved on discovering that the Marquesa had no desire to rob her of her lover, agreed to the suggested merry jest; and the two girls entered the Almedina Palace to effect their change of raiment.

When they emerged again, the masquerade was at its height; and Dolores, disguised in Magdalena's gipsy dress, tripped away to seek out Don Favero and to tell him his fortune in playful zingara fashion.

Magdalena, eager to escape notice until the time of her assignation, stopped for a moment in an alcove near the Cathedral. Here, presently, she was amazed to observe that her father was standing within a few yards of her, gazing upon her unrecognizingly while his glowing eyes were fixed avidly upon the magnificent pearl necklace which the Marquesa had so playfully slipped around her neck as the clue to her disguise.

Malaveda felt his passionate lust once more getting the better of him as he gazed at the beloved pearls again so nearly within his grasp; but with a mighty effort, he crushed down the demon of temptation and rushed away from the masked and dominoed figure he had mistaken for the Marquesa.

Magdalena, shocked by the fearful malignity and unmistakable covetousness revealed in her father's eyes, staggered back, horrified; but just at that moment, she was surrounded by a group of merry revellers who, mistaking her for Dolores, began to serenade her once more. For a short time longer, she was thus caught up in the whirl of the giddy masquerade; but after a while, she managed to make her escape from the lively throng and, as it was now close upon midnight, hurried away alone to keep the assignation made by Lenardo.

As she stood by the statue of St. Sebastian, waiting happily for her lover to appear, she suddenly felt a burning sensation at her throat; and snatching off the necklace, she was amazed to see that the pearls glistened and changed colour as she held them in her hands, gleaming first white as snow and then red as blood.

Just then, unobserved and unheard by her, engrossed as she was by this strange phenomenon, Malaveda the goldsmith appeared from behind the statue where he had concealed himself on his return from the square to watch for the bejewelled revellers passing that way; and beholding, as he thought, the figure of the Marquesa Dolores holding in her hands the marvellous pearls he coveted so passionately, he was no longer able to resist the murderous impulse against which he had fought all evening. With a despairing curse upon the fiend who thus tempted him, he drew his dagger and, springing forward, stabbed the unsuspecting and hapless girl in the back.

Then, as he clutched greedily and gloatingly at the fatal necklace, to regain which his jewel lust had once more driven him to commit murder, he saw to his horror that the limp, bleeding form he held in his grasp was that of his own beloved daughter, Magdalena; and with a great cry of woe, the grief-stricken father fell unconscious across her dead body.

THE TALES OF HOFFMANN   *Offenbach*
(*Les Contes d'Hoffmann*)

ONE evening during the early days of the last century, several gay and noisy young students were drinking together in Luther's famous wine-cellar at Nuremberg. They had come in for refreshment between the acts of the opera which was being performed in the adjacent theatre; and all were merry and ready for any revel which might arise—with the exception of one of their number who sat apart, lost to his surroundings in a deep reverie of sad thoughts.

This latter was Hoffmann, the poet and musician, a man somewhat older than the others—a man who, though blessed with handsome looks, exceptional grace of form and manner, and a fascinating charm of personality, was yet prone to frequent fits of despondency from which his boon companions had the utmost difficulty in rousing him. Not even his lifelong friend, Nicklaus, had the power to call up a smile to pierce through the dark clouds of these gloomy spells; and to no one had he yet related the story of the circumstances which had made him the victim of such an unhappy state of mind. That he had suffered sorely from the adverse effects of more than one deep love-passion was well known; and it was also suspected that he had been drawn into the harmful meshes of some supernatural influence. But the young students, despite their natural curiosity, had always refrained from asking questions which might lose them the friendship of one whom they dearly loved.

This evening, however, to their surprise and pleasure, on being rallied by his companions upon his unusually deep fit of gloom, Hoffmann suddenly roused himself and offered to tell them the stories of his three love episodes. Abandoning the opera for that night, therefore, the students ordered in a fresh bowl of steaming punch and gathered around the romantic Hoffman, eager to listen to the enthralling tales he had to tell.

.   .   .   .

In his first story, Hoffmann appeared as an impressionable and sensitive youth in the throes of an early boyish love-passion.

Having several times observed the form of a pretty maiden standing at the windows of the house of Spallanzani, a famous physiologist, young Hoffmann became so fascinated by her charming looks that he fell in love with her and eagerly sought an opportunity of declaring his passion. With this object in view, he offered himself as a pupil to the scientist, hoping thus to secure an introduction to the dainty young lady, whom he believed to be Spallanzani's child—since the latter talked continually of his wonderful " daughter ", Olympia, speaking always in enthusiastic terms of her many graces, of her clever singing and dancing, and of the grand reception he intended to give shortly in honour of her coming-out.

In reality, however, Olympia was not a human being at all, but was merely a marvellously life-like automaton made by Spallanzani himself, who had been assisted in the work by another scientist named Coppelius—a mysterious individual who had gained a considerable reputation as a wizard and dabbler in the occult arts. Realizing that young Hoffmann believed their wonderful piece of mechanism to be indeed a real flesh-and-blood maiden, the pair conspired together to keep him in this belief, in order to retain him longer as a profitable pupil. They also hoped to amuse themselves and their friends at his expense.

Consequently, they would not permit Hoffmann any closer inspection of Olympia until the night of the party. In addition, the sinister trickster, Coppelius, declared that the young man's sight was bad and sold him a pair of specially-prepared spectacles through which the automaton would appear to him to be indeed a living person.

Coppelius, believing that a large fortune could probably be made by exhibiting the mechanical figure, now claimed a substantial share in the anticipated profits therefrom, he having made half of her body and supplied her with her beautiful moving eyes; and Spallanzani agreed to buy him out. With this object, he gave him a draft on a certain disreputable Jew—knowing the latter to be bankrupt but craftily concealing the fact from Coppelius, whom he believed was about to depart from the country and, consequently, was not likely to discover the fraud in time to rectify it.

Coppelius, quite unsuspicious, accepted the false draft and departed; and on the same day, Spallanzani gave his splendid entertainment in honour of the coming-out of his beautiful "daughter".

When all the guests had arrived, the scientist produced the exquisitely made life-sized doll, dressed daintily in pretty girlish garments; and the automaton, having been wound up beforehand, was led round the ballroom by Spallanzani with great pride. Olympia bowed gracefully to the guests, greeting them in clear, bell-like tones; and presently she sang to them a fine operatic song, full of such finished trills and flourishes that the audience was astounded by the wonderful performance.

The visitors, of course, knew perfectly well that the figure was merely an automaton; but seeing that young Hoffmann—who was wearing the magic spectacles that caused the doll to appear to him more than ever to be an actual human being—thought otherwise, they merrily conspired with Spallanzani to pretend that Olympia was indeed his living daughter.

Becoming more and more enamoured of the pretty "maiden" as he gazed admiringly at her through his strange spectacles, Hoffmann was at last completely bewitched by her pink-and-white waxen beauty; and sitting down beside her, he took the first opportunity that occurred to declare his passion for her—utterly regardless of her stolid attitude, stiff movements, and mechanical replies of "Yes! Yes!" to all he said.

So enraptured was he that he became entirely oblivious of his surroundings, continuing to pour forth tender love speeches into the unheeding ears of the pretty Olympia—to the great amusement of the other guests. When his friend Nicklaus, who was also present, tried to enlighten him as to the true state of affairs, he thrust him aside roughly and devoted himself more assiduously than ever to the unresponsive doll.

When dancing began he engaged her immediately as his partner, lovingly encircling her slender waist with his ready arm; but the doll, having been overwound, now got out of control and whirled the infatuated Hoffmann round and round the room at so dizzy a pace that he at length fell to the ground in a swoon—Olympia spinning on alone until finally caught and placed in the laboratory once more.

At this moment, to the dismay of Spallanzani, the wizard, Coppelius, dashed into the house in a towering rage, having already discovered the fraud which had been practised upon him and returned to wreak vengeance upon his false partner. So indignant was he that he resolved to destroy the mechanical doll; and hastening to the laboratory, he managed to break the wonderful automaton into small pieces before anyone could stop him.

Hoffmann awakened to his senses once more whilst the work of destruction was in progress; and his magic spectacles having been broken in his fall, he now realized, to his shame and mortification, that he had been in love with a mere lifeless doll and had made himself a laughing-stock to all who had witnessed his folly. Full of confusion, he rushed from the room, amidst the derisive jeers of the amused guests; and thus ended his first adventure in the realms of Cupid.

. . . .

A few years later, Hoffmann, now in the first flush of hot-blooded manhood, found himself in Venice, where his ardent nature revelled in the glamour of beauty and sensuous pleasure to be enjoyed there.

Both he and his friend, Nicklaus, were frequent visitors at the luxurious palace of the beautiful courtesan, Giulietta. Hoffmann had conceived a violent passion for his lovely hostess, stubbornly refusing to believe evil of her, despite the warnings of the more prudent Nicklaus, who assured him that she had numerous other lovers and would certainly deceive and cast him aside in the end.

Giulietta, for her own ends, very willingly encouraged the advances of Hoffmann; for the fair courtesan was in the power of a demon-magician calling himself Dapertutto who, by his arts, had gained complete mastery over her. At his command and under his influence, she had already obtained for him the shadow of Schlemil, one of her lovers; and she had now agreed to take the reflection of Hoffmann in a magic mirror her sinister master had given her for this purpose—for it was by this means that the demon secured the souls he coveted.

Therefore, Giulietta encouraged Hoffmann to make love to her; and on one of his visits, after a passionately tender scene with him, she carelessly held up the magic mirror and invited him to gaze within it. Unsuspectingly, Hoffmann did so, though wondering at the triumphant laugh with which Giulietta accompanied her instant withdrawal of the mirror. Presently, however, when Dapertutto equally carelessly placed another mirror before him, he was horrified to find that it gave back no reflection—a sure sign that magic was at work.

A feeling of uneasiness now came over Hoffmann, a feeling which deepened upon the entry of Schlemil—whom he instantly perceived to be his rival and predecessor in the affections of Giulietta. The scheming courtesan, nevertheless, still led her newly infatuated victim to believe that she loved only him, by presently entreating him to secure the key of her chamber from Schlemil—declaring, with pretended distress, that the latter had it in his keeping against her will.

She then cleverly left her two lovers together, in company with Dapertutto, who had just joined them. Hoffmann immediately commanded his rival to give up the key of their hostess's chamber; and upon Schlemil refusing to do so, he furiously challenged him to fight.

The sinister Dapertutto offered his own sword to the unarmed Hoffmann, not wishing the duel to be delayed; and after a few passes with this uncanny weapon, feeling an evil influence enveloping him, Hoffmann, to his horror, stretched Schlemil dead at his feet.

For a few moments, Hoffmann, in a half-dazed state, remained staring at the dead body of his opponent; then, looking up, he saw that Dapertutto had vanished and that he was alone.

Presently, however, a gondola passed by the open balcony; and amongst luxurious cushions lay the faithless Giulietta, already reclining in the arms of Dapertutto, her new lover, and waving a mocking farewell to the deserted Hoffmann—who now at last realized that his love had been scorned and that he himself had been the dupe of a fickle unscrupulous courtesan.

.   .   .   .

Twice had Hoffmann passed through the fire of passion and been scorched by its flames; and he seemed fated never to be a happy lover. In his third adventure—in which he experienced the deepest, purest, and only real love of his life—dire misfortune awaited him once more.

Hoffmann's ardent nature had deepened and matured as the follies and fancies of early youth left him; and when, some years after the Venice episode, he fell in love with Antonia, the lovely but frail daughter of Councillor Krespel, his passion was so strong and overwhelming that every fibre of his being thrilled in his beloved one's presence and when parted from her the whole world seemed empty.

To his joy, Antonia returned his love; and the pair plighted their troth—against the wishes of Krespel who, though anxious to secure his daughter's happiness, yet feared that the excitement of so passionate a love might have a disastrous effect upon her delicate health. For Antonia had inherited from her dead mother a glorious gift of song, together with a strong consumptive tendency; and Hoffmann, not knowing of the latter weakness, encouraged the beautiful girl to sing more than was advisable, taking the greatest delight in her rich voice.

Krespel, therefore, endeavoured to keep the ardent lover away from the house as much as possible. Having occasion to be absent for a few hours one day, therefore, he instructed his servant, Franz, not to admit Hoffmann should he happen to call. Old Franz, however, was deaf and misunderstood his master's words; and Hoffmann found no bar to his entrance when he presently arrived.

When the happy lovers had talked for some time, Hoffmann entreated Antonia to sing to him once more—which she gladly did, though now telling him that her father had forbidden her to use her voice so frequently. During the song, she was attacked by a sudden fit of coughing and faintness, which greatly alarmed them both; and a few minutes later, the pair were further startled by the opening of the street door—and they knew that Krespel had returned sooner than expected.

Hoffmann, not wishing to distress Antonia by an angry scene with her father, quickly concealed himself behind a thick curtain, hoping to depart later when a favourable opportunity occurred. Antonia retired into an adjoining apartment; and immediately afterwards, Councillor Krespel entered the room in which Hoffmann was concealed, followed by a tall sinister-looking man. The latter was known to Krespel as Dr. Mirakel; and the worthy Councillor not only disliked and distrusted his visitor, but was mortally afraid of him likewise—believing him to have been the cause of his wife's early death, and suspecting him now of having designs upon the life of his delicate daughter.

This mysterious Dr. Mirakel was, in reality, the evil genius of Hoffmann—a demon who had dogged his path throughout his three love-adventures, first as Coppelius, secondly as Dapertutto, and now as Mirakel—and from the angry scene that followed between the visitor and Krespel, the concealed lover learned, to his grief, the terrible news that his beloved Antonia had a fatal disease and that her death might be hastened by the exercise of her wonderful gift of song.

When the unhappy father had succeeded in driving Mirakel away from his presence and had himself retired to another room, the lovers met once more for a few moments; and upon Hoffmann now earnestly entreating Antonia to sing no more, she tearfully promised to obey his wishes.

Hoffmann then departed to seek the harassed Krespel, hoping now to gain his approval and confidence; and no sooner had Antonia been left alone for a moment than the mysterious Dr. Mirakel suddenly reappeared and addressed her. Representing himself as the friend of her parents, although unknown to her, he began to chide her for not making more use of her exquisite voice; and on her declaring that her father and lover had both made her promise not to sing on account of her weak health, the wily demon, determined not to be thwarted, resorted to supernatural means to gain his ends. Sternly bidding Antonia to gaze upon her mother's portrait which hung upon the wall, he now invoked the spirit of the dead woman. As in a vision, he caused the latter to speak from the picture and to persuade the girl that she was doing grievous wrong by not making full use of the precious gift so divinely bestowed upon her.

As the vision faded and the portrait resumed its normal aspect once more, the sinister Mirakel vanished from sight. The hapless Antonia, feeling that she had thus received a heavenly command to use her wonderful gift, at once began to sing, quite forgetful of her promise to refrain from so doing; and her rich voice rose in an exquisite song, the clear bell-like notes ringing through the house in a glorious outburst of passionate feeling such as she had never given vent to before.

But the effort and unusual exertion were too much for her frail strength to bear. As Krespel and Hoffmann hastened into the room, attracted by the sound of her wonderful singing, she fell, exhausted, to the ground; and, a few moments later, she breathed her last in the arms of her grief-stricken lover.

．　　．　　．　　．　　．　　．　　．　　．　　．

Such were the adventures of the ever-thwarted, ill-fated Hoffmann in his search for the joys of love; and as the recital of them came to an end, the unhappy hero buried his head in his hands and was once more plunged into his accustomed deep gloom.

The lively students, however, were determined not to allow him to fall back into melancholy that night, at least. After commiserating with him in his misfortunes, they called for yet another bowl of punch; and Hoffmann, grateful for their sympathy, feverishly joined them in draining this likewise to the bottom.

DANTE AND BEATRICE — *Philpot*

IT was May-day in Florence, towards the end of the thirteenth century; and early in the day the light-hearted citizens had gathered in the streets to celebrate the festival.

As the citizens presently followed a procession of priests into the Cathedral, the Ponte Vecchio over the river Arno was deserted for a short time; but presently, the poet Dante—young, handsome, and of noble appearance—approached slowly. He hesitated for a moment, undecided whether to join the worshippers or not; and finally deciding to remain without, he turned towards the bridge and, leaning over the coping, gazed towards the city with a deep sigh.

His reverie, however, was quickly broken by a group of merrymakers. Among these were his friends, Giotto—already the most famous artist of his time—and Cavalcanti, who called upon him to join the festival; and in this they were encouraged by Gentucca, a pretty young girl member of the social circle in which they all moved. When the abstracted Dante begged to be excused, Gentucca saucily declared he must be a woman-hater, if he did not care to join in the merry-making; but the poet assured her that, so far from this being the case, his heart was filled with a great love for a certain beautiful lady—whose name, however, he would not reveal.

On being teased by the young cavaliers, who now declared playfully that she herself might be the object of their love-sick companion's infatuation, Gentucca was filled with confusion and hurried away at once. When she had departed, Dante's continued air of sadness so impressed his friends that they anxiously inquired the reason for this. The poet replied that he had been troubled by a strangely disturbing dream in which he had beheld his beloved one lying dead before him—adding that he regarded this as a fateful portent; and though his friends endeavoured to laugh away his fears, he sent them off to rejoin Gentucca and resumed his former position on the bridge, unable to shake off his feeling of gloom.

At this moment, however, his eyes lighted up with joy once more; for the object of his secret adoration now appeared— Beatrice, the beautiful daughter of Folco Portinari, one of the rich merchants of the city.

Beatrice, though she instantly noticed Dante—for whom she in turn had conceived a secret passion, though as yet unaware that it was returned—did not immediately approach him. Instead, when a number of her friends surrounded and greeted her with congratulations upon her birthday—which happened to fall upon the festival day—she invited them all to attend the splendid banquet her father was giving in her honour that same evening.

Then, approaching the lonely figure on the bridge, Beatrice shyly asked the poet for his congratulations likewise; but Dante, whose love was so overwhelming as to deprive him almost of speech in the presence of his adored one, was so overcome with confusion that he could only utter a few incoherent words. Beatrice, however, with quick intuition, divined the deep devotion and love for her that lay beneath his embarrassed speechlessness; and, though filled with joy at the discovery, a sudden shyness also now assailed her, so that she retired hastily, after inviting him to attend her birthday banquet that evening.

While Dante still remained gazing raptly after the departing form of his adored lady, overwhelmed by her beauty and graciousness, the clamour of a noisy tumult was heard in the distance. Presently, Cavalcanti and Giotto hurried up to the poet with the news that a fierce fight had just broken out between the two rival parties who at that time distracted the city with their quarrels— the Neri and the Bianchi; and a riotous crowd presently burst into the street. Dante and his friends immediately tried to use their influence with the Bianchi—to which faction they belonged—to quell the disturbance; and they were on the point of succeeding when the leader of the Neri, Corso Donati, arrived upon the scene. Corso, an extremely arrogant noble, self-seeking and un- scrupulous, had also conceived a violent and uncontrollable passion for Beatrice Portinari; and having suspected recently that Dante was his rival in her affections, he now seized the present occasion of a factional disturbance to pick a personal quarrel with the poet. With insulting effrontery, therefore, he swaggeringly challenged the latter to a duel.

Dante, eager to preserve peace on the festival day, at first attempted to bring Corso to a more reasonable frame of mind; but seeing that the latter was determined to fight, he accepted his challenge, and the duel began. Corso, in his furious desire to kill his rival, made such wild lunges that Dante quickly disarmed him and held him at his sword's point; but, with great magnanimity, he spared his life. Corso, however, disdained to show gratitude for such undeserved mercy; but, though furiously enraged by his defeat, he was forced by his followers to retire. The citizens now crowded round the victorious Dante, whom they all loved, and crowned him with laurels and flowers; then they raised him upon a shield, hero fashion, and, proclaiming him as their " prince of Chivalry ", carried him off amid delighted cheers.

Towards evening the same day, in the splendid palace of Folco Portinari, a sumptuous entertainment was held in honour of Beatrice's birthday.

Although Beatrice, more beautiful than ever in her exquisite festival robes and jewels, received her guests with her usual charming graciousness, her thoughts were with one only—Dante, for whom her eager eyes constantly sought. However, it was not until the banquet was nearly at an end that the undeclared lovers were able to meet; then, seeing that the poet obviously desired to speak with her, she drew him aside into an alcove, that they might have a few minutes alone.

This time, Dante was no longer speechless, but boldly and fervently declared his love, which Beatrice responded to with an equal fervour; and the lovers plighted their troth then and there in impassioned tones.

From the height of this joyous exaltation, however, they were suddenly recalled to their momentarily forgotten surroundings by the furious ringing of an alarum bell, followed by a fanfare from the city trumpeters. This was a call to all citizens to take up arms at once, as Florence was threatened with a great danger.

As the birthday guests in dismay came pouring forth from the banqueting-hall, the Neri leader, Corso, dashed into their midst, announcing that their enemies, the Aretines, were marching upon the city in great force. Immediately, Cavalcanti and Dante, as chiefs of the Bianchi faction, decided to head the van of their beloved Florence's defending forces; and Cavalcanti departed at once, followed by all his eager adherents among the company.

Beatrice endeavoured in her agitation to detain Dante a little longer by her side, fearful for his safety in the coming struggle; and observing the pair thus unmistakably conversing as lovers, Corso, in raging jealousy, decided to precipitate his own acceptance as the girl's future husband. Demanding an interview with her father, therefore, he was instantly conducted to the presence of Portinari in an inner room.

Meanwhile, after a last passionate embrace, Dante tore himself from the arms of his beloved one and hastened with all speed to join his comrades; and Beatrice rejoined her agitated guests.

Almost immediately afterwards, Corso, on coming from Portinari's private room, had a secret interview with some of his own followers. As general leader of the city's defences, in addition to being head of the Neri party, he arranged with his confederates an unscrupulous plot whereby, whether or not he succeeded in vanquishing their common enemy, the Aretines, he would at least make sure of the total destruction of the rival Florentine faction, the Bianchi, with Cavalcanti and Dante at their head.

Fortunately for the latter, however, this dastardly plot, as unfolded by Corso to his officers, was overheard by the Jester of the Portinari household, who, out of devotion to his beloved mistress and to the Bianchi party, determined to frustrate the scheme by revealing it to the rival leaders. Consequently, when Corso later on sent him forward with a despatch to Cavalcanti and Dante, the faithful Jester hailed the commission with alacrity and set forth eagerly.

Meanwhile, before the departure of Corso, a courier arrived with disastrous news for Folco Portinari. His ships and convoys had been seized by the invading Aretines; and with the confiscation of this merchandise, he was now faced with ruin, his credit being heavily mortgaged. The cunning Corso, learning of this disaster, now offered to rescue Portinari from his financial difficulties as a bribe for the hand of Beatrice in marriage—which had been refused him on his recent interview. The unfortunate merchant, realizing the misfortune that would otherwise overwhelm him, was now reluctantly compelled to consent to this proposal; and the triumphant Corso next insisted that the betrothal should be forthwith announced to the still remaining banquet guests who were now returning from bidding farewell to the fighting cavaliers.

When this totally unexpected announcement was presently made by her father, Beatrice was at first stunned; then, overwhelmed with grief at such a sudden threat to her life's happiness, she tearfully implored Portinari to retract his words and not to force her into a loveless marriage. But the distracted merchant, trapped and bound by his agreement with the powerful Corso and unable otherwise to save himself from ruin, refused to listen to her pleadings; and Beatrice, with despair in her heart, was compelled to submit to the repeated formal announcement of this hated betrothal.

.   .   .   .

The wedding of the unhappy Beatrice was ordered by Corso to take place immediately upon his return from victory; and on the day of the ceremony grand preparations were made in the Cathedral of Santa Maria, where many noble guests arrived at the hour appointed. The battle of Campaldino had already been fought and won by the Florentines, though under curious and unusual circumstances; and Corso's couriers, sent on in advance to hasten the marriage preparations, informed their eager questioners that either Dante or the latter's ghost had been instrumental in saving the city's defenders from disaster—for a persistent rumour had gone forth that the beloved poet had been slain early in the battle.

Their talk, however, was soon interrupted by the arrival of Corso, who seemed strangely agitated and was impatiently anxious for his marriage to be celebrated without a moment's delay. When Beatrice and her bridesmaids presently appeared, the heart-broken bride's courage failed her for the moment; and, falling upon her knees, she uttered despairing supplications to the Virgin for help and protection.

Corso, full of anger at her action, approached and raised her to her feet. Then, half supporting her, he led her forward and commanded the waiting Bishop to pronounce the actual marriage words without further delay and to omit the introductory ceremonial—appearing to be feverishly anxious that not another moment should be lost.

The Bishop at first demurred at such an irregular curtailment of the sacred ritual; but upon the command being angrily repeated by the powerful noble, he consented to proceed with the service.

At that moment, however, the sounds of an approaching cavalcade were heard; and scarcely had the intimidated Bishop uttered the words demanding whether any person could show just cause why the waiting bride and bridegroom should not be united, an armed figure dashed wildly into the Cathedral and cried: "Yes! I!"

The armed man raised his visor instantly and revealed the pale features of Dante to the astonished company—who had believed him to be dead, because of the false report spread abroad by Corso and the Neri.

Dante now sternly denounced Corso as a traitor to the city of Florence, revealing his dastardly scheme for the betrayal of the Bianchi party, which would have given victory to the Aretines had it not been frustrated by himself—Dante; and he brought forward full proofs of this accusation, producing as witness the Portinari Jester who had overheard the whole plot.

Corso, mad with rage at the failure of his plot, rushed upon Dante with his drawn sword; but the latter and his friends quickly beat him off. Nevertheless, he succeeded in hacking his way through the angry crowd into the open square outside; and then he sprang upon his horse and rode away at a furious pace.

A moment later, however, as the Neri were rejoicing at their leader's escape, there came a cry of horror from all. Corso's fiery steed, maddened by the noise, suddenly threw him and dashed on alone at a furious gallop, dragging his rider at his heels, a spur having become entangled in the stirrup. Though they mounted and galloped to his aid, the Neri were too late to save the life of their leader, who was found to be dead when the terrified horse at length ended its mad career by crashing to the ground.

Full of awe, the assembled company in the Cathedral now offered up prayers for the soul of the dead man. Soon, however, their gloom was changed to gladness; and as Dante and Beatrice embraced one another with thankfulness because of their joyful reunion, an involuntary Hymn of Praise broke forth from the whole congregation, proclaiming the Divine Power and the triumph of Love.

.   .   .   .

For a brief spell only did the ill-fated lovers enjoy happiness. Scarcely had another year passed than Beatrice, overtaken by a mortal illness, lay dying.

Her faithful and best-loved friends gathered together in her room, waiting sadly for the end; but when Dante presently entered, they withdrew respectfully, that the lovers might make their final farewells alone.

Dante was prostrated with grief; and as he clasped his beloved one in his arms he recalled the fateful dream which had caused his sadness on the day of their first declaration of love—which he knew now had been a premonition.

As the beautiful Beatrice expired, the grief-stricken Dante made a solemn resolve. With impassioned fervour, the great poet vowed to Heaven that he would devote his remaining life to immortalizing her in verse, and would sing such praises of his beloved one as man had never yet sung of woman—that all the world might thus be stirred by the pure and eternal love of Dante and Beatrice.

LA GIOCONDA _Ponchielli_

In Venice, during the seventeenth century, the dreaded Inquisition was at the height of its power. Nevertheless, the beautiful city, the Queen of the Adriatic, was one of the gayest in Europe.

One festival day, a light-hearted crowd of merry-makers jostled one another in the great courtyard of the Ducal Palace. Sailors, fishermen, gondoliers, and masqueraders fraternized with monks, Moors, and other foreigners; and the holiday folk generally seemed without a care.

Yet a sinister note was given to the gay scene by a notice cut in black letters on the wall at one side, below an opening aptly known as the Lion's Mouth. This notice advised all who had any denunciations to make to the Inquisition to drop their written indictments through the opening. Not far away, too, stood the table of a scribe, who sat there, pen in hand, ready to write any such denunciations.

But only one person in that merry carefree throng had thoughts of a sinister kind on such a happy festival day. This was Barnaba, a secret spy of the Inquisition, who, though dressed in festival attire and occasionally touching the strings of a lute, seemed unable, in spite of his forced gaiety, to inspire confidence in his pretended enjoyment of the scene. People shrank instinctively from him, as though they sensed something dangerous about him.

This was especially the case with the pretty ballad-singer, La Gioconda, who presently entered the courtyard, leading her blind mother, La Çieca, towards the beautiful Church of San Marco. Having conceived a passion for this young girl, Barnaba now blocked her path and began to pour forth violent protestations of love for her.

La Gioconda shrank from this unwelcome admirer in dismay, feeling a natural distrust. She was herself in love with a young noble named Enzo, whom she knew to be in hiding in the city disguised as a sea-captain, having been unjustly proscribed by the Inquisitorial authorities. When, therefore, Barnaba now tried to seize her in his arms, she broke away from him in fear and ran towards the lagoon, hoping there to find her beloved Enzo.

Thus, her mother, La Cieca, was left alone, sitting on the steps of the Church to await her daughter's return. Seeing her there, helpless, the spy quickly concocted a vile plot to get her in his power and thereby to force her lovely daughter to show him the favour he desired. His chance to carry it out soon occurred.

When, presently, the winner of a regatta race was carried shoulder high into the square, Barnaba pretended to commiserate with the loser of the contest. Then he whispered to the latter that his defeat had probably been caused by La Cieca having cast a spell over him, adding that the blind woman was obviously a witch. The supporters and friends of the loser of the race soon took up the cry that La Cieca was a witch; and the helpless blind woman was seized and dragged from the church steps by an angry mob.

At this moment, the disguised noble, Enzo, appeared with La Gioconda who, horrified by what had happened during her brief absence, begged him to save her mother. Calling to his sailor attendants, Enzo quickly rushed to the rescue; and a wild scene ensued. Just as things were beginning to look black, the palace doors were opened and out came Alvise, one of the great lords of the Inquisition, followed by his beautiful wife, Laura.

Immediately, Gioconda flung herself at the feet of this powerful official and implored him to spare the life of her mother, who was no witch but only poor and blind. The beautiful Laura, full of pity, likewise begged her husband to protect the frightened woman; and, at her request, the great lord ordered La Cieca to be set free. Full of gratitude, the blind woman pressed a simple rosary into Laura's hand with humble words of blessing. Then Gioconda took her mother into the church to return thanks.

Now, Barnaba, the spy, had surprised a glance of recognition which had passed between the Lady Laura and the pretended sea-captain, Enzo, this being followed by a lingering look of love. Suddenly he knew what this meant. Before her marriage, Laura had been betrothed to young Enzo Grimaldo, Prince of Santa Fior; but when the latter had been falsely proscribed and forced to flee the city, she had been compelled, against her will, to wed the powerful Alvise.

From her instant recognition of the seeming sea-captain, the spy knew that the latter was actually the fugitive noble. He also realized that Enzo and Laura still loved one another; and he determined to take advantage of these facts.

When the Inquisitor and his wife had departed on their way,

he followed Enzo and, addressing him by his full name, declared with cleverly assumed friendliness that he knew his story. He then promised to bring Laura on board Enzo's vessel that evening —and thus they might elope in safety.

Full of joy, Enzo hurried away to his ship, believing that his pretended new friend desired him out of the way that he, Barnaba, might himself stand more chance with Gioconda. Enzo knew that the charming ballad-singer loved him; but he had been embarrassed by this knowledge, because of his own continued passion for Laura.

But the sinister spy had no intention of letting the lovers get away so easily. He now approached the scribe and dictated a letter to the Lord Inquisitor, Alvise, informing him that his wife intended to elope that evening by ship with a lover, adding that the latter was the proscribed Prince of Santa Fior. When this letter of betrayal was written, he folded it and dropped it into the Lion's Mouth receptacle.

But Barnaba did not know that the dictation of this letter had been overheard by Gioconda, as she came out of the church. Always suspicious of the spy's actions, she had slipped behind a pillar near by and listened to what passed between him and the scribe. Though she did not catch the name of Laura, she heard enough to realize that Enzo loved another woman and was about to leave the city with the latter that night. At first she was full of woe on thus learning that her own love was not returned. Then jealousy seized her, and she determined to challenge her rival and to board Enzo's ship herself.

As the proscribed noble's brigantine lay in the lagoon that night, awaiting orders to sail, a small boat, rowed by Barnaba, came alongside. In it sat the Lady Laura, wrapped closely in a dark cloak and hood. Having helped his victim safely on board, the spy rowed back to a waiting galley, well pleased with his vile plot. Unknown to him, however, another small boat was hovering about the brigantine; and from this La Gioconda had just climbed aboard and hidden in the shadows.

After a rapturous meeting between the lovers, Enzo went below to give final instructions about sailing; and Laura knelt before a little shrine of the Virgin, set up on the deck, to pray for divine protection in their hazardous adventure.

Then, hearing steps behind her, she rose quickly and wrapped her cloak more closely about her once more, hiding her face. Gioconda now hastened forward and poured forth bitter words of reproach upon her rival for having, as she believed, stolen the heart of her beloved Enzo. She was even about to stab her, when she saw that a State galley was approaching and stayed her hand.

In terror, Laura beheld her husband, Alvise, in the galley with Barnaba and the Inquisitor guards; and once more, fearing that all was lost, she knelt before the shrine and prayed to the Virgin for help. Her sudden action caused her cloak to slip back, so that her face was fully revealed; and at the same time, she held up a rosary—the rosary given her by La Cieca earlier in the day.

Instantly Gioconda realized that her fair rival was the noble lady who had interceded for her mother's life; and her jealousy vanished, gratitude only remaining. Quickly she dragged the despairing Laura to the other side of the vessel, where the small boat in which she had herself arrived—manned by a couple of her fisherman friends—still awaited her own return. Into this she helped her trembling rival to drop safely, and ordered her friends to make quickly for the shore.

When Barnaba presently boarded the brigantine, therefore, he found that Laura had escaped; and returning instantly to the galley with this news, he and the furious Alvise began to chase the little rowing-boat.

Meanwhile, Enzo, warned of the approaching galley, had rushed on deck, distracted. To his amazement, he was now met by Gioconda, with the news that she had helped Laura to escape. The unhappy ballad-singer then could not refrain from pouring out reproaches upon Enzo for not accepting her own devoted love. In the midst of her passionate outburst, however, more State galleys were seen to be drawing near, obviously to capture the proscribed noble.

All else was now forgotten in this moment of extreme danger; and Enzo boldly decided to set his ship on fire, rather than submit to capture. He gave instructions to this effect, and bade his men save their own lives. Then, frantically lowering one of the small boats, he and Gioconda managed to escape from the blazing vessel and to make their way back to Venice.

.   .   .   .

Although the unhappy Laura had made a safe escape from the brigantine, she was soon recaptured by her powerful Inquisitor husband and taken back to his palace.

Furious that she had been about to besmirch his honoured name, he announced to Laura that she must expiate her sin by death. With callous cruelty, he caused a magnificent bier to be set up in her chamber; and then he handed to her a vial of poison strong enough to cause instant death. Some passing gondoliers happened to be singing a charming serenade; and he commanded his trembling wife to listen to this music. By the time the serenade came to an end, she must have swallowed the poison. Having delivered himself of this cold-blooded command and waited until his despairing wife had mounted the bier and taken the vial of poison in her hand, the vengeful Inquisitor left her to die alone.

But help was at hand for the beautiful Laura. Gioconda, having landed safely in the city, had soon learned of the latter's capture; and, fearing for her fate, she had managed to conceal herself in the palace. She now entered the captive's chamber and swiftly exchanged the poison for a strong narcotic drug which would cause a deep sleep only—but so deep a trance-like sleep that it would seem like actual death for a few hours.

She made Laura swallow the narcotic, which caused her almost instantly to fall back upon the bier in a deathly trance; and then she departed to conceal herself once more.

When Alvise presently returned, therefore, at the finish of the gondolier's serenade, he believed that Laura was indeed dead—being confirmed in his belief by the fact that Gioconda had taken the precaution to leave the empty poison vial beside the bier, after pouring its deadly contents away.

. . . .

Later that evening, Alvise gave a grand banquet and entertainment to his aristocratic friends. The entertainment was a lavish one. Exquisite dancers performed a marvellous symbolic dance, in which they appeared as the Hours of the Day and Night, and, by their graceful movements, expressed the constant warfare between Light and Darkness, Good and Evil. But though the guests were amazed by the beauty of this performance, they were soon plunged into a shuddering gloom.

Unseen by the host, Enzo, La Gioconda, and La Cieca had entered in disguise and mingled with the guests, hoping to learn something of the fate of Laura.

La Cieca's presence was discovered first; and on being dragged forward by Barnaba, she declared that she had come to pray for the dead Laura. At the same moment, a passing bell was tolled; and the horrified guests now learned from the stern Inquisitor that he had caused his erring wife to take her own life. He drew back a curtain as he spoke, and revealed the motionless form of Laura lying upon her bier.

Knowing nothing of Gioconda's exchange of the vials, Enzo was plunged into frantic despair on thus beholding his beloved Laura lying dead, as he supposed; and, knowing this to be the

work of her vengeful husband, he drew his dagger and rushed
furiously upon Alvise. He was, however, quickly seized by the
guards and carried off by them.

Thus the brilliant scene ended in tragic gloom.

.   .   .   .   .   .

In a ruined ancient palace, La Gioconda had her secret abode.
Here, late that same night, towards dawn, two poorly-clad men
carried the unconscious form of Laura into the ballad-singer's
room. La Gioconda had many friends among the poor; and these
two, at her request, had willingly performed this task for her.
They had crept into the vault where Laura had been laid and had
stolen her away.

Gioconda well understood the power of her own beauty. By
means of it, when Enzo had been captured, she had persuaded
Barnaba—who had been placed in charge of him—to release his
captive. To secure his consent, she had promised, in desperation,
to give herself that night to the spy. She now expected Enzo to
appear any moment.

But she was anxious about her mother, who had also been
captured; and she implored the men who had borne Laura to her
abode to return and seek out La Cieca. No sooner had the men
departed, than Enzo, still in a distracted state, rushed into the
room.

Seeing Laura's motionless form now lying in La Gioconda's
abode and still thinking her dead, he wildly accused the ballad-
singer of having brought about this tragedy. He drew his dagger
and was about to stab her when, suddenly, he heard his name
called softly from the shrouded figure. It was Laura awakening
from her trance-like sleep; and next moment the lovers were
clasped joyfully in each other's arms.

But Gioconda soon bade them be up and doing. She had
arranged for their escape. Two of her gondolier friends were
already waiting to transport them to a swift vessel in the lagoon,
whence they could escape to a place of safety.

Scarcely had the lovers departed with the gondoliers, than the
spy, Barnaba, appeared. He had come to claim his reward. To
his satisfaction, Gioconda declared that she wished to adorn herself for his greater pleasure and to enhance her beauty. She began
to take out from a trinket-box long strings of beads and bracelets
and necklaces of imitation jewels, and to deck herself with them;
but, in doing so, she managed also, unseen, to seize the dagger
which Enzo, in his haste, had dropped on the table.

Gioconda had now determined to die rather than accept Barnaba
as her lover; and when the spy, impatient of further delay, now

moved forward as though to clasp her in his arms, she plunged
the dagger into her heart.

Enraged by having thus been tricked, the spy bent over her
prostrate form and gloatingly hissed into her ears the terrible news
that he had already strangled La Cieca, her mother. But he was
cheated even of this final triumph. His words fell upon unheeding ears. La Gioconda was dead.

LA BOHÈME   *Puccini*
(*The Bohemians—Based on Murger's* La Vie de Bohème)

WHEN Louis Philippe, the Citizen King of the French, was vainly
attempting to retain his seat upon a tottering throne, two young
students might have been seen one cold Christmas Eve at work in
an attic in the Latin Quarter of Paris. They were Marcel, a
painter, and Rudolph, a poet; two carelessly light-hearted young
men who, together with their friends, Schaunard and Colline—
the former a musician and the latter a philosopher—loved to
regard themselves as great artists whom a cold and unappreciative
world had as yet failed to recognize.

Full of buoyant spirits, daring, reckless, and happy-go-lucky,
these four students seemed to pass a charmed existence; a life
which, though full of ups and downs, of joy and sorrow, they
would not have exchanged for any other, being true Bohemians
at heart, over whom the intoxicating atmosphere of the Latin
Quarter had cast its spell of enchantment. Extravagant to the
last degree, they spent their money lavishly when Fortune smiled
upon them, feasting like lords, indulging their sweethearts,
snatching at every joy within their reach, reckless of the morrow.
Then, when rainy days came quickly once more, they cheerfully
returned to work again, no whit dismayed but only eager to
retrieve their fallen fortunes. Nothing could damp the ardour of
their spirits.

Thus it was with Rudolph and Marcel on this Christmas Eve.
Though their fortunes at that moment were at the lowest ebb and
they knew not whence their next meal would come, yet were they
merry and light-hearted, as though the fickle goddess had never
ceased to smile. There was no fire in the grate and their fingers
were so cold that they could neither paint nor write any longer;
so Rudolph triumphantly brought forth the manuscript of an

immature drama with which he had once hoped to astonish the world and proceeded to use it as fuel in the empty grate, declaring gaily that its " pungent wit " and " sparkling dialogue " should give them warmth—even though the world would have to bear the loss as best it could. Page by page, and act by act, the " masterpiece " was recklessly set alight; and as the two friends drew up their chairs and eagerly warmed their hands at the grateful blaze, they laughingly bade one another observe the " dazzling sparks of wit " that flashed from the dusty pages!

While they were thus engaged, Colline the philosopher entered with an armful of musty volumes of the classics for which he mournfully announced no pawnbroker in Paris would give him even a single franc. Seeing the cheerfully blazing fire, however, he ran towards it with joy, helping to feed its greedy flames and hailing Rudolph as the noble benefactor of his freezing friends.

Just as the last few pages were burning, however, there came a pleasant interruption. Schaunard the musician entered, followed by a couple of serving boys, the one carrying abundant fuel and the other laden with rich provisions of all kinds. Their musical companion had just had a happy and unexpected windfall which, with the usual generosity of the Latin Quarter, he was anxious to share with his friends; and next moment, having spread the table to their satisfaction, the four friends sat down to enjoy this timely feast, joyously drinking one another's health and seasoning every dish with laughter and good fellowship.

When their hilarity was at its height, there came a second interruption—an unpleasant one, this time. Their long-suffering landlord appeared with a demand for his overdue rent. But even such a cold douche as this could not damp the high spirits of the students, whose ready wits soon devised a means for dealing with the situation. They hailed the unwanted visitor as though with delight, inviting him to sit down and feast with them; and they plied him with copious draughts of wine and begged him to relate to them the stories of his own giddy youth as a " gay dog ". Then, when he had become half-tipsy and they had led him on to absurd lengths, the wily students suddenly pretended to be highly shocked by his improper stories; and declaring that one so debauched was not fit to breathe the same air with themselves, they seized the braggart and laughingly bundled him out of the room—knowing that they were safe from his unwelcome presence for a few hours, at least.

The four friends now decided that it was folly to remain indoors when Christmas Eve gaieties were afoot without; and Schaunard suggested that they should go forth to spend what remained of his windfall, concluding with a late supper at the Café Momus—one of their favourite haunts when in funds.

Having divided the money equally between them, they set off in high good humour to spend it—with the exception of Rudolph, who remained behind to finish a poem, promising to join his companions later on.

When his three friends had noisily departed, Rudolph brought a candle nearer to his work and tried to finish his poem; but scarcely had he written a few words than he heard a timid knock at the door. On opening it, he was amazed to see a poorly-clad but lovely young girl standing there, holding a key in one hand and an extinguished candle in the other. Her beauty was of that ethereal, refined and exquisitely delicate quality that particularly appeals to the sensitive poetic mind; and as Rudolph gazed upon the young girl's velvety pale skin, slight graceful form, soft dreamy eyes and tiny white hands, a wave of joy flooded his artistic soul at the mere sight of one so fair and yet so frail.

So fragile, indeed, was the young girl that the effort of climbing the stairs had completely exhausted her and brought on a violent fit of coughing; and scarcely had she explained that she had called to beg a light for her candle than she was seized with sudden faintness and would have fallen to the ground had not Rudolph caught her in his arms.

Quickly placing his visitor in a chair, the young student soon revived her with some wine, watching her the while with increasing interest and a strange joy, which he felt instinctively was reciprocated; for when the fair girl opened her eyes fully, she looked upon him with the sweet shy glances of newly-born passion.

Having recovered from her faintness, however, she arose at once and asked again for her candle to be lighted; and when Rudolph had performed this small office for her—trembling with emotion as he placed the light in the tiny hand which seemed to him one of her greatest charms—she bade him farewell and opened the door. Then, remembering her key, which she had dropped when seized with faintness, she turned to look for it; and in so doing the draught from the door blew out the candle once more. At the same moment, Rudolph's candle was also extinguished, so that the room was plunged in darkness; and the young student, moved by a sudden impulse, slipped round to the door and fastened it.

Both were now groping in the darkness, the girl seeking her key—which Rudolph presently found and put in his own pocket, still making no effort to get another light; for he was filled with a sudden fear that this sweet young creature would shortly leave him and he longed above all things to prolong her stay. They talked to each other in a happy way as they continued the search in the dark; and presently, Rudolph, guided by his visitor's soft voice, came closer to her side and caught her little thin hand in his. Thrilled by her touch, the young student could no longer restrain the passion that now filled his heart with such exquisite joy; and, folding her in his arms, he poured forth an eager declaration of his love, to which, to his delight, the young girl as gladly responded.

Having presently lighted one of the candles, Rudolph described his own life and occupation and questioned his companion as to hers; and the girl informed him that her name was Mimi and that she worked fine embroideries for a living.

While they were still talking happily together, the voices of Marcel, Colline, and Schaunard were heard outside, calling loudly upon their friend to come and join them in their pleasure-seeking —to which Rudolph, upset by the interruption, returned an impatient answer; but Mimi, thus learning that he had gaiety afoot, suggested that she should go with him that they might pass the evening together. Rudolph, overjoyed that she was thus willing to acknowledge him as her accepted lover, gladly made ready to go out; and, hand locked in hand, the pair went forth joyously to join in the merry-making of Christmas Eve.

.   .   .   .

Rudolph and Mimi soon reached an open square, at one side of which was the Café Momus, the favourite meeting-place of the Latin Quarter; and here they were joined by the other three students, who received Mimi with a hearty welcome.

The square presented a lively scene and was filled with a merry crowd of students, artists, work-girls, and children with their parents, all bargaining at the brilliantly-lighted shops and open stalls and bent on holiday enjoyment. Rudolph, seeing in one of the shops a pretty bonnet trimmed with pink roses, went in with Mimi to buy it for her, quite regardless of the fact that its price swallowed all his share of Schaunard's windfall; and when the delighted Mimi had placed this fascinating " creation " upon her dainty head, they went to join their companions at the Café Momus for supper.

Finding the café crowded within, the friends seated themselves with Mimi at a table outside, whence they could the better observe the amusing scene taking place in the square; and having ordered an extravagant supper, they began to enjoy themselves with their usual careless abandon.

As they sat there, an extremely pretty, coquettish and smartly-dressed girl approached the café, accompanied by a fussy old gentleman, with whom she presently sat down at an outside supper-table a few yards farther along; and at the sight of the newcomer, Marcel turned pale and began to fidget nervously in his chair. This aggravatingly pretty young woman was Musetta, a former sweetheart of Marcel's with whom he had quarrelled some time past and who had, in pique, quickly found a new admirer. These two really loved one another, but their quarrels and separations were frequent; for Musetta was a born coquette, and also having a passion for fine clothes and luxuries such as Marcel seldom was able to provide for her, she would occasionally desert him for an adorer more richly endowed with the means for satisfying her extravagant requirements. Her latest conquest was this fussy old noble, Alcindoro de Mitonneaux, who had been so flattered by the pretty girl's attentions—bestowed on him while maddened by Marcel's conduct—that, still considering himself to be something of a beau, he had allowed her to twist him round her clever little finger with ease and to drag from him much of his carefully hoarded wealth.

Thus it came about that Musetta was gorgeously attired and filled with elation by the obvious effect her finery made upon all who knew her amongst the Christmas crowd. Upon observing Marcel sitting near by, however, she eagerly endeavoured to attract his attention—for the mere sight of the man she truly loved made her dissatisfied with her present uninteresting elderly cavalier, of whom she had already tired.

But Marcel at first refused to heed the languishing looks and inviting gestures of the coquettish Musetta, despite the fact that he still passionately adored her; so Musetta resorted to a saucy trick to gain her ends. Presently seeing that Marcel was about to capitulate, she took off one of her shoes, pretending that it hurt her; and thrusting this into the hands of her elderly admirer, she imperiously bade him take it to a boot shop in an adjacent street and bring her a pair of shoes one size larger. Then, when the fussy old gentleman had departed—much against his will, but not daring to refuse his skittish charmer's requests—Musetta and Marcel rose simultaneously; and next moment they were clasped in each other's arms.

Whilst the reunited lovers were rejoicing together, a stirring sound of military music was heard as a patrol of soldiers in gorgeous uniforms marched by to attend a tattoo; and most of the merry-makers outside the café hurried away to see the show. The students decided to join this merry throng; but having by this time no money left to pay for their luxurious supper, they were in a quandary. Musetta, however, soon solved this little matter by placing their bill on her table and informing the waiter that old Alcindoro would pay for it along with his own.

Hailing this manœuvre with hilarious laughter, the four student friends, with Musetta and Mimi in their midst, ran off gaily to watch the tattoo—Marcel and Colline carrying Musetta between them, for, having but one shoe, she could not walk.

. . . .

As time went on, the student friends had many more ups and downs in their love affairs as well as in their finances, squabbling and making it up again from week to week.

Marcel and Musetta passed some months happily together, for, though the coquettish girl still took every opportunity for a flirtation with anyone who might happen to admire her, yet she really loved Marcel only. But she would not be tyrannized over, for her high spirit could ill brook restraint; and if Marcel showed signs of wishing to curb her inordinate love of fine clothes and admiration, she quickly resented it. The two, however, on the whole fared better than Rudolph and Mimi, who, in spite of their passionate love, yet spent a miserable existence together.

Rudolph's love was of that all-absorbing and madly jealous nature which caused him to be for ever imagining and fostering suspicion of the object of his affection; not even a glance or a word could he bear Mimi to bestow elsewhere. Consequently, their life together was spent in a constant state of misunderstandings. Though they might be deliriously happy one day, they would often suffer for this by many weeks of misery. Often they were on the point of separating for ever; and, indeed, at last they finally agreed to this.

At the time when Mimi, after a great mental struggle, came to this resolution, she had been avoided by Rudolph for some little time; and having learnt that he had joined Marcel at an inn near the Gate of Customs, she made her way there one cold and wintry morning.

As she waited outside the inn for Marcel, to whom she had sent a message asking him to help her with her resolve, she was seized with a violent fit of coughing; for of late the wasting disease to which she had always been inclined had developed with alarming rapidity, and her frail form was constantly shaken by a racking cough.

When Marcel presently appeared, he was shocked on observing her wasted looks and anxiously tried to draw her into the inn; but **Mimi refused to enter for fear of meeting with Rudolph. She** then told him of her strained relations with the latter and implored him to assist in their final parting.

While they were speaking of this, Rudolph himself appeared in the doorway of the inn; and fearing to meet him just then, Mimi slipped behind a group of plane trees as he approached. As it happened, Rudolph spoke to his friend likewise about his estranged relations with Mimi, declaring, however, that his jealousy was always groundless, being caused only by his passionate love. He then spoke of his deep anxiety regarding Mimi's frail health, adding that her feverish condition filled him with despair as the herald of an early death. The hapless Mimi could not fail to overhear this conversation; and now realizing for the first time of the doom that awaited her, she was so overcome with woe that her sobs quickly made her presence known to her lover.

In a moment Rudolph was at her side with tender words of comfort. Yet another reconciliation took place; and the lovers entered upon a new cycle of delirious joy. But this happy phase, like the many others that had preceded it, also quickly came to an end; and the separation that ensued was the longest they had yet endured. At this time, also, Marcel and Musetta had experienced one of their most serious squabbling periods, owing again to the latter's incorrigible flirtatious tendency; and they likewise kept apart for many weeks.

Rudolph and Marcel, therefore, both thus deprived of their loved ones, joined their student friends once more, endeavouring to heal their sore hearts in a renewed pursuit of art. But neither could forget the joy that had been theirs; and one day as they sat working together in the same old attic in which pretty Mimi had first introduced herself, the thoughts of both returned to the days of their happy love. Every now and again, Marcel would press to his lips a bunch of bright ribbons that once had belonged to Musetta; and Rudolph, when he thought himself unobserved by his friend, would take from a drawer beside him the little rose-trimmed bonnet Mimi had left him as a keepsake and tenderly caress it.

Though it was now many months since parting, the students had seen the girls from time to time and, observing that they were richly clad, knew that they had found new admirers. The pair remarked on this now as they sat at work, making a sorry pretence of not caring about the circumstance—which, however, revived all the pain in their hearts. But this attempt at mutual comfort was a sorry failure; and they gladly hailed the arrival of Colline and Schaunard, who brought with them a very meagre meal, consisting of four small rolls and a herring. For the friends were just at that time going through one of their frequent penniless periods. With their usual careless good-humour, however, they sat down to the scanty food with us much hilarity as though it had been a feast of the highest order, gaily inviting one another to imagine that the crusts were dainty dishes and pledging one another in water as though it had been good wine.

While they were thus making merry, the door was suddenly opened; and, to the astonishment of all, Musetta entered, wearing an anxious face and appearing much agitated. In answer to the eager questions poured upon her, she announced that Mimi was without, but was too weak and exhausted to mount the stairs— being, in fact, in a dying condition. Upon hearing that his beloved one was so near, Rudolph hastened to her assistance; and, with the help of his friends, he soon brought her into the room and laid her tenderly upon the bed.

Mimi and Rudolph embraced one another passionately; and while they were thus absorbed in their joyful reunion, Musetta related to the others the reason for their sudden visitation. Having heard that Mimi had left her rich admirer and was now lying ill in the last stages of consumption, she had hastened to her side; and upon the exhausted girl expressing a passionate desire to see Rudolph once more before her death, she had undertaken to bring her to him and, by half carrying her, had succeeded in this difficult enterprise. Having no suitable food or cordials with which to revive the fainting girl, and no money available for either, Colline and Schaunard presently left the room with an overcoat which they meant to pawn.

Mimi presently motioned Marcel to her side and, placing Musetta's hand in his, begged the pair to be reconciled once more, for her sake; and she was filled with joy when they embraced and declared that they still loved one another dearly.

Then Musetta, anxious to leave the dying girl alone with her lover, that they might have a last happy talk together, took Marcel away with her to fetch Mimi's little muff which she had asked for, being unable to keep her hands warm. So Mimi lay happily in Rudolph's arms and told him again and again that her love for him had never changed; and the young student, overjoyed on thus learning that he was still beloved by the being he himself adored, declared passionately that they would never again be parted—in his gladness failing to realize that his beloved one's little spark of life was even now almost extinguished.

Schaunard and Colline presently returned with food and a cordial they had bought with the money obtained by pawning the coat, saying that a doctor would shortly arrive; and soon afterwards Marcel and Musetta also appeared with the little muff they had gone for.

Mimi placed her tiny hands in the muff with childish pleasure; and presently murmuring that she now felt quite warm, she closed her eyes and seemed to fall asleep.

Rudolph then gently moved away and questioned his friends in a low voice as to when the Doctor would arrive; but when Musetta approached the bed with the cordial she had poured out, she saw to her sorrow that Mimi was already dead.

Hearing her exclamation of consternation, Rudolph ran back and took Mimi's cold little hand in his; then, gradually realizing the sad truth, he uttered a cry of anguish and sank, overcome with grief and despair, beside her lifeless form.

THE CLOAK   *Puccini*
(*Il Tabarro*)

AT a bend of the river Seine, a barge lay at anchor, with a gang-plank thrown from its deck to the wharf. It was a large, strongly-built, well-kept barge; and the longshore men and stevedores had been busily engaged unloading the hold all day. The cabin looked pretty and well tended with its bright green painted window-ledges and the pots of gay scarlet geraniums that stood on the roof. Newly-washed clothes were hanging out on the line to dry; and a canary sang in a cage over the cabin door.

It was sunset, and already the river was losing itself in a grey haze, while the panoramic vista of Old Paris—with the awe-inspiring structure of Notre-Dame which so insistently and clearly dominated the scene in the day-time—was quickly becoming dim and mysterious as the twilight shadows lengthened and darkened.

At the tiller on the top of the cabin, Michele the Skipper sat gazing westward, seemingly so lost in wonderment at the beauty of the fading sunset that his long unlighted pipe hung in the corner of his mouth unheeded and unwanted.

But it was not only the awe-inspiring departure of the sun that kept Michele still and silent. He also had dark and disturbing thoughts; and when his pretty young wife, Giorgetta, presently emerged from the cabin, the glance of passionate longing he cast upon her was mingled ever and anon with a smouldering gleam of suppressed anger, this in its turn giving way to a sudden air of gloomy resentment.

Giorgetta, at first unaware of the presence of her husband, took down her clothes from the line, watered her flowers, and fed her canary; then suddenly noticing Michele, she teased him for having been so lost in contemplation of the glorious sunset as to neglect to light his pipe. She next asked if she might bring out wine to refresh the longshore men who had just finished their heavy job and were now coming away from the empty hold; but when Michele, after consenting and commending her kindness of heart, snatched a kiss, she quickly turned her face away to prevent him from repeating the caress.

Disappointed and angry, Michele went down into the hold just as his three assistants came up, weary after their hard work. With the first of the longshore men, a handsome young man named Luigi, Giorgetta exchanged rapid glances of eager understanding as she vanished into the cabin; but when she returned presently with a goodly supply of wine, she was careful to treat the men all alike, bestowing her favours equally on each.

While the men were drinking and wishing good luck to their pretty young hostess, an organ-grinder arrived on the wharf and began to play such lively tunes that Giorgetta declared merrily that she wanted to dance; whereupon Tinca, a clumsy old fellow, seized her and tried to hop about with her in comical fashion.

Giorgetta, however, soon pushed him aside as he trod on her toes; but when Luigi approached, she gladly resigned herself to his eager arms and the pair were soon dancing happily and with perfect rhythm. On the appearance of Michele, a few moments later, they instantly stopped and separated; and Giorgetta began to chat with her husband, who, however, still seemed gloomy and lost in his own thoughts.

A pedlar selling ballads caused another slight diversion; but conversation between the husband and wife remained strained and difficult. When, therefore, Frugola, the wife of one of the men, drew near to exhibit the contents of a bag she had filled with oddments picked up during her day's collecting of thrown-out unwanted articles from door to door, Giorgetta gladly looked at the things and chatted about them, though the two had nothing in common with one another.

When Frugola presently sighed for a little cottage and garden in the country, where she could dwell alone with her husband and her old Angora cat, Giorgetta laughed derisively at such a tame existence; and she declared that her own idea of bliss was to live in a gay town with plenty of friends, gaiety, brightly-lighted shops, life, and love.

Then she and Luigi, who both came from the same district, joined together in their praises of such a life and tenderly recalled their own early days in Belleville, to which town they both longed to return. So transfigured were they in their united recollections, spellbound by the same thought—secretly longing that they were even now in Belleville together—that they remained for a few moments hand in hand, lost to their surroundings. Frugola, suddenly realizing that these two were lovers, hastened to drag her own man off to his supper; and Luigi and Giorgetta were left alone for a few moments.

After a passionate tirade against their enforced separation and the danger of their hastily snatched moments of blissful inter- course, Luigi moved swiftly towards Giorgetta, longing to em- brace her; but the agitated girl implored him to control himself, declaring that her husband would kill them did he suspect their intimacy. Just as the pair separated, Michele appeared and suspiciously expressed surprise that Luigi had not already departed with the other men. In reply to this, the young man, controlling himself with difficulty, said he had waited to ask the Master of the barge if he would take him on board on his next day's journey and let him land at Rouen to seek work. Michele, how- ever, laughed disagreeably on hearing this, declaring that there was but little or no work to be secured in Rouen; and when he had again moved away to light up the lantern for the night, it being now almost dark, the lovers once more stole a few ecstatic moments together, reiterating their undying love and railing at the unhappy fate that kept them apart. They then arranged to meet an hour or two later in the darkest part of the boat away from the lanterns, according to their recent secret custom. Michele would then have retired to rest; and Giorgetta promised to leave the gang-plank down and to strike a match as the signal of safety. After this, the lovers embraced passionately, and Luigi stepped on to the wharf and was soon lost in the shadows.

Giorgetta remained alone for a short time, in sad contemplation; but presently she was joined by her husband, who suggested that it was time for her to retire to bed. When Giorgetta declared that she could not sleep on the stuffy barge and that she hated this dull life on the river, Michele gently reminded her that but a short year ago she had seemed perfectly contented there with him and their infant son who was now dead. Inflamed by his recollections of that happy time and heedless of Giorgetta's pained gesture at the mention of her dead babe, Michele went on to describe the joy it had been to him to wrap his cloak around the three of them in the evening twilight and to clasp them in one loving embrace. Then, suddenly remembering her present coldness to him, he implored her eagerly to return his own still passionate love once more.

Giorgetta, however, scarcely able to bear his presence now that she loved another, broke away from his proffered embrace and, declaring that she was weary, announced her intention of retiring to bed. As she went, Michele, furious at her rebuff, and taking this as a confirmation of his suspicions of the last few weeks, muttered beneath his breath a term of vile opprobrium. Unknown to the lovers, he had discovered their secret and suspected their clandestine meetings; and, still loving his wife passionately, he could control his raging jealousy no longer and was now determined to wreak his vengeance upon the man who had destroyed his happiness.

As he sat in the darkness near the gang-plank, a feeling of despair came upon him and he was tempted to end his misery by flinging himself into the river; then, regaining control of himself, he mechanically felt in his pocket for his pipe and as mechanically struck a match to light it.

As the tiny light flared, a man crept stealthily across the gang-plank and dropped silently into the boat. This was Luigi, who had mistaken the match light as the signal which Giorgetta was to give him. Instantly, Michele leapt upon him; and realizing that his enemy had been providentially delivered into his hands, he held his throat in a grip like iron. As his victim vainly struggled to escape, Michele furiously forced him to declare his guilty love for Giorgetta. When Luigi, helpless and at his mercy, had gasped out his enforced confession, the outraged husband, in an uncontrollable burst of raging jealousy, increased his vice-like strangling grip upon his rival's throat until the latter ceased to struggle and lay limp in his grasp.

Michele then laid the lifeless form on the bench beside him and covered it over with his dark cloak—that same fatal cloak which had served to enfold his beloved ones to his breast during his ecstatic happiness of a year ago. Then he grimly awaited the coming of Giorgetta, whose voice he now heard calling to him from within the cabin in a tone of alarm.

Next moment, Giorgetta appeared, pale and agitated; and, having heard the sound of scuffling near the gang-plank, she declared in a tone of alarm that she was frightened.

Then, seeing her husband sitting alone, apparently calm and quiet, she controlled herself. Saying she was now no longer frightened, she sat down beside Michele, and made a special effort to please him, in order to dispel his evident distrust of her. She asked him to forgive her for having refused his caresses before retiring; and then, as though to make amends, she suggested coquettishly that she should sit as close to him as even he could desire. When Michele, in a strange suppressed tone, asked if she was now willing to sit under his cloak as in the happy days gone by, she replied tremblingly that she was. Then, thinking to please him further, she added that he had always told her a man needed to carry a big cloak in which to hide sometimes a wonderful joy and sometimes a deep sorrow.

Then Michele, triumphant because of the fearful vengeance he had taken, declared wildly that sometimes a man's cloak might also hide a murderous crime; and rising, he flung aside the dark cloth beside him and revealed Luigi's dead body, which now fell heavily at the feet of the agitated girl.

With a shriek of horror, Giorgetta started back, and would have fled away in terror and with despair in her heart; but Michele, in a fury of passion, rushed upon her and flung her violently down into the limply extended arms of her dead lover.

GIANNI SCHICCHI   *Puccini*

WHEN Buoso Donati, a wealthy old miser of Florence, was attacked by his last illness during the year 1299, he was quickly surrounded in his comfortable mansion by obsequious relatives —all solicitous of administering to his comfort and anxious to impress him with their own worthiness and deserving need. True, they had not troubled much with him in the immediate past; but rumours having gone forth of the considerable riches he had amassed during the course of a miserly life, they felt it was prudent to be with him at the end, hoping in the short time at their disposal to secure goodly mention of themselves in his will.

On the morning when the old man had breathed his last, there-fore—the end having come rather more suddenly than had been expected and before his doctor could again be summoned—they draped his corpse with a crimson cloth and, falling upon their knees, began to pray aloud for his departed soul. They gave vent to extremely forced ostentatious moans and sobs of mourning, in the hope of impressing one another with their simulated grief.

They were a strangely assorted company, old and young, some fairly well-to-do and others obviously poor. The principal relatives of the dead man were his cousin, Zita, an avaricious old woman, whose nephew, Rinuccio, a handsome young man, was also present; Simone, the oldest relative and the most important, having been town sheriff all the year; and a nephew, Gherardo, who had brought his little son, Gherardino, with him. There was also present another cousin, Betto, who came from Signa, and who was so poor and so shabbily clothed that the others looked upon him disdainfully and left him somewhat isolated.

The little boy, Gherardino, totally uninterested in the mournful proceedings, amused himself by playing marbles in a corner of the room. He made himself such a nuisance to the others, however, by bumping into the kneeling figures as he chased his rolling playthings, that he was at last pushed out of the room by his irritated father.

Despite the pretended grief and prayerfulness of the mourners, their thoughts were obviously preoccupied with more mundane matters; and presently, the shabbily-clad Betto attracted the reluctant attention of first one of the more important relatives and then another by whispering of a sinister rumour he had heard to be current in Signa. This rumour was to the effect that old Buoso was believed to have made a will bequeathing all his money and possessions to the Church.

As the adverse significance of such a will to their own interests dawned upon the mourners, they gradually rose to their feet, full of indignation and quite forgetful of their prayers. Simone—to whom they appealed as the eldest and most important—suggested that if Buoso's will had not yet been filed in the town hall, it was probably still in the room in which they were assembled. If so, and they could lay hands upon it, they could prove for themselves the truth of this disturbing rumour.

Immediately, a feverish search for the will began, every drawer, chest, and cupboard being ruthlessly turned inside out. Old Betto did not hesitate to profit by this sudden confusion. Being thrust disdainfully on one side by all, he presently noticed beside him a table on which lay a handsome silver tray bearing a silver seal and silver scissors; and these articles of value, by various furtive manœuvres, he managed to conceal about his person unobserved by the will hunters.

After several false alarms, young Rinuccio, the good-looking nephew of Zita, at last found the fateful document; and holding the parchment aloft, he began to strike a bargain with his aunt before delivering it up. He demanded that, should the will make them all suddenly rich, he should be permitted to wed his sweetheart, Lauretta, the fair daughter of a stranger peasant named Gianni Schicchi—a request hitherto uncompromisingly vetoed by the avaricious old woman, who desired her nephew to make a more advantageous match. In the stress of the present excitement, however, she announced her willingness for him to marry even a witch should the will prove to be in their favour; and Rinuccio, well pleased with his bargain, handed over the parchment to Zita.

All the relatives crowded around the old woman, eager to learn its contents. Upon Simone reading out at the beginning the hopeful words.: " To my dear cousins, Zita and Simone ", the latter was so filled with joyful anticipation as to what was likely to follow that, in an impulse of gratitude, he immediately lighted the three large candles which had been set in readiness near the deathbed but which no one had yet thought it necessary to burn.

He then returned to join in reading the will; and presently, the hopeful looks of pleasing anticipation gradually died out of the faces of the company as they read on and proved for themselves that the horrid rumour heard in Signa by Betto was true. The miser, Buoso Donati, had indeed bequeathed the whole of his money and property to the Church, and nothing had been left to themselves!

Full of indignation and disgust, old Simone, as a sign of protest, savagely extinguished the three candles he had just lighted; and the disappointed relatives flopped down disconsolately in various parts of the room, several of them now weeping real tears.

As they poured forth wrathful abuse upon the dead man and lacerated themselves by thinking of the benefits about to be reaped by monks and priests instead of by themselves, young Rinuccio suddenly sprang to his feet. He announced that there was but one man who could help them with advice in their present dilemma and who could possibly devise a means by which the miser's hoards might yet enter their pockets—Gianni Schicchi, the father of his own beloved sweetheart, Lauretta.

At first Zita angrily declared that she would never permit the threshold to be crossed by a mere peasant who was believed to have come into Florence from the backwoods, adding again that his daughter was certainly not a fit mate for a member of the Donati family; and the others endorsed her opinion. But Rinuccio averred stoutly that they were all wrong to be so snobbish; and he added that Gianni Schicchi was a bright and witty fellow who, despite his humble birth, was well acquainted with the law and knew better how to circumvent the lawyers than anyone in Florence. At last, the downcast relatives, grasping at any straw of comfort in their present need, were about to give their consent when Gianni Schicchi himself arrived at the door, accompanied by his pretty daughter—the sly Rinuccio having already sent the little boy Gherardino to fetch them a few moments earlier.

The relatives, seeing that it was now too late to make further fuss about the matter, bade Rinuccio call in his friends; and Gianni Schicchi and Lauretta entered the room together.

As Lauretta ran to the side of her lover, her father—a merry fellow whose good humour and air of authority at once inspired confidence—quickly overcame the antagonism of the relatives as he inquired into the cause of their disconsolate looks.

The still suspicious Zita, however, endeavoured to drag her nephew away from the side of his sweetheart, declaring again that a match between them was more out of the question than ever now that there was no inheritance for the youth under Buoso's will and since Lauretta, also, had no dowry. On hearing this, Gianni's brow darkened; and he prepared to depart immediately without giving the benefit of his valuable advice to the company.

When, however, his pretty daughter flung herself upon her knees and implored him not to part her from her beloved Rinuccio but, instead, to find some way out of the difficulty, declaring that otherwise she would certainly throw herself into the river, he could not resist the appeal of one he loved so well; and he demanded to be shown the will, which was at once handed to him.

As Gianni Schicchi tramped up and down the room, scanning the document, the relatives, now full of hope once more, eagerly followed him about like hungry chickens waiting for crumbs. Presently a bright and humorous idea occurred to him whereby he could mete out a quaint justice to the greedy and hypocritical mourners and at the same time secure a dowry and consequent happiness for his beloved daughter.

He first of all dismissed Lauretta to feed the birds upon the balcony; and then he set to work to carry out his plan. Having learnt that no one outside the house—not even the Doctor—yet knew of the actual demise of Donati, he ordered the male relatives to remove the body of the old miser into another room for the time being, at the same time directing the women to make the bed afresh and to bring forth a bedgown and nightcap for himself. Then, after despatching Rinuccio to fetch a notary at once, he declared that he would impersonate Buoso Donati as being in a dying condition and thus make a fresh will by which they should all benefit.

Full of joy, the unscrupulous relatives eagerly agreed to the plan. After destroying the unwanted document, the wily Schicchi further secured their absolute silence and obedience to his commands regarding the trick by informing them of the severe penalties the law provided for those who falsified or connived at the falsification of a will—the loss of the right hand, the confiscation of all belongings, and banishment from their beautiful Florence.

As the now jubilant mourners proceeded to dress their new friend in the night garments of old Buoso, they showered praises and flatteries upon him; and each one managed to whisper a special request to be given certain property or goods over and above the bequests to the others, promising him substantial rewards for such favours. Besides the farm-lands, bonds, and cash in hand, which it was agreed should be divided in equal proportions among them, the remaining rich bequests—the comfortable mansion, the finest and most valuable mule in Tuscany, and the prosperous saw-mills at Signa—could not well be divided, though they might be shared. Noting how each relative, filled with eager cupidity, desired to get the better of the other and how they were already squabbling among themselves for these extra " plums " of the will, Schicchi, while seeming to agree to the whispered requests and proposed bribes of all, arranged secretly within his own mind an excellent way of solving this difficulty.

While the conspirators were thus settling their plans, they received two bad shocks which considerably upset their nerves. The first of these was the untimely arrival of the Doctor, who called to inquire after his patient, not having yet learnt of the latter's death during the early hours of the morning.

All were filled with dismay; but Gianni Schicchi, equal to the occasion, instantly ensconced himself in the great four-poster bed and drew the curtains closely around him. When the Doctor entered the room, he was kept near the door by the scared relatives with the excuse that their beloved Buoso was much better but so tired and worn out that he desired to rest a while undisturbed. This announcement, surprising to the Doctor, who had expected to find his patient worse, if not *in extremis*, was confirmed by the audacious Schicchi who, in weak and quavering tones—exactly imitating the voice of the old miser who had been a well-known character in the town—also begged to be left to rest in peace, but asked the Doctor to call again in the evening.

Having thus got rid of the physician, the relatives were about to breathe calmly once more when they received a further shock by hearing the tolling of the church bell announcing a death—which caused them to imagine that Buoso's demise must have become known in some unforeseen manner. To their relief, however, they soon learnt that this passing bell was being tolled in mourning for the mayor of the town, who had suddenly died of a stroke; and their minds were once more set at rest.

Soon after this, Rinuccio returned with a notary and two witnesses—a shoemaker and a dyer; and Schicchi, still keeping himself well hidden behind the bed-curtains—the room having been further darkened by the drawing of the window draperies—continued his impersonation of Buoso. So cleverly did he imitate the voice of the latter, indeed, that the notary and witnesses, though they had known the old man well, were completely deceived.

The relatives, overjoyed at the renewed prospect of securing the undeserved benefits of a goodly inheritance, clustered together in a deferential group, again simulating a mournful aspect—in order to further deceive the notary—because of the supposed quickly approaching demise of a beloved member of the family; and as the weakly quavering voice from the bed now began to dictate the various clauses of his " last will and testament ", they listened with suppressed excitement.

They were delighted when, to conventionalize the proceedings in the notary's eyes, the first items named proved to be a sum for an extremely modest funeral and a meagre gift of five lire to the monastery which, under the real will, would have benefited at their expense to the extent of the entire estate. And when the next clauses dealt with the equal division of the farm-lands, bonds, and ready cash, as before arranged, they each called out in exaggeratedly grateful tones : " Oh, thank you, thank you! " as their names were mentioned. However, all were waiting with intense but prudently subdued eagerness to hear the final bequests of the valuable property which could not be divided, but which each relative so passionately desired—and for possession of which each had, as he or she hoped, satisfactorily bribed the good-natured impersonator of the pretended " dying " man.

Their hopes, however, were presently frustrated by the astute cleverness of their " friend in need ". He quaveringly dictated that the " best mule in Tuscany " he bequeathed to his " devoted friend, Gianni Schicchi! " Full of amazement and indignant alarm, the listening relatives involuntarily uttered impetuous exclamations and made ominous movements towards the bed. But as the disturbed notary looked up in surprise and disapproval from his laborious Latin scribing, they remembered the final warning of their too clever " friend " and drew back again, awaiting, with great anxiety, the dictating of the next item.

To their horror, the feeble voice from behind the curtains proceeded also to bequeath the comfortable mansion in Florence to " my affectionate and devoted friend, Gianni Schicchi! "

When the angry relatives again now loudly remonstrated against the giving of valuable property to " such an accursed rascal ", the voice of the " dying man "—which now had a most disturbingly exultant ring in it—called upon them querulously to be quiet; and the notary, annoyed by such unseemly wrangling, also bade them not to " disturb the final will of Master Buoso ".

The now furious relatives, compelled to silence by their fears of the notary discovering the law-breaking trick they had been parties to, again controlled themselves with difficulty; and they squirmed painfully and ludicrously as they listened in helpless impotence to the final bequest of the ever prosperous and increasingly valuable saw-mills at Signa dictated by the " dying " man also to his " most devoted friend, Gianni Schicchi ". He added moreover that he commanded Zita to pay from her own purse one hundred florins to the notary and twenty florins to each of the witnesses for their trouble.

While the wrathful company still endeavoured to bottle up their rage a few moments longer, the notary carefully finished inscribing the document in the presence of the witnesses, whose signatures were next added; and then, having bidden a grateful farewell to his " dying client ", he departed with his humble companions.

Their safe departure was the signal for a clamorous and furious onslaught upon the astute " friend in need " by the madly disappointed relatives, who began belabouring him wildly with any weapon they could lay hands upon, calling him the while " Traitor! Robber! Scoundrel! Impostor! "

Gianni Schicchi, however, was a powerful man, as well able to defend himself physically as by his wits. In high good humour that he had thus successfully punished the hypocritical relatives of old Buoso for their brazen avarice and at the same time so cleverly—if unscrupulously—secured a goodly dowry for his pretty daughter to enable her to wed her chosen sweetheart, he laid about him vigorously with old Donati's stout stick which still stood beside the bed; and finally, he drove them off.

The wrathful conspirators, bound to uphold the faked will because of their own complicity in it, at last realized their impotence to prevent Gianni from inheriting the lion's share of the miser's estate. Determined, however, to secure at least a little more than their " friend " had bequeathed to them, they began to loot the room of as many of its valuables as they could grab before being compelled to quit by the triumphant new owner.

The lively Gianni, however, finally turned them all out into the street and locked the door upon them; and then he began to set the room in order once more, well pleased with the excellent success of his roguish plan.

And if he had happened to possess an uneasy conscience in regard to his enterprise—which was certainly far from being the case—it would have been entirely relieved and pacified when presently he beheld upon the balcony outside his pretty Lauretta folded in the arms of her lover, Rinuccio, to whom—being well provided with a handsome dowry by her clever-witted father— she might now be united in a happy marriage. And to what better use, mused the delighted Gianni Schicchi, could the money of old Donati have been put?

THE GIRL OF THE GOLDEN WEST   *Puccini*
(*La Fanciulla del West*)

DURING the period of the gold fever in California, about the middle of the nineteenth century, a flourishing mining camp had been set up at the foot of the Cloudy Mountains. Amidst the rough log-shacks in which the gold-seekers lived was a somewhat larger, but equally rough and ready, building known as the " Polka "—the inevitable miners' tavern and gambling-house, without which no camp was complete.

Here, one afternoon, a company of the miners was gathered, drinking, smoking, and playing cards. Nick, the bar-tender, was kept very busy, constantly serving the " boys "; and though most of the campers were lively enough as they joked and laughed, some of the others were quiet and gloomy. These latter were suffering from a bad attack of home-sickness, which was increased by the arrival of the mail with letters from home.

Presently, a squabble arose among the more rowdy members of the company, because of the conceited boast of one of their number, Rance, the Sheriff, that in a short time he intended to marry Minnie, the beautiful young mistress of the " Polka ", who had continued to run the business after the death of her father. Minnie had been brought up among the miners, who all adored her as their " Girl of the Golden West "; and she cared for them with real affection, ruling over them like a young queen and treating them almost as though they were children. She even held a school class for some of the great rough fellows during the winter months, teaching them what little learning she had herself and endeavouring to make them steady and honest. She also permitted them to keep their precious gold in a barrel at the back of the bar.

As to her favours, however, she treated them all alike, permitting none of them to take liberties with her. When, therefore, the boastful Rance declared that their beloved " Girl " would soon become his wife, the miners were very indignant, knowing his boast to be a vain one.

Into the midst of this hubbub, Minnie herself presently appeared —a very beautiful young woman whose strong and affectionate influence over the miners was instantly apparent in the sudden calm that now ensued. She first of all scolded them roundly for their rowdy conduct during her absence; and then, all smiles again, she graciously accepted from them several little gifts they had brought her and now somewhat sheepishly presented—the one a ribbon, the others a bright scarf, flowers, and various other trifles.

Rance, the Sheriff, who had recently conceived a violent passion for the charming mistress of the tavern, soon found an opportunity for leading her apart from the others, and, boldly declaring his desire for her, begged her to accept him as her future husband. Minnie, however, had always distrusted this man, disliking his boastful manner and an innate cruelty which she felt lurked in his disposition; and coldly keeping him at arms' length, she managed to stave off his advances for the time being.

As she turned away from Rance, a good-looking stranger, giving his name as Dick Johnson, came into the bar for refreshment and rest, looking as though he had had a long and rough ride. Minnie at once recognized in the newcomer a stranger whom she had met once before on a lonely hill-side, on which occasion they had struck up a sudden friendship, being mutually attracted by one another; and though Johnson, who also recognized her, seemed somewhat upset on finding that the " Polka " belonged to her, they were quickly engaged in pleasant conversation.

Rance, who was instantly filled with jealousy on realizing that the pair were acquainted, glowered at them from time to time; and the miners were displeased also, not caring that their beloved " Girl " should be so friendly with a stranger unknown to themselves.

Presently, however, a report was brought in by one of the men that Ramarrez, the leader of a gang of bandits who existed at that time by plundering the various gold-mining camps of California, as well as by highway robbery, was known to be skulking in the district with some of his Mexican " greasers "; and the presence of the newcomer was forgotten in this fresh interest. Full of excitement, the miners all hurried off to round up their common enemy, leaving Minnie in charge of their gold, with only Nick the bar-tender, and Billy Jackrabbit, a faithful friendly Indian, for protection. Johnson, who had kept in the background during the general hubbub of the miners' departure, now came forward and had another happy chat with Minnie, the deep mutual interest of their first meeting strengthening with every word they spoke. Minnie, unable to resist the ready response of her own heart to the eager, unmistakable, and quickly growing passion of the handsome and fascinating stranger, but mindful of the presence of Nick and the Indian, presently whispered an invitation to Johnson to visit her that evening in her own little home on the hill-side where they might talk undisturbed; and soon afterwards the pair separated, already undeclared lovers.

.   .   .   .

Later in the evening, Minnie eagerly awaited the arrival of Johnson in her little hill-side cabin, which consisted of one room only, with a loft above it. Here she was attended by an Indian woman, Wowkle, Billy Jackrabbit's squaw, who prepared the supper with many intervals devoted to the rocking of her papoose, while her happy mistress decked herself in various little bits of finery in honour of the expected guest.

Billy also presently appeared, anxious for her safety because of the bandits; but Minnie, laughing at his fears, managed to get rid of him. When her guest arrived a little later, she also dismissed the squaw, who departed to the abode of her lord with her papoose upon her back.

As Minnie and Johnson talked together, their instant attraction and growing interest in one another quickly developed and ended in a passionate declaration of love; and they were so happy that they became quite oblivious of the time. So absorbed were they that they did not at first notice the rising wind which heralded a storm; but when at length they discovered that a terrific blizzard was raging, Minnie invited her visitor to remain the night beneath her roof.

Just then, to their surprise and dismay, their happy conversation was interrupted by a loud knocking upon the door and the voices of some of the miners demanding admittance. Not wishing to arouse the jealous anger of her rough friends by letting them find the distrusted stranger in her home, Minnie hastily made Johnson conceal himself behind her bed-curtains; and she then opened the door to admit the clamouring miners. Rance and several others rushed in excitedly, expressing great relief on finding her safe and well; and in reply to her surprised inquiries they declared they had just discovered that the stranger, Johnson, who had visited the "Polka" early that evening was none other than Ramarrez, the infamous chief of the "Greaser" band. The bandit had evidently intended to rob them of their gold, but, strangely enough, had departed without it—which fact was a mystery to them, though they imagined he was prevented from doing so by the unexpected presence of Minnie. They added that, fearing lest he might have followed her to her home, they had now come along to assure themselves of her safety and then to continue their search for the robber.

Minnie was struck to the heart on thus learning that the man to whom she had given her love was a thieving bandit; nevertheless, being unable to betray him, she controlled her feelings for the moment and eventually contrived to despatch the miners once more on their search.

When they had gone, however, she turned furiously upon Johnson and scornfully denounced him for winning her love under false colours; but the wretched man implored her forgiveness, declaring passionately that his love for her was sincere and deep. He explained that he had been brought up in this evil course by an unscrupulous robber-father; and he added that with the coming into his life of Minnie's sweet and pure influence, he was determined to make a fresh start and earn an honest living—the proof of which was the fact that he had refrained from stealing the miners' gold that very evening because she had caused his better nature to prevail.

Minnie's outraged feelings and pride, however, were not easily soothed; and filled with despair because he believed he had now lost her love for ever, Johnson recklessly dashed outside into the stormy night, intending to give himself up to the prowling miners. Almost instantly there came the sound of a pistol shot in the darkness, and he fell wounded within a yard or two of the doorstep; and Minnie, horror-struck and unable to let the man she loved be taken after all, ran out and dragged him back, half-unconscious, into the hut. With great difficulty, she managed to help him up into the loft above, hoping thus to conceal him from his enemies.

No sooner had she done so than Rance, the Sheriff, entered the hut unceremoniously and angrily commanded her to deliver up the bandit she was hiding—declaring he had himself seen him fall wounded near her doorstep after the pistol shot had been fired.

For a short time Minnie boldly held him at bay; but as they stood arguing drops of blood began to trickle through from above, falling upon the Sheriff, who quickly scrambled up into the loft and dragged forth the wounded man in triumph.

Minnie was now in despair, knowing that summary justice would instantly be meted out to her lover when he was handed over to the miners; then a bright idea suddenly occurred to her. Knowing that gambling was the Sheriff's greatest passion, she made the bold proposal that they should play a rubber of poker—the best two games out of three—to decide the fate of the captive. If the game fell to Rance, his reward should be the man's life and her own hand in marriage into the bargain; but if the game fell to Minnie, then Johnson was to be left in her hands and Rance was not to inform the others of his hiding-place.

As Minnie had rightly guessed, the Sheriff could not resist a gamble of this kind; and when he at once agreed, cards were produced and the game began. So desperate, however, was Minnie, that she dared not trust to chance, after all; and by a clever manœuvre, she managed to conceal a set of cards in one of the stockings she was wearing. Then, having won the first game, she complained of a sudden faintness, and asked Rance to fetch her some brandy from a shelf at the other side of the room; and while his back was turned, she seized the opportunity of placing the hidden cards in such a way that they should fall to her. The consequence was that when the play was resumed on her pretended recovery, the second game fell to her, and she thus won the wager.

Rance, though full of rage and disappointment, nevertheless kept to the bargain made and departed with an ill grace and muttered threats of getting even with his rival eventually.

.　　.　　.　　.　　.　　.　　.　　.　　.

For a week Minnie managed to keep her lover hidden, nursing him tenderly until he had recovered from his wound; and then, suspecting that his hiding-place had become known, Johnson was obliged to take flight. His suspicions proved correct, for he was quickly seen and recognized by the miners, who were still out scouring the country for him. An exciting chase ensued, which ended in Johnson being captured at early dawn on the outskirts of the great Californian forest.

The miners, triumphant but furious because of the many robberies Johnson, as Ramarrez, was known to have committed, thronged about him as he was dragged into their midst, again wounded and with his garments torn; and they at once clamoured that the summary justice of lynch law should be meted out to him.

Rance, the Sheriff, readily enough agreed, his own treacherous information having led to the discovery of the bandit's whereabouts and his consequent round-up; and as the noose was being prepared, he triumphed gloatingly over his fallen rival.

Johnson, pale and haggard, faced his awful position with calm resignation; but he begged the miners, as the only favour he craved, not to tell Minnie of his fate but to let her imagine that he had succeeded in escaping.

Just as the hanging was about to take place, however, Minnie herself rode up at a furious pace, having followed in the wake of the fugitive. Jumping from her panting horse, she flung herself in front of her lover and, drawing her pistol, fearlessly defied the lynchers to tighten the rope.

Though Rance, beside himself with rage, furiously bade the men thrust Minnie on one side and proceed with the execution, no one stirred to displace the brave girl, who now passionately pleaded with the miners for her lover's life, telling them that Johnson had renounced his bandit ways and was even now departing to another country, there intending to earn an honest livelihood. Then, finding the sullen men still obdurate, she begged them for her own sake to release their captive, reminding them of her loving devotion to them in the past which they could now repay by generously granting her request.

This last appeal was effectual; and the miners, melted by Minnie's eloquence and their love for her since her childhood's days, overruled the angry and baffled Rance and set their prisoner free.

They then bade her an affectionate farewell; and as Johnson and Minnie departed, hand in hand, to seek a new and better life elsewhere, the rough men suddenly felt sad and forlorn, being overcome with the deepest emotion as they realized that their beloved " Girl of the Golden West " had now passed out of their lives for ever.

MADAM BUTTERFLY   *Puccini*
(*Madama Butterfly*)

WHEN Lieutenant Pinkerton, a gay young American naval officer, found himself likely to be stationed in Nagasaki for some considerable time, he decided to contract a " Japanese " marriage. Having fallen in love with a charming little geisha, Cho-Cho-San—or Butterfly, as she was more generally called—whose bewitching daintiness and sweet nature had quickly enthralled his heart, he had determined to indulge his passion at all costs.

For this purpose he engaged the services of Goro, an old marriage broker, who was willing enough to arrange this matter for so desirable a client—to whom dollars seemed of little account. Not only did the usefully experienced Goro undertake to draw up the marriage contract—which, however, could be annulled monthly!—but he also secured for his client a quaint little house in which to spend the blissful dream. Set in a flowery garden high above Nagasaki harbour, the house was an ideal love-nest; a nest, however, which the cynical old broker well knew would sooner or later be deserted.

When all was ready and the wedding-day arrived, Pinkerton followed the obsequious agent from room to room of the charming retreat prepared for his pleasure; and he was delighted with all he saw. Goro had forgotten nothing; and the wedding guests— pretty Butterfly's relatives and girl friends—were expected to appear any moment for the ceremony.

Just as Pinkerton was beginning to tire of the old broker's some-what boring loquacity, the first of the wedding guests arrived. This was Sharpless, the American Consul, who had come in his official capacity and also as the friend and compatriot of the bride-groom. He was an older man than Pinkerton, for whom, how-ever, he had much affection; so much, indeed, that he had come thus early with the intention of persuading his friend to abandon this Japanese so-called "marriage", knowing that little lasting happiness was likely to come of it. For one thing, from what he had already seen of her, he felt that the pretty little bride regarded her coming marriage with intense seriousness, not as a temporary amusement; and in his own large-hearted tenderness, it pained him to think that one so sincere and innocent should be called upon to suffer when the inevitable awakening came.

Consequently, he now asked Pinkerton to reflect again before he entered into this connection, declaring that the Japanese maiden's love was so deep that she almost certainly believed her future husband would regard their marriage as a binding one; and he besought his young friend not to gratify what was to him a mere passing fancy at the expense of bruising the wings of the trusting little Butterfly.

Pinkerton, however, was deeply in love at the moment, and refused to listen to his friend's counsel; and he gaily assured the more prudent Consul that no harm was likely to come to the object of his affection—who would readily find a new admirer when he had to leave her. With these careless words, he ran eagerly to greet his dainty little bride, who at this moment appeared, accompanied by a bevy of merry girl friends.

A veritable butterfly in appearance was Cho-Cho-San, sweet and dainty as a freshly-opened flower; sunny-hearted and gay, yet full of quaint and thoughtful fancies; childish and fairy-like, yet possessing a woman's heart, pure, true, and capable of a deep and abiding passion. She had bestowed this treasure of love upon the handsome young Pinkerton with sincere and implicit trust; and her belief in his love for her was so intense that she never gave a thought to the possibility of his affection waning but considered herself the happiest girl in all Japan.

She now greeted him with bright smiles, introducing him with pride to her friends; and then, with artless simplicity, she began to prattle merrily to the two Americans, telling them of her family history—how her mother was poor, and how she herself had been obliged to become a geisha to earn a living. When asked about her father, she grew suddenly sad, and merely stated that he was dead; but later on they learnt that he had met his death honourably by committing "Hara-kiri", a sword having been sent to him by the Mikado for this purpose. Presently, when asking Pinkerton's permission to retain a few girlish treasures she had brought with her, she showed him this very sword which she revered as her greatest possession. As a further proof of her perfect trust in her future husband, she now whispered in his ear the startling fact that she had visited the Christian mission-house and adopted his faith, having been willing to renounce her own religion for his sake—a fact which, if known to her relatives, would cause them to regard her as an outcast.

By this time, the relatives who had been bidden to the wedding had all arrived; and a motley enough group of undesirables they appeared to be in the eyes of Pinkerton—who, however, received them graciously and accepted their flowery compliments with gay good-nature. The Registrar and Commissioner having also arrived, the wedding now took place without further delay—the ceremony merely consisting of the reading by the Commissioner of the conveniently elastic marriage contract and the signing of the same by the bride and bridegroom.

This simple proceeding over, Sharpless and the other officials took their leave; and though Pinkerton was longing to be alone with his dainty little bride, he was obliged to resign himself to the entertaining of his many unwanted guests—who were all eager to feast and enjoy themselves at the expense of the rich American and to do justice to the luxurious food provided by the outrageously thorough old Goro.

When the hilarity was at its height, however, there came an unexpected interruption. An uncouth individual of weird and wild aspect suddenly burst in amongst the guests, brandishing his arms and uttering cries of furious rage. This unwelcome intruder was Butterfly's most important uncle, a Bonze, or Japanese priest who, having already learnt of his niece's apostasy, had now come to denounce her and to call down curses upon her.

Pinkerton had at first laughed at the extravagant speeches and absurd gesticulations of the angry old Bonze; but when the other relatives presently took up the denunciations also, he grew angry and ordered the servants to turn them all out of the house.

Then, as the imprecations of the departing guests died away in the distance, Pinkerton comforted the now weeping Butterfly with tender caresses and soon succeeded in restoring her to joyousness once more.

Night had now closed in, and as they presently wandered out together on to the moonlit terrace, Pinkerton folded his fair bride in his arms in a passionate embrace; and in that moment of ecstasy, the lovers felt that the world was indeed well lost.

.   .   .   .

A period of intense happiness now followed for this ill-matched couple; but, alas! it was but a short one. Pinkerton's love for his little Japanese wife, though passionate at the time, was, as Sharpless had felt, but a passing phase; and when, after a few months had drifted by in this pleasant dream, his ship having received orders to return to America, he had departed with little real regret. Nor did he intend to return to the nest he was thus deserting for ever; and he believed, in his careless way, that the pretty Butterfly would as easily forget him and eventually take unto herself a Japanese husband. Yet, to ease the pain of his departure, he as carelessly promised the weeping girl that he would return to her when the robins began to nest; and Butterfly, believing implicitly in this promise, was satisfied. Every day she declared to her faithful maid, Suzuki—who had no such trusting belief—that this happy event would certainly come to pass.

Later on, when a fair, blue-eyed baby boy was born to her, she rejoiced on the little one's birth because of the additional pleasure she innocently felt was in store for the surely-returning father; and even when three years had passed away since her wedding-day and no word had yet come from the faithless Pinkerton, she still remained confident that her hopes would be realized. It was quite useless for the handmaid, Suzuki—whose knowledge of such "marriages" was wider—to suggest to her mistress that her hope was a vain one; the trusting little Butterfly only grew quite angry and refused to listen to her.

One day when they were talking thus—after having made the disturbing discovery that the funds left by Pinkerton were now almost exhausted—a visitor suddenly appeared; and to the delight of Butterfly, this proved to be none other than Sharpless, the American Consul—who had, however, come on a very different mission. He had just received a message from Pinkerton, who, somewhat unexpectedly, was again being stationed at Nagasaki, his ship being due to arrive that same evening. In his letter announcing this fact, the young Lieutenant stated that he was now married to a beautiful American lady; and he asked his old friend to seek out the pretty Butterfly and to break this news to her as gently as he could.

Butterfly received the Consul with joy; and on learning that he had a letter from Pinkerton, she clapped her hands and became very excited, declaring that her hopes were about to be realized and that her beloved husband was returning to her at last. Her eager anticipation and childish delight quite unmanned the tender-hearted Sharpless, who now saw only too plainly how right he had been in warning Pinkerton that the Japanese maiden regarded her marriage as a binding one and that her love was as the breath of life to her; and though he essayed many times to explain his cruel mission, his efforts to do so were in vain, so that he despaired of ever making her realize the fatal truth.

He was somewhat relieved, therefore, by the unexpected arrival of old Goro, the marriage broker, who brought with him Prince Yamadori, a wealthy Japanese suitor, whom he had for a long time past tried vainly to induce the deserted wife to accept as a legal husband—for one so young and pretty was still a tempting prize to offer to his amorous clients. Yamadori had now come to plead his own cause with the obdurate Butterfly, who, however, still refused to listen to him, indignantly adding that she already had a husband, who was shortly returning to her.

Seeing that argument was useless in her present state, old Goro and his disappointed client withdrew, hoping for better success on their next visit. When they had gone, Sharpless endeavoured once more to explain the real object of his own visit; and having again failed dismally, he next tried to persuade her to accept the wealthy Japanese suitor who desired to make her his bride. Such a suggestion coming from one she trusted so deeply, however, wounded her so much that he did not venture to press the point.

As the final strengthening of her argument and the crowning

proof of the utter uselessness of trying to persuade her that she was forgotten by Pinkerton, Butterfly ran to fetch her pretty baby boy and holding him up before the eyes of the amazed Consul—who had no idea of the child's existence—cried out passionately : " Do you think he could forget *this* proof of our love? "

Sharpless, knowing that Pinkerton had no knowledge that a son had been born to him, was now so overcome with deep emotion that he could scarcely control his feelings of pity for the deserted little Japanese wife; and, utterly unable just then to reveal to her the fact of Pinkerton's legal marriage, he hastily took his leave—inwardly railing at his friend for entrusting him with such a thankless mission.

No sooner had the Consul departed than the roar of cannon was heard from the harbour as a salute to an arriving ship; and hurrying to the terrace, Butterfly saw that the incoming vessel was flying the American flag; and with the aid of a telescope, she made out its name to be the *Abraham Lincoln*—Pinkerton's ship! Full of delirious joy and feeling convinced that her beloved one would be with her within a few hours, she called to Suzuki to gather the fairest flowers from the garden that they might adorn the little home with garlands in honour of his return.

After the two women had placed flowers in every available space, and strewn fragrant petals lavishly upon the floors, Butterfly next dressed her baby boy in his finest clothes and arrayed herself in her wedding garments; and then, calling Suzuki to join her and making three holes in the *shoshi*, the expectant trio settled down to watch for Pinkerton's approach.

Many hours passed, but the longed-for visitor did not appear; and when darkness set in, Suzuki and the child, tired out with watching, fell fast asleep. But Butterfly would not sleep; and all through the long weary night she kept a constant watch, never losing hope but still believing that her beloved one would surely come.

.   .   .   .

When the dawn came, Suzuki awakened and busied herself about the house. Then she returned and begged her tired mistress to rest a while in the upstairs sleeping-chamber; and Butterfly, now overcome with fatigue and wishing to look well when her eagerly-expected husband appeared—as she still believed he would —was at last persuaded to retire.

When she had hastened away, now eager to revive her tired looks, Suzuki sent the little boy out to play in the garden; and then the faithful maid knelt for a few moments before an image of Buddha to pray for her hapless mistress. While she was thus engaged, Sharpless and Pinkerton entered the room. The latter, after hearing of the Consul's unavailing visit of the day before, had come with his friend thus early in the morning to seek advice from Suzuki as to a means of acquainting Butterfly with the true state of affairs.

Suzuki, thinking for the moment that Pinkerton had returned, after all, to claim his little Japanese wife, received him gladly, telling him of Butterfly's preparations for his arrival and of her longing to greet him. Each word spoken by the faithful maid was as a knife in the heart of the now remorseful Pinkerton, who was filled with sincere grief for the additional pain he was about to inflict upon the gentle heart of one who still loved him so truly and deeply.

The handmaid, however, was quickly undeceived upon now observing a tall and beautiful lady waiting in the garden; and, with quick intuition, she realized only too well who the stranger was. The kindly Consul explained to her that Mrs. Pinkerton had come to offer protection and care for the baby boy, that his future welfare might be assured; and he begged her to assist them in this matter.

Pinkerton, having noted with increasing emotion, as he wandered about the flower-decked room, the many signs of Butterfly's deep love for him, now declared that he could not bear the anguish of meeting her; and he hastened away, leaving his legal wife and the Consul to conduct the painful interview as best they could. As he departed, full of grief and remorse, his wife entered from the garden.

Kate Pinkerton was a beautiful and kind-hearted woman, who had been greatly moved by the Japanese girl's sad story; and she also entreated Suzuki to help them to be of service to her unhappy mistress.

While they were discussing this matter, Butterfly was heard calling from the chamber above, having heard the sound of voices; and next moment she appeared in the doorway, full of excitement and expecting to greet her husband. At the sight of Kate, she stopped short, gazing intently upon her; and though no word was spoken, she knew instinctively that this was the woman for whose sake she herself had been cast aside.

Sharpless now expected an outburst of passionate reproach; but, to the surprise of all, Butterfly remained quite calm and bore this sudden shattering of all her cherished hopes with a quiet dignity. When Kate entreated forgiveness for the pain she had so unconsciously been the means of inflicting, she answered gently that she only wished every happiness to be showered upon her and her loved ones. Then, when asked to give up the baby boy to the guardianship of his father for his own future benefit, she promised quietly that Pinkerton should have the child if he would himself come for him in half an hour's time. Having thus succeeded in their mission, Kate and Sharpless quickly departed, unable to bear any longer the heart-rending sight of such resigned suffering.

When they had gone, Butterfly dismissed Suzuki; then, taking up her father's sword, which she had always carefully cherished, she reverently kissed the blade. Now that she at last realized the terrible truth that Pinkerton was her husband no longer, and that for his own good she must also part with her child, she had no further desire for life; and as she lifted the sword, she brokenheartedly read out aloud the words engraved upon it: "Die with honour when you can no longer live with honour!"

At that moment, the door was opened to admit the baby boy, who was pushed within by Suzuki; and, dropping the sword, Butterfly ran forward and clasped her child in her arms in a last passionate embrace. Then, laying him carefully on the ground, she suddenly seized the sword once more and plunged it into her bosom.

When, a few moments later, Pinkerton entered the room to claim the fulfilment of her promise, Butterfly was lying motionless and silent; and the faithful heart that had loved him with such true devotion was at rest for ever.

MANON LESCAUT   *Puccini*

ONE bright summer evening towards the end of the eighteenth century, merry groups of students and idlers were gathered together in the courtyard of an inn at Amiens, near the Paris Gate. As they there awaited the arrival of the diligence, they passed the time pleasantly in joking, drinking, singing snatches of gay songs and flirting with the pretty work-girls who were just returning from their daily labours. The latter were glad enough to join in the merriment of the lively youths, whose favours they very willingly accepted.

One of these students, however, held aloof from the others. The work-girls' loud jollity had no attraction for his sensitive, poetic nature; and despite being rallied by his companions for his indifference to the girlish charms around him, he stood apart, wrapped in his own dreamy thoughts.

This fastidious youth was the Chevalier des Grieux, a young man of high birth and good breeding, who was also possessed of a fine, passionate nature and the true artistic temperament which could only be satisfied with the highest in beauty, art, and love. Though his giddy companions, in their raillery, now declared his gloomy looks portended that he must be a victim to the darts of Cupid, his heart had never yet been touched.

Presently the diligence entered the courtyard; and amongst the passengers who alighted was a beautiful young girl, who was accompanied by her brother and an elderly fop, whose elegantly rich attire and lordly airs proclaimed him to be a person of wealth and importance.

The young girl was Manon Lescaut, a maiden of exquisite loveliness, who, in spite of her extreme youth and beauty, was even now being conducted by her brother to a convent. The life of a nun was the fate destined for her by her parents, who feared that the snares of the world might prove too much for one so fair, whom they believed could only be kept safe from temptation by taking the veil.

Manon, however, had a rich, passionate nature that craved for light, warmth, beauty and all the joys of a happy, full life; and she was sad at the thought that the cup of pleasure which she so ardently desired to drain was to be snatched from her lips ere she had scarce tasted of it.

Her brother, also, felt that it was a mistake to deprive so fair and radiant a young life of the joy that should certainly be its due; and he had already determined to disobey the instructions he had received from their parents and to prevent the incarceration of his young sister's charms. His motive, however, was far from being disinterested, since his nature was a depraved one; and in order to gratify his desire for low pleasures and his mercenary, avaricious instincts, he determined to use his sister's beauty as a decoy for securing wealth for them both.

To this end he had already encouraged the very obvious attentions of the rich, elderly libertine, Baron Geronte de Ravoir, who had travelled with them in the diligence and who had become so fascinated with Manon's young loveliness that he desired above all things to possess her; and when the foppish, amorous Baron presently invited the brother and sister to join him at supper, Lescaut eagerly accepted for both.

Meanwhile the handsome young student, Des Grieux, had no sooner beheld the fair Manon than he had become so enthralled by her exquisite, ethereal beauty and delicate grace, that he could scarce take his eyes from her face. Eagerly making his way towards her, he soon found an opportunity to enter into conversation and to ask her name and destination.

Manon replied simply and shyly; but her tones were so sad and she sighed so deeply as she spoke of the convent life awaiting her at her journey's end, that Des Grieux was filled with pity and distress. He besought her not to think any more of taking the veil, but to allow him to contrive some means of escape for her.

As the pair gazed into each other's eyes and talked thus eagerly together, a deep love sprang up spontaneously in their hearts; for both were young, fair, and of ardent temperaments, and were, moreover, mutually attracted to one another by a strange, but sweet magnetism which neither could resist.

Des Grieux was overjoyed to find in Manon the answering sympathy of a delicate, sensitive, highly-strung and passionate nature such as his own poetic temperament had longed for, and he eagerly besought her to meet him again later in the evening. Manon agreed to do so; and then, hearing her brother calling to her, she hurried away into the inn, leaving Des Grieux to wander apart from the merry throng once more and to indulge in his new rapturous thoughts alone.

Meanwhile the well-seasoned *roué*, Baron Geronte, had not been idling his time. Having already determined to carry Manon off by force with him to Paris, there to become his mistress, he secretly called aside the landlord of the inn and arranged with him to have a post-chaise ready in a secluded spot behind the inn at a certain time during the evening.

It happened, however, that this conversation was overheard by Edmond, one of the young students, who, having noticed the mutual attraction of love between Manon and Des Grieux, now approached the latter and informed him of Geronte's plan for the abduction of the beautiful girl.

Full of dismay at this news, Des Grieux entreated the assistance of Edmond, who declared that the only thing to be done was for Des Grieux himself to make use of the waiting post-chaise and to depart in it with Manon before the old *roué* could complete his plans.

Des Grieux hailed this scheme with relief and joy; and Edmond, eager to help in such a mischievous trick, ran off to make arrangements for the post-chaise to be got ready at once.

Meanwhile, Lescaut, ever ready to satisfy his gambling craze, was already engaged with his new companion in playing cards and dice, and in drinking with some of the wilder students; and so absorbed were both he and Geronte, that they did not notice that Manon had again gone out into the courtyard and was talking with Des Grieux in a quiet corner.

Des Grieux quickly told the beautiful girl of Geronte's plot for her abduction and of his own plans for her rescue; and again declaring his deep love for her, he entreated her to go with him at once to Paris, where they might dwell together in perfect happiness.

At first, Manon tried to resist this temptation; but, finally, her love for Des Grieux overwhelmed every other feeling and she declared she would gladly go with him wherever he wished. The lovers, therefore, crept stealthily to the back of the courtyard, where they found the post-chaise already waiting; and it was not until they had entered the vehicle and were driving along at a merry rate that Geronte and Lescaut saw what had happened.

The disappointed *roué* stamped and raved about the courtyard, nearly choking with rage on seeing his fair victim thus snatched from his grasp under his very nose; but Lescaut soon found a means of pacifying him. Knowing his sister's love of luxury and comfort, Lescaut believed that she could only be happy whilst the means of gratifying her naturally extravagant desires were forthcoming. Therefore, he bade Geronte not to despair of winning her yet, since, when the young student's slender purse was exhausted, Manon might be enticed away from him by the offer of more magnificent living such as Geronte had to offer her.

This, indeed, proved to be the case; for when Des Grieux had lavished all the means at his immediate disposal upon gratifying the artistic longings of the ardent girl whom he had taken under his protection, he found himself unable to provide for so bright a creature within the restrictions of a narrowly-limited purse.

Manon loved Des Grieux passionately; but her voluptuous, pleasure-loving soul craved for luxury and extravagant amusements such as Des Grieux could not possibly gratify in the humble little cottage to which he had taken her. The consequence was that when the Baron Geronte at length arrived on the scene during Des Grieux's absence, his offer of a magnificent house and all the glittering delights that wealth could purchase was too strong a temptation for the sunshine-loving Manon—who thus allowed herself to be lured away from her true lover to become the mistress and petted favourite of one for whom she had no real affection.

Geronte's admiration, however, was pleasing to her; and for some weeks Manon lived a life of continual pleasure and luxury in the Baron's magnificent hotel, where her every whim was gratified and where she reigned almost as a queen.

Her brother, Lescaut, was well pleased with the turn events had taken, since he, also, now lived a life of luxury at the expense of his sister's wealthy protector; but he was clever enough to see that Manon would not long be satisfied with her present luxurious distractions and that satiety must inevitably come. He realized, also, that her love for Des Grieux was not dead, but only awaited his reappearance to burst forth into full bloom once more; and he knew that Des Grieux alone would have lasting influence in his sister's life.

For his own ends, therefore, and for the sake of having future means of gratifying his own expensive tastes, Lescaut sought out the wretched Des Grieux and encouraged him to gamble desperately—enticing him to this course by telling him that he would thus secure the wealth that should eventually enable him to win back the radiant Manon whom he still so fondly loved. He even went further still, and arranged for an interview between the pair; but dire misfortune came of this.

One day Geronte had arranged for a grand entertainment to be given before his beautiful mistress in their hotel, having secured the services of certain musicians and singers to give renderings of some high-flown verses which he had himself composed in praise of her beauty; and he arranged also for a dancing exhibition in the minuet and other fashionable dances of the period. Finding, however, that the spoilt beauty soon showed signs of boredom, he left the hotel with his friends to take a stroll along the Boulevards, somewhat piqued, but intending to return shortly to see how she amused herself during his absence.

This was the very hour for which Lescaut had arranged the meeting between Des Grieux and Manon; and a few minutes after the departure of the Baron, the lovers were in each other's arms.

Manon was overjoyed on finding herself once more in the presence of her beloved Des Grieux; and the latter so quickly fell under the magic spell of her fatal fascination, that his first reproaches were soon forgotten in the passionate words of love and endearment which he could not repress.

So absorbed in their joy were the lovers that, oblivious of their surroundings, they paid no heed to the passing of time; and thus it came about that they were presently discovered by Geronte, still folded in each other's arms.

Madly infuriated by the sight, Geronte instantly ran out from the hotel and denounced Manon to the authorities as a person of ill repute; and, in spite of her tears and entreaties, the unhappy girl was dragged off to prison and subsequently condemned to deportation.

Lescaut, still acting for his own selfish ends, made several endeavours, assisted by the almost frantic Des Grieux, to save the wretched victim from her awful fate; but all their efforts were in vain.

Des Grieux was overcome with grief and despair by the failure of his later attempts to effect Manon's escape from prison on the day before she sailed. Then, rather than be parted from his beloved one, and when the last chance of rescue had vanished, he offered himself as one of the crew on board the vessel that conveyed her to America.

He was thus enabled to be of some small comfort to her on her arrival in the strange land she had dreaded so much. Even here, however, fate was still against the lovers, and Manon's fatal beauty was the means of placing further perils in her path. In order to escape a worse danger than any which had threatened her before, she was compelled to make a sudden hurried flight, accompanied by the ever-faithful Des Grieux.

The lovers now were forced to wander as fugitives in a vast solitary wilderness, far from human habitation and aid; and here starvation soon met them face to face.

All too quickly, poor Manon wasted and drooped, her bright butterfly nature utterly crushed by such terrible reverses; and at last, one day, as the pair toiled on their way, she sank to the ground dying from exhaustion.

Full of despair, Des Grieux vainly sought for water and refreshment to save the precious life he loved so well; but Manon, knowing herself to be past all human aid, called him back to her side once more. Folded closely in his trembling arms, she expired a few moments later, declaring her love for him with her last breath.

Heart-broken, Des Grieux, with a cry of woe, fell senseless beside the dead body of his beloved Manon—that Manon, so fair and so alluring, such a bewildering contrast of passionate love and mischievous coquetry, a fascinating, sunshine-loving butterfly with a tender human heart.

SISTER ANGELICA   *Puccini*
(*Suor Angelica*)

IT was the hour of prayer in a certain Convent in Italy one evening towards the end of the seventeenth century. The sisters were already within the little church singing and praying devoutly; and two postulants, coming late, hurried along the cloisters, in anxious haste to take their places before the service came to an end. Sister Angelica also was late; but as she entered the church, she did not forget, as the postulants had done, to make the customary act of penitence by kneeling down and kissing the ground.

As the evening service ended, the nuns came out of the church two by two, bowing reverently before the Abbess as they passed her in the garden. Having blessed them, the Abbess retired into the main Convent building, while the nuns remained without in a semicircle, waiting for certain penances to be announced by the monitor sister.

This having been done, the monitor withdrew, and the sisters were free for a short time to occupy themselves according to their own devices.

It was almost sunset, though a few bright streaks of sunshine still fell upon the Convent garden; and the warm May evening filled the simple hearts of the sisters with gladness.

One of the older nuns, Sister Génévieve, reminded the others that this was the first of the three evenings in the year when a golden ray of sunshine shone upon their fountain, turning its flowing waters into the semblance of liquid gold; and the Mistress of the Novices added that this was a wonderful sign to them of the great mercy of God, who thus permitted them for three evenings, on their return from prayer, to behold the fountain made golden by the sun. All other times, they were either too late, so that the shadows had already fallen, or too early in full daylight to behold this special golden ray as it fell upon the fountain's tiny stream. As they thus realized that another year had passed since the last time they saw the symbolic ray, they remembered that since that time one of their beloved sisters had passed away; and they arranged that when the glorious ray of sunshine presently fell upon the fountain, they would take some of the water to sprinkle upon the departed nun's grave in the little cemetery beyond.

They then began to talk about the wishes they still could not at times prevent from overwhelming them, though they believed that it was sinful for them to cherish any such hankerings. One sister, who had been a shepherdess in her early youth, declared she often longed, above all things, to behold within her arms once more a little white lamb and to hears its plaintive bleat. Another longed for rich foods to eat; and others confessed also to harbouring forbidden longings.

Presently they observed Sister Angelica—a beautiful and gentle nun who, though she had been with them for seven years, seldom spoke with the other sisters but remained wrapped in her devotions —working among the flowers in the garden; and they began to whisper among themselves that even she had her secret wishes, too. They declared she constantly prayed that she might behold her dearly-loved ones again, but that no one had ever visited her during her seven years' residence in their midst. Another added that the Mother Abbess had spoken of her as being of a noble and wealthy family; and it was believed that she was a Princess who had been compelled to take the Convent vows forcibly in expiation for some sin. She had a rare knowledge of medicinal herbs and seemed to find her greatest comfort in cultivating healing plants for the relief of those who suffered. Even now, being called to the aid of one of the sisters who had been badly stung by wasps, she soon produced some soothing leaves to ease the pain.

While the sisters, a few minutes later, were in the vestibule crowding around a couple of Questuants, who had just arrived on donkeys with panniers well filled with provisions, they were startled to hear the Convent bell ringing to announce the arrival of a visitor; and in an instant they were full of eager interest and anticipation as to which of them the visit was being made. Their curiosity was further raised on being told by the Questuants that they had seen a very splendid coach standing at the door; and on hearing this, Sister Angelica, forgetting her usual reserve, eagerly asked them to describe the coach to her, suggesting its possible colouring and upholstery and particularly its blazoning.

Noting her sudden enthusiasm and heightened colouring the nuns were filled with sympathy, hoping that the visitor might be for her, even though but a moment before their own expectancy had run high.

As they all waited in a tense silence, the Abbess came forth into their midst and announced that the visit was to Sister Angelica, at the same time motioning to the others to withdraw.

When the nuns had retired, Sister Angelica could not refrain from showing her joy that the long silence of her friends was about to be broken, declaring that the seven years she had spent without a word, or a letter, or news, she had offered willingly to the Virgin in expiation of her sin. The Abbess, however, severely reproved her for her present exaltation; and then, as the humbled sister became calm once more, she announced that the visitor was her aunt, the Princess.

As the Abbess withdrew, the Princess, an elderly woman, full of aristocratic dignity but stern of mien, entered, clothed in rich garments and leaning upon an ebony stick. She threw a cold glance of unrelenting severity and disapproval upon her niece; and when Sister Angelica, trembling with intense emotion, almost staggeringly approached as though to embrace her, she merely stretched forth her left hand as the utmost she would condescend to offer in salutation. Sister Angelica, however, quickly seized the outstretched hand and covered it with eager kisses, her seven years' pent-up emotions now breaking forth uncontrollably; and then she sank back upon her knees, unable to speak but keeping imploringly questioning eyes upon her aunt and with tears streaming down her cheeks. But the old Princess still kept her own gaze persistently and severely aloof, while making plain statements of fact.

She announced that she had merely come to secure her niece's signature to a legal document dividing the property and fortune left by the Prince and Princess, her father and mother, upon their death some years ago—this having now become necessary owing to the betrothal of her younger sister, Anna Viola.

Then, as Sister Angelica expressed amazement that the pretty child she had left seven years ago was now grown up and of an age to marry, the Princess added that Anna Viola's suitor had consented magnanimously to overlook the black stain cast upon the family escutcheon by the elder sister's sin.

Sister Angelica, realizing that her aunt's hard heart had not softened with the passing of the years, now tearfully entreated the old aristocrat to show more mercy towards her, declaring that she had expiated her sin many times over by her prayers of repentance and her penances and by offering up to the Virgin all the desires and longings of her heart. But, she added, there was one thing she could not offer up in expiation, and that was forgetfulness of her little son, the precious babe who had been the innocent cause of her disgrace—for she had borne this child out of wedlock to one she had loved too well. She had seen and kissed her little son but once before he was torn away from her, and had pined for him for seven long years; and she now passionately implored her aunt to give her news of her precious child, to tell her how he looked and of the words he spoke.

The old lady, however, did not at first answer a word; but when the distracted mother, now waxing bold in her anxiety, commanded her to speak in the name of the Virgin, she spoke the dreaded words. The child had been seized with a fatal illness two years ago; and, although no care was spared to save his life, he had died.

With a heartrending cry, Sister Angelica fell to the ground, sobbing violently in an abandonment of grief as she realized that her beloved child was now lost to her, after she had waited so long for news of him. The Princess, at first thinking her to be in a swoon, made a movement to aid her; then, hearing her sobs, the momentary feeling of pity vanished and she hardened her heart once more against the niece who had sinned. Calling to the porteress, she ordered writing materials to be brought.

Sister Angelica, hearing the nuns approaching, roused herself sufficiently to affix her signature to the document produced by her aunt—from whom, however, she now shrank as from one who had the plague. The old Princess, having thus secured the object of her visit, then took her departure without another word, leaving misery and black despair behind her.

Darkness had now fallen and the nuns began to light up the lamps within the Convent walls and on the graves in the cemetery beyond; but Sister Angelica remained outside alone in the black gloom of the garden. In the Cloisters beyond other nuns sang songs to the Virgin as they passed from the cemetery into the Convent; and Sister Angelica also now raised her voice in a song and prayer of farewell to these kindly sisters whom she had loved but whom she would not see again on the morrow, since she had determined to live no longer. She now sought among her plants for certain herbs and flowers containing deadly poisons; and these she placed in a jar of water. She next collected a bunch of brambles and twigs and set them alight by means of a flint, placing the jar upon the blaze. When the poison was brewed, she drank it off resolutely, kissing her crucifix as she called out another farewell to the kindly sisters; and then, with a cry to her beloved child in Heaven, whom she seemed now to hear calling to her, she fell dying to the ground.

But though she had performed this deed full of serenity and exaltation, a change now came over Sister Angelica as she suddenly realized the deep wrong she had done in thus taking her own life; and as the pangs of death seized her she frantically called upon the Madonna to forgive her and to show her a sign of grace.

At that moment a miraculous vision appeared to the dying nun.

R

The little church became illumined with a soft mystic light, while a shining cupola of stars encircled it; and through the open portals there issued forth in great glory the compassionate Queen of Consolation, leading by the hand a fair young child—the son of Sister Angelica. Thus, with adoration and gratitude, the departing spirit of the repentant nun went forward gladly to share the heavenly joys of her newly-found little one.

LA TOSCA   *Puccini*

ONE afternoon in the June of 1800, when Napoleon was the terror of Europe, Cesare Angelotti, an escaped political prisoner from the Fortress Sant 'Angelo in Rome, dashed into the church of Sant 'Andrea della Valle. He was breathless with running and the fear of recapture; and his hands trembled as he unlocked the door of a little side chapel with a key sent him by his sister, the Lady Attavanti. He knew that the latter had concealed there a complete set of women's clothing for his disguise.

No sooner had the fugitive hidden in the chapel than Cavaradossi, a painter, came into an adjoining part of the church to work upon a large picture of the Magdalene, the canvas of which was set up upon a dais temporarily erected for the purpose.

As Cavaradossi took up his brushes and began to paint, the old sacristan, who had followed him in, set down a basket of fruit for 'the artist's refreshment. Then, as his eyes fell upon the canvas, he was greatly shocked to recognize in the Magdalene a portrait of the Lady Attavanti, whom he had frequently seen at prayer in her family's chapel.

Cavaradossi laughingly declared that it was the sight of this blue-eyed, fair-haired beauty at prayer that had inspired him; and then, having got rid of the scandalized sacristan, he was about to settle down to his task when he heard the sound of someone issuing from the Attavanti Chapel. Turning sharply, he beheld, to his amazement, his old friend Angelotti—whom he had never expected to see again.

Full of joy, he promised to help the fugitive to get safely away, first taking the precaution of fastening the church door securely from the inside; but before they had been able to decide upon any plan of action, they heard a woman's voice outside calling to Cavaradossi for admission. This was Floria Tosca, a beautiful singer and actress beloved by the artist, whom she visited thus every day. Hastily bidding Angelotti conceal himself once more in the Attavanti Chapel and thrusting into his hand the basket of fruit with which to revive himself, Cavaradossi ran to open the church door.

As Tosca—a dark imperious beauty—entered the church, uttering indignant protests on being obliged to call out for admission, she glanced suspiciously around; for she was of a passionate nature and readily jealous of a suspected rival. Cavaradossi's agitated manner added to her uneasiness; and when she presently recognized in the half-finished picture a portrait of the Lady Attavanti—whose blonde loveliness formed such a piquant contrast to her own dark and brilliant beauty—she could not refrain from uttering jealous reproaches. Cavaradossi, however, soon reassured her by declaring that the Lady Attavanti was only of interest to him as a subject for his present picture. Tosca, all smiles once more, then informed him that she was to sing at the Queen's festival that night in the Farnese Palace; and the lovers arranged to meet after the entertainment and to spend a few blissful hours together. After this, Cavaradossi, anxious because of the hidden fugitive, begged her to leave him to his work once more; and though Tosca again pouted because he wished her to go so soon, she was once more reassured by his loving farewell caresses and at last took her departure.

When she had gone, Angelotti came forth again, somewhat refreshed by the fruit he had partaken of; and Cavaradossi now planned a way of escape for him through the chapel, which opened out into a deserted garden, at the end of which was a path leading to the artist's own villa. He added that near the villa there was an old dried-up well, half-way down which was a secret opening leading to a cave, where his friend might hide in safety. At that moment the sound of cannon fire warned the friends that Angelotti's escape from the fortress had become known; and fearful lest the latter should lose his way before gaining the proposed haven of safety, the painter resolved to accompany him. Snatching up the feminine garments left by the fugitive's sister, the pair hurried feverishly through the chapel into the deserted garden beyond and made their way to Cavaradossi's villa.

Scarcely had they gone than a crowd of townsfolk poured tumultuously into the church, full of excitement as they followed the old sacristan, from whom they had just learned the splendid news that Napoleon had been defeated by their own armies; and while they were joyfully returning thanks, Scarpia, the Chief of the Police, with his agents and guards, appeared in the doorway. Instantly there was silence; for the powerful Scarpia was hated and feared by all, being a man of ill reputation and brutal instincts, cruel and licentious—the very incarnation of evil and corruption.

Announcing that a State prisoner had escaped and was believed to have taken refuge in the church, Scarpia demanded to be shown the Attavanti Chapel, which was found to be open—to the surprise of the now trembling sacristan, who had left it locked. Though the fugitive had vanished, Scarpia presently picked up a fan which had fallen from the bundle of woman's clothes brought for Angelotti by his sister and which bore upon it the arms of the Attavanti family. He also noticed the picture and learnt from the sacristan that it had been painted by Cavaradossi, the lover of La Tosca, the famous singer—whose beauty had also inflamed his own passions to such an extent that he had vowed to possess her as his own mistress, though well aware that she hated and despised him.

With cruel exultation, Scarpia felt that he now had something by means of which he might work upon the singer's well-known jealousy and thus to bend her more readily to his own evil desires. He was well pleased, therefore, when Tosca herself now entered the church—having returned to snatch another few moments with her lover. She was greatly surprised to find that he had already left; and she was even more disturbed on seeing Scarpia there with his satellites. When the Chief of Police presently showed her the fan he held and said he had found it beside the picture—taking care to draw her attention to the Attavanti arms painted upon it—she was filled with the wildest jealousy, being goaded almost to madness by the insinuations of the wily Scarpia. Pretending to sympathize with her, however, the latter escorted her to the door with seeming concern; but when she had departed he sent three of his men to spy upon her movements, hoping that thus he might also discover the escaped prisoner and his own artist rival and so bring them all within his power.

. . . .

Later that evening, Scarpia sat alone at supper in his apartment in the Farnese Palace. Though about to abuse his power as Chief of Police, he had no qualms of conscience. By using Tosca as a decoy, he believed his agents could not fail to find the escaped fugitive; and he determined to bring Cavaradossi—knowing him to be the latter's friend—to the scaffold likewise. Thus he would have a clear field for securing the lovely singer as his mistress.

On finishing his meal, he sent a messenger to Tosca—who had already arrived at the palace to sing at the concert in the royal apartments below—commanding her to come to his room immediately her performance was over. Soon after, his chief agent,

Spoletta, entered and reported that he had followed the singer to the painter's villa, which she had left soon after entering. When he had himself entered the villa with his men, there was no sign of the fugitive, Cavaradossi himself being alone. Having made a thorough search of the villa in vain, he had arrested the painter, whom he now ushered into the presence of his chief.

When Cavaradossi was commanded by Scarpia to reveal the present hiding-place of the escaped prisoner, he resolutely refused to do so—though realizing the danger of his position on being told that he was known to have brought Angelotti to his villa. Even when his questioner next menacingly declared that means were at hand to compel him to give this information, the painter—though shuddering as he remembered the revolting tales he had heard of the cruelties practised in the private torture-chamber of this inhuman Chief of Police—still firmly declined to betray his friend.

Then Scarpia, angered by this opposition from the rival he desired to be rid of, ordered Spoletta to bring the executioner and his attendant torturer with the appointed Scribe to take the victim's deposition. At this moment, the Queen's festival concert having just ended, Tosca appeared in the doorway, having been compelled against her will to obey the peremptory summons of the hated Chief of Police. On beholding Cavaradossi there as a prisoner, she was horror-struck as she instantly realized his danger; and rushing forward, she flung herself into his arms.

Her lover had only time to whisper an agitated injunction to her to say nothing of what she had seen in the villa, passionately imploring her not to betray his friend and guest; and then he was led into the adjoining apartment, which had been fitted up as a torture-chamber. Spoletta and his sinister attendants followed, and the door was closed.

Tosca, though filled with horror and alarm, endeavoured to be brave and to follow out her lover's instructions; and, at first, when questioned by Scarpia as to the whereabouts of the fugitive, she also denied all knowledge of him—though, because of her unexpected arrival at the villa to demand an explanation regarding the dropped fan, the secret had then been revealed to her. When, however, she heard her lover's groans under the first pangs of the torture now being applied to him, she fell on her knees and implored for mercy to be shown to the victim; but her pleadings were in vain. Then she sprang up and rushed to the door of the torture-chamber, beating upon it and calling aloud to Cavaradossi to release her from her promise, when his agony would be stopped—in reply the brave artist again begged her to keep silence.

Scarpia now fiendishly ordered the torture to be applied more violently; and as her lover's groans presently became cries of anguish, Tosca could no longer bear the horror of his sufferings. With a despairing gasp, she murmured faintly that the fugitive was hiding in the well in the villa garden. Satisfied with his victory, Scarpia at once gave instructions for the victim to be released from torture and brought back into the room; and he then despatched guards to capture the hapless Angelotti. As Cavaradossi was brought in, exhausted and bleeding, he heard the directions being given for his friend's capture; and realizing that such information could only have come from Tosca, he sadly reproached her.

As Tosca tearfully entreated his forgiveness, an attendant entered the room to announce that news had come to hand that the reported war victory was false and that Napoleon, so far from being defeated, had gained a great victory at Marengo. This adverse news filled Scarpia with chagrin; but he declared furiously that it made no difference regarding the execution of Cavaradossi as an accomplice in the escape of a State prisoner. The painter, therefore, would be shot at sunrise next morning.

On hearing this terrible announcement, Tosca flung herself upon her lover, entreating to be allowed to accompany him; but she was roughly thrust aside by the guards, who dragged their prisoner from the room to be conveyed to the fortress of Sant 'Angelo.

Left alone with Scarpia, the distracted Tosca, frantic with apprehension and knowing that entreaties for mercy would be of no avail, offered the cruel tyrant her many valuable jewels and treasures as bribes to save her lover's life; but all her offers were laughed to scorn. Then Scarpia, who had known that this moment would come, plainly stated the only terms he was prepared to consider—her own honour, the yielding of herself to his now savage desire, in return for the release of Cavaradossi.

With the most intense scorn, Tosca furiously repudiated such a vile suggestion; then realizing from the burning passion that glowed in his eyes that this hideous alternative was indeed the only one her unscrupulous tormentor would permit, she shrank back shudderingly from his eagerly extended arms.

At that moment, Spoletta entered the room to report that his men had now discovered the fugitive Angelotti—who had, however, taken his own life by swallowing poison before being taken. He then asked if his chief desired the other prisoner, Cavaradossi, to be executed; and the triumphant Scarpia, turning to Tosca, once more whispered his terms and asked her to say whether her lover should live, or die.

Tosca, defeated and eager only to save the life of the man she loved, even though at such a monstrous price, now yielded, and indicated her consent by a despairing nod of her head; then, rousing herself, she demanded the prisoner's instant release in return. The cunning Scarpia, however, declared this request could not be granted because, having been condemned, Cavaradossi's execution must appear to have taken place. He then satisfied Tosca by arranging with Spoletta that a mock military execution should be enacted at four o'clock next morning, but that the firing-party should use blank cartridges, Cavaradossi being instructed to fall and feign death upon the volley being fired—after which he could be taken away by Tosca herself, who would also be present. Unseen by Tosca, however, certain secret signs were given by the villainous Scarpia to his subordinate, whereby the latter readily understood that real bullets were to be used, after all. The wily tyrant had no intention that his rival should ever cross his path again.

When Spoletta had departed, Scarpia was eager to claim his reward and to clasp his beautiful victim in his arms; but Tosca, not yet entirely satisfied and seeking desperately to postpone the dreaded moment of her surrender, now demanded that he should write out a safe conduct for herself and her lover to quit the country on the morrow after the mock execution had taken place.

Scarpia, his good humour restored by the triumph he had gained and realizing that the safe conduct would not be used, at once sat down to write out the document. While he was so engaged, a last desperate hope came into the mind of Tosca; and drawing near to the supper-table, she silently and swiftly seized a sharp-pointed knife lying there and concealed it behind her back, unseen by Scarpia. She then leaned against the table, keeping her eyes fixed upon every movement of the Chief of Police who, upon finishing the document, folded it and sprang up. Unable to restrain his passion longer, he now moved forward with outstretched arms to clasp his victim in a close embrace; but, swift as lightning, Tosca raised the knife and furiously stabbed him in the breast.

With a choking cry, her enemy fell at her feet with a curse, and a few moments later was dead.

The lovely singer, terrified by her own awful deed, was at first stunned; then, taking the lighted candles from the table, she placed one on either side of the body, upon which she also reverently laid a crucifix, which she took down from the wall.

Then, having possessed herself of the safe conduct, she left the room and hurried away from the palace with all speed to attend her lover's mock execution.

.   .   .   .

When Tosca reached the fortress of Sant 'Angelo, the hour of dawn had almost approached. By means of her safe conduct, she readily gained access to the battlements of the fortress, where Cavaradossi had already been brought out to await the arrival of the firing-party.

With a cry of joy, Tosca flung herself into the arms of her lover; and she triumphantly showed him the safe conduct and told him of the plan arranged for his escape from death. Then the now happy pair communed in deep content for a short time longer.

At last full daylight appeared, and at four o'clock the firing-party appeared with Spoletta at their head. With a last fond embrace, the lovers departed, Cavaradossi being led forward to stand by the opposite wall, while Tosca retired to a spot where she was hidden from the soldiers.

As the officer lowered his sword, the volley rang out, and Cavaradossi instantly fell in a crumpled heap. Spoletta, preventing the sergeant from giving the usual *coup de grâce*, covered the body with a cloth; and the firing-party then retired immediately, leaving the singer alone.

As soon as the last soldier had departed, Tosca ran forward, calling eagerly upon her lover to rise that they might get away at once. As Cavaradossi did not move at her call, she snatched away the cloth in agitation; and then, to her horror, she saw that he was dead and that she had thus been cruelly betrayed.

She flung herself upon the corpse of her lover in the utmost grief, weeping and moaning wildly. A few moments later, however, she was disturbed by the loud cries of Scarpia's officers; and realizing from this noise that the murder of their chief had now become known, she sprang to her feet in terror. Almost immediately afterwards a crowd of soldiers rushed into the courtyard headed by Spoletta; but before they could seize her, the heartbroken Tosca sprang upon the parapet and hurled herself into the depths below.

TURANDOT   *Puccini*

A PRINCESS of Ancient China, named Turandot, was so enthrall-
ingly beautiful that she fascinated all who beheld her. Yet
Turandot's heart was as cold as a stone. To all the princes and
great lords who wished to marry her, she gave the same curt
answer, "No!" What was more, she had received permission
from her father, the Emperor Altoum, to do as she would with
them. This is what she did.

Whenever a new suitor appeared at the palace, Turandot would
set him three riddles to answer. If he were able to give her the
correct replies, the Princess promised that she would marry him.
If, however, he proved unable to answer the riddles correctly,
then he must be instantly beheaded.

Because the riddles were so extremely difficult, nobody had
yet been able to solve them correctly. Consequently many handsome young princes had already lost their lives. The old
Emperor himself would gladly have saved them, but was unable
to break his royal word given to the heartless Princess, who
refused to release him from his promise. And so the executions
went on.

On the day when this story opens, the Prince of Persia was to
be beheaded as soon as the moon arose. He had failed to solve
the conundrums set him by the Princess of China; therefore he
must die.

In the late evening a vast crowd gathered in the square just
within the Walls of the Violet City of Peking near the place of
execution. The royal palace rose on one side of the square, its
bastions and porticoes decorated with unicorns, dragons, and
other strange monsters. At the foot of the main portico an
enormous bronze gong was suspended from two arches. When
this gong was struck three times it was the signal that a new
competitor for the hand of the Princess had arrived and was
ready to try his luck.

A noisy rabble had gathered around the highest bastion, from
which a pompous Mandarin was reading out once more the
Princess's Proclamation regarding those who sought her hand in
marriage. He also announced the coming execution of the unhappy young Prince of Persia at moonrise that same evening.
The crowd hailed the proclamation with savage glee. They were
proud of their fierce and lovely Princess. They were also more

than a little afraid of her. It was wise to acclaim her decree.

Caught in this rough rabble were two strangers, an old man, attended by a slave-girl named Liu. Both wore the garb of beggars, and looked weary and worn. When the old man was presently knocked down by the jostling crowd, the girl, terrified, called aloud for help to prevent him from being trampled upon. In answer to her cry, another stranger, a handsome youth—who was, in reality, a wandering Prince in disguise—hastened forward and managed to drag the old man to a place of safety.

To his amazement, the stranger Prince—whose name was Calaf—now recognized in the old man he had rescued his own father, Timur, the dethroned King of Tartary. The latter's throne had been seized by a usurper and Timur had been compelled to make his escape into China, attended only by the faithful slave-maiden, Liu. Ragged and unknown, the pair had wandered from place to place, and had now reached Peking. A happy reunion took place between the wanderers, who had never expected to meet again. But Prince Calaf declared they must be careful to remain unknown, since they were still in danger from the Tartar usurper who sought their lives and had spies everywhere.

It was at this moment, the moon being about to rise, that the execution procession came along—a terrible procession headed by the executioner carrying his gigantic sword. After him came soldiers and Mandarins in gorgeous robes, followed by the fair young Prince of Persia whose life was forfeited. The Princess herself would appear presently to gloat over her victim.

The crowd of onlookers, though they adored their cruel Princess, whose beauty and haughty spirit held them in thrall, now felt a sudden pity for the gentle young Prince. He walked like one in a dream with a sweet smile on his face, willing to lay down his life at the word of the royal maiden he loved.

The stranger Prince, Calaf, was filled with indignation at the sight; and, careless of danger, he began to rail and even to call down curses upon the royal tyrant. The words died on his lips, however; for, at that moment, the Princess Turandot herself appeared on the balcony of the adjoining palace.

With the light of the newly-risen moon shining upon her, Turandot revealed herself to the stranger, a vision of loveliness, as she stood there proudly in her magnificent robes and jewelled head-dress. She was, indeed, a glittering figure, whose slightest movement seemed to send out sparks of fire from the many flashing jewels she wore—diamonds, opals, emeralds, rubies, sapphires, amber, turquoise, pearls. She appeared for a few moments only, a gloating triumph in her eyes. Then, as the crowd fell to the ground with bowed heads, instantly silent under her magic power, she imperiously made the Death Sign by raising her arm, and withdrew.

The procession now proceeded on its way to the place of execution, leaving the square empty save for the unknown royal exiles and their slave-maiden. The young Prince Calaf still remained spellbound by the fatal beauty of Turandot. All his anger against her had suddenly turned to overwhelming love, a joyful light shone in his eyes, and cries of extravagant admiration poured from his lips.

The old King and Liu tried to drag him away with them, knowing the danger of dallying in that spot. Calaf, however, refused to go with them, declaring that he now loved the Princess and would seek her hand in marriage. He would strike the great gong three times, as the signal that he was willing to undergo the test of guessing the three riddles. He scarcely heeded the despairing entreaties of his unhappy father, the frightened pleas of Liu. Even when the grim sound of groans and triumphant cries presently announced that the Prince of Persia no longer lived, he still repeated his resolve.

When the Officers and Court Mandarins returned to the square with the procession, he ran into their midst and demanded to be brought before the Princess at once as her new suitor. Amazed at the young man's eagerness to step into the jaws of death, the Mandarins wisely advised him instead to depart and save his life, declaring that he would never be able to solve the very difficult problems that would be put to him. In particular, three extremely important Court Officials—by name, Ping, Pong, and Pang—tried likewise to dissuade him. Though they lived in such an atmosphere of tragedy, these three ministers had a sense of humour. They painted the tortures and woes of those who offended against the Imperial decrees in a comical fashion, but declared that only a witless fool would wish to endure them, all the same.

Calaf, however, refused to listen to their advice, or to the further pleadings of his father and Liu. He dashed madly to the gong and, seizing the great hammer beside it, struck three resounding blows upon it, at the same time crying aloud: "Turandot! Turandot! Turandot!"

He was then admitted into the palace, to await his trial before the Princess.

. . . .

Next day, the three light-hearted Court Officials, Ping, Pong, and Pang, superintended the preparations for a grand banquet in one of the Royal Pavilions. They took great pains to see that everything was done in the most magnificent manner. It was just possible that this might prove to be a wedding feast—though they felt that a funeral was the more likely event. There was little chance of this foolish new suitor being able to guess their Princess's riddles. Why was he not warned by the fate of the Prince of Persia, who had perished the evening before?

But it was their job to be prepared for a wedding banquet. So they went cheerfully about their tasks, making merry jokes even though wishing themselves safely back in their own peaceful country homes. China had gone mad with these constant executions of crazy lovers! Catch *them* being such fools!

Meanwhile, the Unknown Prince—who refused to give his name to anyone, because of his royal father's danger—now found himself in the midst of a gorgeous scene in the Place of Audience in front of the palace. Here again, massive sculptures of dragons, unicorns, griffins, and giant tortoises were to be seen on every side, together with rainbow-hued lanterns and rich brocade hangings. Calaf, however, was not overawed by this grandeur. Had he not been brought up in the equal magnificence of the royal House of Tartary? When, presently, he looked up and beheld at the top of a wide marble staircase the Emperor Altoum of China, seated upon an ivory throne surrounded by his Court Officials, he merely bowed to him with the simple dignity of one likewise of royal birth.

The old Emperor was full of distress on yet another handsome youth presenting himself as the certain victim of his icy-hearted daughter. Like his ministers, he eagerly begged him to depart while there was yet time. His entreaties, however, were in vain; the young Prince was too deeply in love to be turned from his purpose.

The Heralds now announced the arrival of the Princess Turandot, who entered with her attendants and stood beside the throne. The royal maiden first announced her reasons for not desiring to marry, and for treating her suitors with such severity. In ages gone by, she declared, a Princess of her House had been torn from the throne and slain by a cruel royal invader. It was to avenge that unhappy ancestress that Turandot herself now showed no mercy upon her own princely victims. To modify her cruel acts, however, she had devised her famous three riddles, so that each suitor should at least have the chance of saving his life and of winning her as his bride. She merely smiled coldly when Calaf, still spellbound by her entrancing beauty, declared that his love would help him to solve the problems.

This was the first riddle put to him by Turandot: "What is that which hovers in the night as a phantom, soaring upwards and spreading its wings over all? Everybody calls upon it and implores its aid. The phantom departs at dawn, but is born again and again in every human heart. What is the answer to my riddle?"

After a few moments' silence, the young Prince, full of joy, eagerly cried: "The answer, O Princess, is 'Hope'! Hope is ever born again in the human heart!"

The Wise Men of the Court who stood by with silken scrolls upon which the answers were written, declared that the suitor had replied correctly.

Turandot, though unpleasantly surprised by this quick solution, smiled again in an icy manner as she put her second question: "What have you that is like a flaring flame, but is no flame; sometimes it is madness and burns with fever; and sometimes it languishes! If you lose your life it grows cold; but it flames as you dream of victory! When you listen to its voice, you tremble. Like the sunset it is dyed in a crimson glow!"

What a riddle was this! The young Prince was filled with dismay for a short time; for the Princess's mocking glances were not easy to bear, and her dazzling beauty took his breath away. All thought him doomed already. But, suddenly, Calaf's brain cleared, and he knew what to say. He cried out: "Mighty Princess! The answer is 'Blood'!"

He was right; and Turandot grew alarmed and angry. Nobody had ever before guessed the answers to two of her riddles! She now swept down the steps from the throne, pressed close to the kneeling Prince and ferociously hissed her third riddle at him, almost touching his lips with her own, hoping thus to drive his too-bright wits astray: "Fire gives thee ice, and from thy fire more ice comes! Clear as day, yet not to be found out! The power that wills you free will make you a slave! Yet taking you as slave, will make you king!"

Again Calaf remained kneeling, with his head hidden in his hands, while Turandot repeated in triumph: "What is this ice that turns to fire, O stranger?"

Suddenly Calaf knew what it was, for his love made his wits clearer than ever before. Springing to his feet, he cried out gladly: "The answer is 'Turandot'! The fire of my love shall melt the ice in thy heart, O Princess!"

The Wise Men consulted their scrolls, and declared this third answer also to be correct; and tumultuous applause arose.

Turandot staggered back, furious because the quick-witted Prince had guessed her three famous riddles. Furious, too, because she would now have to keep her royal promise—which the now delighted old Emperor insisted upon! But when Calaf next boldly took her in his arms and kissed her, strange to say, she did not resist, for she felt love in her own heart for the first time.

Nevertheless, Turandot was appalled and passionately angry about the whole matter; and, to mollify her somewhat, Calaf now very foolishly said he himself would ask her just one riddle. He would still give the victory to her if she could find out his name before the next morning—since this was still unknown to all.

And now came a tragic incident. Turandot commanded everybody in the city to spend the whole night trying to solve this problem for her, on pain of torture—she was really a very fierce Princess!

In pursuance of this command, some of her soldiers seized the slave-girl, Liu, whom they had seen talking with the stranger suitor earlier in the day; and they roughly ordered her to reveal this secret. They felt she must certainly know the stranger's name. Fearing that torture might cause her to betray her beloved Prince, the devoted slave-girl quickly snatched a dagger from her captor and stabbed herself to the heart.

Later on, the secret of his name was revealed—again not wisely! —to Turandot by Calaf himself. By means of his dashing approach to her, the young Prince had already won her heart, though she would not yet admit this fact.

Left alone with the Princess—now closely veiled—after the body of the faithful Liu had been carried away, Calaf first of all reproached her sternly for her savage cruelty. Then, his passionate love for her conquering all, he boldly tore off her veil, that he might gaze upon the beauty that entranced him. Furiously denouncing such an act as sacrilege against one known and revered as " the Daughter of Heaven ", Turandot defied him to approach another step nearer—though showing amazement and a strange confusion at his audacity.

But Calaf was now sure of himself, and of her. With a cry of rapture, he clasped her now yielding body in his arms, and kissed her passionately again and again. He knew that he had conquered and that the heart of Turandot now felt the answering warmth of the love she had so long denied herself. Turandot knew it, too; but she still held back. She had not yet learned his name.

When, however, with his loving arms around her, she presently bade him depart with his name still unknown, since she no longer desired to triumph over him, he declared that he, also, had no wish for triumph. He then calmly announced himself as Calaf, son of Timur, the exiled King of Tartary.

For a short time, the former cold, cruel Turandot seemed about to return, and triumph again shone in her eyes. Having now learned his name and thus herself become the victor, she declared that the young Prince must follow her to the Hall of Audience, there to learn his fate! But her triumph was also to be the triumph of Calaf, whose heart was quickly filled with joy.

When the royal pair reached the throne, Turandot announced to the Emperor that she had guessed the name of the princely suitor who had solved her three riddles. Then she added, with a sweet and happy smile revealing that her once icy, cruel heart was now filled with warmth and tenderness: "His name is LOVE!"

ALEKO   *Rachmaninov*

IN a certain peaceful spot on the banks of a river which flowed through vast country wilds a tribe of gipsies had pitched their tents. Here, late one evening, the careless wanderers gathered about their blazing camp-fires, or stood in groups outside the tents, chatting and singing snatches of merry songs as they waited to refresh themselves with the savoury supper which already steamed and bubbled in the huge cauldrons hanging from tripods over the fires.

They were a simple, happy folk, these wanderers, who lived and loved and died amidst the beauties of nature, knowing not the many evils and doubtful joys of civilization. They loved freedom above all things; and their code of honour, while forbidding them to judge any man, would not permit them to dwell with a wrongdoer in their midst.

This evening as the rising moon, silvery and bright, appeared above the glittering stream, a strange feeling of uneasiness had crept over the gipsies. In order to distract their minds and to make the time pass by more quickly while their supper was in process of preparation, the young men and girls called upon the Chief to tell them a story.

The leader of the gipsies was a venerable and dignified old man, whose sad glowering eyes and deeply lined face revealed the passage of passion's fiery touch and sorrow's bitter sting. A host of unhappy recollections having intruded themselves upon his broodings this evening, he gathered the young people about him and told them the story of his own early love and of the grievous wrong that had been done him by a stranger not of his own tribe.

"Years ago," he said, "I loved and wedded the most beautiful maiden of our tribe, and for one short year enjoyed the divine rapture that only those who truly love can know. Had a fabulous fortune or even a kingdom been offered to me in exchange I would have laughed such a gift to scorn; for the love of my fair Marioula was more precious to me than all the wealth and honours that the world could lay at my feet. When our child, the maiden Zemfira yonder, was born, I felt that my joy was almost too great to bear—and alas! I soon found that it was certainly too great to last!

"Marioula, free, loving child of the desert as she was, proved herself to be as fickle as she was fair! Another tribe of wanderers pitched their camp beside ours just after my joy had lasted for a year; and though they rested in our neighbourhood but two days, when they struck their tents my beautiful but false Marioula went with them—her love having been stolen from me by one of their hot-blooded youths, for whom she forsook me, her adoring husband, and her helpless babe! Ah me! The woe of that cruel hour struck deep into my heart and the pain of the still bleeding wound will never depart whilst breath remains in me!"

While the old Chief thus related the story of his life's tragedy, his lovely daughter—the same Zemfira whose fickle mother had deserted her in infancy—shivered slightly as she glanced furtively from her husband, Aleko, to the handsome young gipsy who was now her own secret lover. By a strange fatality the faithlessness of the Chief's wife was actually at that moment being repeated in her daughter—who, whilst inheriting the mother's alluring beauty, also showed an equally capricious and fickle temperament, chafing at restraint, fitful as the wind, and claiming love from all for the satisfaction of her passionate nature.

A year ago Aleko, her husband, had come as a stranger to the tribe and, declaring himself weary of the trials and disappointments of ordinary civilized life, had begged to be allowed to remain for a time with the gipsies, who received him with the courtesy and hospitality of their kind.

Aleko, a disappointed and somewhat melancholy man, past his first youth, soon recovered tranquillity and peace of mind among the simple-hearted wanderers; and, on becoming acquainted with the Chief's beautiful daughter, he had fallen passionately in love with her, loving with all the intensity of a man who had never before felt the magic thrill of a woman's attraction.

The ardent young Zemfira on her part was equally attracted by the stranger, about whom hung an air of mystery and romance; and upon her accepting his love and surrendering her own in return, the pair were wedded in accordance with the quaint gipsy rites and customs.

In one short year, however, the fickle Zemfira tired of the stranger husband who adored her and began to accept the attentions of a young gipsy of her own tribe, whose passionate love-making she eagerly responded to and whom she met in secret whenever the opportunity occurred.

This evening as the Chief's tragic story came to an end and his hearers trooped off to partake of the savoury supper now ready, Zemfira and her lover snatched a few moments' conversation and arranged to steal away together from the camp that night after the moon had set and all was dark.

The young gipsy scornfully laughed away Zemfira's timid expressions of fear lest Aleko should discover their secret plans and her declaration that he was already suspicious because of her coldness and indifference to him. She added that he might prove dangerous in his jealousy, which he had plainly exhibited in a sudden outburst of anger on hearing the old Chief's story—the circumstances of the latter having evidently caused him to doubt still more the constancy of his own fair wife. Her lover, however, succeeded in reassuring her; and after many tender embraces the pair parted, as Aleko was observed to be lurking near.

Zemfira retired at once to her tent, where she sat beside the cradle of her infant child and began to sing a cradle-song. The latter, however, instead of being a gentle lullaby, soon developed into a wild gipsy song, in which she railed recklessly at her husband and hinted audaciously at a secret lover whose embraces she meant to accept.

Aleko, upon entering the tent at this moment, was shocked and angered on hearing the song, which strengthened his suspicions of her change towards himself; and he sternly rebuked the wild Zemfira, who, however, paid no heed to him, but hurried from the tent still recklessly singing her tantalizing song of defiance.

Aleko, now sadly realizing that the love of his beautiful gipsy wife was indeed lost to him for ever, at first gave himself up to despair and grief. Then a fierce, unrestrained anger seized him; and vowing that none other should enjoy the favours of his beloved one, even though these were denied to himself, he hastened after the now flying form of Zemfira, who had vanished in the darkness.

Meanwhile, the lovers had met at the appointed spot. Zemfira, full of fear for the anger of her jealous husband, was eagerly urging the young gipsy to hasten their departure—which the latter continually delayed in order to enjoy the intense joy of the moment—when Aleko himself suddenly appeared before them. He upbraided the pair for their perfidy and threatened the young gipsy in furious accents.

Zemfira bravely met the wrath of the husband whom she had wronged, declaring that true love was free and not to be restrained; and she added that she was willing to die rather than to return to one who no longer held her heart. Almost in the same breath, however, she entreated her lover, in terrified accents, to fly from the vengeance she could read in her husband's flashing eyes; but, ere he could escape, Aleko, in a frenzy of jealous passion, sprang upon the young gipsy and stabbed him to the heart.

Zemfira, with a cry of despairing grief, flung herself, weeping, upon the dead body of her lover, uttering wild curses upon his murderer; and Aleko, still further infuriated, drew forth the dagger again and plunged it into the breast of the unhappy girl.

By this time the whole camp had been aroused by the noise of the quarrel and the cries of the lovers as they fell; and the old Chief and his sacred companions now appeared upon the scene as the beautiful Zemfira expired.

The passion-tossed Aleko, soon filled with remorse and despair, knelt over the corpse of his beloved Zemfira imploring forgiveness; and then, standing bravely before the bereaved and grief-stricken father, he awaited sentence, humbly expressing his readiness to expiate his crime by death.

But the old Chief, with calm and beautiful dignity, merely rebuked him sternly for thus bringing bloodshed and strife into his tribe's peaceful gipsy life. Then, declaring that while he and his simple folk judged not and took no man's life in expiation, they could not permit a murderer to abide in their camp, he commanded the young men to carry away the bodies of the dead lovers. After this pronouncement, he returned to his tent, followed quietly and sadly by the rest of his people.

Thus was the wretched Aleko left alone without love or companionship, to wander forth into the world, an exile, who must expiate his sin and bear his grief as best he might.

FRANCESCA DA RIMINI   *Rachmaninov*

WITHIN the First Circle of the inferno gigantic black rocks led
down into the terrible abyss below. Gloomy darkness reigned for
the most part, but every now and again the sombre blackness was
suddenly illuminated brilliantly by red gleams from the everlasting
flames and steel-blue lightning from the lurid clouds that were
rushing through the storm-riven sky.

When the subterranean rumblings and the ominous rolling of
the thunder ceased for a few brief moments, heart-rending cries
and the hopeless sighs of souls in torment could be heard; these
again would quickly be drowned by the awful crashing of fresh
peals of thunder and the roar of the returning whirlwinds.

Into this awe-inspiring scene, breathing the sultry atmosphere
with difficulty, appeared the great Italian poet, Dante—according
to the wonderful vision he afterwards pictured so exquisitely in
his masterpiece, the " Divine Comedy ". The latter tells of the
imaginary experience of a soul after death in the three stages he
believed it to pass through and described as the " Inferno ", the
" Purgatorio " and the " Paradiso "

As Dante, in his vision, appeared on the fearful rocky heights of
the First Circle of the Inferno, he was accompanied by the Shade
of the Roman poet, Virgil, who was to be his guide through
the wonderful and mysterious paths and by-ways of these subterranean regions. As the two travellers drew near to the edge
of the precipice, the spectral guide suddenly drew back and
shuddered, as though with fear; then, turning to Dante, he
announced that they were about to descend into the yawning
abyss and that his companion must be of a good courage and
follow closely.

Dante replied that it was not encouraging to follow one who
appeared obviously to be afraid of what was before him; but the
Shade of Virgil told him that though he shuddered and drew back
for a moment on approaching the precipice, his action was not
one of fear, but rather of compassion for those unhappy souls
who were suffering torments below. He then called upon Dante
to hasten ere their courage should in truth desert them; and,
without further pause, the pair began their awful descent into the
abyss and were soon lost in the darkness below.

Dense black clouds gathered around and enwrapped them as
in a stifling mantle, and at first nothing could be distinguished

through the thick atmosphere; but after the travellers had descended for a considerable distance the air cleared somewhat, and, though an intense gloom reigned supreme, objects and landmarks could be observed once more.

Dante now saw that he stood with his companion on the summit of a high rock which ran down sheer into the abyss. On every side overhanging rocks were to be seen, while the angry crimson horizon stretched far away in the distance like a streak of blood, whence came the warning sound of a quickly approaching storm, still mingled with the incessant cries and moans of the souls in torment which never ceased.

As Dante discovered himself upon the summit of the rock his spectre guide informed him that they had now arrived at the place where eternal darkness reigned in company with an eternal and terrible tempest. This storm drew in its wake the spirits suffering in anguish and continually gathered in its tumult souls from everywhere with no hope of release from their endless sufferings.

"Who, then, are these unhappy souls?" asked Dante in compassionate tones; and the Shade of Virgil replied:

"These are the tortured spirits of those who, in earthly life, permitted the passions of love and desire to reign uncontrolled so that they dominated over reason and ruined their lives! Behold! Here they come!"

Just then the noise of the approaching whirlwind drew nearer; and, next moment, the tempest burst upon them in all its fury, so that the voices of the travellers could no longer be heard. In the wake of the storm came crowds of phantoms rushing past them, with the loud sighs and lamentations only uttered by those in anguish.

Dante was horrified by this fearful spectacle and drew back, aghast; but the Shade of Virgil was bolder and called to several of the phantoms by the names they had borne in their earthly life.

After a while the storm grew somewhat less violent, there was a slight lull, and the ranks of the suffering spirits became thinner; and presently there appeared the phantoms of Paolo and Francesca, the devoted lovers of Rimini, whose interlocked arms and appearance of loving one another still even in their agony strangely attracted Dante, so that he inquired of his companion their names, expressing a wish to speak with them.

In reply to his request Virgil said: "In the name of the love which has drawn them to this suffering, ask them, and they will speak to you!"

As the spirit lovers came floating by, united still even in the midst of their torment, Dante approached them, therefore, and called out to them compassionately :

"Unhappy spirits, your sufferings make me weep! I prithee, if it is possible, draw nigh unto us, and while there is a lull in this terrible tempest, tell us where you hail from and how you came to fall thus!"

As if in answer to the poet's plea, the lover phantoms drew nearer; and at the same moment the dense clouds descended once more and darkness reigned. But, out of the darkness, the voices of Paolo and Francesca were heard saying: "There is no greater suffering in the world than the remembrance of happy days when happiness has fled!"

Then they related the story of their tragic passion to the sympathetic poet, knowing that he who had also known the joys and sorrows of a beautiful love would have mercy and compassion upon their trials, temptations and sufferings.

THE LOVE OF PAOLO AND FRANCESCA

Within his splendid palace at Rimini the powerful and successful Commander, Malatesta, was engaged in discussing with a famous militant Cardinal his plans for the defeat of the Ghibellines, the great enemies of the Pope. For a long time past these powerful foes had threatened to secure the upper hand; but now a plan of campaign had been formed for their defeat. When this new scheme had been discussed and approved, the mighty leader, Malatesta, entreated the Cardinal to bless him, his sword and his troops. Willingly and with confidence the Cardinal pronounced his solemn benediction upon the enterprise; and then he departed, with his attendants, in pomp and dignity.

After the departure of the prelate, Malatesta addressed his own attendants and generals, desiring them to bid farewell to their wives and friends and to go forth and make their preparations for immediate departure to the seat of war. He then despatched a servant to bring into his presence his wife, Francesca.

As he now waited in the chamber alone a dark frown overspread the stern countenance of the Commander-in-Chief. He was a prey to that torturing malady, jealousy, having reason to fear that his fair wife did not return his love, but that, although her hand was his, she had bestowed her heart elsewhere. So strong a hold had this tormenting suspicion taken upon him that even the sound of the trumpets' fanfare calling the soldiers and strong young men together to go forth to fight the enemies at their gates—a sound which had formerly been wont to thrill him and to fill his heart with rejoicing—had now no power to stir him even slightly, for his jealous thoughts would give him no peace.

Yet he had only himself to blame, having done his wooing by proxy. Having beheld the beautiful Francesca he had immediately desired to wed with her, but, being occupied with military affairs and also unaccustomed to social dalliance, he had sent his young brother, Paolo, as the bearer of his proposals to the maiden's father asking her hand in marriage.

The proposals were willingly accepted; but, whether carelessly or for some reason known only to himself, Francesca's father permitted her to believe that it was Paola himself who was the suitor for her hand. Possibly he may have thought that the maiden would be afraid of the black-browed Malatesta and that he might have trouble in forcing her consent to a marriage with one so much older than herself, and one, withal, of so serious and gloomy a disposition—or, perhaps, on seeing that she was instantly attracted by the grace and charm of the young Paolo and that she seemed naturally to regard him as her suitor, he preferred to leave her thus unenlightened in order to secure her willing agreement with the proposals brought.

However the deception may have arisen, Francesca and Paolo had no sooner looked into one another's eyes than a deep and abiding love sprang up in their hearts. The fair maiden, imagining that it was Malatesta who stood before her, placed her hand in that of the latter's ambassador, declaring that she willingly gave it to him, that her heart was his also and that she would love him for ever.

When the nuptial day arrived, however, and she realized the awful mistake she had made—or had been permitted to make—and that it was the grim warrior who was to be her husband and not the handsome young Paolo, she was overcome with grief and the sunshine of joy left her heart for ever. Although she was compelled to give her hand to Malatesta and went through the marriage ceremony as one in a dream, she could not also give him her heart, having already bestowed her love upon another. She became a dutiful and obedient wife; but her lack of warmth to him was a constant source of disappointment to her gloomy husband, whose own passion was the more strongly kindled by reason of her coldness.

All this passed through the mind of Malatesta as he now sat in his audience chamber waiting for his wife to come and bid him farewell before his departure to the war; and he wondered if, had she never seen Paolo, Francesca would have loved him, Malatesta. Accustomed to compel attention and to carry all before him

Malatesta was inclined to think that the latter would have been the case; and a jealous anger grew up in his heart against his young brother. He decided that he must get rid of the latter by some means or other; and so strong a hold did this dark thought take of him that he even went so far as to invoke the aid of infernal agencies in his evil scheme.

He was interrupted, however, by the entrance of Francesca, who came and stood before him submissively with folded hands and listened quietly and without any emotion as he informed her of his departure that night to fight the Pope's enemies, and that, therefore, he must leave her for a time. Francesca asked that she might be permitted to enter a convent during his absence, but her husband refused her request curtly, saying that he had appointed his brother Paolo to act as her guardian during the wars. He gazed searchingly at her as he made this announcement; but Francesca had her feelings well under control and replied quietly that she would obey him.

Her calmness and apparent resignation served only to exasperate Malatesta. He asked her roughly and fiercely if she ever intended to love him or, at least, to treat him with some degree of the warmth expected by a husband of his wife; and he bade her look upon the havoc she had wrought in him—the wreck of his former self, owing to his unrequited love for her.

To this outburst Francesca replied very gently: "Forgive me, my lord, but I cannot lie by saying that I love you when I do not!"

She then asked him when he would return; and he replied ominously: "When the Pope's foes are beaten and when I have slain *all* my enemies!"

Though still raging with jealousy and unsatisfied passion Malatesta then hastily dismissed Francesca; and after giving instructions to his brother to act as the guardian of his wife, goods, and chattels during his absence, he departed for the wars at the head of his troops.

After the departure of Malatesta a period of great happiness dawned for Francesca and Paolo. Owing to the latter's trust as guardian of his brother's wife and property, they were now able to meet frequently and to pass many joyful hours together. At first they tried to meet as ordinary friends, endeavouring earnestly to avoid the tender intercourse of lovers; but, after a while, they found that it was impossible to resist the imperative call of youth and the passionate love that consumed them both.

The constant fear of her stern lord's wrath and her own sincere desire to fight the temptation of disloyalty to him, caused Francesca to struggle valiantly against the eager pleading and passion in the eyes of Paolo, whom she forbade to speak to her of love; but though she succeeded for a time in crushing down the smouldering fire she could not extinguish it nor prevent it from bursting forth eventually into unquenchable flames. For these two young people, so fresh and so fair, seemed to have been created for one another; and their rapture was so beautiful a thing that it seemed as natural for them to love as for the flowers to bloom and the sun to shine. Cruel, indeed, was the fate which ordained that so perfect a love should be unlawful; still more cruel the temptations placed in their path; and most cruel of them all the vengeance and punishment later meted out to them for following the dictates of their young hearts.

When Francesca found that Paola could no longer refrain from speaking of love in her presence, she brought forth a book and made him read to her instead; and, for a short time, she gained a further respite. But the book she happened to produce told of the immortal passion of those fairest of lovers, Lancelot and Guinevere, and it was not long before these readings added fuel to the fire she thus sought to quench; for the enthralling story of those royal lovers of olden times was a perfect picture of their own love.

Thus the weeks and months went by, swiftly and enchantingly, like a beautiful dream. Paolo and Francesca were so happy that they almost forgot that Malatesta was at the wars and would one day return to claim his own and that gloomy darkness would follow the golden sunshine they now rejoiced in.

The end came with tragic swiftness.

First came the day when Francesca could no longer keep Paolo from declaring his overwhelming love for her and entreating for hers in return. According to their usual custom she sat at her tapestry frame plying her needle while Paolo lay at her feet and read aloud to her from the beautiful story they both loved so well. After reading of the many wonderful exploits performed by the chivalrous knight, Lancelot, in honour of his fair lady, Paolo asked Francesca if she believed that the Queen would receive the hero in answer to his plea.

Francesca replied: "Surely! She would be cruel if she refused to do so."

"You also are cruel, for you often refuse to see me!" began Paolo, but Francesca gently stemmed the coming outburst and bade him read further. Then Paolo read on, describing how the Queen received Lancelot kindly; and both agreed that the loving pair must have been very happy. But when the next few lines pictured how, upon the Queen's inquiry as to what reward Lancelot sought for the deeds he had done and how, for answer, the knight had gazed into her eyes and they both understood the meaning of his gaze, Paolo could read no further. Flinging himself at the feet of Francesca he sobbed forth his own love, which refused to be repressed any longer; and he entreated her to have pity upon him and to love him in return.

Francesca made one more desperate attempt to resist the fierce answering call of her own heart, gently bidding the kneeling youth to remember that though they must suffer renunciation in their present lives, yet joy would be theirs in the next world. Paolo, however, declared that love in Paradise seemed cold and a long way off, and that he longed only for love now in this present life; and he added passionately : " I would gladly renounce Paradise and all it means for one sweet kiss from thee, for that kiss would hold in one moment all that Eternity could give ! "

He endeavoured to draw her towards him as he spoke, but Francesca, pale and frightened, drew back, bidding him remember that she belonged to another; and she added that if she should thus prove unfaithful to her wedded lord—even though she loved him not—she believed that the punishment of the Inferno awaited her and her fellow-sinner.

" What of that ! " cried Paolo, once more drawing her into his grasp. " At least, we should be together ! We were made for one another ! Therefore, let us love and live and suffer together ! Come, love me, my Francesca, and let the memory of our kisses be eternal happiness for us ! "

Francesca could no longer resist the passionate pleading of Paolo and the call of youth within her; and with a cry of joy the lovers fell into each other's arms and resigned themselves to the exquisite happiness of the love that consumed them.

Thus were they found by the returning conqueror, Malatesta, who took up his sword and slew them both as they lay clasped in their first embrace. So passed away, in that moment of perfect joy, Paola and Francesca, from the dazzling golden light of love into the blackness of oblivion, to awaken in the abode of lost souls, as seen in the vision of the poet Dante.

EPILOGUE

As the unhappy Shades of Paolo and Francesca finished the recital of their tale of love and woe and passed on with the other phantoms upon the rushing wind of the eternal storm, Dante, full of compassion for their sufferings, fell back unconscious. At the same moment the sad dirge of the lost spirits could be heard in the distance now chanting in chorus: "There is no greater sorrow in the world than the remembrance of happy days when happiness has fled!"

L'HEURE ESPAGNOLE   *Ravel*
(*The Spanish Hour*)

How quickly an hour can pass! Even in Spain, where, in the eighteenth century, time moved at a more leisurely pace than now. And some hours are so precious that it seems a tragedy to lose a single golden moment of them.

So thought pretty Concepçion, the fascinating young wife of staid old Torquemada, the famous clockmaker of Toledo. This was Thursday, the day on which her elderly husband went out to wind up the town clocks, and she could count on him being away from home for at least an hour or so.

During that magic hour she could always arrange for her handsome young lover, Gonzalve, to visit her in safety—a rapturous hour to which she looked forward all the week. To-day was another of these delectable Thursdays, and her lover was already almost due—but, horrors! Her husband had not yet departed upon his weekly errand! How she longed for him to go!

But Torquemada, though surrounded by clocks in his shop, had forgotten the time. With a clockmaker's magnifying-glass stuck in his eye-socket, he was still busily examining the intricate works of a small jewelled box from which, after a few turns of a key, a dainty little bird would pop out and sing a tune. Various other musical-boxes lay on the shelves beside him; and clocks and watches of all kinds and sizes filled almost every available inch of space.

On either side of the window stood a huge Catalan clock, of which Torquemada was particularly proud, for each was a little taller than a man. The gentle ticking and swinging of pendulums, the chiming of bells, and the striking of hours—often at varying times!—was the music he loved best. And when a cuckoo's cheerful notes were heard at regular intervals, the old clockmaker's heart rejoiced. That cuckoo-clock was his delight

The cuckoo's note, however, should now have reminded him

that he was already due at the clock-tower of the Town Hall; but it didn't.

Just then, too, an unexpected customer, Ramiro, a muleteer, entered the shop. He handed a very big watch to the clockmaker, declaring that it kept stopping. This was awkward, since it was his, Ramiro's, job to drive the government mules at certain fixed hours, carrying the parcel-post on their backs. So he must always be punctual.

Torquemada admired the watch, which Ramiro proudly declared to be a family heirloom. It had once saved his uncle, the famous toreador, from death. The big watch under his belt had stopped the bull's horns from goring him. And now the watch itself had stopped.

Torquemada said he would soon put it to rights. He was just taking it to pieces when Concepçion, his wife, now seriously annoyed by the curtailing of her precious hour with her lover, ran into the shop. Why was her husband still there? Had he forgotten that it was time for him to be winding the government clocks?

In a great flurry of dismay, old Torquemada put down the interesting watch that had once saved a toreador's life and began bustling about looking for his hat and his tools.

To add to Concepçion's annoyance, she now noticed that the two big clocks still stood in her husband's shop. Had not Torquemada promised that she should have one of the fine Catalan clocks in her own room? But the old clockmaker, though always indulgent to his pretty young wife, declared that such clocks were much too heavy for him to carry about.

Then, snatching up his hat and his bag of tools, Torquemada apologetically begged his customer to await his return, when he would deal with the mending of the watch; and off he trotted in a great hurry to attend to the town clocks. This was a much more important matter. He must not lose his government job!

Luckily Ramiro was a good-humoured fellow. He was also delighted with the many charms of the clockmaker's pretty young wife. He had not the slightest objection to waiting an hour or so. What a pity, though, that he had no conversational gifts. He scarcely knew what to say to a lovely lady. But he would certainly do his best and make the most of his waiting time.

His presence, however, did not suit the plans of Concepçion. What bad luck for her that this tiresome customer should remain here, just when her lover, her darling Gonzalve, was about to arrive! She must find the former a job of some kind to do. Ah!

The Catalan clock. He was a finely-built young man, and was sure to be strong.

Very sweetly she asked the muleteer if he would mind carrying one of the Catalan clocks up the stairs into her room. Not at all, it would be a mere nothing to him; he was used to heavy work. So declared Ramiro, delighted to give pleasure to the charming Señora without having to make conversation. Was not every muleteer a sort of amateur removal man? He seized one of the enormous Catalan clocks, heaved it carefully on his broad shoulders and back, and, moving slowly out into the passage beyond, began to mount the staircase with his load.

Concepçion heaved a sigh of relief. The stranger was safely out of the shop for the time being. And here, at last, was her beloved bachelor sweetheart, Gonzalve—that handsome and precious young man!—coming in at the door. She ran to meet him, rapturously flinging herself into his arms.

But what was wrong with her lover to-day? True, he embraced her with his usual fervour; but he kept uttering little singing notes and making every phrase into a poem. He declared the bright flowery enamel of the clocks and musical-boxes to be as a garden of sweet blossoms, of which she was the fairest. So wrapped up in metaphors and the beginnings of poems was he, indeed, that he scarcely noticed her eager desire for caresses and yet more caresses! How tiresome of him to waste time making up absurd poems in which she had no interest! And their precious hour would so quickly slip away—for that silly old Torquemada, because of being late, would be sure to hurry through his work and return sooner than usual! Besides, the muleteer would be back from his job upstairs before there was time for more loving embraces, unless Gonzalve came down to earth a little quicker!

But Gonzalve obviously fancied himself as a poet, and at each single kiss he paused to make a new rhyme. Poor Concepçion became more and more worried as she tried vainly to lure him back to the main point of his visit—love-making! Gonzalve, to-day, was more inclined to verse-making. How tiresome of him! She was getting bored; and no wonder. And now, here came that hefty muleteer into the room once more, smiling broadly! A handsome fellow, too, as well as strong. What *would* her lover think?

Fortunately Concepçion was quick-witted. She announced to the surprised Gonzalve that the newcomer was a removal man who had just come in to move the heavy clocks. Then, apologetically, she told Ramiro that she had made a mistake and had indicated the wrong clock to be moved. Would it be too much to ask him to fetch back the clock he had just taken upstairs, and then to carry up instead the Catalan timepiece now left in the shop?

Ramiro, delighted to go on pleasing this pretty if somewhat erratic lady, at once left the room to bring back the clock from upstairs. He declared that he liked hard work.

Once more Concepçion had time for a little love-making with her bachelor friend. But, to her annoyance, Gonzalve was still wrapped up in the making of poems; and he now began to compose a poem about the caprice of his sweetheart and the two clocks. Concepçion became more and more impatient and worried, knowing that Ramiro would be back again any moment. He must not find Gonzalve still in the shop, lest he guessed rightly that the would-be poet was, indeed, her lover—a fact she had, so far, kept secret from all. The only thing to be done was to hide him.

Explaining all this to the verse-making Gonzalve, she now begged him to get inside the remaining Catalan clock; which he somewhat reluctantly did. No sooner had she closed the clock door upon Gonzalve, than a new admirer entered the shop, to her further dismay. This was Inigo, a wealthy banker who, eager for a flirtation with the "charming Lady of the Clocks", as he now addressed her, had likewise waited until Torquemada was safely out of the way.

Finding her alone, as he thought, he now proceeded to make hay while the sun shone, uttering pretty speeches to the almost distracted Concepçion—taking her by the hand, and trying to steal a kiss. But the banker's ardour did not appeal to Concepçion just then, since she knew that all he said could probably be plainly heard by the hidden Gonzalve. At a more convenient time she might have been flattered and pleased; but the present was decidedly *not* a convenient time! She feared for the anger of her lover—and, merciful heavens! Here was that most unwelcome muleteer again, who now entered and dumped down his burden in its former place, well satisfied with himself!

Hurriedly explaining to the astounded banker that this was a removal man, she asked Ramiro, more sweetly still, if he would now carry the other clock up to her room, as that was the actual timepiece she preferred. True, it was a heavier clock, but the muleteer was so splendidly strong—perhaps he could manage it?

Ramiro, still delighted to be of use to so lovely a lady, declared he could easily carry twice the weight. He lifted up the clock containing the hidden Gonzalve—the latter now alarmed but afraid to speak—and jerked it carelessly on to his shoulders. He vowed it was a mere nothing as regarded its weight; but its pendulum seemed to be rattling about rather strangely!

Afraid of a possible mishap, Concepçion, now nearly worried to tears, followed him upstairs, trying to talk loudly and carelessly to hide the ominous sounds from within the clock.

Thus Inigo the banker was left alone for a few moments. He felt he was not getting on very well with Concepçion. Perhaps, after all, he was somewhat too middle-aged and fat to appeal to such a pretty young thing? He was certainly becoming more corpulent than he liked. But he would make another attempt. He would treat the clockmaker's wife as a child, and play a funny trick upon her to attract her interest. Yes! He would get inside the big Catalan clock just dumped down by the removal man.

He did so; but he was so fat that it was all he could do to squash himself into the clock. He was most uncomfortable.

When Concepçion presently ran back into the shop, hoping to get rid of the banker quickly before Ramiro returned, he opened the clock door and called out childishly " Cuckoo! Cuckoo! "

Concepçion was furious when she found Inigo inside the clock —and so tightly wedged therein that it would be difficult to get him out again. Although he at once began to make love to her, despite this undignified position, she refused to listen to him, bidding him to come out and hurry away at once. But this was easier said than done; and as Ramiro could now be heard descending the staircase once more, Concepçion hastily closed the clock door upon the foolish banker.

Ramiro had brought down again the clock containing Gonzalve. No sooner had it been placed in her own room than Concepçion had decided distractedly that this was a more dangerous place for her lover to be discovered in—as she felt he certainly would be, presently. She had, therefore, made a further flimsy excuse to have the big timepiece brought downstairs once more. This was the clock that never kept time, she declared. Would the muleteer take it back to the shop again and bring up the other one, after all?

The obliging Ramiro had done so only too willingly and quickly; and yet one more journey did he make with each clock. For neither lover, when alone for a brief moment with his charming but now distracted lady-love, would emerge from his hiding-place and depart from the shop, as she desired. The one continued to talk poetry, and the other to make pretty speeches.

Then, at last, when the two big clocks were back in the shop— each with its door closed upon a most uncomfortable lover—

Concepçion played a trick upon both her admirers. In sheer exasperation because her precious hour had thus been wasted and knowing that her husband would be back at any moment now, she had a bright idea. At least she would enjoy these last few minutes before old Torquemada returned.

When the perspiring Ramiro now asked which of the two clocks she finally wished to be taken upstairs, she replied, neither. She then coquettishly invited him to lead the way up to her room, minus the clocks, and smilingly followed him. Ramiro felt he had gained a triumphant success now that he was to be rewarded with a few kisses after all his hard work. He surely deserved them.

Left to themselves, Inigo and Gonzalve each discovered the other. Gonzalve was the first to emerge from his clock-case, still full of the poems he hoped to write. Almost immediately, however, he saw old Torquemada passing the window towards the door. It was too late for him to escape. He rushed to hide once more in a clock—and chose the wrong one. He thus discovered his rival, wedged tightly therein!

With Torquemada now entering the shop, the only thing to be done was for both philanderers to pretend to be purchasers. They declared they had been admiring the beautiful clocks while waiting for the clockmaker to appear. Inigo, helplessly stuck fast, explained that, having slipped inside one of the Catalan clocks to examine the working of its pendulum more closely, he had become wedged, owing to the fullness of his figure. He begged to be helped out.

Torquemada, however, first suggested—with a mischievous twinkle in his eye, for he more than suspected the state of affairs—that as the two gentlemen evidently admired his fine Catalan clocks, he presumed they would each be willing to purchase one. Gonzalve and Inigo could do no less than answer in the affirmative—somewhat sheepishly, to be sure, for the clocks were very expensive.

Then Torquemada, well pleased with his bargain, tried, with the help of Gonzalve, to pull the stout Inigo out from the clock-case in which he was so firmly wedged; but they could not do so, and the chain of the pendulum broke.

At that moment, Ramiro slipped quietly into the shop, followed at a discreet distance by Concepçion, both unperceived at first by the struggling trio. Quickly coming to the rescue, the practical and good-natured muleteer seized Inigo firmly around the waist and lifted him bodily out of the clock.

For a few moments, all the actors in this little comedy looked anxiously at one another. Then all began to laugh. Why make a fuss? No harm was done.

The poet had wasted his precious moments verse-making, when he might have been love-making. The banker had been as foolish as the cuckoo he had imitated. The old clockmaker had got the better of his too-charming wife's admirers. And Ramiro, the plain, hefty muleteer, had succeeded where his more elegant rivals had failed. Pretty Concepçion had smiled on him and had not been chary with her kisses.

And so, a crowded and lightsome Spanish Hour had come to an end.

THE GOLDEN COCKEREL   *Rimsky-Korsakov*
(*Le Coq d'Or*) *A Fantastic Fairy Tale*

On a sunny spring-time day, the famous King Dodon sat upon a gorgeously gilded and feather-bedecked throne in the magnificent open-air audience hall of his palace. He was surrounded by his courtiers and the Boyards or Lords who formed his Council of State; and on either side of the throne were seated his two sons, the handsome young Princes Afron and Guidon. A solemn hush hung over the brilliant assemblage; and all looked eagerly and expectantly towards the King, who seemed buried in anxious thought.

Well might King Dodon be anxious. His country was threatened with warfare; and though in the days of his youthful prime he had always been ready to repel his foes, he had long since ceased to care for warlike pursuits and had no desire to engage in certain serious conflicts which now threatened the peace of his dominions. During recent years the once active King had devoted himself entirely to a life of indolence and luxurious ease and his people had followed his example. Even the young men had ceased to take interest in the profession of arms and had given themselves up to pleasure, to which they devoted more time than to manly exercises.

The rulers of neighbouring countries were not slow to take advantage of this state of affairs; and now, in his advancing years, the splendid and once redoubtable King Dodon was threatened with invasion on every side and could not sleep for fear of possible dangers for which he was not prepared. In great alarm his armies had been gathered together with the utmost difficulty and despatched to the borders; but still the King could not rest in peace, knowing not when the danger might draw nearer and his capital and even his own sacred person be threatened.

The Boyards, therefore, had been called to meet their monarch in the Council, together with the two young Princes; and now, just as the long and solemn hush was beginning to get on everybody's nerves, the King aroused himself with a deep sigh and called upon his elder son, Prince Guidon, for advice in this time of difficulty.

The young Prince—who, though he had been brought up in soft ease and luxury, yet desired to be regarded as a dashing youth full of fiery ardour and brilliant wits—sprang eagerly to his feet; and he declared that he had lain awake all night seeking for some clever ruse to circumvent his country's foes. The plan he had to suggest, however, was a very foolish one. He hated the idea of the army being so far away; and he proposed, therefore, that all the fighting men should leave the frontiers at once and come back to form a guard outside the capital to protect the precious lives within it—especially those of the Royal Family and Court!

Prince Afron's suggestion was even more witless still. Why be worried by the sight of an army at all, he inquired? Surely it would be better to disband the warriors for a time and recall them to the colours just a month before the enemy attacked. Then they could forget about the war until the fighting actually began.

Though the silly and short-sighted advice of the two Princes was extremely pleasing to the doddering old King and his lazy Boyards, it was strongly opposed by Polkan, the aged Voevoda or head of the army. The latter pointed out sarcastically that not only was it more dangerous to have a cruel enemy at close quarters than at a safe distance, but that the invaders were hardly likely to be so obliging as to give timely notice beforehand as to when it was their intention to make an attack.

The King passionately denounced his sage Counsellor for throwing cold water upon plans which had appeared to promise at least temporary exemption from the warlike activity which would so sadly interfere with his own rest and comfort; and a scene of wild uproar now ensued. While the young Princes and the Boyards seemed about to attack the old Voevoda, the King began to wring his hands and to call out for some soothsayer to appear, who might foretell the future for them by magical divination.

As though in answer to the royal cry of despair, there suddenly appeared at the entrance to the hall a very old and venerable-look-

s

ing Astrologer, who wore a tall pointed hat and flowing blue garments sprinkled with golden stars. He carried in one hand an astrolabe and in the other a bag; and as the whole company relapsed instantly into respectful silence, the dignified stranger slowly approached the throne, bowed low before the King, and said :

"Hail, King Dodon! I have come to offer unto thee a magic remedy for thy present woes, so that thou mayest once more sleep in peace! "

So saying, the Astrologer took out from his bag a Golden Weathercock; and whilst the courtiers gazed admiringly upon this enchanted object—which flapped its wings and crowed—its owner continued : " Accept my Golden Cockerel, O Sire, and place it upon the highest spire of thy palace roof; and it shall be a true watchman unto thee! When all is peaceful and quiet, it will make no sound whatever, and thou mayest rest and take thy pleasure in safety and comfort; but if enemies are about to draw nigh to thee, or if thy peace is threatened in any way, then will my magic Golden Cockerel raise his comb, flap his wings, and crow aloud " Cock-a-doodle-doo! Beware! "

King Dodon was overjoyed at the thought of securing such a treasure as this, and begged the Astrologer to say what riches or favour he could bestow upon him for bringing so useful a gift. The Astrologer, however, declared that such ordinary rewards as riches and high rank meant nothing to him, since he regarded love only as precious; but he added that he would call upon the King later on to redeem his promise by bestowing upon him a certain gift which he would then ask for.

King Dodon gladly assured his venerable visitor as to his willingness to redeem his promise when the right time came; and then the Astrologer bowed low before the throne once more and departed as quietly as he had come.

The enchanted Weather-vane was taken away at once and placed carefully upon the highest spire on the palace roof; and as the King came down from his throne and walked about the hall, full of joy as he received the congratulations of his courtiers, the voice of the Golden Cockerel was heard crowing from its lofty perch : " Cock-a-doodle-doo! Eat, sleep, and take your ease! "

The King and his Court quickly followed out this pleasant advice; and singing, dancing, and all kinds of merry-makings took place. The King was delighted to know that no danger could approach him without due warning and that he might now safely forget all his worries; and he decided that first of all he would enjoy a good long sleep. After dismissing his sons and his Counsellors, therefore, he settled himself comfortably upon a luxurious couch of ivory, strewn with fur coverings and the softest of cushions; and then he called for old Amelfa, the Royal Housekeeper, and bade her to bring him some dainty confections and rich wines. While he feasted thus comfortably, he listened to his pet parrot, which had been taught to make flattering remarks to him; and then he settled down to sleep—Amelfa seating herself on the ground beside him with a big flapping fan, ready to chase away the flies from her royal master's nose.

It seemed that, for the moment, even the King's slumber should bring him the joys of peace; for, in his dreams, he was now visited by the vision of a most beautiful Queen, whose alluring charms thrilled him and caused his heart to beat wildly as in the days of his youth.

Following the royal example, everybody in the palace had likewise fallen asleep; and even the guards no longer thought it necessary to keep awake, even though the sun still shone brightly overhead.

Then, suddenly, the voice of the Golden Cockerel was heard loudly crowing his warning cry: "Cock-a-doodle-doo! Arouse yourselves and beware! Beware!"

Instantly, all was hustle, bustle, and confusion in the palace. The guards sprang to their feet in alarm; and the aged Voevoda, Polkan, hastened into the presence of the King, crying loudly: "Awaken, O my King! Awaken! The Golden Cock is crowing, and terrible danger threatens!"

At first, King Dodon, rising sleepily and unwillingly from his comfortable couch, was annoyed on being thus rudely awakened in the midst of the most seductive dream that had ever visited him; but upon hearing from the impatient Polkan that the magic Cockerel was indeed giving lively warning of an approaching enemy, he became resigned. Addressing the frightened people—who were now clamouring wildly around the palace—he bade them prepare their fighting men to set forth to the frontier at once; also to make a generous offer of their riches and goods to provide against the many new expenses that would have to be met.

He then appointed his two sons as leaders of the expedition against the coming foe, bidding them to divide the army between them and go forth to gain glory and renown. The young Princes, however, were in great ill-humour at having been so roughly disturbed from their own enticing dreams; and, being cowards at heart, they grumbled at the prospect of dangers and hardships in store for them and at the cruelty of being separated from their many sweethearts.

King Dodon reproved his sons for their softness and poor spirit—conveniently forgetting his own similar characteristics—and, with a parting embrace and his royal blessing, bade them take command of his hosts forthwith; and the young Princes, though much cast down and full of self-pity, were fain to depart with the Boyards and chief warriors, leaving the aged Polkan and remaining soldiers in charge of the capital.

No sooner had the blare of trumpets and noise of the departing army died away than the voice of the Golden Cockerel was heard once more crowing lustily: "Cock-a-doodle-doo! Rest and take your ease!"

When the people heard this reassuring cry, they gladly returned to their homes again, to eat, drink, sleep, or make merry, as suited them best. King Dodon now gladly dismissed his Court and retired to his ivory couch once more, calling to his housekeeper, Amelfa, to recall to his mind the seductive dream from which he had been awakened by the recent hubbub.

The old dame, though she had no knowledge of what the dream could have been about, knew that it flattered her royal master to be regarded as young enough to play the lover; so she slyly shook her finger at him and declared that he had dreamed of a beautiful Queen with whom he had fallen in love. King Dodon, thus reminded of the charmer of his last ravishing dream and already full of drowsiness, once more settled down into a deep and peaceful slumber, again dreaming happily of the mysterious siren who had before filled him with such joy.

The whole Court, including the guards and even old Amelfa this time, fell into the same heavy yet peaceful slumber, which appeared to be caused by some hypnotic means, since it lasted an unusually long time and affected one and all.

Then, once more, there sounded the clear clarion cry of the Golden Cockerel, crowing insistently and calling out the warning: "Cock-a-doodle-doo! Arouse yourselves, and beware! Beware!"

Again, all was hustle, bustle, and confusion; and the frightened folk ran hither and thither, declaring that the Golden Cockerel's warning could only mean that disaster had already befallen the young Princes' brilliant army before it had even had time to reach the frontiers.

King Dodon, though again furious at being thus disturbed a second time in the midst of a ravishing dream, soon realized that the Golden Cockerel's warning must not be disregarded. He

agreed, therefore, to Polkan's suggestion of calling up the reserves
of old men; and he declared that he himself would lead this
second army and go forth to the rescue of the royal children—
in fact, he now rather fancied himself in the *rôle* of a rescuer.
He then called for his armour and weapons of war; and though
the former had become too tight for his rotund body and his
favourite sword was red with rust, he donned the complete equipment boldly. When ready, after much puffing and blowing, he
was carried forth and mounted upon his white charger—which
had likewise grown dull and decrepit with age and had lost the
fire of its youth.

When the people beheld their King—who certainly had some
spirit left in him—riding at the head of his stout army of greybeards and followed by old Polkan, they raised loud shouts of
joyful pride; and they poured blessings upon their beloved
monarch for thus going forth in their defence. They entreated
him, however, to take care of his own sacred person and to keep
out of all danger, that he might return safely to them once more.

Thus, despite his advanced years, rode forth King Dodon, in
great splendour and comic pride—though mightily afraid of his
staggering old war-horse—to meet the foe, of which he had been
so timely warned by the Golden Cockerel.

.   .   .   .

After marching many weary miles in the wake of the first
splendid, if reluctant, army of young men that had set out before
them, King Dodon and his greybeards were puzzled because
they could find no trace of the youthful warriors, nor of the foe of
whom they had been warned; and as darkness fell, their uneasiness increased. By this time they had reached a narrow gorge
in a wild and desolate spot; and here, at last, they came upon
traces of a great battle. As they penetrated into the gorge, the
moonlight shone down upon the ghastly faces of countless dead
bodies of warriors, lying stark upon the hillocks or among the
bushes. All these dead bodies were those of the handsome youths
of King Dodon's first splendid army; and the mystery of the
hidden foes deepened, as no corpse or even wounded warrior
could be seen of the enemy battalions. The latter had vanished
as completely as though they had never been in the gorge at all.

Among the slain were found the two young Princes, Guidon
and Afron; and from the fact that the sword of each royal youth
was still imbedded into the heart of the other it was soon realized
that the two brothers had killed one another. On examining the
other bodies more closely, it was now plain to all that this
mysterious battle had evidently been fought either with an invisible

foe, or with no foe at all, each warrior having turned upon his neighbour and slain him.

All through the night, King Dodon and his grief-stricken followers poured forth lamentations for the untimely end that had befallen their sons; but though they searched the gorge thoroughly for many hours, they could find no trace of enemy warriors.

Then, to their amazement, as the night mists rolled away and the first rosy glow of early dawn slowly penetrated the entrance to the gorge, the outline of a large silken tent of brilliant colours became clearly visible in one of the wider hollows.

Just as King Dodon, with Polkan and a few attendants, was about to make a sudden raid upon this mysterious tent, he was halted by a remarkable sight. The flaps of the tent were silently moved aside and a queenly woman of dazzling beauty came forth, attended by four female slaves and, regardless of the presence of King Dodon and his elderly army, raised her arms high over her head and addressed a song of welcome to the rising sun.

This dazzling vision of female loveliness was clad in filmy shimmering robes of rose colour, adorned with chains of pearls and priceless jewels; and as the soft tones of her seductive voice reached them, the righteous anger in the hearts of the approaching warriors vanished utterly and they drew back to a respectful distance, leaving King Dodon and his Voevoda to parley with the mysterious siren.

Having finished her hymn of praise, the beautiful singer turned and gazed long and intently upon King Dodon, whose heart began to beat wildly as he recognized in this lovely stranger the seductive maiden of the joyful vision which had twice visited him since his possession of the Golden Cockerel; and when the bewildered monarch asked tremblingly whence she came and whither she was travelling, she replied boldly: " I am the far-famed Virgin Queen of Shemakhan; and I am journeying to make conquest of thy city, King Dodon, and to take it for my own ! "

Then, as King Dodon and the amazed Polkan demanded how she intended to accomplish this feat, when she had no army and was attended merely by a retinue of slaves, she replied with an enchanting smile : " Beauty needs no army ! Beauty provides me with all the weapons I need, and by means of my beauty I conquer one and all ! "

She then clapped her hands and called for goblets of wine to be brought, declaring that the King and Polkan were welcome guests; and next moment a gorgeous carpet had been spread before the tent, and the visitors were invited to sit down upon silken cushions and to partake of delicious sweetmeats and wines. Both elderly warriors hesitated for a few moments only, fearing enchantment, or poison; and then the King, already under the spell of the Queen's alluring beauty, accepted a goblet and drank deeply and with delight of its luscious ruby contents. Old Polkan, somewhat sulkily, followed his royal master's example.

Having soon secured the dismissal of the more matter-of-fact and disapproving Voevoda to the rear of the tent, the Queen of Shemakhan devoted herself exclusively to the further enslavement of King Dodon, making flattering love to him and bringing him completely under the sway of her magical fascination. She even sought to arouse his jealousy by telling him that both the young Princes, his sons, had vied with one another for her love, and had even fought each other to the death for possession of it. As she proceeded with her story, King Dodon realized that, though unaccompanied by an army, yet this siren Queen was the most irresistible of all foes, since her seductive beauty had caused his entire army of youthful warriors to turn on themselves and slay one another for the favour of her smiles. Nevertheless, so completely had he himself likewise fallen beneath her fatal spell that these terrible misfortunes now meant nothing to him—despite his advanced years, all he foolishly desired was the love of the beautiful enchantress beside him, whose every word was already law to him.

Consequently, he forgot his kingly dignity and made himself look ridiculous in the eyes of his followers. When the Queen invited him to sing her a love-song, he did so—in a cracked quavering voice that brought peals of silvery laughter from her rosy lips; and when she insisted upon binding his flowing grey locks with a silken kerchief, he gladly permitted her to do so—caring nothing for the foolish spectacle he then presented. Finally, she compelled him to take part in a wild orgy of dancing which now took place. After the pretty slave maidens had performed many graceful evolutions, the Queen herself performed an entrancing *pas seul*; then she seized her royal victim by the hand and, dragging him into the midst of the whirling mad revel, made him dance to the intoxicating music played by the slaves—which he eagerly did at her command, though he had not danced for many years past and was extremely stiff in his movements.

At last, the foolish old King sank back among the cushions, exhausted, but still full of the strange joy by which he was held in thrall. Then, flinging himself at the Queen's feet, he acknowledged himself to be her slave, entreating her to become his

Consort and to return with him to his capital, there to reign with him.

The wily Queen of Shemakhan had foreseen this offer and played her hand for it, having also certain other desperate plans for the future formulating in her scheming brain; consequently, after coquetting a little longer with her elderly lover, she now made pretence of agreement with his request. Commands were given for the slaves to strike the tent; and—though no one saw whence they came—a grand retinue of gorgeously-clad attendants suddenly surrounded the lovely enchantress. A golden chariot likewise mysteriously appeared for the royal pair to travel in; and all the company moved forward to join in the procession now formed in honour of King Dodon's triumphant return to his capital.

. . . .

Meanwhile, the people left behind in the capital had been full of fear as to what would become of them should their King meet with defeat—which seemed extremely likely. Would they all become the slaves of the victorious enemy; or would the latter destroy them utterly?

After an anxious night and morning, however, signs of much activity were seen to be taking place in the palace—where the old housekeeper, Amelfa, was particularly busy shaking up cushions, rearranging draperies, and giving obvious instructions for a second throne to be erected. Unable to restrain their curiosity, some of the hardier spirits broke into the palace and there learned of what had happened from old Amelfa—who was, herself, nearly bursting with importance. Yes, runners had arrived with wonderful news, the old dame declared. No, there had been no battle this time; but the King had gained a great victory, all the same. What was more, he was returning to the capital that same day with a lovely Queen, who was to be his bride; and he would be accompanied by the most marvellous procession ever seen in the land.

On hearing this astonishing news, the people were plunged into a great state of excitement; and though they grieved for a short time on hearing that their young princes had been slain, they did not hesitate to don their gala attire in joyful anticipation of the forthcoming wedding revels. They soon began to congregate in the streets in great masses, ready to welcome the returning " conqueror ". They even swarmed on to the roofs of the houses and clung to the chimney-pots, in order to get the best possible view of the approaching procession. On the steps of the palace, the oldest of the Boyards—who had been left behind to guard the city—assembled with their wives and children, all garbed in the richest of raiment.

The atmosphere soon became stifling; and although the sun still shone brightly, it was observed that a dense black cloud was creeping up from the east, giving warning that a terrible thunderstorm was approaching. The joyful people, however, refused to have their spirits damped by the ominous appearance of the eastern sky; and since the Golden Cockerel still remained silent and glistened in the bright sunshine, with its wings folded as the sign of peace, they felt no qualms of fear but awaited with eager anticipation the approach of the royal procession.

At last, just before the black thundercloud obscured the sun, the triumphal cavalcade appeared in the distance; and a mighty shout of welcome went up from the thousands of spectators.

First came the hoary warriors, all holding up their heads with pride, as though indeed returning from some mighty feat of arms; and then followed the retinue of the Queen of Shemakhan. Not only did this consist of a gorgeous procession of eastern courtiers and slaves, but also included a vast number of strange creatures never before seen by the shouting spectators—giants, dwarfs, horned and dog-headed freaks, negroes, and tiny black boys. All in this strange company wore brilliant garments and barbaric ornaments; and many of the slaves carried caskets of pearls and precious stones to add to the treasures and wealth of the city.

The enthusiasm of the people, therefore, knew no bounds when, presently, the magnificent golden chariot containing King Dodon and his royal bride came slowly by; and for a few moments, all were struck dumb by the dazzling beauty of the siren Queen. Seeing, however, that the latter only threw haughty scornful glances around her, the people sought to please her by turning somersaults and cutting capers, to prove to her the joy of their welcome. But the strange Queen refused to smile at them.

Nor did King Dodon look happy. Although he constantly gazed sentimentally into the starry eyes of the proud Queen of Shemakhan, the latter only returned his glances of love with cold indifference and disdain. Gone were her allurements of a few hours back; and the unhappy King began to feel that he was but a pawn in some mysterious game that was being played—as, indeed, he was. What was more, the end of this curious game was at hand. As the golden chariot drew up at the steps of the palace, a stranger suddenly appeared thereon, in whom all recognized at once the mysterious old Astrologer who had presented the Golden Cockerel to the King.

Clad in the same star-spangled blue garment and tall hat, the Astrologer stood, motionless and silent, gazing earnestly into the eyes of the Queen of Shemakhan, who returned his gaze long and steadfastly. When King Dodon, delighted at the sight of one who had bestowed upon him so precious a gift, greeted him genially and asked him now to name his price for the Golden Cockerel, he turned swiftly and said: "Give me, O King, this beautiful maiden, the Queen of Shemakhan! I demand nothing more, nothing less!"

Full of dismay, the King sprang to his feet, and, declaring that this price was an impossible one, commanded him to name some other reward, promising him anything else, even to the half of his kingdom. The Astrologer, however, again firmly stated that he desired only to have possession of the lovely Queen of Shemakhan, that nothing else would satisfy him; and he added that since the King had made a solemn promise to grant him his desire, he must certainly redeem that promise now that the time of reckoning had come.

King Dodon, no longer able to restrain his rage, burst forth into a torrent of abuse; and to such a height of excitement did his uncontrollable passion lead him that, raising his royal sceptre, he aimed a violent blow at the Astrologer and stretched him dead at his feet. At the same time, the sun vanished behind the black clouds that had been gathering and a loud clap of thunder was heard, whilst a strange darkness began to creep over the scene.

As the people drew back, awed and horrified by this deed of violence, Dodon was relieved when the Queen of Shemakhan declared coldly that the foolish old man had only got his deserts for his presumption; but when the King endeavoured to continue his love-making and would have embraced her, she repulsed him with equal scorn, saying contemptuously: "Prepare to die, thou hoary-headed old imbecile! This sorry jest has gone far enough! Thy death is at hand!"

As the crestfallen King now turned to mount the steps of the palace, the voice of the Golden Cockerel was heard crowing loudly: "Cock-a-doodle-doo! I will avenge my mysterious master! I will peck this foolish dotard and kill him!"

With these words, the Golden Cockerel flew down from its perch on the spire above, circled over the heads of the people a few times, and then aimed a heavy blow with its powerful beak at the head of King Dodon, who fell instantly to the ground, dead. At the same moment, there was a violent peal of thunder, which struck the terrified people almost dumb; and for a few minutes a veil of black darkness hung over all, through which could be heard the scornful laugh of the stranger Queen.

When at length the storm had ended and the cloud of darkness began to pass away, it was seen that the mysterious Queen of Shemakhan and the Golden Cockerel had both vanished, as though they had never been present—together with the former's brilliant retinue and the slaves carrying caskets of jewels.

Thus did a mighty magician vainly endeavour to bring within his own power a beautiful enchantress through the means of a doting old King and, though failing in his enterprise, repaid the latter for base ingratitude in his own coin.

IVAN THE TERRIBLE   *Rimsky-Korsakov*

ONE summer evening during the latter part of the sixteenth century, a group of light-hearted maidens had assembled to sing and play games together in the grounds surrounding the palace of Prince Youry Tokmakov, the Tsar's Viceroy and Governor of the ancient city of Pskov.

These lively young girls were the guests of Princess Olga, the Viceroy's fair young daughter who, however, had slipped away from them to a clump of bushes, behind which she was now listening eagerly to a message brought by her friend Stesha, with whom she shared a wonderful secret.

The beautiful Olga was already betrothed, against her wishes, to the Boyard Matouta—an elderly suitor of mean disposition, whom she disliked and despised. Recently, however, she had made the acquaintance of a handsome young burgher, named Michael Toucha; and a passionate love having quickly sprung up between the pair, they had plighted their troth in secret. With the aid of Stesha—who acted as messenger and go-between—the lovers were able to meet now and again at twilight in unfrequented parts of the Viceregal gardens, there to snatch brief moments of bliss; though they realized that the future held but little hope for the consummation of their love.

Apart from the fact that Michael Toucha was not of noble birth, there was another formidable reason why he would never find favour in the eyes of Prince Tokmakov. The young man was also an enthusiastic revolutionary and, fired by a patriotic love for his native city and for the freedom and rights of her inhabitants, his soul rebelled against the despotic rule under which she was compelled to exist. He was already an ardent leader of the more advanced and soaring spirits among the community who sought to break away from the tyranny of the all-powerful Tsar, Ivan the Terrible—whose stern belief in the invincibility of "Divine Right" had led him to take fearful vengeance on all those venturesome souls who dared to defy his iron rule and absolute dominion over the vast lands he held.

The message now brought by Stesha to her friend was to the effect that Michael Toucha intended to visit his beloved one that same evening and might arrive at any moment. Full of joy that she was so soon to feel the arms of her lover around her, Olga hurried back to her guests, whom she was now eager to get safely within the house. She had only just succeeded in doing so when there came the sound of a shrill whistle from behind the bushes she had just left—the signal of her lover's approach—and she hastened to meet him.

After their first rapturous greetings were over, Olga was quickly plunged into grief on learning that her beloved Michael Toucha had come to bid her farewell. Realizing that Prince Tokmakov would never consent to wed his daughter to a portionless suitor, the young man announced that he was resolved to journey to the borders of Siberia, where he hoped to trade in furs and silver; then, when he had become wealthy, it was his intention to return and to lay his riches at the feet of the Viceroy, in the hope of securing his favour and the hand of lovely Olga.

Olga tearfully entreated her lover not to risk his precious life by taking such hazardous risks; and, flinging her arms around his neck, she declared passionately that the Prince, though he had betrothed her against her will to the Boyard Matouta, might yet release her from the hated contract when he knew of her secret love. Gently, but insistently, Toucha endeavoured to set aside her clinging arms, knowing only too well that her entreaties would be of no avail; but the more passionately did Olga cling to him and announce her resolve never to be parted from him.

Darkness had now fallen; and whilst the lovers were still discussing the future which looked so gloomy for them, they were startled on seeing two persons approaching from the mansion. To their alarm, they quickly recognized the Viceroy and the Boyard Matouta, who thus sought the cool evening air and the privacy of the gardens as they spoke together upon urgent personal matters. With a hastily whispered farewell, the lovers parted—Michael escaping over the fence and vanishing into the darkness beyond, whilst Olga crouched in the bushes close by, afraid to move away until the nobles had retired. Thus the young girl overheard a piece of news not intended for her ears—news which filled her with an additional sorrow.

At first the two great lords discussed matters of state. They had received information that the Tsar Ivan had just wreaked terrible vengeance upon the neighbouring city of Novgorod because the sons of the freemen and burghers there had rebelled against his rule—fearful massacres having been ordered by the stern tyrant, whereby the innocent had suffered with the guilty and the whole town was filled with lamentation.

The Viceroy expressed the hopeful view that Pskov was not likely to share a similar fate, as he himself had discharged his duties with unblamable loyalty and had so far been able to keep the revolutionary element under reasonable control. Matouta, however, was full of fears, declaring that the young malcontent, Toucha, had already caused much disaffection in the city and might, consequently, bring the wrath of the Tsar upon its inhabitants.

So full of fear was the craven-hearted Boyard, indeed, that he trembled at every sound, even at the rustling of a leaf; but when his host reassured him as to the absolute privacy of the gardens he recovered somewhat and began to speak of his betrothal to Olga, expressing the desire that his marriage to her might soon take place.

Then the Viceroy made a strange confession to his guest. He revealed the fact that Olga was not, as supposed, his own child, but was the daughter of his dead wife's sister Vera, who had died years ago without naming the father of her babe. The little one, he continued, had been taken into his own house and brought up as his daughter and heiress. The mystery of her true parentage had never been revealed—though it was known to Prince Tokmakov that her unnamed father was a person of the highest rank.

The concealed Olga, on thus learning that the Viceroy—whom she loved tenderly—was not her real father, could no longer keep her feelings under control; and she uttered a faint cry of woe. At the same moment, however, there also came the clanging of a great bell, while a distant glow quickly appeared in the sky. Knowing that the pealing of this bell was a tocsin to call the townsfolk together and that beacon fires as a warning of danger accounted for the glowing sky, the Viceroy hurried his now terrified guest away at once; and presently he proceeded with him to the market-place to address the alarmed people already gathering there. Thus the unhappy Olga escaped discovery and, over-come with grief, hastened within doors.

When the Viceroy, with his Boyards and all other persons of authority, had entered the main square of the town and had mounted a dais hastily improvised, he was about to address the clamouring and anxious townsfolk when a dusty, travel-stained courier dashed up with a dread message. He announced that the Tsar Ivan, after having sacked the neighbouring city of Novgorod because its rebellious factions had dared to resist his laws, was even now marching upon Pskov and would arrive at daybreak.

Prince Tokmakov reassured the frightened people by reminding them that they had done no wrong and, therefore, might expect the Tsar to be gracious to them. He next advised them to bake loaves of fine meal, to prepare mead, and to set forth bread and salt in the streets as symbols of welcome against the arrival of their exalted guest, whom he also counselled them to greet with humility and to implore him to show sweet clemency towards them. He then added that the Tsar was passing through their town on his way to pray at the shrines of certain local saints—which they might regard as a favourable sign that he was coming in peace.

Though these words of the Viceroy—whom they loved and revered—brought back hope to the majority of the townsfolk, another section of the crowd called upon Michael Toucha, the revolutionary, to speak also. Michael—who had been chafing impatiently during the Viceroy's address—needed no second bidding; and, mounting the platform, he scornfully repudiated the idea that the people should humble themselves before their tyrant ruler. They had done no wrong, he declared, and so deserved no punishment; nor did they need to crave for mercy. He then boldly called upon his followers to refuse to pay homage to one who did not respect their rights, but, instead, to arm themselves and march out of the city with him to dwell as outlaws rather than abase themselves before the terrible Tsar. He bade them to take this means for striking a blow for the liberty of Pskov, their beloved city.

This inflammatory speech caught the imagination of many of the younger members of the assembly, who, calling upon Toucha to be their leader, now marched with him out of the city. The remainder of the community, however, followed out the instructions of the Viceroy, sitting up all night to bake fine bread and to set out in the streets loaves and salt as the symbols of welcome to their royal visitor; and they brought forth their banners, icons, and crosses to carry in procession as the Tsar entered the city, that he might be pleased with his reception and that his anger might be turned away from them.

Whilst these hasty preparations were taking place in the early hours of the morning, the Princess Olga appeared on the balcony of the viceregal palace, attended by her faithful old nurse, to whom she presently confided the story she had overheard the previous evening between the Viceroy and the Boyard Matouta. Somewhat comforted by the kindly sympathy of her old nurse, she began to look forward to the arrival of the great Tsar Ivan, for whom she had an unaccountably sacred affection and respect. Having been taught from her earliest childhood to regard him as second only to her Divine Father, she had always cherished an intense longing to see him in the flesh.

Even as Olga and her old nurse spoke together, the great square in front of the palace became crowded with a host of excited people, whilst the simultaneous joyous pealing of all the bells in the city and the sound of loud acclamations from the adjoining streets heralded the approach of the dreaded tyrant. As the noise of the tumult drew nearer, the people fell upon their knees, bowing their heads to the ground in sign of their deep humility and reverence.

First came a procession of fierce Tartar warriors clad in full battle array, followed by the celebrated Oprichniki Guards, resplendent in rich trappings and awe-inspiring of aspect. Then, mounted upon a fiery steed, there appeared in the square the mighty Tsar, Ivan the Terrible—a man of noble features and regal bearing, who gazed proudly upon the kneeling populace thus humbly greeting him and pleading that he would show mercy upon them.

With calm dignity the Viceroy approached the silent sovereign and bade him welcome to the city of Pskov; and the Tsar, pleased with his reception, graciously desired his representative to lead the way into the Viceregal palace where he wished to partake of refreshment.

When the party had taken their places within the handsome reception rooms of the palace, Prince Tokmakov standing at the right hand of the exalted guest and the trembling Matouta upon his left with the other Boyards grouped around, the Tsar commanded that a goblet of mead should be presented to him by the mistress of the house. The Viceroy explained that his wife had long since been dead, but that his daughter would be honoured to wait upon her sovereign, for whom she had ever had the utmost respect and affection; whereupon Olga entered the room with eager yet trembling steps and deeply bowed head and, kneeling, presented the goblet of mead to the royal guest. She was followed by her friend Stesha and a bevy of other fair maidens, all bearing salvers of the choicest sweetmeats and rarest foods the city could produce.

As Olga approached him, the sternness of the Tsar's features relaxed. He greeted her gently and inquired her name, afterwards addressing her in a caressing manner by the pet-name "Olenka"; and then he bade her to greet him with a kiss— the privilege of a welcome guest. When the maiden looked up with a startled glance, he stepped back suddenly and gazed into her beautiful face with amazement, as a host of tender recollections suddenly rushed upon him—for Olga was the exact living image of a fair girl whom he had loved with all the strength of a passionate nature many years ago in the romantic days of his early manhood, when the call of youth meant more to him than the powers of kingship and when love was the only thing that mattered.

Olga, on her part, gazed affectionately, yet timidly, at the Tsar, as she replied modestly that it was too great an honour for a humble maiden thus to salute her sovereign. The transformed Ivan, however, still smiled upon her; and, taking off a handsome ring, he slipped it upon her finger. At the same time he stooped to kiss her reverently and gently, for a strange emotion filled him; then, recovering himself somewhat, he greeted the other girls and bade them sing to him.

His eyes, however, constantly sought the sweet face of Olga, whom he kept by his side and continued to caress; and when, presently, she retired with her friends, he dismissed his own attendants and bade the Viceroy remain a while with him alone. He then eagerly demanded of his host : "From what family did you take your wife, Prince? This fair maid, Olga, is the living image of one I loved long years ago!"

Prince Tokmakov replied that he had wedded a lady of the noble house of Nassonov—at which name the Tsar appeared much agitated; and then, too proud to deceive his sovereign, he told him simply that although he had wedded Nadejda, the elder daughter of that house, Olga was not her child but was the daughter of her erring sister, Vera, the name of whose unknown lover had never been revealed.

With feelings of the deepest emotion the Tsar now realized that the fair maiden to whom he had felt himself so strangely drawn was, indeed, his own daughter—the child of the beautiful Vera Nassonov, whom he had loved so passionately in the golden days of his youth and who had gladly shared with him in secret for a brief spell the magic bliss of a stolen joy which her own equally passionate nature had made her powerless to resist. Bowing his head humbly before this realization of the inscrutable workings of the Divine Father, the chastened Ivan registered a solemn vow then and there to engage no more in war and bloodshed; and he now declared devoutly: "God is the Protector of the City of Pskov, and her people may rest in peace!"

Great rejoicings were now held by the inhabitants of Pskov when it became known that Ivan the Terrible had no evil intentions towards them but only fatherly blessings to bestow upon all; and for a short time the softened Tsar remained in the district, engaging in hunting and other peaceful pastimes. Then he determined to carry out his original intention of visiting the local shrines; and he set forth first for the Monastery of Pechersk—whither a number of pilgrims also accompanied him from Pskov, that they might return thanks to the saints for preserving their city. It was while the Tsar's tent was pitched upon the banks of the River Miededna, as he journeyed to Pechersk, that he had another and unexpected meeting with Olga—a meeting destined to end in tragedy.

Among the pilgrims from Pskov who followed in the wake of the Tsar to the local shrines at Pechersk was Olga—still regarded by her friends as the daughter of Prince Tokmakov, Ivan having kept his secret to himself. Olga's object, however, was not a religious one only. She had received tidings again of Michael Toucha, who had asked her to meet him in a certain spot during her pilgrimage journey through the forest. Having managed to slip away from the other girl pilgrims, she made her way to the trysting-place, trembling with fear, as twilight had already set in.

However, she was quickly joined by Toucha, and the reunited lovers clasped one another in a glad embrace, forgetting their troubles for the moment in the intense joy of their meeting. When Olga presently revealed the fact that, having learned she was not Prince Tokmakov's own daughter, she now believed herself free to wed with a burgher, the happy pair rejoiced in the seemingly rosy prospect before them; and Michael declared they would go away together and make their home on the far distant banks of the Volga.

But fate was against the union of Michael and Olga, and their fair castle in the air was soon dashed to pieces. Even as they spoke thus happily together, a gang of armed men suddenly sprang out from the neighbouring bushes and set upon them. Michael bravely struggled to protect his beloved one; but he was

quickly overcome and flung to the ground. At the same time a
cloak was dragged over Olga's head and she was lifted up, half-
fainting, and carried away through the forest.

This outrage had been carried out by order of the Boyard
Matouta, who had learnt by means of the spies he employed that
the young Princess had arranged to meet her outlaw lover in the
forest. In revenge for her unfavourable reception of his own suit
and for the Viceroy's scarcely-veiled contempt for the craven
spirit he had shown at the time of the Tsar's arrival in Pskov, he
had determined to use Olga's present indiscretion as a means of
disgracing her in the eyes of the terrible Ivan—little dreaming that
the latter was the unknown father of the girl.

Therefore, he bade his men carry the captive to the royal camp
on the banks of the Miededna; and securing admission to the
Tsar's tent, he gloatingly related how the young Princess Olga
had been discovered by his men indulging in a stolen interview
with her revolutionary outlaw lover, Michael Toucha. The mean-
spirited Matouta, however, was soon filled with dismay. The
Tsar, furious at the Boyard's covertly insulting accusation against
the fair girl in whom he himself was so intensely interested,
instantly dismissed him from his presence with scornful anger.

Ivan then sent for Olga, who entered weeping and, flinging
herself at his feet, implored his pardon and protection. The unhappy girl confessed her love for Michael and admitted that she
had indeed gone to keep tryst with him that evening when she
had been so roughly taken captive by order of the hated and
despicable Matouta.

At first the Tsar sternly reprimanded her for her foolish conduct, declaring that a revolutionary was no fit mate for her and
that he would have Michael Toucha chained and imprisoned;
and he added that Olga herself must now journey with the royal
party to Moscow and choose a husband from among his nobles
there. His harshness, however, was only temporary. With
passionate words of entreaty, the grief-stricken girl implored him
to have mercy upon her, declaring that she could not believe him
to be a cruel tyrant, having always regarded him as a loving and
gracious father of the people—one who would protect and care
for her as her own unknown father would have done.

On hearing this impulsive outburst and realizing the undoubted
sincerity of the maiden's words, Ivan was deeply moved; and he
now spoke tenderly to her, bidding her to cease weeping and to
have no fear that he would deal harshly with her. He was just
on the point of revealing his true relationship to her when there
came sounds of a disturbance outside the tent, and the voice of

Michael Toucha was heard demanding that Olga Tokmakov should be given up to him.

After Olga's abduction by Matouta's men, Michael had quickly called his own outlaw friends to his aid and followed madly in the wake of the ravishers. Soon learning that his beloved one was in the tent of the tyrant Tsar, he determined to rescue her at all costs. The rebel band was instantly engaged in a hot encounter with the guards, who, imagining that the outlaws were about to make an attempt on the life of their royal master, quickly pushed them back towards the bank of the river. Olga, hearing her name called in agonizing tones by her lover, tore herself from the grasp of the Tsar, and rushed outside.

As the distracted Olga broke away from his grasp and fled outside, the Tsar heard almost immediately afterwards the sound of a shot; and, a few moments later, the unhappy girl's dead body was brought back into the tent and laid at his feet—a bullet intended for one of the rebels having struck her flying form instead.

Thus did retribution seek and find the great Tsar, Ivan the Terrible. He who by his tyrannies had brought woe and despair upon thousands of wretched parents, himself now felt the poignant anguish of a loving father bereft of his child; and as he knelt beside the corpse of the fair young daughter he had found and lost within so short a space of time, the grief-stricken monarch humbly bowed his head beneath the chastening hand of a just God.

THE LEGEND OF TSAR SALTAN   *Rimsky-Korsakov*

In the Legendary days of enchanters, fairies, and magic, there lived in the mystical kingdom of Tmutarakhan three sisters and their guardian, an old cousin named Babaricha. Their home was a very humble one; and because they were poor, they had to do all the work of their house themselves. Not that the two elder sisters ever did anything else but spin and weave; they expected the youngest sister to wash, and cook, and clean for them. As for old Babaricha, she usually sat by the stove all day long, with idle hands; so the Cinderella of the family had to wait upon her, too.

But the youngest sister, Militrissa, was of a happy and sunny nature. She did not mind how hard she worked, if only her sisters were kind to her; but this was not often the case. For Militrissa was very beautiful; and her plainer sisters were jealous of her. So they often treated her unkindly and always spoke to her in a snappy manner.

One day the two elder sisters sat by an open window, spinning and chattering about what they would do should the great Tsar Saltan suddenly decide to marry one of them. This was one of their favourite pastimes. The elder sister declared that if she were to become the Tsaritsa, she would give grand banquets every day, at which the most important people in the world would feed upon the richest food to be bought. She loved rich food herself and, being greedy, felt she would enjoy feasting more than anything else. The second sister loved fine clothes, jewels, and gold; so she declared that if she were married to the Tsar she would have made for her the most exquisite silken and jewel-trimmed robes the world could produce.

Just then, busy Militrissa passed through the room with a broom and a bucket; and hearing what her sisters had said, she cried out eagerly: "Oh, if I were married to the Tsar, I should want only to bear him the most wonderful hero-son in the world!"

Strange to say, this little conversation was overheard by the great Tsar Saltan himself, who happened to be passing by the open window. Like the famous Caliph Haroun-Al-Raschid, he loved to wander about by himself in disguise and to find out how his people lived and talked when they thought themselves alone.

He now entered the humble abode of the sisters, who fell on their knees before him, since they recognized him at once; and they trembled when they knew that he had heard their careless conversation. The Tsar, however, reassured them; and then he declared that he was so pleased with Militrissa's choice and with her gentleness and exquisite beauty, that he would certainly marry her.

So Militrissa rode away with the Tsar, to become his bride; and the two sisters were bidden to follow the happy pair to the palace —the one to become a cook, since she was so fond of good food, and the other to be chief seamstress, because of her liking for fine clothes.

. . . .

The two elder sisters and old Babaricha, who remained with them, were now more jealous than ever of beautiful Militrissa; and they soon hatched a cruel plot, whereby they hoped to get rid of her.

About a year later, while the Tsar was away at the wars, Militrissa's hero-son, Guidon, was born; and the glad tidings was

sent to Saltan by special messenger. But Babaricha and the
Tsaritsa's two jealous sisters managed to stop the messenger and
to make him so drunk that he fell asleep. Then they stole his
letter and substituted another message which gave the false and
shocking news that the lovely Queen had given birth to a monster
in female form, instead of the splendid son hoped for.

The consequence was that when the Tsar Saltan received the
message and learned that his heir was a monster, he was both
alarmed and furious; and he sent the messenger back to the
palace with a terrible command—that the lovely Tsaritsa and her
newly-born child were to be placed in a barrel and flung into
the sea.

The Tsar's word was law; and though none of the Tsaritsa's
attendants could understand why she had thus fallen out of
favour, the command had to be carried out. So the unhappy
Militrissa and her splendid baby son were put into a barrel, which
was taken out to sea and cast therein.

But a kindly Providence was taking care of the royal castaways.
The barrel was flung up on the shores of the desert island of
Bujan; and the baby prince, Guidon, had grown so miraculously
strong that he was able to burst it open and to set himself and
his mother free. What was more, like the infant Hercules, he
continued to gain strength every moment; and soon he contrived
to make a bow and arrows and hunted around for food. He
aimed at a hawk which was attacking a swan, and killed it
instantly. The grateful swan now came forward to offer her
thanks and to explain that the dead hawk was a wicked enchanter
who had transformed her, a princess, into her present form. The
spell being now broken, the Swan-Princess, in gratitude, promised
her aid at any time to her deliverer, and then as the young Prince
and his mother presently fell asleep, exhausted after their recent
experiences, she sailed away, still in the form of a swan. She did
not yet wish to reveal herself in human form.

By slaying the hawk, the baby Prince had broken another
spell, also. A wonderful city presently arose from the depths of
the sea, in which it had been immersed by means of the Wizard's
magic. Now it once more appeared as the centre of the island
of Bujan; and when the royal sleepers awakened, the gates of the
city opened and a splendid throng of courtiers, citizens, heralds,
and soldiers poured forth in a joyous throng. The Counsellors
of the City came forward and offered the crown to the youthful
Guidon, begging him to accept it and become their King—
which, already knowing himself to be of royal birth, he gladly did.

So Prince Guidon and his mother, the Tsaritsa Militrissa,

entered the resuscitated city, amid the rejoicings of the people; and here they lived for many years very happily.

.   .   .   .

When Guidon, King of Bujan, had grown up into a handsome youth, he began to long to visit the land of his birth and to see his father the great Tsar Saltan, of whose mighty deeds he had oft heard from his mother. When a ship from Tmutarakhan called at the island one day on its return journey, his longing became so great that he called upon the Swan-Princess to help him to gain his desire without the risk of becoming known—being well aware that he had enemies in his mother's land. The Swan-Princess—who had magical powers—very cleverly settled the matter by temporarily changing him into a huge bumble-bee; and in this form he flew on board the stranger ship and travelled safely to the land of his birth.

On arrival at Tmutarakhan, the Captain of the ship was entertained by Tsar Saltan, who was eager to hear about the marvellous city which had so magically appeared on the once desert island of Bujan. The young Prince, in his disguise as a bumble-bee, heard and saw all. When he saw the noble mien of the Tsar, his father, he realized that Saltan must have been tricked and deceived when he gave the command for his Queen and her innocent babe to be cast into the sea; and he soon discovered who were the culprits. For the two elder sisters of Militrissa had now managed to make themselves important ladies of the Court, together with their old cousin Babaricha; and they sat near the Tsar at his banquet to the Captain and crew of the newly-arrived ship.

When the Captain described the many wonders of the Island of Bujan, Tsar Saltan was amazed. Among these curiosities was a Magic Squirrel which cracked nuts with golden shells and kernels of priceless emeralds; another was an army of unconquerable warriors ready to rise up from the sea to protect their young King should he ever be in danger. These and many other marvels described by the Captain made Tsar Saltan very eager to visit the island himself; and he announced his intention to do so as soon as his State barge could be made ready. But the two sisters of Militrissa tried to prevent him from making the journey; for they knew that the young King of Bujan had a very beautiful mother, and they did not wish the Tsar to behold her, lest they themselves should lose favour in his eyes. However, a great bumble-bee soon appeared and buzzed so furiously about them that their attention was thus distracted, since they were afraid of being stung. They made such a fuss that soon the whole Court was busily chasing the bee—which enjoyed itself mightily. Meanwhile, the Tsar learned all he desired to know about Bujan from the Captain, and made his plans accordingly.

Next day, Guidon, still in the form of a bumble-bee, flew on to another ship sailing to Bujan; and on arrival there, the Swan-Princess transformed him once more into his natural form.

.   .   .   .

The young King Guidon, before the arrival of his royal father, the Tsar, felt that his happiness would be completed if he could be provided with a wife. He had heard marvellous stories of a certain Princess whose beauty was so dazzling that night became day in her presence; and he longed to make her his Queen.

Once more he called upon the Swan-Princess to help him to gain his heart's desire. In response to his request, the Swan-Princess now transformed herself into her own natural form, and stood before him as the loveliest Princess in the world. She, the Swan-Princess, was the dazzling maiden whose bright beauty made night appear as day. Instantly the young Prince fell in love with her; and the happy pair received the blessing of Militrissa and the acclamations of their people.

While they were still rejoicing, the Tsar Saltan arrived on the shores in great state and was received gladly by Guidon. The lovely Swan-Princess then revealed to him that Guidon was his own long-lost son; and when she also called upon Militrissa to appear, the Tsar's joy was complete. He had never ceased to love the humble maiden he had made his Queen, and had always longed to find her once more.

So great was the happiness of all in this wonderful reunion that even when the two jealous sisters and their old cousin Babaricha—who had travelled with the Tsar as Court attendants— now confessed their wicked plot, they were forgiven, at the request of gentle Militrissa.

MOZART AND SALIERI   *Rimsky-Korsakov*

THE famous Italian Kapellmeister, Salieri, sat alone, buried in deep reflection, in the music-room of his fine house in Vienna one day during the year 1792. Despite the fact that the warm sunshine of fame and good favour now shone brightly upon him— after many years of hard struggling through the gloomy clouds of stupendous labour, disappointment, and continuous perseverance

—his thoughts were not pleasant ones. Although he had attained to so high a position in the world of music and now lived in comfort and honour, happiness and peace of mind were not his. For he, whose talent was greatly admired, who had thought himself so secure in his fame as the premier musician of his day that he could even afford to smile indulgently upon other struggling aspirants and to hear them spoken of without envy, was now plunged into the black abyss of jealousy by the advent of a rival in the wonderful musician and composer, Mozart. The latter possessed the heavenly gift of music genius—and genius is to talent what a planet is to a twinkling star.

Yet, this same Mozart had not his, Salieri's, comfortable and honourable position, but was poor—and never likely to be otherwise, since he had no idea of the value of money, but lived, like all real bohemians, from hand to mouth. True, he had not the Italian Kapellmeister's strength of mind and determination of character to struggle against the difficulties and obstacles in his path; but then he did not need to wear himself out by endless toil and laborious effort in order to produce the divine harmonies with which his imaginative brain teemed. For genius is a thing that cannot be attained merely by the will of man, but is, like physical beauty, the blessed gift of God. Salieri, in his blind jealousy, railed at what he regarded as Divine injustice in thus indiscriminately bestowing this same immortal gift of genius upon certain favoured individuals here and there, to swamp in a moment the loving toil of lifelong devotion to Art given by such lovers of Art as himself, who merely possessed talent.

Mozart lived the careless, happy-go-lucky life of a man whose every action is the outcome of impulse, to whom routine, service, and discipline were things abhorred, and who only worked when he felt inclined to do so. His very labour might also be called a pastime, since he composed without any apparent effort the marvellous harmonies which poured forth from his brain in such rich profusion.

Of what use, then, was it for such an artist as Salieri—highly talented and sound musician though he knew himself to be—to spend months and even years producing and perfecting a composition, admired though it might afterwards be? The careless but heaven-gifted Mozart, the genius, had only to sit down and pour forth in a few hours a perfect flood of divine melody, such as the merely talented Salieri could never hope to equal in a lifetime of laborious work. He railed because the chance gifts of an inscrutable Providence should ever and anon alight upon—in his opinion—some easy-going trifler and so cause him to wear the

evergreen crown of immortal glory, passing by the more industrious and serious devotee of Art—such as Salieri himself.

While Salieri was thus indulging in morbidly jealous reflections
about his mighty rival, Mozart himself entered the room unceremoniously. For Salieri, notwithstanding his envy, received
his rival on a friendly footing. He was as attracted by the latter's
irresistible charm and personality as by his genius—and to listen
to the music of Mozart, played by the composer himself, was to
forget one's earthly surroundings and to pass for the moment within the portals of Paradise.

An illustration of this unwilling but irresistible admiration and
homage to genius—undreamt of by the modest recipient, who was
himself strangely unsusceptible to flattery and adulation—was
quickly forthcoming. Mozart, gay, careless, debonair, and still
young enough to appreciate the mere joy of living, entered the
room with a brisk step and eager greeting, laughing light-heartedly
as though at some merry jest. When Salieri, after a somewhat
strained return of greetings, inquired the cause of his amusement,
the harum-scarum musician told him the reason with another
burst of laughter. On his way thither, on passing the open door
of a tavern, he had heard an old blind fiddler playing an air of
his own—Mozart's—and making such a comical travesty of it
that he had bribed him to come along with him at once and repeat
the performance that Salieri might also be entertained by it.

He thereupon called into the room the decrepit old blind
musician he had spoken of, bidding him play the same composition he had just heard him performing in the tavern. The old
man willingly enough took up his fiddle and played one of the
graceful airs from " Don Giovanni " so execrably that Salieri,
despite his envy of his rival, angrily bade him depart and play no
more. He declared that it hurt him as much to hear such
exquisite music thus murdered as it would to see Raphael's beautiful " Madonna " bedaubed by some novice or to read the inspired
lines of Dante with the impudent additions of some wretched
rhymster.

Mozart, however, still laughing, gave the fiddler a coin—which
he could ill spare, money being ever scarce with him—and after
dismissing the old man told Salieri that he had come to ask his
opinion upon some musical themes that had been worrying him
insistently all morning. He added, casually, that he would come
another time, if more opportune, observing that Salieri did not
seem to be in a favourable mood. The jealous Italian, however,
though filled with fresh envy on thus hearing of this new composition so obviously inspired, could never resist the personality

of the careless, happy-go-lucky Mozart, nor the intense joy of listening to his enthralling music; and he invited him to remain and to let him hear the melody.

Mozart thereupon went to the piano and after describing the subject of his composition in a whimsical fashion—a youth in love with some fair lady, both very happy, when, suddenly, a dark cloud of gloom and mystery envelops them—his fingers strayed over the keys and a flood of exquisite melody filled the room.

Salieri, in spite of the gnawing envy tearing at his heart, was completely carried out of himself and, overcome by spontaneous admiration and delight, poured forth burning words of praise. At the same time he reproached Mozart, the composer of such a priceless gem, for having cared to stop at a tavern door to hear a blind beggar murder another of his loveliest airs—a proceeding which he, Salieri, greatly deprecated as unworthy of an artist, being undignified and belittling.

Mozart, however, who never could be persuaded to take himself seriously and was as modest and as simple as a child—which characteristics naturally annoyed the self-important and flattery-loving Salieri, who, like many merely talented individuals lacking the force of true genius, had a considerable amount of vanity—expressed wondering surprise that his friend should be so deeply impressed and moved by what was to himself a mere trifle. Then, merrily declaring that, whether a genius or not, he was nevertheless mightily hungry, he made as though to retire.

Still under the spell of the wonderful music he had just listened to, Salieri immediately suggested that they should dine together at the " Golden Lion ", a favourite inn. Mozart, nothing loath, cheerfully accepted the invitation and said that he would meet him again at the inn as soon as he had been home to inform his wife that he was dining out.

When his prospective guest had hurried away, singing a merry song, Salieri quickly fell back again into his morose mood, more jealous than ever of his heaven-gifted rival. Again he realized with despair that it was absolutely hopeless for him—Salieri—or any other devotee of musical art even to attempt to reach the golden heights of fame while Mozart, the wizard of harmony, still lived to soar ever above them. In a frantic burst of envious rage he called down curses upon the master musician who had just held his heart in rapturous thrall when playing the simple composition that had come to him as direct inspiration from the Divine Bestower of genius; and he vowed to slay Mozart that same day. No longer should his own path to glory be obstructed by him.

In feverish haste the Italian now drew forth from a secret hiding-place a tiny flask containing a deadly poison which had been given him eighteen years ago by a friend. He had himself been tempted to take this draught on many occasions when luck had gone against him; but he had always set it aside again in the hope of a rosier dawn to come—or for the silencing later on of some deadly foe whose machinations might overcast his life.

"Such a foe is Mozart!" he now cried passionately. "He blights my life and prospects, even while he enraptures me! The contents of this phial shall bring oblivion to him this day and leave me alone on the path of fame!"

Placing the fatal flask in an inner pocket, the Italian Kapellmeister sallied forth to keep his appointment at the sign of the "Golden Lion", where Mozart presently joined him; and the two partook of dinner together.

Salieri was excited and in high spirits and ordered the best foods and the most expensive wines; but Mozart, on the other hand, seemed strangely depressed, having suddenly become sad and silent, so that he spoke little and his thoughts seemed far away. When Salieri presently rallied him on that subject he admitted his abstraction, saying that it was due to the fact that his thoughts were engaged with the composition of the great Requiem Mass he had quite recently received a commission for under strange circumstances, with which he had thought all his friends were acquainted. Finding, however, that his host had not heard of it, he told him the story which has since become so famous. It was as follows.

A mysterious stranger—who afterwards turned out to be a rich nobleman—had called at his house twice during his absence from home, and had been so eager to see him that he had actually called a third time. He then commissioned the famous musician to write for him a Requiem Mass in memory of his wife, whom he had loved passionately and for the loss of whom he was clad in the deepest mourning. Mozart had agreed to do so, and had at once commenced the work to which he had grown so much attached that he did not now wish to part with it, but hoped that the mysterious stranger would never appear to claim it.

Then, as Salieri listened to this tale of a strange commission with increased envy still gnawing at his heart, Mozart added in a hesitating tone as though somewhat shy of confessing to superstition, that ever since he had been writing this work he had fancied that the piece would be his own Requiem. He often felt that the black-robed stranger seemed to be dogging his steps wherever he went—even now he imagined the latter's shadow to be seated at the table beside him.

Salieri, though he shuddered involuntarily, rallied his guest upon his low spirits and for succumbing to such morbid thoughts, bidding him put these idle superstitious fancies away from him. He advised him, when he felt dull, to take a drink of good wine and to read the lively story of " The Marriage of Figaro ".

This chance remark, however, brought up the subject of Beaumarchais, the author of " Figaro "; and Mozart suddenly asked his host if he believed, as was popularly supposed, that Beaumarchais had met his death by poison. To this, Salieri, with a violent start, replied hastily that he did not think so, as that author had ever been of a particularly lively and cheerful disposition and was not likely to have taken his own life nor to have had enemies who might wish to destroy him. Mozart agreed with him, adding that Beaumarchais was also a genius and, therefore, not likely to commit a crime, it being his—Mozart's—belief that genius and crime were never found together.

This last remark sounded unpleasantly ominous in the ears of the envious Salieri, who, however, became even more excited in his manner. Filling up both their glasses to overflowing, he bade his guest drink with him again and again to one another's health and to their lasting friendship.

Under this cloak of seeming hilarity, however, the Italian kept a keen eye upon the master musician; and when the latter's glance again wandered aside and remained fixed as though his thoughts had just strayed into unknown regions far away, he stealthily produced his hidden phial and poured forth its contents into the other's glass. Then, hardly able to conceal his agitation, he called upon his companion to drink yet once again; and after Mozart had, unsuspectingly, swallowed the poisoned draught, he filled up his glass again with fresh wine and bade him drink still more.

But Mozart refused to drink again, and, rising, went over to the open piano, saying he would play to his host some passages from his " Requiem ".

As the glorious music, so perfectly played by the master's loving touch, filled the chamber, Salieri once more fell under its magic spell and, against his will, was moved to such sincere and irresistible admiration that tears rolled down his cheeks. When Mozart stopped for a moment, astonished that his wonderful harmonies should have thus moved his friend to tears, the latter entreated him to continue, declaring that the tears he was shedding, though bitter, were yet consoling.

For a short time longer the magnificent notes of the famous Requiem filled the room. Then Mozart rose, somewhat unsteadily, announcing that he felt suddenly unwell; and, saying that he would go to his home to rest for a while, he bade farewell to his host and retired.

"Yes, rest, Mozart, but from that sleep there will be no awakening in this life!" muttered Salieri, as his rival departed. Then a horrible thought came into the murderer's mind. Suppose, as the master musician had said, that "crime and genius never go together"? If that were the case, then he, Salieri, could never win the fame of a genius, even though he now had no longer a rival to fear. His dark deed had thus been committed in vain!

Then he pulled himself together and endeavoured to comfort himself with the reflection that he had heard it whispered among the common folk of his own country that the great master sculptor, Michelangelo—of whose genius there had never been any doubt—secretly slew the man who designed the Vatican.

But in vain he sought for comfort; and he now realized, with the anguish of a stricken conscience, that for ever afterwards there would ring in his memory the last marvellous harmonies of a true genius as the Requiem for the death of his own peace of mind.[1]

A NIGHT IN MAY — *Rimsky-Korsakov*

ONE warm evening in May lively merry-makings were taking place in a certain village of Little Russia. It was the season of Whitsuntide, known in that country district as the Week of the Water-Nymphs, when the youths and maidens decked themselves in their gayest attire and met to play their national games and to dance and sing together in happy groups.

This was the most joyous season of the year for the young people, for Love was in the air and many a pretty maid secured

[1] There has never been any proof, or even any definite suspicion that Mozart was poisoned by Salieri, or that he met his death by poisoning at all, most of his biographers having written to the contrary. However, the fact that the Italian Kapellmeister was known to be inordinately jealous of his brilliant contemporary and that it was said by some of his friends that Mozart himself believed, when dying, that he had been poisoned, gave rise to the suspicion upon which Poushkin based the poem from which the libretto of this opera has been taken.

a bold sweetheart during these springtime festivities. First one couple and then another would slip apart from the noisy throng to wander away together into the more unfrequented woodland glades to exchange their sweet vows, or to sit by the lake-side waiting, hand locked in hand, for the water-nymphs to appear. These superstitious village folk believed that at this particular festival-time, the spirits of unhappy maidens who had sought oblivion from their sorrows by drowning appeared again in the form of water-nymphs who might be seen dancing in rings on the banks of streams and lakes, weaving wreaths of flowers and singing mysterious songs of love, now sad, now gay.

On this particular evening the young people had chosen for their meeting-place a pretty spot at the end of the village, opposite the cottage of the village belle, Hanna; and there they held high revels. Not very far distant there stretched a large lake, set in somewhat gloomy surroundings; beyond this stood the ruins of a nobleman's ancient castle, once the scene of a grim tragedy and now reputed to be haunted. The shadow of mystery that hung over the sombre lake and castle beyond, however, did not cloud the high spirits of the rustic revellers; and they still pursued their games and dances untiringly as at the beginning of the day, although the shadows of evening were already creeping down the hill-sides.

Special interest was taken in an enthusiastic rendering of the favourite game known as " The Millet ", because, in addition to the combined singing and actions of the performers, intricate solo dances were introduced into the game by a young man named Kalénnik, the best dancer of all the village youths. After this game had come to an end outside Hanna's cottage, the lively players tripped off to begin it again at the other end of the village.

Thus, as twilight deepened, the open space in front of Hanna's abode became silent and deserted; but presently, a graceful youth slipped out from amidst the shadows and, approaching the cottage, began to sing in subdued tones a passionate love-song to the low accompaniment of the bandoora—a native instrument upon which he was a very skilful player.

This serenader was the son of the village Mayor. He was a handsome young man named Levko, and was the favoured admirer of the fair Hanna. He had given the slip to his gay companions in order to steal a few blissful moments with his beloved one, whom he well knew to be waiting within her closed doors for his expected arrival.

When Hanna presently came out, the lovers indulged in happy converse for a short time; and when Hanna tearfully expressed fear that their happiness might not last because she occupied a humbler position in the village than did the Mayor's son, Levko comforted her tenderly and declared stoutly that he would soon gain the consent of his father to their union—even though that all-important person withheld it at present.

By this time the twilight had deepened almost to darkness and the stars were already shining overhead; and as Hanna's gaze travelled back from the glittering heavens and across to the mysterious lake and haunted mansion beyond, she shuddered for a moment. Then, suddenly, she begged her lover to relate to her the story of the tragedy that had happened years ago in the castle before it was deserted and had fallen into ruins—a story of mystery which had never been told to her, but which she knew the old village gossips sometimes spoke of to one another in awed whispers. This was the story which Levko now related:

In the early days of the castle a certain nobleman had lived there with his beautiful daughter, Pannochka, who loved him with such passionate devotion that she had no love left to bestow even upon a sweetheart. As his daughter grew to maidenhood, however, the father, who was a widower, decided to marry again; and one day, to the great grief of the lovely Pannochka, she was bidden to give greeting and place to a stepmother—who, though also of great beauty, bestowed such an evil glance of jealous hatred upon her husband's child that the latter was frightened and fled from her presence in haste.

That night, as Pannochka sat weeping alone in her chamber, a fierce black cat suddenly approached her and, with a snarl of rage, pounced upon her with its sharp claws extended. The maiden sprang to her feet in terror and, snatching up a knife, struck wildly at the strange cat and drove it, still snarling and screeching, from the room.

When the nobleman's wife appeared next day, it was seen that her hands were bound up with linen, as though wounded; and then the dreadful truth was realized by Pannochka. Her beloved father's new wife was a wicked witch.

Pannochka was soon driven forth from the castle gates, cold, hungry, and clad in rags—this cruel deed being done by the nobleman himself at the bidding of his witch-wife, whose evil influence he was powerless to resist. The heart-broken Pannochka wandered but a few steps; and then, in mad despair, she flung herself from the top of a steep bank into the silent lake below and was seen no more in human form.

That was not the end of the tale, however. As the despairing Pannochka plunged into the lake, she was received gladly by the water-nymphs dwelling in its depths and invited to become their Queen. Every now and again, the gossips declared later, she would come out into the castle grounds at night to dance and play in the moonlight with her nymph subjects. On one of these occasions, according to the legend, the wicked stepmother was seen walking on the edge of the lake and was dragged into the water by the nymphs. The witch, however, was quick to save herself from destruction and, by means of her magic, instantly transformed herself into a water-nymph and thus escaped.

Levko finished his fantastic tale by declaring that the old wives of the village believed that Pannochka still danced with her nymphs in the moonlight at intervals and that, if seen by a mortal, she always begged the latter to guess which of the water-sprites was once her witch-stepmother—whose evil spell would remain upon her until this false nymph could be discovered and driven forth for ever.

As the noisy revellers could now be heard returning, the lovers embraced once more and parted, Hanna retiring into her cottage, while Levko slipped away quietly into the shadows of the trees.

When the merrymakers presently appeared, they were livelier than ever; and this time the dancing was fast and furious. Now that darkness had fallen, the fussy old Mayor of the village had commanded that the revels should cease, lest the young folks should get into mischief or indulge in unseemly pranks. The young men, however, thought otherwise, and were determined to keep up their frolics as long as they pleased; and for a short time the girls also lingered to applaud the wild antics of their favourite Kalénnik, who was now in a half-intoxicated condition. Presently, Kalénnik tipsily announced his intention of hunting up the Mayor and defying him in his own house; and with this intention he went reeling down the street in the direction of the latter's abode. The girls, now somewhat alarmed, fled hastily to their homes; but the young men hid in the shadows, waiting, with stifled laughter, to see what would happen next. Very soon they were in the midst of a glorious prank at the instigation of the hidden Levko.

The young serenader had just observed a cloaked figure approach stealthily to the door of Hanna's cottage and knock thereon. Curious to know who this nocturnal visitor could be, he drew nearer, though still keeping himself hidden from view; and he was just in time to hear a declaration of love uttered in extravagant terms by the stranger as soon as the village beauty appeared in the doorway. To his amazement, he recognized the voice as that of his own father; and he realized—at first with indignation and later with amusement—that the pompous and fussy Mayor, though fond of preaching propriety to the youths of the village, was just a vain philanderer himself who secretly ran after pretty girls, despite his advancing age and exalted position.

In his present pursuit, however, this elderly Don Juan met with no success. To the great delight of the hidden Levko, Hanna scornfully refused all the advances of her mayoral admirer and even threatened to reveal his shocking conduct to her own true lover, his son, Levko. The old libertine, however, was not easily got rid of. In wheedling tones he continued to entreat the pretty girl to accept his advances, promising her jewels and gay clothes; and he added that his son Levko was but a foolish boy, too young to know the meaning of love.

This last remark was more than the hidden Levko could stand; and seeking out the other youths lurking in the shadows, he whispered to them a merry plan for making a laughing-stock of the importunate suitor. Instantly, the young men rushed forth and, flinging themselves upon the astonished Mayor, began to hug and kiss him—to the great relief of Hanna, who quickly retired within her cottage and bolted the door. It was not until after much struggling and angry expostulation that her unwanted admirer managed to free himself from the encircling embraces of the boisterous youths and to hasten back to his own home.

But Levko did not mean to let the foolish official off so lightly, considering that such an absurd old humbug deserved a more salutary punishment for refusing consent to his son's marriage and then attempting to make love himself to the latter's sweetheart. So he gathered his boon companions together again and taught them a disrespectful song, arranging that they should presently sing this ditty beneath the windows of the mayoral abode.

Meanwhile, the Mayor had quickly recovered his lost dignity within the safe and respectable confines of his own home; and here, a little later in the evening, he entertained a visitor in the person of a noted distiller. The latter had been sent by the present owner of the haunted castle to make arrangements for the establishment of a distillery upon that ill-omened spot.

The Mayor's sister-in-law, a prim and fussy old maid who had kept house for him since he had been a widower, was paying obsequious court to the guest—who was very desirable in her eyes, despite the fact that he was enormously fat and coarse. All three were making merry together when suddenly the door was burst open and Kalénnik, the tipsy dancer, reeled into the room and, after defying the mayoral authority in maudlin tones, flung himself on to a couch and promptly fell asleep. When the Mayor would have had the roisterer thrown out, the distiller, amused by the incident, quickly dissipated his host's anger by declaring with his fat laugh that such a spectacle boded well for the new distillery.

Before the party could settle down again, however, a stone came hurtling in through the open window; and at the same time, a group of merry revellers outside began to sing the disrespectful song taught them by Levko, in which the pompous Mayor was held to ridicule.

Furious that this should happen in the presence of a guest of importance, the Mayor bustled outside to catch the ringleader—little dreaming that this was his own son; and presently he returned dragging in with him a youth who was indeed Levko, but whom he did not recognize because the mischievous young man's face was now blacked with soot and he had likewise turned his sheepskin coat inside out as a further disguise.

There was a small lock-up cell adjoining the Mayor's parlour; and seeing that his irate father was about to thrust him within this undesirable chamber, Levko managed to wrench himself free and to rejoin his companions outside. At the same time a gust of wind extinguished the candles, so that the angry Mayor, seeking to recapture his prisoner in the dark, seized his sister-in-law by mistake and clapped her unceremoniously into the lock-up and barred the door, heedless of her frantic expostulations.

Just then the Mayor's clerk ran in, puffing and blowing, declaring that the rowdy youths outside had caused a tumult by their ribald singing, but that he had managed to catch the ringleader—whom he had locked up in the penthouse adjoining his own dwelling. "Then who is the rascal in *my* lock-up?" now demanded the bemused Mayor; and, hastily unbolting the door of his own strong-room, he was amazed on being confronted by his infuriated sister-in-law. Nearly choking with rage, the affronted spinster ran out into the street—where she was instantly seized by the rowdy serenaders who, having already effected the escape of Levko from the clerk's lock-up, now hurried the struggling female along and deposited her in the penthouse in place of their merry leader. Then they dispersed quickly, well pleased with their frolic for the time being.

Consequently, a further violent scene occurred when the pompous old Mayor presently came along with the distiller and attended by his triumphant clerk to examine the supposed roisterer within the penthouse and was confronted once again by his outraged sister-in-law. This time the irate spinster, in her venomous vituperations, let fall more than one hint regarding certain peccadilloes of her hypocritical brother-in-law well known to her—in particular his secret philanderings; and as he followed her home in subdued silence, cowed by her insinuations, the Mayor, to his intense chagrin, was obliged to endure the quizzical side-glances of his two companions.

Meanwhile, Levko, the mischievous cause of all this commotion, had escaped from his wild companions for a short spell; and after washing off the soot from his face, he wandered down to the now deserted lake-side to collect his scattered wits. Soon the thoughts of the ardent young lover came back to the object of his passion, his fair sweetheart, Hanna; and presently he brought forth his bandoora and began to play upon it with a tender touch and to sing to its accompaniment a sweet love-song in honour of his adored one.

So engrossed was he in his happy thoughts, he did not at first notice that strange happenings were taking place around him. Then he rubbed his eyes in amazement as his gaze fell upon a marvellous sight—a scene which he had thought until this moment could only be experienced in the dreams of childhood. While he had been serenading his sweetheart, a host of ethereal water-nymphs had emerged from the lake and were now singing and dancing lightly upon the banks and dew-sprinkled lawns beyond.

These pale yet lovely beings were the ghostly spirit-forms of drowned maidens who had sought in watery graves oblivion from the persecutions of the wicked or from the heartlessness of faithless lovers; and it seemed that the sweet music of a human serenader had brought them forth. For the time being they had cast aside their melancholy and were happy once more as they danced and sang, or wove wreaths of the pale spring flowers that gemmed the banks and grassy dells.

As Levko gazed upon this fair company with mingled awe and delight, Pannochka, the beautiful Queen of the water-nymphs, came to his side and whispered: "Find my wicked witch-step-mother for me, good youth! Even now her evil spell is still upon me, so that I cannot swim freely through the waters but am stifled in their depths! She is here amongst the nymphs, but I know not which is she! Find her for me, brave youth, and I will reward thee by giving thee thy heart's desire!"

So full of passionate entreaty was the voice of the drowned Pannochka that Levko longed to grant her request, though he knew not how to do so. Just then, however, the nymphs began to play the old game known as "The Raven", which, as luck would have it, gave him the clue he sought. In this game one of the performers had to represent a raven, which desired to harry and peck the other players, who represented chickens; and at first, none of these pretty nymphs wished to play the part of the cruel raven. Presently, however, a nymph from the outer ring pushed her way forward and eagerly offered to play the raven; and watching her subsequent actions with curiosity, Levko soon noticed that she harried and pecked the harmless "chicks" with such venomous animosity that it was obvious she enjoyed playing so cruel a part. Seeing now a baleful light gleaming in her eyes, Levko cried out accusingly: "The nymph who plays the 'raven' is the wicked witch!"

Full of joy at the young man's discovery, the players seized the spiteful nymph who had played the "raven" and disappeared with her into the depths of the lake; and next moment, the lovely spirit-maiden Pannochka again appeared beside the still gazing Levko and thanked him for having thus released her from the spell of her enemy, so that she could now swim freely in the water for evermore. She then placed in his hand a sealed letter bidding him show it to his father, who would no longer refuse to consent to his marriage with pretty Hanna.

As the Queen of the Water-Nymphs now vanished from sight, Levko wondered whether he had been dreaming. But no! The letter which the drowned Pannochka had given to him still lay in his hand; and the young man, untroubled by its supernatural source, hurried back to the village without further ado to test its magic powers.

He found that the Mayor, followed by a gaping crowd, was still seeking for the ringleader of the roistering youths who had so rudely disturbed his peace of mind; and when Levko suddenly appeared, still wearing his sheepskin coat turned inside out, he was at once seized by the clerk as the culprit and brought before the irate official.

As the Mayor glared sternly at the captive, thus learning with amazement that the saucy rogue was none other than his own adventurous son, Levko calmly produced the sealed document given to him by Pannochka; and the clerk was bidden to read it aloud. To the astonishment of all, including Levko himself, the document proved to be an official letter from the Governor of the district, stating that as the Mayor of the village had behaved himself in an unseemly fashion of late, he must straightway make amends for his misdoings by giving consent to the marriage of his son Levko with the village beauty, Hanr .. The Governor further commanded that the wedding should take place at once, and added that he expected to find this order had already been carried out upon his next official visit to the village—which Levko now mendaciously declared would be the following evening.

Though angry and deeply mortified, the Mayor did not dare to disobey the command contained in this document, which bore the official seal and signature of the Governor. The consequence was that the marriage ceremony of Levko and Hanna took place next morning—to the great joy of the happy lovers and the satisfaction of their many friends, who all came to take part in the wedding festivities.

To Hanna alone did Levko reveal the true origin of the lucky document that had secured their happiness, leading the Mayor and others to believe that the Governor's own messenger had handed it to him. Then, full of joy, not unmingled with awe, the bridal pair knelt to offer up thanksgiving for the miracle wrought on their behalf and to pray together for the soul of the drowned Pannochka.

SADKO   *Rimsky-Korsakov*

FROM the Cycle of Folk-lore Tales of Novgorod comes the legend-story of Sadko, the Master-Musician, who may be described as the Slavonic Orpheus. Just as Orpheus could charm the savage hearts of men and beasts with his lute, so could Sadko perform similar miraculous deeds with his gusslee, the sweet-toned musical instrument of Ancient Russia. His thrilling voice and magic touch upon the strings had power to calm the wildest passions of mortals, to bring peace to troubled minds, and joy to those who had never known joy before.

Many were the adventures of Sadko. Although he attained to great riches and honours by means of his wonderful gift of music, he had begun life as a poor minstrel. He was so poor, indeed, that he was glad to sing songs and to play his gusslee at the fire-sides of the fisher-folk, and to receive a little food in payment. He thought he was in luck's way, too, when he was invited to enter-tain the rich merchants of Novgorod at their feasts and to pick up a few coins afterwards. By so doing, he built up a name and reputation for himself—indeed, he was often spoken of as " the

Nightingale of Novgorod ". Yet he was as poor as a church mouse.

But Sadko did not mean to remain poor all his days. He was a true son of Novgorod, with the same commercial instincts as the rich merchants at whose banquets he played. He was determined to become richer than any of them—so rich, in fact, that he could buy them all up, did he so wish. His courage grew as his musical fame increased; and at last his belief in himself became great enough for him to do a very rash thing.

At one of the grand banquets to which he had been bidden to amuse the guests with his sweet singing and gusslee playing, Sadko surpassed himself. Then, to the astonishment of all, he suddenly changed the tone of his songs, in which he now began to upbraid the merchants because of their greedy love of money and luxury.

When the rich men showed their annoyance and threatened to expel him from their feasts, when he would surely starve, he did not seem in the least disturbed, as they had expected. Instead, he boldly declared that he would soon become even richer than any of them. Then, angered by the burst of derisive laughter which greeted this boast, Sadko rashly offered to lay them a wager. He would go forth to Lake Ilmen, not far away, and catch a bumper haul of golden fishes. He even added wildly that if they would stake all their worldly goods and possessions upon his wager, he, in his turn, would stake his own head upon the result, since he had nothing more valuable to offer.

The rich merchants thought this was a huge joke, and laughingly agreed to accept the wager. Then, still smarting from his reproaches, they announced that they intended to hold him to his bargain. He must go forth at once and catch his golden fishes; and, failing to produce the same, he must, indeed, lose his head.

So Sadko was driven forth from the banquet, while the hired buffoons made fun of him for his foolishness and the guests laughed aloud at the idea of a poor minstrel ever becoming as rich as a prosperous merchant of Novgorod.

.   .   .   .

Sadko wandered alone upon the shores of Lake Ilmen, feeling that he had, indeed, been extremely foolish to make such an impossible wager. He felt that he would never be able to return to Novgorod. But he still had his beloved gusslee with him, and could comfort himself with his own sweet music.

So the poor minstrel laid down the fishing-net he had been made to carry as he set forth upon his hopeless enterprise. Then he took up his gusslee and began to play upon it and to sing i the thrillingly seductive voice that had won for him the name of "the Nightingale of Novgorod".

It happened that Princess Volkova, one of the daughters of the Sea-King, happened to be swimming near the shores of Lake Ilmen that day; and hearing the magical music made by Sadko, she instantly fell in love with the minstrel and greeted him rapturously.

Sadko was amazed at the sight of the lovely sea-nymph; but when she presently offered to give him anything he desired for having charmed her with his music, his wits did not desert him. He suddenly remembered his wager; and he begged the fairy stranger to give him a shoal of golden fishes.

The Sea-King's daughter promised to do so; and when he had once more played and sung to her, she bade him cast in his net as she swam away.

Eagerly Sadko obeyed; and soon, to his joy, he dragged ashore a net full of fishes made of solid gold.

Thus did Sadko win his wager and become the richest man in Novgorod. At first the rich merchants were afraid that they would have to forfeit all their goods and possessions to him, these being the stakes agreed upon. But Sadko was not of a greedy nature, and he was very well content with his own huge new fortune; so everybody was happy.

Sadko was now regarded as a hero by one and all; and he determined to use his wealth wisely and well. He still preferred to be loved for his sweet music rather than for his gold. He chose a fair and kindly wife who loved him dearly; and he had a very happy home.

Nevertheless, in spite of his good fortune, his splendid merchant ships, and his fame as the sweetest minstrel in all Russia, Sadko was of too adventurous a nature to settle down as a quiet merchant, while still a handsome young man. He soon began to grow restless and longed to undertake new enterprises.

At last his love of adventure would be denied no longer. So he bade a temporary farewell to his wife and his friends and set sail in one of his own merchant vessels, followed by an entire fleet of other ships, all his own, as escort.

He was young and bold, and he hoped that he would meet with marvellous adventures. He was not disappointed.

. . . .

Soon after Sadko had set sail with his splendid fleet of merchant ships a dreadful storm arose. The tempest raged for days with terrific force, the wind became a hurricane, and the sea rose in mountainous waves. So terrified became the sailors on board the leading vessel which carried Sadko that they declared the Sea-King's anger must have been aroused for some unknown reason and that a sacrifice must be offered him in appeasement.

But who should be the victim to be tossed into the sea as sacrifice? It was decided to cast lots; and, to the dismay of Sadko, the lot fell upon himself. Of what avail now were his wealth and his exquisite gift of music? To be cast into the raging sea was more of an adventure than he had bargained for!

But Sadko was brave, as well as bold. He clutched his beloved gusslee closely to his breast, resigned to his fate; and he was cast into the sea, with merely a wooden plank as raft. He soon lost this small support, and becoming unconscious, was plunged into the ocean depths.

Almost immediately the storm ceased, and the waves calmed down; and the splendid fleet of merchant ships continued on its way, minus the owner.

.   .   .   .

When Sadko presently recovered consciousness after being flung into the raging waves, he found himself in the Sea-King's palace on the ocean bed.

Here, somewhat to his surprise, he was received as an honoured guest by the King and Queen of the Sea and their many lovely nymph-daughters. He was tended with the utmost care, and entertained in right royal style. He wandered in beautiful coral gardens and beheld brilliantly-coloured fishes of wonderful shapes; and all the riches of the sea were at his disposal.

Best of all, however, he could still play his beloved gusslee and sing sweet songs to its accompaniment. What was more, the magic of his performance was felt as strongly here in the sea as on land. All the sea folk clustered around him and listened in delight as he sang his romantic songs. And when he played gayer and rhythmic dance tunes, they all danced or moved rhythmically to their accompaniment.

The Sea-King was so enthralled by the magical music of Sadko that he was eager to keep so exquisite a performer always in his watery domain. For this reason he desired the honoured visitor to marry one of his many daughters, hoping that by thus domesticating him to an under-sea life, he could keep him there a longer time. He commanded his three hundred lovely daughters, therefore, to parade before the minstrel in a pearl-decked procession; and Sadko was bidden to choose a bride from among these ravishing nymphs.

Instead of choosing the loveliest of the Sea-King's daughters, as most young men in his position would probably have done, Sadko very wisely chose the plainest of them all. Being of a prudent nature, he felt that, by so doing, he would not be so likely to fall in love with his ocean bride. Therefore, he would not suffer so much when the time came for him to leave her—for he still hoped to return to his beloved wife in Novgorod.

Consequently he chose the youngest of these maidens, the Princess Volkova, who, though less beautiful than her many sisters, was, nevertheless, very lovely indeed. He had also recognized in this Princess the kindly nymph whose gift of golden fishes had made him rich; and he felt grateful to her.

The Princess Volkova was full of joy when she knew that Sadko's choice had fallen upon her; for she had loved him in secret ever since the day she had first met him on the shores of Lake Ilmen. It had been owing to her, indeed, that he had been brought safely to the Sea-King's palace, after being cast adrift on the plank; and it was she and her nymph attendants who had tended him as he lay unconscious.

The Sea-King ordered a great festival to be held to celebrate the wedding of Sadko to his youngest daughter, the Princess Volkova; and at the wedding feast he invited the minstrel to play again on his gusslee and to sing to its accompaniment.

Only too gladly did Sadko take up his precious instrument; and the music he now played upon it was so hilariously lively that all the sea folk went nearly mad with joyous glee.

The Sea-King himself was the most hilarious of all. He danced with such gusto and wild abandonment that his subjects quickly followed his infectious example. The consequence was that this delirious movement in the ocean bed affected the waters above, which now rose and fell with an equally wild abandonment, as though stirred up by an earthquake. The ships on the ocean's surface were tossed about like cockle-shells; and there were many wrecks.

Then, quite suddenly, St. Nicholas intervened, and stopped the wild delirium of Sadko's music by breaking the strings of his gusslee. Instantly the mad dancing stopped as the music ended. The Sea-King remembered his royal dignity once more; and a peaceful quiet fell upon his subjects as the waters above became calm and smooth.

Next, St. Nicholas commanded the minstrel to return to his home in Novgorod; and in that same moment, Sadko felt himself borne swiftly upwards and cast upon the shores of his own country once more.

. . . .

As Sadko lay sleeping upon the banks of Lake Ilmen, after

being cast ashore there by St. Nicholas, the Sea-King's daughter, Princess Volkova, came thither to bid him farewell. As a sea-nymph, she could not live on the land with him; and she would not return to the sea without him. Her love was devoted and eternal; it could not be given to another. So she sat beside him and sang to him a low, sweet lullaby of farewell.

Then, with a last look of love, the fair sea-nymph glided away, sadly and lingeringly. As she moved towards Novgorod, silvery drops of water fell from her at every step. When, presently, she vanished from sight, a stream of water remained in her stead—a stream which grew and swelled until at last it became the mighty river Volkova, which was to connect Novgorod with the sea for ever afterwards.

.   .   .   .

When Sadko awoke, he returned to Novgorod, where he was received with great joy by his fair and faithful wife and his many friends.

A grand festival was held by the rich merchants in his honour; and everybody was loud in the praises of their returned hero of music.

But Sadko would take no glory for himself; and he bade his friends give thanks to the good St. Nicholas for his safe return.

THE SNOW-MAIDEN   *Rimsky-Korsakov*
(*Snegourotchka*)

It was Spring-time in Russia; but in the country and forest districts of the Red Mountain, not far from the City of the Good Tsar Berendey, bitter cold and cheerlessness still reigned. The radiant Sun-God refused his golden warmth-giving rays in that particular part of the country.

For sixteen years now the fair land of the Berendeys had been thus afflicted with sunless Springs and Summers. The reason for this was that the great and glorious Sun-God had been offended because the dainty but flirtatious Fairy Spring, in a passing fancy, had lured the icy God of Winter, King Frost, to her arms.

This unnatural union was displeasing to the all-powerful Sun-God—who was likewise rendered jealous, because the lovely Fairy Spring should thus have shown favour to the sparkling King Frost rather than to his own brilliant self. When, too, their beautiful daughter, Snegourotchka, the Snow-Maiden, was born, and was kept hidden by them from his sight in the secret depths of the Forest of Berendey, his displeasure was deeper still.

So greatly, indeed, did the Sun-God resent the presence of this cold-hearted Snow-Maiden on the earth that he had refused to spread the comforting warmth of his own golden rays over the country of Berendey, where she had been kept hidden ever since her birth.

What was more, he had vowed that if ever the secret maiden should come within the orbit of his influence, his rays should quickly cause her icy heart to melt, when she would perish miserably. Meanwhile, he bided his time, knowing that the thing he desired would surely come to pass at last, and that each year brought his triumph nearer.

King Frost knew this, too; and he would fain have kept his secret Snow-Maiden a safe prisoner for ever. But Fairy Spring was not so wise; and when her lovely daughter's sixteenth birthday arrived, she met her icy lover for the last time and arranged with him for their beloved child to mingle with human beings at last.

The Fairy Spring was at the trysting-place in the forest on the Red Mountain. Here a lonely Faun, the Spirit of the Woods, seated like a gnome upon a tree-stump, kept watch for Winter. It was almost dawn, and the distant cocks were already crowing; and as the first streaks of pale light crept through the purple darkness, the birds began to appear, first by twos and threes, but soon in increasing numbers.

Then, seeing the approach of Fairy Spring from the snow-clad Red Mountain, accompanied in her lovely progress by flocks of swans and cranes, the Faun knew that his Winter vigil had ended; and he left his broken stump and crept into the hollow of a tree to sleep.

The Fairy Spring wept because of the still-icy scene, for the still-sleeping flowers, and for the shivering birds who had flown thither from colder lands, expecting her own season's warmth; and she bade her feathered friends dance to keep themselves warm—which they gladly did.

When the birds had warmed themselves with a merry dance, they quickly retired and huddled together once more as King Frost and his icy attendants drew near to greet Fairy Spring.

When the latter declared that it was now time for their daughter to see human beings and enjoy freedom, and that she no longer needed their care, King Frost was still doubtful about the dangers

involved in such a course; but he called forth the hidden Snegourotchka to decide the matter for herself.

The lovely Snow-Maiden, now sixteen years old and eager for
the joys of youth, declared that she had already heard in the
distance the sweet music made by mortals and had been entranced
by it; and she entreated her parents to let her go forth into the
world. Her request was again urged by the Fairy Spring; and at
last, very reluctantly, King Frost gave his consent. He decided
that a good old couple of childless peasants, by name Bobyl and
Bobylicha, should be allowed to care for her in their simple home;
and then he called forth the Faun, his Guardian Spirit of the
Forest, and bade him, with his fellow fauns, to protect the lovely
maiden if ever she should be in danger when wandering in the
woodlands.

Then, bidding their daughter a tender farewell, King Frost and
the Fairy Spring departed—the former vanishing in a flurry of
snow-flakes, and the latter escorted by her attendant birds; and
Snegourotchka was left alone in the forest.

But not for long; for with the early dawning light, there came
the sound of a merry procession approaching with happy laughter
and sweet singing. But though this gay human singing again
filled her with delight, the shy maiden quickly hid herself behind
the old withered tree, into the hollow of which her guardian Faun
had already slipped.

A few moments later, a Carnival procession of peasants from
the neighbouring village came into sight on the woodland path
beyond. They had come out joyfully to welcome the advent of
Spring, although Winter had scarce departed and sunless days
seemed likely to remain. But this was the proper time of the year
to welcome the Spring; and so the peasants of Berendey had come
out in a grand Carnival procession, in accordance with their usual
custom.

Among this merry company was old Bobyl and his wife, Bobylicha; and it was to this honest old couple that Snegourotchka
now presented herself, as though drawn to them by magic. As
the pair gazed upon her in amazement and presently bowed
before her as though she were a Princess, the Snow-Maiden
declared herself to be a lost wanderer seeking a friendly home;
and she begged the old couple to allow her to dwell with
them.

Bobyl and Bobylicha were only too glad to adopt such a lovely
maiden as their daughter; but as they took her along with them
to join in the procession, they were filled with awe when all
the forest trees bowed their branches down before the youthful

stranger. They knew then that she was no ordinary mortal like themselves.

. . . .

In the humble cottage of old Bobyl and his good dame, Snegourotchka lived safely enough for a time. Her wild beauty brought many village admirers; but, to the latter, she had little to say. She was still the Snow-Maiden, whose heart was frozen; and the maiden joys she had craved for seemed denied to her. She was, however, always happy when the handsome young shepherd, Lell, came and sang songs to her to the accompaniment of his pipes, upon which he was a skilled player; for it had been the sweet music of Lell she had heard in her secret retreat in the heart of the forest, which had so entranced her into demanding her freedom to dwell with mortals.

But, one day, when Lell demanded kisses in return for his music, she refused him; and though she offered him service instead—to spread a meal for him in her humble foster-parents' home—he declared he could not sell his music for service. Then she offered him a flower, which he accepted; but when he found that her kisses were still withheld from him, he flung away the flower in anger.

Then, seeing some of the village girls beckoning to him—for the handsome shepherd was eagerly sought by them—he carelessly strolled off to accept their saucy invitations; and Snegourotchka, because of her cold heart, was again left, lonely and sad, though still longing for Lell and his sweet music.

In despair, she now called upon her mother, Fairy Spring, and her father, King Frost, to have pity upon her, and to let the great Sun-God melt her frozen heart with his warm rays; but no answer came to her prayer.

Soon, however, her unhappy reflections were broken in upon by the one village girl who had always showed kindness to her— the others regarding her as a dangerous rival in the affections of their swains.

This newcomer was Coupava, the daughter of the richest peasant in the village. Coupava lived in a prosperous-looking abode opposite the humble cottage of old Bobyl; and seeing Snegourotchka sitting outside, looking sad and lonely, she ran across, hoping to cheer the beautiful stranger with her own glad news. She now told Snegourotchka that she had recently become betrothed to Miskar, a rich merchant of the neighbouring city; and she added excitedly that her lover was coming that day to visit her and to bring gifts for herself and her friends.

Even as she spoke, there came the sound of merry voices and a stir in the village; and next moment, the rich city merchant, Miskar, came into sight, followed by a string of Coupava's youthful friends. Coupava hurried away to greet her betrothed and to help him bestow the gifts he had brought upon her merry young friends, who were all very gleeful because one of their number had secured such a wealthy suitor.

Soon, however, this hilarious rejoicing changed to dismay. The happy Coupava was eager to share her joy with her new friend, the adopted daughter of the old peasants who lived in the cottage opposite her home; but no sooner had she introduced her betrothed to the stranger, than Miskar, fascinated by the Snow-Maiden's unearthly beauty, had eyes for no one else.

Roughly throwing off the clinging arms of the distressed Coupava, Miskar now began to pour extravagant words of admiration upon Snegourotchka and to lay at her feet the rich gifts and trinkets he had brought for his betrothed, to whom he no longer paid any attention.

Old Bobyl and his dame, delighted that their adopted daughter should be thus favoured by the rich merchant, now told the shepherd, Lell, to keep his distance; and greedily gathering up some of the handsome gifts, they urged the coldly silent Snegourotchka to be thankful for her good fortune.

But the Snow-Maiden had nothing to say to the infatuated wealthy merchant kneeling at her feet and pleading for her love; for she wished her cold heart to be warmed by the love of Lell—who no longer seemed to care for her, having departed scornfully on the arrival of her new and unwanted admirer.

Meanwhile, as the enthralled Miskar still pleaded in vain before Snegourotchka, poor Coupava was being comforted by her friends, who were all furious because of the insult she had suffered; and at last they persuaded the despairing girl to betake herself and her woes to the Good Tsar, Berendey, their beloved Little Father, who was always ready to help and advise his peasant children. From him she would surely get redress for the injury done her; and Coupava, with renewed hope, now set forth eagerly for the city, accompanied by her sympathizing friends.

.   .   .   .

In his splendid palace, the great and good Tsar Berendey sat on his golden throne, listening to the sweet music made by a group of blind singers and gusslee-players, who had begged permission to entertain him and his dazzling Court that day.

But, though the musicians were excellent and their music well chosen, it had not the power to drive away the sad thoughts of the Good Tsar, who was just then greatly troubled. Although he had conquered his enemies and his country was at peace, continued contentment and prosperity for his beloved people could not be hoped for unless sunny days returned once more.

For sixteen long years there had been a succession of cold, sunless Springs and Summers, so that the pale blossoms scarce ripened into fruit, and the harvests of corn were so poor as to be hardly worth the gathering. The Sun-God, Yarilo, had removed his favour from the land he once had loved; and the Tsar now determined that something must be done to propitiate the offended God. He decided that, on the morrow, when the Feast of Yarilo fell due, all the unmarried youths and maidens of the land should assemble in the Valley of Yarilo and there utter invocations and songs of praise to the mighty Sun-God at the time of his rising.

While planning this with his ministers, the weeping Coupava was brought in to tell her tale of woe before the throne; and on hearing her story, the Tsar was filled with pity for her disappointment and with indignation against the wealthy merchant, Miskar, and the stranger maiden who had caused all this trouble.

He immediately ordered a Court of Judgment to be held, and caused the culprits to be brought before him. At first, he commanded that Miskar should be exiled from the country; but when he beheld the marvellous beauty of Snegourotchka and learned from her own lips that her cold heart had never yet been touched by love, he decided to give the merchant another chance. He then declared that if Miskar could win the love of Snegourotchka by next sun-rise, when the Feast of Yarilo was to be held, his sentence should be remitted. Since, however, it was necessary that the lovely Snow-Maiden's heart should be touched in any case, he must have a rival who might succeed if he should fail.

With one accord, the ladies of the Court invited the Tsar to allow the sweet-singing shepherd, Lell, to share this charming task, since he was known to be a goodly youth; and this he agreed to.

Thus, Miskar and Lell were chosen as rival competitors for the hand and heart of Snegourotchka; and the Court of Judgment ended with a song of praise for the wisdom and mercy of the great Tsar.

.   .   .   .

That evening, being the last day of Spring and the Eve of the Feast of Yarilo the Sun-God, the peasants of Berendey held high revels in the forest. Everybody came out to one of the sheltered glades; and while the old people sat around on banks and knolls, the youths and maidens danced and sang.

Country dance after country dance was performed; and when

the dancers tired, then acrobats and tumblers took their place. The revels were to last the whole night through, so that all the throng would be ready at dawn next morning at the Feast of Yarilo to join in a mighty chorus of greeting and praise to the great Sun-God on his rising.

Among the revellers were Miskar and Lell, to each of whom had been given the pleasant task of winning their way to the unawakened heart of lovely Snegourotchka.

At first it seemed that handsome Lell would be the favoured one; and had the matter rested with Snegourotchka, that would certainly have been the case.

The Snow-Maiden, though still conscious of her cold heart, knew now that it was Lell whom she desired to love when her heart should soften; and when they presently met in the woodlands, she wove a garland of flowers and placed it over his brow.

But Lell, though he accepted the garland and seemed proud to wear it, was no longer thinking of the lovely but cold Snow-Maiden; and he wandered back to the revellers and, taking up his pipes, began to sing to them one of his sweetest songs. Snegourotchka followed and listened rapturously to his song—for it was the sweet singing of Lell the Shepherd which had first made her eager to leave the secret retreat of her childhood.

The Tsar had now wandered out with some of his Boyards, or nobles, to watch the revels in the forest; and when Lell's sweet tune came to an end, he was so delighted by his performance that he offered to him as a reward the hand of any fair maiden he might choose.

Snegourotchka eagerly hoped that she would be the chosen one; but though Lell hesitated for a moment beside her and gazed admiringly at her exquisite beauty, he passed her by. Then, taking the hand of Coupava, he led her as his chosen bride to the Tsar, who graciously bestowed his royal blessing upon the happy couple.

The Snow-Maiden, now full of woe because the sweet singer had not chosen her as his bride, ran away into the forest, seeking the help of her fairy mother. Here, to her alarm, she was followed by Miskar, whose passion for her was still alive and who was eager to awaken an answering love in her cold heart.

But Snegourotchka was afraid of his eager love-making, and called aloud for help. In answer to her cry, the Guardian Faun and Spirit of the Forest appeared and, seizing the would-be lover in his grasp, held him closely until the maiden had made her escape.

The mischievous Faun next played a fine trick upon Miskar,

leading him a dance through the forest—showing him tantalizing visions of the flying maiden, and then bending down trees to intercept him.

Meanwhile, Snegourotchka, alone once more, now called loudly and pitifully upon her mother for help; and when the Fairy Spring appeared in answer to her cries, she begged that her icy heart might be melted and that she might at last feel the joys of love.

Realizing the despair of her beloved daughter, the Fairy Spring now promised to grant her request. Then, warning the maiden to remain no longer in the forest, since dawn was at hand and it was necessary for her to keep away from the reach of the Sun-God's rays, the Fairy Spring departed to rest another year, since Summer was already at hand; and Snegourotchka now wandered happily through the forest, rejoicing in her newly-softened heart.

Presently she was met again by Miskar, whose teasing by the Faun had now ceased; and at his first renewed words of love, an answering flame sprang up in her own heart, already melted into warmth. At last she loved as other maidens loved; and Miskar felt well rewarded for his eager pursuit of her. Hand-in-hand, the now happy pair made their way to the Valley of Yarilo, where the Sun was beginning to rise in great glory above the heads of the vast company already gathered there to sing the praises of the mighty Sun-God.

The Tsar had enthroned himself on a raised bank near a silvery lake, with his Boyards around him forming his Court; and already the young betrothed couples were passing before him to receive his blessing.

Eager that Miskar should have his sentence of banishment remitted, since he had now won her heart, Snegourotchka joyfully stepped forward with him, ready also to receive the royal blessing.

But, in her eager joy, she had forgotten her fairy mother's warning; and as the first rays of the rising Sun shed a warm golden light upon her, the lovely Snow-Maiden began to wilt and fade away. In that magical moment of experiencing the warmth of the Sun's rays for the first time, she vanished for ever; and with a cry of anguished despair, Miskar, her lover, flung himself into the lake.

But the first horror of the people was quickly changed to joy, as they felt the warmth of the Sun's summer rays; and their songs of praise to Yarilo increased to rapture as they now realized that the curse of sunless days had at last been removed from the fair land of Berendey.

THE BARBER OF SEVILLE   *Rossini*
(*Il Barbiere di Siviglia*)

ONE early morning during the eighteenth century, just as the rosy dawn appeared, the sound of soft, sweet music arose from one of the streets of Seville. A group of picked musicians had been stationed in front of a private house to accompany a serenade to a certain fair lady who dwelt within.

A little apart from the musicians stood the singer, a tall, handsome cavalier, wrapped in a dark cloak. As his song proceeded, the serenader kept his gaze riveted upon a window that led out upon the balcony of the house, as though expecting the form of his adored one to appear in that spot.

This cavalier was the Count Almaviva, a rich nobleman, who, having beheld one day, on a visit to Seville, a lovely maiden upon the balcony of this house, had straightway fallen in love with her. In consequence of this he had left his country estate and taken up his abode in Seville, that he might be near the object of his affections and seek an opportunity to woo her.

He learnt that the young lady's name was Rosina and that she was the ward of a fussy old physician named Dr. Bartolo; and, by means of nightly serenades and frequent strolls past her dwelling-place, the young Count endeavoured to bring himself to the notice of the maiden. Nor was he unsuccessful; for the lovely Rosina, although kept almost a prisoner by her jealous guardian—who desired to wed her himself—managed to obtain sight of her serenader and quickly conceived a romantic passion for him.

In spite of the mutual understanding between them, the pair had never yet met, nor spoken with one another; and to-night the Count had hoped to attain this object. But Rosina was too closely watched by her guardian and her duenna; and when the dawn at length broke Almaviva sadly dismissed his musicians, sending them away with a handsome reward.

After the delighted musicians had departed, the Count remained dejectedly near the abode of his beloved one. Here he was presently accosted by the popular barber and general factotum of the town, a merry roguish fellow named Figaro, whose quick wit and lively mercurial temperament caused him to be in constant request by his many patrons for their practical jokes and intrigues.

Quickly noticing the dejected looks of the stranger cavalier, Figaro entered into conversation with him, offering his services, should he need them; and merrily he described his numerous valuable qualities to the Count. He declared that he was the best match-maker, plotter, and gossip in all Seville—to say nothing of being the most fashionable adept in his more legitimate occupation of chirurgeon-barber.

Almaviva quickly succumbed to the charm of the roguish barber; and seeing at once that Figaro might be of great use to him, he confided to him the secret of his love for Rosina and engaged him to assist in his suit, promising to reward him very handsomely for his services.

Figaro readily agreed to devote himself to the interest of this new patron; and very quickly his inventive wit suggested ways and means for bringing the lovers together. He informed the Count that old Dr. Bartolo desired to wed his charming ward himself, regardless of the disparity in their ages and the indifference of the lady; in which ridiculous project he was being aided and abetted by another equally fussy old fellow, one Don Basilio, a music-master. However, as the barber was constantly in and out of the house, he assured the Count that he would find means to communicate with Rosina and to hoodwink her guardian; and with this assurance the Count departed, greatly cheered.

Figaro's artful plans succeeded so well that Rosina soon learnt that her love was returned by the handsome cavalier who haunted the precincts of her home, whom the barber described as a young student named Lindoro; and she now managed to send him a note, in which she declared that his love was acceptable to her.

The Count was thus filled with joy; and, with the aid of the inventive barber, an interview between the enamoured pair was now devised. At the suggestion of Figaro, the Count disguised himself one evening as a common soldier; and pretending also to be intoxicated, he forced his way with a rowdy, roistering manner into the house of Dr. Bartolo, from whom he demanded a night's lodging as the rightful due of one who served his country. During the stormy altercation that ensued between the indignant Doctor and himself, Rosina, attracted by the noise, made her appearance.

Quickly lurching to her side, the pretended soldier managed to reveal his true identity to her; and though instantly separated by the angry and outraged Doctor, the lovers contrived dexterously to exchange letters. The interview was soon brought to an end by the arrival of the guard, drawn thither by the commotion, into whose charge the Doctor gladly handed over his unwelcome guest. As the officers hurried him away, however, the Count declared to them his real name, and showed them, in proof of his assertion, the high orders and decorations he wore beneath his disguise; upon which they set him free and respectfully departed, the richer by a substantial gift.

Shortly afterwards the indefatigable Figaro devised another scheme for the meeting of the lovers. This time, Almaviva, disguised as a poor musician, was unsuspectingly admitted into the house of Dr. Bartolo, to whom he explained that his name was Don Alonzo; and he added that he had been sent by Bartolo's friend Don Basilio, whom he declared to be ill.

Finding himself not very well received by the old guardian, he handed to him the note he had received from Rosina, pretending he had found it in the inn where Count Almaviva lodged; and he offered to show this to the young lady and declare to her that it had been sent by one of the Count's other numerous admirers, that she might thus become estranged from him.

Dr. Bartolo, quite unsuspicious of trickery, readily agreed to this ruse, being very anxious to put an end to his ward's infatuation for the Count who, as he of course knew by this time, was haunting the neighbourhood; and he thus consented to allow the music lesson to proceed, in order that this disturbing communication might be made to his ward.

He thereupon brought Rosina into the room and introduced her to the supposed Don Alonzo—in whom, however, she quickly recognized her lover. At that moment Figaro most opportunely arrived in his capacity as barber to Dr. Bartolo, in order to keep the old gentleman obligingly occupied with his toilet, while the lovers made arrangements for their elopement which the Count desired to carry out that night.

Very cleverly, also, the barber managed to secure the keys of certain doors usually kept locked at night, so that Rosina, at the appointed time, could reach the balcony, whence, by means of a ladder, she could escape to her lover.

In order to disarm the Doctor's still evident suspicion, the form of a singing lesson was gone through; but, thanks to Figaro's constant chatter and deft manipulation of his client's beard, the lovers managed to exchange confidences between the snatches of music and to make all the arrangements for their elopement and secret marriage that night.

All went well until, quite suddenly, the old music-master himself appeared on the scene, very much astonished on finding his place and occupation usurped by a strange young man. Figaro, however, with his usual versatility, saved the situation by pretending that Don Basilio really looked extremely ill and, feeling his pulse with mock anxiety, declared him to be in a high fever and entreated him to return home to bed. The Count also, by the judicious offer of a well-filled purse, succeeded in persuading the confused professor to depart for the time being.

Dr. Bartolo's suspicions, however, were now fully aroused, so that it became necessary for the Count to make a quick escape; and when he had gone the old guardian fussily produced the letter given him by the pretended musician and endeavoured on his own account to poison Rosina's mind against her lover in the manner agreed upon. Rosina's jealousy against some unknown rival was thus quickly kindled; and angry and distressed at having been deceived, as she supposed, by the Count, she revealed the secret arrangement for her elopement that night.

The wily old Doctor quickly followed up the advantage he had scored and now pressed his own suit; and Rosina, in a fit of pique, gave him her consent. He then hurried away, well pleased, to make arrangements with a notary to unite them that day. Meeting with Don Basilio and now learning from him that the strange musician and Count Almaviva were one and the same, he hurried on his plans with still greater eagerness, feeling that with such a daring rival he could not consider himself safe until his marriage contract with Rosina had been signed. Having arranged with the music-master to bring the notary along that same night, he went away to procure the officers of justice to be in readiness to arrest the Count and Figaro should they appear and endeavour to upset his plans.

But success was to be with love and youth; for the star of the Count was in the ascendant, and, with the aid of the irrepressible Figaro, he was able to accomplish his ends.

Fortunately, the elopement had been planned for the early part of the night; and as soon as darkness set in Almaviva and the barber made their appearance in front of the Doctor's house. By means of a ladder, they soon succeeded in reaching the balcony. Here they were presently joined by Rosina who, though already repenting of her jealous fit, at first repulsed her eager lover, charging him with unfaithfulness; but upon the cavalier explaining the whole matter of the letter, at the same time revealing his true identity as the Count Almaviva, she was quickly reconciled to him.

Whilst the now happy lovers were thus engaged in tender converse, the alert Figaro discovered that the ladder by which they were to reach the ground below had been taken away; and at the same moment Don Basilio appeared on the balcony with the notary, who had brought the contract for the marriage of Rosina with Dr. Bartolo.

Seeing that no time was to be lost, the three plotters hurried forward, the Count declaring to the notary that he and Rosina were the parties who were to sign the document. Then, drawing the amazed Don Basilio aside, he slipped a valuable ring on to his finger and advised him to be amenable to reason, at the same time judiciously showing him a loaded pistol as an even more persuasive argument.

The old music-master prudently accepted the forced situation with a good grace; and the Count and Rosina immediately signed the marriage contract in the presence of the notary, with Figaro and Don Basilio as their witnesses.

Just as the joyful lovers were thus lawfully united, Dr. Bartolo arrived with the officers of justice; and seeing that the Count and Figaro had indeed appeared, as he had suspected they would, he furiously denounced them as thieves and rogues, and commanded the officers to arrest them.

However, Almaviva advanced readily, and, with great dignity, announced himself as a Grandee of Spain and the newly-made husband of the fair Rosina. Eventually, after a somewhat stormy scene, enlivened by the witty raillery of the lively Figaro, the old Doctor acknowledged his defeat and reconciled himself to the inevitable with excellent good-humour—even magnanimously bestowing a fatherly blessing upon the triumphant pair.

Thus did these determined lovers gain their hearts' desire; and when Count Almaviva returned home with his charming bride, he took with him as his confidential body-servant the man whose fertile wit had helped him to win his happiness—Figaro, the merry Barber of Seville.

LA CENERENTOLA   *Rossini*
(*An Italian Cinderella Story*)

ONE summer day, sounds of pettish squabbling came from a room in Don Magnifico's somewhat shabby baronial mansion near Salerno. This fact was not strange, however. The Baron's two extremely plain daughters, Clorinda and Thisbe, seemed to spend most of their time bickering with one another. They only stopped every now and again to grumble and snap at their half-sister who, because she was poor and pretty, they had turned into a domestic drudge. They compelled the latter to wait on them, hand and foot; and they would not allow her to share in any of their own pleasures.

They did not even call this unfortunate girl by her own pretty name, Angelina. They preferred her to be known as " Cenerentola ", which they felt was a more suitable name for her. The kitchen and a stool among the cinders was her proper place, they declared. They were certainly very unpleasant young women—and not too young, either.

But Cenerentola was definitely both young and beautiful; not even rags could hide her many charms. She was also gentle and sweet-tempered, and ready to please everybody. She never grumbled at her hard lot.

To-day, she was bright and smiling as usual, as she made coffee for her step-sisters. It was good coffee, too; but they only scowled when she brought it to them. Nor did they offer any to her. Cenerentola did not mind, however. But when a beggar presently came to the door, she surreptitiously gave *him* a cup of the coffee, and some bread, too. The squabbling sisters saw what she had done, and scolded her snappily.

Little did they dream that this beggar was really Alidoro, the disguised tutor of the handsome young Prince of Salerno, Don Ramiro. Alidoro was doing a little Secret Service work on his own initiative, trying to find a really charming wife for his royal master. He soon decided that Clorinda and Thisbe were much too bad-tempered, but that Cenerentola really had a kind heart. Besides, she was extremely pretty. He decided to keep an eye upon her.

A few minutes later, a group of courtiers called at the mansion. They had brought an invitation for the Baron and his daughters to attend a grand ball which the young Prince was to give at the palace that night. They also announced that when the ball was over the Prince would choose the most charming young lady present to be his bride.

This was great news; and Clorinda and Thisbe were overjoyed to hear it. They danced and sang skittishly as they rushed off to choose their costumes for the ball. They felt sure that one of them would certainly be the chosen of the Prince. They were conceited as well as bad-tempered. Their father, a pompous and foolish old Baron, was delighted, too. He already saw himself established as an important official at the palace.

But Cenerentola felt rather sad. She knew that *she* would not be allowed to go to the ball. Soon, however, a wonderful thing happened to her. Another stranger now appeared unexpectedly in the domestic quarters of the mansion—a stranger with whom she instantly fell in love.

The stranger was dressed in the royal uniform, and announced himself as the Prince's valet-equerry. He was, however, actually the Prince himself. Having heard from his tutor, Alidoro, of the sweet and lovely Cenerentola, he had changed places with his confidential valet-equerry, Dandino, and had determined to win her in this lowly disguise. He liked the idea of such a romantic adventure.

When he beheld Cenerentola as she hurried into the kitchen with the empty coffee-cups, he fell in love with her at first sight. He helped her to pick up the broken cups, which she had dropped, one by one, as she gazed ecstatically at him; then they quickly made friends. He told her his name was "Dandino".

Cenerentola soon had to run away upstairs to help her exacting step-sisters to dress for the ball. But the Prince was determined to see her again—and at his ball, too. So he fixed up a plot with Alidoro, by means of which the latter should act as a sort of Fairy Godmother to her.

Cenerentola was now more eager than ever to go to the ball, hoping that she might there see again her delightful young admirer, "Dandino", the Prince's attendant. But her step-sisters again refused her request. Nor would the Baron listen to her plea. He had already played ducks and drakes with her small fortune—left to her by her mother, his second wife, long since deceased—and he preferred her to remain in the background, fearing lest his trickery should be discovered.

So poor Cenerentola, after helping to array Clorinda and Thisbe in all their finery, sadly saw them depart for the ball, seated stiffly with their fat and pompous father in the dilapidated family coach. Then she returned to the kitchen to weep because she had been left behind.

But she did not weep long. Soon, Alidoro, the old royal tutor, appeared and announced that *he* would take her to the ball! What was more, he had brought her a perfectly ravishing costume to wear, complete with silver slippers, jewels, and bouquet.

Joyfully Cenerentola arrayed herself in these gorgeous clothes, and twisted strings of pearls in her shining curls. When she was ready, she looked a "vision of loveliness", the delighted tutor declared. Then, in great excitement, she drove off to the ball in a splendid coach, with Alidoro sitting beside her. But the latter did not reveal his true identity.

.   .   .   .

At the royal palace the ball was at its height. Clorinda and Thisbe were enjoying themselves mightily, for the Prince, Don Ramiro, was making a great fuss of them both, and paying them much attention. Each felt almost sure of being the chosen bride when the ball came to an end.

Little did they dream, however, that the " Prince " who seemed to be admiring them so much, was really none other than Dandino, the royal valet-equerry, in disguise! Don Ramiro had determined to go forward with his little scheme. He was enjoying himself, too, in his own disguise as royal attendant. When he spoke to Clorinda and Thisbe, they scarcely listened to his words, but soon turned aside haughtily. They had no intention of wasting their time talking with a mere valet-equerry. Was not Don Ramiro, the handsome young Prince, paying them marked attention? They certainly had more important fish to fry!

Soon, however, their house of cards came fluttering to the ground. A lovely newcomer had arrived—Cenerentola in all her borrowed glory. The late arrival's dazzling beauty, glittering jewels, and magnificent robes instantly drew the eyes of all. Especially the eyes of that impertinently forward—but certainly handsome!—young equerry-valet person, " Dandino ", who eagerly approached and was as eagerly greeted by the lovely new guest. They must have met before, declared Clorinda! But, mercy on us, cried Thisbe! The Prince, Don Ramiro—their own devoted " Prince "—was now dancing with the newcomer. But *only* once, thank goodness!

The fact was that the real Dandino, in his disguise as " Prince ", had likewise been swept off his feet by the loveliness of the late-arriving guest and had rushed off at once to claim her for a dance. But the real Prince, in his valet-equerry uniform, scowled so blackly at him from his own less prominent position, that his under-study quickly relinquished her to his disguised royal master—who peremptorily ordered him to devote himself solely to the plain daughters of the Baron.

But the joy of the ball had already departed for Clorinda and Thisbe. They knew they had no chance against the gorgeously-garbed stranger. By the way, the latter reminded them, curiously enough, of that tiresome little slut at home—though, to be sure Cenerentola had not such amazing beauty! But there *was* just a look. . . .

Events now moved rapidly. In an ante-room of the palace, Dandino—still disguised as the Prince—had again surreptitiously secured the exquisitely-dressed Cenerentola as a partner, while his royal master's back was turned for a moment. He had become really infatuated with the lovely stranger; and now, forgetting his present disguise, he declared his infatuation. But Cenerentola—still under the impression that he was actually Don Ramiro, the Prince—told him simply that she loved his valet-equerry and had thoughts for no one else.

These words were overheard by the real Prince, who had soon followed the pair into the ante-room; and he was filled with joy. His little plan had worked well. As he now came forward, the seeming " Prince " departed hurriedly, fearing the royal anger later on.

Then the real Prince, as " Dandino ", declared his own love for Cenerentola, who, though revealing her own in return, suddenly remembered her borrowed plumage and present disguise. In great confusion she declared she could say nothing then, since she was there under false pretences, and that he, " Dandino ", must first discover her true identity. But, to help him, she gave him one of her bracelets, saying that she would be wearing a similar bracelet when next they met. Then, breaking away from his side, she disappeared from the palace as mysteriously as she had arrived.

The Prince, after consulting with his old tutor, Alidoro, now decided to doff his disguise and continue his wooing in his own person. Dandino was, therefore, informed that he must come down from his high perch and resume his true position once more as valet-equerry.

But Dandino enjoyed one more good joke before his play-acting came to an end. Still in his disguise as Prince, he lured the pompous old Baron—already elated and puffed with pride at the imaginary idea of a royal son-in-law—into the ante-room, which his royal master had just left. He then, in a casual tone, inquired what sort of state and privileges the Baron would expect to be provided should he, the " Prince ", choose either Clorinda or Thisbe as his bride.

Boastfully the foolish Baron, thinking only of outside show, replied that, at least, he would expect his daughter to be provided with thirty lackeys; no less than sixteen horses of her own; a magnificent State coach would, naturally, be hers; and she would always have hosts of Dukes and other noblemen swarming around her. And, of course, at all her banquets, plenty of " ices "—to which the Baron himself was particularly partial—would always be served. And the wines! How he smacked his lips at the prospect!

But now he was informed by the gorgeously-dressed young man that only a Prince could provide such luxuries for his bride. As for himself, he was only *playing* at being a Prince. He then revealed the horrid fact that he was merely Dandino, the valet-equerry. Then who was the "Dandino" his daughters had treated so scornfully, inquired the irate Baron? Oh, he, of course, was the real Prince, Don Ramiro, explained his companion, as he strolled away, laughing merrily.

The Baron nearly had an apoplectic fit!

.   .   .   .

Back in the Baron's mansion next morning, black looks were cast at Cenerentola, as, once more in poor attire, she went about her many tasks, still bright and cheerful as usual. How like she was to the lovely stranger at the ball, grudgingly admitted Clorinda and Thisbe. What a good thing they had left her behind!

The weather outside was black, too. A sudden thunderstorm had come up. It had been raised by the magic of old Alidoro, who, travelling with his royal master, had decided that the latter —now frantically searching for his lost lovely guest of the night before—must seek shelter at the Baron's mansion. It would have been quite easy, of course, to have told the Prince plainly that the girl he loved lived there and that all he had to do was to walk in and demand her hand in marriage.

But Alidoro had a reputation to keep up as a worker of magic; and he also wished to appear in a new *rôle* as the discoverer of the Prince's lost lady. Besides, he simply loved to do things in a complicated manner. Hence the sudden thunderstorm—also the overturning of the royal coach just at the door of the Baron's mansion. Strange to say, nobody was hurt. More magic on Alidoro's part, of course! Soon the royal party entered the house —the Prince, Alidoro, Dandino, and attendants, all complete.

The Baron and his two plain daughters were full of excitement —perhaps one of the latter was to be the chosen bride, after all. Then came the big surprise.

Cenerentola, on being sharply commanded by the Baron to place a chair for " His Royal Highness ", promptly set the chair beside Dandino—whom she still took to be the Prince. On being scolded and told to take the chair to the other visitor, she thus learned of the true identity of her own lover.

Full of shy confusion at this realization, she hid her face in her hands. This sudden action caused her sleeve to fall back, revealing a bracelet on her wrist—the fellow to the bracelet she had given her admirer of the night before. Instantly the Prince recognized it and her at the same moment; and taking her eagerly in his arms he kissed her with great joy and announced her as his chosen bride. The happy and smiling Cenerentola was then led away by her royal lover to the waiting coach—now miraculously right side up once more—and drove off with him to the palace.

The dumbfounded Baron and his two plain daughters were thus left, disconsolate. But not for long. Cenerentola's kind heart did not change with her good fortune. When she was married to the Prince, she sent for Clorinda and Thisbe and the Baron, and invited them to share in the luxury which she now enjoyed.

This was certainly more than they deserved. But then, Cenerentola was more than beautiful. She had a beautiful nature, too. So everybody was happy.

THE DEMON   *Rubinstein*

AMIDST the wild, lonely heights of the Caucasus Mountains, a terrific storm was raging. The four winds of Heaven seemed to have been let loose and to have joined their forces into one stupendous hurricane; and while the fierce tempest roared and raged, the ground was rent by a fearful earthquake. Out of the wide chasms that yawned in every direction evil spirits escaped for a brief spell from their abode of darkness, laughing in derision as they passed now and again groups of good spirits appearing through the lightning-rent skies.

Into the midst of this awe-inspiring scene, their master, half-mortal and half-demon, presently appeared upon the highest mountain peak of Kazbec, in answer to the call of the truant evil spirits over whom he ruled. He cursed the world and its Creator and railed at the Spirit of Light Who so often prevented his wicked plans from coming to pass. His curses, however, were futile and seemed to give him but little satisfaction; and presently, wearying of everything, even of his own terrible power, he drooped his head for a moment and appeared to be upon the verge of despair.

Just then, however, in a flash of dazzling radiance, the Spirit of Good appeared, crowned with Light; and instantly the Demon burst forth once again into a passion of vindictive rage, railing at the Light that would destroy his darkness, defying all the hosts of Heaven, and uttering violent curses against the dwellers upon earth.

In spite of the stern rebukes of the Angel of Light, Who warned him again that his evil hatred would never conquer the Goodness of Divine Love, the Demon continued to hurl defiance at the

Creator. His sole satisfaction since he had succumbed to the evil within him had been to offer opposition to everything good and pure and to engage in endless strife with the heavenly hosts. Even when the fury of the present storm abated somewhat and his attendant evil spirits had returned to their own abode, he lingered upon the mountain-tops, still cursing and planning further wickedness into which to plunge weak mortals.

As the hours rolled on, however, and the storm passed, a sudden change came over him, and his fury vanished as the sun rose in the clearing sky. He who had railed at the hosts of Heaven and cursed the dwellers upon earth throughout the tempestuous night now became strangely silent, his rage vanishing with the dawn of a glorious summer day as a new passion took possession of him.

The reason for this sudden change was a remarkable and almost unbelievable one. Down in the valley below, which lay in the district of Grusia, he beheld a mortal maiden of such exquisite beauty that he immediately conceived a wild and violent passion for her—remaining silent, heedless of all nature, as he gazed, fascinated, upon her.

This lovely maiden, who had come forth thus early to gather flowers and to wander upon the banks of a sparkling streamlet that flowed below, was Tamara, the daughter of Prince Gudal, the Ruler of Grusia. As she filled her arms with sweet-scented blossoms and rejoiced in the beauty of the peaceful morning that had succeeded the storm-racked night, her reflections were no less sweet and beautiful—for her thoughts were all of her betrothed lover, the Prince of Sinodal, who was even now travelling with all speed from his distant land to be united to her. He was expected to arrive for the marriage ceremony within the next few days.

So pleasantly were her thoughts engaged in anticipation of her gallant lover's arrival that Tamara wandered somewhat farther afield than was her usual custom, soon leaving her attendant maidens far behind. Presently, to her intense alarm, as she turned to retrace her steps, she was accosted by a stranger, whose unearthly fascination held her in instant thrall. The Demon, having conceived an overwhelming passion for the beautiful maiden on beholding her for the first time in the valley below, had ceased his railings against the Spirit of Good; and, determined to lose no time in securing this new prize, he now appeared before her in the guise of a handsome young man and clad in the rich garments of a great Prince. He addressed her eagerly, and plunged at once into a passionate declaration of his love.

Amazed and terrified at the hot flow of words uttered by the stranger, Tamara's first thought was to fly from his presence; but so fascinated was she by his sinister beauty and by his earnest pleading for her love, that she felt, for the moment, almost powerless to move. As she listened to this wild love-making, all remembrance of her betrothed faded from her mind and an answering passion began to kindle in her own heart for this brilliant new lover who had so suddenly appeared from she knew not whence and whose wooing, though she felt it to be unearthly and unholy, filled her with a strange joy.

When, however, the Demon would have folded her in a passionate embrace as he uttered these extravagant words : " Thou art the Queen of my Love, and I will make thee Queen of all the world! " she was terrified, as she thus realized that the stranger was certainly no ordinary mortal but a being possessed of supernatural powers. She made the sign of the cross, and, with a mighty effort, tore herself away from his inviting arms and fled from his presence—not slackening her steps until she had rejoined her companions and had returned with them to her father's castle.

The Demon, however, was full of triumph; and, satisfied that he had already ensnared the heart of Tamara, he felt that she could not now escape his toils. In order that he might satisfy his sudden desire, he now determined that her betrothed lover, the Prince of Sinodal, should never arrive in Grusia but should meet with an untimely end upon his present journey. By means of his supernatural powers, therefore, he caused terrible disaster to fall upon his rival.

Little dreaming that he had innocently earned the fatal hatred of a supernatural being, the young Prince of Sinodal proceeded eagerly and patiently upon the long and weary journey which he hoped and believed was to bring him to the crowning happiness of his life—his marriage with the beautiful Tamara, whose love he prized more than all the world. The journey had been a troubled one from the first, for the distance was great and the way had been exceedingly rough; and during the night that followed the meeting of his beloved one with her new sinister wooer, final disaster overtook him.

That night the young Prince and his suite encamped near a wayside chapel which, as it happened, had been built many years ago as a memorial to one of his own ancestors who had been treacherously murdered upon that spot by an enemy; and the old body-servant of the Prince, full of superstition and trembling lest the place should be haunted, entreated his royal master to pray for the soul of his murdered ancestors ere he lay down to rest.

The young Prince, however, was too footsore and weary to attempt special devotions at so late an hour. Despite the admonitions and warnings of his old servant—whose fears of approaching danger he endeavoured to allay by promising to pray for the soul of his murdered ancestor when daylight came— he fell asleep within his tent and was soon dreaming of Tamara, his beautiful bride-elect.

But the premonitions of the old servant were well-founded, and what he had feared came to pass. A few hours later, when the whole caravan was wrapped in unsuspecting slumber, a party of savage Tartars—ancient enemies of this particular royal family— brought up swiftly and silently by the mysterious powers of the Demon, made a sudden raid upon the sleeping camp; and the unfortunate young Prince, with his suite and followers, was taken unawares. All were massacred save a few swift runners who managed to escape and to bring the terrible news to Grusia. Thus did the Demon dispose of the rival in his path; and he now hoped that his pursuit of the fair Tamara would end in conquest and joy for himself. Strange to say, the passionate love he had conceived for this beautiful maiden was a real and sincere one; and he even ventured to hope that if he could win her love in return, he might redeem himself from his fallen estate and thus resist the evil influences with which he had encompassed himself.

Meanwhile, the Court of Prince Gudal made all the necessary preparations for the approaching nuptials of the royal maiden; and on the day of the marriage, Tamara stood in the reception-hall of her father's palace, clothed in her bridal robes, awaiting the arrival of her bridegroom—of whose approach news had been received the day before.

While her attendants were full of animation and gaiety, Tamara herself was strangely preoccupied. Though she anticipated with pleasure the meeting with her bridegroom, for whom she had a sincere love, her thoughts were wandering. Ever since her meeting in the valley with the mysterious stranger who had lain such sudden and overwhelming siege to her heart, she had been unable to keep him out of her mind. The beauty of his person, the softly tender tones of his musical voice, his deep admiration and passionate wooing, haunted her constantly, so that his magnetic personality seemed ever present with her though she saw him not; and she could not forget his tempting, pleading words. Consequently, the present sounds of revelry seemed to her far away and to be unconnected with herself. When the lively guests from the banqueting-tables beyond drained goblets of wine in her honour, it was with a great effort that she roused herself sufficiently to acknowledge their greetings and good wishes with a smile. Even when a number of her own girl friends took part in a wild fantastic dance specially arranged and devised for the bridal festivities, she scarcely noticed the mazy rhythm of it. Leaving the applauding guests to enjoy the spectacle, she moved aside to a quieter part of the chamber, allowing her disturbing thoughts free play once more.

It was at this moment that there came a sudden and tragic interruption to the revels. Just as the merry dance came to an end and the guests were about to drain their goblets once more in honour of the nuptials of their host's fair daughter, the news was brought that the gallant young Prince of Sinodal had been surprised and slain by marauding Tartars the night before and that his corpse was even now being brought to the castle.

Immediately the gay music ceased, giving place to wailings and cries of woe; and presently the chanting of a funeral dirge was heard as the body of the dead bridegroom was brought into the chamber.

With despairing cries, the grief-stricken Tamara flung herself upon the body of her beloved one and burst into passionate weeping. Despite the pitying commiserations of her royal father and her many girl friends, she refused to be comforted, begging only to be left alone with her dead lover.

When the guests had all retired, however, Tamara was instantly confronted with a fresh trial. No sooner had she been left alone than she heard tender words of comfort whispered in her ear by the same soft, seductive voice that had haunted her continually since her meeting with the stranger in the valley; and, looking up in alarm, she once more beheld that mysterious being standing beside her with outstretched arms.

Enthralled against her will, Tamara listened with a beating heart as the Demon sought to console her for the loss of her betrothed. When, however, emboldened by her downcast eyes and seeing that she was not indifferent to the lure of his irresistible fascination, the stranger once more hotly pressed his own suit and endeavoured to fold her in a passionate embrace, she was again terrified and fled wildly from his presence.

But, wherever she went, whether alone or in company, the words of the Demon still rang in her ears and his sinister yet alluring presence seemed ever with her, pervading her every thought. At length, feeling that her power of resistance was weakening and that she would not have strength to refuse his evil desires should she meet him in person again—for she realized that he possessed supernatural powers—Tamara sought her father and tearfully entreated him to allow her to enter a convent. She declared that now her betrothed had been taken from her she only sought oblivion, the world and its pleasures no longer having any attraction for her.

At first, Prince Gudal endeavoured to dissuade his daughter from taking the veil, offering first one objection and then another, as he desired to seek for her another bridegroom. Then seeing that she was almost distracted with grief and that the seclusion of a nunnery alone could bring her peace of mind, he finally gave his consent, and the unhappy Tamara was received into the nearest convent.

Even here, however, she had to face another and final terrible conflict ere peace was vouchsafed to her; for the Demon, whose passion for this beautiful maiden was intense and overwhelming, sought her yet once again even in the sanctuary in which she had sought refuge. At the entrance to the nunnery, he found his way barred; but, by means of his supernatural powers, he quickly forced an entrance and made his way to the apartment of the victim he sought.

Once more he made violent protestations of love to Tamara; and, now revealing to her his true identity as a demoniacally possessed mortal, he begged her to have compassion upon him. He declared that if she would return his love he would forsake the ways of evil and would, for her sake, even humble himself and bow down once more to the Will of God Whom, in his pride and disobedience, he had offended. The unhappy girl was now torn by conflicting feelings—believing that this strange being's seeming penitence could not be sincere, yet feeling the warmth of an answering passion, which she seemed powerless to resist, enveloping her on every side.

She was about to succumb to the intoxicating joy of the stranger's unholy love when, as the Demon folded her in a close embrace, she saw the evil light of triumph in his burning eyes and made a last frantic effort to resist his influence and to escape from his toils. At this terrible moment, the Angel of Light appeared at the entrance to the cell; and Tamara, with a cry of relief and joy, was about to fly to Him for protection when, overcome by the fearful ordeal through which she had just passed, her overwrought strength gave way and she fell lifeless to the ground.

The Demon, seeing that his hope of an earthly joy had been thus snatched from his evil grasp, and that, in addition, he had lost the redemption he had sought, was filled with rage and despair; and renewing his curses against mankind and all the heavenly hosts, he vanished from the spot amidst the lightnings and tumults of a terrible storm. At the same moment the Angel of Light departed, bearing aloft with him the purified spirit of the love-rent Tamara to rest in peace at last.

SAMSON AND DELILAH   *Saint-Saëns*
(*Samson et Dalila*)

IN a wide open square of the splendid Philistine city of Gaza in Palestine, the defeated Israelites were bemoaning their sad fate, groaning under the yoke of the invaders. They feared that the God of Israel had deserted them for ever; that never again would they be able to drive forth the powerful enemies who now beset their fair and once-peaceful land.

The all-powerful Jehovah, Who had brought them from bondage out of the land of Egypt, Who had led them miraculously through the Red Sea, had now suffered them once more to become subject to a heathen race; and they could not cast off the hateful yoke.

The wretched captives almost began to believe that their God no longer cared for His Chosen People; and though they still called upon His Name as they huddled together this day in the streets of Gaza, their prayers seemed to be hopeless.

How could they pray with hope in their hearts when they were defeated and were even now herded together, against their will, opposite the magnificent Temple of the false god, Dagon, whom their heathen enemies so foolishly worshipped. Were they not being derided at every turn?

But just as their despair was at its height, they were roused from apathy by their splendid young leader, Samson, a mighty man of valour, who had himself fought like a lion against the Philistines and who, though temporarily defeated, still believed that victory would yet be his. Had not the God of Israel been with him from the day of his birth, and was he not dedicated to His Service? Had not an almost superhuman strength been his since his early youth; and was not his long, uncut hair the sign and symbol of his dedicated service to Jehovah, and thus, the source of his mighty strength? Had he not performed miraculous deeds of strength that had become legends in the land? Why, then, despair because of temporary misfortunes and defeat? The God of Israel would once again come to their aid, never fear.

Thus spoke Samson to the hopeless Hebrew crowds, bidding them not to give way to despair but to continue their prayers; not to doubt, but to gird up their loins and be ready for the renewed struggle which would yet surely come. He, Samson, had seen in a vision that he would certainly lead them to victory.

Now ashamed of their doubts and encouraged by their splendid leader's inspired words, the downcast Hebrews once more prayed and called upon their God for help with renewed hope in their hearts.

It was at this moment of their revived faith that there entered into the square the hated Satrap of Gaza, Abimelech, splendidly attired and accompanied by a group of Philistine soldiers.

Seeing the defeated Hebrews now praying humbly upon their knees, Abimelech began to deride them and to pour scorn and contempt upon them for seeking the aid of an unseen God, Who was powerless to help them. He added that Dagon was the god they should appeal to—Dagon, who had given victory to the Philistines and brought defeat to their enemies.

Instantly filled with righteous anger at such blasphemy, Samson broke forth into indignant reproaches against his heathen enemy's words; and he again called passionately upon the God of Israel to come to the aid of His people.

Furious at this outburst from the defeated leader, Abimelech rushed upon him with his drawn sword. But Samson, with a sudden twist of his mighty arm, wrenched the sword from the Satrap and slew him before the terrified attendants could intervene. Then, calling upon the now ready and eager Hebrews to follow him, Samson dashed out of the square after the quickly retreating Philistine soldiers, slaying each one that stood up against him.

A pitched battle soon ensued; and Samson, joyful in his mighty strength, and now boldly joined by his revived followers, carried all before him as he fought his way through the city and out into the country beyond.

Meanwhile, the High Priest of Dagon, having come forth from the Temple on hearing the commotion, beheld the dead form of the Satrap, Abimelech, lying before the steps; and he called angrily upon the straggling Philistine soldiers now left in the square to follow and bring back the captives. The Philistine soldiers, however, had been terrified by the righteous wrath and mighty strength displayed by the splendid Hebrew leader, believing now that this was supernatural; and they were still too much afraid to follow, despite the furious words of the High Priest.

Then, as the body of Abimelech was being carried into the

Temple messengers came hurrying up to the High Priest, with the alarming news that Samson had so effectively rallied his people that they were now gaining victories on every side; and they were still driving the flying Philistines before them.

The success thus begun with the death of Abimelech continued for the Israelites, with mighty Samson at their head; and after many further successes, they returned once more to Gaza. But this time they returned as victors; and as they stood once more outside the Temple of Dagon, they rejoiced and sang songs of praise and thanksgiving to the God of Israel, Who had delivered them from their enemies by the hand of His chosen servant, Samson.

And Samson himself was greeted with joyful songs of triumph, and was met by all his people with shouts of welcome and by processions of fair maidens carrying garlands of flowers.

Among the latter, there even came forth from the Temple of Dagon a procession of Philistine maidens, to sing the praises of the brave and splendid Samson, even though he was their enemy. At the head of this procession was a beautiful Philistine woman named Delilah, who had come thither for a secret purpose.

Delilah had already enthralled the mighty Samson once before when, in a weak moment, he had been enticed to visit her in her abode; and she now hoped to enchant him further, planning thus to betray him later on when the opportunity should arise. Mighty men had fallen before now by means of the artful guiles of siren women—none more beautiful and glamorous than she!

Delilah, therefore, now approached her victorious enemy-admirer with honeyed words, crowning him with flowers and using every feminine art and blandishment in order to fan into renewed life the flames of passion she had aroused in him at their last meeting.

It was in vain that Samson tried to feign indifference to the sweet smiles of Delilah and to the seductive motions of her lovely form in the undulating dances she and her maidens presently performed before him in celebration of his victory. The mighty man of valour, though he had the strength of a lion on the battlefield, was powerless against the enticements of beautiful Delilah, whose charms he had previously weakly succumbed to against his will and whose present determined assault upon his more developed passions he was now equally unable to resist. During the voluptuous movements of her seductive dance, he tried not to look upon her, but constantly found his burning gaze returning to gloat upon her loveliness; and though the Hebrew elders around him anxiously entreated him to turn aside from the wiles of the heathen woman, lest she should lure him to destruction, his resistance was not long-lived.

When Delilah, in dulcet tones, next invited him to visit her again at her secret abode in the Valley of Soreck he was already caught in her toils once more; and though at first he turned aside involuntarily, the siren had seen the eager look in his longing eyes and knew that her cause was won.

In her richly luxurious abode in the Vale of Soreck, Delilah awaited the coming of her lover, the mighty Samson; this time, with some anxiety. Some weeks had elapsed since she had lured back his passion for her in the square at Gaza; and though he had visited her many times in that interval, she had not yet achieved her purpose—to learn the secret of his strength, that she might destroy it.

Though her dazzling beauty and her sensuous charms had made Samson her lover—sometimes a reluctant one, though always fiercely passionate—he did not always hold himself at her beck and call. He did not need the Hebrew elders to remind him of the dangerous path he trod in visiting this heathen siren. He knew only too well that she could lure him from the path of duty and that it was a sin for one dedicated to the service of the God of Israel to have dealings with an idolatress. Every now and again, therefore, he refrained from visiting Delilah and threw himself all the more eagerly into the constant warfare he waged against the Philistines; and at such times a renewed strength seemed to be given him, so that he then went on from victory to victory.

Meanwhile, the High Priest of Dagon, angry at the turn of events against the Philistines, but chiefly desirous of avenging the death of the Satrap, Abimelech, knew well enough that no further victories for his people were possible while their much-hated enemy, the mighty Samson, continued to lead the Israelite hosts. The terror of this splendid hero's abnormal personal strength seemed to paralyse all who fought against him; and the superstitious awe in which his almost supernatural power was held by the Hebrews and their strange dependence upon it, made the High Priest plot to learn the secret. If only the hidden source of his mighty strength could be discovered, then it might become possible to undermine it and thus bring about the downfall of the hero he hated. The secret of Samson's strength! Delilah must discover this for her people!

On the same night, therefore, that the beautiful Philistine siren was awaiting her enemy lover, the High Priest presented himself first before her. He found Delilah robed in gorgeous garments, a dream of loveliness, as she stood at the open doorway on the terrace of her luxurious abode in the Vale of Soreck, with tall trees and tropical plants making a wonderful background to set off her voluptuous beauty; and she received him graciously.

When, however, the High Priest, after again repeating the hopes of the Philistines that she might lure Samson to his doom, began to suggest that her power over the great hero might possibly be dwindling, since nothing seemed to stop his present victorious progress, she angrily denied such an accusation. She fiercely declared that her power over Samson's passion-torn soul was as great as ever; and though it had seemed lately that he was neglecting to visit her, yet he was still her slave, always bound to return to her even against his will.

All that now mattered was to learn the secret wherein lay his mighty strength; and this she hoped to discover that same night, since she was even now expecting him to visit her.

The High Priest, glad to hear this good news, offered to give her a handsome reward of gold and jewels if she would perform this great service for him; but this suggestion merely angered Delilah, who proudly announced that she wanted no reward for bringing woe upon the enemy of her country. Not only, too, did she desire vengeance upon Samson because of his victories against her people, but because, having loved her, he had forsaken her more than once—a slight to her power as a beautiful woman which she could never forgive.

Nevertheless, he was still her lover and in her toils, and she could draw him back as though by a magic spell—the enchantment of her beauty and alluring glamour. That same night, though he had absented himself for some little time, she knew that he was about to return to her arms; and she would then wrest his secret from him without fail. Though he had resisted her caresses, yet he trembled more and more at her touch; and she had saved her most powerful weapon till the last—her tears! His firm resolve to keep his precious secret would certainly melt before her pearly tears!

Now filled with hope that his enemy would shortly be delivered into his hands, the High Priest hurried away, planning to return later by secret paths and with a number of Philistine guards in readiness to capture the mighty man of valour, when subdued by the entrancements of Delilah.

Scarcely had the High Priest departed than Samson appeared. Again he had come against his better judgment, as though drawn thither by a power stronger than his own will—the power of passion. He loved Delilah and, though he had denied himself the joy of her caresses for what seemed to him an eternity, he could no longer keep away from her beloved presence, which drew him as a magnet.

He had come by secret ways, carefully avoiding the paths where his Philistine enemies might be lurking; for he knew that his movements were watched. As he now drew near the abode of his enchantress, distant lightning began to flicker—an approaching storm, in harmony with the storm of passion now raging in his own breast.

On beholding Delilah standing at her portico with outstretched, eager arms, he was once more overwhelmed by the sight of her exquisite siren-like beauty; but though, at first, he tried to wrench himself away from the sweet encirclement of her arms, he once more found himself powerless to resist such joy.

Using her utmost wiles and allurements, Delilah first of all soothed her lover with great tenderness into a state of ecstatic joy, so that he declared again and again that he loved her with all his being—though he still sorrowfully mourned the fact that, because of his love for her, he was forgetting his people and his God. Then, with subtle guile, the temptress bade him give her a proof of the love he said he bore her—to reveal to her the secret of his strength, which filled her with amazement.

Still unaware of any ulterior motive behind her request, but knowing that he must not divulge this hidden secret even to one so well-beloved as his beautiful mistress, Samson begged her to demand of him anything rather than this.

As he spoke the gathering storm drew nearer and nearer, the flickering lightning became more vivid, and thunder began to rumble; but Samson did not see any warning to him in the rising anger of the elements, though he refused again and again to grant the request of his beloved one.

Then Delilah made use of her last weapon. With tears pouring from her beautiful eyes, she now implored her lover to let her share in his wonderful secret; if he would not do so, then let him begone and see her no more—leave her to languish without his love, since she would never receive him again.

Now torn with anguish at the sight of Delilah's tears and fearful lest, indeed, she should refuse ever to see him again, Samson, forgetful of everything but his passionate love for her, at last allowed himself to be led into the house, promising to grant her request. Here, within her inner chamber, he revealed to the siren that the precious secret of his mighty strength lay in his long, uncut hair—the sign and symbol of his own lifelong vow as a Nazarite to the service of his God.

Full of unholy joy at the priceless knowledge she had thus gained by her alluring arts, Delilah continued to soothe and caress her lover until at last he fell asleep on her couch. Then, stealthily, she cut off the thick, long locks that were the symbol and source of his once mighty strength; and when, presently, she heard the Philistine soldiers approaching, brought thither by the High Priest, she rushed to the open doorway and exultingly bade them enter and secure their now powerless enemy.

Thus was Samson, the mighty man of valour, lured to his doom by the false siren, Delilah, and, shorn of his strength, delivered by her into the hands of his enemies.

. . . .

In the prison at Gaza, Samson, shorn of his locks and blinded by his enemies, was given the labour of a slave—that of turning the heavy grinding-mill. While he thus toiled unceasingly, now enfeebled by the loss of his hair, his Philistine guards mocked and derided him. Worse than this, there came to him from outside the wailing cries of the Hebrews, now captives once more, since he, their mighty leader, had been lured from their midst, so that victory had once more come to their enemies.

Repentant now, and heartbroken because of the woe he had brought upon his people, Samson called constantly upon the God of Israel for forgiveness and for help in his hour of need.

But an even greater humiliation was in store for him. At the great Festival of Triumph held in the Temple of Dagon in honour of their victory, the Philistine chiefs determined that Samson should make sport for them.

The unhappy fallen leader, therefore, was brought into the Temple—led by the hand of a small child, because of his blindness and to prove to the exulting company to what low depths of helplessness he had descended.

Here he was greeted with further jeering cries of derision from his triumphant enemies; and even his false love, Delilah, gloated over him as she presented him with a golden cup of wine and bade him drink to their former joys. Then she poured insults upon him and taunted him scornfully for his foolishness in believing that she could ever have loved him, an enemy, and for permitting himself to be so easily beguiled by one who had only hate in her heart for him.

Next, the High Priest, likewise gloating and triumphant, commanded the wretched captive to offer a libation to the great god, Dagon, who had gained the victory over the helpless, unseen God of the Israelites.

All this time Samson had endured the taunts and insults poured upon him in silence and apparent humility; but, inwardly, he had been praying earnestly for help and renewed strength—and, suddenly, as though by an inward vision, he knew that his repentance had been accepted and that his prayers were about to be answered.

When, therefore, he was commanded by the High Priest to offer a libation to the idol, Dagon, he made as though to approach in humble obedience; but, in a whisper, he bade the child who led him to guide his steps towards the two huge central marble pillars which supported the roof of the Temple. This new position pleased the High Priest and Delilah, since their tormented captive would thus be more plainly seen by all the company; but their satisfaction was short-lived.

When the blinded hero found himself standing between the two great marble pillars, a look of radiant joy suddenly transformed his pain-furrowed countenance. Then, with a little cry of thanks and praise to the God of Israel Who, in answer to his prayers, had miraculously restored his strength for one last mighty deed, he seized the huge columns in his arms and lifted them up bodily. Next moment the splendid Temple of Dagon collapsed and fell in ruins.

Thus perished Samson, the hero of Israel, that Mighty Man of Valour; and with him perished the false woman who had betrayed him, together with the enemies of his people.

THE BARTERED BRIDE *Smetana*

A MERRY scene was taking place in a pleasant country village in happy Old Bohemia. It was the Spring Carnival season; and all the villagers had turned out in festive attire to join in the jollity of a grand fair which was being held on the village green. Later on in the day, there was to be a show of tumblers, acrobats, tight-rope-walkers, and dancing bears; but now, in the early afternoon, the villagers had another matter to occupy their interest.

Kruscina, a rich peasant, and his wife, Ludmilla, had chosen a bridegroom for their pretty daughter, Marenka; and, in accordance with Bohemian custom, they had placed this important matter in the hands of a marriage-broker, who had arranged for the young couple to meet and plight their troth that afternoon.

Kecal, the village marriage-broker, was expected to appear at any moment now with the chosen bridegroom and the latter's parents, together with the marriage contract.

All the villagers, therefore, were looking forward to cheering the newly-betrothed pair and to singing and dancing around them in honour of the event. Already they were gathering in merry groups, chattering together and singing their peasant songs.

But pretty Marenka herself was feeling far from gay; for she had no desire to wed with the bridegroom chosen for her. She had, instead, fallen in love with Jenik, a stranger in the village who, though young and handsome, was very poor, being merely a farm-worker; and she knew that he would never be accepted as a suitor for her.

She had now stepped aside from the merry crowd with Jenik for a few moments before her parents appeared, to tell him of the blow to their happiness now about to fall with the coming of rich old farmer Mischa and his son, Vasek; and she was somewhat surprised when her lover did not seem so greatly concerned as she had expected. Jenik, indeed, appeared to be quite cheerful about this sad business; and he did his best to comfort Marenka, telling her that if only she kept faithful to him all would yet be well.

He then told her that though he was so poor, his home people were quite wealthy. His mother having died young, his father had married again; and this second wife had caused Jenik, the orphan lad, to be sent away to another part of the country to earn his living among strangers. Consequently he had not been home for several years, and so was a stranger there.

Marenka sympathized sweetly with her lover for his homeless and penniless state, though his story made her feel more hopeless still. But Jenik again begged her to believe that all would yet be well.

Then, seeing a merry, cheering crowd drawing near, he slipped away in haste—for Jenik had a secret plan in his mind, which he could not divulge to his sweetheart just then.

Marenka, puzzled and rather hurt by her lover's present curious optimism, soon found herself engaged in a tussle against her parents' will.

The fussy old marriage-broker, Kecal, came bustling up to say he had successfully arranged the match between rich old farmer Mischa's son, Vasek, and Marenka; and Kruscina, the latter's father, declared this was exactly what he wished, since old Mischa was the friend of his youth and could also provide well for his son. Ludmilla, his wife, however, reminded him that they had never yet set eyes on young Vasek; but Kecal now poured forth, with professional fervour and eloquence, a long catalogue of the latter's virtues—though adding that he was extremely bashful.

He then called on Marenka to give her consent and to accept this young paragon as her betrothed husband; and he was astonished when the young girl flatly refused to wed with any other man than her beloved Jenik.

It was in vain that the indignant Kecal and the still more indignant Kruscina stormed and scolded; she still remained obdurate. At last the more considerate Ludmilla suggested that at least her daughter might be permitted to see her future husband before consenting to marry him; and this reasonable suggestion was grumblingly agreed to.

Then Kecal hurried away to produce the bashful bridegroom, and also—unknown to the others—to seek out Jenik and offer him another and less important bride; and the young friends of Marenka, determined not to delay their expected betrothal fun any longer, began to sing once more and to dance a lively polka to show their joy.

While the young people were thus merrily dancing, Kecal, the marriage-broker, presently finding Jenik sitting with some friends in the village inn, anxiously tried to induce him to give up Marenka to the suitor chosen for her by her father. Jenik, though still declaring that love was the only thing that really mattered in life, soon decided that the marriage-broker's suggestion might fall in quite satisfactorily with the secret plot he himself had in mind. He thus pretended to be willing to give up Marenka and to consider the offer of Lily, another girl with a good dowry. Finally, after haggling a while, he agreed to sign a document to this effect: that he was willing for Marenka to marry no one else than Mischa's son—for which he was to be paid three hundred crowns as compensation.

Meanwhile, Mischa, the rich peasant, and his wife, Hata, had arrived on the village green, where they were renewing acquaintance with their old friends, Kruscina and Ludmilla; but their bashful son, Vasek, the prospective bridegroom, had managed, during these greetings, to sidle away to a quieter spot to hide his shyness a little longer.

Here, however, he was presently noticed by Marenka who, seeing a chance to set him against herself, approached and began to talk to him—without, however, revealing her identity.

Vasek was a silly, loutish, half-witted youth, who spoke in such a lisping, halting manner that Marenka soon found her patience sorely tried. She succeeded, nevertheless, in making him believe that the girl he was about to betroth himself to was ill-tempered and would treat him badly and might even murder him; in any case, too, she would certainly soon desert him for her former sweetheart. She then flattered him by declaring him to be a charming youth whom another girl in the village—a sweet and gentle maiden—greatly longed to wed.

The foolish Vasek was so alarmed by her black picture of the bride chosen for him that he vowed, at the dictation of his new friend, to have nothing to do with Kruscina's daughter. Then, scared at the immediate prospect of having to defy the marriage-makers, he rushed off towards the fair-ground, where the acrobatic entertainment was just beginning; and here he was soon enjoying himself.

Marenka, hoping that her ruse would have the desired effect, now returned to the betrothal group. Here she was grieved to the heart on learning of the document, hastily drawn up by the triumphant marriage-broker, in which her lover, Jenik, stated his willingness to give up his promised bride to Mischa's son—though, the contract added, to no one else. Also, the contract contained the proviso that Vasek must take Marenka willingly and not against his own desire; and it added that Jenik was thus willing to barter his promised bride for the sum of three hundred crowns.

Old Mischa and his friend, Kruscina, were delighted by the withdrawal of Jenik in favour of Vasek; but on hearing the final clause in the contract, that he was to receive three hundred crowns in exchange, they and all the company gathered around were amazed at his seeming mercenary callousness and turned from him in disgust. Jenik, however, boldly signed the document in their presence; and then he hastened away, unable to endure the reproachful looks of the now unhappy Marenka.

The marriage-broker was eager to go forward with the signing of the real marriage contract as originally drawn up by him between Marenka and Vasek; but now, to his further annoyance, trouble arose from the latter.

On hurrying away in dismay, after absorbing the alarming description of his bride-elect given him by Marenka, Vasek had been drawn towards the opening performance of the strolling players, whose acrobats, tightrope-walkers, and dancers quickly caused him to stop and gaze upon them with the open-mouthed wonder of a half-witted rustic. He was particularly enthralled by the fairy-like appearance of a Spanish gipsy-girl, Esmeralda, who was a tight-rope dancer and whose abbreviated skirts and small dainty feet filled him with delighted admiration.

Esmeralda soon noticed the gaping youth; and while tripping

around the gathering circle of spectators to entice them to take seats for the show, she came up to Vasek and flattered him by engaging him in conversation, pretending to admire his smart clothes, and, indeed, flirting openly with him.

The foolish Vasek was extremely pleased with her attentions and eagerly offered himself as her sweetheart, completely forgetting his usual bashfulness—also his forthcoming betrothal!—in the unexpected excitement of her charm and pretty looks. This was just the kind of girl he could be happy with, he decided. When, therefore, Esmeralda next begged him, if he really wished to please her, to help her out of a difficulty by temporarily playing the part of one of their actors who had failed to turn up, he was persuaded to oblige her and her distracted manager.

True, he was rather alarmed when he discovered that the part they wished him to play was that of a dancing bear; but when Esmeralda declared that he was exactly suited to such a " clever part ", and that she would love him for ever if he would do it, his inordinate vanity won the day. He consented, therefore, to allow himself to be wrapped up in a bear's skin when it was time for this special show to begin, and to have a long chain put around his neck; after which Esmeralda was to lead him around the fairground, enticing him by her laughing caresses to dance in a comical fashion.

Vasek promised to return in time for this performance; and then he tore himself away from his new charmer for a short time, in order to see what was happening about his bride-elect. The betrothal party was just getting desperate about his absence; and as soon as he appeared upon the scene, he was eagerly seized by Kecal, the marriage-broker, and impatiently bidden to sign the marriage contract already drawn up.

On beholding Marenka in the group, however, Vasek suddenly remembered her warning; and he now quite boldly announced that he would not dream of marrying one so bad-tempered as Kruscina's daughter—one who might even murder him, according to the charming stranger who had so kindly warned him. He pointed to Marenka, as he spoke, as the charming stranger in question; but on being informed by the now irate Kecal that she was the same Marenka chosen as his bride, he quickly changed his tone and said he would sign the contract, after all.

But Marenka still declared firmly that if she could not have the now faithless Jenik, nevertheless she would wed with no one else; but when, with distracted mien, she begged to be left alone for a few minutes to reconsider the matter, her request was granted, since it was felt she was about to change her mind.

As the unhappy girl wandered aside, alone, she was suddenly joined by Jenik, who, again showing himself in a cheerful mood, begged her to smile upon him once more and to trust in his skill to circumvent those who would part them.

But Marenka, now roused to righteous wrath by her lover's apparent callousness, denounced him in no measured terms; and she added, in desperation, that, since he no longer cared for her, she would agree to marry Vasek in accordance with her parents' desire.

Jenik laughed aloud at such a foolish idea, still declaring that she should put her trust in him; but when he was at last about to explain his fine plan to her, she struggled free from his tenderly encircling grasp and rushed away back to the waiting betrothal group. Tearfully she announced that her mind was now made up and that she was ready to marry Mischa's son.

To her amazement and renewed indignant grief, Jenik, who had closely followed her, again expressed his own willingness for her to obey her parents; and he added that he abided by the contract he had signed—that he would give her up to none other than Mischa's son.

And now, at last, Marenka, noting Jenik's still tender glances upon her, understood the secret plan and hidden joke devised by her lover; and she realized that he was not faithless after all.

For when Jenik now joined the betrothal group, he walked boldly up to the rich peasant, Mischa, and hailed him as his own father; and Mischa, astonished into immediate recognition, was bound to admit that this handsome young man was, indeed, his eldest son—the offspring of his deceased first wife, whom his second wife had persuaded him to send away from home.

When, therefore, Jenik had signed the document stating that he was willing for Marenka to marry no one else but the son of Mischa, he had not played her false; and he now asked her to declare before all the company which of Mischa's sons she preferred.

Overjoyed by this happy turn of events and now able to laugh at the merry joke played on the betrothal party by her beloved Jenik, Marenka no longer avoided the latter's eager embrace, but gladly declared that he was her only choice.

Hata, the mother of Vasek, was furious that her husband's elder son—so jealously hated by her—had thus turned up again at such an inopportune moment; and she was now called upon to endure another disappointment. Just as Jenik had exploded his most surprising bombshell, there came a cry from the fair-ground: "The Bear has escaped! The Bear has escaped!"

Next moment, who should appear but Vasek, dressed up in a bear-skin and dancing about foolishly, half in and half out of the thick, heavy skin, and followed merrily by pretty Esmeralda, the acrobatic dancer, from whose restraining chain, in a playful moment, he had escaped.

So ludicrous a sight did the silly, half-witted Vasek now present, that all the betrothal party, including his own extremely annoyed mother, laughed aloud and made fun of him.

Even Kruscina himself admitted that such a foolish fellow was no fit mate for his fair daughter; and he now declared himself in favour of the handsome Jenik, who had been clever enough to play such a fine trick upon them all.

And Mischa, too, rejoiced at this reunion with his elder and best-loved son, whom he had only driven forth at the importunate request of his jealous second wife, Hata. So he likewise gave his consent to the marriage contract being carried out, with Jenik as the bridegroom—the "Mischa's son" acceptable to Marenka, for whom he would also provide a similar marriage portion.

So, the "bartered bride" secured the man of her choice after all; and the merry villagers were now able at last to sing, dance, and rejoice over a pair of really happy lovers.

THE BOATSWAIN'S MATE *Smyth*

HARRY BENN, a conceited and cocksure ex-boatswain, was seated beneath a shady tree outside the "Beehive" Inn one summer evening. Although a mug of the most excellent beer to be got in the whole country-side for many miles around was set before him on one of the scrupulously clean rustic tables, he was feeling anything but contented.

Here was a first-rate little country inn, with a flourishing custom, a well-to-do, widowed, buxom landlady—middle-aged, but still possessed of many attractions; and here was he, a middle-aged unattached bachelor, of quite passable good looks and estimable character—in his own opinion, at least—just pining to become the landlord of the aforesaid flourishing country inn and the husband of its prepossessing buxom landlady. Quite an ideal joining of forces, in the view of Mr. Benn; a rattling good proposition.

But was the lively and desirable Mrs. Waters to be convinced of the many obvious advantages of such an alliance? Not she! Every time it was broached—which was always when this persistent idealist reached his third glass—she ruthlessly turned it down.

Hence the despondency of Mr. Benn on this fine summer evening. An attempt to abstract sympathy from Mary Ann, the coveted landlady's maid-of-all-work—who was sitting on a bench outside the door stolidly waiting to be paid her wages preparatory to spending the night at her own home—met with equal failure. Mary Ann's views on husbands—based upon the wage-snatching propensities of a stepfather addicted to drink—were decidedly uncomplimentary. When the disappointed suitor reproved her for leaving her mistress for the night, alone and unprotected, she replied tartly that the landlady of the " Beehive " was lucky in " not having a husband to look after her ".

Nevertheless, when Mrs. Waters presently appeared in the doorway with her knitting, after having paid Mary Ann her wages and sent her off with strict instructions to return in good time on the morrow, the ex-boatswain yet once again mentioned the important subject which was so closely connected with his own welfare and comfort. He asked Mrs. Waters if she felt safe when alone at night—the " Beehive " being a considerable way out of the village—if she wasn't afraid of burglars; and if she didn't long for the protection of a man about the house.

To all of which now hoary questions the sprightly Mrs. Waters replied carelessly and unfeelingly in the negative. Then, declaring that she wished to transact some business at the village post-office, she consoled the downcast suitor somewhat by asking him to remain in charge of the house and to serve any customers who might call during her short absence.

When the landlady had departed, with a flutter of frills and flower-decked millinery, Benn endeavoured to cheer himself by singing merry sea-songs and by stamping up and down as he fortified himself with the resolution never to take " no " as an answer from one who could provide him with such a comfortable home.

Just then a good-looking and well-set-up stranger—obviously an ex-soldier on the tramp looking for a job—came in through the rustic gate. Mistaking Benn for the landlord, he called for a drink, tendering fourpence—which he jocularly declared was all the capital he possessed.

Benn brought out two mugs of beer; and liking the pleasant looks of the newcomer, who seemed to take a very cheery view of life in general and of his own misfortunes in particular, he began to chat with him. Then, taking him into his confidence, he presently revealed the fact that though not yet the landlord of the " Beehive " Inn he greatly desired to attain to that enviable position.

As he talked to the stranger—whose name was Travers—about the unsuccessful addresses he had paid to Mrs. Waters, a bright idea for another attempt suddenly occurred to him; and fetching out two more mugs of beer, he unfolded his plan and made a proposition to his new " mate ". He proposed to scare Mrs. Waters into accepting his suit that very night in the following manner :

Travers was to pretend to be a burglar and to break into the " Beehive " Inn in the early hours of the morning and alarm the landlady who, on awakening to find a strange man in the house, would naturally scream aloud for help. Benn, who would be waiting outside, pretending to keep watch upon the house of the lonely widow during the absence of her maid-servant, would then rush in, knock down the " burglar " and proceed to comfort the frightened lady—who, thus forced to realize her own helplessness, would surely then consent to accept him as her legal protector. Travers' reward for his share in this scheme was to be the magnificent sum of ten shillings—of which he certainly stood in considerable need.

The ex-soldier, however, did not at first regard the suggested plan with any enthusiasm. He pointed out that not only was he to come off second-best in the scuffle, but he also ran the unpleasant risk of neighbours coming upon the scene and handing him over to the police, with a resultant " five-years'-hard "—a risk for which the earning of ten shillings did not appeal to him. But upon Benn's assurance that there were no neighbours within hail of the lonely inn, that he himself would see that no attempt was made to capture him, and that he would make the reward three " quid "—he reached this amount by easy stages, gradually enticing his much desired assistant—the ex-soldier at length agreed to the proposal. He insisted, however, on the important condition that the boatswain should set down in writing a statement that the whole adventure was a deep-laid plot and that he—Travers—was not a real " burglar " at all. This having been done and all the details of the plan arranged, Travers departed, just as Mrs. Waters returned from the village.

Refusing to pay heed to Benn's reiterated expression of concern for her lonely, unprotected state that night, the bored landlady dismissed her tiresome suitor and began to clear her tables, preparatory to closing the house. Nevertheless, the romantic atmosphere of the sunset hour made her thoughts wander back to the days of her youth when it was her delight to trip down to some trysting-place to meet a sweetheart whose love-making she had no desire to repulse.

These musings of a romantic past were suddenly and rudely broken by a noisy company of country labourers, who came swarming in through the rustic gate, singing ribald songs. Seating themselves at the tables, the newcomers called loudly for drinks all round, despite the fact that they had obviously already imbibed more than was good for them. Their continued calls for liquor, however, met with no response, for Mrs. Waters refused to serve such half-tipsy customers at that late hour in the evening, declaring that she would have no brawling on her premises, and by exercising a tactful firmness, aided by much amiable coaxing, she soon managed to rid herself of this rowdy company. Then, after vainly calling her cat to return from its amorous wanderings, she locked up the house and retired for the night, little dreaming that her slumbers would so soon be disturbed.

Shortly after two o'clock in the morning, the ex-boatswain and his new " mate " appeared outside the inn, both having fortified themselves with a substantial meal at Benn's expense. The latter was extremely nervous as he went round to a side window that opened on to the kitchen and easily managed to slip back the somewhat crazy latch and to throw up the window. But he immediately afterwards shivered with fright; for at that moment the night-roving cat and its boon companions started an unearthly caterwauling and furious spitting.

The two conspirators waited for a few moments in suspense; then, hearing no sound from within, Travers crawled in through the open window, while Benn took up his vigil outside, waiting for the expected terrified shrieks of the lady of the house to break the stillness of the night as the signal for him to take up the *rôle* of rescuing hero.

The amateur burglar soon began to stumble about in the dark kitchen and to make a good deal of noise; and presently he saw a light shining from the bedroom above and was pleased to know that he had effectually disturbed Mrs. Waters and that she was already beginning to descend the stairs. To his alarm, however, he saw that the intrepid landlady, suspecting burglars, was carrying a double-barrelled gun; and this being a development he had not expected and having no desire to stop a bullet, he dashed hastily into a cupboard and closed the door.

Mrs. Waters, with her hair hanging down her back and hurriedly garbed in a petticoat and shawl and bedroom slippers, entered the kitchen at that identical moment; and setting the lighted candle down on the table, she rushed to the cupboard and pressing the gun against its door, declared fearlessly that she would shoot did the intruder attempt to come out.

The scared Travers endeavoured to pacify her by declaring that he had thought it was an angel descending the stairs; but when the irate landlady, refusing to accept such barefaced flattery, announced her immediate intention of firing off one barrel of the loaded gun through the window to arouse the neighbourhood and of keeping the second barrel for him should he dare to move, he quickly changed his tactics. Now full of alarm for his own safety, he begged her earnestly to do nothing of the kind, confessing that he was really no burglar; and he then revealed to her the whole plot invented by Benn, even slipping under the cupboard door the written statement given him by the ex-boatswain.

When Mrs. Waters had read the document and realized that he spoke the truth, she permitted the pretended burglar to issue forth from his cramped position in the cupboard. Being pleasantly surprised with his good looks and agreeable manner, she quickly made friends with him—even coquettishly retiring for a moment behind another cupboard door and hastily adding to her hurried toilet a neat wrapper and mob-cap, twisting up her hair beneath the latter with a few deft touches. Travers likewise made haste to draw on his boots, which he had removed on his entrance; and then he smoothed down his own hair as best he could. As he did so, he felt well pleased at the turn events had taken, regarding the buxom but attractive lady of the house with an approving eye and greatly appreciating the comfort and obvious stability of her establishment.

Mrs. Waters, with a merry twinkle in her eye, now demanded the intruder's assistance in turning the tables on Benn, declaring that she meant to give the latter the lesson of his life. Nothing loath, Travers, at her request, hid himself upstairs, while Mrs. Waters let off the gun, firing it into a doormat so that the sound would not reach the village. Immediately afterwards, she unbolted the front door, shrieking "Murder! Help! Burglars!"

When Benn rushed in, ready for the prearranged scuffle, she seized his arm and told him in agitated tones that she had descended on hearing a noise in the kitchen and, finding a "burglar" hiding behind the door, had fired off her double-barrelled gun pointblank at him and shot him dead.

Completely deceived by her story and nearly frightened out of his wits by this supposed dreadful termination of his fine scheme, the conscious-stricken Benn was dumbfounded and nonplussed;

and in faint tones, he suggested that perhaps the " burglar " was not quite dead but might yet be revived.

Mrs. Waters, however, hysterically refused to allow him to examine the " corpse ", declaring that since she had done this unfortunate deed in self-defence, it was his duty to help her to hush it up by burying the " dead burglar " for her. In pretended deep distress, therefore, she produced a spade and bade him in peremptory but agitated tones to go forth at once and to begin digging a " grave " in the garden behind the potato plot.

The flustered and terrified ex-boatswain at first feebly protested against being set such a gruesome task. Mrs. Waters, however, would take no refusal, but turned him out, neck and crop, bidding him not to return until the " grave " was dug, when she would have the " body " ready for him to bury.

As the discomfited Benn staggered out into the garden, staring ruefully at the spade thrust into his unwilling hands and reflecting dismally upon the awkward fix in which his ambition to become landlord of the " Beehive " Inn had landed him, Travers came down from above into the kitchen and laughed heartily with the merry landlady over the joke she had played upon his late fellow-conspirator. When, however, growing bolder, he ventured to give her a little squeeze, she turned round sharply and boxed his ears.

It was now daybreak; and as Mrs. Waters was about to bundle the late " burglar " out of the house also, she received a bad shock. To her own discomfiture and amazement, she now beheld the rolling figure of Benn coming up the garden path, accompanied by a policeman—the boatswain's terrified conscience having led him to seek out the village guardian of the law, to whom he had made the highly-coloured statement that murder had been done at the " Beehive " Inn, confessing, furthermore, that he himself had been the cause thereof.

The quick-witted landlady, not yet at a loss, now thrust the intruder of the night into the scullery beyond the kitchen; and when the policeman and the quaking Benn entered the house, she confronted them both boldly, indignantly protesting against such an intrusion.

When the man of law demanded particulars of the " murdered burglar ", she assumed a look of innocent amazement, declaring that there had been no burglary and no murder, and that there was certainly not a corpse in the house. She then explained that the whole supposed incident was a cock-and-bull story imagined by Benn under the influence of the large quantity of drink with which she had served him late that evening—the probable evil consequences of which she had given him due warning at the time.

A sound of breaking crockery at this moment issuing from the scullery, she hastened to add that the only person who had been near the place since last evening's closing time was a man who called at daybreak to ask for a job and who she had set to do some necessary plumbing and gas-fitting; and slightly opening the scullery door, she began roundly to scold the individual thus described for doing his work badly and breaking her crockery.

As Benn peeped into the scullery and recognized Travers, he got another bad shock; but being relieved by the sight, despite his discomfiture at the failure of his plot and the evident present success of his fellow-conspirator, he now supported Mrs. Waters' statement that too much drink was at the bottom of the whole exaggerated story he had reported. The policeman, though only half convinced that there was no " gory corpse " upon the premises, was finally overruled by the lively and glib-tongued landlady, who concluded her caustic remarks in general and her withering counter-attack upon the doubtful sobriety of the un-lucky Benn by pushing both the man of law and the downcast and defeated ex-boatswain ignominiously out of the house.

After the dissatisfied pair had reluctantly departed, Travers once more appeared in the kitchen, full of complimentary praises for Mrs. Waters' witty resourcefulness, accompanying these by many openly ardent glances of admiration for her personal charms. To these, the landlady, though smiling and well-pleased with her-self, at first tartly declared that once the coast was clear, he must betake himself off likewise. Then, relenting at his quick and sincere look of disappointment—which caused a glow of satis-faction and a sudden quickening of her own pulses—she invited him to remain to breakfast with her, and proceeded to brew the tea at once.

During the merry meal which followed, Travers did not fail to make hay while the sun shone, even boldly confessing that the one job he coveted above all others was to be landlord of a nice little country inn like the " Beehive "; and when at last his now well-disposed hostess insisted upon his departure, she sent him away happy after a lingering farewell and with the hopeful and highly significant promise to meet him for a walk in the woods that same evening.

Thus did the conceited ex-boatswain over-reach himself and lose the coveted prize he sought to the seemingly simple but wide-awake and astute " mate " whom he had proposed to use merely as a negligible " sprat " to catch a most desirable " whale ". And when Mary Ann, the handmaid of the "Beehive", returned to work later in the morning, she was amazed to find her usually sedate mistress dancing gaily about the kitchen and flourishing a mirror, into which she was coquettishly smiling at her own undoubted and recently well-proved charms.

FÊTE GALANTE　　　　　　　　　　　　　　　*Smyth*
(*Lovers' Festival*) *A Dance Dream*

ON a perfect summer night during the eighteenth century a gay masked ball and festival was taking place in the grounds of a certain royal castle, with all the elegance and gorgeousness of the period.

The scene was reminiscent of a Watteau picture. The moonlit formal garden, with its clipped hedges, neat bushes, ornamental vases, and exquisite flowers, was further illuminated by the flaring lights carried by the torch-bearers who moved hither and thither among the guests; and the brilliantly-lighted windows of the castle in the background threw an additional glow over the scene.

The courtiers and guests were all attired in the wonderful costumes of that most artificial period; and the exquisite colourings of their silks and velvets, the delicate fineness of their lace ruffles, and the dazzling glitter of their priceless jewels accorded harmoniously with their graceful movements and the ease and courtliness of their manners. Some of them had chosen to hide their identity under masks and dominoes; for a summer night's entertainment suggested romantic possibilities, and many lovers hoped to whisper their vows amid the kindly shadows cast by the leafy trees.

When the King and Queen appeared, hand in hand, ready to take part in a sarabande, the guests bowed low before their royal host and hostess; and the stately measure that ensued was the prelude to other and more voluptuous dances by special performers

During the dancing of the sarabande, the King's glances never left the face of his beautiful Queen; and the ardour of his proud gaze revealed the depth of the passionate love he bore for her The Queen, however, was heedless of this constant regard of the King, being somewhat sad and preoccupied with thoughts of her own secret love—for her heart was given to another, a strange lover in exile, whose identity was unknown to her royal lord though his existence was jealously suspected by the latter when piqued by her unresponsiveness.

After the conclusion of the sarabande, the Queen stood somewhat apart in a shadowy corner, while the King moved courteously among his guests; and as she thus mused alone for a moment, she accidentally let her lace handkerchief fall to the ground. Instantly, it was picked up by a tall masked cavalier, wrapped in a voluminous domino, who, as he gracefully returned the dainty trifle, bent forward and whispered a few impassioned words in her ear and then vanished among the company.

Startled, and trembling with sudden emotion, the Queen only recovered her control with difficulty; for this masked stranger was her secret lover, who had dared thus to return from exile and had entered the grounds in disguise to implore his royal mistress to grant him a few moments of her company when an opportunity should occur.

Fortunately for the agitated Queen, a welcome interruption came at this moment with the entrance of a company of pierrot players who had been engaged to entertain the guests with their singing, dancing, and mumming. During the little puppet play enacted by these mummers upon a raised mossy knoll, it was easily seen that Columbine was in love with Pierrot, but that, being of a coquettish disposition, she was ready enough to flirt with Harlequin and other swains, or even with old Pantaloon on occasion. Pierrot, on the other hand, though acknowledged as the sweetheart of Columbine, was allowing his roving eye to rest frequently upon the beautiful Queen, of whom he had become enamoured recently and worshipped from a distance.

As pretty Columbine afterwards danced and pirouetted daintily in and out among the guests, the King, attracted by her light and airy charms, addressed some complimentary remarks to her and invited her to be his partner during the next dance.

While Columbine shyly listened to the King's flattering speeches, the Queen, noting the sad looks of the love-sick Pierrot —unaware of his passion for herself and imagining that he was pining for Columbine—came forward and spoke to him, bidding him to take comfort, since his sweetheart was probably only pretending to treat him lightly.

At that moment, the King's glance fell upon the pair; and instantly jealous even of a mummer, he left Columbine and drawing near to the Queen at once began to reproach her for smiling upon other admirers and yet refusing him—her legitimate lord—the favour of a kindly glance.

The Queen, annoyed and fearful of a scene before their guests, turned aside impatiently and, taking her cloak from an attendant page, moved away haughtily upon the arm of a gentleman-in-waiting. The King, though somewhat chagrined, followed, with a number of the guests; and Pierrot was left alone with his sad thoughts.

But only for a few moments. Almost immediately, as the dance music began again, the lively Columbine returned and merrily besought him to dance with her once more, declaring that, despite the attentions of the King and her play-acting coquettishness, she still loved her dear Pierrot only. Pierrot, however, was in too gloomy a mood to be won back by her pretty wiles just then; and piqued by his seeming churlishness, Columbine turned away from him pettishly. Then, upon the entry of Harlequin—who also loved her—with entreaties for her company, she danced away merrily and carelessly with the latter, leaving the downcast Pierrot to his yearnings and dreaming.

Still occupied with his sad thoughts of a hopeless love that could never be returned, Pierrot was glad to find himself alone for a short time, the guests having all wandered away to another part of the grounds, or into the castle, whence came the sounds of festive music and light laughter. Pierrot, too, sang softly to himself a little song in praise of solitude and love; then, wrapping himself in his black domino, he lay down beside some bushes to rest for a while and to forget his unrequited passion.

A few moments later, the masked cavalier came forward into the moonlight from behind a tree where he had concealed himself; and almost immediately afterwards the Queen hurriedly joined him in great agitation. Full of fear lest her returned lover should be seen and recognized, despite his disguise of mask and domino, the royal lady tremblingly besought him to depart at once, declaring that it was madness for him to have attempted to see her again.

The adventurous cavalier, however, enraptured on finding himself once more in the beloved presence of his royal lady, from whom a cruel fate had so long separated him, passionately declared that since banishment must be his unhappy portion this short precious stolen interview was as a glimpse of paradise—each golden moment of which was worth more to him than an age of weary exile. She had called to him, and he had come; and now he claimed his reward.

The love-lorn Queen, unable to resist such pleading and carried away by the passion that consumed her, now led her lover hastily into a little temple-arbour, near by, where she bade him unmask; and then she abandoned herself to his ardent embrace. As the cavalier's domino fell back, he stood revealed in the costume of a pierrot; and so engrossed was he with the ecstatic joy of clasping his beloved one in his arms that he remained oblivious of the fact that his protective covering thus lay neglected at his feet.

Again the Queen besought him to leave her and to seek safety in flight before his presence should be discovered; and again her secret lover refused to deprive himself of these blissful moments, clasping her all the more ardently, recklessly clinging to the joy of the magic present and uttering bold defiance of approaching danger.

The murmuring of these low but agitated voices disturbed the half-dozing Pierrot who, observing the enraptured pair within the arbour, smiled and muttered indulgently to himself, being full of sympathy for all lovers. At first he was carelessly indifferent as to their identity; but presently, as their voices became louder and more impassioned, he sat up and looked more curiously at the occupants of the arbour. Then, to his dismay and grief, he immediately recognized the Queen; and, fearful of discovery, he rose stealthily and, wrapping himself in his dark cloak, began to move away.

Just as he drew back into the shadows, seeking a hiding-place, he saw Columbine suddenly appear in a gap in the hedge that surrounded the formal flower-garden. She was looking for him, and as her glance fell upon the pair in the temple-arbour locked in each other's arms, she started violently. Recognizing the Queen at once, and seeing her in the embrace of one who wore the costume of a pierrot, she immediately mistook the latter for her own still beloved and one-time sweetheart. She was overcome with grief at the sight, though she had before suspected Pierrot of being attracted by his royal mistress. Then, filled with jealous anger because she now felt sure that Pierrot was faithless and had indeed betrayed her with the Queen, she uttered a cry of woe and rushed away in a paroxysm of jealousy to avenge herself upon her recalcitrant lover by informing the King of his imagined treachery and disloyalty.

The half-dazed Pierrot, guessing at her sinister intention, quickly hid himself behind a bush; and the lovers, disturbed and alarmed by Columbine's cry, indulged in a hurried final embrace and separated—the cavalier masking once more, snatching up his domino, and departing hastily upon the terrified entreaties of his now distracted royal mistress.

Pierrot then deliberately stepped forth from his hiding-place into the moonlight, and began to sing one of the songs from the puppet play enacted a short time ago, which concluded with a warning to lovers in general to beware of treacherous tongues and jealous ears. He gave especial emphasis and deliberate meaning to these last words of his song as he observed the King at this moment approaching in company with Columbine; and the latter winced painfully as she realized that they were intended to apply to her—for she already regretted her hasty action in fetching her royal master to surprise the Queen and her lover. As remorse began to enfold her, she made a movement as though to withdraw from the scene; but the King seized her by the wrist and sternly bade her to question Pierrot as to his relations with the Queen, declaring that she would be able to get the truth from him since she had been his first love.

Having thus given his command, the King approached the pale and trembling Queen who, having composed herself somewhat, was now issuing forth from the temple; and controlling his own jealous feelings for the moment, he bade her return with him to their expectant guests.

As the King thus led away his still agitated Queen in courtly fashion, Columbine ran to Pierrot and began to upbraid him bitterly for his supposed defection. She accused him of having been the Queen's lover ever since their company had been appointed as players to the Court; and she added that her proof for this wild statement was the fact that she had just seen him with their royal mistress in his arms.

Then, as Pierrot—understanding from this tirade that the real identity of the Queen's lover had not been guessed by the angry Columbine but that the masked cavalier had been mistaken for himself because of the disguise adopted by the exile—remained silent and somewhat nonplussed, she again suddenly felt remorse for her blind haste in seeking to betray him by bringing the King's displeasure upon him. She entreated him, therefore, to reassure her by declaring that the scene she had beheld in the temple had been merely a jest on his part, enacted in pique to tease her, as had been her own little flirtation with Harlequin.

Pierrot, however, in reply, only reproached her with cold contempt for her heartless betrayal of one she professed to love; and Columbine, expressing her now firm belief that he indeed loved the Queen and that she—Columbine—consequently rejoiced that she had avenged herself upon him, rushed away in a passion of tears.

The King then emerged from the shadows, whence he had observed this scene, and sternly commanded Pierrot to reveal to him all that he had observed in the temple-arbour between the

Queen and her disguised real lover. He announced that he himself was not deceived in this matter as Columbine had been, and believed Pierrot to be guiltless of having dared to make love to the Queen. However, as the puppet-player, from his hiding-place, had beheld what he had no right to behold, he must pay the penalty by revealing to his royal master the exact story of what he had seen and the whole truth as to who had been with the Queen—when all would be forgiven him.

Pierrot was filled with dismay on hearing this command, fearing lest trouble should fall upon the beautiful and well-beloved Queen. Then, imagining, in his loyalty and devotion to her, that he could preserve her honour untarnished by persuading the King that the royal lady had indeed—as declared by Columbine—been merely flirting for a moment with himself—poor humble Pierrot—he answered lightly as though he certainly had been the culprit who had thus indulged in a stolen kiss.

The King, however, refused to be thus deceived; and full of a raging jealousy against his consort's secret lover, he again furiously commanded Pierrot to reveal to him who had been with the Queen in the temple-arbour—once more promising him forgiveness on his compliance and threatening the drastic punishment of death should he refuse to divulge the truth.

Pierrot, now thoroughly alarmed for the safety of his beloved Queen's honour and inspired by the ecstasy of his loving devotion for her, felt it to be not only his duty but his privilege even to risk sacrificing his life for her sake; and yet again he replied as though he were the culprit, still believing that he could convince the King that this was the fact. He declared that light fooling was a dangerous game, that he had certainly soared too high in his folly that night; and he entreated his royal master to forgive him, a poor mummer, for carrying a jest too far.

But the King was now beside himself with jealous passion; and furious with the chivalrous mummer for refusing to obey his command, he declared angrily that some jests were too ill-placed for forgiveness and that the reckless joker, exceeding his privileges, must serve as an example to teach others a lesson. He then commanded the attendants to seize Pierrot and to hang him immediately in the temple-arbour—the secret of which the puppet-player still declined to reveal.

Then, turning to his guests, who were now appearing from various parts of the grounds and were already gazing curiously upon the actors in this sudden dramatic interlude, he quickly recovered himself. Announcing that so trivial a matter must not be allowed to interfere with their pleasure, he called aloud for the moonlight rout to proceed forthwith, determined to drown his outraged feelings in the maddest of revelry.

A group of dancers, attired as bacchantes and satyrs, at that moment came whirling into the midst of the guests, who joined hilariously in their mad convolutions, dancing after them on to the lawns beyond. The Queen, sad and conscience-stricken at this tragic sequel to her few stolen moments of illicit rapture, would have lingered behind in the hope of yet being able to save the brave defender of her honour; but the King sternly compelled her to follow with him in the wake of the revellers.

The royal pair having thus moved away, the unfortunate Pierrot was dragged off hastily to meet his doom, still half dazed, but resigned to his fate—even in a state of exaltation from the exquisite felicity of giving his life to save the honour of the beautiful royal lady he adored. As the lights near by were momentarily shaded while his quick execution took place, there suddenly came a wild and heartrending shriek from the despairing Columbine, who now realized that by her own impetuous act she had thus lost her lover for ever.

When the lights once more shone forth with renewed brilliancy, the Queen returned alone to the scene of the tragedy, having escaped from the vigilance of her angry lord and from the mad revels of the guests; and she stood transfixed with horror as she beheld the limp body of the chivalrous, ill-fated Pierrot hanging within the temple-arbour, on the steps of which lay the swooning form of the heartbroken Columbine.

THE FOREST   *Smyth*

In the depths of the forest, the peaceful tranquillity and the eternal immutability of Nature seem to be fittingly enshrined as flawless jewels in virgin gold. A sense of worship pervades the atmosphere breathed by ancient trees. It is as though the Spirits of the Forest, the elemental forces of Nature, were ever present, unseen by human eyes. In the guise of fauns and hamadryads, they seem to be performing mystic rites amidst a temple of greenery, the incense from their rustic altar rising in a blue haze and penetrating to the skies above.

Time has no meaning for the Forest Spirits—whose presence is strangely felt, though not seen. One can imagine that they sing constantly in praise of their own everlastingness and in indulgent tolerance—if not contempt—for the uncertainty and brevity of all things human.

To the casual wayfarer, these invisible elemental Spirits are merely a poetic fancy engendered by the solemn hush of Nature in her most secret haunts; but to the dwellers upon the forest borderlands they are very real, being regarded by them as their guardians and friends—so much so, indeed, that in times of trouble or need, they frequently invoke their aid and advice.

This was particularly the case in mediaeval ages. At the time when this story opens, pretty Röschen, a simple peasant maiden who dwelt in a lonely rose-covered cottage on the outskirts of a vast forest, held a firm belief in the power of the hidden sylvan spirits whose curious influence she felt on every side when wandering in the woodland depths. Often she would be filled with reverent awe as she imagined their mystic but benevolent presence pervading her loneliness.

This particular evening, however, she had no time for thoughts of an unseen presence; for her friends from the neighbouring village had come to congratulate her upon her recent betrothal to Heinrich, the woodcutter, and to bring gifts for her wedding which was to take place next day.

As the village maidens were merrily dancing and singing around the shy but happy Röschen, their rejoicings were interrupted by the appearance of a pedlar in their midst, with an intriguing-looking pack upon his back and leading a dancing bear.

At first, the girls, scared at the rough, though comical, antics of the bear, were inclined to run away; but when the pedlar called off his four-footed companion and spread out the contents of his pack, they clustered around him willingly enough, eager to buy bright ribbons, laces, and trinkets with which to bedeck themselves on Röschen's wedding-day.

While the visitors were thus happily engaged, Heinrich, the woodcutter, appeared from a path in the forest; and Röschen, full of joy, left the merry group and ran to greet her lover, who was the handsomest young man in the country-side. When, however, she noticed that he carried a dead deer which he had just killed in the forest and which he announced was his contribution to the wedding feast on the morrow, the gentle Röschen was filled with dismay and alarm for his safety. She feared lest, in accordance with the severe forest laws of those days, he might be condemned to death for thus poaching on the forest preserves of the powerful Count Rudolf who owned the land and whose castle stronghold was no great distance away.

But Heinrich only laughed at the fears of his sweetheart, declaring happily that no one had seen him commit the deed; and then, to satisfy her further, he slipped the deer out of sight down a well which stood near by.

By this time, the pedlar had finished disposing of his gaudy wares; and, packing up his bundle, he went on his way once more with his dancing bear. The village maidens also now departed to their homes, after offering further congratulations to the happy lovers whose wedding they were to attend on the morrow.

As the songs and laughter of the light-hearted villagers died away in the distance, Röschen's fears for the safety of her beloved one, because of his transgression of the forest laws, returned in such force that, to comfort her, Heinrich joined with her in invoking the aid of the Forest Spirits; and the betrothed pair implored the latter to guide and console them in any difficulty or danger that might arise.

It was now sunset; and after a final embrace, the lovers parted, with joyful anticipation of the consummation of their happiness on the morrow. When the pretty Röschen had vanished within her cottage with a last farewell wave of her hand, Heinrich also prepared to take his departure.

Just then, however, there came the sudden blast of a hunting-horn; and next moment, a beautiful woman, mounted on horse-back, appeared from the main forest path. She immediately accosted Heinrich with an air of such complimentary graciousness that the young man was instantly fascinated by her extraordinary charm.

This beautiful stranger he recognized at once to be the Lady Iolanthe, the all-powerful mistress of Count Rudolf, the liege lord of the neighbouring castle and forest lands. Over the latter it was known she held such complete sway and evil influence that she did not even seek to disguise her lofty contempt for him as a weak pliable tool to be used by her for the attainment of her own ambitions and unbridled passions.

Iolanthe, although so beautiful as to inspire involuntary admiration and a magnetic attraction in all beholders, was by nature cruel, unscrupulous, and unrestrained in her unlawful desires. As she was also reputed to be a witch and, consequently, was regarded with dread by the superstitious rustics dwelling about the forest, Heinrich, fearful of her " evil eye ", would have withdrawn at once into the friendly cover of the forest.

Iolanthe, however, was so pleased with the handsome looks of the stalwart young woodcutter that a sudden passion for him began to burn within her with great force; and she determined to exercise her well-practised arts of fascination upon him, hoping thereby to include him in her train of admirers and, by luring him from the simple Röschen—to whom she knew him to be betrothed—to secure him as a new lover for herself. She dismounted, therefore, calling to an attendant who followed to hold her horse at a discreet distance; and with easy graciousness, she entered into friendly conversation with the young rustic Adonis whose handsome appearance had so instantly appealed to the passionate instincts she never sought to control. In persuasive tones and making use of all the seductive wiles in which she was such a complete adept, she invited him to cease the unprofitable occupation of woodcutting and, instead, to enter her service at the castle—by which manœuvre she hoped to have him constantly at her beck and call, and even to compel his love should she continue to desire it.

For a short time Heinrich, flattered by the interest and attentions of the great lady and strangely moved by her passionate appeal—the meaning of which he could not fail to understand—made no attempt to stop the flow of her hot words or to reply to her cunning invitation; and as he felt the subtle influence of her siren-like attraction seizing upon his own simple personality, he began to be dazzled by the picture of ease, light pleasure, and indulgence painted for him did he enter her service.

This sudden temptation, however, quickly passed; and remembering his beloved Röschen with a remorseful pang that he should even for a moment have been enticed into forgetting her loving trustfulness in his integrity, he turned abruptly from the compelling lure of Iolanthe's passion-gleaming eyes and curtly declined her invitation to enter into service at the castle or to accept her personal favours. Then, pointing to Röschen's cottage, he added boldly: "The maiden I love lives there! Her only will I serve!"

Iolanthe, unaccustomed to having her imperious will thwarted, laughed scornfully on hearing this; and, unable to believe that her own dazzling beauty and never-failing allurements could seriously be declined in favour of a simple country wench, she cried out: "Go into the cottage and bid farewell to that chit! Then follow me to the castle to learn my further pleasure!"

Once more Heinrich fell under the spell of the bewitching loveliness and enticing personal appeal of the incomparable stranger; and impelled also by the authoritative tone of her command, he slowly entered the cottage, as in a dream and against the dictates of his own now weakened will.

At that moment further hunting-horns sounded, and Count Rudolf and his huntsmen appeared upon the scene.

Already annoyed by his mistress's desertion of him during the hunt, the Count's anger was further increased on catching sight of Heinrich's handsome figure disappearing into the cottage. His jealous suspicions instantly aroused, he broke forth into a furious tirade, reproaching Iolanthe for leaving him to hunt alone, for her wild conduct in general, and for her present evident pursuit of a new admirer whom he accused of already being her lover.

Iolanthe, well realizing her own power over the weak-willed Count, replied that she was tired of his continual jealous outbursts, that she had ceased to care for him, and that if she chose to take a new lover she should certainly do so.

While the angry pair were thus wrangling, a fresh and hilarious party of huntsmen appeared, dragging before them the pedlar whom they accused, in joking fashion, of having interfered with their sport by scaring them with his dancing bear, and whom they also suspected of poaching. Iolanthe, contemptuous of this trivial occurrence, seized the opportunity it afforded of ending the present dispute; and peremptorily bidding Rudolf to dismiss the brawlers, she unceremoniously entered the cottage to pursue further her seduction of the young woodcutter for whom she had conceived so violent a passion.

The Count, however, sulkily flung himself somewhat apart, leaving his men to do as they pleased with the unfortunate pedlar they had caught in the woodland preserves. Thinking that it would provide them with some rough amusement, the rowdy huntsmen at first decided to tie their victim on to the back of his bear; then, not caring for the possible risks to their own skins involved by this plan, they determined, instead, to duck him in the well. As they proceeded to do so, however, they discovered the dead deer concealed therein, and drew it forth in fear and trembling before the now interested and angry gaze of their liege lord.

The pedlar, as he was about to take the opportunity of slipping away during the confusion that followed, was seized again by order of the Count, who now accused him of being the culprit who had stolen the deer. The wretched pedlar, however, remembered that he had seen Heinrich carrying a deer when approaching Röschen and her girl friends earlier that evening; and he now declared that it was the woodman who had thus broken the forest laws and who was probably at that moment within the cottage of his betrothed.

Rudolf, once more in good humour because he believed that he might now avenge himself upon his tantalizing mistress's new lover, bade his men release the pedlar, to whom he carelessly flung a purse as compensation for such rough handling; and the latter departed, well contented by this unexpectedly happy termination to his adventure.

Then, as Iolanthe was now seen to be issuing from the cottage with an angry frown on her face, having failed to separate the lovers, the Count ordered his huntsmen to enter and search for the real culprit; and a tragic scene immediately ensued. Röschen, pale and tearful, and full of fear for the safety of her beloved one, rushed out; and kneeling at the feet of the all-powerful Iolanthe, she cried out imploringly: "Oh, save him! Save him!"

In answer to her piteous appeal, Iolanthe sarcastically declared that it was a pity the young man had so foolishly declined to enter her service at the castle, where safety, contentment, and pleasure awaited him. But when Heinrich was presently dragged forth by the huntsmen, she made one more desperate attempt to break down the handsome woodman's opposition to her imperious will —her sudden uncontrollable desire to secure him as her lover overwhelming her furious rage at the rebuffs she had already received at his hands.

Calling to an attendant to bring her horse, she began to move away; then, turning to bestow a last enthralling glance of passionate invitation upon the downcast woodman, she said seductively: "If now in wiser mood, then follow me!"

The unhappy Röschen, quickly realizing that to obey this last command was the only means whereby her lover might be saved from death and willing even to surrender him to another if, by so doing, his precious life could be preserved, flung herself upon Heinrich and entreated him to comply with Iolanthe's request.

Heinrich's answer to this unselfish appeal, however, was to clasp his beloved one in a close and fervid embrace; and then, freeing himself finally from the enticing wiles of the passion-torn temptress, he replied to her last inviting call "Are you coming?" by boldly calling down curses upon her.

Mad with disappointment and rage that her desires should be thus denied and her favours flouted, Iolanthe commanded the huntsmen to slay the humble peasant who had dared to defy her will; and then, mounting her horse, she rode away at a furious pace, followed by the well-satisfied Count Rudolf and his attendants.

As Heinrich fell to the ground, stabbed by the knives of his captors, the despairing Röschen also fell lifeless upon his bleeding body.

x

Thus did the Spirits of the Forest, still engaged in their mystic rites, ever watchful though invisible, answer the invocation uttered by the lovers earlier that evening, guiding them in their high resolve of preferring Love, which is immortal and mighty, to Life, which is unstable and transitory.

THE WRECKERS   *Smyth*

IT was Sunday evening; and the inhabitants of a lonely little village on the wildest part of the Cornish coast were wending their way to church, lustily singing hymns and psalms as they trudged along. For this was the middle of the eighteenth century, in the early days of the religious revival inaugurated by John Wesley; and the teachings of the great preacher, together with his stern call to prayer and repentance, had fired the emotional Celtic imagination of these simple village folk to such an extent that their newly-revived religious observances had become a passionate obsession with them.

Nevertheless, there still prevailed among them the traditional and barbarous custom of slaying and robbing the unfortunate victims of the many shipwrecks that occurred along that wild and stormy coast. Strangely enough, not only did these primitive Celts reconcile such violent practices in some mysterious way with their consciences, but they even regarded them as a quite natural proceeding by no means at variance with their strong religious professions. Indeed, they had gradually come to look upon these murderous outrages as their chief means of livelihood, so that they did not hesitate to bring about wrecks artificially by extinguishing the established lights—the lighthouse-keeper being in league with the wreckers.

Nor did these psalm-singing villagers, on their way to church on the Sunday evening on which this story opens, regard it as in any way out of keeping with their conduct as revivalist converts to stop their hymn-singing temporarily before entering the church, while they indulged in drinks and gossip outside the village inn.

Most of them remained gloomy, however, for latterly there had been such a paucity of wrecks—upon which the majority of them depended for their subsistence—that they had been reduced almost to the verge of starvation.

As they now spoke and drank together, Pascoe, the headman of the village—an elderly man, famous among the people as a local preacher under the Revival and as a strict disciplinarian with an unbending attitude towards sinners—came out from his cottage near by, and sternly rebuked the drinkers for thus desecrating the Lord's Day. He declared that God was punishing them for their sins by guiding the ships in safety past the perilous rocks notwithstanding the extinguished lighthouse lamp, so that the sea no longer yielded up to them their accustomed prey; and he added that this curse could only be removed by their humble prayers and repentance.

When the austere Pascoe had continued on his way, Lawrence, the lighthouse-keeper, with his pretty seventeen-year-old daughter, Avis, drew near to the crestfallen group. The last remarks of the local preacher were overheard by the newcomers; and Avis tossed her head in laughing contempt as she asked the crestfallen idlers if they really believed such nonsense. She then called upon her father to tell his friends the true reason for the recent unfortunate lack of wrecks—a discovery which he had just made.

As the men gathered around him in surprise, eager to hear his news, Lawrence told them that he had found in a distant lonely creek the smouldering remains of a beacon in such a position that its flames must certainly have served as a guide to a storm-driven vessel, enabling it to avoid the disaster of foundering upon the treacherous rocks—a positive proof that some traitor in their midst was trying to prevent passing ships from becoming wrecks.

As the amazed wreckers expressed indignation that one of their own people should be thus betraying them by endeavouring to deprive them of the spoils of the sea, Avis further electrified them by insinuating that she could make a good guess as to the identity of the traitor.

With these tantalizing words, however, the spoilt village beauty—who was a shallow-minded girl of ungenerous disposition—turned aside and made her way to a more secluded spot, where she had arranged to meet a young fisherman named Mark. The latter had formerly paid her a considerable amount of attention, being, indeed, regarded by the villagers as her sweetheart and suitor; but latterly he had cooled in his attitude towards her, so that she suspected he had bestowed his affections elsewhere.

Her suspicions were confirmed presently when, as they stood together, Mark coldly stated that their meetings must cease, since she was no longer to him what she had been; and when he left her hurriedly after this announcement, she was at first overcome

with grief and disappointment at such an abrupt termination to a
promising courtship. This feeling, however, her wounded vanity
quickly changed to resentment against him and to bitter jealousy
of her rival—whom she now guessed to be Thirza, the beautiful
young wife of Pascoe, the headman; for she had seen the pair
alone together several times recently.

Thirza had come as a stranger to the village, and was unpopular
and disliked by the wreckers because she had never ceased to be
shocked and horrified by their murderous practices; and she had
not hesitated to express constantly her frank reprobation of their
barbarity and her contempt for their hypocritical professions of
religious fervour in the face of such callous cruelty.

Avis, always jealous of Thirza's unusual beauty, was now filled
with deadly hatred against her because she believed Mark to be
in love with her. She also had an angry grudge against Pascoe as
a kill-joy, because of his fanatical denunciation of all forms of
gaiety, and for regarding pretty clothes, dancing, and merriment
as wiles of the devil; and she determined to seek an early opportunity of revenging herself upon the stern headman and his too
attractive wife.

As she now stood near Pascoe's cottage, Thirza herself came
outside with her husband's fishing-nets, which she began to hang
up on the walls to dry; and noticing how downcast the lighthouse
keeper's pretty young daughter looked, she inquired kindly what
troubled her.

Avis, however, flounced away at once and hurried off to church
and at that moment Pascoe himself came up, having stopped to
visit a sick friend before joining the worshippers. Seeing that
Thirza was busy with the nets, he scolded her for doing such
work on the Sabbath Day, and bade her go to church instead

This was the signal for an angry outburst on the part of Thirza
who, though she had so far modified her denunciations of the
wreckers' barbarous customs in the presence of her husband
could now restrain herself no longer. She passionately told
Pascoe that the hypocritical life of his people was hateful to her
and filled her with disgust and indignation; and she added that
she declined to worship under the same roof with those whose
habit it was to pray or to murder as it suited them.

Though astounded by this outburst from the young wife he so
passionately adored, Pascoe hastened to defend himself and his
wrecker friends with many specious arguments presented with
his usual eloquence. Thirza, however, remained unconvinced
and when, still regarding her as mistakenly hypersensitive, he
would have embraced her with indulgent forbearing, she shrank

from his extended arms with horror and loathing, and fled back to the house, declaring that his murderous presence was hateful to her.

Pascoe was stunned with sincere grief as he at last realized the antagonism of Thirza to the practices he connived at and her personal antipathy to himself; and for some time afterwards his behaviour and speech seemed strange and unaccountable to his companions. Later on, when the worshippers returned from church, full of gleeful enthusiasm because a storm was brewing and might result in a useful wreck for them, he turned aside and moved away, muttering something about a pillar of fire lighting up the night and saving souls alive—quoting from one of his favourite scriptural passages.

Lawrence, the lighthouse-keeper, and his companions were amazed, thinking that Pascoe must be wandering in his mind; but Avis insinuated cunningly that the headman's mutterings probably referred to the lighting of beacons—adding spitefully that she believed Pascoe was the traitor in their midst and that he had been bewitched and corrupted by his unfriendly stranger wife.

Their suspicions thus aroused by Avis's vengeful accusations and by Pascoe's own incomprehensible conduct, the villagers determined to patrol the shore secretly that night; and they arranged to carry horns, so that if any of them should observe the fire of a beacon, he could immediately give warning to the others by blowing four loud blasts.

. . . .

It was now past sunset, and a terrific storm had already blown up; and as twilight fell, there suddenly came the sound of a gun fired out at sea—a signal of distress from a vessel driven out of her course and heading for the rocks. In the wildest excitement and full of unholy joy, the wreckers joined hands and sang songs and danced as they fervently returned thanks to God for remembering them once more by delivering a vessel into their hands. Then, seizing strong ropes, grappling irons, and axes, they hastened down to the shore to take up their appointed positions in readiness for their gruesome task.

Darkness fell quickly; yet no lamp shone forth from the lighthouse. But as the wreckers hung about, waiting eagerly for the doomed vessel to founder upon the rocks, they did not forget to keep watch for signs of the supposed traitor in their midst. Avis, in pursuance of her revenge, was determined to prove to them that it was indeed Pascoe—incited thereto by his unpopular wife—who was aiding the ships. Accompanied by the tavern-keeper's young son Jack—her latest admirer—she hastened to a lonely creek, in hot pursuit of the local preacher, whom she had observed making his way in that direction.

In the neighbourhood of this same wild and lonely spot, Mark the fisherman also directed his steps, alone and as secretly as possible; and drawing forth from a crevice in the rocks some pieces of wood, sticks, and an old barrel he had hidden there earlier in the day, he quickly built these up into a beacon in such a position that its blaze would presently serve as a guide to the distressed ship out at sea. As he worked, he thought happily of Thirza, whom he so dearly loved and with whom he shared the dangerous but blessed secret of thus saving those whom the wreckers would have lured to a watery grave.

Just as he was about to set fire to the beacon, Thirza herself came running towards him and begged him not to light the bonfire that night. She declared that the wreckers were watching every bay along the coast; and despite her sympathy with the unfortunate voyagers and her former eagerness to help them, her anxiety for her lover's safety overwhelmed every other feeling.

But Mark gently reproved her for even permitting such a thought to enter her mind; and he boldly declared that he cared nothing for the spies about him, but that the beacon he had just built should certainly blaze forth that night as his parting farewell to Cornwall. Then, clasping Thirza tenderly in his arms, he besought her passionately to go away from the village with him on the morrow in a vessel he knew to be leaving the harbour next evening.

Thirza, unable longer to resist her lover's pleadings, consented to do so; then, snatching the already lighted torch from his hand, she deliberately set fire to the beacon with her own hands in a passion of triumphant love and defiance. As the flames burst forth, horn blasts could be heard in the distance—the signal that the watching wreckers had already observed the light that spelled disaster to their own evil hopes and safety to the distressed vessel which would now steer clear of the rocks.

Then, hearing the voice of Pascoe, crying out prayers and entreaties to his God as he roamed the shores near by, the lovers reluctantly separated, hastening away into the darkness with joyful vows to meet again on the morrow at the harbour to sail away and part no more.

Presently, Pascoe—still entreating the Divine forgiveness for what he believed to be his idolatrous earthly love for the beautiful young woman who so justly condemned him—drew near to the still smouldering beacon; and suddenly remembering its signifi-

cance to his wrecker confederates, he called out aloud : " Treason!
Death to a traitor! "

Next moment, however, he noticed a shawl lying on the ground
near the beacon which he recognized as belonging to Thirza;
and realizing at once what this portended, he uttered a loud cry
of woe and fell senseless to the ground. Thus was he found
by the wreckers who, amazed and dumbfounded that the accusation of Avis was thus seemingly proved to be the truth, dragged
him away to a cave—where, a few hours later, when he had
recovered consciousness once more, they held judgment upon
him.

.   .   .   .

There are many caves on the coast of Cornwall into which the
sea surges in overwhelming volume at high tide and from which
egress to the cliffs above is only possible through shaft-like
passages in the rocks. In former times smugglers made use of
such dangerous caves for their nefarious purposes; and the exits
from the caves to the passages leading out to the upper ground
they closed in by means of heavy iron gates or doors which could
be shut and bolted at will. When the gates were closed, any
person remaining in such caves could not hope to escape from
drowning at high tide.

It was in one of these caves that Pascoe was brought up for
judgment by the wreckers; and Tallan, the tavern-keeper, con-
stituted himself judge in the informal but grim trial which now
took place, while Lawrence and his daughter were the main
accusers.

Pascoe, though still dazed and overcome with grief because of
his wife's hatred for himself and of his discovery of her evident
participation in the firing of the beacon, could not subdue his love
for her sufficiently to bring judgment upon her; and by his silence,
he led his confederates reluctantly to believe that he must indeed
be the traitor. Avis continually encouraged the wreckers in this
belief by declaring vindictively that the headman had been
seduced into betraying them by his strange witch-like wife.

The wreckers, who also hated Thirza, were willing enough to
believe in any adverse influence she might have wielded over her
husband; and as Pascoe still made no attempt to defend himself,
Tallan now sternly announced to him that he was found guilty
of treason towards his comrades and must pay the penalty—
which was death.

At this moment, however, there came a dramatic interruption
by the entrance of Mark the fisherman who, too noble to permit
another to suffer in his stead—even though that other was the

man he most desired to be removed from his path—suddenly stepped forward and announced calmly that Pascoe was innocent of the charge laid against him. He then declared that he himself —Mark the fisherman—had fired the beacons to warn ships in danger; adding that he was determined to have no traffic with the murderous practices of the villagers, which he had thus successfully foiled.

As the angry wreckers now gladly released their old comrade and seized Mark in his stead, Avis was horror-struck at the dangerous position of her former sweetheart—whom she still loved; and in a desperate attempt to save him she declared that he could not have fired the beacon just discovered, since he had spent the night in her arms as her accepted lover.

This lying announcement, however, was quickly confounded by Thirza, who also now rushed forward and, laughing the distracted girl's statement to scorn, proudly claimed Mark as her own lover with whom she was resolved to die, since they were also confederates in the firing of the beacons.

This latter statement was willingly hailed by Lawrence who, after angrily thrusting aside his despairing daughter, called upon his comrades to pronounce judgment upon the man and woman who had thus not only betrayed their interests but had, in addition, disgraced their religious tenets by daring to love unlawfully; and the pair were condemned to die together by being left to drown in the cave, which was already being quickly flooded by the advancing tide.

This pronouncement of death upon the wife for whom his passion still burned, roused Pascoe from his dazed condition; and he dashed forward and tried to drag Thirza through the gates to the safety of the cliffs above, through which Tallan, Lawrence, and the others had already passed.

But Thirza struggled wildly to free herself from his grasp, declaring passionately that she would never live with him again but longed only to die with the man she loved; and when Pascoe still refused to release her, she became furious and began to call down curses upon him and his confederates, whom she again denounced as murderers.

Her curses terrified the superstitious wreckers to such an extent that they entreated their comrade to leave her to suffer the death to which she had been condemned; and at last, Pascoe, realizing the futility of hoping ever to secure happiness with one whose heart was given to another, recovered his control and dignity somewhat and angrily flung his struggling wife back into the arms of her lover.

By this time the roaring waves of the overwhelming tide were already dashing high up into the cave; and as the wreckers clanged the iron gates behind them and left the doomed pair to their fate, Mark and Thirza passionately embraced and waited with exultant joy in their hearts for the quickly approaching moment when they would be united in death.

SHAMUS O'BRIEN   *Stanford*

AFTER the Irish Rebellion in 1798, there was much suppressed excitement one day in the village of Ballyhamis, in Cork. The most popular young man in the village, Shamus O'Brien, one of the ring-leaders in the rebellion and now an outlaw, was known to be back in his home once more. He was in hiding from the English soldiery, who were even now scouring the country-side for him. There was a price on his head, too; but the villagers loved the handsome and courageous young Shamus too well to betray him—all except one, that is to say.

Mike Murphy had no love for Shamus O'Brien—for the simple reason that he coveted the latter's beautiful wife, Nora. But Nora had scorned his suit, knowing him to be mean and ignoble in disposition. Besides, she had always loved the warm-hearted, brave and merry Shamus and had eyes for no other man.

When the pair had married, amid the rejoicings of all the village, Mike Murphy still cast covetous glances upon lovely Nora. He hoped against hope that the time would come when she would be glad to turn to him in some emergency and seek his aid—at his own price!

After the Rebellion had been quelled, that emergency seemed to have arrived; and Mike Murphy kept his eyes open, knowing there was a price upon the head of Shamus. He intended to claim the one hundred guineas reward offered by the English Government for the capture of the outlawed rebel. Mistress Nora might not be so proud when her gay husband had been hanged at the cross-roads. So Mike Murphy sought out the English soldiery, and turned informer.

While Shamus O'Brien lay hidden in his humble cottage home, as the soldiers drew near to the village, Father O'Flynn, the jolly old Parish Priest, tried to cheer up the despondent villagers by declaring the English soldiers would have their work cut out to catch the gallant young rebel. Even when Nora, who had run outside to take an anxious look around, reminded him that the avaricious, spiteful Mike Murphy was a real danger, he soothingly told her that all would yet be well, since Shamus's bright wits would not fail him in an emergency.

Nevertheless, the good old Priest knew well enough that the soldiers were not far away; and he followed Nora into the cottage to warn Shamus of this fact. Nora's pretty sister, Kitty O'Toole, however, remained outside to keep watch. She took up a position near the cottage, where she could not be seen.

Consequently, when Mike Murphy presently appeared with Captain Trevor, the Officer-in-Charge of the English soldiery, she heard their conversation as they drew near. From this she soon realized that Mike was, indeed, a dastardly informer and had betrayed the friend of his youth.

Captain Trevor was a handsome and pleasant young officer, who found his present duty extremely distasteful. He knew that Shamus O'Brien was a patriot and loved Ireland—that, though he was a rebel, the wrongs of his country were certainly very real ones. Trevor, therefore, had much sympathy for him. Nevertheless, he was a true soldier, faithful to his own country, and had his duty to perform—the hateful duty of rounding up this brave rebel and of hanging him in accordance with his instructions from headquarters. Like all honest men, too, he hated to have to make use of an informer; and he found Mike Murphy a particularly despicable specimen of his kind.

Mike was blatantly gloating over the betrayal of his countryman; also, he was much too anxious about being assured of the certainty of his reward. Besides this, he was obviously a coward, being scared of the consequences to himself from the wrath of the villagers when they knew that he was the betrayer of their beloved hero. After pointing out O'Brien's cottage to the Captain, he was eager to claim his reward and vanish. Trevor, however would not let him go until he had given him a close description of the hidden rebel . . . as for the reward, he could not claim that until the man had been actually captured.

With this, Mike had to be content; and he now hurried away to watch the proceedings from a hidden point of vantage, hoping that he had not been seen.

But young Kitty O'Toole had seen and heard all; and she now boldly stepped forward and intercepted the Captain with a respectful curtsey, hoping to hold him in conversation a while and so give more time for Shamus to make his escape from the cottage She learned from the officer that he was now awaiting the arriva of his men, when a raid would be made on O'Brien's abode; meanwhile, she was glad to see that he did not seem averse to indulging in a little flirtation with her.

The English Captain, indeed, was greatly struck by the charm and liveliness of pretty Kitty, who was a typical Irish beauty; and, being entirely heart-whole, he was inclined to fall in love with her at sight. But Kitty—although she also felt an answering leap in her heart, finding the Englishman equally attractive to herself— kept him at a distance, her main idea at the moment being to gain time. When the Captain presently most reluctantly went off to fetch up his squad of dragoons, she hurried towards the cottage to see what was happening there.

To her dismay, Shamus himself rushed out; and, calling to his neighbours who now came crowding around, he began to harangue them, bidding them to carry on his good work and to rebel again. Soon, however, as the English soldiery could now be seen approaching, he returned to the cottage with Kitty and Nora. Here, using his quick Irish wits, he soon devised a plan of action whereby he hoped to give his enemies the slip.

When the soldiers arrived, therefore, Kitty strolled outside once more and calmly told Captain Trevor that he would be only wasting his time by searching the cottage, since Shamus O'Brien had already made his escape. The only persons left indoors were his wife, his small son, and the village idiot.

The English officer, however, sent his men into the cottage to make a thorough search. As they entered, there came out a ragged and unkempt-looking figure, with tousled hair in which straws were stuck, loosely-hanging limbs, and the open, slobbering mouth and vacant stare of a half-wit. This was Shamus O'Brien, who had thus so cleverly disguised himself as the village "natural" that Captain Trevor and his men were completely deceived. Speaking thickly and foolishly, the pretended "idiot" insisted upon acting as guide to the soldiers in their search for the escaped rebel, declaring that he knew every inch of the country-side better than anybody else in the village—also every likely hiding-place.

As Kitty and her friends vouched for the truth of this statement, declaring that the "poor innocent" was, indeed, a wonderful guide, Captain Trevor decided to take him along with his men to help in the man-hunt.

So the English officer and his dragoons left the village once more on their wild-goose chase, little dreaming that the man they sought was, in fact, the village idiot whom they had brought as their guide—a "guide" who led them a fine dance, landing them

in bogs, and finally giving them the slip at the first likely
opportunity.

Meanwhile, poor Nora came forth, full of anxiety for her dare-
devil husband. Twice she had heard the mysterious "banshee"
wailing outside the house; and she trembled lest she should hear
it a third time—for this would mean dire misfortune, even death
to the one she loved so dearly. She was greatly comforted, however, by cheery old Father O'Flynn, and by the sympathetic
Kitty.

Then, to her joy, Shamus appeared, full of glee because he had
been able to give the soldiers the slip and had then returned on
his tracks. But his joyful relief was short-lived. Even as he
kissed his wife and child, the mournful wailing of the "banshee"
was heard again for the third time by Nora, who now knew that
trouble was in store for her beloved one.

This proved true enough; for treacherous Mike Murphy had
seen the disguised Shamus re-entering his home and had quickly
informed the soldiers of the whereabouts of their escaped "guide".
Captain Trevor and his men, therefore, now surrounded the
cottage; and the gallant rebel was finally captured and carried off
to a temporary barracks-building, to await his trial and execution,
while the despairing Nora fell fainting into the arms of the good
old Priest.

.   .   .   .

And now, Captain Trevor found himself in a greater quandary
than ever. All the young officer's sympathies were with the
captive rebel and his wife—to say nothing of the lively sister-in-
law. Indeed, it was pretty Kitty who occupied his distracted
mind most. He had fallen sincerely in love with this brave and
charming Irish girl—who would certainly hate him for ever if
he caused her sister's bold husband to be hanged! Yet, his duty
as a soldier was clear enough. The young Captain felt himself
very hardly used.

Then, the despicable Mike Murphy was again making himself a nuisance by demanding the reward offered for informing—
his blood-money. Angrily Trevor stated that he would get his
money when the Government felt inclined to pay it. Then, seeing
that Mike was now anxious to sneak away and hide until all
was over—knowing that the villagers were ready to tear him to
pieces—he sternly bade him to remain at hand, since he would
be needed for evidence at the drum-head trial he was about to
hold. So Mike found himself compelled to skulk around; but,
being an arrant coward, he kept in the background as much as
possible.

The unhappy young Captain, torn between love and duty, next had to endure some very bad moments when Kitty and the weeping Nora appeared and begged for a farewell interview with the captive. Although against his instructions, he allowed Nora to be taken in to her husband; and then he begged the waiting Kitty not to think too badly of him, since he was bound to do his duty. Kitty, who was already half in love with the young English Captain, despite the tragic circumstances of his appearance in the village, could not refrain from granting his request; and when he assured her of his own love for her, she gave him reason to hope that she returned it, even though saucily bidding him " not to blarney with an Irish girl ".

As the weeping Nora came away from her pathetic interview with her doomed husband, she was accosted by the base Mike Murphy, who now promised that if she would consent to elope with him, he would give evidence at the trial which would save Shamus from being hanged. But Nora contemptuously declined to listen to such a vile suggestion; and the jealous Mike slunk back, angry and defeated.

The drum-head trial, consequently, though a fair one, went against the prisoner, since the evidence of Mike Murphy as the informer and chief witness could not be over-ridden; and Shamus O'Brien was condemned to be hanged at the cross-roads next morning, one hour from sunrise.

Early next day all the village folk arrived at the cross-roads, where the gallows had already been erected; and here they waited to bid farewell to their hero-friend. It was a sad gathering; and when Nora and her baby boy appeared, attended by Kitty and Father O'Flynn, the crowd groaned and wept with them in sympathy.

Even now, the vile Mike Murphy managed to get a word with the two weeping girls, gloating because his offer of the day before had been rejected. Then, still fearing the anger of the villagers, he hid himself near the gallows, where he could watch the wretched end of his rival in love.

When the cart came along with the bound prisoner and his guards, the weeping and wailing increased. But Shamus O'Brien was brave and had no fear of death; and as the cart halted near the gallows, he made a bold and patriotic speech to his friends, bidding them to go on with the fight for freedom.

Meanwhile, the sympathetic young Captain Trevor was nearly distracted by the tears of Kitty and Nora; and, since he could not prevent it, he was anxious to get the dreadful business over.

When, however, Father O'Flynn humbly begged to be allowed to enter the cart to pray with the condemned man for a few moments, he willingly granted his request. At least his captive should have all the religious comfort he required.

But the good old Priest had not the wits of a lively and patriotic Irishman for nothing. As he now knelt beside the best-loved member of his flock and prayed aloud with him, he very deftly cut the cords that bound the captive, unseen by the guards.

Instantly Shamus leapt over the side of the cart and made a wild dash for liberty. Mike Murphy, from his hiding-place, was the first person to see what had happened; and he rushed forward furiously to stop the daring fugitive. At that moment, the guards fired; and there was a great uproar.

But it was the traitor who received the death-volley, and fell to the ground; while Shamus O'Brien, escaping by inches, dashed into cover and vanished from sight.

Nor was he recaptured; for, all the sympathy being on his side, it was a very half-hearted search that ensued. Nor did Captain Trevor blame his men for their dilatoriness. He was only too thankful that his unwanted captive had got safely away; and he rejoiced sincerely for the sake of his pretty sweetheart, Kitty, and her grateful sister, Nora.

THE TRAVELLING COMPANION   *Stanford*
(*Based on a Hans Andersen Fairy-Tale*)

ONE dark, stormy night during the Middle Ages, a handsome young man named John entered a dimly-lit country church to rest a while. He was an orphan and quite alone in the world. His father had recently died, his little home had been sold. So John had come out to seek his fortune, carrying a traveller's staff. All his worldly goods lay in a wallet strapped on his back.

All that day he had been travelling on foot. Then, as a thunderstorm broke at nightfall, he had crept into this little church for shelter. He flung himself wearily on the first bench he came to and lay listening to the wind and the rain, feeling rather sorry for himself.

Presently, however, as the thunder died away in the distance, he began to feel more cheerful once more. Then it was that he made a rather gruesome discovery. He was not alone, after all.

As he walked up the nave of the church, he saw that a bier, upon which lay the dead body of a man, had been placed in front of the altar—obviously awaiting burial next day. The body was covered with a very richly-embroidered and heavily-fringed shroud, proving that the dead man must have been wealthy and of importance.

At that moment there came an interruption. Two rough-looking men also entered the church; and, not liking their looks, John hid behind a pillar. These men were robbers; and when they saw the bier they determined to steal the handsome shroud, reaching out towards it.

John was horrified by such sacrilege as robbing the dead. He now came forward and bade the men depart. The ruffians, however, were not so easily put off their vile deed; besides, they were two to one. Then John, determined to protect the dead man from being robbed, unstrapped his wallet and, flinging a purse at the robbers' feet, bade them take that instead. It was all the wealth he possessed—about forty golden pieces of money, left him by his father.

The rough men gloated over the shining gold and now asked, rather shamefaced, what price he was willing to pay them for their withdrawal. But John curtly bade them take all he had, depart, and leave the dead with him. Eagerly enough, the robbers gathered up the gold and shuffled out of the church.

John was left alone once more, minus his very small fortune. But he had prevented a dead man from being robbed. It was well. " Good night, Companion! " he said. He knelt before the altar and prayed a while. Then he went outside, lay down on the roadside a little farther along, and fell asleep.

Next morning John was awakened by the merry singing of a party of lively country girls. They sang a curious song about a Princess who caused all her lovers to lose their heads, but who was bound to lose her own, instead, some day, when the right man came along. " And that's the end of the story! " sang the girls.

John was so fascinated by this song, which had a merry lilting tune, that soon he was singing it himself. Then the girls told him what it all meant. Their King had a daughter, a beautiful Princess, whose lovers had either to guess a riddle she set them, or be hanged. If they guessed rightly, they would receive her as a bride and rule over half the kingdom. Otherwise they were handed over to the hangman.

Many young men had already tried the test and failed. The

Princess was so enchantingly beautiful that they had loved her at first sight and had willingly risked their lives—and lost. Consequently a row of skeletons in chains now hung in a certain avenue in the palace garden.

"Why don't you try your luck? You are a handsome young man and she may fall in love with you?" suggested the girls.

John declared he would do so. He felt excited and liked the idea of such an adventure. Besides, he had now no money and must make his fortune somehow.

Then, turning round, he saw a Stranger standing beside him—tall, thin, cadaverous, as though he had but little life in him. He introduced himself as John's Travelling Companion. John thought he had seen him before, but did not know where. The Stranger called him by his name. He also told him that yesterday, he, John, had possessed a purse of gold, but had done a good deed with it so that he was now penniless.

John was startled on hearing this. Was his new friend he who had lain beneath the shroud last night in the church? Perhaps. In any case, he offered his friendship; and John needed a friend.

But when the Travelling Companion advised him to be careful about the Princess and her riddle, John did not heed his words. Instead, he followed the peasants to the royal palace. The Travelling Companion followed behind, at a little distance.

.   .   .   .

In the square outside the palace a flight of steps led up to a terrace in front of the royal abode. It was the day for the Princess to propound her riddle, if any suitor should appear. She hoped that none *would* appear. She hated the young men to lose their lives. She only longed for love; and no suitor yet had inspired her with the love she desired. They all sought her rich worldly dower—not the bride herself, with her loving human heart.

As the King now joined his daughter on the terrace in front of the waiting crowd below, he likewise hoped that nobody would turn up to demand the test. He knew that his daughter was under a spell; and he hated her to give the hangman another victim, though powerless to prevent it.

But disappointment awaited both. As usual, on the stroke of noon, the royal herald stepped forward and called upon any aspirant for the Princess's hand and half of the kingdom besides to stand forth at once. Instantly there was a stir among the waiting crowd. Handsome young John, in his well-worn travelling garb, ran eagerly to the foot of the steps and announced himself as a suitor willing to undergo the test.

In vain the Travelling Companion, who accompanied him,

endeavoured to hold him back; in vain the crowd pointed to the row of skeletons dangling in an avenue near by—the gruesome remains of those who had failed to answer the riddle on former occasions. John had no sooner set eyes upon the fair Princess than he had loved her. He would gladly risk all for her—even his own life.

And as the Princess now stepped forward and gazed into the honest glowing eyes of the gallant but shabbily-clad youth, she likewise felt love awaken in her heart for the first time. But she knew he must die, for he would never be able to solve her riddle. She earnestly begged him, therefore, to depart at once. There was no compulsion for him to remain and risk his precious life. He was so young and fair; would he not go away at once?

But her pleadings had no effect upon brave John. He loved the Princess; and he would try to win her as his bride. "Tell me your riddle, Madam!" he demanded each time she tried to dissuade him.

At last, the Princess could refuse no longer, since the young man's demand was his bounden right. She must keep her royal word. "Tell me my thought!" she said; and, with despair in her heart, she turned and walked slowly back into the palace, followed by the King, equally sad.

This, then, was the famous riddle. What was the Princess thinking of? John must come back to the square at noon next day, with the correct answer, if he hoped to win the Princess and half the kingdom as her dowry. Otherwise, he must join the dismal company in the Avenue of Skeletons.

Everybody felt certain that he would provide yet another job for the hangman.

.   .   .   .

But the Travelling Companion thought otherwise. That same evening, as he walked beside John outside the palace, watching the lights go out, one by one, until only a single light remained—that in the Princess's own room—he bade the love-sick and worried youth to trouble himself no longer. He, the Travelling Companion, would find out the secret for him; and John must now retire to a humble lodging opposite and sleep without a care.

So full of authority was the voice of the Travelling Companion that John was fascinated; and his fears subsided. He went within doors; and the Travelling Companion was left alone in the shadows beneath the Princess's window.

Presently the Princess appeared on the balcony outside. It soon became evident to the Watcher below that the royal maiden knew something of magic. At first she uttered words of sadness, declaring that though joy was in her heart, sorrow was there, too. She knew that her lover must die.

Then she made an incantation. A mist suddenly appeared; and this gradually developed into a wild storm of wind, hail, rain, and thunder.

When the storm was at its height, the Princess spread out her arms and rose into the air, vanishing in the darkness of the clouds. Unknown to her, however, the Travelling Companion likewise rose into the air and followed closely behind her.

.   .   .   .

In a Wizard's cave in the heart of a wild mountain, a large company of goblins and gnomes were singing, dancing, and holding high revels. They were gambolling and cavorting around two rough-looking thrones in the centre of the cave. On one of these thrones, the old Wizard himself was sitting; the other was empty. It awaited the coming of the Princess, who was in the power of the Wizard. He regarded the Princess as his foster-child, and had taught her some of his own magic.

The Wizard soon stopped the revels, telling the goblins that the royal maiden was hastening thither on the wings of the wind. He was anxious, too, for he felt her unexpected coming boded no good. His fears were well founded.

Presently the Princess appeared at the top of the rough steps leading down into the cave from its entrance. A group of goblins danced forward to escort her to her throne. The Travelling Companion had also slipped in, unnoticed, behind the Princess. He hid in the shadows of the rocks, and nobody knew he was there. But he could see and hear all that passed.

No sooner had the Princess seated herself upon the throne than the Wizard knew, from her softened, sad manner, that something had happened to change her. She had fallen in love! Just the very thing he had hoped would never happen! For if this new lover passed the test, she would, by loving him, have broken the spell the Wizard had laid upon her. His magic power over her would then be gone for ever.

But this must not happen, decided the Wizard. He would make it impossible for this new bold suitor to guess her thought —which was to be his test.

"He also has a Magic—the Magic of Love!" declared the Princess. But the Wizard cried out triumphantly: "His Magic of Love will never guess your riddle! I command you to think only of *Me*! I, and I alone, will be your Thought! None can guess that, for nobody knows of Me!"

The Princess, still in the power of the Wizard, promised that he should be her thought on the morrow. Then she once more passed up the steps at the entrance to the cave, rose up into the air, and vanished into the darkness beyond on her return journey to the palace.

The Travelling Companion had heard all that had passed, and knew the secret he had sought. But he still had a deed to perform. He must make an end of this vile Wizard. He now came forth from the shadows, with a drawn sword in his hand. With one mighty stroke of the sword as it flashed through the air, the Wizard's head rolled on the ground; and the goblins all cowered back in craven fear. The Travelling Companion picked up the Wizard's head and wrapped it carefully in his cloak. He was ready to depart now. But these masterless goblins must not be left to do further mischief on their own account. The Travelling Companion raised his sword once more.

Instantly the cave fell in with a mighty crash, burying the goblins beneath it. At the same moment, the Travelling Companion rose into the air once more and followed in the wake of the Princess.

.   .   .   .

Next day at noon, the square outside the palace was again crowded with people. Everybody wanted to know the result of the riddle test.

When the royal party had appeared on the terrace, the Princess once more begged John to depart and not attempt to guess the answer to her riddle. There was still time, and none would say him nay. But if once he replied to the riddle with the wrong answer, his life was forfeited. She could not bear that.

But John had seen the answering light of love in the eyes of his fair Princess, and his own heart leaped at the sight. He boldly demanded his right to reply to the riddle. Very sadly the Princess then repeated her question: "What is my thought?"

Slowly, but still gazing into her eyes, John replied: "Your thought is dead, O Princess! Last night it died! Behold! Bid it farewell!"

He then unwrapped the cloak given him by the Travelling Companion; and the Wizard's head fell to the ground.

The Princess gazed upon those hated features for the last time; then, with great relief and unbounded joy, she fell into the open arms of her lover, John.

At that same moment, a rattling of chains and bones was heard in the gruesome avenue beyond. The skeletons had all disappeared, and, in their place, **an equal number of gaily-dressed** young men appeared, who now ran forward joyfully to dance with the pretty country girls.

The King and his people were likewise full of joy that the spell had been broken; and everybody began to sing once more the lilting song John had heard before. This time, however, they altered the words to this effect:

> " The man has come that *keeps* his head,
> And Madam has lost her own instead;
> So that's the end of the story! "

. . . .

Not quite the end of the story, however. As happy John and his beautiful Princess walked hand-in-hand towards the palace to join in the merry-making already beginning in honour of this joyful occasion, they invited the Travelling Companion to come with them.

But the Stranger shook his head. He said he could not enter the palace, but must return whence he had come.

Then he turned and walked away slowly towards the church; and the Princess and John watched him until he had vanished from sight.

That night, in the church, a lifeless form, still covered with its richly-embroidered fringed shroud, once more lay on its bier before the altar, alone and quiet. The Travelling Companion had paid his debt an hundred-fold. He now rested in peace.

DIE FLEDERMAUS[1]　　　　　　*Johann Straus*
(*The Bat*)

IT was late afternoon in a fashionable watering-place near a great Austrian city, on a certain day during the eighteenth century. An air of unrest seemed to hover over the household of the gay Baron Gabriel von Eisenstein.

Outside, a rich tenor voice was singing a sweet and sentimental serenade. There was no unrest about this singer. His insistent singing, however, soon distracted the attention of Adèle, the Baroness's pretty waiting-maid, from her eager reading of a letter from her sister Molly, a ballet-dancer. The latter had been invited

[1] With kind permission of Josef Weinberger Ltd., London, owners of the stage performing rights.

to attend a grand party to be given that night to the ladies of the
Ballet by a Russian millionaire, Prince Orlofsky; and she suggested that Adèle should join her there. Adèle could pretend to
be an artiste, too; she could also wear one of her mistress's fine
gowns—surreptitiously borrowed for the occasion.

Adèle was delighted at the idea. But her mistress's consent for
her absence must first be secured. This would not be easy; there
was trouble in the house that day. Adèle was worried; and the
singing outside exasperated her. She rushed to the window and
told the singer to leave the garden at once.

At that moment, her lovely mistress, the charming Baroness
Rosalinda, entered the room, equally worried. When Adèle asked
for a few hours' absence that evening, in order " to visit a sick
aunt ", she flatly refused to let her go. She could not be left alone.
Had Adèle forgotten that her master had to go to prison that
evening? The Baron had foolishly managed to get on the wrong
side of the law. Being hot-tempered as well as gay, he had had
a difference of opinion with a sheriff's officer, having struck the
latter with a whip and called him " a donkey ". For this irregu-
larity he had been sentenced to five days' imprisonment, to begin
that evening. So Adèle must stay to comfort her mistress.

As Adèle departed, weeping with disappointment, the singer
from outside slipped in. He proved to be Alfred, the former
singing-master of Rosalinda and likewise a sometime sweetheart.
The pair were delighted to meet again; but when Alfred became
too loverlike, Rosalinda, though flattered, bade him keep his
distance, reminding him that she was now a married woman.
However, she agreed to let him visit her again later that evening,
after her husband had departed for his five days' incarceration.

No sooner had Alfred departed, than the Baron came in,
followed by his lawyer, Dr. Blind, with whom he was having a
violent altercation. By some stupidity or other, Blind had actually
caused his sentence to be extended to *eight* days! No wonder he
was annoyed!

However, when Dr. Blind had gone, he became more resigned.
At least, he had received permission to dine with his charming
wife that evening, before beginning his sentence. But he must
not be long over the meal, or Frank, the Governor of the Gaol,
would himself come to fetch him away.

Eisenstein rang the bell for Adèle and ordered her to fetch in
immediately an expensive dinner from the nearby inn, " The
Golden Lion ". Noticing her red eyes, he asked what was wrong.
On hearing that she wanted leave of absence because her aunt
" was dangerously ill ", he declared that such a statement was

nonsense. He had himself just seen the dame in question riding along on a donkey, as lively as a cricket. Collapse of poor Adèle, who now rather sulkily hurried away to fetch in the dinner!

Dr. Falke, a Notary and an intimate old friend of the Baron's, now arrived. He had come in to help "cheer up the convict", he said. He also had concocted a plot to pay off an old score upon his friend—but this plot he kept to himself for the time being. Three years ago, he and the Baron had attended a fancy-dress Carnival, he as a "Bat" and the latter as a "Butterfly". They had enjoyed a particularly hilarious time, resulting in the "Bat" becoming intoxicated. When driving home together later on, the "Butterfly", as a joke, had stopped the carriage and put out the already snoring "Bat" on the roadside. Consequently, on awakening next morning, the doctor had been compelled to walk home in his tight and uncomfortable Carnival dress, to the accompanying jeers of street urchins and passers-by. Ever since he had been known by the nickname of "Dr. Bat"—to his annoyance. He now hoped, however, to play an equally amusing trick on the Baron, in return.

While Rosalinda was fetching wine to cheer them all, Falke now invited the Baron to go with him to the grand supper-party to be given that evening by Prince Orlofsky to the ladies of the Ballet. He could easily spend a few merry hours at this party and still be in plenty of time to present himself at the prison before next morning. To be on the safe side, too, he could be introduced at the party as the "Marquis de Renaud". His wife, of course, need know nothing of this little jaunt; he could bid her farewell just as though going off to prison.

The Baron, always ripe for a gay escapade of this kind, gladly agreed to accept his friend's invitation; and "Dr. Bat" departed well pleased and looking forward to the amusing development of his secret plot later on.

Instead, therefore, of donning the shabby old clothes produced by Rosalinda as suitable for prison wear, von Eisenstein hastened to dress himself in his most gorgeous evening garb, declaring he meant to let "those Jacks-in-Office" realize that he was somebody of importance and not a Baron for nothing.

When, too, Adèle presently set on the table the appetizing meal of calf's head she had fetched from "The Golden Lion", he refused to touch it. He now said he must not keep the prison authorities waiting any longer—greatly to the surprise of his wife. However, he took the little bouquet of flowers which decorated the calf's head, and stuck it in his button-hole. Then, with a loving farewell to Rosalinda—not omitting to steal a kiss from the pert and pretty Adèle—he very cheerfully departed, ostensibly to prison but actually to the party.

Meanwhile, Rosalinda had already informed Adèle that she could take the evening off, after all. As she now expected her old lover to call, the maid's presence might be embarrassing. Consequently Adèle now gladly rushed away to array herself secretly in one of her mistress's many fine gowns. When ready, she hurried off to join her sister at the Prince's party, without being seen again by the Baroness.

But Rosalinda was soon enjoying a thrilling hour with Alfred, the singing-master who, on keeping his engagement, promptly made himself very much at home. Not only was his love-making somewhat warmer than Rosalinda had bargained for but, entering the adjoining dressing-room, he laughingly donned the Baron's best brocaded dressing-gown and gold-tasselled smoking-cap. He then sat down to enjoy the succulent supper ordered by the Baron and to drink the latter's most expensive wines.

Soon he became extremely lively, and sang loudly in the rich tenor voice which still had power to thrill the heart of Rosalinda.

Then came a sudden interruption. Frank, the Governor of the Gaol, arrived, to the dismay of the Baroness. He declared that as the Baron had not yet turned up at the prison, he had come himself, in a friendly manner, to convey him thither in a private cab.

Very naturally, he took the lively Alfred to be the Baron, seeing him supping there hilariously, most domestically attired in dressing-gown and smoking-cap; and Rosalinda was in a quandary. She would be horribly compromised if she denied that Alfred was her husband. Therefore, he must pretend to be the Baron for the time being!

Fortunately the singer was already in the good-humoured stage of semi-intoxication; and he made no objection to obliging his former sweetheart in her present predicament when she whispered to him to keep up the fiction that he was actually her husband.

Consequently, Frank was completely unaware that, as he presently drove off with his captive, he was about to lock up, not von Eisenstein, but Alfred, the tenor singing-master.

.   .   .   .   .   .

Meanwhile, the hilarious party given by Prince Orlofsky was at its height. The charming ladies of the Ballet had turned up in great force—among them, pretty Molly and her even prettier sister, Adèle. The latter—introduced as "Olga" and dressed richly in her borrowed gown—was a brilliant success and soon proved herself the most popular lady present. She was clever, witty, and naturally a good actress and dancer; and she was soon surrounded by gay admirers.

Among the latter was von Eisenstein, the pseudo " Marquis de Renaud ". Although he had at first recognized Adèle as his wife's maid—and wearing Rosalinda's best gown, too, the pert little minx!—he soon found it convenient to forget this fact and, instead, to enjoy a pleasant flirtation with her. She was the prettiest girl present! He was having an extremely good time.

But Falke—" Dr. Bat "—had not forgotten the trick he meant to play on his old friend. He asked the Prince's permission to send a hurried note to Rosalinda, inviting her also to attend the party. When she presently arrived—glad of a frolic, after her unlucky interlude with Alfred earlier in the evening!—he easily persuaded her to impersonate a Hungarian Countess and, in that guise, to wear a mask. By so doing, she would be able to play a joke upon her husband and get even with him, since the latter had obviously deceived her by coming to a party instead of going to prison.

Rosalinda quickly entered into this prank—being rather indignant with her gay Gabriel for showing such marked attention to her dressed-up maid. She soon lured the susceptible Baron away from " Olga " and had him ensnared by her own vivacious charm. The pretended " Marquis ", having already imbibed plenty of the sparkling wine so generously supplied by his wealthy host, had no idea that the mysterious but fascinating masked lady was his own wife. Before long, therefore, Rosalinda had succeeded in abstracting from him his magnificent jewelled repeater-watch, which he had dangled before her eyes—this being his usual method of impressing pretty ladies of easy virtue. She intended to use this famous watch as evidence against him later on.

Another guest at the party was Frank, the Governor of the Gaol. Likewise at the invitation of " Dr. Bat ", he had hurriedly come to the festive scene after seeing Alfred, the singing-master, safely lodged in a comfortable cell under the name of Baron von Eisenstein. In accordance with Falke's complicated plot, he was announced as the " Chevalier Chagrin ". He was soon introduced to the " Marquis ", having no idea that the latter was the real Baron von Eisenstein who, by rights, should now be languishing in one of his own cells as a " Guest of the State ". The pair got on together famously; but the disguised Baron would not have joked so light-heartedly with this jovial " Chevalier " had he known that the latter was, truly, his gaoler.

As the evening went on, more complications arose; and Falke

began to find his mischievous plot getting somewhat out of hand. Especially was this the case when the Prince and his guests presently demanded to be told the famous story of how he had earned his nickname of " Dr. Bat ". Before he had time to give the story a turn more to his own advantage, the pretended " Marquis " broke in and, taking the words out of his mouth, related the comical incident exactly as it had occurred. He, the " Bat ", was thus more laughed at than ever before.

After this, the fun waxed fast and furious. More and more champagne was consumed; more and more light and airy lovemaking went on; and the music, singing, and gay dancing became more and more deliriously joyous.

But, at last, daylight broke, and the wonderful party came to an end. Hats and cloaks were called for, and carriages came lumbering up for those fortunate enough to own such luxuries. All the other guests, now thoroughly well mixed up and clinging on to one another, singing snatches of lively songs and vowing eternal friendship, found their way home as best they could.

.   .   .   .

Early next morning, when the still champagne-bemused Frank returned to the gaol, he felt anything but Governor-like. As he staggered into his office, his chief gaoler, Frosch—who was likewise somewhat uncertain on his feet, having found some excellent gin in the stores during his chief's absence—met him with the news that his captive of the evening before was singing at the top of his voice. He had also asked to be legally defended, and Dr. Blind, the lawyer, had been sent for.

Both Frank and Frosch still saw everything in double or treble form; but each put down his temporary defective vision to his own individual indulgence of the previous night.

While they were talking together, the outer bell rang, which Frosch answered in person. Next moment he ushered into the office Adèle and Molly.

The unexpected appearance of two of the pretty girls he had flirted with at the party revived the Governor quickly; and, dismissing Frosch, he prepared to continue his amusement of the night before.

The two girls, however, declared that they had come solely to make confession of their little deception, explaining that Adèle was not really a ballet-dancer, but, instead, was lady's maid to the Baroness von Eisenstein. Adèle, however, added that she wanted to become an actress, and felt she would be a good one—and would the Governor help to get her trained? Frank, remembering her success at the party, agreed with her that she was certainly much too bright to be wasting her time as a maid. Adèle, delighted, then began to prove her talents by an exhibition of reciting and singing, acting first the part of a soubrette and then that of a great lady of quality.

Another ring at the bell brought confusion; and the two girls had to be temporarily locked up in a cell to prevent their being seen by this next early visitor.

The new arrival proved to be von Eisenstein, who had come at last to give himself up and serve his sentence. He was amazed to see his latest friend, the " Chevalier Chagrin ", awaiting him; and he was still more amazed on now learning that the " Chevalier " and Frank, the Governor of the Gaol, were one and the same person.

He then announced himself as the Baron von Eisenstein; but this fact the Governor positively refused to believe. The latter declared that he already had the Baron safely locked up, having himself fetched him away from his home the evening before. He had found the Baron, comfortably clad in his dressing-gown and smoking-cap, supping happily with his wife; and he had come away to prison without any fuss. This morning, he had called for a lawyer; and Dr. Blind was expected at any moment.

Von Eisenstein knew now that his pretty wife had obviously been up to mischief during his absence; and he was both angry and upset, since he loved Rosalinda dearly. He determined to find out more about this affair. When, therefore, Frank was presently called away to attend personally to the release of Molly and Adèle—who were now calling out to be set free—and the lawyer, Dr. Blind, had arrived in the office in answer to the request of Alfred, he soon got busy. He unceremoniously hustled the protesting Blind into an adjoining room, made him hand over his wig, lawyer's gown, and spectacles, and then arrayed himself in the same.

Consequently, when Alfred, the singing-master, was presently ushered into the office by the gaoler, it was the Baron who interviewed him in his disguise as a lawyer.

But a further shock was in store for von Eisenstein. Rosalinda herself had now arrived at the prison thus early, hoping to arrange for Alfred's escape before the advent of her husband, the legitimate captive. She rushed into the Governor's office just as Alfred had been brought thither; and the pair were talking excitedly together when the pretended lawyer entered.

Unable to keep up his disguise for long, however, von Eisenstein soon revealed his true identity, and furiously stormed at the culprits—and particularly at his wife for deceiving him.

But Rosalinda had a trump card up her sleeve. She slyly retaliated by producing the splendid jewelled repeater-watch which she had managed so cleverly to abstract the night before. And when von Eisenstein now realized that she was indeed the mysterious and fascinating " Hungarian Countess " he had flirted with so outrageously at the Prince's party, he calmed down immediately. It was a case of the pot calling the kettle black !

At this moment, too, most amazingly, Prince Orlofsky, Dr. Falke—the " Bat "—and a host of the other party guests, came swarming into the room, full of laughter.

Having enjoyed a good joke at the expense of his gay friend, Falke now explained that the whole affair was nothing but a frolic he had planned in merry retaliation of the Carnival incident, when he himself had been the victim and had been compelled to walk through the streets in the garb of a Bat. He had at last, however, been able to prove that " Bats have claws "! And could use them, too! The Prince and his guests had all had a share in this huge practical joke, which had been great fun.

So everybody was satisfied—especially Adèle, who now got her heart's desire. The wealthy Prince, greatly struck by her un-doubted histrionic abilities, undertook to have her trained for the stage, with himself as her patron.

And though the little flirtatious interlude of pretty Rosalinda and her singing-master had not exactly also been contrived by the " Bat ", the Baron himself did not know this, and nobody en-lightened him—so why worry? Rosalinda certainly did not! Instead, she very gladly fell into her greatly-relieved husband's loving arms, well pleased to be there.

ARABELLA[1] — *Richard Strauss*

VIENNA was at its gayest in 1860, and lightsome music, waltzing feet, and merry laughter greeted one on every side.

The dance-salons, concert-halls, promenades, and public gardens were always well packed with gorgeously-garbed officers—nearly all of them bearing titles—accompanied by elegantly-crinolined ladies. This did not mean, however, that these dazzling gentle-men were necessarily suitors of a kind acceptable to certain prudent

[1] Copyright, 1933, by Richard Strauss.

parents with pretty daughters to launch in the matrimonial market.

Such a disturbing thought especially occupied the somewhat calculating minds of Count Waldner and his good lady, the Countess Adelaide; indeed, they were just at their wits' end at this moment.

Waldner was a decidedly impoverished member of the aristocracy, having made severe inroads into his never-too-large fortune during his early days as a cavalry officer; and since his retirement he had become considerably less solvent, owing to his indulgence in high living of various kinds, mainly gambling. He would, indeed, soon have become entirely disreputable had it not been for his foolishly frivolous, but more practical wife. The latter, having two very charming daughters to find husbands for, kept him up to the mark and insisted on the family retaining as fair a position as possible in the best Viennese society, even though their debts continued to mount high.

Consequently, though extremely hard-up, Count and Countess Waldner established themselves during the season in a somewhat shabby apartment in one of the less expensive hotels in Vienna—though they were frequently at loggerheads with the management, owing to their extravagance and lack of means to support it.

Here they concentrated on getting their elder and more beautiful daughter, Arabella, successfully married to someone rich enough to retrieve the family fortunes.

This, however, was no easy matter; for though Arabella was a particularly charming and well-brought-up girl, always obedient to her parents' wishes, she was too modest and ladylike to run after any of the more popular prizes so promptly snapped up by the more audacious girls. True, she had many admirers—in particular, a quartette of smart young officers, three of whom were Counts; but, alas, these young men, though most agreeable, were all ineligibles with no particular prospects. Nor, in their turn, could they afford to marry a portionless beauty—though Matteo, an almost penniless young chasseur, was so greatly attracted by the charming Arabella that he was in almost continual attendance upon her.

As for Zdenka, the younger sister, she had no chance at all until Arabella was firmly established in life. Consequently, when in the public eye, it was decided that she should appear to be a boy; and she was compelled by her parents to masquerade in male attire as a youth in the Vienna apartment.

Zdenka, however, though not so beautiful as Arabella, had all the sentimental yearnings common to any other young girl; and, to her own discomfort, she had already conceived a romantic attachment for Matteo, her sister's most ardent admirer. Mindful of her parent's desire for her own incognito, she carefully kept her secret hidden from all, and, in particular, from Matteo. To add to her woes, however, the latter constantly sought the supposed youth's sympathy and aid in furthering his forbidden pursuit of Arabella—and though the two sisters were passionately attached to one another, poor Zdenka suffered much in thus acting as a go-between.

It was at this time that, finding no sufficiently eligible suitor for his daughter in Vienna, the impecunious Count Waldner, in despair, wrote to an old army friend—by name Mándryka—now living in the wilds of Transylvania, where he had amassed great riches in farming; and to this long-neglected friend of his youth, Waldner suggested his fair young daughter as a possible bride, knowing him to be still unmarried. He also enclosed a picture of beautiful Arabella to clinch the matter.

When the reply to this bold appeal arrived, it announced that Mándryka was already on his way to Vienna, being very willing to consider the suggestion made in the Count's letter.

On the day on which this wealthy stranger was expected to arrive there was great excitement in the Waldner family; and though Arabella had no desire to wed a man as old as her own father, she was sweetly obedient to the latter's will. It was arranged that she should not meet this very eligible suitor until that night at the Coachmen's Ball—a popular function which the *élite* of Vienna was attending; and thus she would be seen for the first time by the stranger in her most attractive festive garb.

While the ladies were dressing for this splendid ball, Mándryka was announced to Count Waldner, who was astounded when a handsome young man walked into the reception-room at his hotel. The young man explained that he was indeed Mándryka, but was the nephew and heir of the older Mándryka who had been the friend and contemporary of the Count. His uncle had recently died, so that Waldner's letter had been opened by the young Mándryka, who had promptly fallen in love with the charming picture of Arabella enclosed within it; and he had now come to offer himself as her suitor.

Though Mándryka was not of noble birth and had not the polished address of the elegant young Viennese gentlemen, he was handsome, presentable, and undoubtedly sincere, honest and straightforward—a " rough diamond " backwoodsman and hunter, who had made good. What was more important, however, was the pleasant fact that he was now extremely wealthy, having inherited his uncle's fortune; and this consideration made him highly desirable in the eyes of the financially worried Count.

Consequently, the latter felt real pride and satisfaction when Mándryka eagerly offered himself as Arabella's husband-elect; and he accepted his suit with great relief. He was delighted, too, when, presently, Mándryka lavishly ordered expensive wines, and made a considerable show with his hussar in attendance and his two menservants.

Later on, at the grand ball which he was invited likewise to attend, Mándryka, on being presented to the exquisitely-attired Arabella, seemed spellbound by her beauty; and from falling in love with her picture, he now averred his love for her in the actual flesh, and was overjoyed when she expressed her willingness to be his bride.

Arabella, herself, was instantly attracted by Mándryka, whose forthright sincerity and reverentially idealistic attitude to love she quickly realized from his conversation; and she rejoiced that by wedding him she could thus do her duty by her parents and retrieve the family fortunes, and at the same time satisfy her own heart, which had so promptly felt an answering love.

Consequently, she now gave the cold shoulder to all her former admirers, one by one, as they presented themselves before her; and she refused to dance with them.

The love-sick Matteo, on hearing the news of her engagement, was plunged into the depths of despair; and in this state of gloom he was presently discovered by Zdenka—the latter still wearing the garb of a youth, though now hoping at last to appear shortly as a young girl on the marriage of Arabella.

Coming upon Matteo in a sheltered alcove of the gay ball-room, Zdenka was horrified to hear the man she herself so dearly loved threaten to take his life because Arabella no longer smiled upon him and had refused to dance with him; but, though her own heart was aching with misery, she did her best to comfort him. Several times before this, in the hope of keeping up the pretence that her sister still loved him, though bound by duty to her parents to await the arrival of a wealthier suitor, Zdenka had made Matteo momentarily happy by handing him love-letters purporting to come from Arabella, though these had all been written by herself.

Now more alarmed than ever by his present despairing condition, she slipped into his hand yet another tender little note ostensibly coming from her sister, but likewise written by herself, together with a key which she mendaciously declared Arabella had sent to him with a request to meet her in the hall of her hotel apartment that night after the ball—for which rendezvous her sister would return alone a little earlier. They would thus be able to enjoy a few blissful minutes together before the return of the rest of the party.

Unluckily this little scene and interview was observed and over-heard by the clean-living Mándryka, who was horrified by such seeming duplicity on the part of one so newly-betrothed; and he sought out Count Waldner at once to inform him of this assignation.

Meanwhile, having given Matteo the key, Zdenka hurried away to her home apartment, already somewhat fearful of the consequences of her rash act—having been anxious only to save her beloved Matteo from taking his life then and there, as he had threatened to do. Now she began to be alarmed lest her equally well-beloved Arabella should suffer because of this dangerously equivocal appointment she had just made in her name. She resolved, therefore, to masquerade in Arabella's clothes, and to keep the clandestine meeting herself, trusting that in the already dimmed hotel lights, Matteo, in his agitation, would take her to be, indeed, Arabella.

Before the resourceful Zdenka could carry out her resolve, however, and before she had even divested herself of her boy's garb, the trouble she feared actually came to pass.

Arabella, on returning from the ball, was the first member of the Count's party to enter her home hotel, where, to her amaze-ment, she found Matteo awaiting her in the hall at the foot of the staircase. She was further amazed when the young officer addressed her in lover-like terms, thanking her for her letter and for the key she had sent to him.

Indignant on finding her former admirer thus awaiting her, fearful for her own maidenly reputation and completely mystified by his declaration that she herself had invited him to come thither and had even sent him the key of her room, Arabella repulsed all Matteo's advances, and bade him a curt good night. She was just about to hurry up the staircase to escape his further importunities, when the outer door was opened once more and her father, mother, and Mándryka entered, all in a state of the greatest agitation.

For Mándryka, furious at the making of the assignation he had inadvertently overheard and at the handing over to Matteo of Arabella's key by Zdenka, had informed Count Waldner and his wife of the infamy of their fair daughter, declaring that he could no longer offer himself as her suitor.

Terribly upset by this disastrous news, which thus wrecked all their hopes of retrieving their fallen fortunes, the Count and

Countess had begged Mándryka at least to return home with them to seek an explanation from their imprudent and foolish daughter, whom they declared could not be at such fault as he described.

But when, on entering the hall of the hotel, they actually beheld Arabella and Matteo talking together agitatedly at the foot of the staircase, the truth of Mándryka's allegation seemed proved beyond the shadow of a doubt. In vain did the mystified and now nearly frantic Arabella declare her innocence. She could not convince the plain and simple backwoodsman from Transylvania that Matteo was not there at her own invitation; and the disillusioned young man was filled with woe on thus seeing his hoped-for idyllic romance fading before his eyes.

The Count and Countess, likewise furious in their disappointment, loudly blamed their unhappy daughter; and a general hubbub of scoldings, accusations, counter-accusations, and recriminations now ensued.

Then, suddenly, there came a strange interruption. When the hubbub was at its height, the slender figure of a fair young girl, clad in a loose feminine white robe hastily gathered around her graceful form, was seen descending the staircase. It was Zdenka, no longer disguised as a boy, who, hearing the commotion below and fearing its cause, had snatched up her sister's *négligé* and hastened down the stairs to explain matters.

In vain the Countess tried foolishly and ineffectually to hide Zdenka's now plainly feminine figure behind her own outdoor cloak. The cat was out of the bag; and it had already been realized by the two young men that this agitated vision of beauty was no stripling but a charming young girl.

In contrite tones, Zdenka confessed to her desperate escapade even admitting her own love for Matteo; and Arabella gladly forgave the sister she loved so dearly—whose pitiful little romance she now guessed for the first time. When, too, Matteo now realized that Zdenka had loved him all the time she had been aiding him in his hopeless pursuit of her sister, he was deeply touched. Knowing, too, that Arabella was lost to him for ever and admiring the now plainly visible maidenly charms of the sportsman-like "boy-girl", he was willing enough to accept the sincere love she had to offer him; and he folded her gladly in his arms.

Meanwhile, Mándryka, likewise contrite, but joyfully relieved by this curious turn of events, humbly begged Arabella to forgive him his temporary distrust of her—which she graciously did, knowing that there had certainly been seeming cause for his doubts of her.

For some little time longer, the Count and Countess stormed at their younger daughter for the trouble she had caused; but at last, seeing that their eager hopes of worldly comfort would still be realized, after all, they smiled once more upon the quartette of now happy lovers, and even gave consent also to the formal betrothal of Zdenka and the ineligible Matteo.

So all was well that ended well, and peace at last descended upon the now rapturously happy Arabella and her family.

ARIADNE ON NAXOS   *Richard Strauss*

IN the large and richly-decorated hall of the splendid town mansion of a great noble, one early evening during the seventeenth century, last-minute preparations were being made for an entertainment which was to follow the banquet already taking place. A stage had been set up at the back of the hall, and various small rooms on either side of it had been converted into dressing-rooms for the performers. All was hustle and confusion in the hall; and the noise of scene-decorators and stage-carpenters putting final touches to their work mingled with the strains of lively music which sounded through the closed doors of the banqueting-hall beyond.

Into the midst of this bustling scene, the music-master, who was responsible for the production of a specially commissioned grand opera that evening, hastened in a great state of perturbation.

Seeing a gorgeously-clad Major-Domo approaching he ran up to him and demanded excitedly the truth of a message he had just received—that the serious operatic work of his pupil on the dramatic subject of *Ariadne on Naxos* commissioned for the evening's festivities was to be followed by a comic dancing interlude, a sort of vulgar Italian opera *buffa* and Harlequinade.

On hearing that this was indeed the case and that, moreover, the two entertainments must be hastily performed and follow one another without a moment's delay, since a grand display of fireworks was to take place promptly at nine o'clock, he indignantly protested against this outrage; and he declared that his pupil, the composer, would never permit his inspired and artistic work to appear in such an unsuitable medley.

The pompous and self-conceited Major-Domo, however, was equally shocked on his part that a mere music-master, or even a

Y

composer, should dare to question the will or whim of his august master—who was paying well for the "crotchets and quavers" supplied to his order. He added that the suppliers should be well satisfied with such payment and the "honour of exhibiting their tricks" at the festivities.

In despair at this vandalism and shocked that a work of high art should be treated with such scant respect, the music-master departed to seek his pupil and to break the dreadful news to him as gently as possible.

Scarcely had he gone, than a gay young officer appeared and, roughly thrusting aside the lackey who conducted him, unceremoniously entered the dressing-room allotted to Zerbinetta, the pretty and flirtatious actress who was to dance and play the part of Columbine in the Harlequinade—of whom he was at present the lover.

As the lackey staggered back, he was accosted by the composer entering hurriedly, who nervously besought him to find the musicians at once, as he desired to have a final short rehearsal that he might make a few changes of certain passages in his opera. He added that he also wished to rehearse some bars with the Prima Donna who was to play Ariadne.

The lackey, however, with an air of insolent contempt for one so obviously poor and unimportant, declared that the musicians were at present playing during the serving of the banquet, and that the Prima Donna was in her dressing-room and must not be disturbed.

Left alone, the composer was very uneasy, though still unsuspicious of the further indignity in store for him and his masterpiece; but he was soon somewhat comforted by the sudden inspiration of an exquisite melody which came into his mind at that moment.

His joy in this inspiration, however, was short-lived. Almost immediately afterwards, the door of another dressing-room was burst open and the principal tenor—already garbed in his costume as Bacchus—appeared, carrying in his hand a wig of light-coloured flowing locks which he flourished in a rage in the face of a protesting wigmaker who followed him, and whose ears he now boxed for bringing him a wig he did not like. After a violent altercation the wigmaker departed in a pet, while the angry tenor retired once more, banging his door and refusing to take the slightest notice of the composer, who timidly asked for some paper on which to jot down his notes.

The music-master now returned, and from him the unfortunate composer heard of the unelevating programme of which his opera was to form a part. A few moments later the various members of the two companies met together in the hall, the operatic singers regarding the other performers with contemptuous disapproval.

Zerbinetta, the leader of the merry Harlequinade troupe, seated herself in the midst of her company and proceeded to daub on her stage complexion, with the assistance of Harlequin, Scaramuccio and the other characters—including her dancing-master producer —with all of whom she flirted with the cool impudence of an acknowledged beauty. This merry company spoke with disparagement of the " dull stuff " of the piece which was to precede their own gay antics; while the tenor and Prima Donna, on their part, expressed lofty disdain for the dancing comedians. The music-master and the dancing-master each endeavoured to comfort their leading ladies with fulsome praises.

While this exchange of discourtesies was proceeding, the Major-Domo entered the hall with a high and mighty air, and made an announcement with greater pomposity than ever. His noble lord had commanded that, owing to the unusual length of the banquet and to the fact that the fireworks must commence promptly at nine o'clock, it would be necessary for the operatic performers and the comedians to combine their efforts and to play their pieces upon the stage at one and the same time. Both must be cut down accordingly; and it was thus necessary to hasten forward any changes the actors might wish to make as the performance must commence within a few minutes. A storm of indignation now burst forth from the composer because his fine tragic opera would thus be made a travesty of; and wildly he declared that he would withdraw his work and company at once. The music-master, though in a terrible quandary, reminded him of the fee of fifty ducats upon which he had counted on living for the next six months; and the dancing-master, eager to arrange the simultaneous performance for a like reason, also begged him to make the necessary cuts and to allow his piece to proceed—declaring that many of the great masters of the past had been obliged to make similar sacrifices in order to secure a first hearing. Thus practically compelled by dire necessity to this miserable course, the unfortunate composer, rumpling up his hair in despair, opened his music score and feverishly began to make the required large cuts, wincing and exclaiming at each as though it were a gash in his sensitive flesh.

Meanwhile, Zerbinetta, having already had the outline of the story of Ariadne's desertion of Theseus related to her in facetious fashion by the dancing-master, declared merrily that in the comned play they must quickly provide this unfortunate classical heroine with a new admirer, since a constant succession of lovers was desired by all women. On hearing this the composer sprang up and declared passionately that Ariadne was a high-souled woman who could love but one man for ever, and so craved for death when he deserted her. When the music-master, however, admitted that Ariadne's prayer was answered by the coming of Bacchus, the god of eternal youth, Zerbinetta laughed gaily and knowingly, declaring she knew that something of this kind would certainly be the case. Though the composer explained that his Ariadne believed that Bacchus was Death coming for her as she had prayed, the lively and coquettish Columbine still clung to her opinion that the deserted one would choose to live rather than die at the approach of a new lover.

In practical fashion she then announced to her company of comic players her own version of the story, and arranged which portions they should enliven with their dances and fooling, heedless of the wretched composer's simultaneously continued relation of a tragic and devoted love. Undeterred, Zerbinetta even tried her coquettish arts upon the latter to such an extent that the simple-minded composer was for the moment deceived into a sudden interest in her, so that he forgot his woes and relapsed into an ecstatic state, extolling the beauties of music and forgetful of his surroundings.

Meanwhile, the music-master had pacified the Prima Donna by declaring that her high artistic performance would stand out all the more prominently in comparison with the silly frivolities of the commonplace little Zerbinetta; and the performance was now ready to begin, the guests of the noble lord having entered and seated themselves in front, the musicians being already in their places.

When, however, the ecstatic composer suddenly came to earth and beheld the fantastic figures of Harlequin, Scaramuccio, and their companions waiting in the wings ready to join in the performance as the opening bars of his beloved opera sounded, it was more than he could endure; and with a despairing gesture he rushed away distractedly. The music-master, though shaking his head sadly in sympathy with his unfortunate pupil, decided to make the best of things; and, giving the signal, the curtain went up. Though the resulting combined entertainment was fantastic and whimsical enough, the exquisite music held its own throughout, the characters in the opera calmly performing their parts and carrying out the classic theme entirely oblivious of the amusing antics of the comic players.

.   .   .   .

When the curtain went up, the Prima Donna, as Ariadne, was discovered lying motionless outside a cave on the desert island of Naxos, while a Naiad and a Dryad on either side of her with Echo in the background described her desertion by Theseus, for whom she had grieved and wept until exhausted. Presently, Ariadne, awakened to a consciousness of her surroundings by their songs, raised herself from the ground; then, remembering the tragedy of her present existence, she began to weep afresh and to pray for Death to bring oblivion to her sufferings and peace to her broken heart.

In the wings, Zerbinetta, Harlequin, and the others, sang songs and choruses to the weeping heroine on the stage, bidding her take a more cheerful view of life. Then, to enliven her further, Harlequin and the three clowns capered on to the stage and performed a lively and fantastically comical dance. As Ariadne took not the slightest notice of these antics, but continued her weeping and her mournful song, still craving for death as she awaited the expected coming of Hermes to lead her to the Land of Shades, Zerbinetta called back her company into the wings and herself danced lightly on to the stage. Approaching Ariadne with a deep obeisance, she sang to her a song, at first sympathizing with her woe and then enticing her to forget Theseus the deserter and to comfort herself instead by taking a new lover—coquettishly declaring that she herself had thus found comfort for the loss of our fickle sweethearts.

As Ariadne still paid no heed to her, she became impatient and diverted herself by indulging in a flirtation with Harlequin who had now skipped on to the stage once more. After this she danced and coquetted with all the other members of her company who had followed in his wake, fooling and playing with each in turn; and finally she flung herself into the arms of Harlequin and disappeared with him, leaving the others to pirouette alone in comic fashion.

As the three clowns, on finding themselves deserted by their charmer and her chosen admirer, presently capered off, somewhat sheepishly, the Naiad, the Dryad, and Echo hastened on to the stage in great excitement, talking together eagerly of a beautiful youth who had just landed upon the island from his boat. This was the tenor, arrayed as Bacchus, the beautiful god of Youth and of Wine. He was described by the nymphs as just returning from a voyage, during which he had nearly fallen into the toils of Circe, whose magic spells, however, he had managed to escape from, though with difficulty.

As the radiant young god now appeared, he sang forth a song of rejoicing in so sweet a voice that it immediately aroused the sorrowing Ariadne, who slowly arose and awaited the approach of the singer.

Gradually, Bacchus drew nearer and nearer towards the cave, still singing his glorious song; and then, as he beheld the drooping figure of Ariadne standing there, he was immediately enthralled by her beauty and entreated her to leave the island with him.

In her song of reply, Ariadne expressed her belief that the dazzling stranger was the messenger of Death for whom she craved and announced her willingness to enter his boat; then, in a tone of curiosity rather than of fear, she gently inquired of him how her translation would be effected, declaring that already he seemed to have worked some magical change in her.

Bacchus, appearing still more enthralled and expressing a quickly growing passion for the fair princess, declared that she herself was the enchantress who had wrought the change; but as he clasped her in his arms, Ariadne still declared that his must be the magic, since her humble cave seemed to have been transformed into the dazzling abode of a goddess.

Bacchus now gradually led her towards the transformed cave, singing her praises as he went, while Ariadne expressed her joy in such an exquisite realization of the death she had prayed for.

As they finally disappeared into the cave, however, Zerbinetta determined not to be out of this final scene, appeared from the wings and declared to the audience that when a new god came to woo, woman was ever ready to be taken captive once again.

Then, as the curtain fell, the voice of Bacchus was heard singing to Ariadne from within the cave his passionate declaration that the stars were more likely to die in their places than that Death should tear her from his arms.

ELEKTRA   *Richard Straus*

AFTER the murder of Agamemnon, King of Mycene, by his own Queen, Clytemnestra, and her paramour, Ægisthos, dark days fell to the lot of the Princesses of the land. Their unnatural mother, after marrying her guilty lover, was determined not to endure the just reproaches of her children; therefore, she degraded them to the rank of slaves, so that they might be kept out of her sight.

Her son, the young Prince Orestes, she had tried to slay at the time of the King's murder; but he had been saved from sharing the same terrible fate by the timely help of his sister, Elektra. He had, however, been forced to leave the country and had taken refuge in Phocis, where he remained for seven years—awaiting a favourable opportunity to return to Mycene and take vengeance upon his mother and her lover by slaying them both.

Meanwhile, his sisters, Elektra and Chrysothemis, were enduring great hardships in the palace at Mycene, where, after being degraded to the level of the slaves, they were subjected to many indignities. But worse than their own personal sufferings was the grief in their hearts, not only for the untimely death of their beloved father but for the banishment of their brother, for whose return they longed passionately.

In the heart of Chrysothemis, grief and the longing for freedom alone reigned; but in the heart of Elektra a desire for vengeance against her mother had obsessed every other natural feeling, and she lived only for the consummation of the vengeance she believed the gods would surely grant her.

She longed even more than did her sister for the return of their brother, Orestes, whom she intended to use as her instrument of justice; but when seven years had gone by she began to lose hope of his assistance. Her thirst for revenge, however, had not diminished one iota, but had increased with the years, having grown to be so completely a part of her being that she lived only to see it accomplished; and when, at the end of seven years, Orestes was still absent, she determined to carry out her fell design without him.

Though for the purposes of her intended crime, she endeavoured to hide her savage passion from the curious eyes around her, she could not altogether conceal it; and the light of burning hate which shone in her eyes when she gazed upon the guilty King and Queen was seen and marked by many. She was carefully shunned by her slave companions—all save one, who still kept to her allegiance and suffered the blows of her fellows for so doing— who despised her for the degraded position she had been forced into and spoke against her haughty behaviour and denunciatory words. Even Clytemnestra herself went in secret fear of her vengeful daughter and avoided her presence as much as possible.

One day, when seven years had gone by and still there came no signs of Orestes, Elektra's passionate feelings so far overcame her that she at last resolved to carry out vengeance upon the murderers of her royal father ere another sun should rise. To this end she sought the assistance of her sister, who was physically stronger than herself and could, therefore, use a weapon with surer effect.

Chrysothemis, however, was of a far gentler nature; and instead of having nursed feelings of vengeance in her heart during the seven dark years that had passed, she only desired freedom from her enforced servitude and the protecting care which a husband's love would give to her. Full of horror at Elektra's bloodthirsty designs, she entreated her to put away such terrible thoughts from her mind—declaring that their guilty mother already suspected her designs and would presently cause her to be cast into prison.

Hearing the Queen even now approaching, Chrysothemis departed, entreating her sister to accompany her; but Elektra was not afraid, and she determined to disarm suspicion from her mother's mind by holding flattering talk with her.

When Clytemnestra presently appeared, therefore, she addressed her in respectful tones, as though speaking to a goddess; and the Queen, completely deceived, desired her attendants to withdraw that she might talk alone with her seemingly humbled daughter, heedless of their whispered words of warning to her against the latter.

When the slaves had retired, Clytemnestra, who had a hunted, frightened look in her eyes, told the ragged Princess that she had been troubled with terrible dreams; and she asked her daughter's advice for recovering her peace of mind. Elektra, in a tone of deep mystery, declared that this could only be attained by the sacrifice of a woman—the deed to be done by a man who must be of noble nature and not base as was Ægisthos.

Immediately Clytemnestra guessed who was in the mind of Elektra—her own son, Orestes, of whom she went in constant fear, believing him to be still alive. Elektra, realizing from her mother's sudden look of fear that the latter had never received definite news of the death of Orestes—though she had caused false reports of the same to be given to her daughters—now flung off her pretended mood of mildness; and once more she furiously denounced the Queen as a murderess and declared that vengeance would surely fall upon her.

Clytemnestra shrank back in terror before her daughter's torrent of passionate words; but at that moment one of her attendants returned and informed her that a messenger had just arrived and had brought with him a report that Orestes was indeed dead.

Relieved by this, to her, welcome news, Clytemnestra retired to her own chamber with a laugh of triumphant scorn. Soon afterwards Chrysothemis ran weeping to Elektra, telling her of the report of their brother's death which had been given to her by the slave who had been sent by the Que n to inform Ægisthos of the fact.

Though stricken with woe at this confirmation of her own fear, Elektra once more earnestly entreated the help of her sister in carrying out her scheme of vengeance against the murderers of their father, telling her that she had already in hiding the great axe with which the guilty pair had done the fell deed. Though she promised her great honours and many gifts afterwards, and even offered to become her slave, Chrysothemis only trembled with horror at the idea of slaying her own mother. Utterly refusing to take part in so terrible a crime, she rushed away, followed by the curses of Elektra who, obsessed by her one desire for vengeance to the exclusion of every other natural emotion, now resolved to carry out her purpose alone and unaided.

As she moved away stealthily to unearth the hidden axe with which she intended to deal the fatal blow, she was accosted by a stranger who, noting her ragged and humble attire, mistook her for one of the slaves, and addressed her as such. When the Princess haughtily demanded his business, he informed her that he was the messenger who had come to announce the death of the young Prince, Orestes, declaring that he had been servant to the latter and had witnessed his end.

Full of grief and anger, Elektra passionately reproached the travel-worn messenger for being so poor-spirited as to be yet alive himself to bring news of the death of the Prince, for whom he should have been ready to give his own life; and the stranger, realizing from her noble bearing and poignant grief that she could be no slave but must be of some kin to the person of whom they spoke, now asked her name.

On learning that it was the Princess Elektra who stood before him, the stranger seemed deeply moved; and he drew nearer and whispered into her ears the words: "Orestes lives!"

At this moment, a party of the late King's own body-servants appeared and, kneeling before the stranger, greeted him as their prince and master.

Thus realizing that it was her own long-absent and dearly-loved brother, Orestes, who stood before her, Elektra greeted him joyfully; and the young Prince's brow darkened with deep anger when he learned from her of the degradation to which she and her sister had been subjected during his enforced absence.

Orestes also desired above all things to avenge the death of his father—having, in fact, spread the false reports of his own death in order to deceive Clytemnestra and Ægisthos into a mistaken sense of security from him, their most dreaded enemy; and he gladly agreed to Elektra's eager request for him to assist her by slaying the guilty pair.

Producing the great axe which her own weak arms would have failed to wield, the Princess quickly led Orestes to their mother's chamber. Next moment, Clytemnestra's screams brought forth her attendants and the Princess Chrysothemis upon the scene; and Elektra stood aside with a triumphant air upon her face, gloating over the fact that the vengeance for which she had lived was at last accomplished.

Ægisthos, hastening into the chamber as the Queen's dying groans pierced the air, was himself met by the avenging Orestes, who instantly dealt him his death-blow. Thus were the murderers of Agamemnon brought to justice by his own son.

The people of Mycene all rejoiced greatly at the deaths of the guilty King and Queen, who had ruled them with much tyranny; and with the wildest enthusiasm, they hailed Orestes at once as their new King, greeting him lustily as he presently appeared in their midst.

Chrysothemis at once joined her brother as he received the acclamations of the people; but Elektra, in her passionate exultation at the consummation of her long-desired vengeance, sang first a hymn of thanksgiving to the gods and then began to execute a marvellous dance of triumph.

All the people ceased their greetings to Orestes and watched the exultant Princess with bated breath, held spellbound by her wild and fantastic movements; but, heedless of them all, Elektra worked herself up into a mad frenzy of triumph, her dance growing ever wilder and wilder until, at last, utterly exhausted and spent, she fell lifeless at the feet of the new King.

FEUERSNOT[1]   *Richard Strauss*
(*Fire Famine . . . Beltane Fires . . . Johannis Fires . . . St. John's Eve*

IT was during the twelfth century that mysterious happening took place in Munich one Midsummer's Eve.

According to their usual custom the children of the town were out collecting wood for the bonfires that were always lighted on that festival night. Beltane Fires they called these special bonfires All the young folk danced around them on Midsummer's Eve, and

[1] Copyright, 1901 and 1928, by Fürstner Ltd., London W.1.

sang and made a great noise. Another thing. If any young man
was bold enough to leap through the flames and to seize and kiss
his sweetheart on the opposite side, he was regarded as a fine
fellow, indeed. Good luck, too, would go with his love-making.

So, good bonfires were necessary; and the children of Munich
saw to that. From house to house they went, collecting wood from
each and piling it into sacks or baskets, or even into hand-carts.

To-night they were in extra good form; and they sang and made
a great commotion as they banged upon the door of the Burgomaster's house. They felt pretty sure they would get a good
supply of wood here. They did.

Diemut, the Burgomaster's pretty daughter, was ready for them.
An enormous basket, full of wood, was instantly lowered from the
balcony; and the kind Burgomaster himself came bustling out and
told them to help themselves. At the same time, Diemut, accompanied by her three special girl-friends, all daintily dressed in their
gayest clothes, came running out of the house, carrying dishes of
cakes and sweetmeats. These they distributed lavishly among the
delighted children and to many of their older friends in the
merry crowds already gathered in the square.

The children, encouraged by this unexpected treat, soon became
somewhat out of hand. From having plenty, they wanted more.
From being noisy, they became clamorous. They now rushed in
a body and hammered loudly on the door of the big house opposite
that of the Burgomaster's, yelling out their cheery, doggerel-
rhymed songs and demanding wood and yet more wood for their
bonfires.

Now, this building was known as the Wizard's House, because
an old Necromancer had once lived there. Though he had been
very wise and learned, the people of Munich had driven him from
their midst. They could not understand or appreciate the many
beautiful things he had wished to teach them. The present owner
of the house was a newcomer, whom very few of the townsfolk
had yet seen, since he spent all his time buried amongst his books.
There seemed to be a mystery about him, too. Some said that,
though a student of magic, he was kind, wise, and learned; others
said that he came of a race of monsters. The Bailiff, or Constable,
however, declared that he was a lord of noble birth, that his
credentials were good and his means substantial; and the Innkeeper said he was a pleasant young man who dined regularly at
his board and paid well for his food, though he spoke with none.

In answer to the clamorous voices of the children and to their
banging upon his door, Kunrad, the new owner of the house, now
appeared in the open doorway, amazed at the crowd outside. He

was a handsome young man in his middle twenties, gentle, shy, and rather dreamy in his manner. He was, indeed, a learned philosopher as well as a close student of magic, who had spent so much time among his books that he knew little of the outside world.

Wonderingly he gazed at the revellers and inquired the reason for their merriment. He seemed never to have heard of the Feuersnot or Beltane Fires, nor of the festivities held on Midsummer's Eve. On now being told of these matters, he suddenly appeared as though awakening from a dream. Delighted at the sight of the revellers, he realized that he had been a fool to spend so much time among his books and thus to have missed so many of the joys of life. But he would now make up for lost time.

He invited the children to enter and take some of his musty old books away for their bonfires; and he bade them break down his doorway and any other wooden objects they could find in his house. Next he began to smash up one of his window shutters and to pile the wood on the hand-cart brought by the now delighted youngsters.

Then, quite suddenly, Kunrad stopped his activities. He had seen Diemut, the lovely daughter of the Burgomaster; and he could not take his eyes off her. His heart began to beat wildly, his blood to race; and in that moment he felt the first ecstasy of love. He had never experienced passion before.

Diemut, too, felt an answering glow in her own heart; but she would not admit that she could thus be stirred so suddenly by this mysterious stranger. While she gazed at him, as though in a dream, Kunrad, on fire with the love that now surged through his veins like a flame, boldly rushed up to the beautiful maiden, clasped her in his arms, and kissed her passionately on the mouth.

Diemut was furious at the liberty he had taken, though inwardly thrilled by his daring. Having freed herself from his grasp, she hurried away with her three friends, planning with them how she could avenge herself upon the young stranger for his impertinence.

Some of the crowd also showed annoyance; others praised the the stranger for being such a venturesome wooer; and for a few moments there was more commotion than ever. Soon, however, the main object of their assembling asserted itself once more. It was Midsummer's Eve; and the Beltane Fires must be lighted without further delay!

Even the Burgomaster had had enough of this noisy clamour outside his house; besides, he, himself, wanted to see the bonfires merrily burning. So he drove the children and the hilarious crowd off into the open spaces beyond, where the bonfires were already beginning to spring up on every side. Then, with his friend, the Bailiff, he prepared to follow.

Seeing Diemut standing aside with her three girl-friends, still looking pale and upset, he called to her to come and join in the fun, as usual. But Diemut declared she would now remain at home; and she rushed inside the house and locked the door, in a pet. Thinking she would soon change her mind, the Burgomaster and the Bailiff hurried along to join the revellers.

Darkness had now fallen, and the sky was glowing red and orange from the dancing flames of the Beltane bonfires. Wild cries and laughter floated back into the square from the happy throng in the distance. The Midsummer frolic was at its height.

But the square was not empty. Kunrad, the love-awakened young student of magic, had no intention of leaving his romance to grow cold. He had seen Diemut return to her home; and he hung about outside, wondering how he could speak with her again. The sound of the Beltane revellers' rousing songs and the sight of the flame-illumined sky increased the excitement in his own breast; and he began to sing a song in rapturous praise of the fires of love.

Presently he heard an answering song softly sung from the balcony of the Burgomaster's house. It was the sweet voice of Diemut who, after lighting a lamp in her room, had come out through the open window to the balcony beyond, where she now lingered, combing her long fair hair. She had staged this little scene, knowing that the bold stranger was still lurking near. In spite of her anger against him, her heart glowed at the remembrance of his audacious kiss. She, too, loved for the first time, though she scarce realized it yet. But she meant to teach the young man a lesson, nevertheless.

When Kunrad presently drew near and, entranced by her beauty, began to whisper passionate words of love, she replied, to his great delight. At first she seemed reluctant to admit the answering flame she so surely felt. But gradually she showed more favour and smiled upon him.

When Kunrad now eagerly entreated her to come down and unlock the door, that he might enter and make his declaration at closer quarters, she refused in shocked tones. Then, as he still pleaded, she suggested that he should get into the large basket in which wood had been lowered to the children a short time since. The basket was on a pulley-rope; and she and her three girl-friends would then haul him up, so that he could enter her room from the balcony.

Suspecting nothing, Kunrad eagerly got into the big basket; and slowly the hidden girls began to haul the pulleys. When, however, the basket with its human load had been drawn up half-way, the ropes were securely fastened, and it was left dangling in mid air. With merry laughter, the three girls then ran away, to join their sweethearts dancing round the bonfires.

Diemut at first pretended to help her would-be lover, first by means of her loosely-hanging sleeve, and then by letting her long hair dangle tantalizingly just out of reach. Finally, however, she let him see plainly that she had played this trick upon him as a punishment for his audacity in stealing a kiss from her earlier in the evening. Then, tauntingly bidding him call his vaunted knowledge of magic to his aid, she left him with derisive laughter and entered her chamber, closing the window behind her.

Kunrad was furious at the trick which had been played upon him. He was fuming with rage when, next moment, a crowd of the townsfolk, told of his plight by the three mischievous girls who had helped to haul him up, now came crowding into the street to jeer at him. How they laughed at the sight of the disconsolate suitor swinging to and fro below his lady love's balcony, so near and yet so far!

The Burgomaster, however, was angry with his daughter and bade her come forth and release the stranger. He had further good reports of the handsome newcomer from his friend the Bailiff, and now considered him a likely suitor for his pretty daughter. But Diemut paid no heed to his commands; and mean-while, the crowd continued to taunt the trapped lover as he hung in mid air.

Then Kunrad, now in a towering rage at this indignity and determined to teach a severe lesson to Diemut—whom he already dearly loved—made use of the magic he had studied so long. He invoked the aid of his late master, the dead Wizard, whose house, books, and wealth he had fallen heir to. He entreated him and his Spirit Powers to extinguish all the lights and fires in the town and not to rekindle them until Diemut had accepted his love.

Instantly, in answer to his despairing cry, the town was plunged into darkness. Every fire, lamp, and candle went out; and all the blazing Beltane bonfires ceased to burn. The children cried with fear; and all the citizens, old and young, were likewise terrified. They could not get a light of any kind; and a deadly cold enveloped all, despite the fact that it was Midsummer's Eve.

And now, the frightened people crowded around the Burgo-master's house, calling out for Kunrad to be taken from his basket and hanged for using his witchcraft against them. But in the darkness they could do nothing.

Suddenly the moon came out from behind a cloud; and in the pale silvery light which now shone upon the Burgomaster's house, Kunrad was seen standing upon the balcony—which, by means of a mighty spring, he had at last been able to reach.

But what a majestic Kunrad was now revealed! He seemed like one inspired, as, without warning, he began to harangue the crowd. He poured scorn on them for having, in their blind narrowness of outlook, cast forth the Wise Wizard, that great Spirit, his Master. But they would not be able to cast out the new and second great Master, himself, who had honoured them by choosing to live in their midst and to carry on the good work of his forerunner. Munich should help him in the person of Diemut, whom he had chosen to be his bride.[1] Until, however, that fair maiden consented to love him—he knew the spark of love was already kindled in her heart—he intended to leave the townsfolk in their present darkness and cold. He thus reminded them that, without love and an appreciation of great Spirits, of the true and the beautiful in Art, there could never be light and warmth.

Even as he spoke, the shadowy form of Diemut appeared on the balcony, coming slowly forth from her window towards him. She also had heard his harangue. No longer could she hold aloof from the bold and handsome stranger whose first glance had enthralled her, even though she had so grievously wounded him by refusing to listen to the true dictates of her heart.

She now came forward and, confessing her love for him, laid her hands in his. At that moment the lamp in the window behind began to glow softly once more; the lights and fires in the town were rekindled; and the Beltane bonfires blazed and crackled as before. Realizing now that light and warmth indeed came from love alone, all the people uttered loud cries of joy as Kunrad clasped Diemut, his fair bride, in his arms.

[1] This is an allegorical reference to Wagner, the great Spirit of Music, the Wizard whom Munich at first refused to recognize. The second great Spirit, his successor, is himself, Strauss, whom Munich—represented by Diemut—now accepts with acclamation.

HELEN IN EGYPT[1]   *Richard Strauss*
(*Die Ägyptische Helena—The Egyptian Helen*)

THE fatal beauty of Fair Helen of Troy did not cease to cause trouble and tragedy, even after the long-drawn-out Trojan War had come to an end.

While the doomed city was still burning, Menelaus, King of Sparta, having regained his erring wife, boarded his royal ship with her and set sail once more for Sparta.

But the triumph of his victory brought Menelaus no joy. Though he still loved the beautiful Helen, his conscience now bade him slay her as a peace-offering to the gods—also that she might thus expiate her sin for having caused the needless sacrifice of so many noble Greek and Trojan lives. This final dreadful deed he planned to enact upon the voyage home; but, strange to say, the tragedy was averted by magical means.

At the time when the royal vessel was passing not far from the coast of Egypt, it happened that on an islet near by, Aithra, the nymph-like sorceress daughter of an Egyptian King, was lamenting the temporary absence of her lover, Poseidon, the mighty God of the Seas. In her rich island-palace, her slaves and attendants sang songs to comfort her; but she scarce heeded them. She listened only to the news and scenes recorded to her by another companion, the All-Knowing Sea-Shell—a mussel-like sprite recently bestowed upon her by her powerful lover.

This mysterious oracular Talking-Shell had the magical gift of seeing events taking place at a distance; and presently she described to her mistress the tragic scene then happening on the passing vessel. The lovely Helen lay sleeping in the ship's hold, and Menelaus had crept down to gaze upon her beauty for the last time, sad at heart, but determined to carry out his terrible resolve to slay her.

Even as the Talking-Shell spoke, she added that the distracted King had now seized his dagger, ready to plunge it into the heart of his fair Queen; and she called upon Aithra to use her magical arts to avert the tragedy.

Aithra, generously eager to save the most beautiful woman in the world, swiftly invoked the aid of the Storm Spirits and Winds ruled over by her lover, Poseidon; and instantly a terrific storm sprang up. The royal vessel was roughly tossed about, and soon

[1] Copyright, 1928, by Fürstner Ltd., London W.1.

foundered; but Menelaus, with Helen in his arms—his love for her triumphing temporarily in this hour of danger—swam safely to the shore. Then, in the darkness, the royal pair stumbled along the beach until they came to the palace of Aithra the Sorceress, who received them very graciously.

Helen would now gladly have made peace with her wronged lord, and longed to win back his love; but Menelaus declined to be moved by the alluring charms which had stolen the heart of Paris. Again he announced himself as an instrument of retribution; and he added that never would he permit her to gaze again upon their pure young daughter.

As, for the second time, he raised his dagger against her and was about to strike the fatal blow, Aithra again came to the rescue of the lovely Queen; and by means of her arts of sorcery, she called up spirits and phantoms to distract the attention of Menelaus. Seeing what he believed to be the spectre of Paris, he rushed out madly into the night to slay him afresh.

Then Aithra, seeing that Helen was likewise in an overwrought state, persuaded her to drink a magic potion, whereby a temporary forgetfulness of her troubles should come to her.

As Helen, after drinking the potion, fell into a reposeful sleep upon a couch, the Sorceress went out to meet the returning King, who was now more distracted than ever and declared wildly that the blood of Paris was dripping from his weapon, recking not that he had been fighting with a spectre. Aithra, however, managed to calm him; and then, by means of her arts, she actually succeeded in making him believe a very strange tale she had invented. She persuaded Menelaus into thinking that the entire period of the Trojan War had been merely a phantasm of his own tired brain, which had been diseased all that time; and she cunningly added that, while he was thus imagining dreadful scenes of carnage, his beautiful Queen, Helen, had been kept secure from harm in this same islet-palace in Egypt. Here she had remained under Aithra's magic spell of slumber, whereby she had retained her early youth and beauty.

Hypnotized into this belief, Menelaus now reverently approached the couch whereon lay the slumbering form of the radiant Helen he had loved in his youth; and when the beautiful Queen presently awakened, he clasped her rapturously in his arms.

Still under the spell of Aithra's cunning story and soothed by her potions, Menelaus became once more as a bridegroom eager for his bride; but Helen, taking Aithra aside, besought the Sorceress in a whisper to transport them first to some quiet spot where the Trojan War and she, Helen, had never been heard of.

Aithra, still full of pity for the most beautiful woman on earth and caring nothing for the troubles and tragedies the latter had caused, promised to do so. When, therefore, the royal pair, now happy in their mystic dream state, had retired to an inner bridal chamber, the Sorceress once more called up her spirit slaves to her aid; and, in their sleep, Menelaus and Helen were wafted on Aithra's own magical cloak, to an exquisite desert oasis not far from the Atlas Mountains.

. . . .

Next day, the reunited royal pair awakened in a rich, gilded tent, surrounded by shady palm trees and with a silvery spring near by. Helen awakened first; and, seeing a jewelled coffer near the entrance to the tent, she realized that Aithra had lavished this gift upon her. With delight, she took from the coffer a jewelled mirror and comb, and a rope of pearls; and she wove the latter skilfully into her shining hair. She felt, indeed, a bride once more.

Her joy, however, was short-lived. When Menelaus awoke and came forth, she found that another hallucination had now taken possession of his distracted mind. This made him regard Helen as a being of divine origin, whom it would be sacrilege for him to touch; and he imagined, too, that he had actually slain the beautiful Helen whom he had once loved. His bemused remembrance of the troubled events of the previous day, though clouded and distorted, had caused the soothing potions of Aithra to have only a partial effect.

When, therefore, Helen, seeking in the tent for a further supply of the same potion to calm him once more, inadvertently picked up a silken cloth from which the sword of her lord fell to the ground, Menelaus seized the weapon instantly. He then dared her to approach him, though still declaring his belief that this same weapon had once destroyed his lovely Queen and bemoaning this imaginary event.

As the royal pair were thus experiencing an unhappy awakening, there approached a splendid cavalcade of horsemen, consisting of a Desert Sheik, named Altair, with his handsome young son, Da-ud, and their retinue. They announced that they had been sent thither by the sorceress, Aithra, to pay homage to beautiful Helen and to entertain her and the great King Menelaus.

A group of black slaves next came forward with caskets filled with priceless gifts; and a rich carpet of cloth-of-gold was spread before Aithra's great jewelled coffer, upon which Helen now seated herself as a Queen upon a throne.

The Sheik Altair, instantly inspired with a fierce passionate love on first beholding the ever-fatal beauty of Helen, prostrated himself before her in worshipful abasement, as though she were, indeed, a goddess; and his son, Da-ud, a beautiful youth, but a mere stripling, did likewise. Helen, however, whose early love for Menelaus had now returned with deep intensity, had eyes for no one else; and she begged the still distracted King to sit beside her on the coffer throne and to share with her the gifts and homage of the Desert Chief and his son.

But Menelaus, in his bemused state, was now further agitated. In the radiant stripling, Da-ud—who had also instantly fallen a victim to the siren-like charms of Helen and was gazing upon her with passionate glances equal to those of his father—he fancied he saw once more his youthful rival, Paris; and again jealousy consumed him. He would have rushed upon him, then and there, eager to destroy him, but that Helen, with soothing words, restrained him for the moment.

The Sheik Altair, disdainful of such ill manners in one he sought to entertain as an honoured guest, and also scheming to secure the beautiful Helen as his own Queen, now announced that a grand hunting-party was about to set forth; and he invited Menelaus to join Da-ud and his young companions and himself in this royal entertainment. Helen eagerly supported the suggestion, hoping that the excitement of the chase would drive this new hallucination from her beloved lord's disturbed brain.

So Menelaus allowed himself to be robed in hunting garb; but before mounting the spirited steed awaiting him, he grasped his famous war-sword once more, refusing to leave it behind, despite the alarmed entreaties of Helen.

When the hunting-party had departed, with Altair in temporary attendance, Helen, to her joy and relief, was joined by the friendly Aithra, who declared she had come to proffer assistance—knowing, by her arts, that all was not well with the lovely Queen and that the magic draughts of the previous night had not had the desired effect upon her lord.

She now offered Helen a stronger potion composed of lotus, the herb of forgetfulness, and begged her to give Menelaus this at regular intervals, so that he should never remember the past, but should worship her only as some divine goddess.

But Helen had no desire to be worshipped as a goddess, and longed only for Menelaus to love her again as the Helen of his early days and as the mother of their fair young daughter, Hermione; and she entreated Aithra instead to supply her, not with the means of oblivion, but with a portion that should bring true remembrance back to Menelaus.

Aithra, horrified, begged her to think again about this, since Menelaus, when restored to his normal mind by the draught of remembrance, would recognize Helen as his faithless wife; and he would then instantly desire to slay her to appease the gods, as on board the ship that had foundered. But Helen was adamant in her resolve. She would rather die as Helen at the hands of Menelaus—for whom her love had blossomed afresh—than be worshipped by him as a goddess too divine to touch. The latter would be a living death to her; and passionately she announced that she would accept nothing but the potion of remembrance.

Realizing that only thus could she bring happiness to the most beautiful woman in the world, whom she desired to serve, Aithra called for her attendants; and the potion was duly brewed.

While Aithra and her slaves were thus busy in the tent, the passion-torn Sheik Altair accosted Helen, having returned secretly from the chase, hoping to find her thus alone; and he began to make eager love to her.

But Helen, thinking only of her own beloved lord, repulsed him again and again; and she was relieved when, presently, there came an interruption to these unwelcome attentions—though a tragic one.

The slaves in attendance around her now grew excited, as they could see the huntsmen in the distance chasing a gazelle; and they began to describe the scene in a kind of chanting song. Suddenly their excitement changed to agitation and cries of alarm. They declared that the royal hunter, Menelaus, was no longer chasing the gazelle but had overtaken the young chief, Da-ud. Now their two swords were clashing fiercely; and then, with a shriek of horror, they saw the youth fall to the ground, dead.

While Altair, scarce heeding the untimely death of his young son, still continued his declarations of love to the now stricken Helen, the horns sounded the end of the chase; and a few minutes later, the dead body of Da-ud was brought by slaves and laid beside the tent. Following them came Menelaus, still carrying his great sword, but dazed, as a man in a dream; and Helen hastened to his side to soothe and comfort him in his deluded state.

Then, as Aithra and her attendants came forth from the tent with the potion of remembrance they had just brewed, Helen snatched up a phial of the magic mixture and boldly invited Menelaus to drink it, firmly ignoring Aithra's entreaties for her to refrain from her purpose. To encourage the bemused King, she drank first of the mixture herself; then she offered the goblet to Menelaus.

Fearing the consequences of this rash deed, Aithra once more called upon her own lover, Poseidon, the Sea-God, to come to her aid; and in answer to her call, thunder and a tempest of wind was heard, together with the sound of tramping feet and the rattling of the weapons of a martial host approaching from behind the tent.

But Menelaus heeded not these strange sounds, as he took the goblet containing the potion of remembrance from the goddess-like being before him and drained its contents. Instantly his brain cleared, his full remembrance of the past returned, and he now recognized in his lovely companion the same Fair Helen whose fatal beauty had been the cause of so many noble lives being sacrificed. Remembering also that his conscience required him to slay her in expiation of her sin and to appease the gods, he raised his mighty sword once more.

Helen, however, unafraid, merely gazed steadily into his eyes, a divine smile upon her lips; and Menelaus, once more enthralled by her perfect beauty, dropped his sword, opened wide his arms, and embraced her gladly in token of forgiveness and renewed love, declaring that never more should they be parted.

Furious at this strange spectacle of reunion, Altair, the Desert Sheik, called wildly upon his slaves to tear the lovers apart. But Aithra's call to the powerful Sea-King had already been answered generously; and scarcely had the slaves rushed upon the royal pair than the back of the pavilion was thrown open, revealing a wonderful sight. There stood a mighty troop of armed horsemen, whose dazzling and noble mien declared their divine origin—on beholding whom all the desert folk, including Altair himself, based themselves humbly.

In the centre of this splendid cavalcade, now forming a vast semicircle, stood a snow-white palfrey, upon which rode a lovely child-maiden, clad in cloth-of-gold and with streaming golden hair forming a cloak around her. This was Hermione, the fair young Princess of Sparta, the daughter of Helen and Menelaus.

Two of the dazzling horsemen now dismounted and lifted the Princess Hermione from her white steed; and the child ran up to her royal parents and greeted them with rapturous joy.

Presently the horsemen remounted the little Princess upon her white palfrey; and when two more snow-white horses, richly caparisoned, next miraculously appeared, Menelaus and Helen likewise mounted.

Then, to the sound of sweet singing, the reunited royal trio rode away joyously towards their home in Sparta.

INTERMEZZO[1]   *Richard Strauss*

IN the charming country house of Hoffkapellmeister Robert
Storch, at Grundlsee, much hustle and bustle was taking place.
It was seven o'clock in the morning, one snowy day during the
winter. The famous conductor was about to set out for Vienna,
to fulfil a number of important concert engagements there. The
sledge to take him to the station was at the door; but the great
Master was not yet ready for departure.

In their bedroom, his pretty wife, Christine, was busily helping
him to pack his bag; and as she was a very careful and somewhat
over-anxious helpmeet, she fussed about him like a hen with an
only chicken. Had he put in the bag all the clothes he was likely
to need? Had he forgotten his gargle, his pills? Would he be
sure to choose a good seat in the middle of the train, where he
would be safer in case of an accident? Would he keep out of
draughts, and remember to change his shoes when he came in and
to wrap up well when he went out?

Robert laughingly reassured his wife on all these points. But
soon, because both were highly temperamental, a little bickering
arose. Christine grumbled because her popular husband always
seemed to have a better time than she. He could go off to Vienna
to gain more fame by his brilliant work as a conductor and composer. But she had to remain at home with their little boy, look
after the house—with the help of several excellent maids, Robert
slyly put in!—pay the bills, go through the same old dreary round,
day in, day out.

Robert, however, pointed out that their home was a charming
and pleasant one, that money was always forthcoming for the
bills, that she had a loving husband, and really had nothing very
much to grumble at! Christine readily enough admitted all this,
but still insisted that he had the better time.

Then came a hurried, but first-rate, breakfast for Robert, a pack
of sandwiches for the journey; the great man was packed cosily
into the sledge, and off he went to board the train for Vienna.

Left behind, Christine still went on grumbling a little, now
seeking sympathy from her maid, Anna. As she dressed her hair
she again declared that it was no joke being the wife of a celebrity.
She would much rather have a less important husband always at
her own beck and call.

Finally, however, after attending to her household duties, interviewing the cook, and so on, she remembered a pleasant social engagement she had made. Thus, all her small worries were quickly forgotten in the ever-absorbing question, what should she wear?

. . . .

Christine, though she loved her husband dearly and longed for his return, had no intention of being dull during his absence. The Winter Sports were at their height; so off went Christine to enjoy herself on the ice and in the snow.

Here, at a new toboggan-run, she had a very lively and interesting adventure. As she was coasting down the run at a fair speed, she collided with another toboggan, in which a handsome young man was likewise coasting at a good speed. They were both tumbled into the snow, and, though not hurt, they did not hesitate to call one another impolite names, each blaming the other for the mishap. Soon, however, they laughed and made friends; and on learning that the stranger was a certain Baron Lummer, Christine was much impressed. She liked the idea of having a handsome young Baron dancing attendance upon her; it would pass the time pleasantly. Soon, they were seen everywhere together—on the toboggan-run, at dances, and in the cafés.

Presently people began to gossip about them—especially as the Baron had another and considerably younger lady friend in the neighbourhood. Christine, however, continued to enjoy herself with her new admirer.

Then, all too soon, the gilt came off her gingerbread. The Baron—who never had enough money for his extravagant needs—tried to borrow a thousand marks from her, sending her a note to this effect. Christine, indignant that he should thus think to sponge upon her, curtly refused his request when next he came to see her. On hearing, however, that her new friend was really extremely hard up and was studying for an examination with the idea of getting work by which he might earn money, she softened somewhat—especially when the Baron, trading on her sympathy, declared that, in consequence of having to " burn the midnight oil ", he also suffered much from migraine. She then said that she would ask her influential husband to find him a job of some kind.

This latter suggestion, however, was not too pleasing to the idle young Baron, who certainly liked play better than work. But, having failed to borrow a thousand marks, he now pinned his faith upon securing at least his expenses to Vienna. Tired of the Winter Sports and of his new lady friend, his one idea now was to get back to the gay city he loved so well. Soon his chance came.

During his sponging interview with Christine, a letter arrived, addressed to the Hoffkapellmeister Storch, which, in the absence of her husband and thinking it might be something of importance about his work, his ever-anxious wife opened and read. She now received a great shock.

The letter contained a tender message from a lady unknown to the reader, demanding tickets for the opera, and making an assignation to meet the donor afterwards in the bar. It was signed "Mieze Meier". What a bombshell!

Of a highly temperamental nature, Christine immediately feared the worst—that her husband was unfaithful to her! The letter began "Dear Schatz"—a false name he had obviously given to hide his true identity!

Raging about the room, the angry wife impetuously declared her intention to seek a divorce at once. She would go to a notary without waiting for explanations from the husband who had deceived her.

Then, seeing that the letter had come from Vienna and that "Mieze Meier" was evidently unaware that her admirer was already in that gay city, another idea occurred to Christine. The Baron should at once travel to Vienna on her behalf—and at her expense—to find out about the whole matter and report to her. This suggestion fitted in well with the bored Baron's own wishes; and off he set, financed freely, as he had desired.

Christine now sent off the following telegram to Robert: "You know Mieze Meier! Your faithlessness has been shown! We are parted for ever." Next, she bade her surprised and greatly annoyed maid to begin packing up, as she intended to leave her deceitful husband's house as soon as possible. Anna grumblingly set to work, as slowly as she could.

Even her little son became annoyed with her when, in an hysterical fit, she clung to him, declaring him to be her sole comfort now that his father had turned out to be such a "bad man". But young Franzl stoutly refused to believe that his beloved father was anything but a "very good man". He was a staunch little fellow.

It was the same with the Notary, whom Christine next visited. The man of Law declared she was acting too hastily and had as yet no grounds for a divorce. But the angry Christine all the more loudly demanded that a divorce she certainly would have. The Notary at last pretended to agree, and wrote a letter to Robert, telling him of his wife's strange request.

Meanwhile, Hoffkapellmeister Storch was enjoying a brilliant success in Vienna. Nor was it all work for him. In between his concerts and operas, he had a pleasant time with his colleagues. In particular, he was able to indulge his fondness for his favourite card-game "Skat", without interference from his beloved Christine. His wife often grumbled that such games with his cronies kept him from her side.

His friends knew of this possessive trend in his otherwise charming wife, and they often teased him about it. They were playfully poking fun at him on this account on the day when Christine's irate telegram arrived. Their teasing increased to hilarity when, in amazement, he read out to them the contents of this most unexpected missive. How they laughed!

So the quiet, shy Hoffkapellmeister was a gay dog, after all! Who would have thought of him as a philanderer? When the puzzled Robert, becoming angry as well as distressed, declared he had never even heard of "Mieze Meier", they pretended not to believe him and chaffed him unmercifully.

But the distracted musician rushed away to send a frantic telegram to Christine, declaring her accusation to be an idiotic one and demanding her reasons for it. He received no reply to this message, however; and though, throughout the next few days he sent many further telegrams, gradually changing their tone from an angry to a beseeching one, still he received no answer. He did, however, get a letter from Christine's Notary about her wish for a divorce, which distracted him still further.

As the time went on, he became more and more agitated and perplexed; for he dearly loved his wife and knew there must be some mistake. He did not wish to leave Vienna at the moment, as several more important concerts still claimed him; yet, he was at his wits' end!

Now, Kapellmeister Stroh, his colleague and immediate second-in-command, had suspected from the beginning that the whole affair was based on a misunderstanding. Stroh himself was the culprit and should have been the recipient of the message. He was only too well acquainted with "Mieze Meier", a pretty little actress of somewhat easy morals, to whom he was at that time showing considerable attention. He quickly realized that his new lady-love had obviously confused his own name "Stroh" with that of his superior, "Storch". But at first he kept this information to himself, as he and his friends were so thoroughly enjoying the temporary discomfiture of the woman-shy great man.

However, a little later on, meeting Robert pacing about the street in a storm, heedless of the rough elements and now really distracted with anxiety because of receiving no reply to the many letters and telegrams already sent to Christine, he realized that the joke had gone far enough; and he now confessed all. He, Stroh, was the admired gentleman-friend of "Mieze Meier", who had obviously mixed up his name with that of Storch and had sent a communication of some kind to the Hoffkapellmeister's house, which must have been opened by Christine. Hence her hysterical anger, her first wild telegram, and her subsequent silence.

Furious that his colleague's light conduct had thus brought about such an upheaval in his own home, Robert now insisted that Stroh should go at once to Grundlsee and explain matters to Christine. He himself would follow in a day or two, when the concerts were over. When Stroh had contritely agreed to this and had departed on his difficult mission, Robert sent yet another telegram to Christine, explaining that the whole affair was a mistake and an unholy mix-up of names.

.   .   .   .

Christine was still packing up her own personal belongings in frantic haste, with Anna's unwilling help. She was in such an hysterical state, she hardly knew what she was doing. She now regretted having sent the Baron to Vienna. As Anna tartly pointed out, he could do nothing without a photograph of Robert —which, in her frantic haste, she had omitted to provide him with. She wept and railed as she packed; and she kept losing things and blaming Anna, who threatened to leave her.

Matters were becoming hectic when, suddenly, the unexpected arrival of Stroh was announced. At first, Christine angrily refused to see him, suspecting that, as her husband's trusted colleague, he would certainly be on his side. Stroh, however, would take no refusal but came boldly into her room and insisted on her listening to his explanation. It took all his wits to convince her that the letter she now showed him from "Mieze Meier" was really intended for himself, Stroh, that his pretty lady-friend had mixed up the names, and was, indeed, entirely unknown to Robert.

Finally, however, Christine realized the mistake that had been made, which had caused her own and Robert's tremendous emotional upheaval; and she was then filled with joy and relief. Her beloved Robert was faithful, after all; she need not leave him; the divorce could be called off; and what a glorious welcome she would prepare for her dear husband on his return! She began to unpack at once, to tidy the house once more, and to get a fine feast ready.

But when Robert at last arrived and had greeted his wife with great joy, graciously accepting her protestations of regret for her hasty suspicions, he also had a bone to pick with her.

What was all this gossip he had heard about her going around with a handsome young Baron during his absence, he wrathfully demanded? Full of confusion, Christine had to explain away the Baron as best she could—a not too easy matter, and one requiring considerable tact.

But Robert's tit-for-tat had no malice in it, and was merely teasing. When the Baron presently turned up again, somewhat dismayed on beholding the great man there before him, the latter, instead of making any more fuss, generously promised to find him a job. The Baron departed, decidedly crestfallen.

So the storm-clouds ended in smoke; and Robert and Christine, after many tender embraces, congratulated one another that theirs was, indeed, a happy marriage. After all, this recent trouble had been merely a rather exciting little Intermezzo—nothing more!

DER ROSENKAVALIER   *Richard Strauss*
(*The Rose-Bearer*)

IN Vienna, during the early years of the reign of Maria Theresa, love intrigues formed one of the chief amusements of persons of quality. Therefore, it was no strange thing that, early one bright summer morning, the Princess von Werdenberg should be enjoying an interview with an ardent admirer in her boudoir, whilst her sleepy, but faithful, lackeys kept watch outside to prevent interruption.

The Princess's husband, Field-Marshal Prince von Werdenberg —an elderly man too much engrossed in matters of war and sport to be greatly interested in the doings of his pretty wife—was away on a hunting expedition. What more natural, then, than for the Princess—still young and beautiful enough to be one of Cupid's victims, though approaching the borderland of sophistication—to invite her young kinsman and devoted sweetheart, Octavian, to visit her and to pour forth into her willing ears the sweet words of love she delighted to hear.

Octavian, a handsome youth, sat at the feet of his beloved Princess in an adoring attitude, every now and again rising to draw her into his eager embrace. The Princess listened indulgently to his extravagant expressions of admiration and adoration—for, in spite of his extreme youth, she loved the boy dearly and delighted in his ardently responsive passion.

Their golden hours of sweet dreaming this morning, however, were doomed to a rough awakening. Suddenly there came the sounds of an arrival in the courtyard below, and the Princess exclaimed in deep alarm, as she heard heavy footsteps approaching: "Ah, woe! My husband has returned unexpectedly! Quick, conceal thyself, my beloved Octavian!"

Octavian hastily retired to a cupboard in a recess; and the Princess paced restlessly up and down her room, listening to the voices of her zealous lackeys arguing with the newcomer—whom she soon realized was not her husband, after all, but a near kinsman, the Baron Ochs von Lerchenau, a middle-aged and dissipated *roué*, for whom she had little affection and less respect.

In a few moments Octavian emerged from the recess, attired in female garments, and entreated the Princess to pass him off to her intruding cousin as a new waiting-maid. His lively *inamorata*, ever ready for a joke and delighted with his charming appearance —for he made an extremely pretty "girl"—gladly agreed to do so.

At this moment the visitor burst into the room, angrily expostulating with the dismayed attendants for having kept him waiting outside so long. Seeing that he was indeed her kinsman, the Princess gave him a gracious welcome and inquired the reason for his unexpected appearance so early in the morning.

The Baron, however, was immediately so struck with the fair, fresh beauty of the dainty "waiting-maid" that he could scarcely take his eyes from her. He kept casting languishing glances in her direction and making inviting signs for her to approach nearer to him—to the secret entertainment of the Princess, who more than once had to bid him keep his hands off the "girl", whom she addressed as "Mariandel". The flirtatious visitor, however, was at last induced to sit down and state his business whilst partaking of a cup of chocolate.

The Baron now explained to his cousin that he had decided to marry and was, in fact, about to enter into a contract that same day with a very young girl named Sophia, the daughter of Faninal, a wealthy merchant who had recently been ennobled. When the Princess expressed surprise that he should stoop to wed with one of such plebeian origin, he airily confessed that the father's moneybags were of more service to him in his present impecunious state than a long pedigree—adding that enough blue blood flowed in his own veins for himself and his wife.

The marriage contract was to be signed later during that day;

but, in the meantime, he required the services of a nobly-born youth to bear to his promised bride a silver rose as the pledge of his love, in accordance with the pretty custom of such ancient families as his own—and he begged the Princess to name one of their kinsmen for this important mission.

The Princess immediately named Octavian as a suitable person to act the part of rose-bearer for her cousin; and she showed him a miniature of the handsome young man. The Baron was quickly struck by the likeness between the pictured youth and the pretty young "waiting-maid"; and his cousin mendaciously informed him that they were indeed related, though the relationship was not strictly "canonical"—for which reason she chose to keep "Mariandel" always about her own person and apart from the other maids.

Having agreed to accept Octavian as his rose-bearer, the Baron next managed to whisper an invitation to the new "waiting-maid" to join him at supper that evening, and even tried to steal a kiss—to the increasing amusement of the Princess; but the disguised Octavian at last managed to make his escape and to slam a door in the face of the amorous Baron.

For a short time later on, the Princess was engaged with her hairdresser and a number of vendors of dress goods; but when she was alone once more, Octavian returned to continue his interrupted love-making. He now found his adored one somewhat sad, however, and was distressed when she sighed and said she feared that their happy meetings must shortly end—that he would almost certainly bestow his affections on some fair young girl sooner or later. Despite the young man's passionately extravagant declarations of undying love, she knew only too well that, as his senior by more years than she cared to count, she could not hope to hold him much longer. Nevertheless, when she presently dismissed him to perform his task as rose-bearer for the Baron, she little realized that the end of her charming romance would come within the next few hours.

. . . .

Later in the day great excitement reigned in the household of the newly-ennobled merchant-prince, Herr von Faninal, whose gorgeous abode glowed with brilliant decorations, which were the envy and admiration of his worthy citizen guests. In the midst of this splendour, his fair young daughter, Sophia, clad in elegant robes, awaited the arrival of her *fiancé's* rose-bearer—a ceremony she had never expected to experience and one which somewhat alarmed her.

For pretty Sophia was a simple, sweet-natured maiden who did not share the ambitions of her wealthy father and had no special desire to marry into the ancient nobility. Nevertheless, as a dutiful daughter, she was prepared to receive the elderly Baron chosen as her husband.

Presently, loud greetings and music announced the arrival of the eagerly-expected rose-bearer; and next minute, Octavian, clad in dazzling garments of silver and white, entered the reception hall. He carried in his hand a lovely silver rose which, upon his bended knee, he gracefully presented to Sophia. He was followed by a party of elegant attendants, who grouped themselves around the room; but Sophia saw no one but the handsome young Octavian, whose glowing eyes instantly held her own enthralled.

In that first long look the two young people felt themselves transported, as it were, to another world—a rosy world of joy and love, in which they two were the only dwellers; and though they gradually came back to the scene around them and talked of ordinary matters, they both felt the glory of a new happiness and knew that true love had dawned, unbidden, in their hearts.

Scarcely had they recovered than the doors were once more flung open and Faninal, with great pomp and ceremony, ushered in the Baron Ochs von Lerchenau who, despite his noble birth, soon proved himself to be nothing but a vulgar boor. He treated the obsequious Faninal first with insolent condescension and next with downright rudeness; and he quickly offended the modest Sophia with the rough boorishness of his wooing and the leering suggestiveness of his bold glances. His coarse words and manners filled the simple girl with disgust; and when he drew her down on to a seat beside him and began to fondle her with easy familiarity, she wrenched herself free from his arms with flaming cheeks, full of indignation, and forbade him to touch her again.

Her resistance, however, vastly amused the licentious Baron, who was now delighted with the loveliness and spirit of his plebeian bride-elect; and he followed her eagerly about the room, to force his unwelcome attentions upon her—to the furious anger of Octavian, who only repressed his rage with the utmost difficulty. It was, therefore, a relief to all when Faninal and the Notary called the Baron into the adjoining chamber to examine the contract document before the ceremony of signing it began.

The remainder of the guests and attendants followed; and for a few moments Octavian and Sophia were left alone.

Full of despair at the now hideous prospect of the marriage which had been arranged for her, the humiliated Sophia turned to the handsome rose-bearer and tearfully entreated him to help her, declaring that she would never wed with the Baron. For answer,

Octavian clasped her tenderly in his arms, passionately declaring his love for her and vowing to spare her at all costs from the fate she dreaded.

Now full of joy, Sophia gladly responded to the ardent declarations of Octavian, shyly avowing her own love in return; and for a few happy moments the lovers indulged in sweet converse, oblivious of their surroundings and of the ambiguousness of their position.

They were soon reminded of this latter fact, however; for, while still locked in each other's arms, they were seen by some spying attendants, who quickly brought Faninal and the Baron upon the scene to surprise them.

The Baron, instead of storming, merely laughed at the confusion of Octavian and Sophia, rallying them upon their speedy love-making and coarsely declaring himself pleased that his bride-elect should have a lover. He then seized Sophia by the arm and endeavoured to drag her into the adjoining room to sign the marriage contract; and when the indignant girl drew back, declaring that she would never wed with him, he tried all the more roughly to force her into the presence of the Notary.

This boorish conduct on the part of his principal was more than Octavian could stand; and, drawing his sword, he furiously challenged the Baron to a duel. The Baron, being a craven, instantly called for his servants; but Octavian compelled him to draw and, after a couple of passes, wounded him in the arm.

Instantly, all was confusion; and a loud hubbub arose. The Baron made a tremendous fuss over his very slight scratches, howling aloud that he was dying; and the obsequious Faninal and his attendants laid him carefully upon a couch and sent for surgeons and nurses. Faninal politely entreated the disturbing rose-bearer to depart at once; and then he packed Sophia off to her own room, angrily declaring that she should yet be married to her aristocratic suitor, willy-nilly.

The cowardly Baron quickly recovered under the ministrations of the surgeons, who scarcely found a scratch or two to bind up; and presently, he was left alone to rest upon a couch. A few moments later, however, a messenger entered and handed to him an intriguing-looking little scented note. Upon opening this eagerly, the reclining Baron found that it was signed "Mariandel" and that it was, indeed, a message from the pretty "waiting-maid" he had flirted with in his cousin's apartments that morning, stating that she had been better pleased with his attentions than she had then allowed him to see. Consequently, she had decided to accept his kind invitation to dine with him that evening; and she named a certain inn as the *rendezvous* and the time she would be there.

The Baron was greatly cheered at the thought of having thus made another conquest; and deciding to keep the assignation, he settled down to rest for a short time.

The young Octavian was blessed with an excellent sense of humour. On thinking matters over, he determined to gain his own ends and to get the better of the Baron by playing on him a merry trick which would lead to the undoing and ridicule of the vain-glorious libertine. It was with this object that he had sent the note to the Baron from the imaginary " Mariandel "; after which he proceeded to the inn named therein, where he made elaborate arrangements for the carrying out of his joke. He hired several rascally-looking loafers and hid them in various parts of the large room he had engaged in the inn, giving them careful instructions to show their villainous faces on signals from himself at a certain set time. He also arranged with a female hanger-on attached to the Baron's entourage to enact a special part in his little farce.

He next sent messengers to Faninal and Sophia, and also to the Princess von Werdenberg, begging them to appear at the inn at a particular time named by him; then, having thus completed all his plans, he proceeded to array himself once more in the clothes of " Mariandel ", the pretended " waiting-maid ", and sallied forth to meet the amorous Baron.

A few minutes later he returned to the inn leaning on the arm of the latter and pretending to be pleased with his elderly admirer's foolish remarks and maudlin love-making. The pair seated themselves at the supper-table in the private room set apart for them; but the Baron was so delighted by his seeming conquest of the pretty and saucy " Mariandel " that he preferred to make love to her rather than to feast.

Presently, however, the enticing " waiting-maid ", after partaking, under protest, of a glass of wine, pretended to grow sleepy; and when the Baron then endeavoured to draw her into his arms, he was startled and alarmed by the sudden appearance of strange, evil-looking faces staring at him from various parts of the darkened room.

The apparitions vanished as suddenly as they had appeared; but the Baron soon experienced another bad fright. There now appeared in the room one of his own disreputable female hangers-on—though he did not recognize her as such—disguised as a widowed lady clad in deepest mourning and accompanied by four young children also garbed in black. This lugubrious female flung herself in the arms of the amazed Baron, declaring herself to be his deserted but still loving mistress; and at the same time the four little youngsters clung around his legs and hung on to his coat-tails, calling out plaintively, "Papa! Papa! Papa!"

The Baron was furious at this interruption to his pleasure—but was at the same time confused, not remembering which of the many victims of his amorous intrigues this particular one could be; but, thinking to bluster the matter out, he ran to the window and called loudly for the watch.

When, however, in answer to his frantic calls, the Chief Commissary of Police appeared on the scene, he found himself in a worse predicament than ever; for the Commissary insisted upon asking him many awkward questions and sternly accused him of having the young girl, "Mariandel", at the inn without the consent of her guardians.

As the now dumbfounded Baron tried to find a way out of this new difficulty, his confusion was still further increased by the arrival of Faninal with Sophia; for he had sought to appease the Commissary by declaring his supper companion to be his *fiancée*. On hearing this statement repeated by the Commissary, Faninal became so furiously angry at the Baron's outrageous conduct that he fell down in a fit and had to be removed to another chamber, where he was attended by Sophia.

Meanwhile, Octavian, having found an oportunity of whispering secretly to the Commissary, retired to a curtained recess, where he hastily discarded his feminine garments; and, presently, he reappeared in his own garb as rose-bearer, just as the Princess von Werdenberg entered the room.

The Baron was now completely nonplussed—for, at this moment, Sophia also returned to announce to him that her father was so disgusted by his loose behaviour that he withdrew his consent to the marriage which had been arranged and refused to have anything further to do with so disreputable a suitor for his daughter's hand.

The Princess next stepped forward and explained to the worsted philanderer that the whole of the evening's proceedings had been a hoax—a diversion which had been planned by the young Octavian, his own kinsman and rose-bearer, who had also enacted the part of the pretty "Mariandel". Finally, the Baron, thus covered with confusion and ridicule, was obliged to beat a discomfited retreat; and he retired from the neighbourhood with the utmost speed.

The Princess now sadly realized that young Octavian's calf-love

z

fancy for herself—which she had so foolishly returned with interest—had been swamped by the real love which he had conceived for the fair and youthful Sophia; and, generously, she bade him woo the latter, while she retired to the inner chamber to secure the consent of Faninal to their union.

Gladly Octavian clasped Sophia in his arms and poured forth his love vows once more into her willing ears; and soon the joy of the lovers was crowned by the ready approval of Faninal—who was delighted to have thus secured a husband of noble birth for his daughter after all.

The party now retired from the inn to join in the rejoicings for the betrothal of Octavian and Sophia; and if, in the midst of the revels that ensued, the heart of the Princess was sad, she did not complain but only sighed regretfully because she had awakened from a fair and rosy dream too sweet to last!

SALOMÉ   *Richard Strauss*

ON the terrace of the Palace of Herod the Tetrarch of Galilee the soldiers and guards were talking together as the evening fell. From the open windows of the banqueting-hall came the sounds of music and the clattering of silver and golden dishes; for Herod was feasting a splendid company that night, including high officials and nobles of Rome who were the ambassadors of Cæsar. From the left of the terrace, however, came every now and again a very different sound, and one in strange contrast to the festive sounds of the banqueting-hall—the voice of Jokanaan,[1] the Jewish prophet of Judea, who was held captive there in an old well or cistern, and who uttered stern denunciations against the crime-stained Tetrarch and his wicked wife, Herodias.

While the soldiers spoke of Jokanaan—of his holiness, of his rough clothing, and how he had lived in the desert subsisting upon locusts and wild honey, of his prophesyings, and of his disciple-followers—their captain, Narraboth, a handsome young Syrian, stood apart with his friend, the page of Herodias, heedless of the words of his men and deaf to the voice of the Prophet. From the raised terrace he gazed down continually into the banqueting-hall; but he had eyes only for the dazzling beauty of the Princess Salomé, the daughter of Herodias. It was in vain that the page

[1] John the Baptist.

spoke of the strange loveliness of the newly-risen moon—Narraboth could see only the beauty of Salomé, which enthralled him and filled his heart with a love and worship that would not be denied. The page, knowing the hopelessness of such a passion, begged him to look no longer, fearing lest harm should come to his friend; but the young Syrian's gaze ever and anon returned to the lovely Princess whose every movement he noted.

Another gaze also fell constantly upon Salomé that night—that of Herod the Tetrarch, whose lustful eyes devoured her loveliness with a hot glow that plainly betrayed the unlawful desire that burned within him.

At length Salomé could bear this burning gaze no longer. Though of a deeply passionate nature herself, she loathed the vicious Tetrarch, her higher instincts being in constant revolt against her evil surroundings. Presently, therefore, she arose from her couch and came forth on to the terrace, glad to breathe the fresh pure air of the evening and to escape for a few moments from the gaze of Herod, whose passion was distressful to her.

As the Princess came towards the edge of the terrace, admiring the beauty of the moon, the young Syrian reverentially approached and spoke with her in trembling tones—unable to keep from the flame that scorched him and heedless of the whispered warnings of the page who feared lest trouble should befall because of his friend's passion.

While they spoke together, the voice of Jokanaan was heard from his prison, again uttering his denunciations and prophesies; and instantly Salomé's attention was aroused by the deep musical tones of his voice.

Eagerly she questioned the young Syrian and his soldiers about the prisoner; and their account of the fearlessness of the stern prophet seized upon her imagination to such an extent that she longed to behold the man who was bold enough to utter the truth about the sins of her mother and the wicked cruelties of the Tetrarch. Here at last was a man who came up to her standard of what splendid manhood should be. As his denunciations again were heard, she listened intently, all her vivid, passionate personality awakened and glowing with a sudden desire to behold the owner of the rich voice that thrilled her as no other man's voice had ever thrilled her.

Greatly disturbed by her obvious interest, the young Syrian endeavoured to divert her attention; but his efforts were in vain, and presently Salomé asked the soldiers to bring forth their prisoner that she might look upon him.

The soldiers replied that they could not do so, since the Tetrarch refused to allow anyone, even the High Priest, to speak with the prophet, of whom he had a strange fear.

But as Jokanaan's deep bold voice broke forth again in outspoken rebukes, Salomé's wild longing to behold the man now knew no restraint. Turning to the young Syrian—of whose love for her she was well aware—she began to use her arts of fascination upon him, begging him to grant her request and promising as a reward for this favour to bestow flowers and smiles upon him when she passed him in her litter on the morrow.

Narraboth—torn between duty and his jealousy of a possible rival in the passing interest of the beautiful Princess whom he loved so devotedly—entreated Salomé not to ask this thing of him; and he invited her to return to the banquet-hall, even though to do so deprived him of the joy of her presence. But when Salomé again insinuatingly repeated her promised reward, with an enthralling smile upon her scarlet lips and a look of witchery in her eyes which none could resist, his resolution melted and nothing remained but the ardent desire to please her, even though it cost him his life. Calling to a soldier, he commanded that the prophet should be brought forth at once.

And when Salomé gazed upon the noble form of Jokanaan as he came forth from the cistern-prison with chains about his hands and feet, and beheld the beauty of his person and the stern accusing glance of his flashing eyes—so different from the soft languorous glances of the effeminate pleasure-seeking men she was accustomed to—she remained for a moment as though spellbound. A passionate love suddenly surged up in her heart for this man—who, however, scarcely heeded her presence as he again called forth denunciations upon the evil Herodias.

Seeing that the young Princess was fascinated by the strong, powerful personality of the stern prophet, the young Syrian was distressed and alarmed and besought her not to speak to the prisoner. But Salomé now had eyes and ears for none but Jokanaan, whose fine bearing and true force of character appealed to her strongly; and she now addressed herself to him in her most seductive tones, making use of all the wiles and powers of fascination she possessed in such superabundance, utterly oblivious of her surroundings and of the presence of the soldiers.

First she praised the beauty of his body, then the blackness of his hair; and finally, losing all restraint, she extolled the redness of his mouth and entreated him to let her kiss his lips, passionately repeating her amorous request and declaring that she would gain her desire, come what might.

But Jokanaan coldly repulsed all the fascinations of Salomé

with lofty contempt, sternly rebuking her; and then, utterly untouched by her exquisite beauty but furious at her proffered love, he finally declared that she was accursed as the daughter of an infamous mother. He then returned to his prison with angry dignity.

During this passionate interview, Narraboth, the young Syrian, had vainly endeavoured to stem the tide of Salomé's amorous declarations; but finally, full of grief, he realized that the fair Princess's passion for the prophet was now beyond control and that his own devoted love for her was in vain. Suddenly, with a cry of despair, he stabbed himself and fell dead at her feet.

Even the tragic death of Narraboth, however, did not stop the flow of Salomé's passionate entreaties to Jokanaan; and it was not until the accusing prophet had returned to his prison, that her hot words ceased.

Then, as she realized that her proffered love had been refused, that her beauty and charms were despised, and that this man she so passionately desired would never love her in return, her love changed to a violent uncontrollable hatred. She now longed to avenge herself upon him, while, at the same time, her agonizing desire for him remained the same.

At this moment, Herod the Tetrarch, with his wife, Herodias, and their courtiers and guests, came forth from the banquet-hall, also seeking the coolness of the night air upon the terrace. As the brilliant company assembled in groups, Salomé still remained apart, pale, drooping, silent, and wrapped in her passionate dream, while the fiery blood raced in her veins.

Herod usually avoided the terrace because of his fear of the prophet he held captive, whose denunciations could not be denied by his guilty conscience, and in whose prophecies he secretly believed, despite the contemptuous railings of Herodias, who would have had him execute the holy man for daring to revile her. To-night, however, he knew that Salomé was there; and, prompted by the burning of his passion for her, he thus sought her bewitching presence once more. Presently observing the dead body of the young Syrian and learning that he had just killed himself, he guessed that Narraboth had thus taken his own life for love of Salomé; and angrily he commanded that the body should be removed. He had drunk deeply at the banquet, but was still full of strange fears and forebodings of coming evils; and when presently the voice of Jokanaan was again heard denouncing in fiery language the Tetrarch and his wicked wife and uttering the most scathing rebukes, as before, he called upon Salomé to entertain him in order to drown his fears, inviting her to eat luscious fruits and to drink wine with him. Salomé, however, turning with disgust from the lustful glances of the Tetrarch, coldly declined all his advances; and she still remained apart, while Herod continued to gaze upon her, heedless of the remonstrances of the jealous Herodias who angrily bade him not to look thus upon her daughter.

For a short time Herod held converse with the soldiers and guests, among whom were Nazarenes, Sadducees, Pharisees and other Jews, who spoke of the prophecies of Jokanaan and of the coming Messiah. Fierce altercations quickly arose between the Nazarenes—who asserted that the Messiah had already come and was performing miracles daily—and the Pharisees and Sadducees, who denied this assertion. Soon, however, the Tetrarch's eyes returned to Salomé, whom he now entreated to dance for him; but the young Princess still declined to give him pleasure—to the approval of her mother, who again angrily bade her husband take his burning gaze from her lovely daughter.

But Herod, intoxicated by Salomé's beauty and charm, still persisted in his request, declaring wildly to the Princess that if she would dance for him he would give her anything she might desire as a reward—his richest jewels and finest treasures, even to the half of his kingdom.

Then, suddenly, Salomé, despite the angry remonstrances of her mother, changed her mind, a fearful thought seizing upon her. Having secured the reckless sworn word of Herod that he would afterwards give to her the thing she demanded, no matter what it might be, she agreed to dance before him her famous and beautiful Dance of the Seven Veils.

Herod, exulting over this defeat of the jealous Herodias, was full of delight that the lovely Princess had at last yielded, as he imagined, to his desire that she should dance for his pleasure; and slaves having brought rich gauzy veils and removed her sandals, Salomé began to dance. Never before had her voluptuous movements been so full of grace or her radiant beauty so bewitchingly revealed; and her whole passionate nature seemed to be expressed in the mazy rhythm of her dance, so that all the company were entranced as they gazed upon her.

When the dance came to an end and Salomé sank amidst her cloudy veils at the feet of Herod, he was almost beside himself with desire of her beauty; and in a hoarse voice half choked with passion, he called upon her to name the thing that he should give to her. Instantly Salomé sprang to her feet and demanded that the head of Jokanaan the prophet—whom she now hated for despising her love—should be brought to her forthwith upon a silver charger.

This dreadful request, though loudly applauded by her mother, so staggered Herod with horror that at first he could scarcely believe he heard her aright, pretending that she was but joking. When Salomé, however, fiercely repeated her request, reminding him that he had sworn his kingly word which he could not break in front of his guests, and he realized that she was in earnest, he desperately endeavoured to dissuade her from her terrible desire, fearing to kill the prophet of whom he stood in the greatest awe. He offered her instead his splendid white peacocks; his richest jewels—ropes of pearls, sapphires as big as eggs, opals full of flashing fire, priceless rubies, emeralds, magic turquoises, topazes, jade—fans and garments made of ostrich feathers; the mantle of the high priest and the veil of the Temple; all that he possessed, even unto the half of his kingdom.

But to all of these feverishly proffered gifts, Salomé turned a deaf ear, coldly but relentlessly demanding the head of Jokanaan; and when Herod protested again and again, bidding her not to heed the wishes of Herodias, who eagerly supported her demand, she declared passionately that she heeded not her mother but desired the head of Jokanaan upon a silver charger for her own pleasure only. She still continued to repeat her awful demand, taunting the Tetrarch by scornfully accusing him of cowardice. At last Herod, unable to escape from his rash promise and goaded to desperation by her stinging words, agreed reluctantly to her wish and commanded the executioner to bring the head of the prisoner to the Princess as demanded by her. As he sank back trembling upon his cushion, Herodias instantly withdrew from his finger the Ring of Death and gave it to the soldiers to bear to the executioner as the symbol and token required for the performance of his dreadful deed; and though he almost immediately repented having given the command it was too late. The executioner had already received the ring and was performing his grisly office.

There was a deathly silence, for the whole company and even the soldiers were filled with horror at the young Princess's terrible request; but Salomé never wavered from her resolve to be revenged upon the man who had disdained her proffered love. She waited with an awful calmness and determination for her wish to be carried out. But though she listened eagerly for a cry from the victim, no sound came up from the dark cistern pit. Impatient at the delay, she presently called wildly and furiously to the soldiers to go and fetch her the thing she had demanded, the thing that had been promised her, and the thing that was hers. As even the rough soldiers drew back, appalled by her unnatural vehemence, the bare black arm of the executioner was presently seen to stretch up above the top of the cistern bearing aloft a silver shield upon which lay the bleeding head of Jokanaan the prophet.

With fierce eagerness Salomé rushed forward and seized the head; and while Herod sank back covering his terrified countenance with his mantle, and the Nazarenes fell upon their knees and began to pray, she devoured its beauty with rapturous eyes and exultingly kissed the red lips that had been so sternly denied to her but an hour ago. Then, remorse and despair seized her as she realized the emptiness of her revenge, her exultance died away; and she now kissed the dead lips with a deep tenderness in her passionate fervour, bemoaning her sad fate as she extolled in extravagantly poetic terms the beauty of the loved one now lost to her for ever.

Herod, trembling in every limb and horror-struck at the fearful deed his own weakness and insensate desire was responsible for, staggered to his feet; and, full of nameless fears, he ordered the lights to be put out as he groped his way indoors. Then, turning upon the threshold, he again beheld Salomé standing in the moonlight fondling the head of Jokanaan and despairingly kissing the dead lips that had scorned her.

Horrified and enraged beyond all control at this dreadful sight, he called furiously to the guards : " Kill that woman."

Instantly his command was obeyed; and the beautiful and passionate Salomé fell crushed beneath the shields of the soldiers.

MAVRA   *Stravinsky*

A PRETTY young girl named Parasha sat at the open window of her home in a small Russian town, working at a piece of embroidery and singing as she worked. She sang of the birds, the flowers, the sunshine, the canary twittering in the cage beside her; and she also sang of the temporary ache in her heart because she had not beheld her secret admirer for seven whole dismal days.

Then, to her joy, a handsome young Hussar almost miraculously appeared at an open window in the house opposite; and he sang an answering song to her own.

This singer was Vassili, the sweetheart she had just been longing to see—a wonderful secret admirer whose existence the romantic girl had so far managed to keep safely hidden from her mother. The latter, a plump and practical dame, would certainly not approve of an impecunious young Hussar as a satisfactory suitor for her daughter. So meetings very few and far between were all that at present could be enjoyed by Parasha and her sweetheart; and when they occurred, they lasted all too short a time.

No sooner had the happy pair now exchanged greetings and Parasha had listened eagerly to the gipsy song sung to her by the ardent Vassili, than the voice of her mother was heard calling her name; and they knew that the latter was about to enter the room.

After making a hurried plan for their next clandestine meeting in the town and at a frantic sign from his beloved one, the young Hussar vanished from the opposite window; and Parasha turned reluctantly to greet her mother.

The latter bustled in, full of laments for the recent death of the excellent domestic helper who had served her faithfully for many years. Good cooks were now almost impossible to get; and, meanwhile, until she secured another, her household was being neglected for lack of assistance.

In worried mood, therefore, the maidless dame now rather crossly demanded that her daughter, instead of sitting embroidering at the window, should go forth instantly into the town to seek for a new domestic—a seemingly hopeless task which filled the latter with dismay. Then, suddenly, a bold but mischievous idea came into the head of Parasha; and now, willingly undertaking the proposed mission, the seemingly obedient daughter put on a smart outdoor cloak and hat and left the house to inquire in the town for that *rara-avis*, a capable maid-servant. But there was an extremely saucy look in her bright eyes as she departed— which, however, was unnoticed by her worried mother.

That good dame now settled herself in a comfortable chair to await the return of her daughter with the new maid; and presently she was joined by a gossiping neighbour, a busy-body lady who had come in ostensibly to commiserate with her on the loss of her excellent maid, but was also eager to chat.

Time thus passed pleasantly enough for the two ladies, who discussed first the particular virtues and value of the recently deceased household treasure and the real difficulty of finding another so perfect yet willing to accept the same reasonable wages. Then they went on gloomily to express the fear that the present bright, sunny, summer weather would all too quickly merge into the dark days of winter.

They seemed, however, to be thoroughly enjoying this somewhat dismal exchange of views, and had just gone on to the more cheerful topic of new bonnets and clothes, when Parasha returned, full of excitement. Not only had she secured a perfectly wonderful new maid, but she had actually brought this treasure back with her, ready to begin work at once.

With amazed relief, her mother praised the girl for her good deed; and she and the neighbour friend bade her bring in the new domestic, that they might question the latter's qualifications for themselves.

The new arrival proved to be an extremely tall and hefty-looking young woman, somewhat angular and awkward in her movements; and she certainly looked strong. True, her voice was rather rough and deep; but she spoke most respectfully and declared that she could cook, and scrub, and was a hard worker. She had the attractive name of " Mavra "; and Parasha declared that she had formerly worked for her mother's old friend, " Ann ".

This latter recommendation was quite sufficiently good for the greatly relieved lady of the house; and when bidden by her elated daughter to admire the charming smiles of the cheerful Mavra and to listen to the renewed recital of her many capabilities, she gladly did so.

Having congratulated her friend upon securing such a fine new domestic treasure, the gossiping neighbour now departed to spread the wonderful news elsewhere.

Then Parasha's mother, happy at being thus so providentially relieved of the tiresome necessity of having to cook the family's next meal, declared her immediate intention of going out for a walk. As she retired to her chamber to don her best clothes for this unexpected little outing, she bade her daughter introduce the new cook to the kitchen and scullery and explain where everything was kept, that work might begin at once.

This command was precisely what Parasha desired. No sooner had she made sure that her mother was safely upstairs and occupied in changing her clothes, than she turned with a cry of joy and rushed into the eagerly opened arms of the new domestic.

For " Mavra " was none other than her own secret sweetheart, Vassili, the dashing young Hussar from the house opposite, with whom, on being sent out to seek for a new cook, she had planned this risky masquerade in accordance with her own bright idea. Having procured, with the aid of Parasha, some suitable feminine garments, the young Hussar, equally eager for the frolic, had hastily dressed himself in them; and he had likewise donned a servant's bonnet-like cap to hide his own hair. Then the two conspirators strolled down the road and up again, as though coming from the town; after which, they had presently entered the young girl's home together.

Neither Parasha nor her sweetheart knew how long they would be able to keep up this masquerade, nor how soon the young Hussar would give himself away by his entire lack of domestic lore; but they determined to make the most of the opportunities for being alone together which they hoped would now occur.

While her mother was still upstairs dressing, therefore, Parasha made no attempt to show the new " cook " any of the details of the domestic paraphernalia. Instead, she gladly listened to the words of love poured forth by her sweetheart, accepting his caresses with eager willingness; and the youthful pair enjoyed a deliriously happy half-hour.

Then, hearing the sound of descending footsteps, the sweethearts instantly separated; and Parasha was , already busily explaining domestic matters to " Mavra " when her mother entered the room, now clad in outdoor garb. After giving some final instructions to the respectfully attentive newcomer, the now cheerful dame called to her daughter to accompany her out walking; and presently the pair set off for their outing—Parasha departing somewhat reluctantly, but unable to find any good excuse for remaining behind.

On being left alone, the pretended " cook ", instead of going into the kitchen and beginning the many tasks which had been enumerated and having no real desire to wash the dishes or prepare a meal—thinking in his masculine inexperience that any time later on would do for these—at first gave himself up to sweet and passionate thoughts of his beloved Parasha and to making clever plans for further stolen interviews with her. Then, as he moved about the room, tenderly touching objects belonging to his fair lady, he happened to catch sight of his own reflection in a mirror; and he fell a-laughing at the strange spectacle of himself in feminine attire.

Presently, on gazing more closely at his reflection in the mirror, he was horrified to observe that, in his eager haste to dress up in feminine garb, he had actually forgotten to shave himself! Realizing that nothing would give him away sooner than the dark shadow of a morning beard on his " girlish " chin, the young man hastily produced some shaving-tackle he had taken the precaution to bring with him and began, then and there, in a great hurry, to shave himself before the glass.

Finding his domestic servant's huge cap-headdress—complete with curls attached—an inconvenience, he threw it aside, thus revealing his own neat masculine short-cut hair. Further tram melled, too, by his unaccustomed voluminous skirt, he likewise tore it off. Then, free and comfortable, he set to work again upon his barbering job.

He had just spread a really good soapy lather upon his face, and was carefully shaving off the offending incipient beard, when the door opened and Parasha and her mother entered the room, having just returned from their walk—which the young girl had purposely manœuvred to make a short one, being eager to return to her beloved Vassili.

But what an alarming spectacle now met the eyes of the two ladies! Instead of finding the excellent " Mavra " busily setting out the expected meal, the astonished lady of the house beheld a strange man in soldierly garb, actually in the act of shaving himself before the mirror in her sitting-room. Uttering loud hysterical cries at the sight of one she immediately supposed to be a burglar, she soon fell back in a swooning condition.

This sudden uproar brought in once more in hot haste the gossiping neighbour-friend. This dame was of a more practical turn; and, instead of swooning, she made a sudden rush to secure the intruder, calling wildly upon Parasha to assist her and loudly crying out " Stop, thief! Stop, thief! "

Seeing that his dangerous game was already up, young Vassili, casting a final loving and reassuring look upon his pretty Parasha —a look which plainly said " We'll meet again soon, my beloved! "—made straight for the window, through which he leapt at a single bound and so disappeared from sight.

Parasha, who was already dutifully tending her hysterical mother and reviving her with water, was glad to realize that no actual harm had been caused by the escapade. Neither of the older women had guessed that the supposed " burglar " masquerading as the new domestic she had secured was known to her, or that he was, indeed, her own secret sweetheart.

When, therefore, the neighbour-friend, still greatly excited by the incident, began to sympathize with and to comfort the now quickly recovering lady of the house by declaring that, after all, she had come off well, since she might easily have " been murdered " by the impudent masquerading intruder, Parasha diplomatically agreed with her.

But, under her breath, the young girl murmured to herself with deep relief: " Vassili, my beloved! Our secret is still safe! "

THE NIGHTINGALE   *Stravinsky*

MANY thousands of years ago there lived a certain mighty Emperor of China, who was the most magnificent sovereign on earth. He lived in a wonderful palace made of precious porcelain; and the throne he sat upon was all of solid gold, studded with sparkling gems. His robes were so richly jewelled and so stiff with gold and silver threads that they would stand alone.

So luxurious were all the appurtenances of this Emperor's Court that no one had ever seen their like before; and the lords-in-waiting were very nearly as dazzling in appearance as the Emperor himself. This was especially the case with the Lord Chamberlain, who was extremely haughty and pompous and held his aristocratic head so high up in the air that he had never seen the ground he walked upon since he was a child; and when anyone of a lesser rank than his own spoke to him, he only condescended to answer " Pooh! "

The most exquisite flowers grew in the palace gardens, and they all had silver bells attached to them, which tinkled in the soft breezes; and the garden was so large that even the head gardener did not know where it ended. The farthest point most people had reached in this enormously large garden had brought them to a beautiful forest, beyond which it was believed that the blue ocean rolled. Here, amongst the tall trees on the borders of·this forest, dwelt a Nightingale, who had the loveliest voice in the world and whose magical song could charm away evil and bring joy to the saddest hearts.

There was a poor Fisherman who came all the way from the seashore every evening for the sole pleasure of listening to the sweet singing of the Nightingale; and the humble folk who dwelt round about loved to listen to her joyous song, which made them forget their troubles for the time being.

Many travellers who came past that way were so entranced when they heard the thrilling notes of the Nightingale that when they returned to their own lands, they wrote entire books about it, declaring it to be the most wonderful thing they had come across on their travels.

Yet, strange to say, neither the Emperor of China himself, nor any of his courtiers, had ever heard of the little bird whose fame had travelled so far and wide. Indeed, it was not until he had read a description of the songstress's powers in a book of travels sent him as a present by the Emperor of Japan, that the mighty Ruler of China learned that such a wonderful creature existed in his dominions.

He was then extremely annoyed that he had never been told of it before; and he commanded the Lord Chamberlain to have the celebrated songstress brought to Court that he might judge her voice for himself.

At first, the pompous Lord Chamberlain declared that, not knowing the abode of the lady in question, he was afraid he could not gratify this sudden wish of his lord and master. When, however, the Emperor announced angrily that unless he produced the bird that evening, he and all his fellow-courtiers should be trampled upon, he bestirred himself at once—for he did not relish the idea of being trodden under foot by the royal elephants, even though the latter had their tusks gilded and wore golden bells around their big ugly feet.

After inquiring in vain from hundreds of people as to the whereabouts of the Nightingale's abode, the Lord Chamberlain was informed by a little kitchen-maid that she knew the bird well and that, as she went to listen to its song every evening, she would gladly lead him to the haunt of the songstress.

So the Lord Chamberlain and a few other courtiers followed the little kitchen-maid, who led them through the palace garden to the borders of the forest beyond. After mistaking first the lowing of a heifer and then the croaking of the frogs in the marshes for the famous singer, they at last heard the wonderful voice of the Nightingale as it trilled through the woodland depths.

The Lord Chamberlain was so amazed and overjoyed as he listened to the magic song, that he lost his breath for quite a minute; but as soon as he had recovered himself, he made a pompous speech and invited the Nightingale to come to Court that same evening, to sing before the Emperor.

"Thank you, I will come with pleasure!" replied the Nightingale. "But my voice really sounds very much better in the green woods, and I hope His Majesty will not be disappointed!"

The coming of the Nightingale to Court was the greatest event of the Emperor's reign; and the excitement in the palace was intense.

When the Nightingale arrived, she took up her stand upon the golden perch which had been provided for her and began to sing at once. Everybody was enchanted with the wonderful charm of her sweet voice, which had the magic power of making people feel intense joy or sorrow as she willed.

There were tears in the eyes of the Emperor when the song

came to an end; and the Nightingale had to sing again to chase the tears away and to make him smile.

The plain little brown and grey bird now became the rage and was established as Chief Musician at Court, with many lords and ladies to wait upon her; and she was only allowed to go out into the garden once at night and twice in the daytime. So much admiration did she attract that all the Court ladies became quite jealous and vainly attempted to sing in shakes and trills that they also might be regarded as Nightingales; and there was nothing else talked of but the new songstress. Even the common people were allowed to hear her occasionally; and the little kitchen-maid often stood at the scullery door to listen while the performance was taking place.

Then, just when the new singer's popularity was at its height, a second gift arrived from the Emperor of Japan. This turned out to be a clockwork Nightingale made of precious gems which sparkled at every turn, and which, when wound up, could sing pretty tunes. True, these tunes were only waltzes and were quite mechanical; but the jewelled bird's outward appearance was so gorgeous and dazzling, and the clockwork apparatus inside its body which produced the tunes appeared so marvellous to the Emperor and his courtiers, that it was at once appointed Imperial Court Singer—being voted much more wonderful than the real Nightingale, whose sombre garb had never been wholly approved of, though her voice had enchanted all.

So the plain little bird, surprised and hurt by the ingratitude of man, flew away to her beloved woodlands once more, where she again sang sweetly every night to the humble Fisherman and to the kindly country folk; and the gaudy artificial Nightingale became the craze of the Emperor and his Court.

The popularity of the new toy lasted quite a long time; and then, one day, its mainspring broke and it was found to be nearly worn out. The royal clockmaker mended and patched it up as best he could; but it was never the same again and its wheels were worn so thin that it was only allowed to be wound up to sing occasionally on the most important festivals.

The Emperor was so upset by this catastrophe that he lost not only his good spirits but his appetite as well; and, at last, he became so extremely ill that he was expected to die any minute. The order was given for his coming funeral, and a new Emperor even was chosen to be in readiness to succeed him.

While these dismal preparations were taking place, the sick Emperor lay upon his bed, pale and wan, with the spectral form of Death sitting at his bedside; and the shades of his Good and

Evil Deeds hovered around and peeped at him from behind the
bed-hangings. It was late at night and the royal invalid was just
on the point of expiring, when, suddenly, he heard the sound of
the most beautiful music floating in through the open window.
To his joy, he recognized the sweet song of the little bird whom he
had treated with such ingratitude.

It was indeed the humble little Nightingale, who, having heard
of her Imperial admirer's illness, had come, out of the kindness
of her heart—and not because he deserved it—to sing to him, and
to heal him with her magical voice; and as the Emperor lay back
in bed and listened to the wonderful sounds, his pains left him,
his vitality returned, and he began to feel better.

Even the gaunt visage of Death showed delight as he listened
to the song of the Nightingale; and the sinister visitor begged her
to continue her song, promising to depart at daybreak if she
would consent to do so. The Nightingale gladly agreed to this
bargain, singing joyfully all the night through; and at daybreak,
Death and his shadowy spirits departed and the Emperor arose
from his couch, cured of his sickness and in the best of health.

As soon as he had arrayed himself in his royal robes and had
put the crown upon his head once more, he thanked the Nightingale for having saved his life by her soothing song, and entreated
her to take up her abode at Court once more; but the humble
songstress replied: " Nay, my lord, I am not a courtier, but a
creature of the wilds, loving the beauties of Nature. My home
must be in the forest; but I will come and sing to you every
night—and I will tell you wonderful secrets, too, if you will
promise never to let anyone know that it is a little bird who tells
you everything! "

The Emperor gladly gave the promise asked by the Nightingale,
and retired to his bed once more. Then, as the funeral procession
approached and his courtiers, robed in mourning garments,
entered the chamber in order to bear him away to his burial—
believing that he must surely have died during the night, as he
had been on the point of expiring when last they saw him—he
thrust aside the curtains and greeted the astonished beholders with
a hearty " Good morning! "

MIGNON   *Thomas*

ONE festal day, during the early years of the last century, a lively scene was taking place in the streets of a certain little German country town. A troupe of gipsy mountebanks had just arrived there; and, seeing that a holiday was in progress, they had quickly set about regaling the idle populace with an impromptu entertainment in the open courtyard of an inn. A merry crowd soon gathered around them, and loud bursts of applause greeted the efforts of the gipsies, who accompanied their wild songs and fantastic dances with the twanging of guitars and tambourines.

Amongst the spectators was one who seemed almost regardless of the gay scene before him; a noble-looking old man with long grey elf-locks, whose shabby, worn-out garments and a harp which he carried proclaimed him to be a wandering minstrel. There was a look of unutterable grief in this old man's eyes, together with a strange restless gleam, as though the soul within sought constantly for some beloved object it never could find. Every now and again he would break forth into wild snatches of song, full of heart-broken sadness, which were received by the bystanders with good-humoured indulgence—for old Lothario the Harper was a familiar figure to them and it was well known that some great sorrow had rendered him half-crazed.

The gipsy mountebanks found their audience an appreciative one. Seeing that the impromptu entertainment was likely to prove profitable, the leader—a fierce-looking rascal named Giarno—announced that Mignon, the fairest and most talented of their gipsy maidens, would now give an exhibition of the famous egg-dance. So saying, he thrust forward a beautiful young girl, in whose soft eyes fear and scornful resistance seemed struggling for the mastery. It was soon plain to all that she regarded the lusty Giarno as a cruel tyrant whom she was at last determined to defy; upon being bidden by him to begin her dance, she utterly refused to do so.

Alas, poor Mignon! Of noble birth, she had been stolen from her home in early childhood by the gipsies with whom she had been brought up. Giarno the Mountebank, seeing in her beauty and grace a means of attracting audiences and securing gain, had compelled her to dance in the streets of every town and village they passed through; and he frequently beat her cruelly when, through fatigue or misery, she failed to please him.

For many years the unhappy child, through fear of her harsh master, was forced to obey his will; but as she advanced to maidenhood, all her natural highborn instincts of refinement and modesty rebelled against the publicity of the life she was compelled to lead. Now, at last, she determined to revolt! Outraged by the free glances of admiration cast upon her by the careless gallants in the crowd, she shrank back and tried to escape. Enraged by her refusal, the fierce Giarno seized his stick and declared he would beat her unless she obeyed him at once; but, despite his threats, brave little Mignon still declined to do his bidding.

The old harper, Lothario, had been watching this scene with growing interest, feeling himself drawn to the pretty Mignon by some unaccountable attraction; and on seeing the young girl shrink back from the upraised arm of her tyrant master, he hurried forward, calling out as he approached: "Courage, maiden! I will protect you!"

Before he reached her side, however, a second defender arrived upon the scene—a handsome youth who, dashing forward and snatching the stick from Giarno's hand, bade him, as he valued his life, not to harm the gipsy girl. Cowed by this sudden onslaught, the bully drew back, muttering apologetically that he did but seek additional gain by the performance of his dancing-girl; and upon receiving from his assailant a few coins in compensation for his loss, he was contented and withdrew with Mignon from the crowd.

The bold cavalier who had thus come to the aid of the gipsy maid was a Viennese student, by name Wilhelm Meister—who, being young, rich, and gay, was for the time being amusing himself by travelling from place to place, eager to see the world and to engage in the excitements of youth. His natural generosity and kindly pity had led him to interfere on Mignon's behalf; and now, as he strolled away to a refreshment garden near by, he felt elated by his encounter and longed for further adventures.

It happened that the whole of this little scene had been witnessed from a balcony opposite by two strangers to the town—an actor named Laertes, and Filina, his leading lady, an actress of much beauty and fascinating but coquettish manners. Being greatly struck by the handsome appearance and gallant behaviour of the young student, the pair made their way likewise to the refreshment gardens, where they soon entered into friendly conversation with Wilhelm. The latter was much amused by the exaggerated conversation of the actor; but he was so delighted with the sparkling beauty of the fair actress that he quickly fell under the spell of her many fascinations. He determined to see more of her later on, despite the fact that Laertes had already warned him that she was a born coquette.

As he came away from the garden, he met the gipsy troupe once more. Recognizing her defender, the grateful Mignon sprang forward at once and, kissing his hand, began to pour forth heartfelt thanks for his protection of her. Wilhelm was touched by her simple gratitude, and began to question her, being struck by her obvious refinement and somewhat ethereal beauty; and only too willingly Mignon told him her pitiful little story—how she had been stolen by the gipsies when a little child and of her harsh treatment by them ever since. She could remember little of her early life; but from her rapturous recollection of flowering orange-trees and everlasting blue skies, Wilhelm guessed that her home had been in Italy.

As they spoke together, the mountebank, Giarno, drew near and, remarking that the young cavalier seemed to have taken a fancy to Mignon, suggested that he should buy the girl's freedom from him. Eager to rescue the girl from so sordid a life, Wilhelm gladly agreed to the proposal, paying over to the gipsy a hundred ducats at once; and Giarno quickly departed, well pleased with the good bargain he had made.

Again Mignon poured forth grateful thanks upon her benefactor —for whom a passionate love was already springing up in her young heart; then turning to old Lothario the Harper, who was also hovering near, she begged him to rejoice with her.

Leaving the now happy girl with Lothario, Wilhelm strolled back to the gardens, where he was soon joined again by Filina and Laertes, who announced that they had just received news of an important engagement. A certain Baron Rosenberg was entertaining a company of noble guests at his castle in the neighbourhood and had instructed the strolling players to give a performance at a splendid *fête* he was giving a few days later; and Filina, eager not to be parted from her new admirer, now suggested that Wilhelm should join them as poet attached to the company.

Wilhelm, just ripe for such an adventure and dazzled by the charms of the coquettish Filina—with whom he already fancied himself half in love—agreed to the proposal, and promised to join them at the *fête*. He then returned to Lothario and Mignon, telling the latter that he intended to place her with some worthy people in the town, who would watch over her welfare.

Mignon, however, implored him not to send her away from him; and she begged to be permitted to accompany him on his travels in the disguise of a page, that she might serve him wherever he went.

When Wilhelm gently shook his head and removed her clinging hands from his arm, the old harper now offered to be her guardian, declaring that if she would roam with him, he would watch over her with loving care. But Wilhelm, seeing the look of intense disappointment upon the face of the gipsy girl, now relented and, touched by her devotion, said that she might remain with him for the present, if she chose. When, some days later, therefore, Wilhelm set off for the castle of Rosenberg, Mignon joyfully accompanied him in the garb of a page; and old Lothario, determined to keep a watch over the beautiful maiden whose sweet looks so strangely moved him, followed to the same neighbourhood that he might be near at hand should she decide to throw in her lot with him, after all.

.   .   .   .

Upon arriving at the castle Wilhelm was joyfully received by the fair Filina, who, as the favourite " star " of the theatrical company, had been allotted a handsome suite of apartments; and the young man, again intoxicated by her subtle witcheries, was flattered and filled with delight.

The timid Mignon, however, after being received with coldness and laughing scorn by the actress, retired to a recess at the far end of the boudoir. As she heard her beloved benefactor's protestations of admiration for the gay pleasure-seeking coquette before him, a dull, hopeless pain came into her heart—for she felt that she, the poor gipsy maid, could never hope now to share in the sunshine of his love.

She wondered childishly whether she could make herself sufficiently like Filina to attract him; and when the pretty actress presently departed to the *salon* with Wilhelm, she determined to try the experiment. Finding herself alone in the room, she drew forth one of Filina's gauzy robes and arrayed herself in it; then, sitting before the mirror, she began to enhance her youthful complexion with the usual accessories to beauty used by the practised coquette, laughing with delight at her altered appearance.

Suddenly, however, she heard the sound of approaching footsteps and, fearing to be discovered in her borrowed finery, she ran into an adjoining room as the intruder entered the boudoir.

The newcomer was a foppish youth, named Frederick, nephew to Baron Rosenberg. Wishing to pose as an admirer of the fascinating Filina, he had now come to pay his court, expecting to find her alone. No sooner had he entered the room, however, than he was followed by Wilhelm, who had returned to speak with Mignon, whom he was about to send back to the town after all, at the request of Filina. When Wilhelm demanded his business, the youth instantly provoked a quarrel with him and furiously drew his sword.

Wilhelm, to humour the youth, whose attempted gallantry amused him, playfully drew his own sword; but at this moment, Mignon rushed in from the inner chamber and flung herself between them. Quickly seeing that a duel had never been seriously intended—Frederick having already sheathed his sword in evident relief—and suddenly remembering her borrowed plumes, she began to make a shamefaced apology for her folly. Then Wilhelm gently took her aside and told her that they must now part, as he had decided to send her back to the town to the protection of the guardians he had named before.

Filina, who had followed her new admirer into the room, mockingly added that since the gipsy maid had obviously taken a fancy to the dress in which she had adorned herself, she might keep it. But Mignon, stung by the laughing scorn of her rival and rendered desperate by Wilhelm's decision, now furiously tore the gauzy robe to ribbons and rushed away in a tempest of tears and angry feelings.

Wilhelm, astonished at this outburst of jealousy on the part of Mignon—whom until now he had regarded as a child—suddenly felt an awakened interest in her and began to wonder at the depth of passion she had betrayed; but as the evening *fête* was now about to begin, he departed to witness the performance.

. . . .

The play chosen for representation that night was *A Midsummer Night's Dream*, and Filina, in the character of "Titania", won golden opinions from all. In her dainty fairy garments she bewitched the hearts of her audience by her charming acting and fascinating coquetry; and the old castle walls rang with the loud bursts of applause constantly accorded to the lovely actress.

Meanwhile, the unhappy Mignon, having passionately torn off her borrowed finery and donned her old gipsy garments once more, had flown from the castle and made her way to the bank of a lonely lake in the grounds. Here, overcome by the grief of her hopeless love and rendered almost frantic by the bursts of applause in praise of Filina that ever and anon reached her, she was just about to throw herself into the water when the timely arrival of Lothario the Harper saved her from her terrible resolve.

The old man had been hovering about the grounds all evening; and he now listened sympathetically to the whole story of the young girl's grief—feeling strangely, as he soothed her, that her sorrows were his own. So much akin to her did he feel, indeed, that when—carried away by her jealous emotions on hearing yet another loud burst of applause ring out upon the evening air—Mignon uttered a rash wish that the building in which her rival now triumphed might suddenly burst into flames, a curious gleam came into the old harper's wild eyes. He left her side at once; and when he presently returned once more, he told her exultingly that, in accordance with her desire, he had set the castle on fire and that the flames would soon burst forth.

Before Mignon could fully grasp the meaning of what her half-crazed friend had done on her behalf, the festive entertainment came to an end, and guests and performers alike came out in the illuminated gardens to refresh themselves in the cool evening air.

The praises of Filina were sung on every side; and as the triumphant actress came forth on the arm of Wilhelm, she was received with great enthusiasm. Wilhelm soon noticed Mignon standing in the gloom with Lothario and, hurrying forward, he greeted her with tenderness and relief for, alarmed by her prolonged absence, he had been searching for her. Filina, hating to see the pair together, soon joined them and haughtily desired Mignon to return to the theatre and fetch a bouquet she had left upon the stage. Mignon, her despair brought back by the solicitous voice of Wilhelm, hurried into the doomed castle at once, remembering old Lothario's wild words and hoping to be overcome by the fumes within.

The interior of the castle was already burning fiercely; and as the startled guests suddenly saw flames bursting forth from the building they had just left, they rejoiced at their own safety.

But Mignon was within the burning castle; and quickly realizing her danger, Wilhelm, with a cry of horror, dashed through the smoking doorway to rescue her. Struggling against the fumes and suffocating heat, he made his way to the theatre and here he found the gipsy girl lying half dazed upon the already burning stage. Snatching her up in his arms—heedless of her frantic pleading that she might be left to her fate—he bore her triumphantly through the blinding smoke into the safety of the grounds beyond.

Here he was quickly joined by Lothario—upon whom he now saw that the recent excitement and shock had had the effect of restoring his reason to his normal balance and clearness. To his surprise, the old harper presently announced in cool, decided tones his intention of conveying the unconscious girl to the palace of Cipriani in Italy, where he had influence to secure her every care and attention.

Realizing that Lothario was in earnest and would not be
diverted from his purpose, Wilhelm agreed to help the old man
to convey Mignon to Italy; for he now felt drawn to the beautiful
young girl by the magnetic power of her own love for him—and
already his passing fancy for the frivolous coquette, Filina, was
dying away.

With every care and tenderness, therefore, the old man and his
young companion bore the hapless Mignon to Italy.

. . . .

Upon arriving at the palace of Cipriani—a stately building upon
the borders of a beautiful lake—the rescued girl fell into a fever,
brought on by the dangerous excitement and mental suffering she
had lately endured.

Wilhelm found, to his amazement, that the directions and
commands of Lothario were all obeyed by the servants of the
palace as though the old harper were their master; but he hardly
found time to wonder at this, all his thoughts being now
centred upon the suffering Mignon. In her delirium, the sick
girl constantly breathed his name, thus betraying her passionate
love for him; and as Wilhelm gazed upon the pale face of the
fair maiden he had rescued and remembered her wonderful
devotion and gratitude to him, an answering passion, deep and
tender, gradually awakened within his own breast. One day,
therefore, when Mignon had sufficiently recovered to be brought
into a large sunny room overlooking the sparkling lake, the
young student told her of his love; and the young girl's faithful
heart was filled with joy and sweet contentment.

Whilst the lovers were rejoicing together, Lothario entered the
room; but, instead of his familiar, way-worn garments, they saw,
to their surprise, that he was now richly clad and moved with the
proud bearing of a noble. He greeted them in courtly tones and
introduced himself as the owner of the palace in which they now
resided, the Count of Cipriani. His only child, Sperata, had
been stolen from him many years ago—since when he had sought
her vainly in his half-crazed state—but he believed she had now
been restored to him in the person of the lovely Mignon.

As he spoke, the Count produced a casket and drew from it a
girdle which he said had been almost constantly worn by his little
Sperata; and at the sound of this name, a chord of memory was
struck in the consciousness of Mignon, and she eagerly drew forth
another relic from the casket. This was a little prayer-book, from
which the Count said his lost child had always spelled her evening
prayer; and Mignon, a whole stream of sweet recollections now
rushing upon her, closed her eyes and repeated from memory the

same simple childish prayer that was contained in the book.

Satisfied at having thus proved beyond a doubt that the beautiful girl before him was indeed his own beloved daughter, Count Lotharia clasped her in his arms with great joy; then, placing her hand in that of Wilhelm, he bestowed his blessing upon them both.

EUGÈNE ONÉGIN   *Tschaikovsky*

IT was a warm evening in the late autumn during the early years of the last century. Madame Larina, a wealthy landowner in Russia, was sitting in the garden of her beautiful country house, busily engaged upon the homely task of peeling fruit. Through the open windows of the mansion close by came the sound of the sweet singing of her two fair young daughters, Olga and Tatiana; and as she listened to them, the mother's heart was filled with tender recollections, for the song was one she had herself sung in the days of her youth.

Presently a band of merry peasants came trooping into the grounds, carrying sheaves of corn, which they presented to Madame Larina—for to-day was the end of the harvesting, and they had come to lay their customary tribute at the feet of their beloved benefactress.

Madame Larina received the peasants with great kindness, inviting them to sing and dance before her and to partake of the refreshment she had ordered to be prepared for them. So the lively youths and maidens, despite their weariness after their long day's toil, began to go through the mazy figures of a country dance upon the lawn, singing a merry harvest song as an accompaniment.

On hearing the song of the peasants, Olga and Tatiana came out into the garden and stood beside their mother, listening to the singing and watching the intricate dance with interest.

The two sisters, though both fair to look upon, presented a great contrast to one another. The elder, Olga, was light-hearted, matter-of-fact, and frivolous, loving gaiety and amusement; Tatiana, on the other hand, was dreamy, romantic, and retiring, caring little for the usual excitements of youth and preferring to wander off alone to read in solitude or to indulge in day-dreams.

When the peasants had finished their dance, they trooped away again to partake of their patroness's hospitality; and immediately afterwards, a fine carriage drove up, from which alighted two young men of noble birth who lived in the neighbourhood. These were Vladimir Lenski, a young nobleman who was betrothed to Olga, and his friend, Eugène Onégin. The latter, although he owned land in the district, was as yet unknown to Madame Larina and her daughters.

At sight of the stranger, the shy and timid Tatiana would have retired to the house, but was detained by her mother; and a few moments later, Lenski came forward to greet the ladies, at the same time introducing his friend.

Onégin was a handsome man, who had seen much of the world and possessed an interesting and fascinating personality; and as the impressionable Tatiana gazed shyly upon him, she was strangely attracted, feeling that he was the very personification of the romantic hero of her girlish dreams. Onégin, too, was interested in the pensive girl, who was more to his taste than the laughing Olga; and, entering into conversation, he presently strolled into the twilit garden with her, leaving Lenski and his *fiancée* to their own sweet devices.

A little later on, Madame Larina called the two couples in to the evening meal; and after the declared lovers had retired to the house, Tatiana and Onégin reluctantly emerged from the shadowy garden, deep in conversation, and passed in after them.

Tatiana, despite her natural shyness, had found intense enjoyment in the society of Onégin. Although his conversation revealed him to be a somewhat world-weary cynic, with little belief in human goodness, yet his personality thrilled her to an extraordinary extent; and her heart already throbbed wildly with a strange delirious joy that would not be suppressed. As the night advanced, this sudden passion grew more and more intensified; and when at last she retired to her chamber, her agitation was so great that she could restrain her feelings no longer.

Her old nurse, Philipjewna, who attended to her personal needs, endeavoured to soothe the young girl, seeing that she was overwrought; but she found her task a hard one, for Tatiana insisted on hearing the story of Philipjewna's own love experiences and betrothal and was not to be diverted from this all-enthralling subject. Tatiana, however, paid little attention to the story she had asked for, being too much engrossed with her own conflicting emotions; and when the recital came to an end, she desired the old nurse to bring writing materials into the room and then to leave her alone.

When Philipjewna had brought the writing materials, she

kissed her nursling tenderly and left the room, hoping that sleep and pleasant dreams would restore the young girl to calmness by the morning.

But sleep was very far from the thoughts of the agitated Tatiana. Unable to quell her now overwhelming passion, she had determined to write a letter to Eugène Onégin, confessing the deep love she had conceived for him and asking him to grant her a private meeting in the grounds next day. For a long time conflicting thoughts assailed her, maidenly modesty and natural reticence struggling vainly with her new-born love and the desire to have it returned; but at length the intensity of her passion overcame all other feelings and, seizing a pen, she began to write. Even now, when her decision was made, she found it a difficult task to set out her feverish thoughts upon the paper; and many were the sheets she destroyed and the new attempts she made.

The night crept on, but Tatiana was heedless of the passing hours; and at length, as the first signs of dawn appeared, she finished the letter and, with trembling hands and much misgiving, placed it in an envelope ready to be delivered.

The letter was characteristic of the girl's disposition, and every line breathed of the sweet trustfulness that had prompted its writing. It was the simple outpouring of a generous, beautiful nature; and the depth and intensity of passion it revealed proved the value of the gift offered—the gift of a pure young maiden's heart.

She was still sitting at the open window when Philipjewna came in to arouse her at dawn; and she begged the old nurse to have the letter conveyed to Eugène Onégin without delay. At first the nurse hesitated and began to scold her for sitting up all night; but realizing that the girl was still in a state of nervous excitement, she decided to humour her. She took the note, therefore, and promised to have it delivered at once. Left alone, Tatiana buried her face in her hands, half regretting that she had sent the letter, and wondering whether Onégin would grant her the interview she had asked for—first hoping that he would accept her rash invitation, and the next moment praying that he would not.

Later in the day, however, as the time appointed for the meeting drew near, she took courage and went out into the grounds with doubt and longing in her heart, trembling at the thought of what would be the result of her interview—fearing lest her love should be scorned, yet equally full of shy fears should it be returned.

When Eugène Onégin duly appeared, Tatiana's little stock of courage entirely forsook her, leaving her trembling in the presence of the man she loved so passionately; and she would certainly have run away again had not Onégin imperiously bidden her to remain. Then, drawing nearer to the agitated girl, he told her gently that he had received and read her letter—adding that since she had been so frank with him, he would, in return, be frank with her.

He then went on to declare in passionless tones, yet half regretfully, that he was too world-weary to accept the fresh young love she had to offer, that he was neither worthy to receive so generous a gift nor had he a like passion to offer in return.

As the trembling Tatiana listened to these cold, yet truthful words, each one of which stabbed her to the heart, she felt full of shame and crushed to the earth. Onégin, though sorry for the pain he was thus inflicting upon the heart of the romantic girl, now bade her, in a more reproving tone than he had yet used, to restrain her feelings, since another, less conscientious than himself, might treat such impulsiveness with less consideration. Then, taking her by the hand, he led her into the house with kindly courtesy.

. . . .

A few weeks later, Madame Larina gave a ball in honour of Tatiana's eighteenth birthday; and amongst the guests were Lenski and Eugène Onégin. The entertainment was an elegant one and the assemblage brilliant; but Onégin found it dull and was frankly bored. He spent most of the time with Tatiana, whose romantic nature still interested him; but the young girl was restless and silent, and, realizing that she seemed ill at ease with him, he presently left her to her own reflections.

Being now more bored than ever, he felt annoyed with Lenski for having persuaded him to attend the party; and presently a means for paying off this small grudge against his friend mischievously presented itself to him. Seeing the pretty, smiling Olga approaching, he promptly invited her to give him several dances in succession, including the cotillion she had promised to her *fiancé*. Olga, by nature a daring coquette, gaily accepted his attentions with such obvious triumph that Lenski's brow grew black with disappointment and jealousy—for he loved her passionately and could brook no rival in his affections. Full of gloom, he watched the pair as they danced through the intricate figures, noting with increasing anger the many roguish glances bestowed by the coquettish Olga upon her handsome partner. When the cotillion ended, unable to restrain his angry feelings any longer, he openly accused Onégin of endeavouring to steal the affections of his betrothed; then, before all the guests, he furiously challenged him to a duel on the morrow.

At first Onégin tried to laugh the matter off, declaring that he had no thought of doing his friend a wrong; and Olga, now frightened and full of remorse that her giddy conduct should have thus been the means of causing strife, also implored her *fiancé* to calm himself and think no more of the matter.

But Lenski's passionate jealousy would not yield to reason; and he continued to pour such angry reproaches and stinging taunts upon Onégin that the latter likewise lost control of himself and, goaded beyond endurance, angrily accepted the challenge. The guests, alarmed and dismayed, at once took a hurried departure; and the ball, which had begun so brightly, ended in confusion and gloom.

Early next morning, Lenski and Onégin, with their seconds, met in a retired part of the grounds; and there, with the usual ceremonial etiquette, the duel was fought. Both felt sad at the thought that their long and happy friendship should end in this terrible way, and each longed to utter the words that would have reconciled them; but pride kept their lips sealed. When the signal was given, they raised their pistols and fired simultaneously.

Lenski fell to the ground at once; and when Onégin, who was untouched, ran forward with the seconds and clasped him in his arms, he found to his horror that the fiery young man was dead.

Full of grief and remorse that he had thus for the sake of a foolish code of honour slain the beloved friend of his youth, Onégin, dazed and miserable, left the neighbourhood at once; and for several years afterwards he wandered restlessly from country to country, vainly endeavouring to drown the tormenting regrets and harrowing recollections that haunted his brain.

. . . .

Neither change of scene nor wildest adventure succeeded in bringing comfort or peace to the remorseful heart of Eugène Onégin. At last, seized by an irresistible longing to return to the scene of his trouble, he travelled to Russia once more; and upon arriving in St. Petersburg, he was sought out by his old friends and induced to remain there for some weeks. On receiving an invitation to a magnificent ball from one of his relations, Prince Gremin, a nobleman of high position and honours, he was persuaded to accept this; and when the evening arrived, he attended the function, though somewhat against his will.

Even such a brilliant scene as this could not bring real distraction to the unhappy man's torn and weary heart; and as he wandered restlessly from room to room, his self-accusing thoughts still haunted him and the memory of the fatal duel was again pictured in his mind as vividly as ever. Presently, however, he noticed a stir among the guests, a subdued murmur of admiration; and following their gaze, he saw that the centre of attraction was a beautiful young woman, richly clad and sparkling with jewels, who was passing from one group to another with easy grace and dignity, bestowing smiles and gracious words on all. A second glance told Onégin that this brilliant figure was Tatiana, the young daughter of Madame Larina, the romantic maiden who had so impulsively offered him her fresh girlish love a few years ago— Tatiana, no longer a dreamy child, but grown into a lovely soulful woman, gracious and self-controlled, a very queen amidst this dazzling array of fair women.

It was indeed Tatiana, who had been taken from her quiet country home to become the admired wife of Prince Gremin who, though many years her senior, yet loved her tenderly and did all in his power to make her happy; and the fair young girl, though she could not give him love, yet made him a dutiful and devoted wife and had soon learned to bear her exalted position with becoming dignity.

As Onégin now gazed once again upon Tatiana—always interesting to him but doubly so now in her matured beauty, with all her natural charms of mind, body, and disposition intensified an hundredfold—his heart suddenly throbbed with a new and strange feeling of exaltation—and he who had thought himself dead to all passion, felt his pulses quicken and a thrill of the keenest joy pass like an electric current through his whole being.

His emotion increased presently when Prince Gremin brought his beautiful young wife forward and introduced her to him with pride and affection. Although Tatiana greeted him with easy calm and even coldness—making no attempt to hide their former acquaintanceship—yet the intense look of repressed passion in her deep tender eyes plainly revealed the fact that her feeling for him had not diminished but, indeed, had deepened with her growth. As she moved away again on the arm of her husband, Onégin felt the sharp pangs of jealousy for the first time in his life and knew that he now loved this woman with his whole heart; and he was seized with a passionate desire to possess the love he had once refused.

Unable, in his turn, to restrain his overwhelming passion, he determined to declare himself at all costs. Making his way to a retired spot, he waited until Tatiana came by alone; then, hastening towards her, trembling with emotion, he told her of his love and implored her to grant him hers in return. Tatiana, however, could not refrain from reminding him bitterly that he had slighted her proffered affection but a few years ago, treating it as the mere passing fancy of a sentimental girl and even reproving her for her impulsiveness.

Cut to the quick by this just report, Onégin sank to his knees and implored her with increasing emotion to pardon him and to bestow upon him the love he now longed for above all things. His pleading was so powerful that Tatiana, unable to keep up her pretence of coldness any longer, admitted that her own passion for him was still the same; and for a few moments a feeling of delirious joy filled her heart at the thought that her love was at last returned.

When, however, Onégin next entreated her to go away with him that they might yet be happy together, since theirs was a great love that would not be denied, the young wife staunchly announced her intention of remaining true to her husband, no matter how difficult it might be to refuse the pleading of the man she loved.

Again and again Onégin passionately besought her to obey the dictates of her heart; but Tatiana, though tempted almost beyond endurance, still brokenly, yet firmly, refused. At last, fearing to remain longer lest her resolution should break down, she fled away from his presence with a last distracted look.

Then Onégin, full of despair and realizing that the happiness he craved for could never now be his, drew forth a pistol and turned it upon himself. Next moment, a shot rang out, and he fell lifeless to the ground!

IOLANTA   *Tschaikovsky*

ABOUT the middle of the fifteenth century, in a secluded valley amidst the hills of Provençe, there was to be seen an exquisite garden, so full of beauty that to gaze upon it seemed almost like taking a peep into the wonderful fairyland of one's childhood days.

In the midst of this flowery garden there had been built a small one-storied château, handsomely appointed within and without. In front stretched a flower-gemmed terrace, beneath which was to be seen a wall overgrown with ivy and other climbing plants concealing a door which led to a summer bower within.

The approach to this little earthly paradise was hidden by the heavy undergrowth and was not readily to be discovered; for all around, even to the distant mountains, the country was wild and rugged and no one would have dreamed of finding so refreshing an oasis in so unlikely a wilderness.

But, though an air of mystery overhung the spot, as though it were the abode of some enchanted Princess in a fairy-tale, joyful life and beauty dwelt therein; and one glorious summer afternoon, the fair maiden whose home it was might have been seen wandering as usual in her blossoming garden with her nurse and girl companions.

Lovely though her surroundings were, the maiden herself was the fairest blossom of all. The fresh pink roses were not more delicately tinted than were her softly rounded cheeks; the tall white lilies were not more graceful than her slender form and could scarcely vie with the purity of her smooth brow; and her soft dewy eyes and shining tresses seemed but reflections of the blue sky and dazzling sunshine.

The divinity to be worshipped at this secret shrine was certainly more than worthy of her surroundings; yet as she moved among her young companions and joined in their games and amusements, the tragedy of her existence became apparent. The girls had brought baskets into the garden and every now and again would stop to place in them various flowers and fruits from the choicest plots; but when their lovely mistress wished to do likewise, they guided her hands in the right directions and gently pulled down the branches and briers until her slender fingers felt and closed over the luscious fruit. The Princess of this fairy-like abode was not enchanted, as one might have readily imagined; but, alas! she was blind. For that reason she had been kept hidden away from the world and brought up in this lonely but lovely spot—the beauties of which, however, were only known to her by her marvellously acute senses of touch and hearing; and she had never learned the truth of her infirmity and did not know the meaning of sight.

Such was Iolanta, the blind daughter of René, King of Naples and Count of Provençe; and as she occupied herself with her companions on the afternoon on which this story opens, the afflicted Princess little dreamed that the uneventfulness of her life was at last to be broken and that within the next few hours her destiny would be changed.

Iolanta had not been born blind; and while she was still an infant, King René had been engaged in an ancient feud that had existed for many years between his family and the Dukes of Burgundy. Both sides having grown heartily weary of the struggle, the reigning Duke proposed at this time to his hereditary enemy that they should agree to bury the hatchet and to seal the compact of their renewed friendship by the betrothal of his only son to the newly-born Princess Iolanta.

The compact was readily entered into by King René, and the betrothal contract of the two children was duly drawn up and signed. Then, shortly afterwards, a terrible misfortune befell the King of Naples, which threatened to destroy all his plans and hopes of a peaceful future and to plunge him once more into a renewed feud with his haughty and powerful neighbour. One night a fire broke out in his palace and the flames gained so rapidly in the apartments of the baby Princess that at first it was feared she could not be saved from death. It was impossible to get her out of the blazing apartment; and, in the last extremity, as a final attempt at rescue, the terrified babe was dropped out of the window from a great height and caught into willing arms below. Her life was thus saved; but, to the grief of her royal father, it was afterwards found that—whether from fright and shock or from the dazzling glare of the flames could not be determined— though her lovely eyes still retained their brilliancy and beauty, the sight had gone from them and she was blind.

Full of woe for the terrible affliction of his beloved and mother-less child, whose bright hopes of a joyous life thus seemed darkened for ever, King René was further plunged in despair as he also realized that his ancient feud was now likely to be renewed. The proud Duke of Burgundy would scarcely desire to wed his only son to a blind girl and might refuse to believe that she had ever been otherwise than blind, being more likely to imagine that he had been purposely deceived at the time the betrothal contract was signed.

In order to preserve peace in his long harassed land, therefore, the troubled King resolved to keep the knowledge of his child's blindness a secret from all save a few faithful servants whom he could trust. With this object in view, he had caused the retreat already described to be prepared for her in an almost unknown valley of the Provençe hills, where she could be brought up away from the sight of the world and in complete ignorance even of the awful fact that she was blind. To the Duke of Burgundy and to all other inquirers it was given out that the child was delicate and had been sent to be brought up in a convent in Spain, where she was to remain until her sixteenth year when her marriage was to be celebrated; and the secret of her true hiding-place and the real cause for her isolation had thus been safely preserved.

To Bertran, a faithful retainer, the guardianship of the royal child had been entrusted; and a careful, loving nurse for her wa found in Martha, the wife of Bertran. This loyal couple also were the custodians of the small château erected in the midst of the beautiful retreat; and, with the addition of a few serving-maids and archer guards, these were the only persons who ever saw the little blind Princess—save her father, who was only able to visit her at long intervals. The latter's true estate was not revealed to her, and she learned to know and to love him as her father under the title of Raymbaut, a troubadour.

At first, the ministrations and companionship of her nurse, Martha, were sufficient for the blind child; but as she grew to maidenhood, it was deemed advisable to provide for her companions of her own age. Therefore, a few maidens of high degree were sent as attendants upon her—all of whom were bound to secrecy and instructed to keep from her the knowledge of her blindness and of her true rank.

Thus Iolanta, sightless herself and accustomed to living and moving in a world of darkness, never having heard of the joys of light and colour and knowing beauty only by her delicate sense of touch and intuition, believed all others to be even as she herself. Therefore, she was happy, despite her dire affliction, and grew up lighthearted as a bird and beautiful as the dawn.

. . . . . .

Throughout the childhood of Iolanta, King René had been resigned to her affliction—though he lived in dread of the time when he would have to reveal the fact of her blindness to her betrothed and thus, possibly, bring warfare once more upon his now smiling land. As the young Princess approached to maidenhood, however, hope revived within him, and he began to think it possible that some wonderful miracle might happen to restore her sight before the time for her marriage arrived. Not content merely to hope, he sought eagerly for means of help. Hearing of a certain Moorish physician, famed for his amazing powers of healing, he sent for him and offered him great rewards if, out of his deep store of Eastern learning—and even of his reputed knowledge of the Dark Science—he could bring back the sight to the young Princess's beautiful eyes.

The physician, Abn Hakia, was willing to devote his talents to this congenial task; and after visiting the blind child, he gave hope that, though it would be necessary to wait until she had attained the age of sixteen years, it was possible that he might then effect a cure—if, in the meantime, his directions were faithfully carried out.

Such tidings of hope revived the drooping spirits of King René; and giving instructions that the directions of the Moorish physician should be strictly obeyed, he looked forward with anxious eagerness to the time when his daughter should attain her sixteenth year, when the final treatments and tests were to be made.

That time had now arrived; and, full of loving anticipation, almost agonizing in its intensity, the King of Naples set forth towards the retreat of Iolanta. As he drew near, he despatched one of his Knights in advance to announce to his daughter's custodians that he would arrive within a few hours with Abn Hakia, the Moorish physician.

Strangely enough, Iolanta, unconscious that her fate and future welfare thus hung in the balance, throughout that day had experienced a strange undefinable feeling that she lacked something —she knew not what, but something she could not name—and for the first time in her life a cloud almost of depression fell upon her. While moving amongst her girl companions in their fruit and flower gathering, she suddenly sank weeping upon a mossy bank. The girls crowded around her, full of distress; and one of them ran to fetch old Martha, the nurse.

The ministrations of Martha soon comforted Iolanta, and presently she fell asleep to the sound of the old nurse's crooning lullaby. Then her companions carried her away to rest upon a couch in the bowery apartment beneath the terrace—the entrance to which was almost hidden by the overhanging roses; and there they left her alone to sleep.

Soon after the sleeping Iolanta had been carried away by her maidens, the sound of a hunter's horn was heard, and the Knight Almeric rode up to the entrance of the well-hidden château and informed Bertran the custodian that his royal master was about to arrive with the Moorish physician. Even as they spoke together a further hunting-horn heralded the approach of the royal party and, a few minutes later, King René entered, accompanied by Abn Hakia.

Well pleased on learning that Iolanta had unexpectedly fallen asleep, the King bade Martha lead the doctor into the presence of the Princess, as the Moorish physician desired to examine the latter's eyes whilst she slept. When Abn Hakia presently returned the King eagerly demanded a report upon the examination, declaring passionately that he would give everything he possessed if his daughter could regain her sight.

In the calm eyes of the Eastern physician—dark, unfathomable and inscrutable—he could read nothing; but his heart leapt with joy when Abn Hakia said: "Have hope, O King, for Allah is great and all things are in His hands! There is a chance that the royal maid may be cured under the special treatment I shall now give her; but it is essential that she be told that she is blind, of which fact she is now ignorant. Unless she has the desire to see, nothing can be done for her!"

On hearing this condition, the King became angry, declaring that he would not permit Iolanta to be told of her affliction lest the cure should not be successful, when this knowledge—so carefully and lovingly kept from her during the past years—might make her unhappy. He even announced his resolve to punish with death any person who should dare to reveal to his daughter that she was blind.

While the King and the Moorish physician thus argued upon this vital point, a stranger in another part of the garden was unconsciously playing into the hands of Abn Hakia. Two handsome young men of high degree, having wandered from the beaten track and lost their way in the surrounding wild district had, accidentally, stumbled upon the hidden retreat. Amazed at the beautifully cultivated grounds in which they so unexpectedly found themselves, they hastened through the luxurious gardens until they reached the rose-hung terrace.

These wanderers were none other than the young Duke of Burgundy—who had recently succeeded his father as ruler of that powerful province—and his friend, Count Vaudemont, who were even now journeying to the Court of King René that the former might claim his affianced bride. In a sudden spirit of adventure, the young Duke had separated himself temporarily from his attendant retinue and proceeded on foot with his friend; and though he had now lost his bearings, he did not seem unduly dismayed—indeed, his present errand had little interest for him.

As the two young men stopped to rest for a few moments by the rose terrace, the bridegroom-elect spoke of his future bride in tones of the greatest discontent. He railed at his late father for having made such a tiresome contract for him, declaring that he had no desire at all to meet his betrothed, having already given his heart to another fair lady, the Countess of Loteringia, whose beauty and wit were far famed.

Presently noticing the half-hidden door amongst the roses, Count Vaudemont pushed it open; and the two young men drew back in amazement, lost in admiration as their gaze fell upon the beautiful form of the Princess Iolanta, who slept upon a couch within.

The young Duke hastened back into the open, full of superstitious alarm and calling his friend to withdraw likewise, declaring that the place must surely be enchanted and that the thereal being within must almost certainly be some dangerous siren who would cast evil spells upon them should she awaken and find them there. Vaudemont, however, remained fascinated, his senses enthralled, and, scorning the fears of the Duke, said softly : " Nay, say rather that she is an angel from Heaven! "

He also stepped back, however; for, at the sound of strange voices, Iolanta awakened and, rising from her couch, came forth and asked in her sweet voice : " Who is here? "

The Count explained that they were weary travellers who had lost their way; and Iolanta said sweetly : " Then I will fetch wine and fruit for your refreshment! "

As she moved back into her apartment to fetch the fruit and wine placed there by her own thoughtful attendants, the Duke—still fearful of being thrown under a spell of enchantment—hastened away from the spot to seek for help; but Vaudemont, already strangely attracted by the lovely maiden, waited, full of eagerness, for her return.

When Iolanta appeared, therefore, with fruit and wine and begged him to refresh himself, he did not hesitate to do so, for fear of offending her. Then, feeling more and more the rapture of her charming presence and realizing that he already loved her, he spoke to her tenderly, yet reverently, admiring her beauty and wooing her very gently. Seeing, however, that the young girl seemed confused and mystified by his words, Vaudemont perceived that she was too unsophisticated to understand him and that he must have patience. He asked her, therefore, to give him a red rose; but when Iolanta had willingly plucked the flower for him, he found that it was a white one. When he again asked her for a red rose, she asked in a puzzled tone : " What is red, and what is white? I know not what you mean by such words! "

When Vaudemont thus realized that this beautiful girl was blind, his pity was so great that he could not speak for some moments. Fearing, from his sudden silence, that she had offended him, Iolanta's tears began to flow; and Vaudemont, with tender gentleness, endeavoured to comfort and cheer her by telling her about the world in which he lived and of the wonderful things to be seen and done therein—amazed that she should be so ignorant of these matters and even of her own infirmity.

Iolanta thus learned from her new friend the fact that she was blind; and she now realized that the strange feeling of something lacking which had possessed her all day was a true feeling. Full of interest in Vaudemont's revelations of wonders and beauties unknown to her, she begged him eagerly to tell her more about these marvels of sunshine, colour, and form—all of which beauties of Nature he declared helped mankind to understand and to realize God, the Creator of all.

"You say beautiful things!" she said. "I, too, understand God by something within myself, by the scent of the flowers and the songs of the birds; but how much greater must be your understanding of Him by the wonders of which you speak!"

So engrossed were the two young people in their happy talk, every word strengthening the strange bond of sympathy between them, that they heeded not the sound of approaching footsteps; and interruption came all too soon.

King René, with the Moorish physician and his daughter's companions, had come to seek Iolanta in her rose bower, where they imagined her to be still sleeping; and they were astounded and bewildered on finding her awake and talking with a stranger.

When the King haughtily demanded of the intruder how he dared to speak with his daughter, Iolanta begged him not to be angry with the stranger, whose company was a delight to her—adding that he had told her of the beauties of the great world and of the mighty wonders of Nature which she had never seen, and had expressed pity for her blindness.

All exclaimed in alarm on thus hearing that their beloved Princess had been made acquainted with her affliction; and the King cried in a fury: "What have you done, rash youth? My child's happiness is destroyed for ever; and you shall surely die for the evil thing you have done!"

The doctor, however, was glad to learn that Iolanta thus knew of her blindness, which was in accordance with his wishes; and he told the King that the maiden now might certainly be cured if only she would desire to see. Otherwise, he could do nothing for her.

A sudden idea now occurred to the King, and his anger began to cool. He announced sternly: "Begin your cure, Abn Hakia, for it is almost twilight, which is the time you have chosen for performing this mighty work. If by the time you have completed your treatment my daughter has not regained her sight, this young stranger shall certainly be slain. If, on the other hand, by your mighty healing art and by her own strong desire to see, she is cured, then shall the young man live and receive my favour!"

Iolanta, who had conceived a deep affection for the young stranger whose sympathetic presence and tender words had already unconsciously taught her the meaning of love, was instantly filled with alarm lest he should lose his life for his rashness. She now longed passionately to see, for his sake, that his precious life might be spared; and she cried eagerly: "Oh, hasten, wise physician, and apply your cure; for I wish above all things in the world that my eyes may look upon the countenance of my new beloved friend!"

Well pleased on hearing these words, the physician now led Iolanta within the château to apply his final tests for her cure; and Count Vaudemont and the King were left alone.

King René immediately apologized to the stranger for the harsh attitude he had been obliged to take, explaining his reason for doing so—which the Count readily understood. The young man then declared his love for the fair Iolanta and begged that her hand might be bestowed upon him, whether she regained her sight or not; and he revealed his name and high rank. Just as King René had replied sadly that his daughter had been betrothed to another since infancy, there came an interruption. The Knight Almeric appeared and announced to the King that the young Duke of Burgundy had arrived and craved an immediate audience; and King René turned to Vaudemont and said: "Behold your rival, who approaches us!"

The Duke now appeared on the scene, and explanations quickly followed; and the two young men were astounded on learning that the beautiful blind maiden whom they had discovered so romantically was King René's daughter and the Duke's betrothed, whom they had come to claim in fulfilment of the contract made so many years ago.

Realizing that his friend had conceived a deep love for the afflicted royal maiden, the young Duke now confessed to the King that his own affections were already bestowed upon the Countess Matilda of Loteringia; and he begged to be released from the contract made by his late father.

King René willingly agreed that the contract with the Duke of Burgundy should be annulled, his past fears of warfare being now set at rest; and he also gladly consented to the marriage of his daughter with Count Vaudemont.

By this time twilight was far advanced and the Moorish physician's tests were completed; and, to the overwhelming joy of all, when the bandages were removed from Iolanta's eyes, it was found that the cure had been successful and that the royal maiden could now see.

Although bewildered at first on beholding the wonders around her, Iolanta quickly accustomed herself to her new powers; and when King René placed her hands in those of Count Vaudemont she smiled with great joy and uttered praises to Heaven for the mighty miracle that had been wrought on her behalf and for the wonderful happiness that now filled her heart.

THE QUEEN OF SPADES
Tschaikovsky
(*La Pique Dame*)

ONE bright springtime day, early in the last century, merry throngs of people might have been seen enjoying themselves in the beautiful Summer Garden at St. Peterburg. Now that the ice and snows of the severe Russian winter had at last melted away and the warm sunshine shone forth once more, everyone was eager to be out in the open air and to inhale the gentle breezes, to admire the beauty of the freshly opened flowers, and to rejoice with the happy singing birds carolling among the branches of the trees.

The Summer Garden presented a specially gay and animated scene, providing as it did a happy recreation ground for many groups of children, who played their merry games while their nurses strolled about and chatted together.

This pleasant spot being also a favourite meeting-place for the wealthy and aristocratic, a number of ladies and gentlemen in fashionable garb contributed a buzz of conversation; and a good sprinkling of military men in brilliant uniforms added further to the brightness of the scene.

Among these latter were two young officers, named Tchekalinsky and Sourin, who, however, were not quite in the best of spirits, having met with bad luck in their card play the night before. They were just consoling themselves with the reflection that their own misfortunes had been capped by the extra bad luck of their friend Herman, a fellow-officer, when they observed the latter approaching, and moved aside on noting his gloomy looks.

Young Herman was indeed in a melancholy frame of mind. Presently, on being rallied for his silence and gloom by his companion, Count Tomsky, he confessed to the latter that his bad spirits were caused by the fact that he had fallen in love, and that he was at the same time filled with despair since he did not even know the name of his beloved one—who, however, was certainly of a noble family not likely to consider the advances of so unimportant a suitor as himself.

Tomsky, deeply interested, asked for further particulars; and Herman, being a young man of ardent and romantic temperament, burst forth into an enthusiastic description of the object of his affections, saying that her beauty and sweetness had never been excelled. Then, to Tomsky's surprise, he declared that he had never yet spoken to her, and that he had only met her a few times walking in the Gardens and accompanied by her constant guardian, a sinister-looking old woman, whose rich clothing, priceless jewels, and haughty bearing, however, proclaimed her to be of high degree.

"Nevertheless," he added, "I know that my ardent glances have made an impression upon this beautiful maiden and that she cannot be insensible to the deep passion she has aroused in me. Her terrible old guardian also has noted me, and, while casting looks of indignation and disdain upon me for presuming to gaze upon her ward with eyes of love, I have remarked a strange look, almost of fear, in her baleful glances!"

As Tomsky, greatly interested in his young friend's mysterious love affair, was about to question him further on the matter, Tchekalinsky and Sourin approached them in company with their friend, Prince Yeletsky. The latter was a wealthy nobleman of great dignity and brilliant attainments, to whom they were at the moment offering their congratulations, his engagement to a certain beautiful young lady having just been announced.

Whilst Herman, still further plunged into gloom at the sight of another man's happiness, drew back a few paces, Tomsky hastened forward to join in the congratulations to Prince Yeletsky. Upon asking the latter to say which of the charming maidens of high degree adorning St. Petersburg society he had chosen for his future bride, the Prince, indicating the approach of two ladies, said with joyful eagerness: "Behold! Here she comes! It is the beautiful Lisa!"

As Prince Yeletsky hastened forward to greet his *fiancée*, the young officer, Herman, fell back with a gasp of despair. The lovely maiden who now approached to place her hand in that of her nobly-born suitor was none other than his own beloved one whom he had so passionately adored from a distance and whose name he now heard for the first time.

The fair young girl was accompanied by her guardian, a weird looking but aristocratic old dame, whose piercing black eyes set deeply in her parchment-like painted face, cast forth almost malignant glances on all around—until they rested upon the stricken Herman, when a strange look of fear instantly appeared in them. With a shudder, she drew Tomsky aside to ask the name of the gloomy young officer, declaring that she had a mysterious fear of him.

Lisa, on her part, was also greatly disturbed on thus coming face to face with her unknown admirer, whose attractive personality already had an extraordinary fascination for her; and th two ladies, unwilling to prolong their strange uneasiness, quickly passed on with Prince Yeletsky.

When they had gone, Tomsky, having guessed at the cause of Herman's agitation and full of pity for the unhappy young man, endeavoured to divert him from his unlucky attachment by telling him of the evil reputation of his beloved one's guardian—who was also her grandmother. He stated that she was a widowed Countess, who, owing to her weird looks, dangerous dabbling in occult matters, and celebrated exploits as a cunning gambler, was usually spoken of as "The Queen of Spades".

He stated further that, in the early days of her youth, the Countess had been a famous beauty toasted in all the capitals of Europe as "The Venus of Moscow". Strange to say, however, though lovers innumerable fluttered constantly around her, eager for her smiles, love made no appeal to her, as she lived only for gambling—for which she had an overwhelming passion. It was further reported by the gossips of the town that her continuous and marvellous good luck at the gaming-table was due to her secret knowledge of a certain combination of three cards which never failed to bring her success—a secret which the tattlers further affirmed had become hers at the price of yielding to the importunities of one of her many adorers. She had been forbidden to reveal the secret to anyone else; but having twice disobeyed this command of her now dead lover, the latter had since visited her in ghostly guise to proclaim that she would surely die when a third man, forced by despair, should try to wrest from her this secret of the three cards.

Tchekalinsky and Sourin laughed at the gossips' tale told by Tomsky, and soon strolled away with the latter, as the rumblings of an approaching thunderstorm came nearer; and Herman, left alone and heedless of the storm which quickly broke with sudden fury, pondered over the strange story he had just heard. His own convictions forced him to believe in its truth, as he now realized that here was the key to the curious fear in the eyes of the old Countess whenever she gazed upon him—proof that she had a presentiment that he was to be the third man who would force her to reveal the fatal secret and thus bring about her death.

The more Herman pondered upon this matter, the more obsessed he became with a strange mad desire to work out what he now regarded as his destiny and to learn the magic secret of the three cards from the ill-reputed old Countess. Thus, by gaining a fortune at the gaming-tables, he might win as his bride the lovely Lisa, who he felt had only been plighted to Prince Yeletsky because of the latter's wealth.

So great a hold did this idea take upon the imagination of the romantic Herman that he determined to put aside his former humility and to pursue an ardent wooing of his beloved one by means of clandestine meetings; and thus, he hoped to induce her to help him in his efforts to persuade the celebrated " Queen of Spades " to yield up her secret to him.

With this object in view, the young officer secreted himself one evening on the balcony outside the window of Lisa's room, to await an opportunity of seeing her and declaring his love.

The fair Lisa, being still but a youthful maiden, had been entertaining some girl friends that evening; and when her guests rallied her upon her somewhat downcast looks, declaring that being but newly betrothed she should be all smiles and liveliness, she had made a special effort to rouse herself and to join in their games and dances.

When the girls had departed, however, a strange feeling of depression and of coming calamity crept over her; and, instead of retiring to rest at once, she dismissed her maid and gave herself up to sad reflections. Ever since her last meeting with Herman in the Summer Garden, she had realized that her love was wholly given to this mysterious young officer whose ardent glances had won her heart against her will. Though she greatly respected the courtly Yeletsky—whose love for her she knew to be sincere—she felt that, despite the honours and dignities she would enjoy as his wife, the sunshine of happiness would nevertheless have vanished from her life now that her love was given to another.

As she wept at this sad thought, a sound caused her to look up; and she beheld the romantic subject of her affections, Herman, stepping into her room from the balcony.

With a stifled cry, Lisa drew back, overcome by mingled feelings of surprise, fear, and a strange joy; but Herman hastened forward with eager steps and outstretched arms, pouring forth an ardent declaration of his passion and entreating her to accept his love and so obey the true dictates of her heart.

At first, Lisa made a movement as of anger, declaring that she would rouse the household unless her intruding lover departed; but upon Herman, half mad with love and doubt, drawing a pistol and announcing that he had but come for one kind word from her ere putting an end to his now useless life, she endeavoured to calm him. Being unable, however, to disguise her own agitation and betraying her love thereby, Herman was emboldened to continue his declaration, being overcome with joy on realizing that his passion was thus returned. At this moment there came an interruption in the form of a sharp knock at the door; and the young officer had only just time to conceal himself behind a curtain when the old Countess entered the room, scolding her granddaughter for not having retired to rest.

The old dame seemed to be haunted by a supernatural warning of her own approaching death, appearing to feel instinctively the unseen presence of one who was to have a fatal influence over her and to bring calamity; but Lisa succeeded in reassuring her and promised to seek her couch at once—whereupon the Countess departed.

Herman then came forth once more, and his wooing now became so intensely ardent that Lisa could no longer resist his pleadings, and with great joy the lovers sealed their compact of love with many tender embraces.

After this mutual understanding, Herman and Lisa had few opportunities of seeing one another—for the latter was kept strictly guarded by the old Countess, who now lived in constant fear of meeting with the mysterious young officer in whose presence she always felt such a strange foreboding of coming evil. Herman, thus realizing that without at least unbounded wealth he could not possibly present himself as a rival suitor to the rich and aristocratic Prince Yeletsky, became more than ever obsessed by the idea of wresting from the notorious " Queen of Spades " the magic secret of the three cards, the combination of which brought such good luck at the gaming-tables.

This idea of his was fostered, unconsciously, by his friends, Tchekalinsky and Sourin, who, knowing of his impecunious state, constantly exhorted him in joking fashion to make friends with the uncanny old Countess and to learn her secret. Finally, the idea took such a strong hold upon the young officer's imagination that he was haunted continually by it and could think of nothing else.

At last, he determined to induce Lisa to help him to gain an interview with her grandmother. With this idea, he attended a masked ball given one evening by a rich dignitary of the city, knowing that Lisa would certainly be attending the ball in company with her *fiancé*, Prince Yeletsky.

Among the brilliant throng attending this function the unhappy Herman wandered in disguise, feverishly awaiting the chance of an interview with his beloved one—from whom he had that morning received a note stating that she desired urgently to speak with him.

Soon, to his relief, he saw Lisa enter on the arm of Prince Yeletsky; and, later on in the evening, after the close of a musical interlude performed by some of the guests, the lovers managed to snatch a few stolen moments together.

After the first joy of meeting was over, Lisa gave to Herman a key of her garden gate, telling him that by means of a ladder she had left there he would be able to gain access to the room of her grandmother, with whom he would thus secure the coveted inter-view. Having thus arranged their plan, the lovers mingled once more with the other guests.

Later that night, just before the ball came to a close, Herman made his way to the home of " The Queen of Spades " and gained entrance to the Countess's sleeping apartment by means of the ladder left outside by Lisa. Here he concealed himself until the old dame returned from the ball—which she also had attended, dressed in gorgeous attire and blazing with jewels.

He had not long to wait ere he heard the arrival of the ladies in the boudoir beyond. After the aged Countess had been prepared for bed, she was brought into her sleeping chamber by a bevy of flattering maids and attendants, who praised her brilliant appear-ance at the ball and then wished her a good night's rest.

The weird old dame looked even more uncanny than usual, a strange light shining in her dark, yet piercing eyes; and, refusing to go to bed immediately, she insisted on being propped up on a couch, where, after dismissing her maids, she indulged in chatter-ing reminiscences of the triumphs and conquests of her youth.

Whilst she thus crooned to herself, Herman suddenly presented himself before her and implored her to make him happy by telling him her famous secret—the names of the three cards that brought good luck to the gambler.

The old Countess, at first full of amazement and anger at the intrusion of a stranger into her room, gazed at him with menacing glances. Then, as Herman, growing reckless in his frantic eager-ness to learn the secret, drew forth a pistol, declaring that he would force her to speak, a sudden change came over her. Overwhelmed with a nameless terror as she now recognized the strange young man whose presence always caused her to shudder with un-accountable fear, the shock was more than she could bear; and, flinging up her shaking arms, she fell back upon the couch dead.

For several moments Herman remained transfixed with horror and overcome by an eerie feeling that supernatural agencies were at work. Then, realizing that the old dame's secret had perished with her, he was filled with despair—which increased when Lisa, entering the room a few moments later and seeing the pistol in his hand, accused him of having murdered her grandmother and drove him from her presence.

The wretched Herman now passed some terrible days, almost mad with grief and remorse and haunted constantly by visions of the dead Countess. Shutting himself up in his room at the barracks, he refused to see anyone or to go out, feeling that nothing mattered if Lisa refused to smile upon him.

Lisa, however, could not long bear to live without seeing her beloved one. Soon believing that she had wronged him by her hasty suspicions, she sent him a note asking for his forgiveness and entreating him to meet her that evening at midnight on the Quay, where they would be unseen, or, at least, unknown.

Herman received the note on the day of the Countess's funeral; and though it brought him some comfort, he could not overcome a strange uncanny feeling which he had experienced all that day. Towards evening, a sudden storm arose and the wind howled around the house; and as he sat in his lonely apartment, shivering with a nameless fear, an apparition of the dead Countess appeared before him, telling him in ghostly accents the names of the three cards he had desired to know—three, seven, ace.

As soon as the spectre had vanished and he had recovered somewhat from his fright, Herman became obsessed with a mad desire to try his luck at the gaming-tables immediately; but refraining for a short time longer from giving vent to his freshly stimulated passion, he set forth at midnight to the Quay to keep his appointment with Lisa, who was already waiting for him by the bridge.

There was a passionate meeting between the lovers. However, Lisa was soon plunged into grief and alarm once more on hearing from Herman that he now knew the secret of the three cards, so that she was again forced to believe that he had indeed murdered the Countess with his own hands; and she imagined him to be raving when presently he told her excitedly of the apparition he had seen and that he was about to make a wonderful fortune at the gaming-tables.

With tearful entreaties Lisa implored him to go away with her and to forget the evil knowledge he had thus gained by supernatural means; but Herman, now indeed raving and quite beside himself with the gambler's passion, tore himself from her side in a frenzy and rushed off to the gambling-house.

Now realizing that her beloved one was indeed mad and lost to her for ever, the unhappy Lisa gave way to a paroxysm of despair: and feeling that life had no joy left for her, she flung herself from the bridge into the river below, there to seek oblivion from the woes she could not bear.

Meanwhile, Herman fled with mad haste to the gambling-house, where he found his rival, Prince Yeletsky, whom he at once challenged to play with him three times for terrific stakes.

His friends, Tchekalinsky, Sourin and Tomsky, who were also present, endeavoured to prevent him from engaging in such a reckless game, reminding him of the bad luck he always experienced at cards; but their efforts were unavailing, and the play began at once.

To the astonishment of all, the first game fell to Herman, who won with his three; and, encouraged by this, he doubled the stakes and won a second time with the seven. Already a large fortune was his; but, not satisfied with this, the rash young officer, elated with his success, insisted upon a third game, staking all upon a single card—and lost!

Instead of turning up the ace, as foretold by the apparition of the Countess, he saw, to his horror, that he held in his hand the Queen of Spades! At the same moment, he once more beheld the spectre of the sinister old Countess—who had been his evil genius and had thus brought him to utter ruin—appearing to smile in triumph at his downfall; and, filled with the madness of despair, the unhappy Herman plunged a dagger into his heart as his ghostly deceiver vanished from sight.

HUGH THE DROVER *Vaughan Williams*

On the last day of April in the year 1805, when England was daily threatened with invasion by Napoleon Bonaparte, a fair was being held outside a small town in the Cotswolds.

The Showman had forgotten nothing that could amuse the people. A cheapjack was selling his wares by auction. Shell-fish, toy lambs, primroses, and many other things were hawked from group to group; there was a shooting-gallery, also a Punch-and-Judy show and a play-booth. All the fun of the fair, in fact, was in full swing, and nobody was worrying about " Boney ".

When, with much banging of the drums, tootling of the fifes, and blowing of the trumpets, a dummy was brought forward, and the Showman, twitching off the covering, revealed it to be Boney himself, but with horns and a forked tail, the crowd only hooted in derision and shouted a chorus to the Showman's patriotic song about what Boney would get if he were caught by the men of the Cotswolds.

When the din had died down, there came by an old Ballad-

Singer who, in response to the entreaties of the rustic youths and maidens for a love-song, began to sing them the famous old ballad "I'm to be married on a Tuesday morning". He had only sung the first verse, however, when a girl's voice in the distance took up the refrain. They all knew that voice. It was Mary's.

Mary was the prettiest and most popular girl in the town, the only child of the widowed chief magistrate, the Constable. She now joined the crowd around the Ballad-Singer, sang one more verse of the ballad, and then burst into tears.

Her father's sister, dear old Aunt Jane, was trying to comfort her when, with much self-importance and pomposity, there came up the great man himself, the Constable. It soon became clear what had upset Mary. With the Constable came John the Butcher, a hulking young brute, who boasted that he was the strongest and richest man in the place and threatened to crack the skull of anyone who said otherwise.

To this man, who openly revelled in his trade of slaughtering, the Constable had promised the hand of his only child; and Mary, who was a gentle, laughter-loving girl, could not bear the thought of being married to such a man. Some of the townspeople sided with John the Butcher; others thought of him as Mary did. The two factions were just coming to blows when the entrance of the Morris Dancers turned their thoughts to merrier things; and they all trooped after the procession.

Mary and Aunt Jane were left alone; and while Mary was explaining how unhappy she was but that she meant to do her duty and obey her father, her words were taken up, half mockingly, by a voice behind her. The two women turned round in surprise; and there stood a stranger, a tall young man, ostensibly engrossed in mending a horsewhip, while he sang, very sweetly and softly, an address to the "little linnet"—Mary herself, who meant to do her duty and hop into the cage.

Asked indignantly who he was, the stranger replied that he was called Hugh the Drover. Now drovers had no good reputation in those days. So Aunt Jane was horrified, and even Mary was rather nervous. But it was no use. It was a case of love at first sight.

The pair drew nearer and nearer to each other; and by the time Aunt Jane, now thoroughly alarmed, had rushed off to fetch the Constable, it was too late. Mary and Hugh felt as though they had been waiting for each other all their lives; and they were soon irrevocably pledged.

When the Constable arrived on the scene, his fury was cut short by shouts proclaiming a fight. A purse of twenty pounds was offered as a prize; and the Showman called for someone to stand up to John the Butcher for the championship of the Cotswolds. But no one offered. Some declared that John did not fight fair; and all hung back.

But Hugh had seen his chance. He whispered to Mary; and just as it seemed as if no one would take up the challenge, he came forward. He would fight the Butcher. When the Showman asked who he was, he replied that he was a Drover, and that his work was to travel about the country buying horses for the Army. "A Drover!" said John the Butcher, with scorn. "He can't produce the stake!"

Then the Drover replied that the stake was too low. Who would sell his life for a mere twenty pounds? He would fight the Butcher, but for no prize less than that girl there, the pretty Mary.

The Butcher had gone too far now to draw back; and he really meant to kill the Drover if he could. The ring had been made ready; the crowd was bent on seeing the fight.

And a great fight it was. The men were evenly matched and both on fire to win. But the Drover was the better man of the two. In spite of John's foul blows—which roused the Showman and the spectators to fury—he could not batter down his agile, lightning-fisted opponent. John fell like an ox, and was counted out. The crowd then went wild with joy, the women pressing round Mary, the men shouldering Hugh and carrying him round in triumph.

Suddenly there was a pause. John the Butcher got to his feet at last and had been taking counsel with the Constable. They came forward. This Drover, declared the Constable, must be a spy. "Ask him how he came by the money in his bag! He is a French spy, Boney's spy! He has sold the secrets of our town, and we shall have Boney here in no time!"

This dreadful accusation was enough to turn the people as much against Hugh as they had just before been in favour of him. They now seized upon him, and dragged him off to be put in the stocks in the market-place of the town.

.   .   .   .

So Hugh the Drover spent the night in the stocks, where he could only too plainly hear the singing and shouting of the Butcher and his friends, who were roistering in the tavern close by. He was very miserable—not for himself, as he could face any fate with courage; but for Mary, who, it seemed now, must be left to be married to such a man as John and be cooped up in the town for life.

Soon after four o'clock, as the sky was beginning to grow light, the old Ballad-Singer, acting now as Night Watchman, came by and rapped on the door of the tavern. John and his friends came roaring out; and as they passed the stocks, they jeered at the prisoner. John struck him with his fists and told him of the soldiers who had already been summoned from Gloucester to come and take him off to be shot as a spy. But Hugh did not reply to this.

When they had gone and the town was all quiet again, the door of the Constable's house opposite opened very quietly, and Mary slipped out. She had managed to secure the keys of the stocks and had come to release her lover. It was not easy. The bar of the stocks was so heavy that she could hardly lift it; and Hugh was so stiff that he could scarcely get up. But at last he was free; and they were just stealing away together when they heard, not far off, the sound of a horn.

Unfortunately for them, this was May morning. All the young people were out early to gather the may-blossoms. On both sides, the way of escape was blocked. Full of fear, Mary now implored Hugh to make a dash for freedom. He might get away, alone; but she could not run so fast and her white dress was sure to be seen. But, to her dismay, Hugh flatly refused to go without her, declaring that life would not be worth living if she were left behind.

Then, seeing him so determined, Mary hit on a plan. They would get into the stocks together, and Hugh should hide her under his cloak. When the May-Day merry-makers arrived, therefore, she would be discovered and her disgrace would be complete. Her father would certainly disown her and John the Butcher would cast her off—thus, she would be free of the hated betrothal and be able to go with her lover, whatever his fate.

All happened just as she foresaw. John and the merry-makers came calling for Mary under her window; but the Constable put his head out instead and shouted that she had gone.

Then there was a hue and cry; and Mary was at last discovered in the stocks, clasped in Hugh's arms. Furious at the sight, the Constable now vowed that Mary was no longer a daughter of his and should never have a penny of his money; and John not only refused to marry her, but also grossly insulted her.

This was too much for the townspeople, who all loved Mary. Indignantly some of them set upon John, intending to duck him in the horse-pond; but others, still afraid of his strength and importance in the town, tried to protect him.

Just as the struggle was at its height, suddenly the sound of a

drum and bugles was heard drawing near. The soldiers from
Gloucester had come; and everyone stood still and silent as they
marched into the market-place. No sooner had they halted than
John the Butcher rushed up to the Sergeant and pointed out
Hugh as the spy. The Sergeant, however, roughly told him to
mind his own business; and then he ordered the Constable, who
was now leaning out of his window—having run into the house,
in a fright, to escape the riot—to come down at once.

Meanwhile, Hugh had whispered something to Mary, and
now wrapped his cloak about him to hide his face from the soldiers.
When the Sergeant called him forward, he still kept his face
hidden. "Ashamed to show it?" asked the Sergeant. "No
wonder!"

At that, Hugh, who had recognized the Sergeant as a friend
of his, whipped away his cloak. For a moment the Sergeant
stared at him in bewilderment. Then, with a shout of welcome,
he began wringing Hugh by the hand and calling his men to
come and see. Hugh the Drover a spy? Why, King George
had no more faithful a servant. What was more, he was an old
friend of the Sergeant's, whose life he had once saved by rescuing
him from a snowdrift!

Then the Sergeant turned in wrath on the Constable. What
did he mean by dragging him and his men out of their beds on a
wild-goose chase? Nevertheless, he had no intention of going
back to Gloucester empty-handed; instead, he would "press"
John the Butcher for the Army, as he had the authority to do.

And so, just as Hugh had been marched off to the stocks, so
John the Butcher was marched off, kicking and shouting, to be
made a soldier. The crowd followed behind, singing and laughing at the crestfallen and struggling bully.

Hugh and Mary were left alone. And now, when the strain
was all over, the young girl's nerve suddenly failed and fears
assailed her. She was afraid to leave her home, afraid she was not
fit for a wandering life, afraid she was not good enough for her
beloved Hugh.

But Hugh's love was strong enough to remove all these fears at
last; and when, presently, the townsfolk came back, and her
father and Aunt Jane and all her friends now begged her to stay
among them, she firmly declined. Her life lay with her lover;
and amid the fond farewells of all, Mary and Hugh the Drover
went away together, with joy in their hearts.

THE POISONED KISS   *Vaughan Williams*

NIGHT was departing and Day was approaching in the heart of a dense forest where, in a clearing, stood a mysterious house.

Here, signs of awakening life were already to be observed. Mingled with the eerie sounds of the whirring wings and cries of owls and bats, there still came the caterwauling of cats, the croaking of frogs, and the swish of witches' brooms; for these creatures seemed reluctant to vanish. They were certainly more a part of that mystic scene than was the dawning sun, equally reluctant to appear.

For this was the abode of the famous Wizard, Dipsacus; and it was encircled by Enchantment, so that the creatures of darkness held their revels there more appropriately than did the creatures of light. Twice the rising sun was driven back by the mischievous forces of darkness; and it was not until the voice of the Wizard himself from within had commanded Night to depart and Day to appear that the sun began to rise in earnest.

Then came a glad chorus of cuckoos, larks, and distant crowing cocks; and the enchanted forest slowly awakened to a magic beauty.

Through one of the still dark forest paths came a gaily-dressed young man, stepping gingerly and gazing fearfully around him, full of alarm at every sound; for he had never been in an enchanted forest before. This was Gallanthus, the attendant of the adventurous young Prince Amaryllus, with whom he had spent a most uncomfortable night, lost in this mysterious forest they had just reached on their travels. At the first signs of dawn he had left his royal master still sleeping behind a bush and had walked on a little way to reconnoitre.

Gallanthus was amazed to find a house here in the heart of the forest, and was alarmed at its strange appearance. He was further scared on observing a large dog-kennel on one side of the house labelled "*Beware of the Serpent*", and a hen-coop on the other side bearing the ominous sign "*The Snakery*". A large sign-board near the door gave the following announcement: '*Dipsacus, Necromancer . . . Consultations daily.*"

While Gallanthus was fearfully noting these not too reassuring sign-boards, a pretty young maid came tripping out from the house, carrying a broom and a duster, ready for her morning's work; and the royal attendant, always eager for a flirtation and greatly fascinated by her dainty looks, soon made himself known to her. He learned that her name was Angelica and that she was employed by the necromancer as maid and companion to his fair daughter, Tormentilla.

This pert young person likewise informed her inquirer that Tormentilla, though dazzlingly beautiful, had curious tastes. Her father, for some secret reason of his own, had brought her up entirely on poison-foods, so that she would eat only such deadly things as carbolic, prussic-acid, arsenic, vitriol, cyanide, and so on, which, since she was herself now immune, had no ill effects upon her. The only pets she cared to have about her, too, were spitting-cobras, adders, and other poisonous snakes—hence, the kennel marked "*Snakery*".

Though he shivered with fright at what she told him, Gallanthus soon won himself into the good graces of Angelica, who was delighted to meet a young man at last, having been kept cooped up in the Wizard's abode for several years with her mistress and deprived of all contact with the outside world. The two young people commiserated with one another regarding their employers —for Gallanthus explained that his master was the son of a very important dame in high society, who likewise practised the arts of sorcery and fortune-telling, with the aid of the usual paraphernalia of mediums, cards, potions, and crystals.

While chatting together happily, however, they were presently startled by sudden thunder and lightning; and as this heralded the approach of the magician, Gallanthus hurried back into the forest, in a panic, while Angelica tripped off into the house.

To the accompaniment of lightning and thunder, Dipsacus the Necromancer now appeared, attended by hobgoblins, witches, gnomes, and wild animals. Clad in a long gown covered with cabalistic signs and wearing a high sugar-loaf hat, the magician looked alarming enough; but, as a matter of fact, his magical arts were no longer of a first-class kind, since he had permitted himself to get rusty and somewhat out-of-date. As he was well aware of this unpleasant fact, it made his temper bad.

Consequently he now roundly scolded his three chief attendant hobgoblins, Hob, Gob, and Lob, for having joined in the unseemly commotion at dawn and for having also neglected to keep his potions ready mixed; and he despatched them, grumbling, to perform extra duties as penance. Then he called Angelica to give him news of his lovely daughter; and when informed by the saucy maid that Tormentilla was walking in the forest with her vipers and pet cobra, for lack of anything better to do, he set forth to keep an eye upon her.

Meanwhile, Gallanthus had discovered his royal master in a great state of excitement. On awakening, Amaryllus had strolled farther into the forest, where he had presently come across the most beautiful maiden he had ever beheld, sitting on a rock beneath a tree. To his horror, however, he saw that a number of adders were crawling about her, while a terrible spitting-cobra was coiled around her neck with its sinister hood reared up above her lovely head.

Instantly falling in love with this goddess-like maiden and fearful for her safety, Amaryllus had snatched up a stout stick and hit the cobra on the head. Then, to his amazement, the girl, instead of being grateful for his deed, had snatched up the limp form of the snake and, holding it closely and tenderly to her bosom, had rushed away uttering loud cries of woe—without even turning to see who had struck the blow.

Alarmed for the consequences of this rash deed, Gallanthus explained to his master the true identity of his forest goddess and of her fondness for venomous reptiles; and he advised him to fly at once before she discovered who had slain her pet cobra. But Amaryllus declared that all would be well, since the maiden had not even stopped to see who had struck the snake; and he added that he already loved Tormentilla and meant to stay and win her love in return . . . not as a royal prince, but as a simple goat herd.

Even when Gallanthus reminded him that he already had a long list of fair conquests to his credit, and likewise pointed out that he had no goats with him to prove his claim to be a goat-herd, his royal master replied firmly that this was the one and only time that true love had come to him—as for goats, he could easily pretend that he had lost his flock.

As, thus talking, the travellers once more drew near to the Necromancer's house, they saw Tormentilla and Angelica approaching; and, to their relief, they noticed that the cobra, still held fondly in the former's embrace, had evidently been merely stunned by the blow it had received and that it was now beginning to writhe about again.

Joyful at her pet's recovery, Tormentilla bade Angelica put the cobra back into the Snakery; and then she turned to greet Amaryllus, for whom an answering love instantly sprang up in her own heart. While reviving her shaken nerves with a cocktail —compounded entirely of several deadly poisons and brought at her request by Angelica—the Enchanter's lovely daughter talked sweetly with the handsome young stranger who had so miraculously turned up to break the monotony of her lonely life.

She listened eagerly to his words of admiration and love, which she gladly reciprocated.

But this romantic interlude was roughly interrupted when Dipsacus the Necromancer presently arrived upon the scene. Furious at the sight of two strangers talking with his daughter and her maid, he called up a sudden hurricane by means of his magical arts, which effectually parted the two pairs of lovers. Just as Amaryllus was about to fold Tormentilla in his eager arms, he was seized by the Wizard's attendant hobgoblins; and thus he missed the fair maiden's first kiss of love—which was fortunate for him, had he but known it. Angelica and her admirer, Gallanthus, however, had been quicker in the uptake and had enjoyed many pleasant kisses before being likewise torn assunder by the hobgoblins.

The two young men, finding that a spell now prevented them from moving another step forward, were compelled to depart into the forest once more along the same path by which they had come; and the Enchanter was thus left alone with his now angry daughter, who indignantly demanded for the first time in her cloistered life an explanation of her weird parent's reasons for keeping her so long a captive in the forest.

The Necromancer, realizing that his once obedient and complacent daughter was no longer content to be a willing tool, found himself compelled to reveal his secret; and it was a strange tale he unfolded. In the days of his youth, he had practised magic and necromancy in Golden Town, the city on the other side of the forest; and here he had received as a pupil a lady of very high degree, also a dabbler in magic arts. To this amateur magician he had revealed much of his own professiónal knowledge; and the pair had likewise fallen deeply in love with one another. Then the high-born sorceress had haughtily declared herself unable to wed with one of such doubtful antecedents; and he had been driven out from the city, while his *inamorata* had chosen a spouse of her own class.

As Tormentilla now carelessly suggested, he might easily have avenged his injury there and then by using his own superior magic arts to slay the pupil who had so callously jilted him—but, alas he loved her still! He decided, however, to take a more subtle revenge at a later date. He also had married and had a beautiful daughter, Tormentilla; and as his high-born ex-pupil had become the mother of a handsome son, he determined that his revenge should, therefore, be gained thus: The handsome son, when grown-up, should be slain by the Necromancer's beautiful daughter, by means of a Poisoned Kiss.

To this end, he had brought up Tormentilla to be herself immune from poisons, by feeding her upon every kind of deadly venom all her life; but she would thus have the power to slay a lover by means of her poisonous kiss upon his lips. Despite his skill, however, only the first kiss would thus be fatal, all succeeding ones being harmless. Nevertheless, if this first kiss should fall upon the lips of his once-loved lady's only son, his revenge would be assured. And this he intended should happen.

Having thus revealed the reasons for her poisonous upbringing, Dipsacus further announced it to be his wish that Tormentilla should now set out with her maid for Golden Town, to carry out his plan; but, to his dismay and anger, his daughter flatly refused to undertake the murderous mission. She declined to be compelled to poison one lover before accepting the caresses of another. Little had she dreamed when about to caress her forest lover that her kiss would be a poisoned one; and she now blessed the hurricane which had separated them so opportunely.

The Wizard, too, would have gnashed his teeth with rage had he also been aware of the identity of the so-called goatherd, who was, in fact, none other than his false one's son. For the Necromancer's youthful sweetheart—though he had not revealed this fact to his daughter—was the Empress Persicaria, the reigning sovereign of Golden Town; and her son was Prince Amaryllus.

When Dipsacus realized that his carefully brought up daughter now refused to obey his will and meant to defy him, he declared that she and her maid should be banished for ever; and he hurried into the house to hunt up in his books a spell that should drive them forth and prevent them from ever returning. His now poor memory failed to supply him with the necessary words of incantation at the moment. Had his magic not become so rusty, too, he would have already discovered the identity of the goatherd and have secured his revenge that morning. Now, many new complications were involved.

Tormentilla and Angelica meanwhile were rather pleased than otherwise at this turn of events, both being extremely bored with their dull forest life; and they decided to make their way to Golden Town, after all, since that was the city of their forest sweethearts. Suddenly, however, remembering that they would need money and new clothes if they were to visit this fashionable city, they at first wondered how this difficulty could be surmounted. Then Angelica had a bright idea. She slipped into the house, and while the Necromancer was still poring over his book of spells, she chipped off a goodly piece of the famous Philosopher's Stone owned by her master—which she happened to know he kept in a tobacco-jar on the mantelpiece in one of his secret rooms.

When she came gaily dancing out again with this treasure, the two girls rubbed the magic chip, and solemnly wished for all the money and clothes they needed.

Instantly a shower of golden pieces fell at their feet; and at the same time, a host of messenger-boys and milliners miraculously appeared, all carrying gay boxes filled with smart new frocks and hats, direct from Paris, Vienna, and other fashion centres. They deposited their parcels on the ground and then vanished as miraculously as they had appeared.

Consequently, when Dipsacus once more bustled out with his spell of banishment completed, the two girls were ready for their great adventure.

First bidding his three hobgoblin henchmen, Hob, Gob, and Lob, to follow and keep an eye upon the exiles, Dipsacus listened to the somewhat indecently joyous farewells of his disobedient daughter and her saucy maid. Then he pronounced the spell of banishment upon them; and the two girls vanished through the forest to an accompaniment of thunder and lightning, with the inevitable and rather tiresome hurricane thrown in as make-weight.

.   .   .   .

With unlimited wealth provided for them by the piece of Philosopher's Stone so neatly chipped off by the practical maid, Angelica and her mistress easily established themselves in great state in a rich apartment in Golden Town.

Here the news of Tormentilla's marvellous beauty quickly spread like wildfire in every quarter of the city; and hosts of admirers swarmed around her new dwelling-place, which was soon filled to overflowing with the flowers, sweetmeats, and other gifts they lavished upon her.

Although Tormentilla certainly enjoyed being the sensation of Golden Town, she was always anxious to keep her admirers at a distance; and so great was her dread lest her goatherd lover should appear and claim the fatal kiss she might not have the strength of will to withhold, that she refused firmly to see any young man alone—thus requiring the almost constant attention of Angelica.

This latter precaution was somewhat irksome to the giddy maid, who, however, managed to have a very gay time, notwithstanding. She had been quickly rediscovered by her sweetheart, Gallanthus, who, with his royal master, had returned immediately to Golden Town after their forest adventure; and this was highly satisfactory to her. Though thrilled to learn from him that her mistress's beloved one was none other than Prince Amaryllus of Golden Town, she begged Gallanthus to keep his master away from Tormentilla, now revealing to him the danger of the latter's first fatal kiss. But she did not forbid Gallanthus himself to visit the apartment; and the pair enjoyed several pleasant secret meetings.

Meanwhile, the Empress Persicaria had discovered by means of her magic arts—which she still practised and, indeed, had kept carefully up-to-date—that the beautiful stranger making such a stir in the city was the lost sweetheart of her beloved son; and since—being an incorrigibly possessive mother—it was her amiable custom to do away with any maiden whom the young Prince specially admired, she determined to dispose of Tormentilla before Amaryllus was likely to meet her. The young Prince, having thoughts for no one else but his lost forest maiden, had so far refused to visit the beautiful newcomer; and thus, he had no idea that she and his beloved Tormentilla were one and the same person.

In great haste, therefore, the royal Sorceress despatched her three best spinster mediums to the rich apartment of Tormentilla, with a huge box of poisoned chocolates as a gift for the fair visitor.

But the Empress's little plan did not have the desired effect, for Tormentilla found the chocolates, with their piquant fillings of arsenic, hemlock, prussic acid, and other charmingly flavoured poisons, very much to her liking—also, being entirely immune from the evils of such substances, she suffered no ill effects from them.

More successful, however, were the secret plottings of the three hobgoblins, Hob, Gob, and Lob, who had been bidden by their Wizard master to keep an eye upon his errant daughter and to cause her to carry out his pet project, after all.

Their first attempt at getting in touch with Tormentilla took place the same day on which the mediums arrived at the apartment with the poisoned chocolates. The three hobgoblins had disguised themselves as reporters who had called to interview the beautiful stranger for their respective newspapers.

Angelica, however, firmly refused to allow the supposed men visitors to see her mistress; and though the pretended journalists were somewhat intrigued by the spinster mediums—who made a considerable fuss of the note-taking trio—they had to abandon any idea of reaching Tormentilla in that disguise.

Then they hatched another plot. Having learned that Angelica intended to meet her lover, Gallanthus, that night after her mistress had retired and that Tormentilla would thus be left alone and unguarded for a short time, the following plan was decided upon. Lob was to put on a Cap of Invisibility, enter the palace unseen, and whisper in the young Prince's ear an invitation to follow the whispering voice which should promise to lead him to his beloved lost maiden. Meanwhile Gob was to keep Gallanthus so occupied with various small mishaps that he would have no chance to tell his master anything about the fatal poison kiss of which he had learned from Angelica, but of which Amaryllus himself still knew nothing. Hob's duty was to scatter a powder of wakefulness on Tormentilla's couch and then to keep watch near by to direct operations in the apartment. The conspirators felt this plan could not fail to succeed.

When Tormentilla had retired early to her chamber that night, Angelica went below and softly admitted Gallanthus, to partake of a quiet little supper with her.

Meanwhile, the hobgoblin, Lob, wearing his Cap of Invisibility, had crept unseen into the royal palace; and making his way to the apartment of the Prince, he whispered enticingly into the latter's ear, bidding him follow his voice which would guide him to the abode of Tormentilla. Joyfully and in haste, Amaryllus sprang up and followed the mysterious voice, eager to behold his beloved one.

On reaching the latter's apartment, Amaryllus, still guided by the mysterious voice, entered the ante-room leading to Tormentilla's chamber; and at that moment, Tormentilla herself, kept awake by the magic powder scattered on her couch by Hob, drew aside the curtains and entered the room.

With a great cry of joy, the lovers rushed forward to embrace one another. Then, suddenly realizing her fatal curse, Tormentilla drew back in fear, and begged Amaryllus to leave her, telling him distractedly that the touch of her lips would bring death to him.

But Amaryllus gallantly declared that he would gladly welcome even death at her beloved touch, but added that he could not believe anything but bliss could come of their embrace; and he pleaded so eagerly for her love that Tormentilla herself began to wonder whether, after all, her fears were not a fantastic dream.

The whispering, enticing voices of the hidden plotters urged her on into forgetfulness of her curse; and at last, unable to resist further and overcome by an answering passion, she sank joyfully into the arms of Amaryllus and received his first eager kiss upon her own sweetly responsive lips.

Thus, the fatal deed was done; and the Poisoned Kiss was given.

.   .   .   .

But the young Prince did not die; nor did the Necromancer's fine long-drawn-out scheme of vengeance have the terrible effect he had anticipated.

And why? Because he had been very cleverly double-crossed by his ex-pupil, the Empress Persicaria, whose amateur sorcery was more than the equal of his own professional skill. The astute royal dame, having imbibed far more magic than was good for her former master's little plot, had soon learned by her own arts all about the subtle vengeance cherished by the latter. Knowing that he was feeding his beautiful daughter upon poisons that she might bestow a fatal kiss upon the lips of her own beloved son, the Empress, in her turn, had most carefully fed the young Prince upon antidotes which would nullify such poisons.

Consequently, though Amaryllus had been brought back to the palace in a sort of trance after his visit to Tormentilla's apartment, he had gradually come back to life. The only thing needed to restore him entirely to health was the voice and presence of his beloved one.

This latter necessity entailed a stormy scene between the Empress and her extremely annoyed ex-tutor and ex-lover, Dipsacus the Necromancer, who now met each other again for the first time in twenty years. This interview took place in the royal palace; and it ended in the two protagonists acknowledging that they had both been beaten by Youth and by Love.

Consequently Amaryllus was allowed to be healed by the now sweet and safe kisses of his beloved Tormentilla, and to receive her as his bride. Then, after sentimentally recalling the happy days of their own youthful romance, the Empress and the Necromancer decided to bury their now blunted hatchet and to make a belated second marriage together instead.

Gallanthus and his saucy Angelica were not long in fixing their own wedding-day; and, not to be left out of the general rejoicings and conscious of deserving reward for their own part in these strange proceedings, the three hobgoblins offered themselves as suitors to the three spinster mediums, being eagerly accepted by the latter—who had long since thought their last chances gone.

Thus came good out of evil—and Joy from a Poisoned Kiss.

AÏDA

Verdi

DURING the reign of one of the great Pharaohs of Egypt, Amonasro, King of Ethiopia, declared war against the Egyptians and invaded their country. Despite their daring, however, the Ethiopians were beaten; for the Egyptian Army was then at the height of its glory and was victorious wherever it went.

After one of his most crushing defeats, Amonasro had to bear yet another bitter blow. Amongst the many captives carried away by the all-conquering Egyptians was his own fair daughter, the Princess Aïda.

Although unaware of their lovely captive's high rank, the conquerors guarded her with especial care because of her dazzling beauty and gentle grace; and upon her arrival in Memphis, the great Pharaoh presented her as a slave to his daughter Amneris. At first, the Princess of Egypt refused to regard the charming girl-captive merely as an ordinary slave, but treated her instead with the familiarity and affection of a sister; and thus, for a time, Aïda's bonds rested lightly upon her and, except for a natural grief for the sufferings of her beloved country and her own enforced exile, she had little to trouble her. After a while, however, when the joy of a great love came into her life, a change took place; and then for the captive maid black storm-clouds of woe quickly gathered around.

Radames, a handsome young officer in the King's Guards, owing to his high position, had frequent access into the presence of the Princess and her attendants; and from the first moment his eyes rested upon the beautiful and gentle Aïda a passionate love for her sprang up within his heart, which deepened and strengthened daily. His love was quickly returned by the captive maid. Although at first her conscience blamed her for loving the enemy of her country, she could not long struggle against a passion that would not be subdued; and presently, she gave her heart unreservedly into the keeping of the handsome young Egyptian.

The lovers' joy, however, though they tried to keep it secret, was not long permitted to remain unclouded. The noble Radames was also beloved by the Princess Amneris, whose proud and passionate nature could brook no rival in her affections. For long the fair Amneris had cherished her passion and had vainly desired to have it requited; but Radames, though he quickly guessed her secret, refused to meet her open advances, being too noble to accept favours from one he could not love. Yet, despite the young officer's coldness, Amneris had always hoped to win his love in the end; but, with the advent of Aïda, her hopes were quickly dashed to the ground. Although Radames and the beautiful slave at first endeavoured to hide their love, the jealous eyes of the Princess speedily detected it; then, determined that her own passion should not be thwarted, she used all the means in her power to obtain her heart's desire.

War was soon again declared between the rival countries, the King of Ethiopia having once more gathered a large army together and already invested Thebes. The Egyptians having also massed their mighty forces, instructions were given to the priests of Isis to learn the will of the goddess as to who should lead them against the foe. On a certain day, the priests declared that the dread goddess had spoken; and then Pharaoh gathered all his court and council together and announced that Isis had chosen Radames as the leader of the Egyptian hosts.

A wave of overwhelming joy swept through the heart of Radames at this glad fulfilment of his own dearest wish; and as he breathed a prayer of gratitude to the goddess who had thus favoured him, a thunder of applause burst from the assembled company—for, though young in years, the chosen warrior leader was honoured and beloved by all.

The Princess Amneris then came forward and placed the royal standard of Egypt in the hands of Radames, bidding him in a voice that trembled with emotion to bear it ever into the paths of victory and renown. She was filled with exaltation that the man she loved was chosen for this honour; and she already looked forward to the time when he should return, covered with glory—a hero for whom even the hand of a Princess of Egypt would not be too great a reward.

But Aïda was filled with despair; and she crept away to her own chamber, weeping with anguish. How could she join in desiring the defeat of her own beloved people; and why had an unkind fate ordained that she should love the enemy of her country?

Meanwhile, a solemn dedication service was held in the Temple of the War God, Ptah; and here Radames was invested by Ramphis, the High Priest, with the sacred insignia appertaining to his new position, all the congregation joining in his own enthusiastic anticipation of success.

Nor were these anticipations and prayers in vain; for the Egyptian forces again carried all before them and defeated the Ethiopians on every side.

Thus it came about that the young Radames returned to Memphis a victorious hero, covered with glory and honour, and followed by a long train of captives to make his triumph complete.

Among these captives—though unknown to all—was Amonasro, King of Ethiopia, who, having gone into the battle disguised as an ordinary officer, had escaped recognition; and though his proud spirit revolted against the degradation of being thus taken prisoner, he yet went to Memphis with hope in his heart that he might there meet with his lost daughter and also learn something of his enemies' plans.

On the day on which Radames was to make his triumphal entry into the city, great preparations were made to receive him with all the pomp and magnificence usually associated with such a pageant. Within the palace, the Princess of Egypt commanded her slaves to sing the praises of her hero as they clad her in her most gorgeous jewelled robes. She was filled with joyous expectations; for she knew that the victor's reward was to be her own hand in marriage and that her dearest hopes would thus be realized.

Nevertheless, her brow darkened upon the entry of Aïda—drooping because of the defeat of her own people; for the beautiful slave's presence at that moment revived the jealous feelings which had remained dormant during the absence of Radames. In order to prove whether Aïda's love for the hero was still the same, she tricked her by falsely announcing that he had fallen in battle. Then, as Aïda's sudden wild grief betrayed her, she sought yet another proof by declaring that she had but jested and that Radames was alive and well. When, on hearing these words Aïda's face became irradiated with joy, the Princess knew that her former suspicions were still valid; and she now poured forth cruel taunts upon the beautiful slave.

At that moment, however, hearing sounds which told her that the festival was about to begin, her mood suddenly changed to glad expectancy again; and she went to join her royal father upon the throne set up at the city gates, through which the triumphal procession had to pass, bidding Aïda attend her with her other maidens.

Radames was received with great favour by Pharaoh, who showered praises and thanks upon him for the mighty deeds he had performed; and as the young conqueror knelt, overcome at the foot of the throne, the Princess Amneris with her own hands placed the crown of victory upon his brow with much tenderness.

The King now desired to see the prisoners taken in battle; and as the captives, one by one, passed before the throne, Aïda uttered a cry of glad surprise and, running into the arms of Amonasro—who was among them—greeted him tenderly as her father. Amonasro, however, whispered instructions to her not to reveal his true identity; and when the company gathered around on thus realizing he was the beautiful slave-girl's father, the disguised King related a feasible story as to his capture—describing himself as an ordinary Ethiopian officer—which was readily enough believed.

Pharaoh now desired Radames to name any favour he pleased, which should be readily granted; and the young victor—whose heart was as yet unhardened by the fortunes of war—besought the King to set all the captives free, as his reward. His request was granted; and the captives were all set free—with the exception of Aïda's father, who, on the insistent demand of Ramphis, the High Priest, was retained as a hostage. Pharaoh then led Amneris forward and placed her hand in that of Radames, declaring before all the people that the hand of the Princess of Egypt was the prize he had destined for the deliverer of the country.

Amneris was radiant with joy, having thus secured her dearest wish and feeling that she need no longer fear Aïda as a rival; but Radames was plunged in despair—for he was determined to wed no other maid but Aïda, whom he loved passionately and for whose sweet sake he had crowned himself with laurels. Aïda, too, was filled with grief; for she felt that, Radames wed, naught remained to her but death.

Radames, however, realized that nothing was to be gained at the moment by refusing to accept the reward offered to him; and he thus permitted himself to be regarded as the affianced suitor of Amneris, trusting to find some means of disentangling himself later on. He still saw Aïda from time to time in the palace, but never alone; and at last, despairing of any other means of securing an interview with her, he arranged for her to meet him secretly on the evening before his wedding day, outside the Temple of Isis.

Now, Amonasro—who was also lodged in the palace—had quickly observed the love that existed between Aïda and Radames; and having learnt from the soldiers about him that the scattered forces of Ethiopia had once more been banded together to invade Egypt, he determined to make use of his daughter's love as a means of securing information as to the Egyptians' war plans. Having overheard the arrangement made for the lovers' secret meeting, therefore, he managed to escape from the palace that same evening, and made his way to the Temple of Isis.

As it happened, the Princess Amneris had also arranged to visit the Temple of Isis that night, in order to offer prayers and incense to the goddess on this the last evening of her maidenhood, in accordance with an ancient custom. Attended by guards, she arrived soon after twilight and was immediately conducted by Ramphis, the High Priest, into the Temple, where she began her vigil.

No sooner had the Princess and her retinue retired within the sacred building than Aïda drew near, trembling with fear; and almost immediately after she was joined by her father, who had awaited her arrival in a hiding-place close by.

Quickly reassuring the frightened maiden, Amonasro informed her of the service he wished her to do for him—to discover from her lover the position from which the Egyptians intended to surprise their newly-invading enemies—a fact which, in the hands of the Ethiopians, meant success to their dangerous enterprise.

At first Aïda indignantly refused to ask her lover to be disloyal to the arms he bore; but upon her angry father playing remorselessly upon her filial and patriotic feelings, she reluctantly consented to do his bidding. Scarcely had the disguised king retired into the shadows than Radames appeared; and next moment the lovers were clasped in a passionate embrace.

When the first joy of meeting was over, the unhappy pair tried to make a plan of escape from their present seemingly hopeless predicament. Radames assured his beloved one that he would never wed Amneris, despite the fact that his marriage with the Princess was believed to be taking place on the morrow; and he declared that he intended to join the Egyptian forces at sunrise. After leading them to victory, he would return again as conqueror and demand the hand of the Ethiopian maid as his reward.

But Aïda was not satisfied with this optimistic view, knowing that the rage and jealousy of Amneris would never permit of their marriage; and she begged her lover to escape with her that same night to some hiding-place, whence they could journey later to another distant land. When Radames hesitated at this suggestion, thinking of his own country's need of him, the unhappy girl turned from him, declaring sadly that only death remained for her and adding bitterly that he had better return to the Princess of Egypt and to the honour and glory that awaited him as the latter's husband.

This outburst was more than Radames could endure; and clasping Aïda in his arms again, he declared passionately that they would indeed escape that night, since her love was more to him than anything else the world could offer.

Intoxicated with the intensity of their passion, the lovers prepared to carry out their resolve at once; but, as they were about to depart, Aïda, suddenly remembering her father's command, asked in a trembling voice : " How shall we escape being seen by the Egyptian soldiers? "

" All will be well," returned Radames reassuringly, " if we avoid the Pass of Napata, where they lie hidden! "

No sooner had he spoken these fatal words than Amonasro, having thus learned the secret he longed to possess, sprang from his hiding-place and, boldly approaching the lovers, announced to the young Egyptian his true identity as the King of Ethiopia.

Radames was now overcome with dismay that he had, though unconsciously, betrayed his country's cause; but Amonasro, declaring that no blame could ever attach to him, now entreated him to join the Ethiopian ranks, where glory awaited him and the hand of Aïda should be his reward.

At that moment, however, the Princess Amneris and Ramphis, the High Priest, emerged from the Temple, having heard all that had passed; and calling to their attendant guards, they bade them seize the three offenders. Radames, wildly calling to Amonasro and Aïda to fly for their lives, engaged the attention of the guards until he knew that the Ethiopian King and his daughter had escaped to a safe distance; then, nobly scorning to avoid the just wrath of the monarch he had so unwittingly betrayed, he yielded himself without a struggle into the hands of the High Priest and his satellites and was carried away captive to meet his doom.

A few days later, Radames was brought to the Hall of Judgment within the royal palace, to be tried as a traitor and to receive the sentence of death; but as the guards were conducting him thither, they were accosted by the Princess Amneris, who imperiously demanded to speak with the prisoner.

The guards having fallen back respectfully, Amneris addressed Radames, asking him whether he preferred to die the death of a traitor or to live on as her consort; for the proud Princess was still unable to repress the love that consumed her, despite her anger that it was not returned, and she hoped thus by her renewed offer of marriage to save the young man's life. In answer to his eager inquiries, she even gave him news of Aïda. Although Amonasro had been slain in the battle that had just taken place, his daughter had managed to escape, though none knew of her whereabouts. Then, with passionate earnestness, Amneris besought Radames

2B

to renounce all thought of Aïda for ever and to accept her own love instead, when she would intercede with the King for his life; but Radames still declared staunchly that no power on earth could induce him to thrust the dear image of his beloved Aïda from his heart.

" Go, then, and die! " cried the Princess, enraged that her love should thus be slighted yet again; then, as Radames passed into the Hall of Judgment, she burst into a wild paroxysm of weeping, knowing that nothing could now save him, since, once in the presence of his judges, his doom was sealed.

To the accusations made against him, Radames answered not a word, for, in spite of his clear conscience, he knew that defence was useless; and when the High Priest pronounced upon him the doom of living incarceration as the traitor's sentence, he bowed his head in resignation, having no longer the desire to live.

It was in vain that Amneris—full of grief and now remorseful that she had not interceded for him with Pharaoh before his doom was pronounced—passionately begged for mercy to be shown to the man she loved; the relentless High Priest passed from the Hall of Judgment, heedless of the wailing curses that followed him from the broken-hearted Princess of Egypt.

Meanwhile, Radames was conducted to the Temple of the War God and ushered into the small subterranean vault in which he was to be buried alive; and as the stone that covered the opening was gradually lowered, the priests began to chant the sacred hymn of death.

Radames stood resigned and unafraid upon the bottom step of the crypt; but just as the stone was falling into its socket, he heard a soft sigh behind him, and, turning, beheld, as the last ray of light faded, the trembling form of his beloved Aïda!

Filled with amazement and horror that one so young and lovely should thus be entombed with him, Radames pressed and beat frantically upon the roof of the vault; but the stone had now fallen into its place and he was powerless to dislodge it. As he sank despairing upon the step, Aïda groped her way through the darkness to his side, and, in a sweet exultant voice, bade him gently to be comforted. Having foreseen his doom, she had of her own free will crept unobserved by the priests into the vault, preferring to die with him rather than to live on alone.

Grateful for such a wonderful proof of love and devotion, Radames passionately embraced the triumphant Aïda. Thus clasped in each other's arms, the lovers calmly awaited their end, rejoicing that, though in life they had been forced asunder, yet in death they were not divided!

DON CARLOS   *Verdi*

ALTHOUGH King Philip II of Spain was a cruel fanatic, during whose reign the dreadful Inquisition rose to the height of its power, his son, Don Carlos, was of an entirely different disposition. The young Prince was tolerant, gentle, and kindly; and he had great pity for the sufferings of the unhappy Protestants whom his stern and fanatically devout father persecuted so relentlessly.

The mother of Don Carlos had died in early life; and just as her son had attained to manhood, the royal widower married again. To the despair and anguish of Don Carlos, King Philip chose as his second wife the beautiful young Elisabeth of Valois, afterwards known as Queen Isabella.

Carlos and Elisabeth had been playmates during their childhood; and as they grew up, their childish affection had developed into a passionate and overwhelming love. They longed to marry; but fate was against them. Philip II no sooner set eyes on beautiful Elisabeth than he desired her for himself. Being extremely powerful, he easily gained his wish—though he received a most unwilling and unhappy bride.

Don Carlos, thus ruthlessly called upon to endure the shattering of his sweet romance, found it necessary to move circumspectly, lest his beloved one should suffer. He was anxious to avoid giving offence to his father—who, though a religious fanatic, was also jealous and exacting where his earthly passions were concerned—by revealing the deep love that still existed between Elisabeth and himself. He, therefore, threw himself more whole-heartedly into the cause he had espoused—that of mitigating the woes and wrongs of the Protestants in the Netherlands, where Philip held considerable sway.

Before leaving for Flanders, however, he called at the convent of San Giusto, to pray at the tomb of his recently dead grandfather, the good Emperor Charles V, whom he had dearly loved and whose noble life he wished to emulate.

As he listened to the chanting of the monks, it seemed to him that through one of the latter—who mysteriously appeared beside the tomb—he received a direct message of hope from the spirit of the dead Emperor; and he was greatly cheered thereby. He was, consequently, ripe for the mission brought him by his great friend, Rodrigo—the Marquess of Posa and a Knight of Malta. Rodrigo

now joined him with the news that the Protestants had decided t
revolt against the rule of their cruel overlord, Philip of Spain, an
were looking to Don Carlos to lead them as the champion of thei
cause. The young Prince was ready enough to accept thi
invitation and so to seek distraction from his thwarted love an
safety for Elisabeth by his own absence from the Court.

He was determined, nevertheless, to see the Queen again befor
leaving on his mission. Hearing that she was even then in th
convent grounds, he easily enough secured his audience with he
while Rodrigo very considerately kept her ladies-in-waiting, th
Princess Eboli and the Countess d'Aremberg, otherwise engage
at a little distance.

But though Carlos had hoped merely to persuade the Queen t
intercede with the King on behalf of his mission—which Phili
might regard as of a treasonable character—neither he nor Elis:
beth could control their overwhelming emotion nor refrain fror
uttering the passionate words of love they had kept back so long
Nevertheless, the danger of their position was too great to b
ignored; and Elisabeth begged her beloved one to depart on h
mission quickly and so to avoid the discovery of their mutual lov

But Carlos rashly put off the evil moment of parting; for th
intensity of his love for Elisabeth was now greater than ever. H
begged the Queen to meet him once again that evening in th
palace gardens; and then he hastened away, just as the Kin
entered the convent grounds.

Finding his royal bride thus unattended, Philip was at on
suspicious; and when, next moment, the Countess d'Arember
hurried forward, he furiously dismissed her from the Court i
disgrace for having neglected her duty. Sadly the Queen followe
the drooping Countess, who was her favourite lady-in-waitin

As Rodrigo likewise now came forward, Philip scarcely listene
to the latter's pleadings for the mission of Don Carlos. H
jealousy had been keenly aroused on realizing that it was his so
who had just parted from the Queen; and he bade Rodrigo watc
the pair constantly. As it happened, Rodrigo, the Marquess
Posa, was his favourite minister; he was also the only human bein
the King had ever had any affection for. At the same time, h
knew that Rodrigo also loved Carlos and might, for that reasor
not keep too strict a watch upon his movements. He, therefor
added the ominous words: " Beware of the Grand Inquisitor!
The Marquess shuddered as he now followed his royal master t
the palace.

Meanwhile, the Princess Eboli had most discreetly kept in th
background when King Philip had appeared in the conven

grounds. Despite the conversational powers of Rodrigo, however, he had observed well the little scene between the Queen and Don Carlos sufficiently for her own suspicions to be aroused. Jealousy also struck at her own heart; for she, too, secretly loved the King's son. She determined to keep a careful watch upon her royal mistress.

When, consequently, at dusk that same evening, the Princess beheld the cloaked figure of Don Carlos moving with somewhat too studied carelessness towards a quiet corner of the Queen's own private garden in the palace grounds, she suspected an assignation. She determined herself to impersonate the royal lady before the latter appeared. Masked and closely veiled, she slipped into the fountain recess where Don Carlos was waiting. Imagining her to be his beloved one, the young man instantly began to pour forth a further passionate declaration of his love for her, addressing her in tender terms.

Thus did the Princess Eboli learn for certain that the man she herself adored was in love with the Queen. Now beside herself with jealousy and disappointment, she flung aside her veil and mask and revealed her true identity to his horrified gaze.

As Don Carlos fell back in alarm because his secret was thus known, the love-sick Princess changed her tone. Declaring her own love for him, she begged him to return it and to think no more of one beyond his reach. Then, as Don Carlos still shrank from her in dismay and repugnance, her angry jealousy broke forth once more and she threatened to expose him to the King. These last words were overheard by Rodrigo, who had followed closely on the heels of his rash young friend, hoping to save him from danger. The Marquess now rushed forward and would have stabbed the Princess Eboli, had not Don Carlos prevented him from doing so by thrusting himself between them.

Thus, the jealous Princess returned to the palace in safety but determined to avenge herself upon Don Carlos for refusing her love—which she regarded as a slight. Knowing that the Queen set great store upon a certain jewel-casket and now believing that the latter probably contained some loved treasure given her by Don Carlos, the crafty Princess placed this box on a table in the King's study where Philip was bound to find it.

Meanwhile, another disaster presently befell the young Prince. Next day, the Inquisition held a grand *auto-de-fé*; and all Madrid turned out to see the sad procession of condemned heretics passing to the place of execution, where they were to be burned alive at the stake.

The King and Queen and all their Court were present, together

with the Grand Inquisitor and other officers and familiars of the
Inquisition; and, as usual, the terrible spectacle was preceded by
full religious ceremonies. The magnificence of the Church digni-
taries matched the gorgeous appearance of the courtiers and the
brilliance of the State Guards; and the entire scene had the air of
a festival, despite the expected horror of its finale.

King Philip, as a fanatic, took a sinister satisfaction in the
dreadful fate of the heretics; and though the tender-hearted Queen
would gladly have absented herself, he made her walk beside him
to receive the plaudits of the populace.

Don Carlos, like his beloved Elisabeth, hated the cruelties of the
Inquisition; and to-day his anger and disgust broke out afresh.
As the chosen champion of the Protestants in Flanders, he now
flung himself boldly at the feet of his royal father, protesting
passionately against the present *auto-de-fé*; and he also begged
permission to go forth and establish a more generous and merciful
rule in the Netherlands.

But King Philip was furiously angry, both at his son's present
protests and at his request; and he ordered his instant arrest as a
traitor to the Church and the State, calling upon him to surrender
his sword to Rodrigo. The latter, full of woe for the fate of the
young Prince he loved but unable to resist the authority of the
King and the anger of the powerful Inquisition, was thus reluctantly compelled to disarm Don Carlos and deliver him over
to the guards.

Then, while the unhappy Queen fell back, half fainting in her
despair, the *auto-de-fé* procession continued and the pyres for the
condemned heretics were set alight.

.   .   .   .

King Philip, autocrat though he was, was yet bound to submit
himself to the even more powerful Inquisition. Thus it came
about that, on the day following the *auto-de-fé*, he was visited by
the Grand Inquisitor, a venerable but sinister Grandee, who now
denounced to him the King's own favourite Minister, Rodrigo
Marquess of Posa, as the instigator of the young Prince's lapse
from grace. He declared that it was the Inquisition's will that
Don Carlos should be pardoned and that Rodrigo, as the arch-
conspirator and more dangerous rebel of the two, should be
condemned to death instead.

Unable, in spite of his regal pomp and power, to defy the decree
of the Inquisition—beyond which there was no appeal—King
Philip was thus compelled to submit to the Grand Inquisitor's
command and to sacrifice the only human being he had ever felt
affection for.

As he sat in his study, alone and sorrowful, after the departure of the Grand Inquisitor, he opened the jewel-casket left on the table beside him by the jealous Princess Eboli; and among its contents he found a miniature of Don Carlos. At that moment, the Queen entered the room, looking for the casket; and, mad with jealousy at the sight of the miniature she had thus treasured, the King now furiously accused her of having accepted Don Carlos as her lover.

In vain the unhappy Elisabeth protested her innocence, declaring that she had never been unfaithful to her marriage vows. Philip was beside himself with frenzied rage; and a terrible scene ensued.

The Princess Eboli was now filled with remorse for her cruel betrayal of the innocent Queen she once had loved; and she sought the latter's pardon. She confessed that her treachery had been caused by jealousy, because of her own unrequited love for Don Carlos. But Elisabeth could not condone such conduct; and she dismissed the false Princess from her immediate circle of Court ladies.

Meanwhile, Rodrigo, knowing that his own hours were numbered, since the Inquisition had already denounced him as the instigator of Don Carlos's revolutionary ideas, hastened to the State prison where the young Prince lay captive. The two friends greeted one another with great tenderness; and Rodrigo revealed the fact that their positions would shortly be reversed. Don Carlos was to be released, and he, Rodrigo, was to become the victim of the Inquisition instead.

He was, however, about to make a desperate bid for freedom. But, even as he spoke with his friend, one of the guards who had followed him to the Prince's cell by order of the Inquisitorial authorities, raised an arquebus and shot him through the heart.

As Rodrigo fell to the ground, dead, King Philip entered the cell, followed by the Grand Inquisitor and other officials; and, announcing to his son that he was now free, he handed him back his sword.

But Don Carlos shrank back in horror from his royal father, loathing him for having consented to the death of the noble, pure-hearted Rodrigo. He refused any longer to call himself the son of such a father.

The cries of the populace outside were now heard, clamouring for the appearance of their beloved young Prince, whom they had known to be in danger. But Don Carlos rushed away into the shadowy lanes, and left King Philip to face the people without him.

. . . .

Before leaving for Flanders, where he hoped to lead the Protestant rising, Don Carlos met his beloved Queen once more in the convent of San Giusto, beside the tomb of the Emperor Charles V.

Elisabeth came first to the trysting-place; and as she waited there, she sadly recalled the happy days of her carefree youth in France—at Fontainebleau, where love had first blossomed for her and the royal youth, Carlos, that sweet love now doomed to bloom no more.

When Don Carlos presently arrived, they spoke quietly of their love and of the sacrifice of the parting they were now resolved to make. When the time came for them to say farewell, they parted, not as the passionate lovers they knew themselves to be but almost as a mother and her young son.

But the resigned restraint of the lovers availed them nothing when, presently, to their dismay, they were discovered by King Philip. The latter, suspecting a last secret meeting between the pair at this sacred spot, had hastened thither with the Grand Inquisitor and his guards.

His jealousy violently reawakened, the King once more denounced his son, not only as the lover of his Queen but as a rebel to his rule in the Netherlands; and the Inquisitor now sternly ordered the young Prince's instant arrest, that he might at last be dealt with by the terrible Inquisition tribunal.

Don Carlos at first desperately resisted the attempts of the Grand Inquisitor's familiars to seize him; then, suddenly, he ceased to struggle and a heavenly calm came over his countenance.

At the same moment, the voice of the good Emperor Charles V was heard, as though spoken by a monk who mysteriously appeared beside the tomb, announcing that the joys of heaven awaited him.

The vision instantly faded, as the comforting voice ceased to speak; and Don Carlos fell lifeless beside the tomb. The Inquisition had lost its victim.

ERNANI   *Verdi*

IN the wild mountainous districts of Arragon, in the year 1519, a large company of bandits and mountaineer rebels were gathered together one day in their stronghold. They had been summoned

:hither at the command of their chief, who, though in reality a
noble fallen under the ban of the King of Castile, was known to
:hem only by the name of Ernani.

These lawless folk gave their leader unquestioning obedience
and loyal service; for Ernani had won their fierce hearts, not only
by his noble and commanding presence, but by his just dealings,
his faithful heart, and his unimpeachable honour. Never had
he bandits known their chief to break his word, to betray a
riend, or to deceive even an enemy; and it was with eager
ympathy that they now listened to his appeal for their help.

Ernani told them that he had conceived a passion for a certain
eautiful lady of Arragon, whose name was Elvira and who
eturned his love, since they had already met on several occasions.
Unhappily for the lovers, however, Elvira had been betrothed
against her will to Don Silva, a Grandee of Spain, who, though
advancing in years, was so eager to be united to her that he
had already found means to convey her to his castle, where the
nuptials were to be celebrated next day. The bandit chief implored the help of his friends to rescue this fair lady from her
unhappy position and to assist him to carry her off from the
castle; and the merry rebels gladly agreed to do so.

Having thus made his arrangements with his followers,
Ernani betook himself to the castle of Don Silva, where he
managed to effect an entrance unobserved. Then, concealing
himself in an alcove near the apartments of Elvira, he awaited a
suitable moment for revealing himself to her.

The captive Elvira was in a most unhappy state of mind; for
though her bandit lover had assured her that he would rescue
her from her fate, she feared lest he should come too late.

As the day wore on, Don Silva was called away for a time;
and, during his absence, Elvira was surprised and dismayed by
an unexpected visit from the young King Carlos of Spain.
Though she knew the latter had professed admiration for her,
she had hoped he would be too much engaged with the con-
spiracies and difficulties arising upon his recent accession to the
throne to find time to press his attentions further.

The young King, however, could not quell his youthful passion
so easily; and, knowing that Elvira was at the castle of Don Silva,
he had made this surprise visit in order to declare his love for
her and even to invite her to share his throne.

But Elvira's heart was already given to Ernani and she begged
the King not to press his suit further, since she could not love
him. This reply enraged Carlos, who had heard of her preference
for the bandit chief, so that he seized her by the hand and would

have compelled her to follow him, had not her cry for help quickly brought forth Ernani from the alcove.

An angry altercation now took place between the rivals; but as they were about to engage with their swords, Elvira flung herself between the pair and besought them to desist.

At this moment Don Silva returned and was filled with grief and indignation on thus finding his betrothed speaking with two lovers in her apartment; and, calling for his weapons, he furiously challenged both intruders, vowing vengeance for the insult.

The royal attendants, however, now arrived on the scene; and when Don Silva thus discovered that it was his King whom he had challenged and addressed so furiously, he was filled with dismay and knelt for pardon. Carlos, who was at that time eager for the support of his chief nobles, could not well refuse; but, as he departed, he warned Ernani to fly from his wrath, since it was his intention to exterminate the bandit hordes of which his rival was the chief.

Don Silva having followed the King to see his royal guest depart, Elvira now begged her lover to escape whilst he could, assuring him that she would remain faithful to their love until he could return and claim her as his own. Since Ernani's honour would not permit him to desert his bandit friends in their hour of peril, he was thus compelled to leave her, though with many misgivings.

The rebels and bandits, however, met with no success, for the King, with his soldiers, pursued them with pitiless zeal and did not rest until he had dispersed the band; and presently a report of Ernani's death was brought to Elvira, who was filled with despair at the news. In spite of her grief, however, she was compelled to listen to the suit of Don Silva once more; and upon the old nobleman now insisting upon her fulfilling her betrothal with him, she was thus forced to consent, being too much dazed and overcome with grief for the loss of her lover to resist.

All arrangements for the celebration of the nuptials were accordingly made; and on the day of the wedding splendid festivities were held at Don Silva's castle.

But Ernani was not dead, though he had been for some time a fugitive. Having at last made his way back to the neighbourhood of his beloved Elvira and hearing of revels to be held at the castle, though he knew not the cause, he disguised himself as a poor pilgrim, and asked for admittance and hospitality.

Don Silva, who took a pride in his hospitality to high and low alike, gave the pilgrim welcome, treating him as an honoured guest; and inviting him to join in the festivities, he informed him that they were in honour of his own marriage, which was about to be celebrated. At this moment the bridal party entered the hall, accompanied by a gorgeous train of pages, high-born ladies, and Grandees of Spain; and, to his utter woe, Ernani saw that the bride was none other than Elvira herself.

Filled with anger and despair at her seeming unfaithfulness, Ernani flung aside his pilgrim's robe and recklessly revealed himself to the company, demanding to be given up to the King for execution since he no longer desired to live.

Don Silva, however, though furious at the intrusion of his hated rival, refused to give him up to justice, declaring that it was a particular point in his code of honour to regard the person of one whom he had received as his guest as sacred from harm or betrayal. With these proud words the old noble retired with his followers to give directions for the extra guarding of his castle, fearing lest a party of fugitive bandits might be lurking near their leader.

Ernani and Elvira were thus left alone for a few moments; and as her angry lover began to pour forth reproachful words upon her, the unhappy bride-elect related to him how he had been reported to her as dead and how she had been compelled to accept Don Silva's suit—declaring, however, that it had been her intention to destroy herself that same day. Finding, therefore, that Elvira's heart was still faithful to him, Ernani clasped her in his arms once more; and the wretched pair bemoaned their sad fate together, knowing that they were in great peril.

At this moment Don Silva returned to the hall; and thus seeing that Elvira still loved the proscribed bandit, his jealousy was roused again and he vowed vengeance upon Ernani. When, however, the proud bandit declared once more that he was willing to die, Don Silva still refused to give him up, hoping for a more subtle and terrible revenge.

The attendants now announced that the King and a company of soldiers were clamouring at the gates for admission; and when Ernani had been hastily concealed in a secret chamber and Elvira had retired to her own apartment, Don Carlos was admitted. The young King announced that he had scattered the bandit hordes and now sought their chief; and adding that he had tracked Ernani to Castle Silva, he sternly demanded that he should be delivered up to him.

This command Don Silva stubbornly refused to carry out; whereupon the King gave orders for the castle to be searched. The soldiers, however, being unacquainted with the secret chamber, were unable to find the bandit; and then Carlos, furious at being defied, declared that if Ernani's head were not forthcoming he would have Don Silva beheaded instead.

Whilst the nobleman was still protesting against betraying one who had been his guest—hoping thus to reserve Ernani for a more cruel fate—Elvira hastily entered the hall and, falling on her knees before the King, besought him not to engage in strife but to have mercy on his foes.

On beholding the beautiful Elvira again the King's suppressed love for her burned fiercely once more; and, taking her gently by the hand, he declared that he would now hold her as a hostage for the good faith of Don Silva, until Ernani should be delivered up to him. It was in vain that Don Silva protested against such a proceeding; and the weeping Elvira was at once taken away by the King to his palace.

When Ernani was at length led forth from his hiding-place and learned that his beloved one was held as a hostage by the King, he was furious; and now regarding Don Silva as a companion in misfortune, he offered to join him in a scheme of vengeance against Carlos, who was their mutual enemy and rival in the affections of Elvira. Regarding his life, however, as forfeited to Silva—to whom he was grateful for having protected him so long—Ernani declared his willingness to die whenever his rival should desire it. As a pledge of his solemn promise, he gave the nobleman his hunting-horn, saying, "By this token, in the hour when thou wilt have Ernani perish, sound this horn, and I shall know it is the hour for me to die!"

Don Silva, thus recognizing that he had Ernani in his power, gladly accepted him as a colleague in taking vengeance on the King; and the pair immediately sought out a band of conspirators who were at that time seeking to assassinate Carlos—who had not yet been unanimously accepted as King—and offered to join them in their enterprise. They were eagerly welcomed by the conspirators; and it was arranged that they should meet on a certain day in the Catacombs of Aquisgrano, and, by drawing lots, decide who should strike the fatal blow.

Meanwhile, Carlos had received information that a conspiracy had been formed against him; and as he was now almost certain of being accepted as King by the majority of the people, he bravely determined to face his secret foes and denounce them. He therefore bade his esquire to cause three salutes of cannon to be sounded should he be accepted as King at the final meeting of Electors to be held that day, that he might thus be sure of his regal power before denouncing his foes. He also gave orders for the Ministers of State, together with the Lady Elvira, to be brought to him in the conspirators' meeting-place.

He then made his way alone to the Catacombs of Aquisgrano and took up a position beside the mausoleum of his illustrious father, Charles the Great; and here many solemn and noble thoughts passed through the mind of the young Prince. The sacred responsibility of his high position impressed itself upon him for the first time, so that a sense of his own frailty and weakness made him humbly conscious of his utter dependence upon a Higher Power than his own. He now solemnly registered a vow that if his kingship should be accepted that day, he would forgo the careless pleasures and passions of youth and devote himself loyally to the service of his country and people—and thereby win for himself a glorious name and virtue's " crown of deathless fame ".

Having made this sacred resolve, the young King now concealed himself in the royal mausoleum, whence he could see and hear all that passed without being observed; and a few minutes later the conspirators entered, all wrapped in long dark cloaks. Don Silva and Ernani had established themselves as the leaders; and after reciting their hatred of the monarchy, they drew lots for the privilege of killing the young Carlos.

The name drawn was that of Ernani; and Don Silva, greatly disappointed, entreated the bandit to resign the right in his favour. Ernani, however, refused to forgo the privilege; and in spite of Silva's warning that the latter's own vengeance would quickly follow, he firmly declared that he alone should kill their royal rival.

Just as the lot had been thus decided, the conspirators were startled by the sound of a cannon shot repeated three times from the fortress of the city; and this being the signal for Don Carlos, he stepped forth from the mausoleum with a stern and regal air. At the same moment there entered from another door six Electors and the Ministers of State, followed by royal pages who bore the crown and regalia; and after these came a retinue of splendidly dressed lords and ladies, amongst whom was the pale and drooping Elvira.

At the bidding of the Electors the crown was placed upon the head of the young King and he was solemnly hailed as the Sovereign; and Carlos, with equally dignified solemnity, accepted the charge laid upon him. Then, turning to the discomfited conspirators, he exposed their plot; and, denouncing them as traitors, he condemned the nobles to the block and the plebeians to prison. Ernani was herded with the latter; but refusing to bear such an insult, he now disclosed his true identity as a Duke of ancient family and haughtily claimed the death of an aristocrat.

Carlos readily granted this plea; but Elvira, in despair at thus losing her lover for ever, fell on her knees and passionately implored the King to pardon Ernani, adding as her plea, " Virtue sublime is mercy in kings! "

As Carlos listened to the pleading voice of the beautiful Elvira, he was reminded of the sacred vow he had so recently made; and, desiring to win the affection of his people by ruling them with love and clemency, he now magnanimously proclaimed a gracious pardon for all the conspirators. Further than this, he steadfastly quelled the longings of his youthful heart and resigned all further thoughts of Elvira; and knowing that her love was given to Ernani, he declared it to be his royal will that the pair should be united.

Thus, the faithful lovers were wedded at last; and Ernani and his fair bride retired to the ex-bandit's ducal palace, where a noble company had assembled to bid them welcome and to join in the bridal festivities. But amongst the merry company of wedding guests there glided a masked stranger, who greeted no one and held himself aloof from all. This stranger was none other than Don Silva, who, less noble than his King, was consumed with fierce jealousy at the happiness of his favoured rival and had now come to indulge in a cruel vengeance.

When the guests had departed and Ernani and his bride were alone, they embraced each other with great joy, thankful that their troubles were over, and marvelling at the unexpected happiness which lay before them; but suddenly they were startled by the loud lingering blast of a hunting-horn.

Ernani became pale as death and his heart stiffened with horror; for he remembered his vow to Don Silva and knew that this was the signal for him to die. Elvira was filled with alarm at his altered looks; and, to deceive her, Ernani declared that he was suddenly unwell, bidding her to fetch him a cordial—intending, during her absence, to brace himself for his fearful act. Full of grief that his cup of happiness should thus be snatched from him as he was about to enjoy it, for a moment he thought wildly of escape; but just as he was about to follow Elvira, Don Silva himself entered the room. The latter calmly bade him fulfil the solemn promise he had made—adding, with fiendish triumph, that one so nobly born and of such high character could not stoop to forswear himself.

Well did Ernani know this; for never yet had he broken his word to any living soul, nor could his high sense of honour permit him to do so now. Just as he drew his dagger, however, Elvira returned to the room; and now hearing of the fearful compact which had been made between the two rivals for her hand she knelt before Don Silva and besought him, with distracted sobs, to release her beloved husband from his vow.

But Don Silva had steeled his heart to withstand this piteous appeal, and coldly announced that he awaited the fulfilment of his rival's vow; and Ernani, knowing well that he could expect no mercy from such a remorseless foe and too proud to tarnish his honourable name by forswearing himself, clasped the weeping Elvira in a last embrace. Then quickly grasping his dagger he resolutely stabbed himself to the heart, faithful to the fatal promise he had made. As Elvira, with a terrible cry of woe, fell senseless beside him, he expired—and Don Silva's vengeance was accomplished.

A MASKED BALL *Verdi*
(*Un Ballo in Maschera*)

In the city of Boston, Massachusetts, during the early colonial period, disturbances were constantly occurring between the two contending parties of Royalists and Puritans. At a reception held one evening at the palace of the Governor, Richard, Earl of Warwick, a party of Puritan conspirators had mingled amongst the guests, in order to gather information as to the forthcoming movements of the Viceroy, against whose life they were plotting.

Amongst these conspirators were two negroes named Sam and Tom, who were the ringleaders in the affair. Though they and their friends regarded Richard as a tyrant and hated him as such, however, they found that he was very strongly guarded by a large majority of devoted adherents and that their chances of making an attack upon him were small.

The Earl's chief supporter and most trusted official was his own private secretary, a Creole named Renato. The latter served his leader with a whole-hearted devotion, loving him as his dearest and most honoured friend; but, though Richard returned his secretary's affection, and was sincerely grateful for his devotion, he had avoided him of late and had seemed to shrink from their customary intercourse.

The reason for this was the fact that Richard had unfortunately conceived a deep and overmastering passion for Renato's beautiful young wife, Adelia; and though torn with remorse for the wrong he thus did to his friend, he yet could not conquer the love that had grown up in his heart. In spite of the fact that he had refrained from declaring his passion, he had not succeeded in hiding it from the fair Adelia, who soon as ardently returned it, although she also felt deep remorse at the circumstance. The unfortunate pair were thus wretchedly situated at the time of the Puritan conspiracy.

On the night of the reception, Richard was too much occupied by his tender thoughts of Adelia to notice that many of his avowed foes were actually present in his own house. In spite of the whispered warnings of the devoted Renato, he continued to regard the strained political position as exaggerated and merely scoffed at the idea of serious trouble.

During the meeting, a petition was presented to the Governor for the transportation of an old negress named Ulrica, who was reported to be a sorceress and dealer in the black art; and, utterly regardless of his own personal danger, Richard laughingly declared that before the witch was driven away he would himself consult her on the morrow under a disguise and urge her to predict his own fate.

The negro conspirators overheard this arrangement; and, hurrying away, they proceeded to gather their party together to plan the assassination of the Governor at the abode of the sorceress, where he would probably be unattended.

In spite of Renato's eager entreaty for him to abandon such a mad scheme of playing into the hands of his enemies, Richard still determined to carry it out. On the morrow, therefore, in the disguise of a sailor and attended only by his faithful page, Edgar, and a few followers, he proceeded to the hut of Ulrica.

Here, surrounded by the usual weird appurtenances of a dealer in magic and sorcery, he found the old hag, who was already granting audiences to certain superstitious folk who had come to have their fortunes told.

As the disguised Earl hung back a while in the gloom of the smoky hut, he observed a veiled lady approach the so-called witch and ask in a low tone for a potion to cure a guilty love; and to his surprise he recognized the soft voice as that of his beloved Adelia —and was filled with joy on thus learning for certain that she returned his passion, even though she sought a remedy to destroy it. In reply the hag bade her cull at midnight a certain herb which grew only in a desolate spot outside the city where murderers were hanged; and as Adelia hurried away, afte declaring her intention to seek the herb that same night, her listening lover vowed in his heart that he would follow her thither, in order to protect her from harm.

It was now Richard's turn to have his fortune told; and to the alarm of his attendants, Ulrica, with dramatic intensity, declared that he would shortly meet his death by violence and that the fatal blow would be struck by the person who should next take his hand. Laughing at the prediction, Richard held out his hand to his friends in turn, who, however, all drew back superstitiously; but when Renato presently appeared on the scene, in order to draw his master away before his disguise should be penetrated, the Earl deliberately seized his hand in defiance of the witch's words, well knowing that his secretary was devoted to him.

Late that evening, as midnight approached, Adelia, in fear and trembling, yet firmly resolved in her purpose, made her way with hurried steps to the murderers' gibbet outside the city boundary. In this wild and lonely spot, which was shunned by all as haunted, she sought the magic herb with which she hoped to quench a love she knew to be disloyal to her husband; and here she was closely followed by Richard, who, as she suddenly uttered an exclamation of terror at the sound of his footsteps, hurried to her side and revealed himself to her. Then, as the moonlight showed him the relief and joy in her face at his greeting, he could no longer retain control of his long-repressed feelings. Folding her passionately in his arms, he declared his love for her; and Adelia, though still announcing her resolve to banish him from her heart, could not but admit that she returned his love.

This brief moment of supreme happiness was soon rudely interrupted; for angry shouts and approaching flashing lights showed that some disturbance was afoot. The terrified Adelia just had time to drop a heavy veil over her face, when her husband, Renato, dashed up to Richard and eagerly besought him to return with all haste to the palace. He declared that the negro conspirators, Tom and Sam, had tracked him to this spot and were now approaching quickly with a party of adherents to assassinate him.

At first Richard flatly refused to make his escape, fearing for the fate of the hapless Adelia; but upon Renato promising to escort the lady back to the city, he agreed to fly from the certain danger that threatened him—binding his friend, however, to a solemn promise not to attempt to penetrate the secret of his charge's identity.

Renato, not having the slightest suspicion as to who the veiled lady might be and anxious only for his revered chief's safety, gave the required promise; whereupon Richard dashed away into the darkness and reached the palace in safety.

When he had gone Renato took the trembling Adelia by the hand and hurried her away also; but the pair were quickly spied by the approaching conspirators, who rushed forward to capture them with cries of triumph, believing that they had secured the prize they sought. When, however, they discovered that instead of the Governor it was Renato they had seized, they were filled with angry disappointment; and upon their indulging in coarse jests and taunts at the expense of the veiled lady, the secretary, eager to defend his master's sweetheart, drew his sword and furiously defied the howling mob.

Upon this, Adelia, afraid for her husband's life, hurried to his side, entreating him not to anger the people; and, in her agitation, her veil became disarranged, so that her identity was revealed to all.

When Renato thus saw that it was his own beloved wife he had surprised in the company of the Governor, whom he consequently supposed to be her accepted lover, he was almost stunned with the shock of the discovery; and in his rage and despairing grief, he could scarcely refrain from killing Adelia, as she now fell on her knees before him. However, her piteous entreaties to be at least permitted to bid farewell to her little child and her passionate declaration of innocence, restrained him for the moment; and sternly bidding her return home with him, he resolved to take vengeance upon the Governor—for whom the love and devotion he had formerly borne was now turned to hate.

With this purpose in view, he quickly pacified the angry conspirators by declaring that he intended to join their ranks; and during the next few days he held secret interviews with them, in order to arrange a successful opportunity for the assassination of the Governor.

Meanwhile, Adelia was plunged in the deepest despair, fearing that her husband's jealous anger would lead him to some desperate deed; and full of anxiety for the safety of the man she loved, she endeavoured to learn all she could of the plot which she guessed was being hatched against his life.

One day, on suddenly entering a room in which Renato was consulting with the negroes, Sam and Tom, she was coldly commanded by her husband to draw one piece of folded paper from three which had been placed in a vase; for the three conspirators, having now arranged to assassinate the Governor at a splendid masked ball he was to give in a day or two, had determined to draw lots as to who should deliver the fatal blow.

Adelia, fearing to disobey her husband's command, drew forth a paper from the vase; and, horrified by Renato's exultant tone as he announced that it bore his name, she hurried away to her chamber, full of terrifying thoughts. She now felt assured that her husband intended to kill Richard; and suspecting that he hoped to accomplish his fell purpose on the night of the masked ball, she determined, though in no mood for festivity, to attend the function, in order that she might seek an opportunity to warn her lover.

In spite of the deep passion he had conceived for Adelia, Richard had never intended that his love should injure her in any way; and after a mighty struggle with himself, he had already determined that they should be parted from each other. To this end, therefore, he made arrangements for the appointment of Renato to a high official position in England. He caused the necessary document making the appointment to be duly drawn up; and on the night of the masked ball he carried it with him, intending to hand it to Renato during the evening.

His friends, knowing that the conspirators had been actively engaged of late, endeavoured to persuade him not to attend the ball; but Richard, ever careless of danger, laughed at their fears as usual. Donning a black domino and mask, he boldly mingled with the merry dancers.

Renato, attired in the conspirators' chosen colours of azure and scarlet, also mingled with the dazzling throng, seeking for the Governor. Not knowing his disguise, he was getting impatient of the delay in his plans, when he happened to meet the giddy young page, Edgar, from whom he gained the information he sought.

Meanwhile, Adelia, masked and enveloped in a white domino, also sought for Richard; and at last, to her joy, she heard his voice and recognized him, in spite of his mask and black domino. Quickly making herself known to him, she eagerly besought her over to leave the ball-room at once, declaring to him her suspicions of the danger that threatened him; but Richard, still careless of his own safety, would not hurry away. Instead, he proceeded to tell her of the plans he had made for their safety from temptation by the appointment in England he had arranged or her husband. He then took a tender farewell of her, resolving not to see her again; but even as he still held her by the hand, Renato, having at last tracked him, dashed forward in a passion of jealousy and stabbed him to the heart.

As Richard fell back, dying, he painfully drew forth the document making the new appointment and held it towards Renato. Then, as the horrified guests gathered round, with his last gasping breath he declared that Adelia was entirely innocent and pure, and that in his love for her he had never designed her hurt nor aimed at her peace.

With these words he expired; and Renato, now filled with agonizing remorse, realized too late that in his jealous frenzy he had slain a man who, so far from being base, had faithfully respected the honour of his friend under a terrible temptation.

OTHELLO   *Verdi*

A HANDSOME Moor, named Othello, a man of noble nature and high intellect, had risen by his own ability and prowess to the envied position of a general in the Venetian Army; and because of his honourable reputation and excellent skill in relating stories of the battles and adventures he had engaged in, he was a welcome guest in many of the great houses of Venice.

But Othello himself cared only to visit at the house of a certain Venetian gentleman named Brabantio, who had a fair daughter named Desdemona; for the beauty, gentleness, and virtue of this beautiful maiden had completely enslaved the heart of the handsome Moor, who grew to love her with all the strength of his passionate nature. And as the fair Desdemona listened to the glowing tales of peril, adventure, and victory related by the dusky visitor, she hung upon his words with eager interest, weeping for his woes and rejoicing at his escapes; and at last she grew to love him so dearly that all her thoughts became bound up in him.

Othello knew that Brabantio would be horrified at the mere thought of giving his daughter to a Moor; and so he very easily persuaded Desdemona to enter into a secret marriage with him.

Brabantio was filled with great indignation when he was afterwards told of their union. Accusing Othello of having resorted to magic spells in winning the affections of the maiden, he took the whole matter before the Duke of Venice for judgment. When however, the royal judge had listened to Othello's simple tale of love and to Desdemona's sweet declaration of trust in her husband, he announced that their mutual affection had come about in a perfectly natural way and that no magic had been used.

Brabantio was obliged, therefore, to give up his daughter to her lawful husband; and almost immediately after the case had been settled, Othello, as leader of the Venetian Army, was sent on a military expedition to the island of Cyprus.

The Moor departed first, leaving Desdemona to follow in the care of his lieutenant, Cassio; and upon their arrival in Cyprus great rejoicings were held.

Now Othello had another confidential officer, whose name was Iago. It happened that Iago, who was of an envious, cruel, and bitter nature, had a grudge against Cassio, because the latter had been made chief lieutenant—a post he coveted himself. He also envied the happiness of Othello; for he himself had cherished a passion for Desdemona and had been filled with bitterness at her preference for the noble Moor. He determined, therefore, to bring Cassio quickly out of favour with his master, so that he himself might be advanced; and with this object he devised the cunning and cruel plan of making Othello believe that Cassio was the lover of Desdemona. Thus, by bringing misery on all, he hoped to satisfy his vengeful and envious nature.

He first of all led the unsuspecting Cassio into the folly of drinking too deeply one night when on guard in the camp; and then, as squabbling arose in consequence of this, he brought Othello upon the scene to learn the cause of the disturbance.

The Moor was so displeased with the foolish conduct of Cassio that he would not permit him to be his lieutenant any longer; but the cunning Iago was not yet satisfied. He determined to use the disgraced officer still further, in order to bring woe upon Othello himself, whose happiness in the possession of the lovely Desdemona he was so eager to destroy.

He now pretended to be Cassio's friend, and advised him earnestly to ingratiate himself with the Lady Desdemona, who might be induced to intercede with her husband on behalf of the erring officer. As Iago's own wife, Emilia, was chief lady-in-waiting to Desdemona, it was easy for the necessary interviews to be arranged.

The gentle Desdemona, with never a thought of evil, received Cassio very kindly, and promised to plead for him with her husband.

Unfortunately, just as Cassio bent to kiss the lady's hand in gratitude as he departed, Othello himself appeared, accompanied by Iago, who cunningly drew his attention to this little scene.

The first faint shadow of jealousy thus crept into the mind of Othello; and when Desdemona presently began to plead for Cassio, although he answered her with fair words, he had already begun to doubt her integrity.

After Desdemona had retired, Iago ruthlessly continued his wicked scheme of sowing the seeds of doubt in Othello's passionate heart; and the Moor quickly began to suffer pangs of jealousy and to cherish a secret wrath against his innocent wife.

> " Good name in man and woman, dear my lord,
>   Is the immediate jewel of their souls :
>   Who steals my purse steals trash; 'tis something, nothing;
>   'Twas mine, 'tis his, and has been slave to thousands;
>   But he that filches from me my good name,
>   Robs me of that which not enriches him,
>   And makes me poor indeed! "

said Iago, in a careless tone; and with such enigmatical, subtle words did he set the poison of doubt to work in his master's mind.

Encouraged by the quick success of his villainy, Iago now bade his wife Emilia to procure for him a certain richly-worked handkerchief belonging to Desdemona, which had been Othello's first gift to her during their courtship. Emilia, having no suspicion of treachery, but humbly obedient to her husband's wishes, secured the pretty trifle for him without the knowledge of her mistress. Iago then found an opportunity to make Othello believe that he had discovered this handkerchief amongst the belongings of Cassio and that it had been given to the ex-lieutenant by Desdemona. He also added casually that he had often heard Cassio murmur the name of Desdemona with loving emphasis in his sleep.

This announcement filled Othello with such rage that he rushed furiously at Iago and flung him to the ground; and when next he met Desdemona he broke out into such a stormy tirade that the gentle girl was terrified.

As the days went on the poison of jealousy so artfully administered by the ruthless Iago began to permeate the whole being of the unfortunate Moor to such an extent that he put an evil construction upon the most innocent remarks of Desdemona. The bewildered wife became very unhappy as she noted the altered behaviour of her husband; and she was quite unable to account for such a change, since her love for him was as deep and true as ever.

One day there came ambassadors from Venice with letters on State matters for Othello, in which he was bidden to return home. Upon the messengers asking for the absent Cassio, who was to be deputed to the Moor's place, Desdemona replied that the lieutenant had been disgraced but that she was constantly pleading for his restoration to favour, since she had much regard for him. On hearing these words, spoken in all innocence and kindly feeling for one in trouble, Othello's mad jealousy was roused again; and in a wild outburst of rage he struck Desdemona a rough blow, and then fell to the ground in a convulsive fit brought on by his deep emotion.

That night, as Desdemona retired to rest, she was filled with sad thoughts and strange forebodings of ill; and as Emilia helped her to disrobe, she sang a low, plaintive song, which she declared had been sung to her mother on her death-bed, and which had haunted the unhappy lady all day. These were the words of the song:

> " The poor soul sat singing by a sycamore tree,
>   Sing all a green willow;
> Her hand on her bosom, her head on her knee,
>   Sing willow, willow, willow:
> The fresh streams ran by her and murmured her moans,
>   Sing willow, willow, willow:
> Her salt tears fell from her, and softened the stones;
>   Sing willow, willow, willow! "

When this sad ditty came to an end, Emilia left her mistress in bed; and the troubled Desdemona at length fell asleep.

Presently Othello entered the chamber with his sword in his hand, intending to kill her; but she looked so fair and tranquil as she slept that he could not bear to shed her blood, though he did not mean to go back from his resolve. He still loved her tenderly, in spite of the overmastering jealousy which had eaten into his heart and his firm belief that she had permitted Cassio to be her lover; and bending over the bed he kissed her sweet lips passionately, murmuring softly:

> " O balmy breath, that doth almost persuade
> Justice to break her sword!—one more, one more—
> Be thus when thou art dead, and I will kill thee,
> And love thee after:—One more, and that's the last:
> So sweet was ne'er so fatal. I must weep,
> But they are cruel tears: This sorrow's heavenly;
> It strikes where it doth love! "

The hot kisses of Othello awakened Desdemona, who was much startled at finding her husband bending over her with such a fierce look in his passionate eyes; nor was she reassured when Othello asked sternly:

> " Have you prayed to-night, Desdemona? "

His unhappy wife assured him that she had offered up her prayers as usual, and asked him the meaning of such a strange question; and then Othello declared that it was his resolve to kill her, again fiercely denouncing her as untrue to her nuptial vows. It was in vain that the hapless Desdemona pronounced her innocence and pleaded piteously for mercy; so firmly was Othello convinced of her perfidy, owing to the false insinuations of Iago, that nothing could now make him believe in her innocence. In a paroxysm of jealous passion he now seized the pillows and bed-coverings and pressed them over his victim until she was stifled.

At that moment Emilia's voice was heard calling loudly for admission; and thinking she had come to bring news of Cassio, whose death he had already ordered, Othello opened the door and let her into the room. But Emilia reported that Cassio was not dead, though wounded; and as she related this news the weak voice of the expiring Desdemona murmured softly, "A guiltless death I die!"

Emilia hurried to the bedside, just as her beloved mistress breathed her last. Filled with horror as she thus understood that Othello had slain his fair wife, she uttered loud cries of grief and alarm, so that a number of attendants hurried into the room, amongst them Iago and the Venetian Ambassadors.

Othello defended his conduct by relating the false tales of Desdemona which he had heard from Iago, more particularly dwelling upon the incident of the embroidered handkerchief. When Emilia heard this, her husband's treachery dawned upon her for the first time, and she declared that she herself had pro-cured the handkerchief for Iago at his own command.

It was in vain that Iago endeavoured to prevent his wife from telling what she knew about this incident and from proclaiming Desdemona's innocence, which was now plain to all; and finding that she would not be silenced and that her accusing words had brought his villainy to light, he rushed upon her in fury and stabbed her to the heart.

The Ambassador immediately ordered his arrest; and then, turning to Othello, who was now filled with agonizing remorse and despair on learning that he had slain his beloved wife without cause, he said:

> "O thou Othello, that was once so good,
> What shall be said to thee?"

And Othello replied humbly and sorrowfully:

> "When you shall these unlucky deeds relate,
> Speak of me as I am; nothing extenuate,
> Nor set down aught in malice: then must you speak
> Of one that lov'd not wisely, but too well;
> Of one not easily jealous, but, being wrought,
> Perplex'd in the extreme; of one, whose hand,
> Like the base Indian, threw a pearl away,
> Richer than all his tribe; of one, whose subdued eyes,

Albeit unused to the melting mood,
Drop tears as fast as the Arabian trees
Their medicinal gum: Set you down this:
And say besides—that in Aleppo once,
Where a malignant and a turban'd Turk
Beat a Venetian and traduced the State,
I took by the throat the circumcized dog,
And smote him—thus! "

With these words the unhappy Moor seized his dagger and stabbed himself to the heart; then, as the attendants sprang forward in horror, he fell back dead beside the corpse of his beloved Desdemona.

RIGOLETTO   *Verdi*

DURING the sixteenth century there reigned in Mantua a handsome young Duke, whose brilliant Court was one of the gayest and most licentious of its age. This youthful ruler cared little for the responsibilities of State or for the welfare of his people. Instead, he chose to gather around him a band of careless nobles of his own age and to pass his time amidst the excitements of wild excesses and passionate love-intrigues.

In all his *amours* the susceptible young Duke was constantly aided by his Jester, Rigoletto, a hunchback, who was, consequently, the most privileged person at Court. Beneath the cap and bells, the buffoon possessed a fertile, scheming brain that never failed to devise cunning ruses to gratify the lawless passions of his unscrupulous master.

As a result, Rigoletto had made many enemies. Besides exciting the jealousy of the courtiers by his privileged position, he was also hated by those haughty nobles whose honour had been assailed by his connivance in his royal master's intrigues. The jealous lords constantly vented their spleen upon the hated Jester by scornful taunts and slights—all of which Rigoletto returned with interest, making the proud courtiers the subjects of his spiteful wit and stinging raillery. Inwardly, however, he triumphed in a joy of which they knew nothing.

For Rigoletto had a beautiful young daughter, named Gilda, whom he loved passionately; and fearing lest the maiden's loveliness should lead to the ruin of her innocence, he had kept the knowledge of her existence a secret even from his most intimate acquaintances. To this end he had placed her in a humble house in a quiet part of the city, under the care of her old nurse, Giovanna; and every evening, after dark, he went to visit and receive the sweet caresses of this darling child—a stolen happiness that more than compensated him for the scorn of his enemies.

Little did the Jester guess, however, that the precious treasure he guarded so lovingly was doomed to become the prey of the very person whose notice of her he most dreaded—that of his royal master. Yet so it was ordained; and this is how it came about.

Every morning Gilda attended matins in the neighbouring church; and here she was at length seen by the young Duke, who quickly became enamoured of her beauty. Every day he stole into the church to watch her at her devotions; and Gilda, though she scarcely dared return the ardent glances bestowed upon her by the handsome cavalier, soon felt an answering thrill in her own heart. Fearing her father's anger, she kept this new sweet joy a secret; and since the Duke did not need his panderer's help in such a simple enterprise, it came about that Rigoletto remained in ignorance that his happiness was thus at stake. Despite the care the Jester took, however, his own secret visits to the humble house at length became known to the jealous courtiers; and this discovery was made soon after the Duke had first seen Gilda at the church.

One evening, during a splendid entertainment at the ducal palace, a group of courtiers, freshly smarting under the spiteful wit of Rigoletto, had gathered together in an ante-room to vent their grievances and to listen to the special complaints of one of their number, Count Ceprano—whose pretty wife was at that moment receiving the undesired attentions of the Duke, thanks to the machinations of the hated Jester.

Whilst they were thus talking angrily together, they were joined by another courtier, Marullo, who declared that he had great news for them. He then told them he had discovered that Rigoletto had a mistress, whom he visited every evening after dark at a humble house in a certain quiet street.

The courtiers all laughed derisively at the idea of the ugly hunchback being in love; but Ceprano, seeing in this incident a means of avenging himself upon the scheming Jester, quickly proposed a plan to them. He suggested that they should repair to the humble dwelling pointed out by Marullo, and, forcing an entrance, carry off the fair lady who dwelt therein; and by this means they would punish the hunchback for the many insults he had heaped upon them.

The other courtiers eagerly fell in with this plan, and, having arranged to meet Ceprano late next evening in order to carry out their enterprise, they returned to the brilliant *salon*. Here, an orgy of dancing, feasting, and merriment was being indulged in with an utter absence of restraint—for it was the delight of the gay Duke of Mantua to pursue his pleasures with an extravagant recklessness.

Suddenly, the revels were interrupted by an uninvited guest who dashed into the midst of the company, wild-eyed and furious. This intruder was the Count of Monterone, whose beautiful daughter had lately been stolen from her home to gratify the evil passion of the libertine Duke. In a voice trembling with scorn and anger, the outraged father now demanded the restoration of his child, calling down vengeance upon her betrayer.

The Duke, impatient at such an unpleasant interruption to the revels, instantly ordered his guards to imprison the Count in a dungeon; and Rigoletto, taking his cue from his master, made merry over the now helpless father's despair, uttering mock quips at his expense. Soon, however, he regretted his words; for, as Monterone was being led away by the guards, he turned upon the Jester and cursed him with great fury.

It happened that Rigoletto was very superstitious; and he was filled with fear as he realized that a wronged father's curse had fallen upon him. Though the revels continued as before, the incident took such a hold upon his imagination that he felt some terrible woe was in store for him.

.   .   .   .

Late next night, these disturbing thoughts were. still in the Jester's mind as he hastened towards the humble abode of his beloved daughter; and when he was presently accosted by a begging bravo, or professional assassin, he stopped to converse with him, thinking that he might have occasion later on for the services of some such desperate rogue.

The bravo, who gave his name as Sparafucile, declared that for gold he would dispose of any enemy in the Jester's path; and he stated that his abode was an outlying lonely inn, where intended victims were easily lured by the attractions of his pretty sister, a gipsy girl named Maddalena. Having agreed to seek the bravo's aid should he need it, Rigoletto hurried into the courtyard of his house; and here he found the beautiful Gilda already waiting for him with her attendant, Giovanna.

So far, Gilda had been kept in ignorance of her father's name and profession; but to-night, after greeting him with her usual joyful embraces, she begged him to reveal to her his true identity, being weary of the mystery that so constantly surrounded his movements and her own.

Rigoletto, however, firmly refused her plea, gently bidding her only to love him and ask no questions; and presently he bade her a loving farewell and departed—for he never dared to remain long with her, lest his absence from Court should be noticed.

No sooner had he gone than the young Duke of Mantua himself appeared in the courtyard, having at last discovered the abode of his new lady-love and determined to seek an interview with her that night. Rushing forward, he clasped Gilda in his arms, declaring passionately that he loved her. Giovanna, having secretly received a purse of gold from the stranger upon his entrance, quietly departed into the house; and the pair were thus left alone.

Gilda was at first alarmed on finding herself alone with the stranger, whom she quickly recognized as the handsome cavalier whose ardent glances had thrilled her at her morning devotions; then, unable to resist the passionate wooing of the Duke, she at length submitted willingly to his caresses and admitted that she loved him in return. The cunning gallant described himself as a poor scholar, who would, nevertheless, make a humble home for her; and Gilda was filled with rapture at the thought that no barrier of rank would thus separate her from her lover.

Presently, hearing approaching footsteps in the street beyond, the Duke, fearful of discovery, bade the maiden a hasty, but passionate farewell and quickly hurried away. Then Gilda, gazing lovingly after his retreating figure, reluctantly entered the house—but not before she had been clearly seen by the newcomers. The latter were none other than Count Ceprano, Marullo, and their companion plotters, who, masked and cloaked, had come to carry out their plan of vengeance against Rigoletto.

They were astonished at the youth and beauty of the Jester's supposed mistress. Ere they had time to comment on this, however, they were suddenly confronted by Rigoletto himself—who, being uneasy in his mind owing to the cursing incident of the night before, had returned to take another look at his daughter's sanctuary.

Marullo, quickly seeing additional zest for their scheme in this unexpected interruption, accosted the Jester and, making himself known, boldly invited him to join in their enterprise; and to deceive the hunchback further, he declared that they were about to carry off the wife of Count Ceprano and take her to the Duke.

Rigoletto, thus imagining that his own treasure was not sought, quickly fell into the trap; for the back of Ceprano's palace jutted out on the opposite side of the street—a circumstance which gave credence to the story. Delighted, therefore, to assist in bringing dishonour upon one of his most hated enemies, he readily agreed to join the ravishers.

Marullo then declared that as the others were all masked, Rigoletto must also have his face hidden; and seizing a scarf, he bound it so tightly over the Jester's eyes and ears that the new accomplice could neither see nor hear. He then made the unsuspecting victim hold the ladder they had brought against the wall of his own house; then he and the other plotters—scarcely able to restrain their mirth at the cruel trick they were playing —climbed up to an open window above and made their entry.

Rigoletto, holding the ladder below, still imagined that it was his enemy's house that was being entered; and when the ravishers presently returned with Gilda—closely rolled in a thick cloak—he rejoiced, believing that the victim was Ceprano's wife. His hearing being dulled by his tightly-bandaged ears, he did not recognize the stifled cries of the unfortunate girl as she was borne away; and it was not until the maskers were far out of his immediate reach that he discovered he had been left alone.

Then, tearing off his bandage with difficulty, he saw that the ladder was leaning against the wall of his own house; and, realizing the dastardly trick that had been played upon him, he was filled with rage and despair. As he rushed madly down the street towards the ducal palace, trembling for the fate of his beloved child, he remembered the curse laid upon him by Count Monterone; and he shuddered with superstitious fear as he ran.

.   .   .   .   .   .

Meanwhile, the plotters had immediately brought their prize in triumph to their royal master, declaring her to be the mistress of Rigoletto; and the Duke had received her with amazement and joy on recognizing the lovely features of his new *inamorata*.

When the distracted Jester reached the ante-room, he passionately demanded to have his precious daughter restored to him; and he was filled with woe on learning that she was even now with the Duke in his private chamber. The courtiers, though astonished to know that the abducted girl was his own child, only met him with derisive laughter, callously disregarding his frantic appeals for mercy and keeping him in agony thus for some considerable time.

At length, however, Gilda herself ran forth from the Duke's room and flung herself into her father's arms, having heard his voice in the ante-room; and their vengeance having thus been accomplished, the well-satisfied courtiers now permitted the hood-winked father and his weeping daughter to depart.

As they hurried towards their home, Gilda poured forth the whole story of her fatal fascination for the handsome cavalier who had admired her in church, of his visit to her that evening, and of her despair on now discovering him to be but a base libertine who desired her only as his plaything. Despite this knowledge, how-ever, the unhappy girl loved him still; and when her father swore vengeance upon her false betrayer, she entreated his pardon for her lover—whom she herself already had forgiven.

But Rigoletto's anger against his royal master was so furious that nothing but the latter's death would satisfy his longing for vengeance; and seeking out Sparafucile, the bravo, he bargained with the assassin for a sum of gold to entice the Duke to the lonely inn mentioned at their first meeting and to murder him there. A few days later, Sparafucile informed him that his sister, Maddalena, had already brought herself before the Duke's notice and had enticed her new admirer to visit her at the inn that same evening—when the murder could easily be accomplished during the night.

The Jester now determined to take Gilda to the spot likewise, that he might thus convince her of her base lover's inconstancy and so cure her of her infatuation for him. When dusk fell, therefore, he and his daughter made their way to a wild district on the outskirts of the city; and on arriving at the bravo's lonely inn, Rigoletto drew the maiden into the shadows near a window, whence they could see and hear all that took place in the room beyond.

Presently, they saw the Duke, in disguise, enter the inn; and as Sparafucile left the room, after serving the guest with wine, the pretty gipsy, Maddalena, took his place. The Duke at once began to make love to the girl, who, however, merely laughed and teased him in return; and when Gilda thus saw for herself how soon her fickle gallant had forgotten her and heard him utter the same sweet love-speeches to the gipsy girl which he had whispered into her own delighted ears a few evenings ago, she was filled with grief and despair.

Rigoletto, realizing that his daughter was at last convinced of her exalted lover's perfidy, was now eager to get her away from the inn, not wishing her to know of the tragic end in store for the false betrayer. Bidding her hasten home at once, he told her to array herself as a youth in certain garments he had already provided for this purpose; and then, thus disguised, he desired her to depart without delay to Verona, where he would meet her later on.

No sooner had the weeping girl gone than Sparafucile came out for his final instructions; and Rigoletto told him that, after murdering the Duke, he was to place the dead body in a sack, ready to be thrown into the river Mincio that flowed close by. He gave the bravo half of the blood-money agreed upon between them; and then, promising to return at midnight with the remainder of the money—when he should expect to find the grim deed accomplished—he departed.

Throughout the evening, the unsuspecting Duke amused himself with the pretty decoy, Maddalena; and he made himself so fascinating to the gipsy girl that the latter felt a sudden pity for the fate in store for him. When, therefore, on the invitation of her brother, the royal guest finally retired to rest in an upper chamber, she began to plead with the bravo to spare the young man's life.

But Sparafucile muttered angrily that a bargain was a bargain and that the hunchback's gold meant more to him than the gay cavalier's worthless life. At length, however, he agreed to spare the Duke's life if some other stranger should happen to call at the inn before midnight, whom he could slay instead and pass off to the hunchback as the latter's victim. With this doubtful compromise, Maddalena had to content herself; but she felt little hope of gaining her wish, for it was a stormy night and strangers were unlikely to call.

It happened, however, that the whole of this conversation between the hired assassin and his sister had been overheard by Gilda. Though the unhappy girl had been back to her home and changed her garments for male attire in obedience with her father's command, she had been unable to resist the temptation of returning to the inn that she might look once again upon the features of the man she still loved so dearly, despite his base treatment of her.

She arrived under the window as the gipsy girl was pleading with her brother for the life of their guest; and quickly realizing that the gay young Duke was about to be murdered, she was overcome with horror. Then, on hearing the condition whereby he might yet be saved, a wild enthusiasm filled her heart; and she now resolved to sacrifice herself for the sake of her faithless lover.

Having commended her soul to Heaven, she calmly approached the door of the inn and knocked; and instantly there was a dead silence within. Maddalena trembled on hearing the sound; but Sparafucile drew his dagger and upon a second knock being heard, he flung open the door and fiercely stabbed the supposed youth standing on the threshold. Gilda fell to the ground instantly; and hastily producing a sack, the brother and sister fastened the body within it.

It was now midnight; and a few moments later, Rigoletto entered the inn and, paying down the remainder of the blood-money, demanded his victim. Sparafucile produced the sack, and, not wishing his trick to be discovered, suggested that the body should be immediately thrown into the river, offering his own assistance for this purpose.

Rigoletto, however, declined the offer, desiring to gloat over his victim alone; and when the bravo had reluctantly relinquished the sack, he dragged it to the river bank, where he sat down to exult over his fallen enemy. At that moment he heard the sound of a voice singing in the upper chamber of the inn; for the Duke had been awakened by the talking below and was now indulging in gay snatches of song.

Instantly recognizing the voice as that of his royal master, Rigoletto was filled with amazement and angry disappointment. Furious at having been thus cheated of his prey, he tore open the sack; and by the light of the moon, he beheld the beloved features of his beautiful daughter!

Horror-struck, the wretched hunchback lifted his child in his arms and wildly implored her to speak to him once again; and Gilda, who was still breathing, opened her eyes and murmured a few words, saying that she had willingly given her life to save that of her lover.

She then sank back in her father's arms, dead; and Rigoletto, remembering the malediction that had been laid upon him for having mocked at a distracted parent's grief, realized that his retribution was just. With a despairing cry of woe, he fell senseless beside the prostrate body of his beloved child.

LA TRAVIATA   *Verdi*
(*The Castaway . . . The Lost One . . . The Courtesan*)

ONE night, on the eve of the Second Empire,[1] no more lively part

[1] Although Dumas' story, *La Dame aux Camélias,* which provides the subject of this opera, has for its setting the eve of the Second Empire, the Italian *libretto* places the date in the latter part of the reign of Louis XIV—likewise changes the names of some of the characters. The opera, however, is now usually given Dumas' original setting, namely, the Second French Empire.

could have been found in the whole of gay Paris than that taking place in the *salon* of the beautiful and fascinating *demi-mondaine*, Violetta Valery. With her accustomed extravagant generosity, the fair hostess had provided an entertainment upon the most lavish scale, so that the guests—feasted thus royally and freed from conventional restraint—found it an easy matter to be merry and to exercise their wit for the benefit of one another.

It was a brilliant company, too, Violetta numbering amongst her admirers many scions of the nobility, besides the devotees of art; and since all were bent on pleasure, there was a constant flow of sparkling humour and joyous mirth on every side.

The beautiful Violetta herself was one of the liveliest of the merry throng; for pleasure was as the breath of life to her, and such a scene as this was her delight. Yet, in spite of natural inclination, her gaiety was not without considerable physical effort. Over-indulgence in pleasure had developed inherent seeds of consumption within her with alarming rapidity; and already her frail form showed signs of the advance of the dread disease. Every now and again a sudden faintness would seize her and the effort of moving amongst her guests was at times almost more than she could bear. For the most part, therefore, she was compelled to recline on her couch—whence, however, she rallied her guests with all her accustomed light-heartedness.

Amongst the gay folk present to-night was a handsome young man of noble family, Alfred de Germont, who, although he had not yet confessed his passion, had given his whole heart to the lovely courtesan and had adored her secretly for many months. Violetta—who, though she had had many lovers, had never yet given her heart to anyone—had always felt a curious thrill of joy when Alfred approached her; and she knew that it was true love she felt at last. She had, however, tried to treat the young man with careless indifference and to conquer the passion that was slowly but surely enveloping her whole being. Though she had not exercised any such scruples with her former admirers, she felt it better, for his own sake, that the young de Germont should not become her lover.

But Alfred was not to be discouraged by any such assumed coldness; and having determined to declare himself that evening, it was not long before he found an opportunity of doing so.

On attempting to lead her guests into the dancing *salon* beyond, Violetta was once again overcome by sudden faintness; but though she was soon surrounded by her sympathetic friends, she would not permit them to interrupt their pleasure on her account, bidding

2c

them with laughing carelessness to begin the dance without her and to leave her to rest alone for a few minutes.

No sooner was she alone than Violetta rose slowly and looked anxiously at herself in the nearest mirror, sighing deeply at the sight of her pale face. At that moment, Alfred returned to the room and, hurrying to her side, besought her to take more care of the life that was now so precious to him. He then boldly declared his passion for her and entreated her to accept him as her lover; and though Violetta at first attempted to treat the matter lightly and with gentle banter, she could not long struggle against the wild throbbing of her own heart, which told her only too plainly that she loved him in return. At last, therefore, she gave way to his pleading; and letting him now see that his love was returned, she determined to renounce her former scruples on his behalf that they might both experience the deep ecstatic happiness which comes once only in a life-time.

After this, the lovers met constantly; and, at length, enthralled in their passion, they retired to a country house owned by Violetta some little distance outside Paris, where they could enjoy their bliss undisturbed. Here they spent several months of perfect happiness; and, enwrapped in one another's sweet presence, they seemed oblivious of the whole world.

But such absorbing joy could not last for ever; and at length the dream was broken.

.   .   .   .

One day, on returning to the villa after a few hours' absence in hunting, Alfred met Violetta's maid, Annina; and noticing that she wore travelling dress and appeared somewhat flustered, he stopped to inquire the reason for this. In distress, Annina replied that she had just returned from Paris, whither she had been sent on business for her mistress; and upon being further questioned she revealed the fact that she had been making arrangements for the sale of Violetta's property and possessions. The luxurious manner in which the villa had recently been conducted was expensive, and more means were needed to keep it up.

Filled with compunction that his own selfish enjoyment should have made him forgetful of such mundane but necessary matters and horrified that Violetta should be about to make such sacrifice on his behalf, Alfred declared that he would himself go to Paris at once to settle the difficulty by paying over a large sum of money to prevent the sales. Bidding Annina to say nothing to her mistress about this plan, he set off immediately for Paris, saying that he would return in a few hours.

While her lover was thus absent, unknown to herself, Violetta received a visit from a stranger. A letter having arrived from her chief friend, Flora Bervoix, inviting her to attend a masked ball in Paris that night, she was just laughingly reflecting that her friend would look for her in vain at this entertainment, when a gentleman was ushered into the room. The visitor was a man of advancing years and of haughty aristocratic appearance, who immediately announced himself to be the father of Alfred de Germont. In the same breath, he added sternly : " Alfred de Germont, whom you are bringing to ruin! "

Then, as Violetta drew back indignantly at these words, Monsieur de Germont, though greatly impressed by her dazzling beauty and proud hearing, went on with the difficult task he had come to perform—that of persuading her to renounce his son and leave him for ever. In eloquent but gentle tones he declared that not only was she injuring Alfred's own social position as heir to one of the proudest names in France, but she was also the means of his sister's hand being refused in marriage—the latter's aristocratic suitor declining to enter their family whilst the son of the house was held in thrall by such a well-known courtesan.

At first Violetta hoped that her separation from Alfred was desired only to be a temporary one, in order that his sister's marriage might be negotiated; but when she realized it was required that they should never meet again, she was overcome with grief and declared passionately that this could never be—she could not bear to be parted from the only man she had ever truly loved.

Though sincerely grieving for the pain he was inflicting upon one so lovely, M. de Germont still continued his pleading. He now implored Violetta to reflect upon the good deed she would be doing by renouncing a lover to whose worldly welfare she was a stumbling-block; and he reminded her that in the years to come, it would be a consolation to her to remember that she had thus restored peace to one home.

By this time Violetta was weeping bitterly, for she knew only too well that M. de Germont spoke the truth and that Alfred's position and prestige were indeed affected adversely by his connection with herself; and her love for him was so great that she determined, for his sake, to make the sacrifice desired. In a broken voice, she declared that she would leave him that same day. Furthermore, to prove her pretended callous indifference, she promised to attend her friend's ball that night.

M. de Germont, overcome with gratitude and admiration for her brave and generous resolve, embraced her tenderly as though she were his own daughter—half regretting the harsh course

he had felt compelled to take. He then retired to another room
there to await the return of Alfred, to whom Violetta promised t
write a farewell message at once.

Having written this heart-rending note, Violetta quickly mad
arrangements for her instant departure; and having handed th
note to a servant to deliver to his master, she entered her carriag
and drove away just before her lover returned. She was, there
fore, well on her way to Paris by the time Alfred, on entering th
villa, received her letter bidding him farewell for ever.

On reading Violetta's pathetic note and realizing that she ha
left him thus hurriedly with the intention of severing their blissf
connection, Alfred was filled with despair. His grief, howeve
was presently turned to jealousy on picking up the note fro
Flora Bervoix, which Violetta had unintentionally left on the tab
in her haste. From the contents of this missive he immediatel
drew the mistaken conclusion that his lovely mistress meant
attend the gay Flora's ball that night with the idea of meetin
there a former admirer, the Baron Duphol, whom he had alwa
regarded as a rival.

It was in vain that his father, who entered the room at th
moment, endeavoured to calm the agitated young man, entrea
ing him tenderly to think no more of Violetta but to return to h
own ancestral home, where a glad welcome awaited him. Alfre
now consumed with bitter jealousy, declared instead that he wou
attend the ball at Flora Bervoix's house that night, there to lear
the truth and to avenge his wrongs. Refusing to listen to e
planations or pleadings, therefore, he set off for Paris at onc
and the elder de Germont, now afraid to leave his headstrong s
in such a disturbed frame of mind, followed him, hoping that
might yet be able to curb the distracted lover's actions in som
measure.

When Violetta arrived at the mansion of Flora Bervoix, sh
found the brilliant ball and entertainment already well in progres
Her old friends greeted her return to their midst with muc
pleasure; and her former admirer, the Baron Duphol, seeing h
unescorted, immediately offered her his arm and moved fro
room to room with her with an air of protective pride.

For a time Violetta endeavoured to quell the dull aching pa
in her heart by joining in the gaiety around her; but whe
presently, on reaching the gaming-tables, she saw Alfred ent
the room, she was filled with dismay. On beholding the ve
man she most wished to avoid, in order to keep her promise
the elder de Germont, she was so overcome with conflicting fee

gs that she drew back, pale and trembling, afraid of what his
reeting would be when he saw her on the arm of his most
etested rival.

Alfred was, indeed, strung up to a high pitch of excitement, his
:alousy and anger increased tenfold on thus beholding the pair—
is suspicions of Violetta's desertion of himself being now seem-
gly confirmed. However, assuming for the moment a carelessly
different tone, he challenged the Baron to play with him—an
vitation which Duphol haughtily accepted.

The stakes were high and were doubled each time; and, to the
mazement of all, Alfred won again and again, his luck being so
henomenal that the announcement of supper came as a relief to
e company.

Violetta, who had watched the contest between her lover and the
aron with the greatest anxiety, feeling that their scarcely sup-
essed hatred of one another would break forth on the slightest
rovocation, now sought an opportunity of attracting Alfred's
tention. Having succeeded in drawing him apart from the
ests now seeking their supper partners, she implored him to
ave the house before a quarrel took place between him and the
aron.

Alfred, however, mistaking her motive and thinking she only
ished to save her former lover from his wrath, repulsed her with
orn. Then, quite beside himself with jealousy, he called the
ests from the supper-table and openly insulted her before them
.. Declaring that he now repudiated the favours he had accepted
om her when she had professed to love him, he flung his heavily-
eighted purse at her feet and called upon the company to witness
at he had thus paid her for all she had been to him.

Overcome with grief and wounded to the heart upon hearing
ese cruel words from one she loved so passionately, the unhappy
oletta fell back fainting into the arms of the sympathetic Flora;
d the Baron Duphol immediately demanded satisfaction for the
sult put upon the fair lady he honoured with his attentions—a
allenge which Alfred furiously accepted, full of despair and
ckless of what might happen to him.

M. de Germont, who had also arrived in time to witness
is dramatic scene, now led his agitated son away; and the
lliant entertainment ended in confusion and dismay.

.   .   .   .

Back in her country villa, Violetta sank quickly, and her con-
ion became weaker from day to day. The fatal disease that
d her in its remorseless grip had been accelerated and alarm-
gly developed by the severe mental anguish she had been called

upon to suffer; and her end grew rapidly nearer, her doctor giving no hope of recovery.

One day, however, as she reclined in bed, being no longer able to rise, she received a letter from M. de Germont which revived her drooping spirits and filled her once more with joy. The proud aristocrat who had once desired her to renounce his son's love, now entreated her to accept it—her heroic sacrifice and generous nature having completely won his heart, so that he now wished above all things to see the pair united.

De Germont also informed her that the duel had taken place, and that though Baron Duphol had been wounded he was already recovering. The letter concluded with a note to the effect that Alfred was even now on his way to the villa to entreat her pardon —having been told of the noble part she had played and of the hasty mistake he had himself made in supposing that she had accepted Duphol as a lover.

She had scarcely finished reading the letter when Alfred himself was announced, followed shortly afterwards by his father. Hastening forward with eager steps, the young man clasped his beloved one in his arms; and the two rejoiced together with full hearts.

But the ecstasy of being with her lover once more was too great an effort for the enfeebled Violetta, who soon fell back fainting and in a dying condition; and her doctor was summoned in anxious haste.

Alfred, full of horror upon now beholding the increased frailty of the doomed invalid, fell on his knees beside her bed, passionately imploring her to revive and live for his sake; and the elder de Germont also added his entreaties, encouraging her by declaring that he proudly hoped to call her his daughter yet.

Violetta, overjoyed on thus finding herself so greatly beloved, endeavoured desperately to cast off the deadly faintness that so constantly assailed her; and upon the arrival of the doctor, despite the latter's look of hopeless pity, she declared that she must now live, since such perfect happiness awaited her.

Scarcely had she thus bravely spoken, however, than she fell back upon her pillows with closed eyes; and as Alfred bent tenderly over her, he uttered a cry of grief and despair. His beautiful and beloved Violetta was dead!

IL TROVATORE or The Gipsy's Vengeance *Verdi*
(The Troubadour)

One late evening during the fifteenth century, the servitors and military retainers of the young Count di Luna were waiting for their lord outside the royal castle of Aliaferia, where the Queen of Arragon held her Court. The Count had long loved and desired the Lady Leonora, one of the most beautiful of all the fair and nobly-born maidens in attendance upon the Queen. Despite the fact that Leonora had no love for him—indeed, she disliked him for a certain cruel strain she had early discerned in his character—he constantly continued his amorous pursuit of her; and he frequently wandered late at night in the grounds outside the palace, in the hope of seeing her at her chamber window.

His attendants found the waiting time dull; and this evening, to beguile their vigil, one of the older servitors, Ferrando, related to his companions a tragic incident connected with the family they served. It was a terrible story he told.

When the present Count was a child, he had a baby brother; and the two children were a great joy to their father, who could not bear to think of ill befalling them. Upon the younger child falling sick, therefore, he was terribly distressed, although the ailment was but a trifling one; and he ordered the nurse to keep awake beside her charge throughout the night. The devoted nurse did so; but, as dawn broke, she found that she was not alone. An old Zingara, or Spanish gipsy woman, had entered the room and stood, with skinny arms upraised, gazing intently upon the sleeping child. So malevolent a figure did the intruder appear that the nurse sprang to her feet, shrieking with terror; and her cries soon aroused the household.

The old gipsy was seized by the servants and held captive; and, later in the day, when the sick child seemed slightly worse, the superstitious Count declared that the intruder had cast an evil eye upon the babe and ordered her to be burned at the stake as a witch. Heedless of the poor creature's cries for mercy and her frantic declaration that she had but come to read the fortune of the sleeping child, she was instantly dragged away and bound to a hastily improvised stake set up in the grounds. Faggots were quickly piled around it and set alight; and as the wretched victim's shrieks rose with the leaping flames, her tormentors answered with howls and execrations.

Amongst those in the crowd was the Zingara's own daughter, a beautiful young gipsy who had followed the demented mob with her babe in her arms, trying vainly to get a last word with her doomed mother. Roughly driven back and helpless to resist, she did not reach the dreadful scene until all was over; then, in her rage and despair, she took a speedy and terrible vengeance. Rushing back to the deserted castle—all the inhabitants of which, including the nurse, had gone forth to watch the burning of the witch—she snatched up the sick child and quickly vanished from the neighbourhood, taking him with her.

When it was discovered later that the babe had been stolen, a great outcry arose. The Count di Luna was distracted with grief, and sent out search-parties in every direction; but all their efforts were in vain.

Ferrando, his chief servitor, however, could have told his master that the child would never be found—or so he believed; and now, many years later, he regaled his eager listeners with the gruesome end of his story. On passing by the place of execution on the day after the witch-burning, he had noticed amidst the heap of human ashes the charred bones of a little child; and from these sinister remains he gathered that the Zingara's daughter had stolen the Count's baby boy in order to burn him in the same fire which had consumed her mother! Though filled with horror, he had decided to say nothing about what he had seen—thinking it more merciful to let the unhappy father imagine that his stolen child was still living. But he stored up in his memory a picture of the young Zingara as he had seen her on the edge of the crowd, that he might know her again should he ever have the opportunity of bringing her to justice. Meanwhile, his grief-stricken master had died shortly after these tragic events, leaving instructions for his elder son to continue the search for the lost child—which the present Count di Luna had not failed to obey.

Such was the dramatic story related to his companions by the old servitor; but Ferrando himself did not know the whole of the drama, which was as follows:

When the young Zingara—whose name was Azucena—had reached the place of her mother's execution, she found that the mad crowd had already departed; but just as she was about to fling the Count's child into the already dwindling flames, he uttered a wailing cry which caused her to hesitate—and she placed him for a moment on the ground beside her own sleeping babe, whom she had likewise continued to carry. Then, seized with vengeful fury once more, she snatched up the child again and flung him into the heart of the still glowing embers, which quickly blazed up hotly—covering her head with her cloak, that she might not hear his cries. When she judged these had ceased, she uncovered her face with a triumphant gesture.

Her triumph, however, was quickly changed to horror. On stooping to pick up her own pretty babe, she found that *the Count's son was still alive!* In that moment of blind frenzy, she had snatched up her own child in mistake and cast him into the devouring flames.

Stunned by this terrible blow, Azucena was now filled with remorse and woe; and tenderly lifting up the helpless babe who had been the innocent cause of two such dreadful deeds, she bore him away to the mountains of Biscaglia to be brought up as her own son in the gipsy tribe to which she belonged and which she shortly after ruled as Queen. But, though Azucena soon grew to love her adopted son with all her heart, she could not forget the past; and she still nursed a deep desire for vengeance against the murderers of her mother.

Meanwhile, the stolen child lived the free and happy life of a gipsy in the mountains of Biscaglia. He was given the name of Manrico; and as he was taught to look upon Azucena as his mother, he had no idea of his true and exalted birth. He loved his supposed mother with great devotion; and as the years went on and he grew up into a handsome and noble youth, Azucena felt as proud of her adopted son as though he had indeed been her own. Nevertheless, she caused him to be trained in the art of swordsmanship and in the ways of those of noble, rather than of gipsy birth.

Manrico, being both brave and daring in disposition, very early had the craving for adventure; and as soon as he had learned how to wield a sword with skill, he left the gipsy band for a while and went off to the wars to seek glory and renown. Success smiled on him from the first; and the brave youth, after distinguishing himself in several campaigns, was spoken of with honour and respect wherever he went.

After many wanderings, Manrico at length found himself with the army he had joined—whose cause he felt to be a just one—engaged in settling a dispute with the powerful kingdom of Arragon; and hearing that a grand Tournament was to be held in the district, he determined to enter the lists himself. Having donned a suit of black armour, with an unblazoned shield, he rode off to the Tournament, where he soon covered himself with glory; his valour and skill, indeed, were so great that he carried all before him and none could overcome him in single combat. Consequently, when the Tournament came to an end, Manrico was awarded the victor's wreath of laurel; and the brave youth knelt to be crowned by the fair hands of the Queen of Love and Beauty—the Lady Leonora, Maid-of-Honour at the royal Court of Arragon.

As Leonora and the young victor gazed into each other's eyes, a deep mutual love instantly sprang up between them; and though they spoke but a few words then, they knew that their hearts were irrevocably united.

On returning to his camp, Manrico thought constantly of Leonora; and he determined to see her again—though he well knew that, being of humble gipsy birth, as he supposed, he could not aspire to the hand of a high-born maiden. Nevertheless, he wished her to know of his continued love and devotion.

Clad in the garb of a Troubadour, therefore, he made his way to the palace of Aliaferia one evening at twilight; and standing beneath the window of his lady-love, he sang a passionate serenade to the accompaniment of a soft-toned guitar.

When Leonora heard the sweet song of the bold serenader, she remembered his voice; and a thrill of joy ran through her as, opening her lattice, she recognized in the Troubadour below the form of her brave hero of the Tournament. Manrico was enraptured when he found that Leonora did not despise his love; and after this, the lovers met frequently for a few blissful moments in the palace gardens after darkness had fallen, caring naught for the risk they ran.

.   .   .   .

While his followers listened to the gruesome story related to them by the old servitor, Ferrando, the young Count di Luna still strolled in the palace gardens near the window of the Lady Leonora. He already knew that he had a serious rival in a certain Troubadour who frequently serenaded the fair lady-in-waiting after dark and that Leonora looked upon this stranger with favour. Full of jealous anger against his unknown rival, he determined to remain in the gardens later than usual that night in the hope of encountering the favoured Troubadour—little dreaming that the latter was his own long-lost brother.

Presently, he heard the soft strains of a guitar; and following the sounds, he beheld the handsome form of the young Troubadour standing in a secluded dell with the moonlight shining upon him. At the same moment, Leonora herself appeared, and, addressing her lover in tender tones, declared that she loved him with her whole heart.

Enraged by this romantic scene, the Count di Luna sprang between the lovers and haughtily called upon the Troubadour to declare his name; and on hearing that his hated rival was none other than the renowned Manrico, the enemy of his country, he at once challenged him to mortal combat.

As the swords of the two men clashed, the proud di Luna soon discovered, to his surprise, that he had met his match; for, in a few moments, Manrico disarmed and held him at his sword's point. Some strange intuition, however, restrained the seeming Troubadour from striking the fatal blow; and, instead, he allowed the dazed Count to rise and rejoin his waiting followers.

Soon after this meeting with his rival, Manrico returned to the wars; and, a little later, he was so badly wounded in a fierce fight that he had to retire to his old mountain home in the gipsy encampment, to rest and recover his strength. Here, with great tenderness, Azucena, the Zingara Queen, nursed him back to health; and, since Manrico had been absent a long time, the reunion was very sweet to her, for she had grown to love him as her own son.

When Manrico presently described to Azucena his recent encounter with the Count di Luna, all the gipsy's old desire to avenge her mother came back with renewed force; and she implored her adopted son to slay the young Count when next he had him in his power. She then told him the dreadful story of how her mother had been so cruelly burned alive as a witch and of the partial vengeance she had herself then taken. But, as she did not inform Manrico that *he* was that same stolen child, but led him to suppose that it was the nobly-born babe she had thrown into the flames, he still regarded himself as her son. When, therefore, she now begged him to continue the gipsy family's feud against the present Count di Luna, he was willing enough to do so—not knowing that this haughty young nobleman was in reality his own brother, but regarding him only as his rival in love.

No sooner had Manrico's wounds healed than he received a command from his army leader to go at once to the defence of the castle of Castellar which was being stormed by the troops of Arragon, led by the Count di Luna. He also received at the same time a message from a friend at the Court of Arragon, informing him that the lovely Lady Leonora, having received no news from her wounded Troubadour lover in the enemy ranks, had believed him dead—she was, in consequence, about to enter a convent near Castellar as a nun, having again refused to wed with the Count di Luna.

Filled with dismay at this latter news, Manrico hastily donned his armour and dashed away to lead the troop of soldiers ordered to the defence of Castellar. Then, hastening on ahead to the convent with a party of men, he hoped to arrive there in time to prevent Leonora from taking the vows that would keep her from him for ever.

It happened that the Count di Luna had also heard the news that Leonora was about to take the vows of a nun; and he, likewise, brought a troop of soldiery to the convent, intending to carry her off from the threshold of the altar itself to be his bride, even though against her will. He arrived there just as the procession of nuns approached, with the beautiful maiden in their midst; and, dismounting, he rushed forward instantly to stop their passage.

Leonora trembled at the sudden appearance of the Count, whom she had always disliked and feared; and when he declared passionately that he meant to carry her off by force to be his bride, she repulsed him indignantly.

At this critical moment Manrico suddenly rode up, and, springing from his horse, flung himself between the pair, who stared at him with utter astonishment—though surprise was quickly changed to joy and relief on the part of Leonora. A fierce encounter instantly followed between the two young men; and upon the timely arrival of Manrico's troops, the Count di Luna and his men were beaten off in defeat.

The victorious and triumphant Manrico soon returned to the fortress of Castellar with his beloved Leonora—who no longer desired to enter the convent now that her lover was thus miraculously restored to her; and here the happy pair once more renewed their vows of love and fidelity. Their happiness, however, was short-lived; and heart-rending grief was yet in store for them at the hands of their dangerous enemy.

The Count di Luna, as leader of the storming party, was determined that the attack on the castle should meet with success and that Manrico should be utterly defeated. With this object, he sent for additional men; and as he stood within the encampment just before the attack, he knew that Castellar was doomed. Yet he felt little satisfaction in this thought and knew that his forthcoming triumph would bring him no real joy. Even with Manrico safely out of the way for ever, Leonora would never love him—though he might force her to marry him, her heart would always remain faithful to her adored Troubadour.

While he was thus musing gloomily, he heard shouts in the camp outside; and next moment, a couple of his followers thrust a woman into his tent, declaring that she had been found wandering about and had been seized as a spy. This wanderer was the Zingara, Azucena, who had followed in the wake of her beloved

Manrico, hoping to help him should he fall into the hands of his enemy.

It happened that Ferrando, the old family servitor, was present with his lord at this moment; and after gazing intently upon the gipsy, he suddenly remembered her features and now declared to the Count that this was the same gipsy woman who had stolen his baby brother years ago and burned him upon the witch's pyre—now relating, for the first time, how he had seen the child's bones amongst the ashes.

Full of horror at what he heard, the Count ordered the Zingara to be kept a captive, declaring that she should burn at the stake after the storming of the castle; and on learning from the unfortunate Azucena's disjointed cries for mercy and help that she called upon the name of Manrico as her son, he exulted cruelly, knowing that he could now give his hated rival additional suffering through the torture of his mother.

Next day, Castellar was successfully stormed by di Luna's superior forces; and Manrico, though fighting bravely till the last, was taken prisoner by his triumphant rival. Leonora, however, with the help of a faithful friend, managed to escape to a place of safety. Thus, di Luna was robbed of his chief triumph—the lovely bride he had hoped to secure; but he marched back as a victor to the royal Castle of Aliaferia, taking with him his captured rival and Azucena the Zingara. He caused the captives to be placed together in a strong tower overlooking a courtyard, where, next day, he intended the gipsy to be burned as a witch and Manrico to be beheaded as a State prisoner.

That evening, as the unhappy captives lay in their tower, speaking sadly of their old peaceful home in the mountains which they would never see again, they heard the sound of sweet singing outside. Instantly recognizing the voice as that of his beloved Leonora, Manrico hastened to the narrow window opening and replied to her with a sorrowful song of farewell. The singer was, indeed, Leonora, who, from her place of hiding, had managed to make her way into the palace grounds, to let her captive lover know that she was near him—in her turn acting the part of troubadour to her beloved one.

Again the lovers' songs were interrupted by the sudden appearance of the Count di Luna; and flinging herself at the latter's feet, Leonora now passionately implored him to spare the life of the man she loved. But, though she offered to give her own life in exchange, her pleadings were refused.

Then, realizing that nothing else would avail with the inexorable Count, Leonora, though she scarce could utter the fatal

words, offered to grant him his heart's desire and to become his
bride, if Manrico's life were spared. At last triumphant, the
Count accepted her sacrifice; and he now bade the devoted maiden
go and set her lover free, sending a gaoler with her to unlock the
door of the tower.

But Leonora did not mean to become the bride of di Luna; and
on her way to the tower, she swallowed some deadly poison from
a ring she wore—preferring to die rather than to wed with her
lover's foe.

The captives in the tower were still speaking sadly of past happy
days when the bolts were drawn and Leonora entered the room.
With surprise and joy, Manrico clasped his beloved one in his
arms; but when Leonora declared that she had obtained his
freedom and besought him to fly at once before his enemy had
time to relent, he drew back and refused to stir. Suspecting how
she had secured so unlikely a favour, he began to pour forth
reproaches upon her, deeming her false to him.

By this time, however, the poison was already doing its deadly
work; and, sinking to the ground, Leonora revealed to her lover,
between dying gasps, that she had preferred to die rather than
yield to his rival.

Overcome with despair and woe at the terrible sacrifice she had
made for him, Manrico sprang forward to receive her in his arms
as she expired; and at that moment the Count di Luna entered the
room.

Realizing how he had been cheated of his longed-for bride,
the Count, furious with rage and grief, now ordered Manrico to
instant execution; and seizing the weeping Zingara by the arm,
he dragged her roughly to the window opening to see her son die.

Azucena was now half-dazed with woe and terror; but when
the axe had fallen and the brave Manrico was no more, she turned
fiercely upon the taunting Count and revealed to him in frenzied
tones the true birth of her adopted son, ending her story by
shrieking wildly : " *Thou hast slain thine own brother!* "

On hearing these terrible words, di Luna's gloating exultation
was turned into the deepest horror, and he uttered a loud cry of
woe as, having avenged the murder of her mother, the gipsy fell
dead at his feet.

THE FLYING DUTCHMAN   *Wagner*
(*Der Fliegende Holländer*)

HERE is the Legend of the Flying Dutchman :

There was once a Dutch sea-captain who was so brave and fear-less that no amount of danger seemed to daunt him. Battling with the wild winds and waves was the greatest joy to him; and his light-hearted daring carried him through many a difficult passage.

At last the crowning test of his courage came. On a voyage round the coast of Africa, there arose the most furious tempest ever known in those seas. All prudent seamen at once sought refuge in harbours and sheltering bays weighing their anchors until the storm should have abated; but the Dutch captain only laughed at the terrified members of his crew when they implored him to do likewise. Casting prudence to the winds, he vowed that, despite the raging hurricane, he would double the Cape of Good Hope without fail, even if he kept on sailing for ever.

It happened that this foolish vow was overheard by the Evil One, who, as a punishment for his vain boast, condemned the rash captain actually to sail the seas for ever and put his vessel in the charge of demons. The only hope of release held out to him was to find a pure and lovely maiden who would be willing to love him faithfully until death; and for this purpose he was allowed to go ashore once in every seven years to seek for such a saviour.

Full of remorse and despair, the unhappy captain began his cease-less voyaging; and the mad recklessness of his speed soon won for him the name of the " Flying Dutchman ". The fame of his terrible plight and of the evil influence surrounding him became world-wide; and all good sailors tried to avoid the doomed ship, crossing themselves devoutly whenever its blood-red sails and black masts appeared in sight.

Once in every seven years the Flying Dutchman went on shore; but he always returned to his ship disappointed and despairing, for no maiden could be found willing to share his fate and to be loving and faithful to him until death. For numberless years, therefore, the ill-fated man sailed the seas unceasingly; and though he daily courted death, yet death came not to him and every danger passed him by.

At length, about the beginning of the eighteenth century, the Flying Dutchman steered his ship towards the rugged coast of Norway; and as another seven years' term had just ended, he determined to go ashore and begin his hopeless quest once more. By this time his vessel was laden with gold and jewels and rich stuffs from many lands; and by bestowing his treasures lavishly, he knew he would not be refused hospitality at least.

As he drew nearer to the shores of a lonely bay, he found a Norwegian ship already there before him, having sought shelter from a passing storm; and presently he entered into conversation with the captain, whose name was Daland. The latter informed him that as soon as the storm abated somewhat, he should eagerly make for his home, a few miles farther along the coast, where his beautiful daughter was awaiting his return.

When the Flying Dutchman heard that the Norwegian had a daughter, he was glad; and presently he offered to Daland the whole of his vast treasures if he would give him in return a few days' hospitality and his daughter as a bride.

It happened that Daland—who was greedy of gold—had long desired to find a wealthy husband for his fair daughter; and, though he knew nothing of the stranger before him and felt somewhat afraid of his wild looks and mysterious crew, he could not resist the temptation to possess the wonderful treasures so glowingly described to him. Therefore, he gladly gave the Dutchman permission to woo the maiden; and a short time afterwards, the storm having passed away, the two ships set sail for Daland's home inlet.

Meanwhile, the household of the Norwegian captain had been eagerly awaiting his return for some time past; and on the day of his expected arrival, his fair daughter, Senta, was spinning with her maidens in one of the large homely rooms. Dame Mary, the old nurse, was in charge of the work; and, under her directions, the pretty young girls were kept busily employed as they sang merry songs to the hum of their spinning-wheels.

Only one of the maidens was idle; and this was the beautiful young mistress—Senta herself—who sat with her hands folded, pensively gazing at a picture upon the wall. The picture was a portrait of the Flying Dutchman—who had been once seen by an artist years ago, and whose strange story told in ballad and legend was well known in Norway; and as Senta looked upon that pale, sad face, a great pity for the unhappy wanderer's terrible fate arose within her.

This face had such a curious fascination for the tender-hearted, dreamy maiden that a deep love and devotion had grown in her heart for the tortured soul she longed to comfort. On the day of her father's return, she gazed upon the picture with more intentness than usual, having dreamed many times of late that its subject stood before her as a real living lover.

Dame Mary, however, did not care to see her sweet young mistress gaze so frequently upon the pictured face of one whom Satan had claimed for his own; and she bade the girl get on with her spinning. Instead, Senta sang a wild ballad to her companions, in which she retold the whole story of her legendary dream-hero and his awful doom; and then, as her song came to an end, she stretched out her arms and cried aloud passionately, as though the spectral seaman himself stood before her: "I am the one who through her love will save thee!"

As she uttered these wild words, which caused Dame Mary and her maidens to cry out in horror, a handsome young huntsman, named Erik, entered the room, having heard all. Erik had loved the fair Senta from childhood and had always believed himself beloved in return; and he now hastened to her side in alarm, imploring her not to forsake him.

He then announced that Daland's ship had just arrived, accompanied by another and unknown vessel; and when Dame Mary and the spinning-maidens had hastily departed to set food ready for their master's welcome, he turned again to Senta. He begged her to assure him once more of her love and to help him to gain her father's consent to their marriage—for he was fully aware that Daland desired for his fair daughter a wealthier suitor than a mere huntsman.

The beautiful Senta only laughed at his doubts; and when he next reproached her for gazing so constantly at the picture on the wall, she declared it was but pity that filled her heart for the subject of it. But Erik was not satisfied; and he went on to describe a vision that had recently visited him, in which he had seen his beloved one give her hand to this same phantom captain, who embraced her rapturously and led her to his vessel. When Senta heard this, the glamour of her strange fascination came over her again, and she cried out wildly: "He seeks for me, and I for him!"

Erik rushed away, overcome with grief and feeling that Senta must be under some evil spell; and at this moment Daland entered the room with his mysterious guest—whom, as yet, he did not know to be the Flying Dutchman. He held out his arms lovingly, expecting his daughter to run into them and embrace him eagerly as was always the case on his return from sea; but Senta, with wide-open, intensely held eyes, was gazing beyond him at the stranger in the doorway.

There, in the living flesh, she beheld the face that had fascinated her all her maiden days; and, spellbound with astonishment, she turned to her father as if in a trance, saying : " My father, say, who is this stranger? "

Then Daland explained how he had met with the captain and taken pity on his loneliness; and he eagerly informed her that the stranger desired to offer himself as a suitor for her hand and to bestow upon her the gold and priceless jewels he possessed.

As he spoke, Daland, with the gleam of avarice in his eyes, spread out upon a table the jewels and gold the Flying Dutchman had already given him from his treasure-laden ship; but, seeing that Senta did not even glance at them, he thought it wiser to retire and leave the stranger to plead his own cause.

When he had gone, the Flying Dutchman, with trembling hope, seized the hands of Senta and implored her to share his lonely fate, declaring that he had seen her in visions long ago and believed her to be the one who should bring him peace and rest at last; and Senta, with rapture, consented to be his bride, telling him that she also had seen him in her dreams and had always longed to release him from his woes.

When the Flying Dutchman thus knew that Senta was acquainted with his sad story and was willing to break the evil spell that had been cast upon him, he was transported with joy; and yet he nobly begged her to consider the sacrifice she was about to make by saving him from perdition. To which the fair maiden replied heroically: " Here is my hand! I will not rue! E'en to death will I be true! "

. . . .

Early that evening, Daland gave a feast to the crew of his ship in accordance with his usual custom at the end of a voyage. When Senta and her newly-betrothed lover arrived upon the scene, they found gaiety on every side. Dame Mary and her merry maidens had already brought food and wine on deck; and the jolly sailors were soon greeting their pretty sweethearts as they feasted, laughed, and sang with thankful hearts.

In strange contrast with this merriment, however, complete silence reigned on board the Flying Dutchman's ship. Though food and wine had also been brought out for the stranger's crew, the latter kept below deck and gave no sound of life at all. It was in vain that the maidens tried to attract their attention; and at length, alarmed by the strange appearance of the silent vessel, they desisted entirely.

Then, when the Norwegian sailors, in their own enjoyment, had almost forgotten the presence of the strangers, the mysterious crew of the Flying Dutchman suddenly came to life. Its weird looking members began to sing, in harsh, unearthly tones, a wild song, in which they told the story of their ill-fated master; and, at the same time, a sinister bluish flame gleamed around them and the loud rumblings of thunder were heard.

At first the startled Norwegians looked on in wonder and tried to drown these ominous sounds with their own gay singing. After a while, however, they became alarmed; then, overcome by the dreadful scene and trembling with horror, they hurriedly crossed themselves and retired to the cabin. On observing this, the crew of the phantom ship burst into a peal of shrill, demoniacal laughter; but presently the ghastly flame faded slowly away, the stormy rumblings ceased, and silence reigned once more.

The Norwegians now knew that the dreaded and shunned Flying Dutchman and his demon crew from the abode of darkness were in their midst; and Erik the Huntsman, shocked and horrified, dashed towards Senta and implored her to renounce the stranger whose evil fate she had just agreed to share. He passionately pleaded his own faithful love, begging her to accept it once again; and he reminded her of the old happy days when she had been contented to love him only.

These tender pleading words were heard by the Flying Dutchman, who was hovering near; and the wretched man, full of disappointment and believing that Senta was about to renounce him, instantly left her side in despair. Hastening on board his own ship, he hurriedly gave orders for the anchor to be lifted, crying out wildly: "Abandoned! All is for ever lost! Senta, farewell!"

But Senta, though torn by Erik's pleading, still found her love and devotion to the Flying Dutchman the stronger feeling in her heart; and she ran forward to follow him, declaring passionately that the vow she had made should be kept.

Erik, Daland, and others seized the distraught maiden as she fled, full of horror at the sacrifice she was about to make for one whose evil doom affrighted them; and as they held her back, the Flying Dutchman, though now utterly bereft of hope, nobly vowed that he would release her from her promise to him and sail away at once.

Senta, however, was determined to share the sad doom of the hero of her dreams and by her faithful love to break the cruel spell that had bound him so long. Struggling from the loving grasp of those who now vainly tried to hold her back, she ran forward to the edge of an overhanging cliff close by, stretching out her arms and crying wildly to the hopeless figure on the departing vessel: "My love till death shall take thy curse away!"

With these heroic words, the gentle, devoted maiden, in a transport of joy, cast herself into the sea; and, immediately afterwards, the phantom ship sank beneath the waves, which arose and receded again in a mighty whirlpool.

As the Norwegians gazed with awed amazement upon this magnificent sight, they saw, in the golden glow of the setting sun two ethereal forms rising together from the sea over the wrecked vessel and floating upwards towards the heavens.

They were Senta and the Flying Dutchman, their arms entwined in a loving embrace and a look of perfect peace and rapturous joy upon their radiant, upturned faces.

The ransom had been paid; and the Flying Dutchman was at rest for evermore in company with the fair, sweet maiden who had loved him faithfully until death!

LOHENGRIN   *Wagner*

WHEN Henry the Fowler was reigning as King of Germany during the tenth century, he gained great renown in all the countries of Europe; and by means of his courage and skill in warfare, he brought many fair cities and large tracts of land beneath his sway. Amongst the latter was Brabant, over which he ruled as Liege Lord.

Arriving one day in Antwerp to raise men for his wars in Hungary, he found the city in a great uproar. He soon learned the reason for this. Some years ago, the reigning Duke of Brabant had died and left his two children, Gottfried and Elsa, under the guardianship of his nearest kinsman, Count Frederick of Telramund, to be protected by him until they were old enough to rule the country for themselves. The brother and sister loved one another dearly and were never so happy as when in each other's company; but as the time drew near for them to begin to rule, they were suddenly parted.

Frederick of Telramund had now come under the evil influence of Ortrud, a Princess of another powerful family of Brabant, rival for the throne with the late Duke. The Princess Ortrud was ambitious and unscrupulous; and she was likewise a dealer in the arts of sorcery—though she kept these latter dangerous powers secret from all. She hated Elsa, who had now grown into a sweet and beautiful maiden; and she determined to get rid of her and

o reign in her stead. With great cunning, therefore, she per-
uaded Telramund that she herself was the rightful heiress of
Brabant—adding that if he would marry her, they would rule
he country together.

Telramund had expected to marry Elsa, whose hand had been
promised him by her late father; but the pure and lovely maiden
only felt scorn for him, knowing him to be unworthy of her love.
Consequently, being weak-willed, he easily gave in to the wiles
of Ortrud—who now proceeded to lay a wicked plot, whereby she
hoped to gain her ambitious ends.

One day, when Elsa and Gottfried were walking in the forest
together, the scheming sorceress, by means of her spells, caused
hem to wander apart; and then, by further magic, she trans-
ormed the royal youth into a bird. Elsa wandered about for
ome time, seeking in vain for her lost brother; and, finally, she
returned to the palace, full of grief and alarm. Then the wicked
Ortrud came forward and declared that she had seen Elsa drown
er brother in the moat; and she soon persuaded Telramund that
he maiden had indeed murdered the young Gottfried. At her
urther instigation, Telramund now renounced the hand of Elsa
nd married Ortrud instead; and very soon afterwards he claimed
he throne of Brabant through his scheming wife.

It was at this time that Henry the Fowler, Liege Lord of
rabant, came to Antwerp to call for aid from his vassals; and
ecause of the accusation against the young Princess, he gathered
he nobles together on the banks of the river Scheldt and declared
hat he would give judgment in the matter that same day.

When the people had assembled on the riverside, Frederick of
elramund came up to the judgment throne and accused the
rincess Elsa of having murdered her brother in order to win the
hrone for herself alone; and then the King called upon Elsa to
efend the charge made against her.

When the royal maiden appeared with her ladies, pale and sad,
he looked so fair and pure that the assembled people gazed upon
er almost with awe; and the King himself was so struck with her
ngelic appearance that he declared she could never have done so
il a deed. Nevertheless, in accordance with the custom of those
ediæval times, he announced that the truth should be decided by
rial by Single Combat between the accuser, Frederick of Tel-
mund, and any other Knight who should now come forward as
he Princess's Champion. If the latter proved to be the victor,
hen she should be declared innocent. So black a case had her
njust and jealous guardians now made against the gentle maiden,
owever, that none of the nobles of Brabant were willing to fight

for her; but King Henry, justly determined to give her every chance, now called upon Elsa to name her own Champion.

Then the young Princess stepped forward, proud and fearless in her innocence, which she again asserted; and she described to the waiting throng a wonderful dream that had visited her. In this vision she had seen a splendid Knight in shining armour, with a golden horn hanging at his side and a flashing sword girt around his waist; and she declared that Heaven would surely send this glorious Knight to be her Champion now, in her hour of need, to fight on her behalf and thus to prove her innocence.

So pure and calmly full of faith did the lovely maiden now appear that many of the nobles seemed no longer to doubt her innocence—though Telramund and Ortrud declared scornfully that her fine dream was but a fanciful tale and that no such Champion would ever appear. The King, however, sternly bade the usurpers to hold their peace; and, at his command, the trumpets were now sounded and the Heralds called out: "Who will do battle for Elsa of Brabant?"

There was a long breathless pause; but no one answered the call. Again the trumpets sounded and the Heralds called out: "Who will do battle for Elsa of Brabant?" Then Elsa stretched out her arms and prayed aloud to Heaven to send her the Champion she sought—the Champion of her dream; and this time the call was answered.

A great shout arose from the people, and all eyes were turned towards the river. There they saw a skiff, drawn by a beautiful white swan, now approaching and moving slowly to the shore. Standing in this graceful skiff was a young and splendid Knight in shining silver armour, with a winged helmet and having a golden horn hanging at his side and a flashing sword girt around his waist—the same "Knight of glorious mien" whom the fair Elsa had seen in her dream. Upon arriving at the water's edge the Knight stepped ashore, then turned and bade farewell to his "trusty Swan"—whereupon the royal bird spread its snowy wings and sailed away once more with its fairy skiff.

The frustrated plotters, Telramund and Ortrud, drew back in angry dismay as the glorious Knight of the Swan now offered himself to the royal maiden as her chosen Champion. Elsa rapturously accepted him, promising him her hand as his reward. The Knight of the Swan next begged her to promise that she would never ask him to reveal his race, name, or whence he came, or he would be compelled to leave her—it being a condition of his knightly service that he should remain unknown; and Elsa already loved him so dearly that she gladly gave this promise.

Then the stranger drew his sword and the fight began; and after a short conflict, he disarmed Telramund, but generously spared his life. Ortrud shrieked with rage and dismay; but the rest of the company uttered loud shouts of joy.

King Henry now declared that as Heaven had given the victory to Elsa's Champion, her innocence was proved; and he commanded the people of Brabant to obey the royal maiden and her Knight as their rulers.

So Telramund and Ortrud were stripped of the powers they had usurped, and were driven forth from the palace as outcasts.

.   .   .   .

While joyful preparations were afoot in the ducal palace for the marriage of Elsa with her Champion Knight, the defeated would-be usurpers quickly hatched another plot against the royal maiden. As the jealous pair lurked in secret outside the palace on the night before the wedding, the sorceress Ortrud informed Telramund that she had learned by her arts that if but a single drop of the mysterious Knight's blood could be spilled, he would lose his obviously magic powers. She persuaded him, therefore, to make an attack upon his rival on the morrow. Meanwhile, she would herself artfully seek means for sowing the seeds of doubt of the Knight's integrity in the mind of Elsa.

The opportunity she sought was soon forthcoming. The royal maiden presently appeared on the balcony above; and Ortrud at once made known her own presence and implored a hearing. Then the wily sorceress began to relate a false story, declaring that she and her husband had been under an evil spell when they accused her of having murdered her lost brother, but that they were now full of remorse and misery. So sincere did the arch-plotter appear that Elsa's kind heart was touched; and presently she came down into the courtyard below and took Ortrud back with her into the palace, generously promising that she would intercede for the outcasts with the King.

This fatal act of kindness, however, was to cost Elsa her hard-won happiness. The cunning Ortrud immediately began to sow in the young Princess's heart the seeds of distrust regarding her noble Champion. The jealous but seemingly repentant plotter declared that the Stranger Knight had probably come to her aid from evil rather than good motives; that nobody knew whence he had come, nor even his race or name; and that he could not truly love the maiden he had fought for or he would be willing to clear up the mystery that surrounded him.

On the morrow, all in the palace were filled with excitement and bustle; for this was Elsa's wedding day and great preparations had been made to celebrate it in fitting style. Elsa was overjoyed at the prospect of her future happiness; but doubt of her brave Champion now mingled with her joy. A fear that she might lose her lover began to fill her with dread, for her cunning enemy had not failed to point out that one to whom magic aid was lent might at any moment vanish from her sight.

When the bridal procession to the church was formed, Ortrud was among the train of attendants; but as they were about to enter, the plotter's haughty spirit could not bear that Elsa should go before her. She furiously commanded the bride to stand back, declaring that she herself should lead as the rightful ruler of Brabant. Elsa stopped, full of surprise as she remembered how humble Ortrud had been the night before; and the angry sorceress again challenged her to name her Champion Knight and to say whence he obtained his mystic powers.

Amidst this confusion, the King and his lords appeared on the scene with the bridegroom; and when the Knight of the Swan saw Elsa in converse with the wicked Ortrud, he begged her not to be led to doubt him. As he spoke, Frederick of Telramund now sprang forward and, before all the bridal party, accused Elsa's Champion of having gained the victory over him in their contest by means of sorcery and evil spells; and he likewise called upon the stranger to declare his name and place of abode if he would be regarded as a true knight.

But the Knight of the Swan still refused to divulge his secret, declaring that Elsa alone could compel him to do so; and he added that the King and nobles must be satisfied with having witnessed his deed of valour—which proved that Heaven favoured him. The King and his lordly followers now declared that they were satisfied for him to remain unknown and would honour and stand by him for the deed he had done.

Having failed with this shaft, Telramund crept round to Elsa and whispered to her the sinister suggestion that she should allow him to wound her lover slightly—declaring that by the shedding of a few drops of his blood, the latter would thus lose his magic power and remain for ever at her side. But the Knight of the Swan came forward and drew his bride away, begging her to have no further doubt of him; and Elsa, gladly placing her hand in his, entered the church with him, and the bridal ceremony proceeded.

Later on, as darkness fell and the wedding revels drew to a close, Elsa and her glittering bridegroom were conducted to their bridal chamber by a splendid company of knights and maidens, who sang to them a joyful wedding-song and then departed.

When, at length, they were left alone, the Knight of the Swan clasped his beautiful wife in his arms; and the two rejoiced together in their happy love. But, joyful though she was, the seeds of doubt and fear in Elsa's heart, planted there by the wily Ortrud, were still growing fast; and when these first blissful moments were past, she begged her newly-made husband to reveal to her his secret, declaring that she would guard it well.

The Champion Knight, his rapture now departing and sorrow taking its place as he thus realized that she no longer trusted him, again entreated his beloved bride not to throw away their happiness by asking him to divulge the secret laid upon him—when he would be compelled to leave her. But Elsa, now curious as well as doubtful, grown reckless by her uneasy fears that he was bound by a magic spell, only entreated him the more passionately to reveal his secret. The Knight of the Swan, though sad and disappointed because of her wild disregard of his eager warning, now knew that he must grant her request.

At this moment, Telramund, with four of his conspirator companions, broke into the room with drawn swords, intending to kill the stranger Knight; but Elsa, quick to see the danger, handed her husband his sword—and, instantly, the ungrateful traitor was slain and the other would-be murderers disarmed.

The noise of the scuffle quickly brought the lords and ladies of the Court into the chamber; and having put the fainting Elsa into the charge of her maidens, the Knight of the Swan declared sadly that in obedience to her request, he would reveal his secret to all at sunrise on the morrow—after which, he would be compelled to depart from Brabant for ever, in accordance with the conditions of his knightly service.

When dawn came, therefore, the King, with Elsa and her husband and the nobles of Brabant, gathered together once more on the banks of the Scheldt. Once more the lovely Elsa was filled with woe—though this time her troubles were of her own making.

The nobles first of all gave their promise to their Liege Lord, Henry the Fowler, to fight for him as faithful vassals against the Hungarians. Then the Knight of the Swan stepped forward to make himself known to them, declaring that because Elsa had asked to know his secret he could no longer keep it from her.

He announced that his name was Lohengrin; he was a Knight of the Holy Grail and the son of Parsifal, King and Keeper of the Grail. It was his work to go forth into the world as the Champion of Innocence; but his power over evil only lasted so long as he remained unknown to those he served. As soon as the latter demanded to be told his name and origin, his instructions were to reveal his secret and then to return to the Knights of the Holy Grail who had sent him forth. He then described to his listeners the sacred relic which he and other pure and stainless knights served so faithfully; and he also told them the miraculous story connected with it.[1]

As he finished speaking, a cry arose from the company: "The swan! The swan! Behold it comes!"

All eyes turned to the river; and there, in the distance, the skiff in which the Champion Knight had arrived was seen once more approaching, drawn by the same beautiful swan. All this time, Elsa had kept apart, pale and silent; but now, with cries of grief, she flung herself upon her beloved husband, distracted by the result of her foolish doubts and fears and entreating him not to leave her.

Lohengrin, however, gently unwound her clinging arms and led her back to her ladies, declaring sadly that he no longer had the power to remain, since he must always obey the orders of the Grail Knights. After embracing her tenderly, he bade her a last farewell and moved towards the skiff. Then Ortrud, triumphant at the misery she had caused, sprang forward and revealed the fact that the swan attached to the skiff was none other than the lost young Gottfried, Prince of Brabant, whom she had thus transformed by means of her magic—adding exultantly that if Elsa could have kept her Champion Knight by her side for one year, her brother would have regained his human form once more.

Ortrud's cruel triumph, however, was short-lived; for Lohengrin now prayed to Heaven for additional powers. His prayer was graciously answered; and as the people gazed in wonder, the fair white Dove of the Holy Grail flew softly down and hovered over the skiff, whilst Lohengrin deftly loosened the golden chain that bound the swan. Instantly, the swan sank into the water; and presently there arose in its place the young Prince, Gottfried, Elsa's lost brother.

Lohengrin led the fair youth forward, declaring him to be the rightful ruler of Brabant. Then, as the nobles were receiving Gottfried with surprise and delight, the stranger Knight stepped into the skiff; and the white Dove, seizing the chain, began to draw it along.

Elsa, who had embraced her brother with great joy, now turned to the river; and seeing Lohengrin standing up in the departing

[1] See the story of *Parsifal*.

skiff signing a last sad farewell to her, she uttered a cry of grief and despair and sank senseless to the ground.

Gottfried knelt in dismay beside her; and at that moment the Champion Knight of the Holy Grail vanished out of sight.

THE MASTERSINGERS OF NUREMBERG   *Wagner*
(*Die Meistersinger von Nürnberg*)

WHEN the Renaissance had once more lighted the way to knowledge and culture, the beautiful art of song was revived in Germany by bands of musical enthusiasts known as The Mastersingers and recruited from the various craft guilds.

True, the dramatic, chivalric conception of life which had been the prevailing spirit of the Minnesingers of old—all of whom had been of noble birth and had exercised their art in the courts of kings—never quite returned. The Mastersingers, being but humble burghers and artisans, could not attain to such courtly grace of expression, and their art was of a stiffer and more pedantic character. Yet they did excellent work, establishing schools and guilds of poetry and song in most of the principal towns of Germany; but by hedging themselves in by narrow rules and conventions, they left little margin for the soaring spirit of that true genius which ever chafes at petty restraints and insists on freedom of fancy.

In Nuremberg, the Mastersingers attained to the greatest excellence of their class. Here, in the middle of the sixteenth century, there flourished the simple-minded, large-hearted Hans Sachs, the truest poet of his time, whose broad views were in refreshing contrast with the more cramped conceptions of art held by most of the Mastersingers.

It was during the time when Hans Sachs was a leader amongst the celebrated Mastersingers of Nuremberg that he and his musical friends were called upon to undergo upon St. John's Eve in a certain year a new and exciting experience in the pursuit of their beloved art.

Veit Pogner, a wealthy goldsmith, had offered the hand of his beautiful daughter, Eva, together with the inheritance of his riches and worldly possessions, as a prize to the poet-singer who should gain the wreath of victory in the grand contest to be held on St. John's Day in accordance with the usual custom.

Amongst the competing masters who felt most confident of success was Sixtus Beckmesser, the town clerk, who occupied the important position of Marker in the society—an officer whose duty it was to mark on a slate the faults of competitors against the established rules and regulations of the Music Guild. Beckmesser, though without talent and no longer young or even possessed of any pleasing personal quality, was so conceited that he fancied none to be his equal in music, poetry, and charm. Despite the fact, too, that Eva was to be free to refuse the prizewinner should the latter prove distasteful to her, he yet felt assured of winning her—though the maiden had never shown him any signs of favour.

Meanwhile, Eva had already fixed her affections upon a handsome young knight, one Walter von Stolzing. Descended from the old Minnesingers—whose glorious achievements he had read of and studied—the truly poetic, romantic, and knightly art was revived in this nobly-born youth so strongly that he had left his ancestral hall in order to find kindred spirits amongst the celebrated Mastersingers of music-loving Nuremberg.

Having business relations with old Pogner in connection with his poverty-stricken estate, Walter had thus made acquaintance with the goldsmith's fair daughter; and the exquisite beauty and pure sweet nature of this maiden quickly kindled a consuming passion in his impetuous romantic heart. Soon realizing that his love was returned by Eva, and knowing that none but a Mastersinger could aspire to her hand, he determined to enter the ranks of the competitors on St. John's Day; and he trusted that his great love would inspire his poetic and musical gifts and so enable his song to gain for him the victor's wreath.

With this resolve, he repaired on St. John's Eve to the Church of St. Catherine, where the Mastersingers held their meetings, to present himself as a candidate for admission to the Song Contest. He was greatly disconcerted on being informed by a lively youth named David, who was apprenticed to Hans Sachs the cobbler, that the musical guild was arranged as a trades' guild with degrees of membership—apprentices, scholars, singers—and that it was usual to spend at least a year in each degree before attaining to the rank of a " master ". He was likewise filled with impatience on hearing of the many petty rules and narrow restrictions in verse and song-making necessary to be observed if he wished to please the Mastersingers—seven faults only against these rules being allowed to candidates for admission to their competitions.

Nevertheless, when the Mastersingers had assembled, he requested permission to prove to them that he was a master of poetic song and thus suitable to enter the competition on the morrow; and, as he was introduced to them by Pogner himself, he was invited to sing a song then and there. The Guild members, however, were horrified on learning that he had never studied in any Mastersingers' school and had no other qualifications than that of a love of Nature and a natural poetic instinct.

Beckmesser, the Marker, having pompously ensconced himself in his accustomed curtained recess, with slate and chalk to mark down the faults of the candidate, announced that he was ready to hear the young Knight's trial, and Walter immediately burst forth into an enthusiastic song in praise of spring-time and maidenhood. So full of true poetry and music was his spontaneous composition that it held the masters spellbound—despite the fact that it completely outraged all their agreed rules of construction.

The conceited Beckmesser, however, was full of indignation that one so unheedful of the forms and conventions of his own accepted theories should dare to aspire to enter the ranks of the Mastersingers; and before the song was half finished, he burst from behind his curtain and contemptuously announced that the candidate had already failed many times over. He had scored his slate at least fifty times with faults against the rules.

Now ashamed of having temporarily enjoyed such original music, the Mastersingers agreed with the Marker's condemnation —with the exception of Hans Sachs, who knew that Beckmesser's verdict was chiefly caused by jealousy. He himself, as a true poet-musician, was able to appreciate Walter's beautiful song; and realizing that the young Knight had a real and lofty genius, he boldly stood up in his defence, declaring to the outraged Guild members that the stranger's music was of a higher order than their own.

But the Mastersingers were not to be convinced, even though their revered Hans Sachs spoke in favour of the audacious competitor; and Walter was declared "outsung" and unfitted to be admitted to their ranks.

. . . .

The young Knight, repelled by the Mastersingers' narrow art, from which he had hoped to derive much pleasure, was filled with disappointment and despair. Finding that he could not hope to gain the hand of his beloved Eva as a Mastersinger, however, he determined to make an attempt to elope with her that evening.

Eva, anxious to learn how her lover had fared at his trial, sent her attendant, Magdalena, to get the news from the latter's sweetheart, David, the apprentice of Hans Sachs; then, returning at dusk from a walk, she remained outside the house to hear what her handmaid had to say. The two girls talked in low tones, observing that Hans Sachs—whose shop stood exactly opposite the house of the goldsmith—was still at work. There was a reason for the latter fact. Honest Hans, suspecting the young Knight's intention with regard to Eva, had determined to keep watch and to frustrate his plan, in kindness to the imprudent pair —for he loved them both.

Eva was in despair when told by Magdalena of her lover's failure; but, seeing Walter at that moment approaching, she sent her maid within doors and awaited him with a joy she could not conceal.

The lovers embraced rapturously; and Eva, enthralled by Walter's love for her, readily agreed to his passionate pleading that they should elope that night. Ere they could escape, however, they heard approaching steps; and hastily concealing themselves behind some bushes, they were compelled to wait there until the intruder should depart.

The newcomer was none other than Beckmesser, the conceited Marker, who, having composed a song to sing at the contest on the morrow, had come now to sing it as a serenade beneath the window of the fair Eva; for he hoped that the maiden would thus be so favourably impressed by his composition that she would accept him when he was adjudged the winner—as he so self-confidently expected to be. Stationing himself beneath his charmer's chamber window, therefore, he began his song—which was, in reality, a very poor one, consisting of inferior poetry and worse melody.

Hans Sachs, hoping to deter Walter and Eva from their rash act by keeping them in their hiding-place—having already spied them from his own window as they crouched behind the bushes —now began himself to sing in a very loud voice a rollicking tune with merry words; an unexpected performance very disconcerting to the serenader.

In a furious rage at this wanton drowning of his sentimental song, Beckmesser shouted in vain to the cobbler to cease singing; and then he resorted to strategy. He invited Hans to listen carefully to his song and to criticize it, that he might correct any faults in the composition before its performance on the morrow. This the cobbler agreed to do, cunningly adding that for every fault he detected, he would hammer a nail into the pair of shoes he was at that moment mending for the crotchety town clerk—who had been blaming him earlier in the day for being behindhand with this important job.

So Beckmesser began his song again, delighted upon observing a maiden's figure appear at the bedroom window—imagining this to be his adored one. In reality, however, it was the waiting-maid, Magdalena, anxiously looking out for the return of her errant young mistress.

The serenader's rage was soon increased tenfold, for his faulty accents and musical discords were so frequent that the cobbler's hammer fell with a resounding thud almost constantly. Ere the song was half over, Hans ran out of his shop, holding up the finished shoes in triumph and calling out mischievously in imitation of the Marker's own manner at the young Knight's examination: "Stop! I've finished the shoes already, thanks to the many faults you have made!"

To add to the discomfiture of Beckmesser, young David, the apprentice, now appeared on the scene, and began to belabour him heartily—for, seeing his sweetheart, Magdalena, at the window above and jealously imagining that the serenader was address-ing her, he determined to teach his supposed rival a lesson.

Taken thus by surprise, Beckmesser yelled aloud for help, for David was a lusty youth and was cudgelling him with a will; and aroused by the sounds of the scuffle, a small crowd quickly gathered, stumbling in the dark and squabbling with one another, not knowing what had happened.

Hoping, in the midst of this scuffle, to effect their escape, Walter tenderly endeavoured to lead Eva around the edge of the crowd; but Hans Sachs, who had kept a watchful eye constantly on the pair, soon frustrated this pretty plan by seizing Walter's arm in his own iron grasp. At the same moment, he pushed Eva firmly up the steps of her father's house—where she was quickly seized and taken within by Pogner himself, who, having opened his door to learn the cause of the commotion, was amazed to find his daughter about to enter.

Satisfied that the scared Eva was now safely in her father's care, and having next seized and flung the angry young David into the shop, Hans Sachs likewise returned to his house, dragging the despairing Walter with him; and by the time a sleepy watch-man presently appeared on the scene, the crowd had melted away.

* * * * *

Next morning, as Hans—attired in gala dress ready for the great Festival of St. John's Day—sat in his workshop, the young Knight rushed in from the chamber where he had been sleeping and announced to his kind friend that he had just awakened from a wonderful dream, which he longed to put into song. The art-loving cobbler entreated him to sing it at once, while fresh in his mind—but in the form of a master-song of the correct form, of which he proceeded to give him some hints. He enthusiastically added that with such a Heaven-sent subject, sung in the richly-flowing stream of melody that was his young friend's own priceless gift, Eva might yet be won by him in the contest.

Encouraged by the large-hearted Hans and inspired by his dream, Walter broke forth into a gloriously-beautiful song, perfect alike in poetic form and flowing melody, which the cobbler eagerly wrote down as he sang. When the song ended, Hans, overcome with emotion and joy, pushed the singer back into the bed-chamber, bidding him put on gala raiment and declaring himself confident of his success in the contest.

While the Knight was thus engaged, Beckmesser entered the shop, stiff from his cudgelling of the night before. He had intended to continue his quarrel with the cobbler; but seeing the newly-written song lying on the table and imagining it to have been written by Hans, his mood quickly changed and he begged to be allowed to sing this in the contest instead of his own composition. He added conceitedly that the latter was no longer likely to please his adored Eva, after its adverse rehearsal of the night before.

Hans, knowing well enough that the unmusical town clerk would never be able to enter into the spirit of Walter's love-inspired words, let him take it away with him, though bidding him to sing it to a suitable melody; and Beckmesser hurried away glad to have secured, as he imagined, a poem by Hans Sachs, who was acknowledged to be the finest poet in Nuremberg.

Later in the day, crowds of merry holiday-makers assembled in the large open meadows on the outskirts of the city, to hear the great Competition of Song so eagerly looked forward to by all. It was a wonderful scene of vivid colour, with procession after procession of the Craft Guilds forming living rainbows on either side of the great daïs of the Mastersinger judges. In the centre of the daïs, upon a throne apart, sat Eva, the fair prize-maiden, more beautiful than ever in her pure white robe; and grouped around her were a number of pretty attendant maids, likewise white-robed and flower-decked.

Amidst a sudden hush of expectancy, Hans Sachs announced again to the people the generous and soul-inspiring prize offered by the art-loving goldsmith to be awarded to the competitor whose song should be unanimously declared the most worthy of praise; and immediately the competition began.

After the candidates of the various trade guilds had been heard, Beckmesser, the town clerk, was called upon to render his contribution to the contest. Nervously unrolling the manuscript he had a morning been vainly trying to commit to memory, the self-satisfied Marker—who was by no means a favourite with the audience—stepped forward pompously and began his song. He sang it to an altogether unsuitable, discordant, and unmusical tune; and, in a frantic effort to remember the sense of what he was singing, he mixed up the words in a most hopeless manner. Finally, plunging ever deeper into the mire of confusion as he proceeded, he completely lost all sense of rhythm and converted the poem into an astonishing medley of ludicrous and meaningless balderdash.

At first the people listened in amazement, thinking that the infallible Marker, usually such a stickler for the correct rules of Mastersinging, had suddenly taken leave of his senses; and then they burst into a loud peal of derisive laughter, which completely drowned the voice of the ridiculous singer.

In a furious rage of disappointment and wounded vanity, Beckmesser flung down the manuscript at the feet of Hans Sachs, declaring that the cobbler had foisted a bad poem upon him in order to disgrace him; and then he rushed away in a storm of vexation—followed by the jeers of the crowd, who were only too glad that the fair prize was not for him.

When Beckmesser had disappeared, Hans Sachs picked up the despised poem and declared that the song was a good one, but could only be properly sung by the person who had composed it —whose name was not Hans Sachs. Then he called upon Walter von Stolzing, its composer, to sing the song and to prove that he was worthy to be called a Mastersinger.

A hum of admiration swept over the vast assembly as the young Knight, clad in dazzling raiment, stepped forward; for here, indeed, was one whose graceful form, glowing eyes, and poetry-visioned brow recalled the resplendent Minnesingers of olden times. With hearts that throbbed with excitement, they listened to the rich flood of joyous melody that now filled the summer air.

Yes, Hans Sachs was right. The song was a noble one and this was a Heaven-sent singer who laid a magic touch upon their hearts and filled them with a rapture almost too intense to be borne. Even the critical Mastersingers who had cavilled at his needless disregard of their petty rules the evening before, were now held spellbound with wonder that song could be so glorious a thing.

As the song came to an end, a deafening burst of applause broke from the assemblage who, with one accord, declared the young Knight to be the winner in the contest; and as the beautiful Eva bent forward to place, with hands that trembled with joy,

2D

the wreath of victory upon the brow of the man she loved, the acclamations broke forth again—for the pair were well matched and made a fair picture as they stood together.

Thus the Contest of Song ended; and the young Knight who had set forth so hopefully in search of Art, found also a fair bride, whose love should henceforth be the magic golden key that should unlock for him the gates of Fame, Honour, and Glory.

PARSIFAL   *Wagner*

THE Legend of the Holy Grail belongs to the early period of Christian Knighthood and Chivalry. The Holy Grail, or Sacred Cup which our Saviour had used at the Last Supper and which afterwards received the blood from His pierced side as He lay upon the Cross, was believed by many to have been brought— together with the Spear which had wounded Him—by a company of angels into the mountainous district of northern Spain. Others averred that the Chalice had originally been brought from the Holy Land by Joseph of Arimathea. Whoever were their final bearers to Spain, however, the holy relics were reverently received with joy and gratitude by the good King Titurel, who built for them a Temple-Sanctuary on Monsalvat, where they were constantly guarded and served by brave knights of stainless purity and integrity.

Great was the reward of the faithful service of these knights, for the Holy Grail possessed miraculous powers, bestowing both bodily and spiritual strength upon its guardians and giving them such means of grace that they were able to perform mighty deeds for the good of mankind. With the Sacred Spear, too, the righteous King Titurel was able to keep at bay all who were opposed to Christianity and who struggled vainly to break down his stronghold.

None but the pure and innocent could approach the holy Sanctuary, or hope to derive benefit from its Sacred Relics; for the Grail Knights, by reason of their own spotless purity, could read the hearts of all comers and would sternly repulse any who were unworthy.

Thus it came about that when the sorcerer Klingsor, the most wicked of all magicians, once sought to join the good knights in a pretended fit of remorse for his many sins but in reality for the means of worldly advancement and power, he was denied entrance to the sacred temple. The Guardians of the Grail saw clearly into the deceitful heart of the sorcerer and, reading there his impious and unholy thoughts, drove him back with horror.

Infuriated by his ignominious defeat, Klingsor determined on revenge. For this purpose he set up an enchanted castle on the southern slopes of the same mountain, surrounding it with luxuriant gardens; and in the latter flowery abodes he placed sirens of dazzling beauty who, with their seductive charms, should ensnare the Knights of the Grail who wandered that way and lure them by unholy passions and evil spells to their destruction. Many were the knights thus enticed from the paths of purity to a life of sinful pleasure and soul-destroying voluptuousness.

Thus many years passed away; and at last, good King Titurel felt himself growing too old to perform the sacred offices of the Holy Grail any longer. Therefore, he invested his son, Amfortas, the handsomest and most glorious of all the knights, with the royal mantle and made him Grail King in his stead.

The young King Amfortas, impatient of Klingsor's evil influence, determined to vanquish the wicked Enchanter and put an end to his dangerous magic. Armed with the Sacred Spear, he went fearlessly forth one day upon his great mission. But Klingsor beheld the royal Knight's approach; and he summoned to his aid Kundry, a strange being who, against her will, had ever been subservient to his power. Bidding her exercise her seductive arts upon his enemy, he had little doubt as to the issue.

Nor was he mistaken. Kundry transformed herself into a woman of such surpassing beauty that Amfortas felt his senses enthralled as he gazed upon her. It was in vain that the young King struggled to maintain his integrity and to fight against the evil influences that closed so surely around him; for Kundry never relaxed her seductions until he was fatally ensnared and locked in her embrace. Instantly stealing unawares upon his victim lying thus entranced, the fiendish Klingsor seized the Sacred Spear and stabbed him in the side with it. Then, with a triumphant cry, he returned to his enchanted castle, bearing the holy relic with him.

The wounded King was found and carried back by his faithful knights to the Sanctuary, full of remorse for his sin and doomed to suffer agonies of pain for many long, weary years; for the wound inflicted by the evil sorcerer throbbed and burned unceasingly. It could never be healed until the Sacred Spear should be reclaimed and brought back to the Sanctuary; thus the unhappy

Amfortas remained helpless and agonized in mind and body, with a wound that would not close.

Once, however, as the King lay groaning in the Sanctuary, the angels of the Holy Grail were heard once more. They proclaimed that the Sacred Spear could alone be regained by " The Guileless Fool "—one who, simple, blameless, pure, and unacquainted with worldly knowledge, should, from whole-hearted sympathy with the sufferer's agony, recognize the pitiful woes of humanity and thus bring redemption. This, then, was the one hope held out and the sublime deed to be performed; and after many long years of woe, the deliverer of Amfortas appeared.

One early dawn, Gurnemanz, one of the oldest and most revered of the Grail Knights, was resting in a glade within the sacred domains, with his esquires and other knights around him. The party awaited the arrival of Amfortas, who was to bathe in the lake near by, that its soothing waters might ease his ever-burning wound for a short time.

As they spoke together of the constant sufferings of the King, a wild female figure was seen riding furiously towards them—who, upon approaching the knights, flung herself from the foaming steed and hastened to them, bearing in her hand a small crystal vial.

This was none other than Kundry, the witch-maiden, who, when temporarily freed from the evil influence of Klingsor, would serve the Knights of the Grail as messenger and perform extraordinary feats of endurance on their behalf—as though trying to atone thereby for the wicked deeds she did when unable to resist her own sinful nature and the commands of her unholy master. She was well known to the knights—some of whom, however, regarded her with scorn and suspicion, knowing her to be a sinner; but Gurnemanz was always gentle and tolerant with her.

Kundry now appeared as a wild, half-savage creature, with long flowing locks of black hair, piercing black eyes, and clad in a fantastic robe fastened by a girdle of snake-skins. She had travelled far in search of a healing balsam for the wounded King; and as the latter was now carried to the lake-side in his litter, she handed the vial to him. The royal sufferer thanked her for the gift, though he knew it could bring him but little relief; and Kundry sank exhausted to the ground.

Presently, there came a cry, as a wild swan slowly sank dying into the thicket near by; and at the same moment, the esquires dragged forth a handsome youth, whose beauty and look of perfect innocence and purity made all regard him with interest and wonder. Yet his bow and arrows proclaimed him as the slayer of the fair bird—a species held sacred by the Guardians of the Grail.

The youth appeared unconscious that his deed was wrong; but seeing that the knights were sorrowful as they gazed at the fallen bird, his own heart was immediately touched. Suddenly breaking his bow and arrows, he impetuously flung them away. On being questioned by Gurnemanz, he declared he knew nothing of his antecedents, save that his mother's name had been " Heart-in-Sorrow " and that they had dwelt together in the forest wilds.

However, Kundry—who, in her wanderings, had gained much knowledge—now came forward and declared that the young stranger's father had fallen in battle and that his mother had brought him up in a desert place, where he could not learn the use of arms nor gain knowledge of the wicked world. Thus the lad had led the pure innocent life of nature and knew not the meaning of evil. Then, having beheld one day a party of knights in glittering armour, he had followed them, full of wonder and forgetful of the mother who so tenderly loved him—and whom Kundry now declared had died of grief at his loss.

On hearing this, the youth, now feeling sorrow for the first time in his life, sprang furiously upon Kundry; but Gurnemanz gently dragged him back. The good Knight—astonished by the utter innocence and primitive simplicity of the handsome stripling and recollecting the prophecy that one who should be a " Guileless Fool ", pure and undefiled, should alone be found worthy to regain the lost Sacred Spear—now regarded the youth with increased interest. Feeling that Heaven must have guided him to Monsalvat, he began to tell him about the Holy Grail and its wonderful powers.

Meanwhile, Kundry had crept away unperceived into the thicket; and, overcome by a deadly weariness, she sank into a deep slumber. This was the means by which Klingsor the sorcerer called her to perform his evil behests—and, struggle as she might, she could not prevail against this fatal sleep.

Having explained to the wondering youth the mysterious nourishment and power given by the Holy Grail, the uncovering of which was about to be performed by the King—who had now left the lake and was being carried back to the Temple-Sanctuary —Gurnemanz invited him to join in the sacred ceremony. He saw plainly that the young stranger had noble qualities latent in him and believed that these would be stirred into actual being by the holy influence of the Sanctuary treasures.

When they reached the magnificent hall of the Temple, the knights were already assembled, waiting with rapt and reverent attention for the customary unveiling of the Grail, by which they received physical and spiritual food and strength. The litter of Amfortas was carried forward and placed beside the holy shrine; and then the voice of the aged King Titurel was heard from a niche in the background where he sat in retirement, calling upon his sick son to uncover the Grail that its blessing might once more be bestowed upon its guardians.

At first, Amfortas, groaning with the agony of his wound, gave forth supplications to be relieved from this duty, the effort of which always increased his pain; but on being encouraged and comforted by his companions, he performed the sacred office. Raising himself painfully, he unveiled the Holy Grail and waved it reverently to and fro, thus consecrating the bread and wine—which was afterwards distributed, that all might partake of the comforting Sacrament.

As the Holy Cup was revealed, a brilliant light fell upon it, causing it to glow with a rich wine-purple colour and to shed a soft heavenly effulgence on all around; and Amfortas, though he took no part in the Love-Feast because of his still unforgiven sin, remained for some time in a state of rapt exaltation. Then, as he felt his wound break out afresh, as it ever did when he performed the sacred office, he uttered a long-drawn cry of agony and sank back, fainting and exhausted.

All this time, the stranger youth had stood apart from the ceremony, still and dazed, as though entranced; but when the wounded King's cry of anguish rang out, he placed his hand with a convulsive movement over his heart, as though filled with an emotion entirely new and strange to him.

But, though pity was thus unconsciously awakened in his breast, he did not yet understand the agonies of a conscious guilt, which was the wounded King's chief woe, nor did he comprehend the meaning of what he had just seen; and Gurnemanz, impatient at such seeming stupidity, thrust him out through a side door of the Temple, bidding him depart to his old wild ways once more—realizing that the youth must himself first experience passion and temptation and conquer the same, ere he could understand and feel sympathy for the woes and sins of others.

Nevertheless, the pity that had stirred the young man's heart so strangely for the first time grew apace; and having already learned from Gurnemanz the story of the lost Sacred Spear, he now determined to make the attempt to regain the treasure which alone could bring relief to the unhappy royal sufferer. With fearless spirit and a joyous step, therefore, he set off, alone and unafraid, to storm the enchanted castle.

. . . .

Klingsor, the sorcerer, observed the approach of the noble youth and at once recognized him as a dangerous foe; for his breast-plate was purity and his shield simplicity. Quickly he called to his aid the witch-maiden, Kundry—whom he had just awakened from the deep slumber of destiny by his magic spells—to work his evil will once more.

Though Kundry could not prevail against the terrible power of Klingsor, she only obeyed his commands in anger and horror, performing against her will wicked deeds for which, when removed from her master's influence, she tearfully endeavoured to atone by acts of mercy and service. She longed above all things to die, but could not. She who had lived through the ages and had laughed at everything good and pure—whose spirit had inspired the savage heart of Herodias and had even mocked the Saviour of the world—was now doomed to a path of evil for ever, compelled to lure all within her snares of passion and sin.

On learning that the simple Fool was to be her victim also, she now asked Klingsor in despair if she was never to be released from his toils and to find rest in eternal sleep; and the sorcerer replied that deliverance for her would only come when someone should be found strong and pure enough to resist her wiles. Feeling that this could never happen whilst she remained in the power of her evil master, Kundry uttered a cry of woe as she prepared to obey him once more; and Klingsor, from his magic tower, watched his approaching victim with malignant zest.

As the eager youth approached the enchanted castle, he found his entry opposed by the fallen knights who had been lured within its precincts by Klingsor's beautiful sirens; but snatching a sword from one of them, he quickly overcame them all. The degraded knights, once so brave and strong, had become weak through indulgence, sloth, and sin; and the fiery ardour and simple fearlessness of the young invader so daunted them that they soon fled and left him master of the situation.

Having thus triumphed over the weak outer guardians of the castle, the handsome stripling gazed proudly around him; and perceiving the magic garden close at hand, he entered it, marveling at its luxuriance. Here he was quickly surrounded by Klingsor's sirens, beautiful flower-maidens who danced before him with enchanting enticements; but the simple youth remained calmly insensible to their soft persuasions—and at last they left him in anger, deeming him to be a fool indeed.

Then, suddenly, Kundry appeared, now wearing the form of a maiden more bewitchingly lovely than any he had yet seen; and she called to him in thrilling tones by the name of "Parsifal". Remembering that this was the name by which his mother had always called him, the youth approached the dazzling vision before him, filled with wonder; and Kundry, after explaining to him that his name meant "Pure-in-Folly", told him again of his mother's love and devotion. Then, using her seductive arts to lure him into the toils of passion, she told him that his mother had entrusted her with a last message for him—and a kiss.

As the youth now sank to the ground, overcome with emotion, the enchantress bent over him passionately and pressed upon his lips his first lover's burning kiss. But this caused Parsifal to spring to his feet once more, pressing his hand to his heart—for it seemed to him that the wound of Amfortas burned there, and the thought of the suffering King's urgent need recalled his wandering senses to the great mission he had undertaken. In that critical moment, his nature seemed to change. In a flash, world-knowledge had come to him and he realized the great truth of redemption by grace—understanding that, by conquering temptation, he could become worthy of bringing salvation to the stricken King whose sufferings had first awakened sweet pity within his heart.

The temptress never ceased her wily arts for a moment, and the youth felt more and more the pangs of desire and passion burning within him; but when she again encircled him in her sensuous embrace and pressed a second long kiss upon his lips, he was awakened to the full consciousness of his danger and repulsed her with horror. Then, having thus triumphed over the desires of the flesh, Parsifal gazed upwards towards the heavens with such rapt ecstasy upon his face, that Kundry was filled with remorse for the vile part she played and looked upon him with awe and wonder.

Only for a moment, however; for the enchantress was still bound in the toils of her evil master and was compelled to obey his will. She continued her temptings, therefore; and now growing more subtle, she offered him worldly power as well as passionate love. Nevertheless, Parsifal resisted all her wiles, remaining true to his own pure and noble nature and refusing to be enticed from the path of duty and mercy which he now so clearly recognized.

Then Kundry, finding that all her arts and lures were in vain, called loudly upon her wicked master to come to her aid. The sorcerer immediately appeared on the battlements of the enchanted castle, bearing aloft the Sacred Spear; and furiously casting the stolen weapon at the youth, he likewise set his evil spells in motion against his defier.

But his magic was powerless when brought into contact with purity and faith; and the holy Spear remained suspended in the air, hovering over the head of Parsifal until the noble youth seized it in his hand and solemnly made the sign of the Cross with it. Instantly, the enchanted castle fell to the ground, shaken by a violent earthquake, while the magic garden suddenly became a desert; and as Kundry sank to the ground with a cry of woe, Parsifal hastened from the place of his temptation, triumphantly bearing aloft the Sacred Spear—with which he was now to conquer the hostile races of the world.

.   .   .   .

For many years Parsifal wandered forth alone to complete his self-imposed mission. At last, when grown to perfect manhood by suffering and sorrow, he returned to the domains of the Holy Grail Temple-Sanctuary at Monsalvat. Here he was gladly welcomed one early morning by the faithful Knight Gurnemanz, now grown to be a very old man, who had taken up his abode in the adjoining forest and become a hermit.

From old Gurnemanz, Parsifal learned that most of the Grail Knights had gradually left the Sanctuary, because Amfortas, in his agony of body and mind, had refused to perform the soul-preserving office of revealing the Holy Grail, which had formerly given them such peaceful nourishment and power. Thus the strength of the noble knights had dwindled and faded; and the aged King Titurel had already died for lack of the Grail nourishment.

Gurnemanz himself was now being served by the saddened and repentant witch-maiden Kundry. Upon being released from the evil influence of Klingsor, the old Knight had found her in her present humbled condition; and he had permitted her to perform the few menial services for him which she gratefully desired to do. Now approaching Parsifal, Kundry humbly and tenderly washed his feet, anointing them afterwards with the contents of a golden vial she drew from her bosom and drying them with her own long hair. Old Gurnemanz then took the vial from her and poured the remainder of its contents over the head of Parsifal, afterwards saluting him as King and Saviour; and the young Knight, filling his hands with water from the sacred spring near by, very gently sprinkled a few drops over the bent head of Kundry as she knelt at his feet—thus baptizing the humble sinner as his first act as the bringer of Salvation.

Gurnemanz now brought forth from the hermitage the rich scarlet mantle of the Grail Knight, with which he and Kundry proceeded to invest Parsifal over the shining armour he already wore; and they also placed in his hand the Sacred Spear from which he had never been parted since wresting it from the evil sorcerer. Then the three very solemnly bent their steps towards the Temple and entered the Sanctuary.

Here they found the Guardian Knights who still remained gathered beside the bier of the dead King Titurel, waiting for the Holy Grail to be revealed to them; but Amfortas, whose agony was now even greater than ever and who longed passionately for the death denied to him, had again refused to perform his holy office. Rising from his litter in a mad frenzy of pain and despair, he tore the covering from his wounded side and wildly implored his faithful companions to plunge their swords into his heart and end his woe.

As the knights drew back in alarm at this outburst, Parsifal stepped forward with noble and calm dignity and gently touched the suffering King's open wound with the Sacred Spear that alone had power to cure it. At the touch of the holy weapon, Amfortas felt his pains vanish and his wound close; and knowing that he was at last forgiven and restored to health, he fell upon his knees in an ecstasy of gratitude and praise.

Parsifal now assumed the office of Grail King, which was henceforth his right; and, uncovering the long-unrevealed Holy Grail, he waved the sacred chalice reverently before the kneeling knights. The Sanctuary was gradually filled with the dazzling purple light that glowed from the sacred vessel; and in the midst of this a white dove was seen to descend slowly from the dome. As the holy bird hovered over the head of the rapt Parsifal, the witch-maiden, Kundry, sank dying to the ground, at last released from the doom of evil by the noble Knight who had been strong enough to resist her wiles. At the same moment the voice of the dead King Titurel was miraculously heard pronouncing a blessing upon the new King of the Grail Knights.

Thus was the Sacred Spear restored to the Sanctuary of the Holy Grail and salvation brought to its guardians by the " Guileless Fool ", the blameless, true, and simple One, whose purity and faith had overcome temptation and whose awakened pity for the sufferings of others had revealed the real spirit of brotherly love

. . . .

It will be plain to all that the story of *Parsifal* is an allegory and that the incidents and characters in it are symbolic of human moral development, of the conquest of Good over Evil, and of the revivified spirit soaring triumphant above the baser instincts that seek to draw it back.

Amfortas represents suffering and guilty humanity. The body of humanity, grievously wounded and throbbing with the burning poison of sin, can be healed only by the restoration and touch of the Genius of Good—symbolized by the Spear—which has obtained mastery over the powerful spirits of Evil. Klingsor represents everything opposed to Goodness and Loving-kindness, being the mainspring and source of all Evil. Kundry, the instrument subject to the power of the instigator of ill, signifies the temptations that beset the seeker after Truth—those incitements against the moral law which the pilgrim can resist only with the strength given by purity and faith. Finally, Parsifal himself is typical of the Saviour of the world, the pure, guileless, and blameless One, the Conqueror of Temptation, Whose pity and love for wounded and guilty humanity brought salvation to all—Who, by redemption, threw open the gateway to eternal Life and Love.

THE RING OF THE NIBELUNGS *Wagner*
(Der Ring des Nibelungen)
Part I. The Rhinegold—(Das Rheingold)

IN the rocky depths of the wild Rhine river three lovely waternymphs—Flosshilde, Woglinde, and Wellgunde—were merrily swimming hither and thither one dusky twilight. Though it was their duty to guard a certain mighty treasure, they found their task a light one, since no one had ever sought to rob them of it.

This evening, however, a visitor came to them at last; and suddenly the Rhine nymphs ceased their gambols in great surprise, on beholding a stranger in their midst. From a deep cleft in the rocks below a hideous black gnome had appeared; for Alberich the Nibelung, being of an adventurous spirit, had wandered upwards from Nibelheim, the underground abode of the gnomes, eager for fresh exploits.

As he now gazed upon the lovely Rhine nymphs, he was suddenly filled with a longing desire to possess one of them as a bride; and, uttering a friendly greeting, he endeavoured to ingratiate himself with them. The water-maidens, however, scorned his advances, laughing at his ugly appearance; and when, incited by the fierce desire within him, he vainly tried to seize first one and then another in his grasp, they swam away merrily, leading him on with teasing taunts from rock to rock until he was quite exhausted.

Presently, on approaching a central rock, upon which the nymphs had ensconced themselves, Alberich was astonished to behold a wondrous gleam of gold issuing from its peak. Delighted by this dazzling radiance, he asked what it was. The maidens replied that the marvellous glow he saw came from the precious treasure they had been set to guard, the Rhinegold, which could only be torn from the rock by one who had forsworn for ever the delights of love. The robber might then shape from it a magic Ring that would gain him mighty power in the world.

On hearing this, Alberich, who had always longed for power, determined to gain the treasure. Loudly declaring that he renounced love and its delights for ever, he climbed the rock and by a mighty effort wrenched the magic gold from its summit. The Rhine nymphs, now powerless to protect their treasure, dived back into the water with cries of despair whilst Alberich triumphantly returned to Nibelheim with his prize.

Soon after this incident, the King of the gods, Wotan, the All-Father, entered into an agreement with two powerful giants, Fasolt and Fafnir, to build him a noble castle in Asgard, the abode of the gods; and in payment for this service, he promised to bestow upon them Freia, the goddess of Youth and Beauty.

Awakening one dawning day upon a flowery mountain-side, where he had been slumbering beside his celestial spouse, Fricka, the goddess of Marriage, Wotan saw the glittering turrets of a glorious mansion upon a distant rocky height and knew that the task was done. Arousing Fricka, he proudly pointed out to her their new abode, to which he gave the name of Valhalla.

Just then, however, the beautiful Freia fled to them for protection; and, closely pursuing her, came the two giants, demanding her as the payment agreed upon for the task they had just completed.

But Wotan now refused to give up the beloved Freia; and when the giants, furious at his refusal, again demanded their rights, he turned eagerly for help to Loki, the god of Fire and Deceit, at whose mischievous instigation he had entered into the compact. Loki had promised the great god to assist him in preventing the giants from obtaining the reward agreed upon for their labours; and he now cunningly related the story of how the Rhine nymphs had lost their magic gold to Alberich the gnome, hoping to excite the giants' interest in a treasure that could secure the holder such mighty power.

His ruse succeeded. The two giants now declared that they would accept Alberich's treasure in lieu of the goddess Freia; and they desired Wotan to set forth and rob the gnome at once.

Wotan, however, was furious on being asked to turn thief; and he angrily refused to do their bidding. Upon this, Fasolt and Fafnir suddenly seized Freia and ran off with her, declaring that they would hold her in pledge until the Rhinegold treasure was delivered to them.

A dreadful misfortune now befell the dwellers in Asgard; for Freia was the guardian of a magic apple-tree, the fruit of which, eaten daily, alone preserved their youth and immortality. Deprived of the beautiful guardian's care, the apples began to fade and die; and the gods, consequently, quickly found themselves growing old and withered as their radiant strength departed.

Full of horror, Wotan was now forced to secure the return of Freia at the price named by the giants; and, accompanied by Loki, he descended through a rocky cleft to Nibelheim.

Here the pair made their way to the cave of Alberich, whose brother, Mime, they found crouching beside his blacksmith's forge, smarting from recent blows. By this time Alberich had shaped from the Rhinegold a magic Ring of marvellous power, and by means of it had made himself the ruler of Nibelheim, forcing the unhappy gnomes to slave day and night amassing treasure-hoards for him. He had also compelled his brother, Mime, the most skilful smith in that land of forges, to make him a *Tarnhelm*, or wishing-cap, by means of which he could render himself invisible or take on the form of any creature he chose.

Having learnt this from Mime, who was even now smarting from the blows of his tyrant-brother, the two gods laid their plans; and when Alberich presently appeared, they greeted him in friendly tones and invited him to show them the wonderful powers of his *Tarnhelm*.

The gnome, proud of his new treasure, at once put on his wishing-cap, and changed himself into a dragon; and then, at the request of the cunning Loki, he unsuspectingly took on the form of a toad. However, no sooner did the toad appear, than the gods instantly seized it; then, binding their captive securely, they triumphantly bore him off to Wotan's mountain-side.

Here Alberich, though he had quickly regained his own shape, found himself a prisoner indeed, his precious *Tarnhelm* having been put out of his reach; and the exultant gods refused to set him free until he had agreed to yield up all his mighty treasures

The wretched dwarf, therefore, in order to gain his freedom, was compelled to call upon his gnome-subjects to bring forth the precious hoards they had laid up for him and to pile them in a heap upon the mountain-side.

When the *Tarnhelm* had been added to the glittering heap of gold and gems, Alberich entreated to be allowed to retain the magic Ring; and upon the request being refused, he passionately laid a curse upon the circlet, declaring that it should bring disaster and death upon every person who should afterwards own it. But, in spite of the curse, the Ring was snatched from his finger by Wotan; and then, on being set free, the hapless gnome, robbed of his power, fled back to his own land, vanishing through a cleft in the rock.

A concourse of gods and goddesses had now arrived upon the scene; and presently the giants, Fasolt and Fafnir, also arrived to claim their wages, bringing their hostage with them. At first Wotan also endeavoured to retain the Ring for himself; but the gods refused to yield Freia until they possessed this wonderful talisman as well as the other treasures. Then Erda, the wise goddess of Earth, rose slowly from the ground and warned the great god that disaster was in store for him the longer he held the now fatal talisman; and, at last, overcome by this warning, Wotan tore the Ring from his finger and flung it upon the treasure-heap.

The giants now took possession of their prize; and upon Freia being set at liberty, all the gods at once regained their pristine youth and strength.

But Alberich's curse had not been a vain one. No sooner did the giants obtain their treasure than they began to quarrel as to which should have the Ring; and, in the fight that quickly ensued, Fasolt was killed. Fafnir, the survivor, then secured the mighty hoard, together with the Ring and *Tarnhelm*, and retired to a certain gloomy cave in a wild, deserted spot; and here, in the form of a huge fiery dragon, he guarded the prize he had won.

Wotan, overawed by this immediate proof of the terrible power of Alberich's curse, began to wonder how he could preserve himself and all the gods descended from him; for he, also, had owned the fatal Ring for a time, and, god though he was, his powers were limited. Even when Fricka reminded him that the dazzling abode, Valhalla, was still left to him as a Castle of Refuge, he was little comforted, knowing that it had been obtained at a shameful price that would at length bring about the destruction of the gods —for even he, their All-Father, could not escape the curse laid upon the Ring. Nevertheless, he agreed to take possession of the castle.

As the glittering mansion was separated from the gods by the great yawning valley of the Rhine, Donner, the god of Thunder, came forward to their aid. First clearing the cloud-laden, misty air by means of a thunderstorm, he set up a dazzling rainbow-bridge from one mountain top to the other.

The bridge completely spanned the valley; and upon this beautiful arch of radiant light, the gods passed over to take possession of the glorious halls of Valhalla.

THE RING OF THE NIBELUNGS — *Wagner*
(*Der Ring des Nibelungen*)
Part II. The Valkyries—(*Die Walküre*)

ONE wild and stormy evening, Siegmund, a noble warrior-hero, flying weaponless and shieldless through a dark forest, sought refuge from his pursuing enemies in the first lonely homestead he came to. Opening the door with eager haste, he unceremoniously stepped within.

He found himself in a strange-looking room; for the house was built around a mighty ash-tree, the huge trunk of which stood as a pillar in the centre. Finding that the room was empty, Sieg-mund strode forward to the hearth; and, utterly exhausted by his late exertions and flight, he stretched himself upon a bear-skin before the fire and sank into a sweet, refreshing slumber.

Soon afterwards, there came forth from an inner chamber a beautiful but sad-looking young woman—Sieglinde, the mistress of this curious dwelling-place. Full of surprise on seeing a stranger lying upon the hearth, she called to him in a low tone.

The sound of the woman's sweet voice aroused Siegmund; and raising his head, he asked for a drink. Sieglinde quickly filled a drinking-horn with water and handed it to the warrior, who drank thirstily. Then, as Siegmund gazed upon the fair beauty of his benefactress, a thrill of delight passed through him and he asked who it was who thus restored him to life.

Sieglinde, through whose veins an answering thrill had also sped, replied that she was the wife of Hunding, a warrior, in whose house he had found shelter; and to show that he was wel-come there, she brought him a horn of foaming mead, and begged him to drink again. When Siegmund returned the horn, their eyes met in a long, passionate gaze; for love had suddenly entered their hearts and both felt that their fates would be for ever inter-twined.

As they talked together there was a quick step outside, and next moment Hunding, the warrior, entered the room. He was of a fierce, stern, and gloomy countenance; and as his eyes fell upon the stranger standing beside his hearth, a dark scowl swept over his brow. Sieglinde explained in a trembling voice that the stranger had sought shelter in their house and that she had given him refreshment; and then, extending a somewhat tardy welcome to his guest, Hunding doffed his weapons and bade his wife spread supper for them.

When the three were seated at the table, Hunding curtly demanded his guest's name and history; and Siegmund replied sadly that he was known to the world as " Woeful ", owing to his misfortunes, and that he and a beloved twin-sister had been born to a famous hero. One evening, when Woeful was still but a child, on returning from a forest·hunt with his father, a terrible sight had met their eyes. Their home had been burnt and laid waste by enemies, the beautiful mother lay dead, and no trace whatever remained of the tender little maid who had been the sunshine of their lives. Some years later, the warlike hero also suddenly disappeared; and then his unhappy son was left to struggle as best he could with the ill-luck that had followed him all his life. That evening, on passing through the forest, he had rushed to the aid of a weeping maiden, whose kinsmen were seek-ing to wed her to a man whom she abhorred; but, being over-whelmed and disarmed by the fierce tyrants, he had been com-pelled to flee for his life and take refuge in the first homestead he came to.

On hearing the last part of this story, Hunding's brow grew dark; and he declared with suppressed anger that they were his own kinsfolk whom Woeful had attacked. He added that he himself had been called to their aid, but, arriving too late to be of assistance, had returned to his house—only to find the flying foe upon his own hearth.

Siegmund, seeing that he had thus unwittingly sought shelter in the abode of an enemy, felt that his last hour had come, since he had no weapons for his defence; but Hunding, being bound by the laws of hospitality not to harm his guest till the morrow, declared that he was safe for that night, but should die with morning light.

Hunding then bade his wife prepare his evening draught and retire for the night; but as Sieglinde moved towards the inner chamber, she threw a tender, sympathizing glance upon the despondent Siegmund. Then Hunding, having seen that the door was fastened, took up his weapons with a triumphant look at his doomed guest and also departed to the sleeping-chamber; and Siegmund, left alone, sank upon the hearth with troubled thoughts.

Presently, as he lay gazing into the dying embers of the fire, the door of the inner chamber was softly opened and the beautiful Sieglinde came towards him in haste, declaring that he might now depart in safety, since Hunding lay wrapped in helpless slumber, she having mixed a narcotic with his evening draught. She added that a wonderful weapon also lay ready to his hand; and then, returning the tender glance bestowed upon her by Siegmund, she began to tell him a strange story.

On the day she was wedded to Hunding against her will—having been forced to the deed by fierce ravishers who had stolen her from her home in early childhood—a stranger, wrapped in a dark cloak, had suddenly entered this very hall. Plunging a shining sword deep down to the hilt in the ash-tree's stem, he had declared it possessed magic qualities—adding that it should become the prize of the first hero who should pluck it forth. All the warriors at the festive board had attempted to wrench the sword from its deeply-imbedded position; but in vain. Sieglinde next revealed to her rapt listener that she now realized from the kindly glance bestowed upon her by the stranger—whose features had instantly reminded her of the father from whom she had been stolen—that the magic weapon was reserved for some brave hero who should one day come to offer her his love and assistance. This hero, she added softly, her heart whispered now stood before her.

These words filled Siegmund with an intoxication of joy; and, no longer able to quell the love that already surged in his heart, he clasped the gentle speaker in his arms with rapture. Then, as Sieglinde gazed upon him with answering love in her eyes, his features and glances suddenly reminded her of the stranger who had plunged the sword in the tree; and on learning from Siegmund that his father had been known as Volsung, she exclaimed that that was the name of her own father, whose features had been so curiously reflected in those of the stranger who had appeared at her wedding feast.

Siegmund, quickly realizing that it was his long-lost twin-sister who stood beside him and whose love he had won, embraced her with even greater joy than before. Also understanding that his mysterious father, Volsung, had placed the sword in the ash-tree to be plucked thence by his own son only, he hastened to the

mighty tree and triumphantly drew forth the weapon, announcing
its name to be "Needful". Then, the enraptured lovers, hand
locked in hand, unfastened the door and rushed forth joyously
into the sweet spring night.

.   .   .   .

When Wotan had realized that the curse of the Nibelung's Ring
would eventually bring about the doom of the gods, he sought
to put off the evil day by filling Valhalla with mighty hero-
protectors. With this idea, he created a band of Valkyries, or
warrior-maidens, whose duty it was to snatch up the bodies of
fallen heroes slain in battle and carry them on their winged horses
to Valhalla. Here the dead heroes lived again and gradually
formed a mighty company of splendid warriors for the protection
of the threatened gods.

The Valkyries were nine in number and were all the daughters
of Wotan himself by the Earth goddess, Erda. They were beautiful, powerfully-built maidens of the Amazon type, wearing long
flowing robes with scintillating breast-plates and winged helmets;
and they carried shields and javelin-like spears. They uttered
awe-inspiring war-cries as they rode tempestuously through the
storm-tossed clouds on their fiery winged steeds; and they were
fearless and faithful in their service.

Despite the formation of his Valkyrie band, however, Wotan
still feared the curse of Alberich; and he began to realize that,
possibly, the final downfall of the gods could only be averted by
restoring the magic Rhinegold to the still lamenting Rhine
maidens from whom it had been wrested. For this purpose, a
hero of heroes would be required to regain the fatal treasure now
held by the dragon-giant, Fafnir.

To ensure the coming of such a mighty hero at the right time,
therefore, Wotan left Valhalla in human form as the hero Volsung
and entered into marital relations with a fair maiden of the
earth; and, though they knew him not as a god, Siegmund
and Sieglinde were his twin children by this union. Nor did
the latter know that they were destined to be the parents of the
great hero who should remove the curse of the Ring—of which
they likewise knew nothing.

As the happy lovers now fled through the moonlit forest, seeking
a place of refuge from the vengeance of Hunding—who, they
knew, would quickly follow them on awakening from the effects
of the narcotic administered by Sieglinde—they thought only of
their immediate joy. Their happiness, however, was short-lived; and
naught but disaster and misery fell to the lot of the ill-fated pair.

As soon as Wotan's celestial wife, Fricka, the goddess of

Marriage and the upholder of conjugal bonds, knew of the unholy love of Siegmund and Sieglinde and of their flight from Hunding, she was filled with indignation. Summoning her roving and inconstant husband, she poured forth angry reproaches upon him for countenancing this violation of her laws. She demanded that the recreant lovers should be overtaken and punished, and that Siegmund's magic sword should be broken; and knowing that Wotan had already despatched one of his attendant war-maidens, the beautiful Valkyrie, Brünnhilde, to assist his son against the pursuing Hunding, she bade him instantly recall her.

It was in vain that Wotan, who really loved his earth-born children, pleaded for the unhappy lovers; the angry goddess gave him no peace until he promised to cause Siegmund to be vanquished by his avenger.

So the great god reluctantly called back the Valkyrie, Brünnhilde; and when the beautiful war-maiden appeared before him, clad in dazzling mail, fully armed and mounted on her fiery celestial steed, he sadly commanded her to give assistance to the wronged Hunding instead of to Siegmund as he had at first bade her. Brünnhilde, who knew that Wotan still longed to help his son, went forth upon her mission with a heavy heart and soon came up with the fleeing lovers.

After wandering onwards for many days, only stopping for necessary rest, Siegmund and his stolen bride had at length come to a wild, rocky height; but even here they did not feel safe, for they knew that Hunding was quickly following on their track. But Sieglinde was so much exhausted by her long journey that she could go no farther; and sinking upon a sheltering ledge, she presently fell into a troubled sleep.

As Siegmund watched beside the sleeping form of his beloved one, he suddenly beheld the dazzling figure of the beautiful war-maiden, Brünnhilde; and knowing that the Valkyries only appeared to heroes doomed to fall in battle, he asked in trembling tones whom she sought. Brünnhilde answered solemnly that she had come to bear him, Siegmund the Volsung, hence with her to Valhalla, at the command of Wotan. When Siegmund eagerly asked if Sieglinde could accompany him there, she replied that the maiden must remain on earth.

Then Siegmund passionately declared that he would forgo all the celestial glories of Valhalla if he might not share them with his beloved one; adding that with his magic sword, Needful, he would gain the victory in the approaching fight and thus defeat Wotan of his prey.

When Brünnhilde thus realized what a passionate love it was that bound these two young hearts, she was filled with tender pity; and at last, after a short struggle with herself, she resolved to disobey the command of Wotan and to give her assistance to the lovers, instead of to their enemy.

Presently, the young warrior heard the sound of horn-calls coming nearer and nearer; and soon afterwards Hunding came in sight. A violent thunderstorm now began to rage and the sombre gloom of the wild scene was constantly illumined by the awful glare of lightning; but, heedless of the warring elements, Sieg-mund dashed forward to meet the vengeful Hunding as he appeared on the craggy height and quickly clashed swords with him.

The noise of the storm awakened Sieglinde; and she uttered a shriek of terror as a brilliant flash of lightning revealed to her the furiously fighting forms of Hunding and Siegmund, with the Valkyrie soaring defensively over the latter and guarding him with her shield. At this moment there was an unexpected interruption; for Wotan himself, enraged by Brünnhilde's disobedience to his will and bound by his oath to his celestial spouse, suddenly swooped down upon the combatants, with anger in his mien.

Terrified by this awful apparition of the all-powerful god, Brünnhilde retreated before him; and, as she did so, Siegmund's magic sword broke upon the outstretched mighty spear of Wotan, leaving him thus the prey of the triumphant Hunding, who quickly buried his own weapon in the defenceless breast of his enemy.

As her vanquished lover uttered his last dying gasp, Sieglinde sank senseless to the ground; but Brünnhilde snatched her up instantly, and, mounting her fiery steed that stood waiting near, rode wildly away with her prize.

For a few moments Wotan gazed down sorrowfully upon the prostrate form of the hero-son he would so gladly have saved; then, in a terrible outburst of wrath and grief, he killed the conquering Hunding and disappeared on the wings of the storm in pursuit of the flying Brünnhilde.

The beautiful war-maiden rode at desperate speed; but, after travelling an immense distance, her noble steed at last fell ex-hausted at the top of a high rocky mountain. Upon the summit of this mountain, a band of mounted Valkyries in full armour had gathered to rest on their way to Valhalla, each with the dead body of a fallen warrior lying across her saddle-bag. Mounted upon their fiery winged steeds, they had arrived there only a few moments earlier, after a thrilling ride through the furious tempest raised by the angry Wotan. To these war-maidens, her sisters, Brünnhilde hastened to beg assistance, bearing Sieglinde with her.

She quickly told them her story, and begged for a horse to continue her flight; but when the Valkyries knew that she was flying from the wrath of their beloved All-Father, they refused to give her aid, fearing lest Wotan's anger should fall upon them also did they protect one who had disobeyed him. Uttering their wild war-cries, therefore, they leapt into the air once more and soon vanished from sight.

Realizing that she could thus no longer protect the now conscious Sieglinde, Brünnhilde bade her fly onwards alone, towards a certain forest ever shunned by Wotan; and when the unhappy maiden declared that she no longer desired to live, the inspired Valkyrie earnestly besought her not to despair, for it was ordained that she should become the mother of Siegfried, the greatest hero of the world. At the same time she placed in her hands the broken pieces of Siegmund's magic sword, which she had seized as he fell to the ground; and she desired Sieglinde to keep the fragments for her son, who would forge them once more into a weapon of wondrous power.

Comforted and filled with joy on hearing this prophecy, Sieglinde was now eager to save herself from harm; and, bestowing a grateful blessing upon her self-sacrificing protector, she hastened away towards the gloomy forest indicated.

Amidst appalling thunder and lightning Wotan now appeared upon the mountain top; and as Brünnhilde stood humbly before him with downcast mien, the angry god declared that, because of her disobedience to him, she should be a Valkyrie no longer. Instead, deprived of divinity and the sweet joys of Valhalla, she should be doomed to lie in an enchanted sleep—a prize for the first passing churl to awaken and call his own.

On hearing her terrible sentence, Brünnhilde sank upon her knees. With a despairing cry, she implored the All-Father not to leave her to become the prey of any mere braggart, but to place a circle of fire around the rock upon which she must lie in charmed sleep, that she might at least not be awakened by any but a hero valiant enough to brave the flames to gain her.

For some time Wotan refused to grant her plea; but at last he yielded, overcome by the tenderness he still felt for her—for Brünnhilde had ever been the best beloved of all his war-maidens. He declared that he would call forth such fiery flames to protect her slumbers as should scare away all timid cravens; and he added that only one who had never known fear should awaken her— the greatest hero of the world. Brünnhilde was thus filled with joy and gratitude, realizing that this mighty feat was reserved for the yet unborn hero-son of Siegmund and Sieglinde.

Wotan now gently kissed the beautiful Valkyrie upon both eyes, which instantly closed in slumber; and bearing her tenderly in his arms, he laid her upon a low, moss-covered rock, covering her graceful mail-clad form with the long shield she had borne so bravely. Then, striking the rock three times with his spear, he uttered an invocation to the Fire-god Loki to come to his aid. Out leapt a stream of fiery flames, which quickly surrounded the mountain top; and with a last long look of affection at the sleeping maiden, the god returned to his celestial abode.

For years the fair Brünnhilde lay wrapped in peaceful slumber upon her fire-encircled couch; and though many bold travellers longed to possess the lovely maiden, none were found willing to brave the scorching flames—a deed that awaited the coming of the world's greatest hero, Siegfried the Fearless.

THE RING OF THE NIBELUNGS   *Wagner*
(*Der Ring des Nibelungen*)
Part III.   *Siegfried*

MIME the Nibelung stood working at his forge one summer day in the gloomy forest cavern that served him as a dwelling-place. As he hammered at a fine long sword he had laid upon the anvil, he was filled with despondency—knowing that, in spite of all his skill in forging, he could not make a sword that would not be splintered at the first mighty stroke of the noble youth for whom it was intended.

Mime, though but a hideous gnome of evil disposition and full of guile, had been the means of preserving the precious infant life of Siegfried, the promised hero-son of Siegmund and Sieglinde; and he had nourished him with great care, knowing that this child was destined, in years to come, to slay Fafnir, the giant dragon that guarded the mighty treasure of his Nibelung brother, Alberich.

He cunningly hoped by means of Siegfried to obtain this coveted treasure for himself; and so he kept the child ignorant of the secret of the Rhinegold and of his own high birth. As Siegfried grew to manhood, he had no knowledge of his true parentage, though he utterly refused to regard Mime as his father:

in spite of his protecting care, he hated the dwarf, feeling unconsciously that he had only preserved him for his own evil ends.

Mime knew this and feared him accordingly; and as he now
stood working at his forge this summer day, he trembled as he
thought of the youth's wonderful strength. Every sword he had
yet made for him, Siegfried had only contemptuously snapped
asunder.

Just as he finished the sword, Siegfried himself dashed boister-
ously into the cave, leading by a leash a great bear he had caught
in the forest; for fear was unknown to the hero-son of Sieglinde
and savage beasts he but regarded as his play-fellows.

He was a noble-looking youth of dazzling beauty, mighty
strength, and dauntless courage as befitted a descendant of the
great god, Wotan; and his contempt for the puny Mime was
quickly shown by the careless manner in which, in mere wanton
mischief, he drove the fierce bear round the cave after the wretched
gnome, who shrank back in abject fear.

At last, having laughingly driven the growling beast back to
the forest, Siegfried returned and demanded the new sword he
had bidden Mime forge for him; and the dwarf timidly handed
him the blade he had just finished, which would have been
regarded as a mighty weapon by any ordinary mortal.

But Siegfried laughed derisively as he took up the sword to test
its strength; and striking it but once upon the anvil, the steel
immediately shivered to pieces.

To stem the torrent of wrath that now burst upon him, Mime
whiningly implored Siegfried to remember the loving care he had
ever shown for him since infancy; but the youth declared that he
hated the sight of the gnome and despised the pretended love he
professed for him, since he knew him to be at heart false and evil.

He then demanded to be told who were his parents and how he
came to be left in the charge of a puny dwarf; and Mime,
terrified by the authoritative flash in the eyes of Siegfried and not
daring to deceive him longer, told him in trembling tones all that
he knew. He said that he had found in the forest one day a
beautiful woman, named Sieglinde, who lay in tears and deep
suffering; and carrying her to his cave, he had tended her with
care. She gave birth to a child during the night, and, dying
almost immediately afterwards, had left the babe to the care of
Mime, bidding him to call her son by the name of Siegfried.

Filled with emotion as he listened to this sad story, Siegfried
next demanded some proof of its truth; and very reluctantly Mime
presently produced the pieces of a broken sword, which he said
the dying woman had also left in his charge for her son—whose

hero-father, she declared, had used it in his last fight. Overjoyed by the possession of this great treasure, which proved that his father had been a noble warrior, Siegfried now commanded Mime to forge the pieces afresh into a mighty sword once more. Enthusiastically declaring that with his father's weapon he would win himself renown, he rushed forth into the forest to tell his joy to the birds and beasts he loved so well.

But Mime was left in despair; for though he had many times in secret tried to weld the broken pieces of the magic sword, Needful, he had never yet succeeded and knew it was beyond his skill to do so.

As the dwarf stood despondently at his anvil, a stranger, wrapped in a dark mantle, suddenly entered the cave and sat down to rest by the hearth; and though he called himself a Wanderer, Mime soon learnt to his terror, from the stranger's huge spear causing thunder to mutter as it struck the ground, that it was in reality the great god Wotan who had thus invaded his dwelling.

Although ill-received by the dwarf, the Wanderer calmly kept his seat; and in the course of conversation, he announced that Mime should fall a prey to the just wrath of one who had never known fear and who alone possessed the power to forge the mighty sword, Needful.

With these ominous words the stranger vanished; and as Mime shrank back to his forge, trembling, Siegfried returned from the forest and demanded his sword. The dwarf declared that he had not skill enough to forge the broken blade; and he added that it could only be restored by one who had never felt fear.

Upon Siegfried eagerly demanding what fear was, Mime tried to describe the feeling to him; and the youth declared that he had no knowledge of such tremblings but was curious to experience them. Then Mime craftily remarked that he knew of a terrible giant dragon, named Fafnir, who would quickly teach him what fearing was; and Siegfried exclaimed impetuously that the dwarf should conduct him to this monster without delay.

He then took up the fragments of the magic sword, declaring that he alone, who knew not fear, would restore the weapon; and filing down the steel, he melted it in a crucible and began to forge it afresh. Amidst the roaring of the bellows and the clang of the falling hammer, Mime sat lost in meditation, wondering how he could turn the youth's power to his own purposes; and at last an evil idea flashed across his brain.

He would let the hero slay the dragon and even secure the treasure; and then, when exhausted by his exertions, he would offer him a cooling draught containing a deadly poison, which should instantly cause his death. The great prize would thus fall into the hands of Mime the Nibelung.

Siegfried had now fashioned his sword and was singing gleefully as he hammered it on the anvil, calling it lovingly by name and finishing it off with wondrous skill; and, by the time the gnome had brewed his fatal draught, the magic blade, Needful, was completely restored.

With a loud shout of joy Siegfried seized the mighty weapon and struck it with all his force upon the anvil to test its strength; and the blow was so great that the anvil split from top to bottom and fell asunder with a terrible crash.

But Needful remained bright and unscratched; and, swinging the wonderful sword exultingly over his head, Siegfried rushed out of the cave, calling on the awed and shrinking Mime to lead him to the dragon's den. The dwarf, quickly recovering himself and remembering the prize in store for him, took up the horn containing the fatal draught he had brewed; and joining Siegfried immediately, he led him unerringly through the forest to the wild spot where Fafnir's cave was situated.

Here Alberich the Nibelung had been awaiting the dragon's death for many years; and having learnt this same day from Wotan, the Wanderer, of the near approach of Siegfried, he had slipped back into a rocky cleft to watch what happened.

Soon afterwards, Siegfried and Mime came forth from the forest; but the timid dwarf did not dare to remain long near the cave and quickly departed to hide, after telling the youth that the dragon would soon appear. The young hero presently blew a long, loud blast upon his hunting-horn; and almost immediately afterwards the terrible giant dragon, Fafnir, came out from his cave, demanding who summoned him.

Siegfried stared at the great beast in amazement; but not a single spark of alarm was in his brave heart as he boldly announced that he had come to learn what fearing was. Fafnir replied that he was overbold, since he should now serve him as food; but upon this, Siegfried, having no mind to provide a meal for the unwieldy creature, though fearless still, drew his sword, Needful, and smilingly sprang forward to meet his enemy.

With fire and poisonous fumes issuing from its nostrils, the dragon rushed upon him; but as it raised its huge body, Siegfried slashed boldly beneath the gaping jaws and buried his sword in the monster's breast.

As the dragon rolled over, dead, Siegfried drew his sword triumphantly from its body; but, in so doing, he accidentally tasted the creature's blood. Suddenly he discovered, to his joy, that he could now understand the language of the birds around him; and being especially attracted by the notes of one of them, he went nearer to listen to what it had to say. The bird told him to enter the cave and possess himself of the dragon's treasure, adding that if only he gained the *Tarnhelm* and magic Ring, he could make himself lord of the whole world.

Full of joy, Siegfried dashed into the cave; and at that moment Mime and Alberich came forth from opposite directions, scowling with surprise and anger as they recognized each other. They instantly began to quarrel as to which should have the treasure; but when Siegfried presently issued from the cave, with the Ring on his finger and the wishing-cap tucked into his belt, Alberich departed, content to let his curse take effect upon the spoiler.

As Siegfried passed under the trees, the same pretty bird again spoke to him : and this time his feathered friend warned him that Mime was his enemy and meant to poison him in order to obtain the treasures he had won. The youth, having always suspected the dwarf of evil intentions, was thus put upon his guard; and when Mime presently drew near with an insinuating smile and pleasantly offered him the horn of poison as a " cooling drink ", he instantly plunged his sword into the traitor's heart.

As the crafty dwarf fell dead at his feet, the friendly bird spoke yet once again; and in sweet, thrilling tones, it now told him of a glorious bride whom he might win—the beautiful fallen Valkyrie, Brünnhilde, who still slept upon her rocky fastness, surrounded by fire and waiting for the one fearless hero of the world to brave the flames and possess her.

Filled with rapture at the thought that the joys of love might thus be his, Siegfried eagerly desired to know in which direction so fair a prize lay; and for answer, the pretty bird spread its wings and fluttered along in front to show him the way. Through miles and miles of forest depths the feathered guide flew without resting. Then, when night had passed and the rosy dawn appeared, it suddenly vanished; and Siegfried, finding himself at the foot of a wild mountain, the rocky top of which was encircled by fire, knew that he had arrived at his goal.

As he approached the mountain-side, however, his path was suddenly blocked by a stranger. This was none other than Wotan, the Wanderer, who still roamed the world, conscious of his approaching doom, which should be brought nearer by this same radiant Volsung youth. Having vainly sought advice from the wise goddess Erda, he now half-heartedly hoped to oppose the hero himself.

Seeing a stranger barring his path with extended spear, Siegfried drew his magic blade, Needful, and with a mighty stroke hewed the spear in two pieces—upon which a blinding flash of lightning rent the air, followed by a loud crash of thunder. Knowing now that it was useless to withstand this hero-youth who had thus destroyed his weapon of power, Wotan vanished in a cloud of darkness. Retreating in despair to Valhalla, he there awaited the Twilight of the Gods, which he knew was now quickly approaching, since he, the mightiest of them all, had been defeated in combat.

But Siegfried, free to pursue his way once more, dashed joyfully up the mountain-side, and, plunging fearlessly through the fierce encircling flames, reached the rock beyond in safety. Here the Valkyrie, Brünnhilde, still lay peacefully slumbering; and, gently removing her protecting shield and helmet, Siegfried, entranced, stood gazing in breathless silence upon her dazzling loveliness. A passionate love surged up in his quickly-beating heart; and, kneeling beside the fair maiden, he pressed a tender kiss upon her lips.

Instantly Brünnhilde opened her beautiful eyes, and, rising from her rocky couch, greeted Siegfried with joy, telling him that she had loved him all through her charmed sleep, knowing that he alone should awaken her to life once more.

Then Siegfried, enraptured, clasped her in his arms, entreating her to accept his love; and though Brünnhilde at first shrank back, offended at the touch of a mortal, she could not long fight against the answering passion awakened in her own breast. Remembering that her divinity was now lost for ever, she placed her hand in Siegfried's with joy; and as the hero held his beautiful bride in his arms, he felt that the dark night-time of his early years had at last dawned into a glorious day-time of light and joy.

THE RING OF THE NIBELUNGS *Wagner*
(Der Ring des Nibelungen)
Part IV. The Twilight of the Gods—(Die Götterdämmerung)

WHEN night-time fell after the meeting of Brünnhilde and Siegfried, the three Norns, or Fates, appeared on the Valkyrie's fire-encircled rock, and, crouching amidst the rugged stones, began to sing as they spun their golden cord of the runes of Destiny. Although the radiant lovers slumbered sweetly in a neighbouring cave and all the world around seemed calm and peaceful, the weird song of the three dread Sisters was full of gloom and sadness; for they knew that, owing to the fatal power of the Nibelung's curse, disaster was about to fall—not only upon these lovers, but also upon the dwellers in Asgard, whose doom was quickly approaching.

Suddenly, as they sang, their skein of Destiny broke asunder; and, with wild, despairing cries the three Norns disappeared, knowing now that the Twilight of the Gods would soon begin.

The night wore on, and, as daylight appeared, the lovers issued from the cave: Siegfried, in full armour, with his mighty sword girdled about him, and Brünnhilde leading her horse by the bridle. For the beautiful Valkyrie would not keep her hero, dearly though she loved him, from gaining glory and honour in the world; and Siegfried, having already learned much of her divine wisdom, was now about to set forth in search of fresh exploits and adventures.

As a parting gift and as the sign of their troth, Siegfried placed upon his beloved one's finger his hard-won magic Ring, not yet knowing anything of its fatal curse; and Brünnhilde, in return, bestowed upon him her noble horse, Grani. The lovers swore to be true to one another; and then, after a passionate farewell, they parted.

After many wanderings, Siegfried, following the course of the Rhine, came to the country of the Gibichungs, or Burgundian tribe. Here a powerful King, Gunther, reigned; and with him lived his beautiful sister, Gutrune, and their half-brother, Hagen. The latter's father was none other than the crafty, avaricious Nibelung, Alberich.

Hagen, though so keen-witted as to be the chosen adviser of his royal half-brother, had also inherited the evil qualities of his greedy gnome-father. Hearing of the approach of the hero Siegfried, whose wonderful exploits were by this time world renowned, he laid a cunning plan whereby the Gibichungs might win—or at least share—the fearless one's power and wealth.

Relating the story of the fire-encircled Valkyrie, he pointed out to Gunther that Brünnhilde would make the King a radiant bride also, if Gutrune could be wedded to Siegfried, they would thus secure the Nibelung's treasure, which would bring them mastery of the whole world. He suggested that, in order to carry out this plan, they should give Siegfried, on his arrival, a magic draught they possessed, by means of which he would forget Brünnhilde and conceive a passion for Gutrune instead. Gunther and his sister, dazzled at the prospect of both being so nobly mated, gladly agreed to the scheme; and Hagen cunningly kept back from them his knowledge of the love-pact and vows of the god-like pair.

Consequently, when Siegfried arrived in the Gibichung's land, he was met on the banks of the Rhine by Hagen and conducted at once to the royal Hall; and here he received a joyous welcome from King Gunther and his fair sister.

Siegfried was greatly pleased with his kindly welcome; and when Gutrune presently offered him a well-filled drinking-horn in token of friendship and hospitality, he gladly drank off its contents to the health of his beloved Brünnhilde.

But the magic love-potion had been mingled with the draught, and no sooner had he set down the horn than the likeness of Brünnhilde faded from his mind and all memory of his love for her became a blank. It seemed to him that the fair Gutrune was the first maiden he had ever beheld; and a passionate desire to possess her suddenly grew up within him.

Gutrune beheld his ardent glances with great joy, for an answering love had quickly sprung up in her own heart for the noble hero before her. Taking her willing hand in his, Siegfried led the maiden, who now possessed his whole heart, to her royal brother, and eagerly requested her hand in marriage; and to this Gunther gave his consent on condition that the Valkyrie, Brünnhilde, was secured as a bride for himself. Siegfried gladly agreed to go through the fire once more and to woo Brünnhilde for his new friend; and when the two had sworn an oath of brotherhood, they set out together to begin their enterprise at once.

In a royal barque they sailed down the Rhine a certain distance; then when the Valkyrie's rock came in sight, Siegfried bade Gunther remain in the boat whilst he himself went forward alone to climb the mountain. By means of his *Tarnhelm*, or wishing-cap, he took on the form and appearance of Gunther—the two having agreed that the martial maiden must be wooed and won by Siegfried in the likeness of the King—and promising to be loyal and faithful to his oath, the young hero began to climb the rocky height.

Brünnhilde had just received a visit from her Valkyrie sister, Waltrauta, who had come to entreat her to restore the Nibelung's fatal Ring to the Rhine maidens once more, as the only remaining hope of saving the dwellers in Asgard. With the return of the soul-destroying magic Gold to the Rhine, its curse upon men and gods would become void.

Brünnhilde, however, cut off as she was from the joys of Valhalla, refused to part with her love-token, which was now her most cherished possession; and, despite the passionate entreaties of Valtrauta, she utterly declined to give up the Ring.

Finding that her pleading was in vain, the despairing Valkyrie was compelled to depart; and no sooner had she gone than Siegfried, in the form and garb of Gunther, sprang fearlessly through the zone of fire. Advancing towards Brünnhilde—whom he regarded as a stranger, owing to the potion he had been given by Gutrune—he announced calmly, in a disguised voice, that, having braved the flames, he had come to possess her as a bride.

Full of horror on being thus wooed by a stranger in the absence of her hero-lover, Brünnhilde shrank back and indignantly refused to yield herself to this bold intruder, receiving strength from her magic Ring; but upon her talisman being wrested from her by the superior force of Siegfried, she became powerless and was compelled to submit to his will. Siegfried now led her to the cave as their bridal chamber; but, mindful of his oath and loyalty to Gunther—whose wooing he had thus so strangely undertaken —he laid his sword, Needful, between them.

Next day, at dawn, the disguised Siegfried took the bride he had won for another by the hand and led her safely through the flames and down the mountain-side; and on being met at the river side by Gunther, he instantly vanished by means of his *Tarnhelm* and transported himself to the Gibichungs' Hall. When the true Gunther took her by the hand, therefore, Brünnhilde regarded him as her wooer of the night before; and the pair entered the barque.

*   *   *   *   *   *   *

During the absence of Gunther and Siegfried, Hagen was visited in a vision by his gnome-father, Alberich, who besought him to seek quickly an opportunity to kill Siegfried and so secure from him the magic Ring by means of which the Nibelung might regain his lost power; and Hagen gladly agreed to use his craft for this purpose.

When Gunther returned with Brünnhilde to the Gibichungs' Hall, great preparations were made to celebrate the two marriages in splendid state; and the vassals and warriors quickly assembled to join in the revels.

All this time Brünnhilde had remained submissive and downcast; but now, on entering the Hall with Gunther and finding herself confronted by Siegfried, who led Gutrune by the hand, she started violently and gazed on him with utter astonishment. Suddenly observing the magic Ring upon his finger, the true identity of the bold wooer who had intruded upon her rocky fastness

ness flashed across her mind. Full of furious anger at the discovery, she announced to all the company that she had been betrayed and that Siegfried, in his wooing of her in disguise, had dishonoured their King.

Siegfried fearlessly defended himself, declaring that he had been loyal to his trust; but his explanations were designedly confounded by Hagen, who, for his own evil purposes, used his cunning wit to persuade all that the great hero had indeed acted as a base traitor.

Siegfried, however, having a clear conscience, still declared his innocence; and taking the hand of Gutrune, whom he now loved passionately owing to the effect of the love-potion—he led her forward to join in the revels, followed by most of the company.

But Brünnhilde and Gunther remained in their places, overcome with indignation, and still believing Siegfried to be false. Seeing them alone, Hagen joined them, and with cunning words strengthened their suspicions and persuaded them that it was their duty to avenge themselves for the ill that had been done them. He at last obtained their consent to the slaying of Siegfried in retribution, which he agreed to carry out himself at a hunting-party next day; and having arranged this, they rejoined the revellers and the wedding rejoicings went forward once more.

Next day, a grand royal hunt was organized; and Siegfried, in eager pursuit of prey, found himself at one time alone on the bank of the river. As he stood there a moment, gazing into the water, the three lovely Rhine maidens, Flosshilde, Woglinde, and Wellgunde, swam towards the shore and gave him glad greeting, knowing that this was the great hero who now possessed their long-lost treasure; and in coaxing tones they entreated him to restore the magic Ring to them.

Siegfried, however, refused to listen to their pleadings, even when the nymphs told him that if he retained it longer, the talisman would quickly bring death upon him; and as the Rhine maidens swam away disconsolately, he laughed aloud at their warning.

At that moment, Gunther, Hagen, and the rest of the hunting-party joined him; and sitting down to rest upon the river bank, the huntsmen began to feast and make merry together. To amuse his new friends, Siegfried began to tell them the story of his life and adventures; but just as he was relating how he had scaled the fire-encircled mountain, Hagen crept softly behind him and suddenly stabbed him in the back with his hunting-spear—announcing to the dismayed onlookers that the deed was done in retribution for the hero's betrayal of their King.

Siegfried sank to the ground immediately; and the effect of the magic potion of forgetfulness waning as his life-blood welled forth, all his old love for the beautiful Valkyrie he had so innocently betrayed returned to bless his last moments and with Brünnhilde's name upon his lips, he died.

The dead hero's body was quickly borne back to the royal Hall; and when the fair Gutrune beheld the lifeless form of her husband of a day, she fell senseless to the ground, overcome with despair.

Hagen and Gunther now began to quarrel as to which should possess the magic Ring; and in the furious fight that ensued Gunther was killed.

Loud cries of woe quickly arose, and in the dismay and confusion that followed, Brünnhilde hastened forward. At sight of the dead Siegfried, she was filled with utmost grief; and learning from the reviving and sorrowing Gutrune of his innocence and remembering naught but her passionate love for him, she firmly resolved to perish with her hero.

In a commanding tone none dared to disobey she silenced the noise and confusion around her, and bade the warriors instantly to build up a funeral pyre upon the banks of the Rhine; and when this had been done, the dead body of Siegfried was laid upon it. She then tenderly placed his magic Ring upon her finger, and seizing a lighted torch, set the faggots ablaze.

She now understood that through her alone the sin of the great All-Father must be atoned for, and that by her sacrifice of Love the world should be redeemed. The curse of the Ring would also be removed by her death, for with her ashes the fatal Gold would be restored to the Rhine.

Thus nobly resolving to sacrifice herself, she desired two Ravens hovering near—the messengers of Wotan—to return to the great god so sadly awaiting his end and announce to him that his destiny was about to be fulfilled. Even the return of the magic Gold to the Rhine could not save the gods in Valhalla—whose ancient and sordid rule must now cease and give way to the new era of human Love. She next invoked the god Loki—who still guarded the rock upon which she had lain in her long charmed sleep—and bade him to depart instantly with his flames of fire to Valhalla.

Having thus resolved upon her act of expiation, Brünnhilde then mounted her faithful steed, Grani; and as the flames of the burning funeral pyre sprang brightly upwards, she leapt high with him into their midst to perish beside the corpse of her beloved hero-lover. As the flames died down, the river suddenly rose and overflowed its banks, covering the remains of the funeral pyre; and at the same moment the three Rhine maidens swam up to secure their long-lost Gold.

Hagen made a last frantic effort to reach the talisman by plunging into the flood; but, being seized by the nymphs, he was dragged beneath the waves and drowned.

So the Rhine maidens at last regained their precious treasure, and the curse of the Ring was removed—too late, however, for the doomed dwellers in Asgard, for Loki had already accomplished his mission.

Suddenly, a fiery, crimson glow appeared in the heavens, ever spreading and increasing to a dazzling brilliancy; and as the warriors and mourners gazed with awe upon this wondrous sight, they saw that Valhalla, with its glorious array of gods and heroes, was engulfed in an ocean of leaping flames.

The Twilight of the Gods had come!

TANNHÄUSER *Wagner*

DURING the thirteenth century there dwelt in Thuringia a handsome and noble young Knight, Henry of Tannhäuser, who was famed for his wonderful gift of song.

In a country where music was the delight of high and low, where minstrelsy and knighthood went hand in hand, Tannhäuser was the sweetest minstrel of all; and when contests of song were held, it was he who most frequently carried off the wreath of victory.

The Landgrave, or ruling Prince of Thuringia, had a beautiful niece, the young Princess Elisabeth, whose gracious custom it was to bestow the prizes won at the Tournaments of Song. Surrounded by her Court of fair maidens, she would listen with delight to the joyous strains of the minstrels.

But when Tannhäuser sounded his harp with the soft and tender touch that was his gift and the notes of his exquisite voice rang forth, the heart of the royal maiden was thrilled through and through; and she grew to love the Minstrel Knight with her whole being. And Henry of Tannhäuser trembled with joy when her fair hands placed the winner's wreath upon his brow; for he also loved, and Elisabeth of Thuringia was the queen of his heart.

Then, a curious change came over Tannhäuser. So far from

2 E

being made happy by his love, he gradually became discontented and weary of the life he was leading. It seemed as though an evil spirit tempted him from his knightly duties; and he began to long for a life of everlasting pleasure and delight. A strange but powerful enchantment had fallen upon him.

In Thuringia, there was a mountain known as the Hörselberg or Hill of Venus, within which the heathen goddess of Love and Beauty had taken up her abode and established her Court, holding everlasting revels and seeking to destroy the souls of erring men who fell into her power.

Tannhäuser was finally caught in the toils of this enchantment as he wandered along the mountain-side one day. Lured by the sound of a wonderful love-song he could not resist, sung by the tempting sirens within, he had presently found himself in the midst of the beautiful goddess's bright Court. Here, in this enticing place, many dazzling pleasures soon made him forgetful of all else.

He vanished so suddenly and entirely that none knew whither he had gone; and though his friends and companions sought him long and lovingly, they could not find him.

The Princess Elisabeth was so full of grief at his loss that she hid herself away in her own chamber to weep in secret; and though the minstrel knights still continued to hold their contests she no longer graced the festivals with her presence.

. . . .

Meanwhile, Tannhäuser was living a life of soft pleasure and voluptuous delight in the enthralling Court of Venus; and the beautiful goddess hoped that her loveliness and tender caresses would satisfy the wild longings of the handsome Minstrel Knight whose soul she wished to ensnare for ever.

For a time the young man felt that he had, indeed, found the peace and happiness he had vainly sought. The constant indulgence of his senses deadened his conscience and made him forget that duty, labour, striving, and suffering are the only true means whereby a man can attain to his highest level.

Thus, a year swiftly passed by in this abode of monotonous joys and delights, where no count was kept of days and seasons. Then, at last, a passing return of his better nature came over Tannhäuser and he awakened, as though from a trance, to the knowledge that a wasteful life of selfish pleasure cannot satisfy the longings of a noble nature.

He was kneeling, at the time, beside the fair goddess, as she reclined on a couch within the glittering abode where she held her Court; and on every side were the sights and sounds that had enthralled him so long. A wide shining lake stretched out in the distance; and in its rippling blue waters graceful Naiads disported themselves, whilst Sirens of dazzling beauty reclined on the mossy banks, their sweet silvery voices filling the air with enticing songs.

Tender lovers, wrapped in ecstasy, were reclining here and there; and a number of dainty Nymphs constantly danced around them, joined ever and anon by a train of wild Bacchantes, who brought a whirl of tumult into their movements and excited all to a perfect frenzy of joy. The sound of sensuous music never ceased for a moment; and over the whole dazzling scene a soft rosy light was shed.

Fairest of the fair and Queen of all this Love and Beauty, Venus sat enthroned in its midst; and as Tannhäuser reclined at the feet of the goddess, he felt for the moment that the world was indeed well lost.

Then, suddenly, with this passing thought of the life he had left, the Minstrel Knight awakened from his dream of bliss and seemed to hear the silvery chime of bells from the world outside, bringing back to his remembrance the fair things now lost to him—the radiant sunshine of day, the splendour of night, the renewing life of spring-time, the nightingale's song of hope and promise, the delight of joy after sorrow and of light after darkness —that only mortals know.

In a flash he saw what an evil choice he had made, how cloying were the selfish delights that now held him captive. Instantly weary of such voluptuous pleasures, he longed to be in the world once more with its mingled joys and pains—understanding now that to strive with evil and conquer was the highest human aim.

The deceptive veil of glamour was thus torn from his eyes; and full of remorse for the time he had already so foolishly wasted, he implored the beautiful goddess for freedom to return to earth.

But Venus was angry when she heard his request and re-proached him with ingratitude; and she bade him instead to take his harp once more and sing to her his songs of love and praise. To this request, Tannhäuser replied that he would evermore sing her praises; then, determined to be freed from her enslaving toils, he once more entreated her to let him return to the world, declaring that otherwise he would surely die.

When Venus thus realized that the cloying delights she had to offer could no longer hold the newly-awakened soul of Tann-häuser, she at last reluctantly granted his request—warning him angrily that he would only meet with scorn and disappointment and be glad to return to her sweet joys again. But the Minstrel

Knight announced that he could never return to her, since repentance and his hope of Heaven would now fill all his days; and with these words he bade her an everlasting farewell. Swiftly he fled from the lovely Enchantress and her glittering Court; and then, stumbling blindly into the outer darkness, he fell unconscious on the hill-side beyond.

.   .   .   .

When Tannhäuser recovered his senses, he found that it was morning and that the sun was already shining brightly. On the mountain-side a flock of sheep were feeding, whilst from a rocky peak above a joyous young shepherd piped a merry lay. The fresh green grass was spangled with early flowers and the birds were singing in the budding trees; for it was spring-time and all the world seemed full of joy.

Overcome with gratitude, Tannhäuser sank upon his knees to return thanks to Heaven for his release from selfish pleasures; and he humbly resolved to lead a new life of repentance and devotion to duty.

Whilst he thus knelt in prayer, a band of pilgrims on their way to Rome came by and wound along the mountain path above, singing a hymn of confession and repentance; and when they had gone, Tannhäuser repeated the hymn and continued to pray.

A few minutes later, it happened that the Landgrave of Thuringia and his minstrel knights passed that way on their return from a great hunt; and observing the kneeling Knight, they drew near to learn who he was and whence he came. When Tannhäuser rose and faced them, they at once recognized him as their long-lost brother minstrel, whom they had sought so vainly; and receiving him joyfully, they eagerly demanded of him where he had hidden himself so long, begging him to return with them to the castle.

Tannhäuser merely replied that he had wandered forth in search of peace and rest; and he added that he could not rejoin their beloved ranks because he had resolved to lead a pilgrim's life of devotion. Then a noble young Knight, named Wolfram, who had been his dearest friend since childhood, stepped forward and said that the fair Princess Elisabeth still mourned the absence of the favourite minstrel, whose sweet music had filled her heart with love and rapture; and he begged him to return for her sake.

The name of Elisabeth acted like a charm upon Tannhäuser; for love of this sweet royal maid still filled his whole heart, strengthened by the struggle he had recently passed through. He now flung aside his thoughts of a pilgrim's life and said that he would return to the castle with his friends.

Then the brilliant cavalcade rode forward gaily with Tannhäuser in their midst; and when the castle was reached, high revels were held in honour of the favourite Minstrel Knight's return. The chief of these was a grand Tournament of Song; and it was announced that the prize of the victor was to be the hand of the Princess Elisabeth—who, overjoyed at the return of Tannhäuser, had gladly agreed to be present and to offer her hand as the reward, knowing full well who would gain it.

When the day of the contest arrived, the whole Court assembled in the famous Hall of Song within the royal castle; and as the Princess Elisabeth entered with her train of fair maidens, she was greeted with great joy.

But Elisabeth had eyes for no one but Tannhäuser, who humbly dropped on his knees before her; and raising him gently from the ground, she told him of the woe she had suffered during his absence and of the joy she now felt at his return. When Tannhäuser heard these gracious words and knew that he might now win the hand of his dear Princess, he was full of happiness; and he told her that it was his great love that had always made his music so sweet in the old days.

The Landgrave now announced that the theme of the contest was to be the Nature and Praise of Love; and, one by one, the minstrel knights stepped forward to sing their songs.

The noble young Wolfram began the contest; and as he vainly loved the Princess Elisabeth with his whole heart, he addressed his song to her as a humble worshipper whose only desire was to adore her from afar and to live and die in her service.

The other minstrels described the nature of their pure and virtuous love in a similar strain, addressing their songs to their own lady-loves. Then Tannhäuser sprang forward and passionately disputed all that the other singers had indicated in their poems. Having loved profanely himself, he quickly grew scornful of their restrained and more spiritual conception of love. Then, impelled by a reckless audacity, he outraged the whole company by describing the voluptuous ideas of love he had gained from his recent sojourn in the Court of Venus; and, led away by his exaltation, he addressed his song to the fair goddess herself, declaring that only those who had dwelt in her abode and had experienced the joy of her enchantments were worthy to speak of love.

When his wildly sensuous but beautiful song came to an end, a loud chorus of dismay and indignation arose from the company;

and full of horror that one of their noble order had actually sojourned in the Court of the heathen goddess, the minstrel knights rushed upon Tannhäuser with drawn swords, uttering curses and declaring that the gates of Heaven were now closed on him for ever.

Instantly, the beautiful Elisabeth sprang in front of her lover; and, though utterly crushed with disappointment by his unworthiness, she bade the angry knights stand back and refrain from cursing, since repentance was still left to the unhappy sinner.

The Landgrave now pronounced sentence of banishment upon Tannhäuser; but since Elisabeth had interceded for him, he declared hers to be the voice of Heaven that held out one ray of hope. Therefore, he commanded the fallen Knight to join the band of pilgrims now passing through the land on their way to the holy shrine at Rome, and, repentant and humble, to seek forgiveness from the Pope—and not to dare to return unless such holy forgiveness was forthcoming.

Elisabeth again besought her lover to repent and to set his thoughts alone on Heaven; and Tannhäuser, full of despair, departed at once to join the ranks of the pilgrims, humbly praying as he went.

.   .   .   .

When the pilgrims had left the country, Elisabeth gave herself up entirely to Heavenly thoughts and devotions; and every day she went to kneel before a shrine at the foot of the mountain to pray that forgiveness might be granted to her lover and that he might be restored to her.

Slowly and sadly the months went by; and at last the day came on which the pilgrims were expected to pass by once more on their return from Rome.

Early in the morning Elisabeth went to the Virgin's shrine in the valley to pray; and the faithful Wolfram—who loved her still in vain—kept watch on the path above, nobly praying that Heaven would send the lovers a happy meeting.

At length a holy chant was heard in the distance; and soon afterwards the band of pilgrims came trooping down the mountain path and passed along the valley, singing songs of thankfulness because their repentance had been accepted and their sins forgiven.

Wolfram and Elisabeth eagerly scanned the passing pilgrims with anxious eyes; but Tannhäuser was not amongst them.

Full of grief and disappointment, the royal maiden now resolved to leave the outside world and seek peace in the pur calm life of a nun; and, kneeling once more before the shrine, she solemnly consecrated herself to the Virgin.

Then Elisabeth arose in peace and returned to the castle; but her heart was broken, and—woe claiming its victim—a few hours later she died in the arms of her weeping maidens.

When twilight fell, Wolfram, sad at heart, stood alone on the mountain-side; and still thinking of his lost Elisabeth, he presently broke forth into a low sweet song, calling upon the evening star to greet the passing soul of his beloved one.

The sound of the minstrel's singing caused a crouching figure, bearing a pilgrim's staff, to draw nearer. It was Tannhäuser, who had returned with the pilgrims, after all, but had kept himself apart from them, because he was still unforgiven.

On first beholding him, Wolfram drew back; but when Tannhäuser assured him that he had indeed visited the sacred shrine at Rome and had returned uncomforted, a great pity for his unhappy friend filled his heart. Tannhäuser told him that when the Pope had listened to his confession, he had said that his sin was too great for pardon. He had even declared that it was as impossible for one who had dwelt in the Court of Venus to hope for Heavenly forgiveness as it was for the rood in his own hand to put forth green leaves.

Then, scorned by one and all, with his sin still unabsolved and the hand of Elisabeth farther away from him than ever, the wretched Tannhäuser had followed in the wake of the homeward-bound pilgrims. Having finished his sad story, he now turned from his friend; and, full of despair, he called wildly upon the goddess Venus to receive him into her dazzling Court of Love once more.

In answer to his call, the sounds of enchanting music were distinctly heard issuing from the direction of the Venusburg, upon the side of which, as in a vision, the lovely form of the Enchantress became dimly visible; but Wolfram implored the despairing Knight to refrain from again sharing those evil joys that would ruin his soul, bidding him still to think only of repentance.

At this moment, the solemn funeral procession of Elisabeth came slowly by, accompanied by mourning knights and weeping maidens singing a low requiem hymn. At the same time a fresh band of pilgrims appeared on the heights above and announced that a miracle had taken place on the night of Tannhäuser's departure from Rome. The Pope's rood had burgeoned and put forth fresh green leaves by morning light; and, taking this as a sign of Heaven's favour, the Holy Father had sent messengers in haste to every part to proclaim that Tannhäuser's repentance was accepted and his sin forgiven.

Full of thankfulness that the prayers of Elisabeth had thus been answered, Wolfram joined the pilgrims in their rejoicings for the forgiven sinner; and as the dim vision of Venus vanished within her mountain depths, Tannhäuser, now filled with a wonderful peace, sank dying beside the bier of his beloved one.

TRISTAN AND ISOLDE *Wagner*
(*Tristan und Isolde*)

In the glorious days of chivalry, when King Arthur and his knights were gaining honour and renown by their noble deeds, a stately barque might have been seen one golden noontide swiftly approaching the shores of Cornwall. Tristan, a valiant Cornish Knight, far-famed for his prowess and untarnished honour, was bringing the beautiful Princess Isolde of Ireland as a bride for his uncle, King Mark, whose castle was at Tyntagel, in Cornwall. As they drew near to their native shores, the sailors broke forth into a glad song of greeting, rejoicing at the safe conclusion of their honourable mission.

But there was no joy in the heart of Tristan, who stood at the helm, silent and full of gloom. He, himself, loved this fair Princess of Ireland; but a dark blood-feud between them had forced him to stifle his own passion and to secure her as a bride for another.

A tumult was also raging in the heart of the proud Isolde. She resented the alliance that had been made for her, and was filled with anger against the Knight who came as ambassador to bear her away. They had met before, these two, and a dread secret lay between them.

For many years there had been war between Ireland and Cornwall; but at last the King of Ireland had felt himself powerful enough to claim tribute from King Mark.

Morold, the cousin and lover of Isolde, was sent to levy the tax; but he met with a sorry reception.

Tristan, the nephew and bravest Knight of King Mark, indignantly resented the claim and challenged Morold to mortal combat on the shore. To his joy, he defeated and slew the Irish

Knight, whose head was sent back as the only tribute the subjects of King Mark would pay to Ireland.

But Tristan, himself, had also been grievously wounded by his adversary; and after searching in vain for a healer for his hurts, he crawled into a small boat and set it adrift in his feverish despair. The wind and waves bore the frail craft far out from the coast; and at last the wounded Knight found himself cast upon the shores of Ireland.

Here he was hospitably received by the Irish King and his beautiful daughter, to whom he gave his name as Tantris; and the Princess Isolde, being greatly skilled in leech-craft and famous for her knowledge of balsams and simples, set herself the task of healing the stranger's wounds. His noble appearance and pitiful plight soon won her heart; and Tristan, loving the fair Princess directly he beheld her, was quick to vow fealty to her.

One day, however, as Isolde sat watching beside the couch of her charge, she noticed in the sick man's discarded sword a curiously-shaped notch, which exactly fitted a splinter of steel that had been found imbedded in the skull of Morold—whose head had lately arrived from Cornwall as a ghastly token of defeat and defiance.

Knowing now that it was the world-renowned Tristan, the slayer of her cousin and former lover, Morold, who lay before her and whom she had nursed so tenderly, Isolde was filled with scorn and anger; and seizing the tell-tale sword in her hand, she rushed furiously forward, intending to plunge it in his heart. But Tristan's eyes met hers in such a pleading, helpless glance that the angry Princess was quickly filled with pity and felt she could not harm him as he lay thus in feebleness; and letting the sword drop gently to the ground, she crushed her revengeful feelings and continued her nursing of the sick man. Yet Tristan did not dare to speak of love to her again, feeling that Isolde would now regard his slaying of Morold as a blood-feud and barrier between them; and as soon as his wounds were sufficiently healed, he returned to Cornwall.

Soon after this, peace was declared between the two countries; and as the crowning pledge of the truce, King Mark was persuaded by his knights to ask the hand of the Princess Isolde in marriage. Tristan joined heartily in pressing forward this plan; believing that Isolde was now lost to him, he felt that he could reward her best for her kindness to him by making her Queen of Cornwall.

But King Mark was growing old, and, being childless, had decided to make Tristan his heir; and it was not until his beloved nephew likewise entreated him to heed the desires of his counsellors that he at length gave consent. Then, when peace and friendship had been sworn by both nations, and the King of Ireland had willingly agreed to bestow his daughter upon King Mark as the pledge of their truce, Tristan was despatched in a gilded barge to conduct the lovely bride to her new home.

Isolde submitted to her father's will with due filial obedience and reverence; but her heart was filled with scorn and hot anger against the brave Knight she had nursed back to life and health. As she now reclined in her curtained recess within the stately vessel that bore her so swiftly away from her native land, she declared passionately to her attendant handmaid, Brangæna, that she had been betrayed by Tristan; after vowing fealty to her in Ireland, he had but returned to demand her in marriage for his kinsman. Brangæna, alarmed by this outburst, attempted to sooth her mistress's angry feelings by assuring her that Sir Tristan had doubtless meant to show his gratitude by making her Queen of Cornwall; and she added that King Mark, though advancing in years, was good and noble in disposition and worthy of admiration and regard.

But Isolde gazed impatiently beyond the curtains at the silent, motionless figure of Tristan, wondering sadly how she could support a loveless life so near that glorious Knight, who now seemed so indifferent to her; for Tristan, struggling to repress the love in his heart, had kept sternly aloof from his fair charge throughout the voyage, fearing to trust himself in her presence. This studied coldness enraged the proud and unhappy Princess to such a pitch that she determined they should die together before landing in Cornwall; and she sent Brangæna to the helm to command Tristan's immediate presence in her recess.

At first Tristan refused to leave the helm, remembering his duty and loyalty to his royal uncle; but when, just as they were approaching the shore, Isolde sent another message, imperiously declaring that she would not land in Cornwall unless he sought her pardon first, the unhappy Knight was forced to yield to her request.

Isolde meanwhile opened her casket of drugs and simples, saying she desired a potion that would cure her of all her woes; and selecting a phial containing a deadly poison, she bade Brangæna pour it out into a golden cup.

But Brangæna was horror-struck; and, determined to save her beloved mistress from the consequences of so rash a resolve, she poured away the poison, unseen by Isolde. She then filled the golden cup instead with a love-philtre that the Queen of Ireland skilled in sorcery, had placed in the casket for the young Princess to drink with her husband on her wedding-night.

When Tristan appeared within the recess, Isolde began to pour forth bitter words of reproach upon him, declaring that though she had preserved his life when he lay in feebleness before her, she had still sworn vengeance upon him. Then, offering him the golden cup, she bade him drink its contents with her as a final truce to all their strife. The ship was by this time at the landing-stage, where King Mark already stood with his lords, waiting to receive his lovely bride; and, full of despair, Tristan took the proffered cup and began to drink.

When he had swallowed half the draught, Isolde snatched the goblet from his trembling hand and drank the remainder; and then the two stood and gazed into each other's eyes in wonder and bewilderment. The strange potion was coursing wildly through their veins like a fiery stream, changing all their dull despair into the glow of passion and filling their hearts with uncontrollable love and desire for one another; and at last, utterly powerless to fight against the ecstasy within them, they fell into each other's arms, overcome by a rapture they could not quell.

Brangæna, dismayed by the dire result of her fond deed, implored the lovers to recollect their duty and the scene that was going on around them—for the lords and attendants on shore were now waiting for Tristan to conduct his royal charge to King Mark.

The pair seemed wrapped in a sweet dream from which the joyous cries of greeting gradually awakened them; and then, when they realized what had happened, they were filled with despair and Isolde sank back half-fainting into Tristan's outstretched arms.

But Brangæna, eager to prevent the immediate discovery of their hapless love, quickly roused her mistress and hung upon her shoulders the gorgeous royal mantle that had been provided for her nuptials. Then Tristan, as in a trance, with woe in his heart, led his beloved one forth from the ship and delivered her into the hands of his Sovereign.

. . . .

Isolde and King Mark were immediately wedded, amidst great rejoicings; but although the unhappy victims of the fatal love-potion had strength loyally to fulfil this pledge of peace between the two countries, they could not long keep their devouring passion within bounds. With the help of the devoted and remorseful Brangæna, they frequently met in secret; and the rapture of these stolen interviews was as balm to their bleeding hearts.

But Tristan had an enemy, a knight named Melot, who, under

the guise of friendship, had gained his confidence and learned the secret of his hopeless passion. This false knight, having no real love for the man he called his friend, determined to use the woeful secret for his own base ends. For Melot was jealous of the renown and noble qualities of Tristan and longed to supplant him in the regard of their royal master. Having now discovered a weapon to his hand, he eagerly sought and found an opportunity for betraying him.

Having persuaded the King to arrange a royal hunt one beautiful summer night, the crafty Melot easily induced Tristan to remain behind and thus secure a long sweet interview with his beloved Isolde. Then the false friend himself departed to join in the chase, intending to return in a short time with the King to entrap the lovers.

When the hunting-party had disappeared into the depths of the forest, Isolde emerged from the silent castle, followed by her handmaid; and bidding Brangæna keep watch near the forest, she flung a lighted torch to the ground, this being the signal for Tristan's approach. She then ran eagerly towards a moon-lit avenue, and in another moment the lovers were clasped in each other's arms.

It was a moment of intense joy; and the enraptured pair poured out to one another in tenderest phrases the passionate love they were compelled to keep pent within their hearts before the eyes of the Court. It was midnight; but the happy lovers cared naught for time and would gladly have remained in such sweet converse for ever.

Suddenly, however, there was a cry of alarm from Brangæna, who ran towards them declaring that they were betrayed. Next moment, King Mark and a few of his lords broke hastily into the avenue, having been led to the spot by Melot—who had found an opportunity during the progress of the hunt to inform his royal master of the lovers' intended meeting.

At first King Mark had refused to believe that his noblest and best-beloved Knight could thus seek to tarnish his honour. As he stepped into the avenue, however, and the living proof of it met his gaze, he was filled with deepest grief and began to pour forth bitter reproaches upon the betrayed Tristan.

Stung by the just reproaches of the King and enraged by the cruel treachery of his false friend, Tristan drew his sword and challenged Melot to fight. In his despair, caring little to defend himself, he allowed his adversary to overcome him and soon fell to the ground, mortally wounded.

Isolde was borne back, dazed and despairing, to the castle,

followed by King Mark and his lords; and Tristan was carried, in a dying condition, on board a vessel by his faithful henchman, Kurvenal, who quickly set sail for Brittany, where his master owned a castle overlooking the sea.

Having brought the wounded Tristan in safety to his castle in Brittany, Kurvenal vainly endeavoured to restore him to health. Soon realizing, however, that his beloved master's wounds were too serious for him to heal and that he grew worse instead of better, the devoted henchman was in despair. Then, at last, he bethought him to send for Isolde, whom he knew to be greatly skilled in leech-craft. Thinking only of his master's immediate bodily needs, he despatched a messenger in a swift vessel to entreat the beautiful Queen to come and heal her almost dying lover.

For several days longer, Tristan remained in an unconscious state; but upon being brought out on to an open terrace one sunny noontide, he awoke from his torpor and feebly asked for Isolde. Kurvenal answered that he had sent for her to come with healing balsams for his wounds; and, running to the walls, he exclaimed joyfully that the vessel was even now returning with Isolde on board.

Tristan was overjoyed at this glad news; and when Kurvenal presently went to receive the welcome guest at the castle gates, the wounded man's excitement knew no bounds. In his eagerness to see his beloved one once again, he endeavoured to crawl from the couch; but the effort of moving caused his terrible wounds to open afresh. Just as Isolde rushed through the gateway, he uttered her name with a gasping cry of joy and fell back dead upon the couch.

Isolde, with a loud shriek of woe, fell fainting upon his prostrate body. At that moment Kurvenal was hailed from a second vessel that had immediately followed in the wake of the first. On this barque were King Mark with his knights, and also Brangæna; and quickly surmising that they were come with hostile intentions, the brave henchman barricaded the entrance to the castle and refused admittance to the newcomers, who had instantly landed.

When the knights, by their superior force, broke through the barricade, Kurvenal sprang furiously upon them and fought desperately, in spite of their cries that they came in peace. The first to enter was the traitor, Melot; and with a cry of triumph, Kurvenal thrust him through the heart. Then receiving a mortal wound himself, the faithful henchman crawled to the couch of the dead Tristan, and, feeling for his beloved master's hand, sank dying beside him.

King Mark and his party now pushed forward, unhindered; and Brangæna, raising her still breathing mistress in her arms, besought her to revive, declaring she had good news for her. Upon the flight of the latter to the aid of Tristan, the handmaid had, in desperation, revealed to King Mark how, quite unconsciously, Tristan and Isolde had swallowed the magic potion that had made them lovers for life. Rejoicing thus to learn that his best-loved Knight and his beautiful Queen were free from blame—being powerless to struggle against the mighty philtre—the noble-hearted King was filled with pity for the sufferings they had endured. He resolved generously to renounce Isolde and permit the lovers to be united; and immediately entering a ship, he had followed with Brangæna and his knights in the wake of the unhappy Queen.

But the vessel arrived too late, for Tristan was already dead; and, overcome with grief, King Mark knelt with bowed head at the foot of the couch. It was in vain, too, that Brangæna tried to raise the quivering form of her beloved mistress. Isolde's heart was broken; and, with a last despairing cry, she fell back lifeless to the ground.

Thus had the magic philtre wrought destruction; and in death only were the lovers united.

LURLINE   *Wallace*

BENEATH the billows of the great Rhine River dwelt the King of the Water Spirits, Rhineberg the Powerful. For him the gnome of the underworld and the sea had gathered together wonderful treasures of gold and jewels, such as were not even dreamed of by mortals; and here in his palace of crystal and pearl he held mighty sway.

It was a merry Court he held; for his beautiful daughter, Lurline, the fairest of all the river nymphs, loved to dance upon the sparkling floors with her attendant nymphs and to sing to the music of the flowing waves.

But at last there came a change, and Lurline was merry no longer. One evening, the fair nymph rested upon the Lurleberg, a rock that jutted over a whirlpool, playing upon her harp and singing the thrilling song of enchantment with which she lured her mortal victims to destruction at the bidding of her powerful spirit father. Presently, a handsome young nobleman named Rudolph sailed by in an airy skiff; and as Lurline gazed upon the exquisite beauty of this youth, a passionate love for him grew up in her heart. Dropping her harp just as her song had begun to enthral him, she could no longer bear to lure him to his doom.

After this she grew sad and sighed for the Count Rudolph with every breath; and when the Rhine King knew that his daughter loved a mortal, he was filled with dismay and anger. Finding, however, that in spite of his reproaches Lurline could not forget the beautiful youth she had seen, he gave her permission to seek him out in his own home—hoping that she would quickly discover mortal love to be but a frail, unworthy thing and would then renounce it. The water maiden gladly availed herself of her father's permission, and went forth to seek her earthly lover.

Meanwhile, the young Count Rudolph was passing through a time of difficulty and trouble. Having spent his wealth on the gay pleasures of youth, he had no longer the necessary means to keep up proper state in his ancient castle home. Thinking to mend his fortunes by making a wealthy marriage, he began to pay his addresses to Lady Ghiva, the daughter of an old Baron whom he believed to be very rich but who was in reality quite as poor as himself; and his wooing was acceptable to the haughty Ghiva, who had long cherished admiration and affection for the handsome youth, believing him also to be rich enough to satisfy all her wants.

When, however, at a festive ball given by the Baron in his honour, Rudolph laid his heart at her feet but declared that he had no great wealth to offer her, the disappointed lady refused him with disdain; and Rudolph returned to his castle in chagrin. His merry companions, however, sought to cheer his drooping spirits with lively songs and revelry; but Rudolph found comfort from another source.

There suddenly came into his mind the memory of that evening, when, as he rowed himself in his skiff upon the Rhine, he had heard the thrilling, enticing voice of a water nymph; and as the words of her sweet song now came back to him, he began to sing them to his companions, who listened to him in delight.

But soon their delight was changed into dismay. As the young Count sang the words of this strange sweet song, Lurline herself suddenly appeared in the banqueting-hall, as though in answer to his call.

The lovely water nymph at once approached Rudolph and began to weave a spell of enchantment over him; and having placed a magic ring upon his finger as a talisman against all danger, she disappeared as suddenly as she had come.

But her thrilling voice, singing to the accompaniment of a magic harp, could be heard calling from the river; and Rudolph, on recovering from the stupor into which he had been thrown, now became so violently enamoured of the beautiful nymph that he sprang from his seat and rushed down to the shore, following the sound of her luring song with ecstasy.

His friends, fearing that he was being enticed to destruction, endeavoured to check his impetuous course and to hold him back from danger; but Rudolph, reckless of what lay before him and intoxicated with the charm of the water maiden's irresistible song, flung all detaining hands from him and plunged eagerly into the river. The waves of the Lurlei-berg whirlpool flowed over him, but were powerless to harm him because of the magic ring he wore; and Lurline, full of joy, conveyed him to her own palace of corals, where they spent together a period of delirious happiness.

Then, one day, Rudolph heard the voices of his old companions mourning his loss as they sadly rowed overhead in their skiffs; and, longing to greet them once again, he begged the lovely Lurline to permit him to leave her for a few days, promising to return to her.

Lurline, though fearful of being parted from the mortal lover she adored, yet could not bear to cause him pain by refusing his request; so she gave her consent, declaring that she would await his return at the end of three days on the Lurlei-berg.

Rudolph now desired to take back with him some of the lavish wealth he saw around him; and Lurline, having been given the keys of her father's treasure-chambers during the latter's temporary absence, took him therein to take his fill.

As it happened, Rhineberg returned at that moment and was enraged on discovering what the lovers were about; but when Lurline pleaded for pardon he could not resist her sweet charm. Finally, at her request, he gave Rudolph vast treasures to take back with him to his castle.

The young Count then departed; and on his arrival at his home the news of his altered fortunes quickly spread. The Baron and his daughter Ghiva were now very anxious to encourage the suitor they had formerly rejected; and to them Rudolph revealed the secret of his newly-acquired wealth, showing them the magic ring he had received from Lurline and singing the praises of the lovely water nymph so rapturously that the Baron's daughter was quickly filled with a consuming jealousy. Snatching the ring from his finger, she furiously flung it into the midst of the river.

With the loss of the magic ring the spell of Lurline departed also; and Rudolph, forgetful of his love for the fair nymph, began to find pleasure in the advances made by the cunning Ghiva and to engage in revellings and feastings once more.

In the meantime, fair Lurline sat upon the Lurlei-berg rock, singing her sweet love-songs as she patiently awaited the return of the mortal she adored. One day, however, when a slave-gnome of her father's brought to her the magic ring she had given to Rudolph, having found it in the river, she could not help but believe her lover to be faithless.

Filled with woe, yet enraged that her love should have been slighted by a mortal, she resolved to seek out Rudolph once more and to reproach him for his faithlessness.

Accordingly, she appeared at a splendid festival which was being held on the banks of the Rhine, in honour of the young Count's birthday. Quickly approaching Rudolph, she began to pour bitter reproaches upon him for deserting her loving arms for the sake of his mortal companions—some of whom, she informed him, were even now plotting his assassination that they might seize his treasures.

Her wrath, however, vanished when Rudolph explained how his magic ring had been taken from him by force and declared that he still loved her with his whole heart; for the magic charm of her sweet presence had once more enveloped the young Count and he felt that her love alone could satisfy the longings of his heart.

Meanwhile, his false companions, as he had been warned by Lurline, were even now hatching a plot to murder him and seize his wealth. Their plans, however, were overheard by the Lady Ghiva and her father, who quickly informed Rudolph of his danger and besought him to save his life by instant flight.

But the young Count declared that he would rather die by the side of his beloved Lurline than run away as a coward; and, boldly drawing his sword, he met his enemies undaunted.

Then Lurline, knowing that her lover's life was in utmost danger, took up her harp, and sang a wild song of invocation to the Spirits of the Rhine. In answer to her call, the river suddenly rose in a mighty flood and immersed the would-be murderers.

When the waters had once more returned to their accustomed bounds, Rhineberg, the River King, appeared; and, to the great joy of the lovers, he now gave his gracious consent to their union.

Thus did Lurline, the lovely Daughter of the Rhine, secure her heart's desire; and as she gazed into the eyes of her mortal lover, she knew that she had not lived in vain, since she had gained the greatest of all treasures—the jewel of Love.

MARITANA   *Wallace*

TOWARDS the end of the seventeenth century, when Charles II was reigning in Spain, a wandering tribe of gipsies appeared in the romantic city of Madrid. Every day they were to be seen in the streets and public squares, amusing the light-hearted populace with their merry songs and dances.

With this tribe there came a beautiful young girl named Maritana, who possessed a voice of unusual charm and sweetness; and in a short time the enchanting singing and fair looks of the pretty gipsy maiden had won the hearts of all. Every day Maritana sang and danced before delighted crowds; and even the Queen, as she drove by with her ladies, would stop her State coach to listen for a few moments to the dainty gipsy.

As for the gay young King of Spain, Charles II, he was so enchanted by the dazzling beauty of Maritana that he could not get her out of his mind; and several times he went into the streets in disguise, mingling with the crowds that applauded the gipsy maid, in the hope of gaining acquaintance with her.

On one of these occasions he was seen and recognized, despite his disguise, by the Chief Minister of State, Don José de Santarem; and this wily nobleman, realizing that his royal master was infatuated with the fair Maritana, determined to turn this fact to his own advantage by aiding the King in the latter's clandestine love adventure.

It happened that Don José secretly loved the cold and stately Queen, whom the pleasure-loving King had already begun to neglect; but, so far, his efforts to gain her favour had proved in vain, for the proud, exalted lady refused even to smile upon him. However, on observing the King paying court to the pretty gipsy girl, a cunning scheme presented itself to the unscrupulous Minister. By encouraging this temporary infatuation and bringing it to its logical conclusion, might not the Queen, when made aware of her royal husband's faithlessness, be persuaded to take a lover herself in reprisal? If so, that lover should be Don José de Santarem!

Having thus resolved, Don José sought an early opportunity of making friends with Maritana and of gaining her confidence. He praised her beauty and her lovely voice; and on learning that she longed to become a fine lady and to wear jewels and rich raiment he promised to secure for her all these things if she would trust her fortunes to him and let him advise her.

Maritana merrily replied that she would gladly accept any such good fortune he might offer her; and then she ran off to sing and dance in another street.

No sooner had she departed than a handsome, but dissipated-looking roisterer—whose once gay garments showed signs of poverty and riotous living but who yet preserved a certain dignity and charm of manner—issued forth from a tavern close by, declaring to the bystanders that he had just lost his last coin to gamblers. Don José, to his amazement, recognized in this shabby, yet debonair cavalier an acquaintance of his early youth, Don César de Bazan, a nobleman of equal rank with himself. Thinking he might be useful to him, he quickly made himself known.

Don César, who was of a sunny-hearted, careless disposition, soon explained to his old acquaintance the reasons for his present poverty—declaring candidly that gay living and over-generosity to friends had quickly exhausted the fine fortune he had inherited, and that, in order to escape his numerous creditors, he was now compelled to travel from place to place.

As it was some years since he had been in Madrid, he asked if there was any news in the city; and Don José replied: " None; except that the King has issued an edict against duelling. Every survivor of a duel is to be shot—unless it takes place in Holy Week, when he is to be hanged instead."

It happened that Don César was an expert duellist and famed for the number of his encounters. On hearing this news, therefore, he said with a laugh and a shrug of his shoulders: " Why, then, I must avoid a quarrel; for it is Holy Week now and it would be a dire dishonour for the last of my family to be hanged! "

At this moment there was a loud outcry as a boatman appeared in the square, dragging with him a wretched youth whom he had just rescued from attempting to drown himself; and close upon his heels followed the Captain of the Guard, into whose hands he was about to deliver the culprit to be brought up for punishment.

The unhappy boy—whose name was Lazarillo—begged wildly to be set free, declaring that a harsh master's ill-treatment had made him long to destroy himself but that he would make no more such attempts if he could be released.

On hearing his pitiful story and sad cries, Don César, who had a tender and generous heart, hastened to his assistance and freed him from his captor. The Captain of the Guard angrily commanded this unexpected champion to deliver the boy up for judgment, that he might be punished for his offence; but Don César, furious on being thus addressed by one he deemed his social inferior, instantly drew his sword and haughtily declared that he meant to protect the helpless youth.

A hot quarrel now ensued, and a few moments later the two were engaged in a duel—despite Don José's repeated warnings about the King's edict and the special penalty of Holy Week. Don César, with a few skilful strokes, easily despatched his adversary; but before he had time to escape, he was surrounded and captured by the city guards, who quickly bore him off to the prison-house. Here he was thrown into a cell, together with the unfortunate youth whose cause he had championed so recklessly and who now refused to leave him; and having thus flagrantly defied the King's edict, he was immediately condemned to death and sentenced to be hanged the following morning at seven o'clock.

Don José, so far from grieving for the terrible misfortune that had befallen his one-time friend, at first cared naught about the matter; then, suddenly seeing in this incident a means of furthering his own base schemes, he determined to make a strange offer to the doomed man. If he could arrange to have the beautiful gipsy girl married to Don César de Bazan within the next few hours, all his plans would go well. As the widow of a Grandee of Spain, Maritana would be entitled to a high position at Court and thus be brought into daily contact with the King—who would then be constantly under the spell of her fascinating beauty.

Having carefully made his plans, the wily Minister repaired to the prison-house at five o'clock next morning; and, armed with all authority as the King's Chief Minister, he made his way to the condemned Count's cell. He found Don César already awake and talking cheerfully to the young Lazarillo in his usual gay and careless manner, quite regardless of his quickly-approaching end; and, hurrying forward, he greeted him pleasantly, announcing that he had come to serve him.

Don César replied merrily that there was little in which a dying man could be served; but he added that he should be grateful if the Minister would take the boy, Lazarillo, into his service and protect him. Don José readily agreed to this; and next he cunningly asked if the Count were satisfied to die by hanging—the death meted out to outcasts and low-born rogues.

The haughty family pride of Don César was stung by this subtle taunt, for it was galling to him beyond measure to bring such a disgrace upon his ancient name; and he eagerly besought his old friend to entreat the King to grant him the privilege of being shot instead of hanged, as befitted a noble of Spain—adding dramatically: " Yes, let me like a soldier fall! "

Then Don José announced that he could obtain this favour for him, but only on condition that he married before his execution and that he asked no questions whatever about his bride, who would be thickly veiled; and Don César, glad to secure a soldier's death even upon such strange terms as these, willingly agreed. He at once retired to a small inner chamber to dress himself in the handsome wedding garments which the cunning Minister had already ordered to be brought there. He also requested that his guards and executioners might be permitted to join him in his last meal; and Don José, delighted by the success of his scheme, gave instructions for a fine feast to be served immediately. He then hurried away to find Maritana.

Just as he was leaving the prison a sealed packet was handed to him; and, upon opening it, he found that it contained a free pardon from the King for Don César. Knowing that this unexpected development would spoil all his fine plans, the ruthless Minister determined that the pardon should not arrive at the prison until the execution had already taken place; and thrusting the document within the folds of his tunic, to be forwarded later, he went on his way.

On hearing that such a brilliant marriage with a Grandee of Spain was in store for her, Maritana was at first filled with joy—or, although she had seen the capture of Don César the day before and had even pleaded for his release, she had not heard his name spoken and knew naught of his death sentence. When, however, Don José added that, for certain State reasons, she must immediately go through the ceremony thickly veiled and not behold her bridegroom until some days later, she grew suspicious and said she did not like such mystery.

Then the cunning Minister, to relieve her fears, declared that it was the express wish of the Queen that she should go through this ceremony and obey all his directions, however strange they might seem; and Maritana, who was grateful to the Queen for noticing her singing in the streets, now willingly gave her consent—innocently believing that even such an unusual marriage as this must be in order if it was the royal command. Consequently, she allowed herself to be dressed in a fine wedding-robe and to be so heavily veiled that her features were completely hidden. Then Don José took her to the prison-house, together with a priest.

It was now about six o'clock; and Don César was already carousing merrily with the soldiers who were to shoot him an hour later. The doomed man was quite in his usual good spirits and determined to enjoy the last minutes of his life; but the boy, Lazarillo, was too sad to join in the feasting. Within the youth's heart there had blossomed such deep gratitude and love for his generous and kindly protector that he could not bear to think of the latter's quickly-approaching death; and he longed to discover some means of saving him. As he gazed helplessly around the prison-room, his eyes fell upon the arquebuses with which the fatal volley would presently be fired; and at the sight of these dreaded weapons piled carelessly in a dark corner, a sudden thought flashed through his quick brain. Making his way quietly, with seeming carelessness, to the arquebuses, he dexterously managed to extract all the bullets, unnoticed by any of the merry feasters; then, delighted with his clever trick, he awaited an opportunity of informing the intended victim of what he had done.

When the Minister entered the room with the trembling, closely-veiled Maritana, the revellers received them with gay acclamations; and quickly the bride and bridegroom were led into the prison chapel to be wedded. Neither could behold the other because of the thick veil that enveloped Maritana; but Don César felt that his mysterious bride must be fair and charming to look upon, because several long locks of bright hair had managed to escape confinement, the hand she placed in his was small and soft, and her voice was full of music.

Maritana also was thrilled by the touch and voice of Don César and when, after the ceremony, she was hurried away by the exultant Don José, she longed for the time to come when she should see her husband face to face—for the cunning Minister had told her nothing of Don César's doom, but led her to suppose that she would soon enjoy his company.

The hour had now arrived for the execution of Don César, who went forth to his mock death with a gay heart—for, by this time, Lazarillo had found an opportunity of telling him of how he had tampered with the arquebuses. Therefore, though inwardly full of mirth, he pretended to be suitably subdued and bade a sorrowful farewell to all around him; then, when the volley was fired, he fell to the ground at once, feigning death.

The executioners did not approach to examine the supposed corpse, but returned to the prison immediately; and when they had gone and the coast was clear, the bold Don César calmly got up and walked away! He kept in the shadows and finally managed to get safely away from the prison grounds. Having thus escaped with his life, he determined to find his mysterious bride and hurry from Madrid before recapture became possible.

Knowing nothing of the pardon that had been granted to him, he dared not show himself in daylight, but kept in hiding until evening; then he issued forth cautiously in search of Lazarillo, whom he knew would now be in the service of the Minister.

Don José had laid his plans with great skill. Knowing that a certain dependant of his, the Marquis de Montefiori, upon whom he had bestowed a remunerative appointment, was holding a grand reception that evening, he decided that Maritana should be introduced to this assembly as the Marquis's niece.

Accordingly, when evening fell, he repaired with the gipsy girl, splendidly attired, to the festive scene; and after an amusing argument with the Marquis—who declared that he had no niece!—the bewildered Maritana was accepted by the latter and led by him to the *salon* to be introduced to the assembled guests.

Don José was just about to follow, when a stranger, muffled in the robe of a monk, suddenly entered the ante-room; and, to his surprise and dismay, he quickly recognized in this intruder the handsome features of Don César de Bazan! Gaily relating the story of Lazarillo's trick and of his own feigned death, the elusive Count announced that he had come for his bride.

For a moment, Don José was nonplussed, knowing that if Maritana were taken away now, his own base plans regarding the Queen would fall to the ground. Quickly devising a means of escape, however, he sought out the Marchioness de Montefiori—likewise one of his tools—and bringing her into the ante-room, introduced her with much ceremony as the Countess de Bazan.

It happened that the Marchioness was elderly, ugly, silly, and frivolous; and when Don César understood that he had been wedded to such an unattractive person, he was filled with dismay. He agreed, therefore, to sign a contract suggested by the quick-witted Minister whereby he undertook to relinquish his newly-made wife and to quit Madrid for ever in exchange for a yearly sum of money to be paid in compensation.

Before the paper was signed, however, Maritana's sweet voice was heard singing in the *salon* beyond; and, instantly recognizing the voice as that of his mysterious veiled bride, Don César, knowing now that he had been cheated, flung the pen away and declared that he would have his true wife at all costs.

Once more foiled, Don José now caused the irate Count to be re-arrested and carried back to prison; and shortly afterwards he had Maritana conveyed to a villa adjoining the palace.

Here the gipsy girl pined in lonely state, guarded by the youth, Lazarillo; for, though gorgeously attired and surrounded by luxury, she felt that her position was a false one.

After several days, however, Don José appeared once more; and when the anxious girl demanded of him the whereabouts of her husband, he replied triumphantly: "He is here!"

At the same moment, the King of Spain entered the room. Don José had kept his royal master fully acquainted with his movements regarding Maritana; and he had now brought him to make love to the fair gipsy maiden whose fascinations had so completely enthralled him.

Leaving Lazarillo outside to guard the entrance, Don José went off to seek an interview with the neglected Queen, whom he now expected to convince of her husband's infidelity. But again his plans went awry.

When the King entered her room, Maritana recognized him at once as the stranger who had admired her in the streets; and from the deference shown him by the retreating Don José, the knowledge of his true identity flashed upon her and she drew back in surprise and alarm. Charles advanced eagerly, and, taking her hand, began to pour forth passionate protestations of admiration and devotion, offering her dazzling prospects of wealth and luxury if only she would accept his love. But Maritana was pure and, realizing the danger into which she had been snared, she utterly disregarded the King's protestations and endeavoured to restrain his further advances; and presently she was greatly relieved by a sudden interruption—the sound of voices and a scuffle at the entrance.

The King quickly hurried the girl into the next room; and on returning to the *salon*, he found himself face to face with the intruder.

This was none other than Don César de Bazan, who had regained his freedom—the prison authorities having no power to detain him owing to the King's belated pardon, which had arrived there after his first escape—and had come to demand his wife once more, having learnt from a friendly lackey that she was held captive in the royal villa. He was recognized with delight by Lazarillo; but on learning from the latter that the King was within, he was troubled, now guessing at the whole vile plot of the Chief Minister. Nevertheless, he determined to rescue his unknown bride; and now addressing the King as a stranger, he calmly demanded his name.

Charles, having no idea of the true identity of his questioner and thinking only of shielding himself from scandal, answered in haughty tone: "I am Don César de Bazan! And pray, who are you?"

Instantly, Don César, whose keen wit and happy resourcefulness never deserted him for a moment, replied promptly: "Señor, if *you* are Don César de Bazan, then *I* am the King of Spain!"

The King was so much amused at the quick-witted boldness of the intruder—whom he instantly realized must be the real Don César—that he kept up the farce for a short time; and then, to his annoyance, there came a second interruption to his love-making. Lazarillo entered to announce that the King's presence was urgently needed at the palace; and Charles had to depart, much chagrined.

No sooner had he gone than Maritana entered, drawing back at the sight of another stranger. Don César, however, knowing that he was at last face to face with his bride and full of joy on beholding her beauty and charm, hurried forward with outstretched arms, explaining rapidly that he was her own true husband and that he had come to claim her. When Maritana heard the rich voice of Don César, she instantly recognized it as that of the unseen bridegroom with whom she had knelt at the altar; and since their love was mutual, the happy pair embraced with great joy.

Maritana now begged her husband to seek an interview with the Queen—whom she had observed walking in the palace gardens close by—and to induce her to intercede on their behalf; and Don César hurried away at once.

A short time after, the King returned to the *salon*, having despatched his business at the palace; and he was immediately followed by Don César, who looked greatly disturbed and had a strange story to tell.

He announced that he had found the Queen walking with Don José de Santarem and had waited behind some bushes until she should be alone. From his place of concealment he had overheard the Chief Minister announce that the King was to meet his new mistress that night in the adjoining villa. Then, as the royal lady uttered a cry of distress, the unscrupulous plotter had immediately declared his own passion for her and had begged her to accept him as her lover in order to avenge herself upon her faithless husband. Enraged by this proof of the baseness and treachery of the trusted Minister, Don César had then sprung forward and challenged him to a fight—and, in a few moments, Don José had fallen, to rise no more.

When the young King thus learned how nobly his honour had been upheld by the very man whose own good name he was selfishly seeking to destroy, he felt heartily ashamed of the unworthy part he had just played; and, immediately relinquishing his pursuit of Maritana, he offered the bold Count the wealthy Governorship of Valencia.

"Granada is also vacant, your Majesty, and would be farther away from my creditors!" suggested the irrepressible Don César; and the King laughingly agreed to let him have that appointment instead.

Thus were the base designs of the unscrupulous Chief Minister brought to naught; and Don César de Bazan, restored to favour and a high position, retired with honour to Granada to live in great happiness with his beautiful gipsy bride, Maritana.

COLONEL CHABERT   *Waltershausen*
(Oberst Chabert)

IT was summer-time in Paris; and, late one evening during the year 1817, thousands of pleasure-seekers paced the streets and filled the theatres and cafés. Yet, lights still burned in the office of Derville, the famous lawyer, where work seemed always in progress.

Not that Derville himself was to be found there in the early evening; for he was a young man who, though brilliant in his profession, yet desired to enjoy the good things of life and sought pleasure whilst he might. His two clerks, however, worked on unceasingly, preparing deeds and documents against the return of their master at midnight. Derville himself would then take his turn, remaining up till early dawn to con the papers they had left for him.

Old Boucard, the elder clerk, would grumble now and again at the late hours he was compelled to keep; but Godeschal, his companion, never complained; for he was an old soldier and afraid of no hardships, after the vicissitudes he had been through as sergeant in Napoleon's army. Napoleon was now in exile at St. Helena, but though peaceful days were now his lot, Godeschal often looked back with regret to the stirring past and sighed for the days when he had fought side by side with Chabert, his beloved Colonel. How he had loved Chabert; and how grief-stricken he had been when the brave Colonel fell at the battle of Eylau!

Nor was Godeschal alone in his grief. When the news of

Colonel Chabert's death was brought to Paris, there was general grief for the loss of so gallant a man; and his fair young wife, Rosine, became the chief object of sympathy in Parisian society.

In a very short time, however, Chabert was forgotten; and Rosine presently became the wife of the fascinating young Comte de Ferraud, a peer of France. The pair had a deep love for one another; and when two children were born to them as the years went by, their happiness was complete.

But now, on this hot night in June, ten years after the battle of Eylau, their happiness was about to be shattered.

For Chabert was not dead, as had been believed; and he was even now entering Derville's office with the double object of proving his identity and of claiming his wife. He had been struck down at Eylau, terribly wounded; and after the battle his unconscious body had been picked up for dead and cast into a huge grave or charnel pit with the other slain; but later, on recovering consciousness and realizing his awful situation, he had managed by almost superhuman efforts to free himself. Then, as he lay on the ground above, he had been found by a poor peasant woman, who had given him shelter until his wounds were healed.

Better for him would it have been had he never effected so miraculous an escape from living burial. When, at length, after many weary months of suffering, he went forth to tell his tale and seek assistance to return to his wife and home, no one would believe his story. All laughed to scorn the idea that the gaunt, disfigured, and ragged beggar before them could be the gallant Chabert—whom, besides, they knew to have been slain and buried at Eylau.

Stunned by the helplessness of his position, Chabert lost his senses for a time and was locked up in a mad-house for declaring himself to be the dead Colonel. Then, finally securing his release by giving up his claim and calling himself instead Hyacinth the Beggar, he began to wander on foot through many towns and country wilds; and though he frequently wrote letters to his wife, imploring her aid on his behalf, he never received a reply.

Many further disasters fell upon him; but, at last, after ten years' wretched wanderings, he managed to earn sufficient money to enable him to make his way back to Paris—there to learn the despairing news that his beloved Rosine was now the happy wife of another man.

Though grief-stricken by this additional crushing blow, the unfortunate Chabert yet determined to establish his identity at all costs and to claim his wife; and for this purpose he sought the assistance of the most famous lawyer in Paris.

Nearly a dozen times that day had he called at the offices of Derville, only to find the great man absent or engaged; but when he finally appeared again late at night, he was permitted to wait inside by old Godeschal, the ex-sergeant—who was interested in the ragged client, whose scarred features seemed vaguely familiar to him, though he could not yet place him in his book of memory. His puzzled musings, however, were cut short by the arrival of Derville.

No sooner did the disreputable-looking client declare himself to be the famous Chabert so long believed to be dead, than the young lawyer became intensely interested; for the beautiful Comtesse Rosine—the supposed widow of Chabert and now the wife of Comte de Ferraud—was also his client and one of the most fascinating of his many lady admirers. Therefore, he invited the unhappy man before him to tell him his whole story; and by the time the heart-rending recital came to an end, he felt entirely convinced that the shabby stranger was indeed the same Chabert who had been mourned as dead.

At this moment, Godeschal entered to inform his master that the Comtesse Rosine had unexpectedly arrived and desired an immediate interview; and upon hearing that his beloved one was about to enter the room, Chabert became violently agitated—forgetting, for the instant, that she was now the wife of another man and longing only to clasp her in his arms.

Derville, however, though now more than ever satisfied as to the truth of the story he had just listened to, thrust Chabert into an adjoining room, bidding him to be patient a little while longer; and then he gave orders for the Comtesse to be admitted, at the same time scolding Godeschal for staring after the mysterious shabbily-garbed stranger—for the old sergeant had started violently on hearing the raised voice of Chabert, which had brought back to him a flood of recollections. Half dazed, he admitted the Comtesse Rosine, retiring from the room as she entered; and Derville turned readily to receive his beautiful client, kissing her hand with his usual charming courtesy and leading her to a seat.

That Rosine was agitated, he could easily perceive; and though she began her interview by an attempted flirtation with the handsome young lawyer, Derville skilfully evaded her advances and led her to relate her troubles to him.

He was not greatly surprised to learn that Chabert was the cause of her late visit; and he soon discovered that, though terri-

ied, Rosine desired him to believe that she was merely annoyed
by the threats of a blackmailer. She declared that an impostor
calling himself Chabert had written to her many letters, in which
he claimed to be her first husband who had experienced a wonderful escape from death and living burial; and she added that this
person had now come to Paris and had even called at her house
during her absence.

Derville's quick brain instantly realized that the Comtesse
secretly believed the so-called impostor to be indeed her first
husband—having, doubtless, recognized his handwriting on the
letters—but that she was determined to refuse to acknowledge his
identity. The truth of his surmise was instantly forthcoming; for
Chabert, unable to restrain himself longer, now burst into the
room, and, seizing Rosine's trembling hands in his, greeted her as
his wife in passionate terms of love.

Rosine turned deadly pale; and, thus taken unawares, she
unconsciously proved to the watchful Derville the true identity of
Chabert by her instant shrinking away from his eager embrace
and by the hoarse murmur of his name under her breath. Next
moment, however, in despair at the thought of losing her beloved
Ferraud, she passionately denounced him as an impostor and
utterly repudiated the idea that she had ever beheld him before.
Chabert, crushed again by her unexpected denial of him, now
feverishly recounted to her all that he had done for her in the
past—how he had rescued her when destitute and about to drown
herself in the Seine; how, loving her from that first tragic encounter, he had married her; and how, until the time of his
departure to the wars, he had loaded her with every kindness and
had sought nothing but her happiness.

To all this, Rosine still stubbornly refused to admit any confirmation whatever. Despite her continued repudiation, however, undeniable proof of the stranger's identity was again established by the sudden entry of old Godeschal who, full of emotion,
flung himself at the feet of Chabert and tearfully addressed him
as his long-lost and revered Colonel, whom he now completely
recognized, despite his scars and haggard looks.

Finding herself thus defeated, Rosine uttered a distracted cry
and ran out of the office, determined to cling to her beloved
Ferraud, for whom she had a sincere passion. When Chabert,
infuriated by her cruel denial of him, would have followed with
intent to kill her, Derville held him back and proceeded to calm
his rage and to lay before him plans for his future actions.

.   .   .   .

Meanwhile, Rosine reached her home and passed a restless

night, seeking a loophole of escape from her terrible position. Sh
dared not yet make any statement to Ferraud, without whose lov
she felt she could not exist; but next day, as she sat alone in on
of the *salons* in her beautiful home, a plan came into her mind
Realizing that Chabert still loved her, she selfishly thought that h
might be willing to put her happiness before his own; and sh
determined, therefore, to make an appeal to him to forgo his claim

Elated by this idea, she was about to set forth in search of
Chabert when Derville entered the room, unannounced.

Rosine, though last evening willing enough to win to her sid
the handsome young lawyer by exercising her arts of fascination
now resented his intrusion; for she already realized that he ha
never for an instant believed in her denial of Chabert's identit
and even suspected her of further deceit—and she feared him
accordingly.

Her fears were well-founded. Derville declared that he ha
come to acquaint the Comte de Ferraud with the fact of her fir
husband's existence; and he now openly accused her of havin
received all the imploring letters which Chabert had sent to h
during his wretched wanderings, and even of having been i
possession of his first communication before her marriage wit
Ferraud took place.

The white-faced Rosine, realizing that further denial was us
less, now foolishly sought to purchase his silence by the offer of
gold; and drawing from her writing-table a bag containing
thousand louis d'or, she entreated him to take it and have n
further dealings with Chabert.

But Derville was not to be bought; and he sternly bade th
agitated woman put back her gold, declaring that her action w
but a further proof of the truth of his allegation.

As Rosine bowed her head in humiliation, the Comte de Fe
raud—young, handsome, and full of gaiety—entered the roo
having brought in from the garden a bouquet of flowers for h
beloved wife. Derville, ignoring Rosine's imploring glances, in
mediately asked for an interview; and as the two men retired in
Ferraud's study and closed the door, the distracted wife listen
outside for the words that should seal her doom.

She heard Derville relating the story of her first husban
return; and when the pair came out of the room and the lawy
had departed to fetch Chabert, she hastened, sobbing, to Ferrau
who clasped her in his arms in a passionate embrace. To her jo
she found that Ferraud refused to believe the story he had be
told; and the pair remained for a few happy minutes in th
lovers' paradise. All too soon, however, they were interrupted

the return of Derville with Chabert and the faithful ex-sergeant, Godeschal. The latter refused to leave his newly-found and well-beloved Colonel, fearing lest some conspiracy might be made against him.

Ferraud met the newcomers with dignity, haughtily challenging Chabert to substantiate his claim; and Rosine again stubbornly repudiated the fact that the changed man before them was indeed her first husband. On hearing this, old Godeschal sprang forward and furiously denounced the unhappy woman as a traitress, accusing her of having been in possession of Chabert's first letter announcing his escape from the grave before she was married to the Comte.

Derville, out of pity for the wretched wife, had withheld this latter information from Ferraud, who was now thunderstruck on hearing the accusing words of Godeschal; and seizing Rosine's hands in an agitated grip, he commanded her to declare on oath that the accusation was false. In vain Rosine, half fainting, endeavoured to utter the words of denial that Ferraud longed to hear; but, conscience-stricken, she could not swear on oath that which she knew to be untrue. With bowed head, she now admitted that the returned stranger was indeed her first husband, Chabert, and that she had known him to be alive on the day on which she had been married to Ferraud.

She entreated the latter to forgive her, her deep love for him having been the reason for her guilty silence; but Ferraud, crushed by the blow which must lay his family honour and pride in the dust and enraged by the deception practised upon him, flung the weeping Rosine into the arms of Chabert and rushed out into the open air. The lawyer and the ex-sergeant followed him; and Chabert and his despairing wife were left alone.

Rosine, half dazed, now made a passionate appeal to Chabert to resign his claim to her and to declare himself an impostor. Then, seeing her two children by Ferraud entering from the garden, she called them to her side, fondling them and tearfully bewailing the dishonour that must now fall upon their innocent heads.

Chabert was deeply moved by the sight of the pretty children; and Rosine, perceiving this, now sped her last shaft and declared boldly that she had never loved him in the past but had felt only gratitude for him, adding that the real love of her life had been given to Ferraud, the father of her children.

Entirely crushed on thus realizing that his own deep faithful love had never been returned, Chabert staggered from the room for a few moments to recover his senses; and Rosine seized the

opportunity to take out from a secret drawer in her writing-tabl
a phial containing a deadly poison—determined to die rather that
be compelled to leave her beloved Ferraud.

Ere the poison reached her lips, however, Chabert returned and
seeing what she was about to do, snatched the phial from he
trembling hand and thrust it into his breast pocket. Rosine
baulked in her purpose, again repeated that she had never love
any man but Ferraud; then, taking her children by the hand, sh
hurried from the room.

Chabert, left alone, became a prey to despair; and, completel
broken as he realized the fact that Rosine had never loved hir
but that he himself must yet love her to the end of his days, h
now determined to go back to the oblivion of death and thus t
interfere with her happiness no longer. Deliberately, he sat ;
the desk and wrote a note, in which he declared himself to be a
impostor who had posed as Chabert for blackmailing purpose
but who was, in reality, merely Hyacinth the Beggar. Ther
feeling for his pistol, he stepped out into the garden, cautiousl
hiding behind the bushes and keeping from the sight of th
watchful Godeschal.

Meanwhile, Rosine had met with Ferraud once more; and ju:
as she was again imploring him not to cast her off but to kee
her story from public knowledge for the sake of their children,
shot rang out from the garden. Fearing the worst, Derville an
Godeschal, followed by Ferraud, hastened outside to look fe
Chabert, whom they presently found, already dead.

Reverently, they bore the body into the house; and Rosin
horror-struck by the tragedy, was overcome with grief and remor:
as she now realized that Chabert had died for love of he
Despairing also because her own deception had alienated Ferraud
affections, she flung herself upon the prostrate body of the r
turned wanderer; and, feeling for the phial of poison he had take
from her, she hastily swallowed its contents before her han
could be stayed.

Overcome with horror and grief, the Comte rushed forward
catch her swaying body as it fell back; and the unhappy Rosir
uttered a deep sigh and expired in his arms, with Chabert's nan
on her lips.

DER FREISCHÜTZ or THE SEVENTH BULLET   *Weber*
(*The Free-Shooter*)

OUTSIDE a country inn on the outskirts of the Bohemian forest, a group of young foresters, mountaineers, and peasants were gathered one evening during the eighteenth century. They had just finished firing crack shots at a target in preparation for a festival to be held on the morrow when a competition for a master-shot was to take place, the winner of which would earn the title of King of the Marksmen.

All were singing the praises of Kilian, a peasant, who had been carrying all before him that day. Having already won several minor competitions, the latter was now inclined to be boastful and conceited regarding his unexpected success. In his triumph, he was especially eager in gloating over the ill-luck that had attended the shooting of Max, a young forester, whose shots had all gone astray and who now sat gloomily apart at a table with a mug of beer in front of him.

Well might young Max feel sad and angry with himself; his whole happiness and future career depended upon his performance in firing the master-shot on the morrow. He loved and was betrothed to Agatha, the fair daughter of Cuno, the Prince of Bohemia's Chief Ranger, whose consent to the marriage and consequent adoption of him as his heir and successor was conditional upon his becoming King of the Marksmen. If all went well, the wedding was to take place immediately after the final competitions; but now, though regarded as the best shot in the whole country-side, his luck had suddenly deserted him and he had made the wildest shots all that day. Cuno, though he had a great affection for the young forester as one of his best assistants, was much annoyed by the poor exhibition just made by the latter; and he warned Max that unless he gained the coveted prize on the morrow, he would certainly not receive Agatha as his bride.

The real cause of Max's recent failure was that he had fallen under the evil influence of one of his older comrades, a forester named Kaspar. Kaspar had been dabbling in black magic and had sold himself to Zamiel, the forest Demon-Huntsman, who had supplied him with seven unerring magic bullets, cast in diabolical circumstances. He had bargained to lure another victim into the Demon's power within a certain period, when his own life would be prolonged for a further spell; and the new-

2F

comer was likewise to be tempted with magical bullets. As the allotted period was now nearly ended, Kaspar had been eagerly trying to get Max within his toils, so that he might deliver him over to the Demon as a substitute for himself.

This evening, therefore, after Cuno had departed and the rustic youths and maidens had gone to dance on the village green, Kaspar came back to the table outside the inn, where young Max still sat alone in a depressed and almost despairing mood. At first he rallied him in a lively manner and, enticing him to drink, ordered wine—into which he secretly put some potent drops which soon had the effect of exciting the unhappy lover. When Max had become thoroughly aroused and exhilarated by the fiery drink, Kaspar began to talk to him about the hidden forces of nature which might be used to assist him; then, thrusting his own gun into the youth's hand, he bade him take aim at an eagle soaring aloft in the sky. Max scoffed at the idea of hitting a bird at such a tremendous height; but, under the influence of Kaspar, he raised the gun and took a random aim—with the result that the next moment the eagle fell dead at his feet.

As Kaspar plucked off the eagle's wing feathers and put them in the youth's hat as a trophy, Max, in trembling tones, knowing that black magic must be at work, begged him to say where more of these wonderful bullets could be secured, that by means of them he might make the master-shot on the morrow and win his bride and inheritance. In reply Kaspar invited the youth to meet him at midnight in the ill-reputed Wolf's Glen in the forest, when he would show him how to obtain the magic bullets. Though Max at first hesitated to come within the influence of the evil spirit said to haunt that spot, he finally agreed to keep the assignation on being reminded by the wily Kaspar that his beloved Agatha would droop and die if he failed to win the master-shot next day

. . . .

Meanwhile, the pretty Agatha was also in a sad and troubled mood as she sat at home putting the finishing touches to her bridal garments. Though her lively cousin, Annchen, who had come to help her with her preparations, tried to cheer her with merry talk, she could not overcome a feeling of coming misfortune. A picture of an ancestor had fallen; and taking this as an evil omen, she was full of unhappy foreboding. In particular a good and revered old Hermit, whom she had visited that morning to receive a blessing upon her forthcoming marriage, had warned her of approaching evil; and though he had presented her with a wreath of consecrated white roses to wear as a personal protection, she was still troubled in her mind. She now anxiously awaited the coming of her lover, who had promised to visit her that evening.

But when Max arrived her anxiety increased because of his agitated and wild appearance. When he told her that he could not remain as he wished to visit the Wolf's Glen in the forest that night to retrieve a stag he had shot, she was filled with alarm; and she implored him not to visit that evil spot, fearing lest harm should come to him.

Despite her entreaties, however, Max declared that a forester must be prepared to brave all dangers; and soon he bade her a loving farewell and hastened away to keep his dread appointment.

. . . .

In the Wolf's Glen—a wild and craggy spot surrounded by high mountains with many blasted trees upon which roosted owls with great eyes that glared and glowed in the fitful moonlight—Kasper stood at midnight upon a jutting rock. Here he had built up a fire within a circle of black stones, in the centre of which stood a skull, a crucible, a bullet-mould, and an eagle's wing.

Having completed the circle, he drew his hunting-knife and struck it violently into the skull. Then, holding the skull aloft, he turned round three times and called upon Zamiel to appear.

In answer to his incantation, the terrible Demon-Huntsman suddenly sprang out from the centre of a rock; and Kaspar immediately implored his evil master to grant him another short respite before his already bought soul should be claimed.

At first Zamiel sternly refused his request; but upon being told by Kaspar that another victim was even now approaching, he agreed to accept Max in exchange. He also gave permission for seven more magic bullets to be moulded, these to be fired during the competition on the morrow—though he reserved to himself the destination of the seventh bullet to be guided in whatever direction he desired.

Having thus bargained, the Demon vanished; and immediately afterwards Max appeared on a crag above.

The young forester was horror-struck by the awful aspect of this lonely and weird spot; but, though warned by a passing vision showing his mother and Agatha plainly pictured on the opposite rocks, as in a dream, he gathered his courage together and boldly descended to the circle of stones. He did not wish to be regarded by Kaspar as a coward.

Kaspar then began to cast the magic bullets, fanning the fire with the eagle's wing, dropping quicksilver and various charms into the crucible, and uttering strange words of incantation as he

mixed the ingredients to the magic formula given to him by
Zamiel. During the whole of this time fearful noises were heard,
as though all the demons of Hell were let loose. The moon
vanished; and the awe-inspiring scene was lighted only by the
fire, the glaring eyes of the owls, the phosphorescent decayed
wood of the blasted trees, and the lightning-flashes of a sudden
violent rainless thunderstorm. As each bullet was cast, some
terrifying object or portent appeared before the unwilling gaze
of the already remorseful Max—a flock of flapping night birds,
a black wild boar, wheels of fire, mysterious forms of phantom
huntsmen, strange beasts, falling meteors, hail, thunder, and
lightning.

As the seventh bullet was cast, in answer to the wild call of the
excited and overwrought Kaspar, the Demon-Huntsman himself
appeared; and, with a shuddering cry of horror at the sight of
the fiend, Max fell senseless to the ground.

. . . .

Next morning, Agatha arrayed herself in her bridal garments
and awaited the coming of her bridesmaids with a heavier heart
than she had ever known before. She had been troubled by
frightful dreams all night and was still anxious about her lover
and fearful of how he would acquit himself at the competition
that was to decide their fate.

Annchen endeavoured to cheer her with merry songs and
raillery; and when the other bridesmaids presently arrived, she
put the finishing touches to her cousin's bridal dress and veil.
When, however, the box containing the bridal wreath was opened,
all the girls started back in horror on discovering that instead of
the expected myrtle and orange blossoms, a silver wreath for the
dead had been sent by mistake. But Agatha, though at first upset
by this circumstance, now recovered herself quickly and declared
that she would wear the consecrated white roses given her by the
good old Hermit, which she felt would be a safeguard and a
blessing to her. The bridal-party then set forth towards the
shooting-ground to await the firing of the master-shot.

Meanwhile, all the villagers and foresters had gathered together
near the pavilion of Prince Ottakar of Bohemia, their liege lord,
whose courtiers and retainers made a brilliant assemblage. Soon
after the usual feasting and merry-making had proceeded for some
time, the Prince gave orders for the master-shot to be fired; and
he graciously expressed the hope that Max, as the chosen candidate
for the office of his future Chief Ranger and as the affianced lover
of Cuno's fair daughter, would succeed in proving himself the
best marksman of all. The young forester had already fired some

wonderful shots earlier in the day, which had been greatly admired by the royal visitor and his attendants.

Max, who had been amazed but elated by the success already gained by his magic bullets, now took out the last one and prepared to make the master-shot, while Kaspar climbed into a tree near by to watch the effect of this all-important bullet.

The Prince, noticing a white dove fluttering about in the tree-tops, bade the young marksman fire at the flying bird as his final test.

As Max took aim, the bridal-party came in sight beneath the trees; and Agatha, seeing her lover with his gun levelled in her direction, sprang forward quickly to warn him. But her cry was too late, for Max had already fired, having followed the movements of the dove as it flitted from tree to tree.

As the gun was fired, both Kaspar and Agatha fell to the ground, Agatha in a faint and Kaspar fatally wounded—for this was the seventh bullet, the free shot claimed by the demon Zamiel, who, having no power over the fair maiden wearing her wreath of consecrated roses, had directed the bullet upon Kaspar as his victim already forfeit to him. Max was thus safe from the power of the demon—who demanded but the one victim in payment of his claim and had cynically deceived Kaspar by reserving his own free shot for him.

At first all thought that Max had accidentally shot his bride; but Agatha quickly recovered from her faint, and the horrified Max clasped her thankfully in his arms with great relief and joy.

Meanwhile, Kaspar, in his last writhing agonies, beheld Zamiel rising from the earth behind him, triumphantly eager to claim his own; and as he expired, he uttered a wild curse upon the demon who had deceived him and whom he was now compelled to serve for evermore.

Max now came forward and confessed that, tempted by the devil-possessed Kaspar, he had made use of magic bullets secured by unholy means; and he expressed great remorse for his sin. Prince Ottakar, greatly shocked by the circumstance, at first commanded that Max should expiate his sin by banishment for his whole life; but in response to the tearful pleadings of Agatha and to the gentle intervention of the good old Hermit—who had likewise appeared with the wedding-party—his sentence was reduced to one year's probation. At the end of that time, after due repentance and penance, he would be permitted to return and wed his beloved one.

Full of deep joy that they would thus be united at last, Max and Agatha embraced with grateful hearts; and the rustics concluded their festival with songs of praise and thankfulness for the clemency of their Prince and for their escape from the evil influences that had been at work in their midst.

SCHWANDA THE BAGPIPER   *Weinberger*
(*A Fantastic Story of the Seventeenth Century*)

SCHWANDA, the famous Bagpiper of Strakonitz, was the happiest man in Old Bohemia. Though not rich, neither was he very poor; and the fame of his brilliant playing of the bagpipes had spread far beyond his own country-side. There was no wedding or festival in any rural district of Bohemia at which Schwanda the Bagpiper did not play his merry tunes, which always brought joy to the hearts of all. His very name spelled happiness.

But, although Schwanda was indeed a happy man and had recently been married to the prettiest girl in the country-side, he sometimes sighed for a wider and fuller life—the excitements of cities and even the gaieties of palaces, to which he felt his wonderful gift of music might some day give him access. Then he met with a strange adventure, from which he learned that love was greater than fame. After this, he no longer wished to roam.

One day, Schwanda was away working in the fields as usual—for, being a countryman, this was his usual daily occupation, music being his spare-time joy and relaxation. Towards evening, his pretty young wife, Dorota, was busily setting out his supper on a table beneath a linden tree. Her charming cottage beyond was tidy and ready for her husband's return; at any moment now he might be seen coming from work.

She was just a little anxious. Only a few minutes earlier, a couple of forester friends had called to warn her that the famous robber, Babinsky, was in the neighbourhood.

As the foresters hurried off to continue their search for the robber, Dorota wished her husband would return. Instead, however, a stranger, dressed entirely in black except for a huge white collar and cuffs, swung himself down from the linden tree, and began to talk to her.

Not imagining for a moment that this respectably-dressed stranger could be the robber—though it was, indeed, Babinsky himself—Dorota invited him to sit down and await the return of her husband. She was surprised and rather offended when he declared that he had never even heard of Schwanda the Bagpiper. But he looked at the Piper's wife with real admiration.

Presently Schwanda arrived and invited the stranger to join himself and his wife at supper under the tree. On hearing from Dorota that the famous Babinsky was in the neighbourhood, the stranger declared that he knew the robber well and that he was a kindly fellow who merely robbed the rich to help the poor. He added that wherever Babinsky went, he always left one of his cuffs behind with a message written upon it.

When Dorota had gone back to the cottage to attend to her household duties once more, the stranger tried to induce the Bagpiper to seek better opportunities for his talents elsewhere. He suggested that he might, for instance, be well received in the palace of Queen Ice-Heart, a royal lady whose heart had become frozen and who had never smiled since her diamond-studded sceptre had been stolen—probably by the famous Babinsky himself! "Your gay music would melt her frozen heart and make her smile again; then your fortune would be made!" declared the stranger. "Come with me!"

Always eager to see more of the world and thrilled by this story, Schwanda decided to go away with the stranger who seemed to have bewitched him. But they must go before Dorota returned, or he would never be able to tear himself away from her!

So Schwanda took up his beloved pipes once more, while the stranger hastily scribbled a farewell message on one of his cuffs, which he left on the table. Then the runaways hastened down the forest glade and were soon lost to sight.

When Dorota presently came out once more and found on the table the white cuff with the farewell message written on it, she realized, to her dismay, that she had been entertaining the famous robber Babinsky and that it was he who had enticed her husband away. But she did not despair. She loved Schwanda and knew that he loved her; so she determined to track him down and bring him back. She followed the wanderers down the forest glade.

. . . .

In the gorgeous palace of Queen Ice-Heart, everybody was trying in vain to amuse the frozen-hearted royal lady. The courtiers and ladies-in-waiting sang and danced a complicated ballet before her; but she scarcely looked at them. Where was the Court Magician? Had he, by means of his magic, found her lost lily sceptre studded with diamonds? He had not; and the Queen was furious. What was the use of a Magician whose magic wouldn't work? Queen Ice-Heart would not smile; her heart remained frozen.

But what was happening now, the Queen suddenly asked? A
gay and handsome young man, dressed in country clothes, had
danced into the audience chamber piping a merry tune as he came.
It was Schwanda the Bagpiper, who played such a lively polka
that quite soon all the lords and ladies were dancing to it. Nobody could help being jolly when Schwanda played his pipes.
Even the Queen smiled; consequently her icy heart began to melt.
She ran forward with delight and begged the merry Bagpiper to
stay with her always and to become her consort. Nobody had ever
pleased her so well.

Carried away by his sudden and tremendous success, Schwanda
was, for the moment, inclined to take advantage of this royal offer.
He had never expected to have the chance of becoming a king.
He placed his bagpipes down on the throne and turned to kiss
the Queen—after first desiring the courtiers to look the other way.

No sooner had the kiss been given, however, than there came
an interruption. The distracted Dorota, who had been following
closely on the truant's heels, now rushed into the hall, and
demanded that her husband should be restored to her.

A great commotion ensued. The Queen was furious when
Schwanda left her side and ran to embrace his beloved wife—thus
proving that he had no love for the royal lady; and she ordered
them both to be seized and executed on the morrow. Her soft-
hearted interlude had been a very short one.

Next day, the Queen and her Court gathered around the place
of execution outside the city walls, where the block was already
set up, the executioner standing beside it with his axe. Schwanda
and Dorota were brought forward, both very doleful at their sad
fate. Then Schwanda had a bright idea. He begged to be allowed
to play his bagpipes for the last time; and after considerable
opposition from the Court Magician, the Queen granted his
request and the pipes were sent for.

Meanwhile, the robber Babinsky had by no means deserted the
young Bagpiper he had lured away. In disguise, he had mingled
with the crowd; and he now began to play tricks upon the
executioner. When the latter's attention was withdrawn for a few
moments, he snatched away the axe and substituted for it a broomstick with one of the famous Babinsky white cuffs fastened upon
it. The astonished and dismayed executioner sent off his assistant
hastily to fetch another axe. Meanwhile, however, Babinsky had
stolen the bagpipes from the messenger sent to fetch them, and he
now slipped them into Schwanda's hands.

Without a moment's delay, the Bagpiper began to play his
merry polka; and instantly, as before, everybody began to dance

The Queen, the judges, the executioner, the guards, the courtiers, and the spectators all found the magic tune so infectious that they could not stop dancing the polka. They all seemed mad with joy.

But there was method in Schwanda's mad playing. Gradually he lured the people towards the city gates once more; then, as they all danced into the city, he slipped back, still playing his merry polka, whilst Babinsky—who had cleverly abstracted the keys from the girdle of the dancing City Warden—locked the gates behind them. As a final flourish, the robber tied one of his white cuffs on to the huge key.

But trouble soon arose once more. As the trio hurried away from the city of Queen Ice-Heart, Schwanda sought forgiveness from the injured Dorota, making light of his recent flirtation and declaring that he never even kissed the Queen. He added, mendaciously: " May the Devil carry me away, if I did! "

Instantly he was taken at his word; and the unlucky Bagpiper vanished into the ground to the accompaniment of thunder, lightning, and sulphurous fumes.

Babinsky now tried to comfort the horrified Dorota for the loss of her husband by offering his own love instead—for he was greatly attracted by her beauty and charm. When, however, Dorota indignantly repulsed him, his better nature prevailed and he promised to rescue Schwanda—whose sin was a very small one —from the infernal regions, where he was himself fairly well known. He warned her, nevertheless, that she might find her husband changed after his strange experiences. But Dorota felt that all would be well; and she now returned home, full of hope.

. . . .

Meanwhile, down in the infernal regions, the Devil was extremely annoyed with the new arrival in his domain. He wanted to hear the famous bagpipes played; but Schwanda flatly refused to oblige him. He sat sulkily in a corner, watching a weirdly fantastic ballet of witches, bats, and phantoms, but was not the least entertained thereby. He had to put his fingers in his ears when his host borrowed the pipes and tried to play a tune on them himself—for the music made by Satan was merely a horrible succession of discordant noises. Nobody could play sweet music upon the magic pipes but Schwanda himself. And Schwanda refused to play in such a place.

So the Devil was forced to amuse himself by playing Patience. Nobody would play cards with him, because he always won. Soon, however, he tried again to induce Schwanda to give him some music. He knew he had at present no real hold upon the

Bagpiper, who had committed a mere peccadillo. He now tried to
secure him as a permanent victim, whom he could then always
compel to play the pipes at his command. He produced a document whereby, on appending his signature, Schwanda would sign
away his soul. Then the artful Devil next conjured up a vision of
the lovely Dorota, promising that she should be his—Schwanda's
—once more, as soon as he had signed the parchment.

Eagerly Schwanda signed the document—only to find that he
had been cunningly deceived; for no Dorota appeared. What was
more, the Devil no longer entreated him to play the bagpipes,
but now *commanded* him to do so. When he still refused, a host
of demons suddenly appeared, ready to torture him.

At this moment, however, the robber Babinsky suddenly arrived,
full of gaiety, ready to divert the Devil and to put him into a better
humour. He offered to play cards with him, but warned him that
his stakes were high.

The Devil was delighted, agreeing willingly to every stake
suggested; and the game began. Satan soon discovered, however,
that he was no match for the cunning Babinsky, who could cap
all his best tricks with better ones. The robber won all before
him, until the entire wealth of the infernal regions was his.

Finally, as the last stake of all, the soul of Schwanda was
gambled for, with the bagpipes thrown in as make-weight. Once
more, Babinsky won; and gladly he tore up the document signed
by the Bagpiper. The Devil was now poor, indeed. His once
rich domain was worth no more than scrap-iron.

But Babinsky the robber was a generous soul. All he had
come for was Schwanda and his bagpipes. He gladly returned to
the Devil all the other treasures he had won from him. He
declared that he had no wish to deprive poor Satan of his riches,
his feastings, his wines, and his other little comforts.

The Devil expressed himself as highly appreciative of such
splendid magnanimity. He would certainly never forget it and
would always look upon the robber as one of his own family
friends. Only one thing marred his perfect enjoyment of the day
—that Schwanda the Bagpiper had not played to him.

On hearing this, Schwanda felt he could no longer be un-
gracious; so he took up his beloved pipes once more, and played
the Devil a merry tune. Then he and Babinsky gladly departed to
the upper world; and the Devil settled down once more to another
lonely game of Patience.

. . . .

Babinsky the robber tried to play one more trick upon Schwanda
the Bagpiper, as they returned to the latter's home. He put on a

alse moustache and then pretended that he and the piper had
een away about twenty years, declaring that his friend's wife
vould no longer be young and pretty. By this statement he
oped that Schwanda might be induced to look elsewhere for
:male companionship—then he, Babinsky, would try to win
)orota for himself.

But Schwanda stoutly declared that, no matter how much older
)orota might look, he would still love her just the same.

However, when, presently, in answer to their knock at the
ottage door, Dorota came running out, as young and pretty as
ver, Schwanda realized that his friend had only played upon him
nother of his sly tricks. As the reunited pair gladly rushed
ito each other's arms, the robber ruefully pulled off his false
noustache. True love was more than proof against such simple
·ickery. After receiving their warm thanks for his aid in their
:cent adventures, he departed and left the happy pair to live in
·eace and contentment. He had learnt something beautiful from
1em.

And Schwanda the Bagpiper had learnt *his* lesson, too—**that**
)ve is a more precious thing than fame.

HE JEWELS OF THE MADONNA *Wolf-Ferrari*
' Giojelli della Madonna)

---

t was the day of the Festival of the Madonna; and all the
leasure-loving folk of Naples had turned out to enjoy the
oliday in honour of the event, eager to have a good view of
1e great Church Procession and to join in the wild Carnival
in that would follow.

In one of the public squares facing the sea, a more than
sually merry crowd had collected—to the annoyance of young
·ennaro, the blacksmith. The latter had no intention of joining
a the Carnival pranks but desired only to pursue his usual daily
·ork in peace and quietness, having many disturbing thoughts
> occupy his mind.

For Gennaro was in love; and the object of his adoration was
 wild, wilful maiden, whose beauty and charm enthralled him
 distraction but who could not be persuaded to look upon him
 any other light than that of a brother—as a brother, moreover,
·hose prudence and restraining authority she scorned.

The lovely Maliella longed for excitement and light pleasures
and her high spirit resented the wise restraints imposed upon he
by Gennaro's worthy mother, Carmela—with whom she ha
lived as an adopted daughter since earliest childhood.

Only too well did Gennaro know this; and he was just nov
torn between his brotherly sense of duty in keeping the madca
girl from the temptations of frivolity and his new lover's longin
to grant her every desire. The former had prevailed to-day, s
far. His mother and he had determined to keep Maliella withi
doors, so that she might not be exposed to the careless licence c
the Carnival crowds; but as Gennaro plied his work in the smith
adjoining the house, he knew that Carmela had her hands fu
in keeping the disappointed and angry girl occupied with th
domestic tasks she abhorred.

In the distance, the church bells were already ringing; and a
the sound of singing now proclaimed the fact that the splendi
Procession of the Madonna had been formed and was no
parading the streets, most of the holiday-makers ran off to watc
the approaching cavalcade.

The square was thus left somewhat quieter for a short tim
and Gennaro, at last overcome by his conflicting feelings, ha
just seized this opportunity of a peaceful moment to sink upo
his knees beside his anvil and offer up a short prayer to the Virgi
for guidance in his dilemma, when he was disturbed once mor
The beautiful Maliella herself impetuously burst forth from tl
house beyond, closely followed by the distracted Carmela, wh
held in her hand a comb with which she had been endeavourin
to straighten the girl's unruly locks.

But Maliella was in a rebellious mood and refused to allow he
guardian to make her neat and presentable if her fair looks we
to be kept hidden from the appreciative eyes of the outside worl
She had roughly broken away from Carmela's restraining hand
and now appeared in the square with disordered dress and he
jet-black hair streaming over her shoulders, calling out passio
ately: "No! No! You shall not make me fair for the bene
of my mirror only! This is a Festival Day, and I mean to enj
myself with all these merry folk! I will be held in no longer!

Shocked and pained, Gennaro ran to expostulate with tl
wilful girl, only to receive fiery words of scorn in reply. Despi
his and Carmela's entreaties, Maliella flitted here and there abo
the square, on her head a paper cap dropped by one of tl
holiday-makers; and as the vanguard of the procession began
pass by with the merry crowd in attendance, she struck
coquettish attitude and called out audaciously: "Here am

oung and pretty, and longing for kisses! Who will oblige
1e?"

Instantly, there was a rush to seize the seductive young beauty,
ll the youths being eager to accept her invitation; but Maliella
1errily eluded them all and ran out of the square, only to be
losely pursued by her new admirers.

A band of Camorrists now appeared on the scene, headed by
handsome youth, Rafaele, their dashing leader; and, quickly
aking in the enticing situation, they joined in the pursuit of the
air truant.

Gennaro sought comfort from his shocked and dismayed
1other, now telling her of his love for Maliella; and Carmela
ade him think no more about the unruly girl, but advised him
1stead to seek guidance by praying before the now approaching
:atue of the Madonna.

No sooner had Gennaro departed to meet the approaching
rocession, than Maliella appeared in the square once more,
losely pursued by the handsome Camorrist leader, Rafaele. The
atter's ardent nature had been instantly magnetized by Maliella;
nd he was already in love with the pleasure-loving girl, whose
antalizing elusiveness fanned his sudden passion at every
arn.

Hoping to please their leader, the Camorrist followers began to
ance in a circle around the pair, calling merrily upon the girl
redeem the invitation she had given; but Maliella, now somewhat alarmed by the situation in which her saucy audacity had
laced her, still tried to escape from the inevitable embrace of the
namoured Rafaele—though at the same time elated and pleased
y the hot words of love and admiration which he poured upon
er when, at last, by a skilful manoeuvre, he seized her in his
rms. Ere the victorious youth had time to snatch the kiss he
ungered for, however, Maliella pulled out a long, dagger-like
in from her hair and dared him to the deed at his peril.

Not to be put off by such a threat, Rafaele boldly seized her
ound the waist—only to receive a sharp stab in the hand from
Maliella's stiletto-pin. The girl's daring, however, but inflamed
is passion the more; and after kissing the bleeding wound, he
eized the opportunity of Maliella's hands being engaged in
:placing the pin in her hair to thrust a red rose into the bodice
f her gown.

Determined not to admit herself won, even though secretly
esponsive to the advances of the handsome stranger, Maliella
lucked out the flower and flung it to the ground; nevertheless,
s the main procession at that moment appeared in the square,

she allowed Rafaele to help her on to a chair that she might ge
a better view of the dazzling spectacle.

Rafaele never ceased for a moment to pour words of admiration
upon her; and, incensed by her seeming scornful indifference
he cried out passionately as the Statue of the Madonna was born
by: "Shall I commit sacrilege to please you? Would you wea
the dazzling jewels of Our Lady? I will snatch them from th
passing statue now, if you will but smile upon me!"

But Maliella was terrified by this outburst, and uttered a cry o
horror at this last daring suggestion made by Rafaele. Just then
Gennaro caught up with her and again entreated her to return t
the house, declaring that the lawless Camorrist leader was no f
person for her to be seen talking to. This aroused the anger c
Rafaele; and the two young men were only prevented from flyin
at one another's throats by the timely return of the processio
with the Madonna statue in its midst, which compelled then
with the entire crowd of merry-makers, to sink upon their knee
in reverent obeisance.

As the procession passed on its way to the accompaniment c
the Carnival rejoicings, Rafaele flung his red rose a second tim
at the feet of Maliella, who now picked it up, kissed it, and flashe
a tender glance at the eagerly expectant Camorrist. She then fle
back to the house with a joyous laugh, followed quickly by th
unhappy Gennaro.

. . . .

Soon after supper that evening, as the three members of he
household sat in the garden, Carmela tried to persuade Maliell
to retire to rest earlier than usual—even though the festive sounc
of the Carnival were still heard in the square beyond; but neithe
the girl nor Gennaro heeded her words, both keeping a sulle
silence until Carmela, with a deep sigh, bade them good nigl
and retired to her own chamber.

No sooner had the elder woman departed than the two your
people renewed their dispute; and Maliella, again crying ou
against the restraints of her life, declared she could endure suc
an existence no longer but would run away and seek a hom
elsewhere.

Half stunned by this announcement, the young blacksmit
rose and clasped her in his arms, now boldly declaring his secr
love for her and entreating her to stay and love him in returr
but Maliella, utterly unable to regard Gennaro in any other ligl
than that of a brotherly protector, repulsed him with laughin
scorn and unbelief. Then, when he continued to pour out h
unwelcome protestations of devotion, she boldly declared he

love for Rafaele. When Gennaro, with jealousy raging in his heart, made a disdainful gesture at the mention of the outlaw Camorrist's name, she passionately announced to him her preference for one whose love for her was such that he was even willing to risk his immortal soul by offering to steal the Jewels of the Madonna for her adornment.

Staggered that such sacrilege should even be imagined, Gennaro renewed his efforts to prevent the departure of Maliella, who now tried to escape from the garden; and after a fierce struggle, the girl was compelled to retreat and ran up a little outside staircase to her own room—though with a jaunty step and carelessly defiant laugh.

Darkness had now fallen; and, left to his own devices, Gennaro gave himself up to the gloom and misery engendered by his unrequited love. Then, suddenly, one tempting thought began to take hold of his imagination until his whole being became obsessed with the taunting suggestion.

Had she not expressed admiration for one who would even commit sacrilege for her sake? The Camorrist, despite his boast, had not yet proved his audacity by actually committing the deed he had suggested: then, why should not Gennaro himself steal the Jewels of the Madonna this very night and, by laying them before his adored one, win her love and admiration away from his rival?

In his present feverish state of mind, Gennaro was utterly unable to resist the temptation of this overwhelming thought. Crushing down his horror at the sacrilege he would thus commit and thinking only of the joy of winning approbation from his beloved Maliella, the passion-racked youth staggered to his tool-chest and took therefrom some files and other necessary implements; and then he made his way from the garden by a seldom-used postern-door, which, however, he carefully locked behind him.

Almost immediately after Gennaro's departure, a band of the Camorrists appeared on the outside of the large, securely-fastened garden gate, headed by the dashing Rafaele, who had brought his companions thither to assist him in serenading his newly-found lady-love; and on hearing the sounds of seductive music, Maliella presently appeared on the little staircase that led down from her chamber. She was now clad in a loose white garment, over which she had flung a scarlet shawl; and seeing who the serenaders were, she hastily ran down the stairs and made her way to the gate.

Rafaele greeted her with rapturous delight; and his renewed

protestations of love and his eager invitation for her to leave her present dull abode and join him in the haunts of the Camorrists were so enticing that she could no longer restrain the responsive chords in her own heart. The thought that Gennaro might be lurking near, however, filled her with alarm; and entreating Rafaele to depart at once, but promising to meet him in the Camorrist abode on the morrow, she tore herself away from the gate.

As Rafaele withdrew with his companions, she stood for a moment as though in a reverie, still feeling the joyous thrill of her lover's presence. Then, hearing the sound of approaching steps, she turned hastily and cried out in alarm at the sight of Gennaro, who now stumbled into the garden through the little postern-door, his face white and haggard and his whole appearance strangely wild.

On beholding Maliella, Gennaro's sunken eyes lighted up with passionate adoration; and, approaching her with trembling steps and sinking upon his knees, he flung a bundle at her feet, murmuring brokenly: "For you! For you I did it!"

But Maliella sprang back, horror-struck; for the silvery moonlight revealed that the bundle contained the glittering Jewels of the Madonna!

Full of awe, she gazed upon the sparkling gems until she became fascinated by their rich colour and beauty. Gennaro poured forth the story of how he had broken into the church and had stripped off the shining ornaments from the statue that had been borne through the streets that morning; and he added that he believed the Madonna had already forgiven his sacrilege in consideration of his overwhelming love.

As he spoke, the half-dazed Maliella mechanically began to array herself in the jewelled ornaments, placing the diadem upon her head and hanging the chains, necklaces, and bracelets upon her white neck and arms. The form of the kneeling Gennaro seemed to fade away from her sight altogether, and the glittering jewels conjured up before her mental vision the picture of her beloved Rafaele only. As in a trance, she began to murmur words of love, bidding her visionary sweetheart to admire her dazzling appearance as though he were, indeed, at her side.

Gennaro, in his own overwrought state of mind, now believed that the tender smiles and gentle love phrases of the entranced girl were actually addressed to himself; and, full of joy that, as he imagined, his passion was at last returned, he clasped the jewel-decked form in his arms in a loving embrace.

Maliella, still under the strange spell of the mental vision of

Rafaele which her vivid imagination and passionate desire had conjured up, yielded herself unresistingly to the mystical atmosphere of love which enveloped her senses. As Gennaro—quite unsuspicious of her mistake and almost mad with the unexpected joy of possession—held her in a close embrace, the half-dreaming girl, lost to her surroundings, uttered a deep sigh of unconscious content and surrendered herself to him in a half-swooning condition.

. . . .

Meanwhile, Rafaele and his companions had returned to the meeting-place of the Camorrists. Here, in a lonely house on the outskirts of the city, a merry throng of outlaws had gathered to pass the remainder of the Festival night in an orgy of feasting, dancing, and love-making.

Rafaele was soon the centre of attraction; but the bold pretty girls who surrounded him were presently piqued when, instead of bestowing kisses upon them as was his usual custom, he chose to sing to them a happy love-song in which he set before them the charms of his beautiful new sweetheart, Maliella. When they teased him spitefully because he had not succeeded in carrying off the fair maiden he eulogized, he laughingly told them she would certainly appear in their midst before long; and he bade them go forward with their wild bacchanalian dances.

Just as the hilarity was at its height, a loud knock was heard on the outer door, with cries for help; and upon the bolts being drawn, to the astonishment of all, in rushed Maliella, still in her night attire and adorned with the Jewels of the Madonna.

On recovering her mental equilibrium as her curious visionary obsession gradually left her, Maliella had been filled with dismay when she found herself in the arms of Gennaro and realized that she had, unwittingly, yielded herself to the passion of one suitor when her love was given to another. Overcome with shame at this discovery and still horrified by her recollection of the sacrilege which had been committed for her sake, she had struggled free from the detaining embrace of the young blacksmith; and escaping from the garden, she had frantically hastened with all speed to seek protection and comfort from Rafaele.

As the exhausted girl now sank fainting to the ground after breathlessly announcing that she had fled from Gennaro, who was even now following her, Rafaele bent over her in concern, while some of his men ran out to round up Gennaro. Stung by the curious glances cast upon him by the saucy Camorrist girls, their young leader quickly succeeded in rousing Maliella and sternly demanded an explanation of her present distraught condition; and the unhappy girl was compelled to confess that she had unconsciously surrendered herself to the passion of Gennaro whilst under the spell of her mental visionary picture of Rafaele.

On hearing this strange story, derisive laughter arose on every side from the girls whose kisses the handsome Camorrist leader had refused a short time before. Stung to madness by their sneers and ridicule and believing that he had been fooled purposely by Maliella, Rafaele now spurned the wretched girl, thrusting her from him with such force that she fell again to the ground—thus revealing more conspicuously the dazzling jewels she still wore.

At sight of the Madonna Jewels—which they quickly recognized—and realizing that an act of sacrilege had been committed, an awed silence fell upon the revellers; but on hearing the voice of the now approaching Gennaro as his pursuers chased him, Maliella, in self-defence, declared that the ornaments had been stolen by him from the sacred statue in the church.

Full of horror at such a deed, the women and most of the men fled from the house; and as Gennaro staggered in, closely pursued, Rafaele sprang forward to slay him—but suddenly recoiled superstitiously from one whom he now believed to be accursed.

Maliella, distracted by the sin which had been committed for her sake and in despair because Rafaele now disdained her love, poured forth passionate words of reproach upon the equally distracted Gennaro; and snatching from her neck and arms the flashing Jewels of the Madonna, she flung them to the ground at his feet. Then, in a demented state and resolving to drown herself, she rushed from the house, crying wildly: "To the sea! To the sea!"

Rafaele and all the revellers now left the house, shudderingly, as though it had been visited by the plague; for, wild and lawless though they were, their supersitious fears still had power to make them look upon sacrilege with dread.

Gennaro was thus left alone. Already repentant and only longing for pardon, he crawled upon his knees towards a fresco figure of the Virgin which had been drawn on one of the walls above a tiny shrine, and, prostrating himself before it, prayed earnestly for forgiveness.

A streak of rosy light from the rising sun at that moment pierced the gloomy twilight; and taking this as a miraculous sign in token of the Madonna's pardon Gennaro uttered a cry of thanksgiving.

Then, still not deeming himself worthy to live after his deed of sacrilege and overwhelmed by the despairing hopelessness of his unhappy love passion, he seized a knife from a table close by and plunged it into his heart.

At this moment, some of the Camorrists, accompanied by an angry mob of the townsfolk who had just discovered the crime that had been committed, burst into the house to wreak their vengeance upon the perpetrator of sacrilege—but one and all stopped suddenly upon the threshold and dropped their weapons in silence as they gazed upon the limp form of the unhappy Gennaro lying dead before the little shrine amidst the scattered jewels of the Madonna.

THE SECRET OF SUSANNA *Wolf-Ferrari*
(Il Segreto di Susanna)

COUNT GIL dashed out of one of the handsome apartments in his palace in Piedmont in a great state of excitement. Through the window he had just caught sight of his pretty young wife, Susanna, hatted and cloaked, returning down the road from some mysterious errand of which he knew nothing. Having forbidden her to go out unattended, he was disturbed by the sight. Lately, too, he had noticed the unmistakable odour of tobacco in her private apartments; and as he never smoked himself and knew that Susanna, aware of his strange dislike of any form of nicotine, also refrained from smoking, his jealousy was stimulated to such an extent that he firmly believed he had a rival in her affections. Some strange man must be visiting the house when he was absent; and his beautiful Susanna, whom he loved so passionately, had a secret lover!

As the Count left the room, full of angry suspicion, the pretty Countess Susanna hastily entered through the open french window, looking about her fearfully. Breathless and in great agitation, she handed a small parcel to the old family servant, Sante, who had been on the watch for her; and bidding him not to say a word to his master about her having just been out, she retired to her adjoining boudoir in much relief. She believed that her stolen excursion was unknown to anyone save the old retainer who adored her and would keep her secret.

Scarcely had she vanished than the Count returned to the room; and again sniffing the obnoxious odour of tobacco, his hasty suspicions were quickly redoubled. Calling to Sante, he questioned him as to whether he had dared to disobey his orders against smoking; but the old servant—who was a mute—made indignant and surprised signs of denial. Observing the agitation of the Count, however, while the latter's back was turned for a moment, he managed by gesticulations to convey to the eagerly listening Susanna through the open door of her boudoir, that her husband's suspicions were aroused; and he then departed to make chocolate in obedience to his master's instructions.

When Susanna presently issued forth from her boudoir, with an air of great innocence, the Count was still disturbed and hinted that he thought he had seen her in outdoor attire coming down the country road a short time since. Susanna, however, declared sweetly that he must have been mistaken, since she was not likely to go out unattended against his orders; and she was so charming to him, that Gil's suspicions were lulled for the moment. The pair then spent a happy interlude together as they partook of the chocolate brought by Sante, even indulging in delightful recollections of their first declarations of love.

Presently, however, as Gil held his wife in a close embrace, he again noticed the strong smell of tobacco, even in her clothes and hair; and he suddenly thrust her away from him in quick anger. Susanna, afraid that he had discovered her secret, shrank back in confusion; and the Count, taking her heightened colour and telltale countenance as a sign of a guilty conscience, burst forth into an angry accusation, declaring that she had a secret which she was hiding from him and putting the worst possible construction upon this.

Susanna spiritedly replied that she *had* a secret, but meant to keep it to herself, adding that she had only been amusing herself at home while he was amusing himself at his Club; and when Gil declared that he would question her mother about her conduct, she replied saucily that her mother was quite as bad herself.

A violent quarrel ensued, which ended in Susanna running tearfully into her own room and banging the door, leaving her husband storming up and down the room and furiously demolishing everything that came in his way—flinging books, ornaments, vases, and flowers on to the floor.

The Count, however, gradually calmed down somewhat and flung himself into a chair, burying his head despairingly in his hands, lost in his unhappy jealous thoughts and more convinced than ever that his beloved wife had a secret lover. Presently old Sante crept into the room and, unnoticed by his absorbed master, quietly picked up the fallen objects and put them in order once more.

A little while later, Susanna, all traces of tears and anger removed, entered the room, calm and serene, and carrying Gil's hat.

gloves, and umbrella, which she handed to her husband, reminding him that it was time for him to go to his Club that evening as usual. The Count, seeing her so sweet, gentle, and devoted, as he loved her to be, gladly made up their quarrel, especially as Susanna expressed penitence for her angry outburst and entreated forgiveness.

But even as he kissed and fondled her, Susanna begged to be warned as soon as he returned later on; and regarding this request as suspicious, he again sprang from her impatiently and rushed away as though about to depart to his Club. Secretly, however, he determined to return in a short time, unannounced, to prove for himself whether or not she received a lover in his absence.

As twilight had now fallen, Susanna drew the curtains and lighted the lamp, sighing as she did so at the thought of her husband's unreasoning jealousy and regretting the necessity for her present secrecy, hating to deceive one she so truly loved. Then, calling to Sante to bring her the precious parcel she had brought in under such difficulties, she extracted therefrom a cigarette, lit it, and puffed at it with a sigh of deep content.

For this was the harmless secret which, aided by the devoted old Sante, she had managed to keep hidden from her old-fashioned husband—who, never having himself acquired the habit of smoking, would, she knew, be horrified by her own indulgence—and smoking was one of her greatest joys, though now a stolen one.

But scarcely had she enjoyed a few puffs at the longed-for cigarette than Gil returned. There was not time even for Sante —who had remained to light her cigarette and to laugh with her over their wonderful secret—to retire; and making him hide behind the curtains, she stood up, holding the cigarette behind her, as her husband burst into the room.

Her look of alarm was instantly observed by Gil, who, all his jealous suspicions reawakened, declared that his " enemy " was in the house; and he immediately began to search for the imaginary intruder, calling loudly for Sante to assist him. Sante, who had cleverly managed to make good his escape from behind the curtains, pretended to help his master in the search; but finding no one, the Count once more rushed out of the house in a rage, intending to return yet again unexpectedly.

Thinking herself safe for a little while, Susanna once more lit up her cigarette, thoroughly enjoying her stolen pleasure in spite of the risk she ran of her secret being discovered—for she still did not realize that her husband seriously suspected her of concealing a lover in the house but only feared his anger because of her smoking against his wishes.

Scarcely had she indulged in a few more puffs, however, than Gil once more burst into the room, this time through the french window, the sudden inrush of air putting out the lamp. Enraged by the renewed odour of freshly-smoked tobacco—which immediately greeted his nostrils—he shouted wildly to the hidden lover to come forth; and seizing Susanna's hand in the semi-darkness, he burnt himself with the lighted cigarette she held therein.

Realizing now that her secret could no longer be hidden, Susanna, in a sudden panic of fear, fell upon her knees and entreated forgiveness as though for some terrible fault. Clinging to her husband, she confessed her deception tearfully and declared her willingness to give up her stolen indulgence should he still desire it.

But Gil, full of relief at the discovery of so harmless a secret and ashamed of his unjust suspicions, now humbly implored pardon for himself. He declared that, so far from her giving up the pleasure he had forbidden owing to his old-fashioned notions, he would himself learn to smoke the fragrant weed with her.

And so, with a loving embrace, the husband and wife each lit up a cigarette and enjoyed their first smoke together.

SHORT BIOGRAPHIES OF THE COMPOSERS

AUBER

DANIEL FRANÇOIS ESPRIT AUBER was born at Caen, Normandy, 29th January, 1782 : died at Paris, 13th May, 1871. He was the son of a Paris print-seller, and was sent in early youth to acquire business knowledge in London; but whilst in England, he began to devote himself assiduously to the study of music. Later on, after his return to Paris, he made the acquaintance of Cherubini, whose pupil he became. He soon began to compose operas, a brilliant series of triumphs for him beginning with the production in Paris of *La Bergère Châtelaine* in 1820. He wrote over forty operas, among the best known of which are :—*Fra Diavolo* (Paris, 1830), *Masaniello* (Paris, 1828), *The Bronze Horse* (Paris, 1828), *The Crown Diamonds* (Paris, 1841), *Zerline* (Paris, 1851), and *The Black Domino* (Paris, 1837).

Masaniello (or *La Muette de Portici*), a highly dramatic opera, is considered to be Auber's finest work; but the amusing and frivolous *Fra Diavolo*, with its light sparkling music, has always been his most popular opera and still is included in many operatic repertoires.

BACH

JOHANN SEBASTIAN BACH was one of the greatest composers of all time. He was born in Eisenbach, Thuringia, 21st March, 1685; died 28th July, 1750. His father, Johann A. Bach, who was Court Musician at Eisenbach, taught him the violin; and later, when ten years old, he went to live with his brother, J. Ch. Bach, who gave him instruction on the clavichord. As a chorister at St. Michael's, Luneberg, he worked hard at these instruments, at the organ, and at composition, often studying the whole night through. He became organist at Arnstadt in 1703, and later was appointed organist at Mülhausen. In 1708 he became Court Organist and in 1714 was appointed Concertmeister. In 1717 he went to Köthen as Kapellmeister. In 1723 he became principal Cantor at Leipzig; and here he remained for twenty-seven years, though in frequent strife with Church conventions, his great genius and noble ideals receiving little encouragement. In 1747 he was commanded to visit Frederick II of Prussia; and during this memorable visit he improvised on the various pianos in the palace. He also played on all the chief organs in Potsdam, on one of which he improvised a six part fugue on a theme set by the King. Bach promoted the adoption of equal temperament and also initiated the style of fingering still in use; and as a master of counterpoint and fugue he was supreme. His compositions were very numerous and chiefly of a sacred character, his Church cantatas alone occupying ten volumes. Among the most famous of his works are his Passion Music, his *Mass in B Minor*, a large number of fugues, songs, chamber music, etc. His little operetta-cantata, *Phœbus and Pan*, was written in 1749 as a musical satire, and in this charming composition he poked fun at certain of his critics and rivals. Bach always suffered with his eyes, being near-sighted; and an operation he underwent in 1749 resulted in total blindness. He died the following year.

Between 1850 and 1900, Bach's compositions were issued at Leipzig in fifty-two volumes by the Bach Society, which was established for this purpose. They include the magnificent *Mass in B Minor*, *The Passions of St. Matthew and St. John*, over two hundred cantatas, sacred and secular, and a great number of other pieces. In London there is a Bach Choir, founded in 1876, which exists to give performances of his works. Bach is believed to have had a family of twenty children, all of whom had musical talent. Four of his sons became well-known musicians. The eldest, Wilhelm Friedrich, was the most talented, and became organist at Dresden and Halle. He composed some charming music, as did his brother, Carl Philip. The latter, indeed, was a prolific composer; he was patronized by Frederick the Great.

BALFE

MICHAEL WILLIAM BALFE was born at Dublin, 15th May, 1808; died at Rowney Abbey, 20th October, 1870. He displayed remarkable musical talent as a boy; and when only sixteen conducted the orchestra at Drury Lane Theatre. Later he studied music in Italy; and in Paris he met Rossini, who engaged him as a baritone singer there.

On his return to England, he began to write operas in the Italian style popularized by Rossini. In 1845 he was made conductor of the Italian Opera, Covent Garden. He wrote a great many operas, the best known of which are :—*The Bohemian Girl* (Drury Lane, London, 1843), *The Rose of Castile* (Lyceum

Theatre, London, 1857), *Satanella* (1858), *The Maid of Honour* (1847), *Joan of Arc* (1837), etc. *The Bohemian Girl* was one of the most popular operas in the English repertoires throughout the whole of the Victorian era. None of his other operas attained such world-wide popularity. Balfe also was a famous song-writer, the best known of his songs being :—*Come into the Garden, Maud, The Arrow and the Song,* and *Killarney.*

SIR GRANVILLE BANTOCK

GRANVILLE BANTOCK was born in London, August 7th, 1868. He received his musical education at the Royal Academy of Music, where, in 1889, he became the first holder of the Macfarren Scholarship for Composition. He launched a journal known as *The New Quarterly Musical Review*; and he was for a time conductor of a theatrical company, in which capacity he travelled in many parts of the world. Later he held an appointment as Musical Director at New Brighton, near Liverpool; and in 1908 he became Professor of Music at the Birmingham University and Principal of the School of Music in that city, also Director of the Midland Institute. In 1934, he became Chairman of the Corporation of Trinity College, London. He was knighted in 1930.

Bantock's compositions are of a very high order; and he has written a great number of excellent songs, in which the Gaelic spirit often prevails. His orchestral and choral music include symphonies, cantatas, oratorios, and various suites. Among these may be mentioned his Eastern work, *Omar Khayyám*, his *Hebridean Symphony*, *English Scenes*, and his *Pagan Symphony*.

His opera *The Seal-Woman*, produced in Birmingham, September 28th, 1924, is on a Hebridean folk-lore theme, and is full of the mysticism of those lovely islands. The libretto is by that famous collector of Hebridean folk-songs, Mrs. Marjory Kennedy-Fraser.

BEETHOVEN

LUDWIG VAN BEETHOVEN, one of the greatest of musicians, was born at Bonn, 16th December, 1770; died 26th March, 1827. He was the son of a tenor singer in the service of the Elector of Cologne. His wonderful talent for music was early displayed and cultivated, and even in his eighth year he delighted all who heard him by his truly astonishing execution on the violin. He began to compose sonatas in his thirteenth year, and these promising signs of genius caused the Elector of Cologne to send him, in the character of his Court-Organist, to Vienna, Schenk, and Albrechtsberger. Here, except for some few years spent in the new Court of the King of Westphalia, Beethoven passed the remainder of his life, latterly retiring to the village of Mödlingen, near Vienna. Most of his principal works were composed after 1801. He did not hold musical offices, but devoted himself entirely to composition; and though at first he appeared as a pianoforte player, he afterwards withdrew entirely from the world and lived in a solitude enhanced latterly by almost total deafness. Beethoven was essentially a composer of instrumental music, which received from his work an entirely new and original character, and he developed the symphonic art to a surprising boldness and breadth of form and outline, filling this in with a truly marvellous wealth of grand melody—the landmark of a completely new phase in the history of music. Beethoven wrote one opera only, *Fidelio* (first entitled *Leonore*), and one sacred cantata, *The Mount of Olives*; but, original and beautiful as these are, they still show us that this great musician was at his greatest in his instrumental works, upon which his chief fame rests. *Fidelio* was produced in Vienna in 1805. Besides his noble symphonies and overtures, his quintettes, quartettes, and trios for stringed instruments, his numerous sonatas, variations, and other pieces for the pianoforte, all show the great richness, power, and originality of his imagination. Beethoven died in the village of Mödlingen on 26th March, 1827.

BELLINI

Vincenzo Bellini was born at Catania, Sicily, on November 3rd, 1802. He died at Puteaux, near Paris, September 24th, 1835, in his thirty-fourth year. He received his musical education at the Conservatory in Naples, where he studied under Zingarelli. In 1833, he went to Paris. He produced a number of operas, his style being chiefly founded on that of the then fashionable Rossini, but with the defects of that successful composer's florid style somewhat exaggerated. Rossini was, however, a good friend to the young Bellini, and gave him much valuable advice and encouragement.

Bellini's first opera of importance was *La Sonnambula*, which created quite a sensation when produced in Milan in 1831; and it was an equal success when given in London later on that same year, the heroine's part being played frequently by Adelina Patti, Madame Malibran, and Madame Albani. *Norma* was likewise produced in 1831, at Milan; and it quite astonished the musical world. It was followed by *Beatrice di Tenda*. Other operas of

ellini were *La Straniera* (1828), *Zaira* (1829), *Capuletti ed i Mon-
cchi* (a version of the *Romeo and Juliet* story) which had a
ccess in Venice in 1830. His last opera was *I Puritani*, produced
Paris in 1835. Bellini still holds the operatic stage with *La
onnambula* and *Norma*, with which he charmed the music-lovers
his day; and there is no doubt that had his life not ended in his
rly thirties, he would certainly have done much more important
ork in the realms of opera. His music is very melodious.

BENEDICT

R JULIUS BENEDICT was born at Stuttgart, 27th November, 1804;
ed 5th June, 1885. In his early years he studied with J. C. L.
beille, and was also under Hummel at Weimar, where he was
esented to Weber, who then took him entirely under his charge,
eating him more as a son than as a pupil. At the age of nineteen
ars, he was appointed conductor of the Karnthnerthor Theatre
Vienna. From there he went to Italy, and was appointed Chef
Orchestre at the San Carlos at Naples. Here he produced his
st opera, *Giacinta ed Ernesto* (1829). In 1835, he went to
ngland, which country he made his home for the remainder of
s life. Here his finest operas were written and produced, *The
ides of Venice* being produced in 1843, and *The Crusaders*,
46; and in 1836 he was made musical director of the Opera
ffa at the Lyceum Theatre. In 1850, he accompanied Jenny
nd to the United States, as director of her concerts. On his
turn in 1852, he was appointed conductor of the Harmonic
nion. In 1862 he produced in London his popular opera, *The
ly of Killarney*, a musical version of Dion Boucicault's play,
he Colleen Bawn*. In 1871 he was knighted; and he died in
ngland on 5th June, 1885. Besides his operas, Benedict also
rote some very charming cantatas, chief of which are *Undine*
860) and *Richard Cœur de Lion* (1863); also *Graziella* (1882),
terwards performed as an opera. He also wrote the oratorios,
. *Cecilia* (1886) and *St. Peter* (1870); and a number of other
aller musical pieces.

BENJAMIN

RTHUR L. BENJAMIN, the Australian composer, was born at
dney, New South Wales, in 1893. He received his musical
ucation at the Royal College of Music in London, to which he
turned later as a member of its staff, after spending some time in
dney as a Professor of the pianoforte at the Conservatory there.

One of his earliest works, a *Pastoral Fantasy*, received publicatio
by the Carnegie Trustees. In 1933, his *Violin Concerto* (dedicate
to William Walton) was given its first hearing at a B.B.C. Concer
He has written a considerable amount of music of various kind
and in recent years he has composed a good deal of excellent musi
for films.

Benjamin's best known work is his delightful one-act opera *Th
Devil Take Her*. This was first produced at the Royal College c
Music under the conductorship of Sir Thomas Beecham. Late
on in 1932, this gay little work (the libretto of which is based on a
old folk-song) was put into the repertory of the Old Vic an
Sadler's Wells, where it has proved a very popular success.

Another of Benjamin's operas is *Prima Donna*, written in 193

LORD BERNERS

LORD BERNERS (Gerald Hugh Tyrwhitt-Wilson) was born
Bridgnorth, September 18th, 1883. He succeeded to the Baron
in 1918, and is the ninth Baron. He was educated at Eton, ar
entered the Diplomatic Service, being an honorary attaché fro
1909 to 1920, during which period he composed under his nam
of " Gerald Tyrwhitt ". For a time he was a pupil of Stravinsl
and of Casella; and his style is essentially modern. In addition
being a composer and a diplomat, he is likewise an author and
painter, having exhibited oil-paintings. Among his publishe
books are *First Childhood* and *The Camel*.

Lord Berners' opera *Le Carrosse du Saint Sacrement* was fir
performed in Paris in 1923 at the Théâtre du Champs-Élysée
where its subtle music was well received by a highly critic
audience. He has also written several very successful balle
among which are the *Triumph of Neptune*, given by Diaghile
in 1926, *Luna Park*, a fantastic work included in the Cochr
Revue of 1930, *Wedding Banquet* and *Cupid and Psyche*, bo
produced at Sadler's Wells. The Intermezzo and Hornpipe fro
the *Triumph of Neptune* have been since arranged as pianofor
solos. Among other well-known works are his *Valses Bourgeois*
the *Fantasie Espagnole*, and *Fugue*. A sense of irony, almost
parody, appears in some of his musical works; and he is a wit
and entertaining writer.

BIZET

ALEXANDER CÉSAR LEOPOLD BIZET (known as Georges) was bo
at Paris October 25th, 1838; died there June 3rd, 1875, in l

irty-seventh year. He was brought up in an artistic atmosphere,
eing the son of a singing-master, his mother and an uncle also
eing musicians (the latter founded the Delsarte system). He
ntered the Paris Conservatoire at the age of nine years; and when
nineteen gained the *Grand Prix de Rome* and went to Italy to
udy. While in Rome he wrote his suite *Rome*, and a number
operettas. On his return to Paris, Bizet began to write operas,
s first important success being *Les Pecheurs de Perles*, which
as produced at the Théâtre Lyrique in 1863. It was coldly re-
ived, as were also *La Jolie Fille de Perth* (1867), *Djamileh* (1872),
d *L'Arlèsienne*—incidental music to Daudet's play of that
ame (also in 1872). Then, in 1875 *Carmen* was produced at the
péra-Comique; and this masterpiece gained for Bizet world-wide
me and placed him in the front rank of operatic composers.
rangely enough, however, the Parisians at first showed no
thusiasm for the opera; and it was not until eight years later,
hen it had been acclaimed everywhere else, that they at last
cognized its extraordinary charm and genius. It is possible that
Spanish subject did not appeal to them. Once they had accepted
however, they quickly made up for their former lack of
terest. It was produced in London in 1878.
Carmen was the last work of Bizet. Three months after its first
oduction, just as success was within his grasp, the gifted com-
ser was seized with sudden illness and died.
Carmen, like *Pagliacci*, is regarded as one of the most perfectly
nstructed operas ever written; and its delightful **music shares**
e world-wide popularity of Gounod's *Faust*.

BOÏTO

RRIGO Boïto was born at Padua in 1842; and he died at Milan in
18. He studied at the Conservatory in Milan for nine years;
d for several years he was musical critic to a number of impor-
nt Italian journals. For a time it seemed doubtful whether he
uld devote himself entirely to music or to literature, for which
seemed to have an almost equal genius; and in both spheres he
et with great success. He had a wonderful sense of the theatre,
d not only did he write his own libretti, but provided extremely
amatic libretti for Verdi's *Otello* and *Falstaff*, Ponchielli's *La
ioconda*, and Mancinelli's *Ero e Leandro*. He also wrote poems
d a novel.
Boïto's two most famous operas are *Mefistofele* and *Nerone*, for
th of which he studied for many years. For his libretto of

Mefistofele, he built up his dramatic story from not only th
Goethe legends, but also from the same legend as treated b
Marlowe, Widmann, Lenau, Blaise de Bury and others. He wa
a great admirer and follower of Wagner, and for a time share
the earlier condemnation of that great master's revolutionar
methods. When *Mefistofele* was first produced in Milan at L
Scala in 1868, it was unsuccessful and was adversely criticize
Later on, however, when Wagner also had been accepted, Boït
brought out his splendid opera once more at Bologna in 187
where it was immediately an immense success. In 1926 the gre
Chaliapine scored an enthusiastic triumph as *Mefistofele* at Cover
Garden. It came first to London in 1880.

Nerone was not completed until nearly forty-two years late
Mefistofele having occupied the composer's mind for fifty year
He maintained great secrecy about it. It was produced po
thumously at La Scala, Milan, on April 30th, 1924, with Tosc
nini conducting. It is a stupendous work, and its enthusiast
reception was an undoubted triumph.

Few composers have led so full a life as Boïto. He wrote a gre
number of witty comedies as a side line; he talked and wro
perfect French; he was given honorary degrees at both Oxford ar
Cambridge; and he even entered politics, becoming in 1912
Senator of the Kingdom of Italy. He likewise fought und
Garibaldi.

BORODIN

Alexander Porphyrievich Borodin was born at St. Petersbur
12th November, 1834, and died there 28th February, 1887. F
belonged to the princely family of Imeretinsky; and his mus
shows unmistakable signs of his Eastern antecedents. As a you
he was given by his mother every educational advantage; and fi
of all he adopted medicine as a career, gaining much honour ar
repute in that profession. But his intense love of music was not
be denied, and though he firmly declined to desert Science f
Art, he devoted an almost equal portion of his time to music
composition—and, by thus serving two exacting masters, cut sho
a valuable life.

Borodin composed many symphonies, songs, quartettes, and
good deal of chamber music—all of which secured much atte
tion. The most popular of these lesser works was his symphor
sketch *In the Steppes of Central Asia*. But it was his wonderfu
melodic oriental opera, *Prince Igor*, that has secured for Borod

world-wide fame. This amazingly colourful opera was not quite completed at Borodin's death, but was afterwards finished by Rimsky-Korsakov and Glazounov, and produced posthumously at the Imperial Opera House, St. Petersburg, in 1890. It was first given in London at Drury Lane during the Beecham Season in 1914. His unfinished opera-ballet, *Mlada*, was likewise orchestrated by Rimsky-Korsakov, and produced at the Mariensky Theatre, St. Petersburg, 1892.

Borodin was one of the famous group of musicians interested in establishing nationalism in Russian musical art—to which group also belonged Moussorgsky, Rimsky-Korsakov, Cui, Serov, Arensky, Glazounov, Balakirev, and Dargomijsky. This nationalistic school, however, did not include Tschaikovsky, who preferred a more universal art.

RUTLAND BOUGHTON

Rutland Boughton was born in 1878 at Aylesbury, in Bucks. He received his musical education at the Royal College of Music, where he was a student of Stanford and Walford Davies; and he was a Professor of Music under Bantock at the Midland Institute of Music, Birmingham, from 1902 till 1911. In 1914, he founded the Glastonbury Festival School of Music Drama, of which he is the Director. His delightful music drama, *The Immortal Hour* an operatic setting of " Fiona Macleod's "—William Sharp—poetic work), was first produced at Glastonbury in August, 1914. Upon its later production in London in 1922, it met with remarkable success, and enjoyed one of the longest runs of any British opera, firmly establishing itself in popular favour. In January, 1924, his serious opera, *Alkestis*, was produced in London, and, though not so popular as *The Immortal Hour*, was well received and marked a considerable advance. In December, 1923, *Bethlehem*, a Choral Drama (adapted from the Coventry Nativity Play) was produced—though this little work had previously been given in December 28th, 1915, at Street, Somerset, during the Christmas Festival of the Glastonbury Festival School. In August, 1924, his dramatic opera, *The Queen of Cornwall* (with Thomas Hardy's poetic drama as its libretto) was produced at Glastonbury. The late Sir Edward Elgar regarded *The Immortal Hour* as " a work of genius "; and Mr. Ernest Newman, the well-known music critic, has described it as " one of the loveliest and most original English works of our time ".

CHARPENTIER

GUSTAVE CHARPENTIER was born at Dienze, Alsace-Lorraine, 25th June, 1860. His parents removed to Tourcoing after the Franco-Prussian War; and at the age of seventeen, Charpentier entered the Lille Conservatoire, where he won many prizes. Later on he entered the Paris Conservatoire, where he studied under Massart and Massenet. Here he captured the *Prix de Rome* in 1887 with *Didon*, a scène lyrique. Here also he composed the suite, *Impressions d'Italie*, and a symphonic drama, *La Vie de Poète*. His beautiful romantic opera of Paris life, *Louise*, was produced in Paris at the Opéra-Comique in 1900, and was first heard in London at Covent Garden in 1909. Another opera, *Julien*, is a sequel to *Louise*. Other operas are:—*Orphée, Tête Rouge, La Couronnement de la Muse*. Among many other important work are *Fleurs du Mal* to Baudelaire's Poems and an orchestral suite both produced in 1894; *Serenade à Watteau*, 1896; *Impression Fausses*, etc. Charpentier is ranked with the best of the modern French composers.

CUI

CÉSAR ANTONOVICH CUI was born at Vilna, 18th January, 1835 and died at St. Petersburg, 14th March, 1918. He was the son of a French officer who remained in Poland upon the retreat from Moscow in 1812 and who afterwards married a Lithuanian lady. The young César early showed great musical ability and was famed as an infant prodigy. His father's military gifts, however were likewise strongly developed in him, and he entered the Military Engineering School at St. Petersburg, and afterwards became an authority on that subject. He soon began to compose operas, which quickly gained for him an ever-growing musical reputation. His third opera, *William Ratcliff*, firmly established him as an operatic composer; and though he never became a master of difficult orchestration as did so many of the great Russian composers, his work being more of the delicate, miniature like order of composition, he exhibited much passion, grace, and real lyrical force. Besides a very considerable output of lesser orchestral works, songs, and pianoforte music, Cui produced ten operas, the best known of which in this country are :—*The Captive in the Caucasus, Mam'zelle Fifi* (first produced at the Hermitage Theatre, Moscow, 1903; *William Ratcliff, Angelo The Saracen*.

Cui was one of the famous group of Russian Nationalist

musical composers, of whom the following were likewise members:—Dargomijsky, Moussorgsky, Borodin, Serov, Glinka, Arensky, Balakirev, Glazounov, and Rimsky-Korsakov. Tschaikovsky did not belong to this group, his art being of a more universal quality.

DARGOMIJSKY

ALEXANDER SERGEIVICH DARGOMIJSKY was born 2/14 February, 1813, in a country district of Toula. He early showed great musical gifts, and his parents removed to St. Petersburg for the sake of his musical education. Though he entered the Government service on completion of his general education, he gave up his appointment after a few years in order to devote himself entirely to musical composition. He travelled abroad a good deal, making the acquaintance of the French composers of his day, having already made friends with his own great national contemporary, Glinka, and, later, with Cui and Rimsky-Korsakov. With these, he belonged to the famous group of Russian Nationalist musical composers, among whom were also Cui, Serov, Balakirev, Arensky, Glazounov, and Borodin. After producing a good many songs, he wrote an opera on the subject of Victor Hugo's *Notre Dame de Paris*, entitled *Esmeralda*; and its charming and graceful music brought him great success— -though Dargomijsky was already devoting himself to more serious work, his ideas being greatly in advance of his time. It was not until 1856 that his next opera, *The Roussalka* (*The Water-Nymph*) was produced in St. Petersburg, though he had meanwhile written an opera ballet, *The Triumph of Bacchus*; but *Roussalka* proved too revolutionary a composition for the popular taste of the day. Dargomijsky's fourth and greatest opera was *The Stone Guest*, based on the Don Juan story treated by Poushkin; but he died before it was quite finished, the orchestration being completed by Cui. It was produced in St. Petersburg in 1872, and in it, this composer reached his zenith and revealed his greatest originality.

DEBUSSY

CLAUDE ACHILLE DEBUSSY was born August 22nd, 1862, at St. Germain-en-Laye. He died in Paris, March 26th, 1918. He studied at the Paris Conservatoire, where he won the *Grand Prix de Rome* with his operatic cantata *L'Enfant Prodigue* in 1884. This entitled him to study in Rome for three years. Here he composed the setting of Rosetti's *Blessed Damosel*, which was

2G

rejected by the French authorities. In 1893, his extremely origina tone-poem, *L'Après-midi d'un Faune*, was produced and im mediately aroused great controversy, owing to the new distinctiv style this composer had already made his own. Discussion in creased with the production of his opera *Pelléas et Mélisande*, a the Opéra-Comique, Paris, in 1902, which has Maeterlinck' beautiful poetic drama as its libretto. This opera is remarkabl for its absence of set melody and movement, replaced by almos continuous recitative. Some years later, his small opera, describe as a " Lyrical Episode ", *L'Enfant Prodigue*, was produced i England at the Sheffield Music Festival in 1908, and at Coven Garden in 1910.

Other important works of Debussy are *Chimène*, an opera to libretto by Camille Mendès; incidental music to d'Annuncio' *Martyrdom of St. Sebastian* (1911); *Ariettes to Poems of Paul Ver laine*, *Poèmes de Baudelaires*, *Chanson de Bilitis*, *Nuages*, *L Mer*, *St. Cécilia Ode*, *Iberia*, *Rondes de Printemps*, *Soirée dan Grénade*, *Serenade for a Doll*, *Golliwogs' Cakewalk*, *Gardens i Rain*, *Reflections in the Water*, *Goldfish*, *Dead Leaves*, etc., etc

For some years Debussy was engaged in journalistic criticism

The music of Debussy is remarkable for the new chords pro duced by the employment of the higher overtones to enrich th harmony—a method foreshadowed by Berlioz. His art is re garded as being in revolt against the Classics and the Romantics yet there is a certain amount of classicism in his work, which ofte shows careful balance and restraint. He was the founder of wha is known as the *Impressionist School in Music*, in which sug gestion rather than *statement* is regarded as the ideal and in whic the obviously dramatic, formal, and conventional give place t especial emphasis regarding *tone*. Debussy's was one of the mos original musical minds of modern times.

DELIBES

Clément Philibert Léo Delibes was born at St. Germain du V (Sarthe), 21st February, 1836. He received his musical educatio in Paris, being admitted to the Solfège Class at the Conservatoir in 1848. He studied under Le Couppey, Benöist, Bazin, an Adolphe Adam. He became the accompanist at the Théât Lyrique in 1853; and later on he was appointed organist various important churches. He wrote several short operas fo the Théâtre Lyrique, and a number of operettas, choruses, et He became accompanist at the Opéra in 1863, and was afte wards appointed as Chorus Master. Here a new career in mediately opened for him, and he wrote a number of ballets and *divertissements*, the chief of which was *Coppélia*, produced in Paris in 1870. His first full opera was *Le Roi l'a Dit*, produced in Paris in 1873, which has always been a favourite in Germany. His mythological ballet, *Sylvia*, was produced in 1876, in Paris; and he also wrote for the Opéra-Comique, Paris, two other dramatic works, *Jean de Nivelle*, produced March, 1880, and his beautiful romantic opera, *Lakmé*, which was produced in 1883. He was made Chevalier of the Legion of Honour in 1877. He died in 1891.

DELIUS

FREDERICK DELIUS was born in Bradford, Yorkshire, in 1863. Though practically self-taught he received his later musical education in Leipzig, where he studied for two years at the Conservatoire. His opera, *A Village Romeo and Juliet*, was first produced in Berlin, 1907. His music drama, *Fennimore and Gerda*, appeared in Frankfort-on-Main, 1919. His incidental music to the drama *Hassan*, or *The Golden Journey to Samarkand*, with Flecker's beautiful poem for its subject, was produced in Darmstadt, June, 1923, and in London, September, 1923. Delius' many other vocal and instrumental compositions have all met with very great success. Among these may be mentioned :—*Sea-Drift*, *A Mass of Life*, *Requiem*, *Brigg Fair*, *A Dance Rhapsodie*, *The Song of the High Hills*, *Songs of Sunset*, *In a Summer Garden*, *Paris, the Song of a Great City*, *A Late Lark*, etc. A Companionship of Honour was conferred upon Delius·in 1929, when a grand and most successful festival of his works was held in London under the auspices of Sir Thomas Beecham and Mr. Peter Warlock; and, though then blind and paralysed, the great musician was happily able to attend this belated national recognition of his genius. Delius died in 1934, at Grez-sur-Loing, France.

DONIZETTI

GAETANO DONIZETTI was born at Bergamo, Italy, September 25th, 1798; died there April 8th, 1848. His musical education was conducted at Bologna and Naples; and at first, at his father's wish, he devoted himself to Church music. He had, however, no taste for the latter, and, to evade his father's influence, he entered the army. While thus away from home, he wrote his two first operas, *Enrico di Borgogna* (1818), and *Il Falegname di Livonia*, very soon after. The latter was so successful that he was able to leave the army and to devote himself seriously to operatic work. His first successful opera was *Anna Bolena*, produced in Rome, 1830 He wrote with great ease and rapidity, and produced nearly seventy operas. His style, like that of Bellini, was founded on that of the then popular Rossini, though his work was far more dramatic than theirs; and his rich flowing melodies have attained great popularity. After 1844, Donizetti's talent seemed to have utterly exhausted itself, and he began to suffer from melancholia, which finally developed into insanity and paralysis.

Donizetti's chief operas were: *The Daughter of the Regimen* (Paris, 1840), *La Favorita* (Paris, 1840), *Don Pasquale* (Paris, 1843) *Lucia di Lammermoor* (Naples, 1835), *L'Eliser d'Amore* (Milan 1832), *Lucrezia Borgia* (Milan, 1834), *Linda de Chamoun* (Vienna, 1842). Of these, *Don Pasquale*, *Lucia di Lammermoor* and *The Daughter of the Regiment* still hold the stage with frequent revivals.

Lucia di Lammermoor is now generally regarded as Donizetti' finest work, and its many exquisite melodies are highly descriptive of its tragic subject. The famous Mad Scene in Act III is an example in point, and likewise provides the coloratura soprano with a beautifully melodic means of exhibiting vocal acrobatics of a highly technical quality.

DUKAS

PAUL DUKAS was born in Paris in 1865, and died there in 1935 He received his musical education at the Paris Conservatoire where he later became a professor of composition. He gained the second *Grand Prix de Rome* with his cantata *Velleda*. One of his most renowned works is the brilliant symphonic poem *L'Apprenti Sorcier*, which has been received with great success everywhere. His ballet *La Peri* has likewise proved a very popular work.

It is, however, by his exquisitely symbolic opera, *Ariane e Barbe-Bleue*, produced in Paris, 1907, that Dukas has become more widely known. This is based on Maeterlinck's well-known romance, the touching humanity and delicate symbolism of which gives great scope to a composer of such vision and understanding

Dukas is regarded as having influenced the modern Spanish school by means of his friendship for Albeniz. He was a very sincere critic of music, and edited the works of Rameau and of Scarlatti. So severe a critic was he of his own work that, just before his death, he made a bonfire of most of his compositions written after middle life, none of which he would permit to be published. It is believed that the loss to the world of music by this drastic action was probably very considerable.

DVOŘÁK

ANTONIN DVOŘÁK, the famous Czech composer, was born September 8th, 1841, at Nelahozeves, near Prague. He died May 1st, 1904. He was the eighth son of a butcher and innkeeper and received his early musical instruction from the village organist. At the age of eight he played at various festivals and was a member of the parish choir. At the age of twelve he began his serious study of music at Zlonice, under Liehmann, who gave him a sound foundation for his subsequent brilliant career. He became organist at St. Adalbert's, in Prague, in 1873; and he was also a member of the Bohemian Theatre orchestra there. Later on he became acquainted with Wagner, Schumann, and Liszt, all of whom exercised considerable influence upon his own composition, though the foundation of his art was primarily laid on the Beethoven tradition.

Dvořák is regarded as a great master of instrumentation; also is one of the most gifted and versatile composers of the nineteenth century.

With Smetana, he identified himself closely and enthusiastically with the national music of Bohemia. In his operas, this strong national element is very evident—also in many of his symphonies. His chamber music is notable for its great charm and purity of style.

Dvořák wrote many symphonies, choral works, chamber music, and pianoforte pieces and songs, in addition to a number of operas. The operas, however, are at present little known in this country, with the exception of *Rusalka* (*The Water-Nymph*). The latter is a very striking work, based on an old Czech legend. It was first produced at Prague on March 31st, 1901, at the National Theatre, and at Covent Garden, London, in 1938. It is the most popular of all his operas. Among his other operas may be mentioned *Dmitrj*, *Vanda*, *The Cunning Peasant*, *The Devil and Kate*, etc., most of these being strongly national in character.

Among other well-known works of Dvořák are his *Stabat Mater*, *St. Luidmila*, *Slavonic Dances*, *Slavonic Rhapsodies*, *The Dumky Trio*, *Carnaval Overture*, and many pianoforte solos and duets—of which the famous *Humoreske* is one of the best known.

For over six years Dvořák was Director of the National Conservatory of Music in New York, 1892-8; and in 1901 he became Director of Music at Prague.

BARON D'ERLANGER

FREDERIC D'ERLANGER, born in Paris in 1868, came to England, his country of adoption, as soon as he had completed his literary and musical studies.

His energies during the earlier days of his career were chiefly devoted to opera; and it may be noted that two of his works were performed at Covent Garden, London, namely *Indes Mendo* in 1897, and *Tess*, based on Thomas Hardy's novel *Tess of the D'Urbervilles*, in 1910. *Tess* was first produced in Naples in 1909.

Nevertheless, he did not neglect other fields of music, and is the author of a number of symphonic and choral works, the most notable amongst the latter being a *Requiem Mass*.

Two ballets, *Les Cent Baisers* and *Cendrillon*, figure amongst Frederic d'Erlanger's later compositions. They form part of the permanent repertoire of the Russian Company which appeared every summer at Covent Garden between 1934 and 1939.

Baron d'Erlanger died April 25th, 1943.

FLOTOW

FRIEDRICH VON FLOTOW was born at Teutondorf, Mecklenburg Schwerin, 26th April, 1812; died at Darmstadt, 23rd January, 1883 He received his musical education at Paris, where he early begar to write operas. His first real success was scored with *Stradella* produced at Hamburg in 1844. *Martha* was produced in Vienna in 1847, and quickly won the composer world-wide fame. It wa produced in England at the Royal Italian Opera, Covent Garden London, in 1858, and instantly obtained popularity with the Eng lish public. Flotow wrote several other operas, none of which are well known in England. In 1838, he wrote and brought out ir Vienna a new opera, *The Duc de Guise*, the libretto being basec on Dumas's *Henry III*. The special performance of this oper: was organized by the Princess Czartory for the benefit of th Poles; and most of the characters in it were sustained by amateur —princesses, duchesses, and other Society ladies of Paris. Nothing however, was heard of this opera afterwards.

GATTY

DR. NICHOLAS COMYN GATTY (B.A., Cantab.) was born Septembe 13th, 1874, near Sheffield. He received his musical education a the Royal College of Music in London, studying under Sir Charle

Stanford. He was for a time organist to the Duke of York's Royal Military School at Chelsea; and he was also music critic on several important London newspapers, notably *The Pall Mall Gazette*.

He has written five operas : *Greysteel* (produced Sheffield in 1906); *Duke or Devil* (Gaiety Theatre, Manchester, December 16th, 1909); *Prince Ferelon* (London, May 21st, 1921); *The Tempest* (April 17th, 1920, at Surrey Theatre); *King Alfred and the Cakes* (London (R.C.M.), December 1930, Falmouth, 1938). Most of these operas have been revived in recent years at Sadler's Wells, and are now in the repertory of that theatre. This composer has a very good sense of the theatre, and his musical style is direct and melodious.

Nicholas Gatty has also written and produced a number of smaller orchestral and choral works with great success.

GIORDANO

Umberto Giordano was born at Foggia, Italy, on August 20th, 1867. He received his musical education at the Naples Conservatory, under the special tuition of Paolo Serrão.

When twenty-three years old he competed in the same prize offered by the Music Publishing House of Sonzogno for a one-act opera, which was won by Mascagni in 1890 with the brilliant *Cavalleria Rusticana*. The opera he submitted, *Marina*, though it failed to win this particular prize, brought its young composer into notice. He received a commission for a three-act opera. This was *Mala Vita*, which was produced in Rome two years later, in 1892.

Giordano's best known opera—and by many considered his finest work—is *Andrea Chénier*, produced at La Scala, Milan, March 23rd, 1896. It was given at Covent Garden, London, in 1903. In 1898, *Fédora*, based on Sardou's drama, was produced in Milan. This opera has also been heard at Covent Garden.

A successful light opera was *Madame Sans-Gêne*, first produced at the Metropolitan Opera House, New York, January 25th, 1915.

Among Giordano's more recent operas may be mentioned *La Cena delle Beffe*, first given at Milan December 21st, 1924, and *Il Re*, produced also at Milan, January, 1929. The latter met with brilliant success.

GOLDMARK

Karl Goldmark was born at Keszthely, in Hungary, May 18th, 1832. He died in Vienna in 1915. He received his musical education in Vienna, where he studied with the violinist, Jansa afterwards entering the Vienna Conservatoire. He began to compose at a very early age, and was a very hard worker. As the son of a poor Jewish Cantor, there was little money to spare to develop his genius, and his future success depended entirely upon his own efforts and enthusiasm. However, a few friends who believed in him sent him to Vienna; and his early success more than justified their faith. He soon established himself as a piano teacher in Vienna, composing in his spare time. He was a great admirer and defender of Wagner.

The first composition to gain for Goldmark definite recognition was his *Sakuntala* overture. Then, with the production of his magnificent opera *The Queen of Sheba* in Vienna on March 10th 1875, his reputation soon became world-wide. This highly dramatic work has been performed in most parts of the musical world. His second opera, *Merlin*, was produced at Vienna November 17th, 1886, and has likewise proved a brilliant success some critics regarding it as superior to *The Queen of Sheba*. A third opera, *The Cricket on the Hearth* (with a libretto based on Dickens' well-known story), was produced in Berlin in 1896. *The Country Wedding* is another of his operas.

GOOSSENS

EUGENE GOOSSENS was born in London May 26th, 1893. As was the case with his father and grandfather of the same name, he was for a time one of the conductors of the Carl Rosa Opera Company He received his musical education at the Liverpool College of Music and the Royal College of Music, London; and he also studied at the Bruges Conservatoire. He gained the " Liverpool " scholarship at the Royal College of Music; and he studied composition under Sir Charles Stanford.

Goossens soon made a name as a violinist; and very early, too he became known as a distinguished conductor, not only of orchestral and concert music, but also as a conductor of opera and ballet. In the latter capacity, he served with the Beecham Opera Company, the British National Opera Company, and with the Russian Ballet. In 1923, he went to America, where he became conductor of the Rochester Symphony Orchestra, New York, and also visited many other orchestras as guest conductor. Later, he became conductor of the Cincinnati Symphony Orchestra, being held there in the highest esteem.

As a composer, Goossens' work is fresh and original, clear-cut and full of imagination. His compositions embrace all mediums

—orchestral, chamber, pianoforte music, and opera. His fine operas *Judith* and *Don Juan de Mañara* are both extremely dramatic; and he has a real sense of the theatre. *Judith* was produced at Covent Garden, London, in 1929; and *Don Juan de Mañara* received its first hearing in 1937, likewise at Covent Garden. Each of these operas has a libretto by the late Arnold Bennett.

GOUNOD

CHARLES FRANÇOIS GOUNOD was born at Paris, June 17th, 1818. He died there, 18th October, 1893. He entered the Paris Conservatoire in 1836, and was twenty-one years old when he won the *Grand Prix de Rome* in 1839. In Rome he was appointed Honorary Maestre di Capella for life. His first work of importance was a *Messe Solonnelle in G*, some portions of which were brought out in London in 1851. He spent some time in Germany, studying Bach, whom he greatly admired, and the religious element developed in him by these studies influenced him all his life. He held in Paris, from 1852 to 1860, the post of conductor of the *Orphéon*.

Gounod's world-renowned opera, *Faust*, was first produced at the Théâtre Lyrique, Paris, in 1859, and instantly gained fame for its composer, placing him in the front rank of operatic composers. The success of *Faust* has never diminished; and it is still one of the most popular operas ever written. Among his other best-known operas are *Roméo et Juliette*, produced in Paris, 1867; *Philémon et Baucis* (Paris, 1860); *Mireille* (Paris, 1863); *Sapho* (Paris, 1851) : *Cinq-Mars* (Paris, 1877); *La Colombe* (Paris, 1866); *La Reine de Saba* (Paris, 1860)—afterwards brought out in England as *Irene* (1862). His oratorios, *The Redemption* and *Mors et Vita*, were produced at the Birmingham Festival. *Philémon et Baucis* was performed in the ancient Roman Theatre at Orange, in Provence, in 1928.

Gounod also wrote many lovely songs, of which *Ave Maria* and *Nazareth* are among the most famous. He also wrote a tremendous number of smaller orchestral pieces, among which are the popular *Méditation, Saltarello, Funeral March of a Marionette,* &c.

HALÈVY

JACQUES FRANÇOIS FROMENTHAL HALÈVY was born in Paris, 27th May, 1799; died at Nice, 1862. Showing great musical ability in his early years, he entered the Conservatoire when only ten years old, and studied under Cavot, Berton, and Lambert, and for five years received lessons in counterpoint from Cherubini. He also studied for two years at Rome, and later became a popular teacher, numbering amongst his most celebrated pupils, Gounod and Bizet. He met with no important success until the year 1835, when he produced in Paris two operas :—*La Juive*, presented 23rd February, and *L'Eclair*, presented 16th December. *La Juive* was an immediate success, and won for its composer a first place amongst French musicians. Fifteen years later, this opera was produced at Covent Garden, where it also met with great appreciation and success. *La Juive* is the only one of Halèvy's operas that still enjoys European fame, though he wrote many others, the most worthy of mention being *La Reine de Chypre* (1841), *Les Mousquetaires* (1846), *Guido et Ginevra*, and *Le Val d'Andorre*.

HOLBROOKE

JOSEF CHARLES HOLBROOKE was born on 5th July, 1878. He studied first with his father and also at the Royal Academy of Music, London, and began composing music at an early age. He has written six operas, his most important works being the music dramas contained in his fine trilogy, *The Cauldron of Annwn*, founded on the dramatic poems of Lord Howard de Walden (" T. E. Ellis "). The three portions of the trilogy are entitled respectively :—*The Children of Don* (produced London, 1912), *Dylan, Son of the Wave* (produced London, 1913), and *Bronwen*. *Bronwen* was produced with great success by the Carl Rosa Opera Company during their 1928-29 tour. His other operas are :—*The Stranger* (*Pierrot and Pierrette*) (produced London, 1910), a lyrical drama in three acts and a ballet; *The Enchanter*, an opera-ballet in three acts (produced Chicago, 1915); and *The Snob*, a comic opera in one act. He has also written several successful ballets :—*The Moth, Coromanthe, The Enchanter, The Red Masque*. Among his most celebrated orchestral works are :—*Poems, The Raven, The Viking, Ulalume, Queen Mab, The Bells*, and *Byron*. Other important orchestral works are a dramatic symphony *Apollo and the Seaman*; *Les Hommages*, suite; variations : *Three Blind Mice, Auld Lang Syne*, and *The Girl I Left Behind Me* and a large number of orchestral and pianoforte compositions and a great many songs. Holbrooke's works have been performed at the Berlin and Vienna Philharmonic Concerts, by the Boston Orchestral Society, and in Madrid, Paris, Milan, Rio de Janeiro etc.; and he has produced British music in the West Indies and in many other countries.

HOLST

GUSTAV THEODORE HOLST was born at Cheltenham, 21st September, 1874. He received his musical training at the Royal College of Music, London. His first opera was *Sita*, and this was followed by his charming Indian opera, *Savitri*, which was produced in London, first at the London School of Opera in 1916, and at Covent Garden in 1922. This was followed by a comic fantastic opera, *The Perfect Fool*, which was produced in London the following year. Both these operas have met with instant appreciation and success. A third successful opera, *At the Boar's Head*, was produced in Manchester, April, 1925, by the British National Opera Company, and deals humorously with various Falstaffian scenes from Shakespeare's *Henry IV*. Among the best known orchestral and vocal works of Holst are:—*The Planets*, *The Cloud Messenger*, *Beni Mora*, *Choral Hymns from the Rig-Veda*, the *Hymn of Jesus*, and many other shorter choral and instrumental works. This greatly admired composer was Teacher of Music at St. Paul's School, London, and at Morley College; and in his work in these establishments he did much for the revival of Elizabethan music and also for the greater appreciation of the works of Purcell. Holst's music had great originality. In 1929, he was presented with the Gold Medal of the Royal Philharmonic Society. Holst died on May 25th, 1934; and as a memorial to him a Fund was established to assist in the development of the study of music at Morley College for working men and women, where his enthusiastic leadership had inspired students for so many years.

HUMPERDINCK

ENGELBERT HUMPERDINCK was born 1st September, 1854, at Siegburg, in the Rhine Provinces. His musical education was received first at the Gymnasium of Paderborn and afterwards at the Cologne Conservatoire, where he was entered in 1872. In 1876, he won the Mozart Stipendium and proceeded to Munich. In 1879, he won the Mendelssohn Stiftung of Berlin; after which he visited Italy, where he made the acquaintance of Wagner at Naples and became so friendly with the great composer that he afterwards helped him with the production of *Parsifal* at Bayreuth. In 1881, he won the Meyerbeer prize at Berlin; and, after having produced a number of compositions for the orchestra, he composed his masterpiece opera, *Hänsel und Gretel*, the libretto of which was written by his sister, Adelheid Wette. This beautiful fairy opera was produced first at Weimar in 1893; and the first production of it in London was in 1895. It met with great success, and was followed in 1896 by *Sieben Geislein*, and in 1902 by *Dornröschen*. In 1896, Humperdinck was created Professor by the Kaiser; and in 1905, his opera, *Die Heirath Wider Willen*, was produced at Berlin. He also wrote the incidental music for Maeterlinck's beautiful allegorical play, *The Blue Bird*. In 1910, his charming allegorical fairy opera, *Die Königskinder* (*Kings' Children*) was produced in New York; and in 1911, it was given with equal success at Covent Garden, London. Humperdinck's operas are remarkable for the beauty and simplicity of their subjects and for the exquisite delicacy of their musical treatment. He glorified youth, and he himself never seemed to grow old. His students' opera, *Gaudeamus*, which was produced in 1922, was a work of real joy and happiness. The opera was based on students' lives about the year 1820, and the work was enthusiastically received. Humperdinck died in Berlin on 27th September, 1921.

LEONCAVALLO

RUGGIERO LEONCAVALLO was born at Naples, 8th March, 1858. He studied at the Neapolitan Conservatoire, and afterwards gave singing lessons and went through many hard struggles. He gave several concert tours as a pianist. His first opera, *Medici*, being part of a trilogy, *Crepusculinis*, was not produced until after *I Pagliacci* (produced at the Teatro dal Verme, Milan, 21st May, 1892) had won great success for him. *Medici* was given in 1893, but proved unsuccessful, and the remaining portions of the trilogy, *Savonarola* and *Cesare Borgia*, were not produced. The other operas that followed were:—*Der Roland* (1894), *Chatterton* (Rome, 1896), *La Bohème* (Venice, 1897), *Zaza* (Milan, 1900), but none of these have met with the brilliant success of *I Pagliacci*, which is regarded as being one of the most perfect short operas ever written, both musically and dramatically. The libretto was written by the composer. He also wrote the libretti for his other operas. Another opera, *Maia*, was produced at Rome, January, 1910, and *Malbruk* was given a few days later. Neither of these likewise proving successful, Leoncavallo may be regarded as a one-opera composer—but that one little gem was a brilliant masterpiece. Leoncavallo died August 9th, 1919.

LLOYD

GEORGE LLOYD was born at St. Ives, Cornwall, June 28th, 1913, of north country parents. He was first taught the violin by his mother; and later he went to London, where he studied that instrument under Albert Sammons, and composition under Harry Farjeon.

A first Symphony was played at Penzance, when he was nineteen years old, and repeated at Bournemouth. A Canon for orchestra was shortly afterwards played at Eastbourne, where a second Symphony was also produced. A third Symphony was performed at the B.B.C. Contemporary Music Concerts, November, 1935.

His first opera *Iernin*—on a Celtic subject, with a libretto by his father, William Lloyd—was tried out in 1934 at Penzance. In the following year it was produced at the Lyceum Theatre, London, where it ran for a couple of weeks—one of the longest runs of any English opera this century, receiving a fine reception and a good press. His next opera, *The Serf*—dealing with outlaw life in the reign of Stephen, and with a libretto likewise by his father—was produced at Covent Garden in October, 1938, under the conductorship of Albert Coates; and this also met with an excellent reception.

MASCAGNI

PIETRO MASCAGNI was born December 7th, 1863, at Leghorn. His father, a baker, intended him for the legal profession and discouraged his many efforts to learn music. The music-loving youth, however, encouraged by his friend, Signor Bianchi, a singing-master, secretly entered himself at the Instituto Cherubini, his chief instructor being Alfredo Soffredini. Later on, he was adopted by an uncle; and he was then permitted to devote himself entirely to music, being afterwards sent to the Conservatoire at Milan.

Unable to bear the restrictions of Conservatoire life, however, young Mascagni joined various travelling operatic companies as conductor, and for a time lived in great obscurity. Then, seeing that the Music House of Sonzogno had offered a prize for a one-act opera, he entered for the competition in a great hurry—working at fever heat and completing the opera within a week—and carried off the prize with the now famous *Cavalleria Rusticana*. The opera was produced at the Costanzi Theatre, Rome, May 18th, 1890, and received an enthusiastic success, which was repeated all over the musical world. Everybody clamoured for the opera; and the young composer quickly became world-famous and prosperous.

Mascagni's next opera was *L'Amico Fritz* (Rome, 1891); after

which there followed *I Rantzan* (1892), *Guglielmo Ratcliff* (1895)
Silvano (1895), *Zanetto* (1896), *Iris* (Milan, 1898), *Le Mascher*
(1901), *Amica* (1905). None of these, however, proved so brillian
as *Cavalleria Rusticana*, and, with the exception of *L'Amico Frit*
and *Iris*, have not met with any remarkable success. A late
opera, *Lodoletta*, was produced in Rome in 1917; and *Isabeau* wa
produced in 1929 in Verona, at the great festival in the aren
there. Then, in 1933, Mascagni's grand opera, *Nero*, was pro
duced at La Scala, in Milan, with great magnificence. This reall
fine opera was received enthusiastically and has added a fina
laurel crown to the achievements of its composer. It is ver
beautiful and melodious, and contains many intense climaxes. I
proves that in Italy, at least, lyricism and the spirit of *bel cant*
still remain supreme.

MASSENET

JULES EMILE FRÉDERIC MASSENET was born on May 12th, 1842, a
Monteaux, near St. Etienne. He died in Paris August 13th, 1912
He received his musical education at the Paris Conservatoire an
secured the *Grand Prix de Rome* at the early age of twenty-on
with his cantata, *Rizzio*. He remained two years in Rome an
composed, according to the conditions of the Prix, an opera, *L
Grande Tante*, produced at the Opéra-Comique in 1867. Hi
orchestral suites, *Scènes du Bal* and *Scènes Hongroises*, were com
posed during his travels in Germany and Hungary. By th
production of his opera *Don César de Bazan*, in Paris 1872, h
gained such success that he afterwards ranked among the for
most of French composers of his day. The following operas wer
produced at the Opéra-Comique in Paris : *Manon Lescaut* (1884
Werther (1893), *Thaïs* (1894). His two sacred dramas, *Mari
Madéleine* and *Eve*, were produced in 1873 and 1875 respectivel
Among his other famous operas are : *Le Roi de Lahore* (1877
Le Jongleur de Notre-Dame (Monte Carlo, 1902), *Esclairmond*
(1889), *Hérodiade* (1885), *The Cid* (1885), *Sapho* (1897), *Cléopâtr*
(1914), *La Navarraise* (1894), *Grisélidis* (1891), *Don Quichott*
(Monte Carlo, 1910), *Cendrillon* (Paris, 1899). *Manon Lescau*
based on the Abbé Prévost's famous novel (as is also Puccini
opera of the same title), is the most popular of all Massenet
operas; and probably *Thaïs*, *Le Jongleur de Notre-Dame*, and *L
Roi de Lahore* are the next favourites.

Massenet's music is noted for its grace, wealth of melody, an
deep emotionalism.

MEYERBEER

GIACOMO MEYERBEER was born at Berlin, 5th September, 1791 : died at Paris, 2nd May, 1864. He was a pupil of Lauska, and also had lessons from Clementi and the Abbé Vogler. In 1815 he went to Italy to study musical composition, and there he began to write operas. He first took Rossini as his model, the best example of which was *Il Crociata* (1824). In 1831 he struck out in a new style with *Robert le Diable*, produced at the Grand Opera, Paris. This beautiful and fantastic opera was received with the wildest enthusiasm, and quickly brought fame to the composer. His masterpiece was *Les Huguenots* (Paris, 1836), and his other best known works are :—*Le Prophète* (Paris, 1849), *L'Étoile du Nord* (Paris, 1854), *Dinorah* (Paris, 1859), *L'Africaine* (Paris, 1865), etc. Meyerbeer is regarded as being the founder of the modern French Grand Opera. He loved elaborate spectacular scenes, and great dramatic effects and finales; but, apart from his encouragement of the highly dramatic side of opera, he did much to develop and enrich the instrumental score in operatic composition, by striving for effective tone colour. He had a thorough understanding of the human voice, and knew well how to write effectively for it.

MOUSSORGSKY

MODESTE PETROVICH MOUSSORGSKY was born March 16/28, 1839, at Karevo, in Pskov. He early showed great musical gifts, but entered the army, where he was a popular officer in the famous Preobranjensky regiment, his singing and musical improvisation attracting much attention. Making the acquaintance of Dargomijsky, however, he became one of the New Russian Nationalist School of musical composers. Other members of this group were, besides Dargomijsky and Moussorgsky, Borodin, Cui, Serov, Glinka, Rimsky-Korsakov, Arensky, Balakirev, and Glazounov. Tschaikovsky, however, did not join the group, his own art being more universal. Resigning from the army at the age of twenty-two, in order to devote himself to music, Moussorgsky had a long struggle with poverty, which lasted all his life, at one time compelling him to enter a Government office—which post, however, proved so irksome that he began to live an irregular life of wild excitement, which injured his health. During this period, nevertheless, he produced his splendid national music drama, *Boris Godounov*, based on Poushkin's fine historical drama, which was first given at the Mariensky Theatre, St. Petersburg, on

January 24/February 6, 1874. This opera was first given in England during the Beecham Season at Drury Lane, 24th June, 1913. Moussorgsky's next opera was *Khovantschina* (St. Petersburg, 1885, and Drury Lane, London, 1913), which added to his fame. The only other operatic works of Moussorgsky were *The Matchmaker*, a one-act opera-dialogue, and an opera to be based on Gogol's *The Fair at Sorochintsky*, which was completed after his death by Cui and Tcherepnin. This opera was produced at St. Petersburg in 1923; and in London in 1941. Moussorgsky wrote a great many beautiful songs and orchestral pieces. His songs are regarded as perfect human documents faithfully reflecting the psychology of the Russian people. But it is with *Boris Godounov* that Moussorgsky has gained world-wide fame as an operatic composer of genius; and the dramatic character of the usurper-king became more famous still after the magnificent presentment of it by the great Russian singer, Chaliapine, during the Beecham productions in London in 1913. Moussorgsky died at St. Petersburg on his forty-second birthday, March 16/28, 1881.

MOZART

JOHANN CHRYSOSTOMUS WOLFGANG AMADEUS MOZART was born at Salzburg, Austria, on 27th January, 1756 : died at Vienna, 5th December, 1791. He showed a precocious genius for music when but three or four years of age, and composed before he was six. His father, a musician also, guided his efforts, and from 1762-65 took the child to many European cities to exhibit his talents. In 1768 Mozart was made Concertmeister at Salzburg; and here his first opera, *La Finta Semplice*, was produced, written when about twelve years old. In 1777 he went to Paris and other places, failing to obtain anything but empty applause; and in 1779 he returned to Salzburg as Cathedral organist. From 1781 he lived in Vienna, where he remained until his death. He reaped but little pecuniary benefit from his compositions, in spite of his great genius; and he was seldom free from the anxieties of poverty. In 1791 he received the famous commission from a mysterious stranger to write a *Requiem Mass*; and in enfeebled health he began it, declaring that it was for his own funeral. This was his last great work, and he died ere it was quite finished. There were no ceremonies at his grave, and he was buried in the common ground of St. Mark. Many years later a monument was erected to him by the city of Vienna. As an operatic writer Mozart is considered by many to have no equal. His chief operas are :—

Le Nozze di Figaro (Vienna, 1786), *Don Giovanni* (Prague, 1787), *Idomeneo* (Munich, 1781), *The Magic Flute* (Vienna, 1791), *The Seraglio* (Vienna, 1782), *Cosi Fan Tutte* (Vienna, 1790), *La Clemenza di Lito* (1791), *Bastien and Bastienne* (Vienna, 1768), etc. Besides the exquisite *Requiem* he wrote many other Masses, and a great number of symphonies, sonatas, concertos, quartettes, etc. Very little of his music was published during his lifetime.

NICOLAI

CARL OTTO EHRENFRIED NICOLAI was born at Königsberg, 9th June, 1810 : died at Berlin, 11th May, 1849. He had an unhappy home life, but found a good friend in Justizrath Adler, of Stargard, who sent him to Berlin to study music. In 1833 he went to Rome as organist to the Prussian Embassy Chapel, where he studied both the old and the modern masters. In 1841 he became Court Kapellmeister at Vienna, where in 1842 he established the Philharmonic Society. In 1844 he became Director of the Domcher and Court Kapellmeister of the Opera in Berlin. His chief operas were :—*The Templar* (1840), *Il Proscritto* (1841), and *The Merry Wives of Windsor* (Berlin, 1849). The latter met with a brilliant success, which, however, the composer did not long live to enjoy, as he died two months after its first production.

OFFENBACH

JACQUES OFFENBACH (originally Levy) was born 21st June, 1819, at Offenbach-on-Main, and was the son of the Jewish Cantor of the Synagogue at Cologne. Though of German birth, practically the whole of his life was spent in Paris, and he was a true Parisian at heart. When quite a youth, he was entered at the Conservatoire at Paris, studying in the violoncello class under Professor Vaslin. So quick was his progress, that he entered the orchestra of the Opéra-Comique in 1834, where he played the 'cello; and in 1849, he was appointed conductor of the orchestra at the Théâtre Français. In 1855, he opened the Bouffes-Parisiens Théâtre; and having already written a number of comic light operas, many of these were produced at his own theatre. He became manager of the Théâtre de la Gâité in 1872; and in 1877 he came to England, where he made a most successful tour. As a composer of light opera, Offenbach occupied on the Continent very much the same position as Gilbert and Sullivan in England, his works being extremely popular. From the long list of just over one hundred pieces of this kind for the stage may be mentioned the following of the best known in England :—*La Grande Duchesse de Gérolstein* (Paris, 1867), *Madame Favart* (Paris, 1878), *Orphée aux Enfers* (Paris, 1858), *La Princesse de Trébizonde* (Paris, 1870), *La Belle Hélène* (Paris, 1865), etc. So great was the popular demand for light opera and so eager was Offenbach to meet the same that, unfortunately, he left behind him only one serious operatic work, *The Tales of Hoffmann*. Offenbach longed to see this opera produced; but, after completing it, he became ill and died at Paris on 5th October, 1880, having failed to realize his great desire. The opera was produced the following year at the Opéra-Comique, Paris, and proved an immense success. The libretto was by Jules Barbier and Michel Carré, and was adapted from three tales by E. T. A. Hoffmann. It was produced in London in 1907. *The Goldsmith of Toledo* was produced posthumously in London in 1922. This opera was built up and edited by J. Stern and A. Zamara from an uncompleted opera and other posthumous writings of Offenbach.

PHILPOT

STEPHEN R. PHILPOT was born at London. He received his musical education at the Royal Academy of Music, London, where he carried off a number of coveted medals and certificates. His first opera, *La Gitana*, was produced at the Grand Theatre, Birmingham, in 1904, with great success, and was a popular favourite for many years with the Turner Opera Company. His second opera, *Nigel*—dealing with the subject of Roundheads and Cavaliers—was also produced in Birmingham in 1910, and later on was given in London. After this came his delightful romantic opera, *Dante and Beatrice*, which was produced first at the Shaftesbury Theatre, London, in June, 1918, where it was excellently well received. In 1920 it was successfully produced at Covent Garden Opera House by the Carl Rosa Opera Company, who also took it on tour, during the course of which it met with gratifying receptions wherever it was given. Two lighter works, *The Algerian Girl* and *Bill Adams*, have also proved very successful and enjoyed good runs, the latter having proved a great favourite during a long Australian tour. Mr. Philpot has also composed a great many songs and some very charming music for children's voices, his many fairy operettas being extremely popular.

PONCHIELLI

AMILCARE PONCHIELLI was born at Paderno Fasolaro, near Cremona, on August 31st, 1834; and he died at Milan January

16th, 1886. He studied at the Conservatoire in Milan, and later became organist at a Cremona church, and a bandmaster. In 1856, he became leader in the cathedral at Piacenza; and as he was then devoting himself seriously to composition, he wrote a certain amount of Church music. He soon discovered, however, that operas and stage work were more suited to his particular talents; and he soon began to devote himself entirely to this work.

Ponchielli's first opera was *I Promessi Sposi*, produced at Cremona, 1856; and others quickly followed.

La Gioconda—with a libretto by Arrigo Boïto—was produced at La Scala, Milan, April 8th, 1876. This was a huge success, and has been produced since in many countries. None of his other operas were so successful. Among them may be mentioned *I Lituani* (1874), *Il Figliuol Prodigo* (1880), and *Marion Delorme* (1885).

Ponchielli was one of the first of the Italian operatic composers to be affected by the modern influences of the more advanced style of lyric drama, just then being produced by Wagner; and he did much to build up a more virile type of opera in his own country. Puccini was one of his most famous pupils and followers.

PUCCINI

GIACOMO ANTONIO DOMENICO MICHELE SECONDO MARIA PUCCINI was born at Lucca June 22nd, 1858, and died November 29th, 1924, at Brussels. He came of a family of musicians. He studied first at Lucca, and afterwards at the Milan Conservatoire, his chief teacher being Ponchielli. His first opera, *Le Villi*, was produced at the Teatro dal Verme, Milan, May 31st, 1884, with such success that it was afterwards enlarged and produced at La Scala, Milan, January 24th, 1885. His next opera, *Edgar*, was produced at La Scala in 1889. *Manon Lescaut*, produced at the Teatro Regio, Turin, 1893, showed very considerable development; and with the production of *La Bohème* at the same theatre in 1896, he was at once placed in the first rank of modern composers. His exceptional genius was hailed with delight; and the wealth of passion and exquisite melody in his music has made him world-renowned as a romantic operatic composer. His next opera, *La Tosca* (Rome, 1900), met with an equal success. *Madam Butterfly* (La Scala, Milan, 1904) is regarded by many as the finest of Puccini's works; yet, when first given, for some unaccountable reason, it was not well received. On its second production at Brescia, however, it was received with the greatest acclamation. Since then it has been enthusiastically welcomed wherever it has been given, being now, with *Tosca*, *Bohème*, and *Manon*, a universal European favourite.

Puccini's American opera, *The Girl of the Golden West*, was first produced in New York during 1910, where it met with an immense success. Puccini's remarkably strong vein of humour is expressed in his one-act comic opera, *Gianni Schicchi*, produced at New York, 1918. Two other one-act operas, *The Cloak* and *Sister Angelica*, likewise produced at New York in 1918, have also met with much appreciation and success—a well-contrasted trio. Another opera, *La Rondine*, was produced at Monte Carlo in 1917; but this has never proved so popular as the others.

Puccini's last great opera, *Turandot*, on a Chinese legendary subject, was produced, posthumously, at Milan 1926, London 1927, by Toscanini, with great splendour. It was practically completed before Puccini's death, but some unfinished orchestration was added by Franco Alfano. This dramatic and gorgeous opera was a fitting climax to the work of the most popular Italian composer of our age. Puccini's music has a luscious and passionate quality that makes an instant appeal to all lovers of romantic melody.

RACHMANINOV

SERGEI VASSILIEVITCH RACHMANINOV, the famous Russian pianist and composer, was born on April 2nd, 1873, at Nijni-Novgorod, Russia. He studied at the Moscow and St. Petersburg Conservatoires under Zvierev, Siloti, and Arensky. His many compositions include operas, orchestral works, concertos, chamber music, and pianoforte works. His pianoforte works are probably the best known—especially his preludes, of which he wrote over twenty. The most famous of the latter is the *Prelude in C Sharp Minor*. Among his choral works are the cantata *Der Frühling*, Op. 20; and the operas *Der geizige Ritter*, *Aleko*, and *Francesca da Rimini*. In 1892, he won a Gold Medal with his opera *Aleko*, which was produced in Moscow in 1893. This very dramatic little opera—which is on a gipsy subject—was given in London in 1915 at the London Opera House. Rachmaninov gave recitals in almost every land; and at one time so far apart were his engagements within one month that he had to have two pianos travelling in separate directions in order to fulfil them. In 1903, he was Conductor of the Imperial Opera; and from 1912 to 1913, he conducted the Moscow Philharmonic Symphony Orchestra. After the Russian revolution, he escaped to Sweden and eventually settled in America. This highly gifted composer died on March 28th, 1943.

RAVEL

MAURICE RAVEL, the distinguished French composer, was born March 7th, 1875, at Ciborne, near St. Jean de Luz; he died in Paris in 1937. He received his musical education at the Paris Conservatoire, where he studied under Fauré, Gédalge and Bériot. He was also influenced by Chabrier, and by Satiem; and though no disciple of Debussy, his style is often spoken of as akin to that of the latter—both being in opposition to the " heavier " Wagnerian style so long admired. Both are essentially " modern ".

He competed several times for the Rome Prize, and though he won the second prize, his failure to gain the coveted first prize led to a hot controversy in the press, since he had already secured wide recognition by his published works—one of these being the popular *Pavane for a Dead Infanta*, a remarkably fine *String Quartet*, and the charming *Jeux d'eau*.

Among other well-known works of Ravel are the suite *The Tomb of Couperin*, *Gaspard de la Nuit*, *Boléro*, and the ballets, *Mother Goose*, *Daphnis et Chloe*, *The Valse*, a great number of songs (some of these set to poems of Verlaine, Mallarmé, Verhaeren, etc.). He also wrote a great many compositions for the pianoforte.

His delightful fantastic one-act opera, *L'Heure Espagnole*, was produced in Paris in 1911; and it met with much success when given in 1918 at Covent Garden, London. In 1926, another one-act opera, *L'Enfant et les Sortilèges*, was produced in Brussels, this likewise being on a charmingly fantastic subject. Both operas have a delicacy and clarity of style that seem to call almost for a marionette production. The latter, in particular, may be regarded as the perfect example of a marionette opera. His puppets, nevertheless, are provided with delightful music; and the orchestration of the little work is immaculate.

RIMSKY-KORSAKOV

NICOLAS ANDREIEVICH RIMSKY-KORSAKOV, one of the greatest of the Russian operatic composers, was born March 18th, 1844, at Tikhvin, in Nijni-Novgorod. He died at St. Petersburg on June 21st, 1908. He entered the Navy, and remained in the Service for many years. In 1873, he became a professor at the St. Petersburg Conservatoire; and for a time he was the teacher of Stravinsky and Arensky and also trained a large group of the younger Russian composers in operatic art. He belonged to the famous group of musicians interested in establishing nationalism in Russian musical art; to which also belonged Balakirev, Borodin, Moussorgsky, Cui, Serov, Dargomijsky, Arensky, Glazounov, and Glinka. This nationalistic school did not include Tschaikovsky, whose art was more universal.

The operas of this great composer are remarkable for their vivid colourfulness and barbaric gorgeousness; and they are all extremely popular in Russia. They deal mainly with Russian folklore and fantastic Eastern legends. The best known in this country are the following:—*Ivan the Terrible*, a highly dramatic opera produced at St. Petersburg January, 1873, and heard in London for the first time at Drury Lane in 1913, during the brilliant Beecham Season. In 1913, also, *Mozart and Salieri* was produced in London, having been heard first in Moscow in 1898. In 1914, the humorous fantastic folk opera, *A Night in May,* was given at Drury Lane, London, having been produced in St. Petersburg in January, 1880. In 1914, also, *The Golden Cockerel*, a satirical fantastic opera (which had been first produced posthumously in Moscow in 1910), was given at Drury Lane, with wonderful Bakst decorations, and met with immediate success.

Other well-known operas of Rimsky-Korsakov are:—*Tsar Saltan* (Moscow, 1900), *The Snow-Maiden* (St. Petersburg, 1882), *Sadko* (Moscow, 1897), *The Tsar's Bride*, *Scheherazade*, *Mlada*, *Pan Voyede*, *Boyarinya Vera Sheloga*, *Sevilia*, *The Christmas Night*, *Invisible City of Kitezh and the Maiden Fevronia*, etc.

ROSSINI

GIOACCHINO ANTONIO ROSSINI was born at Pesaro, Italy, February 29th, 1792, of very humble parents, his father being the town trumpeter and horn-player at the theatre. He died near Paris, November 13th, 1868. As a child he showed such great aptitude for music that, in spite of the troubles and poverty of his parents, an excellent teacher was found for him in Tesei. In his boyhood, he appeared on the stage as a solo singer. He also sang in church as soloist. In 1806, he entered the Conservatoire at Bologna, under Mattei; and here his progress was so rapid that he took a prize for a cantata after his first year there. In 1810, he began to write operas, of which he produced no less than fifty within twenty-six years. He went to London in 1823, and sang in a series of concerts. He then went to Paris, where he remained until his death. He wrote nothing further after 1836; and having at that early period of his career gained great fame and wealth, he devoted the remainder of his life to luxurious living. He is said to have regarded Meyerbeer as a possible rival, and to have refused to write again after hearing the latter's *Les Huguenots*.

Rossini's florid, but melodious, style of operatic composition remained the standard model for Italian opera for a great number of years. He wrote with the utmost facility, and his music is famous for its melodiousness.

His most celebrated operas were:—*La Cambiale di Matrimonio* (Venice, 1810), *Tancredi* (Venice, 1813), *The Barber of Seville* (Rome, 1816), *Semiramide* (Venice, 1823), *William Tell* (Paris, 1829), *Cenerentola* (Rome, 1817), *L'Italiani in Algieri* (Venice, 1813), etc. His brilliant *Barber of Seville* is still as popular as Gounod's *Faust*. *Cenerentola* has been recently revived at Covent Garden.

Rossini also wrote the famous oratorio *Moses in Egypt* (Naples, 1818), and a *Stabat Mater* (1842).

RUBINSTEIN

ANTON GRIGORIEVICH RUBINSTEIN, the celebrated pianist and composer, was born of Jewish parents in 1830 at Wechwotynetz in Bessarabia. Like so many musicians of the highest order, Rubinstein began his career at an early age. He was only nine years old when he made his first tour as a concert pianist. In 1848, he settled in St. Petersburg and became a professor of music. When he was twenty-seven years of age he made his second visit to England— where some of the music critics censured him severely for playing without a score! His reason, however, for the then unfashionable feat of memorizing all music played at public concerts was the fact that his eyesight was always weak; and in his latter years he became blind. Rubinstein had an emotional style of playing which, coupled with his remarkable technical equipment, rarely failed to exercise an almost electrifying effect upon his audience.

He founded the Russian Musical Society at St. Petersburg in 1861, and, in the following year, the Conservatoire of Music—of which he was also the Director from its inception until 1867. He again became Director of the Conservatoire twenty years later.

Nearly every branch of music was written for by this versatile composer. His style, to a very marked degree, displayed the influence of Mendelssohn and Schubert. The *Ocean* and *Dramatic* are two of his best known symphonies. He wrote much pianoforte music. Of his operas the best known are *Dimitri Donskoi* (1852), *The Children of the Heath* (1861), *Feramors* (1863), *The Maccabees* and *The Demon* (St. Petersburg, 1875), and *Nero* (Hamburg, 1879).

Rubinstein died in 1894, at the age of sixty-four years.

SAINT-SAËNS

CAMILLE SAINT-SAËNS, one of the most famous French composers, was born at Paris October 9th, 1835. He died in Algiers in 1921. He came of an aristocratic Normandy family. He studied at the Paris Conservatoire under Stamaty, Malèden, and Halèvy at various periods; he also received some private tuition from Gounod. He gained a prize in 1867 at the opening of the Paris International Exhibition, with his cantata *Les Noces de Prométhée*. He was organist at the Madeleine for nearly twenty years. He was also an excellent pianist and was engaged in concert work for many years, visiting London many times and receiving an honorary degree at Cambridge.

Saint-Saëns made his name first with his chamber music, piano concertos, and, in particular, with his fine symphonic poems, *Omphale's Spinning-Wheel*, *Phaeton*, *Danse Macabre*, *The Youth of Hercules*. The first-named was the first symphonic poem to be written by a French composer.

His first opera was *La Princesse Jaune*, produced in 1872; his second was *Le Timbre d'Argent*, brought out in 1877. The same year, 1877, saw also the production at Weimar of *Samson et Dalila*, with which he gained world-wide fame as an operatic composer. Later came *Etienne Marcel* (1879), *Henri VIII* (1883), *Proserpine* (1887), *Ascanio* (1890), *Phryné* (1893), and *Frédégonde* (1895). After *Samson et Dalila*, the most popular of his operatic works are probably *Henri VIII* and *Proserpine*.

Saint-Saëns was extremely versatile, and was an author of some note. He published his own very interesting Reminiscences in several volumes. He was an enthusiastic believer in the earlier French School of Music; he also defended the Romantics, and much disliked the ultra-modernists. At one time he accused Wagner of influencing French music, though he admired Wagner in his own particular sphere.

Saint-Saëns was a very prolific composer, and wrote in almost every medium, symphonies, concertos, pianoforte, violin, violoncello, and chamber music of every kind; the majority of these being now standard works. His music is noted for its exquisite beauty of melody and the easy elegance of its style. Yet his masterpiece, *Samson et Dalila*, was a failure when first produced at Weimar under Liszt; and it was not until fifteen years later, when produced in Paris, that it proved the brilliant success it deserved—a popularity it has firmly held ever since.

SMETANA

Bedrich (or Friedrich) Smetana was born at Litomysl (or Leitomischl), in Bohemia on March 2nd, 1824; and he died at Prague in 1884. For a while he studied under Liszt, and later on established himself as a popular teacher in Prague. In 1856, he became conductor of the Philharmonic Society at Gothenburg in Sweden. Meanwhile, he was composing; and he soon established himself as the national composer of Bohemia, all his work being intensely national in character. He is regarded, indeed, as being the main originator of Czech national opera, which he definitely established. He was also interested in a new school of musical thought then growing up and known as " The Music of the Future ".

Dvořák was his contemporary, and both were deeply interested in each other's work, though Smetana was a man of greater intellect and general culture than his friend. They lived, too, in different social and political circles; but both were united in the intensely " national " character of their music, which Dvořák continued after Smetana's death.

Smetana, in addition to his fame as an operatic composer, is also admired for his magnificent symphonic poems, the most widely known of which are *Vltava, From Bohemia's Woods and Fields*, and *Vysehrad*. His best known opera is *The Bartered Bride*, a humorous work, which is as melodious as it is national in character. It was produced at Prague in 1870. The lively polka at the end of the first act is famous the world over. *The Kiss* is probably the next best known of his operas in this country. *The Secret* is another.

Unhappily Smetana did not live to see the full glory of his genius. First he became deaf, and then he became mad; and he died in poverty. His great genius is now fully recognized, however, and the centenary of his birth was celebrated at Prague in 1934 with great rejoicings, by repertory performances of his operas and symphonies.

SMYTH

Dr. Ethel Mary Smyth, D.B.E., was born April 23rd, 1858, and is classed in Grove's Dictionary of Music and by musicians as amongst the most eminent composers of her time, and easily at the head of all those of her own sex. She received her musical education under Heinrich von Herzogenberg, in Berlin and in Leipzig. She wrote several operas, produced with great success in Germany and in England:—*Fantasio*, produced in Weimar and Carlsruhe by Motti in 1906; *The Forest*, produced in Dresden in 1901, Berlin, 1906, and in London, 1902; *The Wreckers*, produced in Leipzig in 1906, and in London, June, 1909; *The Boatswain's Mate*, produced in London, 1915; *Fête Galante*, produced in Manchester and in London in 1923. In 1922, she was created a Dame of the British Empire. Dame Ethel Smyth also wrote much successful chamber music, symphonies, choruses, songs, and a Mass. The latter is a fine outstanding work, virile, masterly in construction and workmanship, and particularly remarkable for the excellent and rich colouring of the orchestration. Another humorous opera, *L'Entente Cordiale*, a worthy military counterpart to the amusing *Boatswain's Mate*, and with a lively libretto by the versatile composer herself, was produced in London in July, 1925. In addition to writing music, this composer had a very delightful literary gift, her books, *Impressions That Remain*, *Streaks of Life*, and *A Three-Legged Tour in Greece*, showing the strong touch of real humour so apparent in some of her musical compositions—in particular *The Boatswain's Mate* and *L'Entente Cordiale*.

Dame Ethel Smyth died May 9th, 1944.

SIR CHARLES VILLIERS STANFORD

CHARLES VILLIERS STANFORD was born September 30th, 1852, at Dublin; and he died in London March 29th, 1924. He came of a legal family, and himself studied law for a time, and was a Doctor of Civil Law, as well as a Doctor of Music and a Master of Arts of Cambridge. He showed musical gifts at a very early age, and when only eight years old composed a march, which was later played at the Theatre Royal, Dublin. He was educated at Cambridge, and studied music at Leipzig and in Berlin. He became Professor of Music at Cambridge, and was organist of Trinity College; and he conducted the Cambridge Musical Society's productions from 1872 to 1893. He was also conductor of the Leeds Festival from 1901 to 1910. He produced several operas in Germany, and conducted concerts there and in other parts of the Continent. The honour of knighthood was conferred upon him in 1902.

Stanford was one of our most prolific British composers. He wrote operas, symphonies, chamber music, orchestral and choral works, and many pianoforte and violin solos, and songs, besides much Church music—among the latter being the popular Service, *Stanford in B Flat*.

His first stage work was the music for Tennyson's *Queen Mary*, produced at the Lyceum Theatre, 1876, at the age of twenty-four. His Irish opera, *Shamus O'Brien*, was produced at Covent Garden in March, 1896. His delightful four-act opera, *The Travelling Companion* (which has an excellent libretto by Sir Henry Newbolt), was first produced in this country by the Liverpool Repertory Opera Company at the Theatre Royal, Bristol, in 1926; and it has since been revived very successfully at Sadler's Wells in 1936, being now in the repertory of that theatre. It was actually written in 1917, and was published by the Carnegie Trustees.

Stanford wrote a book on Musical Composition, as well as an entertaining book of Reminiscences.

JOHANN STRAUSS

Johann Strauss II, son of Johann Strauss I, the "Waltz King", was born at Vienna October 25th, 1825. He died there June 3rd, 1899. He inherited his father's genius for light music, but soon surpassed him. Few of the senior Strauss's waltzes are now remembered, but Johann II's waltzes have the lasting brilliance and beauty that time seems only to increase. They will never be out of date. *The Blue Danube* is still the most famous of all waltzes.

His father's established fame no doubt helped him in the beginning of his amazing career—though Johann I was not at first anxious for his son to continue in his footsteps. But the gay genius of Johann II was not to be suppressed, and he rapidly made a brilliant reputation for himself. *The Blue Danube* created a tremendous furore; and other waltzes almost equally successful were *Tales from the Vienna Woods*, *Wine, Woman, and Song*, *Voices of Spring*, *Morgenblätter*, *Roses of the South*, etc. Altogether he wrote over four hundred waltzes.

But Johann Strauss's fame was not confined to waltzes alone. He wrote a number of very successful light operas, of which the most famous is *Die Fledermaus* (The Bat), which is packed with sparkling music, and in which waltz tunes again predominate. It is one of the most animated and sprightly works of its kind ever written, and, though a light comedy subject, is included in the repertoires of most grand opera companies. It was first produced in Vienna in July, 1874.

Other well-known brilliant light operatic works of Johann Strauss are *The Gipsy Baron* (Vienna, 1885), *The Queen's Lace Handkerchief* (Vienna, 1880), and *The Merry War* (Vienna, 1881), all of which proved immensely successful.

RICHARD STRAUSS

RICHARD GEORG STRAUSS was born June 11th, 1864, at Munich. He showed great musical gifts from his earliest years, having composed several pieces before leaving school. In 1882, he studied composition with the Court Kapellmeister, composing almost ceaselessly interesting works of many different kinds, most of which were performed and received as promising productions. He was at the University during 1882-3, and in 1885 began to conduct, being appointed Musical Director at Meiningen, and proceeding to the Munich Court Theatre in 1886. He was next appointed Musical Director at Weimar in 1890, and became Court Kapellmeister at the Berlin Opera House in the same year.

Strauss's first opera, *Guntram*, was produced at Weimar on May 12th, 1894; and in the same year he became Court Kapellmeister at Munich. He again occupied the same position at Berlin in 1899. About this time he undertook a number of tours, and in 1903 a " Strauss Festival " was held in London. Later, he conducted some of his operas in London.

Strauss continued to produce more and more important works —*Symphony in F Minor, Sinfonia Domestica*, a sonata, a piano quartet, and many songs—all of which illustrated his extraordinarily original gifts and paved the way for the remarkable operatic works which were to follow. He always had a great admiration for Wagner, as whose successor he is sometimes regarded. His next opera, *Feuersnot*, produced at Dresden in November, 1901, showed Wagner's influence had waned. His passionately dramatic opera, *Salomé*, based on Oscar Wilde's drama, was produced in Dresden on December 9th, 1905, and created a great sensation, placing Strauss immediately in the highest rank of modern operatic composers. This was followed by *Elektra*—by many considered his finest serious work—produced in Dresden in 1909, and at Covent Garden, London, in 1910. His charming light opera, *Der Rosenkavalier*, was produced at the Royal Opera House, Dresden, on January 26th, 1911, and in London January, 1913. It was enthusiastically received and showed this highly gifted composer in a new and unexpected light. His clever " freak " opera, *Ariadne on Naxos*—first written as an incidental musical interlude to Molière's *Le Bourgeois Gentilhomme*, and afterwards very considerably enlarged and revised— was produced in London at His Majesty's Theatre on May 27th, 1913, having been previously heard at Stuttgart in October, 1912. It was afterwards revised and produced in Berlin, 1916.

Among Strauss's later works are:—*The Legend of Joseph* (a ballet), produced 1914; a humorous light opera, *Arabella*, produced at Dresden July, 1933, and at Covent Garden May, 1934; *Intermezzo*, another light opera, produced in Dresden November 4th, 1924. These two works, with *Whipped Cream* (a Fantastic Ballet), April 10th, 1924, and *Teresina*, another ballet, have proved that a pleasant comedy subject suits this composer excellently well. Indeed, many critics consider he is at his happiest with such material, and that *Rosenkavalier* is undoubtedly his finest operatic work. *The Woman Without Shadow* was produced at Vienna, 1919. *The Silent Woman* was produced at Dresden, 1935. *Helen in Egypt*, a truly gorgeous opera, was produced with great magnificence at Dresden in October, 1928; and his sincere one-act serious opera, *The Day of Peace,* produced at Munich June 24th, 1938, in his seventy-fourth year, was received with great acclamation by a vast and enthusiastic audience. A one-act opera, *Daphne,* was produced with it.

Strauss is justly regarded as the greatest German composer of his age; and he is remarkable for a surprising versatility.

STRAVINSKY

IGOR FEDOROVITCH STRAVINSKY was born June 5th, 1882, at Oranienbaum, near St. Petersburg. He came of a musical family, his father being a famous opera singer. Though at first trained for the legal profession, he soon decided to devote himself to a musical career, and studied for a time under the direction of Rimsky-Korsakov. He is a distinguished pianist. He produced his first work in 1906, and was early held in high esteem in Russia. His original style soon began to cause discussion; and with *The Rite of Spring*, a ballet produced in 1913, this increased rapidly, since he ignored all the existing conventions of the day as regards harmony, rhythm, and form. His romantic fairy opera, *The Nightingale*, based on the subject of Hans Andersen's story, was produced in London June, 1914.

Very early in his career, Stravinsky began to devote himself to ballet work; and in Paris he wrote many original compositions for Diaghileff, the famous impresario of the Russian ballet. Among the most famous of these highly original ballets may be mentioned *The Fire Bird* (1910), *Petrouchka* (1912), *The Nightingale* (1914) (adapted from the opera), *The Soldier's Story* (1917), *Les Noces* (1923), *Apollo Musagetes* (1928), *Renard* (1915), *Game of Cards* (1937).

Another opera of Stravinsky's is *Mavra*, a light fantastic work produced Paris, 1921; and *Persephone*, produced 1934, is described as an opera-ballet. He has also written a secular oratorio on the subject of *Oedipus Rex* (1928), a choral-orchestral *Symphony of Psalms* (1930), a *Violin Concerto* (1933), and other works, all of which have aroused much controversy.

As a composer—and a modern of the moderns—Stravinsky is still somewhat of an enigma to many musical critics, who are, however, ready to admit his courageous originality. Time alone will prove his ultimate position in the world of music.

THOMAS

CHARLES AMBROISE THOMAS was born at Metz, 5th August, 1811; died at Paris, 12th February, 1896. Born of musical parents, he entered the Paris Conservatoire at the age of seventeen, becoming director of that institute in 1871. In 1832 he won the *Grand Prix de Rome*; and whilst studying in Italy was very active as a composer. On his return from Rome he began to write operas, the first of which, *La Double Echelle*, produced at the Opéra-Comique, Paris, in 1837, met with considerable success. Others followed; and with *Le Caïd* (1849) and *Le Songe d'une Nuit d'été* (1850), his name was finally established, and gained him a high place amongst French composers. The operas that followed met with little success; but in *Mignon*, produced at the Opéra-Comique, Paris, in 1866, the musical world recognized a masterpiece, and paid enthusiastic tribute to the genius of its composer. *Mignon* was first given in London, at Drury Lane, in 1870; and in New York in 1883. It is still popular in many operatic companies' repertoires. Other operas by Ambroise Thomas are:—*Hamlet* (1868), *Le Carnival de Venise* (1857), *Raymond* (1851), etc.

TSCHAIKOVSKY

PETER ILJITSCH TSCHAIKOVSKY was born in Wotkinsk, 7th May, 1840: died at St. Petersburg, 6th November, 1893. He early showed his bent for music, and though trained for the law, abandoned that profession, and, determining to study music alone, entered the Conservatoire at St. Petersburg, where he studied with Anton Rubinstein and Saremba. After studying three years in St. Petersburg, Tschaikovsky was appointed a teacher at the new Moscow Conservatorium, established by Nicholas Rubinstein, where he produced a number of orchestral works and three operas. His first opera, *The Voïevoda*, produced in Moscow in 1869, was a failure; and of the list of eleven operas which he produced, but few retained lasting popularity, with the exception of *Vakoula the Blacksmith* (St. Petersburg, 1876), *The Oprichniki, Mazeppa, The Queen of Spades (Pique Dame)*, and *Eugène Onégin*. The latter is the most famous of all his works, and is extremely popular in Russia, being full of delightful melodies. *Eugène Onégin* was first produced in Moscow in 1879. Amongst his other operas are :—*The Enchantress, The Queen of Spades* (St. Petersburg, 1890), *Joan of Arc, Mazeppa* (St. Petersburg, 1892), *Iolanta* (St. Petersburg, 1893), *Undine, The Oprichniki* (St. Petersburg, 1874). Besides these, Tschaikovsky wrote a great number of brilliant orchestral works, deservedly popular throughout Europe, being noted for their fine tone-colouring, spirit, and beauty of melody : amongst the most celebrated of these being the rich *Overture* "1812", composed in memory of Nicholas Rubinstein, the *Fifth Symphony* and the *Sixth Symphony, The Pathètique*, and the charming *Casse Noisette (The Nutcracker Suite)*. His operas show a decided Italian influence, and are highly emotional. In *The Queen of Spades* he is regarded as having touched his zenith.

Tschaikovsky did not belong to the famous group of musicians interested in establishing Nationalism in Russian musical art—of which Rimsky-Korsakov, Cui, Dargomijsky, Serov, Balakirev, Borodin, Arensky, Glinka, and Moussorgsky were such enthusiastic members. Tschaikovsky preferred his own art to be of a more universal character.

DR. VAUGHAN WILLIAMS, O.M.

RALPH VAUGHAN WILLIAMS was born October 12th, 1872, at Down Ampney, Gloucestershire. He was educated at Charterhouse and Trinity College, Cambridge; and he received his musical education at the Royal College of Music, London. He secured his Mus. Doc. at Cambridge in 1901; and in 1919, Oxford University conferred the Honorary Degree of Mus. Doc. upon him. He has received many other honours. The Gold Medal of the Royal Philharmonic Society was conferred upon him in 1930; and he received the Order of Merit in 1936.

Dr. Vaughan Williams is regarded as one of our most outstanding British composers. His output has been very large; and he has written a great deal of music which has become extremely popular. Among his most famous songs are *Orpheus with His Lute, Linden Lee, The Roadside Fire, The Vagabond, Silent Moon*, etc.

Among his other notable compositions are :—*The London Symphony, A Sea Symphony, The Wasps, The Norfolk Rhapsody, Concerto Accademico*, the *Folk-Song Suite* (this is a most charming composition, illustrating this composer's keen interest in English folk-songs); *Flos Campi* (performed at the International Festival at Geneva in 1929); *Fantasia on Sussex Folk-Songs, Fantasia on a Theme of Tallis, The Shepherds of the Delectable Mountains, Four Hymns,* etc., etc.

Vaughan Williams has written three operas, *Hugh the Drover, Sir John in Love,* and *The Poisoned Kiss. Hugh the Drover* was produced at His Majesty's Theatre July, 1924, and proved extremely successful—a success which has been maintained on its more recent revivals. It is an intensely English work, teeming with folk-songs, and having its setting in the Cotswolds. Its librettist is Harold Child, who takes as his period the time when "Boney" and his possible invasion was the nightmare of the peaceful English country-side. *Sir John in Love* was first produced London, 1929. *The Poisoned Kiss* was produced at The Arts Theatre, Cambridge, May 12th, 1936. It is a light fantastic opera, with a witty libretto by Evelyn Sharp, and is replete with charming airs. It has since been heard at Sadler's Wells.

VERDI

Giuseppe Verdi was born at Rancola, near Busseto, in the Duchy of Parma, Italy, October 10th, 1813; and he died at Busseto January 27th, 1901, at the age of eighty-eight years. He received his musical education at Busseto and Milan. Strange to say, he was actually refused a scholarship at Milan Conservatoire on the ground that he showed no aptitude for music! Yet he was eventually to be recognized all over the world as perhaps the greatest of all Italian operatic composers. He was appointed organist at Rancola at the age of ten years; and when but twenty years old he became Director of the Philharmonic Society at Busseto.

Verdi settled in Milan in 1838, and there his first opera, *Oberto di San Bonifazio* was produced at La Scala in 1839. The opera that first brought him European fame, however, was *Ernani* (Venice, 1844). *Rigoletto* was produced in Venice, 1851, and *Il Trovatore* in Rome, 1853. These two operas, through all changes of taste and style, still continue to hold their own in popular favour. He wrote many other operas, the best known of which are:—*La Traviata* (Venice, 1853), *Aida* (Cairo, 1871), *Otello* (Milan, 1887), *Macbeth* (1847), *Falstaff* (Milan, 1893), *I Lombardi* (1843), *Un Ballo in Maschero* (Rome, 1859), *Simon Boccanegra* (1855), *Les Vespres Siciliennes* (1855), *Forza del Destino* (1862), *Don Carlos* (Milan, 1884). His final opera was *Falstaff* (Milan, 1893), which he composed when he was eighty years old. The works which Verdi composed in later life are held by some to be far greater than those of his earlier or middle life. *Aïda*, *Otello*, and *Falstaff* are said to show the influence of Wagner. Verdi himself showed distinct preference for his earlier works.

Verdi's *Requiem Mass*, composed in memory of his author and patriot friend, Manzoni, was produced at Milan in 1874. He also composed a *Stabat Mater* and a *Te Deum Laudamus*, both of which are very beautiful settings.

The contents of the Verdi Museum are now permanently housed in the Opera House at Milan. Until 1929 these precious relics were kept at the house which Verdi had built for aged musicians outside the city. Recently there has been mooted a projected scheme for the establishment of a Memorial Theatre at Busseto, where Verdi was born and died, which would express the Italian master as the Bayreuth Festival Theatre does Wagner.

WAGNER

RICHARD WAGNER was born at Leipzig on 22nd May, 1813 : died at Venice, 13th February, 1883. He was educated at Dresden and Leipzig, where he also studied music. Poetry was a passion with him as a boy; and verse and play-writing occupied his mind until a great enthusiasm for Beethoven turned it into a musical direction. He was Musical Director at the Magdeburg Theatre from 1834-1836, Conductor at Königsberg in 1836, Music Director at Riga in 1837-39, and lived in Paris in 1839-42, where he struggled in vain to obtain a footing. His opera *Rienzi* was produced at Dresden in 1842 with a success which obtained for him the post of Kapell-meister at the opera-house there. *The Flying Dutchman* was produced the following year at Dresden, and marked a new epoch in his artistic history. *Tannhäuser*, the first of his creations from the German myth-world, was also produced at Dresden in 1845. After this he got into pecuniary difficulties; and his sympathies also being with the revolutionary movement of 1849, he was proscribed and escaped to Paris. By the efforts of Liszt, *Lohengrin* was produced in 1850 at Weimar. After ten years of exile, Wagner was pardoned and took up his residence at Munich, where King Ludwig of Bavaria became his enthusiastic and generous patron. *Tristan and Isolde* was produced at Munich in 1865; and this great music-drama marked a new epoch in operatic art. *Die Meistersinger von Nürnberg* followed in 1868. Wagner was now world-famous, and his colossal genius began to receive the support it deserved. In 1872 his own great theatre at Bayreuth was

2 H

founded; and upon its completion in 1876, his remarkable tetralogy, *Der Ring des Nibelungen*, was produced there in its entirety. *The Ring* was first given in London in its entirety at Covent Garden in 1882; and in New York in 1889. His last dramatic effort and crowning achievement, *Parsifal*, was produced at Bayreuth in 1882. Wagner's early years were full of struggle, opposition, and strife; but through all his disappointments he clung firmly to the new ideals of art he had formed, and in the end he conquered, his latter years being crowned with success and enthusiastic appreciation. Wagner's second wife, Cosima von Bülow, was the daughter of Liszt; and her devotion to the great master was the admiration of all. It was owing to her efforts that the great Bayreuth Festival Theatre, where the works of Wagner are regularly performed, was finally established on a firm financial basis. She died in 1930.

WALLACE

WILLIAM VINCENT WALLACE was born at Waterford, Ireland, 1st July, 1814; died at the château of Bayen, in the Haute-Garonne, France, 12th October, 1865. His father, a bandmaster, gave him his first instructions; and at an early age he could play most military instruments, besides being very proficient on the violin. At the age of fifteen he became Director of the Philharmonic Society in Dublin. In 1835 he set forth on a professional tour through Australia, New Zealand, India, South America, and the United States, meeting with enormous success as composer and performer. He was Director of Music at the Italian Theatre, Mexico, 1841-42. In 1845 *Maritana* was produced at Drury Lane, London, and for many years shared with Balfe's *Bohemian Girl* the highest popularity in Britain of any lyrical drama. Other well-known operas of Wallace's are:—*Lurline* (Covent Garden, London, 1860), *The Amber Witch* (1861), *Matilda of Hungary* (1847), *The Desert Flower* (1863), etc.

VON WALTERSHAUSEN

HERMANN WOLFGANG VON WALTERSHAUSEN was born in Göttingen in 1882, and was the son of a Strasburg Professor of National Economics, A. Sartorius von Waltershausen, being descended from a well-known Göttingen family of scientists. He was the pupil of I. Erb, in Strasburg, Alsace, and Ludwig Thuille, afterwards passing to the University of Munich, where he studied in particular the History of Art and also made a special study of the characteristics of the German peoples. His first musical work was the unpublished music-drama, *Pelegrino*, and his second effort was *Else Klapperzehen*, a musical comedy dealing with a farcical subject taken from the German Middle Ages. It was produced in May, 1909, by Ernst von Schuch at the Court Theatre, Munich, with success. His third work, the tragic opera, *Oberst Chabert*, was given under the conductorship of Hans Schilling-Ziemssens Leitung, at Munich, 18th January, 1912, and, being immediately successful, found its way very quickly into all the more important theatres. In addition to these works, Herr von Waltershausen has also written purely literary works, amongst others the festival play, *Die Abschiedssyphonie*, produced in Munich in 1908, the comedy in verse, *Heidhart Fuchs von Reuenthal*, as well as portions of a translation of Horace in very modern form.

WEBER

CARL MARIA VON WEBER was born 18th December, 1786, at Eutin, Germany. He studied under Henschkel, the conductor of Duke Friedrich of Meiningen's orchestra, and later under the Abbé Vogler. His first opera, *Das Waldmadchen*, was written at the early age of fourteen, and was performed several times. In his eighteenth year he became conductor of the Breslau Opera; and when his studies under Vogler came to an end he was appointed Director of the Opera at Prague. His first important opera, *Rubezahl*, was written about this time; and his cantata, *The Lyre and Sword*, was received with great enthusiasm. In 1816 he went to Berlin, where he had a great reception; and a little later, he became Hofkapellmeister at Dresden. His celebrated *Invitation to the Dance* was inspired by his wife, an actress and singer. His famous and most popular opera, *Der Freischütz*, was produced in Berlin in 1821. It was in this always greatly admired opera that melodies from the actual work itself were introduced into an operatic overture for the first time. Other successful operas followed:—*Preciosa* and *Euryanthe*, produced in Vienna, 1823, and *Oberon*, produced in London at Covent Garden, 1826. He also wrote a large number of cantatas, masses, concertos, and brilliant pianoforte pieces. Weber is regarded as the founder of the Romantic School in music; and by many operatic students also he is regarded as the forerunner of Wagner—who had the greatest admiration for his work. Weber died in 1826.

WEINBERGER

JAROMIR WEINBERGER, a popular and greatly admired Czech composer, was born at Prague in 1896. He was a pupil of Jaroslav

Kricka and Karel Hofmeister; and he began to compose when quite young. In 1922, he became Professor of Composition at the Conservatoire in Ithaca, U.S.A.

Weinberger made a very brilliant success with his first opera, *Schwanda the Bagpiper*, produced at Prague in April, 1927, following this with equally successful performances in Germany and Austria the following year. It had, indeed, an amazing success, and has since been translated into nearly twenty languages. It was given at Covent Garden in May, 1934. This light-hearted fantastic opera is full of merry tunes, some of these being based on Bohemian folk-tunes and dances. The main idea of the story itself is based upon an old Bohemian legend; while the character of the robber Babinsky is likewise drawn from life. The librettist is Milos Kares.

A later opera, *Wallenstein*, produced in 1937, has not proved so successful.

Weinberger has also written many orchestral compositions, among which may be mentioned *Don Quixote* and a *Scherzo Giocoso*. He has also written a *Pianoforte Sonata* and *Colloque Sentimental*. In 1917, he wrote a Pantomime, *The Abduction of Eveline*. His future work is awaited with much interest, after the amazing success of *Schwanda the Bagpiper*.

WOLF-FERRARI

ERMANNO WOLF-FERRARI was born on 12th January, 1876, at Venice. He studied under Rheinberge at Munich from 1893 to 1895; and in 1902 he was appointed Director of the Liceo Benedetto Marcello in Venice, from which position he resigned in 1909, as he desired to live in Germany. He produced his first opera, *La Sulamita*, at Venice in 1889 before he went to Munich, this work being the result of his own self-teaching. Other operas followed :—*Cenerentola*, produced at Venice in 1902; *Le Donne Curiose*, in 1903. The latter was afterwards produced with much success in America. His fine opera, *La Vita Nuova*, dealing with the subject of Dante and Beatrice, was brought out in 1903. His charming light opera, *The Secret of Susanna*, followed this, and was produced at Munich in 1910, and at Covent Garden, London, in 1911; and his dramatic opera, *The Jewels of the Madonna*, was produced in Berlin, 1911, and was given at Covent Garden, London, during the summer of 1912. Another fine opera, *Amanti Sposi* (Married Lovers), produced in Venice, March, 1925, has likewise achieved remarkable success.

ALPHABETICAL LIST OF OPERAS

(With Composers, Librettists, and Dates of First Production)

OPERA	COMPOSER	LIBRETTIST	FIRST PRODUCTION	PAGE
Aida	Verdi, Giuseppe	Mariette Bey } Antonis Ghislanzoni } Camille du Locle	Cairo, 1871 Milan (La Scala), 1872 New York, 1873 London (Covent Garden), 1876	740
Aleko	Rachmaninov, Sergei Vassilievitch	Adapted from Poushkin's poem *The Gipsies*	Moscow (Imperial Opera House), 1893 London Opera House, 1915	503
Alfred and the Cakes, King	Gatty, Dr. Nicholas Comyn	Reginald Gatty	London (R.C.M.), 1930 Falmouth, 1938	195
Alkestis	Boughton, Rutland	Adapted from Gilbert Murray's translation of Euripides' *Alcestis*	Glastonbury, 1920 London, 1924	83
Amico Fritz, L' (*Friend Fritz*)	Mascagni, Pietro	Suaratoni (Suardon) from story by Erckmann-Chatrian	Rome, 1891 New York, 1894	324
André Chénier (*Andrea Chénier*)	Giordano, Umberto	Luigi Illica	Milan, 1896 London, 1903	202

941

		Katel Sabina	Prague, 1866 Prague (Revised), 1870 London (Covent Garden), 1931	593
... Friedrich				
Bat, The (*Die Fledermaus*)	Strauss, Johann	Haffner and Genée (from Meilhac and Halévy's *Le Réveillon*)	Vienna, 1874 New York, 1874	636
Beltane Fires (*Feuersnot*)	Strauss, Richard	Ernst von Wolzogen (from an old Dutch Saga)	Dresden, 1901	658
Bethlehem	Boughton, Rutland	From the Coventry Nativity Play	Street, Somerset, Christmas, 1915	89
Boatswain's Mate, The	Smyth, Dame Ethel Mary	By the Composer (from W. W. Jacobs' story *Captains All*)	Frankfort, 1914 London, 1915	599
Bohème, La (*Bohemia*)	Puccini, Giacomo	Giacosa and Illica (from Murger's *La Vie de Bohème*)	Turin, 1896 London, 1897 New York, 1898	449
Bohemian Girl, The	Balfe, Michael William	Alfred Bunn	London, 1843 Paris, 1869	10
Boris Godounov (Opera in four Acts and a Prologue)	Moussorgsky, Modeste	Adapted by Composer from Poushkin and Karamzin	St. Petersburg (Mariensky Theatre), 1874 London (Drury Lane), 1913 New York, 1913	376
Bronwen (Part III of Trilogy *The Cauldron of Annun*)	Holbrooke, Josef Charles	Lord Howard de Walden (T. E. Ellis)	On Tour, Britain, 1928-29	263
Butterfly, Madam (*Madama Butterfly*)	Puccini, Giacomo	Illica and Giacosa (from David Belasco's drama)	Milan, 1904 London, 1905 Washington and New York, 1906	473

944

		By the Composer		
Chabert, Colonel (*Obersı Chabert*)	Waltershausen, Hermann Wolfgang von	By the Composer	Munich, 1912	866
Chénier, André (*Andrea Chénier*)	Giordano, Umberto	Luigi Illica	Milan, 1896; London, 1903	202
Children of Don, The (Part I of Trilogy *The Cauldron of Annun*)	Holbrooke, Josef Charles	Lord Howard de Walden (T. E. Ellis)	London, 1912	250
Cloak, The (*Il Tabarro*)	Puccini, Giacomo	Giuseppe Adami (adapted from Didier Gold's *La Houppelande*)	New York, 1918; London, 1919	457
Coach of the Holy Sacrament, The (*Le Carrosse du Saint Sacrement*)	Berners, Lord Gerald Hugh Tyrwhitt-Wilson (Gerald Tyrwhitt)	Based on play by Prosper Mérimée	Paris, 1923	51
Contes d'Hoffmann, Les (*The Tales of Hoffmann*)	Offenbach, Jacques	Jules Barbier and Michel Carré (from three tales by E. T. A. Hoffmann)	Paris, 1881 (posthumously); London, 1907	430
Coq d'Or, Le (*The Golden Cockerel*) Satirical Fantastic Opera in three Acts	Rimsky-Korsakov, Nicolas Andreievich	V. Bielsky (from poem by Poushkin)	Moscow (Zimini's Opera House), 1910 (posthumously); London (Drury Lane), 1914	520
Cornwall, The Queen of	Boughton, Rutland	Adapted from Thomas Hardy's poetic tragedy	Glastonbury, 1924	99
Cosi Fan Tutte (*They All Do It*) or The School for Lovers	Mozart, Johann Chrysostomus Wolfgang Amadeus	Da Ponte	Vienna, 1790	390

946

Don Pasquale	Donizetti, Gaetano	Salvatore Cammarano (after *Ser' Marc Antonio*)	Paris, 1843; London, 1843; New York, 1846	148
Drover, Hugh the	Vaughan Williams, Dr. Ralph (O.M.)	Harold Child	London, 1924	726
Duke or Devil	Gatty, Dr. Nicholas Comyn	Ivor Gatty	Manchester, 1909	185
Dusk (Twilight) of the Gods, The (*Die Götterdämmerung*) Part IV of *The Ring of the Nibelungs*	Wagner, Richard	By the Composer	Bayreuth, 1876; London, 1882; New York, 1888	835
Dutchman, The Flying (*Der Fliegende Holländer*)	Wagner, Richard	By the Composer (from Heine's version of the legend)	Dresden, 1843; London, 1870; New York, 1877	791
Dylan, Son of the Wave (Part II of Trilogy *The Cauldron of Annwn*)	Holbrooke, Josef Charles	Lord Howard de Walden (T. E. Ellis)	London, 1913	257
Egyptian Helen, The (*Helen in Egypt*) *Die Ägyptische Helena*	Strauss, Richard	Hugo von Hoffmannsthal	Dresden, 1928	664
Elektra	Strauss, Richard	Hugo von Hoffmannsthal	Dresden, 1909; London (Covent Garden), 1910; New York, 1910	654
Enchanter, The (*The Wizard*)	Holbrooke, Josef Charles	By the Composer	Chicago, 1915	269

		...of same name	tage (Vienna Theatre), 1903 London Opera House, 1915	111
Figaro, The Marriage of (*Le Nozze di Figaro*)	Mozart, Johann Chrysostomus Wolfgang Amadeus	Da Ponte (based on comedy by Beaumarchais)	Vienna, 1786; Paris, 1793; London, 1812; New York, 1823	405
Fledermaus, Die (*The Bat*)	Strauss, Johann	Haffner and Genée (from Meilhac and Halévy's *Le Réveillon*)	Vienna, 1874; New York, 1874	636
Flute, The Magic (*Die Zauberflöte*)	Mozart, Johann Chrysostomus Wolfgang Amadeus	Schikaneder	Vienna, 1791; Paris, 1801; London, 1811; New York, 1833	400
Flying Dutchman, The (*Der Fliegende Holländer*)	Wagner, Richard	By the Composer (from Heine's version of the legend)	Dresden, 1843; London, 1870; New York, 1877	791
Fool, The Perfect	Holst, Gustav Theodore	By the Composer	London, 1923	284
Forest, The (*Der Wald*)	Smyth, Dame Ethel Mary	By the Composer	Dresden, 1901; London, 1902; Berlin, 1906	612
Fra Diavolo	Auber, Daniel François Esprit	Eugène Scribe	Paris, 1830; London, 1831	1
Francesca da Rimini (*Francesca of Rimini*)	Rachmaninov, Sergei Vassilievitch	Adapted from drama of Gabriele d'Annunzio on the famous Romance	Moscow, 1904	507

949

OPERA	COMPOSER	LIBRETTIST	FIRST PRODUCTION	PAGE
Freischütz, Der (The Free-Shooter) or The Seventh Bullet	Weber, Carl Maria von	Friedrich Kind (from old legend in Popular Tales of the Northern Nations)	Berlin, 1821 London, 1824 New York, 1825	873
Fritz, L'Amico (Friend Fritz)	Mascagni, Pietro	Suaratoni (Suardon) from story by Erckmann-Chatrian	Rome, 1891 New York, 1894	324
Gianni Schicchi	Puccini, Giacomo	Gioachino Forzano	New York, 1918 Rome, 1919 London, 1919	461
Gioconda, La	Ponchielli, Amilcare	Arrigo Boïto (from Victor Hugo's drama The Tyrant of Syracuse)	Milan, 1876 London, 1883 New York, 1883	443
Giovanni, Don (Don Juan)	Mozart, Johann Chrysostomus Wolfgang Amadeus	Da Ponte (from tale by Tirso de Molina)	Prague, 1787 London, 1817 New York, 1826	393
Girl, The Bohemian	Balfe, Michael William	Alfred Bunn	London, 1843 Paris, 1869	10
Girl of the Golden West, The (La Fanciulla del West)	Puccini, Giacomo	Carlo Zangarini and Guelfo Civini (based on drama by David Belasco)	New York, 1910 London, 1911	468
Godounov, Boris (Opera in four Acts and Prologue)	Moussorgsky, Modeste	Adapted by Composer from Poushkin and Karamzin	St. Petersburg (Mariensky Theatre), 1874 London (Drury Lane), 1913 New York, 1913	376

Golden Cockerel, The (Le Coq d'Or) Satirical Fantastic Opera in three Acts	Rimsky-Korsakov, Nicolas Andreievich	V. Bielsky (from poem by Poushkin)	Moscow (Zimini's Opera House), 1910 (posthumously) London, 1914	520
Golden West, The Girl of the (La Fanciulla del West)	Puccini, Giacomo	Carlo Zangarini and Guelfo Civini (based on drama by David Belasco)	New York, 1910 London, 1911	468
Goldsmith of Toledo, The	Offenbach, Jacques (built up and edited by J. Stern and A. Zamara)	Carl G. Zwerenz (founded on Hoffmann's Tales)	London, 1922 (posthumously)	422
Götterdämmerung, Die (The Twilight [Dusk] of the Gods) Part IV of The Ring of the Nibelungs	Wagner, Richard	By the Composer	Bayreuth, 1876 London, 1882 New York, 1888	835
Greysteel	Gatty, Dr. Nicholas Comyn	Reginald Gatty (from Icelandic Saga Gisli the Outlaw)	Sheffield, 1906	190
Guest, The Stone (Opera in four Acts)	Dargomijsky, Alexander Sergeivich (completed by Cui)	Poushkin's version of the Don Juan story	St. Petersburg, 1872 (posthumously)	117
Hansel and Gretel (Hänsel und Gretel)	Humperdinck, Engelbert	Adelheid Wette (from Grimm's fairy tale)	Weimar and Munich, 1893 London, 1895	295
Helen in Egypt (The Egyptian Helen) Die Ägyptische Helena	Strauss, Richard	Hugo von Hoffmannsthal	Dresden, 1928	664
Heure Espagnole, L' (The Spanish Hour)	Ravel, Maurice	Poem of Franc-Nohain	Paris, 1911 London, 1918	514

952

Title	Composer	Librettist	Place and Date	Page
Iris	Mascagni, Pietro	Luigi Illica	Rome, 1898; Milan, 1899; London, 1918	333
Ivan the Terrible, or The Maid of Pskov (Opera in three Acts)	Rimsky-Korsakov, Nicolas Andreievich	From drama by the poet Mey	St. Petersburg (Mariensky Theatre), 1873; London (Drury Lane), 1913	531
Jewels of the Madonna, The (I Giojelli della Madonna)	Wolf-Ferrari, Ermanno	Carlo Zangarini and E. Golisciani	Berlin, 1911; London, 1912; New York, 1912	883
Jewess, The (La Juive)	Halévy, Jacques François Fromenthal Elias	Eugène Scribe	Paris, 1835; London, 1846	244
Johannis Fires (Feuersnot)	Strauss, Richard	Ernst von Wolzogen (from an old Dutch Saga)	Dresden, 1901	658
Jongleur de Notre-Dame, Le (Our Lady's Juggler)	Massenet, Jules	Poem of Maurice Léna	Monte Carlo, 1902	339
Juan, Don (Don Giovanni)	Mozart, Johann Chrysostomus Wolfgang Amadeus	Da Ponte (from tale by Tirso de Molina)	Prague, 1787; London, 1817; New York, 1826	393
Juan de Mañara, Don	Goossens, Eugene	Arnold Bennett	London, 1937	212
Judith	Goossens, Eugene	Arnold Bennett	London, 1929	219
Juive, La (The Jewess)	Halévy, Jacques François Fromenthal Elias	Eugène Scribe	Paris, 1835; London, 1846	244
Khovantschina (Opera in five Acts)	Moussorgsky, Modeste	Stassov and the Composer (from Russian History)	St. Petersburg, 1885; London, 1913	384

953

OPERA	COMPOSER	LIBRETTIST	FIRST PRODUCTION	PAGE
Killarney, The Lily of	Benedict, Sir Julius	Oxenford and Boucicault (from latter's play *The Colleen Bawn*)	London, 1862	40
King Alfred and the Cakes	Gatty, Dr. Nicholas Comyn	Reginald Gatty	London (R.C.M.), 1930 Falmouth, 1938	195
Kings' Children (*Die Königskinder*)	Humperdinck, Engelbert	Ernst Rosmer (from fairy tale by Elsa Bernstein)	New York, 1910 London, 1911	299
King of Lahore, The (*Le Roi de Lahore*)	Massenet, Jules	Luigi Gallet	Paris, 1877	343
Königskinder, Die (*Kings' Children*)	Humperdinck, Engelbert	Ernst Rosmer (from fairy tale by Elsa Bernstein)	New York, 1910 London, 1911	299
Lakmé	Delibes, Clément Philibert Léo	Gillé and Gondinet	Paris, 1883, London, 1884, New York, 1886	131
Legend of Tsar Saltan, The	Rimsky-Korsakov, Nicolas Andreievich	Bielski (after Poushkin)	Moscow, 1900 London (Old Vic), 1933	539
Lily of Killarney, The	Benedict, Sir Julius	Oxenford and Boucicault (from latter's play *The Colleen Bawn*)	London, 1862	40

Opera	Composer	Libretto	First performances	
Lohengrin	Wagner, Richard	By the Composer	Weimar, 1850 New York, 1871 London, 1875	796
Louise	Charpentier, Gustave	By the Composer	Paris, 1900 London, 1909	105
Lucia di Lammermoor (*Lucy of Lammermoor*)	Donizetti, Gaetano	Cammarano (after Scott's *Bride of Lammermoor*)	Naples, 1835 London, 1838 Paris, 1839 New York, 1845	153
Lucrezia Borgia	Donizetti, Gaetano	Romani (after Victor Hugo's tragedy)	Milan, 1834 London, 1839 Paris, 1840 New York, 1847	158
Lurline	Wallace, William Vincent	Fitzball (after old legend of the *Lorelei*)	London (Covent Garden), 1860	854
Madam Butterfly (*Madama Butterfly*)	Puccini, Giacomo	Illica and Giacosa (from David Belasco's drama)	Milan, 1904 London (Covent Garden), 1905 Washington and New York, 1906	473
Mademoiselle Fifi (*Mam'zelle Fifi*)	Cui, César Antonovich	From Guy de Maupassant's novel of same name	Moscow (Hermitage Theatre), 1903 London Opera House, 1915	111

955

OPERA	COMPOSER	LIBRETTIST	FIRST PRODUCTION	PAGE
Madonna, The Jewels of the (*I Gioielli della Madonna*)	Wolf-Ferrari, Ermanno	Carlo Zangarini and E. Golisciani	Berlin, 1911 London ((Covent Garden), 1912 New York, 1912	883
Magic Flute, The (*Die Zauberflöte*)	Mozart, Johann Chrysostomus Wolfgang Amadeus	Schickaneder	Vienna, 1791 Paris, 1801 London, 1811 New York, 1833	400
Maid of Pskov, The (*Ivan the Terrible*)	Rimsky-Korsakov, Nicolas Andreievich	From drama by the poet Mey	St. Petersburg (Mariensky Theatre), 1873 London (Drury Lane), 1913	531
Mam'zelle Fifi (*Mademoiselle Fifi*)	Cui, César Antonovich	From Guy de Maupassant's novel of same name	Moscow (Hermitage Theatre), 1903 London Opera House, 1915	111
Manon Lescaut*	Puccini, Giacomo	Adapted by the Composer from the Abbé Prévost's novel of same name	Turin, 1893 London, 1894	480
Mariana	Wallace, William Vincent	Fitzball and Alfred Bunn	London (Drury-Lane), 1845	858

956

Marriage of Figaro, The (*Le Nozze di Figaro*)	Mozart, Johann Chrysostomus Wolfgang Amadeus	Da Ponte (based on comedy by Beaumarchais)	Vienna, 1786 Paris, 1793 London, 1812 New York, 1823	405
Martha (*Marta*)	Flotow, Friedrich von	St. Georges and Friedrich	Vienna, 1847 New York, 1852 London, 1858 Paris, 1865	179
Masked Ball, A (*Un Ballo in Maschera*)	Verdi, Giuseppe	Somma (based on Scribe's libretto for Auber's opera *Gustave III*)	Rome, 1859 London, 1861 Paris, 1861 New York, 1861	759
Mastersingers of Nuremberg, The (*Die Meistersinger von Nürnberg*)	Wagner, Richard	By the Composer	Munich, 1868 London, 1882 New York, 1886	803
Mavra	Stravinsky, Igor Fedorovitch	Based on a tale by Poushkin	Paris, 1921	688
Mefistofele	Boïto, Arrigo	By the Composer (from Goethe's *Faust* and other *Faust* legends)	Milan, 1868 London, 1880 New York, 1880	65
Merry Wives of Windsor, The	Nicolai, Otto	Mosenthal (from Shakespeare's comedy)	Berlin, 1849 New York, 1863 London, 1864	417
Mignon	Thomas, Charles Ambroise	Barbier and Carré (from Goethe's *Wilhelm Meister*)	Paris, 1866 London (Drury Lane), 1870 New York, 1883	697

957

• The story of Massenet's *Manon* is not included here, as it deals with the same subject, being likewise based on the Abbé Prévost's romance of same name.

OPERA	COMPOSER	LIBRETTIST	FIRST PRODUCTION	PAGE
Mirella (*Mireille*)	Gounod, Charles François	Based on the Provençal poem of F. Mistral	Paris, 1863	228
Mozart and Salieri (A Dramatic Episode in Operatic Form)	Rimsky-Korsakov, Nicolas Andreïevich	Poushkin's dramatic poem-duologue	Moscow (Hermitage Theatre), 1898 London (Drury Lane), 1913	543
Nerone (*Nero*)	Boïto, Arrigo	By the Composer	Milan, 1924 (posthumously)	70
Nibelungs, The Ring of the (*Der Ring des Nibelungen*)	Wagner, Richard	By the Composer	Bayreuth, 1876 London, 1882	819
Part I. The Rhinegold (*Das Rheingold*)	Wagner, Richard	By the Composer	Munich, 1869 London, 1882	819
Part II. The Valkyries (*Die Walküre*)	Wagner, Richard	By the Composer	Munich, 1870 London, 1882	823
Part III. Siegfried	Wagner, Richard	By the Composer	Bayreuth, 1876 London, 1882	830
Part IV. The Twilight (Dusk) of the Gods (*Die Götterdämmerung*)	Wagner, Richard	By the Composer	Bayreuth, 1876 London, 1882	835
Nightingale, The (Opera in three Acts)	Stravinsky, Igor Fedorovitch	M. Mitousoff (adapted from Hans Andersen's fairy tale of same name)	London (Drury Lane), 1914	693

Night in May, A (Une ... Mai) Humorous fantastic opera in three Acts	Rimsky-Korsakov, Nicolas Andreievich	Adapted from one of Gogol's South Russian Tales	St. Petersburg (Mariinsky Theatre), 1880 London (Drury Lane), 1914	549
Norma	Bellini, Vincenzo	Romani	Milan, 1831 London, 1833 Paris, 1833 New York, 1841	28
Nozze di Figaro, Le (The Marriage of Figaro)	Mozart, Johann Chrysostomus Wolfgang Amadeus	Da Ponte (based on comedy by Beaumarchais)	Vienna, 1786 Paris, 1793 London, 1812 New York, 1823	405
Oberst Chabert (Colonel Chabert)	Waltershausen, Hermann Wolfgang von	By the Composer	Munich, 1912	866
Onégin, Eugene (Romantic Opera in three Acts)	Tschaikovsky, Peter Iljitsch	Modeste Tschaikovsky and Shilovsky (from Poushkin)	Moscow Conservatoire, 1879 London (Olympic), 1892	704
Othello (Otello)	Verdi, Giuseppe	Arrigo Boito (from Shakespeare's tragedy)	Milan, 1887 New York, 1888 London, 1889	764
Our Lady's Juggler (Le Jongleur de Notre-Dame)	Massenet, Jules	Poem of Maurice Léna	Monte Carlo, 1902	339
Pagliacci, I (The Clowns, The Players, or The Mountebanks)	Leoncavallo, Ruggiero	By the Composer	Milan, 1892 London, 1894	307
Parsifal	Wagner, Richard	By the Composer (after epic by Wolfram von Eschenbach)	Bayreuth, 1882	810

959

Title	Composer	Libretto	First Performances	
Prince Igor (Opera in four Acts and Prologue)	Borodin, Alexander Porphyrievich (completed by Rimsky-Korsakov and Glazounov)	By the Composer and Stassov (from old Slav Chronicle The Epic of Igor)	St Petersburg (Imperial Opera House), 1890 (posthumously) London (Drury Lane), 1914	77
Prodigal Son, The (L'Enfant Prodigue)	Debussy, Claude Achille	Ernest Guinand	Sheffield (Music Festival), 1908 London, 1910	128
Puritani, I (The Puritans)	Bellini, Vincenzo	Count Pepoli	Paris, 1835 London, 1835 New York, 1844	31
Queen of Cornwall, The	Boughton, Rutland	Adapted from Thomas Hardy's poetic tragedy	Glastonbury, 1924	99
Queen of Sheba, The	Goldmark, Karl	Mosenthal	Vienna, 1875 London, 1885 New York, 1885	206
Queen of Spades, The (La Pique Dame) Opera in three Acts	Tschaikovsky, Peter Iljitsch	Modeste Tschaikovsky (after Poushkin)	St. Petersburg (Mariensky Theatre), 1890 London Opera House, 1915	719
Rhinegold, The (Das Rheingold) Part I of The Ring of the Nibelungs	Wagner, Richard	By the Composer	Munich, 1869 Bayreuth, 1876 London, 1882 New York, 1889	819
Rigoletto	Verdi, Giuseppe	Piave (after Victor Hugo's Le Roi s'Amuse)	Venice, 1851 London, 1853 Paris, 1857 New York, 1857	769

OPERA	COMPOSER	LIBRETTIST	FIRST PRODUCTION	PAGE
Ring of the Nibelungs, The (Der Ring des Nibelungen)	Wagner, Richard	By the Composer	Bayreuth, 1876 (in its entirety) London, 1882 (in its entirety) New York, 1889 (in its entirety)	819
Part I. The Rhinegold	Wagner, Richard	By the Composer	Munich, 1869	819
Part II. The Valkyries	Wagner, Richard	By the Composer	Munich, 1870	823
Part III. Siegfried	Wagner, Richard	By the Composer	Bayreuth, 1876	830
Part IV. The Twilight (Dusk) of the Gods	Wagner, Richard	By the Composer	Bayreuth, 1876	835
Robert the Devil (Robert le Diable)	Meyerbeer, Giacomo	Scribe and Delavigne	Paris, 1831 London, 1832 New York, 1834	362
Romeo and Juliet (Roméo et Juliette)	Gounod, Charles François	Barbier and Carré (from Shakespeare's tragedy)	Paris, 1867 London, 1867 New York, 1867	239
Rosenkavalier, Der (The Rose-Bearer)	Strauss, Richard	Hugo von Hoffmannsthal	Dresden, 1911 London, 1913 New York, 1913	675
Rusalka (The Water-Nymph)	Dvořák, Antonin	Jaroslav Kvapil	Prague, 1901 London, 1938	166

Title	Composer	Libretto / Source	Place, Date	Page
	Andreievich	of Russian folk-lore tales	St. Petersburg, 1901	
St. John's Eve (*Feuersnot*)	Strauss, Richard	Ernst von Wolzogen (from an old Dutch Saga)	Dresden, 1901	658
Salomé	Strauss, Richard	Adapted from Oscar Wilde's poetic drama	Dresden, 1905; New York, 1907; London, 1910	682
Samson and Delilah (*Samson et Dalila*)	Saint-Saëns	Fernand Lémaire	Weimar, 1877; Paris, 1892; New York, 1892; London, 1909	586
Savitri	Holst, Gustav Theodore	By the Composer (from an old Indian legend, an episode in *The Mahabharata*)	London School of Opera, 1916; London (Covent Garden), 1922	292
Schicchi, Gianni	Puccini, Giacomo	Gioachino Forzano	New York, 1918; Rome, 1919; London, 1919	461
Schwanda the Bagpiper	Weinberger, Jaromir	Milos Kares	Prague, 1927; London (Covent Garden), 1934	878
Seal-Woman, The	Bantock, Sir Granville	Mrs. Marjory Kennedy-Fraser (on a Hebridean folk-lore theme)	Birmingham, 1924	17

Title	Composer	Libretto/Source	Place and Date	Page
Spades, The Queen of (La Pique Dame)	Tschaikovsky, Peter Iljitsch	Modeste Tschaikovsky (after Poushkin)	St. Petersburg (Mariensky Theatre), 1890 London Opera House, 1915	719
Spanish Hour, The (L'Heure Espagnole)	Ravel, Maurice	Poem of Franc-Nohain	Paris, 1911 London, 1918	514
Star of the North, The (L'Étoile du Nord)	Meyerbeer, Giacomo	Eugène Scribe	Paris, 1854 London (Covent Garden), 1855	369
Stone Guest, The (Opera in four Acts)	Dargomijsky, Alexander Sergeivich (completed by Cui)	Poushkin's version of the Don Juan story	St. Petersburg 1872 (posthumously)	117
Stranger, The (Pierrot and Pierrette)	Holbrooke, Josef Charles	Walter E. Grogan	London, 1910	281
Susanna, The Secret of (Il Segreto di Susanna)	Wolf-Ferrari, Ermanno	Max Kalbeck (from the French of Enrico Golisciani)	Munich, 1910 London, 1911 New York, 1911	891
Tabarro, Il (The Cloak)	Puccini, Giacomo	Giuseppe Adami (adapted from Didier Gold's La Houppelande)	New York, 1918 London, 1919	457
Tales of Hoffmann, The (Les Contes d'Hoffmann)	Offenbach, Jacques	Jules Barbier and Michel Carré (from three tales by E. T. A. Hoffmann)	Paris, 1881 (posthumously) London, 1907	430

965

OPERA	COMPOSER	LIBRETTIST	FIRST PRODUCTION	PAGE
Tannhäuser	Wagner, Richard	By the Composer	Dresden, 1845 New York, 1859 Paris, 1861 London (Covent Garden), 1876	841
Tess	d'Erlanger, Baron Frederic	Luigi Illica (from Thomas Hardy's novel *Tess of the D'Urbervilles*)	Naples, 1909 London, 1910	172
Thaïs	Massenet, Jules	Louis Gallet (from romance by Anatole France)	Paris, 1894 London, 1911	349
Toledo, The Goldsmith of	Offenbach, Jacques (built up and edited by J. Stern and A. Zamara)	Carl G. Zwerenz (founded on Hoffmann's Tales)	London, 1922 (posthumously)	422
Tosca, La	Puccini, Giacomo	Illica and Giacosa (after drama by Sardou)	Rome, 1900 London, 19. ? New York, 1901	490
Travelling Companion, The	Stanford, Sir Charles Villiers	Sir Henry Newbolt (based on tale by Hans Andersen)	Bristol, 1926 London, 1936	630
Traviata, La (*The Castaway, The Lost One, The Courtesan*)	Verdi, Giuseppe	Francesco Maria Piave (based upon *La Dame aux Camélias* by Dumas fils)	Venice, 1853 London, 1856 Paris, 1856	776

967

OPERA	COMPOSER	LIBRETTIST	FIRST PRODUCTION	PAGE
Wald, Der (*The Forest*)	Smyth, Dame Ethel Mary	By the Composer	Dresden, 1901 London, 1902 Berlin, 1906	612
Walküre, Die (*The Valkyries*) Part II of *The Ring of the Nibelungs*	Wagner, Richard	By the Composer	Munich, 1870 Bayreuth, 1876 London, 1882 New York, 1877 and 1885	823
Water-Nymph, The (*Rusalka*)	Dvořák, Antonin	Jaroslav Kvapil	Prague, 1901 London, 1938	166
Windsor, The Merry Wives of	Nicolai, Otto	Mosenthal (from Shakespeare's comedy)	Berlin, 1849 New York, 1863 London, 1864	417
Wizard, The (*The Enchanter*)	Holbrooke, Josef Charles	By the Composer	Chicago, 1915	269
Wreckers, The (*Les Naufrageurs*)	Smyth, Dame Ethel Mary	H. B. Brewster	Leipzig, 1906 London, 1909	618
Zauberflöte, Die (*The Magic Flute*)	Mozart, Johann Chrysostomus Wolfgang Amadeus	Schickaneder	Vienna, 1791 Paris, 1801 London, 1811 New York, 1833	400